Africa

Africa

A Modern History

Guy Arnold

Atlantic Books
London

Published in Great Britain in 2005 by Atlantic Books,
an imprint of Grove Atlantic Ltd.

Copyright © Guy Arnold 2005

9 8 7 6 5 4 3 2 1

A CIP catalogue record for this book is available from the British Library.

ISBN 1 84354 175 0

Designed by www.carrstudio.co.uk

Printed and bound by Bercker in Germany

Atlantic Books
An imprint of Grove Atlantic Ltd
Ormond House
26 – 27 Boswell Street
London WC1N 3JZ

CONTENTS

Part 1: The 1960s Decade of Hope

Part II: The 1970s Decade of Realism

Part III: The 1980s Basket Case?

PART IV: The 1990s New Directions and New Perceptions

ACKNOWLEDGEMENTS

From 1960 to 2000, the period covered by this book, momentous changes occurred throughout Africa to transform the continent from being a colonial extension of Europe into fifty independent nations. Following independence these new nations, struggled to achieve an identity of their own, faced the pressures of the Cold War, witnessed the emergence of the one party state and the charismatic political leader, watched the rise of their armies as major political players who carried out coups on a scale unequalled anywhere else and saw their continent wracked by wars that inevitably attracted interventions by the world's leading powers – in the Congo, Angola, the Horn and elsewhere. Lack of trained personnel and economic weakness rendered most African countries deeply vulnerable to external manipulation by the former colonial powers, the new superpowers, part of whose ideological confrontations were conducted in Africa, and the western controlled World Bank and IMF, a process famously described by Kwame Nkrumah as neo-colonialism. The Africa which established the Organization of African Unity in 1963 had changed out of recognition by the beginning of the 21st century. By any reckoning the events of these years amount to an historical revolution.

During 40 years of travelling in Africa and writing about its political and economic development I have drawn upon the knowledge and experience of a wide range of people whom it would be impossible to name. Their insights have influenced my own growing understanding and attachment to Africa over my professional writing life and this book reflects that influence though the arguments and conclusions are entirely my own.

I wish to record my particular thanks to Toby Mundy, my publisher, who has backed this large project with enthusiasm; and Louisa Joyner who has overseen each stage in the preparation of the book for publication. I am particularly grateful to Sue Hewitt and Ruth Weiss for their careful reading of the text and suggestions as to facts, presentation and clarity, and to Derek Ingram for a final appraisal.

Guy Arnold
2005

LIST OF ILLUSTRATIONS

SECTION 3:

SECTION 4:

LIST OF MAPS

1940s

1945   End World War II

Establishment of United Nations

Sixth Pan-African Conference
(Manchester, England)

Setif Uprising, Algeria

Only four African countries
independent – Egypt, Ethiopia
Liberia, South Africa

1948   National Party wins South African
election; implements apartheid

1950s

1951   Portugal transforms its African
colonies into overseas provinces

Egypt abrogates 1936 Treaty with
Britain; British troops occupy Canal
Zone

Libya independent

1952   Army coup in Egypt; King Farouk
goes into exile

Ahmed Ben Bella forms Algerian
Revolutionary Committee in Cairo

1952-1959 Mau Mau rebellion in Kenya

1953   Trial of Jomo Kenyatta for managing
Mau Mau backfires, helps create
myth of Kenyatta the nationalist
leader

Britain forms Central African
Federation (CAF): Northern
Rhodesia, Southern Rhodesia,
Nyasaland under white minority rule

1954   Col. Nasser takes full control in
Egypt

National Liberation Front (FLN)
launches Algerian war of
independence

1956   Sudan, Morocco, Tunisia
independent

Suez Crisis

French Loi Cadre gives universal
suffrage in French West and
Equatorial Africa

1957   Gold Coast independent as Ghana

1958   De Gaulle tours Francophone Africa;
offers self-government within a
French Community

Guinea under Sekou Touré opts for
full independence; France breaks
relations

1960s

1960   Harold Macmillan gives 'Wind of
Change' speech in Cape Town

21 March, Sharpeville Massacre in
South Africa

30 June, Belgian Congo independent;
descends into chaos

'annus mirabilis' – most of
Francophone Africa – Cameroon,
Central African Republic, Chad,
Congo (B), Dahomey (Benin),
Gabon, Ivory Coast (Côte d'Ivoire),
Madagascar, Mali, Mauritania, Niger,
Senegal, Togo, Upper Volta (Burkina
Faso) – independent

Ethiopia, abortive coup against
Emperor Haile Selassie

British Somaliland joins former
Italian Somaliland to form
independent Republic of Somalia

Nigeria independent

1961   Patrice Lumumba murdered in
Katanga (Congo)

Casablanca (radical) and Monrovia
(moderate) groups threaten to divide
Africa into rival camps

Portugal claims its African subjects are full citizens of Portugal

Liberation struggle launched in Angola

Sierra Leone, Tanganyika independent

South Africa leaves Commonwealth

Death of UN Secretary-General Dag Hammarskjold

ECA study: "Impact of Western European integration on African trade and development" – EEC a threat to African exports

1962   Algeria, Uganda independent

Haile Selassie ends Federation of Eritrea and Ethiopia, incorporates Eritrea in Empire – prelude to 30 years' warfare

UN general assembly calls upon all members to break ties with South Africa; special committee against apartheid is established

1963   Katanga secession ended by UN forces

Addis Ababa conference of 30 independent African states creates Organisation of African Unity (OAU)

Early OAU resolution calls on all members not to establish any relations with South Africa until apartheid is abandoned

Amilcar Cabral launches independence struggle in Portuguese Guinea (Guinea-Bisau)

First Yaounde Convention between the EC and African countries with ties to EC (former colonies of members)

Kenya, Zanzibar independent

Central African Federation dissolved

1964   revolution in Zanzibar (January); Zanzibar joins Tanganyika to form United Republic of Tanzania (April)

British forces quell army mutinies in East Africa

First OAU summit held in Cairo

FRELIMO launches liberation struggle in Mozambique

French troops reverse coup in Gabon to keep M'Ba in power

The Shifta border war between Kenya and Somalia – to 1967

Rivonia treason trial in South Africa: Mandela, Sisulu and other African nationalist leaders get life sentences, sent to Robben Island

Nyasaland and Northern Rhodesia independent as Malawi and Zambia

Zhou en Lai in Mali enunciates Eight Principles of Chinese aid

1965   Coup in Algeria: Ben Bella deposed; Boumedienne becomes head of state

The Gambia independent

White minority government of Southern Rhodesia makes unilateral declaration of independence (UDI) 11 November

OAU resolution calls on members to break diplomatic relations with Britain by 15 December unless it has taken action to reverse UDI; only 11 countries do so

Joseph Mobutu carries out second coup in the Congo (24 November) – to rule to 1997

1966   Commonwealth summit in Lagos devoted to UDI in Rhodesia

Coup in Nigeria: military rule replaces civilian government

UN imposes sanctions on Rhodesia

Coup ousts Nkrumah in Ghana; military rule

UN General Assembly proclaims 21 March (Sharpeville day) International day for the Elimination of Racial Discrimination

UN terminates South Africa's mandate over South West Africa (Namibia)

SWAPO launches armed struggle in Namibia

Assassination of Prime Minister Verwoerd of South Africa

Botswana, Lesotho independent

1967   Formation of East African Common Market (Kenya, Tanzania, Uganda)

Col. Ojukwu proclaims independent state of Biafra (May);

Nigerian civil war begins (July)

Egypt humiliatingly defeated by Israel in Six day War

Arusha Declaration, Tanzania

President Banda of Malawi enters into diplomatic relations with South Africa

1968   Spanish Guinea independent as Equatorial Guinea

Britain passes Commonwealth Immigration Act restricting immigration from Commonwealth countries

Mauritius, Swaziland independent

1969   Coup in Somalia brings Siad Barre to power

Coup in Libya brings Muammar al-Gaddafi to power

Coup in Sudan brings Jaafar Nimeiri to power

Hardline Afrikaners break with National party in South Africa to form Herstigte Nasionale Party under Albert Hertzog

Second EC-Africa Yaounde Convention

Pearson Report

1970s

1970   Rhodesia proclaims itself a republic

UN strengthens arms embargo against South Africa; urges members to terminate all relations with the Republic

Non-Aligned Summit in Lusaka, Zambia

China begins construction of 1,100-mile TANZAM railway linking Tanzania and Zambia; opens 1976

1971   Commonwealth summit in Singapore debates decision of Heath

Government to resume sale of arms to South Africa

Idi Amin mounts coup in Uganda to oust Milton Obote (in Singapore for Commonwealth summit)

Mobutu assumes absolute power in the Congo, renames Zaïre

International Court of Justice rules that South Africa is illegally in Namibia

President Banda of Malawi on state visit to South Africa

US Polaroid corporation experiment in South Africa: improved work conditions for black employees break apartheid rules

Ovambo strike in Namibia (to 1972) brings country to a standstill

1972   Opening of Orapa diamond mine in Botswana signals rapid development of mineral wealth

Pearson Commission to Rhodesia reports (April) that Africans overwhelmingly reject constitution proposed by Britain

Sudan: Addis Ababa Agreement ends North-South civil war:

Nimeiri grants regional autonomy to South

Burundi: 100,000 Hutus massacred

Uganda: Amin forces all non-citizen Asians to leave; Britain receives 30,000

Rhodesia: commencement of sustained guerrilla warfare in north-east by forces of Zimbabwe African National Union (ZANU)

1973   Rhodesia closes border with Zambia

Britain joins European Community: opens way for EC aid to Anglophone Africa under Lomé Conventions

Sahel drought

British journalist Adam Raphael, in Guardian, reveals that only three of the top 100 British companies in South Africa pay their African workers above the poverty datum line

24 September: PAIGC declares Guinea-Bissau independent; recognized by a majority of UN members

Yom Kippur War: almost all African countries break relations with Israel

Algeria hosts Non-Aligned summit (September) and Arab summit (November): Boumedienne calls for Algeria and Arab world to take control of their economies

African economies hit by fourfold increase in price of oil

1974 Portugal: 25 April Revolution; Caetano government overthrown;

Gen. Spinola recognizes right of African territories to independence

UN General Assembly rejects South Africa's credentials and South Africa ceases to participate in UN deliberations

South Africa sponsors détente with its neighbours to ease tensions in the region

UN Sixth Special Session held in Algiers: launch of New International Economic Order (NIEO) initiative

General Assembly adopts Declaration and Programme of Action on the Establishment of an NIEO

Ethiopia: fall of Haile Selassie; military Dergue to rule

1975 End of Portugal's African Empire: Mozambique (June), São Tomé and Principe (July), Cape Verde (September), Angola (November) independent

Mozambique: civil war between ruling FRELIMO and rebel RENAMO – to 1992

South African force invades Angola; a PR disaster for Pretoria

Formation of Economic Community of West African States (ECOWAS)

Nigeria launches Third Development Plan, at Naira 32 billion the largest ever in Africa to that date

Nigeria: Gen. Gowon ousted in coup by Gen. Murtala Muhammad Lome I

Comoros independent

1976 Nigeria (February): Muhammad killed in coup; Olusegun Obasanjo becomes head of state

South Africa: Soweto uprising heralds year of violence

Spain gives up control of Spanish (Western) Sahara: Morocco and Mauritania claim the territory and mobilise forces to seize it

Seychelles independent

1977 Ogaden war between Ethiopia and Somalia – to 1978

Haile Mengistu Mariam assumes full control of Ethiopia and purges opponents; implements Marxist policies; US ends aid

The two superpowers (US and USSR) become engaged in the Horn: USSR supports Ethiopia, US supports Somalia

Zaire: Shaba wars (1977 and 1978) launched by exiles in Angola threaten Mobutu's hold on country; France and Morocco provide military assistance

President Bokassa of Central African Republic crowns himself emperor in lavish ceremony

Djibouti independent

Rhodesia: Gen. Peter Walls argues publicly for negotiations, says Rhodesian government cannot win the war

1978 Amin launches attack on Tanzania through the Kagera salient

French mercenary Bob Denard leads 50 white mercenaries from South Africa to carry out coup in Comoros

Algeria: death of Boumedienne; Chadli Benjedid succeeds him

South Africa; Muldergate scandal destroys Vorster's political career; P. W. Botha becomes Prime Minister

Kenya: death of Kenyatta; Arap Moi becomes President

1979 Commonwealth summit in Lusaka: Britain convenes constitutional conference in London to settle future of Rhodesia

Lome II

Africa 2000: analysis of Africa's economic problems, leads to

Lagos Plan of Action 1980

Tanzanian army in support of Obote invades Uganda; fall of Amin

Central African Republic: coup supported by France ousts Emperor Bokassa

Ghana: Jerry Rawlings seizes power in coup: three former military heads of state executed

Nigeria: Obasanjo returns the country to civilian rule

Egypt isolated in Arab world following the Camp David Accords

South Africa explodes nuclear weapon in South Atlantic

1980s

1980 Brandt Report

Rhodesia becomes independent as Zimbabwe; Robert Mugabe Prime Minister; 30,000 dead in guerrilla war (official)

Wars in Africa 1980-1990 result in 5 million refugees, one-third of world total

Liberia: Samuel Doe seizes power in coup; President Tolbert killed; 13 members of his government publicly executed

South Africa: policy of destabilizing its neighbours – to 1990

Southern African Development Coordination Conference (SADCC) formed by Frontline States

1981 World Bank Report: Accelerated Development in Sub-Saharan Africa An Agenda for Action

1982 Zimbabwe: Mugabe wages 'Dissidents' War' against Ndebele to 1987; destroys Joshua Nkomo's power base

US President Ronald Reagan bans import of Libyan oil

1983 South Africa: Botha introduces constitutional reforms which establish a tricameral racial legislature; leads to increasing protests and violence through to 1986

Sudan: resumption of North-South civil war

Nigeria expels two million foreign workers from Ghana (majority), Cameroon, Chad, Nige,

Nigeria: New Year's Eve army ousts civilian government of Sheu Shagari; Gen. Muhammed Buhari head of state

1984 UN General Assembly rejects new South African racially segregated tricameral constitution

Lome III

OAU: 30 member states (a majority) recognize the legitimacy of the Sahrawi Arab Democratic Republic (SADR) occupied by Morocco, which quits the OAU rather than accept its decision

Ethiopia: tenth anniversary of revolution: formation of the Workers' party of Ethiopia; country affected by famine

World Bank report: Toward Sustained Development in Sub-Saharan Africa: A Joint Program of Action; calls for more aid

1985 OAU adopts five-year plan (1986-90): African Priority Programme for Economic Recovery (APPER); this is followed by UN Programme of Action for Africa's Economic Recovery and Development (UNPARED)

Tanzania: Nyerere retires as President; succeeded by Ali Hassan Mwinyi

Western business disinvests from South Africa

South Africa: 15 August at Durban President Botha delivers 'Rubicon' speech – makes no concessions; Rand loses 35 per cent of value in 13 days

Group of South African businessmen go to Lusaka to talk with Oliver Tambo and other ANC leaders about the future of South Africa

Libya: Gaddafi says: We have the right to fight America, and we have the right to export terrorism to them

Sudan: Nimeiri ousted by military

December: five-day border war between Burkina Faso and Mali

1986   Yoweri Museveni wins control of Uganda after years of civil strife

United States bombs targets in Libya

Mozambique: death of President Samora Machel in air crash

South Africa: government repeals 34 laws and regulations as it begins to abandon apartheid

South Africa: the Eminent Persons Group (EPG) established by the Nassau Commonwealth summit of 1985 to sound out opinion in South Africa quits the Republic when Botha orders cross-border raids into Botswana, Zambia and Zimbabwe

World Bank report: Financing Adjustment and growth in Sub-Saharan Africa, 1986-90

1987   Angola: battle of Cuito Cuanavale (into 1988) in south of country involving South African and Cuban forces destroys myth of South African superiority

Tunisia: Gen. Zine al-Abidine Ben Ali replaces 84-year-old Bourguiba as no longer competent to rule

1988   Algeria: rise of Front Islamique du Salut (FIS)

1989   Egypt: President Sadat assassinated; Hosni Mubarak president

Ethiopia: military coup against Mengistu fails

South Africa: Botha has stroke; F. W. de Klerk becomes President

Liberia: Charles Taylor and his

National Patriotic Front of Liberia launches civil war

1990s

1990   End of Cold War

South Africa: de Klerk unbans ANC and 33 other black political organizations; announces determination to end apartheid (2 February) ; week later releases Nelson Mandela

Namibia independent (March 21); Sam Nujoma becomes President

Angola: MPLA government abandons Marxism-Leninism

UN Secretary-General sends mission to South Africa to report on progress towards dismantling apartheid

ODA (aid) to Sub-Saharan Africa falls by 21 per cent from 1990 to 1996

Chad: civil war ends; Hissène Habré flees country; Idriss Deby president

Ethiopia: Eritrean people's Liberation Front (EPLF) launches final offensive against Ethiopian forces

Côte d'Ivoire: Houphouet Boigny (aged 85) wins presidential election after 30 years of continuous office

1991   South Africa: remaining apartheid laws repealed

Somalia: Siad Barre quits country as it collapses into chaos

Zambia: elections – Kaunda is defeated by Frederick Chiluba who becomes president.

Algeria: first round of elections on 26 December bring FIS close to victory; army cancels second round (due 15 January 1992) which FIS would have won; prelude to civil war (1992-2000)

1992   Dissolution of USSR removes alternate court of appeal for aid and political systems

Brazil: Rio Earth Summit on environment

Mandela addresses UN: calls upon it to lift sanctions because of progress in South Africa

Somalia: 28,000 US marines deployed in 'Operation Restore Hope'

1993 Eritrea independent

Burundi: civil strife to 2000 kills 200,000

Côte d'Ivoire: death of Houphouët Boigny ushers in period of political instability

1994 South Africa: (April 27) first national non-racial one person one vote elections; ANC victory; Mandela becomes President; formation of Government of National Unity

Malawi: elections bring an end to Banda's rule

Rwanda: extreme Hutus carry out systematic genocide of Tutsis, April to September, 800,000-1 million slaughtered; international community fails to intervene

1995 Nigeria: execution of human rights protester Saro Wiwa by Abacha government causes international outrage

Publication of Our Global Neighbourhood

1996 Somalia: UN withdraws its peacekeeping mission UNOSOM

1997 Zaire: Mobutu ousted; Laurent Kabila President; country renamed Congo Democratic Republic; country descends into war

Africa's Great War; estimated three million casualties (dead);

Neighbouring states – Uganda, Rwanda, Burundi, Angola, Namibia, Zimbabwe – become involved in one or other side

Congo (Brazzaville): civil war

Zimbabwe: Land Redistribution Act – white-owned farms designated for compulsory purchase

1998 Border war between Eritrea and Ethiopia – to 2000 – 70,000 Dead

1999 South Africa: Thabo Mbeki succeeds Mandela as the country's second black president

Nigeria: return to civilian rule; Olusegun Obasanjo president

Côte d'Ivoire: growing divisions between north and south bring the country to the brink of civil war; France sends troops

2000s

2000 Sierra Leone: Britain sends troops as peacekeepers in civil war

Zimbabwe: Mugabe holds referendum to alter constitution; a 55 per cent 'no' vote is recorded

2001 Ghana: elections return John Kufuor for second term

Democratic Republic of Congo: Laurent Kabila is assassinated (January 16); his son Joseph appointed president

Nigeria: at Abuja summit the concept of a New Partnership for African Development (NEPAD) is launched

2002 OAU dissolves itself; replaced by African union (AU) with greater powers to intervene in individual states in reaction to genocide, ethnic cleansing or abuse of human rights

2003 Zimbabwe leaves the Commonwealth

US President George W. Bush visits Africa

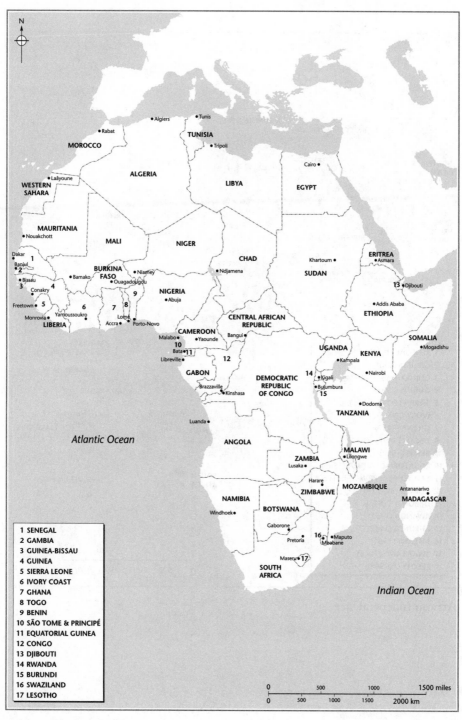

N

Rabat •
• Algiers
• Tunis
MOROCCO
TUNISIA
• Tripoli

Laâyoune •
ALGERIA
LIBYA
• Cairo
EGYPT

WESTERN
SAHARA

MAURITANIA
• Nouakchott
MALI
NIGER
CHAD
• Khartoum
SUDAN
ERITREA
• Asmara

Dakar •
1
Banjul •
2
BURKINA
FASO
• Niamey
NIGERIA
13 • Djibouti

• Bamako
• Ouagadougou
• Abuja

Bissau •
3
Conakry •
4
9
CENTRAL AFRICAN
REPUBLIC
• Addis Ababa
ETHIOPIA

Freetown •
5
6
7 8
Yamoussoukro •
Monrovia •
Accra •
Lomé •
Porto-Novo •
LIBERIA
CAMEROON
• Bangui
SOMALIA
• Mogadishu

Malabo •
10
• Yaoundé
UGANDA
KENYA

Bata •
11
12
• Kampala
• Nairobi

Libreville •
GABON
14
• Kigali
DEMOCRATIC
REPUBLIC
OF CONGO
15
• Bujumbura
• Dodoma

Brazzaville •
• Kinshasa
TANZANIA

• Luanda

Atlantic Ocean
ANGOLA
MALAWI
• Lilongwe

ZAMBIA
• Lusaka

Harare •
ZIMBABWE
MOZAMBIQUE
Antananarivo •
MADAGASCAR

NAMIBIA
BOTSWANA

Windhoek •
Gaborone •
16
• Maputo
Pretoria •
Mbabane

Maseru • 17
SOUTH
AFRICA
Indian Ocean

1 SENEGAL
2 GAMBIA
3 GUINEA-BISSAU
4 GUINEA
5 SIERRA LEONE
6 IVORY COAST
7 GHANA
8 TOGO
9 BENIN
10 SÃO TOME & PRINCIPÉ
11 EQUATORIAL GUINEA
12 CONGO
13 DJIBOUTI
14 RWANDA
15 BURUNDI
16 SWAZILAND
17 LESOTHO

0   500   1000   1500 miles
0   500   1000   1500   2000 km

African Nations 2005

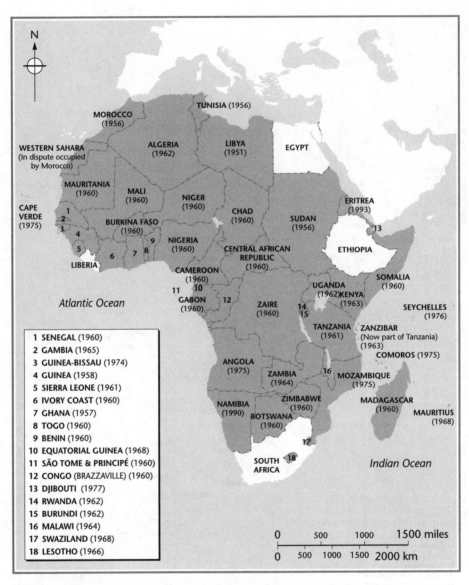

N

MOROCCO
(1956)

TUNISIA (1956)

WESTERN SAHARA
(In dispute occupied
by Morocco)

ALGERIA
(1962)

LIBYA
(1951)

EGYPT

MAURITANIA
(1960)

MALI
(1960)

NIGER
(1960)

ERITREA
(1993)

CAPE
VERDE
(1975)

BURKINA FASO
(1960)

CHAD
(1960)

SUDAN
(1956)

13

NIGERIA
(1960)

CENTRAL AFRICAN
REPUBLIC
(1960)

ETHIOPIA

LIBERIA

CAMEROON
(1960)

UGANDA
(1962)

KENYA
(1963)

SOMALIA
(1960)

SEYCHELLES
(1976)

Atlantic Ocean

GABON
(1960)

ZAIRE
(1960)

TANZANIA
(1961)

ZANZIBAR
(Now part of Tanzania)
(1963)

COMOROS (1975)

ANGOLA
(1975)

ZAMBIA
(1964)

MOZAMBIQUE
(1975)

MADAGASCAR
(1960)

MAURITIUS
(1968)

NAMIBIA
(1990)

ZIMBABWE
(1960)

BOTSWANA
(1960)

SOUTH
AFRICA

Indian Ocean

1 SENEGAL (1960)
2 GAMBIA (1965)
3 GUINEA-BISSAU (1974)
4 GUINEA (1958)
5 SIERRA LEONE (1961)
6 IVORY COAST (1960)
7 GHANA (1957)
8 TOGO (1960)
9 BENIN (1960)
10 EQUATORIAL GUINEA (1968)
11 SÃO TOMÉ & PRINCIPÉ (1960)
12 CONGO (BRAZZAVILLE) (1960)
13 DJIBOUTI (1977)
14 RWANDA (1962)
15 BURUNDI (1962)
16 MALAWI (1964)
17 SWAZILAND (1968)
18 LESOTHO (1966)

0	500	1000	1500 miles
0	500	1000	1500	2000 km

African Independence

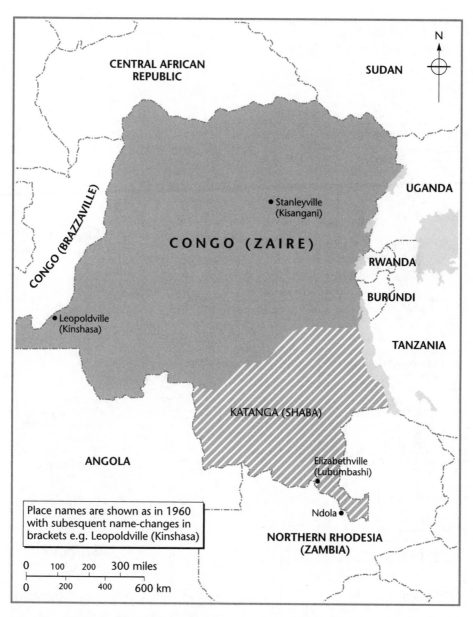

The Congo Crisis *(See Chapter Two)*

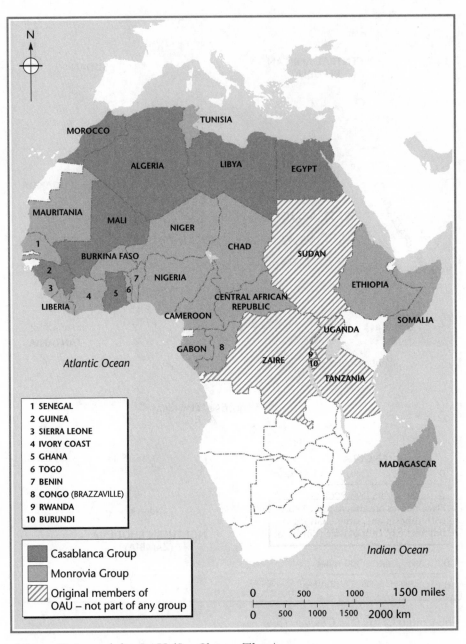

1 SENEGAL
2 GUINEA
3 SIERRA LEONE
4 IVORY COAST
5 GHANA
6 TOGO
7 BENIN
8 CONGO (BRAZZAVILLE)
9 RWANDA
10 BURUNDI

Casablanca Group

Monrovia Group

Original members of
OAU – not part of any group

African Unity and the OAU *(See Chapter Three)*

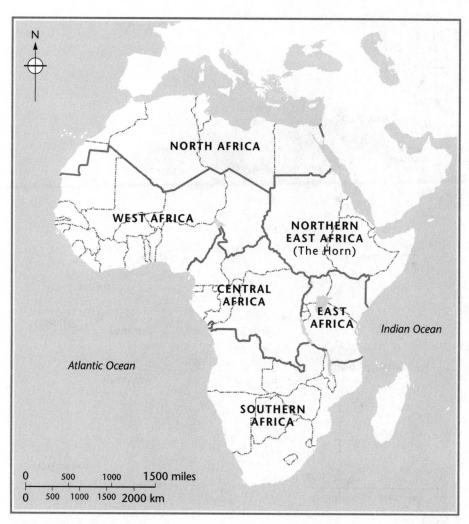

Africa's Regional Divisions

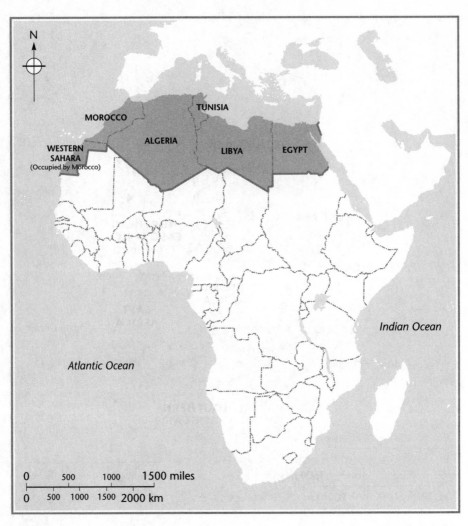

Arab North Africa *(See Chapter Six)*

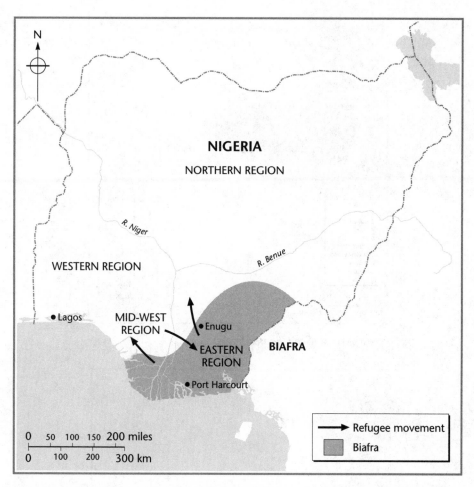

The Nigerian Civil War *(See Chapter Seven)*

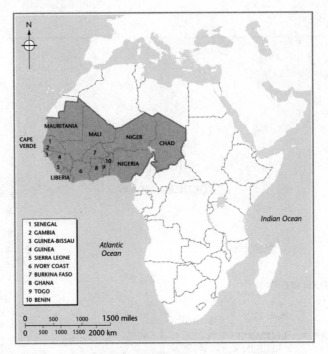

West Africa *(See Chapter Eight)*

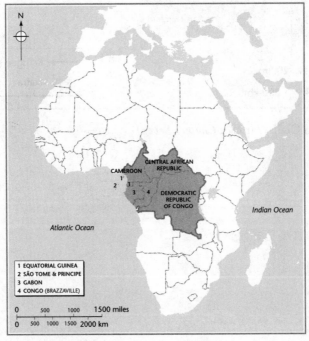

Equatorial Africa *(See Chapter Eight)*

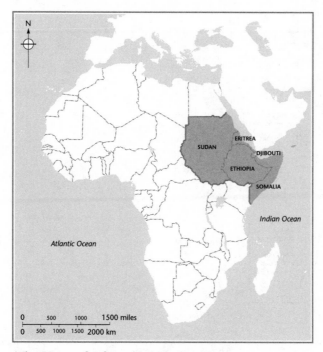

The Horn of Africa *(See Chapter Nine)*

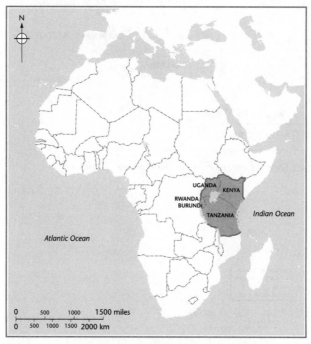

East Africa *(See Chapter Ten)*

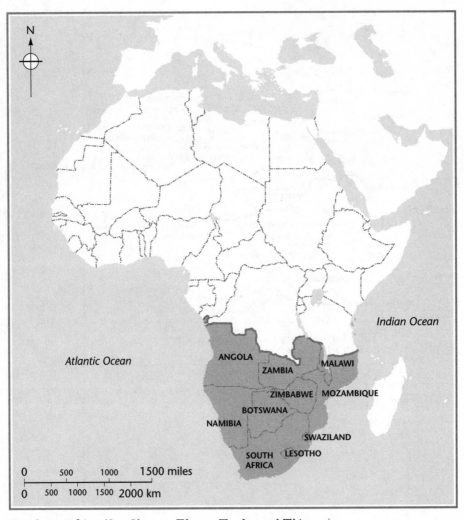

Southern Africa *(See Chapters Eleven, Twelve and Thirteen)*

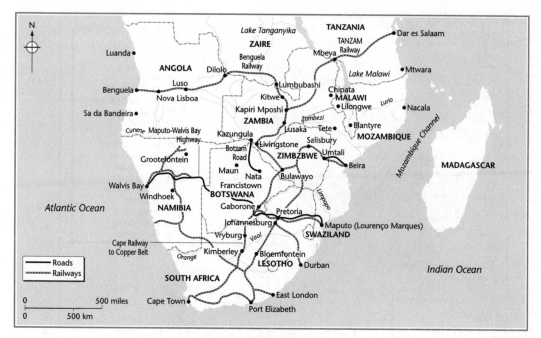

Highways of Southern Africa *(See Chapter Thirteen)*

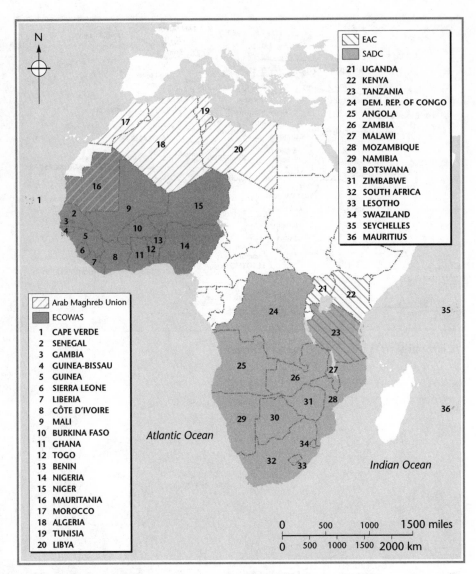

Regional Development Communities *(See Chapters Fourteen and Fifteen)*

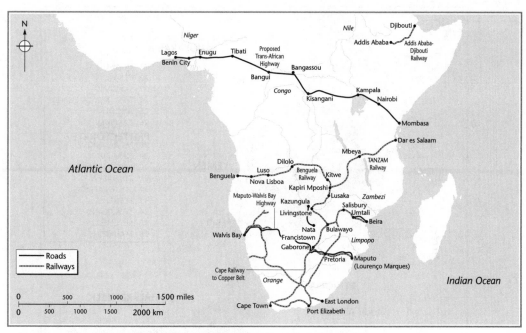

Strategic Highways (*See Chapter Eighteen*)

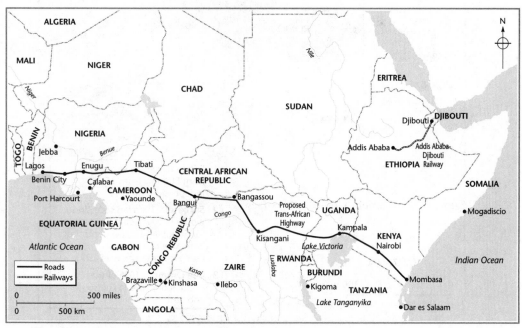

Proposed Trans-Africa Highway (*See Chapter Eighteen*)

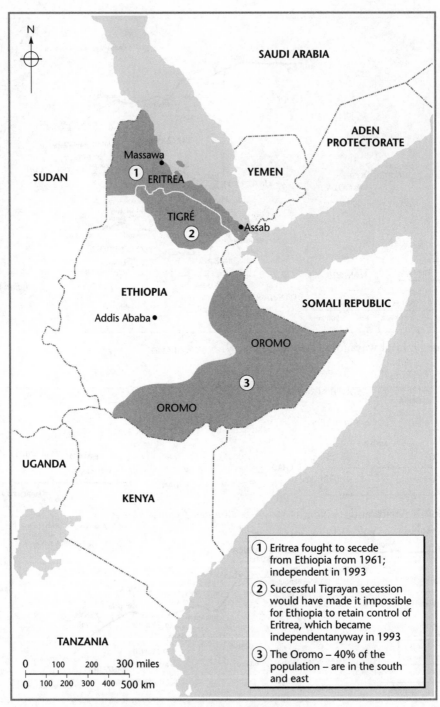

N

SAUDI ARABIA

ADEN
PROTECTORATE

Massawa
① ERITREA

YEMEN

SUDAN

TIGRÉ
②

•Assab

ETHIOPIA

SOMALI REPUBLIC

Addis Ababa •

OROMO

③

OROMO

UGANDA

KENYA

TANZANIA

| 0 | 100 | 200 | 300 miles |
| 0 | 100 200 300 400 | 500 km |

① Eritrea fought to secede
from Ethiopia from 1961;
independent in 1993

② Successful Tigrayan secession
would have made it impossible
for Ethiopia to retain control of
Eritrea, which became
independentanyway in 1993

③ The Oromo – 40% of the
population – are in the south
and east

War in the Horn of Africa *(See Chapter Nineteen)*

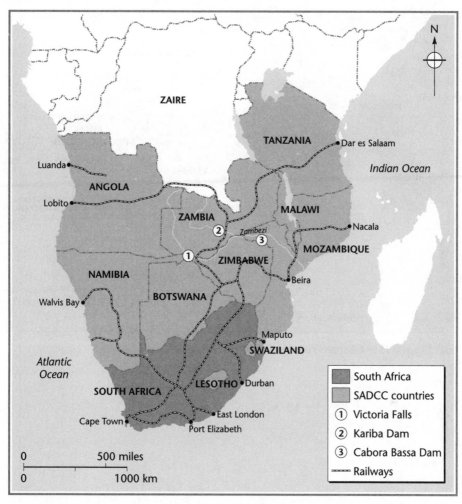

South Africa and its Neighbours *(See Chapter Twenty-Three)*

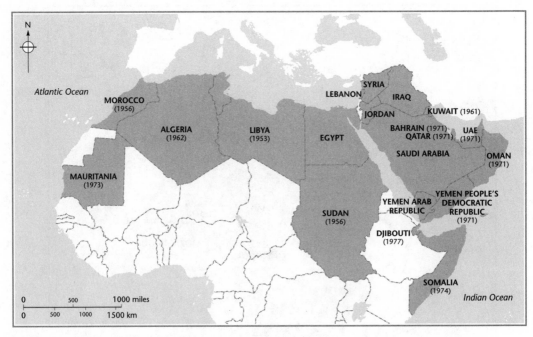

The Arab League *(See Chapter Twenty-Six)*

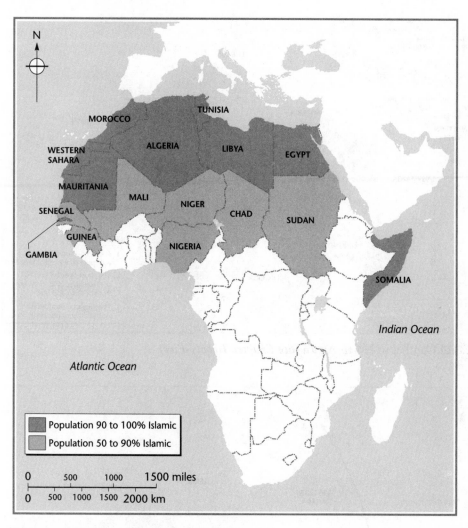

Islam in Africa *(See Chapter Twenty-Five)*

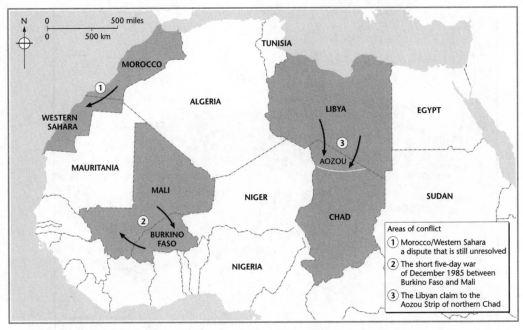

Areas of Conflict in North Africa *(See Chapter Twenty-Five)*

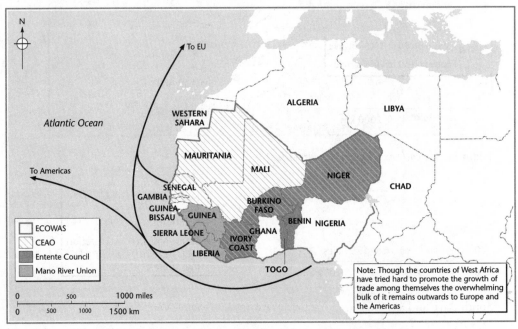

West African Economic Groups *(See Chapters Eight and Twenty-Seven)*

South African Destabilisation Tactics *(See Chapter Twenty-Nine)*

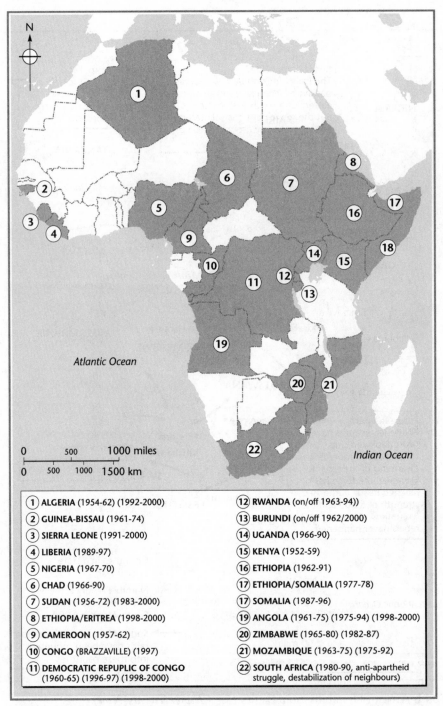

Atlantic Ocean

0   500   1000 miles

0   500   1000   1500 km

Indian Ocean

① **ALGERIA** (1954-62) (1992-2000)	⑫ **RWANDA** (on/off 1963-94))
② **GUINEA-BISSAU** (1961-74)	⑬ **BURUNDI** (on/off 1962/2000)
③ **SIERRA LEONE** (1991-2000)	⑭ **UGANDA** (1966-90)
④ **LIBERIA** (1989-97)	⑮ **KENYA** (1952-59)
⑤ **NIGERIA** (1967-70)	⑯ **ETHIOPIA** (1962-91)
⑥ **CHAD** (1966-90)	⑰ **ETHIOPIA/SOMALIA** (1977-78)
⑦ **SUDAN** (1956-72) (1983-2000)	⑰ **SOMALIA** (1987-96)
⑧ **ETHIOPIA/ERITREA** (1998-2000)	⑲ **ANGOLA** (1961-75) (1975-94) (1998-2000)
⑨ **CAMEROON** (1957-62)	⑳ **ZIMBABWE** (1965-80) (1982-87)
⑩ **CONGO** (BRAZZAVILLE) (1997)	㉑ **MOZAMBIQUE** (1963-75) (1975-92)
⑪ **DEMOCRATIC REPUBLIC OF CONGO** (1960-65) (1996-97) (1998-2000)	㉒ **SOUTH AFRICA** (1980-90, anti-apartheid struggle, destabilization of neighbours)

Africa's Wars *(See Chapter Thirty-Six)*

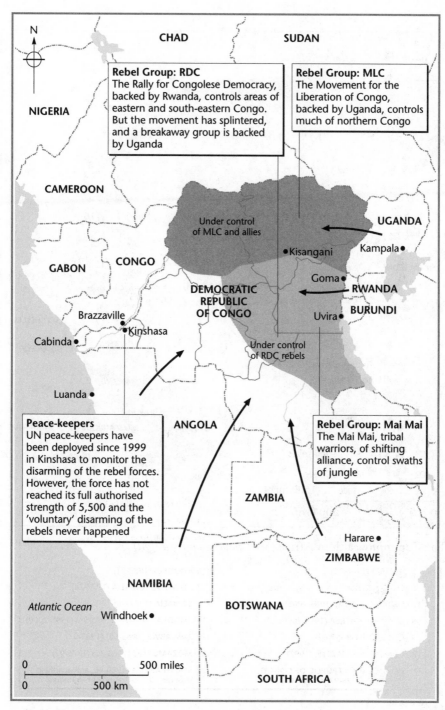

Rebel Group: RDC
The Rally for Congolese Democracy, backed by Rwanda, controls areas of eastern and south-eastern Congo. But the movement has splintered, and a breakaway group is backed by Uganda

Rebel Group: MLC
The Movement for the Liberation of Congo, backed by Uganda, controls much of northern Congo

Under control of MLC and allies

Under control of RDC rebels

Peace-keepers
UN peace-keepers have been deployed since 1999 in Kinshasa to monitor the disarming of the rebel forces. However, the force has not reached its full authorised strength of 5,500 and the 'voluntary' disarming of the rebels never happened

Rebel Group: Mai Mai
The Mai Mai, tribal warriors, of shifting alliance, control swaths of jungle

CHAD

SUDAN

NIGERIA

CAMEROON

UGANDA

Kisangani

Kampala

GABON

CONGO

DEMOCRATIC
REPUBLIC
OF CONGO

Goma

RWANDA

BURUNDI

Brazzaville

Uvira

Cabinda

Kinshasa

ANGOLA

Luanda

ZAMBIA

Harare

ZIMBABWE

NAMIBIA

Atlantic Ocean

Windhoek

BOTSWANA

SOUTH AFRICA

0 — 500 miles
0 — 500 km

Africa's Great War *(See Chapter Thirty-Seven)*

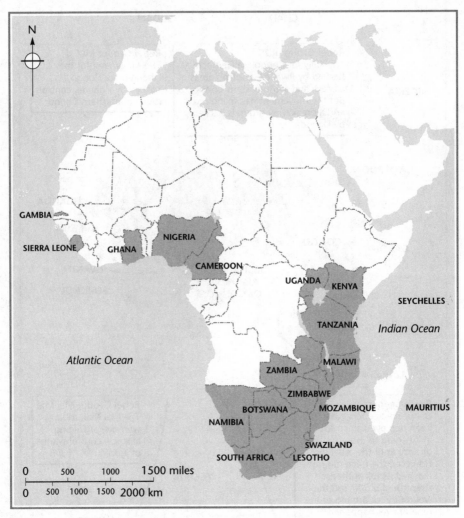

The Commonwealth in Africa *(See Chapter Thirty-Eight)*

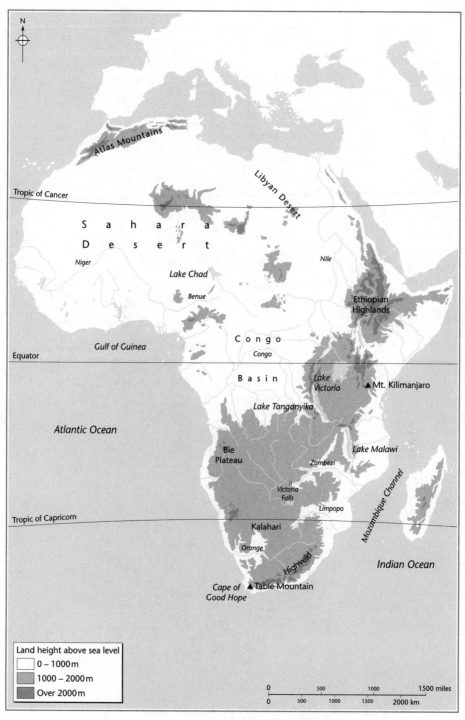

A Geographical Map of Africa

1945

THE IMPACT OF WORLD WAR II

When World War II came to an end in 1945 the European colonial powers thought to resume business as usual in their empires; but this was not to be. Huge changes in the world's power structures were about to take place while the climate in which the maintenance of European empires appeared to be part of the natural political order was disintegrating under a range of new pressures. These included the marginalization of Europe by the emergence of the two superpowers, the coming of the Cold War and, everywhere, nationalist demands for independence. Moreover, much of the groundwork necessary for the transition to independence had been laid during the war even though this had not been the intention. Britain may have fought its last imperial war, as historians were later to suggest, but it was the last imperial war in more senses than one.

When the war began in 1939 the African empires of the European powers were intact and few colonial administrators or politicians of the metropolitan countries had given much thought to the possibility of African independence or, if they had, it was in vague terms of a long-distant future. The war was soon to change such perceptions; indeed, it would call into question the very existence of colonialism:

> In the first place, the spectacular reverses suffered at the beginning of the war by the two main colonial powers effectively destroyed their semi-conscious assumption that they had a natural right to rule the 'uncivilized' world. In Africa this assumption had been strengthened by a widespread acceptance of it even among the natives – to the extent at least that white power was assumed to be invincible.[1]

The collapse of France in 1940 dealt a massive blow to French prestige in Africa, and the struggle for colonial loyalties that followed between the Free French

1

and the Vichy regime did not help. And though black Africans rallied to France's defence, the relationship between the French and their colonial subjects had been profoundly altered: 'But the realisation that she actually needed their help, that they were no longer being lectured like children but appealed to as brothers, was clearly going to make it difficult to retain an authoritarian system of government after the peace.'[2] From 1940 onwards progress for a French imperialist 'would imply closer integration with the mother country, and political maturity would mean not the rule of Africans by Africans – which after all had existed before the imperial power arrived – but the participation of Africans as Frenchmen in the government of a greater France.' Or so, for a while, it was to seem.[3]

The crisis for the British came early in 1942 with the fall of their impregnable, as they thought, bastion of Singapore to the Japanese. This was not just a traumatic defeat but, far more significantly, the defeat of whites by non-whites. *The Times* described the fall of Singapore as 'the greatest blow, which has befallen the British Empire since the loss of the American colonies... British dominion in the Far East can never be restored – nor will there be any desire to restore it – in its former guise.' Moreover, another blow to imperialism in Asia, the bulk of the Asian populations remained spectators from start to finish of the war while Churchill, the arch-imperialist, was obliged to promise independence to India in return for its co-operation during the hostilities. The fact that Britain, though battered, had not been invaded by Germany and was carrying on the war made it easier for it to call for assistance from its imperial subjects to help save the Empire. Ironically, the response of many Africans to this call ensured that after the war the empire was doomed since, during the course of the struggle, Britain had forged an instrument for its termination by teaching its black soldiers the nationalism essential to its demise. Another factor arising out of the war was the rapid increase of British demand for colonial products – for example, spices from Zanzibar to replace those normally imported from the Dutch East Indies, which had been overrun by the Japanese. The added flow of money to the colonies that resulted became an extra source of confidence for the breed of new nationalists that was emerging.

In British East Africa, the outbreak of war led to a suspension of politics, both white and black, and when Italy entered the war on the side of Germany in 1940 the government of Kenya suppressed a number of African political organizations, including the most important one, the Kikuyu Central Association, and interned their leaders. On the other hand, Commander F. J. Couldrey, editor of the *Kenya Weekly News,* was the first leading European in a colony dominated by white settlers, to say openly in a BBC broadcast to East Africa, that the colony could not achieve self-government by Europeans alone but that it had to be on the basis of all races 'co-operating'.[4] Indeed, World War II was to prove an event of major importance for the peoples of Kenya: 'Out of a total of 280,000 men recruited in the East African Forces (including men from Nyasaland, Northern Rhodesia and British Somaliland, as well as from the East African territories proper), some 75,000 came from Kenya, a figure representing a little under 20 per cent of its total adult male African population.'[5] Over the war years a considerable amount of money in family allowances was paid into the African reserves; at the same time the demand by the army for agricultural and livestock products ensured a steady market for the tribes that were able to supply them.

But the main consequence was certainly the immense widening of the experience of most of the men recruited. Many served in the Middle East and the Far East, as well as nearer home in other parts of Kenya, Madagascar and Ethiopia. They came into contact with men of other tribes, and with Europeans, Indians and Arabs of all classes. They saw that the traditional superiority of European and Asian was by no means accepted outside East Africa. And in their army training they were given both formal and informal education – it was, for example, the policy of the army to make as many *Askari* as possible literate and also able to speak basic English. Many soldiers received technical training of various kinds, and after the end of the Japanese war the army opened schools of general and technical training, at a simple level, for soldiers before their disbandment.[6]

Another outcome of the war for the three territories of East Africa was the growth of co-operation between them. It was necessary to co-ordinate a plan of defence and to develop joint action in providing manpower and foodstuffs. On 1 August 1940, an East African Economic Council was created. Ironically, foreshadowing events that still lay in the future, the Ugandans complained that such co-operation was working too much in favour of Kenya.

As Waruhiu Itote, better known as the Mau Mau General China, was to write in his book *Mau Mau in Action*, 'Several of our leaders had been in the Kenya African Rifles during World War II, including Dedan Kimathi and myself.'[7] In Uganda 'The Second World War did much to disturb [the] state of unruffled calm. There was, in the first place, some draining away of manpower. At the peak of recruitment in 1944 nearly 55,000 men were serving in the army, and many more spent short periods in military labour organizations.'[8] During the years 1919 to 1945 there was no African political activity against colonial rule in Uganda but in 1945 disturbances in Buganda indicated that Uganda, like much of Africa, was moving into a more hostile political stance although there had been little evidence of open hostility towards Britain while the war lasted and many Ugandans (a total of 76,957) had enlisted in the Pioneer Corps, the East Africa Medical and Labour Services and the King's African Rifles. Tanganyika became similarly engaged in the war effort as Kenya and Uganda. Its soldiers, serving with the King's African Rifles, took part in the campaigns against Italy in Somaliland and Ethiopia that destroyed the Italian empire in East Africa. Later troops from Tanganyika were involved in the campaign of 1942 to overthrow the Vichy French Government in Madagascar. In June 1943 soldiers from Tanganyika formed part of the 11th East African Division that sailed to Ceylon in preparation for the Burma campaign. It was the first occasion in which the King's African Rifles were to serve in active operations outside the African continent. Altogether, 87,000 Tanganyika Africans were conscripted for war service; it was assumed by the colonial authorities that when they returned home demands for African rule would become more insistent. Given its small size, Zanzibar made a substantial contribution to the imperial war effort and large numbers of Zanzibaris served in medical, signals, transport, docks and education units of the armed forces. The sum of £12,000 was raised for war charities and an additional £15,383 was subscribed for fighter aircraft for Britain. Zanzibar also raised a local naval force, a volunteer local defence force, and turned the police into a military body.[9]

It was a somewhat different story in British West Africa where the army had a bad reputation as a symbol of foreign rule. Nonetheless, in the Gold Coast, over the years 1946–51, ex-servicemen played a critical role in the general political upsurge that occurred in that territory. Despite the fact that the West African colonies did not have white settler minorities to contend with and were generally seen as more politically advanced than those of East Africa, official white attitudes were no further advanced. 'Though African soldiers had rendered distinguished service to the Commonwealth in World War II, little consideration was given at that stage to the possibility of commissioning officers from the ranks.'[10]

The war also eliminated two European powers from the African colonial scene. It ended any possibility of Germany making a colonial comeback, an outcome that would certainly have been on the cards had Hitler been victorious, and Italy lost its African empire. Instead, 'British, Indian, white South African and Rhodesian troops, as well as Sudanese, King's African Rifles and soldiers from the Royal West Africa Frontier Force, invaded Italy's East African possessions. By July 1941 the last Italian forces surrendered in Ethiopia.' By May 1945, the total number of Africans serving in British military units (combatants and auxiliaries) came to 374,000 while the total from all colonies (excluding

India and the Dominions) came to 437,000 so that Africans formed the majority of these colonial forces. White soldiers from South Africa numbered 200,000 while Southern Rhodesia contributed 10,000 whites, 14,000 Asians and 76,000 black soldiers in auxiliary services. South African losses amounted to 8,681 men, the combined losses of the colonies to 21,085 men.[11]

Many of these black soldiers learned new skills, for example, as clerks or truck drivers, and they travelled widely to India, Burma, Palestine and other countries where they learned new ideas and obtained a broader outlook on the world and its politics. Another aspect of the war was an increase in colonial government controls: for example, trade through government marketing boards set the foundations for the state infrastructures of the future. All together 'The importance of overseas experience in India and Burma in World War II by both East and West African troops can scarcely be overestimated: more than any other single factor this exposure helped to bring the colonies politically into the modern world.' Contacts took place with the Indian Congress Party but 'the total effects of Asian service were to open the eyes of African soldiers to developments in other territories under imperial rule, to dispel the notion of European invincibility and to develop personal maturity. The respect which ex-servicemen afterwards commanded both in urban and rural areas gave them an important status in subsequent political, social and economic development.'[12] This was certainly true but, as the returned African soldiers also found, they were not accorded the respect as fighting men by Britain that they deserved. In November 1945 *West Africa* magazine published letters from West African soldiers still in India, under the heading 'Appeal for more recognition'. One such letter, signed 'Yours very faithfully, R.W.A.F.F. Boys in India', began as follows:

> Sir: -We have been reading in the *Times of India,* and other allied newspapers since V. J. Day. Once and again we have heard it beamed to the world on the wireless – a phrase, *'and others.'* This embarrasses us and hundreds of our country-mates who hold this view; that causes tears to becloud our sense of vision when we ask to who on earth these six letters – 'others' – might refer...

Later in the letter they list the numbers of allied prisoners released from Japanese camps – British, Australian, Dutch, American, Indian, Others. According to a note from Delhi, the Indian press revealed that

> more than 77,000, and 49,000, West and East African troops respectively took part in most of the strongest battles, fought under the worst

conditions, at one time or the other in Burma since late in 1943 up to V. J. Day.

Later, in this revealing letter, the writers continue as follows:

> We were only too pleased, however, when the *RWAFF News* Victory Supplement of Sept. last carried pictures of our regiment and national heroes and 'happy warriors'. Equally when *West Africa*, on 22 September, revealed, under the heading: 'You have learnt to be leaders' that 'A special correspondent of *The Times,* present on the occasion, commented acidly the other day that, at the Japanese surrender after the Burma campaign, the Indian Army was not officially represented; although out of a million troops engaged, about 700,000 were Indians – and nearly 80,000, he added, were West Africans (whose ultimate total in the Far Eastern campaign substantially exceeded 100,000, making it the largest of any of the Colonial Forces engaged)…

Africans, they discovered, were not the only imperial subjects to be downgraded or to have their contributions ignored on such occasions.[13]

DE GAULLE AND FRENCH COLONIAL AFRICA

On 30 January 1944, General Charles de Gaulle presided over the opening session of a conference in Brazzaville, the capital of French Equatorial Africa, to discuss French colonial policy after the war, most especially that relating to sub-Saharan Africa. De Gaulle had called the conference in his capacity as chairman of the Free French 'Committee of National Liberation'. Back on 18 June 1940, when de Gaulle had broadcast that France was not finally defeated, he had done so on the basis of the existence of an empire as yet untouched by the Germans. 'Had there been no empire, there would have been no Free French territory. For two and a half years Brazzaville, capital of French Equatorial Africa, was also the provisional capital of what claimed to be the government of France.'[14] De Gaulle was able to draw much support from French Equatorial Africa (AEF) and many Africans volunteered for service with his forces. AEF came to be described as 'the cradle of the French resistance movement.' By 1942 there were 10,000 men from AEF alone serving with General Leclerc's Free French Army and many of them were to take part in Leclerc's trans-Saharan march from Chad to Bir Hakeim. In Dahomey in 1948, 58 per cent of the electorate of 54,000 were either ex-servicemen or serving soldiers whose military service had given them French citizenship rights and thus the vote. African soldiers from areas with strong martial traditions had a high respect for their French officers whom they regarded much as they did their chiefs. Their officers responded to this regard with a paternalistic sense of responsibility.

Thus, although in general both Britain and France (the two principal colonial powers in Africa) had received remarkable support during the war from their African colonial subjects, this was not true everywhere, and at Setif in Algeria an ominous incident warned of grim times ahead. Situated in the Tell Atlas range, Setif was the centre of the Setif province of Northern Algeria. In 1945 it was the scene of an angry uprising against French rule that acted as a prelude to the Algerian war of 1954–62. On 8 May 1945, riots broke out in Setif when the police challenged Algerian Muslims who were carrying nationalist flags during the celebrations of the Allied victory over the Germans in Europe. Their action was a protest at continuing colonial rule. In the disturbances, which followed the first demonstration, about 100 European settlers were killed; then, in retaliation, between 6,000 and 8,000 Muslims were massacred. Official French statements claimed that 88 Frenchmen and 1,500 Algerians had been killed as a result of the anti-riot operations carried out by the police and military. On the other hand, the nationalists claimed that 45,000 Algerian people were killed. Independent observers placed the death toll at between 10,000 and 15,000, which was far higher than the official French figures but much lower than the nationalist ones. The accuracy of the figures was less important than the fact of a massive and brutal reprisal, which 'gave notice' that the French settlers and the colonial authorities would oppose ruthlessly any moves towards independence. Ferhat Abbas, then the outstanding Algerian nationalist figure, was arrested and his organization, *Les Amis du Manifeste et de la Liberté* (AML), was proscribed. Further disturbances took place in October 1945 and May 1946. A pattern of violence had been established which would erupt again in 1954 to dominate Algeria for the next eight years.

By the end of the war the African colonies faced two kinds of challenge: the need to rebuild and redirect economies and services that had been geared to a war effort; and the fact that vast new horizons had been opened up to those Africans who had served with the British or French forces, sometimes thousands of miles away from the African continent. 'Although the prognostications of many officials in 1945 – that the experiences of the troops would lead to immediate disturbances after their return to the reserves – were not fulfilled in the event, none the less these experiences were to have a lasting effect.' One immediate result was the remarkable growth of African associations in the various colonies. Though, as historians have noted in relation to Kenya[15]:

In 1945 there were many lines of dissension apparent – pastoralists against agriculturalists, Bantu Kavirondo against Luo of Kavirondo, all other tribes against the Kikuyu. This last antagonism became very apparent when the Mau Mau movement failed so signally to spread beyond the borders of the Kikuyu. In short, the tribalist had become the nationalist – had had to become so if he were ever to be more than a petty local politician.

Here indeed was one of the most fraught questions that would face the new generation of African leaders that was soon to make its bid for independence from colonial rule. Only as nationalists could they appeal across tribal divisions for solidarity against the common colonial enemy. And, once successful, they were likely to find their new nations again splitting along tribal lines.

INDEPENDENT AFRICA

In 1945 only four African countries – Egypt, Ethiopia, Liberia and South Africa – were independent and even in these cases independence was only partial. Although Britain had formally ended its protectorate over Egypt in 1922, the country had remained within its 'sphere of influence' and was to continue to do so until Nasser's rise to power in the 1950s. The Anglo-Egyptian Treaty of 1936, which allowed Britain to station troops in the country, only came to an end in 1954 when Britain agreed, reluctantly, to remove its Suez base to Cyprus. During World War II Egypt had been a major British base and from it British forces had eventually driven the Germans out of Libya, which Britain then occupied to end Italian imperial control. The Suez Crisis of 1956 represented a final attempt by Britain to employ old-style imperial gunboat diplomacy in order to dictate policy to Egypt. It was a spectacular failure and thereafter Egypt was fully independent.

Ethiopia's independence goes back to antiquity, at least as far as the Kingdom of Aksum (circa 500BCE). A powerful nation had been created in the nineteenth century and alone in Africa Ethiopia was able to repel the European advance during the Scramble for Africa when Menelik II defeated the invading Italians at Adowa in 1896. Mussolini's Italy avenged this defeat when his forces invaded Ethiopia in 1935 although they only established their control over the country in 1936 after protracted fighting. Ethiopia was liberated from the Italians in 1941 and South African forces captured Addis Ababa on 6 April. Haile Selassie (who had fled as an exile to Britain in 1936) wished to enter the capital at once but was held back by the British on the grounds that they feared the Italians in the city would be massacred. Haile Selassie decided to ignore the British and went ahead to enter Addis Ababa on 5 May 1941, just five years after the Italians had seized the city in 1936.

Immediately, difficult relations developed between Selassie and the British liberators who now became the effective occupying power. Prior to the fall of Ethiopia (January–March 1941) the British had rejected the idea of a protectorate but once they found themselves in control of the whole country they procrastinated over recognizing full Ethiopian sovereignty until 1948, thus proving Haile Selassie to have been right in mistrusting their motives. When the Emperor appointed his first cabinet on 11 May 1941, the British representative Brigadier Lush said this could not be effective 'until a peace treaty had been signed with Italy'. Later, Britain chose to regard the Emperor's ministers as no more than advisers to the British administration. Meanwhile, the South African troops who had liberated Addis Ababa tried to maintain the colour bar that had been instituted by the Italians. Sir Philip Mitchell, chief British political officer in the Middle East, urged a hard line on London and pressed the Emperor to abide by British advice 'in all matters touching the government of Ethiopia' and to levy taxes and allocate expenditure only with 'prior approval of HMG'. Haile Selassie regarded these and other proposals of Mitchell's as intolerable and telegraphed Winston Churchill to ask why a treaty between the two countries was so long delayed. Finally, on 31 January 1942 an Anglo-Ethiopian agreement recognized Ethiopia as an independent sovereign state.

This was not the end of the story. Haile Selassie reluctantly agreed that a 'reserved area', a stretch of country adjacent to the French Somali Protectorate (the Territory of the Afars and Issas – later Djibouti) which was then under Vichy rule, should remain under British military administration, as well as another stretch of land along the line of the Addis Ababa–Djibouti railway, and the Ogaden region, which had been Ethiopian until 1936 when the Italians annexed it to Italian Somaliland. At the time of these negotiations the British were organizing the Ethiopian Army and police on modern lines. British reluctance to quit Ethiopia continued after the end of the war and the British occupation was bitterly resented after 1946 when wartime strategic considerations no longer applied. In that year the British Foreign Secretary, Ernest Bevin, proposed that the British occupied areas except for the line of rail should be severed from Ethiopia and joined to British Somaliland and to former Italian Somaliland, then a trusteeship territory under British control. Only on 24 July 1948 did Britain at last agree to withdraw from the Ogaden, although withdrawal from the other reserved areas did not take place until November 1954.

An independent republic of Liberia was proclaimed in 1847; its creation as a state had been the work of American philanthropists who wished to assist freed slaves of the American south find a home in Africa. Although it was never to be an American colony, for most of its existence Liberia remained an economic colony of US interests and was to be deeply influenced by the American connection. Finally, of these four independent African countries, South Africa under white rule had become fully independent in international law with the passing of the Statute of Westminster in 1931 although it remained a Dominion of the British Empire and Commonwealth. From 1910 (the Act of Union) through to 1990 the whites demonstrated their determination to hold onto power exclusively and in the process created the apartheid state which became the focus of bitter and long intractable problems in Southern Africa.

PAN-AFRICANISM: THE MANCHESTER CONGRESS 1945

The concept of pan-Africanism was born at the beginning of the twentieth century when the first Pan-African Congress, sponsored by the Trinidad barrister H. Sylvester Williams, was held in London during 1900. A second congress was held in the immediate aftermath of World War I at Paris in 1919; this Congress called upon the Allied and Associated Powers to establish a code of law for the international protection of the natives of Africa. Independence at this time was simply not on the agenda. There were three more congresses between the wars – in 1921, 1923 and 1927. Then, in October 1945, just after the end of the war, the Sixth Pan-African Congress was held in Manchester, England, and was attended by such notable leaders-in-waiting as Jomo Kenyatta of Kenya and Kwame Nkrumah of the Gold Coast. The atmosphere had changed markedly since 1919 and the scent of independence was in the air. The Congress was to call for an end to colonialism, its members declaring in their manifesto, 'We are determined to be free.' The Congress became a landmark, a starting point for the coming independence struggles. The Congress rejected colonialism in all its forms, its participants equating economic with political imperialism and determining to crush both forms of alleged exploitation so as to achieve their independence. As the leading African participants were to discover when they returned home, they had achieved considerable prestige by taking part in the event.

A number of African and black leaders visited Britain at the end of the war to take part in a world trade union conference and some of them agreed to organize a Pan-African Congress: they included George Padmore, C. L. R. James, Peter Abrahams, Kwame Nkrumah and Jomo Kenyatta. The latter spent much of the summer of 1945 in Manchester helping the joint secretaries, Padmore and Nkrumah, to organize the Congress. In the end 200 delegates attended the Congress, which was opened by the Lord Mayor of Manchester.

The Congress chairman was the American Negro, Dr W. E. B. duBois. Kenyatta attended in his capacity as General Secretary of the Kikuyu Central Association (KCA), although this was still banned in Kenya. Kenyatta was chairman of the credentials committee and rapporteur of the East African section. The Congress was not militantly anti-European and recognized the value of European contributions in Africa. Although duBois, an icon of the Negro struggle in America, was there, the Congress was dominated for the first time by African leaders and not American Negroes. Kenyatta was elected President of the Congress, and in this role he was described as 'sane, humorous and intelligent'. The congress convinced Kenyatta that it no longer made sense to struggle for piecemeal reforms: 'He firmly decided, therefore, even at this time, that the paramount design must be to unite all the people of Kenya, and the purpose must be nothing short of independence.'[16] Later, when he returned to East Africa, 'Like Nkrumah, who returned to the Gold Coast in 1947, Kenyatta found a fertile field for his activities. In both of these British territories there was much post-war discontent. From both, men had gone to serve in the Army. In service overseas they had become aware of the aspirations of the nationalist movements in Asia. But their horizons had been widened in another way: they had learned simple skills such as driving and hoped to maintain the higher standard of living they had in the Army.'[17]

The Congress was as important to Nkrumah as it was to Kenyatta. Nkrumah had gone to the United States in 1936 and taken a degree in economics and sociology at Lincoln University in 1939. In June 1945 he arrived in London. Almost at once he became involved in the forthcoming Pan-African Congress. George Padmore from Trinidad was then the leading figure in the Pan-African movement and Nkrumah became joint organizing secretary for the Congress with him. Although the West Indian figures, led by W. E. B. duBois, then aged 73, Padmore and James, were veterans of such events they did not dominate the proceedings at Manchester; rather, a younger more dynamic African contingent of men, who would shortly rise to fame as nationalist leaders in their own countries, took the lead. The list of participants (in hindsight) was impressive: from the Gold Coast came Joe Appiah and Ako Adjei; from Sierra Leone Wallace Johnson; from Nigeria Obafemi Awolowo, later to be the leader of the Action Group, Premier of Nigeria's Western Region and a towering political figure in his country; from Kenya Jomo Kenyatta; from Nyasaland Hastings Banda; the black novelist Peter Abrahams from South Africa; and Amy Garvey, the widow of Marcus Garvey. The previous Pan-African Congresses had been dominated by middle-class intellectuals but at Manchester there were workers, trade unionists, a radical student element and no representation from Christian organizations. The emphasis was on African nationalism.[18] The Congress argued for Positive Action *à la* Gandhi, preferably without violence. There were demands for economic independence to prevent imperialist exploitation and hopes were expressed for an African and Asian resurgence to end colonialism and resist both imperialism and communism. The conference called on Africans everywhere to organize themselves into political parties, trade unions, co-operatives and other groups to work towards independence and political advance. DuBois proposed the first resolution: that colonial peoples should determine to struggle for their freedom, if necessary by force. Nkrumah proposed the second resolution: a demand for independence for all colonial peoples to put an end to imperialist exploitation, this to be backed up by strikes and boycotts if needed. It was Nkrumah who coined the final phrase: 'Colonial and Subject peoples of the World Unite.' The Congress was a success: it brought together Africans who would change the face of the African continent over the next 20 years and it called on Africans everywhere to prepare themselves for political change. Nkrumah was to remain in London for two years, and became deeply involved in pan-African and West African causes. He became secretary of the West African National Secretariat (WANS), which had been established in 1945 to co-ordinate plans for the independence of British, French, Portuguese and Belgian territories. Then, in November 1947, he returned to the Gold Coast to become secretary of the United Gold Coast Convention (UGCC) and so began the political career that would make him the first leader of an independent Ghana.

West Africa, then as later the journal of the politics of the region, gave the Manchester Congress a cool reception, questioning the wisdom of the programme and wondering whether their radical ideas would receive support back in Africa. It asked whether nationalist leaders would be 'more likely to get redress of grievances by agitation at large or by concentrating effort on particular areas which are under one government, perhaps even individual matters within such areas'. Later, the same editorial suggested that 'Calling for national independence, in its old sense of unfettered freedom of action, is unreal. It is now a meaningless term. This Kingdom has not got it. Really no country has. Far more to the point is the proposal of a central secretariat to link and organize reform movements in various countries.' An accompanying article covering the main activities of the conference referred to the conditions of 'coloured' people resident in Britain. 'Speaker after speaker protested against the operation of a colour bar against Africans. Mr J. Kenyatta (Kikuyu Central Association) proposed a resolution, which was carried unanimously, "that the pan-African Federation should take all practicable steps to press the British Government to pass an Act of Parliament making racial discrimination illegal".' Many speakers appealed for unity and co-operation among Africans. 'Mr. W. Johnson (Sierra Leone) said: "African students in Britain should not go back to their homes in Africa assuming a role of superiority, but should co-operate with the workers' movements for the advantage of all coloured peoples.'" The largest African contingent came from West Africa and many grievances were aired, especially the problem of illiteracy. 'Mr. W. Johnson dwelt on what he stated as the main problems of Sierra Leone. The first was mass illiteracy. After 157 years of British rule only five per cent of the people were literate, and he estimated that the average number of children each school is expected to serve is 5,000... He described the medical facilities of the Colony as almost nil.'[19] Many of these concerns would remain at the centre of Africa's development problems to the end of the century. In their manifesto at the end the delegates said: 'We are determined to be free... Therefore, we shall complain, appeal and arraign. We will make the world listen to the facts of our conditions. We will fight in every way we can for freedom, democracy, and social betterment.'

The participants in the Manchester Congress were in the vanguard while the policy makers of the Metropolitan powers still hankered for a return to the status quo *ante* 1939. The euphoria of the peace was succeeded all too quickly by the rising tensions of the Cold War that would soon become the all-absorbing priority of the United States and Europe. Indian independence in 1947 acted as the spur to independence demands everywhere else. And as Britain and France, the greatest of the colonial powers, at once discovered in the new world climate, the Americans were either hostile to or uncomprehending of European imperialism and the arguments to justify it. The Soviet Union was even more hostile to colonialism in all its forms (except its own) and was to gain considerable mileage in the years that followed championing liberation movements. The Cold War accelerated nationalist trends while the hostility of the two superpowers to European imperialism put extra and unwelcome pressures upon London and Paris.

THE UNITED NATIONS

An additional pressure for change came from the newly created United Nations which was to play a vital role in bringing about African independence, though it is unlikely that its founding fathers, the victorious Allied leaders, saw this as one of its principal justifications. Winston Churchill, Britain's wartime leader, who had crafted the Atlantic Charter that became the model for the United Nations Charter, certainly did not. As he had famously said shortly after the American entry into the war, with US President Franklin D. Roosevelt as his prime target: 'I did not become his Majesty's first minister in order to preside over the liquidation of the British Empire.' Nonetheless, the liquidation was to come quickly enough. African nationalists were quick to see the importance of the new world body: as a court of appeal in their struggles; as a positive ally in dismantling imperial controls; and as a link to the two superpowers that were both, for their own realpolitik reasons, opposed to the old European empires. Although the primary emphasis of the United Nations in 1945 was upon the maintenance of world peace and this is reflected in its Charter, Clause 2 of Article 1 (chapter one), Purposes and Principles, was crucial to nationalists seeking independence: 'To develop friendly relations among nations based on respect for the principle of equal rights and self-determination of peoples, and to take other appropriate measures to strengthen universal peace.' However, it is Chapter XI, Declaration Regarding Non-Self-Governing Territories, Article 73, which was to prove crucial to the independence process:

> Members of the United Nations which have or assume responsibilities for the administration of territories whose peoples have not yet attained a full measure of self-government recognize the principle that the interests of the inhabitants of these territories are paramount, and accept as a sacred trust the obligation to promote to the utmost, within the system of international peace and security established by the present Charter, the well-being of the inhabitants of these territories...

After this preamble, five clauses cover actions promoting self-government and require the colonial powers to 'transmit regularly to the Secretary-General for information purposes' details of progress under these heads. Chapter XII, International Trusteeship Council, deals with the status of the former mandates of the League of Nations, and Chapter XIII sets up The Trusteeship Council. In the years after 1945 the United Nations would be appealed to again and again by African nationalists as they escalated their pressures and demands for independence from the colonial powers and saw the United Nations as their most important ally in this regard.

In British Africa much was expected of the new Labour government that came to power in 1945. Its prime minister, Clement Attlee, was committed to Indian independence, which was achieved in 1947. What would his government do about Africa? It ended the system of indirect rule when it called for efficient democratic local government in the colonies and encouraged the formation of trade unions and co-operative societies. In 1946 new constitutions were introduced in the Gold Coast and Nigeria. As Lord Hailey commented: 'The Constitutions ordained for the Gold Coast and Nigeria in 1946 were the most typical expressions of [the] attempt to effect a reconciliation between the underlying principles of Indirect Rule and that growing body of African opinion in West Africa which saw the attainment of self-government based on parliamentary institutions as the objective of Colonial rule.'[20] In Nigeria Nnamdi Azikiwe had founded the National Council of Nigeria and the Cameroons (NCNC) in August 1944 and in 1946 he launched an all-out campaign against the new (Richards) Constitutions (which he claimed would move the country towards independence too slowly) even before they came into force. In August 1947 J. B. Danquah and other professional and businessmen launched the United Gold Coast Convention (UGCC) party in the Gold Coast Colony with the slogan 'Self-Government in the shortest possible time'. In 1949 the UGCC was to be superseded by Nkrumah's Convention People's Party (CPP) with the even shorter slogan: 'Self-Government now'. On the other side of the continent Jomo Kenyatta, who had greatly enhanced his prestige by his prominent role in the Manchester Congress, returned to Kenya in 1946 to take the Manchester ideas back to Africa and work out the political struggle there.

BELGIUM AND PORTUGAL

In the Belgian Congo the official policy in the 1940s and 1950s was to gear the *évolués* (Africans considered to have achieved minimal European standards) to be accepted by Belgians and initiated into European ways. Progress was slow and as the colonial lawyer, M. Piron wrote of *évolués* in a paper submitted to the Colonial Congress of 1947: 'Although they daily apply themselves to drawing nearer to the European, the latter often snubs them, pokes fun at their efforts or at the very least, is unaware of them'. Slowly, Belgian attitudes began to change with the end of the war. 'The provisions of the United Nations Charter on dependent territories jolted official thinking in Belgium, as elsewhere. It was decided that something must be done for the *évolués*.' Not a great deal was done, however, while the patronising tone in which *évolués* were addressed could only have given offence. Thus, in 1949, the provincial commissioner of Equateur addressed a *cercle des évolués* in the following terms: 'Have no illusions; it is not you who will profit from the true civilization... Your children will attain a higher degree of civilization than you, but will still not profit integrally from it. Only your children's children will be (truly) civilized.'[21]

Portugal's approach to its African Empire in the 1930s and 1940s took little account of Africans. They were there to perform a task. In its plainest terms this policy 'meant the perpetuation of Portugal in Africa – the prolonged presence of a culturally superior Christian community in a backward, if not barbaric, land. Certainly the African population had no place in the practical policies Lisbon wanted to implement in Africa.'[22] Over this period the number of Portuguese settlers in Angola and Mozambique was increased rapidly: in Angola from 30,000 in 1930, to 44,000 in 1940, to 78,000 in 1950, and 170,000 in 1960; and in

Mozambique from 18,000 in 1930, to 27,500 in 1940, to 48,000 in 1950, and 85,000 in 1960. Even as the leading colonial powers were coming to terms with nationalist demands for independence, the Portuguese were moving in the opposite direction. Overpopulation and poverty in Portugal, the promise of financial success in Africa, and the government's subsidies had their effect at last. 'In the 1950s Angola and Mozambique took on more and more the aspect of white colonies.' More Portuguese women came to make their homes in Africa. The preamble to the second Overseas Development Plan of 1958 stated: 'We must people Africa with Europeans who can assure the stability of sovereignty and promote the "Portuguesation" of the native population.' No item in the budgets for the development plan had direct relevance to African interests or necessities. The *regime do indigenato* was fundamentally neither to encourage nor to suppress: it was to maintain. 'The African world in Angola and Mozambique was to exist in a kind of limbo while the Portuguese got on with their job of making a success of white colonial development. Under the regime Africans had few rights but many responsibilities, the most important being to pay taxes, to farm as directed, and to supply Portuguese private and state enterprises with cheap labour.'[23]

In 1943 Colonial Minister Vieira Machado wrote: 'It is necessary to inspire in the black the idea of work and of abandoning his laziness and depravity if we want to exercise a colonizing action and protect him... If we want to civilize the native we must make him adopt as an elementary moral precept the notion that he has no right to live without working.' Such thinking was to show little advance over the succeeding 20 years, despite events elsewhere on the African continent. The Galvao Report of 1947 revealed the true state of affairs in Portuguese Africa. Henrique Galvao was a Colonial Inspector and Deputy for Angola in the National Assembly in Lisbon. His revelations of corruption, forced labour and bad administration were at first ignored. He then delivered them in the National Assembly in 1948, which led to his downfall, and in 1952 he was arrested for subversive activities. Galvao had attacked the retarded development of Angola and Mozambique, the absence of health services, forced labour and under-nourishment, the migration of 2,000,000 African workers to the Congo, the Rhodesias and the Union of South Africa. His report put the infant mortality rate at 60 per cent, the workers' death rate at 40 per cent. The natives, he said, were simply regarded as beasts of burden, and special condemnation was reserved for the practice of herding workers off to government projects huge distances from their villages.[24]

Basil Davidson, who was to become identified with the liberation movements in the Portuguese African colonies, argued that the vast majority of Africans could in no way benefit from Portuguese racial tolerance. On the contrary, they were subject to the closest possible regulation as 'natives' (though distinguished from the one per cent – plus or minus – *assimilados*). They were available for impressments to forced labour or migrant labour under contractual conditions over which they had no control of any kind and when Portuguese voices were raised in protest at such treatment they were either ignored or repressed as mischievous or subversive. In 1951, expecting admission to the United Nations, the government of Dr Salazar introduced constitutional changes, which abandoned the use of the word 'colonies', and transformed these territories, at least in juridical terms, into 'overseas provinces.' That portion of their populations accepted as being of civilized status – less than one per cent of blacks – was at the same time empowered to send elected deputies to Lisbon's single-party parliament.[25]

HOLDING ON

In 1945 Britain, of the colonial powers, emerged from the war best able to set the pace in decolonization and undoubtedly gained great kudos by its withdrawal from India in 1947. Despite this, however, many colonial attitudes were rooted in the past and much of the prevailing wisdom assumed that India was a special case (there had been no sensible option) and that the rest of the Empire would continue under British rule into an indefinite future. In 1941 the indefatigable Africanist, Lord Hailey, had advised the government that African politics were quiescent with little sign of discontent apart from pockets in the Gold Coast and southern Nigeria. And in May 1943 a British War Cabinet committee minute stated: 'many parts of the Colonial Empire are still so little removed from their primitive state that it must be a matter of many generations before they are ready for anything like full self-government.' When the war ended plans existed to build an imposing new Colonial Office; the view was long term. Over 1945–46, as a result of the war with Japan, British forces were to be found in French Indo-China and the Dutch East Indies, sometimes with surrendered Japanese troops under their command, and these forces held the fort for these other European imperial powers until the former rulers could return in sufficient strength to resist local demands for independence. In Indo-China the British were able to hand over to French troops (hurrying to the East) in October 1945 but in the Dutch East Indies they had to wait until November 1946 before Dutch forces came to relieve them.

As a Colonial Office official put it as the Indian Empire slid away: 'Africa is now the core of our colonial position; the only continental space from which we can still hope to draw reserves of economic and military strength.'[26] Professor John Gallagher, delivering a lecture at Oxford in 1974, said:

Britain's decision to quit India was not intended to mark the end of empire. Quitting India has to be seen in the light of the simultaneous decision to push British penetration deeper into tropical Africa and the Middle East… so the same Labour government, which had liquidated most of British Asia went on to animate part of British Africa. Africa would be a surrogate for India, more docile, more malleable, more pious… No one really knew what geological jackpots Africa contained, because general neglect had skimped the necessary surveys. Here might be God's Plenty which would rescue the Pilgrim British economy from the Slough of Despond.[27]

Despite growing African demands for self-government the British Labour government was far more imperialist in its outlook and intentions than popular myth ever suggested. In December 1950 in Washington for a meeting concerning the Korean War and rearmament, Britain's Prime Minister, Clement Attlee, asked the Chief of the General Staff, General Sir William Slim, who was accompanying him, how long it would take him to create from the African colonies an army comparable in size and quality with the Indian Army, an army which Britain could use to support its foreign policy just as the Indian Army had done. Slim, who had spent his life in the Indian Army, said he could do something in eight or 10 years, but to do anything really worthwhile would take at least 20 or probably more. Thus, though Labour had given India independence, it had no intention of abandoning the rest of the Empire and saw Britain controlling its African colonies for many years to come.[28]

Independence

NIGERIA SETS THE PACE

The Federation of Nigeria became a fully independent state and a sovereign member of the British Commonwealth on 1 October 1960. The country then had a population of 32 million. The transfer of power from Britain to Nigeria, which took place on the Lagos Race Course, was a grand affair. Ministers arrived by motorcade in ascending order of importance with the Federal Prime Minister, Alhaji Abubakar Tafawa Balewa, coming at the end. Princess Alexandra, representing the Queen, came last of all, escorted by mounted police. In the ceremony that followed the Princess handed the bound Nigeria Independence Act of the British Parliament to the Prime Minister. In his speech of acceptance, Abubakar said:

> At last our great day has arrived, and Nigeria is now indeed an independent sovereign nation... This great country, which has now emerged without bitterness or bloodshed, finds that she must at once be ready to deal with grave international issues. This fact has of recent months been unhappily emphasized by the startling events, which have occurred in this continent. (He was referring to the Congo.)

Paying a compliment to the departing British, Abubakar said:

> Today we have with us representatives of those who have made Nigeria – representatives of the regional governments, of the missionary societies, and the banking and commercial enterprises... Today we are reaping the harvest which you have sowed... May God bless you all. This is an occasion when our hearts are filled with conflicting emotions...
>
> But do not mistake our pride for arrogance... we are grateful to the British officers whom we have known, first as masters, and then as leaders, and finally as partners, but always as friends.

That night the Union Jack was lowered for the last time to be replaced by the green and white flag of Nigeria, and Britain's largest and grandest African colony had become independent.

Two years earlier, broadcasting to Nigerians on the occasion of New Year 1958, the new Federal Prime Minister Abubakar had said: 'It is no good blaming the British any more when things go wrong: these days are gone... we must blame ourselves, because we shall have made the wrong decision. And remember too that... the world is watching us, waiting to see whether we can rise to the occasion.' At the beginning of 1960, independence year, Shell-BP announced that oil had been found in commercial quantities in Nigeria and that the company hoped therefore to remain in the country for many years. The (combined) company then had a 50–50 profit-sharing agreement with the Nigerian government. In July 1960 the British Parliament passed the Nigeria Independence Bill. During the second reading the Secretary of State for the Colonies, Iain Macleod, said:

> The Nigerian Government have made great progress in the training of their own Civil Servants and are following the practice of this country of insulating the Civil Service from politics by establishing executive public service commissions. The need is going to exist for substantial numbers of overseas officers to continue giving the devoted service they have rendered to Nigeria over the years.

The basis of this new member of the Commonwealth was all the better, he said, because 'what he was putting before the House was primarily the work of Nigerians'. Mr Macleod went on to wish Nigeria well and said he was sure they could speed it on its way to independence with utter confidence.

> I have great admiration for that magnificent country and for her noble people. I am convinced that the world will be a better place for the emergence of Nigeria in its own sovereign right as a country, and I rejoice to think that this great country, in complete friendship with ourselves, is going now to take its place on the stage of world affairs.[1]

The handover of power by Britain to Nigeria went very smoothly yet even as Nigeria was preparing for independence in mid-1960 those preparations were overshadowed by events in the Belgian Congo which erupted into civil chaos in July, just three months before Nigeria became free, to affect all perceptions of African independence both inside and outside the continent for years to come. Moreover, Western attitudes to Africa, then and later, would be dominated by

Cold War considerations that persuaded the West to regard the new states as its protégés and to treat them after independence much as they had treated them when they were still colonies.

THE CONGO CATASTROPHE

Independence for Nigeria and 15 other African colonies during 1960 may have been achieved with considerable aplomb and many ceremonies – it was, after all, the *annus mirabilis* of African independence (some Africa enthusiasts spent the year travelling from one independence ceremony to another) – but it was a very different story in the Belgian Congo. The territory had had a benighted history: created as a personal fief by King Leopold II who employed the explorer Henry Morton Stanley as his agent, its recognition as the Congo Free State by the main powers had enabled Leopold to exploit it with such ruthless brutality that, following the revelations of the British Consul, Roger Casement, of endless mutilations and other atrocities, the Belgian parliament finally, in 1908, deprived the king of control and turned his territory into a colony. The Belgians were not good colonialists and when the Belgian Congo achieved independence in 1960, the Belgians acted as though little had changed in reality and assumed that they would remain to control it, or at least to control its vast mineral wealth.

In the immediate period prior to independence Patrice Lumumba emerged as the only nationalist with an appeal beyond his own ethnic group, unlike the other contenders for power. Lumumba had become an *évolué* in 1954 at a time when he believed in Western values and had not yet become critical of Belgian colonialism. In 1955, when King Baudouin and the Belgian Minister for the Colonies visited the Congo, Lumumba's prestige rose when he had talks with them. But his new status made him bitter enemies among both the Belgian administrators and his political rivals and from 1956 onwards the administration kept him under constant surveillance. He was invited by the government to visit Belgium in 1956 but on his return to the Congo was arrested on charges of embezzlement when he had worked in the Post Office. He claimed that he had only taken the responsibility for thefts by his staff, but the authorities were determined to get him out of the way and he was sentenced to two years in prison; the Minister for the Colonies, however, reduced his sentence to one year. His term in prison served only to enhance Lumumba's reputation in the eyes of the nationalists.

On 5 October 1958 Lumumba founded the *Mouvement National Congolais* (MNC), an anti-tribal pan-African political party that drew its support from across the country. Earlier that year, when in August President de Gaulle of

France had offered the French Congo across the river membership of the French Community or full independence, Lumumba had at once drafted a demand for full independence for the Belgian Congo. Over the next two years Lumumba attempted to organize a mass party but was thwarted by the tribalism of his opponents. Belgium tried to bring an end to the growing nationalist pressures and unrest by finally moving towards independence. A round table conference was called in Brussels for January 1960. By then Lumumba was again in prison, blamed by the authorities for an outbreak of violence in Stanleyville the previous October. It was soon obvious to the Belgians that the conference could not succeed without Lumumba's presence and so he was released from prison and arrived in Brussels on 26 January. At the conference only Lumumba insisted upon a single Congo while Moïse Tshombe, whose power base was the mineral rich Katanga Province, proposed an independent Congo made up of a loose confederation of semi-autonomous provinces. The Belgians reconciled themselves to Lumumba's stand and set 30 June as the date for independence. By this time Lumumba had become a thoroughgoing nationalist. At the end of December 1959 he had said: 'Independence was not a gift to be given by Belgium, but a fundamental right of the Congolese People.' In the general elections of May 1960 Lumumba's MNC won 37 of 137 seats and, with its allies, formed the strongest block. The other parties were regional and tribally based. On 23 June Lumumba was asked to form a government. He made Joseph Kasavabu president. Lumumba had no experience of government. Once it was clear that the Belgium Congo was about to become independent the big powers moved to fill the vacuum that was about to be left by the departure of the Belgians. What concerned them were the Congo's immense mineral wealth and its strategic position straddling the centre of the African continent.

King Baudouin came to preside over the Congo's independence on 30 June and gave a speech that even an ardent Belgian royalist must have recognized as biased and undiplomatic. He said: 'The independence of the Congo is the crowning of the work conceived by the genius of King Leopold II.' He lauded Belgian achievements and then concluded with a lecture: 'The dangers before you are the inexperience of people to govern themselves, tribal fights which have done so much harm, and must at all costs be stopped, and the attraction which some of your regions can have for foreign powers which are ready to profit from the least sign of weakness...' After listening to Baudouin's speech Lumumba, who had not been scheduled to speak, nonetheless took the podium and replied to the King. After a brief introduction, he said:

For, while the independence of the Congo has today been proclaimed in agreement with Belgium, a friendly country with whom we deal on an equal footing, no Congolese worthy of the name will ever be able to forget that independence has only been won by struggle, a struggle that went on day after day, a struggle of fire and idealism, a struggle in which we have spared neither effort, deprivation, suffering or even our blood.

The struggle, involving tears, fire and blood, is something of which we are proud in our deepest hearts, for it was a noble and just struggle, which was needed to bring to an end the humiliating slavery imposed on us by force.

Such was our lot for 80 years under the colonialist regime; our wounds are still too fresh and painful for us to be able to forget them at will, for we have experienced painful labour demanded of us in return for wages that were not enough to enable us to eat properly, not to be decently dressed or sheltered, nor to bring up our children as we longed to.

Lumumba went on to speak of the contempt with which blacks had been treated, the despoliation of their land, the use of different laws for black and white, the treatment of black politicians, the difference in housing conditions, the exercise of a colour bar, shootings and imprisonment. He finished by saying all this was now at an end.[2]

King Baudouin was not amused.

Five days later the *Force Publique* (the Army) mutinied and locked up its Belgian officers. Belgium sent troops to restore order as though the Congo were still a colony and Lumumba, who was shocked by this Belgian reaction, appealed to the United Nations to help him restore order. On 11 July, encouraged by the Belgians and the mining conglomerate *Union Minière du Haut Katanga,* Moïse Tshombe declared the secession of Katanga Province from the Congo. On 14 July Lumumba broke off relations with Belgium and demanded the immediate withdrawal of all Belgian troops. The United Nations Security Council voted to intervene and on 16 July began sending troops to the Congo. Lumumba toured African states seeking help but only Ghana responded with a token force. On 5 September President Kasavubu dismissed Prime Minister Lumumba who responded by dismissing the President. On 14 September Colonel Joseph-Desiré Mobutu, whom Lumumba had made chief of staff of the army, seized power in the first African coup of the independence era.

At this point Lumumba had only four months to live. He would probably not have been a great leader. He had no experience, and the Congo, at that time and later, required a ruler with a ruthlessness that he did not possess. He had fire and a certain vision that placed him above the tribalism of his rivals and he wanted to create a country that would rise above narrow parochial concerns. But he was never given a chance and the Western powers, led by a resentful Belgium that had not wanted to grant independence in the first place, and the United States whose Cold War concerns and determination to safeguard the Congo's wealth for the West made it indifferent to democratic forms, between them masterminded the destruction of Lumumba. However he might have performed, had he been left alive to run the Congo, in death Lumumba became a martyr to the African nationalist cause and a constant reminder of the cynical big power politics that would be directed at the continent in the following decades as its newly independent states struggled to find their place on the world stage. The name Lumumba became synonymous with African distrust of the West's intentions.

In a letter to his wife, written from captivity shortly before his murder on 17 January 1961, Lumumba said:

> All through my struggle for the independence of my country, I have never doubted for a single instant the final triumph of the sacred cause to which my companions and I have devoted all our lives. But what we wished for our country, its right to an honourable life, to unstained dignity, to independence without restrictions, was never desired by the Belgian imperialists and their Western allies who found direct and indirect support, both deliberate and unintentional amongst certain high officials of the United Nations, that organization in which we placed all our trust when we called on its assistance.

At the end of the letter, he said:

> History will one day have its say, but it will not be the history that is taught in Brussels, Paris, Washington or in the United Nations, but the history which will be taught in the countries freed from imperialism and its puppets. Africa will write its own history, and to the north and south of the Sahara, it will be a glorious and dignified history.[3]

The true and brutal story of Lumumba's death was only fully revealed in 2000 – 40 years after his death when all Africa, finally, was independent – and then as the result of a book, based on newly declassified Belgian archives, by Ludo de Witte.[4] The Belgian Prime Minister, Guy Verhofstadt, and the Foreign Minister, Louis Michel, who came from a different political generation to those who had presided over independence in 1960, were so shocked by the revelations in the book that they persuaded the Belgian parliament to set up an official inquiry.

Uncompromisingly, de Witte says: 'Belgium bears the greatest responsibility in [Lumumba's] murder. Belgians had the leadership of the whole operation – from [Lumumba's] transfer to Katanga, to his execution and the disappearance of the body.' It was only a week after independence that Belgian officials decided to eliminate Lumumba. On 14 July 1960 the Belgian ambassador to NATO told participants in a North Atlantic Council meeting: 'The situation (in the Congo) would be better if the Congolese President, Prime Minister and Minister of Information all disappeared from the scene.' The Belgians did not forgive Lumumba for his unscheduled speech at the independence ceremony on 30 June when, in the presence of King Baudouin, he accused Belgium of having brought 'slavery and oppression to the Congo'. A few days later the Belgians were again outraged when Lumumba dismissed the Belgian officers of the *Force Publique* and demanded the immediate withdrawal of Belgian troops who, on 11 July, had bombarded Matadi after some Europeans in the town had been killed. The United States, also, was determined to prevent Lumumba from calling in Soviet troops to help him reverse the secession of Katanga (11 July) and Kasai (8 August). At a meeting of the National Security Council (NSC) on 18 August President Eisenhower personally gave the go-ahead to the CIA to work out how to eliminate Lumumba.[5] Minutes of the NSC sub-committee on covert operations for August 1960 were to the point: 'It was finally agreed that planning for the Congo would not necessarily rule out "consideration" of any particular kind of activity which might contribute to getting rid of Lumumba.' According to Madeleine Kalb[6], on 26 August 1960 Richard Bissell, the CIA special operations chief, asked his special assistant for scientific matters, Dr Sidney Gottlieb, to prepare biological materials for possible use in the assassination of an unspecified African leader. This plan did not proceed.

There are a number of accounts, more or less sensational, that both the Americans and the Belgians were determined on the elimination of Lumumba and were not concerned as to the method. The Americans wanted him eliminated for Cold War reasons, the Belgians more from a sense of pique and the desire to see the independent Congo ruled by a more pliable figure more favourable to their interests. At that time Cold War considerations were rarely absent from any Western approach to African affairs and Lumumba's nationalism was seen by the West as a threat to its strategic interests in the region, not least because of the country's enormous mineral wealth encompassing, as it did, copper, diamonds, rubber, uranium and cobalt. As de Witte claims, the Belgian Foreign Minister Pierre Wigny wrote on 10 September: 'the authorities have the duty to make Lumumba unharmful.'

On 14 September Colonel Joseph-Desiré Mobutu, supported by the CIA, carried out a coup to neutralize Congolese politicians. He was provided with funds by Belgium. Various plans were considered while Lumumba was under house arrest, guarded by Ghanaian UN troops who, in turn, were surrounded by Mobutu's soldiers who had orders to arrest him. On 27 November Lumumba escaped from house arrest and headed for Stanleyville (Kisangani), his main support base, but he was seized on 2 December by some of Mobutu's soldiers at Port Francqui (Ilebo) on the Kasai River. The UN forces made no attempt to rescue Lumumba, instead obeying orders from the UN High Command in New York not to intervene 'to hinder Lumumba's pursuers' or to take him into 'protective custody'. It was a sordid story with many unsavoury ramifications but at the heart of it was the determination of the United States (through the instrument of the CIA) and Belgium to eradicate Lumumba, whom they regarded as a Communist and a threat to their geopolitical and economic interests. In the end Lumumba was handed over to his arch-enemy Moïse Tshombe in Katanga; he was sent there on 17 January 1961 in company with Maurice Mpolo, one of his ministers, and Joseph Okito, the deputy president of the senate. After being tortured the three men were shot dead that night. Washington had known since 14 January the plan to murder Lumumba and did nothing to prevent it. Tshombe's government did not announce his death until 13 February. Belgian officers were involved in the murder plan and assisted at the execution. Swedish UN soldiers at Elizabethville airport witnessed the arrival of Lumumba and saw him taken away but did not intervene. Four days after Lumumba's execution the Belgian police commissioner Gerard Soete and his brother cut up the bodies of Lumumba, Mpolo and Okito and dissolved them in sulphuric acid.

The US interest in the Congo was in its mineral wealth. In 1958 the Congo produced 50 per cent of the world supply of uranium, most of which was purchased by the United States, 75 per cent of the world's cobalt and 70 per cent of its industrial diamonds.[7]

Forty years after the events described here Belgium formally apologized for its role in the assassination of Lumumba in 1961. In a symbolic gesture of reconciliation with its former colony, the Belgian Foreign Minister, Louis Michel, read the apology during a parliamentary debate on a report into the killing of Lumumba. The parliamentary report had been released in November 2001 and though it failed to link the Belgian government directly to the killing, it found that ministers bore a 'moral responsibility' by failing to act to prevent the assassination. M. Michel said: 'The government believes that the time has come to present the family of Patrice Lumumba and the Congolese people its profound and sincere regrets and apologies for the sorrow that was inflicted upon them by this apathy.' He said Belgium would donate £2.3m to create a Patrice Lumumba Foundation to finance 'conflict prevention' projects and study grants for Congolese youths. Not exactly a fulsome apology but better than nothing.

NORTH AFRICA: THE IMPACT OF WORLD WAR II

The imperial tradition in North Africa differed substantially from that to the south and much of the region had been fought over during the war. Egypt had been Britain's Middle East headquarters throughout World War II, and though never a British colony, it had been very much part of Britain's sphere of influence. Libya had been conquered by Italy, not without difficulty, over the years 1911–1914, and became part of its African empire. The French had proclaimed a protectorate over Tunisia in 1881 while in Algeria, the jewel of their African empire, they had fought a 50-year war from 1830 onwards before they mastered the whole vast territory. France had also established a protectorate over Morocco, in 1912, after a confrontation with Germany. In Sudan, Britain and Egypt had established a Condominium in 1898, following the defeat of the Khalifa's forces at the battle of Omdurman, although for the ensuing 60 years it was the British who became the effective rulers of the country. Demands for independence swept across this whole vast region in the immediate aftermath of the war and in most cases had been realized before Harold Macmillan delivered his 'Wind of Change' speech in South Africa at the beginning of 1960, the *annus mirabilis* of independence.

LIBYA

Following Montgomery's victory over Rommel at the battle of El Alamein in November 1942 the German forces were driven out of Egypt and British forces then occupied Italian Libya while Free French forces moved into the Fezzan region. The British administered Libya until 1950. The United Nations, which had undertaken overall responsibility for Italy's former colonies at the end of the war, finally decreed that Libya should become independent on 24 December 1951 under King Idris, the former Amir Muhammad Idris, a hero of the resistance against Italian rule. The country immediately faced serious political, financial and economic problems – it was then rated one of the poorest territories in the world – while it was necessary to foster a sense of national unity and identity since loyalties were predominantly to the village and tribe rather than to the newly independent state. In March 1953 Libya joined the Arab League and then in July of that year it concluded a 20-year treaty with Britain: in return for bases Britain would grant Libya £1 million annually for economic development and a further £2.75 million annually for budget expenses. In

September 1954 Libya concluded similar base agreements with the United States for US$40 million over 20 years. A friendship pact with France was signed in 1955 and a trade and financial agreement with Italy in 1957. During these years, as the parameters of the Cold War were established, all Libya had to offer was its strategic position, hence these arrangements with the Western powers. However, over the years 1955–56 Libya granted concessions to prospect to several US oil companies and by the end of 1959 15 companies had obtained petroleum concessions in Libya. In June 1959 the first major oilfield was discovered at Zelten in Cyrenaica, and by July 1960 there were 35 petroleum wells in production, giving a yield of 93,000b/d. Further discoveries and a huge increase in oil output between 1962 and 1966 transformed the future prospects of the country.

THE ALGERIAN WAR OF INDEPENDENCE

The Setif uprising of 1945 served as the prelude to the Algerian war of independence, which was to be one of the most savage of Africa's freedom struggles. In 1946, the *Parti du Peuple Algérien* (Algerian People's Party) emerged from underground to transform itself into the *Mouvement pour le Triomphe de Libertés Démocratiques* (MTLD) (Movement for the Triumph of Democratic Liberties). However, a year later Ahmed Ben Bella and a group of militants broke away to form the *Organisation Secrète* (OS) (Secret Organization), which advocated armed struggle. Agitation and violence increased over the next few years and then, in March 1954, nine members of the OS led by Ben Bella and Belkacem Krim formed the *Comité Révolutionnaire pour l'Unité et l'Action* (CRUA) (Revolutionary Council for Unity and Action) to prepare for an armed struggle. CRUA soon changed to become the *Front de Libération Nationale* (FLN) (National Liberation Front). The FLN advocated democracy within an Islamic framework and said that any resident of Algeria would qualify for citizenship in the new state. On 1 November 1954, the FLN and its armed wing, the *Armée de Libération Nationale* (ALN) (National Liberation Army), launched the revolution in the city of Algiers with attacks on police stations, garages, gas works and post offices. FLN strategy consisted of widespread guerrilla action with raids, ambushes and sabotage that would make the administration of the colony unworkable.

Abroad the FLN carried on a diplomatic offensive directed at the UN and at securing Arab support. The civil war that followed saw the authorities resort to torture to obtain information, and the nationalists to using terrorist tactics. Events in Algeria and the course of the war dominated the policies of every French government for the next eight years. In February 1955 Jacques Soustelle came to Algeria as governor general and attempted some reforms, but these proved too few and too late. Massacres of Europeans were followed by summary executions of Muslims. At the beginning of 1956 Guy Mollet became prime minister in Paris. He appointed the moderate General Georges Catroux as governor general of Algeria but when Mollet himself visited Algiers, angry Europeans bombarded him with tomatoes. Mollet subsequently gave way to European pressures, and Catroux's term as governor general was ended abruptly. He was replaced as governor-general by the pugnacious Socialist Robert Lacoste, who initiated a policy of pacification or forcible repression. During 1956 the FLN obtained growing support from the Arab world, especially from Nasser's Egypt. Following the independence of its neighbours, Morocco and Tunisia, the FLN was able to seek sanctuary across the borders in those two countries. France had hoped to gain friends in the Arab world by giving independence to these two Maghreb countries, allowing it to concentrate upon holding Algeria (which by then was known to have oil and natural gas resources) but the strategy did not work. By mid-1956 the active, militant FLN was probably no more than 9,000 strong though it received support from a large part of the Algerian population. France, on the other hand, had built up its armed forces in Algeria to about 500,000 troops.

In 1957 the French government refused to contemplate independence for Algeria, instead sending large numbers of additional troops to crush the rebellion. Apart from the wealth Algeria represented and the presence in it of one million *colons* (white settlers) the attitude of the French government and of the army had undoubtedly been hardened by the defeat in 1954 at Dien Bien Phu in French Indo-China. The army, in particular, was determined not to suffer another such humiliation. Both sides now increased the ferocity of their fighting and responses while the extensive use of torture by the French 'paras' to obtain information helped the army win battles but lost it the struggle for 'hearts and minds'. The French authorities erected barbed-wire barriers along the borders with Morocco and Tunisia, where, by then, an estimated 25,000 to 30,000 FLN troops were based.

The war was responsible for great brutalities: whole populations were moved so as to cut them off from the FLN guerrillas, and by 1959 an estimated two million Arabs (25 per cent of the population) had been forced to leave their villages. Many of the whites in their territorial units became brutal in their tactics and indiscriminate in their targets, while in certain police stations and military detention centres a new breed of torturer appeared. The members of the FLN could be equally brutal toward the *colons*. During the last days of April 1958 the Maghreb Unity Congress, consisting of representatives from Morocco, Tunisia and the FLN, met in Tangier, Morocco. The Congress recommended the creation of an Algerian government in exile and this was proclaimed on 18 September 1958 in Tunis with Ferhat Abbas as its leader. In Paris the Algerian war had provoked a full-scale political crisis, which brought Charles de Gaulle to power on 1 June 1958. Though at first de Gaulle gave the impression that he was the strong man who would secure the future of the *colons* in Algeria, in fact he recognized the inevitable and presided over a French withdrawal. After holding a referendum to approve the new French constitution, de Gaulle offered to negotiate a ceasefire with the FLN and on 16 September 1959, he promised self-determination for Algeria within four years. A series of secret meetings between the FLN and the French government followed and a cease-fire was finally signed on 18 March 1962 at Évian-les-Bains. Meanwhile, the *colons,* who felt they had been betrayed, and sections of the army turned to extreme methods that included an army insurrection in April 1961 led by General Raoul Salan. De Gaulle assumed emergency powers and the revolt was crushed.

In a referendum of 1 July 1962, 91 per cent of the Algerian electorate (6 million) voted for independence and only 16,000 against. President de Gaulle declared Algeria independent on 3 July and the Algerian government in exile came to Algiers in triumph; three days of rejoicing by the nationalists followed.

The European population of Algeria now departed on a massive, very nearly total, scale and the majority, nearly one million, returned to France. These included most of the country's senior administrators, although about 10,000 teachers courageously decided to remain, often finding themselves in exposed positions. In addition, there were the Algerians (*harkis*) who had remained loyal to the French and had often fought for them as well; many of these also quit independent Algeria and settled in France. Official French estimates of the casualties of this war were 17,250 French officers and men killed and a further 51,800 wounded between 1954 and the end of 1961, with an additional 1,000 French civilian casualties. This same estimate suggests that 141,000 nationalists were killed, although the FLN was to claim that Muslim casualties were four times that number. Other FLN claims suggested a high of one million killed altogether – fighting, in concentration camps, under torture or during the removal of populations. The war also witnessed massive destruction of property – schools, bridges, government buildings, medical centres, railway depots, social centres and post offices, as well as farms and great damage to crops. The war, which straddled the events of the *annus mirabilis* of1960, was to have a long-lasting and traumatic impact upon Franco-Algerian relations for decades to come.[8]

MOROCCO AND TUNISIA

As the violence escalated in Algeria from 1954 onwards France felt obliged to accelerate moves towards independence in the neighbouring states of Morocco and Tunisia in the hope (unfulfilled) that this would appease the Arab world and so make France's continued hold on Algeria easier to maintain. In fact, once they were independent both countries provided support for the FLN in Algeria and France was obliged to construct barbed-wire frontier barriers to prevent Algerian nationalists moving back and forth across these borders.

In 1939 the Moroccans rallied to the cause of France and in 1942 to the Free French Movement. The *Istiqlal Party* (Party of Independence) was formed in 1943. It demanded full independence for Morocco with a constitutional form of government under Sultan Muhammad ibn Yusuf. Demands for independence were low level for some time after the end of the war but tensions between traditionalists and modernists came to a head in 1953. Sultan Muhammad, who supported the nationalist movement, fell out with the French administration and then, in May 1953, a number of conservative Pashas and Caids asked for his removal and backed the traditionalist leader Thami al-Glawi, the Pasha of Marrakesh, to replace him. Berbers from the countryside moved on the towns in the Pasha's support. As a result, on 20 August 1953 the Sultan agreed to go into exile in Europe but not to abdicate. There were assassination attempts against Muhammad in both 1953 and 1954. Meanwhile, a prince of the Alawi house, Muhammad ibn Arafa, had been appointed Sultan. There were outbreaks of violence through 1954 and into 1955 when Sultan Muhammad ibn Arafa renounced the throne. On 5 November 1955 Muhammad ibn Yusuf was again recognized as Sultan of Morocco and returned to the country from exile. On 2 March 1956 a joint Franco-Moroccan declaration stated that the French protectorate that had been established in 1912 had become obsolete and that the French government recognized the independence of Morocco. France undertook to provide aid to Morocco and to assist in the re-assertion of Moroccan control over the zones of Spanish influence. On 12 November 1956 Morocco became a member of the United Nations.

The pre-independence years in Tunisia were more fraught than in Morocco. After the fall of France in 1940 Tunisia came under Vichy rule; Bizerta, Tunis and other ports were used by Germany and Italy to supply their armies in Libya. The defeat of the Axis in Africa in 1943 saw the restoration of French authority. The Bey of Tunisia, Muhammad al-Monsif, was accused of collaboration and deposed, to be replaced by his cousin, Muhammad al-Amin, who was to rule until 1957. Nationalist agitation for political change, which had been growing throughout the 1930s, was renewed in 1944 but French repression forced the principal nationalist, Habib Bourguiba, to leave Tunisia and establish himself in Cairo. Bourguiba had created the Neo-Destour (New Constitution) Party in 1934.

In 1945, according to a decree issued by the Bey, the French reorganized the Council of Ministers and the Grand Council, which was an elected body with equal French and Tunisian representation, and extended its authority. However, in 1946 the nationalists made an unequivocal demand for independence at a meeting of their national congress. In 1949 Bourguiba returned to Tunisia from Egypt and the following year the Neo-Destour Party proposed the transfer of sovereignty and executive control to Tunisians, with a responsible government and a prime minister appointed by the Bey. The French responded reasonably to these requests and a new Tunisian Government was formed in August 1950 with equal numbers of Tunisian and French ministers. The object of the new government, it was stated, would be the restoration of Tunisian authority in stages in co-operation with France. The European settlers, who represented 10 per cent of the population, opposed all these moves towards independence and more especially in 1951 when the French advisers to Tunisian ministers were removed. These advances, however, collapsed towards the end of 1951 due to a combination of settler opposition and French procrastination.

There were strikes and demonstrations at the beginning of 1952 and in February Bourguiba and other nationalist leaders were arrested on orders of the new resident-general, Jean de Hauteclocque. Violence then spread throughout the country and France responded by imposing military rule. The Neo-Destour Party was proscribed and France then produced new reform proposals. Neo-Destour, however, took its case to the United Nations General Assembly. Further reforms were halted in response to increasing acts of terrorism on the one hand and French repression on the other. However, in December 1952 the Bey, under threat of deposition, signed new French reform proposals but these were repudiated by Neo-Destour. A secret settler counter-terrorist organization, the 'Red Hand', was formed and during 1953 the country came close to civil war.

On 18 June 1954 Pierre Mendes-France was elected prime minister in Paris on promising to make peace in Indo-China within a month. His election and promise followed the surrender of the French at Dien Bien Phu on 7 May that year. African deputies supported Mendes-France with enthusiasm since he showed a genuine interest in reaching an understanding with overseas peoples on their own terms. He succeeded in making peace in Vietnam. Mendes-France then began negotiations that would lead to full internal self-government in Tunisia and he allowed Bourguiba's outlawed Neo-Destour Party to come to power. It was over this policy that the government of Mendes-France was overthrown in February 1955.[9] However, talks between the two sides were resumed in March 1955 and a final agreement was signed in Paris on 2 June.

The agreement gave Tunisia internal autonomy while protecting French interests and leaving foreign affairs, defence and internal security in French hands. Although the majority of the Neo-Destour Party supported this agreement, it was opposed by the extremist wing headed by the exiled Salah ben Youssef, the Communists and the settlers. A split then occurred between the main Neo-Destour Party, led by Bourguiba who had returned to Tunisia in June 1955, and the extremists under Salah ben Youssef, who had returned in September. In October ben Youssef was expelled from Neo-Destour and in November the party Congress confirmed the expulsion of ben Youssef, reaffirmed the position of Bourguiba as party president and accepted the agreement with France while restating its demand for total independence. Following clashes between the two factions of Neo-Destour and the discovery of a plot to prevent the implementation of the agreement, ben Youssef fled to Tripoli in January 1956. Bourguiba began negotiations for full independence at Paris and in a protocol of 20 March France formally recognized the independence of Tunisia. A transitional period followed. Elections were held on 25 March in which the Neo-Destour party won 98 seats in the legislature. Bourguiba became prime minister on 11 April. In the immediate period after independence relations between Tunisia and France deteriorated because France held on to its base at Bizerta to facilitate its war in Algeria, while Bourguiba's attempts to broker a peace that would allow Algeria to achieve independence were not acceptable to France.

THE SUDAN

In 1924 Britain had launched its 'Southern Policy' in the south of Sudan. This had two objectives: to prevent the rise of nationalism, which had already taken root in Egypt, from spreading from Northern Sudan to the south and thence to British East Africa; and to separate the three southern provinces from the rest of the country with a view to their eventual assimilation by the governments of the neighbouring British territories into a great East African Federation under British control. Muslims from the north who were then in the south of Sudan were evicted and a strict regime of permits was introduced to prevent other northerners coming south. In 1948 a legislative assembly was created for the whole of Sudan. Two political groups emerged and one of these, led by the Umma party and supported by the Mahdists, decided to support the colonial (British) government because they suspected Egypt's motives. The other group, led by the Khatmiyye, stood for 'The Unity of the Nile valley' and close co-operation with Egypt. This group distrusted British intentions.

The 1952 revolution in Egypt changed all the plans that had been formed by the British and Egyptians for Sudan. The new Egyptian regime of army officers disowned the King and the pasha class for whom 'The Unity of the Nile Valley under the Egyptian crown' had been an article of faith and the way was cleared for the settlement of the Sudan question between Egypt and Britain. The British position had been to insist that it meant to secure self-determination for the Sudanese as opposed to imposing upon them unity with Egypt as the Egyptians had long desired. Many Sudanese, in any case, would have resisted union with Egypt by force. The new Egyptian regime declared that it was equally willing to grant the Sudanese the right of self-determination. As a consequence of this changed situation an Anglo-Egyptian declaration was signed in 1953, which provided for the Sudanisation of the police and civil service and the evacuation of all British and Egyptian troops over three years in preparation for independence. An international commission supervised elections and the National Unionist Party (NUP) won them with the result that in January 1954 its leader Ismail el-Azhari became the first Sudanese prime minister. The Egyptians had supported the NUP in the elections on the assumption that el-Azhari favoured a union with Egypt. By the time the British and Egyptian troops had been withdrawn Sudanisation was well under way and el-Azhari, who had shifted his position somewhat, made plain that he stood for total independence. Most members of the NUP, in any case, had regarded solidarity with Egypt as a means to an end and not as an end in itself. Further, any suggestion of union with Egypt would have been violently opposed by the Mahdists.

In August 1955 southern troops at Juba mutinied as the prelude to an attempted revolt by the South in which 300 Northern Sudanese officials, merchants and their families were massacred. The disorders were confined to Equatorial Province and did not spread to either Upper Nile or Bahr el Ghazal provinces. Although order was restored the problem of the relations between the South and the North remained unsolved. The representatives of the South said they would only vote for independence if a federal form of government was fully considered and a promise to this effect was made. Although the agreement of 1953 had prescribed a plebiscite and other pre-self-determination procedures, el-Azhari, with the support of all parties, now ignored these conditions and on 19 December 1955 the Sudanese parliament unanimously declared Sudan to be an independent republic. Faced with this *fait accompli* Britain and Egypt recognized the independence of Sudan and this was formally celebrated on 1 January 1956.

EGYPT AND THE SUEZ CRISIS

The close British relationship with Egypt over a period of 80 years began in violence with the bombardment of Alexandria by a British fleet in 1882 and ended in violence with the Anglo-French invasion of the Canal Zone in 1956. The British withdrawal from Egypt and the ignominious collapse of the 1956 attempt to regain control of the Suez Canal marked a turning point in the story of African independence and the end of British pretensions to big power status alongside the United States and the Soviet Union. Suez represented the last British attempt to impose its will on Third World countries by old-fashioned gunboat diplomacy. Britain and France, the two greatest colonial powers, were defeated by Nasser's Egypt, which, in extraordinary circumstances, was supported by both the United States and the Soviet Union, the world's two superpowers.

On 23 July 1952 the 'Free Officers' seized power in Cairo and forced King Farouk to abdicate (he went into exile on 26 July). They then invited Ali Maher, the veteran politician, to form a government under their control. However, another government under General Muhammad Neguib soon replaced that of Maher although real power remained with the nine officers of the Revolutionary Command Council (RCC). On 18 June the monarchy was abolished. Meanwhile, land ownership had been limited to 300 acres a family so that at a stroke the power of the old feudal classes was destroyed. On the abolition of the monarchy the Revolutionary Command Council declared Egypt to be a republic and General Neguib became its first president, prime minister and chairman of the RCC. Colonel Gamal Abdul Nasser, who to this point had remained in the background, although he was the real leader of the Free Officers, became deputy prime minister.

A power struggle followed between the Free Officers and Neguib who was essentially conservative in his politics. He was relieved of his posts, except the presidency, on 24 February 1954 while Nasser became prime minister and chairman of the RCC. In October 1954, following an assassination attempt against Nasser by a member of the Muslim Brotherhood, its leaders and several thousand of its supporters were arrested; in subsequent trials a number of its members were sentenced to death. The event marked the downgrading of the Brotherhood and the beginning of a long confrontation between Nasser and his political successors and the extreme or conservative Islamicists. On 14 November 1954 Neguib was accused of conspiring with the Muslim Brotherhood, relieved of his final post as president and placed under house arrest. Nasser became the acting head of state.

In the meantime, Egypt had relinquished its claim to a joint Egypt/Sudan monarchy while an Anglo-Egyptian agreement of 12 February 1953 ended the Condominium over Sudan and offered the Sudanese the choice of independence or union with Egypt. Although Egypt had believed that Sudan would opt for a union, the overthrow of Neguib, who was half-Sudanese, as well as the suppression of the Muslim Brotherhood had the effect of heightening old Sudanese suspicions of Egypt's motives. A second Anglo-Egyptian agreement of 19 October 1954 provided for the withdrawal of all British troops from the Canal Zone over a 20-month period. Nasser, once in full control, sought influence for Egypt in three areas: the Islamic world, the African world and the Arab world. He also was to play a prominent role in the 1955 Bandung Conference in Indonesia, which led to the formation of the Non-Aligned Movement, and he led Arab opposition to the formation of the Cold War-inspired Baghdad Pact of 1955.

In September 1955 Nasser announced an arms deal with Czechoslovakia, a member of the Communist bloc, and this angered the US Secretary of State John Foster Dulles who adopted the approach that a country was either 'with us or against us'. Nasser also sought funds for his cherished development project, the Aswan High Dam, which was to supply power and extend irrigation for the needs of the country's rapidly increasing population. In February 1956 the World Bank offered a loan of US$200 million for the dam on condition that the United States and Britain lent a further US$70 million and that the Nile riparian states agreed to the construction of the dam. Egypt would provide local services. However, over the following months, growing Cold War strains, Nasser's avowed policy of non-alignment and opposition to the Baghdad Pact, and acceptance of arms from Czechoslovakia between them persuaded the United States and Britain, followed by the World Bank, to withdraw their offers of aid for the dam on 20 July. On 26 July, in reaction to their withdrawal, Nasser nationalized the Suez Canal, claiming he would use the canal dues to finance the Aswan High Dam. The Suez Crisis followed. After prolonged and fruitless negotiations by Britain and France to retain a measure of control over the Canal, the two countries entered into a secret conspiracy with Israel's Prime Minister David ben Gurion. On 29 October Israeli forces occupied the Sinai Peninsula up to the Suez Canal. The next day Britain and France called on Israel and Egypt to cease hostilities and allow their forces – temporarily – to occupy Port Sudan and Ismailia. Egypt refused. At the United Nations Britain and France vetoed US and Soviet resolutions calling upon them to refrain from the use of force. Anglo-French air operations against Egypt began on 31 October and land operations on 5 November. On 6 November, after only 24 hours, Britain's Prime Minister Anthony Eden, under intense US pressure, called a halt to the invasion. A UN peacekeeping force was rapidly assembled and put in place on 15

November, allowing the British and French to withdraw their forces. The Israelis withdrew from the Sinai Peninsula but retained control of the Gaza Strip and Sharm el-Sheikh which commanded the sea approach to Eilat, until they also relinquished control of these two regions, again under intense US pressure.

Despite defeat by the Israelis and invasion by Britain and France, Nasser emerged with immense prestige throughout the Arab world, as though he rather than the two superpowers had defeated Britain and France. For the next ten years his influence and the impact of the Voice of Cairo radio in subsequent Arab and African independence struggles were to be among the most important political factors in the Middle East and in Africa. For Britain the failure of Suez was traumatic, bringing to an abrupt end the illusory period 1945–56 when it had behaved as one of the Big Three with the United States and the Soviet Union. The failure of the joint intervention also led to a deterioration in Anglo-French relations and subsequent French suspicion of the US-UK Anglo-Saxon alliance. Above all, it marked the decline in world influence of the two major imperial powers just as pressures for independence mounted and, by providing a much-needed fillip to nationalists everywhere, accelerated the process of decolonization. Finally, the Suez Crisis led to an increase in Soviet influence in the Middle East and Africa as the USSR undertook to build the Aswan High Dam in the place of the British, Americans and World Bank.

ANGLO-FRENCH RIVALRY IN AFRICA

A factor of permanent importance before, during and after the independence era in Africa was the rivalry between Britain and France, the two great imperial powers, which stretched back to the days of the Scramble for Africa. They vied with each other to demonstrate that the systems they bequeathed their colonies, when finally they were obliged to grant independence, were superior to one another's. At the same time they were allies in sympathy with each other because of the necessity to decolonize. Both, as declining imperial powers, nevertheless wished to perpetuate what influence they commanded. However the subject of imperialism is viewed, the retreat from Africa for Britain and France was hard to accomplish and provoked bitter emotional regrets that were often paralleled by efforts to hold on longer than made political sense. Racism was the worst legacy of imperialism. Superior power allowed the European nations to carve up Africa, and the subsequent control of colonial peoples gave rise to the belief on the part of Europeans that they were innately superior and, therefore, had some special right to rule over other peoples. Such a belief was especially strong in the colonies of white settlement such as Algeria, Kenya and South Africa. This sense of superiority, combined with the settler determination to hold on to a lifestyle that was the direct result of imperialism, produced a resistance to change that in places was to prove explosive, bloody and bitter.

The 1956 French Loi Cadre introduced universal suffrage in French West and Equatorial Africa. But the suffrage was applied to individual territories rather than the two main French blocs and some African politicians saw this as a deliberate move to divide and so enable France to maintain control over weak segments of a vast area. In a final attempt to prolong French control and delay full African independence, de Gaulle organized a referendum throughout the sub-Saharan French territories in 1958 to approve self-government within a French Community. This move was to be thwarted by Guinea's leading nationalist, Sekou Touré, who persuaded the majority of Guineans to vote 'no'. Sir Anthony Eden, Britain's prime minister from 1955 to January 1957, could not adapt to the new anti-imperial age as his disastrous actions over Suez were to demonstrate. Harold Macmillan, who succeeded him, was the first British prime minister to come to terms with the new age and to realize that a multiracial Commonwealth of equals had to replace the British Commonwealth and Empire, yet even for this subtle politician the process was far from easy. Through his son-in-law, Julian Amery, Macmillan learnt of de Gaulle's attitude towards Africa. 'On one occasion, de Gaulle's Prime Minister, Michel Debré, had observed to Amery that, in Africa, either the French and the British – as the two principal colonial powers – had to decide *jointly* to stay, or *both* to clear out. There could be no halfway house, or one future for the British and another for the French.'[10] In September 1958 de Gaulle attempted to create a French African Community, while a year later he offered self-determination to the Algerians. These French moves had a big influence on Macmillan.

TOGO

Togo caused particular problems between Britain and France since the territory had been taken from Germany during World War I and divided between them as a mandate of the League of Nations. Then, after 1945, it became a Trusteeship Territory of the United Nations so that the two colonial powers did not exercise unrestricted jurisdiction over their portions of the territory. After Kwame Nkrumah had come to power in the Gold Coast in 1951 British policy was to support his claim to integrate British Togoland with the Gold Coast in a single independent state. This ended the possibility that Britain might sponsor a single united Ewe state or a reunification of the parts of former German Togoland. Britain, therefore, had to persuade the two British sections of Togoland – the lesser in extent – to accept integration in a greater Gold Coast under the

Convention People's Party (CPP) of Nkrumah. This British policy presented France with an opportunity to demonstrate that it was giving its mandate of Togo a better deal than Britain was to its mandate. France, therefore, made Togo the 'shop window' of the French Union. Between 1951 and 1954 France introduced reforms in Togo, sidelined the more radical nationalists and installed pro-French leaders in office. These developments were carried out under Robert Buron, Minister of France d'Outre-Mer, whose aim was to embarrass Britain and impress the United Nations. Following careful manipulation, France held elections on 12 June 1955 to a new Territorial Assembly in Togo. The *Union des Chefs et des Populations du Nord* (UCPN), which was a pro-French party that had merged with the Progress Party (PTP) of Nicolas Grunitzky, won 92 per cent of the votes in the north while the PTP won 95 per cent of the votes in the south. The radical nationalists boycotted the elections. Grunitzky became a hero – for France. Although Grunitzky demanded full autonomy and an end to UN Trusteeship, he favoured continued membership of the French Union. However, the results of this manipulated election were not going to endure. An article in *Afrique Nouvelle,* the Dakar missionary paper, showed that known supporters of the PTP in Lomé had been enabled to vote 20 or more times while their opponents were prevented from obtaining voting cards.[11] The result was to drive the opposition underground, not to destroy it. On 4 July 1955 Togo's new Territorial Assembly gave its support to Grunitzky's policy and called for full internal autonomy while 'categorically rejecting any form of reunification (with British Togoland) which would result in a loosening of its ties with France'. The Assembly also asserted its intention of remaining 'within the French system'. The opposition, consisting of the *Comité d'Unité Togolaise* (CUT) and its youth wing JUVENTO, was not prepared to accept this defeat. JUVENTO sent an able advocate, Maitre Anani Santos, to present their case before the United Nations. As a result a UN mission toured Togo in August and September 1955, collected 200,000 petitions and noted that public opinion remained divided. On the advice of this mission the UN General Assembly decided in December 1955 that Trusteeship status in both the British and French halves of Togo should not be ended before a plebiscite had been held. In the end the United Nations set 27 April 1960 as the date for French Togo to become independent under Sylvanus Olympio. Prior to 1960 Olympio had worked to make Togo economically independent although his earlier hopes of creating a pan-Ewe state had been defeated by Nkrumah, who had made the counter suggestion that the Ewe could only be united if French Togo joined Ghana. As a result of these manoeuvres relations between Ghana and Togo became strained and Nkrumah accused Olympio of fomenting discontent among the Ewe of Ghana. This defeat caused Olympio to draw closer to France and to suggest a

'Commonwealth *français*' though he refused to join the French Community.[12]

DE GAULLE IN AFRICA

Apart from the three Maghreb territories of Algeria, Morocco and Tunisia, Madagascar in the Indian Ocean and the Territory of the Afars and Issas (Djibouti) on the Red Sea coast, France had ruled its vast African empire as French West Africa from Dakar and French Equatorial Africa from Brazzaville. As the old system became untenable and the concept, first of a regional federation and then of a French Community, was advanced, France fragmented its empire into a number of colonies with the result that a French Community, inevitably, would mean a Community dominated by France – empire in another guise.

The summer of 1958 was eventful for both France and French Africa. On 1 June General Charles de Gaulle was elected prime minister and one of his first concerns was to produce a new constitution that would allow autonomous 'colonies' to become members of a French Union or 'Commonwealth'. A great deal of political manoeuvring followed as de Gaulle pushed his idea of a modern federal state that would include France's African possessions. There was clear threat in his message to African leaders: 'But what is inconceivable is an independent state which France continues to help. If the choice is for independence, the government will draw, with regret, the conclusions that follow from the expression of that choice.' African leaders saw this as blackmail and objected to being forced to choose between independence and the Franco-African Community.[13] As it was finally envisaged, the Community would allow member states to change their status and become fully independent at a future date, but if they did so they would cease to be members of the Community.

The Constitution of this Community was to be submitted to the people of France and Africa on 28 September 1958. As it stood, the constitution failed to meet all the aspirations of the confederalists since full independence and membership of the Community were incompatible. De Gaulle considered that a 'no' vote by a colony would mean it would at once become a foreign country without any special relationship with France. Between 21 and 28 August 1958 de Gaulle toured much of French Africa to explain his concept of a Franco-African Community and the choice he was putting before Malagasies and Africans. He visited Tananarive (now Antanarivo) on 22 August, Brazzaville on 24 August, Abidjan and Conakry on 25 August and Dakar on 26 August. The leading question for Africans was whether they would preserve the right to independence if they voted 'yes'; if not, then they would find it impossible to vote 'yes'. At the same time, few wished to face the economic consequences of a 'no' vote. As Philibert Tsiranana, the head of the government in Madagascar, explained: 'When I let my heart talk, I am a partisan of total and immediate independence; when I make my reason speak, I realize that it is impossible.'[14] De Gaulle, employing his usual elliptical style, avoided giving any clear indication of what evolution, if any, would be possible for member states within the Community. At Brazzaville he said: 'If within this Community a given territory in the course of time, after a certain period which I do not specify, feels itself able to undertake all the burdens and duties of independence, that is its affair, for it to decide through its elected representatives... I guarantee in advance that in such a case metropolitan France will raise no obstacles.' A study of de Gaulle's language shows him as entirely paternalist in his attitudes to France's African subjects – *de haut en bas* – and this had its impact, especially and crucially upon Sekou Touré of Guinea. Abbé Barthelemy Boganda of Oubangui-Chari (Central African Republic) apparently convinced de Gaulle that at least five territories (Oubangui-Chari, Guinea, Senegal, Dahomey and Niger) would vote 'no' if a 'yes' vote was taken to mean an irrevocable renunciation of independence.

In the event, all the French territories except Guinea voted 'yes' to de Gaulle's proposed community but this in fact was only to last for two years because Guinea's vote for immediate full independence spelt the end of the Community before it began. Two years later it disintegrated when all those members who had voted 'yes' opted for full independence. With the exception of Guinea, the referendum throughout French West Africa obtained 'yes' votes in the high 90 per cent range except in Niger where the figure was 78 per cent. Similarly in French Equatorial Africa the vote was a resounding 'yes'. In Oubangui-Chari, Boganda, who was then one of the most influential figures in French Black Africa, secured a 'yes' vote after de Gaulle had assured him that the door to independence would not be irreversibly closed.

THE ROLE OF SEKOU TOURÉ

Sekou Touré was born at a crucial time in Africa's history. He led Guinea's struggle for independence and rejected the idea of membership in a French Community, instead opting for immediate independence in 1958. He was an exponent of Marxism, the one-party state and the cult of personality – he himself had immense charisma, energy and dedication – and his action in rejecting France earned the plaudits of the developing world even if no one else followed his example. Later, sadly, he became a repressive tyrant. The West, at the height of the Cold War, and the former colonial powers in particular, reacted angrily to such rejection of their tutelage, for newly independent African states were expected to behave as grateful allies of the new Cold War order.

When in 1958 de Gaulle decided to hold a referendum throughout France's black African territories, he offered the choice of autonomy within the French Community or total independence and, at first, Sekou Touré was prepared to accept regional federation. But he also wanted to show that he was the one African leader prepared to stand up to the French colonial master. In the negotiations that took place prior to the referendum, France made a number of concessions to the *Rassemblement Démocratique Africain* (RDA), which was the main African party representing all the colonies, so as to ensure a 'yes' vote. The relationship between de Gaulle and Touré was not unimportant. When de Gaulle visited Conakry on 25 August 1958, he gave an ambiguous speech in which he said Guinea could vote 'no', and in which case France would raise no obstacles to Guinea's independence: 'Naturally she [France] will draw the conclusions, but she will raise no obstacles…' In his reply Touré, who regarded de Gaulle's speech as a threat, failed to compliment de Gaulle or show gratitude for what France had done as a colonial power. Instead he made harsh criticisms of French colonial behaviour and referred to Africa's united, independent future. Touré bitterly resented what he saw as de Gaulle's haughty patronage and in September was to say: 'We prefer poverty in liberty to riches in slavery.' But he did not believe that de Gaulle would sever all relations between the two countries, and before the referendum said: 'I shall say "no" to the constitution but "yes" to France.'

In the referendum, under the guidance of Sekou Touré, the voters rejected the idea of a community of self-governing overseas territories by a massive 95 per cent. Guinea 'took' independence on 2 October and as the leader of the *Parti Démocratique de Guinée-Rassemblement Démocratique Africain* (PDG-RDA), Sekou Touré became president. His action and the 'no' vote of one of the smallest countries of the French African Empire effectively undermined de Gaulle's plan for France's overseas territories and through 1960 all the other African territories demanded full independence, although most of them were to remain tied to France economically and militarily.

After the referendum and proclamation of Guinea's independence, Touré tried to present the first government of the new state to the representative of the French government, Governor Jean Risterucci, as if to an acting head of state. De Gaulle, however, was determined to show that to vote against him earned retribution. Risterucci informed the Guinea government that France intended to transfer all French civil servants out of Guinea within two months and that Guinea would receive no further public investment or budgetary aid from France. The Guineans had not believed that de Gaulle would take such action.

Alioune Drame, the Finance Minister, said shortly before the referendum of 28 September: 'France will not dare. It's not in her interests. It would cost her more than it would us.' Neither Drame nor Touré believed that France could cut all its connections with Guinea but, as a French journalist told them, they did not know de Gaulle. On two occasions Touré sent cables to René Coty, the President of France, with copies to de Gaulle; the first was only answered briefly after five days, the second received a longer, more pointed reply to the effect that France's attitude would depend on whether the government of Guinea could cope adequately as a government. This was a damning exposure of France's attitude of superiority towards an ex-colony.

Although there was an obvious element of pique on de Gaulle's part, he also had to demonstrate to those who had voted 'yes' that there was a clear advantage to them for doing so in the form of aid that was not available to those who had voted 'no'. And de Gaulle had to placate his greatest African ally, Houphouët-Boigny, who felt humiliated and angered by Touré for breaking ranks, which action he saw as the beginning of the end of the federal Franco-African Community. De Gaulle believed that the only hope of holding the union together lay in a convincing demonstration of the advantages of being inside as opposed to outside and, therefore, that the sight of Guinea outside and in poverty and chaos would prove the point. Thus, de Gaulle was not prepared to allow an intransigent Guinea to receive the aid and investment open to the other Francophone territories. Although Houphouët-Boigny embarked upon an anti-Touré propaganda campaign, this was not welcomed by the other African leaders who, either secretly or openly, had favoured a 'no' vote but had not felt sufficiently secure to urge such a vote upon their people. These leaders included Abdoulaye Diallo of French Soudan (Mali) and Modibo Keita. Houphouët-Boigny's anger was wasted for Guinea became wildly popular and Touré's action marked the end, or rather the rapidly approaching end, as soon as it had come into being, of the French Community. De Gaulle shrugged off suggestions that his treatment of Guinea would simply drive it into the Soviet camp. By 30 November 1958 Risterucci had completed his task: everything possible had been removed from the country – the crockery had been smashed, the telephones removed, all portable government property taken. Where things were too big to be taken away, they were destroyed. Only 150 French personnel remained of whom 110 were voluntary teachers who lost their job security in France as a result. The French Government also tried to persuade, though mostly unsuccessfully, private firms to stop investing in Guinea.[15] In March 1960 France excluded Guinea from the franc zone.

As a result of its independence the new state was boycotted by France for many years. Between 1958 and 1960 some attempts, mostly by Guinea, were made to heal the breach but they were unsuccessful. Touré moved the country to the political left, partly from conviction and partly as a response to the French reaction to its determination to be independent when the rest of Francophone West Africa opted for association. During 1959 he turned to the Communist countries for support, while urging members of the Community to seek total independence.

Although other Francophone countries all voted 'yes' in the referendum and Touré was expelled from the RDA, it was Touré who became a hero both at home and throughout the colonial world as the man who had dared to say 'no' to de Gaulle, and who, with Kwame Nkrumah, became one of the leaders of the radical Casablanca Group of states.

FRANCOPHONE INDEPENDENCE 1960

Much changed during 1959. Once de Gaulle had offered independence to the FLN in Algeria he recognized the inevitable break-up of his Community. Thus the French Community in Africa lasted only from the time of the referendum of 28 September 1958 when all but Guinea voted 'yes' until the first breakaway in 1960 when Mali became independent on 26 June, to be followed by the rest over the next few months. These developments were probably hastened by the impact of Harold Macmillan's 'Wind of Change' speech delivered at the beginning of February 1960 in South Africa. The end of the French Community, which had been achieved in the first place by France 'balkanizing' its territories of West and Equatorial Africa, came in 1960. The pro- and anti-politics of the French Community became highly complicated and in Niger, for example, the French engineered the fall of Bakary Djibo, who was opposed to the Community but wanted a West African Federation whose members could secede if they wished. It became obvious that with all its talk of autonomy within the Community, France in fact wanted to perpetuate its control and the more obvious this became the more irresistible were the demands for independence. The result, in 1960, was the year of independence. Cameroon became independent on 1 January 1960 and Togo on 27 April but these were Trusteeship Territories of the United Nations and so had escaped the 'yes/no' dilemma of the full colonies. Other territories which achieved independence during 1960 were: Mali and Madagascar on 26 June, Dahomey (Benin) on 1 August, Niger on 3 August, Upper Volta (Burkina Faso) on 5 August, Côte d'Ivoire on 7 August, Chad on 11 August, the Central African Republic on 13 August, Congo (Brazzaville) on 15 August, Gabon on 17 August and Mauritania on 28 November. The final act in this brief story came in September 1960 when France sponsored the admission to the United Nations of 12 independent black

African states (Côte d'Ivoire, Dahomey, Upper Volta, Niger, Senegal, Mali, Chad, Central African Republic, Congo (Brazzaville), Gabon, Cameroon and Togo). Mauritania was vetoed for UN membership by the USSR because Morocco, then pro-Moscow, claimed Mauritania as part of its territory. And so 'The attempt to find a formula which would rationally unite the lands and peoples irrationally conglomerated by French colonial expansion, which would end colonialism but preserve the empire, was at last abandoned.'[16] It was Sekou Touré who had effectively undermined de Gaulle's Community when he secured a resounding 'no' vote in Guinea on 28 September 1958. Apart from the 14 Francophone countries that achieved independence in 1960, the Belgian Congo became independent on 30 June, Somalia on 1 July and Nigeria on 1 October. It was no wonder, therefore, that the year was described as the *annus mirabilis* of African independence.

THE IMPACT OF NKRUMAH'S GHANA

Kwame Nkrumah had returned to the Gold Coast in November 1947 and just short of 10 years later, on 6 March 1957, he led his country to independence as Ghana. It was the first black African colony to achieve independence from its colonial master. During the preceding 10 years Nkrumah had conducted a classic independence struggle, breaking with the United Gold Coast Convention (UGCC) to form his own Convention People's Party (CPP), serving a term in prison, and finally developing an excellent relationship with the colony's last Governor, Sir Charles Arden-Clarke, before the Gold Coast became independent. Ghana created a pattern that was to be repeated, more or less, over the next few years as more than 30 colonies, British and French, also achieved their independence.

Suitable independence celebrations were arranged for more than 100 official guests: there was an independence race meeting, church services, a Miss Ghana contest, a Governor's State Dinner, Convocation at the University, the opening of the National Museum, laying a wreath on the War Memorial, a sailing regatta. On 5 March the Duchess of Kent arrived to represent the Queen and unveiled the new National Monument. Then the Legislative Assembly met towards midnight and Nkrumah made a final statement, concluding: 'By twelve o'clock midnight, Ghana will have redeemed her lost freedom.' The hour struck, the Union Jack was lowered in silence, 'graciously and peacefully', and the flag of Ghana – red, green and gold with the black star of African freedom – was hoisted to a roar of 'Freedom'. Then, having been carried shoulder high on a platform to the old polo ground, Nkrumah made his historic announcement: 'Ghana will be free forever.'[17] The next day was filled with ceremonial, after which the guests departed and Ghana had to face the realities of freedom. In the years that followed Nkrumah's greatest contribution to Africa – though not to Ghana – was to become the focus of the push for African unity. In a prescient comment on Ghana's independence, the director of the London Africa Bureau, Michael Scott, wrote:

> It is likely to have far-reaching effects on French colonial policy which has always been directed hitherto towards the integration of her African territories into the French Union. This aim of policy is being increasingly repudiated by Africans. Already the creation of Ghana and the fulfilment of Britain's mandate in Togoland, by its participation in Ghana's self-government and independence, have brought about a reversal of French policy towards French Togoland and its Constitution as a republic. The demand for self-government independently of the French parliament has been given impetus first by the events in North Africa and now by the creation of the State of Ghana.[18]

Ghana was to be the first stop for Britain's Prime Minister, Harold Macmillan, on his Africa tour of January/February 1960. He spent five days in Ghana. In a forthright editorial, the *Ghana Times* said that Africa has now been 'catapulted to a position where it compels attention, even by those who formerly merely turned up their noses at it'. Mr Macmillan would have to listen to and respect African opinion. It continued: 'British prestige in Africa is at a dangerously low ebb; the treatment being meted out to Dr Hastings Banda and his colleagues of the National Congress in Nyasaland is a disgrace to Christian Britain. The continued imprisonment of Jomo Kenyatta can only be likened to an act reminiscent of Victorian imperialism. This visit offers a wonderful opportunity to retrieve Britain's honour which the Devlin report has discredited in a rather devastating manner.'[19]

THE CENTRAL AFRICAN FEDERATION

After the Conservative Party had won the elections of October 1959 with an increased majority, Macmillan appointed the young, radical Iain Macleod as Colonial Secretary with a brief to 'get a move on in Africa'. As Macleod was to write in the *Spectator* of 17 January 1964: 'It has been said that after I became Colonial Secretary, there was a deliberate speeding-up of the movement towards independence. I agree, there was. And in my view any other policy would have led to terrible bloodshed in Africa. This is the heart of the argument.' Under Macleod's predecessor, Alan Lennox-Boyd, the assumption had been that the colonies of East and Central Africa would take 10 to 20 years to evolve to full independence. Macleod changed that and pushed the pace as he recognized the inevitability of quick independence for East and Central Africa and for his pains was to be denounced as 'too clever by half' by Lord Salisbury, the patriarchal Tory leader in the House of Lords who believed Macleod had betrayed the whites in the Central African Federation as a whole.

The demise of the Central African Federation may be dated from March 1959 when riots in Nyasaland precipitated a crisis. As Macmillan noted in his diary: 'It looks as if the federation plan, although economically correct (since Nyasaland is not "viable") is regarded with such great suspicion by "advanced" native opinion as to be politically unacceptable.'[20] Subsequently, the report on the causes of the riots by Mr Justice Devlin exerted serious pressure on the Macmillan Government since it argued that there was no evidence to support the contention of the Nyasa colonial government that the Nyasaland Congress Party had been plotting massacre and assassination (a bloodbath of the whites) and that Nyasaland, no doubt temporarily, was a police state 'where it is not safe for anyone to express approval of the policies of the Congress Party'. The Devlin Report set off a series of events that culminated in the dismemberment of the Central African Federation at the end of 1963. Although Macmillan initially reacted angrily to the report, which the Government rejected, it may well have sown the first doubts in Macmillan's mind about the future of the Federation. In his brief to Lord Monckton, who was to lead the Commission bearing his name that was sent to work out a new *modus vivendi* for the Central African Federation, Macmillan wrote: 'I am sure that this is one of the most important jobs in our long history for, if we fail in Central Africa to devise something like a workable multi-racial state, then Kenya will go too, and Africa may become no longer a source of pride or profit to the Europeans who have developed it, but a maelstrom of trouble into which all of us will be sucked.'[21] This reflection reveals just how much the sense of 'white' Africa then dominated the British approach to independence even on the part of so subtle a mind as that of Macmillan. Later in his letter, Macmillan continued: 'The cruder concepts, whether of the left or of the right, are clearly wrong. The Africans cannot be dominated permanently (as they are trying to do in South Africa) without any proper opportunity for their development and ultimate self-government. Nor can the Europeans be abandoned. It would be wrong for us to do so, and fatal for African interests.'

The publication of the Monckton Report on the future of the Central African Federation (majority report) stated that the Federation could not be continued in its existing (1960) form, although to break it up would be an admission that there was no hope of survival for any multiracial society on the African continent. The main arguments for the Federation were economic. However, Mr H. Habanyama and Mr W. M. Chirwa (African members of the Monckton Commission), did not sign the majority report because they were unable to accept the continuation of the Federation not based on consent and they considered the majority dealt inadequately with the all-important question of territorial constitutional advance. They recommended a referendum in each territory to discover whether or not the inhabitants wished their territory to remain in the Federation. Their conclusion was that the Federation should be dissolved forthwith.

MACMILLAN'S AFRICA TOUR 1960

Macmillan was obliged to give a great deal of attention to African problems and his African tour of January/February 1960, ending with his 'Wind of Change' speech in Cape Town, marked a turning point in British African policies. On 5 January 1960 Macmillan embarked on the six-week tour of British territories in Africa. His principal concern was the question of independence in West, East and Southern Africa. Despite his stance as an 'Edwardian' grandee, Macmillan's sympathies were with black Africans rather than the white settlers with whom he always felt ill at ease while he had difficulty understanding their viewpoint. As early as 1942, when briefly he held the job of Colonial Secretary, Macmillan had suggested that the big, rich European farms in Kenya should be bought by the Crown and run as state companies for the ultimate benefit of whites and blacks. He said this would be less expensive than civil war and ten years later in 1952 the Mau Mau rebellion erupted. At the end of 1959, prophetically, Macmillan had written to Norman Brook, the cabinet secretary, 'Africans are not the problem in Africa, it is the Europeans'.

Macmillan's first two stops were in Ghana, which by then had been independent for three years, and Nigeria, which was to become independent on 1 October. At a banquet in Accra Macmillan first used the phrase 'wind of change' but it attracted no attention, perhaps because Ghana had already experienced its own wind of change, although Nkrumah was certainly in the vanguard, advocating independence for the rest of Africa. In Nigeria Macmillan reflected that the territory had suffered from arbitrary, imposed frontiers, which he thought were 'criminal' in the way they cut through tribal territories; wherever he went in Nigeria he sensed a looming regional/federal crisis and this, after he had passed from power, was to erupt in the Nigerian civil war. From Nigeria he went on to Salisbury, the capital of the Central African Federation, where the atmosphere was very different. In Lagos, in an unguarded reply to a journalist's question about the future of Nyasaland and

Northern Rhodesia, Macmillan had replied: 'The people of the two territories will be given an opportunity to decide on whether the Federation is beneficial to them. This will be an expression of opinion that is genuinely that of the people …' This 'gaffe' had not been well received in Salisbury. In the Federation Macmillan faced white hostility and was generally depressed, especially by what he saw in a two-day visit to Nyasaland, and he left the Federation feeling that the future was ominous and reflecting that had he foreseen how the three territories would come to regard each other and the Federation he would have opposed it in 1953. At the time he did not believe that anything could be achieved until Hastings Banda, the leader of the Malawi Congress Party, was released from detention.

Macmillan arrived in South Africa just after the *Pied Noir* ultras in Algeria had reacted against liberal policies emanating from de Gaulle in Paris: they killed 14 gendarmes and wounded 123 in a number of confrontations, the first French killings of other Frenchmen. Macmillan believed that South Africa was potentially similar. After visiting Durban, Macmillan and his wife Dorothy arrived in Cape Town on 2 February where they were guests of Prime Minister Hendrik Verwoerd at Groote Schuur. Macmillan liked little that he saw in South Africa and in his conversations with Verwoerd found that nothing he said had any effect upon his host.

Macmillan had agonized over the speech he intended to deliver in Cape Town and had polished and re-polished it all the way from London with the help of Norman Brook, while his Private Secretary, Tim Bligh, had dropped hints that something special was to come. In the first part of his speech to the South African parliament, Macmillan drew elaborate historical parallels, going back to the break-up of the Roman Empire. Then, after paying fulsome compliments to South Africa for its development and courage in the two world wars, he approached his main theme, that African nationalism was unstoppable. Then, having spoken of the constant emergence of independent nations in Europe, he said:

> Today the same thing is happening in Africa, and the most striking of all the impressions I have formed since I left London a month ago is the strength of this African national consciousness. In different places it takes different forms, but it is happening everywhere. The wind of change is blowing through this continent, and, whether we like it or not, this growth of national consciousness is a political fact. We must all accept it as a fact, and our national policies must take account of it.

Later in the speech Macmillan clearly dissociated Britain from the apartheid policies of South Africa. 'It is a basic principle of our modern Commonwealth that we respect each other's sovereignty in matters of internal policy. At the same time we must recognize that in this shrinking world in which we live today the internal policies of one nation may have effects outside it.' At the time, Macmillan's audience was more impressed by his praise for South Africa than bothered by the wind of change. That, however, came later. The *Daily Service* (newspaper of the Action Group in Nigeria) commented: 'The hypocrisy of advocating a non-racial policy in British colonies while conniving at the apartheid policy of South Africa is ripe for abandonment, and it was a good thing that Mr Macmillan chose South African soil to do a *volte-face*. Secondly Mr Macmillan has strengthened the confidence of African states and of all right-thinking people in the future of the Commonwealth. And thirdly, it is reasonable to hope that his address will lead to serious heart-searching and active re-thinking of policies in South Africa. For the knowledge that he is alone should have a sobering effect on Dr Verwoerd. Mr Macmillan has only one step more to take to instruct the British delegate at the United Nations to vote at all times against the policies from which the British Prime Minister has dissociated himself and his country.'[22]

Speaking in the South African budget debate of early March, Verwoerd said the process then taking place in Africa was well known in English as appeasement. The countries of the West were prepared to leave the white man in Africa in the lurch and tell him he should accept black majority rule. This would mean absorption of the whites by the black masses of Africa. He went on to say that Britain, the US and others should realize they were sacrificing the only real and stable friend of the West for something they could not achieve.

On 21 March 1960, as African crowds demonstrated against the pass system in many parts of South Africa, the police fired on the crowds at Sharpeville, Transvaal, and at Langa, Cape Province. At Sharpeville 69 Africans were killed and 182 wounded. According to the South African Department of External Affairs, the crowd at Sharpeville numbered 20,000, but press reports put it much lower at 3,000. Six Sabre jets and eight Harvard planes, as well as Saracen armoured cars, were used to intimidate the demonstrators. The local police commander, Colonel Pienaar, said: 'It all started when hordes of natives surrounded the police station. My car was struck by a stone. If they do these things they must learn their lesson the hard way.' A Johannesburg news photographer said, 'I took pictures of more bloodshed than I have ever before seen in South Africa.' Dr Verwoerd commended the police for the courageous, efficient way they handled the situation.[23]

ELSEWHERE ON THE CONTINENT

The United Nations General Assembly agreed unanimously to the holding of a second plebiscite for the British Cameroons between September 1960 and March 1961 in which the people would have a choice of either union with Nigeria or union with an independent (French) Cameroon. On 12 January 1960 the Mau Mau emergency in Kenya was brought to an end by the Governor's proclamation. On 15 May Kenya's African leaders decided to call on all African elected members to resign unless the Governor allowed them to visit Jomo Kenyatta, who had been chosen as president in exile of the new Kenya African National Union (KANU). The Republic of Somalia was formed on 1 July 1960 by the merger of the former British Somaliland Protectorate with the UN Trust Territory (the ex-Italian colony of Somalia). Britain had assumed control of the northern regions of Somalia in 1886 with the object of safeguarding the trade links with Aden, especially to ensure the supply of mutton, and to keep out other interested powers, especially France. Following the defeat of Italy in World War II, Italian Somaliland and Eritrea were placed under British control. In 1950 Italy had returned to Somalia as the Trusteeship authority to prepare the territory for self-rule by 1960. Similarly, Britain prepared what had been known as its 'Cinderella of Empire' for independence at the same time. The transition was effected smoothly.

In all the excitement of these dramatic years a number of Africans had risen to prominence as the independence struggles intensified. Some fell by the wayside in the sense that they never achieved power in their countries after independence while others became heads of state. Among the outstanding leaders were Boganda of the Central African Republic, Lumumba of the Congo, Danquah of the Gold Coast, Mboya of Kenya, Nasser of Egypt, Nkrumah of the Gold Coast, Kenyatta of Kenya, Awolowo of Nigeria, Touré of Guinea and Houphouët-Boigny of Côte d'Ivoire. Each of these men made their imprint upon the new Africa that was rising out of the old colonial system. Some such as Barthelemy Boganda (now largely forgotten) or Tom Mboya died before their time (Boganda was killed in an air crash, Mboya was assassinated). Others ruled their newly independent states briefly (the ill-fated Lumumba) or for many years (Kenyatta until he died of old age, Houphouët-Boigny into the 1990s) but all, in their different ways, were hero figures of the independence struggles that swept the continent at that time.

The triumphs of Black Nationalism, however, sparked off pressures for independence in the white south of the continent, where a different story was to unfold. Rebellions in the Portuguese territories – Angola 1961, Guinea-Bissau

1963, Mozambique 1964 – were to be met by years of repression and warfare. In 1958 Dr Verwoerd, the architect of 'grand apartheid', came to power in South Africa to preside over a country retreating steadily into isolation as its white minority attempted to stem the tide of history while Ian Smith and the Rhodesia Front attempted to do the same in Southern Rhodesia.

The rapid end of the European empires – British, French, Belgian and Portuguese – all in the course of a few years and all on the same continental landmass, where the affected territories were contiguous to one another, meant the creation of a power vacuum that was bound to lead to years of violence in the decades that followed as rival groups fought to gain control of the political prizes left by the departing colonial powers. None of the new states was economically strong and most were economic pygmies in world terms. Furthermore, as a later generation of leaders would discover, the inherited state structures were often fragile and gave little guarantee of stability against hungry power-mongers. The result was the phenomenon of the 'failed state' that emerged in the 1990s. These problems, however, lay in the future. The immediate reaction to the *annus mirabilis* of independence was one of joy: freedom had been achieved at last.

In the years that followed it was often suggested that independence had been granted too soon to countries that were not ready for it. When he was in Nigeria on his tour, Harold Macmillan asked the Governor-General, Sir James Robertson, whether the Nigerians were ready for independence. The Governor-General said the Nigerians were not ready and needed another 20 years but he still advised that independence should be granted in 1960. In response to Macmillan's query as to why, he said that any attempt to hold on would alienate the intelligent who would rebel and have to be imprisoned so 20 years of repression would follow. Therefore they should be given independence at that time and begin to learn to rule themselves. It was a paternalist argument but it made sense. Another former imperial administrator, Sir John Johnston, said in 1988: 'You can rule by force or by consent and consent can be pretty attenuated. But once consent is withdrawn, you can't rule by force in the middle of the twentieth century, you've got to hand over.' And another former colonial official, Sir Leslie Monson, quoted the succinct remark of Paul Marc Henri of the French Colonial Service: 'You either shoot or you get out.'[24]

PART I

The 1960s

Decade of Hope

CHAPTER ONE

Problems of Independence

At the beginning of the 1960s Africa was the world's most precarious region, its vast geographic centre 'empty' of power, its northern and southern extremities (Algeria and South Africa) in the grip of forces that appeared irreconcilable to the rest of the continent. Its newly independent states with their fragile infrastructures and minuscule economies desperately required help, but help that would not be accompanied by political demands and 'strings'. Political power depends upon economic strength, and economic strength was what Africa lacked. There were also complex psychological problems associated with independence: African nationalist leaders had to demand and take independence; they could never appear just to receive it. Moreover, the scars of colonialism ran deep for, as Nigeria's Dr Azikiwe had said back in 1948: 'My country groans under a system which makes it impossible for us to develop our personalities to the full.' And as another young nationalist said to a European at this time: 'You have never known what it is to live under colonialism. It's humiliating.'

During the decade that followed the euphoria of 1960, two parallel searches took place. The first was for political stability, the best system to encompass the needs of the new societies; and the second was for economic growth and development, in most cases starting from tiny under-developed bases. The political leaders had, at once, to learn the art of compromise, both with the various forces that had been released in their new states and with the departing colonial powers. One view on the art or necessity for compromise comes from Frantz Fanon[1]:

This idea of compromise is very important in the phenomenon of decolonization, for it is very far from being a simple one. Compromise involves the colonial system, and the young nationalist bourgeoisie at one and the same time. The partisans of the colonial system discover that the masses may destroy everything. Blown-up bridges, ravaged farms, repressions and fighting harshly disrupt the economy... Compromise is equally attractive to the nationalist bourgeoisie, who since they are not clearly aware of the possible consequences of the rising storm, are genuinely afraid of being swept away by this huge hurricane and never stop saying to the settler: 'We are still capable of stopping the slaughter; the masses still have confidence in us; act quickly if you do not want to put everything in jeopardy.'

Fanon's advice went unheeded in Algeria as it did in the Congo.

A more orthodox approach to Africa's problems comes from the American academic, Gwendolyn Carter, who hoped that a united Africa could overcome some of the consequences of Balkanization: 'African countries themselves are eager to have multilateral economic arrangements rather than bilateral ones, and they prefer United Nations aid to that from individual states.' She advanced the idea that African countries should co-ordinate their efforts so as to avoid rivalry for aid and not play one donor off against another. This lofty idea never had a chance. She also suggested, on behalf of the West, that 'In two other ways must we move if we are to give the new African states the opportunity to evolve in terms of their potentialities as well as of their aspirations: we must work to keep the Cold War out of Africa; and we must strive to settle our own racial problems and to aid the multiracial states in settling theirs.' This did not happen either.[2]

Unsurprisingly, the leaders carried over into the new dimension of freedom their passionate anti-colonialism, not least because though they had achieved their political freedom they found themselves prisoners of their countries' weakness and poverty. In any case, at the beginning of the 1960s, despite freedom for some, the continent was racked by explosive problems: in the north the bitter Algerian war was still being waged with one million *colons* supported by 500,000 French troops ranged against nine million Algerian Muslims; in central Africa the Congo was descending into chaos; in Angola Portuguese authority was being challenged as the long war of liberation got under way; and in South Africa, following Sharpeville, the white minority was entrenching its power for what was to be a 30-year struggle to maintain its control over the black majority. Another factor of immense importance was the way the British and French, the two principal departing colonial powers, would continue to behave after the independence of their African colonies had been achieved. They would continue to be guided by all the considerations that had impelled them to empire in the first place: the expansion of trade and investment, securing their interests, safeguarding their migrants in the territories of white settlement such as Kenya, the Rhodesias or South Africa, and their need in a world where their power had been obviously diminished to retain what prestige and influence they could.

Another problem for Africa, one that had long preceded independence, was the absolute need to acquire an African personality, something that had been part of the imperative to decolonize. Guinea's Sekou Touré spoke of the need to 'reconstruct the African personality' while others, and most notably Aimé Cesar and Leopold Senghor, had propounded the concept of negritude. And while Africans thought along such lines, outsiders were then developing their ideas of what the newly emerging Africa was about: 'Everybody forms his own image of Africa in accordance with his preferences or his illusions rather than the realities.'[3] In the preface to his book *Voices of Negritude,* the Afro-American Julio Finn says: 'Negritude has been inextricably involved in a long, give-no-quarter war with colonialism and racism. And it is this which makes Negritude unique: it is the only artistic movement of modern times whose express creed is to redeem the spiritual and cultural values of a people... On the cultural level, Negritude vaunts the inimitability of Black civilization; on the human level, it proclaims the innate dignity and beauty of the race – the right of Black peoples proudly to cast their shadows in the sunlight.'[4]

The fact that the concept of negritude had to be propagated is in itself an indictment of the colonial system and explains the depths of the humiliations for which that system was responsible. As Senghor put it, independent Africa wished to assimilate with the rest of the world in its own way: 'What all these distinguished minds want, whether they are Westerners or Easterners, is to superimpose a European civilization upon us, to impregnate us with it in the name of universality. Hence exotic peoples such as ourselves would be eternally condemned to be not the producers but the consumers of civilization.'[5] Thus, forging a sense of shared nationality was a primary post-independence task.

Despite the *annus mirabilis* of independence, much opinion in the West, especially among the colonial powers, was against it; or, perhaps more accurately, felt that if independence had to come the question then was how these new states could best be controlled. At the time the imperial powers had a straight choice: either to assist the African revolution by lending their technical skills and capital; or to stand alongside the white racialists. Many new opportunities opened up to the African leadership at this time, yet many of the old structures and habits remained firmly in place. Indeed, some of the constraints on freedom were worse than they had been before independence because of the Cold War and the reluctance of the imperial powers fully to relinquish control. The ex-imperial powers and the other industrial democracies were prepared to co-operate with the new Third World countries but only in ways which would do as little as possible to undermine the existing distribution of power and influence within international society, and that constraining approach was to last down to the twenty-first century.

> The truth is that it is not neutralism or socialism that the West distrusts, as much as independence. And there is a peculiar anger displayed by the West when an African state flexes its independence. In part it is the anger of disappointment, of an affronted service. The West knows what is best for an Africa that it governed so long, bringing peace and law and order and the ceaseless productive demands of the modern world; to reject its standards, its institutions, its continuing supervision is not just stupidity, it is ingratitude.[6]

For Britain and France, the relationship with their ex-colonies posed the question as to how, in a fiercely competitive world, they could transform the legacies of pre-eminence and empire from liabilities to assets.

The departing colonialists assumed that their former subjects should accept their values (they still do). Britain left behind mimic institutions – whether in the field of education or politics – and believed that democracy to the African politicians meant a British form of democracy with all its institutional trappings. As Britain found that it had no empire, there followed an emotional reaction accompanied by the assumption that former colonial subjects would remain subservient in outlook to British leadership. 'The British people tended to judge African events by exclusively British values. The euphoria, which grew during the 1950s as Britain was thought to be adopting a magnanimous policy of voluntarily ending her imperial powers and setting up miniature Westminsters all over Africa, quickly evaporated... It was assumed that these British institutions would continue to reflect the glory of the British political system.'[7] In fact Britain and France, by resisting African advance, were denying the roots of their own democracy. For France, total withdrawal from Africa represented an even greater defeat than for Britain since Africa by the 1960s remained the only area of the world where France retained sufficient influence so as to guarantee its claims to middle-power status in the international system.

Speaking on behalf of Africa, Fanon said: 'Humanity is waiting for something other from us than such an imitation [of Europe], which would be almost an obscene caricature. If we want to turn Africa into a new Europe, and America into a new Europe, then let us leave the destiny of our countries to Europeans. They will know how to do it better than the most gifted among us.'[8] He added that it is always easier to proclaim rejection than actually to reject. Writing at the height of the Cold War, Fanon argued that other (non-African) countries of the Third World tried to overcome their problems of poverty by using their strategic positions – one that accorded them a privileged position in the struggle between the two blocs – to conclude treaties and give undertakings with the result that the 'former dominated country becomes an economically dependent country'. It was not to be long before many African countries had become hopelessly economically dependent.

The 1960s, understandably, was the decade for blaming colonialism as the new leaders came up against constraints that inhibited their actions or found they could not easily escape from the patterns of the past. The colonial system had been concerned only with certain forms of wealth and only with those resources that provisioned its own industrial and commercial growth. As a result the departing colonial powers left their colonies in economic strait-jackets, designed to ensure that they continued providing the resources – primary products – that the metropolitan powers required. At the same time, blaming colonialism was also convenient: to do so got governments off the hook when they had made mistakes and provided political leaders with an exciting basis for rousing rhetoric. The human haemorrhage inflicted on Africa by the slave trade, which has been estimated at a loss of between 60 and 150 million Africans, remained the greatest indictment of the Afro-European relationship; the African continent which in the eighteenth century had about the same population as Europe had been reduced by 1960 to only a twelfth of Europe's population.

René Dumont, the French agronomist, examined the failures due to the historical framework in which independence took place. In most cases, for example, African states, which had been carved out of the continent during the European 'scramble' are not based on either geography or ethnic unity but, instead, are the result of the rivalry of the European powers at the end of the nineteenth century. Further, Dumont argued, the inherited imperial institutions, administrative structures and education systems were to lose most of their relevance once independence had been achieved. Above all, the Balkanized state of Africa at independence required regional co-operation, especially if economic progress was to be achieved and the existing divisions, especially those between Anglophone and Francophone Africa, did not assist this process.

Demands for equality, the desire to be treated as the white civil servants that were made by the rising elites prior to independence, meant that these elites were widely separated from the masses they were to rule once independence had been achieved. As the new governments accepted much-needed economic aid from the former metropolitan powers they also had to determine how the aid should be used and here they came in contact with a new breed from the former colonial power, the ubiquitous aid experts, many of whom defended and built upon the colonial record and opposed any deviation from ground rules for development that had already been established. In any case, in terms of the size of their economies, most African countries at independence were hardly viable and therefore were unable to sustain self-supporting development according to the European model.[9] If the economic shackles left by the colonial systems were to be changed this should have been attempted at once when the charismatic leaders were at the height of their influence and popularity. Unfortunately, they were almost all concerned to follow Nkrumah's advice and seek first control of the political kingdom, and those who later turned their attention to economic control found that the inherited strait-jacket had been substantially tightened.

The African states that emerged to independence during the 1960s did so at the height of the Cold War and were warned about the dangers of Communism by the West. Unsurprisingly, in the circumstances, the African response was that if the West, represented by the departing colonial powers, was so opposed to it, Communism must have something to offer them! And so the 1960s witnessed the departure of the colonial powers, at least in their ruling capacity, and the arrival of the USSR and its allies as the purveyors of alternative aid. Marxism had played an important role as an instrument of resistance as well as a symbol of Soviet successes, but as a social philosophy it made little real headway in Africa for it was contrary to the orientations of traditional thought. The Soviet impact was first felt in Africa at the time of Suez and subsequently when Russia had provided aid in West Africa, especially to Ghana, Guinea and Mali. In the early 1960s, however, Russian influence in Africa met with fierce competition from China following the split between the two Communist giants. In 1961, for example, a Soviet trade delegation to Lagos and other approaches to Senegal, Dahomey (Benin), Niger and Upper Volta (Burkina Faso) were rebuffed, and in 1962, despite earlier aid to Guinea (which had included the extension of the runway at Conakry airport), Sekou Touré refused permission for Soviet planes to use the country as a halfway fuelling stop during the Cuban missile crisis.

At the Afro-Asian People's Solidarity Organisation (AAPSO) conference held at Moshi, Tanzania, in February 1962, the split between the USSR and China became apparent as they argued about aid to Africa, prompting President Nyerere, the host, to issue a warning about a 'second scramble for Africa'; he said that both the rich capitalist countries and the 'rich socialist countries' were using their wealth not to wipe out poverty but to gain might and prestige. Nonetheless, China and the Soviet Union vied with each other in their offers of aid and by the end of 1963 Soviet credits to Ghana, Guinea and Mali had exceeded Chinese promises by US$100 million while China was importing only one third the amount imported by Russia from the same three countries. Then, at the Sixth AAPSO meeting in Algiers during March 1964 the Chinese onslaught on the USSR was so vitriolic that it led to an open rebuke from the

African delegates that China risked splitting Afro-Asian ranks. The USSR was learning the limitations that constrained the 'progressive' African states and the extent to which they could turn to it for assistance, and those who argued that the USSR would be able to help progressive leadership overcome imperialist subversion exaggerated either the power or the determination of the USSR. The relative ability of the USSR as opposed to the Western powers to intervene in Africa on behalf of its allies or protégés was illustrated to its disadvantage when in 1964 the armies of East Africa mutinied and Britain sent troops to restore order, or when the ousted President M'ba of Gabon was able to call on French paratroopers to restore him to power; on the other hand, when Nkrumah was overthrown in Ghana, or Keita in Mali, the USSR was unable or unwilling to come to their assistance.

During the 1960s the USSR became a modest supplier of arms in Africa and as such remained no more than a marginal great power in relation to the continent. Its real impact as an arms supplier would come in the 1970s, especially in relation to Ethiopia and Angola. The state of relations between the USSR and Africa in reality depended upon two factors: the enthusiasm of the Soviet Union and the receptiveness of the partner and by and large both the enthusiasm and receptiveness were on a moderate scale during the 1960s and, despite Western propaganda about Soviet penetration of the continent, nowhere did the USSR impose a presence on an unwilling African partner. The USSR sought diplomatic and economic recognition everywhere but was not engaged in Communist subversion: that was largely a figment of Western imagination. Membership of the Communist camp may have been the theory but the practice was big power pragmatism. 'There is no evidence of the single minded pursuit of well considered objectives that form the backbone of the "Communist subversion" arguments.'[10] What the 1960s witnessed was little more than a modest advance of Soviet influence in Africa.

Many of the newly independent African states proclaimed foreign policies that veered to the left as though this would compensate for the lack of necessary internal reforms. The rhetoric of socialism was really meaningless when the elites enjoyed European standards while the majority of the population continued to live on a scale of one fifteenth or more below their elite leaders. The end of empires left a series of power vacuums across Africa and those leaders who succeeded in replacing the departing imperial rulers proved exceedingly reluctant to let go once they had control of the levers of power and, notwithstanding all the demands for democracy that they had levelled at the colonial authorities prior to independence, were more concerned to entrench themselves and their supporters in permanent control than ever they were to have a genuine democratic dialogue with the masses. Thus, many members of the small elites that had provided the vanguard of the independence struggles now installed themselves in place of the departing whites and assumed all their privileges, although without justifying this by either work or dedication in building their new societies. As René Dumont claimed: 'Too many African elites have interpreted independence as simply meaning that they could move into the jobs and enjoy the privileges of the Europeans.' It then became necessary to decolonize these new leaders themselves. There was for these new elites another very African problem, which they had to face. This concerned the African tradition of hospitality and the expectation of poor relatives that those with jobs would find them places or keep them. Sometimes the descent of parasitic kin upon someone who did have a job deprived the wage or salary earner of any chance to invest his money or use it for himself and his immediate family, and pressures of this kind often forced those who were employed to seek a post in another part of the country so as to escape the attentions and demands of tribal kin. Western accusations of nepotism against members of the new elites, including the top political figures, often ignored what could be overwhelming pressures from kin, however distant in a Western sense; if a man did have influence, the easiest way to rid himself of what could be an intolerable burden was to obtain posts for them.

The fruits of office have always beguiled even those who began as dedicated revolutionaries. Arguably, the greatest achievement of the colonial powers was to create a brainwashed elite whose members felt more at home in the metropolitan countries than in their own and who, at home, wanted all the appurtenances of Western culture and material comforts at the expense of indigenous African style. Meanwhile, the steady movement to the towns of young men seeking a better future denuded the countryside of its most able people while, all too often, those who reached the towns did not find work but instead ended up in the shanty towns that rapidly mushroomed round the principal cities. While this human drama was taking place, political leaders felt impelled to construct what were seen as the essential hallmarks of an independent nation: monuments to national heroes, new stadiums, conference halls, luxury hotels to accommodate visiting dignitaries, presidential palaces if the residence of the former governor was not considered grand enough, while motorways and new airlines or grandiose industrial ventures such as steel mills provided the outward show of an independent state even though the workers and peasants found they were little if at all better off. Such extravagances were, perhaps, inevitable, an expression of African personality at the highly visible state level. After all, the struggle for independence had been aimed at eliminating expatriate privilege, which was the symbol of colonial subjugation since the alien enjoyed a lifestyle so far removed from that available to the

Africans over whom he ruled. Yet one of the great post-independence ironies was the extent to which this situation did not change: foreign business and commercial personnel, as well as the rapidly growing body of aid experts and representatives of international organizations, flourished as never before, enjoying an expatriate lifestyle that would rarely be within their grasp in their home countries. The enjoyment of the fruits of independence was understandable and yet 'It would be dangerous, however, if enjoyment of the fruits and wines of power were to cause the enormous and urgent tasks to be forgotten'.[11] And soon the radical, dissenting student would appear on the scene demanding 'fewer foreign cars and more rice'.

There was a tendency in both Britain and France at this time to argue that they had taken centuries to evolve their political systems and Africa could hardly be expected to reach the same position overnight. In part this was arrogance; in part an unconscious admission that they had done very little to prepare their colonies for independence; and finally a genuine realization of the enormity of the tasks facing the new rulers. In any case, African countries had to be free and only then could they construct institutions and devise systems that answered their needs. The charismatic leaders who had led their countries to independence quickly had to learn how to deal with new opposition from within, as opposed to the old external colonial enemy. Such opposition could be based on sectoral or separatist ambitions and this raised the question of whether such opposition should be given a chartered liberty to disrupt, entrench disunity or replace the new government. It was only possible for the departing British and French to leave behind what they knew: that is, replicas of their own systems. They could not bequeath something 'made for Africans' even had it been more appropriate since that would have been seen as insulting.[12] Obafemi Awolowo of Nigeria said that any Western tendency to excuse deviations from democracy was only another insulting colonialist assumption that Africans were too primitive and barbaric to conduct what he called 'this beneficent and ennobling form of government'. That, however, is exactly what the Western powers would do through the years of the Cold War when it suited them to ignore the principles they claimed to believe for reasons of realpolitik.

Almost without exception African leaders immediately before and after independence were immersed in the political process to the exclusion of all else. They might speak eloquently of their country's development needs; in practice they were entrenching their political power and, given the struggle that had preceded independence and the fragile bases upon which that independence rested, this was perhaps not surprising. It meant, however, that huge opportunities were lost for ever. As Frantz Fanon said, 'Everything can be explained to the people, on the single condition that you really want them to understand', an aphorism that ought to be on a plaque in the office of every leader worldwide. Meanwhile, one of the first problems to face the new leadership, parties aligned themselves with tribes so that it became the tribe that made itself into a party. Nkrumah once said that only three or four members of his entourage were capable of understanding what 'is going on' in the area of economic and political change. As for the masses that gave the government its power, they had literally been seduced. They shouted 'Freedom, Freedom, Freedom!' which for them meant freedom to be African without shame.

Following independence, a number of countries such as Ghana, Nigeria and Kenya practised Westminster-style multiparty systems, although it was not long before these were modified, while in the Francophone territories single-party regimes with highly concentrated presidential systems were installed. In both cases, it soon became apparent, these systems were liable to be overthrown by the military: either when they broke down, for whatever cause, or more simply because power-hungry soldiers saw an opportunity to seize control. Where the presidential form of government emerged (at first especially in Francophone Africa) the president as head of state and head of government possessed overriding powers and he also ruled the dominant and often, by law, the sole party. In a number of countries such as Côte d'Ivoire, Dahomey (Benin), Niger or Upper Volta (Burkina Faso) the constitutions were virtually identical and the president held exclusive executive power.[13] As the one-party system of government emerged to replace the bequeathed colonial systems, African leaders sought justifications for the changeover to presidential or one-party rule. They argued that the single party reflected a basic consensus among populations of both individual countries and the continent as a whole in order that they might better tackle the tasks of national reconstruction and development that needed so urgently to be addressed. The argument ran as follows: 'In the anti-colonial period the mass nationalist party had been an expression of the united needs of the African people to struggle against colonialism. In the post-colonial era, once the colonialists had gone, there was no remaining division between rulers and ruled, and therefore no need for conflicting parties.'[14] Why create an opposition when all were, or should be, united in a new national solidarity? It was a neat theory but it assumed too much. The single party, it was claimed, should represent all shades of opinion. The multiparty system, on the other hand, was repudiated since it was open to manipulation and misuse by regional or tribal interests or was liable to be subverted by neo-colonialist pressures. Such a political theory opened the way for the dominant group in the single party to control and if necessary suppress the minority groups or interests.

By the mid-1960s the one-party system had become the predominant form of government in Africa and institutions of government had been transformed into instruments to serve the party and the ruling elite and by presumption the people. The mass mobilization parties to be found in Ghana, Guinea or Mali at this time did aim to transform the inherited political systems and economies. The more elite parties were conservative and tribalist. The mass parties were radical and espoused 'scientific' socialism while the conservative parties said they stood for 'African' socialism. No one at this stage claimed to be capitalist whatever actual policies may have been pursued. Much effort went into the search for a political system that could deal with the challenges faced by the new political leadership. These included fragile state structures, tribal divisions, ambitious politicians who had been excluded from the new power structures, military establishments that were soon to understand their strength in relation to weak political systems and the demands of unity in the face of economic underdevelopment and political inexperience. It became plain in state after state that the inherited political traditions passed on from Britain and France were not the answer. Instead, inexorably, Africa's leaders moved towards the creation of the one-party state and the military moved towards the coup. It may be a matter of debate as to which came first, but once the one-party state structure was in place the coup became the natural alternative to the ballot box election. The move towards the one-party state began prior to independence for though during the struggle political militants had argued for the formulation of programmes for the future, yet 'under the pretext of safeguarding national unity, the leaders categorically refused to attempt such a task. The only worthwhile dogma, it was repeatedly stated, is the union of the nation against colonialism'.[15] In retrospect it is truly remarkable how Frantz Fanon foretold at the beginning of the 1960s so many of the problems that would bedevil Africa in the years to come, and the following passage is worth quoting at length.

> In these poor, under-developed countries, where the rule is that the greatest wealth is surrounded by the greatest poverty, the army and the police constitute the pillars of the regime; an army and a police force (another rule which must not be forgotten) which are advised by foreign experts. The strength of the police force and the power of the army are proportionate to the stagnation in which the rest of the nation is sunk. By dint of yearly loans, concessions are snatched up by foreigners; scandals are numerous, ministers grow rich, their wives doll themselves up, the members of parliament feather their nests and there is not a soul down to the simple policeman or the customs officer who does not join in the great procession of corruption.[16]

Exploitation by the new rulers leads to contempt for the state and discontent among the masses. In turn, this leads the regime to become harsher and, in the absence of any parliamentary checks upon the ruler, it is the army that becomes the national arbiter. And so the new Africa faced a political paradox: that with the coming of the one-party state and military rule the freedom that had just been gained in the independence struggle might be lost again.

Altogether some 26 military coups were executed during the independence decade of the 1960s, to set a pattern that would continue for a further two decades. The coup became the crucial, most frequent means of effecting political change or of preserving a system that favoured a particular elite and coups were mounted against every kind of system. The countries affected by coups included Algeria, Burundi, Central African Republic, Chad, Congo (Brazzaville), Congo (Kinshasa), Dahomey (Benin), Equatorial Guinea, Gabon, Ghana, Guinea (unsuccessful), Lesotho, Mali, Nigeria, Sierra Leone, Somalia, Sudan, Togo, Uganda and Upper Volta (Burkina Faso) and they were mounted against both Western-style parliamentary governments and those committed to social revolution. According to Ruth First: 'The wave of coups d'état and the range of governments affected by them suggested that political instability was the expression of profound and generalized economic problems and social conflict, and that many seemingly dissimilar political systems shared an incipient state of crisis because political independence alone had not enabled Africa to break the circle of dependence that was the condition of colonialism.' Some coups were pay strikes by soldiers acting like trade unions. Some were the army stepping in to keep a particular regime in power. Some were by sections of the army identifying with sections of the political spectrum. A number of coups were met by counter-coups that demonstrated the conflicts within the armies themselves so that, for example, senior officers would be pitched against junior officers, or NCOs would be pitched against officers. Whatever first prompted these army coups, once armies had stepped into the political arena they became competitors for power in their own interest.

This endless succession of coups in the first 10 years of the independence era suggested several things: that the bequeathed systems did not work for the new states; that a variety of underlying tensions threatened to tear the new societies apart; that the African choice was for strong central government; that a system of power pillage (later to be exemplified by Mobutu in the Congo – Zaïre) had been released by independence. Increasingly, therefore, African politicians sought how to regularize the new one-party systems and give them a permanent stamp of legitimacy. There appeared to be both a rejection of democracy by the political leaders and, at first at least, an acquiescence in this rejection by the mass of the people. Were the justifications for the one-party state – the desire for unity, the imperative of concentrating upon development, the need for strong central government to counter tribalism – also justifications for military take-overs? In Tanzania Julius Nyerere was able to create a one-party state structure that was not taken over by the military; he did so by ensuring a real measure of democracy that gave electors a choice of candidates within the one-party system. What is undisputed is that by the end of the decade the concept of the one-party state had been accepted in a majority of African countries while the military coup had also come to be seen, in many if not all one-party states, as the means of changing the government or the head of state. Freedom, nevertheless, was contagious and while more perceptive politicians and intellectuals saw the dangers and limitations of the one-party system, the people at large were sufficiently enamoured of the sense that at last colonialism had passed and that they were 'free' that they were prepared to accept all-powerful leaders in control of one-party systems. For a time at least the political leaders who had fought the colonialists and emerged as the first presidents of their newly independent countries enjoyed great popularity. Such popularity, however, would wear off sharply as continuing poverty reminded the mass of the people that their expectations had not been met. And as disillusion grew so the politicians began to fear the people whom they saw needed to be kept constantly in check – by increasingly hollow claims about the need for unity and the external threats to African development or, in the last resort, by the police. The party, meanwhile, acted as a barometer of public opinion and as an information service for the government. Opposition parties were banned and persistent opponents of the regime imprisoned and sometimes liquidated while elections for the single party achieved uniformly high turnouts.

In his seminal work *False Start in Africa* Dumont examined the one-party system from both the political and development angles.

> The one-party system helps avoid the spectacle of parties out-doing each other with extravagant campaign promises; but this can occur anyway. And the system tends towards the abuse of power by the ruling group, if there is no minimum opposition to make its protests heard. To be truly acceptable and effective, the party must have a real popular base, organize the peasants, and help them to stand up for themselves; their complaints must be heard by the government. The system should facilitate the 'dialogue', between the base and the summit, in both directions: first, to transmit to the peasants the provisions of the plan and necessary crop and economic disciplines; and also to find out what the peasants think of it, what they need to carry it out, and what organizations are best able to put all of them to work.[17]

At the beginning of 1961, following the *annus mirabilis* of independence, 27 African countries were independent. Thereafter, the pace was slower: two in 1961 – Sierra Leone and Tanganyika; four in 1962 – Algeria, Burundi, Rwanda and Uganda; two in 1963 – Kenya and Zanzibar; two in 1964 – Malawi and Zambia; one in 1965 – The Gambia; two in 1966 – Botswana and Lesotho; three in 1968 – Equatorial Guinea, Mauritius and Swaziland; so that by the end of the decade there were 43 independent African states. Of these states Algeria, Burundi, Sierra Leone, Uganda, Zanzibar, Lesotho and Equatorial Guinea were to undergo coups before the decade was over. Kenya, Malawi, Tanganyika (later Tanzania) and Zambia would become one-party states (without the assistance of their armies) and in the case of Tanzania under Nyerere would provide the intellectual as well as the practical justification for adopting such a system. The Gambia, which became independent under a coalition government led by Sir Dawda Jawara, was to enjoy a long period of stable government under a multiparty system, as would Botswana and Mauritius. Swaziland, under its semi-feudal system, enjoyed what might be described as limited democracy until its King carried out his own coup in the 1970s.

Whatever the systems they opted for, the new African rulers had to deal with problems of immense poverty and their people's huge expectations that, once freedom had been enjoyed, independence would mean a better standard of life. The majority of rulers tackled questions of structure first (at least in the sense of exercising control over the political system) and then turned to development.

A primary objective was to Africanize the civil service and here the problems were intensely personal as well as political. In the immediate pre-independence period there had been the returning student who had proved himself academically only to find that he was downgraded and paid less back at home than the white expatriate, or failed to get a job at all. The resulting bitterness rankled. One result of this kind of situation was that no new government could reduce civil service salaries as the economy in most cases required. Another problem that reflected the snobberies of the colonial systems that had just passed was that Africans were loath to take jobs as technicians or tradesmen. They wanted desk jobs. Thus, when Africans began to take over the senior jobs they expected also to receive all the same symbols, such as secluded housing and cars, that had pertained to colonial officials so that in a traditionally egalitarian society, European class barriers were introduced that set the civil service apart as a class. When raised to a senior appointment, for example, an African civil servant at once obtained a government loan to purchase a car for this was required by the status of the job rather than foregone because of the state of the economy. 'It was inevitable that as local persons invaded the senior ranks of the service, their emoluments should bear a close relation to those of their expatriate colleagues in the same or similar posts. This had a distorting effect on the whole of the salary structure.'[18] Meanwhile, rapid constitutional advancement or change in the new states outstripped the development of many institutions including the civil service. All governments recognized the need for a sound, efficient, loyal and stable civil service and gave high priority to its reconstruction and development. But, as with everything else, money was in short supply and corners had to be cut.

There was a quite different political problem. Thus, the British concept of a civil servant not identifying himself with any political party, so as to respond to the policies of the party in power, came under heavy fire in those countries that became one-party states, where the concept of an impartial civil service was abandoned in favour of loyalty to the ruling party. Sometimes, too, ministers did not understand the responsibilities of their top civil servants and would attack them for acts performed in their official capacities. Most civil services in any case are hierarchical and the general European pattern required a high university education for its senior members. But in some new states there were demands that posts should be open to civil servants who lacked university education provided they had the necessary ability to work their way up through the ranks. The British approach differed from that of the French. Although it was proposed that colonial civil servants should be put on a permanent basis with careers, emoluments and pensions guaranteed by the British government and that they should then be seconded on request to the new governments to help maintain existing services, this was not followed through. Furthermore, the British made the new governments responsible for paying compensation to the departing civil servants, a requirement that was deeply resented. France, on the other hand, did better. Its Overseas Service was kept in being with salaries and career prospects guaranteed. The members of the service were then offered under technical assistance to the newly independent states. Other expedients were tried in the run-up to independence: these included job-splitting, promotion on trial, paying less attention to the possession of formal certificates of education or allowing senior Africans to shadow the expatriate whose job they would soon assume. Some of these expedients worked better than others but the need to Africanize the civil service, the speed at which in most cases it was carried out and the lack of experience of the incoming Africans presented huge problems during the initial years of independence.

There was much debate about the educational systems that the colonial powers had left and the extent to which these were appropriate for the new states. Apart from the incongruencies of lessons that referred to 'our ancestors the Gauls' the real argument, often stressed too much by the departing British and French, was that their African subjects had wanted the same education that they themselves had enjoyed, even though this assumed a perpetuation of colonial values. The situation might have been different had the original intention of the colonial powers been – what they often claimed – to prepare their subjects for independence. As Dumont claimed, present education obstructs progress. 'For most African children, in town and country alike, school represents above all a means of entering the elite class. Even in the most backward areas of the bush everyone has grasped the fact that the official with clean hands earns more and works much less.'[19] Inherent in this statement by an outsider, although one deeply sympathetic to African independence and development, is the assumption that every African wants to do what will best assist national development. Every African, like people the world over, wanted to improve his own lot and that of his family.

The concept of development as applied to the newly independent countries led to a number of assumptions about people's behaviour that simply do not operate in a normal society whether such a society is rich or poor. Development is an abstract concept of governments or aid donors. Ordinary people concentrate upon their own needs and ambitions: the politicians about how to rule and stay on top, the elite how to enjoy the best possible lifestyle, the majority about survival and bread. Meanwhile, the real problems of education were those of scarcity: there were not enough schools; where schools existed there were insufficient teachers and lack of equipment; there was never enough money for a full educational programme and, in any case, a national education programme encompassing primary and secondary education for all takes many years to create, even with a reasonable starting base, and few colonies had more than that. Then came the question of higher education – technical colleges or universities. Although every new state wanted its university, politicians learnt early the threats that could be posed by unruly students. Most important of all at independence was the simple lack of enough people in almost all fields with the skills required to make the system work efficiently. The Congo in 1960 – the legacy of a deliberate Belgian policy – had only a reputed 14 university graduates out of a population of fourteen million; and Botswana in 1966 had 26 sixth formers. The lack of skilled personnel meant the necessity of importing aid personnel under technical assistance programmes and though these were forthcoming and their ranks were swelled by the sudden proliferation of non-government (volunteer) organizations (NGOs) providing young people of doubtful skills, such as the British Voluntary Service Overseas (VSO) or the American Peace Corps, these represented no more than a short-term gap-filling expedient. The crucial consideration was how long it would take before the indigenous education system would be able to produce graduates or other trained people at a level that would begin to meet national requirements.

Tribalism presented a range of political problems that were acute before independence and threatened political structures after it had been achieved. During the 1960s, in particular, African leaders shied away from using the word tribe at all and tried to persuade their people to think of themselves for the first time, and only, as Kenyans or Zambians. A principal justification for the one-party state was to prevent the alternative of a multiparty structure whose different parties would be appropriated by rival tribes and so would perpetuate tribal rivalries. But the pretence that tribes could be subsumed in a greater nationalism was doomed to failure. They were and remain a necessary calculation in politics throughout Africa. Colonialism, in any case, had exacerbated tribal antagonisms and suspicions. 'The frontiers generally correspond neither to language nor indigenous tradition, but to nineteenth-century European rivalries or mere subsequent administrative convenience; they bisect some tribes with a long history of antagonism. It is the tribe that largely held popular allegiance before, and if it has a rival now – one, indeed, of persistently mounting appeal – it is much less the nation than the race. And how should this not be so?'[20]

Early in the independence era political leaders made plain that they expected the press to support the government; they became easily offended or vindictive when uncomplimentary reports were published about their policies or doings, however fair such reports may have been. Before long, leading newspapers had been acquired, either directly by the state or by the ruling party, and these at least became mouthpieces of the official line while editors quickly learnt how far they could go before they risked some form of reprisal, reprimand or worse from the government. 'The politicians have put forward several excuses to back up their demand for a "moderate" and "co-operative" press in Africa. "Africa needs all the energies of her sons and daughters for nation-building and therefore cannot afford the luxury of encouraging dissident newspapers" is one excuse.'[21] Such attitudes represented one of the earliest indications that opposition, whether of parties or of opinions, was likely to receive short shrift in the new Africa. The classic 1960s approach to the press came from the Information Minister of Ghana in 1962:

> The African journalist is fully conscious of the responsibility that rests on the shoulders of Africa's new journalists – that of keeping the people informed of the new developments in the country, the continent and the world; exposing imperialism and neo-colonialist machinations; projecting the African personality and contributing to the African liberation struggle and building of African unity.
>
> The new African journalist keeps cheap sensationalism out of his duties and lays emphasis on the positive things that go to help in building the new

Africa – he does not relish the stories which do no credit to the advancement and education of the people.

This Orwellian description of a nationalist paragon of journalistic rectitude does credit to the Minister's imagination if not to reality; behind it, however, is the mailed fist. Journalists in the new Africa were expected to toe the party line.

Writing at the beginning of the 1960s when the world had become conscious, as never before, of the gaps between rich and poor, a gap that was emphasized by the rapid appearance of new African states, many of which had gross national products the equivalent of the income of a medium-sized British or French city, René Dumont argued prophetically:

> Two separate worlds are forming; soon they will have nothing in common, and they may one day confront one another even more tragically than East and West. The idea that an American businessman's son and the son of a Congolese or Indian peasant have an 'equal opportunity' at birth cannot be seriously entertained. The rich world calls itself the free world, and thereby thinks that its conscience is clear; but a 'defence' of liberty which is allied with defence of privileged status is fairly suspect.[22]

Meanwhile, the ex-imperial powers instructed the new African leaders and people to work selflessly for development – something never achieved in Europe – and then complained when they failed to do so.

It was during the 1960s that the world really learnt about development: Western governments established aid ministries, NGOs came into being in order to send volunteers to work in under-developed countries, universities set up departments to study development problems, and aid and development became a growth industry while newly independent countries were invaded by experts, both invited and uninvited, to tell them how to deal with their problems. African leaders saw that they were in an economic strait-jacket and obliged to use the economic channels that had been created by the colonial regimes for their own ends. How to break this pattern was (and remains) a crucial test of independence. Was it possible, for example, to change the nature of a country's exports, and not just their destination, in the sense of finding new, non-traditional markets? If the new states were to achieve even a modicum of economic independence they required capital at all levels, technicians, engineers, skilled mechanics – in fact trained personnel for just about every occupation conceivable. And, realistically, they knew they could not do this on their own. They needed help, and help in the form of aid, whether financial or as technical assistance, came only at a price. The price was to maintain the economic strait-jackets left in place by the departing colonial powers. The question of the value of aid, or of the damage it can inflict, will recur throughout this book. In the 1960s there was still a belief in some quarters in the donor countries that the right injection of aid would enable countries to reach the point of take-off while most African leaders saw aid as a right, a necessary compensation for past exploitation. In order to obtain the help they needed, the new African leadership was obliged to make up to the capitalist countries of the West – and sometimes to the Communist countries of the East – and they soon learnt to play one side off against the other in their search for assistance.

As aid began to flow the recipient governments had to decide how to use it. A gulf soon appeared since 'The overwhelming majority of nationalist parties show a deep distrust towards the people of the rural areas'. Fanon, indeed, saw the process of aid as a debilitating one that would always threaten true independence:

> The economic channels of the young State sink back inevitably into neo-colonialism lines. The national economy, formerly protected, is today literally controlled. The budget is balanced through loans and gifts, while every three or four months the chief ministers themselves or else their governmental delegations come to the erstwhile mother countries or elsewhere, fishing for capital.[23]

Education in the colonies had essentially been for the elites, modelled on British and French university systems, and it had paid scant attention to anything to do with development let alone development needs at the lower levels of society. As a result the formulation of development plans was given over, almost entirely, to foreigners, the new breed of experts who became the ubiquitous expression of ongoing Western interest in the new states of Africa. Such foreigners had a sufficiently difficult task establishing a relationship with the political leadership that was all the more suspicious of them because it needed them so badly. The same experts made no contact with the mass of the people; neither did they learn, even at second hand, what those masses might see as development priorities. While development plans were being forged the new governments had to face the rising expectations of the people who had voted them into power and at least appear to be doing something to meet those expectations. And though Ghana's Nkrumah and Guinea's Touré had attempted, with considerable success, to break the pattern of ongoing dependence upon the West, most of Africa, either willingly or unwillingly, found it was unable to do so.

A final problem, one whose repercussions would last through to the end of the century, was the question of white racialism and the white settler enclaves.

These included Algeria, Congo (Kinshasa), Kenya, Southern Rhodesia, Angola, Mozambique and South Africa, while smaller white minorities were to be found in about a dozen other countries. In Kenya the Mau Mau rebellion of the 1950s was more than the settlers could cope with on their own, with the result that British forces were sent to the colony to deal with the rebellion. This return of the imperial factor meant that, although Mau Mau was defeated, the possibility of a universal declaration of independence (UDI) by the settlers had also been pre-empted and at independence the 45,000 settlers were forced to come to terms with the reality of black majority rule. Further south, however, the white rearguard action was to be fierce and brutal, lasting until 1994 when Nelson Mandela became the first black president of South Africa, and lingering beyond that date with the latent conflict between white and black surfacing in Zimbabwe at the very end of the century. Given the history of white settlement in Africa, these rearguard actions were to be expected. What made them infinitely more dangerous, threatening the entire relationship of Africa with the former colonial powers, was the determined and deeply hypocritical way in which the West, and most notably Britain, defended blatant racism at the United Nations and elsewhere as long as it was remotely possible to do so.

Western racial attitudes became clear from 1960 onwards in the reporting of the Congo (Kinshasa) crisis: black atrocities against whites were always emphasized and the death of one white was given more attention than the deaths of hundreds of blacks, while the repeated use of such phrases as semi-civilized rulers, petty kingdoms or barbarism became stock usage for reporting from the Congo. White atrocities, especially by the mercenaries, and the fact of ruthless white intervention to destroy a government that did not suit Western interests, were ignored, glossed over or represented as necessary measures to restore law and order. Africans were soon appalled by the overt double standards: black racism wherever it appeared was denounced, white racism in Rhodesia, Angola or South Africa was inverted to become 'upholding civilized values'. Margery Perham, whose study of colonial Africa and support for African independence, earned her the invitation to give the BBC Reith Lectures of 1961, said of South Africa: 'They have their backs to the wall, but they dare not turn to read the writing on it. Yet all the rest of the world can read it. Their state rests upon the foundation of absolute power over the black population.' She certainly did not foretell the manner in which Britain over the coming years would use its influence and power through the Commonwealth or in the United Nations to prevent the kind of pressures that might otherwise have brought an end to apartheid sooner than was to prove the case. Perhaps such Western behaviour was inevitable. Empire, after all, had been about the spread of white power and much of its *raison d'être* had been explained in terms of racial superiority and the natural right of Europeans to rule over barbaric or uncivilized races. As empire slipped away the overt sympathies of the British and French ruling elites, not to mention the Portuguese, were with their remaining white minorities in Africa. Had the colonial powers been less racist and insisted upon black majority rule, as Britain surely could have done in 1965 when Ian Smith in Rhodesia carried out his unilateral declaration of independence (UDI), much of the subsequent history of Africa could have been less violent and more constructive.

The problems facing independent Africa, as the new states rapidly discovered, were daunting in their range and variety. They included the search for suitable political systems, the need to Africanize, controlling – or failing to control – the military, the need for aid at almost all levels of development, coming to terms with the artificial boundaries bequeathed by the colonial powers, the tiny size of most African markets and their inability to compete in the world economic system, the lack of skills of almost every description and the huge expectations of their people. At the same time the new states had to take their place on the international stage, they needed to do so proudly and with assurance and they soon discovered just how little power they possessed and just how small even their collective influence was in the world at large. Internal problems – that is, internal to Africa – included boundary adjustments, the search for unity, the need to establish economic unions or common markets, the problems attaching to the white minority controlled states and the need to see the rest of Africa achieve its independence. Such problems were enormously exacerbated, as they soon discovered, by the impact of the Cold War and the determination of the major powers to intervene and manipulate whenever it suited their interests to do so.

The problems were formidable by any standards and yet the 1960s were a wonderful decade for the continent: Africa was free at last, colonialism was over and by 1970 43 African states were independent and members of the United Nations. The decade, despite everything, was one of hope, and the freedom that had just been won was to be enjoyed.

CHAPTER TWO

The Congo Crisis

The murder of Patrice Lumumba in January 1961 marked the end of the first phase of the Congo crisis. The second phase would last until Mobutu seized power in his coup of November 1965. Few events in Africa during the 1960s better illustrated the hypocrisy of the Western powers or their determination to control the newly independent countries of Africa by any means at their disposal. They manipulated the United Nations, they facilitated the deployment of mercenaries, they worked through the great mining groups such as *Union Minière du Haut Katanga* or Tanganyika Concessions, which they controlled, and by threats, bribes and overt political pressures they made certain that a puppet system beholden to them rather than any fully independent political leadership came to power in the mineral-rich Congo. The Cold War was one excuse for this behaviour – preventing the spread of Soviet or Communist influence in the region; greed was another – the Congo was too rich to be allowed to escape from Western corporate controls; and deep resentment on the part of the Belgians at loss of control of their colonial empire in Africa was the third. The end result was to consign the Congo (later Zaïre) to more than 30 years' dictatorship under Mobutu Sese Seko (as he became) who was to make state kleptocracy fashionable. More than any other actions at this time, Western behaviour in the Congo crisis gave substance to Kwame Nkrumah's accusations about neo-colonialism.

A leading article in the *Manchester Guardian* of December 1960 examined the chaotic situation in the Congo as follows:

> The Congo has become so fragmented that a more realistic basis on which to act would be a (UN) resolution seeking to reunite the provinces of Leopoldville, Orientale, Kasai, and Katanga. All four are now under governments operating without any common purpose… Politics were not allowed to develop naturally in the Congo: if they are to develop now some midwifery will be needed. It can be supplied either by the United Nations

as a whole or – and this would have a greater chance of success – by the Afro-Asian coalition. It should, however, be the major aim of United Nations' policy.[1]

At the same time the Prime Minister of India, Mr Nehru, criticized the course the United Nations had been following (there were Indian troops in the Congo, acting under UN auspices). While the whole country was going to pieces, the United Nations was 'sitting there passively', he said, carrying its policy of non-intervention to an extreme. He wished that the United Nations would take a more positive role, using its forces and powers to enable the Congo Parliament to meet in spite of Colonel Mobutu, seeing that the Belgians left the country, and obtaining the release of political prisoners, including Lumumba, to the protection of the United Nations. The Prime Minister put great emphasis on the importance of the Congolese Parliament meeting as soon as possible. This, he said, was the obvious step, but it had been prevented by Colonel Mobutu, who had been encouraged in his opposition to parliament by various authorities and various countries.[2]

THE CRISIS DEEPENS

During the early months of 1961 the situation became increasingly chaotic. The African summit in Casablanca early in January devoted much of its attention to the situation in the Congo. Delegates had a common approach in which they saw colonialism's resurgence: a 'manifestation of neo-colonialism'. With the exception of Ghana, every state present that had troops in the Congo decided to withdraw them, although Ghana wanted to give the UN Command another chance. In the end a compromise was reached: a threat by every state, including Ghana, to withdraw troops from the Congo unless the UN Command acted immediately to support the central government. The Katanga government announced the death of Lumumba on 13 February and claimed that he had been murdered by tribesmen in Kolwezi. On 18 February Nkrumah advocated the creation of a new UN command, which must be African; disarming the Congolese; the expulsion of non-African personnel then in the Congo army; the release of political prisoners; and the temporary removal of diplomatic representatives. Violence through February included attacks on the UN forces whose Canadian, Sudanese and Tunisian troops suffered casualties. By the end of the month a total of 18 countries – Canada, Ireland and Sweden from Europe, and 15 Afro-Asian countries – Ethiopia, Ghana, Guinea, India, Indonesia, Liberia, Mali, Malaya, Morocco, Nigeria, Pakistan, Senegal, Sudan, Tunisia and the United Arab Republic (Egypt and Syria) – were part of the UN operation.

Following the announcement of the death of Lumumba the position of foreign nationals, especially Belgians, became more difficult in Orientale and Kivu provinces, which were strongly Lumumbist. Urging various nations to take their fingers out of the Congo pie, the London *Observer* argued:

> This applies particularly to Belgium, Britain and the United States, all of which have played an active and influential role. Unlike the Soviet *bloc* and France, these three countries overtly support the role of the UN in the Congo. But while they have defended Mr Hammarskjold from the attacks of the Communists, they have, at the same time, helped to undermine the UN authority in the Congo.[3]

On 23 April 1961 President Kasavubu and Prime Minister Joseph Ileo met with 'President' Moïse Tshombe of the breakaway Katanga Province at Coquilhatville in Equateur Province in the hope of working out a settlement of their differences. But after two days Tshombe walked out, declining to co-operate unless Kasavubu renounced his agreement with the United Nations. When Tshombe attempted to leave Coquilhatville, however, he was arrested. At this conference it was decided to divide the Congo into 19 states: Leopoldville province would become four states, Equateur three, Eastern three, Katanga two, Kivu two and Kasai five. Antoine Gizenga, whose base was in Eastern Province, refused to accept these conference decisions. Since the death of Lumumba, whose close associate he had been, Gizenga had claimed to be the legal prime minister and at this time he was backed by the Afro-Asian and Communist blocs. His position was denied by the central government of Kasavubu. Far greater powers than those envisaged at an earlier conference of political leaders that had taken place in Tananarive, Madagascar, were assigned to the federal government and the president. When the first anniversary of the Congo's independence came on 30 June 1961, *West Africa* magazine said, among other things: 'In the first week of independence Tshombe appealed for help from the Rhodesian Army; Lumumba appealed to the UN and later to the Russians; Bomboko intervened and Lumumba re-embraced the Belgians; Tshombe began forming the Katanga Army; the *Force Publique* mutinied and started a campaign of pillage and rape; the Belgian Army retaliated. From abroad the whole process seemed incredible and pathetic, but it was the beginning of disintegration which eventually led to Lumumba's murder, Gizenga's execution of political innocents – including Ghanaian soldiers.' *West Africa* had more to say but the picture it conveyed was one of massive confusion, distrust, factional fighting and dubiously motivated interventions.

On 2 August 1961 President Kasavubu established a new government in

Leopoldville: he appointed Cyrille Adoula as Prime Minister and brought in Antoine Gizenga as deputy. Adoula was to be prime minister for three years. A month later, on 13 September, the United Nations forces attempted to take control of Elizabethville (Lubumbashi), the capital of Katanga, but they met with strong resistance and considerable fighting at Jadotville. Peace talks were then scheduled to be held at Ndola, Northern Rhodesia, on 17 September but the flight carrying the UN Secretary-General Dag Hammarskjold to Ndola crashed in circumstances that have never been adequately explained and he and all on board were killed. A provisional ceasefire was arranged on 20 September between the central Congo government (the UN forces) and Katanga. However, from mid-November 1961 to mid-January 1962 heavy fighting took place as UN forces attempted to end the Katanga secession. At one stage Britain agreed to supply the UN with bombs but then the government refused to do so after heavy pressure from its own right wing. A new flare-up rook place in January 1962 between the forces of the central government and supporters of Gizenga in Stanleyville (Kisangani); Gizenga at this time, though supposedly part of Kasavubu's government, had been absent from Leopoldville for three months. On 15 January the Congolese Parliament passed a motion of censure on Gizenga and the following day Adoula sacked him from the government. Gizenga agreed to return to Leopoldville under UN protection. The UN then handed him over to the government in Leopoldville.

There had been a rapid increase of concern in white-dominated Southern Africa once it had become clear that the Congo would achieve its independence in June 1960 and prior to that date a Salisbury–Elizabethville airlift of arms to Katanga had been mounted with the knowledge of the Belgians. Lumumba had increased white fears when he proclaimed that the liberation of the Congo would be the first phase of the complete independence of Central and Southern Africa. He made clear that he would support liberation movements in Rhodesia, Angola and South Africa. 'A unified Congo, having at its head a militant anti-colonialist constituted a real danger for South Africa. … Lumumba, because he was the chief of the first country in this region to obtain independence, because he knew concretely the weight of colonialism, had pledged in the name of his people to contribute physically to the death of that Africa. That the authorities of Katanga and those of Portugal have used every means to sabotage Congo's independence does not surprise us.'[4]

Dag Hammarskjold, whose untimely death tended to create for him a status he did not deserve, was never held in much esteem in Africa. As Ronald Segal wrote scathingly of him: 'Hammarskjold's report to the Council (UN Security Council) that the dispute with Katanga "did not have its roots in the Belgian attitude" was clearly absurd, and his treatment of the Tshombe regime as a factor outside the scope of the central government was a virtual accession to the wishes of the West. The truth is that the Secretariat, for all its outward deference to the Afro-Asian states during the Congo crisis, was dominated by the West, especially the United States, and responsive to its view of events.'[5] When the Tshombe regime, assisted by Belgian troops, pacified the hostile Baluba north region, its assaults were ignored by the West, but when Lumumba turned to Moscow for support this was importing the Cold War into Africa while the continuing presence of Belgian troops and administrators in Katanga was part of the struggle to sustain peace and good government in the troubled Congo. Radical African states became disenchanted with Hammarskjold's performance in the Congo but since they also saw the United Nations as a protection against the great powers they were reluctant to attack him openly. An Afro-Asian motion in the General Assembly (17 September 1960) while saving the face of the Secretary-General had requested him to 'assist the Central Government of the Congo in the restoration and maintenance of law and order throughout the Republic of the Congo and to safeguard its unity, territorial integrity and political independence'. Hammarskjold had tried to persuade the Belgians to remove their forces from Katanga, although he got no response from them. When he attempted an accommodation with Lumumba the US State Department protested. 'It was clearly one thing to support the UN when it acted as the West desired, and quite another when it took uncongenial directions.'[6]

In many respects, Katanga was central to Western concerns over the Congo since it was both the mineral heartland of the country and the geographic-strategic link with the Central African Federation (through Northern Rhodesia) and the white-dominated south of the continent, which for years to come would be shielded where possible from African nationalism by the West. An article in the *Saturday Evening Post* of 8 September 1962 had this to say of the Congo crisis.

In one of the more ironic twists of our times, ultra-conservatives who pride themselves on being more anti-Communist and more devoted to the cause of freedom than others are clamouring for UN troops to withdraw from the Congo. They are urging the US Government to put its trust in wily, opportunistic Moïse Tshombe, secessionist President of Katanga province. An organization called the 'American Committee for Aid to Katanga Freedom Fighters' in a full-page newspaper advertisement recently proclaimed, 'It's time for the UN Army to get out of the Congo' and asked the question, 'Why not let the Congolese settle their own affairs?'.

That, needless to say, was the last thing that any outsider was prepared to countenance. Addressing a special session of the UN General Assembly in New

York on 2 February 1962, the Congolese Prime Minister, Cyrille Adoula, said that the first concern of his government was national unity and to 'bring Katanga back to legality' and to free the province of mercenaries. Katangan secession would not have lasted without outside help.

> In the Katanga case, real power remained in the hands of former colonial officials, who received the full backing of the Belgian state, and who were assisted in their rape of the Congo and its resources by a host of white adventurers and mercenaries from all over Europe and Southern Africa.
>
> Britain, France and apartheid South Africa gave active support to the secession, as their ruling classes shared the Belgians' fear of Lumumba's commitment to genuine independence and radical social change. The cynicism of the Western powers became evident once the major threat to their interests in the Congo was removed. After the assassination of Lumumba and the elimination of the Lumumbists from the political scene in Kinshasa, Belgium and the Western alliance determined that they could do profitable business in the Congo with the anti-Communist and pro-Western moderates they had helped put in power. Given the worldwide disapproval of the Katanga secession, particularly in Africa and the Third World generally, there was no compelling reason to support it. They pulled the rug from under Tshombe's feet, and the secession was ended by UN military action in January 1963.[7]

U Thant succeeded Dag Hammarskjold as UN Secretary-General and he did what Lumumba had demanded: bring an end to Katanga's secession. However, 'This became possible after President John F. Kennedy gave the UN a green light in December 1962 to end Tshombe's rebellion by force. In this regard, it should be noted that the so-called "U Thant plan" for Katanga's reintegration in the Congo was entirely drafted by Congo experts at Foggy Bottom in Washington and sent to the top floor of the Secretariat through the US mission to the UN.'[8] On 15 January 1963 Katanga's secession was formally ended and Tshombe went into exile in Spain.

Under pressure from the United States and the pro-US moderates of the Binza group (named after a suburb of Leopoldville where they met) – every effort was made over the years 1961–63 to eliminate the Lumumbists from the Congo political scene. The Binza group consisted of five men: Mobutu, Victor Nendaka, Justin Bomboko, Albert Ndele and Damien Kondoko who worked closely with US, Belgian and UN officials and between them controlled President Kasavubu. After his return to Leopoldville under UN auspices in January 1962, Gizenga, the deputy prime minister, was sent to the island prison of Bula-Bemba. By October 1963 most of the ministers from the Lumumbist camp had been sacked; in any case, on 29 September 1963 Kasavubu dismissed parliament so that he, Adoula and the Binza group were able to operate without any legislative or parliamentary checks. The Lumumbists then united under an umbrella organization – the *Conseil National de Libération* (CNL) – which established its headquarters across the Congo River in Brazzaville where, the previous August, a popular revolution had ousted the reactionary government of the Priest-President Youlou who was replaced by the more radical Alphonse Massamba-Debat. What the West wanted in the Congo, and what its collaborators were prepared to accept, was the continued exploitation of the country's resources. As a Congolese intellectual would describe the process many years later: 'The neo-colonial situation involves the uninterrupted exploitation of the country's resources by the metropolitan bourgeoisie, but this time in collaboration with national ruling classes. The primary mission of the latter is to maintain the order, stability and labour discipline required for meeting the country's obligations to the international market.'[9]

In a letter to the UN Secretary-General of December 1963, President Kwame Nkrumah of Ghana called for an all-African force to take over from the United Nations Force in the Congo when the UN mandate expired. He argued that unless this was done the withdrawal of UN forces would be followed by a military coup engineered by either General Mobutu or Moïse Tshombe, 'the puppet of the Union Minière'. Nkrumah saw the Congo's political importance as very great because of its position between independent Africa to the north 'and the territories of colonialism and white supremacy in the south'. He disputed that the Congo had to be in hands friendly to the West. He said that 'any form of foreign control over the Congo Republic constitutes an immediate and substantial threat to the independence of every African leader'. Nkrumah was correct in his assessment of what was happening – from an African point of view – but his arguments were not going to carry weight in a United Nations dominated by the Western powers.

NATIONALIST REVOLTS AGAINST THE CENTRE

The overall situation in the Congo continued to deteriorate through 1963 into 1964; there was no effective government and a general growth of lawlessness. Two groups launched more or less simultaneous armed struggles against the central government. The first of these were the Mulelists; the second the *Conseil National de Libération* (CNL), which launched its armed struggle in those areas where the *Mouvement National Congolaise* (MNC) and other parties of supporters of the Lumumbists were strong. Pierre Mulele, who had briefly been minister of education under Lumumba, was the first prominent Lumumbist to return to the Congo, in 1963, and the first to launch a revolutionary struggle against a neo-colonialist state in Africa. He had spent 15 months in Cairo as the representative of the Gizenga government and then a further 15 months in China where he received training in revolutionary guerrilla warfare. After returning to Kwilu he spent six months preparing the groundwork for a revolutionary struggle and training the first group of his partisans. He taught his guerrillas to respect the people with whom they came in contact and not to mistreat them or deprive them of their property. He saw the major task as being the radical transformation of society from the bottom up, based upon the solidarity of village life. He launched a full-scale guerrilla war in January 1964 and at first his forces succeeded in controlling a major portion of Kwilu; these early successes turned Mulele into a national legend. Most of his followers, who came to be called the Mulelists, were aged 13 to 18. However, he never succeeded in expanding his operations beyond the areas occupied by the two ethnic groups that formed the basis of his insurrection. These were the Mbundu (Mulele's ethnic group) and the Pende (Gizenga's group). In theory the Congolese Army, then numbering 30,000, should have had little difficulty in dealing with the Mulelists who were poorly armed and numbered 4,000 at most. In practice, threats to central government elsewhere in the huge country, as well as the increasing unreliability of most of the army, allowed the Mulelist revolt, which was a genuine nationalist one, to develop into a major threat to government. Mulele held his ground for five years against central government forces sent against him and was so popular on his home ground that despite a government offer of a US$10,000 reward for his capture, he was never betrayed. However, in 1968 he went to Brazzaville for medical treatment and from there Mobutu managed to lure him back to Leopoldville with promises of an amnesty and national reconciliation, where he was murdered on 3 October 1968.

The CNL, on the other hand, was rent by ideological and personality differences from the beginning. Even so, it was a genuine second liberation movement, based upon mass support, and its *Armée Populaire de Libération* (APL) had considerable success during 1964. In two and a half months under General Nicolas Olenga the APL siezed control of North Katanga, Maniema, Sankuru, the entire Eastern province and parts of Equateur Province. Kisangani fell to the CNL on 4 August and by November it controlled half the national territory. On 5 September its leader Christopher Gbenye established a people's republic with himself as president, Gaston Soumialot as defence minister, Nicolas Olenga as army forces commander and Thomas Kanza as foreign minister. However, it was soon obvious that the CNL leadership were less revolutionary intellectuals than concerned to recover the power they had lost earlier to the moderates and they wanted to settle scores with their political enemies. Most of their troops, who became known as the Simbas (Swahili for lions), were youths who went into action under the influence of hemp (cannabis) and behaved towards the people they were supposedly liberating as though they were operating in conquered territory. The collapse of the CNL was brought about by the US-organized counter-insurgency operation of November 1964. Once the CNL revolt had been crushed Mobutu was to lure most of its leaders back from exile and allow them to engage in private business. He did not fear them as he did the charismatic and dedicated Mulele.

Meanwhile, the last UN toops had left the Congo on 30 June 1964, exactly four years after independence, and at once the country erupted into further violence, especially in Kwilu and the most easterly and northerly regions. In July Kasavubu, under US pressure, invited Tshombe, whose pro-Western stance was only too well attested, to return from exile to become prime minister, and forced Adoula to resign. Tshombe at once raised a force of European mercenaries to fight the rebels in the east of the country. By the end of July, after intense fighting, the rebels held about 500,000 square kilometres (200,000 square miles) of territory. The Congolese Army, on the other hand, had virtually disintegrated, leaving at most 5,000 men that could be used to any effect.

THE RETURN OF TSHOMBE

The repeated defeats of Mobutu's army by the Simbas, the departure of the UN troops at the end of June and threats from Tshombe's former mercenaries, then in Angola, to invade Katanga, had rendered Adoula's government increasingly unstable. In July 1964, therefore, Tshombe was brought back from exile in Spain to replace Adoula as prime minister; the change of leaders was engineered by Belgium and the United States. Tshombe, who in the meantime had been in contact with all sectors of public opinion including the Gbenye-led CNL faction through Thomas Kanza, set up a provisional government of 'public salvation'. Since early 1964, before it was decided to bring back Tshombe, the CIA had been conducting a paramilitary campaign against the insurrections in Kwilu and the east. By that time the CNL was receiving help from Nasser's Egypt and Eastern bloc countries while the United States and Belgian military experts and white mercenaries made up the counter-insurgency forces and these combined with the Katanga gendarmes, once Tshombe had brought them back from Angola, so that the mix by mid-year was very much a Cold War affair. The United States committed itself to full support of the Tshombe government. US President L. B. Johnson listed the disturbances in the Congo as one of his major foreign policy problems and said he would 'attempt to see that the people of the

Congo have as good government as is possible'. (What they got in fact was 30 years of Mobutu.)

In September 1964 Organisation of African Unity (OAU) foreign ministers from 34 member countries met in Addis Ababa to consider the Congo question. The Secretary-General, Diallo Telli, said that the 'Congolese Drama' should be 'insulated effectively by the OAU from the Cold War' although by then it was already too late. The foreign ministers passed a six-point resolution calling for an end to the recruitment of mercenaries and the expulsion of those already in the Congo; an immediate ceasefire; an appeal for the creation of a Congolese government of unity; the creation of an ad hoc committee to help leaders achieve reconciliation, bring about normal relations with neighbours and decide on aid requirements; an OAU mission to visit the capitals of countries interfering in the Congo to ask them to desist; and for OAU members to cease any action that might aggravate the situation. An OAU Reconciliation Commission under President Jomo Kenyatta of Kenya was established and Kenyatta appealed to the Congolese for 'immediate and maximum cooperation'. Tshombe, however, said he would not co-operate and would not meet with the rebels. Then, on 23 September, President Kasavubu informed the OAU that the Congo would no longer conform to the organization's decisions and he accused it of 'manifest interference in the purely internal affairs of the Congo.'

Stanleyville was the principal CNL-held city and the rebel headquarters, so the forces of counter-revolution (the Belgians and Americans, aided by a force of 700 mercenaries on the ground) decided to make it their primary objective. *Operation Dragon Rouge* (Red Dragon) was conceived as a combined land–air offensive; it culminated on 24 November with a US-Belgian parachute drop on Stanleyville that coincided with the arrival in the town of the mercenaries, a successful operation from which the CNL did not recover. This operation was carried out even as African countries, working through the OAU, attempted to broker a peace, but the United States and its Western allies did all they could to undermine these African diplomatic moves. President Johnson, under the humanitarian pretext of rescuing white hostages, authorized an airlift of Belgian paratroopers while the Congo Reconciliation Commission was meeting in Nairobi under the chairmanship of Jomo Kenyatta. Kenyatta, indeed, felt the Americans had deliberately deceived him in the person of their ambassador, William Attwood, who tries unsuccessfully in his subsequent book *The Reds and the Blacks* to justify the deception that he clearly employed. Thus, in a co-ordinated action, a column of mercenaries and elite Congolese troops from the military base at Kamina, under Colonel Frederic Vandewalle, advanced on Stanleyville to arrive at the town on 24 November as US planes flew in Belgian paratroopers from the British Ascension island. About 60 of the white hostages and 1,000 Congolese were massacred by the Simbas during the ensuing battle. The intervention was intended to safeguard Western interests in the Congo and prevent the establishment of an independent government that might not co-operate with the West. It succeeded in this objective. However, the CIA campaign against the Mulele maquis in Kwilu and the Kabila rebels in the east was to last for another four years. The CIA employed anti-Castro Cuban and European mercenaries who were used to fly T-6 training planes, T-28 fighter planes armed with rockets and machine guns, C-147 military transports, H-21 heavy duty helicopters and B-26 bombers. The US Air Force provided air support for government troops and the mercenaries and used napalm on ground targets.

Meeting in New York in December 1964, in the aftermath of the US-Belgian intervention of November 24, the OAU Council of Ministers asked the UN Security Council to condemn the Anglo-Belgian-American intervention in Stanleyville. They appealed for an end to hostilities in the Congo and an end to foreign intervention. Speaking on 15 December in the Security Council debate, Kenya's Joe Murumbi said:

> How can one speak of a blood bath which one has designed and caused, in one breath, and of humanitarianism in the other? Where is this humanitarianism when the white mercenaries are allowed full licence to murder innocent African men, women and children? Where was this humanitarianism when Patrice Lumumba, later brutally done to death, was held hostage? ... What happened to this self-same humanitarianism when innocent Africans were butchered in Sharpeville in South Africa? ... It is a peculiar brand of humanitarianism coming from countries whose record and international behaviour do not entitle them to boast about their achievements.

Atrocities were only atrocities, it seemed, when they were perpetrated against whites, not when they were carried out by whites against blacks. Earlier that month, on 6 December, Connor Cruise O'Brien who had served with the UN forces in the Congo in the early days of the crisis, wrote an article in the *Observer* in which he asked:

> Are white people in Africa to be regarded as covered by a sort of Caucasian providence insurance policy, with a guarantee that if the natives get rough, the metropolitan forces will once again come to the rescue? And if so, will this doctrine, in the long run, increase or decrease the security of white people in Africa and elsewhere? Similar policies in China contributed

eventually to the total exclusion of all white influence, missionary or other, from that country.[10]

The rebellion in the east continued into 1965, although early in the year the government had gained control of all the main towns. Katanga had its gendarmes back from the bush and Kasai was brought under full central control. By this time the going rate for mercenaries had risen to £200 a month. By March 1965 the Congo National Army, with its mercenary leaders, was winning the war. A great deal of slaughter took place as the army terrorized the population while relying upon the mercenaries to lead military actions. By July it had become clear that the rebellion was coming to an end. The mercenaries were responsible for a growing list of brutalities and carried out horrific tortures on prisoners before killing them. By November the war was finally over.

THE DAMAGE TO THE CONGO AND AFRICA

Any assessment of the damage to the Congo, both immediate and long term, can only be approximate. An estimated 20,000 Congolese had been killed by December 1964. Many more died in reprisals though no figures are available. The mercenaries carried out indiscriminate killings in villages through which they passed. Although the Western press emphasized the killing of Europeans it appeared likely in the end that no more than 300 had been killed altogether since 1960, though many more had been wounded. Perhaps 30,000 Congolese, a figure that has often been quoted, were killed altogether though the actual number of deaths may have been far higher. The damage to mining activity (then the principal source of national income) was enormous as was the damage to property. The Congo's huge mineral wealth and Western, especially Belgian and British, investments were the principal reasons for intervention together with Cold War strategic considerations. The generally savage conduct of the white mercenaries from Europe and Southern Africa became notorious and did the white cause in Africa great harm. The five years of chaos, revolt, disruption and foreign interference in the Congo from 1960 to 1965 made the country's name synonymous with the idea of breakdown in independent Africa with the result that it coloured Western perceptions of Africa for a generation. No one emerged from the crisis with credit. The Congolese divided into warring factions; the Belgians, whose efforts to prepare the country for independence had been minimalist, had been only too ready to return and manipulate the situation so as to safeguard their investments; the crisis brought the two superpowers into black Africa where Cold War policy considerations rather than concern to assist the Congolese overcome their problems was the guiding principle. In Katanga

British and Belgian capitalist interests – *Union Minière du Haut Katanga* and Tanganyika Concessions – used their influence in support of Tshombe's secession. In a felicitous phrase Tshombe was described as the 'darling of imperialism of all kinds' until he was discarded by the imperialists he had served. The United Nations, dominated by Western interests and most notably the United States, became tainted and its refusal to rescue Lumumba, who was considered by the West to be a dangerous pro-Moscow Marxist and too independent, was long seen by the Afro-Asian bloc as a black mark against the UN and its Secretary-General Dag Hammarskjold.

A revealing assessment of the impact of these events upon Africa comes from Attwood, the US Ambassador to Kenya at the time. He wrote as follows:

> Even more galling to the educated African was the shattering of so many of his illusions – that Africans were now masters of their own continent, that the OAU was a force to be reckoned with, that a black man with a gun was the equal of a white man with a gun. For in a matter of weeks, two hundred swaggering white mercenaries had driven through an area the size of France, scattered the Simbas and captured their capital; and in a matter of hours, 545 Belgians in American planes had defied the OAU, jumped into the heart of Africa and taken out nearly two thousand people – with the loss of one trooper.
>
> The weakness and impotence of newly independent Africa had been harshly and dramatically revealed to the whole world, and the educated African felt deeply humiliated: the white man with a gun, the old plunderer who had enslaved his ancestors, was back again, doing what he pleased, when he pleased, where he pleased. And there wasn't a damn thing Africa could do about it, except yell rape.[11]

Attwood, it must be added, clearly enjoyed the scenario he had painted.

THE MERCENARY INVOLVEMENT

The *Sunday Telegraph* of 26 November 1961, with breathtaking distortion, described mercenaries in the Congo as 'unlikely unshaven Galahads [who] alone in this tortured continent are ready to shed their blood in the cause of non-racialism'. Such cynical disregard for the truth tells us a good deal about Western attitudes to Africa at that time, and the role of the mercenaries in the Congo needs close scrutiny, not simply for what they did on the ground but for what they revealed of the European and American response to a situation for which they must shoulder most of the blame.

The Congo crisis was the first major upheaval with international dimensions in post-colonial black Africa and it witnessed the first appearance of white mercenaries on the continent where their conduct left a lasting impression of racism and brutality. Secessionist Katanga was to last from July 1960 until January 1963 and throughout this time Tshombe was in the market for arms and mercenaries and was largely financed by *Union Minière du Haut Katanga*. The number of mercenaries employed during the Katanga secession averaged 400 although later, when mercenaries were employed by the central government to fight the Simba revolt, their numbers rose to 1,500. The mercenaries were drawn from a range of backgrounds that included British soldiers from the old British-Indian Army, combat experienced French from Algeria, World War II RAF pilots from Rhodesia and South Africa and Belgian paratroopers.[12] The Congo, in fact, represented the first opportunity since 1945 that mercenaries came to be employed as fighting units, and as whites fighting in a black country they provided a conspicuous and explosive element in an increasingly race-conscious world. At independence there were about 100 Belgian officers with the *Force Publique*; by December 1960 there were about 500 'volunteers' as well as large-scale military aid in the form of arms and equipment supplied to the Katanga leader, Moïse Tshombe. As the confusion in the Congo escalated with the UN forces trying to maintain order, the Belgians pursuing their own pro-Katanga agenda, and mounting chaos in much of the rest of the huge country, the opening for mercenary activity became steadily more apparent. On 7 February 1961, South African technicians and pilots were being recruited to serve in the Katanga Air Force. On 10 April 1961, UN Ethiopian troops captured and disarmed 32 Katanga white mercenaries in the north Katanga town of Kabalo where the UN forces subsequently seized a charter aircraft bringing in seven tons of arms and ammunition. As the *Manchester Guardian* pointed out: 'Politically Tshombe has done immense harm by bolstering up an anti-Congolese State by European army officers and advisers. Whether or not he is a Belgian puppet he has behaved like one, and relations between Black and White in Africa are so delicate that any suspicion of European domination in a new form serves only to prevent true co-operation between the races coming about.'[13]

According to the British Labour MP, Philip Noel-Baker, *Union Minière* and Tanganyika Concessions (TANKS) between them had provided the Katanga government with £15 million over 1960–61. He asked:

If Mr Tshombe had not been paid this money, could he have paid his white mercenaries, his Katangese gendarmerie, and the foreign arms firms who have supplied him with aircraft, weapons and ammunition? Could he have started, or continued, the movement which has so greatly increased the cost of the United Nations?[14]

By mid-1964 the situation in the Congo had changed radically as the Simba revolt threatened to bring about the collapse of the government. In these circumstances President Kasavubu invited Tshombe to return from his exile in Spain to replace Cyrille Adoula as prime minister and take control of the war against the Simba rebels. Tshombe complied with this request and at once raised a new force of European mercenaries: he possessed the necessary contacts and there were plenty of willing mercenaries waiting for work. These mercenaries were to play their most effective role in the two months of October and November 1964 when the Simba rebellion was effectively ended although it continued into 1965. Mercenaries continued to play a leading role in the Congo yet, however effective they might have been, the presence of white mercenaries in the Congo, especially those from South Africa, was universally condemned by the rest of Africa.

One of the most damning revelations about mercenary behaviour was revealed in an *Observer* story after a senior mercenary had produced a series of photographs showing atrocities committed by his men. The pictures (two were published in the *Observer*) showed how mercenaries not only shot and hanged their prisoners after torturing them, but used them for target practice and gambled over the number of shots needed to kill one. The officer, who by then had returned to South Africa, said he took the pictures 'for the men to send home to their families'. Subsequently, he claimed to have become so disgusted at the atrocities that he decided to expose them.[15]

After he had dismissed Tshombe on 13 October 1965, President Kasavubu announced that he intended to dismiss the mercenary force, which then consisted of 800 white mercenaries attached to the Congolese army. In fact, the mercenary presence was to continue in the Congo for a further two years and it was only in 1967 that a partly rejuvenated army was strong enough to round them up and expel them from the country. The Congo crisis produced high emotions in Africa and Europe. In Africa the activities of the mercenaries were seen as a form of neo-colonialism while their brutality served only to reinforce anti-white and anti-imperialist views. Moreover, direct and indirect evidence of Western government support for the mercenaries ensured that they came to be regarded as an arm of Western policy and not simply as maverick individuals who could not be controlled. The image of *les affreux* – the horribles – as they came to be called coloured the African response to mercenaries for years to come.

In Europe the Congo crisis was seen by the political right – racists whose starting point was an automatic assumption of white racial superiority and those who opposed African independence – as a struggle to maintain 'civilized' values and they regarded the mercenaries as heroes, an attitude that was greatly reinforced when the lives of whites in the Congo were at risk. Many press articles at the time talked of a return to barbarism and the word Congo became synonymous with the belief among this group that Western control was needed in Africa for a long time to come. Such attitudes also greatly reinforced support for white minority rule in the south of the continent and the continuation of apartheid in South Africa. What also clearly emerged was the fact that none of the principal European countries involved – Belgium, France, Britain and Portugal – could escape responsibility for the actions of the mercenaries. In later years, when mercenaries appeared in other parts of Africa, especially in Nigeria, Rhodesia and Angola, Africans, who had not forgotten the events in the Congo, reacted with anger and revulsion at their reappearance.[16]

1965–70: MOBUTU TAKES CONTROL

On 24 November 1965 Mobutu carried out his second coup, as Nkrumah had predicted. He suspended President Kasavubu and Prime Minister Evariste Kimba, who had replaced Tshombe, and took full executive power into his own hands. The Mobutu coup marked the beginning of the Second Republic and the re-establishment of a minimum of law and order. It also marked the commencement of 30 years of autocratic rule by Mobutu. Maj.-Gen. Joseph Mobutu (as he then was) brought an end to the power struggle between President Kasavubu and ex-Prime Minister Moïse Tshombe when he deposed the President and appointed Colonel Leonard Mulamba as Prime Minister. He told the press that he intended to remain President for five years. In parliament Mobutu gained overwhelming support with a vote in his favour of 259 to 0 with only two abstentions. He then inaugurated a campaign of national reconstruction. The period 1965–67 was one of transition as Mobutu consolidated his power. He became head of state with Mulamba as his Prime Minister while the 1964 constitution was kept as a framework for the time being. The real source of authority, however, was the Army staff.

On 17 April 1966 Mobutu established the *Mouvement Populaire de la Révolution* (MPR) with himself as founding president. Those who wished for political or other advancement soon recognized that they had to join the new organization or party. Mobutu set about the task of eliminating all opposition, whether from politicians, students, workers or rebels. Ex-President Kasavubu retired to his farm, Tshombe was exiled to Spain again. Others, including Evariste Kimba, were accused of plotting and executed. In the beginning the students and labour were pro-Mobutu who promised 'true independence'. In the east of the country the rebels were virtually eliminated during 1966 though only because the army was still assisted by mercenaries at this time. However, when the mercenaries rebelled in mid-1967 the army, which had been reorganized, was strong enough to deal with them and forced them to flee across the border into Rwanda. While engaged in the process of eliminating or nullifying opposition, Mobutu centralized all decision-making in his own hands and created a Secretariat to the Presidency, which concentrated all power close to the Head of State. The Secretariat became an advisory organ for national policy and all decisions or contacts with the President were channelled through it. In October 1967 the Secretariat became the Bureau attached to the Presidency. A new constitution was approved by referendum (by 98 per cent of the voters) in 1967 and this established a presidential regime. The decline of parliament followed as well as an end to all legal opposition. Former political figures who had worked with Mobutu such as Cyrille Adoula, Justin Bomboko, Cleophas Kamitatu and Victor Nendaka were first appointed to overseas embassies, then accused of plotting and dismissed, their political roles finished. By 1970 there was no one in a position to challenge Mobutu's power and political pre-eminence. However, over the period 1967–70 substantial clashes occurred with the students who had become disillusioned with Mobutu. Their power was broken, as was that of the trade unions, which became supine supporters of the regime, counselling patience to their workers who wanted to strike for better conditions, and sometimes did so in defiance of their leadership. In 1970 carefully orchestrated elections for President were held; Mobutu was unopposed and the number of ballot papers collected was greater than the registered electorate. A total of 420 candidates who had been carefully vetted and selected by the political bureau of the MPR were presented on the only list to the electorate and these approved candidates received 98.33 per cent of the vote. Thus by 1970 the stage was set for the ensuing years of Mobutu's presidentialism.

Given its huge resources the Congo should have become one of the richest states in the new Africa. In 1959 the GNP stood at US$1,300 million; by 1975 it had increased to US$3,695 million. The principal agricultural exports were palm oil, coffee, cotton, timber and rubber; and the principal minerals were copper, cobalt, diamonds, tin, gold and uranium with many more besides. This huge range of primary exports had played a major role in the crisis of 1960–65, as had the country's strategic position in the centre of Africa: the West was determined to prolong its control indefinitely.

CHAPTER THREE

African Unity and
The Formation of The OAU

The period immediately preceding and following the independence year of 1960 saw a bewildering series of African conferences taking place as the continent's new leaders sought to map out joint policies for the future. Groups were formed and positions – both radical and moderate – were adopted as the countries which had achieved independence tried to sort out their relations with each other and with the world beyond Africa. Everyone paid lip service to the ideal of African unity even though the realities of power diminished the possibility of any real union being achieved. The concept of pan-Africanism had developed through the first half of the twentieth century until, in the aftermath of World War II, the focus shifted from Black America and the Caribbean to Africa. The first Pan-African Conference had been sponsored by the Trinidad barrister, H. Sylvester Williams, and was held in London during 1900. A second Pan-African Congress was held in Paris in 1919 and called upon the Allied and Associated Powers to establish a code of law for the international protection of the Natives of Africa. Further conferences were held between the wars. Then came the great flowering of the pan-African movement. Its beginning was marked by the Sixth Pan-African Congress of 1945, held at Manchester in England and attended by such notable future African leaders as Jomo Kenyatta and Kwame Nkrumah. It reached its culmination in the late 1950s and early 1960s as the tide of independence began to sweep away the colonial empires of Africa.

The British colony of the Gold Coast became independent as Ghana on 6 March 1957 under the leadership of Kwame Nkrumah who became Africa's leading exponent of continental independence and unity. Other African leaders, however, resented his powerful personality and his interference in their affairs, and suspected his motives. Even so, he gave real impetus to the continent-wide demand for an immediate end to colonialism and the need for African unity. The series of conferences that were held from 1958 through 1961 covered the necessary groundwork that led to the formation of the Organisation of African

95

Unity (OAU) in 1963. Two major external considerations dominated African thinking at this time. Could the new states achieve real independence and throw off the neo-colonialism of the former imperial powers? Nkrumah's answer to that was yes, provided they united. Second, could they confront the Cold War pressures being exerted upon them, especially by the United States, and not be drawn into the East-West confrontation that was then at its height?

Commenting upon pan-Africanism in 1961, D. K. Chisiza, who was then the Parliamentary Secretary to the Ministry of Finance in Nyasaland (three years before it became independent), argued as follows:

> Pan-Africanism as a strategy for emancipation, is unquestionably effective, but we must build from down upwards, not from up downwards: the fabric of the regions must be knitted together not merely tacked. ... The writer suggests the following:
> 1. Attainment of independence.
> 2. Vigorous modernization of economies.
> 3. Encouragement of regional economic co-operation and regional consciousness.
> 4. Political regrouping of neighbouring countries.[1]

This pragmatic approach was very different from that of Nkrumah and held greater appeal for the majority of the emerging African leadership, which was conservative rather than radical despite the rhetoric that was employed at the time.

The First Conference of Independent African States was held in Accra, Ghana, during April 1958. Eight countries took part: there were three monarchies – Libya, a newly formed federation, Ethiopia and Morocco with ancient monarchical foundations; there were two parliamentary democracies, based on the British model – Sudan, a republic with a council of six as 'head of state', and Ghana; and three states headed by presidents – Liberia, Tunisia and the United Arab Republic. Their differences were political, racial, religious and historical – five were Muslim, two – Egypt and Ethiopia – had long histories, that of Egypt being one of the most ancient in the world, Ghana was the creation of the European Scramble for Africa and Liberia the creation of American philanthropists. Between them these eight countries represented the range of problems and aspirations that would dominate Africa in the decade of the 1960s. A first consideration was simply that of getting to know one another, an elementary objective that had not been possible during colonial times. Of the main heads of the agenda for this conference, four were concerned with international affairs, two with these states' relations with each other. Principal subjects for discussion were how to safeguard their sovereignty and independence, foreign subversive activities in Africa, the future of dependent territories in Africa, the war in Algeria and the black-white racial problem. The conference faced a difficulty over its approach to the dependent territories since not all colonial leaders admitted the claim of some politicians in the independent states to provide leadership on their behalves.

Dr Nkrumah opened the conference on 15 April and read messages of good wishes from, among others, the US Secretary of State, John Foster Dulles, and the Prime Minister of China. The conference worked to five main subject headings that reflected then, and later, the principal concerns of the new African states. These were:

1 Exchange of views on foreign policy especially in relation to the African continent, the future of the dependent territories of Africa, the Algerian problem, the racial problem, and the steps to be taken to safeguard the independence and sovereignty and the territorial integrity of the independent African states.

2 Examination of ways and means of promoting economic co-operation between the States 'based on the exchange of technical, scientific and educational information, with special regard to industrial planning and agricultural development'.

3 Formulation of concrete proposals for exchange of visiting missions both government and non-government, which may lead to first-hand knowledge of one country by another and to mutual appreciation of their respective cultures.

4 Consideration of the problem of international peace in conformity with the Charter of the United Nations and the re-affirmation of the principles of the Bandung Conference.

5 The Conference to consider setting up permanent machinery after the Conference.

Egypt pressed the conference to include the question of Israel; this was not accepted at the time though the issue of Israel would recur repeatedly in the years to come. Most speakers, though not Emperor Haile Selassie of Ethiopia or President Tubman of Liberia, condemned France for its Algerian policy.

At the closing session, the declaration that gained the most applause was that of Dr Nkrumah who said the conference had killed the old notion that Africa was irrevocably divided into 'Arab' and 'Black' Africa, into 'Mediterranean' and 'tropical' Africa, into 'Muslim' and 'non-Muslim'. Emperor Haile Selassie said 'Africans are beginning to discover Africa'. 'The real significance of the conference is that states so diverse, which have long been separated or have never known each other, have met for discussions, have learned each other's ways and felt that African countries can on certain matters present a united and influential voice.'[2] The principal subjects discussed on this occasion would recur at all the subsequent conferences, though the number of newly independent countries would rapidly increase, and while some problems would go off the agenda others – such as the Congo – would replace them to take up a great deal of debate. This conference set the tone for much subsequent debate and despite inevitable flights of rhetoric most of the discussions were sober appraisals of the tasks Africa had to face and revealed an acute awareness of what Africa ought to do and what lay within the scope of its power, a power that was strictly limited even when unanimity of approach could be attained.

The next conference of significance was the first All-African Peoples' Conference, which opened on 5 December 1958 in Accra. The conference was non-governmental and had some 500 delegates from all over Africa including many from nationalist organizations. There were also observers from Europe and America. It was set to discuss colonialism, racialism and tribalism in contemporary Africa. An important recent development that influenced the conference was the successful drafting of a charter on 23 November 1958 to create an African Union of States, beginning with Ghana and Guinea. Kwame Nkrumah and Sekou Touré, the sponsors of the charter, hoped it would be the beginning of a wider union; President Olympio of Togo had expressed an interest in joining. The conference gave dramatic emphasis to the possibilities of the Ghana–Guinea Union even though only a few of the important leaders of French or British West Africa expected to be present. A number of delegates spoke of union in general terms and all those from French-speaking West Africa were in favour of working together. On the other hand, President Tubman of Liberia had declared, in a speech the previous November, his opposition to the idea of federation, which he described as 'utopian' while drawing attention to important differences in foreign policy between West African leaders. However, he did emphasize the need for treaties of friendship and other forms of association among West African states. As *West Africa* commented:

> Political interest in West Africa now swings away from relations with European powers to those between West African territories and the new relationships will prove a more serious test of African statesmanship than the old. Earlier this year we point out that independence reopened the frontier problem throughout the area, and it is clear that between territories there are innumerable possible grounds for dispute. If the Ghana-Guinea union offers a pattern for peaceful settlement of disputes,

and a framework for free trade and movement, it will give a lead which others are certain to follow. But there is no single solution to West African unity, and rigid arrangements may perpetuate dis-unity, by making the admission of new states unlikely or impossible.[3]

President Nkrumah opened the conference: he declared this to be the decade of African independence and urged the delegates to achieve first 'the political kingdom: all else will follow' and he warned them to recognize imperialism which might arise 'not necessarily from Europe'. Tom Mboya from Kenya was elected chairman of the conference. Fraternal delegates included six Soviet writers; both Khruschev and Chou En-lai sent greetings to the conference. Western reporting of the conference tended to highlight Western Cold War paranoia: what was the significance of the Soviet writers attending and what did Tom Mboya mean in his speech when he emphasized Africa's indifference to great power quarrels and said that Africans would not tolerate interference from any country 'and I mean any'? As *West Africa* commented:

The Conference is best seen as a demonstration of strength and intention. Even if east and central African visitors have heard from Ghana's United Party spokesman that he thinks treatment of Africans by Africans can be as bad as that of Africans by Europeans, from Liberia's True Whig Party that there is no need for an ideology for all Africa, and from the powerful Action Group delegation that no slogan can fit all the diverse conditions now obtaining in Africa, the visitors go away with a vision of United Africa which, even if little is done towards accomplishing it, can be a powerful stimulant. Any mention of the Ghana-Guinea union – which at present can be described as a close alliance – aroused the Conference's enthusiasm.[4]

The final resolutions were similar in tone and style to those of the previous conference. As *West Africa* summed up: 'Many outside Africa will resent or regret the wording of the Conference resolutions, many will wonder just how concrete its achievements will be. But the Conference's success or failure will owe nothing to outsiders in spite of the crowd of fraternal delegates and observers from Europe and the United States. This may be a strident voice; but it is African.'[5]

In January 1960 President Habib Bourguiba of Tunisia opened the second All-African People's Conference in Tunis; there were delegates from 30 countries and observers from Britain, the US, Russia, China, India, Greece, West Germany and Yugoslavia. In his welcoming speech President Bourguiba said that under-developed countries must co-operate with the industrialized powers if their standard of living was to be raised. On African unity and freedom he said: 'This is the moment of African independence. All the paths towards independence are valuable – whether they are through political stages or by armed conflict. Personally, I favour the pacific ways but I cannot refrain from helping Algeria in its war for liberty.' The conference lasted for four days. Significantly, the largest delegation to the conference came from Ghana whose policy remained the most determinedly pro-African unity.

In June 1960 the second Conference of Independent African States was held in Addis Ababa just over two years after the first one in Accra. The number of independent states attending had increased to 11 while delegations from a number of states approaching independence also participated. In his welcoming speech Emperor Haile Selassie emphasized that the conference was meeting at a moment of crisis in the relations of the Great Powers and that the breakdown of the Summit between Eisenhower and Khruschev was a matter of concern to Africans, as well as to the rest of humanity. Peace was essential to Africa's prosperity and progress. Reverting to a familiar African refrain of the time, the Emperor said that 'While co-operating with all states and international organisations, African states must not accept formulae that perpetuate colonial regimes or sow seeds of divisions among our countries'. He urged the establishment of an African Development Bank, and concluded that the fate of the African continent was passing into African hands. The leader of Africa's oldest independent state called delegates to rise to new responsibilities. Many of the delegates claimed that though the ranks of the independent African states were growing rapidly, relatively little had been done to meet some of their more important problems such as African unity, South Africa and South West Africa, the Algerian war and the French use of African soil for nuclear experiments.

On the question of African unity the Ghana delegation took the lead and Ako Adjei, the foreign minister, urged 'a complete change in our traditional attitudes and a drastic reorganization of our thinking habits'. He proposed the establishment of a Community of Independent African States that would not conflict with the national identity or constitution, or interfere with their policies, relations or obligations. However, Malam Maitama Sule, for Nigeria, said that rapid advance towards African unity seemed improbable. He said they had to be realistic and that though pan-Africanism was 'the only solution to our problems in Africa' a union of African states was 'premature'. Nigeria proposed no more than an Organization of African States with a permanent secretariat. Many delegates emphasized the need for economic co-operation. Support for independence movements throughout Africa was a constant theme. As Ahmed Taibi Benhima, the Moroccan delegate, declared: 'We must not rest until there is no longer mention in our African continent of British Kenya, of British Cameroons, or Portuguese Angola, of Spanish Sahara, of French Algeria or French Somaliland.' Algeria and South Africa remained at the top of the agenda. At the end of the conference the chief resolutions were agreed unanimously. All African states were called upon to apply a total boycott on South Africa and all the colonial powers were to be invited to set a timetable for independence for their colonies. The question of African unity was deferred.

What became known as the Brazzaville Group was formed in December 1960 when 12 Francophone countries met in Congo (Brazzaville). The 12 were Congo (Brazzaville), Côte d'Ivoire, Senegal, Mauritania, Upper Volta (Burkina Faso), Niger, Dahomey (Benin), Chad, Gabon, the Central African Republic, Cameroon and Madagascar. The Brazzaville Declaration called for peace in Algeria, favoured mediation in the Congo and upheld Mauritania's independence. It opposed a political union that would require integrated institutions but accepted a permanent Inter-State Economic Secretariat. The importance of the Brazzaville Group lay in the fact that it introduced two new elements into African politics at that time: it was the first occasion when invitations were extended to a restricted list of independent states; and a deliberate attempt was made to create a bloc of African states as opposed to regional groupings.[6]

In January 1961 leaders of Ghana, Guinea, Mali, Libya, Egypt and the Algerian Provisional Government met in Casablanca where they adopted what came to be known as the Casablanca Charter. Their object was the creation of a joint military command and an African Common Market. The group, which advocated a socialist path of development for the continent and a strong central authority, came to be seen by the rest of Africa as radical.

The movement received expressions of support from the newly formed Pan-African Movement for East, Central and Southern Africa (PAFMECSA). The first problem facing the Casablanca Group was the fact that although its decisions probably reflected much African opinion outside the countries taking part in the meeting, it did not include Nigeria, independent the previous October, which opposed the idea of an African High Command. Thus, the Casablanca Conference emphasized the growing divisions in Africa rather than unity. Other countries that had been invited to attend the conference but had not done so were Tunisia, Ethiopia, Liberia, Sudan, Togo, Somalia, India and Indonesia, the countries from outside Africa then having troops in the Congo under UN Command. Another group of countries, notably the French Community states, which had just participated in the Brazzaville meeting the previous month and were supporters of Kasavubu, had not been invited. The Congo, in effect, was acting as a divisive factor in Africa.

Casablanca was very much a working conference with little time for receptions or public occasions. King Mohammed of Morocco had convened the conference and acted as chairman and the Crown Prince led the Moroccan delegation. Ghana, Guinea, Mali and Egypt were led by their heads of state, the Algerian Provincial Government by Ferhat Abbas, Libya by its Foreign Minister and Ceylon by its ambassador in Cairo.

The main theme that dominated the conference was the deteriorating situation in the Congo. Nkrumah persuaded the other countries at Casablanca who wished to withdraw support from the UN in the Congo to give the UN Command another chance. He argued that there was no real alternative and that outside support for rival Congolese 'governments' would create the very conditions that the pan-Africanists sought to avoid – the unleashing of a full-scale Cold War confrontation in Africa. At the same time, Nkrumah was persuaded by his West African partners that the way to change the UN was to present it with an ultimatum. At that time Lumumba was still alive though he would be murdered a few days after the conference had come to an end. President Nasser succeeded, for the first time, in persuading the African states to condemn Israel 'as an instrument in the service of imperialism and neo-colonialism not only in the Middle East but also in Africa and Asia'. All the participants agreed on the potential value of the UN and on its Congo failure although they differed as to just what had to be done. The result was a compromise: the threat by every state, including Ghana, to withdraw troops from the Congo unless the UN Command acted immediately to support the 'Central Government'. They laid down a detailed programme, which included disarming Mobutu's army, expelling all Belgians and others not under UN Command, and reconvening the Congo Parliament. The conference resolution also reserved the right to take appropriate action 'if the purposes and principles which justified the presence of the UN Operational Command in the Congo are not realised, and respected'. The radical nature of the conference was most obviously apparent in its attitude towards the Congo crisis and the role of the UN.

The African Charter of Casablanca included provisions for the creation of an African Consultative Assembly, which would have under it four committees: a political committee, an economic committee, a cultural committee, and a joint African High Command. Resolutions covered the questions of Israel, Mauritania (which Morocco claimed), Ruanda-Urundi (the demand for an immediate Belgian withdrawal), apartheid and racial discrimination, French nuclear tests in the Sahara, Algeria (opposing any unilateral French solution to the war) and a communiqué on the situation in the Congo. The decisions arrived at by the Casablanca Conference were among the most forthright to emerge from Africa up to that date and set out or reinforced the objections of the more radical African states to the continuing interference in the continent's affairs (neo-colonialism) of the great powers.

The third All Africa People's Conference met at Cairo in March 1961. As with all these conferences, concern about neo-colonialism came top of the agenda – neo-colonialism was defined 'as the survival of the colonial system in spite of formal recognition of political independence in emerging countries which become the victims of an indirect and subtle form of domination by political, economic, social, military or technical means' – and the conference warned independent African states to beware of neo-colonialism which was associated with Britain, the United States, France, West Germany, Israel, Belgium, the Netherlands and South Africa. President Kennedy's new 'Peace Corps' was to be 'mercilessly opposed' since its aim was to 're-conquer and economically dominate Africa'. There were rowdy demonstrations by Somali students against Ethiopia. The forceful resolutions against neo-colonial activities demonstrated the deep awareness of the all-pervasive influence of the major powers in Africa alongside a sense of frustration that most African states simply did not have the ability to resist many of these pressures. Thus, the conference denounced the following manifestations of neo-colonialism: puppet governments represented by fabricated elections and based on some chiefs, reactionary elements, anti-popular politicians, big bourgeois compradors or corrupted civil or military functionaries; regrouping of states before or after independence by an imperial power in federation or communities linked to that imperial power; Balkanization as a deliberate fragmentation of states; economic entrenchment of the colonial power; direct monetary dependence; military bases. It added that the agents of neo-colonialism were colonial embassies and missions serving as nerve centres of espionage and pressure; so-called foreign aid and UN technical assistance which ill-advises and sabotages natural development; military personnel (foreign) who serve above all colonial interests; and the malicious propaganda controlled by imperial and colonial countries. These conference strictures on neo-colonialism may have appeared excessive yet by March 1961 the neo-colonialist activities of the major powers in the Congo had become a principal topic for discussion throughout Africa. At the end, conference resolutions included a call to the 'anti-imperialist' bloc to assist in the development of African economies by granting long-term loans at low interest rates to be repaid in national currencies; the expulsion of South Africa from the UN; the dismissal of Dag Hammarskjold; the immediate release of Jomo Kenyatta; the immediate independence of the Rhodesias and the dissolution of the Central African Federation.

Opposition to the Casablanca Group (its Charter had been published in

January) was not slow to appear. President Tubman of Liberia called a meeting in Monrovia for 8–12 May 1961, which was attended by 19 other independent African states. These were Cameroon, Central African Republic, Chad, Congo (Brazzaville), Dahomey (Benin), Ethiopia, Gabon, Côte d'Ivoire, Libya, Madagascar, Mauritania, Niger, Nigeria, Senegal, Sierra Leone, Somalia, Togo, Tunisia, Upper Volta (Burkina Faso). When the same group of countries met again in Lagos in January 1962 they had become known as the Monrovia Group. The Group adopted a draft charter for an Organisation of Inter-African and Malagasy States. Opening the conference Monrovia President Tubman outlined seven points for consideration. These were:

1 Contributions of African states to world peace.
2 Threats to peace and stability in Africa.
3 Promotion of better understanding, unity and co-operation among African states.
4 Development of permanent machinery to provide for consultation among African states.
5 Formation of general policy on the attitude to people striving for independence.
6 The Congo situation.
7 Working out general principles for border disputes, which arise from the emergence of independent states.

President Tubman added that economic ties were the best way to political unity. He said the conference should endorse the decisions of other conferences 'which we know to be in the best interests of Africa and the world' – he included Casablanca in this statement. The Monrovia Conference was more important for the attitudes it revealed than for any concrete decisions it reached. The formation of the Casablanca and Monrovia groups emphasized the dangerous nature of the ideological divisions that Africa faced before the Ethiopian Emperor, Haile Selassie, and others tried to resolve the differences, which had surfaced between the two main groups. In 1961 Nkrumah was still the mouthpiece of the genuinely independent African states. 'There was some truth in Nkrumah's criticism that the Francophone group were the puppets of French neo-colonialism, since France provided 80 per cent of their budgets. Similarly, some moves by the European Economic Community were regarded with suspicion as a new form of imperialism.'[7] Barbara Ward, who might be described as a 'soft' Cold War warrior as opposed to a 'hard' one, advised President Kennedy not to back the Monrovia group since its members were seen as only partially independent. The Monrovia Conference did not reach any clear conclusions over the Congo or French nuclear tests in the Sahara. The members were only really united in their dislike of Ghana's more radical and, therefore, divisive attitude. As Nigeria's *West Africa Pilot* claimed in an editorial of 18 May 1961, 'The truth is, Dr Nkrumah must be at the head of anything or outside it… He must be told that his reckless pursuit of his own ambitions for expansion will lead him nowhere'.

These African conferences had allowed the growing number of independent states to air their views and their leaders to interact with each other and though there were wide differences as to how problems should be tackled there was fairly consistent agreement as to what the problems were. Neo-colonialism and freeing the remaining African colonies were at the top of the list. At the same time, despite all the talk of unity, it was becoming increasingly clear that Africa was in danger of dividing into rival groups rather than uniting. West Africa had led the way and Nkrumah had led West Africa. Even before the Casablanca and Monrovia meetings of 1961, on 23 November 1958, Ghana and Guinea had drafted a charter, which was later also signed by Mali, to create an African Union of States. This led to the Conakry Declaration of 1 May 1959 in which Ghana and Guinea agreed to establish a union between their two countries. On 1 July that year Mali also joined the 'union' although in real political terms this union never amounted to anything. However, on 19 July 1959, at the village of Saniquellie in Liberia, Presidents Tubman, Nkrumah and Touré formulated the principles for achieving a Community of Independent African States. These meetings, whether of only two or three countries as in the cases of Conakry and Saniquellie, or the much larger meetings that have been examined above, between them created the situation that led to the formation of the Organisation of African Unity (OAU). Laying bare the problems was a necessary preliminary to achieving some form of unity. As Colin Legum wrote in 1961:

> Modern Pan-Africanism is reacting realistically to Africa's fundamental problem: its disunity. Tribalisms, a plethora of unviable states, vying nationalisms, rival ideas, and divergent loyalties are part of Africa's disorder. Everywhere the need is for unity: unity within the new states still struggling to become real nation-states; unity between states; unity in economic programmes to allow for a swift, co-ordinated effort to lift Africa out of its poverty; unity in the fight to get rid of the remnants of colonialism, and to ward off neo-colonialism; and unity to establish Africa's voice in international affairs.[8]

Another, similar statement was made by Julius Nyerere to the Second Conference of Independent African States in 1960:

We know that even after our independence has been achieved that *African Personality* which we would build up will depend upon the consolidation of our *unity*, not only in sentiment but in fact. We know that a *balkanized* Africa however loudly it might proclaim to the world its independence and all that, will in fact be an easy prey to the forces of neo-imperialism. The weak and divided can never hope to maintain a *dignified independence* however much they may proclaim their desire to be strong and united; for the desire to unite is a very different thing from actual unity. One can see the forces of neo-imperialism manipulating these little states in Africa, making them complacently smug in this mere sentimental desire to be one, and at the same time doing everything possible to prevent the realisation of that unity.[9]

Nkrumah was the dominant force working for African unity but in many ways he was his own worst enemy for his genuine idealism and vision were countermanded by his personal ambition. 'At first Nkrumah was revered as the leader of Pan-Africanism but as he pushed eagerly to achieve his ambitions the governments of other African countries became increasingly suspicious of his motives, methods and interference. The more conservative African states were particularly worried when he set up a Bureau of African Affairs which encouraged subversion against other African states considered to be too close to the colonialists.'[10] Nkrumah specifically rejected progress towards pan-Africanism by stages and through existing regional organizations. What he wanted was an all-embracing union where he could use his charisma to emerge as the leader. When the majority of conservative states produced the OAU charter in 1963 they rejected all Nkrumah's pan-African ideas in favour of state status quo and the non-interference in another state's affairs. As a consequence of their deep suspicions of Nkrumah's motives, the heads of state created a largely powerless organization that, among other things, enshrined all the colonial boundaries without questioning their relevance to the people on the ground. Already, in 1960, Nkrumah had stepped up the activities of the Bureau of African Affairs which then had more than 100 agents trained in ideology and subversion, operating all over Africa against what Nkrumah considered were bourgeois regimes. Moreover, 'because of his obsession with a union government for the whole of Africa, Nkrumah made vigorous attacks on any proposed regional groups'.[11] Many Africans wanted unity and understood clearly how weak Africa must continue to be if it remained in its balkanized state but they were not prepared to cave in to Nkrumah's interventions and pressures. In any case, as the eventual reality of the OAU would prove, the nationalist leaders who had led – or shortly would lead – their countries to independence wanted to enjoy the fruits of that independence and not surrender part of it, as they believed they must, to an African Union that would be greater than the individual parts.

As much as anything, the African conferences of 1958–1961 represented a search by the leaders of newly independent countries for a *modus vivendi* both with regard to each other and as a bloc in relation to the outside world. The fact that Africa was likely to achieve unity as much or as little as the Arab world, Europe or Asia was beside the point. The search was certainly worthwhile even if it only revealed the obstacles to real unity. In fact it did much more. Perhaps Haile Selassie's greatest contribution to independent Africa was his role as chairman at the meetings in Addis Ababa, which finally led to the formation of the OAU.

In May 1963 the foreign ministers of 30 African countries met in Addis Ababa to prepare an agenda for a meeting of their heads of state. They discussed the creation of an Organisation of African States, which would be concerned with matters of collective defence, decolonization, and cooperation in economic, social, educational and scientific matters. Inevitably, the meeting also dealt with apartheid in South Africa and racial discrimination. Then, on 23 May, the heads of state or government of 30 African countries came to Addis Ababa and, under the chairmanship of Haile Selassie, approved a Charter to create an Organisation of African Unity (OAU). The Charter was signed on 26 May 1963 by 30 heads of state (Chad and Togo signed later to become founder members). The OAU represented a compromise between a strong federal type of structure that had been favoured by the Casablanca Group and a looser association of states favoured by the Monrovia Group. The founder members of the OAU were: Algeria, Burundi, Cameroon, Central African Republic, Chad, Congo (Brazzaville), Congo (Leopoldville), Dahomey (later Benin), Ethiopia, Gabon, Ghana, Guinea, Côte d'Ivoire, Liberia, Libya, Madagascar, Mali, Mauritania, Morocco, Niger, Nigeria, Rwanda, Senegal, Sierra Leone, Somalia, Sudan, Tanganyika, Togo, Tunisia, Uganda, United Arab Republic (Egypt), Upper Volta (later Burkina Faso).

The Charter of the OAU was similar to that of the United Nations but without a Security Council and without any veto powers. All African states as well as Madagascar and surrounding islands, should they wish, would be eligible to join. Its institutions were: Assembly of Heads of State and Government; Council of Ministers; General Secretariat; Commission of Mediation, Conciliation and Arbitration; and Specialized Commissions. A number of leaders called for the OAU to provide assistance to liberate those states still under colonial control. Nyerere, for example, said: 'The time for allowing our brethren to struggle unaided has gone; from now on our brethren in non-independent Africa should be helped by independent Africa.' He said that Tanganyika was willing to contribute one per cent of its budget and willing to 'die a little' to remove the 'final humiliation of colonialism'. Nkrumah, who had pressed for too much too quickly, was generally isolated but he put on a brave face and said: 'The decisions we have taken here have made African unity a reality and we can see clearly a Union Government of Africa on the horizon. This is the goal, which we set ourselves when we struggled in our separate states for independence. It is also the compelling force which brought us together at Addis Ababa.' The majority favoured gradualism. Immediately, however, as Haile Selassie told the conference, there would be a co-ordinated drive against continued white rule in Southern Africa, supported by the resources of the whole continent. A 'Liberation Bureau' was established and entrusted to a committee composed of Ethiopia, Algeria, Uganda, Egypt, Tanganyika, the Congo (Leopoldville), Senegal and Nigeria with headquarters in Dar es Salaam. Nyerere said that the signing of the Charter meant the ending of all power blocs, such as the Casablanca and Monrovia groupings. President Touré of Guinea was constrained to deny any rift between himself and Nkrumah though their paths had been diverging. All the decisions of the conference had been arrived at unanimously. He said: 'Africa is above personalities now. I affirm here that we entirely trust President Nkrumah. We admire him for his real and active contribution to the evolution of Africa. We know of Ghana's contribution to the speeding up of liberation on this continent and we are also aware that on the economic and political level Ghana's dynamic proposals contributed to the intellectual awakening of Africa.' This might be seen as an obituary to Nkrumah's influence at that time. However, if it was an obituary, a handsome tribute to his vision, if not to his political behaviour, was paid him by the British journalist Keith Kyle. Writing in the *Spectator* he said:

It is now generally accepted that the African summit meeting at Addis ended as a considerable victory for the gradualists. The success of the new Pan-African institutions, which were set up, will largely depend upon the calibre and drive of the permanent secretariat and how sincerely they are backed up by the member States. But before too much speculation about this, it is worth paying heed to the temporary loser at Addis, Kwame Nkrumah, and his one faithful supporter, Milton Obote, for despite all the moderation and common sense at the conference, the real insight and inspiration still seems to be theirs. Theirs is the real radicalism and one should not underestimate its appeal.

He went on:

The diplomatic pattern that preceded the conference had two main strands – the 'militant diplomacy' by which President Sekou Touré of Guinea led the other French-speaking States, many of them hitherto classified as 'neo-colonialist stooges' in Pan-African circles, and sponsored their leaders in the nationalist club; and the increasing alienation of Ghana and Nigeria. Going against the trend represented latterly by Touré of accepting African governments as they are and trying to talk them into line, Nkrumah has energetically backed those forces within African countries which endorsed his views. He has simply been caught out too often. Recently the Congo and Nigeria have drawn very close. During Adoula's official visit to Lagos he and the Nigerians exchanged notes about Ghanaian interference in their internal affairs. In his attitude to Togo, Nkrumah has caused even greater offence by appearing to want to violate the great self-denying ordinance whose adoption by all (or nearly all) African independent states has been the supreme demonstration to date of their international maturity; the resolve to preserve the artificial colonial boundaries, lest ethnic irredentism open up endless occasions for war.

It was unfortunate that his actions as opposed to his ideas had made Nkrumah more enemies than friends and by the time the meeting convened in Addis Ababa he was much distrusted. Nonetheless, as Kyle argued:

Yet the sweep and logic of his speech at Addis, delivered in the full knowledge that it could not make immediate converts, invites a suspension of prejudice. Basically his argument is this: Africa is a rich continent, but her riches are unevenly distributed. So long as her States remain separate political units, most of them will not only be poor, but will have little prospect of escaping poverty. This is because most of them depend on the sale abroad of primary products and as far as one can see into the future the terms of trade will move against them. Moreover, as population rises and technological improvement is applied to the land, the number of landless will multiply. African governments will then not be able to do more for their people than colonial governments and 'all the resentment which overthrew colonialism will be mobilized against us'.[12]

Nkrumah had concluded his speech by advocating the development of heavy industry at the same pace as agriculture although this could only be done on a continent-wide scale: 'Unless we can establish great industrial complexes in Africa – which we can only do in a united Africa – we must leave our peasantry to the mercy of foreign cash-crop markets and face the same unrest which overthrew the colonialists.'

In the year following the establishment of the OAU the member states began to grapple with the many problems the organization would be called upon to settle. In November 1963 OAU delegates met in Accra where they discussed a number of problems. Ghana's suggestion that the OAU should create an African High Command to control army, navy and air forces met with little support. The OAU, in its first major test, set up a commission to arbitrate the border dispute between Algeria and Morocco. Then in February 1964 OAU foreign ministers met at Lagos where they discussed the border dispute between Ethiopia and Somalia, the army mutinies that had occurred in East Africa in the previous month, the rebellion in Gabon, the continuing Algeria–Morocco dispute, the killings in Rwanda and the question of freeing the non-independent states.

The second OAU summit met in Cairo at the end of July 1964. Moïse Tshombe, who was then Prime Minister of the Congo, was excluded from participation. The most important resolution was to boycott South Africa and the Portuguese territories of Angola and Mozambique. It was decided to refuse both over-flying rights and port facilities to any aircraft or ship going to or from South Africa and a special bureau was set up to co-ordinate the boycott. A second bureau was established to co-ordinate an effective boycott against Portugal. Other resolutions were a blow to Nkrumah and it seemed that the majority of OAU members were determined to sideline both his ideas and Nkrumah himself. Nkrumah was opposed to establishing a permanent OAU headquarters and Secretary-General but this was done anyway: Addis Ababa became the OAU headquarters, and the Guinean Diallo Telli the first Secretary-General. Finally, Nkrumah pressed for the proclamation of a continental Union Government within six months, but all the heads of state were prepared to do was set up an ad hoc committee to investigate the fundamental points of this proposal.

Even so, one of the two most important speeches at this conference came from Nkrumah; the other, in direct opposition to his stand, was delivered by Nyerere. Nkrumah said that only Union Government of Africa could guarantee African survival. The imperialists were pouring vast sums of money into South Africa and Portugal to make them militarily and economically stronger. In particular, he attacked the performance of the Liberation Committee in Dar es Salaam which, he said, had failed to make the best use of its resources while some military specialists (from Egypt and Algeria) had been excluded on ideological grounds. Further, under the Liberation Committee the 'freedom fighters' had no real security and were not given instruments for their struggle, nor were food, clothing and medicine given the men in training. The training scheme, he said, had collapsed in two months. 'By raising a threat at Addis Ababa and not being able to take effective action against apartheid and colonialism we have worsened the plight of our kinsmen in Angola, Mozambique, Southern Rhodesia and South Africa. We have frightened the imperialists sufficiently to strengthen their defences and the repression in Southern Africa, but we have not frightened them enough to abandon apartheid supremacy to its ill-fated doom.' Nkrumah concluded by arguing that to say a Union Government for Africa was premature was to sacrifice Africa on the altar of neo-colonialism. 'We should get together, think together, plan together, and organize our African economy as a reality.'

In a bitter and caustic reply to Nkrumah, Nyerere suggested that part of the failure of the Liberation Committee was due to lack of funds because the Conference had committed the unforgivable crime of not including Ghana on the committee and of choosing Dar es Salaam as its headquarters. Nyerere then set out to demolish Nkrumah's concept of a Union Government of Africa. What was needed, he said, was not more preaching about unity, but more practising of unity. The habit of unity must be encouraged in West Africa and East Africa. He attacked Ghana, in part, because the Ghanaian ambassador to Tanganyika had expressed satisfaction over the humiliation suffered as a result of the East African army mutinies.

The spectacle of two of the most eminent African rulers in bitter dispute did not augur well for the performance of the OAU or for the concept of unity. During the remaining years of the decade the OAU faced two major conflicts – first in the Congo and then the civil war in Nigeria – but hardly acquitted itself with distinction in either case. What it had to learn were the lessons that had also faced the United Nations since its inception in 1945: it was one thing to create an Organisation of African Unity; it was something else to achieve unity among more than 30 nations at that time, a figure that would eventually rise to more than 50.

CHAPTER FOUR

The Coup d'Etat and the One-Party State

COLONIAL MILITARY STRUCTURES

The 1960s may have been an exhilarating time for Africans, as the bastions of colonialism fell and independence spread across the continent, yet it was soon apparent that the political kingdom, which Nkrumah had insisted should be sought first, held many pitfalls. Independence was not simply a question of changing flags and replacing the colonial administration with an African one. The systems inherited from the departing British and French often did not fit: they did not answer to either the conditions that existed on the ground or the ambitions of the new leaders. Moreover, 'Colonialism was based on authoritarian command; as such, it was incompatible with any preparation for self-government. Africa was the continent of bureaucratic rule. In that sense, every success of administration was a failure of government. Government was run not only without, but despite the people.'[1] When Africans replaced the departing Europeans, therefore, they did not move into ready-made democratic systems that they had already been practising for some time; they took over authoritarian structures that had been created to enable the colonial authorities to rule their subjects without their consent. Colonial officials had been a class to themselves: set apart from those they ruled and an anachronism back in the rapidly changing metropolitan societies from which they came. All the assumptions of colonial societies were based upon the conviction that the administrator was both right and superior: right in that he knew what was best for the country; and superior because the people over whom he ruled accepted his judgements and were content with the good government he dispensed. Even when it became plain that independence was approaching few changes to the administrative structures were made, while the apparatus of coercion, such as the state of emergency, which was the ultimate means of colonial control, remained intact at the time of handover so that, for example, at the end of the century in troubled Zimbabwe President Mugabe could use the same colonial measures of coercion that had been deployed by Ian Smith and previous Rhodesian governments. According to Ruth First, 'More than anything else, colonial administrations resembled armies. The chain of authority from the top downwards was untouched by any principle of representation or consultation. For long periods in some territories, indeed, the colonial administration not only resembled armies, in their paramilitary formation and ethos; they were, as in the Sudan, the instruments of military men.'[2]

Once they had taken control of these structures the new rulers had to decide what to do with them and to what extent they could and should be altered to accord with the political freedom that their followers believed they had at last attained. They had to do this, moreover, against a wave of new external pressures that included those emanating from the old colonial powers, anxious to retain as much ongoing influence as possible while safeguarding their economic interests, and from a number of new players in Africa, most notably the United States, the Soviet Union and China. The United States had had little involvement in Africa prior to 1957 but this changed rapidly thereafter and, for example in 1958, when the representative of the British chiefs of staff, General Lathbury, visited Washington he found extraordinary interest among US officials in the developments which the War Office was then promoting in Africa. By 1961 the US had become deeply involved in Africa, in the first instance through the Congo. Although at first a majority of conservative leaders were content to take the colonial structures as they found them, a few desired to institute radical changes at once and in four cases – those of Ghana, Guinea, Mali and Tanganyika – the leaders created mass parties as instruments to change their entire societies and lead them away from the colonial structures they had inherited. Despite these radicals, in a majority of cases there was an identity of interest between the new elites and the departing colonial administrators that made a peaceful transfer of power that much easier to carry out. In most cases there had been no real preparation for independence, only an eleventh-hour scramble to provide 'an ideology of delay'. The point became clear over the first years of independence when few of the models of government that had been bequeathed lasted for more than a few years. Thus, from the end of 1960 to the beginning of 1962, 13 states either revised their constitutions or produced new ones. Another aspect of the handover that quickly became apparent was that the departing colonial authorities were prepared to hand over political power as long as doing so did not affect their economic stakes. Rapid Africanization then provided jobs for the new elites, few of which had any inclination to change the system that placed them in the positions of prestige and power, which had formerly been occupied by the departing whites.

The military coup d'état had already become a feature of African politics in 1960, the *annus mirabilis* of independence, with the overthrow of Lumumba and the first army takeover under Mobutu in the Congo. In the Congo, moreover, these changes, which defied the legitimacy of the colonial inheritance, were done with the connivance of the West and the United Nations under Western pressure, to set a precedent of external interference in support of government changes that would continue into the indefinite future. Nigerian and Ghanaian army officers who served in the Congo under UN auspices saw at first hand the power of the soldiers to arbitrate or coerce politicians and took such lessons home with them. African armies soon learnt that their intervention could be decisive while the politicians learnt that foreign intervention could be even more decisive.

Few colonial armies had been prepared for independence in the sense of having a trained African officer corps. The first officer cadets from the Gold Coast were only sent to Britain in 1953, from Uganda in 1959, from Tanganyika in 1961. In fact, the last functions of colonial rule transferred to African control were those concerned with internal security and defence so that African armies after independence were still largely officered by whites, a cause of deep resentment that played its part in the army mutinies in the Congo, Kenya, Tanganyika and Uganda. Different kinds of military coup would emerge during the 1960s but the first was the pay mutiny or, more generally, a strike for better conditions that included anger at the slow rate of Africanization for officers. This was the case initially in the Congo and East Africa. However, the sheer number of coups that were mounted during the 1960s, averaging just under three a year, suggested that a great deal was wrong with state structures that were clearly fragile and perhaps unworkable as they stood. In two months over 1965 into 1966, for example, five states experienced military coups: Dahomey (Benin) in December 1965, Central African Republic, Upper Volta (Burkina Faso) and Nigeria during January 1966, and Ghana in February 1966. Armies had no tradition of standing apart from politics while the loyalties of the soldiers, for example to different regions or tribes, would prove easy to exploit. Power seekers, whether military men or politicians, soon recognized the need to cosset their armies. At the same time the more fragile the state the greater the need for external help and the more such aid was sought and relied upon the greater the discontent within the ranks of the army. In 1968, for example, a total of 1,400 senior officers and NCOs of the French army, marines and air force, the medical corps and the gendarmeries were employed as technical assistants in 12 Francophone countries. These were in addition to the 6–7,000 troops of the French army actually stationed in Senegal, Chad, Niger, Côte d'Ivoire, Central African Republic, Gabon and Madagascar. This was overt neo-colonialism, accepted nonetheless by weak governments that on a number of occasions were obliged to turn to these forces to keep themselves in power. The African armies were the creation of the colonial powers and were moulded to the needs of the West. In the post-colonial period they remained bound to the West for training, equipment and aid. It soon became clear, moreover, that African armies were in the best position to obtain more than their share of the state's limited resources.

When assessing how post-independence politics developed in Africa, it is impossible not to return, again and again, to what the colonial powers developed, or failed to develop, before they departed. There were a number of reasons why so many of the colonial-bequeathed systems broke down so quickly after independence. These included: challenges to the legitimacy of the government that actually succeeded to power; vulnerability of the government to outside interference; weak or poorly tested state structures in the face of internal challenges (such as those by the military); and regional pulls against the centre based upon tribal loyalties. The new rulers had to work out their own concepts of a viable state that would take into account the strengths and weaknesses of their societies in a way that the colonial authorities had never attempted to do because to have done so would have destroyed the premises upon which colonial authority rested. Once a territory had been subdued the colonial rulers saw law and order in economic terms: how to organize the people to provide the labour required for the mines and plantations that produced what the metropolitan powers sought from their empires. Otherwise, they were content to leave traditional activities and their leaders alone, always provided these became their allies in maintaining a status quo that served colonial interests. The new rulers, on the other hand, had to reorganize their entire societies and bring them into a modern, competitive world from which they had been sheltered by the colonial system. There were huge economic gaps – primarily in industrialization – that had been ignored by the colonial authorities; and there were the expectations on the part of the elites for career prospects and on the part of the mass of the people for an improved life that would lift them out of poverty. In these circumstances the new regimes automatically saw their military establishments as instruments to be used in nation building and that, if necessary, included controlling opponents of the government. This view of the military's role came before the more traditional view that the army existed first and foremost for national defence purposes.

In many African states the military came to be seen as central to the nation-building process:

At the heart of many African ambitions for the development of a state which will provide the basis of order, is the belief that the methods of consultation used in the 'stateless societies' of pre-colonial Africa can be adapted for modern use. The justification of the 'one-party state' has always contained an element of appealing to past tradition (the consensus of the tribe).

The political ideals of populist thought confuse distinctions between civil and military. By stressing the need to mobilize the population in support for the regime and in work to improve the wealth of the country, each government attempts to inculcate some of the virtues of military organisation.[3]

African armies found themselves – or forced themselves – to the forefront of the political process in the early stages of the independence era. Sometimes thereafter, as in 1966 in Ghana, they seized power to protect their position. Both the British and the French had encouraged stereotypes of warrior tribes and had recruited their colonial armies from such tribes. There was, moreover, keen competition among the peasantry to enter the army, which was both comparatively well paid and seen as a life of relative privilege. At independence the British had come to regard their local defence forces as the national forces of each territory, but if the majority of the soldiers had been recruited from a particular tribal group (or groups) this presented problems for the future in an independent state. It was to be resolved in Kenya under Kenyatta by apportioning a quota system for recruitment from different tribal regions. The French, on the other hand, had created regional colonial armies and at independence had to divide up existing regiments according to the origin of their personnel in order to establish national forces for each territory that emerged to independence in 1960.

French military involvement in Africa remained substantial for many years after independence. At the request of governments French forces intervened at least 12 times in Africa between 1960 and 1963: several times in Chad, in Cameroon, in Niger, in Mauritania, in Congo (Brazzaville) and in Gabon. In the late 1960s French troops were used in Central African Republic to prevent a counter-coup against President Bokassa who himself had come to power by means of a coup. Throughout the 1960s France sustained President Tombalbaye of Chad in power: partly because Chad was strategically placed in the centre of the continent and the French air base and communications centre at Fort Lamy (N'Djamena) was the centre of French military organization in Africa. The 1967–68 budgets of eight out of 15 Francophone countries allotted between 15 and 25 per cent of their finances to their armies which by then were able to exercise a powerful leverage on the political system to obtain more than their share of what, in most cases, were extremely limited resources. Writing at the end of the 1960s Ruth First could argue: 'Within a decade of independence, and in some countries less, Africa has travelled from colonial government to a very close copy of it. Lugard and Lyautey of the last century have given way to Mobutu, Gowon and Bokassa of this one. Once again the pattern of rule is military-bureaucratic in type.'[4]

In the immediate post-independence years what African states needed most of all was a period of uninterrupted peace in which they could re-forge the instruments of government and work out the paths of political and economic development they wished to follow. This they did not get. Instead, they were overwhelmed with pressures from outside the continent: the Cold War was brought to Africa through the 1956 Suez crisis in Egypt and the 1960 Congo crisis as the United States and the Soviet Union vied for influence in a world confrontation that Africa could not escape. The two superpowers were soon followed by China, which was determined to spread its influence in a region that it considered to be ripe for revolution. At the same time the departure of the colonial powers was more apparent than real as they increased their economic grip on their erstwhile colonies to compensate for the loss of direct political control. Moreover, Africa found itself the target for a burgeoning new class of modern empire builders in the form of United Nations, World Bank and national aid agencies and advisers as well as a new breed of non-government organizations, all seeking to guide the new states along development paths more in the interests of the external world from which they came than those of the new states.

Nkrumah's readiness to interfere in countries that he considered inimical to his obsession with African unity, and US determination to prevent the spread of Soviet influence in Africa, both helped to destabilize regimes that at best were based on brittle foundations. According to one military commentator 'Nkrumah's reception of freedom fighters into special training camps inside Ghana, where they received instruction from Chinese training teams, was based upon the principle that havoc could be caused in the political system of an unfriendly regime by a few men with a few primitive weapons. The Chinese in their aid to the revolutionary movements in the Congo, channelled largely through Burundi or through Congo (Brazzaville), concentrated on guerrilla methods.'[5] And in the Congo the US determination to intervene against Lumumba, whom Washington viewed as dangerously 'red', led to Mobutu's two coups – of 1960 and 1965 – which were both supported and part engineered by the CIA, provided a precedent for future interventions throughout the years of the Cold War. Even so, these Cold War reasons for intervention were only part of the story: 'The issue was not whether the Congo should have a government headed by Lumumba, Kasavubu, Mobutu or Tshombe; but whether an African state should seek an option other than dependence on the West.'[6]

COUPS IN WEST AFRICA

During the 1960s the military coup became a habit in West Africa, affecting Ghana, Mali, Upper Volta, Togo, Dahomey, Nigeria and Sierra Leone. In Ghana, Kwame Nkrumah determined to entrench his power by creating a one-party state in which the Convention People's Party (CPP) would dominate all aspects of public life. A national referendum, held over 24–31 January 1964, returned an overwhelming majority for a one-party state. Electors were asked to approve amendments to the constitution to make Ghana a one-party Socialist State with the CPP the sole national party. The amended constitution would also give the President the right to dismiss judges of the Supreme Court and High Court at any time. In Britain the *Guardian* commented that if the voting were free Nkrumah would be hard put to win the referendum. 'It would probably do more damage than good to the Commonwealth for Britain to take any initiative on seeking Ghana's expulsion.'[7] The Ghanaian High Commissioner, Kwesi Armah, took exception to the *Guardian* comment and said the referendum would be free and that observers were welcome to attend. 'I remind you that the Convention People's Party has gone to the country four times within twelve years. We have gone to the polls more often than any nation in the world, because we realize that our mandate to govern must always be derived from the people.' In the event, an overwhelming majority of Ghana's electorate supported the creation of a one-party state: out of 2,877,464 registered voters, 2,773,920 voted yes, 2,452 voted no. There was criticism of the way the poll was conducted and correspondents doubted that it was either free or fair. The CPP had canvassed for a 100 per cent 'yes' vote and government papers had warned voters that all ballot papers must 'find their way into the "yes" box'. In nearly 104 constituencies the 'no' boxes were completely empty and in many areas, according to *The Times*, voters were not given a choice: either the 'no' boxes had been removed by polling officials or the slits for ballots had been sealed. *West Africa* said of the referendum that while in the past the CPP had been identified with the state, now the state was to be identified with the party. Party officials would be regarded as State officials, just as much as civil servants. The Party's governing body would have the same standing as the cabinet.[8] In December 1964 the government tightened its grip further when it set up a committee with powers of censorship over publications in bookshops, libraries, schools, colleges and universities. The committee 'will work out a system to ensure the removal of all publications which do not reflect the ideology of the Convention People's Party or are antagonistic to its ideals'.

On 24 February 1966, when Nkrumah was on a visit to China, the Army announced it had seized power and had established a National Liberation Council (NLC) under General J.A. Ankrah. The Police Commissioner, J.W.K. Harlley, was the general's deputy. The coup had been planned at Brigade Headquarters in the north of the country and then carried through under the guise of a routine training exercise. MPs and CPP officials were rounded up. Colonel E. K. Kotoka, Commander of the 2nd Brigade, led the actual takeover. Guards of Flagstaff House loyal to Nkrumah resisted for two days. Nkrumah's statue outside Parliament was demolished. The day following the coup *The Times* recognized that 'Ghana would be worth salvaging again; it had swung back to reliance upon the West'.[9] An attempted coup against the Ankrah regime on 17 April 1967 was crushed after an hour of heavy fighting in which Lt-Gen. E.K. Kotoka, promoted to commander of the armed forces, died of wounds received in the fighting. In an editorial the following day, the *Guardian* said: 'Military regimes are irksome and even Ghanaians, so recently delivered from a worse one under Nkrumah, are getting understandably restive under theirs... To replace the still broadly popular NLC with another set of soldiers would have served no purpose, and most people, inside and outside Ghana, will welcome the defeat of the attempt.'[10] Subsequently, three junior officers appeared before a five-man military tribunal in Accra accused of subversion and murder during the coup attempt. Two of them – Lt Samuel Benjamin Arthur (the leader) and Lt Moses Yebouh – were sentenced to death and executed by firing squad on 9 May before a crowd of 20,000. In 1969, a rare event then and later, the coup-makers of 1966 returned the country to civilian rule and the Progress Party of Dr Busia won 105 of 140 seats with 59 per cent of the poll.

Guinea's radical leader Touré outlasted Ghana's Nkrumah by many years. His defiance of de Gaulle and refusal to join the French Community, opting for complete independence instead, made him a hero in much of Africa. Like Nkrumah, he created a mass movement, turned Guinea into a one-party state and was numbered among Africa's radical leaders. But the harsh realities of economic power, or rather its lack, which were exacerbated by the decision of France to cut off all aid and other ties, led to increasing problems. France had been developed as the export market for Guinea and when Touré turned to the Communist bloc for assistance this simply meant less interest from the West and a growing sense of diplomatic isolation. Between 1961 and 1973 there were some six internal challenges to Touré, including alleged plots against the regime, though none succeeded in overthrowing it. A sense of paranoia developed as Touré saw, in turn, the USSR, the US and Portugal – and always France – as enemies attempting to overthrow the state. The paranoia certainly had a basis in fact and in November 1970, at the very end of the decade, there was a two-day

Portuguese-inspired invasion of Conakry in which the President's summer palace and the local offices of the *Partido Africano de Independência da Guiné e Cabro Verde* (PAIGC) were destroyed. A number of Guineans and foreigners were killed and some captured Portuguese soldiers and opponents of Touré were released from prison. Guinea, to use the Maoist term, was 'ripe for revolution' but in this case a revolution from the right rather than the left. The lessons from Ghana and Guinea were the same: that a centralized, all-powerful one-party system that did not encourage some genuine form of debate within its ranks could only be challenged by means of the coup.

When Mali became independent in June 1960 it was briefly federated with Senegal but Senegal broke the connection after two months. Modibo Keita, another of the radical group of leaders, worked quickly after independence to eliminate all opposition. He wanted and proclaimed a socialist state. He had the two principal opposition leaders arrested in 1962 (they were to die in custody). At the same time he took Mali out of the franc zone and extended government control into most aspects of the economy. Although elections were held in 1964 opposition candidates were not allowed to present themselves to the electorate. As with Guinea, economic weakness proved to be Keita's Achilles heel: he found it impossible to develop a full socialist economic policy and in 1967 had to come to terms with France and negotiate re-entry into the franc zone. France imposed harsh conditions including 90 per cent devaluation and the imposition of extensive French supervision of the economy. Unsurprisingly, given earlier socialist rhetoric and denunciations of France, the return to the French fold provoked opposition from militant students and youths who claimed, correctly, that the regime was bowing to colonialist pressures. The position worsened when the government imposed economic austerity measures. Then the newly formed People's Militia, which Keita had created as a radical counter-weight to the army and to provide support for himself, arrested several army officers, provoking immediate fears in the military that Keita intended to reduce the size of the army. Apparently, the army was to be sent on 21 November to help bring in the harvest while the militia would seize the barracks. The army, therefore, had to carry out a pre-emptive strike to save itself and on 19 November 1968 carried out a bloodless coup and deposed Keita. A 14-member Military Committee of National Liberation (CMLN) was established with Lt (later Brig.-Gen.) Moussa Traoré as President and Captain Yoro Diakite as Head of Government. Keita failed but as a militant socialist he had tried to reduce Mali's dependence on overseas aid and free it from French influence. What happened in Mali was a classic illustration of the conflict between radical politics leading to economic crisis that could only be overcome by turning back to the metropolitan power (in later years to the IMF) for an economic rescue operation.

Jean-Marie Koné, a former minister, became foreign minister in Diakite's government. He claimed that the army had seized power to put an end to 'the radicalization of the Marxist regime' of Keita who, he said, after following a policy of balance between the moderates and the Marxists had decided in August 1967 to govern with the backing of the toughest Marxist theoreticians who had forgotten Malian realities. The Chinese trained militia, which had become armed ruffians, were disbanded.[11]

Upper Volta (later Burkina Faso) followed a similar path to that of Mali. The *Union Démocratique Voltaique* (UDV), with Maurice Yameogo as President, formed the government, which turned out to be autocratic and made opposition parties illegal soon after independence. Single list elections were held in 1965, giving Yameogo's UDV 99 per cent of the vote. This result led to mass demonstrations with civil servants and trade unionists being joined by radical students who opposed the government's dependence upon France. In January 1966, with a general strike threatened, the army intervened and deposed Yameogo, a move that received much popular support. The Constitution was suspended, the National Assembly dissolved and a government was formed under Lt-Col. (later Gen.) Sangoule Lamizana. The new government worked to restore the economy. Although the military said they would restore civilian rule and held round table talks with the politicians, failure to achieve reconciliation and further threats of disturbances led the army to announce in December 1966 that it would remain in power for four years. Commenting upon the army takeover, the *Guardian* reflected more generally upon what had occurred in the former French colonies:

> The former French colonies followed a very different path from that of their English neighbours. Their culture and civilization has been so involved with that of France that their independence was more a gesture to world opinion than a genuine expression of nationalism. For a time they have adhered closely to France, but France has indicated that she is unwilling to prop them up indefinitely. As the French attitude has changed, so nationalism has caught up with them. They are hopelessly unprepared for it. Few of the States are economically viable. National income is absurdly distributed. In Upper Volta, for example, over one-third of the budget is spent on educating 7 per cent of the school-age population. In these circumstances it is hardly surprising that adjustment to a changing situation will take place painfully. We sometimes grumble about the way the British former colonies behave, but compared with French Africa they seem positively English in their stability.[12]

Although much of this comment was valid, the smug *Guardian* comparison between Francophone and Anglophone Africa was soon to be overtaken by events in Nigeria, Ghana and Sierra Leone.

The tiny West African states of Togo and Benin were both to suffer their shares of army takeovers during the 1960s. In the case of Togo, the end of the Algerian war in 1962 saw the demobilization from the French army of some 600 Togolese soldiers, who had served the French on individual enlistment, being repatriated to Togo. They wanted to be absorbed into the Togo army but the government could not afford either to enlist them in the army or provide them with other employment; so they joined up with the army and mutinied on 13 January 1963 when the Olympio government was overthrown and the President shot dead. Nicolas Grunitzky formed a coalition government but this turned out to be an uneasy affair and was opposed by Olympio's party, *Comité de l'Unité Togolaise* (CUT). After several uneasy years the army, under Lt-Col. Etienne Gnassingbé Eyadéma, seized power in January 1967, Eyadéma citing fears of civil war as his justification. A Committee of National Reconciliation was set up which, within three months, would create 'the institutions which will lead to free and democratic elections, after which the Army will undertake to withdraw from the political scene'.

Following independence in 1960 Dahomey (Benin) was to experience six bloodless coups in 12 years and in this case economic problems were the principal cause of the upheavals. As it happened, Dahomey had a well-developed educational system and had exported much of its trained manpower during colonial times to neighbouring Francophone countries. After 1960, however, most of the Francophone territories passed legislation to exclude foreign nationals with the result that many Beninois had to return home so that the country faced an influx of highly trained personnel looking for employment. Many found jobs in a rapidly expanded civil service and tended to be good fodder for coups. The President of Dahomey at independence was Hubert Maga whose main support came from the north of the country. He was allied to Sourou-Migan Apithy whose base was in the south-east. Their alliance became increasingly strained and, following trade union and student riots, the government was overthrown by the army, which then created a new civilian government under Justin Ahomadegbe, who represented the south-west region, and Apithy who was appointed President.

This government lasted until November 1965 when the army intervened for a second time and General Christophe Soglo (who had also led the army coup of 1963) first presided over a series of consultations between the different political factions and then, when no agreement was reached, formed a government of soldiers and technical experts on 22 December 1965. The Soglo government, in its turn, was overthrown in December 1967 by a group of younger army officers, led by Maj. Maurice Kouandeté, who appointed Lt-Col. Alphonse Alley head of state to prepare the way for a return to civilian rule. A strong presidential constitution was submitted to referendum in March 1968 and presidential elections were held in May but they were annulled because the three main candidates – Apithy, Maga and Ahomadegbe – were disqualified. In July Dr Emile Zinsou was made President by the army. Eighteen months later, on 10 December 1969, the army deposed Zinsou and Lt-Col. Maurice Kouandete became head of state. He broadcast to the nation that Zinsou had failed in his task of reconciliation obliging the army, once more, to assume its responsibilities. Elections in 1970 in which Apithy, Maga and Ahomadegbe again stood brought the country close to civil war between north and south. A presidential commission of these three was then established; it was transformed into a presidential council and each man, by rotation, was to serve for a two-year period. None of this political-military manoeuvring during the 1960s brought the country any closer to solving its economic problems.

In Nigeria, the giant of West Africa, the increasing strains between the three great regions – east, west and north – occupied respectively by the Ibo, Yoruba and Hausa-Fulani finally destroyed the creaking federal structure that had lasted since independence in 1960. The tribal factor now came to dominate the political-military scene and 'In Nigeria, the minority Ibo group inside the army struck first, and thus destroyed the existing regime and endangered the whole coherence of the army itself'.[14] On 15 January 1966 the first Nigerian military coup brought about the downfall of the Federal Government of Alhaji Sir Abubakar Tafawa Balewa to spark off the events that would lead to the civil war. Immediately, Maj.-Gen. Johnson Aguiyi-Ironsi became head of a military government that would last until the second coup of 1966, which took place in July when Ironsi was killed and succeeded by Lt-Gen. Yakubu Gowon. Nigeria would descend into civil war in 1967.

When Sierra Leone became independent in 1961 the Sierra Leone People's Party (SLPP) under Sir Milton Margai formed the government. When he died in 1964 his brother, Sir Albert Margai, became Prime Minister. The SLPP drew its main support from the chiefs and people of the interior: that is, the conservative elements in the country. The more progressive opposition formed round the All-People's Congress (APC), led by Siaka Stevens. In February 1966 Sir Albert Margai established a committee to consider whether the country should become a one-party state. Resistance to the idea came principally from the Creoles (descendants of the resettled slaves) of Freetown and the APC. Sir Albert was more interested in adopting the Ghanaian model for a one-party state rather than the model that had been established in Tanzania where choice of candidates was permitted and encouraged. Opponents of Sir Albert assumed that he wished to keep himself permanently in power. In the elections of March 1967 the APC won a majority of seats, Stevens gaining five more than Margai. Many people had voted against Margai because they opposed both a one-party system and turning Sierra Leone into a republic. The Governor, Sir Henry Lightfoot-Boston, suggested that a coalition should be formed, but Stevens refused. The Governor, therefore, swore in Stevens as Prime Minister and the members of his cabinet but then troops under the Army Commander, Brig. David Lansana, a supporter of Margai, surrounded State House and detained the leaders of the new government. Lansana reinstated Margai in office. Two days later, however, a group of officers arrested Lansana and Margai and established the National Reformation Council, which suspended the Constitution, dissolved all political parties and prohibited all political activity. The Council claimed that Brig. Lansana had been overthrown because his attitude 'was not to bring about the creation of a national government but to impose Sir Albert Margai as Prime Minister of this country'. A military government under Col. A. J. Juxon-Smith ruled Sierra Leone until April 1968 when it was overthrown in a revolt of private soldiers assisted by some NCOs who arrested the officers and promised a quick return to civilian rule. One week later Siaka Stevens, who had been ousted in March 1967, was again sworn in as Prime Minister. The SLPP went into opposition.

The coups of Sierra Leone were at three different levels. The first coup was carried out by the army commander who on his own initiative used the army to prevent Siaka Stevens from coming legitimately to power. The second coup was conducted by senior officers who overthrew the commander in order to establish the National Reformation Council. The third coup was carried out by warrant officers and privates who denounced the policy that had been pursued by the National Reformation Council. These coups demonstrated that there was little solidarity within the ranks of the army.

CENTRAL AND EQUATORIAL AFRICA

The army of Congo (Brazzaville) received over a sixth of the state's revenue in the first 56 months after independence, 25 billion out of 150 billion Congolese francs, making it the most favoured organization in the country. At independence Abbé Fulbert Youlou became president and a new constitution gave him extensive powers. His policies exacerbated tribal tensions while his pro-Western stance and support for Tshombe's breakaway state in neighbouring Congo (Kinshasa) were not popular. On 13 August 1963 strikes and riots took place in Brazzaville where demonstrators set fire to the prison and released prisoners. Troops were obliged to intervene when the police failed to quell the riots. On 15 August the resignation of President Youlou was announced. A spokesman for the French forces stationed in Brazzaville said that President Youlou's resignation ended the armed support given to him (or rather not given to him) by the French garrison at the start of the disturbances. Power was entrusted to the National Congolese Army pending a new constitution and a new government. Youlou's plan to create a single-party system was at the root of the disturbances. At first the trade unions had co-operated in negotiations with the government but that co-operation collapsed when a government decree banned all political meetings until the *parti-unique* had been created. The unions claimed that the government was depriving the people of their rights under the UN Charter. Alphonse Massamba-Debat, former planning minister and Speaker of the National Assembly, became Prime Minister. Commenting on these events, the *Observer* said: 'Democratic forces in Africa have won a significant triumph by overthrowing Abbé Fulbert Youlou's government in the French Congo. If the populist revolt can consolidate its success – and so prevent the one-party rule of President Youlou – the storming of the Brazzaville prison may come to acquire for Africa the significance of the fall of the Bastille.'[15] This upbeat assessment of the Congo revolution was capped a week later by *The Economist*: 'It was neat, less expensive than it might have been, and instructive. In three eventful days, from August 14 to 17, the people of the ex-French Congo rioted, brought down President Fulbert Youlou and replaced him by a man with a reputation for honesty, M. Massamba-Debat. Four of the rioters were killed and ten times as many wounded; sundry houses and cars belonging to M. Youlou's ministers were burnt.'[16] These enthusiastic British reactions to the fall of Youlou and the forestalling of a one-party system were to be echoed a few years later at the fall of Nkrumah.

A new constitution established a two-man executive, the President and the Prime Minister, in this case Alphonse Massamba-Debat and Pascal Lissouba respectively. This government marked a break with the earlier pro-Western approach and a swing towards a revolutionary policy. The National Revolutionary Movement (MNR) was formed in 1964 and its youth wing, *Jeunesse du Mouvement National de la Révolution* (JMNR) created a paramilitary force, which became increasingly powerful. The government launched the country's first five-year plan for 1964–68. An attempted military coup in 1966 failed. This led to an increase in the influence of the JMNR over the next two years and the development of a 'people's militia' led by Cuban and Chinese instructors. The result was another confrontation with the army in August–September 1968. Violence erupted on 30 August, and on 4 September President Massamba-Debat resigned. The commander-in-chief of the army,

Captain Marien Ngouabi, became the President of the National Council of the Revolution, which set up a provisional government under Captain Raoul Alfred. At the end of the year, however, the army took full control and Ngouabi became head of state. The sequence of events is instructive. A right-wing authoritarian president, Youlou, attempts to create a one-party state and consolidate his power. He is thwarted by a popular uprising and democracy continues, with the leadership veering sharply to the left. The French, who might well have considered Youlou as more sympathetic to their interests, nonetheless stood back and did not deploy their forces in the Congo to keep Youlou in power. The radical youth wing then creates a militia, calling for Cuban and Chinese assistance with training, and this frightens the regular army, which sees itself being replaced, so the army takes over and the country gets a one-party (military) system after all.

Events in neighbouring Gabon were undoubtedly influenced by the occurrences in Congo (Brazzaville) during 1963. Léon M'Ba was the first President of independent Gabon and his foreign minister was Jean Hilaire-Aubaume. Both men were from the Fang tribe but Aubaume was the more radical and they soon fell out. M'ba began to reduce Aubaume's influence and on 17 February 1964, supported by the military, Aubaume ousted M'Ba in a coup; the army set up a Revolutionary Committee under Aubaume. President M'Ba, the President of the Assembly, and several other ministers were taken prisoner while French and Gabonese staff officers were disarmed. The coup-makers took control of the airport, the post office and the railway station in Libreville but did not block the airport runways. They also released 450 prisoners who at once set about pillaging so that some had to be rearrested. A broadcast by one of the military coup-makers claimed the Army had 'put an end to the police regime'. M'Ba, reportedly at gunpoint, announced that he had resigned. However, French troops from Dakar and Brazzaville were flown into Gabon where they seized strategic points and by the evening of 19 February President M'Ba was back in Libreville from Lambaréné where he had been held. There was little resistance to the French forces: a total of 27 people were killed and 44 wounded. The 150 French soldiers who had been stationed in Gabon were now reinforced; the Gabon army numbered only 600.

The French intervention was highly significant and was compared with the British intervention in East Africa the previous January and the non-intervention of France in Congo (Brazzaville) the previous August 1963 when Youlou was ousted. A French statement claimed that the subversive group, which had attempted to oust M'Ba, had not had the support of the Gabonese people. France had an obligation to give assistance to the legal government of Gabon as a result of its standing defence agreement with that country. M'Ba's vice-president, M. Yembib, had requested help through the French Embassy while M'Ba was in captivity. At the time of the coup M'Ba was one of the staunchest friends of France then remaining in Africa; the opposition had been trying to prevent him establishing a one-party state. No doubt France's readiness to intervene was influenced by the fact that Gabon, with a small population of only 500,000, was one of the wealthiest states in Africa and the richest French-speaking state with per capita exports of US$100, a balance of payments surplus and a balanced budget. Oil was its most profitable export and by 1962 it was producing 800,000 tons a year. The oil was exploited by the *Société des Pétroles d'Afrique Equatoriale* in which the French state-controlled *Bureau de Recherche de Pétrole* held a 43 per cent stake while the French *Caisse Centrale de Co-operation Economique* held another 14.5 per cent. On the whole French-speaking African states, including Niger, Madagascar, Central African Republic, Côte d'Ivoire and Senegal, were favourable to the French intervention. M'Ba then ruled without further troubles until his death in 1967 when Vice-President Albert-Bernard Bongo succeeded him. On 12 March 1968 Bongo instituted one-party government and created a single new party, the *Parti Démocratique Gabonais*.

In Chad confrontation between the Black south and the Muslim north would increase rapidly after independence in 1960 to lead to nearly 30 years of civil war that would be immensely prolonged as a result of French military support for the south and (after 1969) Libyan interventions under Gaddafi in the north. Francois Tombalbaye, Chad's first president, managed with French help to hold onto power through the 1960s.

Central African Republic became independent in 1960 under David Dacko, who presided over a stagnating economy and a deteriorating financial system. On 31 December 1965 the military, led by Colonel Jean-Bédel Bokassa, the Army Chief of Staff, overthrew President Dacko who was placed under arrest. Bokassa justified his coup on the grounds that the government was guilty of profiteering and corruption as well as turning to Communist China. On 6 January 1966 Bokassa gave all the ex-members of Dacko's government eight days to declare their support for the new regime, after which they would be regarded as dangers to the state. The revolutionary council announced a campaign to 'clean up morals': there was to be no drum playing or lying in the sun except on Saturdays and Sundays. Diplomatic relations with China were broken off.

The tiny, impoverished Spanish territory of Spanish Guinea became independent, as Equatorial Guinea, in 1968 after 10 years in which Spain had attempted to turn black Guineans into Spaniards. Francisco Macias Nguema became the country's first president. There was an abortive coup against him in

1969 launched by his Foreign Minister, Atanasio Ndong, who however was killed. Then, on 2 February 1970 all political parties were fused in the *Partido Unico Nacional* (PUN) and President Nguema emerged as an authoritarian, ruthless dictatorial ruler.

THE HORN OF AFRICA

One of the earliest attempted coups of the independence era came on 14 December 1960 when a broadcast from Addis Ababa said Crown Prince Asfa Wassan was heading a new government following a coup. At the time, Emperor Haile Selassie was on a state visit to Brazil. The following day the Crown Prince was proclaimed king (negus). Fighting started after Col. Mengistu, the chief of staff, had issued a proclamation stating that the armed forces remained loyal to Haile Selassie. On 16 December Haile Selassie returned to Addis Ababa where he was met by a guard of honour of army, navy, air force and police. The national anthem was sung and the crowds shouted long live Haile Selassie. However, 5,000 dissident members of the Imperial Guard refused to surrender and their stronghold was bombed and machine-gunned. Haile Selassie promised an amnesty to all who admitted error and said that statements by the Crown Prince had been made under duress. Casualties were substantial: 29 members of the armed forces were killed and 43 wounded; 121 civilians were killed and 442 wounded; 174 members of the dissident Imperial Guard were killed and 300 wounded. The Emperor received messages of support from Liberia, Sudan, Britain, Yugoslavia, the US and the USSR and all the Ethiopian missions abroad except from the Chargé d'Affaires in Stockholm who had been dismissed. However, the revolt had been fuelled by a number of grievances including poverty and the lack of advancement of non-aristocrats, for in many ways Ethiopia remained a feudal state and Haile Selassie's approach to reform was one of extreme caution. As *The Times* said: 'Yet the coup failed – perhaps fundamentally because it came too soon. The Emperor, therefore, at the age of 68 has won more time to bring his country into line with African developments.'[17]

The nature of Somali society, with its divisive clan rivalries, made rule through a party system difficult at the best of times. There was a further complication arising out of the merger of British Somaliland and Italian Somaliland in 1960, to form an independent Somalia upon the structures of two distinct colonial systems which, among other things, had left behind two languages, English and Italian. By 1969 there was an upsurge of clan rivalries following the failure of Somalia's policy of unification to take over those parts of Kenya and Ethiopia which it claimed. In 1967 President Kaunda of Zambia mediated a détente with both Ethiopia and Kenya.

Over 1,000 candidates contested the 123 seats in the 1969 elections in which the Somali Youth League (SYL) won a majority (with the help of gerrymandering). Mohamed Haji Ibrahim Egal was re-appointed Prime Minister by President Abdirashid Ali Shirmake and a clan coalition government was formed; all but one member of the opposition members then crossed the floor of the house to join the government and, hopefully, to get jobs for themselves, with the result that Somalia became a de facto one-party state. This apparent monolithic support for the government was an illusion, self-seeking splinter groups rather than party supporters made up the assembly. The hundreds of disappointed candidates were another factor and the public at large became increasingly discontented, a discontent that was aggravated by the autocratic style now employed by the President and Prime Minister.

On 15 October 1969 President Shirmake was assassinated in a factional quarrel. The Prime Minister, who was abroad at the time, hurried back to Mogadishu in order to ensure the election of a new president favourable to himself. On 21 October, when it appeared that the assembly would do as Egal wanted, the army seized control in a bloodless coup. The coup was brilliantly organized; Gen. Karshel, the police commandant, was arrested but won his freedom when he promised police support for the army. Members of the government were detained, the National Assembly was dissolved and the Constitution suspended. A Supreme Revolutionary Council (SRC) was formed, composed of members of the army and police. The SRC renamed the country the Somali Democratic Republic and the President of the SRC, Maj.-Gen. Mohammad Siad Barre, became head of state. The SRC announced that all those arrested would stand trial, mainly for corruption. Over Somali radio it was announced that the coup had been achieved without injury or loss of life and that the army and police would struggle against corruption amongst the leaders of the country. The SRC said it would develop Somalia as a socialist country and, though political parties were banned, democratic elections would be held 'at an appropriate moment'. The country, an amalgam of British Somaliland and the Italian-administered Somalia, had faced immense difficulties welding the two systems together. Civil service appointments had been based upon patronage and it was in urgent need of aid. Now, as it soon became clear, it was to be ruled by a strong man.

When Sudan became independent in 1956 it was already as a country deeply divided between the Muslim north and the Black south, the existing divisions having been emphasized and increased as a result of British policy. Before the 1960s began Sudan experienced its first coup when on 17 November 1958 Gen. Ibrahim Pasha Abboud launched a coup, which he justified on the grounds that political parties and parliamentary democracy had gone for good in Sudan. Subsequently, he assured the country that he would return it to civilian rule as soon as stability was restored – a familiar statement that was to become all too well known through much of Africa during the ensuing decade. Commenting on the coup a month later, *The Times* correspondent wrote: 'The parliamentary system is generally dismissed as being corrupt, unworkable and alien. What concerns people generally is not the fact that the soldiers are in power, but whether the soldiers will in fact be able to produce better results. On this score there are naturally doubts, and even humility. For the rest, the regime, though arbitrary, is certainly not tyrannous.'[18] Abboud handed power back to the civilians, under pressure, in 1964. However, the decade ended with a second, bloodless coup on 25 May 1969 when a group of army officers and civilians, led by Col. (later Gen.) Gaafar Mohammed Nimeiri, seized power.

EAST AFRICA

The pattern of events that unfolded in the first half of the 1960s in East Africa was substantially different from the series of coups which troubled West Africa or the Horn, though the causes were similar. The army mutinies that occurred in January 1964 in Kenya, Tanganyika and Uganda were quickly suppressed with timely assistance from Britain. Subsequently, at an early stage of their independence, both Kenyatta of Kenya and Nyerere of Tanganyika were able to come to grips with the problem of how to control their military establishments. First, however, came the revolution on the island of Zanzibar.

Zanzibar became independent on 10 December 1963 and a month later, on 12 January 1964, a revolt by the African majority overthrew the government of Sheikh Muhammad Shamte, the Prime Minister, and the Sultan, as constitutional head of state, was deposed. The strange figure of self-styled 'Field Marshal' John Okello emerged as the coup and revolution-maker. However, the leader of the Afro-Shirazi Party, Abeid Karume, became the new head of state and President. He was strongly anti-Arab. The speed with which the new government was recognized by Russia, China and other Communist states set alarm bells ringing in the West. The revolution in Zanzibar acted as a prelude to the army mutinies in Kenya, Tanganyika and Uganda and caused crises in all three countries. At first the mutinies were treated as industrial disputes for better pay and conditions and were considered settled after three days. Then the Tanganyikan army mutinied a second time and British assistance was called for – it had not been the first time round even though those in Kenya and Uganda had already been put down with British assistance. This second Tanganyikan mutiny almost turned into a coup. At the heart of the

Tanganyikan dispute was the slow pace of Africanization. At independence there were only three African commissioned officers (a further 15 were in training) while a few weeks before the mutiny a request for a crash officer-training programme produced a scheme by the commanding officer (a Briton) that would only have achieved full Africanization over 10 years. In the event, the mutineers were court-martialled and the Tanganyika African National Union (TANU) Youth League was instructed by President Nyerere to create a new army.

TANZANIA BECOMES A ONE-PARTY STATE

Prior to the events of January 1964 Tanganyika was preparing to turn itself into a one-party state. In January 1963 the Annual Conference of TANU made a new call for unity and opened its membership to all Tanganyika citizens. It invited those who had campaigned against the party to return to it. TANU decided in principle that Tanganyika should become a one-party state and the President was authorized to appoint a commission to investigate what constitutional or other changes would be required. President Nyerere, who soon also came to be called Mwalimu (the teacher), said at this time: 'Democracy in Africa or anywhere else, is government by the People. Ideally, it is a form of government whereby the people – ALL the people – settle their affairs through free discussion... And in African society, the traditional method of conducting affairs is by free discussion... The elders sit under the big tree, and talk until they agree.'[19] After describing the two-party system, or party basis, of Representative Democracy, Nyerere continued: 'I am now going to suggest: that where there is one party and that party is identified with the nation as a whole, the foundations of democracy are firmer than they can ever be where you have two or more parties, each representing only a section of the community! ... For the politics of a country governed by the two-party system are not, and cannot be, national politics; they are the politics of groups, whose differences, more often than not, are of small concern to the majority of the people...' Nyerere argued that, unlike European and American parties that came into being to fight particular social and economic causes, 'Our own parties had a very different origin. They were not formed to challenge any ruling group of our own people; they were formed to challenge the foreigners who ruled over us. They were not, therefore, political "parties" – i.e., factions – but nationalist movements. And from the outset they represented the interests and aspirations of the whole nation.' Nyerere's core argument was that provided the single party was identified with the nation as a whole, then the foundations of democracy could be firmer and the people could have a greater opportunity to exercise real choice, than where two or more parties existed, each representing only a section of the people. Strengthening his case further, Nyerere said:

> I would say that we not only have an opportunity to dispense with the disciplines of the two-party system but that we would be wrong to retain them. I would say that they are not only unnecessary where you have only one party but that they are bound, in time, to prove fatal to democracy. We have already seen how severely these disciplines must limit freedom of expression in a two-party parliament.

Then, on the subject of civil servants, he said: 'For, once you begin to think in terms of a single national movement instead of a number of rival factional parties, it becomes absurd to exclude a whole group of the most intelligent and able members of the community from participation in the discussion of policy simply because they happen to be civil servants.'[20]

In a Guide to the One-Party State Commission of January 1963 Nyerere set out guiding principles to include: Tanganyika to be a Republic with an executive Head of State; the Rule of Law and the independence of the Judiciary to be preserved; there to be complete equality for all Tanganyika citizens and maximum political freedom for all citizens within the context of a single national movement; that there should be maximum participation of the people in their government and ultimate control by them of the organs of state through universal suffrage; and that there should be complete freedom for the people to choose their own representatives on all Representative and Legislative bodies, within the context of the law.

Nyerere came to be regarded as the intellectual defender of the African one-party state at its best and his arguments would be widely quoted in the coming years. Following this speech in which he argued that Tanganyika should become a one-party state, Nyerere was at once faced with powerful counter-arguments of equal intellectual weight from Miss Frene Ginwala, then the editor of *Spearhead* (a pan-African review published in Dar es Salaam). Throughout his arguments, she said:

> President Nyerere emphasizes the need for discussion as a fundamental characteristic of democracy. He implies that with the removal of two-party disciplines there will be an immediate sprouting of self-criticism and discussion. This may be true in so far as parliament and its members are concerned, but what of the rest of society? Can one believe there will be an atmosphere conducive to the expression of dissent from the norm?
>
> President Nyerere himself says that opposition parties 'tend to be

regarded as traitors to the majority of our people'. Might this not also apply to those who differ in any way from official policy, or who express disagreement with any government action? There is, in fact, an unfortunate tendency, especially amongst certain TANU officials to regard any criticism of the Party, particularly from a non-official, as tantamount to treason.

The whole argument that a one-party system would not in any way limit discussion or criticism of shortcomings, falls to the ground, unless steps are taken to ensure firstly that the atmosphere for discussion and self-criticism is created, and secondly that there are avenues and channels for it to flourish and be effective. The atmosphere for free unfettered discussion must be actively fostered by the TANU leadership. The problem of how that criticism can be made to be effective raises the whole question of the institutions that will be required within the new system.[21]

It was perhaps not unconnected with this article that in May 1963 Miss Ginwala was declared a prohibited immigrant with no explanation as to why! Under the one-party system that was adopted, presidential and parliamentary elections were held in Tanzania in 1965, 1970, 1975, 1980, 1985 and 1990, all being carried out peacefully and, despite the party's executive influence in the nomination of candidates, these elections were competitive as each constituency was contested by two candidates. Thus, the elections often contributed to significant changes in the composition of the political elite.[22]

KENYA AND UGANDA

Prior to announcing on 14 August 1964 that Kenya was to become a Republic on 12 December 1964, Kenyatta told the House of Representatives that the country would also soon have a one-party system, 'because we do not subscribe to the notion of the government and the governed in opposition to one another, one clamouring for duties and the other crying for rights'. Kenyatta said he would not justify the one-party state by using the fragile and perennial argument that parties were the expression of social classes, and therefore that there must be only one party. He said that the necessity for a one-party system in most parts of Africa stemmed from two predominant facts. First, traditionally, African society evolved around the family tree, the wider pattern of blood brotherhood and the wider networking of clans and tribes, all of which acted in concert in times of emergency. Secondly, to the African, the supreme authority was the tribal council, which was at once a government and an expression of the personality of every citizen. African leaders were advised by elders, and by obeying the tribal councils, the people maintained that they obeyed themselves, and their true will. 'Constructive opposition from within is therefore not an alien thing in so far as the traditional African society is concerned.'[23]

On 10 November 1964 Kenya became a one-party state by consent when Ronald Ngala, leader of the Kenya African Democratic Union (KADU) and salaried Leader of the Opposition, led his party across the floor of the house to the government benches, or rather, to scenes of jubilation, was carried bodily across the House to the government benches. At an earlier press conference Ngala said: 'This is one of the times when we must be prepared to sacrifice our political dignity for the peace and harmony of Kenya.'

Uganda became independent in October 1962 with an alliance of Milton Obote's Uganda People's Congress (UPC) and Kabaka Yekka (KY – 'the King Alone') party, which won all the seats in the Kingdom of Buganda. It was an uneasy alliance from the start. By 1964 the UPC, aided by defectors from the Democratic Party and the KY, had gained an overall majority in Parliament that enabled Obote to dispense with the KY members of his government. A power struggle then developed between the UPC and Buganda with the latter trying to resurrect its position as a kingdom. In February 1966 a KY Member of Parliament accused government ministers of smuggling gold from the Congo, an accusation that was interpreted as an indirect attack upon Obote, and a motion to that effect was passed unanimously. It looked as though Obote must fall. Obote, therefore, carried out his own coup, arresting five of his ministers at a cabinet meeting. Then he suspended the constitution and took full executive powers. In April he introduced a new constitution and made himself President. He abolished the federal status of Buganda and the other kingdoms as well as the official estates held by the chiefs. The Lukiko (Council) of the Kingdom of Buganda reacted to the coup by demanding that the central government should leave Buganda's soil: in other words, it declared itself independent of Uganda. Three days later, as rumours spread that the Ganda were taking to arms, the regular army under Obote's orders stormed the Kabaka's palace. Following heavy fighting and casualties, the Kabaka (King Frederick Mutesa II) escaped to exile in England, the Kingdom of Buganda was brought to an end and was divided into four districts and placed under a state of emergency.

There were other coups during the 1960s: in Algeria where Houari Boumedienne ousted Ahmed ben Bella in 1965; in Burundi in 1966 where Michel Micombero deposed King Ntwane V to make the country a Republic with himself as President; in Libya in 1969 when Muammar Gaddafi seized power from King Idris; and in Lesotho in 1970 when Chief Leabua Jonathan, who was losing the election, suspended the constitution and ruled by decree. The pattern varied but the end result was the same: the creation of a one-party state and, too often, the military replacing the civilians as the rulers. Over these years a growing number of leading Africans claimed that there was no place for the two- or multiparty system on the continent and that their people did not wish to be dominated by a majority but wanted, instead, a system that allowed decisions to be reached by consensus. In Francophone Africa, 10 years after independence, only seven of the 17 statesmen who had led their countries to independence were still in power, while eight of the new presidents were army officers; and in Gabon and Dahomey, where civilians held power, the army played a significant 'watcher' role in the background. The army, indeed, had become a crucial power broker in half the states of Africa. In former British West Africa the army had brought an end to Nkrumah's nine-year rule, had intervened, ruled briefly, and then returned Sierra Leone to civilian rule while in Nigeria the civil war came to an end with the end of the decade though the army would rule for most of the succeeding 30 years. Yet no rule of thumb could explain the emergence of the one-party state or the predominance of the army. In 1968, for example, in both Dahomey and Sierra Leone the army returned the government to civilian rule while the following year the army in Ghana also stepped aside in favour of civilian politicians. Although the soldiers who carried out coups justified their actions on the grounds of general misrule and corruption on the part of the politicians, discontent soon surfaced when it became clear that the soldiers were unable to do any better. There was an obvious link between deteriorating economic conditions and the military coup. As Moussa Traoré, the Mali coup-maker of 1968, put it, it was no longer possible to acquiesce in the 'deterioration of the country's economy' while 'revolutionary demagoguery' could no longer disguise the true facts. The principal indices of discontent were student revolts and trade union protests and strikes and in 1968, for example, substantial student troubles occurred in Senegal, Upper Volta, Côte d'Ivoire, Ethiopia, Egypt, Tunisia, Algeria, Morocco, Kenya and Madagascar.

Several general conclusions can be drawn from this decade of coups and the emergence of the one-party state. The first, that many of the countries that came to independence were woefully unprepared for it, a fact that reflected on the colonial powers rather than the new African states. Second, that the armies of the new states saw themselves, almost at once, as players in the political game and not as impartial instruments of state. Third, that the political systems and constitutions bequeathed to their ex-colonies by the departing colonial powers were not suited to many of the conditions prevailing at the time of independence; neither had they taken into account the African approach to consensus that was the main justification for the one-party state. There were other arguments but what the colonial powers never understood was the fact that only after independence could African politicians and leaders work out what would best suit their countries and their people and that the process of finding the appropriate system would be both long-drawn-out and painful.

CHAPTER FIVE

Problems of Development

THE DIFFICULTIES TO BE FACED

A t the beginning of the 1960s most of the newly independent African states had underdeveloped, fragmented economies based principally upon small-scale agriculture and craft industries. Colonial economic activity had concentrated upon export-import enclaves concerned with plantation agriculture or the extraction of minerals. The bulk of the profits from these activities, including surpluses that might have been invested locally, were remitted overseas. Without exchange control, moreover, the new African states could not prevent a continuing flight of capital, including both foreign and domestic savings. A respected British aid commentator at this time opened a pamphlet *Aid to Africa* with the following words: 'Little is known about the population of Africa south of the Sahara. In very round figures the area may now contain about 200 million people.'[1] After a century of colonialism it might have been reasonable to expect a somewhat more precise appraisal but from the viewpoint of the newly emerging aid donors the continent presented a virtual *tabula rasa* upon which to operate. The same author continued: 'In a continent the size of Africa, in which agricultural yields are so low, where other natural resources are not lacking and where industrialization hardly exists, the scope for development is enormous.' He enumerated three problems: the general weakness and high cost of administration; lack of clear purpose in economic planning; and the difficulty of stimulating indigenous enterprise. He elaborated further upon the small absorptive capacity of the new states, how aid should be used and supervised, and queried donor policies. Most aid was then 'tied' to the procurement of goods from the donor. There was plenty of finance available at the time; the question was how it should be used. And little noticed at first was the growth of the debt problem. At that stage, immediately after independence, all returns on the extraction of raw materials ought to have been used to finance other aspects of development including industrialization. This did not happen for several reasons: because most such profits were remitted to the metropolitan powers in the form of profits and interest; and because of limited market size, the absence of an educated, skilled labour force, and the inherited patterns of colonial export-import growth instead of national development. Moreover, there was urgent need to co-ordinate inter-state transport systems to facilitate development on a regional scale.

At the time, as these problems surfaced, there existed a clarity of thinking among African leaders, both about the intentions towards Africa of the big powers and about what they ought to do in order to be truly independent, that was not apparent at the end of the century. At the same time, the predominant Western motive was to retain control over the levers of economic power on the continent. The background to these considerations was the Cold War. As the British economist Andrew Shonfield shrewdly observed: 'The habits of totalitarian tyranny both in the rulers and the ruled take a long time to correct. That is no justification for running to the opposite extreme and trying to use economic aid as a weapon in the Cold War... Letting a country go communist is a risk that we must feel able to afford to take; otherwise the West is likely to be the permanent object of blackmail by all the least worthwhile and most oppressive governments.'[2] That sage advice was ignored and in the years that followed, Western aid, too often, was deployed for Cold War rather than for development reasons and African leaders quickly learnt how to use Cold War arguments to ensure a constant flow of aid. Another examination of the continent's problems at this time included this judgement: 'What is needed in Africa today is a thorough-going reconstruction of the entire economy. It is not the details of production, which are wrong, not marginal adjustments which are needed. The entire structure of production is a colonial creation, with an emphasis on primary exports that inhibits any sustained economic growth.'[3] In his seminal book *How Europe Underdeveloped Africa* Walter Rodney lays bare what, in essence, was the starting point for independent Africa:

> It is fairly obvious that capitalists do not set out to create other capitalists, who would be rivals. On the contrary, the tendency of capitalism in Europe from the very beginning was one of competition, elimination and monopoly. Therefore, when the imperialist stage was reached, the metropolitan capitalists had no intention of allowing rivals to arise in the dependencies.
>
> Many irrational contradictions arose throughout colonial Africa as a result of the non-industrialization policy: Sudanese and Ugandans grew cotton but imported manufactured cotton goods, Ivory Coast grew cocoa and imported tinned cocoa and chocolate.[4]

Although diamonds were produced in Africa the cutting, which enhanced the value, was done in Europe: 'No Africans were allowed to come near that kind of technique in the colonial period.'

Rodney writes from a Marxist point of view; he might have added that there were no serious capitalists in Africa at the time of independence except for the whites in South Africa. There was, therefore, an urgent need for Africans to regain power and the consequent decision-making capacity that had been lost during the colonial period.

Some post-colonial problems had been deliberately created. Thus, when independence became inevitable, France, which had administered its sub-Saharan African Empire as the two large regions of West and Equatorial Africa, split them into a dozen states that were hardly viable economically. Both Senghor of Senegal and Boganda of Central African Republic wanted to retain the Community that had been proposed by de Gaulle, not to pander to his political ambitions but in order to bargain with France on a single, united basis. Instead, France kept its former colonies in the franc zone and was therefore able effectively to control their financial decisions. Britain, on a somewhat looser rein, maintained the sterling area for some years thereafter and kept the sterling reserves of its ex-colonies in London, using them to bolster Britain's account when faced with periodic sterling crises. The French Minister of Finance and Economic Affairs said the franc zone had been created with a 'clearly defensive character, conceived essentially for the profit of a metropolis which assumed, at the same time, in an authoritarian and centralized fashion, all the responsibilities of a geographically heterogeneous and dispersed group' – which, of course, France had created.[5]

The French agronomist, René Dumont, produced one of the most important studies of agriculture in Africa at this time.[6] He argued that the problem of mechanization was crucial because African elites were seduced by the idea of modern machines and that it was difficult to convince them that agricultural progress did not depend on immediate and complete mechanization. Rather, he argued, the vocational training of the peasants would constitute the most effective lever for agriculture and general progress in tropical Africa. 'Agricultural development must go beyond its colonial framework. Until now the main emphasis, sometimes the exclusive one, has been on export crops. Efforts in this direction must, of course, be continued as capital resources beyond those offered by foreign aid must be increased to buy equipment.' Unfortunately, as Dumont pointed out, 'The schoolboy son of an agricultural worker is taught to have only one desire, to escape the land and his dependence on it.' In Senegal, for example, agriculture was the last profession school children chose. The colonial powers had neglected education in the rural areas;

their African successors did the same thing.

WHAT IS DEVELOPMENT?

Growth is not the same thing as development and this was to be illustrated in a number of ways during the 1960s. At the beginning of the decade only a very few newly independent states, and then only with the assistance of substantial aid inputs, were in a position to enhance their productive power in any meaningful sense. At that stage it was a question of absorptive capacity, which, in turn, depended upon skills or, rather, their absence. Aid, therefore, moved to the centre of all development arguments; could it create an economic momentum that would continue once the aid had ceased?

A major source of income both during and after the colonial period came from the export of tropical foods in which Africa had a clear economic advantage and it was argued very strongly at the time that maximizing such exports would provide capital needed for development. The process was not that simple. Efforts to increase agricultural exports meant neglect of food crops for home consumption with the result that a continent where 80 per cent of the people lived on the land found itself spending a steadily increasing amount of foreign exchange to import food that it failed to produce for itself. A different case concerned copper in Northern Rhodesia (Zambia). Between 1930 and 1964 (the year of Zambian independence) copper production boomed and the GDP expanded; yet at independence 80 per cent of the population still lived and produced exactly as they had done prior to the copper boom. This posed the question of just what benefit to the people of the colony had been the huge production of copper over these years. 'What this kind of boom really meant can be demonstrated by two facts. About half of the total capital surplus generated in the Northern Rhodesia economy was annually transferred abroad, mainly as copper-mining dividends. Secondly in 1964 on the day of independence, Zambia inherited exactly one secondary school capable of carrying Africans to the level of the Senior Cambridge certificate.' Further, the new states 'remain dependent on world markets in which they have little or no say on prices; and the terms of trade have continued (with some exceptions) to move against them'.[7] By the time Africa became independent the world economic system had created a huge gap in wealth and power between a minority of rich countries at one end of the scale and apparently ever-increasing poverty at the other end. Sometimes the gains that appeared to accrue from growth in a particular sector of the economy were cancelled out by other factors. As Basil Davidson argues in relation to Ghana: 'Thus the annual quantity of cocoa produced in Ghana during the past ten years or so has repeatedly passed all previous records. But so has Ghana's annual burden of foreign indebtedness, and, in consequence, Ghana's helplessness within the general system that was shaped in colonial times.'[8]

Development plans were very much in fashion during the 1960s but only continental planning would have ensured that the gains from economic growth that such planning produced could be evenly distributed. Smaller common markets – the East African Common Market was a good example – were likely to result in the strong sectors (in that case Kenya) getting stronger at the expense of the others. Plans, in any case, were about classifying priorities; in most cases development plans were drawn up by foreigners who believed they must be dependent upon aid inputs. In fact, what tended to happen was that the donors ignored the plans and chose the desirable projects that best suited their aid policies. The plan was no more than a framework. Although it would have made macro-economic sense to draw up a plan to cover the whole continent there were insuperable obstacles to doing so at the time. Vice-President Rashid Kawawa of Tanzania explained this very well: 'The real problem is that each of the separate nations has the fear that in a United Africa it might become a backward and neglected area, exploited for the benefit of another part of this great continent. This is not a stupid objection or a selfish one.' At one level the proliferation of plans through the 1960s appeared rather like a process of wish fulfilment, as though the mere existence of a national plan would make things happen. The economist, Professor Arthur Lewis, wrote as follows towards the end of the decade:

> Development planning has not made much contribution to economic growth. This is partly because most plans are so grandiose and unrealistic that nobody takes them seriously, including the people who draw them up. But there is also the more fundamental reason that the rate of economic growth depends not so much on government expenditure as it does on whether farmers plant more, the businessmen build more factories, and the mines increase their investment. If conditions are favourable to the expansion of such activities, the economy will grow rapidly whether there is a Development Plan or not.[9]

If we examine a few sample countries at the beginning of the decade the extent of the problems becomes clear. The violent upheavals in the Congo dominated the political headlines about Africa for the first part of the 1960s, yet economics, and above all the Belgian determination to maintain its grip on the country's wealth, lay behind the politics. 'Authoritarianism was the basic vice of the system, as of all Belgian colonialism. It was based for too long on the monstrous slogan, "no elites, no problems". As an application of this principle, higher education was closed to the Congolese until 1955. They were forbidden to go elsewhere for study, and unable to do it at home.'[10] Ghana, which as the first black African colony to achieve independence drew much attention to itself at this time, also suffered under colonialism though not in the extreme form of the Congo. 'In no case were the Africans themselves permitted to achieve anything like full development of their own resources. Education and social services lagged, and the African was limited predominantly to unskilled wage labour or to the traditional sector.' This judgement stands despite the generally better educational achievements of British West Africa than elsewhere on the continent.[11]

There were plenty of signs in Ghana immediately after independence that Western businessmen at once expected the Ghanaian government to conform to Western, capitalist policies, even though the country was determinedly neutralist and had adopted a socialist path of development. The West, the source of most aid and investment, believed that in the end the pressures it could mount would overcome African attempts to pursue indigenous African development paths. And when Nkrumah was overthrown in February 1966 economists 'sorted' out the 'chaotic inheritance' so as to present a case for help to the IMF. Between 1959 and the end of 1965 Ghana's foreign debt had risen from £6 million to £237 million. At this point Western Africa watchers and economists could, perhaps, have been excused for saying 'I told you so' and yet by 1971, Ghana's moderate pro-Western leader Kofi Busia could say plaintively that he, or rather Ghana, had done everything the West had told it to do but was not receiving the assistance it needed. 'They had been lectured, but endlessly, on the absolute need to eschew "experiments", to refrain from "adventures", to accept obediently the patterns of behaviour of their senior partners overseas.'[12] When African states in trouble did do what their senior partners overseas told them to do the rewards appeared to be minimal.

Nigeria had much greater potential. An indication of its industrial possibilities can be gained from the fact that between 1947 and 1958 exports grew from £44 million to £136 million and imports rose even more sharply from £33 million to £167 million while keeping pace with this expanding economy were the per capita earnings of the population. Even so, despite average income per head rising by one or two per cent a year between 1950 and 1960, it was still low by any common sense yardstick; at the beginning of the decade it stood at approximately £30, less than one tenth the average for every man, woman and child in Britain at that time. The total national product of Nigeria at £1,000 million then exceeded the combined products of Kenya, Uganda, Tanganyika, the Rhodesias and Nyasaland to make Nigeria the largest economy on the African continent after South Africa. In March 1960 the Shell–BP Development Company of

Nigeria Ltd said it hoped oil output might reach 10 million tons a year by 1970 to make Nigeria one of the Commonwealth's major oil producers, second only to Canada. Nigeria in fact was to become a much larger oil producer than was then envisaged, but in its case the politics of tribalism were to intervene before any serious advances in the economy would be possible.

At the other side of the continent Kenya had the best potential economy although it was still primarily an agricultural country, relying upon coffee, tea, sisal, wattle products, pyrethrum, wheat, meat and dairy products and soda ash as its main exports. Some light engineering had also been developed, and food processing. Its most valuable agricultural exports were coffee, tea, sisal, maize and pyrethrum. It also had a substantially better transport and commercial infrastructure than its two neighbours – Uganda and Tanganyika – and this was to be a cause of problems once the East African Common Market had been formed. To the north of Kenya, Ethiopia entered into a substantial trade agreement with the Soviet Union in 1960, giving Russia the rights to undertake extensive geological surveys throughout the country, to construct gold mining installations and gold processing plants, to build an oil refinery at Assab on the Red Sea and so to break the Western oil firms' (Shell, Caltex, Agip, Standard) monopoly of supply. Writing in the *Guardian* at the beginning of September 1960, Clyde Sanger said that Tanganyika needed to double its national income within 10 years. He was optimistic. 'The value of exports is more than 13 times what it was in 1938 and in 1959 the national income increased by 6 per cent to £177 million. Nevertheless, this country of nine million people is still appallingly poor, with a per capita income of less than £20 a year.' These and other country assessments demonstrated the range of problems to be overcome.

AFRICAN ECONOMIC UNIONS

A number of mainly economic unions were formed in the early 1960s among the Francophone states. They were over-ambitious, they reflected the former colonial ties with France, and they did not have much impact. Nonetheless, they demonstrated an awareness of the possibilities that a union offered even if they also showed up fairly rapidly the constraints that limited the effectiveness of such unions.

The African and Malagasy Union (*Union Africaine et Malgache* – UAM) was formed in September 1961. It grew out of a meeting held in Brazzaville the previous December when 12 Francophone countries agreed to maintain close ties with each other and a special relationship with France. The 12 countries were Cameroon, Central African Republic, Chad, Congo (B), Dahomey (Benin), Gabon, Côte D'Ivoire, Madagascar, Mauritania, Niger, Senegal and Upper Volta

(Burkina Faso). The aims of the UAM were over-ambitious: a common stand on international issues, the promotion of economic and cultural co-operation and the maintenance of a common defence organization. It soon became obvious that the 12 were too diverse, too geographically widespread and too immersed in their individual development problems to allow the UAM ever to achieve any real significance. In March 1964 the UAM reorganized itself as the Afro-Malagasy Union for Economic Co-operation (*Union Africaine et Malgache de Co-opération Economique* – UAMCE) and confined its role to economic affairs. By 1966 it had become moribund. Its successor, the African and Malagasy Common Organisation (*Organisation Commune Africaine et Malgache* – OCAM) had already been formed in May 1965 at Nouakchott, Mauritania, by the 13 Francophone countries: Cameroon, Central African Republic, Chad, Congo (B), Dahomey, Gabon, Côte d'Ivoire, Madagascar, Mauritania, Niger, Senegal, Togo and Upper Volta. They were subsequently joined by Rwanda and Congo (Kinshasa) to make 15 but Mauritania (the original host country) dropped out and the OCAM Charter between the 14 countries was signed on 27 June 1965 at Antananarivo, Madagascar. OCAM's aims were co-operation in economic, social, technical and cultural development. OCAM had a troubled history. Mauritius joined in 1970, Congo (K), by then renamed Zaïre, withdrew in 1972 as did Congo (B) in 1973 while a further three members – Cameroon, Chad and Madagascar – withdrew in 1974, followed by Gabon in 1975. Some of these countries retained their membership of OCAM's various agencies.

Other unions included the Equatorial Customs Union (*Union Douanière Equatoriale* – UDE), which had been created back in 1959. This was replaced by the Customs and Economic Union of Central Africa (*Union Douanière des Etats de l'Afrique Central* – UDEAC), which was established at Brazzaville in December 1964 and included Cameroon, Central African Republic, Congo (B), Gabon and Chad. In 1968 Central African Republic and Chad withdrew from UDEAC to join with Congo (K) in the Union of Central African States (UEAC). Gabon denounced this as cutting across the existing UDEAC. This new union raised interesting issues of neo-colonialism. Paul Lewis, writing in the *Financial Times*, said: 'There is little doubt that the idea of linking up the old Belgian Congo with two franc area countries originated in Kinshasa and the first question anyone asked in an attempt to elucidate the aims of the operation was who had put President Mobutu up to proposing it. According to some, the villain of the piece is General de Gaulle, who is anxious to attract the Congo into his sphere of influence as Africa's biggest French-speaking country and a natural counter-weight to Nigeria.'[13] In December 1968 Central African Republic rejoined UDEAC. These bewildering formations and re-formations were part of a search for a customs union that would work while the expressions of greater political intent, though no doubt genuine at the time, simply did not represent the existing realities.

In East Africa the three Anglophone countries of Kenya, Uganda and Tanzania formed the East African Common Market (EACM) on 6 June 1967 with the object of strengthening the economic, industrial and trade links between the three countries. The EACM headquarters were established at Arusha in Tanzania, the Railways headquarters in Nairobi, Kenya, Harbours at Dar es Salaam, Tanzania, and Posts and Telecommunications at Kampala, Uganda. The three territories had a good deal in common. As British-administered territories they shared similar administrative structures and they came to independence over the two years 1961–63. They were comparable in size and at the same general levels of development. In 1948 Britain had established an East African High Commission to co-ordinate activities in the three territories and in 1961 the High Commission was replaced by the East African Common Services Organisation (EACSO) so that the framework for a possible common market already existed when the three territories became independent. However, (a recurring theme in putative common markets) between 1961 and 1967 Tanganyika and Uganda complained that a majority of the economic benefits of EACSO went to Kenya, which had a more advanced infrastructure and a better-developed industrial base than its two partners. In 1967, therefore, when the East African Community (EAC) was formed, attempts were made to compensate for this imbalance by channelling a greater proportion of community revenues to Tanzania and Uganda, the two weaker partners. However, the EAC foundered during the 1970s over political differences as well as continuing economic imbalances.

In May 1967, in yet another attempt to create a regional union, delegates from 12 West African states met in Accra under the auspices of the Economic Commission for Africa (ECA) to set up a West African Economic Community. This was the first attempt to create a union that would include both Anglophone and Francophone states: those taking part were Dahomey, Ghana, Côte d'Ivoire, Liberia, Mali, Mauritania, Niger, Nigeria, Senegal, Sierra Leone, Togo and Upper Volta. It was not until 1975 that such a union would come into being.

These union manoeuvres, which were a feature of the 1960s, did little to strengthen African trade or the collective ability of their members to deal with the economic world beyond Africa. As much as anything they indicated African awareness of its general weakness: a continent of tiny, fragmented economies was never going to be able to match the external economic pressures to which it was constantly subjected.

The African Development Bank (ADB), on the other hand, was a precise institution that belonged to all independent African states. The idea for such a bank had first been mooted at the All Africa People's Conference of January 1960 held in Tunis. A draft agreement for a development bank with a basic capital of US$200 million, the money to be entirely subscribed by African states, was drawn up in 1963. A formula for subscriptions of members was based on a combination of population, gross national product, foreign trade and government revenue; minimum subscription was set at US$1 million, the maximum at US$30 million. The bank would finance investment projects and programmes relating to economic and social development and would give special attention to those that affected several countries; it would also promote public and private capital investment and provide technical assistance. The Bank came into being in September 1964 after 20 countries had ratified the agreement to set it up. The Bank's headquarters were established in Abidjan in 1965 and became operational on 1 July 1966. The capital of the ADB was entirely subscribed by African countries in order to preserve the African nature of the Bank's operations and the ADB was the only such regional bank to do this. The drawback to this was the limitation placed on available funds in view of the small size of most African economies.

UNITED NATIONS AGENCIES

The Economic Commission for Africa (ECA) was established by the Economic and Social Council of the United Nations on 29 April 1958 in order to promote economic and social development in Africa. It was open to all independent African countries that were also members of the United Nations but on 24 July 1963 South Africa was barred from membership by the Economic and Social Council until 'conditions for constructive co-operation have been restored by a change in its racial policy'. The ECA was sited in Addis Ababa with sub-regional offices in Yaoundé, Gisenyi, Niamey, Tangier, Lusaka and Kinshasa. Its chief officer was an executive secretary. The ECA paid special attention to agriculture and the problems of transition from subsistence to market agriculture and co-operated with the United Nations Food and Agriculture Organization (FAO). In real terms the ECA was an advisory body with only limited resources at its disposal. It promoted co-operation between Africa's sub-regions and inter-African trade. It became a source of African statistics and undertook manpower training, looked at the social aspects of development, transport, communications and natural resources.

From its inception the ECA became involved in arguments between Anglophone and Francophone Africa. The second meeting of the ECA was held in Tangier at the end of January 1960 (when most of Africa had yet to achieve independence) and on that occasion there was a discussion about the impact of the European Economic Community (EEC) upon Africa. A group of states, led by Nigeria, Ghana and Guinea, argued that the association of the Francophone states and the Congo with the EEC through the Yaoundé Convention would widen the divisions between associated and non-associated states. Therefore, they insisted, Africa should create an African Common Market. These mainly Anglophone states wished to counter the stratagem of France and Belgium to maintain an economic stranglehold over their former possessions and so perpetuate divisions between former British and French Africa. Most delegates to the Tunis meeting favoured multilateral over bilateral aid although the French African members of the Community were lukewarm and expected to continue receiving French aid. The ECA then adopted a motion on International Aid to Africa that favoured multilateral aid since bilateral aid involved political pressures. (At this time few people foresaw the extent to which the multilateral agencies would become the tools of the rich Western nations led by the United States.) The delegates from Guinea argued that international assistance should 'liberate' the African continent economically, otherwise political independence would be a 'façade'.

Nearly ten years after the foundation of the ECA, in mid-December 1967, a Conference of African Planners was held in Addis Ababa; it was called to consider the effects of planning in Africa over the preceding years. Between 1960 and 1967 out of 40 independent African countries, including South Africa, 34 had launched development plans. The conference headings included: assessment of development potential, plan implementation, foreign aid, requirements of trained personnel, planning advisory services and the African Institute for Economic Development and Planning (IDEP). On aid the Conference had this to say: 'Although foreign assistance was valuable in giving a push to the process of economic development, it could not be a substitute for local resources. African countries needed to aim at achieving national self-reliance, and avoid drawing up plans in which external assistance had a preponderant share.' The African and Malagasy Common Organisation (OCAM) presented a paper to the Conference of African Planners on planning in French-speaking Africa: 'The authors of the first national development plans of the African countries seem to have been victims of the illusion that it was enough to plan a slowly developing economy to give it the dynamism it lacked. To this illusion there was later added another, namely that financing of foreign origin would in all circumstances be a substitute for national efforts proper.'

Speaking at Geneva in July 1968, Robert Gardiner, the Executive Secretary of the ECA, reviewed the 1960s to that date.

In developing Africa, where the greatest number of the poorest and least-developed countries are to be found, growth has been slower than in other regions. African total output, measured in 1960 prices, grew by 3.4 per cent annually during the first six years of the decade; and income per head grew by about 1 per cent per annum over the same period. As a consequence the poverty and the harsh conditions which characterized much of the continent at the beginning of the decade were but slightly alleviated in the succeeding years.

The gap between Africa and elsewhere was widening. Gardiner said that the work of the ECA was a beginning, 'a promotional and development effort to improve material well-being'.

An Economic Survey of Africa since 1950 published by the United Nations in 1962 suggested that there were two model types of economies in Africa into which most countries fitted. Model One was a country in which commercialization had been brought about chiefly by the transformation of part or parts of the traditional economy usually by peasant agricultural producers for export; where there was relatively little foreign investment in large-scale enterprises; and where the outflow of workers as wage earners from the traditional economy to the modern economy was relatively small. Model Two was a country in which the exchange economy had been brought about largely by foreign capital and enterprise, mainly in mining and by foreign settlement; it was a highly capitalized modern economy (in parts) and its techniques were advanced; the modern economy, and consequently the exchange economy, depended heavily on capital provided by non-Africans, and in most cases upon foreign capital; and there was a relatively large outflow of workers as wage-earners from the traditional economy to the modern economy while in the preceding 10 years there had been a sustained increase in real national incomes in most such countries. At the time of this survey per capita incomes varied between US$70 in Sierra Leone to US$346 in South Africa although strict comparisons were not possible because of the difficulty in measuring subsistence incomes.

By the mid-1960s the World Bank accounted for over half of all multilateral financing. 'The World Bank, however, is in two respects a less than independent ideologically indifferent body. It is for all practical purposes a lending agency controlled by Organisation for Economic Co-operation and Development (OECD) members and it is committed to patterns of development that include large private sectors.' Moreover, in the 1960s voting power gave the United States a third of the total vote while the United States, Britain, France and West Germany had a virtual majority.[14] Addressing the Development Assistance Committee (DAC) of the OECD in Washington on 20 July 1966, the President of the World Bank, George D. Woods, said: 'Today the average terms of assistance are harder than they were last year or the year before, and the prospects are disturbing. At the same time, more and more of the flow of finance is being counterbalanced by the debt service paid by the developing countries. Service on public and publicly guaranteed debt more than doubled between 1961 and 1965. More than half the inflow of development finance is now being offset by the return flow in the form of amortization, interest and dividends. Paradoxically, at the same time that the relative volume of aid has been dwindling, the capabilities of the developing countries have been growing.' That last sentence, at least, appeared to demonstrate that aid had had some positive impact. The 'soft' arm of the World Bank, the International Development Association (IDA), had difficulty in obtaining its triennial replenishments since the rich nations, and especially the United States, were reluctant to provide finances that obtained such low returns. George Woods had asked for refinancing at the level of US$1,000 million a year for the period 1968–70 but obtained only US$400 million a year. *The Economist* commented:

> It was obviously difficult for the US, in the present climate of opinion there and balance of payments troubles, to commit its 40 per cent share of the total, but it has been pretty uncompromising about the strings to be attached; it has managed in the end to get a delaying arrangement, whereby IDA will call upon the American contribution during the three years only for the amount needed to finance procurements in the US (eventually the amount deferred can be called up). This is against IDA principles and Britain, which gives 13 per cent of the total, has kicked up a hell of a fuss about it. On the other hand, the British are always fond of saying that they get back 30s. for every £1 they give to the IDA, which gives them no right to point the finger at other people.[15]

During 1968, when Robert McNamara succeeded George Woods as President of the World Bank, there was a growing sense of the need to reappraise aid. According to *The Times*, 'Unless something is done urgently to shock the donor countries out of their growing cynicism and prevarication, the "have-nots" must inevitably lose patience and attempt to take the law into their own hands. A world so divided, not only economically, but also politically by a bottomless gulf of suspicion, incomprehension and bitterness, would be a world doomed to self-destruction.'[16]

Earlier in the decade the First UN Conference on Trade and Development (UNCTAD) had deliberated for three months in Geneva during 1964. While Britain had suggested a standstill on the imposition of new tariffs against the trade of less developed countries, and the IMF had proposed providing temporary assistance when a fall in the prices of exports from poor countries occurred, and France had suggested raising prices for primary products to reasonable levels, the United States had taken an altogether different line. George Ball, the US Under-Secretary of State, said that America would be prepared to help those who helped themselves. US officials explained that this was to prick the inflated hopes of some delegations and to separate reality from fantasy. The developing countries should create a better climate for private capital, as the private investor controls a large share of available resources and can supply more practical experience and technical knowledge than 'officials'. By the time the Second UN Conference on Trade and Development was held in New Delhi in March 1968 the rich-poor divide had widened. When we examine these public arguments about aid and the relationship between aid donors and recipients it is possible to discern the entire pattern of growing cynicism and reluctance to expand the aid effort on the one hand and the equally disillusioned frustration and anger at an unequal world on the other. The parameters that would dominate the aid debate to the end of the century were laid down at this time.

INDUSTRIALIZATION, INVESTMENT AND THE TERMS OF TRADE

Education is constantly advanced as a prerequisite for rapid economic development and yet the British industrial revolution was accomplished on an extremely narrow base. This raises questions about education in Africa at this time. Is education in fact the key to an industrial-economic breakthrough? Or does it create individual expectations that lead its beneficiaries away from participating in growth for the nation only to seek positions for themselves? British capitalists who exported to the Empire never resolved the predicament that if they concentrated on colonial markets they had also to create modernized industrial systems in those colonies so as to expand their market resources. In fact, the British were reluctant to build genuine industrial complexes overseas and preferred instead to sell consumer goods and leave the industrial bases in Britain.

René Dumont (already quoted) foresaw all the difficulties that new African states would face when embarking upon industrialization. He suggested that they should begin with cotton goods, one of the largest items to be imported that it would be easiest to manufacture in Africa. However, beyond that he enumerated a list of problems: 'Any new industry in Africa will have a difficult enough time getting established, and it is almost bound to fail without vigilant and effective support from the government. Customs protection on a national level, and later on the creation of an African Common Market, itself protected, will be virtually essential in order to overcome a whole series of handicaps: weakness in infrastructure, lack of African technicians, high transportation costs, high cost of spare parts, and the inevitably small factories to begin with.'[17] Through the 1960s a number of countries were disproportionately dependent upon mining revenues from foreign-controlled companies: these included South Africa, Zambia, Angola, Swaziland, Congo (Katanga), where in each case most of the profitable value adding was done outside the continent. Mining accounted for the great bulk of Western investment in these and other countries and as a cynical Guinean remarked of the bauxite extraction from his country, all they were left with were the holes.

A new development during the decade was that of assembly manufacturing whereby all the component parts of a product were exported to Africa to be assembled by cheap labour and then returned to the metropolis of origin; this was sometimes promoted as a first step in establishing an industrial base; in fact it was a sham. The new African countries were being turned into satellite economies: they drew all their capital from abroad and only developed those branches of production whose output was entirely exported. Most of the capital imports came from one source and the bulk of exports went to one destination. An appraisal of Africa's industrialization prospects in 1964 was not encouraging: 'Many developing countries, particularly in Africa, are dangerously dependent on one or two export crops. Frequently the volume of exports is too small a proportion of the world output for the country to have any control over price. The terms of trade, too, always seem to be moving against primary producers.' They produce more and prices fall so they are confined to inelasticity of supply. As a consequence they turn to industrialization.[18] Industrialization for small countries would never be easy. As industries grow there is a parallel increased demand for imports so that industrialization does not mean a reduction of dependency on overseas countries. If new industries are tailored solely to the home market, demand is likely to be too small to sustain it. At a time when Europe was creating the EEC to ensure its ability to compete, it was difficult to envisage successful industrialization of individual African countries. The continent as a whole had a population of 250 million, on a par with that of the EEC plus Britain, but it was divided between 35 sovereign countries. Nigeria, with a population of 50 to 55 million, about the same size as that of Britain, could industrialize successfully, but Gabon with 500,000 could not do so. The development of African regional markets would make industrialization easier to sustain but the experiments with unions during the 1960s were not encouraging.

Over three quarters of the manufactured goods used in the continent are imported. Africa, however, is peripheral to the world economy: only a tenth of the world's primary products originate in Africa, while Africa's imports of manufactured products are little more than a twentieth of the world total.

In concrete terms, low productivity and lop-sided economic development have meant inadequate education, poor food, little medical attention, sub-standard housing, frequent illness and a low life-expectancy for the vast majority of Africans.[19]

None of this augured well for African industrialization and all these negative facts suggested the absolute necessity of tackling the task of industrialization on a continental basis.

There was, as Africa soon discovered, a big difference between obtaining new investment from their former colonial powers and being overrun with aid experts telling them how to manage their economies. The French had long been hesitant about investing in their African territories and on the continent were readier to invest in Nigeria and Congo (K) where they believed the biggest returns were to be made and 'since independence, except in the Ivory Coast, their hesitation has hardened into extreme reserve'.[20] On the other hand, in 1962 there were 25,345 French technical personnel working in Africa and more than 3,000 Africans were studying in France on bursaries. Writing in the *Bulletin de L'Afrique Noire* André Philip argued that methods of development lay between liberalism and planning, and agriculture and industry, and suggested that financial aid should be given for investment, taking the Marshall Plan in Europe as the model. The benefiting country must then make its own effort while external aid should always be used to overcome the inevitable bottlenecks.[21] This advice was not followed. Comparisons between the British and French approaches to investment were often made at this time, more it would seem in a sense of rivalry between the two ex-colonial powers than in a search for the best way to help. 'The Franc Area was... always much more tightly organized than the Sterling Area, which was created at approximately the same time, being in essence a monetary expression of the old French policy of binding colonies to the mother country in a closed economic system, whereby France guaranteed a market for their produce at higher-than-world prices, while they took her manufactured exports.'[22] From the African point of view the principal value of the franc area was that it allowed France to provide substantial aid while absolving the African governments of the need to balance their budgets. In the long run it would prove debilitating to economic independence. Most of the French aid, in any case, was repatriated either by channelling their imports from the mother country, or by the French owned firms which still dominated the economic and commercial life of these countries.

Statistics for this period show the extent to which Africa had to progress before it could break free of the colonial economic heritage. Between 1960 and 1966 the growth rate in African exports was only 4 per cent compared to over 6 per cent for imports, while nearly four times as many consumer goods were imported into Africa as were produced there and a huge proportion of goods that could be made in Africa at that time were imported instead. In 1967 Africa's share of world exports was only 5 per cent. Francophone dependence upon France as an export market was far too high: Senegal sent 86 per cent of its exports to France, Dahomey and Niger 71 per cent each; while imports from France were at a comparable level – Mauritania taking 68 per cent of all its imports from France, Ivory Coast 66 per cent, Senegal 63 per cent, Dahomey 62 per cent and most other Francophone countries in excess of 50 per cent. Britain's ex-colonies were less dependent than those of France and exports to Britain in 1967 for selected countries were as follows: Ghana 13 per cent, Nigeria 37 per cent, Kenya 13 per cent, Uganda 14 per cent, Tanzania 25 per cent; imports from Britain were somewhat higher except for Nigeria: Ghana 25 per cent, Nigeria 32 per cent, Kenya 25 per cent, Uganda 27 per cent, Tanzania 24 per cent.

One of the most enlightened Western analyses of the impact upon Africa of the terms of trade came from Barclays Bank in 1962:

> All the aid recently given underdeveloped countries has been neutralized by the changed terms of trade which have almost without interruption moved against the producers of primary commodities for nearly ten years. It is natural that the underdeveloped countries should have a feeling that assistance is of little or no value if the benefits of aid are cancelled out in this way.

After examining the impact on various countries, the article concluded:

> The immediate duty of the industrialized countries is twofold. First, they should remove the obstacles, which they have erected in the past rather than consider new forms of obstruction. Tariffs and internal taxes on primary commodities should be swept away at once; an immediate start should also be made on getting rid of tariffs and quotas on the processed goods and cheap manufactures produced in the underdeveloped countries. The second duty of the industrialized countries is to increase aid on a multilateral basis, possibly with some new form of price insurance or compensatory finance tied to the terms of trade of the borrowers.[23]

NEW PLAYERS ON THE AFRICAN SCENE

The Soviet Union, China and the EEC each pursued their own political and economic agenda in Africa during the 1960s. Apart from its involvement in the construction of the Aswan Dam in Egypt following the 1956 Suez Crisis, the Soviet Union became involved in West Africa at the beginning of the 1960s when it became a trading and potential aid partner to the three West African 'socialist' states of Ghana, Guinea and Mali. In 1958, when Guinea was isolated by France, Soviet exports to it were negligible but they rose rapidly thereafter to be worth Guinea francs (GF) 134 million in 1959, GF2,000 million in 1961 and GF3,000 million in 1962 by which time the Soviet Union had become the country's most important source of imports. In broad terms no African country had diplomatic relations with the USSR at independence; however, during the 1960s almost all received Soviet diplomatic missions while there were frequent exchanges of delegations. The USSR announced that it was prepared to give aid to all African countries and trade with them.

African countries that approached the Soviet Union sought assistance on two fronts: help to strengthen their bargaining positions *vis-à-vis* their main Western trading partners; and economic and technical assistance to supplement Western aid. They did not regard the Communist centrally planned economies (CPEs) as alternative partners to the West, but as additional ones. As the Russians realized very quickly, they could not replace the West but only supplement what it did and what it offered. 'The chief advantage of the Soviet Union and other CPEs in the field of trade was that they were prepared to deal independently of the free market. By selling produce directly to them, Africans hoped that supplies to the free market could be reduced sufficiently to raise the price prevailing there.'[24] This was more complicated than it might seem though it did bring benefits to some countries. At this time African states saw aid as the prerequisite for establishing manufacturing capacity. The development sections of their plans included aid for manufacturing and it was hoped that the USSR would help in this area particularly as Soviet aid normally took the form of credits for the purchase of machinery and equipment to be repaid in kind by shipments of the recipients' exports. The first Soviet technical assistance agreement with an African country was with Egypt on 29 February 1958; by 1966 the USSR had concluded such agreements with a total of 16 African countries – Ghana, Guinea, Ethiopia, Egypt, Algeria, Cameroon, Congo (B), Kenya, Mali, Morocco, Uganda, Senegal, Somalia, Sudan, Tanzania and Tunisia. All Soviet aid was 'tied' and, for example, an agreement worth US$30 million meant that if suitable projects could be found the USSR would make available up to US$30 million in goods and services to facilitate construction.[25] By the late 1960s the Soviet Union had become concerned over the cost of its aid and emphasized the importance of self-generated development and the peripheral role of foreign aid. The USSR often made gifts to African countries although these were small and did not form a significant part of its assistance.

Aid from the two sides in the Cold War was not mutually exclusive. However, where African countries relied on one side only, it was always the West while approaches to the Soviet bloc were most likely to be made after it had become apparent that the West was unwilling to meet particular aid requirements. Western scare stories about Communist penetration of Africa were out of proportion to the reality. Three African leaders made plain their suspicions of Communist advances. In 1966 President Nasser told the United Arab Republic (UAR) National Assembly that while the UAR and USSR had been 'linked by mutual interests... I do not claim our thoughts and positions were always identical'.[26] And both Presidents Kenyatta and Nyerere warned forcefully that socialist state international economic policies – like those of capitalist states – were primarily related to their own perceived national interests 'which may or may not coincide with those of African states'.

During the 1960s both Africa and the USSR learnt the limitations of Soviet aid. The Soviet Union 'had to recognize that limitations exist in African countries even where there is a leadership that is anxious to overcome them ... In none of the three countries (Ghana, Guinea, Mali) has the Soviet bloc been the major provider of aid (if US public and private activity in the Guinean mining industry is included). Thus all three tried to build socialism with capitalist funds.' Neither Soviet bloc aid nor the markets it offered were sufficient to make an economic break with the West practicable for the majority of underdeveloped countries. There was simply no alternative to Western aid and investments or to western markets.[27] Both the West and the Russians came to accept 'non-alignment' and were prepared to offer aid without insisting on bases or military alliances. In real terms, however, Western aid became irreplaceable. Although it came to be argued that no aid meant no development, what was less clear was whether aid really did mean development.

China was only to become a significant player during the 1970s when it undertook to construct the TANZAM railway, although it had already become embroiled in ideological arguments with the USSR when the two antagonistic Communist powers faced each other in Africa on various occasions after their break at the beginning of the 1960s. Early Chinese advice to underdeveloped countries was to expropriate all foreign capital and to accept no more – because poor countries should rely on their own efforts and mutual co-operation and shun any aid from the rich. This stance was not to last. Instead, China soon began to compete as an aid donor in Africa, not least as a means of pursuing its dispute with the USSR. During the Cultural Revolution of 1966–69, China's external activities declined and its aid only really took off at the end of this period. Aid to African countries increased from 13 to 27 with a huge boost in the amounts disbursed in 1970 due to the US$400 million grant to Tanzania and Zambia for the TANZAM railway. At this time China had two political objectives: to rival the Soviet effort in support of the Aswan Dam in Egypt; and to provide aid to any government, even conservative ones, in return for diplomatic recognition.[28]

After the watershed of African independence, Europe determined that Africa should continue to supply what it wanted from the continent on its terms. The emergence of the European Economic Community (EEC) or Common Market in 1958 provided a new framework that would permit Western Europe as a whole (though without Britain) to impose conditions upon the new states of Africa under the guise of collective benevolence. 'For Africa, an area of weak economic bargaining power, it appears difficult to see the European Common Market as other than a guarantee of continued under-development along existing lines.'[29] EEC associate status was a mirage for it certainly did not give African participants any control over their export prices. Rather, it perpetuated European control. There was much discussion at the beginning of the decade (1961–63) when Britain was negotiating, unsuccessfully as it turned out, to join the EEC about the impact of the EEC upon Africa. In 1961, for example, the ECA issued a study *The Impact of Western European Integration on African Trade and Development* which saw the EEC rather than the looser British dominated European Free Trade Association (EFTA) as a threat to African interests even though the exporters of coffee, cocoa, vegetable oils, bananas and tropical timber were likely to make gains in the EEC market over non-associate members. At the time, the demands of the non-associated African countries (Anglophone Africa) for imports from the original six EEC members were rising more rapidly than from the associated states as a result of these generally larger and more advanced economies. As the ECA reported: 'Measures reducing obstacles to export of manufacturers may be of less direct concern to countries at the stage of economic development reached by the African associates of the EEC than provisions concerned with the growth of manufacturing industries working for the local market. Competition from imported (EEC) manufacturers is a more immediate problem in these countries than exports of manufactured goods.' Commenting on the ECA report, the *Africa Digest*[30] said:

> No form of association with industrial countries will, in itself, be sufficient to solve the long-term economic problems of African countries. But a country which maintains or seeks association with EEC should not

dissipate the short-term benefits gained. It should deliberately aim at using them for decreasing its economic dependency, mainly by reducing its import prices and internal costs, by diversifying the geographical pattern and commodity composition of its trade and by channelling as much investment as possible towards productive purposes. If this is not done, association with EEC can easily tend to perpetuate economic dependency and thus turns out to be a long term disadvantage to the country concerned.

In East Africa, EACSO laid down guiding principles for deciding the attitude of the East African territories to the EEC (although this was before they had achieved independence). They demanded that any British agreement with the EEC should not involve them in any political alignment with Europe. In West Africa, Nigeria, Ghana and Sierra Leone opposed associate status with the EEC for political reasons, Ghana most of all. They believed that 'associated status' was a French device designed to maintain French influence within its former colonies. It was one thing to oppose associated status; it was something else to oppose it effectively. The advice of *The Economist* to the Anglophone states was 'to accept associated status (this could hardly result in Accra voting the French way at the United Nations), and set about replacing the ties that bind francophonic Africa to France and Europe with new ties that would bind the African states to each other. The economic and culture ties to France are not weakening.'[31] Nigeria alone was big enough to 'hold out' against EEC entanglements and was then trying to build up a West African group of countries that included Francophone states. As Britain continued its negotiations for entry into the EEC, Ghana, Nigeria and Tanganyika were most fearful of the political implications of associate membership. Dr Nkrumah, as ever, insisted that Africa's real need was for a Common Market of its own, so that Africans could bargain collectively with the industrial countries.[32] The difficulty with such arguments was that Africa's main exports to the EEC were almost entirely confined to agricultural and mineral commodities. Anglophone African concern at the possible impact of Britain joining the EEC was expressed continually throughout 1962 until de Gaulle vetoed the British bid at the beginning of 1963. At the same time *West Africa* argued that both the Casablanca and Monrovia groups (the OAU would not be formed until mid-1963) favoured the formation of an African Common Market.

While these debates went on the EEC drew up a new five-year association convention between the Six and the Eighteen African associated states to run from 1963 to 1968 under which the EEC would provide aid worth US$800 million (US$730 million for the associated states and US$70 million for dependent states) compared with US$581 million that had been provided under the 1958–63 agreement. This Second Yaounde Convention was ratified in 1964. It did not involve any real reassessment of Euro-African relations; rather, the Eighteen, at the behest of France whose former colonies they were, became the clients of the Six. Associate status in essence combined a customs union and an area in which private enterprise from the Six could enter relatively freely along with the transfer of public capital in the form of aid. The consequence of this new Yaoundé Convention was simply to broaden the dependence of the consenting African states to include the Five as well as France; it certainly did not achieve any fundamental reconstruction of the relationship that would have promoted African economic independence. Instead, the overall development strategy of the African associates would now be subject to decisions taken in Brussels as well as in Paris.

THE GROWTH OF THE AID INDUSTRY

Between 1958 and 1963 the aid industry – that is, the creation of structures to facilitate the provision of aid by the rich developed donor countries to the poor developing countries – gathered momentum and took off. During those years the EEC set up the European Development Fund (EDF), the World Bank established its 'soft' arm for finance on easy terms – the International Development Association (IDA), and the OECD countries established the Development Assistance Committee (DAC). The United Nations proclaimed the 1960s the First Development Decade. Between 1960 and 1962, Canada, Kuwait, Japan, Britain, Denmark, Sweden, Norway, France and West Germany each set up aid departments or ministries. Aid had become an international fashion and the whole of Africa, as its individual colonies emerged to independent status, became a principal recipient region, a status that, for good or ill, would continue to the end of the century.

The first question for Africa to pose about the sudden determination of the rich nations to provide aid was why had this not been done sooner? If at independence every African state was in need of aid, then they must also have been in need of aid while still colonies, yet prior to 1960 this had only been supplied, if at all, on a limited and selective basis. Was the new readiness to provide assistance done from a guilty conscience because the colonial powers had failed to develop their colonies adequately when they were in control? Or was it motivated by considerations of Cold War strategy since there was nothing to prevent the newly independent states from turning to the Communist world for assistance and partnership if this suited them? Or, as Nkrumah first insisted, was aid a necessary weapon of neo-colonialism, a means of perpetuating economic control after the surrender of political control? Whatever they said publicly, African leaders did not believe that the new generosity was solely motivated by concern with their development.

After independence, in theory, all decisions by the new states should have been solely in the hands of Africans. In practice, aid ensured that this did not happen. In 1960 foreign aid was practically the only source of investment capital and its donors could impose political conditions that did not necessarily coincide with the development needs of recipients. At this crucial time for African development too many Africans were going to Europe for training and then working to extend their training instead of returning home to develop their own countries. When they did return home they only wanted to work in the capital city. Problems related to the aid process soon surfaced. 'Distortions in the use of aid may arise from two sources: the intrusion into planning decisions of African political calculations that are incompatible with economic rationality, or the donor's desire to sell as much equipment, machinery and technical assistance, or receive as much short-run prestige as possible irrespective of its effects on the recipient's economy.'[33] When the UN Development Decade was launched in December 1961 the average annual increase of African per capita incomes was at the rate of 3–3.5 per cent; the UN target was to increase this to 5 per cent by 1970. By the mid-1960s, however, there was little sign that this would occur despite the growth in aid that had taken place. A 1965 OECD survey of aid suggested it needed rethinking. The 1964 flow of US$10 billion of aid worked out at US$4 per head in recipient countries that were obliged to generate 85 per cent of the capital they required for modernization. Nearly half of this aid was in the form of grants or near grants, 25 per cent was in the form of official loans, private capital and trade credits accounted for another 20 per cent and World Bank loans for a further 10 per cent. Already at this stage in the aid relationship repayments at US$1 billion a year represented 10 per cent of the aid flow. Pleas for more multilateral aid had as yet made little headway while bilateral aid was too often linked to the donor's goods and thus was open to the suspicion of being given primarily to serve the political ends of the donor. Development in Africa was greatly handicapped by poor transport and communications systems so that productive areas often lacked any adequate access to markets with the result that valuable natural resources remained unexploited. At this time over half World Bank and IDA loans were provided for the transport sector. Technical assistance was generally seen as the best form of aid, provided it meant imparting skills and then departing; too often, however, it came to mean providing certain kinds of skills on an ongoing, indefinite basis.

At the centre of the aid relationship was the growing dependence of African countries upon aid inputs, and a parallel perception that aid would be available indefinitely. At the same time, African governments wished to extend their relations to countries that formerly had been closed to them: essentially this meant the Communist bloc. The West, however, exerted strong pressures to keep Africa tied to it. In his study, *The New Societies of Tropical Africa*, Guy Hunter examines the impact of the Cold War on the aid process.

> Finally, all the newly independent States naturally wish to get to know the international commercial world, after a long period in which their contacts were confined mainly to the commerce of the colonial power. No doubt they will have varying experiences. It certainly ill behoves the British or French, who still occupy so dominating a position in the field, to complain about the still trivial sections of African economies which are directed towards the Eastern bloc; their main task is to prove as efficient as any competitor.
>
> America on a world scale has partly destroyed the credit she might have gained from her real generosity by openly expecting the recipients (of her aid) to keep to the West in the Cold War – it is hard to expect American taxpayers to adopt any other attitude.
>
> Yet it would be difficult for an African government to make an effective protest – such as the freezing of assets – against a major Power upon which it was economically dependent. It is unrealistic to suppose that aid can be altogether divorced from political interest, and it is better either to accept this openly or to channel aid through the United Nations, as many Africans would prefer.[34]

The main donors, however, did not want to channel their aid through the United Nations and only in a later age did they discover the advantages of the multilateral approach. Africans meanwhile, from a position of weakness, saw clearly enough how economic dependence upon a single power would distort the type and direction of trade into forms that suited Europe rather than the individual African economies. Neo-colonialism became a guiding principle of European and American behaviour in Africa throughout the decade. It simply meant the continued dominance of Western controls by other means once the transfer of formal political power had taken place. In any case, 'Relations based on economic weakness acquire a character of dependence, no matter whether the objectives of the dominant interest are limited or total; whether the dominant interest controls the economy or earns 10 per cent of the gross national product, finances what *it* thinks sound development or keeps a subservient government in office. The large dominates the small simply by being large, quite apart from its specific aims, which in turn may have far broader impact than intended.'[35] Throughout the 1960s, consciously or not, development in Africa was harnessed to the flow of aid in all its forms from the developed world. The former colonial powers each had their particular interests to defend in their ex-colonies and designed their aid to this end. The Cold War warriors comprising the United States, the USSR and China used aid as a weapon in their confrontations with each other. The specialized agencies of the United Nations, and most especially the World Bank and IMF, imposed concepts of development that reflected the wishes of the principal Western donors who controlled the votes, on the one hand, and gradually, by the increasing sophistication of their expertise, became the arbiters of all major development decisions on the other hand. Africa, the world's poorest, least-developed region, divided into 50 weak states, found itself the recipient of these variously motivated attentions and though its leadership collectively recognized what was happening found, by and large, that it was too weak and too disunited to prevent the triumph of such aid machinations directing the course of its post-independence development.

NYERERE AND THE ARUSHA DECLARATION

Although most African leaders, starting with Kwame Nkrumah of Ghana, were alive to the neo-colonial threats posed by aid, President Julius Nyerere of Tanzania was the one who most clearly articulated the basic dilemma posed by the need for aid and the baggage that came with it. Speaking at a state banquet in Beijing on a visit to China in February 1965, he said: 'Those who give us loans... must do so because they wish to take part in man's human development, not because they wish to control our young state. Tanzania is not for sale.' Nyerere was articulating what became one of the basic arguments in the Arusha Declaration. He was also naïve in two senses: in his belief, if he held it, that big powers would act in any way other than in pursuit of their own interests; and in the underlying assumption that all African leaders would place the interests of their countries ahead of their determination to hold onto power. One sentence from the Arusha Declaration judges the immediate colonial past that was the heritage of all Africa. 'We have been oppressed a great deal, we have been exploited a great deal, and we have been disregarded a great deal.'

The Arusha Declaration was published on 5 February 1967 and marked a turning point for Tanzania. The first part dealt with the Tanzania African National Union (TANU) political creed and the second part with the policy of socialism. It is part three of the declaration, The Policy of Self-Reliance, that concerns us here. In it Nyerere spells out what for most of Africa would become the aid trap.

But it is obvious that in the past we have chosen the wrong weapon for our struggle, because we chose money as our weapon. We are trying to overcome our economic weakness by using the weapons of the economically strong – weapons which in fact we do not possess.

External finances are then analysed: gifts, which are a form of charity; loans that have to be repaid with interest; and private investment, the bulk of whose profits are repatriated. Gifts and loans, it is argued, endanger independence.

Independence cannot be real if a nation depends upon gifts and loans from another for its development. Even if there was a nation, or nations, prepared to give us all the money we need for our development, it would be improper for us to accept such assistance without asking ourselves how this would affect our independence and our very survival as a nation.

Examining gifts and loans further, the declaration continues:

Gifts which increase, or act as a catalyst, to our own efforts are valuable. But gifts which could have the effect of weakening or distorting our own efforts should not be accepted until we have asked ourselves a number of questions.

Loans, at least in theory, are better than gifts:

A loan is intended to increase our efforts or make those efforts more fruitful. One condition of a loan is that you show how you are going to repay it. This means you have to show that you intend to use the loan profitably and will therefore be able to repay it. To burden the people with big loans, the repayment of which will be beyond their means, is not to help them but to make them suffer. It is even worse when the loans they are asked to repay have not benefited the majority of the people but have only benefited a small minority.

On investment by foreigners:

Could we agree to leave the economy of our country in the hands of foreigners who would take the profits back to their countries? Or suppose they did not insist upon taking their profits away, but decided to reinvest them in Tanzania; could we really accept this situation without asking ourselves what disadvantages our nation would suffer? Would this allow the socialism we have said it is our objective to build?

This part of the declaration concludes as follows:

> How can we depend upon gifts, loans and investments from foreign countries and foreign companies without endangering our independence? The English people have a proverb, which says: 'He who pays the piper calls the tune.' How can we depend upon foreign governments and companies for the major part of our development without giving to those governments and countries a great part of our freedom to act as we please? The truth is that we cannot.[36]

The Arusha Declaration speaks for itself. It was certainly one of the most important and thoughtful documents to come out of Africa during the decade of the 1960s. If few African leaders or governments followed its precepts this was not simply from either lack of understanding or jealousy of the source – Nyerere was seen as a prophet outside Africa rather than on the continent – but because of economic weakness. Most African states emerging to independence were desperate for the means to develop and aid in its various forms seemed the immediate and attractive answer. Later when the pitfalls of the aid trap had become apparent it was too late; and also, sadly, too many African leaders were happy to depend upon aid, no matter what it meant for the long-term future of their countries, as long as it helped keep them in power as it too often did and was designed to do.

At the end of the decade Lester Pearson, the former Canadian prime minister, was invited to lead an international commission on the prospects and problems of aid and development assistance and to make recommendations. The Report by the Commission on International Development, *Partners in Development*, was published in 1969 and set the apparently reasonable target of 1 per cent of the GNPs of the rich nations as the figure they should devote annually to aid for the developing world (at a later date this target was reduced to 0.7 per cent). At that time 21 out of the 40 countries designated by the United Nations as the world's poorest were on the African continent. As the Pearson Report stated: 'In Africa with its very large number of relatively small countries, economic co-operation is a fundamental factor for swifter development.' The Pearson Report was generally well received by donors: Britain and West Germany said they hoped they could meet the target, Norway announced that it would treble its aid, New Zealand pledged to meet the target, Japan to double its aid. France was already exceeding the 1 per cent figure when private investment was included. With the exception of the United States, all the main donors appeared ready to meet the Pearson target.

By 1968, with few exceptions, most African economies showed little growth and in some cases deterioration. Mineral discoveries, however, had wrought major changes in Libya and Mauritania while expectations had been raised in Botswana, Central African Republic and Niger as a result of mineral finds. Apart from South Africa, the economic pacemakers at that time were Côte d'Ivoire in West Africa, Kenya in East Africa and Zambia in Central Africa. However, a disturbing feature in much of the continent was the steady increase in military expenditure, especially in Cameroon, Ethiopia, Sudan, Ghana, Congo (B), Senegal, Zambia, Kenya, Uganda, the UAR and Nigeria (then engaged in the first year of its civil war). In too many cases the soldiers had seized power after mounting coups, and though they were not responsible for the underlying economic conditions that had often produced the situations that 'justified' a coup, they, too, had much to answer for and by the end of the decade most African countries, whether under military rule or not, had to spend more than they could afford on maintaining their armies.

By the end of the UN Decade of Development not a great deal of development had been achieved while the rich-poor gap was widening rather than being bridged. The United States, the world's largest and richest economy, was becoming disenchanted with aid to the extent that Canada, Europe and Japan went ahead to replenish the resources of the IDA without the United States. Martin Rosen, the Executive Vice-President of the International Finance Corporation (IFC), said in Paris on 4 December 1968 that increased private investment was essential to economic growth in the less-developed countries but added that it could only be investment that was justifiable to shareholders. There was little sign of much investment going to Africa. A Report, *A Study of the Capacity of the United Nations Development System*, better known as the Jackson Report, sharply criticised 20 years of aid, and spoke of 'great inertia' and elaborate administrative structures incapable of change and called for the rich to do more to co-operate with developing countries. The Report expressed the hope that the trend towards using multilateral aid channels would grow. In February 1970, speaking at Columbia University, the President of the World Bank, Robert McNamara, said: 'Perhaps one of the most wasteful mistakes that both developing countries and aid agencies can make is to proceed on a random project-by-project basis, rather than first to establish an overall development strategy, and then select projects that mutually support and interlock with one another within that overall plan. Our new programme for Country Economic Reports is designed to provide a foundation for such a strategy.' Perhaps the best 'epitaph' on the decade came from *West Africa,* which pointed out that little had been done over the decade of the 1960s to bridge the gulf between French- and English-speaking countries in West Africa. 'The two currency areas find economic co-operation as difficult as ever, the division between the EEC associates and the rest remains. All the examples of co-operation across national boundaries cannot alter the fact that the sovereignty of even the most unviable of these states is now entrenched, while xenophobia between them is more significant than any hostility to or from non-African states.'[37] That judgement could well be extended to the continent as a whole.

CHAPTER SIX

North Africa

N orth Africa, comprising Morocco, Algeria, Tunisia, Libya and Egypt, is distinguished from the rest of the continent by the fact that its people are Arab or Berber, and that the vast majority of them have adhered to the religion of Islam since the conversions that followed the Arab conquests of the seventh and eighth centuries. Each of the countries of North Africa, apart from Morocco, had formed part of the Ottoman Empire at its height several centuries before coming under European control during the imperial expansion of the nineteenth and twentieth centuries: Morocco partly Spanish, mainly French control, Algeria and Tunisia under French control, Libya under Italy and Egypt under Britain. In the post-independence era of the second half of the twentieth century, these five countries looked more to the Arab world of the Middle East as their natural focus rather than to Africa south of the Sahara. They are also part of Mediterranean culture and many of their links historically have been northwards and pre-dated any sense that they belonged to a greater Africa to the south. As a result, these five countries are regarded internationally, and regard themselves, as Arab states first and then as African states. To the south of North Africa lie the countries of the Sahel and Horn whose peoples are intermingled: part Arab or Tuareg, part black African, where Islam tends to be the dominant religion. Of the 20 members of the Arab League, nine (Algeria, Djibouti, Egypt, Libya, Mauritania, Morocco, Somalia, Sudan and Tunisia) are also African countries and members of the African Union (formerly the OAU). During the immediate independence era of the 1960s the Arab states of North Africa took part in all the groupings and negotiations that led to the creation of the OAU in 1963 with Morocco and Egypt playing especially important 'radical' roles at that time. Egypt, particularly, made a vital contribution to emergent African nationalism and its President, Gamal Abdul Nasser, was a hero to nationalists in both Africa and the Arab world during the 1950s and 1960s when the Voice of Cairo radio became the 'spokesman' and encourager of African nationalism and independence.

Israel, an external factor of huge importance, helped shape the polices of North Africa at this time for as Arab states they were inexorably drawn into the confrontation between the new state of Israel, created in 1948, and the whole Arab world that would periodically erupt in warfare – the Suez War of 1956, the Six Day War of 1967, the Yom Kippur War of 1973 – and though Black Africa generally would have preferred to avoid participating in the Israeli-Arab confrontation, it found this increasingly difficult to do. Nasser raised the issue of Israel at the 1964 OAU Conference which was held in Cairo in an attempt to persuade the OAU to adopt a pro-Arab stand on the issue and in the coming years African states were to equate Zionism with racism.

The Arab-African relationship was often uneasy and always required delicate handling on both sides. Egypt, occupying the geographic hinge that joined the African and Asian continents, played a pivotal role in this relationship and throughout the 1960s under Nasser acted as a positive link between the two worlds.

EGYPT

Under the leadership of Nasser between 1952, when he led the coup that toppled King Farouk, and 1970, when he died, Egypt assumed the leadership of the Arab world and played a significant role as the advocate of both Arab and African nationalism. This role made Nasser especially unpopular in the West whose leading imperial powers, Britain and France, were fighting a long rearguard action to retain their influence. The 1956 Suez Crisis and the humiliation of Britain and France allowed Nasser to emerge as the leading political figure in the Middle East. His predominant position only came to an end following the disastrous defeat of the Arab states by Israel in the 1967 Six Day War.

By 1961 Nasser appeared to have eliminated any serious opposition to his regime in Egypt: the Communists were shattered and the power of the Muslim Brotherhood destroyed so that only the Pan-Arab Socialist Ba'ath Party, although illegal, offered any opposition. The union with Syria, proclaimed as the United Arab Republic in 1958, was not destined to last long, and in fact was terminated in 1961 following an army takeover in Syria; in any case, at one level it had been little more than an expression of Arab solidarity. Wisely, Nasser did not attempt to reverse the Syrian decision. During 1961 a series of decrees were passed to give the State control over most major industrial and financial concerns. Over 300 industries were compelled to sell a half-share of their capital to the government; in addition, the government took a controlling interest in a further 95 companies and acquired all share holdings worth £10,000 or more.

Nasser was then at the height of his influence and popularity.

> President Nasser's revolutionary energy, which ran badly off course during the late nineteen-fifties, has now been redirected to the problems of social change in his own country. If the West, resenting the nationalization measures, sits back to enjoy a coming economic muddle, it may find itself sharing its smirk with the communist world. The reaction of the Arab communist parties, together with earlier warning grumbles from Moscow, indicates that the communists, at least, have recognized President Nasser's brand of socialism as one of the more formidable barriers to the Soviet Union's political penetration of the Arab world, and possibly of the African world too.[1]

Coming as it did from *The Economist*, this was praise indeed for the man who was still generally seen as an anti-British, anti-Western dictator. Nasser's prestige at this time was further enhanced by his pan-Arab and pan-African activities and his destruction of the power of Egyptian landowners. Nasser saw Egypt as an African as well as an Arab state and became deeply involved in the struggle for African emancipation and unity. He provided support for various African liberation movements, and argued on behalf of the doomed Lumumba in the Congo. He attended the January 1961 Casablanca summit whose participants became known as the 'radical' group of African states and refused to attend the subsequent rival conferences at Monrovia in May 1961 or Lagos in January 1962. His standing, especially with African Muslims, was very high. His main African opponent was the moderate Habib Bourguiba of Tunisia, though they became reconciled in 1961 following the Bizerta crisis between Tunisia and France. As *The Times* Special Correspondent wrote in 1961: 'Cairo today is the most important town in Africa – a sort of political Tangier, a free port for politicians and political ideas (so long as they keep within strictly anti-colonial lines, of course).' Continuing hostility between Egypt and Israel, however, was to prove a constant burden for Egypt and the military requirements of this confrontation were a severe handicap to development. Nonetheless, 'Though the revolution may have fallen far short of its promises and popular hopes, it has extricated Egypt from the economic apathy and political corruption that had imprisoned it for centuries'.[2]

Egypt's position as a leading African country at this time – a member of the radical group of countries, an opponent of colonialism in all its forms and supporter of the liberation movements, and the fact that it had stood up to the imperial powers first at the time of Suez and then in 1958 in opposition to the formation of the Baghdad Pact – was due more than anything else to the charismatic leadership of Nasser. However, despite his radicalism Nasser was also a realist and this applied to his reading of the African search for unity.

> Between 1961 and 1963 Egypt became increasingly involved in African affairs through its association with Morocco, Mali, Ghana and Guinea in the 'Casablanca' group of radical African states which in 1963 established on paper a joint military command and a common market. But by the time of the first OAU Conference at Addis Ababa in May 1963 Nasser had concluded that there was nothing to be gained and much to be lost through the polarization of the African continent between radicals and moderates. Henceforth Nasser was a moderating, almost conservative influence in the OAU. He constantly affirmed that the African states should seek the spirit of unity before adopting any constitutional form.[3]

It was appropriate that the first OAU meeting after its inauguration in Addis Ababa in 1963 should have been held in Cairo the following year.

The Aswan High Dam, constructed through the 1960s with Soviet assistance, was not just a major development project; it represented Nasser's determination to modernize his impoverished country and even more than that it was a political statement made at the height of the Cold War. Since the West had reneged on its agreement to finance the building of the dam, Nasser had turned to the Soviet Union both to obtain the aid he needed and to make plain to the West that he would go his own way and not be forced into the Western camp. The dam, which cost US$1 billion, was completed in 1970 – the year of Nasser's death – and formally opened in January 1971. Its reservoir, Lake Nasser, stretched 200 miles in Egypt and a further 100 miles in Sudan. It would sustain a substantial fishing industry and irrigate enough land to provide food for an estimated one million people. It involved the relocation of 90,000 people as well as the re-positioning of the ancient tombs of Abu Simbel. It was the largest development project then being implemented in Africa. At the same time, the dam was to create problems for the future. By holding back the flow of silt it reduced the fertility of the downstream riparian lands whose richness had depended since time immemorial upon the annual flooding of the Nile. Moreover, the circumstances in which the Western powers – the United States and Britain, with the World Bank – had withdrawn their offer of aid to precipitate the Suez Crisis of 1956, and their subsequent replacement as donors by the Soviet Union had created a pattern that would play a significant part in the aid process for the ensuing 30 years: playing off one side in the Cold War against the other, a tactic that would be employed with much success by African leaders such as Mobutu.

The devastating defeat of Egypt by Israel in 1967 was a deep humiliation for Nasser and brought to an end his position of primacy in the Arab world. For the last three years of his rule he had to rebuild his armed forces, whose losses of military hardware had been extensive and collapse of morale even worse, and still more important rebuild the national confidence. Isolated at home and only just surviving politically (Tunis Radio, for example, broadcast stories of Egyptian 'Free Officers' wanting to oust him), condemned by other Arab leaders for his spectacular failure to make any showing at all against Israel, and in ill health, Nasser, nevertheless, set about the mammoth task of reconstruction and recovery. Reluctantly he allowed the army to be retrained by the Russians who at the same time pressed him to accept a political settlement over Israel while demanding, in return for their assistance, his total backing for their military intervention in Czechoslovakia, a backing which was to strain his relations with non-aligned Yugoslavia's Tito. Nonetheless, he demonstrated remarkable resilience. The strength of the air force, now equipped with MiG21s and TU16 bombers, was doubled and the MiGs were secreted in giant underground hangars. On 30 March 1968 Nasser announced a new political programme, which he claimed was designed to transform Egypt into an open society; this was to be tested in a referendum on 2 May when he obtained a 98.2 per cent vote for his reforms. The Egyptian journalist Hasanyn Heikal, who had close contacts with Nasser, wrote on 3 October 1968: 'Time is on our side. A solution [to the Israel question] is not the first priority now. The rebuilding of the Arab military force and specially the Egyptian force, is the incomparable priority.' The conflict or confrontation with Israel now dominated Egypt's foreign policy and though the country was non-aligned in theory, in practice it became totally dependent upon the USSR to rebuild its armed forces. Despite the huge setback of 1967, Nasser did not alter his general African policy but continued his support for the liberation movements in Southern Africa and embarked upon a major initiative when he agreed to allow Egyptian pilots to fly Soviet-supplied fighter aircraft for the Nigerian Air Force against Biafra in the Nigerian civil war. Egypt was determined in its support for a united Nigeria.

On the economic front recovery went well despite the loss of oilfields to the Israelis in the Sinai Peninsula. New oilfields were discovered at this time while work on the Aswan Dam was well advanced with £E96 million of the £E113 million Soviet loan spent and 85 per cent of the construction completed. In May 1968 an agreement was concluded with the USSR for the construction of an iron and steel complex at Helwan; this was the second largest development project in the country after the Aswan Dam. By 1969 the economy had recovered from the setback of 1967 and the GNP for 1969–70 rose to £E5031.8 million which was £E325.3 million above the 1968–69 target. In June 1969 Andrei Gromyko visited

Cairo and reaffirmed the Soviet Union's 'complete support of the just struggle of the United Arab Republic and other Arab countries in order to eradicate the consequences of the Israeli aggression'. The population of Egypt at this time was 30 million, by far the largest in the region, and in the years to come its annual increase tended to consume all the economic advances that were achieved so that the country appeared always to be running to stay in the same place.

The political balance in the region was altered in 1969 as a consequence of coups in two of Egypt's neighbours. In Sudan a bloodless coup of 25 May 1969 was carried out by a group of officers and civilians led by Col. Gaafar Mohammed Nimeiri who initiated a more radical political programme; and in Libya at the beginning of September another coup brought the young Muammar Gaddafi to power. One year later, in September 1970, Nasser died of a heart attack.

ALGERIA

After eight years of bitter civil war (1954–62) against the French-backed *colons* (settlers) Algeria won its independence in 1962, at which time almost all the *colons*, about one million in number, left the country for France. Thereafter, Algeria pursued a broadly socialist policy, first under Ahmed Ben Bella and then under Houari Boumedienne. Surprisingly, perhaps, for the rest of the 1960s Algeria enjoyed good relations with France; in fact the two countries needed each other: Algeria had oil and natural gas which France needed, France had the technical expertise and could provide the aid which Algeria required for its development. The withdrawal of one million *colons* meant the disappearance of most technical and other skills while the country faced unemployment levels as high as 70 per cent of the working population. Some two million Algerians had been interned in camps during the war and a further 500,000 had become refugees in Morocco and Tunisia. The new Algerian President, Ben Bella, was both militant and radical. During the summer of 1962, following independence, most of the European estates were taken over, the balance being nationalized in January 1963. Ben Bella greatly increased his hold on the mainsprings of power in 1963: in April he took over the post of General Secretary of the *Front de Libération Nationale* – FLN (National Liberation Front); in September a new constitution, approved by referendum, confirmed Ben Bella as President for five years and made him Commander in Chief of the Army so that he was both head of state and head of government. Ferhat Abbas, one of the country's leading nationalists, feared a Ben Bella dictatorship and resigned his post as President of the Assembly. The Berber minority became increasingly fearful of its position in the new state and there were Berber revolts in 1963 and 1964.

On 19 June 1965 Ben Bella was arrested and deposed in a bloodless coup led by his Minister of Defence, Boumedienne, and a new Council of the Revolution, with Boumedienne at its head, took supreme power into its hands. Boumedienne announced a return to the principles of the revolution from which Ben Bella had been deviating but he did not seek a popular mandate for his actions. The Council of the Revolution was austerely socialist and set about the task of increasing state control and participation across a range of economic activities. Boumedienne was cautious in his relations with the big powers and, for example, despite developing strong ties with the USSR, still gave top priority to relations with France. In 1968 – ahead of schedule – France evacuated the naval base of Mers-el-Kebir, which it had leased for 15 years in 1962 under the terms of the Evian agreements on Algerian independence, and, despite fears in Paris, Algeria did not then lease it out to the Russians. In 1967 Algeria had sent troops to aid Egypt in the Six Day War but this was over before they could become engaged. Subsequently, Algeria denounced Nasser for 'treason'. Boumedienne pursued a radical line in Africa and Algeria took a lead in denouncing colonialism; it was one of only nine countries to break diplomatic relations with Britain in 1965 over UDI in Rhodesia. These were restored in 1968. In 1969 Boumedienne made an official visit to Morocco to end the border confrontation between the two countries that had lasted since 1963.

Boumedienne's centralizing tendencies did not go unopposed and there was an uprising against him in 1967, which was put down, largely due to the loyalty of the younger army officers. There was further unrest in 1968 and in April an attempt was made upon his life. At the end of 1967 the journal *Révolution et Travail* commented that Algeria had had no parliamentary institutions since 1965 and that the political situation would not return to normal until the 'political machine is made really democratic'. At the beginning of January 1968 Boumedienne announced a purge of all 'incapable persons' in the FLN and a series of national reforms: the country was to be given 'definitive political institutions'. The reforms included agrarian reform, including the liquidation of large properties, 'rigorous control' of state machinery, especially in the economic sector, educational reform, Arabization and compulsory military service. The militant trade union organization, *Union Générale des Travailleurs Algériens* (UGTA), argued for revolutionary ideas as opposed to pragmatism while Marxist students sought a trial of strength with the small group of politicians who really ran the country and were known as the Oujda group. This consisted of the President, the Minister of Finance Kaid Ahmed, the Foreign Minister Abdelaziz Bouteflika, the Minister of the Interior Ahmed Medegrhi and Sherif Belkacem, a former co-ordinating official of the FLN. These and other instances of opposition represented the dissatisfaction of a highly politicized people at the authoritarianism of the government, which was emphasized during the year by a purge of army officers and a reorganization of the ruling FLN.

On the economic front the Boumedienne government pushed ahead with socialist reforms that were about equally dependent upon inputs from the Soviet Union on the one hand and France on the other. One aim was to make agriculture self-financing but the collapse of the colonial structure and withdrawal of the *colons* had produced massive and chronic unemployment of 50 per cent of the workforce. On the other hand, oil and natural gas production was rising and had become the principal foreign exchange earner. A number of foreign, mainly French companies in banking, chemicals, mining and building materials were nationalized in 1968 to exacerbate what were never easy relations with France. Even so, 70 per cent of Algeria's trade was with France and in July the Foreign Minister, Bouteflika, went to Paris to discuss a range of problems including immigration, the nationalization of French companies, compensation and France's refusal to continue purchasing Algeria's wine. Meanwhile, major development projects were being accelerated. A phosphate fertilizer complex at Annaba was designed to produce 500,000 tons of phosphates a year. A Soviet-aided irrigation scheme was proceeding in Greater Kabylie while other Soviet-backed projects included a steelworks at Annaba and a number of food-processing activities.

Boumedienne went a long way towards creating a managerial revolution and the new elite that appeared at this time consisted mainly of young and often highly competent technocrats who began to achieve considerable influence and authority. Real power, however, remained in the hands of the older FLN leaders and the army. Boumedienne appeared far more confident in 1969 than at any time since he had ousted Ben Bella in 1965, following the proceedings in 1968 against those who had plotted against him. He had embarked upon a constitutional policy of constructing a pyramidal structure of elected bodies from the base upwards that would be able to survive changes in government and leadership at the top. This included People's Communal Assemblies (APCs) (set up in 1967) and then in 1969 elections at departmental level when the 15 departments were renamed Wilayate (units that had been used by the FLN during the war). Like almost all African governments at this time, that of Boumedienne saw the trade unions as a separate and therefore threatening source of power. The UGTA had criticized the government for compromising the principles of the Algerian revolution; in 1969 its powers were curbed and UGTA branches with reputations for militancy were dissolved. Single-party solidarity had become the keystone of policy and a government statement said the party was 'unable any longer to tolerate... the confused situation in the unions (in the Algiers district) or the acts of indiscipline shown by some elements towards the concept of a single party'.

During 1969 Algeria made determined efforts to create closer ties with its Maghreb neighbours. Over 11–16 January Boumedienne went on his first official visit to Morocco and the two countries concluded the Treaty of Ifrane which provided for better co-operation between the two countries and ended their border dispute. Later in the year economic negotiations with Tunisia led to complete agreement on all 'pending questions' and also dealt with their – lesser – border dispute. Algeria may also have played a part in helping resolve the dispute between Morocco and Mauritania which led to a *détente* between the two countries in September (until that time Morocco had laid claim to Mauritania as part of Greater Morocco). Algeria had also concluded a treaty of 'brotherhood, good neighbourhood and co-operation' with Libya in February although the coup of September that brought Gaddafi to power installed a regime in Libya that was much closer to that of Algeria than the monarchy of King Idris. An Algerian delegation to Libya after the coup expressed 'deep admiration for the sincere efforts of the revolutionary leadership in Libya in achieving the hopes of the Libyan people and solidarity with the Arab people in their battle of destiny against Zionism, imperialism and colonialism'. The Algerian position at this time was one of resolute support for the Palestine liberation struggle. Boumedienne attended both the Islamic Summit Conference of September 1969 and the Arab Summit Conference of December, both held in Rabat, Morocco. Algeria also convened the first Pan-African Cultural Festival at this time.

By the end of the decade Algerian policy seemed set on a socialist but not communist path. Numerous exchange visits and co-operation agreements marked the close Algerian-Soviet relationship and in March 1970 the President of the Supreme Soviet of the USSR, Nicholas Podgorny, visited Algeria. At that time there were an estimated 2,000 Soviet technicians and teachers working in the country and an equal number of military advisers. Problems with France related to the treatment of Algerians in France and of Frenchmen in Algeria. The government aim was to construct a socialist society that would include state control over most sectors of the economy and to this end the nationalization of most foreign trade activities had been completed in 1969 when import and distribution firms were nationalized. Oil and natural gas, meanwhile, accounted for 69 per cent of export earnings to provide the base for a programme of industrialization whose main targets were for Algeria to produce its own cast iron, crude steel, wheeled tractors, machine tools, manufactured fertilizers and cement, and expand its electricity supply. The biggest part of this programme was the US$300 million iron and steel complex at Annaba. However, 70 per cent of the country's petroleum output was still produced by French companies. Soviet trade with Algeria had increased to an annual level of US$125 million.

The Boumedienne government adopted a consistently anti-colonial line and provided training and other facilities for the liberation movements of Southern Africa as well as the Eritrean Liberation Front and the National Liberation Front of Chad. Emerging at the beginning of the decade from a long and devastating civil war and moving steadily through the 1960s to create a socialist society, Algeria in 1970 appeared to be on the threshold of an economic breakthrough of its own choice.

MOROCCO

King Mohammed V earned great prestige for his role in achieving independence from France in 1956 and though he pursued conservative policies at home he blunted criticism by a militant foreign policy that was exactly suited to the general mood of nationalism sweeping through Africa at the time. During 1959 and 1960 he aligned himself with the revolutionary camp and presided at the January 1961 Casablanca summit of the 'radical' states. However, he died unexpectedly on 28 February 1961 while undergoing an operation and was succeeded by his son Hassan II. Under his father Hassan had been proclaimed Crown Prince in 1957 and appointed Commander-in-Chief of the army, which he completely reorganized. In 1960 he was made Vice-President and effective head of the government. Assumed to be rigidly conservative, he nevertheless won over his critics on his accession to the throne by continuing his father's radical foreign policy and by announcing on 5 March 1961, less than a week after coming to power, that all French forces must leave the country by the following October, two years ahead of schedule. Apart from uneasy relations with France, Hassan II sought good relations with the West and especially with the United States, which he was to visit in 1967. Hassan demonstrated his dictatorial tendencies early in his reign when he made plain his belief that the country needed a 'responsible leader' working with a small team of devoted advisers. He soon came under criticism from radical students and trade unionists and his exercise of 'personal power' was strongly condemned. His principal support came from the army, which he had personally reorganized before his accession, and from the rural traditionalists. Already by 1962 he was distancing himself from the left-wing Algerian government and beginning to consolidate good relations with the United States and Spain.

In 1959, when Mohammed V was still on the throne, a new political party had been formed by Mehdi Ben Barka, who broke away from the dominant Istiqlal party to create the *Union Nationale des Forces Populaires* – UNFP (National

Union of Popular Forces). The UNFP soon attracted repressive measures from the police and army, which were under the control of the King, and in 1960 UNFP formed the opposition to the government. In 1962, under Hassan II, a new constitution turned Morocco into a constitutional monarchy and guaranteed personal and political freedoms. The king then formed his own party, the *Front de Défendre des Institutions Constitutionelles* – FDIC (Front for the Defence of Constitutional Institutions). Elections were held in 1963 but the FDIC, which won 69 seats, did not have a clear majority; Istiqlal and UNFP, both in opposition, won 41 and 28 seats respectively and there were also six independents. Following an alleged coup attempt some of the UNFP MPs were arrested, imprisoned and tortured and a number were sentenced to death. The King began to rule through a government composed of FDIC loyalists, but growing unrest at the limitations upon political activity led him to proclaim a 'state of exception' in 1965, when no political parties or trade unions could form a parliamentary majority, and the King assumed full legislative and executive powers. Later that year, while on a visit to France, Ben Barka, the UNFP leader, disappeared and was never seen again. General Oufkir, a close associate of the King, was accused by France of being implicated in Ben Barka's disappearance and relations between France and Morocco plummeted as a result. Ben Barka had been abducted and killed in Paris with the collusion of the French police and the affair caused an international scandal. The French at one stage suggested that the CIA was responsible for the disappearance. The emergency remained in place until 1968 and despite mounting pressures the King continued his direct rule.

Although he practised political repression at home, Hassan II was far more flexible in his foreign policy. He adopted a moderate line in the councils of the Arab world, a stance made easier by the fact that Morocco was geographically far removed from Israel and could not be seen as a front-line state in relation to the Arab-Israeli confrontation. While he developed close relations with the United States that resulted in a substantial flow of US aid, he also made successful overtures to the USSR, which concluded an aid agreement with Morocco in1966 that began to take shape in 1967 when Soviet designers started work on a hydroelectric project on the Draa River. As a pro-Soviet gesture, or as a tactic to create further disunity on the left, the government permitted the establishment of the *Parti de Libération et du Socialisme* under Ali Yata, the former secretary-general of the Moroccan Communist Party.

Morocco's claims to neighbouring territory, at this time and later, were to cause much friction with Algeria and Mauritania and then, in the 1980s, with the OAU. Morocco argued that an historic Greater Morocco had included Mauritania, although the latter had become independent in 1960, and a large part of Algerian Sahara, as well as Western Sahara, then still under Spanish control. Together these claims amounted to a larger landmass than the existing state of Morocco. Algeria, in response, contended that Moroccan rule over the Sahara regions had been sporadic and short-lived and that Algeria had inherited the territory that France had delineated and that the colonial borders should be maintained. A brief border war between Morocco and Algeria in 1963 over the Moroccan claim had attracted international attention and led to OAU meditation that produced an agreement under which Morocco vacated the territory it had occupied while Algeria consented to an 'examination' of the Moroccan claim. However, at the 1964 OAU summit the organization adopted a general resolution on border disputes that called upon all member states to accept their inherited colonial boundaries. In the circumstances Morocco felt it had been cheated out of the promised examination of its claim. The border quarrel with Algeria was finally settled in 1969 on the occasion of the Boumedienne visit to Morocco. Later that year Morocco came to amicable terms with Mauritania, which it had refused to recognize up to that time, instead regarding it as an integral part of its own territory. The government's hand had been forced when in September 1969 the Islamic Summit Conference was held in Rabat and the conference secretariat insisted that Mauritania's President Ould Daddah should be invited. The two countries entered into full diplomatic relations with each other in 1970. Morocco also achieved a *rapprochment* with France in 1969 after de Gaulle resigned. The rumbling Ben Barka affair was finally allowed to die out. In April 1970 President Podgorny visited Morocco to cement the relations between the two countries that had been growing stronger ever since 1966 when Hassan had visited Moscow.

By 1970 Hassan had established both his political power at home – he would become increasingly autocratic in the coming years – and his international position. He was non-aligned and had achieved good relations with both the United States and the Soviet Union and, after the passing of de Gaulle, an improved relationship with France. He was seen as a moderate in the councils of the Arab world but increasingly conservative in terms of Africa to the south. The border conflict with Algeria appeared settled though Morocco had little sympathy with the more radical politics of either Algeria or Libya under Gaddafi, its radical new ruler. The economy was doing reasonably well at the end of the decade: the agricultural sector had profited from good harvests with cereals, olives and citrus fruit output all increasing; there had been a rise in mineral production, especially phosphates which accounted for 30 per cent of export earnings; and under the 1968–72 Five Year Plan a programme of light industrialization was under way though development generally was hampered by insufficient financial resources and a shortage of foreign aid.

TUNISIA

Tunisia, which achieved independence in the same year as Morocco, came to be regarded as a moderate in both the Arab world and Africa. On 12 April 1956 Habib Bourguiba was voted Chairman and first Premier of independent Tunisia. On 25 July 1957 the Constituent Assembly abolished the monarchy, proclaimed a republic and made Bourguiba President. He was careful to maintain friendly relations with France even while Tunisia was drawn into the civil war in neighbouring Algeria. In January 1960 the second All-African People's Conference was held in Tunis at which Bourguiba showed himself to be more moderate than such African leaders as Nkrumah and Touré. He believed, contrary to them, that African countries should establish their stability before engaging in political union. At the same time he favoured some form of Maghreb association. He fell out with Morocco over its claim to Mauritania, which it advanced at this time, and did not attend the January 1961 Casablanca Conference.

Although he desired good relations with France Bourguiba was uncompromising over colonialism and on 5 July 1961, in a calculated move, Bourguiba formally demanded the return to Tunisia of both Bizerta, which France had maintained as a base after independence, and a stretch of Saharan territory in the south-west although it was occupied by French troops. Fighting between Tunisians and the French around Bizerta and the disputed Saharan territory broke out; Tunisia broke diplomatic relations with France and appealed to the United Nations. By 22 July, when the fighting ceased, 800 Tunisians had been killed while the French remained in control of both Bizerta and the Sahara strip. On 26 August the UN General Assembly declared that French troops at Bizerta violated Tunisian sovereignty and called on France to negotiate. Negotiations with France occupied much of the rest of the year, but following the Algerian ceasefire of March 1962 the atmosphere rapidly improved and on 30 June 1962 France handed over its base installations at Memzel Bourguiba near Bizerta. Over the six months from July 1961 when the Bizerta crisis erupted a third of the 95,000 French community of settlers left the country while thousands of Italians, mainly in the mechanic trades, prepared to do so. In March 1963 an agreement was reached with France on the transfer of 370,000 acres of French-owned land. Tunisia's stand against France led to an improvement in its relations with the more radical Arab states, for Tunisia generally took a moderate line in Arab politics. One of Tunisia's complaints, first against the UAR and then against newly independent Algeria, was the support these countries gave to the 'Youssefists', followers of the radical opponent of Bourguiba, Salah ben Youssef, who at independence had gone into exile in

Cairo. However, an agreement was signed with Algeria in July 1963.

The Bizerta crisis had a destabilizing impact upon the economy but the government went ahead with its plans to increase Tunisian participation in business and commerce: all foreign businesses, except banks and petroleum distributors, were given one year in which to admit 50 per cent Tunisian participation. The process of taking over French-owned land continued in 1964 with legislation in May to expropriate all foreign-owned land, which meant a further 750,000 acres. France retaliated by cancelling all financial aid that had been agreed. The Neo-Destour party changed its name to emphasize its socialism, calling itself the *Parti Socialiste Destourien* – PSD (Destour Socialist Party). French relations with both Tunisia and Morocco deteriorated at this time, not least because of the growing attachment of their leaders to close relations with the United States. The following appraisal of Tunisia's performance in international affairs during the 1960s shows how essentially conservative the Bourguiba regime was in its foreign policy:

> Tunisia is one of the United States' most faithful allies, and receives very generous American aid. This special attention has undoubtedly affected Tunisia's international policy, and the line that she has taken both in her relations with the Arab states and with the Third World in general. She has broken off her short-lived diplomatic relations with China, and has taken the American side in the Vietnam conflict. This alliance, reinforced in 1966, still constitutes the basis of Tunisian policy. She has normal relations with the eastern countries of the Soviet Bloc, but they are not particularly cordial.[4]

There was growing opposition to the government in 1968 although for the 12 years since independence Bourguiba and the renamed Socialist Destour Party had achieved a reasonable level of stability. Bourguiba's moderate stance over the Israel–Palestine question – that Israel and the Palestinians were 'naturally' the negotiators – made him enemies with the more radical Arab states, and especially Egypt. His ideas had been rejected by a conference of Arab kings and presidents in 1965; they opted instead to wage a sacred struggle against Zionism in Palestine, to work for the removal of Israel and to support the Palestinian Liberation Organization (PLO). Following the disaster for the Arabs of the Six Day War, Bourguiba changed to the extent of saying that strength did not lie just in armies and equipment but in unity of heart and rank: 'We do not want the extermination of the Jews but we are defending a right and just cause.' Later, however, when the emotions that the Six Day War had aroused receded, the Tunisians blamed Nasser for his unilateral action and for imposing his viewpoint on the Middle East, claiming that his ambition and determination to be the leading Arab was insulting to others and divisive. In 1968, as a consequence of this line, Tunisia was refused permission to present its condemnation of Egypt's 1967 role at the meeting of the Arab League Council. There was, at least, an agreement in 1968 with Algeria that settled the border dispute between the two countries although statements of Maghreb solidarity at this time did not lead to any closer union. Tunisia found herself to be relatively isolated in the Arab world at the end of the decade and so began to show greater interest in Africa south of the Sahara. Bourguiba established especially warm relations with Houphouët-Boigny of the Ivory Coast, both men sharing similar views. Houphouët-Boigny visited Tunisia in March 1968. Bourguiba also sought closer ties with Congo (K) Republic and Senegal, two other like-minded countries.

Agricultural co-operatives had been created out of the land bought from the *colons* and in 1969 the area was extended through the seizure of the remaining French-held land; these co-operatives accounted for 50 per cent of agricultural production but the workers were wage earners, when they were paid, and their wages were low. Tunisia had achieved a reasonable level of industrialization by this time with 20 per cent of the active population working in the industrial sector. This covered phosphates and superphosphate production, the Bizerta oil refinery, cement, lime and petroleum products. In January 1968 a joint Tunisian-French commission, meeting in Tunis, expressed the wish for closer co-operative relations between the two countries after the difficulties of the previous years, especially relating to the expropriation of land from the French settlers. The *rapprochment* with France resulted in an invitation to Bourguiba to visit France in 1970. Tunisia was upset by the coup that brought Gaddafi to power in Libya since it had regarded the government of King Idris as a moderate ally to counter-balance socialist Algeria and Egypt. By the end of the decade Bourguiba had become more concerned with maintaining his power than carrying out further reforms. 'In the early years of his rule he was a secular modernizer, advancing women's rights and curbing the powers of the Islamic fundamentalists, but he was never able to find the right economic balance to make his country grow and prosper and entered a long struggle with the unions.'[5]

A MAGHREB UNION?

One of the first OAU arbitration missions was undertaken in 1963 to stop the fighting between Algeria and Morocco over their disputed border. Emperor Haile Selassie and Ghana's Foreign Minister Kojo Botsio, accompanied by

Ghana's provisional representative at the OAU, Kwesi Armah, visited North Africa to talk with the two sides. Following their efforts at mediation, Algeria's Foreign Minister Bouteflika requested a meeting at Foreign Minister level of the OAU and this was arranged for 16 November. The frontier fighting had begun on 8 October with clashes at Colomb-Bechar and by 10 October Moroccan forces had taken control of two frontier oases – Hassa Beida and Tinjoub, which were 18 miles inside Algeria. A ceasefire was agreed after two days of talks held in Bamako, the capital of Mali, and signed by King Hassan of Morocco, President Ben Bella of Algeria, President Modibo Keita of Mali and Emperor Haile Selassie. Darsie Gillie of the *Guardian* commented as follows on this mediation effort:

> The conciliators, Emperor Haile Selassie and President Modibo Keita, were both passionately convinced of the grave danger to all Africa, including themselves, of a war between two African states so soon after liberation. Were the foreigners so recently thrown out as conquerors to be brought back again as peacemakers to run Africa on the basis of a new plea?...
>
> It is not expected that the laying down of arms will in itself mean a co-operative state of peace. The Algerian inclination to cause revolution in Morocco, and the Moroccan desire to press claims right across the Western Sahara, have been too evident. The most that is hoped for is that the two men will have learned that the game of seeking solutions to internal troubles by pressing adventures abroad can prove even more dangerous than the original trouble at home.[6]

At this stage the policies of the three Maghreb countries appeared too divergent for a union to make sense. Algeria was firmly ranged with the 'revolutionary' countries while Morocco, and even more Tunisia, were among the 'moderates'. Over the first decade of Maghreb independence from 1956 to 1965 the three countries witnessed – and hastened – the departure of the French and other settlers only subsequently to feel the economic and social impact that their departure entailed. In 1955 the non-Muslim population of the three was 1.8 million; by 1965 it had been reduced to 0.6 million; and by 1970 to 0.3 million. The settlers had exercised major control over the economies of the three territories and without them the prospects of obtaining sufficient aid for effective development had receded. Algeria had major oil and natural gas deposits that would provide the economic base for modernization but the other two countries did not, although in 1964 some oil was found in the south of Tunisia near the Algerian border at El Borma. Although the three had somewhat more developed economies than most African countries to the south, apart from oil and mining they depended mainly upon agriculture and, if anything, competed with one another in their exports to Europe. Local financing for development would remain modest for years to come while there was little sign that they could obtain finance from abroad on the scale required to achieve successful economic take-off.

Nonetheless, as with other potential regional groups the ideal of a Maghreb Economic Union had its appeal and in 1964 the Maghreb Permanent Consultative Committee was established with headquarters in Tunis. Its object was to investigate all problems relating to economic co-operation in member countries and to propose measures to reinforce co-operation and bring into being a Maghreb Economic Community. Its members were Algeria, Mauritania, Morocco and Tunisia. The possibilities of closer Maghreb union improved in 1969–70 when there was a *rapprochment* between Algeria and Morocco, a *rapprochment* between Morocco and Mauritania, and a treaty between Algeria and Tunisia in December 1969, which solved 'all outstanding problems' and was followed in January 1970 by a visit to Tunisia of Algeria's Foreign Minister. In real terms, however, despite their common backgrounds of religion, language, ethnicity and French colonialism the Maghreb countries were no closer to an effective economic union at this time than were any of the other groupings that came and went in sub-Saharan Africa.

LIBYA

A major battleground during World War II, Libya became independent in 1951 under Idris el-Senussi as one of the world's poorest countries. The discovery of oil in great quantities at the end of the 1950s transformed its prospects and during the 1960s Libya enjoyed an oil boom that would change both the economy and the political standing of the country. In 1961 the government decreed that Libya should take a 50 per cent share of all oil profits. When he came to power Idris faced the daunting task of coalescing into one the three different provinces of Tripolitania, Cyrenaica and Fezzan. He was a shrewd statesman who had led the opposition to the Italians, but in 1951 Libya had few trained personnel to operate a modern state. Idris, who turned out to be an enlightened autocrat – he created a vigilant police force – disapproved of political parties. In February 1962 87 people were imprisoned for 'forming in Libya cells of the Arab Socialist Ba'ath Party and carrying on subversive activities aimed at overthrowing the political, economic and social system'.

During the 1950s, before the discovery of oil, Libya turned to the West for financial support, offering base facilities in return. An agreement with Britain in

1953 and another with the United States in 1954 made available to them base facilities for financial subventions for the budget and development assistance. Libya signed a friendship pact with France in 1955 and a trade and financial agreement with Italy in 1957. This overt dependence upon the West was to change following the discovery of oil in 1959. The problems that came with rapidly increasing oil wealth led the King to appoint a new cabinet in 1963 under Dr Mohieddin Fekini who, as Prime Minister, first made Libya into a unitary state on 27 April 1963. In May of that year Libya closed its ports to the shipping of South Africa and Portugal because of their racial policies. Pacts entered into with Morocco in 1962 and Algeria in 1963 marked a move away from close ties with the West. In 1964 a new Prime Minister, Mahmud Muntasser, said he did not intend to renew the base agreements with Britain and the United States but would terminate them by negotiation. At the same time as he announced this policy the Chamber of Deputies passed a resolution to the effect that if negotiations were unsuccessful it would pass legislation to abrogate the treaties anyway. In response Britain withdrew the bulk of its forces in 1966 and the Americans indicated they would do the same. The 1967 Six Day War greatly heightened tensions throughout the region and the political attitude in Libya changed from one of moderation to one of virulent anti-Westernism. The British and US embassies were attacked, and Jewish minorities were persecuted so that many Jews left for Italy or Malta. Libyan and Algerian troops were moved to Egypt but the war was over before they could be deployed. On 16 June the Prime Minister requested the United States and Britain to liquidate their bases and withdraw their forces from Libya as soon as possible. On 28 October, after dismissing two prime ministers in quick succession, the King appointed Abdul Hamid Bakhush who initiated a policy of rapid modernization, including the purchase of up-to-date military equipment from Britain. In the aftermath of the war Libya agreed to make annual payments of £30 million to Egypt and Jordan to help them recover from the effects of the war. Oil output in 1967 came to 627,137,968 barrels, equivalent to 1.7 million b/d and by 1968 Libya had become the second-largest oil producer of the Arab world. In August 1968 a final agreement was reached for the evacuation of the British and American bases. Meanwhile, fresh oil discoveries led the government to devise a new policy to control oil concessions through the state-run oil company, the National Libyan Petroleum Corporation.

On 1 September 1969, when King Idris was undergoing medical treatment in Turkey, the Free Officers Movement that Gaddafi had founded as a student at the Benghazi military college mounted a bloodless coup to oust the old King. On 13 September Gaddafi became Chairman of the Revolutionary Command Council to inaugurate a new era in Libya.

Like the rest of the continent, the countries of North Africa had all been colonized by the European powers, but unlike the countries to their south their first loyalties were to the Arab world of the Middle East. Arab unity, the confrontation with Israel and Islam were always their priorities and though they played their part in the formation of the OAU and in encouraging the general solidarity of African countries in relation to the great powers there was always a sense, however well disguised, that they were only part committed to the new independent Africa that was emerging. This split personality, half Arab, half African, was understandable but it did mean that extra care was needed to foster Arab-African relations and this necessity continued down to the end of the century. Nasser was the outstanding exception, one of the most impressive figures of the decade. Although Nasser 'temporarily gained personal leadership in the region, Egypt was never strong enough to dominate the Middle East nor to prevent the interference of the great powers. He could never find a formula to accommodate the Palestinians or the Israelis'. Many judgements have been passed on Nasser but at the height of his powers in the first half of the 1960s he stood head and shoulders above his peers in the Arab world. One judgement of his home achievements is as follows: 'At home he did achieve some social and economic success. He modernized his country, built the Aswan High Dam and improved agricultural productivity. He created a fairer society and transferred some land to the fellahin, but his centralized, nationalized, socialist economy was a recipe for failure and did not survive much beyond his lifetime.'[7] A more upbeat assessment of his achievements acknowledges a far wider impact upon his country, the Arab world and Africa:

> Gamal Abdul Nasser was a remarkable man. Future ages will look upon him as one of the two or three key figures of the middle years of the twentieth century. For all the diplomatic and military failures of his later years, which cost some of Egypt's hard-won independence by placing it heavily in debt to the Soviet Union, Nasser's influence on the Middle East and much of the Third World was profound. Radical young army officers as far away as Latin America have been called 'Nasserists' as the best way of describing what they stand for.

He achieved for Egypt some of the attributes of a great power though his greatest achievements were at home:

> ... the body of pragmatic social and economic policies which became known as Arab Socialism. The dismantling of the powers of the old bourgeois and feudal classes, land reform, big strides in industrialization,

the building of the High Dam and above all the instillation into the Egyptians of the feeling that development could be a national enterprise, were the real legacies of the Nasserist revolution, and certainly there was no part of the Arab world that was too remote to be influenced by them.[8]

His death in 1970 marked the end of an Arab era of resurgence.

The Nigerian Civil War

The state of Nigeria was an artificial creation of British imperialism and its near disintegration during the latter half of the 1960s bore out the doubts that Macmillan expressed on his visit in January 1960 during his tour of Africa. From the moment of independence, indeed in the run-up to it, there had been fierce pulls away from the centre by the three regions of the North, the West and the East with the two smaller southern regions fearing domination by the North. Each region had a population greater in size than those of most other African countries. When Britain extended its power over what later became Nigeria it created separate colonies, which were only amalgamated to form a single Nigeria by Lord Lugard in 1914. Thereafter, the British colonial administrators fostered strong regional governments and, if anything, encouraged a sense of rivalry between the component parts of its colony while maintaining a balance from the centre. In 1914 there was no historical basis for Nigerian unity except British imperial convenience. At independence, therefore, the new Nigeria was based upon three largely autonomous regions whose interests tended to pull against any central authority and both before and after the British had departed there was intense rivalry as to which group or combination should control the centre. A further complication resulted from the fact that about two million of the Ibo people from the Eastern Region were dispersed in other parts of Nigeria, many of them holding jobs in the more conservative Islamic North where their presence was often resented. This structure, with its inbuilt tensions, that the new state inherited at independence produced increasingly divisive strains in the years 1960–66. Efforts to balance the claims and counter-claims of the three regions failed to satisfy the aspirations of any one of them and the federal political system began to fall apart.

The complexities of Nigeria's history need to be understood in order to explain what occurred after independence. For centuries, until modern times, the North, the great majority of whose people were Muslims, had looked overland across the Sahara for its inspiration. In the South, the forests had isolated and fragmented the tribes and though there developed a clear North-South division, there were also many other divisions including the Yoruba kingdoms in the West, the Benin kingdom in the mid-West and the Ibos of the East who were less hierarchical and more democratic than any of the others. Then came the Europeans: at first on the coast as traders and slavers, then as imperialists who extended their influence into the interior by trade. It is one of the great ironies of West Africa's colonial history that while the French have been accused of 'balkanizing' their vast territories of West and Equatorial Africa prior to independence so as to ensure their continuing post-independence influence, the British in Nigeria were accused of the opposite – the creation of a huge artificial state whose three main ethnic groups ought to have had individual countries of their own.

When Nigeria became independent on 1 October 1960, the stage-managed grandeur of the state occasion and the resultant euphoria briefly acted to mask the inherent contradictions that the new government had to face. Earlier that year Macmillan had remarked on the arbitrary imposed frontiers, which he described as 'criminal' in the way they divided tribal territories, and his political antennae sensed a looming regional-federal crisis. He was not alone in his forebodings about the stresses that Nigeria would face once independence had become an accomplished fact. At least the discovery of oil in the late 1950s gave rise to hopes of rapid economic developments although oil could create as many problems as it solved: 'Shell alone is estimated to have invested a greater sum in Nigeria than the total manufacturing investment in that country. By 1964 the company claimed to have sunk £130 million in its Nigerian industry.'[1] Since most of the oil was found in the East, in what would become Biafra during the civil war, it was to play a significant role in that war, persuading the Ibos that they could create a viable state of their own, and ensuring that the Federal Government would make every effort to obtain control of the oilfields as quickly as possible once hostilities were under way. By 6 September 1968 most of the oil-producing areas of Biafra had been taken by the Federal forces so that Biafra thereafter did not even have oil as a bargaining counter.

CIVIL GOVERNMENT 1960–66

In 1960 the three leading politicians were the Ibo Nnamdi Azikiwe, the Yoruba Chief Obafemi Awolowo and the Hausa Alhaji Abubakar Tafawa Balewa. As politicians prior to independence they had each demonstrated remarkable political talents yet between them they failed Nigeria in the post-independence years. Balewa as the Federal Prime Minister did his best to achieve a balance between the regions but he was never strong enough to hold the country together. Two other powerful political figures were the northern hereditary ruler, Ahmadu Bello, the Sardauna of Sokoto, who was a champion of Northern rights and never thought in terms of a greater Nigeria, and Chief Festus Okotie-Eboh, the Federal Minister of Finance. Given its background, what would best have suited Nigeria at independence would have been an authoritarian, radical regime capable of overriding the regional concerns of most other politicians. Unfortunately, the only real radicalism produced in Nigeria had been against the British and once they had departed politics descended into an argument about how the national 'cake' should be shared and the cake was in any case severely limited. A federal system ought to be used to unite a range of people who have in common more than the differences that separate them. Unfortunately in Nigeria, it appeared to work the other way round: 'When self-government came, it came separately, at different times to the North and the South. Independence was possible only because the federal system enabled the various peoples to keep each other at arm's length. Above all, the system was intended to provide a guarantee that no one tribe could easily dominate the rest.'[2] Underlying political tensions were the problem, peculiar to all Africa at that time, of rising expectations that the government could provide jobs for all its citizens. 'The government is the only substantial employer; and the output of school-leavers continually outstrips the number of new jobs available. This makes politics ruthless. Office means a livelihood not only for a politician but for his "extended" family and, beyond that, his village, town and tribe. In office, politicians will do almost all they can to stay there; out of office, they will do almost anything to get in.'[3]

Nigeria's problems were in no sense unique. Every African country that came to independence in the 1960s faced rising expectations that were stymied by limited resources, the need for development on all fronts that was held back by the absence of anything like an adequately trained professional or technical class, and the need to attract investment funds. What placed Nigeria on a different plane to most other African countries was the size of the population: it simply had more people to educate, train and employ than anyone else. At the end of World War II illiteracy was almost total. In 1955 the Western Region became the first African government to introduce universal free primary education and by 1960 three million children were in 17,000 schools. At the same time the North, with half Nigeria's total population, had hardly begun an educational programme and in 1959 its primary school population was only 250,000. At that time the Northern Region had an estimated 25 million population, the Western Region seven million, the Eastern Region 12 million and the Mid-West two million.

The easy task had been persuading the British to leave. 'It was only when they had held power themselves for some time that the Nigerian political class began to appreciate how scarce were the resources that a government in a poor country could mobilize, and how few in numbers and how thinly spread through the country was the administrative service that had once (under the British) looked so all pervasive. But before they had made those shattering discoveries Nigerian politicians had over-committed their resources and personnel. They had also opened Pandora's box of aspirations with welfare schemes that whetted people's hopes at least as much as they fulfilled their expectations.'[4] At least Nigeria did not face race problems of the kind that afflicted Southern Africa: there was no segregation and Nigerians were to be found on the boards of expatriate companies while half the managerial staff of big expatriate companies were Nigerian by the early 1960s. Corruption, however, was a different matter and resentment against politicians who became rich overnight was certainly a contributory cause of the widespread jubilation at the overthrow of the Federal Government at the beginning of 1966. Another problem concerned the continuation at independence of colonial salary scales for civil servants: these created a glaring differential between the new ruling elite and the mass of the people whose per capita income averaged £30. When the collapse came in 1966, 'The peoples of Nigeria had never before been jointly disenchanted by the same government. While the people of other countries might have resented colonialism together, the peoples of Nigeria had not even shared a joint feeling of anti-colonialism together. The North especially had been too suspicious of the South, and too cautious in her assessment of independence, even to get worked up into a strong feeling of nationalism.'[5]

Although Nigeria attracted much goodwill at independence this was insufficient to ensure an adequate inflow of development capital on the scale required to create employment for all the new school-leavers. The country's rate of economic growth, it soon became clear, would depend, at least in part, upon events both political and economic in Britain, the European Economic Community and the United States, and to some extent the Soviet Union as well, and stabilizing commodity prices – a policy much advocated at the time – was no substitute for expanding markets. Given liberal trading policies abroad and political stability at home, there was then no reason to believe that Nigeria would not emerge from the 1960s with a stronger and better-balanced economy, but the proviso was essential. In 1961 Chief Festus Okotie-Eboh, the Minister of Finance, led an economic mission to visit 23 countries. In London he said he wanted to increase the flow of capital between Nigeria and the countries he was visiting. Nigeria faced three major economic problems: how to increase exports to pay for the ever-rising flood of imports; how to attract overseas investment for industry, to meet balance of payments and provide employment for the swelling numbers of school-leavers; and how to attract financial and other assistance for government development plans.

The proposed 1962–68 National Development Plan aimed to spend £600 million on Federal and Regional projects. Optimistically, Hella Pick wrote in the *Guardian*: 'The various governments have always drawn up separate development programmes, and although there has been some co-operation through the National Economic Development Council these plans have covered differing periods, and very frequently there has been intense competition between the regions for the limited resources available. Now, however, a miracle has occurred: for the first time there will be a national plan, incorporating both regional and Federal plans.'[7] The Federal Government was to spend nearly £60 million on road development and give top priority to improving communications with Niger and Chad to the north, its practical way of advancing towards closer regional union. The Plan, with increased allocations to bring it to £676 million, was launched at the end of 1962 and the aim was to raise £300 million for public expenditure and £200 million for private investment from outside, with the United States, Britain, West Germany, Canada, Israel and Japan each making pledges of financial or technical assistance, Czechoslovakia offering credits and Russia scholarships, as well as further assistance from various UN bodies. All this aid did not cover the targets set by Lagos. A survey in 1963 revealed that there were 5,000 Nigerians at the upper levels of government working alongside 2,500 expatriates; there were also 600 senior Nigerian engineers, 1,000 accountants and auditors, 425 registered doctors and dentists although senior staff in the universities were mainly expatriate.[8] On the eve of the first coup in January 1966 the expatriate community consisted of about 40,000 British and a further 20,000 French, German, Dutch, Italian, Greek, Lebanese, Swiss and American expatriates, representing the rapidly growing international aid community and mainly in commercial and technical posts.

POLITICS

In his book *Mr Prime Minister*, published in 1960, the fiery Chief Awolowo said: 'The defects in British administration have turned out to be a blessing in disguise. For if British rule had been less inept than it was, the opportunity for Nigerians to demonstrate that they are qualified to manage their own affairs would have been correspondingly reduced.' This may have applied to the pre-independence period but it failed convincingly to cover the performance of Nigerian politicians after independence, including Awolowo himself. There was, perhaps, a year from October 1960 before there was a distinct downturn in the political scene. At the end of February 1961, addressing the Action Group Conference in the Mid-West, Chief Awolowo, ever determined to lessen British influence, argued that Nigeria should become a republic. He also criticized the Federal Prime Minister, Tafawa Balewa, and called for the creation of more states. On 1 June that year Northern Cameroons, the former British Trusteeship territory with a population of 750,000, voted in a UN-supervised plebiscite to join Nigeria rather than the Francophone Cameroon Republic. In 1963 Awolowo got his wish when Nigeria changed its constitution so as to become a republic within the Commonwealth on 1 October.

Awolowo, the leader of the Action Group in the Western Region and often seen as a man in a hurry, got into serious political trouble in 1962 after he fell out with the Premier of the West, Chief Samuel Akintola, who sought a *rapprochment* with Northerners. There were in any case personality differences between the two men. On 2 November 1962 Chief Awolowo and 18 other members of the Action Group were charged with treasonable felony after the discovery of an ill-conceived plot against the Federal leadership. After an 11-month trial Awolowo was found guilty on 11 September 1963 and sentenced to 10 years' imprisonment. His appeal against the sentence was dismissed in 1964. In the same trial Chief Anthony Enahoro, the leader of the Action Group in the Mid-West, whose popularity there was as great as Awolowo's in the West, was also sentenced, in his case to 15 years for treasonable felony, conspiracy and possession of firearms; he fled to Britain where he became the focus of attention in an extradition case. It was a pity that these two most able men should descend to conspiracy when they might have used their talents more constructively. In the event Awolowo spent only three years in prison where he wrote *Thoughts on the Nigerian Constitution* before he was released by General Gowon who told him, 'We need you for the wealth of your experience' to join the Federal Military Government during the civil war.

Part of the root problem in Nigeria was too many people pursuing too few jobs and each (they were known as applicants) looking to those in his own group or tribe to help him. 'The real trouble is caused by the rivalry of the few large groups, especially the Hausa-Fulani of the North, the Yoruba of the West and the Ibo of the East. Each of these groups has a common origin, a common history, a common language and a common way of life. They are not only nations but big ones.' This view recurs again and again over these years as both Nigerians and outsiders tried to find a way to bring the three groups into a working partnership rather than maintaining a permanent state of suspicion with one another. The same observer, quoted above, put the problem into the job perspective that counted most with the average Nigerian: 'If an Ibo were appointed chairman of the railway corporation, it was automatically assumed that every possible stoker, linesman and railway clerk would be Ibo.'[9]

Nothing illustrated better the inter-tribal suspicions and rivalries than the Nigerian census. Both the census of 1963 and later ones became matters of acute controversy since the size of a regional population determined the number of seats it would be allocated for elections and the proportion of revenues it could claim from the Federal Government. Numbers, in other words, meant power and the regions constantly accused each other of inflating the size of their populations. A first post-independence census was attempted in May 1962, but abandoned after regional disputes in which North and South accused each other of inflating their numbers. On that occasion, after several months of counting, the North claimed a total population of 30 million against 23 million for the South. A new national census was completed on 8 November 1963. According to Clyde Sanger, writing for the *Guardian*, the census could become the greatest threat to Nigeria's unity since independence: 'Proportions are particularly crucial, since a new delimitation of seats in the federal legislature before next year's elections depends on the population. In the 1959 elections on the basis of the old figures the North was given 174 out of 320 seats.'[10] The 1963 census showed Nigeria to have a population of 55,653,821. Compared with the census of 1952–53, the North had increased its numbers by 76.8 per cent, the East by 71.6 per cent, the West (including the Mid-West) by 100 per cent, Lagos by just over 90 per cent. Much unease followed the publication of these results and Dr Michael Okpara, the premier of the Eastern Region, said the figures disclosed 'inflations of astronomical proportions'. It was doubtful that any census results would be acceptable to all groups. The political significance of these 1963 figures was that the Northern People's Congress (NPC), then the senior partner in the coalition government of Sir Abubakar Tafawa Balewa, emerged in a very strong position that should make it possible to rule the Republic on its own. The controversy following the census results led to a realignment of the parties. The National Council of Nigerian Citizens (NCNC) governments in Eastern Nigeria and the Mid-West rejected the census results. The Northern Region accepted them, as did the Western Region, where the government was a coalition of the NCNC and the United People's Party whose leader was Chief Akintola, the Western Region premier.

The atmosphere of suspicion created by the census was carried through to the Federal elections at the end of 1964. These were held on 30 December. There were disputes over the conduct of the election, frequent accusations of fraud and subsequent disputes over the results. The NCNC and its allies attempted to boycott the elections; and the Federal Prime Minister, Balewa, fell out with President Azikiwe. Eventually, a compromise was worked out though no one expected this to last. The country had been effectively divided on North-South lines. Of an electorate of 15 million only four million had voted. The NPC won 162 seats to give it a narrow absolute majority; its electoral ally, the Nigerian National Democratic Party (NNDP), won 36 seats of 57 in the Western Region. A compromise solution of 7 January 1965 saw the creation of a new coalition government with Balewa continuing as Federal Prime Minister and Festus Okotie-Eboh as Finance Minister. A leader in *The Times* said the situation did not encourage the view that the crisis had been resolved rather than postponed.

In general, though with exceptions, the post-independence government pursued a conservative foreign policy. However, there was intellectual disaffection with the government, which was seen repeatedly to break African ranks and take stands congenial to the West. In November 1960 Nigeria signed a defence agreement with Britain; the Action Group denounced the agreement, accusing the government of being too pro-British. It was a familiar argument at the time and many Nigerians were more radical in their attitude towards the former colonial power than the government was. Little more than a year later, on 21 January 1962, the treaty was abrogated, mainly as a result of Nigerian apprehensions that the pact would inhibit its independence of action, although in real terms Nigeria was simply beginning to cut imperial ties that Britain would have preferred to maintain. As another Africa observer was to write of this short-lived defence pact: 'What is not revealed, and indeed what the British Government is at some pains to conceal, is that a pet project of the Ministry of Defence has proved – as predicted – to be politically explosive, diplomatically embarrassing and, practically, useless. It may come as some kind of bitter satisfaction to wiser heads in Whitehall – the experts of the Colonial Office who advised against such a military pact at the time – that their predictions have come true, and sooner than they or anyone else expected.'[11] On the other hand, Nigeria had taken a radical stand in December 1960 when France exploded its third atomic bomb in the Sahara. Then, alone of African states, Nigeria broke diplomatic relations with France and said the test had shown 'an utter disregard for the Africans, and constituted a grave insult to the Government and peoples of this country'.[12] Relations with France were not resumed until 1966. Lack of African support for Nigeria's lone stand against France rankled and undoubtedly influenced the Nigerian decision in 1965 not to break diplomatic relations with Britain over UDI in Rhodesia when the OAU was calling upon its members to do so. Even so, the last political act of the Balewa Government before its overthrow was to organize the special Commonwealth conference to consider UDI that met in Lagos in January 1966.

Following the flawed elections at the end of 1964, a sense of developing crisis was apparent all through 1965. The President, Dr Azikiwe, wrote an article in the US quarterly *Foreign Affairs* in which he advocated major changes to the Nigerian constitution that included judicial reform, unification of the local government system, enlargement of the scope of the Federal Government's authority, diversification of the federal system, a change in the patterns of suffrage, including the enfranchisement of women in the North, the reinforcement of the constitution and the granting of specific powers to the president – in other words a virtual rewrite of the constitution. In particular, Dr Azikiwe urged the need to divide Nigeria into more regions. 'In order to evolve into a near perfect union, the whole of Nigeria should be divided and so demarcated geographically and demographically that no one Region would be in a position to dominate the rest.'[13] In response, the *Nigerian Citizen*, a newspaper sponsored by the Northern Nigerian Government, called for the President's resignation, and said that if he refused a vote of 'no confidence' should be passed in Parliament. As crisis loomed most of the country's oil, then being extracted at the rate of 200,000b/d, came from the Eastern Region although large new deposits had been discovered in the Mid-West and estimates then suggested oil revenues would reach £100 million by 1967. Writing shortly after the fall of the Balewa government Ali Mazrui would castigate its failures: 'Nothing had helped the movement for a unitary state in Nigeria more dramatically than the mess in which the previous regime up to 1966 left the federal structure… Perhaps Nigeria is too pluralistic a country to be ruled on any basis other than that of quasi-federalism. But the very fact that there is now a quest for *tighter* integration was substantially attributable to the errors of the previous regime.'[14]

THE FIRST COUP 15 JANUARY 1966

By 15 January 1966, when the first coup was mounted, the political class in Nigeria had been deeply discredited. It was associated with corruption, nepotism, tribalism and inefficiency rather than good government so that the military takeover, when it came, was greeted with relief by a disenchanted population. The performance of the Balewa government had proved dismal rather than inspiring though it should not alone be blamed for what occurred: from its inception it had faced the near insurmountable regional demands that always threatened national unity. Several coups had been planned for January 1966 although the one that succeeded in overthrowing the government in the South did not bring its perpetrators to power. Five Ibo majors who sought to remove all the politicians of the leading parties and regions planned the coups. The leading coup-maker of 15 January was Major Chukwuma Kaduna Nzeogwu who broadcast to the nation that the aim of the coup was 'to establish a strong, unified and prosperous nation, free from corruption and internal strife'. The North, however, was the only region where the coup went as planned. On the afternoon of 15 January, Nzeogwu broadcast a proclamation 'in the name of the Supreme Council of the Revolution' and declared martial law over the 'Northern Provinces of Nigeria'. He said the constitution was suspended, the regional government and assembly dissolved, the departments to be run by permanent secretaries for the time being. He also said: 'Our enemies are the political profiteers, swindlers, the men in high and low places that seek bribes and demand 10 per cent, those that seek to keep the country permanently divided so that they can remain in office as Ministers and VIPs of waste, the tribalists, the nepotists, those that make the country look big for nothing before international circles.'

As Commonwealth leaders departed from Lagos, following the special conference to consider UDI in Rhodesia, some actually heard the gunfire that heralded the coup. Junior army officers assassinated the premier of the Northern Region, Sir Ahmadu Bello, the Sardauna of Sokoto, the premier of the Western Region, Chief Akintola, the Federal Prime Minister, Sir Abubakar Tafawa Balewa, and the Federal Finance Minister, Chief Festus Okotie-Eboh. Federal ministers then asked Maj.-Gen. Johnson Aguiyi-Ironsi, the army commander, to take control of government. The new government he formed suspended the constitution. The young army officers responsible for the coup denied that they had been motivated by ethnic considerations and claimed they had only acted to bring an end to a corrupt regime, but the fact remained that they were virtually all Ibos and those they killed were not, thus greatly exacerbating fears in the North of Ibo dominance.

There was an immediate readiness to let Ironsi attempt to overcome the regional antagonisms that had bedevilled Nigeria since independence. He reassured the North when he chose Maj. Hassan Katsina, the son of a powerful Northern emir, as Northern Military Governor. Ironsi himself was non-political. He had worked his way up through the ranks to become a company sergeant major at 24 and had been appointed Equerry to the Queen on her 1956 visit. In February 1966 the Ironsi government released a statement: 'It has become apparent to all Nigerians that rigid adherence to "regionalism" was the bane of the last regime and one of the main factors which contributed to its downfall. No doubt the country would welcome a clean break with the deficiencies of the system.' However, the welcome that had greeted the Ironsi regime did not last long. As a fellow Nigerian soldier and later head of state, Olusegun Obasanjo said: 'But in addition to his failure to take advantage of the initial favourable reaction to the coup, he did not know what to do with the ringleaders of the coup who had been arrested. He could not decide whether to treat them as heroes of the "revolution" or send them before a court-martial as mutineers and murderers.'[15] Ironsi was handicapped by his own intellectual shortcomings.

In early May 1966, the diplomatic correspondent of the *Financial Times* could write 'that Nigerians were still delighted with the ending of the Federal Government and the Army's popularity remained high'. But this was not the same thing as governing. Optimistically, he wrote of the absence of tribal strife.[16] At the time there was a kind of phoney peace as Nigerians waited for the next development. This came at the end of May. The overriding question was what kind of political structure should replace the Federal structure that had broken down. Returning to Kaduna from a Supreme Military Council meeting in Lagos, the Northern Governor Hassan Katsina said to reporters in late May: 'Tell the nation that the egg will be broken on Tuesday.' He was correct. Ironsi had tried hard in the appointments he made to be impartial and not favour the Ibos but such impartiality displeased the hard-liners on both sides of the divide. He was under pressure from the Yorubas to unify the country and abolish the old regional structure. On 24 May he broadcast to the nation details of a new constitution. The former regions were to be abolished and Nigeria was to be grouped into a number of territorial areas to be called provinces. The country would cease to be a federation and instead become simply the Republic of Nigeria. The public services were to be unified under a single Public Service Commission and civil servants were to function anywhere in Nigeria where they were needed. 'For Nigeria it amounted to another coup – executed by the stroke of a pen. The country was no longer to be called a federation, simply "the Republic of Nigeria", ruled by a "national" instead of a "Federal" military government; the regions were abolished and replaced by groups of provinces; the Federal and regional civil services were unified and to be administered from Lagos; political and tribal organizations were dissolved and political activities banned for the next two and a half years.'[17] The reaction in the North was violent. Some of the changes were only cosmetic, such as the regions being turned into provinces that in any case coincided with the former regions, but the two-and-a-half-year ban on political activity was another matter entirely and raised the question of how long the military proposed to stay in power. It was Decree 34, the unification decree that amalgamated the federal and regional civil services, that was regarded as a major threat to the North since it was seen as the beginning of possible domination of the North by the South: with an 'end' of politicians, at least for the time being, civil servants would control both the administration and the distribution of jobs. Ironsi admitted that the change was a drastic one. In a broadcast to the nation, he said: 'Every civil servant is now called upon to see his function in any part of Nigeria in which he is serving in the context of the whole country. The orientation should now be towards national unity and progress.'[18]

Between Tuesday 24 May and the following weekend hundreds of Ibos were killed in pogroms in the Northern cities of Kano, Kaduna and Zaria; some of these pogroms were spontaneous, others had been organized by civil servants, ex-politicians, local government officials and businessmen whom the change of regime deprived or threatened to deprive of their jobs. These pogroms were followed by calls for the North to secede and condemnations of Ironsi. He called the four regional governors to a conference in Lagos, which appointed a commission of inquiry into the killings. They backtracked on Decree 34 and announced there would be no change to the regions. Then, believing all had quietened down, a mistake he later regretted, Col. Ojukwu, the Governor of the Eastern Region, broadcast an appeal to Ibos who had fled from the North to return to their homes 'as the situation is now under control'.

THE SECOND COUP 29 JULY 1966

On 29 July 1966 a group of Northern soldiers arrived at the Western Region military headquarters in Ibadan where Ironsi was staying with Colonel Fajuyi, the West's Military Governor, at Government Lodge. The two men and an aide were taken outside Ibadan, tortured and then killed. The revolt then spread to Ikeja barracks outside Lagos and the rebels seized the international airport. Brig. B. Ogundipe, the most senior officer after Ironsi, tried to prevent the coup spreading and sent a detachment of troops from Lagos to quell the mutiny but they were ambushed and suffered heavy losses. The Northern garrisons supported the revolt although no coup was attempted in the Eastern Region. This counter-coup of 29 July, which followed riots in the Northern Region, had two aims: revenge upon the East by the North for the first coup; and the break-up of Nigeria by Northern secession. The Northern soldiers soon found themselves in effective control in Lagos, the West and Mid-West but not in the East. It did not take long for cooler heads in the North to reject secession as a solution to their problems since it would make the North landlocked and dependent for communications upon the South and cut it off from the country's new oil wealth. Revenge killings of Ibos were to continue through August. Brig. Ogundipe sent Col. Yakubu Gowon to parley with the mutinous troops at Ikeja barracks. Ogundipe, a Yoruba, was an old soldier who, like Ironsi, had worked his way up through the ranks and could expect to find little support in an army split on tribal lines – there were few Yoruba in the army. He summoned whoever was available of the Supreme Military Council to a conference at police headquarters where those who met were in a state of shock.

Meanwhile, the rebel soldiers came out of Ikeja barracks and proceeded to kill Eastern soldiers or civilians. The Hausa soldier Lt-Col. Murtala Muhammed emerged as the principal spokesman of the mutineers whose immediate demands were the renunciation of the unity decree and the total separation of Eastern and Northern soldiers then in the army. They then demanded secession and the creation of a Republic of the North. Ogundipe broadcast a state of emergency.

The coup-makers were unwilling to surrender power to Ogundipe, the Chief of Staff, and now the highest-ranking officer in the army. They felt he did not 'belong'. He therefore, gracefully in the circumstances, gave way to Gowon and was subsequently appointed Nigerian High Commissioner to London. Gowon was the most senior officer of Northern origin although he came from the small Angas tribe of the Middle Belt of the northern plateau region and was a Christian rather than a Muslim. For the second time that year the country faced the question: what would happen next? Was the Federation to continue and who would lead it? The two obvious contenders for the leadership at this point were the cautious Gowon and the hot-headed Murtala Muhammed who at that stage was demanding secession for the North although opposition to the idea was crystallizing, especially among civil servants, lawyers and the police. Northern families then in the south were flown back home and civil servants were told to prepare to do so. A confrontation between Gowon and Muhammed led the majority of senior officers to choose the former as Supreme Commander; they did not want to break up the Federation; rather, it should continue under its existing form with a Northerner as head of state. This 'consensus' was arrived at over three days when Nigeria had no head of state. The Northern troops acted as arbiters of the country's fate. Gowon, who was to lead Nigeria for nine years, was an interesting choice. A Northerner from a minority tribe, he was a Christian, non-smoking, non-drinking soldier who had been educated at Zaria in the North and in Ghana and Sandhurst. He had served in the Congo and then attended a course at Camberley Staff College. He was very much a 'one Nigeria' man who loved the army and knew how it worked. He also knew how to take advice and reach a consensus. He won the backing of those who saw the dissolution of the Federation as a disaster, especially the civil service, and he and his supporters soon became known as 'New Nigerians'. Subsequent controversy about the legitimacy of Gowon's elevation obscured the crucial fact that at the time what was needed was to stop the bloodshed, get the soldiers back to barracks and prevent the country disintegrating. This Gowon achieved.[19]

Gowon's first recommendation of 13 August was to order all troops from Eastern Nigeria to be released and posted to Enugu in the Eastern Region and troops of non-Eastern origin in Enugu to be reposted to Kaduna and later to

Lagos to form the 6th Battalion of the Nigerian Army. That action 'broke the last thread and split the last institution symbolizing Nigeria's nationhood and national cohesion, which had been regularly tampered with by the politicians since 1962'.[20] Gowon and Muhammed were to clash about the coming war with the Eastern Region, even before the formal proclamation of Biafra. As early as April 1967 Muhammed was convinced that civil war was inevitable and that any delay was simply to put off the evil day but Gowon was more cautious. However, between July 1966 and May 1967 Ojukwu had built up the East's forces and boasted: 'We possess the biggest army in Africa.' During this period he had secured arms and ammunition from French, Spanish and Portuguese sources while he had also obtained assurances of mercenary support from France and South Africa.

A second series of massacres of Ibos in the North took place over the end of September into October when between 10,000 and possibly 30,000 were killed. At the time there were about one million Ibos still in the North. A huge movement of population now took place as more than a million Ibos poured into the Eastern Region. There, for their own safety, Col. Ojukwu ordered all non-Easterners to leave the Region. Ibo refugees now came from the West, the Mid-West and Lagos as well as from the North. As the crisis worsened 'and the possibility of a complete breakdown became imminent, the refugees from Lagos came to include senior civil servants of the Federal Government. These were to constitute a powerful pressure group behind Ojukwu, urging him to secede from the Federation'.[21] By late November 1966 Gowon was facing the possibility of war with the East: 'If circumstances compel me to preserve the integrity of Nigeria by force, I will do my duty,' he said.

In January 1967 the military leaders met at Aburi in Ghana under the chairmanship of Ghana's General Ankrah. Gowon wanted to maintain a single Nigeria, Ojukwu argued for separation. The meetings were taped at Ankrah's suggestion to 'avoid' argument later. At Aburi Gowon made some concessions towards confederalism but no solution was reached and he then spent the next six months trying to persuade Ojukwu to turn away from secession, but without success. Following the Aburi conference, in a bid to keep Nigeria whole, the North agreed to the creation of more states, something Ojukwu had argued for and the North, to that point, had opposed. When Biafra seceded at the end of May 1967 Gowon declared an emergency and then divided Nigeria into 12 states, abolishing the old regions, a move that won wide support and removed the fear of domination by the North. War was then inevitable although a final peace bid was led by the Federal Chief Justice Sir Adetokumboh Ademola who flew to Enugu though the possibility of a last-minute reconciliation was an illusion. At 2 a.m. on 30 May Col. Ojukwu made an announcement at State

House Enugu: '...do hereby solemnly proclaim that the territory and region known as Eastern Nigeria, together with her continental shelves and territorial waters, shall henceforth be an independent sovereign state of the name and title The Republic of Biafra'.

THE CIVIL WAR

Once war had become inevitable the attitudes of the major external powers became a matter of great importance to both sides. A united Nigeria had great economic potential, as a market with its population of more than 56 million people, as a rapidly developing source of oil as well as natural gas in an oil-hungry world, and as a substantial producer of coal, iron ore, cotton and rubber. These resources, as well as significant hydro-electric power potential, gave it a base for industrialization. It was then the world's largest producer of groundnuts and the second-largest producer of cocoa (after Ghana). Britain found itself in a dilemma: most of its business was centred upon Federal Nigeria but not the oil, and Ojukwu at once insisted that oil royalties should be paid over to Biafra by Shell-BP The British Government told the oil companies to make a token payment but the Federal Government proceeded to blockade the oil shipments. Britain was then the principal source of small arms for the Federal Government and while continuing to supply these refused to supply more substantial armaments, most notably aircraft, with the result that Nigeria turned to the Soviet Union. On 6 July 1967 Federal troops advanced into Biafra, and Nigeria was at war with itself.

When asked at the outbreak of hostilities what US policy towards Nigeria would be, Secretary of State Dean Rusk told a press conference, 'We regard Nigeria as part of Britain's sphere of influence.' It was a monumental gaffe, reminiscent of nineteenth-century big power attitudes towards the lesser countries of the world, and understandably infuriated the Nigerians. Even so, the big powers saw Nigeria as a 'prize' and determined to remain involved, with Britain, France, West Germany and the USSR in particular taking sides in pursuit of their interests. At the beginning of the war, when the British refused to do so, the Russians sold the Federal Government small, obsolescent aircraft; later, they supplied MiG 17s, Ilyushin bombers, heavy artillery, vehicles and small arms. The Soviet presence in Nigeria grew in other ways as well and in November 1968 it agreed to construct Nigeria's first steel mill and provided a loan of £60 million for the purpose. The Soviet Embassy doubled in size and there was a growth of Nigeria–Russia friendship societies.

Biafra benefited from the image, which it carefully cultivated, of a small, embattled country being bullied by a large one. An abundance of relief supplies was available – the problem was one of delivery. International assistance for Biafra came from a number of sources and for a variety of reasons. Its supporters included humanitarian agencies, four black African states which recognized it, Rhodesia (then embarked upon UDI), South Africa and Portugal because it was in the interests of the white regimes in Southern Africa to prolong the war in Nigeria since chaos and breakdown in Africa's largest, most promising black state boosted their claims to maintain white minority control. There was considerable international sympathy for Biafra as a 'small loser' and the Federal Government was criticized for not having made greater efforts to find a peaceful solution. Tanzania recognized Biafra on 13 April 1968, Gabon on 5 May, Côte d'Ivoire on 14 May and Zambia on 20 May. In the case of Tanzania President Nyerere defended his decision to do so with his usual intellectual skill on the grounds that the Ibos had been artificially included in Nigeria by the British for imperial reasons and had the right to secede if that was the wish of their people. Zambia's President Kaunda followed the Nyerere line. Côte d'Ivoire and Gabon were generally seen as acting on behalf of French interests. Haiti, for reasons that remained obscure, recognized Biafra on 23 March 1969. France supplied weapons for Biafra through its surrogates, Côte d'Ivoire and Gabon; Portugal did so through Portuguese Guinea. The principal sources of humanitarian aid, though there were others, were the International Committee of the Red Cross (ICRC), Church Aid and Caritas. Biafra obtained a number of old DC-class aircraft from Rhodesia. Both Portugal and Spain supported Biafra to stifle aspirations for independence in their own African territories while a motley range of gun-runners and other dubious arms dealers became overnight friends of Biafra. As Gen. Obasanjo was to say in his account of the war, 'The main paradox of the Nigerian civil war was that Tanzania, Zambia, Rhodesia, South Africa, Portugal and Spain all found themselves in the same camp supporting secession in Nigeria.'[22] President Houphouët-Boigny of Côte d'Ivoire, who had a pathological fear of Nigeria, assisted Biafra with financial support and persuaded de Gaulle to be more open in his support for it. De Gaulle, in any case, had not forgiven Nigeria for breaking diplomatic relations over the French nuclear tests in the Sahara at the beginning of the decade. In a realistic assessment of external support for Biafra, Obasanjo wrote: 'The effective rebel propaganda and phoney battle victories on Radio "Biafra" coupled with open diplomatic recognition and other support by four African countries, Tanzania, Zambia, Gabon and Ivory Coast, one West Indian country, Haiti, and covert support by one of the major world powers, France, and the double-dealing by some countries in Africa and Europe, Republic of Dahomey, Sierra Leone, West Germany, Spain, Portugal, Switzerland and Sweden, had strengthened the rebellion almost to the point of permanently sustaining it.

Cynics all over the world had started to deride the Nigerian Army and saw no hope of Nigeria becoming a united country again.'[23] Mobutu, on the other hand, gave open support to the Federal Government as did Ethiopia, Kenya, Uganda, Senegal and Congo (Brazzaville).

Ojukwu's decision to invade the Mid-West Region in August 1967 changed the course of the war. Had he played a wholly defensive role, defending Biafra against Nigerian attack, he might have lasted longer and gained more sympathy within Nigeria itself, but by attacking the neighbouring region he showed his readiness to threaten non-Ibo Nigerians and, as a result, he lost overnight the support and sympathy he might otherwise have had from many of the Yoruba. Instead he could now be branded as arrogant, power-hungry and over-ambitious and the slogan 'one Nigeria' in opposition to the threat he posed became highly popular.

The fall of Enugu to Federal troops on 5 October 1967 raised the hope that the war would soon be over but this was not to be. A description of Enugu after its capture suggested that Ibos, fearful of what might follow the fall of their city, had simply fled. And that being the case, the war was likely to continue for some considerable time. 'It is not so much the war damage; in fact, compared to Asaba the destruction has been comparatively mild. It is rather the complete absence of people that unnerves. There are Federal troops by the score, guarding key positions, but of civilians there are no sign. The limited nature of the damage makes it, if anything, more uncanny. With so many houses so recognizably recently lived in, you almost expect the bad dream to end and all the people suddenly to return. It is rather like one of those mystery stories about abandoned ships, like the *Marie Celeste*, found with signs of evident recent habitation, only with nobody on board.'[24] On 20 October Federal troops took the port of Calabar and the government in Lagos announced plans for post-war reconstruction. An OAU mediation mission arrived in Lagos to be told by Gowon: 'The most valuable contribution the mission can make in the present circumstances is to call on the rebel leaders to abandon secession. Your mission here is not to mediate.' More to the point for the Federal Government, Emperor Haile Selassie said that the mission's cardinal objective was to discuss ways and means, 'with the help of the Federal Government, whereby Nigerian national integrity is to be preserved and innocent Nigerian blood saved from flowing needlessly… We believe a solution needs to be urgently sought to accommodate the varying interests in Nigeria, but it must be specific enough to ensure the steady development of the Nigerian state'.[25]

By the beginning of 1968 the dense Ibo population had become concentrated in the eastern heartland round Aba and Umuahia and the Ibos, with nowhere to run, were fighting for survival. It seemed that a second, more desperate and bloody phase of the war was about to begin. As *West Africa* was to editorialize at the end of the year:

> The grim fact... remains. This is a civil war in which international appeals sound like international interference and in which the Federal Government is no more ready than any other sovereign government to accept instructions from outside. The Federal Government, in fact, has gone further in its response to international opinion than some of its supporters like. Wisely it has extended the stay of the international observers, whose reports refute the accusation that the Federal Forces are bent on 'genocide' (which would, if true, leave the Biafrans no alternative but a fight to the death)...[26]

The Federal side had its own problems, not least among some of its military commanders. After capturing Onitsha early in 1968, Murtala Muhammed, who was a difficult, power-hungry man, walked away from his Division, accusing the Commander-in-Chief (Gowon) in particular and Army Headquarters in general of deliberately starving his division of arms, ammunition and necessary equipment to prosecute the war effectively. He refused to return and expressed his lack of confidence in Gowon. On 19 May 1968 troops of the Federal 3 Marine Commando Division entered Port Harcourt where they witnessed a disorderly and dispirited Biafran exodus under way. After this defeat a flurry of diplomatic activity by friends of Biafra followed to keep the increasingly beleaguered 'state' in being.

As in the Congo (K) a few years earlier, Nigeria had to deal with the mercenary factor. The civil war was the first since the Carlist wars in Spain during the nineteenth century in which mercenaries fought one another from opposite sides; or rather, they did not fight one another which was part of the problem.

Mercenaries had earned such a bad name for themselves in the Congo that it was a political risk to use them at all. The Federal Military Government in Lagos, in any case, wanted to demonstrate its ability to deal with Biafran secession on its own. Biafra, however, was promoting the image of an embattled underdog fighting for its existence and so could legitimately seek outside help including that of mercenaries. In the end both sides used mercenaries but were able to exert far greater control over them than had been the case in the Congo. In July 1967 the Federal Government hired British, Rhodesian and South African pilots at a reported fee of US$2,800 a month tax free to be paid into numbered Swiss bank accounts. However, since Britain refused to supply warplanes, Soviet and Czech planes were purchased and flown by mercenary pilots from Czechoslovakia and Egypt as well as pilots from Britain. The Federal Military Government employed between 12 and 20 such pilots throughout the war – there was a rapid turnover – and employed them to fly Russian MiG17s since the Egyptian pilots proved inadequate. In November 1967 Biafra hired 83 French mercenaries under Col. Roger Faulques. Their task was to train Biafran troops. Faulques was soon joined in Biafra by the already legendary Bob Denard, who came fresh from his activities in Angola and Katanga, with another 200 mercenaries. Then a third group of French mercenaries arrived under Michel Declary. The Biafran decision to recruit French mercenaries followed the refusal of the British mercenary Mike Hoare to accept the Biafran offer for he wanted more money than Biafra was prepared to pay. Many of the French mercenaries quit when they discovered that the equipment needed for training the Biafrans was not forthcoming. By the summer of 1968 the French contingent had dwindled to five and by then it was apparent to the mercenaries that Biafran secession was doomed. In any case it was by then apparent that Biafra's compelling need was for pilots to ferry supplies to its only remaining airstrip at Ulli. Some of these supplies were in the form of humanitarian aid provided by such non-government organizations as Caritas, the World Council of Churches or the ICRC.

Before the main Federal onslaught on Biafra, Gen. Gowon issued a 'Code of Conduct' to his troops in which it was stressed that the Ibo people were not the enemy. At the same time it laid down that mercenaries 'will not be spared: they are the worst enemies'. The stated reluctance to employ mercenaries despite the fact that both sides did so was in part because senior Nigerian officers on either side in the civil war had formerly served with the United Nations in the Congo and had been up against mercenaries there. References to mercenaries almost always led to headlines in the African and Western press. When mercenaries were engaged the assumption was that they possessed military skills that the Federal or Biafran armies lacked; in the end this special advantage came down to pilots. Three kinds of mercenary were employed in the civil war: pilots on the Federal side; pilots and soldiers in Biafra; and relief pilots employed by the humanitarian organizations assisting Biafra. Combat mercenaries charged huge fees but gave poor returns and were rarely worth the money they were paid. The reputation of mercenaries suffered during this war. They were not seen as invincible forces; rather, man for man, the white soldier was no better than the black soldier although he wanted maximum pay while exposing himself to minimum risks. Disreputably, the mercenaries on the two sides engaged in a pact: the Federal pilots did not destroy Ulli airstrip, which they could have done, and avoided engaging with one another since they did not wish to forego their lucrative jobs. Their deliberate failure to destroy the Ulli airstrip greatly prolonged the war: 'Without Ulli Biafra would have collapsed in a matter of weeks, perhaps days'.[27] The French government actively supported the French mercenary role in Biafra, which was persuaded to use French mercenaries by Jacques Foccart, the French secret service chief, and it was his office that recruited Roger Faulques. Later in the war, when the French mercenaries had left, Biafra harmed its image by recruiting mercenaries from South Africa and Rhodesia. In real terms, whether in fighting or training, Biafra got very little value out of the mercenaries upon whom it spent vast sums of money, the greater part of which was wasted. Moreover, despite continuing support for mercenary activity, especially from France, they did little to retrieve the reputation that they had acquired in the Congo.[28]

A number of peace initiatives were mounted during the course of the war: by the United Nations, the OAU, the Commonwealth, Prime Minister Harold Wilson and the Vatican, but none succeeded in bringing an end to the fighting. The Nigerians had to find their own solution and this was only possible once the Federal Military Government had won the war. For any peace talks to take place, Gowon first insisted that Biafra should renounce secession. The OAU, under intense pressure from its members, insisted that peace had to be within the context of 'one Nigeria', which in the circumstances of a war fought for secession and later 'survival' was bound to be rejected by Biafra.

AN APPRAISAL OF THE WAR

At the time of the war and into the twenty-first century a recurring subject of debate in Africa and between Africa and Europe has been about the extent to which European colonialism can and should be blamed for Africa's post-independence problems. In 1968 Dame Margery Perham was the doyenne of British Africanists whose deep knowledge of and love for Africa, and particularly Nigeria, equipped her as a formidable critic. That year she wrote an important essay, *Nigeria's Civil War*[29], that provides a classic historical analysis of the background that made the war inevitable. It is worth examining this piece in depth not only for the light it sheds on Nigeria at that time but also because her arguments have much relevance to other aspects of post-independence Africa, both then and later. Dame Margery argues: 'It cannot be said, however, that the Nigerians rushed altogether recklessly into independence or that the British government wholly neglected to prepare them for it. For some ten years before 1960 there had been almost continuous argument and experiment, with conferences between British ministers and officials on one side, and Nigerian leaders of all parties and regions on the other, hammering out the lines upon which independence was to be achieved.' The author then examines how, in the nineteenth century, Britain expanded its trade, influence and ultimately its power from the coast into the interior.

In 1861 Britain annexed Lagos and made it a colony and from Lagos created a Protectorate of the Yoruba hinterland. East of Lagos Britain created the Oil Rivers protectorate to control the traders of the region and then granted a charter to the Niger Company under Sir George Goldie who became the first creator of what became the British Nigerian empire. Perham describes the historic differences between the Yoruba grouped within states based upon cities; and the Ibo isolated in their forest region who had prevented political organization above the family and clan level, and points out how the British tried and failed to create any form of chieftainship among them. The Niger Coast Protectorate was proclaimed in 1891. As Perham then says, though the Ibo were hard to organize, under the system of British control over the whole of what had become Nigeria, during the 1940s and 1950s they became the most active, Westernized group in Nigeria and 'streamed out of their poor and overcrowded land to employ their energies and their newly-gained skills and education in other parts of the protectorate'. The third major group of Nigerians were in the North where the open country and climate had encouraged the development of city states; they had also been open to Islam and influences from across the Sahara while a religious revival early in the nineteenth century had reinforced the influence of Islam. Lying between the North and the South were a number of pagan groups that formed what came to be called the Middle Belt of Nigeria.

In 1900 the British Government took over from the Niger Company, Lord Lugard was sent as administrator and over six years evolved the system of indirect rule. In 1906 the two contrasted southern regions were brought together and in 1914 Lugard returned to unite North and South. But, and this was the crucial event or non-event, 'This was a union of three British administrations rather than three populations.' There lay the key to what was to follow. For 30 or more years thereafter there was no British policy from above or African pressure from below to stimulate a real unity. Each of the three administrations worked separately from the other two and showed no urge to assimilate, while indirect rule in the North was carried to such an extreme as to preserve the differences between the Hausa-Fulani and the rest rather than help break them down. The result of this colonial approach was that the three peoples came to independence in different ways from different backgrounds and held little in common with one another. Unlike Tanzania where a range of tribes united in a single party, TANU, to demand independence from Britain, in Nigeria separate regionally based political parties were formed to fight for independence. The Yoruba under Awolowo formed the Action Group, yet even so divisions remained among their city states. The Ibo under Azikiwe formed a single democratic party, the National Council of Nigeria and the Cameroons (NCNC) (later the National Council of Nigerian Citizens). They wanted a unity that would allow them to migrate all over the region. Both the Southern parties saw the need to extend their influence outside their tribal bases. On the other hand, the Northern emirs, fearful of the more politically advanced Southerners, created a monolithic northern party, the Northern People's Congress (NPC). The result, as Macmillan perceived during his visit of January 1960, was a vast country that should not have been united at all; or, if it had to be united, this should have been done in a very different way to that which the British had pursued. Two of the three regions had to combine to form a government and in 1960 it was the North and East that did so, leaving Awolowo and his Action Group out in the cold. There was no natural affinity between the Northerners and the Ibos and this soon became apparent. As Perham says towards the end of her essay, 'The troubles, which broke out only two years after independence, were only a prelude. It was now dangerously clear that control of the federal centre and its finances would fall to the party, which in practice meant the region, with the majority of members. The census of 1962 not only recorded a population of 55.6 million… but placed 29.8 of these in the north, thus endowing it with a built-in majority over the other regions.' From that time onwards, unsurprisingly, a census in Nigeria was cause for controversy.

This historical prelude to the civil war should explain why there was much criticism of Britain then and later. The colonial system was about maintaining imperial control; it was not designed to create a nation. Margery Perham could be described as the British establishment 'radical' on African affairs at that time, yet as understanding as she was of African problems and developments and as clear and concise as is her analysis of Nigeria, she is never able, nor does she try, to explain why the British neither attempted nor intended to weld their multifaceted creation of Nigeria into a nation. Indeed, to do so, under the imperial system, would have been to create a nationalist force that would have proved irresistible long before 1960 and imperialism was not about such an approach. In her scrupulous account of how Britain united and yet kept Nigeria divided, Margery Perham lays bare the extent of British blame for the civil war. After reading such an analysis it becomes easier to understand the endless African diatribes against colonialism of the 1960s. At the end of the twentieth century thoughtful Africans could claim that many of the continent's problems still resulted from the colonial era. It may be an easy way out of current dilemmas to blame the colonial past just as the ex-colonial powers dismiss such claims as a sign of Africa's refusal to face present realities. But the debate cannot easily or quickly be made to disappear and the more we examine the decisions and policies of the colonial powers prior to independence, the more apparent it becomes that they have bequeathed to their former colonies an uneasy inheritance.

THE END OF THE WAR, NIGERIA REMAINS UNITED

By the beginning of 1969 the war had become curiously indecisive, a situation that led supporters of Biafra to argue, prematurely, that there could be no Federal victory. At the same time a rift had developed between the Federal field commanders and staff headquarters in Lagos with the former complaining that the latter were too complacent. By this stage in the war the strategy of the Federal Army, which in any case enjoyed huge superiority in numbers and arms, was to blockade the shrinking enclave of Biafra and bring about its surrender by starvation. Towards the end Biafra was confined to a small enclave of territory that was served by the single airstrip of Ulli to which supplies were brought by mercenary pilots. Over December 1969 and the first days of January 1970 the Federal Army deployed 120,000 troops for its final assault on Owerri and the Ulli airstrip. These fell to the Federal forces over 9–10 January and the war was over. At that stage the total strength of the Federal Army was 200,000 troops. Biafra, despite its handicaps, had demonstrated astonishing resilience: its propaganda had fostered the idea that surrender meant genocide, creating a fear that persuaded the Biafrans to fight almost to the end while, at the same time, engendering international sympathy and support. During the final year of the war Nigeria's foreign policy was hard pushed to prevent other countries following the four African states that had recognized Biafra, while strengthening Western and Soviet support in supplying its military requirements. Increased Soviet military supplies arrived in the country in October 1969 and this allowed the Federal Chief of Staff, Brig. Katsina, to announce in November that final orders had been issued to the Federal forces to liberate the remaining rebel-held areas. At the same time Gen. Gowon suggested that the end of the war was in sight and accused 'foreign meddlers' of having prolonged the crisis by using the pretext of providing humanitarian relief. The final assault on what remained of Biafra was launched on Christmas Day.

In a statement *Ibos in a United Africa Federal Policy* the Federal Government said: 'It must be stated quite clearly that the civil war has not been directed against the Ibos as a people but against an unpatriotic and rebellious clique. The Head of State, General Gowon, considers the unimpeded return of the Ibos into the Nigerian family the keystone of his policies and programmes.' With three million Ibos crowded into 1,500 square miles it was malnutrition and starvation that forced them to surrender, plus the increasing difficulty of obtaining ammunition. Even so, the Ibos had kept going with great ingenuity and endless expedients.

One of the most devastating civil wars in post-1945 history came to an abrupt end on 12 January 1970. On 10 January 1970 Lt-Col. Ojukwu handed over control to his Chief of Staff Lt-Col. Philip Effiong and fled to Côte d'Ivoire where he was accorded asylum. On 12 January Effiong instructed the Biafran forces to disengage. On 14 January the *New York Times* reported: 'Nigeria's future as a united nation and a respected member of the international community depends heavily on the compassion and wisdom displayed by her leaders in the wake of their military victory.' As Gen. Obasanjo, who led the final assault, was to say later: 'The task was honourably discharged by all Nigerians in form of relief, rehabilitation, reconstruction and reintegration, and success was accomplished, as in the civil war itself, to the amazement of friends and foes alike.' On 15 January at Dodan Barracks in Lagos, the headquarters of the Supreme Military Council, Lt-Col. Effiong signed the formal act of surrender and declared: 'We accept the existing administrative and political structure of the Federation of Nigeria. Biafra ceases to exist.'

The war, with its terrible suffering, had nevertheless kept Africa's largest black state intact. In the post-war period that followed, Gowon's greatest achievement was the way in which he presided over the reintegration of the defeated Ibos into the mainstream activities of Nigerian life. The war proved a traumatic affair for Africa as a whole; just as the continent was emerging from colonialism it was both daunting and humiliating to contemplate the possible collapse of Africa's largest and potentially most powerful state. The war provided comfort for the white racists in the south who could argue that independence merely brought chaos while it gave Nigerians pause to think at the readiness of the big powers to interfere in pursuit of interests that often had little to do with Nigeria's needs. Britain and the USSR were the two main sources of arms for the Federal Government while France was the principal source of arms for Biafra, supplied mainly through its proxy, Gabon. International observers were unanimous that the reports of genocide were unfounded, which provided a boost for Gowon and his policy of rehabilitating the Ibos. A unique aspect of this war was the high rate of success achieved by Biafran propaganda and the widespread belief it fostered in the West that the Federal Military Government was pursuing a policy of genocide although no proof was ever adduced in support of the claim. The war was prolonged unnecessarily by two factors: the Ibo belief, cultivated by its own propaganda, that genocide would follow surrender; and the part played by international charities, which continued to provide relief when otherwise Biafra would have been forced to surrender. The war became a cause for various charities whose propaganda 'to feed the starving Biafrans', however well intentioned, prolonged both the war and the extent of the suffering. Estimated casualties were 100,000 military (on both sides) and between 500,000 and two million civilians, mainly as a result of starvation, while 4.6 million Biafrans became refugees. In the end, 900 days of warfare had not destroyed Africa's largest black state, while Biafra's bid for secession and independence had failed.

West and
Equatorial Africa

The countries of West and Equatorial Africa (excluding the Congo and Nigeria, which have already been examined in chapters two and seven) are considered here as they faced their first decade of independence. The region covered is vast: the 17 countries of West Africa – Dahomey (later Benin), Upper Volta (later Burkina Faso), Cape Verde, Chad, Ivory Coast (Côte d'Ivoire), The Gambia, Ghana, Guinea, Portuguese Guinea (Guinea-Bissau), Liberia, Mali, Mauritania, Niger, Nigeria, Senegal, Sierra Leone and Togo – have a total area of 7,342,000 square kilometres (2,835,000 square miles). The countries of Equatorial Africa – Cameroon, Central African Republic, Congo (Brazzaville), Equatorial Guinea, Gabon and São Tomé and Principe – cover another 1,743,142 square kilometres (670,646 square miles) to make a grand total of 9,085,142 square kilometres (3,505,646 square miles), approximately the size of the United States. The two Portuguese territories of Cape Verde and Portuguese Guinea remained colonies throughout the decade while Spanish Guinea became independent as Equatorial Guinea in 1968. Half the population of these 23 countries resided in Nigeria. The estimated populations as at the end of the decade were as follows:

COUNTRY	POPULATION (,000)	DENSITY (sq.km.)[1]
Gambia, The	364	32
Ghana	9,026	38
Liberia	1,171	11
Sierra Leone	2,512	35
Nigeria	55,074	60
Dahomey	2,686	24
Guinea	3,921	16
Ivory Coast	4,310	13
Mali	4,438	4

Mauritania	1,171	1
Niger	4,016	3
Senegal	3,925	20
Togo	1,862	33
Upper Volta	5,384	20
Cameroon	5,836	12
Central African Republic	1,612	3
Chad	3,706	3
Congo (Brazzaville)	936	3
Gabon	500	2

'The great contrast in West Africa is between the southern forest zone and the northern savannah lands. The forest has here been the area of difficulty – difficult to penetrate and difficult to settle without the importation of alien food crops.'[2] Apart from this distinction, the vast size of some of these countries with their tiny populations made effective central government extremely difficult to exercise. In political terms the crucial factor setting immediate post-independence parameters for the whole region was the colonial background that had seen West Africa divided between the British and French. Most of this huge area had belonged to French West and French Equatorial Africa and almost all the Francophone states, the exceptions being Guinea and, for a time, Mali, maintained close post-independence relations with France, which was to keep military bases in Central African Republic, Gabon, Ivory Coast and (sometimes) Chad. Most of these states would also remain bound to France economically through the franc zone, which provided for the free movement of currency among its members and gave them a guaranteed franc exchange rate. Members of the franc zone were Dahomey, Upper Volta, Cameroon, Central African Republic, Chad, Congo (Brazzaville), Gabon, Ivory Coast, Mali, Niger, Senegal and Togo although Mali left the franc zone in 1962 to establish its own currency but was obliged to rejoin it in 1968. Guinea was punished for its intransigence in 1958 by being expelled and Mauritania also decided to leave.

The exceptions to France's dominance of the region were the British enclaves along the West African coast: Nigeria, the colossus of West Africa, Ghana, Sierra Leone and The Gambia; Liberia; Portuguese Guinea (later Guinea-Bissau), Cape Verde, São Tomé and Principe; and Spanish Equatorial Guinea consisting of Rio Muni and the island of Fernando Po. Any consideration of political problems and slow economic development must take account of the size of these territories related to their populations and their spread.

AN ECONOMIC OVERVIEW

It is impossible to over-emphasize the extent to which the pattern of economic development had already been set along lines favourable to the metropolitan powers prior to independence. This was not simply a question of the direction of trade but of who had been given control: 'In all the West African territories, with the exception of Guinea and possibly of Mali and Ghana, the colonial Power not only set a ceiling upon the economic potentialities of Africans but also largely determined who would be given access to political power... overall economic control remained in the hands of expatriates. The possession of political power was not the same as the possession of economic power.'[3] Moreover, the colonial governments were only prepared to hand over power on a territorial basis, within the frontiers that they themselves had once drawn on the map. During the 1960s almost all oppositions disappeared and by 1967 only Sierra Leone and The Gambia had legal oppositions and in those two cases they were totally ineffective. In general the new leaders played down tribalism as a threat to the new state. The real division, which quickly became apparent, was that between the new elites and the rest and already by the middle of the decade there were growing signs of popular disillusionment with the new rulers. Attempts to change the inherited patterns of trade were made especially by Ghana, Guinea and Mali but the more conservative states such as Nigeria also tried to alter the balance of their trade relations. The expatriate presence remained pervasive in government, educational and commercial levels for years after independence and in some cases was crucial to the smooth working of the state. There were considerable differences in the British and French approaches.

> British policy was on the whole pragmatic, able to accommodate both Kwame Nkrumah and the Sardauna of Sokoto and the very different parties they led. French policy was in contrast guided by doctrine and attempted to treat its possessions in West Africa as a whole. Both powers were, of course, attempting to ensure that any African leaders to whom they handed political power would be sympathetic to their long-term economic and strategic interests.[4]

By 1967, with the fall of Nkrumah, the collapse of Mali's independent economic experiment and Guinea entering a period of crisis, the West could relax for the would-be radicals were in disarray. Instead, moderate pro-Western leaders were in the ascendant: Presidents Houphouët-Boigny in the Ivory Coast or M'ba in Gabon were the guardians of French interests in the region while Gen. Ankrah had brought Ghana back into the Western capitalist fold. By this date, moreover, the process of aid-giving had been formalized and the rich countries were providing enough to 'buy off' the poor revolutionaries whose anti-Western instincts were reduced by a relatively small inflow of dollars, pounds or francs. More important for the future were the changes to its aid policy announced by the US Agency for International Development (USAID) in April 1967. Following the Korry report of the US Ambassador to Ethiopia, USAID decided, as far as possible, to co-ordinate its aid programmes with other donors through the international agencies such as the World Bank and the International Monetary Fund and either channel aid to the few countries that had the most favourable prospects (from a Western point of view) or concentrate on regional projects. This new policy signalled the rise of the international agencies as the arbiters of development in the Third World. The failure of the radical states to keep to their independent development paths and the growth of aid dependency suggested that few states in this whole vast region could be considered as economically viable.

The belief that a constant inflow of foreign investment was crucial to development was generated at this time and for small economies such investment becomes a far more significant planning factor than it does for larger ones. Most West African countries were also subject to export instability because they were mainly dependent upon primary exports of agricultural commodities or minerals while a large part of their import expenditure was on manufactures and services whose prices were less changeable than those of primary products. Although in the 1960s the GNP growth rate was fairly rapid and more or less in line with the growth of populations, this did not provide an accurate measure of developing wealth whether nationally or on a per capita basis. Agriculture, which accounted for 50 per cent of GDP in the region as a whole in 1960, had been reduced to less than 30 per cent by 1979 while industry – mining, manufacturing, construction and public utilities – had expanded from 15 to nearly 40 per cent although this was a lopsided picture resulting from the huge structural changes in Nigeria as a result of oil. In 1960 Nigeria contributed 45 per cent of West Africa's GDP but by 1979 this had risen to 70 per cent. As a general rule aid inflows were more than compensated for by net outflows. This is well summed up as follows: 'Some of the countries in the region, such as Upper Volta, dispose of more income nationally than they produce domestically. In others, like the Ivory Coast and Liberia, there are large net outflows of factor payments and current transfers, attributable to their employment of foreign owned capital and immigrant labour.'[5]

Although self-sufficiency in agriculture was generally accepted as desirable, many countries of the region faced rising import bills for food products that were the result of rising living standards and the demand for foods which could not be economically produced at home. A majority of staple exports were agricultural and while countries such as Ivory Coast were efficient producers of food commodities for export they were not similarly efficient in substituting for the rising list of food imports. Throughout the 1960s and into the 1970s the composition of exports, agricultural commodities and minerals, did not change very much for most West African countries. Only Nigeria with its rapidly expanding oil industry provided a major exception to this rule. Thus, in 1960 Nigeria's main exports were cocoa, groundnuts and palm produce, which together accounted for 80 per cent of exports. By 1980 they had been reduced to only 2.5 per cent. What did persist throughout these years was the huge differential in pay made to expatriates and Africans working in comparable formalized employment. The Francophone economies were far smaller than the two leading Anglophone economies in 1960 when Nigerian exports accounted for 36 per cent of total West African exports while Ghana came next with 22 per cent.

Aid at this period probably made less impact upon the economies of West Africa than it did upon education or health programmes although most countries were acquiring all the techniques necessary to impress would-be donors with their needs. Even then, unfortunately, the belief that aid was essential to development had been implanted in the thinking of the political elites and the consequent debt trap was a rapidly growing problem. Donor governments, with occasional exceptions, used their aid programmes for political purposes: to repay debts, to undermine political (which generally meant radical) opposition and to maintain behind the scenes political controls and more overt economic ones. Aid was not in fact given either to relieve poverty or to reduce inequality. The concept of aid was closely aligned to the idea that foreign direct investment was crucial to development although at least one economist rejected this approach: 'The doctrine that investment governs growth is both unhistorical and, from a strictly economic standpoint, untheoretical. It survives not only because of intellectual conservatism, but also because commercial interests are entrenched in flows of government contracts and international aid.'[6] Aid and the commercial interests of the donors went hand in hand from the beginning.

The United Nations was becoming increasingly concerned with the rapid increases in population then taking place in many countries of the Third World. Such increases were seen as an added burden upon small developing economies and development assistance had to take predicted increases into account. However, an altogether different view of population growth is given by the economist Douglas Rimmer: 'Increase of population through maintenance or increase of a rate of fertility in face of falling infant and child mortality rates may be a source of values far greater, to those personally concerned, than any loss sustained in economic output averaged per head.'[7] In fact, the growth of population was not a matter of great concern in West Africa at this time. Of far greater importance was the growing migration of job seekers and those wishing to improve their general standard of living from the rural to the urban areas. They swelled the ranks of the urban unemployed, caused labour shortages in the rural areas, and strained resources, which were used to deal with social problems at the expense of productive investment. Such problems did not prevent the rural exodus. The towns attracted the rural migrants for sound social reasons: they offered greater educational opportunities and health care, as well as greater availability of electricity, water and sanitation and such opportunities, as primitive as they might be, were still better than anything that was available in the rural areas.

Assessments of development are too often and too readily determined by figures for GDP growth yet parallel developments are as important. In West Africa during the 1960s there were significant advances in education and these are reflected in figures for educational enrolments over the years 1960 to 1979. Between those years enrolments as a whole rose from approximately 4.8 million in 1960 to 16.4 million in 1977: that is, a 30 to 60 per cent increase in primary enrolment, and a 3 to 12 per cent increase in secondary enrolment. Primary enrolment over this period increased from 4.6 million to 14.1 million; secondary enrolment from 200,000 to over 2 million; teachers in training from 37,000 to 159,000; and students in higher education from 6,000 to 117,000. Much of this increase was in Nigeria where, in 1960, primary school enrolments stood at 2.9 million, secondary enrolments (including trainee teachers) at 160,000 and students in higher education at 3,000. Official Nigerian statistics for 1978–79 showed the new figures to be 11.5 million, 1.5 million and 108,000 respectively while projected primary enrolment then stood at 17 million for 1984–85.[8]

GHANA AND THE NKRUMAH FACTOR

We have already seen Nkrumah the political visionary pushing for African unity; at home, however, the story was different. 'Inside Ghana his slogan was "Seek ye first the political kingdom". He was quick to seize and hold power, but he was far too impatient and dogmatic for the hard slog of day-to-day government. His regime, born of naïve idealism, sank into single-party authoritarianism. He ruined the Ghana economy as his grandiose foreign policy initiatives collapsed one by one.'[9] Constantly and foolishly Nkrumah managed to upset other African leaders. He broke up various West African joint boards such as the West African Airways Board, which he considered to be relics of colonialism. Other more pragmatic West African states such as Nigeria saw these boards as a means of fostering closer regional union. In part Nkrumah's huge influence in both West Africa and beyond had arisen as a result of Ghana's independence ahead of other colonies in the region (and that was certainly his own achievement) but when in 1960 a further 14 West African countries became independent the balance had changed and other leaders, who wished for their own limelight, were not content to live in his shadow and 'While he had from the first offered to surrender part of Ghana's sovereignty in the cause of African unity, few others were ready to give up any vestige of their newly won independence, and regarded Nkrumah's claims for African unity with suspicion'.[10] Even so, Ghana was to continue in the role of mouthpiece for the genuinely independent African states for some time after 1960 and there was at least some truth in Nkrumah's claim that the Francophone states were puppets of France, which continued to provide 80 per cent of their budgets. As all his overtures for unity were repulsed – Nkrumah offered aid in turn to Mali, Guinea, Upper Volta in part at least to induce them to support his unity plans – he became increasingly isolated. He met the nadir of his unity hopes during the OAU Summit Conference at the end of July 1964 in Cairo. On that occasion when he had argued that only a Union Government of Africa could guarantee the African's survival, his concept of African unity was demolished by President Nyerere of Tanzania. Nyerere had once translated Julius Caesar into Swahili and on this occasion he used Mark Anthony's technique in his funeral oration over Caesar, periodically referring to 'the great Osagyefo' (the title meaning Redeemer that Nkrumah had begun to apply to himself) and then pulling apart Nkrumah's arguments. Nyerere rather than Nkrumah had the support of the majority of the OAU and the occasion must have been a humiliating one for Nkrumah.

In any case, by then, the tide was turning against Nkrumah in Ghana itself. There had been an assassination attempt on him at Kulungugu in August 1962 and the trial of the three principal suspects had lasted for more than a year. The pro-Nkrumah press had assumed a conviction but at the end of 1963 the Chief Justice, Sir Arku Korsah, handed down a verdict of not guilty. Nkrumah reacted angrily by dismissing the Chief Justice and pushing a bill through the Assembly to give the President (himself) the power, in the national interest, to set aside any judgment in the country's courts. Huge protests, from both within and outside Ghana, followed and many erstwhile friends assumed that he was now intent on setting up a dictatorship. By 1965 it seemed that everything was going wrong for Nkrumah: there had been two assassination attempts, his state enterprises were failing, there were growing pressures from the left, he was in urgent need of Western aid for the completion of the giant Volta Dam project and his overtures were constantly rejected by other African leaders. One of his last constructive acts, which gained him prestige in Africa, was his suggestion at the Commonwealth Summit of 1965 in London that a secretariat should be created – and this was adopted. He also managed to have the question of UDI in Rhodesia (declared on 11 November 1965) brought before the Security Council. Despite these positive achievements Nkrumah continued in the face of the rest of African opinion to insist that everything that went wrong did so because there was no union government for the continent. In fact Africa faced more mundane problems at the time, most notably those connected with the establishment of sound government. In his last attempt to play a major role on the world stage, Nkrumah left Ghana on 21 February 1966 for China and Hanoi on a peacekeeping mission for Vietnam. The effort was doomed to failure for the day after his departure the Ghanaian Army carried out a coup and seized power.

Nkrumah was derided after his fall and his enemies, who were many, proceeded to tear his reputation apart. His impact, nonetheless, had been profound: in Ghana as the architect of independence; in Africa as the (ultimately rejected) idealist; and in the West as a dangerous radical, not because he turned to the Communists but because he refused to be subservient to Western interests. Indeed, Western paranoia about Nkrumah was demonstrated by the lengths to which the West, led by the CIA, went to get rid of him. The ex-CIA agent John Stockwell, testifies to this in his book *In Search of Enemies* in which he says, 'The CIA station in Ghana played a major role in the overthrow of Kwame Nkrumah in 1966...'[11], while a detailed investigation by *West Africa* in 2001 revealed the extent of the Western conspiracy to destroy him.[12] A different kind of judgement about Nkrumah was made by John Hatch, a main-line member of the British Labour Party, who said: 'Since independence, Ghana has on several occasions been the butt of hostile criticism in the British press. Much of this has been malicious, expressed by the same people who have never been reconciled to accepting Indians or other non-whites as full and equal members of the Commonwealth.'[13] Nkrumah's determination to throw off the post-independence shackles of a reluctantly departing imperialism made him many enemies, including African ones who were content to allow such shackles to remain if they kept them in power. As another commentator put it: 'Since the fall of Nkrumah in Ghana in 1966, less had been heard of European interference in African affairs, and more of inadequate European support for Africa.'[14]

Whatever the long-term judgements of Nkrumah's impact, he managed during the first half of the 1960s to bring the Ghana economy close to a standstill. Ghana had been one of the first countries to develop a cash economy that was based on a wide distribution of wealth through the production of cocoa on small farms. However, something like two-fifths of Ghana's imports over the years 1961–65 were financed by the depletion of reserves or by commercial credit and when the coup was mounted against Nkrumah in February 1966 the country faced short-term external debts of US$112 million and medium-term debts of a further US$423 million. The troubled politics of Ghana during the first half of the 1960s and the parlous state of the economy that resulted illustrate, as in few other cases, how politics that take an economic base for granted will erode or ruin that base no matter how sound it may have been. Few African countries had achieved independence with a better economic outlook than Ghana which then had accumulated reserves of £200 million in London; it was the world's largest producer of cocoa and a significant producer of coffee, palm kernels, copra and bananas for export.

Nkrumah's ambition to modernize the Ghana economy was on a parallel with that of Nasser in Egypt; his great project was the Volta Dam. Officially known as the Akosombo dam, the Volta River Dam was completed in 1965. It had an especial importance because it was regarded as an early example of the new approach to development that was being promoted at that time: the concept of massive development projects that would enable newly independent countries to break old (colonial) economic patterns and achieve economic take-off. The dam had been conceived at the time of Ghana's independence, pushed by Nkrumah and jointly financed by Ghana, the World Bank, the United States and Britain. The dam created Lake Volta, one of the largest man-made lakes in the world with a capacity of 148,000 million cubic metres. The lake changed the ecology of much of Ghana and created a new and extensive fishing industry. The Volta Aluminium Company (VALCO), a joint US venture with very extensive US and Ghana Government aid, built a smelter in Ghana to which bauxite from the United States or the West Indies was to be transported instead of using Ghana's own 200 million ton bauxite resource or bauxite from neighbouring Guinea. Furthermore, US loans for the project were provided on condition that the power made available to VALCO was low-cost. Ghana, which had provided half the capital, expected to repay the loan out of power sales. Interestingly, Nkrumah failed to see that the deal illustrated all the characteristics of neo-colonialism that he so readily decried in other areas. Ghana, it is true, gained the necessary capital and technical input for the construction of the hydro-electric project that would provide power for the national grid and agriculture, and the lake for irrigation, fisheries and transport. On the other hand it had to agree that the VALCO smelter could use imported alumina and also guarantee that total taxes should not be increased over a substantial period and that there should be full convertibility of all net profits for 30 years. These conditions made full Ghanaian control impossible and represented a high price to pay for the dam. 'Nothing could more clearly demonstrate the precautions taken by international firms to ensure that control of the total productive process should never be entrusted to one of the new states – nor better illustrate the need for regional planning in Africa itself.'[15]

FRANCOPHONE WEST AFRICA

In 1958 Guinea represented the extreme nationalist wing of French African politics and Sekou Touré's brave statement 'It will fall to us to preserve, for Guinea and for Africa, the honour of African man... We shall vote "No" to a community which is merely the French union re-christened... We shall vote "No" to inequality' had to be paid for and the price was to be a high one. Guinea at a stroke lost its main overseas market in France and had to turn for help to a reluctant USSR. Traditional agriculture accounted for just under half the GDP and still accounted for 43 per cent in 1976 but luckily Guinea possessed 30 per cent of the world's known bauxite reserves as well as iron ore and diamonds. During the 1960s it concentrated upon rapid development of its power potential for the mining sector; otherwise, its manufacturing base was small. Having rejected French patronage, Touré was forced to go it alone. He was both a radical and a Marxist and became a leading exponent of the one-party state and the cult of personality (his own). Although he was famous in Africa for his stand against de Gaulle, at home he became unchallenged political leader but only as the result of increasing oppression. In his first speech after independence Touré asked citizens to spy on each other. He suppressed liberty of information while private newspapers and radios were banned and citizens had to declare the extent of their wealth. His socialist policies ensured that little foreign capital was available for investment and the economy declined. He 'discovered' a number of plots against himself during the decade and used these to eliminate his opponents while also blaming France, the Ivory Coast and Senegal for fomenting discontent. By the end of the 1960s his dictatorship had reached its zenith but he had driven 500,000 of his people into exile and lost the confidence of the rest.

Neighbouring Mali was the third of the radical states of West Africa (with Ghana and Guinea). In April 1959 Mali joined briefly with Senegal in a Federation, which became independent on 20 June 1960. However, Senegal seceded two months later and the Republic of Mali was proclaimed on 22 September 1960. The new President, Modibo Keita, rapidly established a one-party state that accorded him full presidential powers. He tried to create a socialist economy in a country that geographically was huge and landlocked and had a tiny population most of whose people were subsistence farmers. There were some minerals but these were not exploited since they were small in quantity and in remote parts of the country. By mid-1966 the disbursement of foreign loans had reached the alarming figure of US$120 million, nearly equivalent to a third of the GDP, so that the country was accumulating huge debt service obligations for the future. Keita was obliged to come to terms with the non-socialist world he had hoped to eschew when in 1967 he felt compelled to renegotiate entry to the franc zone, which he had left in 1962. Leaving aside any shortcomings on the part of Keita, the abandonment of his socialist path was dictated by the fact that Mali's economic base was so small and weak that it precluded effective independence of action.

Senegal was France's oldest black colony and its capital Dakar had been the military and administrative headquarters of French West Africa. Leopold Senghor had opposed the constitutional changes introduced with the *loi cadre* of 1956, which had established local government for the constituent colonies of French West Africa but not for the region as a whole. This prevented the creation of a federation – something opposed by the influential Houphouët-Boigny of the Ivory Coast – and in effect meant the balkanization of the whole French territory. Senghor had favoured the unity of French West Africa and some form of federation that would have given it real bargaining power after independence and in this respect he was closer to Nkrumah than most other Francophone leaders. Because of its administrative role under France, Senegal was one of the most developed of the French territories at independence and its commercial and manufacturing sectors allowed it to compete with Ivory Coast, though both countries were heavily dependent upon agriculture as the source of their wealth. However, Senegal's strategic situation had always been more important than its economic wealth and Dakar was one of the best ports in Africa and served the hinterland beyond Senegal. One of the most interesting of the new leaders, Senghor was a writer and poet, the proponent of the idea of negritude and deeply influenced by his love of France. His failure to establish a federation meant that Senegal lost the advantages of its former administrative role for the region and had to fall back upon an economy largely dependent upon the production and export of groundnuts, although it also had the most important textile industry in French black Africa. Senegal briefly joined with its neighbour in the short-lived Federation of Mali but this did not work out. Thereafter, Senghor worked with the Brazzaville Group of moderate countries and restored his relations with Houphouët-Boigny which had become strained over the argument about a federation.

The richest of the Francophone West African territories at independence was Ivory Coast whose agriculture and fisheries were the source of its wealth; exports included coffee, wood, cocoa, bananas, cotton and pineapples and in contrast to Ghana, where economic and political neglect allowed its vital cocoa sector to decline, Ivory Coast by good management would later replace Ghana as the leading cocoa exporter. The economy had grown rapidly over the years 1950 to 1960 although the manufacturing and mining sectors remained insignificant on any continental reckoning. Félix Houphouët-Boigny who ruled Ivory Coast from independence in 1960 to his death in 1993 was one of the most influential figures in Francophone Africa. 'The architect of the Brazzaville and so of the Monrovia bloc, his policy is the antithesis of Dr Nkrumah's, canvassing the close co-operation of independent African states instead of their federation or union.'[16] Towards the end of his long rule Houphouët-Boigny was to be criticized for his extraordinary extravagance in building a vast basilica at Yamoussoukro but he always insisted upon a show to support the dignity of his office and the extravagance of the Presidential Residence in Abidjan shocked many outsiders and Africans in 1961 when they entered it although 'an Ivorian journalist who inspected the palace on the day after the big reception, exclaimed: "My God, anyone could live here – the Queen of England, President Kennedy. It makes me feel thrilled to be an Ivory Coast citizen."'[17] Houphouët-Boigny had served as a cabinet minister in France for 13 years before he became President of Ivory Coast and was equally at home in France as in Africa. In his pragmatic way he gave Ivory Coast stability and growth. He was always pro-French and pro-West and totally opposed to Nkrumah's concept of African Union. Writing at the beginning of the 1960s Ronald Segal provides an accurate vignette of this extraordinary man: 'Indeed, if a bloc of modern African states exists, pro-Western and maintaining close political and economic links with France, Houphouët-Boigny is more than anyone else responsible. His history is the history of France's *rapprochment* with Africa, and his policies constitute an alternative to the vigorous African nationalism of the Casablanca states.'[18]

Dahomey (later Benin) as we have seen experienced no less than six coups in the first 12 years of independence although, happily, these were bloodless. They resulted from the economic difficulties the country suffered during these years and the hope, unfulfilled, that a new government would be better able to balance the budget than its predecessor. More than the other countries of French West Africa, Dahomey suffered from the break up of the federation and 'never recovered from this balkanization, for not only were the years which followed to show the difficulty both of improving agriculture and industrializing this little state, but also the return of the Beninians who had been expelled from other territories was to make more difficult the proper management of public finance'.[19] The economy was overwhelmingly dependent upon agriculture with only tiny manufacturing and mining sectors. Like the rest of the region its principal markets were in Europe.

Togo had been split under the mandate system of the League of Nations between Britain and France and at independence in 1960 the British mandated territory was joined to Ghana. An agricultural economy, Togo's staple exports were cocoa and coffee. Mining and the export of its substantial deposits of phosphates began in 1961. The first six years of independence were politically troubled and the country only achieved greater stability under Col. Etienne Gnassingbé Eyadéma who came to power by means of a coup on 13 January 1967. By that time the coup had become the most familiar means of changing governments in West Africa.

Like Togo, the former German colony of Cameroon had been divided under the mandate system of the League of Nations between Britain and France. Following independence in 1960 and the subsequent integration of Southern Cameroons, the British Trusteeship territory, into the new state (the other British section of the country, Northern Cameroons, elected to join Nigeria) the new Federal Republic of Cameroon emerged on 1 October 1961. French Cameroon, consisting of 166,489 square miles of territory with a population of 3,225,000 people, was by far the larger, dominant part of the new state; the former British Southern Cameroons covered only 16,581 square miles and had a population of 814,000 people. The President, Ahmadou Ahidjo, began the task of political and economic integration and between 1961 and 1971 federal services were expanded in the English and French states with greater federal responsibilities in particular for education, economic planning, finance, transportation and agriculture. In addition, most of the existing political parties were merged in the *Union Nationale Camerounaise* (UNC), though not until 1966 when President Ahidjo felt strong enough to carry through this measure, and then he made himself president of the new party. At this time Cameroon had one of the more diversified economies of Africa while also providing sea communications for landlocked Chad and Central African Republic. Though agriculture provided the economic base Cameroon possessed a wider manufacturing sector than most West African countries and during the 1960s and 1970s was to meet 50 per cent of its manufactured requirements from internal production. Ahidjo inherited a nation divided racially, ethnically and by language and for two decades he concentrated on securing control by centralization and by boosting the importance of the single ruling party and his own presidential powers. He was largely successful in this aim but at the price of curtailing civil liberties, individual rights and the freedom of the press. Ahidjo pursued a pro-Western and especially pro-French foreign policy and maintained a mixed economy in order to attract foreign investment. 'He created a quiescent "stable" state in which private enterprise, foreign capital and the economy as a whole was able to flourish.'[20]

Gabon, which became independent in 1960, was very much the creation of Leon M'ba. In 1952 he had gained election to the territorial assembly and in 1953 he reorganized the *Mouvement Mixte Gabonais* and turned it into the *Bloc Démocratique Gabonais* (BDG), which remained the local division of the *Rassemblement Démocratique Africain* (RDA). In 1956 he became mayor of Libreville. M'ba was a strong supporter of Houphouët-Boigny and like him opposed a federal structure for French West Africa at independence and favoured, instead, each country preserving its own system and maintaining its own links with France, a policy that was appreciated in Paris. In 1958 Gabon had voted unanimously for autonomy within the French Community rather than for complete independence; when in 1960, like the rest of French West Africa, Gabon became fully independent, M'ba became the country's first president. M'ba was conservative in his policies and very pro-France whose African policies he served well. He was consistent in his opposition to any form of federalism and, moreover, discouraged all links among the independent states of Equatorial Africa that went beyond loose economic and military co-operation. The population of the country was a mere 500,000 at independence and when in 1964 a coup temporarily toppled M'ba from power France intervened militarily to restore him. Most of the country's agriculture was at the subsistence level and the economy depended upon the exploitation of Gabon's rich mineral resources and its forest products. Minerals included petroleum (Gabon became a member of the Organization of the Petroleum Exporting Countries), uranium and manganese export of which during the 1960s gave the country one of the highest per capita incomes on the continent. There were also huge iron ore deposits at Mekambo in the interior but exploitation had to await the construction of the Trans-Gabonais railway. When M'ba died in March 1967 he was succeeded by his young Vice-President and firm supporter Albert-Bernard Bongo who continued his policies and close alliance with France. Bongo believed that private enterprise provided the right answer for Gabon's development and adopted the slogan: 'Give me a sound economy and I will give you stable politics.'

Gabon's neighbour, the Republic of Congo (Brazzaville), was more developed though far poorer than Gabon. Its greatest asset was the Congo River on which the capital Brazzaville was situated to serve as a port and junction for traffic using the Ubangui and Congo rivers. The other major city, Pointe Noire on the Atlantic, was also a port and the services these two ports provided made a significant contribution to the country's GDP. Brazzaville had been the administrative centre of French Equatorial Africa and the dissolution of this federation faced Congo with a difficult period of adjustment. The country's first President, Abbé Fulbert Youlou, soon made himself unpopular with his pro-

Western policies and support for Moïse Tshombe's secession in Katanga. Prior to independence Youlou had proposed a Union of Central African Republics but negotiations broke down because of Gabon's reluctance to sacrifice its economic strength to a federation. In 1963, following a confrontation with the unions and a general strike, Youlou resigned on 15 August. The army maintained order until a new constitution had been devised which established a two-man executive comprising the President and the Prime Minister. The new President was Alphonse Massamba-Debat and his Prime Minister was Pascal Lissouba. The country moved sharply to the left politically, away from its colonial inheritance, and began to follow more radical, revolutionary paths of development. Apart from palm products, sugar and tobacco, most agricultural production came from small farms. Minerals did not become important until the 1970s. There was an unsuccessful coup attempt in 1966 but in 1968 the army effectively became the supreme authority and the soldier Marien Ngouabi became head of state. He continued the radical policies of Massamba-Debat.

The third French Equatorial African territory was Central African Republic, which was almost exactly in the centre of the continent. With an area of 238,000 square miles it was slightly larger than France although supporting a mere 1.2 million people at independence. Before independence Central African Republic had been dominated politically by Barthelemy Boganda who, unfortunately, was killed in an air crash in 1959. David Dacko then became leader of the ruling *Mouvement pour l'Evolution Sociale de l'Afrique Noire* (MESAN) and subsequently President in 1960. In 1962 Dacko told the National Assembly that the country should dispense with the French subsidy to the budget because every year receipts had exceeded expenditure and the favourable balance of £575,000 was greater than the usual French subvention. Apart from diamonds the country's wealth came from cotton, coffee and cattle. Dacko soon followed the growing number of precedents elsewhere on the continent to make Central African Republic a one-party state. At independence Dacko had asked Jean-Bédel Bokassa, who had fought for the Free French and risen to the rank of captain in the French Army in Indo-China, to create a Central African Army. This Bokassa did successfully to become Commander-in-Chief in 1963 and Chief of General Staff in 1964. When in 1966 Dacko faced opposition while he attempted to prune his corrupt, overpaid civil service whom he accused of 'negligence, corruption, even sabotage' Bokassa stepped in to seize power on New Year's Eve 1966. He imprisoned Dacko, abrogated the constitution and made himself President. His coup led to immediate poor relations with France. Bokassa's only real consideration, it soon became clear, was to perpetuate his own rule.

The last of the small French West African territories that became independent in 1960 was Upper Volta: impoverished and landlocked, it had a larger population than its richer neighbour Ivory Coast and its economy was almost entirely based upon agriculture. The first President of Upper Volta was Maurice Yameogo, a political lightweight who had to play a balancing act between the pressures exerted by his more powerful neighbours, the radical Nkrumah of Ghana and the conservative Houphouët-Boigny of Ivory Coast.

Four giant French territories were Mauritania, Mali, Niger and Chad whose combined area covered 4,821,300 square kilometres (only a little short of 2 million square miles) stretching from the Atlantic (Mauritania) to Sudan (Chad). In 1960 their combined populations came only to 13,331,000 people, averaging three to the square kilometre. Extending from the Sahara southwards through the Sahel region to the richer savannah country of the south and divided between Arab or nomadic Tuareg peoples in the north and sedentary black Africans in the south they could hardly be described as nations at all. It is simply that the laws of imperial expansion had persuaded the French to move into this huge 'empty quarter' during the nineteenth-century Scramble for Africa and work out subsequently how to divide and administer the territories. Mauritania with just over one million people at independence was by population the smallest state of French West Africa and consisted largely of desert which, in any case, was claimed by Morocco; most of the 1960s were to pass before Morocco admitted Mauritania's right to exist as an independent state. Moktar Ould Daddah, the country's first President, turned Mauritania into a one-party state in 1967. At least Mauritania had large mineral resources in the form of 100 million tons of iron ore and rapid development of this after independence gave the people one of the higher per capita incomes of the region. Mali (see above), with Ghana and Guinea, was for a time one of the three radical states of the region. Niger, slightly larger than Mali, was the second largest of all the West African states though with only three people to the square kilometre as opposed to Nigeria's 60. Over a million of its people were Hausa and enjoyed close cross-border relations with the people of Northern Nigeria. Niger was – and remains – one of the poorest countries in the world; two-thirds of it is desert and large areas in the northeast uninhabitable. The economy is based upon traditional agriculture and the rearing of livestock although important uranium deposits gave it strategic importance, especially at independence during the height of the Cold War.

The most remote of these four countries, and one of the most remote in all Africa, is Chad. Covering 495,000 square miles its population was under three million at independence. The country suffered from poor communications both internally and with its neighbours while its centres of economic development lay between 1,400 and 2,800 kilometres from the sea. The vast northern region was mainly desert inhabited by a sparse population of Arab nomads; the south was more advanced under black Africans. There were longstanding historical tensions between north and south, the northerners having traditionally raided the south for slaves. The economy depended upon livestock in the north and east and the cultivation of cotton in the south and economic survival depended upon continuing French aid after 1960. It had the least developed industrial sector of Equatorial Africa. The *Parti Progressiste Tchadien* (PPT) became the local branch of the RDA and formed the first African government after elections in 1957. Francois Tombalbaye became the leader of the party in 1959 and the country's first President in 1960.

It is one of the ironies of the African story that this huge harsh bleak under-populated land, a vacuum seized by the colonial French, should have witnessed a quarter of a century of civil war from the mid-1960s to the late 1980s. The war witnessed three occasions when France sent in troops to support the south; old territorial claims between France and Italy, dating from the 1930s, were resuscitated by Libya's Gaddafi to the 50,000 square mile Aozou Strip in the north (it contained rich deposits of uranium); and US financial support was provided to ensure that Gaddafi did not succeed in his designs. Like other Sahel countries, Chad suffered from the problem of land divided between a black, 'Christian' south (in this case the most prosperous section of the population) and a poorer north, which was mainly inhabited by nomadic, Arab or Arabicized peoples who were Muslims. In 1962 President Tombalbaye took steps to turn the country into a one-party state under the PPT, and though representatives of both groups – southerners and northerners – were members, Tombalbaye was its dominant force. A French garrison had remained in the north of Chad at independence, but in 1964 these French troops were withdrawn to be replaced by elements of the Chad national army, which soon became embroiled in local disputes. Although the one-party state was accepted in the south, this was not the case in the north. A first revolt, partly in reaction to heavy taxes, took place in 1966 at Ouaddai and was supported from across the Sudanese border. This and other early rebellions were haphazard: in part against taxation and the southern civil service, and in part the result of long-standing northern suspicion of and antipathy to the people of the south. Gradually the northern rebels organized themselves and formed the *Front de Libération Nationale du Tchad* (FROLINAT) (Chad Liberation Front) in 1966. Frolinat became the spearhead of a revolt, which up to that time had been sporadic and without obvious purpose. The situation was complicated in 1966 when an anti-government revolt occurred in the south at Salamat, while in the far north the Toubou nomads, acting as government guards at Aozou, mutinied in sympathy with northern aspirations. The first leader of FROLINAT, Dr Abba Siddick, was soon replaced by Goukouni Oeddei, who introduced another factor into the war when he turned to Libya for support. In 1968 the French air force transported government troops to Aozou, then in 1969 1,600 French troops were sent to Chad in support of Tombalbaye. The number was reduced in 1971 and the troops were removed altogether in 1972 without having made much difference to the growing power of FROLINAT, which at that stage was undefeated. By the beginning of the 1970s the war was set to continue for two decades.

THE NON-FRENCH TERRITORIES OF WEST AFRICA

A number of tiny enclaves along the West African coast had been seized as strategic footholds by the British and Portuguese: these included Sierra Leone and The Gambia, and Portuguese Guinea (later the independent state of Guinea-Bissau). The exception was Liberia. Liberia had been founded by American philanthropists for freed slaves and had become independent in 1847. In 1960, after more than a century of independence for most of which time it had been ruled by the True Whig Party, Liberia had a population of 1.5 million people and an economy dominated by the export of iron ore and rubber. In 1943 William Tubman, who came from an old Americo-Liberian family, became President. A natural conservative, he refused to join the Ghana–Guinea Union of 1958, favouring instead a loose confederation of West African states. Tubman was to rule Liberia until his death in 1971 and despite his insistence on state occasions of dressing in a black morning coat and top hat pushed Liberia into the modern era. He gave all Liberians the vote for the first time and began the difficult task of eliminating the distinctions between the Afro-Americans of Monrovia and the Africans of the hinterland. There had been little development in Liberia before Tubman came to power, so he introduced a series of five-year plans and opened the country to foreign investment with his 'open door policy' which led to rapid economic growth and a big increase in government revenues (these had amounted to only US$2 million in 1944 but had reached US$200 million by 1971). Concessions to foreign companies led to an improvement in the country's technical and social infrastructure but otherwise did little for general economic development. Even so, under Tubman the first deep-water port was opened at Freeport and the iron ore port at Buchanan while arterial roads and a power grid were extended nationally and better education and health services were introduced. Tubman played a leading role in rallying the moderates – the Monrovia Group – as opposed to the radical Casablanca Group at the beginning of the 1960s and with Haile Selassie of Ethiopia helped formulate the principles of the OAU.

Sierra Leone, founded by British philanthropists for former slaves, represented the early stirring of British unease at the slave trade from which the country had long profited. After achieving independence in 1961 it passed through a troubled decade that saw the emergence of different layers of military coup-makers. Its economy depended upon alluvial diamonds, a large proportion of which were illegally smuggled out of the country, and iron ore. The Gambia, stretching like an attenuated finger into Senegal, between 13 and 30 miles wide and 300 miles long on both banks of the Gambia River, is a geographic absurdity, part of the fragmentation of the continent carried out by the European colonialists. Dawda Jawara became the Prime Minister of this tiny state in 1963 when it achieved self-government and remained so after full independence in 1965, only turning The Gambia into a republic in 1970. Jawara followed constitutional practices and won successive elections at the polls. Portuguese Guinea descended into a long liberation war during the 1970s and this was only resolved in 1974. One other tiny territory in this region was Spanish Equatorial Guinea, which became independent in 1968.

PARTY POLITICS

Although the military coup emerged as the most popular basis for a new government in West Africa over these years, political activity in the region had a long history. A myth, carefully fostered by the colonial powers, grew up in the post-war era that only after 1945, affected by the momentous changes taking place world-wide, did the colonial peoples of Africa begin to demand independence. Political agitation against the colonial system went back much further although mass voting, which is the necessary basis for a fully effective political party, came only after 1945. Moreover, as the new generation of nationalist politicians such as Kwame Nkrumah soon realized, whoever got in first reaped the harvest, for the one certain basis for mass support was opposition to continued colonial control: this hostility to the existing colonial system was as widespread as its companion enthusiasm for self-rule. As demands for independence grew so too did Western alarm that the successor governments to colonialism would turn to the new model of Communism, for Western thinking at this time was dominated by Cold War calculations. As Houphouët-Boigny, the most pro-Western of emerging leaders, is reputed to have said: 'If you send your son to the University of Paris he comes back a communist, but if you send him to the University of Moscow he comes back a conservative.'[21]

Parties could break down political apathy but to do so they had to establish cells in every town and village and create a flow of information both ways: that is, from the leadership to the people and in return from the rank and file to the leaders. Although political parties did do this – or try to do it – by the beginning of the 1960s only those in Mali and Guinea were still making serious efforts to keep close touch with the rank and file. More ominously for genuine party politics, 'Ghana's party pays lip service to this objective, but does not really try. The parties have agents all over the country, but their job is to keep the populace in line, rather than to stimulate discussion and transmit opinion upwards.'[22] Arthur Lewis, the eminent West Indian economist and political commentator, who made this judgement, was perfectly correct, but what he did not do was draw a parallel with such behaviour in the new states of Africa and similar behaviour in the old democracies of the West. Over the 40 years from that time to the end of the twentieth century a stream of criticisms of African political behaviour have been made from outside the continent as though Africa is a showcase of bad political behaviour unrelated to patterns that exist elsewhere. Political parties in multiparty systems may pay lip service to the need for opposition but they always try to hold onto power as long as possible. In the Africa of the 1960s where the departing colonial powers left behind multiparty systems even though for their own purposes they had put their support behind a particular party and its leadership, the party that held power at independence had an opportunity which would not recur to consolidate its position on the once-off basis of having led the country to independence. Unsurprisingly, in the circumstances, the new ruling parties chafed at the presence of an opposition party and worked to eliminate it. Where practicable, they absorbed the opposition; otherwise they suppressed it and created a one-party state. This happened with quite remarkable regularity so that by the mid-1960s only Nigeria, which was about to explode, Sierra Leone and The Gambia retained multiparty systems. The suppression of opposition parties necessarily meant other suppressions as well. Criticism of the ruling party that had become synonymous with the state became treason so that criticism by individuals, trade unions, rural organizations or any other groups was suppressed and those making it harassed. In turn this led to control of the press with leading newspapers becoming organs of the ruling party. As a result of this progression of controls in the name of loyalty to the ruling party and government, there was a steady erosion of civil liberties and curtailment of the rule of law.

African politicians who achieved supreme power at this time were little different from politicians elsewhere: they wanted power for themselves and meant to hold on to it for as long as they were able to do so, for personal love of power has always been a principal motivation for all politicians. What made a huge difference and enabled so many to become absolute so quickly was the sudden switch from colonial control to national control and the 'nationalist' who had led his people to independence found himself to be in a unique position. In any case, the modern democracy of mass parties that genuinely tolerate one another when in opposition is not only a recent political phenomenon but a relatively rare one as well. A majority of West African politicians coming to power in the circumstances of the 1960s decided against the system that the West had only offered them selectively and late in the last days of colonialism. This immediate rejection of multiparty democracy by parties and leaders who had fought a political battle on the single issue of independence was hardly surprising. Another factor that had to be taken into account – and still needs to be understood – was the utterly beguiling attraction of ministerial power. Men who only a few years earlier had been fighting their battles from small offices, being harassed and sometimes imprisoned, found themselves enjoying all the trappings of power and, moreover, being treated as above the law by their followers and more generally by the populace at large. The decisions they took were often of less importance than the fact of taking them at all. These heady days did not last long: ministers who were overthrown or lost their jobs discovered how quickly they could be forgotten; and those smart or tough enough to hold on to power soon discovered other means of bolstering their positions – suppression and if necessary oppression – always, of course, in the name of national unity. A number of African leaders found little difficulty in making the transition from popular nationalist fighting the colonial oppressors into one-party rule dictator who believed himself to be above the law and would indeed be all powerful until his turn came to be overthrown in a coup. The fact that such behaviour was all too apparent gave much satisfaction to reactionaries in the former metropolitan powers who had argued that their colonies were not ready for independence and the fact of their satisfaction led many Africans to support their tyrants since they could not bring themselves to agree with their former colonial masters. In general, though there were to be significant exceptions, Africa would sustain one-party systems of greater or lesser dictatorial tendencies for another two decades, and was to be supported in this by its supposed friends in the West on the grounds that African development required unity from below if it was to work. Such arguments were self-serving: against the background of the Cold War with the need to accumulate allies on the one hand and the Western determination to maintain its economic stranglehold on its former colonies on the other, a one-party system under a dictatorial leader was often easier to deal with, especially if the leader needed external financial support to survive, than would have been a more fractious democracy. Although there were many genuine grounds for rejecting Nkrumah's persistent calls for a union of all African states, one reason for rejection undoubtedly was the determination of the new leaders to enjoy their freshly won powers without hindrance.

It was often forgotten or overlooked in the aftermath of independence that the colonial powers, Britain and France, had bequeathed to their successors highly centralized states that assisted the creation of one-party rule or dictatorship. They had not, for example, developed much local government because up to the end they were determined to keep power in their own hands. In Guinea, Sekou Touré identified the party with the people and elevated it to a position of superiority over the government so that major decisions were taken out of the hands of ministers and cabinet and made instead by the Party's Executive Committee. In recent history at that time such elevation of a single party had only been carried out in Communist countries. It could be very effective; it was, in the end, profoundly anti-democratic.

> The idea that a single political party should have the right to monopolize political discussion, whether in West Africa or anywhere else, is so absurd, in the light of human history, that it is hard to take it seriously... The single-party thus fails in all its claims. It cannot represent all the people; or maintain free discussion; or give stable government; or above all, reconcile the differences between various regional groups.[23]

The political problem that affected almost all the new states was what form of democracy was best suited to a plural society? The Western system of first past the post was clearly not the answer if the winners were then seen to impose their will upon the plural minorities that had lost. Democracy, to work effectively, must provide all sections of opinion with an opportunity to be represented in decision-making. This has been hard enough to achieve in the relatively more unified countries of the West where divisions have been on class and economic rather than ethnic lines; in West Africa at this time, with its many ethnic sub-divisions, the process was far harder and often seemed unattainable. And so we return to the one-party state. Justifications for this form of government were much discussed in the Africa of the 1960s. It was seen as the best available system for uniting the people behind a new and inexperienced government whose first, overriding concern was development. A multiparty approach that insisted upon an official opposition would simply create divisions that could and should be avoided in the name of development and national unity. There were other justifications but these were the core arguments and they were greatly reinforced by the realities on the ground: the fact that Nkrumah or Touré, or in a quieter but no less ruthless and effective way, Houphouët-Boigny, controlled all the levers of power and had every intention of holding onto them indefinitely.

Western reluctance to be more critical of the new governments stemmed from two broad causes. The first was the all-absorbing concern with the Cold War, which coloured all Western dealings with Africa at this time. The fear that new radical governments would turn to the Communists persuaded the United States and the ex-colonial powers to support non-democratic and sometimes tyrannical regimes provided these remained in the Western camp. The second cause was more cynical: that Western interests, especially economic ones, would be best served by one-party state leaders who did not have to go through democratic processes before entering into agreements with Western commercial interests that in turn were bolstered by the rapidly growing new arm of foreign policy, the aid business. These foreign considerations were bolstered from within by other, quite different considerations. In politics, 'what counts is having one's own man in a position of authority, whether in political office, the party hierarchy, the public service, or a parastatal body. The dominant purpose of electoral activity in West Africa has therefore been the control of such preferment. The disappearance of party politics makes little if any difference. Indeed, one-party states have resulted not only from the intolerance of governments for opposition, but also from the disinclination of the oppositions to be automatically excluded from government patronage.'[24] If there was loot to be had in the new state, everyone wanted his share and that was a powerful personal motive, which led many opposition politicians to acquiesce in the one-party state and join the ranks of the ruling party.

One final, some would argue overriding, argument in favour of the one-party state at this time was the need for political stability and when it was achieved under a strong man it was hailed as a justification for his subversion of wider liberties.

CHAPTER NINE

The Horn
of Africa

No other region of the African continent faced such immediate problems of boundary adjustment following independence as did the Horn of Africa whose legacy of imperial manipulation was to be more than 30 years of warfare. The tiny territory of French Somaliland (later Djibouti) was as senseless a creation as the equally tiny and absurd Gambia on the other side of the continent. The French had taken it to match Britain's Aden on the Arabian side of the Red Sea and it only made sense as an entry port for the railway to Addis Ababa. After its defeat at the battle of Adowa in 1896 Italy had been obliged to content itself with its colony of Eritrea, which effectively made Ethiopia landlocked. The British Protectorate of Somaliland on the Red Sea shore of the Horn and the Italian colony of Somalia on its Indian Ocean shore meant different administrations and different languages during the colonial era for two Somali regions that would only be united in 1960. When in 1941 British forces defeated the Italians in Ethiopia after the five-year Italian occupation that had followed Mussolini's 1935 onslaught, the Emperor shrewdly dashed ahead of his country's 'liberators' to enter Addis Ababa first. He was well aware of Britain's imperial ambitions concerning his country and, as it transpired, fully justified in not trusting the British who spent the next 10 years trying to bring Ethiopia under their control. Part of the traditional Somali grazing lands had been incorporated in the British colony of Kenya as the Northern Frontier District (NFD) and this led to the Shifta war of the 1960s between Somalia and Kenya.

In the big power manipulations in this region from 1942 to 1950 the Emperor Haile Selassie watched the old colonial powers – Britain, France and Italy – manoeuvre for renewed influence; but in the end it was a newcomer to the African scene in the form of the United States, one of the world's two emerging superpowers, that became the new 'guardian' of Ethiopia, principally to secure the military base at Kagnew in Eritrea to oversee America's new strategic interests in the Indian Ocean. When British Somaliland and the UN Trusteeship territory of former Italian Somaliland were united as the independent Somali Republic in 1960, the flag of the new state had as its centrepiece a five-pointed star: two points represented the former British and Italian colonies, now united; the other three points represented French Somaliland, the huge Ogaden region of Ethiopia and the NFD of Kenya respectively, a conceit that automatically placed Somalia in confrontation with its three land neighbours. The Somali Republic refused to agree to the 1964 OAU ruling that the new states of Africa should accept their inherited colonial boundaries and embarked instead upon years of near or actual warfare with its neighbours. The UN decision to federate Ethiopia and Eritrea in 1950 and the subsequent Ethiopian incorporation of Eritrea in 1962 produced what was for years to be described as Africa's longest war. Finally, British colonial policy in the Sudan that enhanced the divisions between North and South meant that in 2000 the two parts of Africa's largest country were still fighting what had by then become both the longest and possibly also the most devastating war on the continent.

ETHIOPIA

In 1960 the Emperor Haile Selassie had a high reputation in Africa. As an exile following Mussolini's invasion of his country in 1935 he had upheld African demands for independence at the League of Nations. He was the proud descendant of the only African leader, Menelik II, who had defeated one of the great powers during the Scramble for Africa, while the Jamaican Rastafarian movement, a mixture of black nationalism and religion, saw him as its spiritual leader. During the 1940s he had successfully defied British attempts to subvert Ethiopia's independence and had made plain his desire to modernize a country that was regularly described as medieval. As the longest-ruling head of state in Africa he enjoyed great prestige and was shortly to take a leading role in the formation of the Organisation of African Unity. The only blot on this reputation was his readiness, though the pressures had been greater than he could withstand, to allow the United States to create its military base at Kagnew and become the country's principal aid donor and, as Washington liked to believe, political mentor. In 1962, a decision that would ultimately cost Ethiopia dear, Haile Selassie ended the Federation of Ethiopia and Eritrea, which had largely been engineered by the United States in order to secure the base it wanted at Kagnew, instead incorporating Eritrea into Ethiopia. This act led the Eritrean Liberation Front (ELF), which had been founded at Cairo in 1958, to launch what became a 30-year struggle for secession and independence. During the remaining years of his long reign until his overthrow in 1974 the Emperor faced growing opposition, especially from students, and demands for more radical reforms than he was prepared or able to grant; the growing tension between the traditionalists and the radicals was to be made worse by the escalating guerrilla activities of the ELF in Eritrea where the developing war steadily absorbed more and more government resources.

In May 1960, even before the Somali Republic became independent in July, Haile Selassie held discussions with the Ambassadors of Britain, the United States, Russia, France, Yugoslavia and the UAR about the situation in the Horn, which he described as 'very grave'. He was referring to the claims already advanced by the Somalis for a union of the so-called Somali territories, including the Ogaden Province of Ethiopia. He said these claims were a first step aimed at the dismemberment of Ethiopia and that the 'so-called Somali demands' constituted a thinly disguised conspiracy which he would oppose with all means in his power.[1] Thus the scene was set for years of conflict, sometimes erupting into full-scale war, between Ethiopia and Somalia. Indeed, border clashes with Somalia occurred immediately after that country's independence in July and the Ethiopian press accused the new Somali Republic of refusing to reciprocate Ethiopia's desire for friendly relations by at once exchanging ambassadors. The Ethiopian papers speculated as to whether there was not 'some hidden foreign hand' behind the Somali attitude.

The attempted coup against Haile Selassie of 14 December 1960 when he was on a visit to Brazil (see above, chapter four) failed; it was, however, symptomatic of growing Ethiopian restlessness and desire for change that reflected the continent-wide demands for a break with the past and rapid development and progress. As a leading article in *The Times* put it, personal loyalty to Haile Selassie was not enough: 'This idea of personal loyalty has been one of the Emperor's constant themes since his return. But although many of his ignorant subjects may offer him such loyalty, the time has come when his country must make the transition to the nation state, in which loyalty to kings becomes at best a symbol for loyalty to country.'[2] Assessments of Ethiopia's progress at this time were all the same: the pace of economic development was slow when compared with that of other African countries and expectations were not being met. Ethiopia, more than most African countries, depended upon agriculture with 90 per cent of the population working on the land while only five per cent of the GDP was derived from industry. There had been some advances: in road construction, for example, and the development of a modern port at Asab. But these advances were not enough to satisfy the radicals. In 1961 the government decided to establish a civil service recruited on the basis of merit through open competitive examinations. What was urgently needed was land reform and greater autonomy for the provinces as well as expansion of agricultural production.

A good many Western observers visited Ethiopia during the 1960s and their reports reflect an almost conscious sadness that what the Emperor stood for could not last. James Morris, writing for the *Guardian*, described Ethiopia as

> just awakening from a long aloof dream, and disgruntled by the daylight. It is the view of the Emperor of Ethiopia that you can best make haste very slowly indeed. He has repeatedly proclaimed his intention to modernize the country, and to give the people a fair voice in the conduct of their own affairs, but the speed at which he is advancing towards a constitutional monarchy is distinctly sluggish. Thanks to his firm conservative hand, Ethiopia has so far escaped the welter of cross-values, the hodge-podge of immature politics, that has overcome most of Africa.[3]

In an interview with Andrew Wilson of the *Observer* early in 1962, Haile Selassie said he would end feudalism in Ethiopia. 'One cannot imagine,' he said, 'what hard work must be faced in order to end feudalism without bloodshed. But our future is to move from feudalism to democracy. To remove all difficulties will take some time. There are those who must be convinced.' The Emperor declined to name a date for the formation of political parties – which had never existed in Ethiopia – but said he was 'always finding new ways'.[4] There spoke a tired man; Haile Selassie was then approaching 70, and had spent the 20 years since regaining his throne trying to modernize one of the most conservative countries in the world against the vested interests of powerful semi-independent hereditary rulers who would surrender none of their privileges willingly. Clyde Sanger, one of the most sympathetic Afrophiles of that time, described for the *Guardian* the establishment of a new university in October 1962 and then reflected upon the current unease in Ethiopia. 'In an uneasy atmosphere of discontented rumblings and threats from the Army, disillusionment over governmental changes among young intellectuals, the banishment of a Supreme Court judge and a score of suspected fellow plotters, and the dismissal of local editors for indiscretions, the establishment of a proposed University of Ethiopia... is a crucial move.' The establishment of the University may have been an advance but too many other developments arose out of old-fashioned fear at radical change. There was a growing consensus that the situation could not last.

Interestingly, despite the large US presence as the country's most important donor, the Emperor had lost none of his old skill at playing the great powers off against each other. Thus, in August 1963 a £37 million loan offered by Russia to cover the design and construction of an oil refinery at Asab was accepted by the Ethiopian Chamber of Deputies but only after a heated debate. In the division

11 voted against, 33 abstained, and 124 were in favour.[5] Reviewing progress in Ethiopia, Norman Bentwich, another sympathetic British journalist, first described slow but steady reforms, touched on the problem of 400,000 Somalis in the southern province, and then said: 'One of the Emperor's most skilful achievements is the geographical and ideological distribution of foreign assistance. Since his restoration to the throne, he has been determined to avoid any aid imperialism and to be neutral in receiving benefactions and advisers from the Western and Eastern blocs. The Soviet Union has just completed the building of a big technical college at Bahar Dar at the southern end of Lake Tana, a small town which the Emperor envisages as an industrial centre because it is near the source of power from the falls of the Blue Nile.'[6]

The problem, and it would become acute in the early 1970s, was simply that no major decision was made except by the Emperor, and by the end of the decade he was in his mid-70s. At that time the rebellion in Eritrea was in full swing and the army, as a result, was becoming larger and more influential. Like many long-lasting leaders, Haile Selassie turned his attention, increasingly, to continental affairs in which he saw his role as one of mediation. He worked hard through the OAU, first to prevent and then to end the Nigerian civil war. At home, however, he became ever more conservative in the face of growing student and other unrest. In 1969 coups from the radical left in two of his neighbours brought Siad Barre to power in Somalia and Gaafar Nimeiri to power in Sudan.

ERITREA

Following the United Nations' decision to create a federation of Ethiopia and Eritrea in 1950, the United States had effectively replaced the European powers in the domination of Ethiopia. Currency reform had severed the Ethiopian dollar from the pound sterling and tied it to the US dollar while US aid, especially for civil aviation, had become the country's largest source of external funds. The change had been entered into willingly enough by Ethiopia which had rejected ties with the European colonial powers – Britain, France and Italy – that had each been ready to interfere and had opted instead for a close alliance with the United States. Washington had devised the federal idea because what it really wanted was a base in Eritrea. The USSR condemned the federation as a new form of Western colonialism. John Foster Dulles, soon to become President Eisenhower's Secretary of State, said at the time: 'From the point of view of justice the opinion of the Eritrean people must receive consideration. Nevertheless, the strategic interests of the United States in the Red Sea basin and consideration of security and world peace make it necessary that the country has to be linked with our ally, Ethiopia.' The Federation of Eritrea and Ethiopia formally came into being on 6 August 1952.[7]

In 1953 Eritrea came under the sovereignty of the Ethiopian Crown though retaining semblances of autonomy. The Americans then constructed a multi-million-dollar complex at Kagnew. This base 'was among the most crucial of the US National Security Agency (NSA) bases in the world. It primarily served US military and intelligence objectives in the region. It was used to promote the "command and control" of the American ballistic missiles in the Indian Ocean. It also served in the conduct of what are known as "cryptologic" activities. These included operations of jamming and telecasting coded information.'[8] US aid to Ethiopia, up to 1970, came to US$250 million, the highest figure for American aid to any African country.

The Federation of Eritrea and Ethiopia came to an end in 1962 when the Eritrean legislative assembly voted itself out of existence. It was by then an emasculated body controlled by the Emperor. Four years earlier at Cairo in 1958 Eritrean dissidents who were determined that their country should not be subsumed by Ethiopia had founded the Eritrean Liberation Front (ELF) and they had turned to armed struggle in 1961 when in September the first shots were fired in what came to be known in the 1980s as 'Africa's longest war'. On 15 November 1962 Haile Selassie issued Order No. 27 in which he announced that 'the federal status of Eritrea is hereby terminated' and that Eritrea was 'hereby wholly integrated into the unitary system of administration of Our Empire.'[9] By mid-1965 the ELF was reported to have a guerrilla force of 2,000 troops and these were often better trained and equipped than the Ethiopians opposed to them. Ethiopia, therefore, raised the number of its troops in Eritrea to divisional strength at 7,000. Eritrean resistance to the central government was sporadic and uneven during the 1960s, although the ELF gained considerable publicity from hijackings. By 1965, a further complication for Ethiopia, the ELF was receiving support from Sudan. In 1962 the ELF had moved its headquarters to Damascus and was always to receive substantial Arab (Muslim) backing in its struggle. For a decade the ELF was the most significant Eritrean liberation group, although others, such as the Popular Liberation Front (PLF) with Marxist leanings, came into being in the early 1960s. Both were committed to full independence for Eritrea. But by 1969 young militants in the ELF accused the leadership of feudalist or reactionary tendencies and moved towards a more socialist stance; they were supported by radical Arab governments – Iraq, Libya, Syria – as well as by Al Fatah (the Movement for the Liberation of Palestine) and the stage was set for the young militants to gain control of the Eritrean Liberation Army (ELA) and then from bases in Sudan develop a systematic guerrilla campaign across the border into Eritrea.

SOMALIA

The Somali coastline of 3,025 kilometres is the longest in Africa and facing onto both the Gulf of Aden at the entrance to the Red Sea and the Indian Ocean has enormous strategic significance. The oil supply from the Arab world passes Somali waters, either *en route* for the Suez Canal or for the Cape. Its three land neighbours were French Somaliland, Ethiopia and Kenya, each of which occupied territory that Somalia claimed. The most fertile region of arable land lies in the south along the Shibeli and Juba rivers, while the area between them is permanently irrigated to allow extensive and continual agricultural production of bananas, sugar and maize. The Somalis are a Hamitic people, related to the Galla, Danakil and Afars of Ethiopia, although Bantu influence is important in the riverine region in the south. However, 75 per cent of the people are nomads moving constantly with their herds in search of seasonal pastures, and this movement, which had encompassed large tracts of land outside the boundaries of the modern state that came into being in 1960, lay at the root of the Somali 'problem'.

Between 1950 and 1960 (when British Somaliland and former Italian Somaliland, which had become a UN Trusteeship territory after the war, were joined to form the Somali Republic) little development had taken place. During the first decade of independence, Somalia was one of the rare democracies in Africa, although the political system gradually deteriorated until by the end of the decade the system had been reduced to near anarchy. 'At the time of independence in 1960, Somalia was touted in the West as the model of a rural democracy in Africa. Tribalism and extended family loyalties and conflicts were the core of the government, and by the late 1960s more than 60 parties campaigned for election to a Parliament of 123 seats. Democracy had degenerated into anarchy. Somalian corruption astounded even Afrophiles. The last Prime Minister was playing roulette in Las Vegas at the time of the national uprising led by General Mohamed Siad Barre in October, 1969.'[10]

An aspect of Somali behaviour that constantly causes outsiders to pause is the readiness of its clans to fight each other when few peoples in Africa have a more obvious basis for national unity than the Somalis. 'It is a very homogeneous population, both ethnically and religiously, which makes for a nationalism quite unusual in Africa. Ninety per cent are of the Somali ethnic group (Hamitic), which has a strong sense of cultural identity despite internal (clan) distinctions.'[11] Too often, however, in the years that followed independence clan differences threatened the unity of the country rather than racial homogeneity binding it together.

In the immediate aftermath of independence, despite differences between north and south, the national unifying factor was the Somali desire to achieve its dream of Greater Somalia that would embrace the areas of neighbouring territory traditionally seen as Somali lands, and this made for dangerously explosive relations with both Ethiopia and Kenya. These Somali pressures for territorial aggrandisement, exerted through the 1960s, had no success: there were border incidents and confrontations with Ethiopia, a guerrilla war along the border with Kenya, while in French Somaliland the voters rejected independence which the pro-Somali faction favoured. At least in 1967 Prime Minister Ibrahim Egal changed policy and sought a *détente* with both Ethiopia and Kenya, leading the three countries to embark on a series of talks to find a settlement. Internally, however, growing differences began to divide the country so that for the 1969 elections 1,000 candidates representing 68 parties contested 123 seats. The Somali Youth League (SYL), which was the best-organized party and had dominated the country's politics since independence, won the election and Egal was again appointed Prime Minister. Then virtually all the opposition members joined the government in pursuit of office. Shortly thereafter Siad Barre seized power in a coup.

If we examine political developments through the 1960s it soon becomes clear that internal affairs took second place to Somalia's irredentist claims against its neighbours. The first Prime Minister, Dr Abdirashid Ali Shirmake, began well when on 13 August 1960 he described the government's programme to the National Assembly: 'The future of the country is linked up with a balanced, gradual, realistic and substantial economic development; it is so because, in the first place, if a nation's economy is continuously dependent on foreign aid, she cannot be considered as really independent, and in the second place, because the realization of an effective social justice, intended to diminish the disparity between the different areas, categories and citizens is really the indispensable prerequisite for a well-ordered life and, above all, for establishing that sense of human and national solidarity which, more than any other political or juridical element, becomes a cement of union, brotherhood and peace.'[12] Such high-minded sentiments about development and nationhood would all too quickly take second place to the more immediate problems of border confrontations. Heavy fighting between Somali tribesmen and Ethiopian troops occurred on the Ogaden–Damot border in December 1960, just before the New Year, when as many as 180 Somalis were killed and Ethiopian aircraft strafed several Somali villages. In a speech at Hargeisa in the north on 15 April 1961, President Aden Abdulla Osman responded angrily to an Ethiopian broadcast that claimed no one had turned out to meet him on his tour; he went on to say that so far only two of the five Somali territories represented by the five-pointed star on its flag had as yet been unified and that there should be no relaxation of Somali efforts to achieve the freedom of the remaining three territories. He concluded his speech by calling upon Ethiopia to allow Somalis in the Ogaden to determine their future.

In November 1961 the National Assembly warmly supported and welcomed the request of the population of the NFD of Kenya to seek to obtain the union of that region with the Somali Republic before the independence of Kenya. In February 1962 the Somali Embassy in London, on the authority of the Prime Minister, stated that Somali claims for unity were based on religious, ethnic and other ties, but it was also important to remember the necessity for an effective and democratic system of government for all countries. In the light of living conditions and grazing needs of the Somali people, only a Somali government was capable of affording such a system to any Somali community. The people and government of the Somali Republic supported suitable forms of African unity. At the same time they were satisfied that African unity as a whole could make but little sense unless there was reasonable homogeneity in each state within a larger Federal system.[13] In the years that followed Somalia was to find little support for its stand among other African states.

Meanwhile, it had made its position all too clear to its two principal neighbours, Ethiopia and Kenya. In September 1962 the *Somali News* attacked the United States for giving military aid to Ethiopia and claimed that between 1954 and 1962 US$107.3 million was earmarked to help African nations 'almost entirely for the maintenance of internal security or internal stability of the newly emergent nations of Africa' but of this US$67.4 million had gone to Ethiopia. In the summer of 1962, Jomo Kenyatta who had finally been released from detention in mid-1961 to assume the leadership of the Kenya African National Union (KANU) had visited the Somali Republic (26–30 July). Replying to a farewell speech by the Somali Prime Minister Shirmake, who had raised the question of the NFD Somalis joining the Somali Republic, Kenyatta said: 'I might as well say that we and especially KANU regard the NFD as part of Kenya. We also regard Somalis in Kenya as our brothers. They are part and parcel of Kenya and we will like them to live in Kenya in that fashion. They have lived there for many years and there has never been any quarrel or any friction between the people of the other groups in Kenya, between them and the Somalis who live there... this being a domestic affair of Kenya.' He could not have made Kenya's response to Somali demands any more straightforward.[14] At the end of 1962, as Somalia continued to mount pressures upon Kenya, Masinde Muliro, the Vice-President of the Kenya African Democratic Union (KADU) and Minister of Commerce and Industry in the pre-independence coalition government with KANU, said: 'No matter what the Northern Frontier Province Commission reports, this Government will never allow the province to join Somalia. This is not the time to start dismembering Kenya, and if the present colonialists were to allow secession we would declare war to regain the territory immediately after *uhuru*.' The Somali government protested to the British government at this and a similar statement by Tom Mboya, the general secretary of KANU and Minister of Labour. Once it was clear that Britain supported the Kenya stand Somalia broke diplomatic relations with Britain (12 March 1963). On 14 March, still nine months before Kenya's independence, Kenyatta, who by that time had become Prime Minister, said that he would not contemplate 'any secession or handing over of one inch of our territory'. Kenya became independent on 12 December 1963 and over the next three years to December 1966 the Kenyan government estimated that casualties in the border war with Somalia came to 1,650 Shifta bandits killed, 69 Kenyan military and police personnel and 500 Kenyan civilians. The economic burden for Kenya of policing the area over this period had been considerable.

Fresh border fighting between Ethiopia and Somalia occurred in February and March 1964. In July 1964 the OAU meeting in Cairo ruled that member states' 'present [existing] frontiers should be maintained'. The Somali National Assembly, however, decided that Somalia would not be bound by this policy and after much debate said that the OAU resolution 'is in no way binding on the Somali Republic or applicable to the present disputes the Somali Republic has with Ethiopia and Kenya'. In 1965 at the United Nations the Somali representative raised the issue of French Somaliland on the grounds that France refused to allow the people of that territory to proceed to independence and exercise their right to self-determination.

A major political change took place in 1967 when the former Prime Minister, Shirmake, became President and Mohamed Ibrahim Egal became Prime Minister. He switched Somali foreign policy from a virtual state of war with her neighbours, coupled with resentment of the Western powers, to a policy of peaceful co-existence. Egal accepted mediation by President Kaunda of Zambia in Somalia's disputes with its neighbours and a period of easier relations followed. Kenya lifted its trade ban on Somalia following the Arusha agreement brokered by Kaunda and in January 1968 the two countries restored diplomatic relations.

In 1968 Egal launched the 1968–70 Development Plan, which concentrated outlay upon the public sector with 70 per cent of expenditure going to infrastructure projects. But the continuing erosion of democracy, rising levels of corruption and a weakening of the judiciary all suggested a coming crisis and this was sparked off by the assassination of President Shirmake on 15 October 1969. When Prime Minister Egal returned from an official visit to the United States to secure the election of a new president favourable to his interests the army stepped in on 21 October and carried out a bloodless coup. A radio announcement by the military stated: 'In view of the maladministration of the country and the violations of the established laws in the country, such as the constitutional laws, and in the administration of the Civil Services which endangered the existence of the nation and were due to the mischievous and bad practices of the so-called responsible authorities, the National Army, supported by the police, this morning at 0900 Mogadishu time, took over the administration and political power of the country.' A 25-man Supreme Revolutionary Council (SRC) under chairman Gen. Siad Barre announced its goals: the suppression of tribal (clan) divisions and nepotism and the establishment of scientific socialism. The government moved sharply to the left and a policy of nationalization was announced. The new regime said it would adapt scientific socialism to the needs of Somalia and drew heavily from the traditions of Communist China: 'volunteer' labour planted and harvested the crops, and built roads and hospitals, and in May 1970 all foreign banks, oil companies, electricity and sugar companies were nationalized. Barre said that full compensation would be paid but that it was time for Somalis to take over. An entirely new script for the Somali language was introduced. West Germany and the United States suspended aid to Somalia and though they claimed they were doing so because of new links Somalia had established with East Germany and Vietnam respectively, the real reason was their objection to Barre attempting to develop economic independence.

SUDAN

The North-South divide became central to Sudanese politics even before independence. The Southern Army Mutiny of 1955, on the eve of independence, represented the culmination of growing Southern suspicion of Northern intentions. The South, in any case, was ill-prepared for new political developments while the mistakes of the Northern political parties were the result of inexperience and ignorance of conditions in the South rather than of bad intentions. When in 1955 the Northern political parties agreed to consider a federal solution to overcome North-South differences the Southern representatives in parliament in turn agreed to the declaration of independence on 1 January 1956. For just under three years Sudan was to be ruled by a civilian coalition of the National Unionist Party (NUP) led by Abdallah Kalil (who soon replaced Sudan's first Prime Minister, Azhari); the Mahdists of the Umma Party (UP) led by Sadiq al-Mahdi; and the Khatmiyya, led by Sayyid al-Mirghani. Elections in early 1958 were inconclusive, with the result that the country continued under a weak and increasingly divided coalition. On 17 November

1958, a coup was launched by the army, led by Gen. Ibrahim Abboud, and both Sadiq al-Mahdi and Sayyid al-Mirghani gave the new military regime provisional backing, with the proviso that they did not stay in power too long. The regime was to last for six years. 'The military regime may have achieved in the North what was considered by foreign observers as stability during its first four years of existence. It was, however, a superficial stability, the price of which was oppression of political opposition and the imprisonment of a number of politicians, trade unionists, students and communists.'[15] It did not have much success in the South. On 27 February 1962 the Ministry of the Interior announced the expulsion of all Christian missionaries in the Southern Sudan. At that time there were 617 missionaries in the whole of Sudan. The military government saw their activities as being political as much as religious and against the government. By 1964 the crucial question about the South was whether it should become independent or remain within the Sudan Republic. The Northern political parties opposed Southern independence. The new civilian government of 1965, led by the UP's Muhammed Ahmed Mahgoub as Prime Minister, increased military operations against the Southern rebels (the Anya Nya) and decided that it would co-operate with those Southerners who favoured unity. '... the desire for separation arose as a result both of the colonial policy and of differences between the North and South, some of which are natural and some man-made. History, economic disparity between North and South, mistakes and blunders of inexperienced politicians and the activities of the missionary societies – each has contributed to the problem.'[16]

The divide between North and South in Africa's largest country has highlighted other problems than the strictly national one of unity. Is Sudan a bridge between Arabic and English-speaking Africa, between Muslim and Christian Africa, between Africa of the ethnic divide as opposed to the unified state? According to Ali Mazrui[17] Sudan is less a bridge than a demonstration of how the chasm cannot be bridged. It is often forgotten that 60 per cent of the Arab community and 72 per cent of the Arab lands are in Africa and that one of Africa's enduring problems is the need to reconcile the Arab North of the continent with the Black South. Arabs constitute the most important link between Africa and Asia while the Sudanese form the most important point of contact between Arab Africa and Black Africa. 'There is first the very phenomenon of racial mixture and inter-marriage in the northern parts of the Sudan, coupled with the fact that a large proportion of Arab Sudanese are in fact Arabized Negroes, rather than ethnically semitic. For many of them the Arabness is a cultural acquisition, rather than a racial heredity.'[18] It is not possible to discuss cultural differences between North and South without including the religious dimension and as Mazrui points out, 'No other African country has been as closely identified with a schism between Islam and Christianity as the Sudan has been.' Dealing with the factor of external Christian pressures in the South, Mazrui says: 'Perhaps only the arrogance of a Christian press could describe a population which is only one-tenth Christian as being "basically Christian". ... Western commentators do sometimes assume that while it is fair game to let Christian missionaries loose among simple African villagers, it is sometimes approaching religious persecution to let Muslim missionaries loose within the same population.' Prior to independence British policy sought to keep both the Arabs and Islam out of the South. The result was predictable: if the gap between North and South was to be bridged on the withdrawal of British rule, it was inevitable that the North would seek to break the educational and proselytizing monopoly which Christian missions had long enjoyed.[19] Religion as a point of debate in Sudan is not to be avoided. A number of divisions separate North and South, including religion, and the experience from independence in 1956 to the end of the century would suggest that any capacity as a bridge that Sudan might have possessed has so far failed miserably.

In March 1965 the government called a conference to find a solution to the North-South divide and though it came up with no long-term answers it did agree on repatriation of refugees, freedom of religion and a training programme for the South to allow its people greater participation in the army, police and civil service. In July 1965, a month after the Mahgoub government had come to power, rebel fighting round the Southern city of Juba was met with severe reprisals: many Southerners were killed and the divide widened. On 25 July 1966 the Mahgoub government was defeated on a censure vote and replaced by a new government under the young Sadiq al-Mahdi. It halted the current economic decline but was defeated in its turn in 1967 when Mahgoub returned to power. He was then to remain as Prime Minister until the coup of 25 May 1969 that brought Nimeiri to power.

The rebellion in the South, like most such rebellions, was at best sporadic in its early stages until properly organized. In October 1962 a strike in Southern schools led to anti-government demonstrations, which prompted many students to flee across the borders into neighbouring countries. Then some 500 former soldiers of Equatoria province came together to form the Anya Nya movement. This guerrilla organization began without arms and without much obvious purpose except opposition to Northern domination, and its members lived off the country. But in 1963 a former lieutenant in the army, Emilio Tafeng, became its leader; he organized the guerrillas and made them into an effective movement. It was Tafeng who first used the name Anya Nya (a snake poison) for the guerrillas. Growing disillusionment with the military government in the

North and the desire for a return to democracy persuaded Northerners to use the issue of the South as a weapon against the government even if they had little real sympathy for Southern problems. From 1963 onwards Anya Nya maintained training camps outside Sudan in the Congo and Uganda, while inside the country it waged a guerrilla war, which consisted largely of ambushes of government forces. By the end of 1964 membership of Anya Nya had reached 2,000 and the greater part of the Sudan army had been moved to the South to deal with it. In 1967 a political figure of southern Sudan, Aggrey Laden, set up a Southern Sudan Provisional Government and established administration in the areas which by then were controlled by Anya Nya. From this time onwards the guerrillas called themselves the Anya Nya Armed Forces (ANAF), and by 1968 they had an estimated 10,000 members. By 1969 the government took Anya Nya sufficiently seriously to use the air force to seek out and attack the rebel hideouts; at the same time the numbers of Southern refugees were greatly increased as a result of the Northern policy of razing villages that had sheltered the rebels, a policy that did nothing to reconcile the government of the North to Southerners who were not necessarily in sympathy with Anya Nya tactics.

Efforts to reconcile North and South over these years were not helped by articles in the British press, especially those that insisted upon the religious dimensions of the civil war. Thus, referring to an article which had appeared in the *Guardian* the Chargé d'Affaires for Sudan in London, Bushra Hamid Gabreldar, described it as misleading: 'Since 70 per cent of the Southern population are pagans and more than 25 per cent of the rest are Muslims, and since the terrorists in question belong equally to the three groups, it seems strange to refer to a Christian-persecuted South.'[20] At the end of October 1966 the Prime Minister, Sadiq al-Mahdi, visited the South hoping to find new ways of reconciling the North-South conflict. The rebel leaders had already said they would reject any constitution that ensured the predominance of Islam throughout the country.

In 1968 Sudan still lacked a workable constitution and divisions over the Southern question had become sharper. In the North there were also other divisions, not least between members of the Ansari and smaller Khatmiyya sects, but also about whether Sudan should become a Muslim state, about its relations with Cairo and its attitude towards East and West in the Cold War. The elections of that year did not produce any clear majority so that an ineffective coalition government continued in power. By then the rebellion in the South had created 55,000 refugees in Uganda, Ethiopia was supporting the rebels and Sudan was supporting Somalia in its ongoing quarrel with Ethiopia. Then, on 25 May 1969 young revolutionary-minded army officers carried out a bloodless coup. Their leader was Col. Gaafar Nimeiri who became the Chairman of the

National Revolutionary Council and Commander-in-Chief of the Armed Forces. The coup was a response to a situation in which there was no constitution, the political system was dominated by sterile sectarian interests, the economy was stagnant and there was no sign of an end to the war in the South which involved the non-Muslim peoples of Equatoria, Upper Nile and Bahr-el-Ghazal provinces. The coup-makers arrested politicians and senior army officers. Only the Muslim Brotherhood mounted demonstrations against the coup. On the anniversary of the coup (25 May 1970) the government nationalized all foreign banks and followed this measure the next day by nationalizing a range of foreign companies. Commenting on these nationalization measures, Roy Lewis of *The Times* wrote: 'While the right of any government to nationalize foreign firms, subject to "fair, prompt and effective compensation" is not contested, the Sudanese measures are without doubt the most sweeping and precipitate attempted in Africa since the Zanzibar revolution. They amount to virtually complete suppression of any substantial private enterprise.'[21] Compensation was offered in the form of 4 per cent bonds on valuation of the business seized, repayable over five years after a moratorium of 10 years, that is between 1980 and 1985, an offer that was regarded as outrageous by the affected companies.

In the first statement he made Col. Nimeiri listed the Southern problem as one of the reasons prompting the coup and on 9 June he issued a policy statement in relation to the South. He claimed that he wished to follow the line adopted by the government in 1964, which had recognized for the first time that the Southern problem existed and had attempted to solve it by means of a round table conference. Nimeiri said his government was committed to the same objectives. All Southerners, abroad and at home, were called upon to see that peace and stability prevailed in the South and that life should return to normal conditions so as to enable the new government to carry out its policy. The need to build a broad socialist-oriented democratic movement in the South as part of the revolutionary structure in the North was an essential prerequisite for the application of regional autonomy. The Southern people should have the right to develop their respective customs and traditions within a united socialist Sudan. Regional autonomy was seen as the target after certain prerequisites and a programme of action had been drawn up. This would involve five objectives: the continuation and further extension of the Amnesty Law; economic, social and cultural development of the South; the appointment of a Minister for Southern Affairs; the training of Southern personnel to shoulder the new responsibilities; and the creation of a special economic planning board and the preparation of a special budget for the South. This declaration and programme of action on the South was hailed by both North and South as the most important single action of the new regime. The appointment of Joseph Garang, a leading Southern Communist, as Minister for Southern Affairs was a source of assurance to both sides since he was an advocate of union (the Sudan Communist party, prior to independence, had advocated autonomy for the Southern Provinces). In August 1969 Nimeiri toured the South to explain the new policy. He emphasized the need for peace and economic development. The Amnesty Law of 1967 was renewed in October 1969 to extend to October 1970. There followed an immediate increase in the populations of Southern towns as refugees returned home.

DJIBOUTI

At the end of World War II the port of Djibouti (in what was then French Somaliland), which handled 60 per cent of Ethiopia's trade on the railway to Addis Ababa, found it was losing trade to the rival port of Asab in Eritrea. It was further adversely affected by the closure of the Suez Canal, first as a result of the 1956 Suez Crisis and then over the period 1967–75 following the Six Day War. In 1956 French Somaliland was made an overseas territory of France. In 1958 it voted to become a member of the French Community. When Somalia became independent in 1960 it campaigned for the independence of French Somaliland, which it saw as part of Greater Somalia. President de Gaulle visited the territory at the end of August 1966. 'On its own Djibouti could hardly exist as an entity. Its mineral wealth is minimal and unexplored and its climate is murderous. But as a sort of East African Tangier – and as the entrepôt for largely land-locked Ethiopia – Djibouti is a prize of great value. Not unnaturally Ethiopia and the Somali Republic are both candidates for its ownership, even though France – so far – has not indicated that it intends to withdraw.'[22] In 1967, in a move to pre-empt Somali designs, France held a referendum which was carefully weighted in favour of the northern Afars, so as to reduce Somali influence – many Somalis were expelled from the colony at this time – and a majority of those who voted wanted to continue the French connection. Following the referendum the name of the territory was changed from French Somaliland to the French Territory of the Afars and Issas. Louis Saget, the French High Commissioner – the post of governor was now abolished – nonetheless held reserve powers covering foreign policy, defence, internal security, the currency, justice and broadcasting so that not a great deal was left outside French jurisdiction. The Popular Movement opposed continued association with France and demanded full independence. In elections the following year (1968) for a new chamber of deputies, the Afars under Ali Aref and his *Regroupement Démocratique Afar* (RDA) won 26 of 32 seats. France had managed to ensure the exclusion of many Somalis from the voting with the result that tensions were heightened. Over the next 10 years mounting pressures for independence came from the Somali-dominated *Ligue Populaire Africaine pour L'Indépendence* (LPAI), which was supported from outside the country by Somalia, while the OAU also exerted increasing pressure on France to grant the country full independence. In July 1976 France changed its policy and replaced Aref as head of government with Abdallah Mohamed Kalil (an Afar married to a Somali) whose government contained leading members of both ethnic groups. The Territory of the Afars and Issas became fully independent on 27 June 1977 as Djibouti with the LPAI leader, Hassan Gouled Aptidon, as President and Ahmed Dini (an Afar), the Secretary-General of the LPAI, becoming Prime Minister. By agreement, France stationed about 4,500 troops of the Foreign Legion in Djibouti, 'at the disposal of the government'.

CHAPTER TEN

East Africa

Kenya, Tanganyika and Uganda form the core of this region and the three territories came to independence within two years of each other between December 1961 and December 1963. They had a good deal in common, sharing a British colonial background, language and administrative institutions. They were comparable in size and resources, and had roughly equal populations while their levels of development were on a par with each other except that the presence of a substantial settler population in Kenya had acted as a magnet for considerably greater capital inflows, a fact that would cause problems between them in the immediate post-independence years. The impact of the Mau Mau rebellion in Kenya during the 1950s, despite its defeat by British imperial forces, had nonetheless hastened the regional momentum for independence with the result that the handover in all three territories had gone relatively smoothly. Jomo Kenyatta, whom the penultimate British Governor, Sir Patrick Renison, had described as the leader 'to darkness and death' had been transformed into 'Good Old Mzee' and came to be regarded in Britain as a 'moderate' African leader, as was Julius Nyerere in neighbouring Tanganyika. The transition from colony to independent nation appeared to have been accomplished very smoothly, especially in relation to the turbulent 1950s in Kenya.

The first problem facing the leadership in each country was to establish sound political control. In Tanzania Nyerere set out to create a one-party state and was to provide intellectual justifications for this exercise that found adherents throughout the continent. The more pragmatic Kenyatta allowed developments to take their course with much the same result: within a year of independence the dissolution of the opposition Kenya African Democratic Union (KADU) led to the emergence of a *de facto* one-party state. In Uganda Obote faced a somewhat different problem: how to create a unified state against the claims of the old kingdoms, and particularly the most powerful, Buganda, which was a state within a state.

Creating a one-party system was relatively easy but a single party must have an ideological purpose beyond providing stable government and herein lay its greatest challenge, for a two- or multiparty system, at least in theory, offers alternative policies. In the case of Tanganyika (transformed into Tanzania in 1964 following the union with Zanzibar) Nyerere justified the one-party system as a means of continuing the unity that had been achieved in the battle for independence and by 1965 had come to see the multiparty alternative as positively dangerous and destructive. As the masses in all one-party systems would soon ask: who controls the controllers? What checks and balances are required in a one-party state and how can these be created? Part of the solution, Nyerere suggested, was to allow members of the ruling party, in Tanganyika's case the Tanganyika African National Union (TANU), to run against official TANU candidates at elections although no non-TANU candidate had any chance of being elected. Another political problem, a crucial and necessary aspect of nation building, was to endow the head of state with awesome charisma so that in the early days he was first the hero of the independence struggle while later developing into the all-powerful presidential figure not to be questioned.[1] Both Kenyatta and Nyerere earned this status, though in very different fashions, but Obote, who lacked the inherited charisma of the Kabaka of Buganda, never managed to achieve such a standing in Uganda.

In his early political life, which included a long spell in Britain and the publication of his book *Facing Mount Kenya*, Kenyatta had come to be regarded as a dangerous man of the left by both settlers and colonial authorities. In a famous trial he had been convicted (on perjured evidence) of managing Mau Mau and sent to an isolated prison in the north of Kenya. At the end of the 1950s and into the 1960s his release from detention became a central political objective in the independence struggle. When finally he achieved power and became first Prime Minister and then President of an independent Kenya, Kenyatta's image was reversed and he came to be seen as moderate, pragmatic, subtle and as a symbol of national unity. He presided over a smooth transition from white settler to black rule and achieved a high level of racial reconciliation while his tolerance reduced tribal rivalries. His rallying cry 'Harambee' – 'Let's pull together' – became the catchword in the new Kenya. During the remainder of the 1960s, despite a number of political crises, Kenyatta ruled over a comparatively free and prosperous society although his critics claimed that he was too conservative and *laissez-faire* in his policies. His admirers, however, called him Mzee, the old man, and elevated him above politics as the 'Father of the Nation'. Julius Nyerere, by contrast, was an austere idealist who certainly earned his title Mwalimu, the teacher. Although he could be as tough as Kenyatta when the need arose, his approach was very different. 'He was an idealist and his economic policies were hardly successful, but he did create a moral and social climate superior to the rest of Africa.'[2] The Arusha Declaration of 1967 became one of the most famous landmarks in the continent's political thinking. In his speech of 7 February 1967 in which he outlined the Declaration's main purposes, Nyerere put forward the concept of *ujamaa* (familyhood or family sharing). It was a philosophy of self-help that led in 1970 to the policy, ultimately rejected, of villageization. Both Kenyatta and Nyerere achieved a status in their own countries and on the continent that was never earned by Uganda's political leader of the 1960s, Milton Obote. He was a politician renowned for his skill at political infighting and he needed all his skills in his fight to create a centralized state following independence. With patience and skill Obote overcame the opposition of the Kabaka (King) of Buganda, Frederick Mutesa II, and his traditionalist supporters, first by offering them an alliance and then by manipulating them. By the end of the decade he had destroyed the power of Buganda and the lesser kingdoms, created a unified political system and then turned it into a one-party state with himself as President. However, once he had achieved his objectives, Obote found he was isolated with no real power base and he succumbed, as did so many of Africa's new leaders, to the temptations of absolutism.

It was events in the island of Zanzibar that upset the apparently smooth early phase of independence in East Africa. Zanzibar, a separate British colony, became independent on 10 December 1963. At the beginning of the 1960s there were 40,000 Arabs on the island who owned the land, a few thousand Asians who ran the businesses and 300,000 Africans who did the work. Yet in 1963 Britain effectively handed over power to the Arab minority and then wondered why there was a revolution six weeks later when the Africans seized power. The revolution in Zanzibar, carried out over 12–16 January 1964, brought Abeid Karume, the leader of the Afro-Shirazi Party, to power as President. The Arab Sultan, Seyyid Jamshid bin Abdulla, left the island unharmed, with a retinue of followers in a yacht. He was subsequently declared banished for life. Kenya and Uganda recognized the new revolutionary government, which was also quickly recognized by the USSR, China and other Communist powers. John Okello, a Ugandan by birth, was the extraordinary figure responsible for leading the revolution, the self-styled 'Field Marshal' who proclaimed a people's republic and said that a14-man Revolutionary Council had been set up. His own powers, he claimed, were 'equal to that of the whole government'. He said that he had conceived the idea of the revolution without consulting the other leaders. On 17 January armed units of the Tanganyika police, numbering about 200, were despatched to Zanzibar to maintain law and order until the island's police force had been reconstituted. In his autobiography, Okello described the contempt with which Arabs on Zanzibar treated Africans and told how in his presence one spoke to another, not believing that he understood what they said, 'We know these Africans are fools and they will remain under our control forever; but don't pay any attention to these mainland Africans because they don't understand KiSwahili.' This conversation, according to Okello, took place on 8 January when he was 'making a routine reconnaissance of the town' prior to the revolt, which he launched four days later. Okello was too unreliable and erratic a figure to be acceptable to the mainland rulers and he was rapidly sidelined. The official version of the revolution does not mention him at all: 'The story of the Zanzibar Revolution of January 12 1964 is the answer of the people of the islands of Zanzibar and Pemba to the intrigues and plots of the Sultan and his political henchmen to prevent a popular democratic regime coming to power when Zanzibar cut free of British colonial domination on December 10, 1963.'[3] The article went on to describe how the revolution had been led by the Afro-Shirazi Party and its leader, Sheikh Abeid Amani Karume. As Okello, who dropped from sight, says in his autobiography: 'Now that my name has been omitted entirely from the "official" version of the Revolution I believe there is *nothing* about me or my part in the Revolution which makes East Africa's leaders comfortable.'[4] On 20 January 1964 the 1st Battalion Tanganyika Rifles mutinied.

THE ARMY MUTINIES

The January 1964 army mutinies in Tanganyika, Uganda and Kenya (see chapter four above) were inept affairs although only the intervention of British troops prevented the revolts overturning the governments of Kenya and Uganda. The British intervention in its three former colonies raises the question as to why Britain did not intervene in Zanzibar whose Prime Minister Sheikh Muhammad Shamte also appealed for help. The answer to this question concerned the British assessment of its interests in the region. The British government must, by then, have realized its mistake in handing over power to the Arab minority in Zanzibar although it must also have been wilfully dense to do so in the first place. Apart from that, however, British intervention in Zanzibar would have meant overturning a revolution while in Kenya, Tanganyika and Uganda it only meant coming to the assistance of the legitimate governments and restoring order on their behalves. The mutinies had a traumatic if different impact in the three countries. 'Neither could the newly independent governments afford, as Nyerere put it, the national humiliation of using outside forces to suppress their own people. Kenyatta was not quite so reluctant as his neighbours to accept outside help and in March 1964 he signed a defence agreement with Britain.'[5] Undoubtedly, Nyerere felt most deeply the double humiliation of the new state being held to ransom by its mutinous army and then the need to ask the ex-imperial power to come to the rescue. As he responded to these events in a radio broadcast, Nyerere said: 'I call on all members of the TANU Youth League, wherever they are, to go to the local TANU office and enrol themselves. From this group we shall try to build a nucleus of a new army for the Republic of Tanganyika.'[6]

Ali Mazrui, an acute observer of the East African scene, said of the mutinies, 'The new states of Africa have virtually the same basis for military troubles as they have for political troubles – they are no longer adequately tribal and are not yet fully national. Their armed forces are inspired neither by the dedication of tribal warriors nor by the patriotism which comes with a long-established national consciousness.'[7] As he went on to say, the great irony of the East African mutinies, which were principally about pay and conditions, was that the new nationalist governments in East Africa were driven to seek the aid of former imperial troops to force their own troops into submitting to African rule. Assumptions about Africa at this time centred upon independence as though the achievement of it would solve all other problems. In fact it created as many as it solved. The idea of loyalty to the African governments in East Africa was invoked at the time of the mutinies; this demand raised an even greater question that would dominate political thought for years to come, that of the one-party state versus the multiparty state. The multiparty system that much of Africa was abandoning at the time provides the basis for a distinction between loyalty to the government and loyalty to the country. The single-party system, on the other hand, does not provide room for manoeuvre on this question of loyalty. It was one thing for Nyerere to call upon TANU youth to enrol in a new army that would secure the future of the state but what would happen when a political alternative to TANU appeared?

Unlike both Kenyatta and Obote, who regarded the mutinies as dangerous political problems to be solved by whatever means lay to hand, which meant British military assistance, Nyerere clearly felt obliged to explain his action in calling upon Britain for support to Africa as a whole. He summoned an OAU meeting, which convened in Dar es Salaam on 12 February when some 200 delegates from 28 countries came to discuss the implications of asking British troops to intervene. As Nyerere explained:

Our national humiliation arises from the necessity of having non-Tanganyikan troops do our work for us; it is not very much affected by their nationality. But the presence of troops from a country deeply involved in the world's Cold War conflicts has serious implications in the context of

African nationalism, and our common policies of non-alignment, because these policies may depend not only on remaining outside such conflicts but also on being seen to remain outside them.[8]

Here speaks the Mwalimu, almost certainly over the heads of many in his audience who would have taken the more practical view that the means were less important than the fact that the mutinies had been put down. Obote officially dissociated himself from the resolution on the East African mutinies that was then passed by the OAU Foreign Ministers and criticized Nyerere for calling the conference at all. And as the delegates made plain, the OAU was not prepared to accept any automatic responsibility for interventions in such situations. Kenyatta had stated on 7 February that the calling in of extra British troops (there were already some stationed in Kenya) had not embarrassed him or his government. Only Nyerere of the three East African leaders felt the need for public soul-searching

FEDERATION AND AN EAST AFRICAN COMMUNITY

In June 1960, prior to independence, Nyerere delivered a paper that was later accepted at the October meeting in Mbale, Uganda, of the Pan African Freedom Movement for East and Central Africa (PAFMECA). In it he said: 'The unity and freedom movements should be combined, and the East African territories achieve independence as one unit at the earliest possible moment. This means a Federation of the Territories now administered separately.'[9] Having pointed out that Tanganyika was closer to independence than the other two territories, Nyerere then said:

I also believe that the attainment of complete independence by Tanganyika alone would complicate the establishment of a new political unit. If the British Government is willing to amend their timetable for the constitutional changes of the other territories and then these territories expressed a desire for Federation, I would be willing to ask the people of Tanganyika to join that Federation with the others.

The hope did not materialize. On 5 June 1963 in Nairobi Kenyatta, Nyerere and Obote issued a statement: 'We, the leaders of the people and governments of East Africa assembled in Nairobi on 5 June 1963, pledge ourselves to the political Federation of East Africa.' At the end of that June Kenyatta addressed a mass rally at the Clock Tower, Kampala, at which he said: 'Uganda's kings and hereditary rulers should not have any fears about a Federation of East Africa because there will be room in the federation for everyone.'[10] These apparently unequivocal calls for federation became more cautious in 1964. Replying to a delegation of representatives of the KANU and TANU Parliamentary Groups in May, Nyerere said: 'We must also be quite clear about one thing. Once a federation has been established, it is established for all time. It can move for greater unity but it cannot disintegrate. There can be no question of dissolution in relation to a federation of East Africa, which is freely established by the will of the people. The federation will become the sovereign unity which has to be defended at all costs, just as our separate countries are now the units to which all citizens owe allegiance.'[11] The strength of Nyerere's statement suggests that doubts were growing on the part of his audience. In the same month Uganda refused to be pressured by Kenya and Tanzania to proceed with federation. 'Kenya and Tanganyika backbenchers were trying to push the East African leaders into federation before many important issues had been settled. If Tanganyika and Kenya wished to go ahead and federate now, Uganda would wish them well, but would not be forced into any hasty union.'[12] Pressures against federation mounted in all three countries and gradually it fell off the political agenda. Instead the possibilities of an East African Community (EAC) moved centre stage.

In 1948 Britain had established the East Africa High Commission to co-ordinate activities in the three territories. In 1961 the Commission was replaced by the East African Common Services Organization (EACSO). At least by the beginning of the 1960s the groundwork for operating a successful common market existed when the three countries became independent and conditions were about as favourable as could be expected. Yet, between 1961 and 1967 Tanzania and Uganda complained that a majority of the economic benefits of EACSO went to Kenya, which had a more advanced infrastructure than its two partners and a better developed industrial base. The majority of investment was in Kenya, mainly in Nairobi and Mombasa, with cement, tobacco products, brewing, textiles, food processing and petroleum refining the main components of the sector. Furthermore, the investment policies of the three were very different. Kenya hoped to attract significant inflows of investment capital and passed regulations to attract them. On the other hand, the Uganda development programme, Work for Progress, placed little emphasis upon foreign private investment except for the partial reinvestment of profits. Instead, private domestic firms were expected to provide the means of expansion. Tanzania, meanwhile, was pursuing a definite socialist policy that included taking control of foreign companies so that no inward flow of investment was expected. 'By the mid-1960s, net gains from the East African economic union (or quasi-union, since agriculture and economic planning had never been integrated) approached £17 million a year; but this represented under 2 per cent of the combined domestic product of the three countries. Half of the net gain represented economies on joint services; rather less derived from the creation of a common market for industry and partially for agriculture.'[13] A number of factors worked against closer economic co-operation: there was no formal structure to control and direct the common market; there was little harmonization of import, income and excise taxes and monetary and exchange control; the gains were unevenly divided – and this was the crux of the problem – with Kenya making substantial gains while the other two faced losses; and in any case the total gains were too small to allow fiscal redistribution or relocation of production to ensure net gains for each state. As a result Tanzania, a net loser, initiated moves to reform the EACSO and warned that without them it might have to safeguard its future development by partial or total withdrawal. As a result of these imbalances the three members entered into the Kampala Agreement of 1964 (amended at Mbale in 1965), which provided for industrial relocation of certain industries such as beer, shoes, cement; agreed quotas to protect new industries in Uganda and Tanzania from Kenyan competition; and agreed the allocation of a few new industries designed to cater for the overall East African market. By mid-1965 Nyerere was warning that speedy political union was no longer in prospect and that if economic union was to continue major institutional reforms were necessary at once. At the same time it had come to be realized that economic union was as much political as it was economic.

A Commission on East African co-operation was established with three senior ministers from each country under the chairmanship of Professor Kjeld Philip (a former Finance Minister of Denmark) from the United Nations. It reported in May 1966 and its recommendations formed the basis of the June 1967 Treaty. The smallness of the actual East African market was always a matter of concern; it would, for example, remain smaller than was necessary to create certain critical industrial complexes and it would be more likely to succeed if it formed the core of a wider economic union. An important innovation of the 1967 Treaty was the restitution of a transfer tax. This allowed Tanzania and Uganda, under certain conditions, to tax imports of manufactures from Kenya so as to protect their own infant industries. When the East African Community (EAC) was formed in 1967 an attempt to rectify the imbalance between Kenya and the other two members was made by channelling a greater proportion of community revenues to Tanzania and Uganda.

The EAC comprising Kenya, Tanzania and Uganda was formally established on 6 June 1967. Its object was to strengthen economic, trade and industrial ties between the three countries. Like other similar 'communities' in Africa or elsewhere, its provisions were unexceptionable. These included a common excise tariff, no internal tariffs and the establishment of an East African Development Bank (EADB). Its main organs were the Common Market Council, the Common Market Tribunal, the Secretariat and the East African Authority (consisting of the three heads of state), which was the ultimate authority of the EAC. Other aspects of the EAC were five councils, an East African Legislative Assembly, a General Fund, the East African Railways Corporation, the East African Harbours Corporation, the East African Posts and Telecommunications Corporation and the East African Airways Corporation. The EAC headquarters were sited in Arusha, the Railways at Nairobi, Harbours at Dar es Salaam, Posts and Telecommunications at Kampala.

From 1967 to 1976 Kenya enjoyed a trade surplus with its two partners. In 1977 the EAC ceased to exist. It foundered over political questions and these were sparked off by the coup that ousted Obote and brought Idi Amin to power in Uganda at the beginning of 1971. Perhaps, however, the EAC really failed because the time was not ripe. It had been launched when pressures for both unity and regional markets were very strong, yet, as its three members discovered, each had its own distinct approach to development and each faced different political problems and, apart from anything else, these differences were reflected in the three men – Kenyatta, Nyerere and Obote – who brought the EAC into being, while Nyerere refused even to meet with Amin when the latter replaced Obote.

KENYA

Kenya became independent on 12 December 1963 with Kenyatta as Prime Minister. A year later a new constitution to make Kenya a republic had replaced the complex regional independence constitution while the opposition party KADU had dissolved itself, its members crossing the floor of the House to join the ranks of the ruling KANU and turn the country into a *de facto* one-party state. Ronald Ngala, KADU's leader, had at first resisted the disintegration of his party but the trend was against him; already in early 1964 members of KADU had begun to cross over and join the government side of the Assembly and by April it was clear that KADU was dying: by then there were 102 KANU members to 23 KADU in the House of Representatives. Tom Mboya, the Minister of Justice and Constitutional Affairs, addressing the Nyanza Regional Assembly at Kisumu, said that the 'opposition mentality' must be ended. 'There was one Central Government to whom all owe loyalty and the country was being run by this government and not by the political party that put it in power.'[14] This was the reverse of the approach that elevated party above government but it would have the same effect as far as Kenyatta was concerned and soon he was able to act in a genuine sense as a national leader, making nonsense of the argument that he led only a Kikuyu–Luo alliance, and though two of his most prominent ministers, Odinga and Mboya, were Luo, other ministers included a Kamba, a Kisii and a Margoli.

Recognizing the inevitable, on 10 November 1964 Ronald Ngala announced the dissolution of KADU and amid scenes of jubilation was carried shoulder high across the Assembly. He told the Assembly: 'I have a full mandate to declare today that the official Opposition is dissolved. KADU is joining the government under the leadership of Mzee Jomo Kenyatta and the Opposition today will vote with the government for the new Constitution in the Senate.' Kenyatta replied: 'I welcome our brothers wholeheartedly... I regard this day as a great day, not for KANU but for the people of Kenya.' Asked later to explain his change of heart, Ngala said: 'This is one of the times when we must be prepared to sacrifice our political dignity for the peace and harmony of Kenya.' Early in 1965, after Kenya had become a republic, there was a debate in the House of Commons in London in which tributes were paid to the way in which during the preceding three years Kenyatta had transformed the atmosphere in Kenya from one of disunity and despondency into one of buoyancy and unity. The necessary corollary to becoming a one-party state is that while official opposition is banned, opposition will instead be found within the ranks of the ruling party and this was to happen soon enough in Kenya. Nonetheless, during the period 1965–66 when Kenya was a *de facto* one-party state there was a great deal of open debate, both in Parliament and in the country; but in 1966, after the Kenya People's Union (KPU) was formed there followed reduced candour in public debate while challenges to government policy became less effective.

Given the bitterness that existed between the white settlers and the African nationalists over the Mau Mau years it was inevitable that Kenyatta should pay particular attention to the white minority as he took over the reins of power. A photograph, taken from the stage of the Nakuru Town Hall on 12 August 1963 when Kenyatta met and addressed the white settlers for the first time, showing the range of expressions on their faces is extraordinary: suspicion, through doubt, apprehension, bewilderment, disbelief, contempt, fear, reluctance and a tentative desire to accept. The meeting was a decisive moment in black-white coming to terms prior to independence.[15] The *East African Standard* of 13 August reported under the headline 'Farmers Join Premier in Harambee, Europeans asked to Forget Suspicions, Historic Speech Cheered.' This was Kenyatta's 'forgive and forget the past' speech.

We want you to stay and farm in this country. We must also learn to forgive one another... There is no society of angels black brown or white, we are human beings and as such we are bound to make mistakes. If I have done a mistake to you it is for you to forgive me, if you have done a mistake to me it is for me to forgive you, the Africans cannot say the Europeans have done all the wrong and the Europeans cannot say the Africans have done all the wrong. We are all human beings and as such likely to do wrong. The good thing is to be able to forget and forgive one another. You have something to forget just as I have.

(This theme, of forgiving and working together for the future of the country was employed 17 years later by Robert Mugabe on the eve of Zimbabwe's independence in 1980.)

Kenyatta kept his word to the whites whose contribution to the economy he knew was essential. 'Kenyatta was no multi-racialist and his conciliatory mood was no sign of weakness. Like all Kikuyu he was essentially a realist, and he knew that for the present, and for some years to come, he could not run the economy without the European farmers and businessmen. Kenyatta's authority over the country was unquestioned, but he had behind him men who were still bitter and for whom Kenya was a country for black Africans and for nobody else... Kenyatta was strong enough to trounce his own back-benchers in the National Assembly and tell them that he would keep his white officials as long as they were efficient and competent Africans were lacking; yet a time would come when pressure for complete Africanization in government, land and business would be too great even for Kenyatta to withstand.'[16]

On the occasion of independence Kenyatta was generous in his remarks addressed to the British, perhaps taking his cue from Balewa's speech at Nigeria's independence in 1960. 'We do not forget the assistance and guidance we have received through the years from people of British stock...' Kenyatta the realist did not allow the occasion of independence, with the world's attention briefly on his country, to pass without an appeal for outside help. Nation building, he said, needed the co-operation of outside investors: 'To our overseas friends we offer a stable political environment and expanding market in Kenya and East Africa.' He also said that Kenya would not really be free until all Africa was free. And in a warning to would-be troublemakers, showing his iron fist, he said: 'The fact that the Imperialist Government is dead does not mean that the people can do as they please. There will still be police and there will still be prisons.'

Despite insistence upon Kenya's non-alignment, Kenyatta's sympathies were with the West. They were to be tested sorely in November 1964 over the Congo crisis when Kenyatta was chairing the OAU Commission to find a peaceable resolution to the white hostages then held by rebels in Stanleyville (Kisangani). A joint US-Belgian military rescue operation was planned and mounted even as the US Ambassador to Kenya gave the impression that Washington supported the OAU peace initiative. William Attwood, the US Ambassador, subsequently wrote an autobiographical account of his time in Kenya[17] and of this affair he arrogantly claims, 'As I walked out [of seeing Kenyatta], Ambassador Lavrov [of the USSR] was waiting to come in: the campaign to confuse and capture Kenyatta was really in high gear.' Attwood clearly missed the irony of his statement. When the full extent of American duplicity became apparent there was deep African anger. 'That Mzee Kenyatta had been making every effort to save the hostages by peaceful negotiated methods when, behind his back, the Americans and the Belgians launched a different type of operation. It was evident that the Americans had appealed to Kenyatta to use his good offices only as a stalling tactic while they and the Belgians made other arrangements.'[18] Attwood titled his book *The Reds and the Blacks* and as he says in the blurb, 'As the title suggests, it is essentially about what I saw of Soviet and Chinese efforts to penetrate and subvert Africa, and what we and the Africans and others did to counter these efforts.' Attwood, a Cold War warrior, is clearly incapable of impartial thought: the subversion of Africa had been a Western achievement and anything the Communists did was mild by comparison. When Attwood went to see Kenyatta after the US-Belgian intervention had taken place, he said, 'I knew that he felt I had deceived him and that we'd pulled a Pearl Harbour on the OAU.'[19]

The Cold War, in any case, affected both the internal as well as the external policies of Kenya. There was the affair of a convoy of lorries full of Chinese arms that passed from Tanzania through the south-west of Kenya *en route* for Uganda. The convoy was intercepted and seized by the Kenya authorities to cause a crisis between Kenya and its two neighbours, and only after Obote, accompanied by two ministers, had flown to Nairobi to apologize to Kenyatta did the affair subside. In June 1965, however, Kenyatta said: 'It is naïve to think there is no danger of imperialism from the East.' He said Kenya rejected Communism and went on: 'It is natural that we should detest Western colonialism and associate the word imperialism with the West. But if we are truly non-aligned we must not avoid making friends with those Western countries who extend an honest field of co-operation and trade.' Kenyatta in fact was always pro-Western.

Oginga Odinga, the Luo nationalist whom Kenyatta had made his Vice-President, was considerably more radical than the President and, if not a

Communist as his enemies insisted, was certainly inspired by Marxist theories. Growing distrust between the two men and various policy confrontations made a split more and more likely; in any case, Odinga had soon discovered that he had little real power. When the army mutinied in January 1964 Kenyatta personally telephoned Odinga and told him not to leave Nairobi for Kisumu because the British Army was blocking the road: this was a personal warning, an order for Odinga to stay at home. Communist arms were supposedly being smuggled into the country, and in April 1965 Kenyatta refused a shipload of Russian arms on the grounds of obsolescence. He then became increasingly concerned with the activities of the Lumumba Institute, created as an instrument of KANU, and Odinga's name was linked with both Russian arms and the activities of the Institute, which Kenyatta closed. Then Kenyatta, under pressure from the British, replaced Odinga as the head of the Kenya delegation to the 1965 Commonwealth Conference in London. In the two years following independence Odinga found himself isolated within the structure of KANU. Their antagonism came to a head in 1966 when Kenyatta relieved Odinga of his portfolio of Home Affairs, which he gave to Daniel arap Moi, a former leader of KADU. (It was one of the ironies of one-party politics that former KADU members became the true Kenyatta loyalists.) Odinga resigned as Vice-President and left KANU, accompanied by Bildad Kaggia and Achieng Oneko, two of the more radical KANU leaders, while 28 members of the Assembly followed Odinga to create an opposition party, the Kenya People's Union (KPU). Kenyatta suspended all the dissidents and called by-elections in their seats; this became known as the 'little election'. When it became clear that they might lose their seats 21 of the dissidents returned to the KANU fold and only seven stayed with the KPU. The election took place on 2 June 1966 and resulted in an overwhelming victory for Kenyatta although Odinga kept his Central Nyanza seat with a big majority. After 20 months of an effective one-party system Kenya had returned to two-party politics. Kenyatta followed the 'little election' by introducing a Public Security Act, which gave the government powers of detention without trial, censorship and control over aliens.

ECONOMIC CONSIDERATIONS: TRADE UNIONS, LAND RESETTLEMENT AND ASIANS

At the beginning of 1964 the problem of unemployment was acute and affected 10 per cent of the labour force. Following tripartite talks between government, business and labour, legislation was introduced to enable the government to employ an additional 15 per cent more personnel while private employers agreed to add a further 10 per cent to their labour forces. It was clear soon after independence that the government would clamp down on union activity and Kenyatta used Mboya as the instrument of this policy. Tom Mboya had come to prominence in the 1950s as a trade union leader: he was Secretary of the Local Government Workers' Union and acted as Director of Information and Treasurer of the Kenya Africa Union (KAU) before it was banned when the Mau Mau emergency was declared. In September 1953 he had been elected General Secretary of the Kenya Federation of Labour (KFL) and of this he later said: 'The KFL became the voice of the African people, in the absence of any other African organisation to speak for them.' This remained the case until the emergence of KANU just before independence. The strength that the KFL acquired through its political role led Mboya to make a bid for the complete independence of the unions and by the late 1950s it looked as though the unions were powerful enough to successfully dictate their own terms to the emerging political parties. At the same time, the KFL was the only truly national organization without evident traces of regional or tribal conflict. At the 1960 Annual Conference of the KFL Mboya said: 'The trade union movement must have a right to pronounce on political matters and even to take appropriate action to assist during the struggle for independence... If the movement must be free and independent of government and employers, that movement must be capable of formulating its own policies on those problems that affect the workers either as employees or as a class that lives and occupies a certain position in the society and community in which it exists.'[20]

Mboya's blueprint for free and powerful trade unions, as he was quickly to discover, was anathema to KANU (and other African ruling parties) as it worked to gather all power to itself and saw the trade union movement as a rival and potentially dangerous centre of power. Kenyatta's government was to brook no opposition from independent power factions and Mboya as a minister of his government was given the task of undermining the trade union movement that he had largely created. And just as Kenyatta cut the union movement down to size so too did Nyerere tackle the power of organized labour. Nyerere saw organized wage earners as a potentially privileged class whose members had to be persuaded to direct their energies towards raising productivity and the living standards of the whole people. This utopian approach to wage earners, whose wages in any case were hardly substantial, was unlikely to make much headway. Nonetheless, when in 1962 he addressed TANU on socialism, Nyerere compared diamond miners and their wages with peasant farmers producing food and suggested that part of the wealth from the mines should go to the community and not all be retained by the mineworkers. Although he conceded that it was the purpose of a trade union to ensure for its workers a fair share of the profits of their labour, a fair share, he argued, had to be fair in relation to the whole society. Nyerere, in a somewhat different way to Kenyatta, saw the unions as posing a possible threat to his socialist society – as well as to the one-party state. Historically, unions have been seen as the vanguard of socialist movements, yet as Africa discovered this was not necessarily the case. 'Trade union leaders and their followers, as long as they are true socialists, will not need to be coerced by the government in to keeping their demands within the limits imposed by the needs of the society as a whole. Only if there are potential capitalists among them will the socialist government have to step in and prevent them putting their capitalist ideas into practice.'[21] Such a reasoned judgement was more academic than real.

Land remained a central political question after independence. At one stage in the colony's history Europeans owned 25 per cent of all the arable land in private hands. In the period after independence about 1,500,000 acres were voluntarily sold at fair prices to Africans by the settlers and the process was carried out with little public debate. Kenyatta always paid special attention to land questions and in his speeches he repeatedly called for hard work on the land. In the period 1963–66 more than 170,000 Africans were settled on former European holdings, and the scale of this settlement alone gave some indication of the size of the European land stake in Kenya. At independence Britain had provided £27 million to buy out white farmers and settle Africans in the White Highlands and the programme was carried out with a minimum of either rancorous debate or publicity. Kenyatta, in one of those twists for which he was famous, appointed a former hard-line settler, Bruce Mackenzie, as Minister of Agriculture and Land and made him responsible for this land transfer.

Conflict between aspiring Africans and the minority Asian community was bound to cause problems after independence. Only about 40 per cent of the Asians had either qualified for or taken out Kenya citizenship during the two-year grace period after independence. Unemployment, the demand for Africanization and feelings of resentment against the Asians, as well as the announcement of Britain's intention to curb immigration, combined to produce the crisis of February 1968, when pressures against the Asians led to their mass migration to Britain.

On 18 February Malcolm Macdonald (the last British Governor and first High Commissioner to Kenya after independence) went to Nairobi on a special mission to talk with Kenyatta, ostensibly to persuade him either to halt or at least to slow down measures against the Asians. Meanwhile a British Bill was prepared and rushed through Parliament, depriving Asian holders of British passports of any automatic right because of that fact to move to Britain. The official Kenyan view was that the Asians were 'the responsibility of the British Government'. Kenyatta said: 'Kenya's identity as an African country is not going to be altered to the whims and malaises of groups of uncommitted individuals.'

Kenyan politics during the first decade of independence were often turbulent while MPs, even if they toed the general party line, could be deeply critical as well. Kenyatta's powerful position raised him above the need for party support; in consequence, he neglected KANU and some of its members resented this. In 1968 one member of parliament said Kenya MPs were 'the most underprivileged, demoralized and ignorant in East Africa', while Cabinet Ministers were 'the richest, most arrogant and most miserable people'.[22] The assassination on 5 July 1969 of Tom Mboya, by then the Minister of Economic Planning, at the age of 38, deprived Kenya of one of its most able political figures. The assassination set off a spate of rumours and a political crisis. Mahason Isaac Njenja Njoroge, a Kikuyu, was convicted of the killing but it was widely assumed that he was no more than an instrument of someone much higher. Anger among the Luo was met by a spate of Kikuyu oathing in support of the government and, for example, three British journalists were expelled for reporting the oathing, which was illegal. On 25 October riots broke out in Kisumu, the heart of Luo country, when Kenyatta visited the town. The disturbance gave him the excuse to have Odinga and his deputy in the KPU arrested along with six other opposition MPs and on 30 October the KPU was banned. In what had again become a *de facto* one-party state elections were held on 6 December 1969 in which 620 candidates contested 158 seats. The final results showed that even if only KANU candidates could stand that was no guarantee that the bad ones had seats for life: five ministers, 14 assistant ministers and 79 backbenchers lost their seats.

As Kenya entered the 1970s Kenyatta's supporters, outside the country as well as inside it, could argue that he had presided over some remarkable achievements. The whites had been mollified to become some of his staunchest supporters; the land question was well on the way to being solved; the economy was not doing too badly and Kenya had become one of the most favoured aid recipients in Africa, while it was also regarded by the West as a firm ally in the Cold War despite its pretence at non-alignment. On the other hand, radical Kenyans argued that Kenyatta had betrayed everything the independence struggle had been about. 'After 1963, the losers were those who had fought for liberation, the winners those eager to "eat". The African President assured the former colonial rulers that "the government of an independent Kenya will not be a gangster government". A "gangster government" was presumably one which would repossess the stolen lands for the use of all the people and preside over the creation of a more egalitarian society.'[23] The authors of this statement and others below published their views anonymously for they would undoubtedly have landed in prison had their names been known. As they went on to say: 'As our politicians orbit endlessly around the President, they compete with each other to sing his praises loudly and attract his favour. Obsequious loyalty brings its own reward – a position closer to the warming power of the sun with all the economic privileges that go with membership of the inner circles. A loss of favour could put the politician out of orbit altogether, into limbo or extinction.' This savage but accurate description went very near the bone and could be applied widely in the Africa of that time. These critics argued that elections were held from time to time so as to allow friendly foreign nations the opportunity to hold up Kenya as the showpiece of democracy in Africa. There is much more in the same vein: the corruption of politicians, the loss of autonomy of such bodies as the legislature or judiciary, a president who rules as a kind of sultan. At the same time the Western powers had soon realized that the President would not flirt with Communism but, rather, had created conditions for capitalist countries to have a free-for-all in Kenya so that Kenyatta was seen as a valuable ally against 'foreign ideology': 'Anything which threatened imperialist control of our economy came into the category of "foreign ideology"… The Americans and British tutored Kenyatta and the young KANU government on "anti-Communist" tactics.'[24] These strictures upon the Kenyatta government have to be taken in perspective; his critics were radical Marxists yet the picture they paint was a recognizable one and could be applied to other countries with their untouchable leaders surrounded by their obsequious courtiers.

TANZANIA

In the last hours before Tanganyika became independent on 9 December 1961, Nyerere revealed that his greatest anxiety was the people's expectation that independence would bring rapid changes, and that the government would be unable to fulfil their hopes. Nyerere was to puzzle his admirers as much as his opponents and not least when in January 1962, less than two months after independence, he stepped down as Prime Minister to work with the party. Few were certain as to what he intended. The British expected that an independent Tanganyika would accept a close relationship of dependence and so were shocked when he resigned to strengthen the party (TANU). They began to understand that he had embarked upon a policy of self-reliance. It was also believed that the decision had been a TANU rather than a government one, adding strength to the view that like other African states Tanganyika was moving towards a one-party structure. 'Those who had type-cast the TANU leader as a "moderate" were alarmed at the change as a sign that the country was taking a leap to the left. They refused to accept the genuine declaration of the new Prime Minister, Rashid Kawawa, that Nyerere remained the "father of the nation"… Cynics looked behind the straightforward explanation for sinister causes, but were unable to find any of substance.'[25] *The Times* opined: 'What may happen to Tanganyika if Mr Nyerere does not keep control can only occasion the gravest misgivings. African talent is desperately thin on the ground; few African countries can less afford to bully or frighten expatriates and capital away. Extremism in foreign policy, furthermore, besides injuring a very weak economy, would worsen an already difficult outlook for East Africa as a whole.' This considered appraisal of the possible consequences of Nyerere's decision, like many similar Western appraisals of Africa at that time, is apparently only concerned with what is good for Tanganyika; in fact it betrays the interests uppermost in Western thinking: the position of expatriates in Africa and the future of Western investment. There was a more radical view of the event: 'Sir Ernest Vasey's translation from Finance Minister to financial adviser, on the excuse that he was not eligible for citizenship, followed criticism of him by the left wing of TANU for his adherence to Western capitalist techniques and attitudes and for the involvement with the West which his policies were producing.'[26] In July 1962, just halfway through the year in which Nyerere was reorganizing TANU and preparing to launch the country upon a radical socialist path, with ill-judged timing the Arthur D. Little Report, the result of a three-man mission for the Agency for International Development (IDA), was presented to the government with its recommendations for the future industrialization of Tanganyika. The country could not become a manufacturing centre processing imported materials for re-export, the report argued. The country's industrial future should be based on the partial or complete processing for export of domestic raw materials, or manufacture for the local market. The report also suggested that investment uncertainty could be reduced if the government entered a guarantee programme concerning repatriation of earnings and capital for foreign investors. External advice then and later would inhibit African attempts to industrialize and keep them as sources of raw materials while at the same time ensuring the best possible conditions – maximum repatriation of profits – for external investors.

On 8 December 1962, the eve of his installation as President of Tanganyika which would become a republic on that day, Nyerere said in his speech that he intended to change the country quickly and raise the standard of living and that 'he might have to push people around'. Indications that TANU was not prepared to tolerate opposition were not slow to appear. There had been incidents during the Presidential election when TANU 'strongmen' had disrupted African National Congress (ANC) meetings and subsequent ANC meetings had been banned rather than the 'strongmen' being disciplined. Later,

Nyerere was to warn that opposition should be constructive and not merely annoying. Freedom of speech, he said, ought not to be misused. It was not in order that some people might be able to abuse others that such freedom was granted. As always in a one-party state – at this stage Tanganyika was a *de facto* rather than *de jure* one-party state – the old question recurred: who controls the controllers?

Unlike Kenya, Tanganyika did not have large white or Asian minorities to accommodate after independence and Nyerere rejected any attempt to give whites or Asians special political rights, although he was determined that they should not be discriminated against. In fact race relations were sufficiently equable that African elected members, anxious to ensure the protection of minorities, proposed reserved seats for them under the independence constitution while the Europeans and Asians objected to this, expressing themselves satisfied that such a measure was unnecessary and that politics could be conducted in a non-racial atmosphere. This harmonious beginning was marred in January 1962 when, following some racial incidents, a number of whites were expelled for racial discrimination. Nyerere defended the expulsions: 'Our people have expected much from independence which it is impossible to give them. But I am determined that they will get one thing and that is personal respect.'

More ominous for the future was the growth of an authoritarian attitude in the ranks of TANU. This, perhaps, was hardly surprising once the emphasis had been put upon the role of the single party, first in bringing about independence and then as the national instrument for development. Thus, in 1962, several small political parties were harassed out of existence by TANU. Moreover, when Nyerere first suggested competitive elections within the one-party system, he found little support for the idea within the ranks of TANU. Authoritarianism came early to most newly independent African countries under a variety of guises. On 27 September 1962 the National Assembly passed, without dissent, the Preventive Detention Bill: persons threatening the stability and security of the State could be detained and no detention order could be questioned in any court. Detainees were to be told within 15 days of the grounds for their detention and could make written representations to the Minister of Home Affairs. The Prime Minister, Rashid Kawawa, said the Bill was desired by the people: 'We do not want democracy to be lost, and therefore democracy must defend itself. Tanganyika was prepared to be condemned by the whole world in order to defend democracy.'

Mr Wilbert A. Klerrun, the Publicity Secretary of the TANU Parliamentary Party, felt the need to justify this measure in a letter published in the *Guardian*:

We have a very strong government – strong in the sense that it is so popular as to be virtually irremovable through the ballot box. We are convinced, however, that there are people both within the country and outside it who would like to circumvent the ballot box. Persons to whom the will of the people is an obstacle and who, therefore, are prepared to resort to any other means to reach their objective. And while we agree that, politically, it would be better for the government to wait until this danger became obvious both inside and outside Tanganyika, our government rightly believes that it would be the height of irresponsibility to take such a risk without security. We prefer present criticism for *possible* authoritarianism to future pangs of conscience for *certain* irresponsible negligence.[28]

Since, as the writer claimed, the government was so strong such measures were surely unnecessary but authoritarianism is the natural companion of strength. The measure received immediate support from the country's neighbour Kenya. The *Kenya Weekly News* editorialized to the effect that the measure came as no surprise. The signs that the government of Tanganyika needed the bill were apparent: defections from TANU, the creation of opposition parties, demonstrations by University students against one-party rule, the burning of TANU party cards, apathy of voters registering for the Presidential elections. 'In this matter one had to weigh the arguments of justice and morality against the hard facts of political life in Tanganyika today. TANU had a frighteningly massive task to undertake, the transformation of a backward poor country into a dynamic nation.'[29] The article concluded by asking whether outside observers could point to an alternative to TANU. The answer, at that time, was no and since that was the case why was the measure necessary at all?

DISILLUSION WITH THE WEST

Over the years 1961–65 most aid for Tanzania came from the West but the country's pro-Western stance was to be shattered by four issues: 'The four issues which caused this "loss of innocence" in foreign affairs were the continuing support given by the Western powers to the racist regimes in Southern Africa, American and Belgian intervention in the Congo, the direct intrusion of cold-war politics following the union of Tanganyika and Zanzibar and the British failure to intervene in Rhodesia when its white-dominated regime unilaterally declared independence.'[30]

The West's continuing support for the white racist regimes in Southern Africa, and most especially for South Africa and its apartheid system, led

Nyerere to give his full support to the various liberation movements. These were obliged to turn to the Communist countries for arms as the only available source and this allowed the white South and the West to claim that the liberation movements were Communist and therefore that the white minority regimes were fighting Communism. The Zanzibar revolution of January 1964 opened the door to the Eastern powers, which to that date had found few opportunities of influencing East Africa. They moved into Zanzibar with a vengeance, however, to raise fears in the West that were only partially allayed when Nyerere brought about the union of the two countries in April 1964 as the United Republic of Tanzania. Even so, this led to a break with West Germany, which refused to continue its aid programme since there was East German diplomatic representation in Zanzibar, even though Nyerere reduced this to consulate status. The crisis brought out clearly the readiness of the West to use its aid as an instrument of political blackmail. Thirdly, Nyerere referred to American duplicity towards Kenyatta over the US/Belgian intervention in the Congo in November 1964 as 'an action reminiscent of Pearl Harbour'.

The final disillusionment came when Britain failed to intervene following Ian Smith's unilateral declaration of independence (UDI) in Rhodesia. An OAU resolution called upon all members to break diplomatic relations with Britain by 15 December 1965 unless adequate action had been taken to reverse UDI: in the event only 11 countries did break relations with London, and Tanzania was one of them. Britain retaliated by freezing a newly negotiated loan of £7.5 million. These events constituted a most important learning process for Nyerere and other African leaders as well: that the West was far more committed to the racist white minorities on the African continent than it was amenable to majority African opinion. At the same time, African states were obliged to swallow their pride because they were still in desperate need of Western aid. And this gave the Communist countries their chance. 'By 1968 Nyerere accepted that Tanzania had become an ally of the Communist powers in regard to the liberation of Southern Africa. On that issue the policies of the Western powers had left Tanzania with no other option to this alliance save a humiliating acceptance of the permanence of racial oppression in Southern Africa.'[31] As it turned out Tanzania was to have a good experience with Communist China (rather than with the USSR or Eastern Europe) culminating in Chinese aid for the TANZAM railway.

Over the first years of the 1960s Nyerere saw his vision of an egalitarian and democratic society being eroded by over-dependence upon foreign aid, a growing elitism among the TANU leadership and increasing divisions between the urban and rural areas. It was in reaction to these developments that TANU produced the Arusha Declaration. The interesting aspect of Nyerere and

Tanzania at this time is that though he was admired personally for his determination to produce an incorruptible, utopian society few others really wanted anything of the kind. Although not making direct condemnations of the elite generation, the Arusha Declaration set forth a stringent leadership code: Every TANU or government leader must be a peasant or worker and not associated with capitalism or feudalism; no leader should hold shares in any company; no leader should hold directorships; no leader should receive two or more salaries; and no leader should own houses he rented out to others. 'The leadership code caused immediate and widespread concern within the party, the trade union movement, and the government bureaucracy. Leaders were allowed to convert their assets into trust funds for their children and to retain and employ hired labour on their farms. In spite of these concessions and the party's formal approval of the Declaration as a whole, the leadership code was neither widely supported nor vigorously implemented in the first few years.'[32] Following the proclamation of the Arusha Declaration the government embarked upon the task of gaining control over the economic 'commanding heights' by nationalizing the banks and the major agricultural processing companies, insurance and export trading companies. Later, the sisal estates and primary industries were also taken over by the state. However, the new search for national self-reliance that Nyerere launched was heavily circumscribed because Tanzania remained dependent upon the workings of an international system that was economically and politically weighted against small countries. National interests might be determined in Dar es Salaam but the attainment of these national goals was inhibited by decisions taken outside Africa. Nationalization, self-reliance, austerity and anti-corruption measures and the determination to take total control of the country's economy were never enunciated better anywhere else in Africa. The successful achievement of these aims was another matter.

Was Nyerere being impossibly utopian? His experiment in socialism during the 1960s and 1970s acted as a magnet for Western intellectuals, many of whom went to teach in the University at Dar es Salaam, and for many more Nyerere became the 'guru' of how Africa's problems ought to be tackled. All the new states of Africa faced the task of achieving rapid economic development while they also attempted to create their own political values to replace those left behind by the departing imperialists. Many of the new leaders opted for a one-party authoritarian system that gave them immense power though all too often they ended up employing all their talents to maintain the system that kept them in place. Nyerere set forth the kind of society he wanted to create as one based upon *ujamaa*, which did not draw its inspiration from either East or West. As he argued, *ujamaa* was opposed to both capitalism and doctrinaire socialism because the latter sought to build its happy society on a philosophy of inevitable conflict between man and man while the former sought to build a happy society on the basis of exploitation of man by man.[33] This was all very well but Nyerere never really discusses how his socialism could be attained in practice and given all the anti-socialist developments in Tanzania prior to the Arusha Declaration this represents a major failing. He sets out a stringent leadership code, but then undermines it by concessions that allow his TANU leaders to hold onto their capitalist wealth. He enunciates a creed of self-reliance and demonstrates how aid will create a dependence mentality but continues to seek aid on a scale that is far greater than the 'catalyst' function he assigns to it. In each case Nyerere was bowing to political realities that were far more powerful than his socialist creed. But even if it failed in the end, Nyerere's socialist creed was like a breath of fresh air in a continent where too many of the new leaders allowed themselves to be corrupted by the allure of power.

UGANDA

Uganda, which came to independence in 1962, faced a very different set of problems to those of its two East African neighbours. The Ganda peoples of the Kingdom of Buganda constituted 28 per cent of Uganda's population and controlled the richest lands producing 90 per cent of the country's high-quality coffee crop, the principal export. The first loyalty of the Ganda was to their traditional ruler, the Kabaka, rather than to the British-created state of Uganda and when in 1953 the British Colonial Secretary Oliver Lyttelton hinted at the formation of an East African Federation they reacted with deep hostility, assuming that as with the Central African Federation farther south this would give control to the white settlers of Kenya. The Kabaka demanded that Buganda should be transferred to the Foreign Office, that is, be detached from Uganda and granted independence separately. He refused to co-operate with the British government over developing Uganda as a unitary state and would not nominate Buganda Ministers to the Legislative Council. The British response was to exile the Kabaka to London on 30 October 1953. This was the beginning of a fight against a unitary state that would only be resolved by force in 1966. When Uganda became independent in 1962 nothing had been satisfactorily resolved: not only was Buganda a state within a state but it had uneasy relations with the other smaller kingdoms, the most important of which, Bunyoro, claimed the 'lost counties' that had formerly been part of Buganda and were then part of Uganda.

As a consequence of this background the first years of Uganda's independence were taken up with a struggle between the kings who demanded a federal system under which they would retain substantial local power and the political radicals who wanted a centralized, unified state. Under the terms of the 1955 Constitution the Kabaka of Buganda, King Frederick Mutesa II, had been made a constitutional monarch but by 1962 he had consolidated his position and exercised not merely political influence but real power within his kingdom. In the run-up to independence a complicated pattern of political alliances resulted in a coalition between the Uganda People's Congress (UPC) led by Milton Obote and the Kabaka Yekka (KY or King Alone) party of Buganda forming the government that came into being at independence in October. A year later when Uganda became a republic the Kabaka was elected President while Obote remained Prime Minister. A power struggle ensued between Buganda, which had abandoned none of its separatist ambitions, and Obote's government, which was determined to create a modern centralized state. Uganda's post-independence constitutional crisis arose out of the fact that four kingdoms with substantial regional powers were not prepared to give them up without a struggle while Obote was equally determined to destroy their independent authority and create a unitary state. The UPC-KY alliance broke down in 1964 over the issue of the lost counties – Buyaga and Buyangazi – which the Kabaka insisted should be returned to Buganda. In a referendum the counties voted to return to Bunyoro and not Buganda, a result that emphasized the differences between the conservative Kabaka faction and the modern centralists. Finally, the issue of dual power came to a head in February 1966 when Obote first carried out a putsch against right-wing members of the UPC (he had five ministers arrested) and then forced through an interim constitution which ended most of Buganda's federal privileges, while also withdrawing autonomy from the three smaller kingdoms of Bunyoro, Ankole and Toro. Under the new constitution the President (Obote) was given full executive powers and then, when the Lukiko (parliament) of Buganda demanded that the central government quit Buganda, Obote sent in troops under Col. Idi Amin Dada to storm the royal palace. The Kabaka fled to England. In September 1967 a new unitary constitution was enacted. Obote's problems, however, were far from over. In order to consolidate its power the UPC was also obliged to tackle the left-wing Youth League as well as the trade unions; this was successfully accomplished. But Obote had no real power base. He developed close relations with the 73,000-strong Asian Community, many of whom were prominent in government service and largely controlled the manufacturing sector. Obote's government came increasingly to rely upon armed oppression and detention as a normal response to opposition, with the General Service Unit (GSU) under Akena Adoko as a principal means of maintaining control.

In his search for wider national support Obote moved to the left and in 1969 announced a 'Common Man's Charter' as well as further nationalization measures and redistribution of incomes. In May 1970 plans for 60 per cent nationalization of 80 major companies were announced. In the meantime, however, Obote was losing his grip on the army, which by 1969 was overspending its budget by 28 per cent. Amin, now a Major-General, was assisting the Israelis to channel military aid to the Anya Nya in southern Sudan and he continued to do so, despite a reversal of policy on this issue by Obote. In December 1969 Obote was wounded in an assassination attempt, an event that gave him an excuse to ban all opposition parties. There were indications that Amin had been involved in the attempt. The death of the Kabaka in London on 22 November 1969 (of acute alcoholic poisoning) led to unrest in Buganda. On 1 May 1970 Obote announced that his government was taking immediate control of oil companies, banks, insurance, mines, transport, manufacturing and plantation industries. In explaining these major takeovers, Obote referred to his Common Man's Charter of October 1969 and explained:

> The basic reason, really, behind the measures I announced on May Day is that we are trying to prevent a development of a violent conflict between the masses who produce coffee and cotton and the managers and directors of big companies who really are engaged in a line of activities to which the people find themselves as spectators.[34]

BURUNDI AND RWANDA

The huge imbalance in population between Hutu and Tutsi in Burundi and Rwanda has meant that the Tutsis, the minority, have always felt threatened unless they were the rulers with the result that they have gone to great lengths to dominate the majority Hutus. This imbalance has raised fundamental questions about democracy since any universal franchise election must always result in a Hutu majority. Checks and balances are essential if the two people are to live in harmony. The unhappy history of these two small landlocked and overcrowded states has, too often, been in the form of violence by the one group against the other. The two states of Burundi and Rwanda, the former Belgian Trusteeship Territory of Ruanda-Urundi, signalled before they became independent in 1962 the deeply troubled path of brutal Hutu-Tutsi antagonism that would plague their independent existence down to 2000. The Belgians had followed the German practice (Ruanda-Urundi had been part of German East Africa until 1919) of working through the established system of chiefs and retaining the Tutsi monarchy, which meant accepting the inequalities resulting from Tutsi domination over the Hutus, so that by independence deep-seated

Hutu resentments, which the colonial administration had done nothing to assuage, had instead become more entrenched.

In Burundi a new political party, the *Union pour le Progrès National* (UPRONA) (Union of National Progress) was formed but it proved ineffective and unable either to contain or control the ethnic tensions and suspicions that mounted on the approach of independence. In January 1962 self-government was granted by Belgium and at that point the monarchy appeared to be the most acceptable form of government to both Hutu and Tutsi. Burundi, by then fully separated from Rwanda, became independent on 1 July 1962. The *mwami* or king, Mwambutsa IV (who had reigned since 1915), attempted to balance the rival claims of the two ethnic groups by the alternate appointment of Hutu and Tutsi prime ministers. Even so, there was a Hutu uprising in 1965 though this was suppressed. In July 1966 Mwambutsa IV was ousted in a coup by his son, who became king as Ntare V. The new king appointed Michel Micombero as his Prime Minister, but after only four months the latter deposed the King and proclaimed a Republic with himself as President. Micombero then systematically purged the government and civil service of Hutus, entrenching Tutsis in all the important offices. By 1971 the ruling *Conseil Suprème de la République* (CSR – cabinet) consisted of 23 Tutsis, only two Hutus and two others. At independence the Hutu accounted for 80 per cent of the population and the Tutsi for 13.5 per cent.

In 1916, during World War I, Belgian troops from the Congo had occupied Ruanda and following the peace the newly formed League of Nations created the mandate of Ruanda-Urundi, which was placed under Belgian control. During the years of their mandate the Belgians on the one hand ruled through the traditional kings and chiefs but on the other hand encouraged the rise of Hutu aspirations, with the inevitable result that they brought about the collapse of the system so that in 1959 a violent Hutu-Tutsi civil war erupted when the Hutus rose in revolt against the dominant Tutsis. The civil war ended in the collapse of the monarchy and the exile of Kigeri V who was later deposed. The Belgians, who had eventually restored order, introduced a series of democratic reforms, which favoured the majority Hutu; in the municipal elections of June–July 1960 the *Parti de l'Emancipation du Peuple Hutu* (Parmehutu) won an overwhelming victory. A referendum of 1961 recommended the abolition of the monarchy and subsequent legislative elections gave the Hutu massive political control, while the leader of Parmehutu, Gregoire Kayibanda, became the country's first President at independence on 1 July 1962.

Much of Rwanda's history following independence concerned Hutu-Tutsi rivalries, which periodically climaxed in bloodshed and massacres. In the immediate aftermath of independence the Hutus carried out a consistent policy of depriving Tutsis of positions of political influence; then, in December 1963, following an invasion carried out by émigré Tutsis, the Hutus massacred about 10,000 Tutsis and caused many more to flee the country. Thus the Hutus had established total political control and in 1965 made Rwanda a one-party state. In the elections of 1965 and 1969 Parmehutu candidates were returned unopposed, and Kayibanda was re-elected as President. His regime became more authoritarian and isolated. At independence the Hutu (who were farmers) accounted for 90 per cent of the population while the Tutsis (who were cattle herders) accounted for 9 per cent.

CHAPTER ELEVEN

White Racism
in Central Africa

Few issues during the 1960s caused as much African anger as did the 1965 unilateral declaration of independence (UDI) by the white minority in Rhodesia. The declaration itself, the fact that it had not been pre-empted by earlier British action and the realization that even the British Labour Party, which had always been seen as friendly to African aspirations, would refuse when in power to deal effectively with the rebels, confirmed long-held African fears that the West would always come down on the side of the white minorities. When the immediate drama that followed Smith's declaration of independence on 11 November 1965 had subsided and his rebel regime was in place it soon became apparent that the series of 'talks about talks' and the British Prime Minister Harold Wilson's meetings with Ian Smith on board HMS *Tiger* in 1966 and HMS *Fearless* in 1968 had everything to do with finding a face-saving formula that would relieve Britain of its imperial responsibility, and nothing to do with resolving the problem as it ought to have been resolved in favour of African majority rule. The British had always had the knack of distancing themselves by one remove from events for which ultimate responsibility was theirs. They had done this – and were still doing it – with regard to South Africa and now they did it over Rhodesia.

THE CENTRAL AFRICAN FEDERATION

The Central African Federation of Northern and Southern Rhodesia and Nyasaland had been created in 1953 and had always been seen by the whites in Southern Rhodesia and by the Africans in all three territories as a device to perpetuate white control in the region. There was no attempt on the part of the Federation's white founders to hide their contempt for the Africans who were supposed to be their 'partners' in a new imperial venture. Sir Godfrey Huggins (later Lord Malvern) the long-time Prime Minister of Southern Rhodesia dominated the two-day conference of white politicians who met at Victoria Falls in February 1949 to consider the proposed Federation of the three territories. He left no doubt in the minds of the delegates from Northern Rhodesia about how the Federation should be implemented. He said, among other things, 'The natives must be ruled by a benevolent aristocracy in the real sense of the word... Our democratic system does not embrace mob law.' Later, for good measure, he added: 'The history of the world suggests that there is *prima facie* evidence that there is something wrong with the Bantu branch of the family.'[1] It was Sir Godfrey Huggins, the principal architect of the Federation, who propounded the concept of racial partnership as 'the rider and the horse' and the Africans were to be the horse. As the debate about implementation proceeded in the years following this meeting, Huggins was to say of the Federal Constitution, when it was being drafted in 1951, 'Once the Imperial government have granted this constitution they have lost all control – don't forget that... In practice the reservations [about African rights] are not worth the paper they are written on.'

Huggins' principal political partner in the Federal story was the rough diamond Roy Welensky (knighted in 1953) who became the Federal Prime Minister. He too made plenty of pronouncements about white supremacy. 'It has got to be recognized, once and for all, that when we talk of maintaining high standards in the federation... we mean white standards. People who have in their minds that we might abdicate in 10 or 15 years... ought to prepare themselves for a rude shock.'[2] As opposition to Federation grew so Sir Roy and other whites put down their markers to make plain their determination to hold onto power at all costs. In 1956 Sir Roy said: 'We Europeans have no intention of handing over the Federation to anyone, because we have no intention of getting out. We believe that the African should be given more say in the running of his country, as and when he shows his ability to contribute more to the general good, but we must make it clear that even when that day comes, in a hundred or two hundred years' time, he can never hope to dominate the partnership.'[3] The history of Rhodesia is the history of Anglo-Saxon racialism in Africa. Two factors operated throughout the colonial period: white control of African education in order to limit advance and white control and demarcation of the land. The open expression of these racial views was the prelude to inevitable repression, conflict and bloodshed. In the retrospect of a later 'forgive and forget' culture about imperialism it is important to recall the sheer demeaning contempt such attitudes conveyed. At the same time, the growth of African nationalism and the inexorable pressures it exerted lent a kind of desperation to such pronouncements, which, for all their arrogant certainty, reflected a growing sense of white unease at a less than secure future. 'The white leaders of the Federation realized more clearly than any other Europeans in Africa, except the South Africans, that once the principle of African advancement is admitted there can be no halt in its progress to eventual majority rule.'[4] And so, over these years, the groundwork was established that would form the background to UDI, and growing white extremism became the order of the day. Garfield Todd and Edgar Whitehead were the last two white leaders prepared to make any concessions to the African majority before the white extremists took control. 'Todd was the last European political leader at all prepared to work with African political leaders; Whitehead was to disregard nationalist leaders and sponsor an African middle class of what he called "responsible" African leaders; the Rhodesian Front were to turn to the chiefs for support. From this time forward "partnership" was dead as far as politically conscious Africans were concerned. The steady flow of repressive legislation and the repeated banning of African Nationalist parties by the Whitehead government only served to emphasise that the races had parted ways.'[5]

Southern Rhodesia had done very well out of the Federation since it had siphoned off the greater part of the wealth from Northern Rhodesia's copper industry for the development of its own economy. 'The Copperbelt was the milch cow and Northern Rhodesia suffered a net loss in the years 1953–63 of nearly £100 million – the bulk of which was used to develop Southern Rhodesia and the rest to prop up Nyasaland. As though this were not enough, when the £280 million Federal debt was divided up at the end of 1963, Northern Rhodesia was saddled with £96 million – for which it had relatively little to show in the way of assets; it was more than five times the territory's national debt in 1953.'[6] Further, despite Northern Rhodesia's United National Independence Party leader Kenneth Kaunda's protests when the Federation was broken up, almost all the military equipment went to Southern Rhodesia and so passed under white control. The end of the Federation on 31 December 1963 saw the three territories going their separate ways: Northern Rhodesia and Nyasaland would soon become Zambia and Malawi respectively on independence while Southern Rhodesia, whose white politicians were moving even further to the right than their already hard right position began to prepare for UDI. Both before and after the end of Federation Britain had ultimate responsibility for these three territories and at no stage can it be exonerated of blame for what happened. As Lord Malvern said in retirement in 1962: 'No bill that had not been agreed with the British government ever saw the light of day in Southern Rhodesia.' Both Kenneth Kaunda of Zambia and Hastings Banda of the Malawi Congress Party (MCP) had fought to end the Federation, which they saw as a device to perpetuate white control. Ian Smith had resigned from Sir Edgar Whitehead's government in 1961 because the Constitution that Whitehead had worked out with the British Commonwealth Secretary Duncan Sandys allowed the possibility of 'premature African dominance'. Smith proceeded, with other racial extremists, to found the Rhodesian Front. Once it had become clear that the whites in the Federation could not maintain control over Northern Rhodesia and Nyasaland without British help, British interests quickly turned to making their peace with the rising African leaders.

From the beginning of 1964 events in Southern Rhodesia moved sharply into crisis gear. When he became Prime Minister in 1964 Smith said: 'I cannot see in my lifetime that the Africans will be sufficiently mature and reasonable to take over... If we ever have an African majority in this country we will have failed in our policy, because our policy is one of trying to make a place for the white man.' Clifford Dupont, another hard-liner, shortly followed with the terse statement: 'We can and will halt the wind of change.' On the African side, the Zimbabwe African People's Union (ZAPU), the successor to the Rhodesian African National Congress, had been founded in 1961 by Joshua Nkomo; it was banned by the white majority government in 1964. It then set up headquarters in Dar es Salaam in Tanzania, later moving to Lusaka in Zambia. From 1964 to 1969, while Nkomo was detained, its external leader was James Chikerema. Like the other liberation movements, ZAPU had to turn to the Communists for support and at first ZAPU accepted aid from the People's Republic of China but in 1965, after entering into an alliance with the African National Congress (ANC) of South Africa, it switched to the USSR. However, under Nkomo ZAPU was never sufficiently militant to satisfy its more radical members; this led to a split in 1963 (before it was banned in Rhodesia) when Ndabaningi Sithole left it to form the Zimbabwe African National Union (ZANU). In 1967 ZAPU launched its first guerrilla raids into Rhodesia from Zambia though these had only a limited impact. Faction fights between Ndebele and Shona members again split ZAPU at the end of the decade when Chikerema, a Shona, deserted ZAPU to form the Front for the Liberation of Zimbabwe (FROLIZI). ZANU was a more radical nationalist movement than ZAPU and early adopted a policy of guerrilla warfare against the white regime, especially after Ian Smith came to power in 1964. It was outlawed that year.

MOVES TOWARDS UDI

The British Labour Party came to power in October 1964 under the leadership of Harold Wilson. It was said at the time that the Rhodesia file was at the top of the urgent business awaiting the new Prime Minister's attention. The Federation had been dissolved at midnight on 31 December 1963. Nyasaland became independent on 6 July 1964 as Malawi, and Northern Rhodesia followed on 24 October to become Zambia. In April 1964 Winston Field was ousted as Prime Minister of Rhodesia by his followers, because of his apparent unwillingness to carry out a UDI. He was replaced by Ian Smith and once he had taken over it was clear that Rhodesia was set upon the course that would lead to UDI in 1965. The Smith regime could not be accused of hiding its intentions either to follow the South African apartheid pattern or to break the British connection and seize independence illegally. By mid-February 1965, having taken the measure of Wilson, Smith became increasingly open as to his agenda. 'If you persist in standing in the way of our just request,' he wrote to Wilson, 'I shall have no alternative but to take such steps as may be necessary...'[7] In elections of 7 May 1965 Smith and the Rhodesian Front won all 50 of the A Roll seats to make his position impregnable on the political front. In Britain, as emotions on both sides of the debate ran high, the Duke of Edinburgh entered the debate when, in a speech at the University of Edinburgh, he said: 'I think everybody recognizes that the ultimate result is inevitable. But I think a few years here or there do not matter if we can achieve this result peacefully and quietly.'[8] As negotiations were carried on between the British government and the Rhodesians the British position was set forth in what came to be known as the Five (later Six) Principles:

1 The principle and intention of unimpeded progress to majority rule, already enshrined in the 1961 constitution, would have to be maintained and guaranteed.
2 There would also have to be guarantees against retrogressive amendments to the constitution.
3 There would have to be immediate improvements in the political status of the African population.
4 There would have to be progress towards ending racial discrimination.
5 The British Government would need to be satisfied that any basis for independence was acceptable to the people of Rhodesia as a whole.
6 It would be necessary to ensure that, regardless of race, there was no oppression of majority by minority or of minority by majority.

These proposals would clearly leave the white settlers in full control of the country into the foreseeable future. It was calculated that Africans under these conditions might achieve majority power over 50 years.

The question of the use of force by Britain now moved to the centre of the debate. No minority in history possessing economic, political and social power and prestige ever willingly surrenders these advantages to the majority; it has to be coerced. There was always only one method open to Britain to do this: to place armed forces in Rhodesia and take back political control. The year preceding UDI witnessed growing African anger that Britain was clearly not ready to use force against the Rhodesian minority on behalf of the four million strong African population of the colony, although in November 1964 the Americans and Belgians had used force to rescue a handful of whites in the Congo. On 24 October 1964 Britain's new Commonwealth Secretary, Arthur Bottomley, attended the Zambian independence celebrations where he had every opportunity to sound out African opinion although on his return to London he said that the use of force against the Rhodesians was not being considered 'at the moment'. He also said of the Rhodesian nationalists, 'like all people who are struggling to get their rights, if you are not allowed to do it by lawful means sometimes other methods have to be employed'. At least Bottomley kept Britain's options open. But Africans argued that Britain had used force in Kenya, Aden, British Guyana, so why not in Rhodesia? The demand for the use of force became steadily more insistent.

THE UNILATERAL DECLARATION OF INDEPENDENCE (UDI)

On 11 November 1965 Rhodesia's white minority government made its unilateral declaration of independence. In a radio broadcast Ian Smith said: 'We Rhodesians have rejected the doctrinaire philosophy of appeasement and surrender. The decision which we have taken today is a refusal by Rhodesians to sell their birthright. And, even if we were to surrender, does anyone believe that Rhodesia would be the last target of the Communists in the Afro-Asian bloc? We have struck a blow for the preservation of justice, civilization and Christianity; and in the spirit of this belief we have this day assumed our sovereign independence. God bless you all.'

In Britain there was to be much pretence of tough action but none of it was going to alter what was happening on the ground in Central Africa. The despatch of a squadron of RAF Javelins to Zambia in December 1965 for defensive purposes only gave heart to opponents of Smith and angered pro-Smith Tories. But in the House of Commons, when pressed by the Tory leader Edward Heath, Wilson gave the real explanation: 'It is a fact that if we have to maintain the position that we have asserted, that Rhodesia is our responsibility, we should do everything in our power to prevent the stationing of other forces in Zambia, wherever they may come from, as a means of providing air cover for President Kaunda.'[9] As Kaunda soon realized, their purpose was to pre-empt alternatives and not to threaten Smith.

On 3 December 1965 a meeting of the OAU was called in Addis Ababa to consider the Rhodesia crisis; unfortunately, it did more to demonstrate African disunity than to put pressure upon the illegal Rhodesian regime. Some African leaders wanted to send an OAU force to the Zambezi but the British Javelins were already in place to forestall such a move, to the relief of many OAU delegates. In its communiqué the OAU claimed that UDI had been proclaimed 'with the connivance of the government of Britain' and asserted that the OAU had determined to bring an end to the Smith regime though it did not explain how this would be done. The one precise commitment made by the OAU was a call for all the 35 states represented at Addis Ababa to break diplomatic relations with Britain on 15 December if it had not by then ended the Rhodesian rebellion. In the event only 11 African states broke diplomatic relations with Britain. Nigeria refused to do so on the grounds that it would not achieve anything; Somalia borrowed a guide to diplomatic practice from the British embassy in Mogadishu to ascertain how to break relations with Britain; President Nyerere of Tanzania did break relations with Britain and lost £7 million aid then in the pipeline for his pains.

The next development on the diplomatic front came on 11 January 1966 when 19 Commonwealth countries met in Lagos for a special summit to consider Rhodesia. Wilson initially was reluctant to go and said off-handedly that he 'might drop in' but he went and scored a tactical triumph. He presented the meeting with forecasts of the Department of Economic Affairs on the likely impact of sanctions. In their final communiqué the Commonwealth leaders said: 'The Prime Ministers noted the statement by the British Prime Minister that on the expert advice available to him, the cumulative effects of the economic and financial sanctions might well bring the rebellion to an end within a matter of weeks rather than months.' A number of those present clearly did not believe this assessment. However, despite British threats of financial action and sanctions, the key lay with South Africa. Two days after UDI South Africa's Prime Minister, Dr Hendrik Verwoerd, said: 'We will continue to deal with one another in economic and other matters as before.' Once it had become plain that UDI would take place, Verwoerd knew that from South Africa's point of view sanctions must not be allowed to take effect for if they could be made to work against Rhodesia they might later also be applied successfully against apartheid South Africa. Meanwhile, the imposition of a naval blockade by Wilson on the Mozambique port of Beira from which an oil pipeline ran to Umtali (Mutare) in Rhodesia was seen almost at once to be a farce since Rhodesia was obtaining all the oil it needed through Lourenco Marques (Maputo) or South Africa. Moreover, half the oil delivered at Lourenco Marques arrived in British tankers, whose owners were defying sanctions and claiming the oil was destined for the Portuguese in Mozambique.

On 15 October 1964 the British Labour party had won a narrow electoral majority and formed the new government and through to March 1966 Wilson had often used the excuse of this tiny majority to explain away his cautious actions over Rhodesia, especially as it was a topic on which the Tory opposition was especially pressing and hostile. However, on the last day of March 1966 Wilson had won a second election, which gave him a majority of 100. Kaunda, who to that point had been fooled by Wilson, told his cabinet colleagues: 'Now you will see. Harold will do the right thing.' What Wilson did in April was initiate a series of secret visits to Salisbury by high-ranking civil servants to conduct what became known as 'talks about talks'. Arthur Bottomley, the Commonwealth Secretary who had not been consulted, was amazed at Wilson's action and warned him that there would be a furious African reaction, which there was. The talks represented a major retreat by Wilson from the apparently strong stand he had taken to that date. Bottomley was not intellectually brilliant but he was honest. Wilson moved him from the Commonwealth Office shortly afterwards and then dropped him altogether in 1967. When it became clear in Lusaka that Wilson was no longer treating Smith as a traitor but talking with him in order to work out a face-saving deal for the British government, Kaunda was appalled and from that time lost his faith and trust in Wilson. Kaunda had first heard the news of the 'talks about talks' on a BBC broadcast, which had increased his anger, but in any case, once Wilson had his majority of 100 he no longer felt the need to appease Kaunda and treated him with indifference if not contempt. Kaunda reacted by describing Britain's handling of the Rhodesian crisis as 'shifty and evasive' – he meant Wilson.

It had been agreed at Lagos that a full Commonwealth Conference would be held in July 1966 but Wilson now tried to delay this to September and in May despatched Malcolm Macdonald, Britain's 'special representative', to persuade African leaders to allow the delay to September. In Lusaka, however, he was met by an angry and distrusting Kaunda and failed to mollify him. Kaunda threatened that Zambia would leave the Commonwealth but this only earned him the retort from Wilson that British assistance in implementing sanctions might be withdrawn. Another dimension was added to the London–Lusaka row when in 1967 Ali Simbule, an old-style Zambian nationalist, was appointed High Commissioner to London from his post in Dar es Salaam. Asked in Tanzania what he thought of UDI, he said Britain was shirking her moral and constitutional responsibilities and then added, in a memorable phrase, 'Britain is a humbled, toothless bulldog, wagging its tail in front of Rhodesia Premier Ian Smith and fearing him like hell.' The British Government reacted furiously and demanded an apology but none was forthcoming and at the end of May Simbule went to London anyway, thus making his point.[10]

During the years 1964–67 both Zambia and the Rhodesian Africans had hoped for outside action – by Britain, the United Nations or the OAU – but by 1967 such hopes had evaporated and a ZAPU representative could say: 'At no time in history has a police state peacefully given up the reins of control... One way remains – the African people must use force to achieve majority rule. Force by the African people will be promptly replied to by the regime's security forces. The conflict can thus not be limited and will inevitably escalate into civil war. This is the tragedy of the Rhodesian crisis.'[11]

SANCTIONS, TALKS AND GUERRILLAS

The first British response to UDI was to impose limited sanctions in November 1965 and further sanctions in December 1966, which were endorsed by the United Nations Security Council. At the same time the 'kith and kin' argument, always somewhat spurious, was used as one of the reasons why Britain could not use force in Rhodesia, though it was never explained why, if white British troops who were sent to Rhodesia would not fire on their white Rhodesian kith and kin why the latter would fire on their British kith and kin. Nonetheless, there were many Britons at the time who were pro-Smith and the white minority. Meanwhile, despite Wilson's statement at Lagos that sanctions would work in a matter of weeks rather than months, other appraisals suggested at the very least it would be a long haul. 'The United Nations mandatory sanctions on Rhodesian exports effectively applied, even only to those selected items – asbestos, iron ore, chrome, copper, meat and meat products, hides, skins and leather – might eventually be another matter. But even these could only be effective if South Africa's links with Rhodesia were broken and the Zambian market completely closed. In 1967 neither seemed particularly likely...'[12] By 1969 the most obvious result of sanctions had been the diversification of the Rhodesian economy. Moreover, the apparent lack of forward planning by Britain gave the impression that the government was not serious in its attempts to bring down the illegal regime. This British attitude probably influenced the attitudes of UN member states and other nations outside the UN, such as Switzerland, West Germany and Japan, to the imposition of UN mandatory sanctions, introduced as they were in two stages more than 12 months and 30 months respectively after UDI.[13] On the other hand, the Rhodesian regime had taken many anticipatory actions prior to the imposition of sanctions. These had included moving foreign reserves out of London and Switzerland in anticipation of Britain blocking them, while stocks of vital goods had been built up inside Rhodesia. However, South Africa became Rhodesia's lifeline and, for example, held Rhodesia's foreign reserves. At the same time the regime benefited from Zambia's dependence on imports coming through it and the need to export copper via Rhodesia. Even so, Zambia managed to reduce its imports through Rhodesia from £35.5 million in 1965 to £23.2 million in 1966 and down to £12 million by 1968. Although arguments about the impact and effectiveness, or non-effectiveness, of sanctions and the extent to which sanctions busting was carried out became part of the ongoing Rhodesia story, the difficulties of exporting encountered by the regime were enormous. In the end it was South Africa, which in its own terms could not allow sanctions to work, that ensured the regime's survival. South Africa was Rhodesia's main source of petroleum.

The most revealing aspect of the talks about talks and the two set-piece meetings between Wilson and Smith on HMS *Tiger* and HMS *Fearless* was that the Labour party hierarchy in Britain was prepared, and in some quarters anxious, to support what was very clearly a political surrender to the hard-line white racists in Salisbury. No one in the British Cabinet resigned or, as far as is known, even contemplated doing so as a protest at policies that in theory if not in practice went against Labour principles. In December 1966 Wilson met Smith on board HMS *Tiger* and put forward proposals under which Smith could return to legality. The key points of the '*Tiger*' settlement were a new Independence Constitution which would establish an open road, which could not be blocked or impeded, for African political advancement to majority rule within a reasonable period of years; the essential parts of the Constitution to be protected by the most effective possible safeguards to prevent changes which could stop or impede this advancement; and that any Independence Constitution on these lines must be demonstrated by appropriate democratic means to be acceptable to the people of Rhodesia as a whole. This in fact would have given Smith the legality to do what he was doing anyway without the burden of sanctions. From an African viewpoint it represented a total sell-out. Smith rejected it. Despite this, two years later, in November 1968, Wilson arranged the meeting on HMS *Fearless* and proposed even more shameful terms that included dropping the Six Principles. As his political colleague Richard Crossman was to observe, Wilson was thrilled at the prospect of the '*Fearless*' meeting, 'longing to be off, loving having the press all round him, loving being the centre of world attention, feeling that at last he must win when he faces Smith eyeball to eyeball'. It was a maliciously accurate picture of the Prime Minister.[14] This second attempt to achieve a settlement would have given Smith legal independence on a series of promises that the Six Principles would be met, which they would not. Smith again said no.

At the time of the Fearless talks Wilson tried to obtain African support and three ZANU leaders – Sithole, Leopold Takawira and Robert Mugabe – were brought from detention to the Officers' Mess at New Sarum Air Force Base for a meeting with the Commonwealth Secretary George Thomson and the Minister of State Maurice Foley to secure ZANU approval for the *Fearless* offer. After the meeting Sithole smuggled out of prison to London a document denouncing the *Fearless* proposals as 'an attempt to sell the inalienable right to self-determination of the 5,000,000 Africans of the country to the 220,000 white settlers. The proposals are unacceptable as a basis for any constitution'. At the meeting Takawira ridiculed the Labour government's sensitivity to the use of force and Thomson replied, weakly: 'The reason for not using force is that it would be an invasion. It would have to be done from Zambia if it were decided to use it. We have no near base. We had one in Aden, but we no longer have it. The reason is that the whole of Southern Africa would be plunged in a war. There would be lots of bloodshed. It is easy to start a war. But a war is like a bushfire, which once it has started flares up and spreads. You don't know where it will end.'[15] In a devastating editorial, the *Observer* castigated the *Fearless* proposals as follows: 'Though the immediate effects of an agreement with the Smith regime might be only the loss of all the non-white members of the Commonwealth, a handful of British embassies and libraries burnt by angry African crowds and perhaps some British firms expropriated by African governments – the long-term impact would be likely to be infinitely more damaging. It could be the single act of policy which began an alienation of all African and most Asian countries from both Europe and America...'[16] The editorial continued that if the proposals were accepted Africa would assume that all the West was on the side of the white racists. In January 1969 Commonwealth leaders met in London at their delayed biennial summit and declared that the *Fearless* proposals were unacceptable. The British government accepted this position since Smith had in any case refused the proposals and saved Britain from the onus of having carried through a total sell-out.

Wilson's performance over Rhodesia infuriated many of his supporters and delighted the Rhodesians who must have been amazed at their easy victory. Despite his own proclaimed anti-racism views Wilson always put political advantage at home first and was fearful of upsetting the 'kith and kin' lobby which was certainly vocal at the time. Moreover, the 1964 elections had seen the surprise victory of Peter Griffiths at Smethwick who had overturned a Labour majority of more than 7,000 to defeat the former Labour Commonwealth Secretary Patrick Gordon Walker with the slogan 'If you want a nigger neighbour vote Labour'. Race issues clearly carried votes. Drama without objective appeared to be the hallmark of Wilson's approach to Smith. In October 1965 Smith went to London at Wilson's request more for form's sake than anything else and at the end of the second day's talks said the Rhodesians 'had no option now but to take their independence'. Wilson's reaction was to make an appeal on television: 'I know I speak for everyone in these islands, all parties, all our people, when I say to Mr Smith, "Prime Minister, think again."'[17] It would be hard to think up a more fatuous way of responding to Smith. Ben

Pimlott, Wilson's biographer, paints an unsavoury picture of Wilson's desperate scrabbling to obtain an agreement at almost any cost, making plain that the only principle motivating the Prime Minister was to show how clever he could be, but Smith proved his nemesis because he was uninterested in an agreement and knew he could obtain what he wanted by calling Wilson's bluff which he did in no uncertain manner. On 19 October 1965 the Rhodesian Security Council secretly decided to declare independence 'at the first opportunity'.[18] Then, 'On 30 October Wilson finally and irrevocably threw away "what little advantage he had"... in a fateful broadcast to the British nation and the world. In this he clearly announced: "If there are those in this country who are thinking in terms of a thunderbolt, hurtling through the sky and destroying their enemy, a thunderbolt in the shape of the Royal Air Force, let me say that this thunderbolt will not be coming.' At this time, according to Smith's Security Chief Ken Flower, 'Smith was holding fewer cards at this stage, knowing that neither his Army nor his Air Force would oppose force with force.'[19] So Wilson let pass one of the best ever opportunities for Britain to take the right action in Africa, in both moral and political terms, and gain the goodwill of its newly independent states to Britain's long-term advantage. Instead, there followed 15 years of crisis, deep suspicion of Britain's motives and accusations of racism, and a guerrilla war in which 30,000 people lost their lives.

Guerrilla activity against the Smith regime began shortly after UDI. On 29 April 1966 ZANU guerrillas and troops of the Smith regime clashed at Sinoia. The military engagement was of minor importance but it did serve to illustrate the growing differences between ZANU and ZAPU that would be a permanent feature of the Rhodesia story both up to independence in 1980 and subsequently. The ZANU action took ZAPU by surprise and angered its leaders because their rivals had got in the first blow and made plain their intention of launching a full-scale guerrilla war. The next year, on 19 August 1967, only hours after their joint forces had crossed the Zambezi River into Rhodesia, Oliver Tambo, leader of the South African ANC, and James Chikerema of ZAPU called a press conference in Lusaka to announce a military alliance between their two movements. The group penetrated to within 60 miles of Bulawayo to cause a panic in Salisbury and the government turned to South Africa for aid. The presence of South African blacks from the ANC inside Rhodesia with ZAPU justified the prompt despatch of South African Police with helicopters to boost the European and African mercenary forces then at the disposal of the Smith regime. From this time onwards South African paramilitary units were to be stationed in Rhodesia and the Zambezi became the front line of the white-controlled South. By 1967, though guerrilla action was only beginning to make any impact, there was every indication that the struggle would develop into a bitter racial confrontation. By 1968 the activities of ZANU and ZAPU led the Rhodesian Commissioner of Police to warn: 'It would be wrong to minimize the dangers which Rhodesia faces from terrorist infiltrations; these are now employing more sophisticated tactics and are well armed.' In July 1968 South Africa experienced its first white casualty when police constable Daniel du Toit was killed on the Zambezi. The South African Prime Minister J. B. Vorster threatened Zambia which was applying sanctions to Rhodesia as well as permitting the guerrillas to pass through its territory: 'If you want violence, we will hit you so hard you will never forget it.' Rhodesian troops were deployed along the Rhodesia–Zambia border throughout 1969; by that year the different guerrilla groups had established a number of training camps inside Rhodesia. There were then approximately 2,700 South African forces in Rhodesia supporting the white regime which had 1,800 white regular troops and 1,800 black mercenaries of its own as well as several thousand white reservists. In June 1969 the Rhodesian Secretary of Defence said: 'Should terrorist infiltration continue on the increasing scale evidenced to date, it will be necessary for further money to be found to maintain the army at the standard that will be required to meet this contingency.' On 2 March 1970 Rhodesia became a republic and Clifford Dupont became its President. By this time the liberation movements realized that they and their cause would get no help from the West: 'The Labour Party's performance in office between 1964 and 1970 was a clear indication to the African liberation movements that they have little to expect from any British government except opposition. In the words of Labour Defence Secretary Denis Healey: "There is no such thing as a socialist foreign policy. There is only a British foreign policy."'[20]

The crisis and drama of UDI over these years tended to obscure the development problems of the other two 'partners' of the former Central African Federation, Zambia and Malawi, both of which became independent in 1964 and found, almost at once, that their policies had to be geared to events in Rhodesia.

ZAMBIA

'As guests for the independence celebrations converged upon Lusaka, somebody coined an expression about Zambia: "Africa's second chance." It might be able to succeed where others were failing.'[21] Throughout the 1960s Zambia was to enjoy high revenues from copper, its principal export, and this enabled it to embark upon ambitious development plans. There was a Transitional Development Plan covering the years 1965–66; this was followed by the First

National Development Plan (FNDP) for 1966–70 whose principal aims were as follows:

1 To diversify from copper.
2 To create 100,000 new jobs.
3 To increase per capita income from £61 to £100.
4 To maintain price stability.
5 To minimize the urban-rural imbalance.
6 To raise educational levels.
7 To improve living accommodation and welfare.
8 To develop new communications, sources of energy and transport.

Hopes for rapid development were high and offers of aid substantial. Like other newly independent African countries Zambia regarded the trade unions as one of the only two nationwide organizations (the other was the armed forces) that might pose a threat to central government power; this was particularly the case with regard to the powerful Mineworkers Union of Zambia (MUZ) on the Copperbelt where, in any case, the mineworkers had long acted as a powerful political lobby. As the Rhodesian crisis unfolded, Kaunda feared a major military confrontation with the South that would be both racial and ideological and that Zambia would be unable to withstand on its own, hence his constant appeals to Britain to take firm action and his bitter anger at Wilson's refusal to do so, which he saw as support for the white regimes. On a visit to Britain in July 1968, for example, Kaunda asked for ground-to-air missiles. He knew that the support he required would not be forthcoming from Africa; he wanted British or American support and did not want to turn to the Communists. Over the confrontation with Rhodesia he was always dependent upon British decisions and these were not made in his interest.

At the end of his long political career Kaunda's reputation rested far more upon his role in international affairs and as the leader of the front-line states than for his home policies, yet in the early years after independence he was both liberal and imaginative in his approach to the country's many problems and did not, for example, imitate his neighbour and friend Julius Nyerere by imposing a one-party system upon Zambia. Despite the arguments for a one-party state, then routinely deployed in much of Africa, for eight years Kaunda resisted pressures to make UNIP the sole party, insisting that any such demand had to come through the ballot box and not be imposed from above. In 1967 he said: 'We go further and declare that even when this comes about we would still not legislate against the formation of opposition parties because we might be bottling up the feelings of certain people, no matter how few.'[22] Although much influenced by Nyerere, Kaunda's 'humanism' was not derived simply from the Arusha Declaration and *ujamaa*. As a friendly critic puts it: 'There are marked differences between the intellectualism and grasp of doctrine shown by Nyerere and the earnest high-mindedness of Kaunda.'[23]

In terms of aid there was a growing Zambian relationship with China over these years: China provided assistance in constructing a road to the remote Western province; in 1965 Zambia accepted China's first military mission to Africa; eventually, with Tanzania, it entered into an agreement for China to finance and construct the TANZAM railway linking Dar es Salaam with Kapiri Mposhi in Central Zambia; and in July 1969 China opened its New Chinese News Agency (Hsinhua) in Lusaka. If UDI stimulated economic diversification in Rhodesia it also acted as a spur to make Zambia reduce its dependence upon the South. The Mwaamba coalmine in the Southern province was developed to replace coal and coke from Wankie in Rhodesia. A new hydro scheme was developed on the Kafue River and a second power station was built on the north bank of the Kariba Dam, financed with a £35 million loan from the World Bank to make Zambia independent of power from the South. To the east an oil pipeline was completed in 1968 from Dar es Salam to Ndola and the Great North Road to Dar es Salaam was fully tarmacked. Despite many important developments, the Zambian economy remained overwhelmingly dependent upon copper. In 1968 production reached a record 595,000 tons with exports earning £300 million or 95 per cent of total export earnings to contribute £104 million to government revenues. In 1969 Kaunda announced plans to take a 51 per cent stake in all the copper mines, effectively those of Anglo-American and Roan Selection Trust. At the same time that Zambia was making these development advances it was attempting to impose UN sanctions upon Rhodesia and even with substantial reductions was still obliged to take imports from the South.

From independence to the end of the decade a principal Zambian concern was always transport and communications. The country was landlocked and its traditional exit routes all passed through the white-dominated-South – Rhodesia, Mozambique and South Africa. There was the alternative route through Angola along the Benguela railway but in Angola, too, a war was being waged against the Portuguese and transport along that route become increasingly precarious. These facts formed the background to the search for an alternative that would ultimately be provided by the Chinese-built TANZAM railway, although that would not be opened until 1976. The export of its bulk copper was Zambia's top priority. In December 1965 Zambia imposed sanctions on Rhodesia and Rhodesia retaliated by cutting off oil supplies to Zambia. The United States, Canada and Britain then began to airlift oil from Dar es Salaam to Elizabethville in the Congo, only 60 miles from the Copperbelt. The airlift was reduced in April 1966 when the United States and Canada withdrew from the operation. Meanwhile the 1,200-mile 'Hell Run' dirt road from Kapiri Mposhi to Dar es Salaam was tarmacked and this allowed the oil to be transported more cheaply by road tankers. In October 1966 Zambia awarded a contract to ENI to construct a pipeline from Dar es Salaam to Ndola. In May 1966 Rhodesia demanded advance payment in convertible currency for all Zambia's freight (coal and copper) and Zambia refused in a move that was seen as a bid to force Britain to act against Rhodesia. The other routes into Zambia could not cope with the demand, however, and in July Zambia had to give way and pay for 'limited' tonnages being carried once more by Rhodesia Railways. The ENI pipeline was completed in 1968 and opened by Kaunda on 2 September, allowing Zambia to end petrol rationing on 31 October after three years.

These development, transport and UDI-related problems were overshadowed by the disloyalty of a significant proportion of the whites then resident in Zambia. 'The bitter heritage of pre-independence race relations in Zambia is aggravated by the continued existence of a large white minority within the country, many of whom make no attempt to identify politically with Zambia, and some of whom have engaged in spying and sabotage on behalf of southern African regimes which Zambia regards as immediate threats to its security.'[24] As a direct result of pre-independence race relations, one of the first acts of the independent National Assembly was to pass the Penal Code (Amendment) Act of 1964, which made it a criminal offence 'for any person to utter any words or publish any writings expressing or showing hatred, ridicule or contempt for persons because of their race, tribe, or place of origin'. In 1966 Kaunda had to dismiss almost his entire special branch (they were white officers) for leaking secrets to Salisbury or withholding information from him. In April 1967 the British government was reported to be 'coldly furious' at the arrest of a number of Europeans who were put on trial in May on charges of spying when an extensive spy network was uncovered. Britain did not apologize when the spying accusations were proved to be true. In September neighbouring Malawi established diplomatic relations with South Africa to bring another South African presence to a third Zambian border (after Rhodesia and the Caprivi Strip of Namibia). In September 1967 Zambia requested Britain to take appropriate action over the South African police presence in Rhodesia; instead, Britain expressed concern that Zambia might be used as a base for guerrillas. By 1968 Zambia's foreign policy had become increasingly concerned with the growing South African involvement in Central Africa, as well as the continuing guerrilla activity along Zambia's borders, and threats of retaliation from all of

Zambia's southern neighbours. The 1960s proved to be a fraught decade for Zambia: it began with the battle to dismantle the Central African Federation and the achievement of independence; Zambia then had to face all the political and development problems of a new state and on the whole coped with them remarkably well; but its achievements were constantly overshadowed by the pressures of UDI and the growing fear of a racial and ideological war that could engulf the entire region.

MALAWI

Dr Hastings Banda had been outside Africa for 40 years when he finally returned to Nyasaland in 1958 to lead the fight against the Central African Federation. As a young man he had gone to South Africa to earn money; from there he had gone to the United States and put himself through university, to Britain where after qualifying as a doctor he had worked for years as a general practitioner and won the affection of his poor patients whose fees he had often waived. He had returned to Africa in the 1950s to practise medicine in the Gold Coast and was there when it became independent as Ghana. His successful fight against the Federation made him a hero to Africans throughout the continent yet after independence he was to act in a very different way to the orthodox socialist nationalists who had become the norm elsewhere on the continent. He rapidly eliminated all opposition in the form of his younger, more radical colleagues, including the men who had gone to Ghana to beg him to return and lead the fight against the Federal Government, and he then proceeded to create one of the most autocratic systems in Africa with himself as the principal arbiter of Malawi's fortunes, a position he maintained in highly idiosyncratic style until the 1990s.

Malawi became independent on 6 July 1964. Eight weeks later Banda faced a hostile cabinet in which his younger, more radical colleagues wanted to accept a loan from Communist China, which Banda described as a 'naked bribe'. This was the ostensible cause of the split but there were others: they wanted Banda to speed up the process of Africanization and take a tougher anti-colonial line. There were also differences of style, personality and outlook. Banda had imbibed none of the nationalism or radicalism then sweeping Africa, which affected his younger colleagues. He dismissed three ministers – Kanyama Chiume (Foreign Affairs), Orton Chirwa (Justice and Attorney-General) and Augustine Bwanausi (Works, Development and Housing); a further three ministers – Yatuta Chisiza (Home Affairs), Willie Chokani (Labour) and Henry Chipembere (Education) – resigned in sympathy to deprive the cabinet of virtually all its leading members. Subsequently, they launched unsuccessful revolts against Banda. Shocked by a degree of opposition he had not expected, Banda reacted by giving greater responsibilities to white expatriates and turning for support to the less educated masses as opposed to the radical intelligentsia. The events of September 1964 represented the parting of the ways that set Banda on his lone authoritarian course. From being regarded as the leader of one of the most militant nationalist movements, Malawi under Banda now came to be seen as one of the most conservative countries in Africa. In any case, at independence Malawi was rated as one of the poorest countries in Africa and was heavily dependent upon the white South with many thousands of Malawians working in Rhodesia and South Africa. The main aim of the Malawi Congress Party (MCP) prior to independence had been to destroy the Federation; the party emerged after independence without any development blueprint for the new country, 90 per cent of whose people lived on and by the land.

Through the 1960s Banda showed himself to be at odds with most of black Africa's leaders though, except for a powerful individualist streak in him, it was never clear as to just why he should have behaved in this fashion. He laid claim to large stretches of Mozambique, Tanzania and Zambia as parts of the former Maravi Empire though these claims only succeeded in antagonizing his neighbours and he took to lecturing the rest of Africa about its attitudes towards the white-controlled South. In 1966, for example, Banda warned that any attempt by African states to use force against the white-ruled states would end in disaster since neither singly nor in combination were they able to match Rhodesia, South Africa and Portugal and he warned the Malawi Parliament that an attack on South Africa would be seen by the Europeans of the whole southern region as a threat to exterminate them so that they would be driven to desperate measures.[25] In October 1967 Yatuta Chisiza, who had resigned in 1964, led an abortive anti-government raid in the north of the country after Banda had announced that Malawi was to establish diplomatic relations with South Africa. It was easily defeated and Yatuta and 14 others were later executed. Banda appeared to be secure and the other ministers who had opposed him now abandoned the struggle. The pace of Africanization remained slow and at the end of 1967 expatriates still outnumbered Malawians in the higher grades of the public service although that year saw the appointment of the first three African permanent secretaries. This slow pace may have annoyed aspiring Malawians but it reassured the 8,000-strong expatriate community. However, what really set Banda apart from other African leaders was his policy towards the South. 'Banda's alienation from his fellow African leaders and his authority within Malawi formed the backdrop to the development of his policy towards South Africa. The constraints which contact with the mainstream of African thought would have imposed on him were absent; in his own country there was no one to contradict or question the schemes he set in motion. The adage remained in force, "Kamuzu knows best."[26] On an official visit to Kenya in September 1967 Banda gave a speech in which – bravely – he said, 'South Africa could not be boycotted or isolated into liberalism.' Threats by African countries merely accelerated the 'laager' mentality of whites in the South. Perhaps only in Kenya under Kenyatta with whom he had a good deal in common could Banda talk like this.

Between 1966 and the end of the decade Banda had enacted the constitutional changes that made him a formidably powerful president of a one-party state. In May 1966 he was elected first President of the Republic by the National Assembly, acting as an electoral college, and on 6 July Malawi became a republic and the MCP became the only legal party. The President was authorized to appoint up to three persons as cabinet ministers who were not MPs. In February 1968 this limitation was removed. In December 1970 the constitution was amended to provide that Dr Banda should hold the office of President for life.

Banda's open policy of engagement with white Southern Africa was unique and provocative and led to especially hostile relations with his two neighbours, Tanzania and Zambia. Before independence, at the beginning of the 1960s, Banda had assumed (wrongly) that Mozambique would also soon be independent and he had denounced the Portuguese for their repressive policies, while the *Malawi News* had described Portugal as 'a country of 4ps (Poverty, Prostitutes, Priests and Police).'[27] Meanwhile Banda, who faced the same problems of dependence for communications upon his neighbours as did Kaunda, had been flirting with the possibility of closer ties with Tanzania and using Mwanza as a principal outlet and port of entry for Malawi. The possibility of using Mtwara had been discussed with Tanzania in August 1961 before either country became independent. However, Banda was already inclined towards co-existence with the Portuguese in Mozambique and in May 1964, six weeks before independence, he paid a one-day private visit to northern Mozambique during which he appears to have sealed an agreement with the Portuguese to construct the Nacala railway through to Malawi (as it was shortly to become). He had been advised, meanwhile, that the northern route through Tanzania could not be justified economically. What made Banda choose to turn southwards was never easily explicable and, for example, in 1969 he claimed that he had had a pre-independence agreement with Nyerere about the use of Mtwara and that a railway was to be built from Central Nyasaland around the end of the Lake (Lake Malawi) to Mtwara, but that Kaunda had persuaded Nyerere to go for the TANZAM railway instead. Banda had wanted the railway to pass through northern and central Nyasaland and cross the border at Fort Jameson into Zambia though that would have made it much longer.

Chipembere was to claim that the collapse of this scheme gave Banda the excuse to promote closer links with the Portuguese, which was what he favoured anyway.[28]

By March 1967, when Malawi signed a trade agreement with South Africa, its relations with Zambia were at an all-time low and, for example, Banda was to reply to criticisms of his decision in the Zambian press: 'While they are criticizing me for trading with South Africa openly they themselves are trading with South Africa secretly.' Six months after sending a goodwill mission to South Africa, in September 1967, Banda announced that he was opening diplomatic relations with Pretoria. The first Malawian representative in the Republic was to be a white civil servant, Philip Richardson, with a black understudy. Banda attacked his principal critic – Kaunda, and Zambia – in vitriolic terms: 'As for my critics in neighbouring countries, I treat them with utter contempt, because they are physical and moral cowards and hypocrites… While they are decrying South Africa, they are doing so on stomachs full of South African beef, mutton and pork… They are doing so while allowing South African financiers and industrialists to invest heavily in their mines, industries and agriculture.'[29] On 12 December 1967 a South African career diplomat, Jan Francois Wentzel, became his country's Chargé d'Affaires in Malawi. South Africa quickly followed its breakthrough in Malawi with a loan of £4.67 million for the new capital at Lilongwe; this was followed by a second loan of £6.4 million to Malawi Railways for the Nacala link through Mozambique.

Banda's biographer explains his switch to the South as follows: 'Yet for all the unpopularity of Banda's plain speaking, and of his policies towards the white South of Africa, Malawi's gradual move into isolation at the end of 1965 and beginning of 1966 was not entirely involuntary. No less important was Banda's own disenchantment with the unrealism and discord which seemed to him to be becoming endemic, not only in African affairs and at the OAU, but also at the United Nations.'[30] In March 1968 South Africa's Foreign Minister, Hilgard Muller, made a formal visit to Malawi where he spoke of 'co-prosperity' and warned of the dangers of Communism. By 1969, experts loaned from Pretoria were helping to control some of Malawi's key institutions, including the broadcasting services which were audible in parts of Zambia, and in February of that year a new director of the Malawi Information Services began work: he was David van der Spuy from the South African information department. Malawi Air services increased their flights to Johannesburg to cope with the increased two-way traffic. By May 1970 when South Africa's Prime Minister J. B. Vorster visited Malawi, Banda's isolation in Africa was almost total. In a speech at the official dinner for Vorster, Banda said: 'What I do know is simply this: your way of life is your way of life. Our way of life is our way of life. There are certain things on which we agree, let's think more of those things, let's work more from the basis of those things on which we agree, on which we see eye to eye... Those things on which we do not agree, on which we do not see eye to eye, will take care of themselves.'[31] Banda was to remain adamant in his determination to co-exist peacefully with the apartheid state and not to support any form of violence.

Portugal
in Africa

In 1960, as the two principal colonial powers, Britain and France, were conceding independence to their colonies, Portugal was making plain it did not see self-rule, let alone full independence, as an option for its African possessions and was entrenching itself, apparently determined to hold on at almost any cost. The British and French, no matter how much they subsequently employed neo-colonialist tactics to manipulate and, where practicable, to control their former colonies, had at least bequeathed political structures, which their successors could develop, or not, as they chose. The Portuguese, on the other hand, had prepared nothing that could be bequeathed to their successors because they had no intention of quitting the continent. They did not believe in a 'civilizing mission' and they did not go through the motions of preparing their subjects for a future in which they would rule themselves.

The white question, what to do about the European settlers in Africa, was and would remain a major stumbling block in the path of African development for years to come. 'The self-deception of Europeans in multi-racial societies is undoubtedly the major political problem still facing Africa. European supremacy is firmly maintained on an elaborate structure of propaganda both intentionally and unintentionally designed to reassure the white rulers of the justice of their cause, and to prevent the outside world from understanding what is really happening.'[1] If that applied to South Africa and Rhodesia, it applied still more to the Portuguese in Angola and Mozambique. When at the beginning of the 1960s it became clear that Portugal was determined to hold on in Africa, the West demonstrated its collective racism by supporting Portugal's efforts even if for form's sake it also protested at some of the more blatant manifestations of Portuguese colonial brutality. Arms supplied to Portugal for NATO purposes by the United States, Britain, France, West Germany and Italy were to be regularly diverted without concealment or pretence for use in Portugal's African wars. As Amilcar Cabral, the charismatic leader of the revolt in Portuguese Guinea, was to write of Portugal's colonial policy at the beginning of the decade, 'While hastily modifying the Portuguese constitution so as to escape the obligations of the UN Charter, the fascist colonialism of Portugal also took care to suppress all means of non-official information about its "overseas provinces". A powerful propaganda machine was put to work at convincing international opinion that our peoples lived in the best of all possible worlds, depicting happy Portuguese "of colour" whose only pain was the yearning for their white mother-country, so sadly torn from them by the facts of geography. A whole mythology was assembled.'[2] In the struggles that erupted at the beginning of the 1960s two themes dominated Portuguese propaganda: its defence of Western values and its fight against the spread of Communism.

PORTUGAL'S STAND

Antonio de Oliveira Salazar, the dictator who governed Portugal for 36 years from 1932 to 1968 and was the creator of the New State (Estado Novo), was responsible for his country's Africa policy, announcing in 1961 in the face of escalating world opposition that Portugal would defend its African possessions; at that time he personally assumed control of the Ministry of War. Salazar's colonial policies were based upon a narrow political and economic nationalism and a total refusal to contemplate self-government at a time when the rest of colonial Africa was undergoing rapid decolonization. The Portuguese ignored the lessons of Algeria, the Congo and Kenya and 'It took over a decade of colonial wars, the collapse of the dictatorship and the return to democracy in Lisbon, before Portuguese Africa was set free. Here again, this singularly violent process of decolonization marked out the Portuguese colonies from the rest of Africa.'[3] On 20 June 1960, as pressures mounted for independence throughout Africa, Salazar said: 'Portugal will never agree to discuss self-determination for its overseas territories.' In 1961 Dr Adriano Moreira, Minister for Overseas Provinces, announced that Africans in Portuguese territories were now full citizens of Portugal, effectively bringing an end to the *indigenato* system under which a minority could become *assimilados*. However, he said that power should always be exercised by those most fitted for it and the law should define the conditions under which anyone might intervene actively in political life. At that time, of Portugal's 10.5 million African subjects, 99 per cent were illiterate, less than 4 per cent in Mozambique and less than 8 per cent in Angola could speak Portuguese, less than 5 per cent in Mozambique and less than 10 per cent in Angola lived in or around the white towns. Portuguese interest in the Africans of these territories was entirely centred upon their economic usefulness as labour.

When on 27 September 1968 Marcelo Caetano became Prime Minister, following Salazar's incapacitating stroke, he appeared set to continue Salazar's African policy.

Although miscegenation in Portuguese Africa was usually free of the sense of white shame that was too often a part of it elsewhere on the continent, it was still seen as an 'erotic experience' and was only turned into an aspect of colonial policy in retrospect. In the late nineteenth century, for example, the limited numbers of Africans who had achieved *assimilado* status found they faced increased racial discrimination as more Europeans came to settle in Angola. Whatever the stated aims of Portuguese colonialism, the pace was excruciatingly slow. In 1950, there were 30,000 *assimilados* in Angola out of a population of four million, and only 4,353 *assimilados* in Mozambique out of a population of 5,733,000. Thus, when the Angolan war began in 1961 less than 1 per cent of the African population had been 'assimilated'. Although Salazar could tell the National Assembly proudly in 1960 that the Portuguese had been in Africa for 400 years, only 0.74 per cent of Angolans had become *assimilados* by that date, and only 0.44 per cent of Mozambicans and only 0.29 per cent of Guineans. Up to 1961, when the *indigenato* system was ended, an African applying for *assimilado* status had to be 18 years old, able to speak Portuguese, and be of good character (with a clean police and military record); then he could submit his application for the privilege. However, if he had a job in the colonial bureaucracy, had a high school education or was a merchant, in industry or business, those conditions were waived. As the Frelimo leader Eduardo Mondlane claimed: 'The most that the *assimilado* system ever sets out to do is to create a few "honorary whites", and this certainly does not constitute non-racialism.'[4]

When the process of decolonization got under way in the 1950s, Portugal (with Ireland and Greece) was one of the three poorest countries in non-Communist Europe and it needed its colonies both as a source of wealth and as lands to which poor Portuguese peasants could be sent to start a new life. As far back as 1928 an editorial in the South African *Cape Times* had suggested that Portuguese Africa was a guarantee of 'any permanent and expanding national prosperity for which Portugal may hope' and that, although Angola and Mozambique were then undeveloped and, in effect 'costly hobbies', the future held promise. The idea was to persist that Angola was a kind of national saviour of the modern era. By the beginning of the 1960s Angola and Mozambique had become profitable, 'and because they have become profitable they have given Portugal, and not only the government there, a positive sense of accomplishment as a world power. These were to be significant considerations in the decisions of 1961'.[5]

The United Nations exercised considerable international authority during the 1950s on the side of the nationalists, in Africa and elsewhere, who were demanding an end to colonialism and by Christmas 1960, after five years of UN pressures, Portugal felt its isolation acutely. As a colonial power it stood very much alone since all the others (except for Franco's Spain whose African possessions were negligible) had accepted decolonization in principle and were implementing it in practice. On 9 June 1961, after the explosion in Angola, the UN Security Council voted nine to nil, with Britain and France abstaining, to call upon Portugal to end its repressive measures against the African population of Angola. Salazar gave a defiant reply in the Portuguese National Assembly. On 30 January 1962, the UN General Assembly, by 99 votes to two (South Africa and Spain), with France abstaining, condemned Portugal's 'armed action against the people of Angola as the denial to them of human rights and fundamental freedom'. The Assembly called on Portugal to take immediate steps to speed the process of self-government. On 17 December 1962 the UN General Assembly by 82 to 7 (Belgium, Britain, France, Portugal, South Africa, Spain and the United States) with 13 abstentions and 8 absentees condemned Portuguese colonial policy as 'inconsistent with the Charter of the United Nations' and called on all states to cease selling military equipment to the Portuguese government. The resolution upheld 'without any reservation' the claims of the Portuguese territories to immediate independence. These and similar UN pressures would be exerted upon Portugal until its final withdrawal from Africa in the mid-1970s.

The 1950s witnessed the dissolution of the British, French and Dutch empires though the process was to continue throughout the 1960s, but Salazar viewed with extreme scepticism the British hope of transforming the empire into the Commonwealth. His own policy was clear: 'Portugal's overseas territories were "Portugal Overseas", an extension of Portuguese soil, and not colonies. To a hostile world, this proposition was simply a device for evading Portugal's obligation under the UN Charter to lead her subject peoples to independence and thus to terminate her empire.'[6] The Portuguese had first landed in Africa (and the Far East) five centuries earlier and a century before the other Western powers (except Spain) had even begun to envisage the creation of overseas empires. As a consequence, the Portuguese believed that he 'belonged' to the places he had settled. Although such intellectualization of Portuguese colonialism might be justified in relation to early settlements it could not be applied to the large groups of poor Portuguese peasants who had been sent out to Angola and Mozambique under government schemes in the years after 1945. In fact, the Portuguese ruling hierarchy followed three basic traditions: colonialism, authoritarianism and nationalism. In the early 1960s, 'The Portuguese government blamed the rebellion on Communists without and Protestant missionaries within, and applied its propaganda efforts to establishing the image of a civilized and white Christian Portugal confronted by a savage heathen and black Africa. This was race war undisguised. There were public references to a war of extermination, and the Minister of Defence, presiding at the embarkation of soldiers for Angola, proclaimed: "You are not going to fight against human beings, but against savages and wild beasts."[7] The conflicts in the Portuguese territories lasted as long as they did precisely because Portugal refused to entertain the idea of any negotiations to end colonialism. While soldiers were being despatched to Angola to fight 'savages and wild beasts' Moreira, the Minister for Overseas Provinces, was encouraging Portuguese settlers to go to Angola and on 28 August 1961 said, 'We believe it necessary to increase the settlement of our Africa by European Portuguese, who will make their homes there and find in Africa a true continuation of their country.'[8]

There was a curiously hypocritical reaction to Portuguese obduracy on the part of Britain and the United States. The British who were then decolonizing at speed resented the Portuguese stand almost as an affront: if the greatest of all the colonial powers was obliged to decolonize then surely backward Portugal should do the same. The United States, at that time, still posed as the champion of oppressed peoples who should be freed, though always provided they were freed to the right side in the Cold War. Yet neither Britain nor the United States, despite these resentments, exerted any meaningful pressures upon Portugal; to the contrary, they supported its increasingly impossible stand since this suited their pro-white, anti-Communist policies in Southern Africa. A different view was offered by a Protestant missionary who had spent many years in Angola: 'Another seemingly universal false assumption that one meets everywhere among the Portuguese, and especially among the better educated is that they, the Portuguese, in their dealings with the Africans are superior to all other colonizing peoples. They wholeheartedly believe that they have a unique natural gift for understanding the African, for establishing rapport with him, and for making him an adoring, obedient and grateful ward.'[9] As late as 1969 Dr Franco Nogueira, Portugal's Foreign Minister, saw Portugal's future rooted in Africa where there was 'vast economic potential and political unity' and this attitude was shared by many Portuguese. Portugal's support for Biafra during the Nigerian civil war was an attempt to discredit black independence by emphasizing tribal differences, which, as Portugal argued, made an African state without white sovereignty totally unviable.

Portugal responded to outside pressures with inflated propaganda, both as to how the wars in Africa were proceeding and how, on a wider canvas, Portugal had a special world role to play. In 1969, for example, the assassination of Eduardo Mondlane in Dar es Salaam was followed by a number of defections from the upper ranks of FRELIMO and these were presented as being more significant than in fact they were. At the same time Portuguese casualties were carefully played down. On the wider canvas there was something slightly ludicrous about Portuguese claims. Thus, when in July 1969, Caetano went on a visit to Brazil, the Portuguese *Diario de Noticias* argued: 'The South Atlantic is a Luso-African-Brazilian sea. Cape Verde is there for the defence of the South Atlantic with the Azores for the communications in the North Atlantic. And as Portugal's African provinces on the west coast face Brazil, so are they the key to a defence strategy which Brazil cannot ignore at a time when Soviet ships make frequent incursions along the coast of Brazil and Angola and it has been proved that they unload war material destined for subversive elements.' This extract is a curious mixture of bravado, appeal to Brazilian friendship and portrayal of Portugal as a bastion of a Western stand against Communism.

THE ATTITUDE OF THE WEST

Although over the years 1955 to 1960 condemnation of Portugal mounted in Europe, Asia, Africa and the Americas and liberal non-government organizations in the West became quite vociferous in their attacks upon Portuguese colonialism, the countries that could really bring pressure to bear upon Portugal – the United States, Britain and France – in fact did little other than register occasional protests, while at the United Nations they usually abstained or opposed motions that condemned Portuguese practices. More powerful colonial rivals saw Portugal's claims to a special relationship with Africa as no more than a smokescreen for 'excessive colonial ambitions and deficient colonial achievements'.[10] What the Western powers really stood for is brought out in Minter's *Portuguese Africa and the West*.

> The struggle of the peoples of Angola, Mozambique, and Guinea Bissau is not just an isolated fight against an anachronistic colonial power. As they have fought, they have discovered that they fight also against white rule in Southern Africa, from Zimbabwe and Namibia. They have discovered that they fight also against an imperial system, in which many countries are involved and of which the United States is the head. They fight knowing that others struggle against the same enemy, in Asia, in Latin America, in the Middle East, and even in the heart of the system, in the United States of America.[11]

If this sweeping accusation of what might be described as a worldwide conspiracy appears exaggerated it nonetheless contains the core of many accusations that would be levelled at the West to the end of the century among efforts to explain the manifest failures of Africa to overcome so many of its development problems.

Almost to the end of its African wars Portugal received active British support: by diplomatic means as when the Foreign Secretary Sir Alec Douglas Home visited Lisbon in mid-1961; at the United Nations when Britain abstained or voted against resolutions that were hostile to Portugal; and by the supply of arms, including two frigates, ostensibly for NATO purposes even though the British government was perfectly aware of the uses to which they would be put. Britain, in any case, had extensive economic interests in both Portugal and its colonies and in 1968, for example, its investments in Portugal accounted for 25 per cent of all foreign investment while Britain was Portugal's most important trading partner. During the 1960s West Germany also became one of Portugal's most important trading partners and established close diplomatic and military relations with Lisbon. West Germany was a major source of small arms while German intelligence officers reportedly were made available to the *Policia Internacional e de Defesa do Estado* (PIDE) (the Portuguese security police) and co-operated in the campaign against FRELIMO, which culminated in the death of Mondlane. German firms and capital provided an important component in ZAMCO, the consortium created to construct the Cabora Bassa Dam in Tete province of Mozambique.[12]

In general, Britain, France and West Germany maintained close business, investment and military ties with Portugal, including its African empire, and their reasons – even at the height of anti-Portuguese criticisms – were a mixture of profit, solidarity (white racism) and anti-Communism. These powers, whose investments were crucial to apartheid South Africa at that time and were also present in the profitable sectors of Angola and Mozambique, helped sustain Portugal in both Angola and Mozambique, as did South Africa whose white minority government had more obviously compelling reasons for doing so. There was little pretence on the part of these Western countries and 'wars in three colonies did not discourage Western support for a member of the North Atlantic Treaty Organisation, whose signatories are "determined to safeguard the freedom, common heritage and civilization of their peoples, founded on the principles of democracy, individual identity and the rule of law".'[13] They were more than willing to shore up Portugal's military power against African freedom.

The NATO connection was especially important, indeed sustaining, for Portugal. Portuguese officers on training with NATO would subsequently serve in Angola or Mozambique and then return to further service in NATO where they would provide information about what was happening in Africa, always from the Portuguese viewpoint. Although the NATO powers insisted that the range of arms they provided for Portugal were strictly for NATO purposes and therefore should have been retained in Europe, such bans were easily overcome by technical arguments when parts were shipped to the producers' factories in South Africa before assembly and onward delivery to the Portuguese forces in Angola and Mozambique. Such activities were part of what cynics would describe as a new 'great game'. Most of the naval vessels employed by the Portuguese, either to move troops and supplies or to operate along the African coast, came from the United States, Britain, France and Germany despite Portuguese assurances that they would only be used for NATO purposes. There was a long-sustained pretence in the West that military aid to Portugal had nothing to do with its wars in Africa. The Portuguese did not reciprocate such hypocrisy. Like South Africa, Portugal constantly emphasized its value to the West in fighting Communism. It had a good ally in Dean Acheson, President Truman's Secretary of State and later an adviser to succeeding US Presidents. In 1961 he suggested that the Azores bases were 'perhaps the single most important we have anywhere', surely something of an exaggeration. Throughout the 1960s Acheson acted as an apologist for white racism in Southern Africa and, for example, wrote an introduction to *The Third World*, a book by Portugal's Foreign Minister Nogueira justifying Portuguese policies. In 1969 Acheson could write: 'Hostile harassment with our help of three friendly countries in Southern Africa is still going on... these acts of harassment and folly were designed in the United Nations to coerce Portugal into setting adrift territories which it has political responsibility for twice the time of our own country's independent life.'[14] Given the fact of Portugal's long period of responsibility, just what had the Portuguese accomplished for their African wards? The United States supported the Portuguese stand throughout the 1960s and refused to attack its colonial policies. Instead, as Seymour M. Finger, the US Ambassador to the United Nations, argued in 1969, 'while such peaceful change remains possible – however slow it may be – we are convinced that such peaceful means are in the best interests of everyone concerned'. Given US support for Portugal, the effect of advice to Africans to have patience and refrain from violence simply allowed the monopoly of violence to remain with the established colonial government, with its police and armed forces.[15] The supporters of colonialism always argued thus.

Meanwhile, Portugal was fighting its African wars and each year through the 1960s saw an escalation of costs so that by 1968 defence and security absorbed £160 million, equivalent to 45 per cent of all state spending. On paper only £90 million of this went to Africa but this excluded the cost of training recruits in Portugal prior to their overseas service or the cost of troop movements to Africa.

The Portuguese armed forces, integrated into NATO, were not trained for colonial wars although after 1961 they had to operate in three different areas in Africa that were separated by immense distances posing huge transport and logistics problems. In the end the Portuguese began to Africanize their armies: that is, recruit African troops to serve alongside Portuguese forces. The much-feared PIDE penetrated almost all the nationalist movements in Africa to do them considerable damage. (In 1969 PIDE became the General Directorate of Security in the Ministry of the Interior.) Racism, despite the non-racist image the Portuguese had long tried to project, was fundamental to Portuguese colonialism.

> With the growing Portuguese population has come a sharpened colour-consciousness; not only has the Portuguese immigrant – himself a labourer from an economically depressed country – sealed off the African's economic opportunities at the lowest level, but his own insecurities have led him to justify his privilege on the basis of his colour. Any notion of racial integration, of a new Brazil, in Portuguese Africa is fantasy.[16]

As the two wars in Southern Africa escalated in intensity so South Africa became more deeply involved: in Angola this began with military advisers; in relation to Mozambique Pretoria was to give serious consideration to the possibility of moving into the southern half of the territory in the event of a military defeat for the Portuguese. On the border between Angola and South West Africa (Namibia) a major hydro-electric project was developed jointly by the Portuguese and the South Africans on the Cunene River; and in Tete province in Mozambique a vast dam and hydro-electric project was developed at Cabora Bassa with the principal object of supplying power to the Republic and the further (Portuguese) object of tying South Africa into a defensive alliance against the growing successes of FRELIMO.

An important question in relation to Portugal's three mainland African colonies – Angola, Guinea Bissau and Mozambique – is why the revolutionary quality of the anti-Portuguese liberation movements was more absolute than elsewhere in Africa. The *Movimiento Popular de Libertação de Angola* (MPLA) in Angola, the *Partido Africano de Independencia da Guine e Cabo Verde* (PAIGC) in Guinea and FRELIMO in Mozambique each claimed a revolutionary or Marxist perspective different to what had been tried – and failed – elsewhere in Africa. The most dedicated socialists were to be found in these three territories both during the struggle and long afterwards. In part this may be explained by the fact that the Portuguese held on so long and in doing so with the support of the West left little alternative to the liberation movements other than to turn to the Communists for both support and an ideology that was most obviously opposed to Western capitalism. Nowhere else in Africa during the liberation struggles did the Communist powers have such a clear field of operations. There was, it is true, the long-standing alliance between the African National Congress and the Communist Party in South Africa but the background to this alliance was very different. Certainly, by the time the Portuguese finally quit Africa aspects of Marxism had become deeply entrenched in all three territories.

ANGOLA

Colonial exploitation depended upon not teaching skills to colonial subjects, for once such skills had been passed on they would free the subject races from dependence upon their colonial masters. European exploitation of Africa began with the slave trade, which reached its height between 1650 and 1700 to create a gap between European and African cultures so that when Europeans arrived in Africa after 1850 they believed that Africans had stood still in history. 'There are at least strong grounds for thinking that the overseas slave trade, itself the very core of the white-black connection, was among the most influential of them. But nowhere else in Africa was its influence so long-enduring and destructive as here in Angola.'[17] A regulation of 1899 codified the Portuguese settlers' assumption that blacks had a 'duty' to work for whites and that only when they did so could they be regarded as better than brutes. 'So they raised to the rank of benevolent doctrine the settler notion that Africans were working only when they worked for whites. They accepted forced labour under the pretence of rejecting it.'[18] As Basil Davidson argued, there was a great colonial contradiction: 'Leave things as they were and there was no "civilizing mission". Take the latter seriously, and you had trouble on your hands.'

Angola, the largest and wealthiest of Portugal's colonies, was certainly worth holding; it produced coffee, oil, a range of minerals, diamonds, cotton, sugar and maize. Its main cities were situated on a 1,000-mile coastline and offshore it had rich fisheries. Portuguese aid to this storehouse of potential wealth was almost entirely directed to the needs of the white settlers. Marcelo Caetano, later to become Prime Minister of Portugal, gave a series of lectures on Africa over 1952–53 when he was a professor at Coimbra and then said: 'The natives of Africa must be directed and organized by Europeans, but are indispensable as auxiliaries. The blacks must be seen as productive elements organized, or to be organized, in an economy directed by whites.' In the face of such attitudes an explosion was inevitable and by 1959 the Portuguese in Angola expected trouble for they imported large quantities of arms and did so again in 1960. As a British Baptist missionary wrote of the situation, 'Angola is not only a haven but a heaven for Portuguese peasants and merchants who have come from a land of toil and abject poverty to an affluence of which they had previously only dreamed. The African is the source of their wealth. In Europe they were labourers who barely subsisted. Here the African does the work and on his toil and sweat they have grown rich. But the African with even high-school education is a menace to their privileged position.'[19] More than 100,000 white working-class immigrants were to arrive in Angola after 1961 and many, despite the government's intention that they should become farmers, worked instead in the towns, often at menial jobs, and became slum dwellers; they worked as waiters, bar girls, bus conductors and were better off than they had been at home. As a consequence they resisted any African advance that would threaten their jobs.

The second and most crucial white group, also about 100,000 strong, consisted of small traders and those working in small-scale plantation agriculture who saw their future in Angola. Both groups were geared to resist any African advance. Portugal's determination to hold onto Angola was reinforced by its unfolding mineral wealth – oil and diamonds, its rich agricultural potential, and its ability to absorb poor Portuguese peasants. The great cause of anger in Angola was the system of forced labour; otherwise, 80 per cent of Africans remained in subsistence agriculture.

Meanwhile, various radical groups including a Communist party had developed and in 1956 these merged to form the *Movimento Popular de Libertação de Angola* (MPLA). Illido Tome Alves Machado became its President and Viriato da Cruz its Secretary-General. Other nationalist parties also formed and merged. These included the *União das Populações de Angola* (UPA), under Holden Roberto, and the *Frente de Unidade Angolan* (FUA), which was launched in 1961 by Europeans in Benguela. In 1959 Dr Agostinho Neto, whose nationalist sympathies were already known to PIDE, returned to Angola from Lisbon (where he had received training as a doctor). He was arrested in his surgery at Catete in June 1960 for his nationalist activities with the result that many of his patients and supporters marched to Catete from Bengo village to demand his release, sparking off a confrontation in which troops fired on the demonstrators, killing 30 and wounding more than 200. The troops then marched on Bengo and Icolo villages, which they destroyed while killing or arresting all the inhabitants. Dr Neto was imprisoned in Cape Verde, and later taken to Portugal. He escaped and returned to Angola to rejoin the MPLA in 1962.

The Baixa revolt of 1960–61 was launched by labourers, who earned no more than US$20–US$30 a year per family, against obligatory cotton production: they were forced to produce cotton in place of foodstuffs and sell their produce to the government at a fixed price below the world price. In November 1960 the cotton-growers stopped work and refused to pay their taxes. In January 1961 the Portuguese army went on intimidatory manoeuvres that resulted in a major confrontation in which many thousands of Africans were killed – by mid-1961 the British Baptist Missionary Society, then operating in Northern Angola, concluded that as many as 20,000 Africans had perished. On 15 March the Africans massacred whites in the region; the Portuguese retaliated with equally brutal and indiscriminate massacres of Africans. A *Daily Mirror* correspondent quoted a Portuguese army officer as saying, 'I estimate that we have killed 30,000 of these animals... There are probably another 100,000 working with the terrorists.' The Portuguese troops could not leave Luanda because they feared an uprising in the shanty towns that surrounded the city; instead, they carried out arrests and executions and conducted a witchhunt of African ministers, *assimilados* or other potential leaders. By the end of August, however, the Africans had become increasingly disoriented: they lacked effective leadership and they had no arms. The total African casualties for 1961 have been variously estimated at 8,000, 25,000 or 50,000 with the latter figure probably more accurate than 8,000. Most of these died of disease and famine following the fighting. Portuguese civilian casualties were estimated at 400. In May 1961 the government mounted a big offensive against the rebels. The *Observer* reported the disappearance of arrested Angolan Africans. 'Wave after wave of Africans have been arrested, 1,500 of them in the Lobito area alone. There are no known camps in the area. The local prison holds only 100, and the total disappearance of the arrested Africans has given rise to the most sinister fears.'[20]

A storm of international indignation greeted the oppressive measures taken by the Portuguese although this failed to alter their approach to the rebels. Portugal controlled information coming out of Angola and suppressed political opposition. Foreigners who had extensive capital investments in Angola did not want to put these at risk and Lisbon hinted to Washington that it might not renew the base facilities it had made available to the Americans at Azores. 'The Portuguese point of view was clear. Portugal was at home in Angola; it faced a foreign invasion and threatened nobody; Angola was not a colony and Portugal was not going to leave.'[21] By the end of 1961, 150,000 Africans had fled across the border into the Congo to escape further Portuguese reprisals. The war was fought over a vast area that was sparsely populated and difficult to move in, facts that would affect the fighting for the rest of the decade. By the closing months of 1961 it had become clear that the Angolan scene had been transformed for ever although over the next few years the Portuguese attempted to persuade both themselves and the outside world that the revolt was a one-off affair and that the territory could return to normal, an attitude that they reinforced by sending many thousands more settlers to Angola through the 1960s. However, in November 1961 a British correspondent wrote from Leopoldville as follows: 'Until recently, White home-rulers were Portugal's only political problem in Angola. They are what accounts for the intricate security service. Black nationalism is something new. It has startled the mother country, but has not destroyed its blind, superb optimism. Portugal, says Portuguese officialdom, cannot even envisage giving up Angola and Mozambique, because Portugal is too poor to do without them; and Portugal is too poor to be indispensable to either after independence.'[22]

The lack of general development coupled with the treatment of the African population explains the ferocity of the rebel explosion while also raising the question as to why had it taken so long. After more than 400 years of the Portuguese presence Angola only had 250 miles of tarred roads, almost no health services outside the main towns and one of the highest illiteracy rates in the world. Although the Portuguese had defeated the uprising they presided over a territory simmering with discontent with none of the causes addressed or ameliorated. 'Their success [the Angolan rebels] is considerable. They are pinning down a Portuguese army and air force of 20,000 men. And by mustering support at the United Nations, they have enfiladed Portugal's Western alliance, dependent on the diminishing value of the Azores naval base.'[23] This relatively optimistic appraisal of the nationalist impact did not foresee the divisions that would split the nationalists over the next few years as the UPA under Holden Roberto refused all co-operation with the MPLA. In March 1962 the UPA joined with the *Partido Democratico Angolana* (PDA) to form the *Frente Nacional de Libertação de Angola* (FNLA) and the following month (April) the FNLA established a government in exile in Leopoldville – *Governo Revolucionario de Angola no Exilo* (GRAE) with Holden Roberto as Prime Minister. A year later the Congo (K) government officially recognized the GRAE as the government of Angola, forcing the MPLA to close its offices in Leopoldville and move to Brazzaville. However, the apparent triumph of the GRAE in the internecine fighting was short-lived for in 1965 the FNLA Foreign Minister Jonas Savimbi left the movement to found a more traditionalist nationalist movement, the *União Nacional para a Independência Total de Angola* (UNITA). But as the subsequent history of Angola was to demonstrate, purely ethno-nationalists were not to succeed. There was a broad consensus between colonial powers and nationalists that independent Africa should be composed of nation states based on existing colonial boundaries, a development that suited both sides for different reasons. Although Savimbi had accused Holden Roberto of tribalism when he defected from the FNLA, his own support was based upon the Ovimbundu people, the most populous group in Angola, so that he too, effectively, was a tribalist. Meanwhile, the MPLA petitioned the OAU to reverse its decisions taken at Dakar and Leopoldville to recognize the GRAE as the legitimate representative of the Angolan people.

At the beginning of 1964 the *New York Times* (20 January) reported that a feeling of security had returned to Angola. The army had reoccupied the main towns, which the rebels had held, and the Portuguese civilians had returned to them. A crash programme in road building had been started although this was largely for military purposes while the substantial numbers of Portuguese troops and their families had given a fillip to the economy, which Portugal had decided to open to foreign investment. Optimistic claims by both the MPLA and the GRAE that a resolution of the Angola problem could not be far distant were premature. On 7 August 1964 the Portuguese government announced that the fighting was over and that action in the north had become 'sporadic and very limited'. There were 300,000 Angolan refugees in the Congo (K). Despite apparent Portuguese optimism about the course of the war, a range of sophisticated armaments continued to be supplied to Portugal under NATO agreements and these regularly appeared in Africa. West Germany became of particular importance, notably in providing air support and in 1966, for example, sold Portugal 40 jet fighters for US$10 million. By agreement they were to be used exclusively in Portugal for defence purposes within the framework of the North Atlantic Pact, but instead were deployed in Africa. A spokesman for the Portuguese Foreign Ministry explained their use in Africa as follows: 'The transaction was agreed within the spirit of the North Atlantic Pact. It was agreed that the planes would be used only for defensive purposes within Portuguese territory. Portuguese territory extends to Africa – Angola, Mozambique and Portuguese Guinea.'[24]

On the nationalist side, the guerrillas received small arms and ammunition, grenades, light automatics, mortars, artillery and ground-to-air missiles from the USSR and China, Czechoslovakia and one or two other Communist countries, as well as a small amount of humanitarian aid from private – non-government – sources in the West and considerable government assistance from Sweden. By 1966 the MPLA was able to open up the eastern front, adjacent to Zambia, and mount military operations over a huge area of the country while the Portuguese found that they were unable to contain the insurgents. Angola has long porous borders with the Congo and Zambia and these were proving ideal for guerrilla operations and unfavourable for regular army manoeuvres. Portuguese military losses increased during 1966 and 1967 as a result of renewed activity by the MPLA and the emergence of UNITA as a new anti-government guerrilla movement.

Portuguese policy during the 1960s, while the army and police held the population down, was to develop the territory to a maximum so as to secure the future of the increasing number of whites who were still being persuaded to settle in Angola. There was oil in the Cabinda enclave and iron ore at Cassinga and Angola appeared to have the best development prospects south of the Sahara, apart from South Africa. Development was inhibited, however, by the sheer size of the country, which could not be controlled, even by an army of 50,000. Few of these development projects were designed to improve the lot of the Africans who remained the necessary auxiliaries of white prosperity. Slowly through the 1960s the Portuguese began to realize that they could not hold Angola by force alone; they would have to reform institutions and win over the African population. But the realization came too late. At the end of the decade, in 1970, the struggle became far more intense with the rebels pinning down 60,000 Portuguese troops and slowly winning the war, which was a war of attrition rather than one of set battles.

MOZAMBIQUE

The sudden end after World War II of more or less universal European imperial dominance laid bare many aspects of racial arrogance that had become so ingrained as to seem natural to those afflicted by them. The Portuguese, it seemed, suffered from this sense of superiority in inverse proportion to their real imperial power. In a pastoral letter of 1960, Cardinal Cerejeira, the Patriarch of Lisbon, wrote: 'Schools are necessary, yes; but schools where we teach the native the path of human dignity and the grandeur of the nation which protects him.' This nation, Portugal, was then an impoverished European backwater whose people enjoyed an average per capita income of no more than US$250. It was little wonder, therefore, that it was so anxious to hold onto its two prized African possessions, Angola and Mozambique. The Portuguese had established forts on the coast of Mozambique in the sixteenth century although major settlement had only occurred in the twentieth century and much of that just prior to the outbreak of the colonial war. Mozambique, despite the sudden realization in Lisbon of its potential worth, was exceptionally poor and relied for over half its income upon providing rail and port services for Rhodesia and South Africa and remittances from its workers in the South African mines. An added grievance to the normal nationalist resentments lay in the fact that education was minimal and jobs, even semi-skilled ones, were reserved for the Portuguese, thus preventing even quite limited African advance. Writing in 1961 on the 'Colonizing Traditions, Principles and Methods of the Portuguese' Marcelo Caetano appealed to British imperialism in the following exculpatory passage: 'Portuguese policy places on parallel lines the interests of Europeans as leaders in the transformation of backward regions and the interests of the natives as a mass prepared to become part of a future civilized people. Thus Portugal cannot accept in absolute terms the principle "paramountcy of native interests", rather on the contrary her traditional methods come closer to what Lugard called "Dual Mandate".[25] By the time Portuguese leaders began to deliberate on their colonial policies, their African subjects had had enough. They wanted liberty.

The starting point of the war in Mozambique was the massacre of demonstrating Africans by the Portuguese at Mueda in June 1960. Three small exile groups then opened offices in Dar es Salam. In 1962 they merged to form the *Frente de Libertação de Mocambique* (FRELIMO) under the presidency of Dr Eduardo Mondlane, who had been a professor of anthropology at Syracuse (NY). FRELIMO was fortunate in its leadership and was to be the only viable group throughout the struggle, so Mozambique was not faced with the three-way division between competing liberation groups that was to afflict Angola. On 10 August 1962 the UN Special Committee on Colonialism asked the General Assembly to support 'immediate independence' for Mozambique. In September the newly formed FRELIMO held a conference in Dar es Salaam at which Mondlane urged his followers 'to act, work and organize that we may free our continent from foreign oppression'. On 29 September the *Johannesburg Star* reported that the Portuguese government had begun a massive defence build-up, which included the construction of 15 military airfields on the country's borders, to prevent guerrilla infiltration into Mozambique. At the same time it had announced development plans for the Zambezi valley to include a hydro-electric project and the opening up of agricultural land for 13,500 whites and 60,000 Africans.

FRELIMO was quickly recognized by the OAU and subsequently received funds from it. It was also to obtain financial support from the Soviet bloc, China, Tanzania, Algeria, Egypt, Sweden, Denmark and NGOs such as the Rowntree Trust and the World Council of Churches. In June 1963 Mondlane appeared before the nine-nation African Liberation Committee in Dar es Salaam and appealed for training facilities in Tanzania. Up to this date little fighting or even skirmishing had taken place. Over July and August 1964 President Americo Tomas of Portugal visited Mozambique where he was given a tumultuous welcome by whites and blacks (according to Portuguese sources) and watched a military parade of 5,000 out of the 25,000 troops then in the country. Reporting the Tomas visit, the London *Financial Times* (30 July 1964) said that Mozambique was unique of Portugal's African territories: there was no revolt against white supremacy. Despite Portuguese optimism at the time of Tomas' visit to Mozambique, time was running out. FRELIMO launched its war on 25

September 1964 with a proclamation to the people of Mozambique by the Central Committee of FRELIMO: 'Mozambican People – In the name of all of you FRELIMO today solemnly proclaims the general Armed Insurrection of the Mozambican People against Portuguese Colonialism for the attainment of the complete independence of Mozambique.' Mondlane himself describes the advances that were made over the next three years: 'On 25 September 1964, FRELIMO had only 250 men trained and equipped, who operated in small units of from 10 to 15 each. Towards the middle of 1965, FRELIMO forces were already operating with units of company strength, and in 1966 the companies were organized into battalions. By 1967 the FRELIMO army had reached a strength of 8,000 men trained and equipped, not counting the people's militias or the trained recruits who were not yet armed. In other words, FRELIMO increased its fighting strength 32 times over in three years.'[26] By the latter year the Portuguese were deploying up to 50,000 troops against FRELIMO, which by 1968 claimed to control one fifth of Mozambique and 800,000 people. At that time the fighting was mainly confined to the two northern provinces – Cabo Delgado and Niassa – though there was also some fighting in Tete province.

As always at that time the West saw Africa in Cold War terms. In 1965 Mondlane had stated plainly where he stood: 'We are Mozambican nationalists of the same kind that Tanzania and most Africans are and most Africans are trying to be. We don't really think that the Cold War ideological struggle is relevant to us. We want to free Mozambique, and our policies are going to be Mozambique policies.'[27] Portugal's allies on the other hand tried to present the war in Mozambique in Western strategic terms which, conveniently, supported white racial policies in Southern Africa. Writing in *Le Figaro* in October 1967, General Bethouart first referred to the blocking of the Suez Canal as a result of the Six Day War, the fact that large oil tankers would not be able to use Suez in the future anyway, the turmoil in the Arab world, and the Soviet menace, then continued: 'Faced with this situation the West must revise its policy towards South Africa and the Portuguese provinces which, through their great seaports, control the outflow of the prodigious mineral, agricultural and industrial riches to be found in large quantities in that part of the continent.'[28] In the meantime, Portuguese annual military expenditure was steadily escalating and by 1968 had reached US\$217 million for its colonial wars

On 3 February 1969 Dr Eduardo Mondlane was killed by a parcel bomb delivered at the house where he was staying in Dar es Salaam. This was a grievous blow to FRELIMO which he had led with much success since its creation. He was replaced at first by a triumvirate of Uria Samango, Samora Machel and Marcelino dos Santos but this was soon dissolved: Samora Machel became President of FRELIMO, dos Santos Vice-President while Samango was expelled from the party. Despite the setback caused by Mondlane's death, in 1970 the war took on a new intensity as FRELIMO forces began to press southwards and attacked the zone where the Cabora Bassa Dam was being constructed while Portugal sent out further reinforcements to its army in Mozambique. By this time Portugal, not unwillingly, had been drawn into the regional strategies of South Africa, the final bastion of white rule. It had found an unlikely African ally in Hastings Banda of Malawi whose determination to maintain good relations with the white regimes of Southern Africa had isolated him from the rest of black Africa. His attitude was of huge importance to the FRELIMO war since the southern spur of Malawi cut into northern Mozambique, in part isolating Tete province where the vital Cabora Bassa Dam was being constructed and ensuring that 400 miles of Mozambique's frontier was free of guerrillas since these were not permitted to operate from Malawi. The contract for the construction of the Cabora Bassa Dam had been awarded in September 1969 to the ZAMCO consortium of South African, West German and French companies; its principal economic object would be to supply South Africa with power while its political aim was to ensure South African support for the Portuguese war effort in the region.

PORTUGUESE GUINEA

The tiny West African colony of Portuguese Guinea was another of the colonial anomalies, an impoverished wedge of territory in French West Africa. It had been ruled jointly with the Cape Verde islands from 1836 to 1879; its land boundaries had been fixed in 1891 by a series of conventions with Britain and France. Unlike Portugal's larger African colonies – Angola and Mozambique – Guinea was too poor to attract many white settlers, but there had always been opposition to Portuguese rule and by the 1950s the colony was infected by the nationalism then sweeping through Africa. In 1952 Amilcar Cabral had founded the *Partido Africano de Independência da Guiné e Cabo Verde* (PAIGC) as a discussion group, but by 1956 it had developed into a well-organized country-wide movement run by a central committee of which Cabral was Secretary-General. Given Portugal's rigid attitude towards its colonial empire, a violent uprising in Guinea seemed inevitable. 'A few leaders may understand, from the start, this necessity to use violence both in self-defence and as the only means of opening the door to a better future. But they remain powerless until and unless large numbers of people also feel and acknowledge it. Only then can the bitterness and hope take fire.'[29] As with the other Portuguese colonies, advance for the African majority had been minimal and the number of *assimilados* in this case was less than a third of a per cent of the population. The practical outcome of Portuguese rule was one doctor for every 100,000 Africans, only 300 hospital beds (almost all in Bissau), only one hospital outside Bissau and a minimal supply of nurses and midwives. Educational provision was as backward as health with only one per cent of the population in any sense literate and in the only government secondary school 60 per cent of the pupils were Europeans. In 1960 a total of 11 Africans had acquired graduate status as 'assimilated Portuguese' in Portugal.

In July 1961 guerrilla raids were launched against administrative and military targets in the north-west of the country, forcing the Portuguese to deploy troops to guard such targets. In August 1961, from Conakry in neighbouring Guinea, Cabral formally announced that the PAIGC was resorting to armed struggle and from that time onwards constant attacks were mounted against such targets, obliging Portugal to send military reinforcements to the territory. As early as 1962 the PAIGC held elections inside the territory in which 52,000 people out of a total population of less than 500,000 voted to back the PAIGC. The movement obtained the backing of the OAU Liberation Committee as well as full support from neighbouring Guinea. In 1963 the Portuguese admitted that the PAIGC had infiltrated 15 per cent of the countryside. In May 1963, with another 10 years of fighting yet to come, the PAIGC shot down its first Portuguese plane. The PAIGC intensified the armed struggle in 1964 when it formed its military wing – *Forças Armadas Revolucionárias do Povo* (FARP) – while its guerrillas were sent for training to the USSR, China, Cuba, Algeria, Senegal, Ghana and Guinea. On a visit to London in April 1965 Amilcar Cabral claimed that 40 per cent of Guinea was in rebel hands, despite Portuguese denials of success. He quoted the official Portuguese newspaper *Diario de Manha* which had published articles earlier that year congratulating the Portuguese troops in Guinea because they faced an enemy 'not to be held in contempt' and one that had given proofs of its intelligence and spirit of initiative, while concerning local loyalties it had said: 'It is anyone's guess how many of the peasants digging in the fields do not at night exchange their hoes for guns, or have a PAIGC badge in their house.'[30]

The PAIGC was the most accomplished of the Lusophone anti-colonial movements primarily because it performed best on the five necessary criteria: the extent to which the nationalist movement was achieved and maintained; the ability to motivate the rural population politically; the degree to which armed action was profitably subordinated to political objectives; the ability to defend the liberated areas from counter-insurgency campaigns; and the capacity of the nationalists to secure international (especially UN) support.[31] It should be recognized, however, that unlike Angola and Mozambique, the PAIGC had a small country and a small, more cohesive population in which to organize and operate.

The year 1968 was a turning point in the war. President Tomas visited Guinea in February and insisted that it would remain one of the 'sacred portions of national territory'. In May General Antonio de Spinola was made Governor-General. By the end of the year the PAIGC claimed to have killed 1,700 Portuguese soldiers, destroyed 200 military vehicles, 60 boats, 10 aircraft and taken 24 prisoners. In 1969 the PAIGC claimed to control two-thirds of Guinea's area and 45 per cent of the population. At the time Portugal had an army of about 35,000 troops in the territory together with an additional 3,000 African mercenaries. The PAIGC placed great emphasis upon education and established educational programmes in all the liberated areas. During 1965–66 it had established 127 primary schools, operated by 191 newly trained teachers with 13,361 pupils; in the following year, 1966–67, the numbers were increased to 159 schools with 220 teachers and 14,386 pupils. Eighty per cent of these pupils had completed two years' schooling; their average age was 12 years. Some 50 young men and women were sent to Europe in 1967 for technical training in a variety of fields. Several printed school books, prepared by the PAIGC staff, were available for use and others were being prepared for publication.[32] This was a considerable achievement for the liberation movement of such a small country while engaged in an all-out war.

Portugal's two island territories, Cape Verde islands and São Tomé and Principe, were not involved in any actual liberation struggle as such. They were too small and in the case of Cape Verde too tightly controlled by the Portuguese while São Tomé was a closed society entirely dependent upon a plantation economy. However, there were close ties between Cape Verde and Guinea and as the war in Guinea intensified, Portuguese repression of nationalist activities in Cape Verde became more ruthless. Even so, the PAIGC enjoyed overwhelming support from the people of the islands to form an independent government with Guinea-Bissau. The PAIGC, for its part, had a twofold policy: to win independence for Cape Verde and Guinea-Bissau; and to bring about a federation of the two territories.

When Salazar suffered his stroke in 1968, Marcelo Caetano became Prime Minister in his place and while no major changes of policy were expected, there were several reasons to believe that change could not be long delayed as *West Africa* pointed out: 'The PAIGC, FRELIMO and MPLA have pushed the Portuguese regime to the brink of financial and social disaster. The second reason lies in the nature of the regime. This is not so much a political system as a police and administrative structure. Its trouble now lies not simply in the fact that for nearly four decades there have been only the narrowest openings for new talent to make itself felt and heard.' The third reason was the exit of Salazar; his successor did not possess his iron determination.[33] Despite the huge costs in wealth, lives and suffering expended by Portugal during the 1960s in order to hold onto her African possessions, the next decade would see this last of the European African empires collapse.

CHAPTER THIRTEEN

South Africa

No other situation on the entire continent excited so much concern, antagonism or condemnation as did the racist policy practised by South Africa at the time that most of the rest of Africa achieved independence. Opposition to apartheid united independent Africa as nothing else did. One of the first resolutions of the OAU after its formation in 1963 called upon all its members not to establish diplomatic or other relations with South Africa until apartheid had been abandoned while condemnations of apartheid became axiomatic at any African conference. Moreover, opposition to apartheid had far deeper significance than merely the condemnation of an obnoxious policy in a particular country. It also affected Africa's relations with all those white Western countries that were seen either negatively or positively to support the status quo in South Africa. The racist arrogance of apartheid was not only regarded as an insult to all Africa but also as the natural outcome of white imperialism, a view that was to be borne out in the post-independence years by the consistent way in which Britain in particular and the other Western powers more generally shielded South Africa in the United Nations, if necessary by the use of their vetoes, from African attempts to impose sanctions upon it. White support for South Africa from 1960 through to the late 1980s came to be equated with Western regrets at the passing of the European imperial system. Apartheid was akin to a state of mind, not just on the part of the white South Africans who imposed it on their African majority, but also on the part of its external supporters who regretted the passing of white supremacy. For Africans, therefore, only its eradication from the continent would satisfy their sense that at last the imperial age had come to an end. Its ramifications went deep: 'For South Africa is not a private obsession of Africa and the West. From India to Brazil colour sees in "apartheid" the subjugations of the past and the still subjugated present. South Africa is an expression on the face of the white world in history, and one which even yet the white world does not care to erase.'[1]

In 1909, when Britain drew up the Act of Union, it became clear that the government at Westminster intended to hand power to the white minority in South Africa without safeguarding the future of the black majority and when an African deputation went to London in the hope of persuading the British government to reject the colour bar in the constitution, it was told by the Colonial Secretary that the question must be settled in South Africa itself. When the House of Commons considered the bill only the Labour Party and about 30 Liberals opposed the colour bar. 'The rest, although they unanimously regretted it, sent the Act on its way "respectfully and earnestly" begging White South Africa, sooner or later, to modify its provisions.'[2] This hypocritically pious 'respectful and earnest' request, delivered at the height of Britain's imperial power, gave a foretaste of the many ways in which over the coming years Britain would fail to exert the pressures that it could and ought to have exerted upon South Africa. As so often in its imperial history, Britain was distancing itself by one remove from direct responsibility for the outcome of its imperial policies.

> The Act of Union was seen by Africans as an act uniting white South Africans against black. The African organizations scattered through the four provinces were shocked by the British Government's abuse of trust in surrendering all power to a white minority government which, as a fundamental principle, opposed the extension of democratic rights to the non-white majority. But their people remained divided into many separate tribes, thinking tribally, and most of them, illiterate.[3]

Having got the colour bar entrenched in the constitution, the whites went on to demand more rights to ensure that South Africa would be a 'white man's' country; what they sought next was absolute control over the land, and since land was the only security the African had, its seizure on behalf of the white minority meant that the African majority had neither political nor economic security. Under the terms of the Native Land Bill the million whites would have access to more than 90 per cent of the country while the four million Africans would be restricted to only 7.3 per cent of the country and freehold ownership or leasehold was only possible in the reserves. As Gen. Smuts was to claim in a speech at the Savoy Hotel in London in 1917, 'It has been our ideal to make it [South Africa] a white man's country.' In 1945, by which time he had become South Africa's only major international figure, the friend of Churchill, the supporter of the worldwide British Commonwealth and Empire, and part architect of the United Nations Charter, Field Marshal Smuts revealed himself to be as racist as any Afrikaner of the looming National Party (NP) when he said: 'There are certain things about which all South Africans are agreed, all parties and all sections, except those who are quite mad. The first is that it is a fixed policy to maintain white supremacy in South Africa.'[4]

Following its election victory in 1948, the National Party began to consolidate its power and institute comprehensive apartheid and for the next three decades it had the overwhelming support of the majority of the Afrikaner people while by the election of 1966 it also began to win substantial support from the English-speaking whites who were attracted by the government's determination to maintain control in the face of increasing black unrest and foreign criticism. Although the NP worked hard to achieve external acceptance, it was also shrewd enough to see that the more the policy of apartheid led to South Africa's isolation in the world so the more its 'embattled' white community would draw together in support of the government. The new government lost no time in appointing its Afrikaner supporters to senior as well as junior positions in all state institutions – the civil service, the army, the police and state corporations. South Africa's mineral wealth and economic potential also worked in the government's favour for external capitalist interests were quick to seek an accommodation with the new Afrikaner regime. Two issues were vital to both sides: economic expansion; and gaining the political and financial confidence of the West. Further, from the outset of its long period of political control, the National government grasped the importance of elevating Communism to the status of its number one enemy and threat so as to appeal to the West as an ally in the Cold War which at that time had only just got under way. In 1950 it passed the Suppression of Communism Act which effectively gave the government power to designate as a Communist anyone who tried to bring about social or political change, allowing the Minister of Justice to 'name' any whom he thought Communist and to ban them from participating in meetings or organizations.

J. G. Strijdom, who succeeded Daniel Malan as Prime Minister in 1954, said, 'Either the white man dominates or the black man takes over... The only way the European can maintain supremacy is by domination... And the only way they can maintain domination is by withholding the vote from the non-Europeans. If it were not for that, we would not be here in parliament today.' The policy could not be clearer. On 20 June 1957, Strijdom said: 'If the white man is to retain the effective political control in his hands by means of legislation, then it means that the white man must remain the master... We say that the white man must retain his supremacy.'[5] The previous day the leader of the United Party, Sir de Villiers Graaf, had said: 'When we get into power again there will also be discrimination.' He might make the language sound less aggressive; he meant the same thing. The introduction of apartheid – that is, the legalized separation of the races – from 1948 onwards was not so much a new policy, for by then racial segregation had become ingrained in the South African system, but, rather, the formal entrenchment of the system to ensure the continuation of white political and economic control over all aspects of South African life. The NP, which won the 1948 election under Dr Daniel Malan, was to enjoy uninterrupted political power until the 1990s. There were several clearly defined periods in the apartheid era: first (1948–61), the establishment of what became known as classical or grand apartheid, ending with the Sharpeville massacre of March 1960 and South Africa's withdrawal from the Commonwealth in 1961; second (1961–76), the period of growing isolation as Africa to the north became independent; and third (1976–94), sparked off by the Soweto uprising of 1976, the period of increasingly embattled 'holding on' until an accommodation with the black majority became inevitable. The attitudes of the White leaders, quoted above, for all their arrogance, were based as much upon fear as upon certainty and were in marked contrast to the 1955 Freedom Charter which became the basic policy statement of the African National Congress (ANC): 'South Africa belongs to all who live in it, black and white, and that no government can justly claim authority unless it is based on the will of the people.'

Chief Albert Lutuli best personified the non-violent approach to political change that the ANC had pursued from its inception in 1912 through to the beginning of the 1960s. In 1952 he had been elected President-General of the ANC and on 22 October 1961, after a lifetime of counselling non-violence in the face of violent oppression, he was awarded the Nobel Peace Prize for 1960. A reluctant government, after considerable international pressure, allowed him to go to Oslo to receive his honour but *Die Transvaaler* described the award as 'an inexplicable, pathological phenomenon', while *Die Burger*, the Cape Nationalist daily, considered the award a 'remarkably immature, poorly considered, and essentially un-Western decision'. The term 'un-Western' used here went to the heart of white South African fears; the recognition that a black South African merited such an award for his stand against white racism was intolerable. Chief Lutuli said: 'Who will deny that 30 years of my life have been spent knocking in vain, patiently, moderately and modestly at a closed and barred door? What have been the fruits of moderation? The past 30 years have seen the greatest number of laws restricting our rights and progress, until today we have reached a stage where we have almost no rights at all.'[6]

Lutuli might be moderate but the grand architect of high apartheid, Prime Minister Verwoerd, was not. After his election as Prime Minister he said, 'I believe that the will of God was revealed in the ballot.' Asked by a Nationalist newspaper whether he ever felt the strain of his responsibilities, Verwoerd replied: 'No, I do not have the nagging doubt of even wondering whether, perhaps, I am wrong.'[7] On his memorable visit to South Africa in 1960, Harold Macmillan had found Verwoerd an extremely narrow-focused, totally obdurate man, 'Consistent to his principles, Verwoerd refused to have a single African servant in the house (Groote Schuur)' and as Macmillan noted in his diary, to Verwoerd apartheid 'was more than a political philosophy, it was a religion; a religion based on the Old Testament rather than on the New... he had all the force of argument of some of the great Calvinist leaders of our Scottish kirk. He was certainly as convinced as John Knox himself that he alone could be right, and that there was no question or argument but merely a statement of his will...'[8] As Verwoerd justified the implementation of apartheid in every sphere of South African life, allotting the Africans to their appointed Bantustans or homelands, it became clear that the divided South Africa which he was creating was piling up impossible problems for the future that, if maintained, must tear the country apart.

The turning point or divide between the old South Africa in which the Africans, against increasing odds, had striven for change by argument and a new bleaker, more brutal South Africa in which repression and violence would become the norm came over the years 1960–61. Following the Sharpeville massacre (see above, Introduction) the ANC and the Pan-Africanist Congress (PAC) were banned; both organizations then turned to more violent methods of protest with the formation of their two militant wings – *Umkhonto we Sizwe* (Spear of the Nation) and *Poqo* (Blacks Only) of the ANC and PAC respectively – that were created to use sabotage against white property. South Africa's withdrawal from the Commonwealth in 1961 marked the beginning of the country's increasing international isolation. In 1963 17 *Umkhonto* and ANC leaders were arrested and put on trial, including Nelson Mandela and Walter Sisulu. Mandela and the others were charged with treason (he had previously been charged with the same offence in 1956 and after a trial which had dragged on for years been acquitted in March 1961). Subsequently, he had organized a massive stay-at-home protest at the decision that year to turn South Africa into a republic. After several months in detention he had gone into hiding to become known as the 'Black Pimpernel' as he worked to organize the ANC. He left South Africa illegally in August 1962 and addressed a conference of African nationalist leaders in Addis Ababa. He then went on a brief visit to London. On his return to South Africa he was arrested and sentenced to five years' imprisonment. Meanwhile, the ANC conspirators, in astonishingly amateur style, met at Lilliesleaf farm, Rivonia, and the security services had no difficulty following their movements and, when the time came, arresting them along with much written evidence. Mandela and Sisulu were the leading defendants with seven other ANC and Communist leaders in what became known as the Rivonia treason trial. The charges of sabotage were not disputed but the defendants denied the intent of armed rebellion. The inept prosecution by the prosecuting lawyer Yugar allowed Mandela to turn the occasion into one of a statement of black ideals and in the process he obtained world attention. The Rivonia trial of 1964 was a landmark in South Africa's story and Mandela's condemnation of the apartheid system became an historic judgement of an indefensible creed. On 20 April 1964 he gave a four-and-a-half-hour speech in which he enumerated simply and clearly what Africans wanted: to be paid a living wage, to live where they obtained work, to own land where they worked, for men to have their wives and children to live with them. 'We want a just share in the whole of South Africa; we want security and a stake in society. Above all we want equal political rights, because without them our disabilities will be permanent.' In an historic peroration, Mandela concluded:

> During my lifetime I have dedicated myself to this struggle of the African people. I have fought against white domination, and I have fought against black domination. I have cherished the ideal of a democratic and free society in which all persons live together in harmony and with equal opportunities. It is an ideal which I hope to live for and to achieve. But if needs be it is an ideal for which I am prepared to die.

He was condemned to life imprisonment, along with other African leaders, and sent to Robben Island.

APARTHEID

By 1960 the word apartheid had become an international term of abuse and so South Africa's rulers resorted to euphemisms: separate development, parallel streams, self-government, Bantu homelands within a South African Commonwealth. Dr Verwoerd described the policy as 'four-streamed vertical separate development'. The apartheid legislation turned black distaste for the Boers into detestation while those whites who could not stomach 'Christian Nationalism' emigrated to Britain or elsewhere. There was a considerable loss of white professionals at this time. Throughout the 1950s and 1960s the government extended its repressive legislation to outlaw all forms of African political activity. The 1950 Suppression of Communism Act was one of the most repressive pieces of legislation. This was followed by the Criminal Law Amendment Act of 1953 and in 1967 the Terrorism Act with many others in between. Crucial to the whole concept of the separation of races was the 1959 Promotion of Bantu Self-Government Act that laid the foundations for the separate homelands or Bantustans. These were to be farming communities, providing sustenance and acting as dormitories and retirement homes for the black men whose labour was needed in the white towns. In 1967 the Department of Bantu Administration and Development stated its policy of herding blacks into the homelands with chilling bluntness: 'It is accepted government policy that the Bantu are only temporarily resident in the European areas of the Republic for as long as they offer their labour there. As soon as they become, for one reason or another, no longer fit for work or superfluous in the labour market, they are expected to return to their country of origin or the territory of the national unit where they fit ethnically if they were not born and bred in their homeland.'[9] The 1963 Bantu Laws Amendment Act in effect reduced the country's seven million Africans, living and working in the 87 per cent of the country designated for whites, as guest workers or loan labour, to the level of chattels.

During Verwoerd's premiership apartheid became the most notorious form of racial domination that the post-war world was to know. One of the greatest evils under the apartheid system was the government's policy of eliminating 'black spots': that is, land owned or occupied by Africans in white areas. The numbers involved is uncertain but the Surplus People Project, which studied the removals, estimated that 3,548,900 people were removed between 1960 and 1983; 1,702,400 from the towns, 1,129,000 from farms, 614,000 from black spots, and 103,500 from strategic development areas.[10] The endless stream of repressive apartheid legislation gave the police virtually unlimited powers of arrest and those arrested could be held indefinitely without trial in solitary confinement without access to anyone except government officials.

> South Africa in the apartheid era was unique. It became increasingly distinctive from other countries as decolonization and desegregation spread elsewhere. South Africa was a partly industrialized society with deep divisions based on legally prescribed biological criteria. As the economy expanded, industry absorbed more and more black workers, but racial categories continued to define primary social cleavages.[11]

The relative longevity of the apartheid experiment was ensured because there was no powerful economic interest willing to oppose the system. Apartheid ensured a virtual white monopoly of skilled jobs, high wages and the right to industrial (trade union) bargaining. Despite the argument that became much more important in the 1980s – that the requirements of capitalism – labour and markets – would erode apartheid, during the 1960s capitalism thrived on apartheid and sustained it.

Between 1948 and 1970 the NP increased its strength at each election. The United Party gradually disintegrated – it had no alternative policy to offer – and the small Progressive Party, which was eventually reduced to the solitary figure of Helen Suzman who became the lone voice of liberalism in the apartheid state, honoured by Africans as their spokesman in Parliament against racial segregation. Prime Minister Verwoerd was assassinated in 1966, stabbed to death in the parliamentary chamber by a temporary messenger, Demetrio Tsafendas, a Mozambican of mixed racial descent. J. B. Vorster became Prime Minister in his place; he was an equally dedicated white supremacist, who stamped ruthlessly upon any opposition and used the 90-day detention rule extensively. In 1962, while Minister of Justice, Vorster (who on taking office had used the memorable phrase that 'rights are getting out of hand'), said: 'United Party policy held the same future for South Africa as that of Progressives and Liberals: total destruction of white leadership.'[12] In 1968 security controls were centralized under the Bureau of State Security (BOSS). The NP, for all practical purposes, had become the monolithic wielder of all power in South Africa.

The preamble to the 1961 Republican Constitution began: 'The people of the Republic of South Africa acknowledge the sovereignty and guidance of God.' The constitution was conceived, drawn up, discussed, approved and adopted as an Act of Parliament by whites only, to the deliberate exclusion of all other South African inhabitants, and its provisions expressed their wishes and nobody else's. White hopes during the 1960s were based increasingly (and they worked hard at it) on the assumption that the Republic was and would remain essential to Western interests. As a consequence, the government relentlessly projected two themes: the mineral wealth South Africa had to offer; and the strategic value to the West of having the southern tip of the African continent in friendly hands. The first of these themes was sustained by apartheid, which was the cornerstone of investment profitability; the result was the creation of a vicious circle in which the interests of both sides in the equation depended upon the maintenance of a brutally unjust system. After he became Prime Minister, Vorster expanded the so-called 'outward looking' policy to make allies in Africa. The exchange of diplomats with Malawi and the subsequent offers of substantial aid were seen as an important breakthrough. His hopes of making equal breakthroughs with the three High Commission territories after they became independent as Botswana, Lesotho and Swaziland were not to be realized, however. At the end of the decade the hard-line NP supporters of apartheid opposed any policy that would dilute it and did not look with favour upon a policy that would allow black diplomats white privileges in South Africa. They became known as the *Verkramptes* (cramped ones) as opposed to the *Verligtes* (enlightened) but in the election of 1970 the hard-liners were annihilated. As a result they broke away to form the *Herstigte Nasionale Party* (Refounded National Party) under Dr Hertzog. This represented the first break in the monolithic power of the NP but it made little difference to the overall position.

The homelands policy was Verwoerd's most distinctive contribution to apartheid. In 1958 he offered 'separate development' as a formula to save South Africa from political integration and external intervention. It promised the white man *baaskap* (racial domination) in 87 per cent of the country (the white areas) while blacks would achieve eventual *baaskap* in 13 per cent of the country. However, partition in any meaningful sense was never intended for the Bantustans were not viable political or economic units. They were designed to provide the white economy with its black labour. From 1960 onwards the projected Bantustans – Bophutatswana, Ciskei, Gazankulu, KaNgwane, KwaNdebele, KwaZulu, Lebowa, Qwaqwa, Transkei and Venda – were created and encouraged to pursue separate development. In fact, the most dramatic aspect of the homelands policy was to be the mass removal of black populations from the white areas of South Africa to the various homelands. The hardships involved in this policy were usually appalling and the brutality with which it was pursued focused increasing international attention upon the inequities of the apartheid system, despite the fact that the government now spent more money on development in the homelands while also allowing (a reversal of earlier policy) white investments in them as well. The homelands continued to be seen as labour reserves for white South Africa. The homelands policy allowed the denial to Africans of equal rights to be justified on the grounds that they were aliens only temporarily sojourning in South Africa for purposes of work, rather than South African citizens of inferior race, which was the basis of apartheid. The fallacy inherent in this policy was always the need of white South Africa for black labour on the one hand, and the fact that the 13 per cent of the land area which had been assigned to the homelands was not only totally inadequate in terms of the size of the black populations it was meant to serve, but was also the least viable land agriculturally, and by and large lacking in mineral resources. In 1963 Transkei was given internal self-government with Chief Kaiser Matanzima as Prime Minister.

ECONOMIC SUPPORT FOR THE APARTHEID STATE

External funds in the 1960s found their way most readily into the white-controlled territories of Africa – South Africa, Rhodesia, the Portuguese territories – rather than the newly independent black states. There were two explanations for this pattern: the first, that investors were doubtful of the long-term political stability of the new states; the second, that investors preferred dealing with longstanding partners which, in the case of South Africa, meant established white-controlled enterprises. Such attitudes were reinforced by overtones of racism, the assumption that white business partners were more likely to be dependable. Official South African estimates in 1961 indicated that US$1,507 million had been invested there by Britain, US$590 million by the US, US$235 million by France. Other estimates put the figures higher: US$2,800 million for Britain, US$840 million for the US with West Germany and Japan rapidly increasing their stakes in the country. Despite apartheid and the white determination to enforce segregation, South Africa had become an integrated industrial society in which the four races – African, Indian, Coloured and White – could not survive without each other. Economic differentials, however, were vast with an average African income of US$75.50 a year against a White income of US$1,398 a year, then the third-highest in the world after the US and Canada. The emergence of the modern, non-mining, sector was heavily dependent on foreign investment and the growth of this sector was essential if the country's prosperity was to be maintained and increase. In the early 1960s over 300 British companies had associates or subsidiaries in everything from mining to textiles and engineering and 7 per cent of Britain's overseas investments were then in South Africa. US manufacturing investment in Africa was primarily concentrated in South Africa, which was the most industrialized country on the continent, with mining and smelting as the most profitable areas. According to M. D. Banghart, the Vice-President of American Metal Climax which was then expanding its operations in both South Africa and South West Africa, American firms could make an average profit of 27 per cent on investments in South Africa, more than double the profit from comparable investments in the US, principally because apartheid depressed the African wage bill. The low cost of labour provided a built-in incentive to Britain, the United States and other Western countries to invest in South Africa; they condemned apartheid, but lightly, while doing nothing to bring it to an end. In 1963 wages earned by South African black miners were US$216 a year, while Zambian miners earned US$810 a year and American white miners earned US$2.70 an hour. Apart from ethical considerations, South African labour policies made bad economics; had the system been an open one the economy would probably have been twice as strong as it was when black majority rule was finally achieved in 1994. The outflow of investments that followed the scare of Sharpeville in 1960 had largely ended by 1965 when it was clear that the government had regained control and equilibrium; thereafter, Western money flowed back into the system, further encouraged by strategic considerations concerning South Africa's role in the Cold War.

South Africa's economy was then, and later, enormously dependent upon inflows of foreign capital. Between 1965 and 1970 it received a total of US$2,546 million from the West: the average annual net inflow rose from US$260 million a year in 1965/67 to US$562 million in 1968/70 and reached a record US$786 million in 1970. Western business was attracted to South Africa because investments obtained such large returns, sometimes (according to *American Business Week*) between 17 and 26 per cent. Apart from the major Western investors, South Africa also attracted smaller ones and, for example, by 1970 Canada had invested Canadian $70 million there. By the beginning of the 1970s the number of British companies operating in South Africa had risen to 500 and those from the US had increased to 300, including most of the best-known names from both countries.

The United Nations 1963 arms embargo on South Africa might have made a substantial dent in Western exports but in fact it was either ignored or largely circumvented. It was totally ignored by France, which as a result became a major new investor in the country. Other countries, and notably Britain, found ways round the embargo by the indirect licensing of South African firms to produce British arms. As the South African Defence Minister, Jacobus Fouché, said in 1963, the problem was no longer that of getting the arms manufacturers of other countries to produce arms in the Republic, but rather one of deciding whose requests to establish factories should be allowed. There was clearly an element of bravado in this statement but not a great deal. French exports to South Africa rose from US$33 million in 1960 to US$100 million in 1970 while its investment rose at a faster rate. The attitude of British commercial institutions and companies towards South Africa was instructive. Sir Charles Hambro of Hambro's Bank said in 1963 that he had 'not lost confidence in the long-term future of the country' and that 'one of the best ways of strengthening Western civilization in Africa is to strengthen South Africa'. ICI argued slightly more guardedly that while in theory it would be possible to withdraw from South Africa in practice it was not and, in any case, ICI was contractually bound to partnerships with South African interests. In 1968 the Palabora Mining Company (an offshoot of RTZ) announced an Educational Bursary Scheme of up to 10 bursaries for a maximum of £647 a year, open to all European children. Its annual report the following and succeeding years said: 'A scheme is being formulated for African children.' Many industries saw South Africa as the base for expansion into the rest of the continent and in 1969 Lord Stokes of Leyland said in Johannesburg: 'You have to take the long-term view in business. We want, therefore, to be established here in our own right.' In a remark that gave away more, perhaps, than intended, Sir Val Duncan of RTZ said his company confined itself to the 'mature democracies', which for him included South Africa with 80 per cent of its population denied the vote by law while its African workers were paid desperately low wages. By the end of the decade South African companies were establishing themselves on the borders of the

Bantustans for convenience of access to black labour. 'The example of the border areas is only one more confirmation that apartheid is an extremely flexible device for using Africans in the white economy while denying them political power. Mr Harry Oppenheimer put it well when he said: "There is no evidence so far that economic integration has led to any improvement in political or social integration."'[13] A purely economic view of apartheid made a great deal of sense: 'Apartheid is not primarily about the separation of the races at all, since the economy has always been, is now, and probably always will be dependent on African labour; apartheid is a device for making sure that that labour is in constant supply and total subjection.'[14] As Prime Minister Vorster told the House of Assembly on 24 April 1968: 'It is true that there are blacks working for us. They will continue to work for us for generations, in spite of the ideal that we have to separate them completely... The fact of the matter is this; we need them because they work for us... But the fact they work for us can never entitle them to claim political rights. Not now, nor in the future... under no circumstances.'

Harry Oppenheimer succeeded his father as head of the global 'empire' that comprised the Anglo-American Corporation and De Beers Consolidated Mines in 1957. His empire 'controlled forty per cent of South Africa's gold, eighty per cent of the world's diamonds, a sixth of the world's copper and it was the country's largest producer of coal'. He subsidized the Progressive Party, launched in 1959, recommended the incorporation of educated Africans into the political system, yet he had no respect for African culture and though admitting the migrant labour system was bad in principle, saw it as essential to the gold-mining industry.[15] Oppenheimer was South Africa's leading industrialist and commanded great economic power; he was, in fact, essential to the regime although he adopted the stance of a moderate opponent of the NP. His principal object appeared to be the immediate safeguarding and expansion of his economic empire. He was a prominent supporter of the South African Foundation, set up in 1959, to project South Africa's name abroad, and by so doing he roused the antagonism of non-white leaders. Always careful to cover his position – liberal but never too liberal – he was in fact a paragon of accommodating capitalism. In his chairman's statement to the shareholders of Rhodesian Anglo-American Ltd, on 17 November 1960, he said: 'Whether African nationalism is really irresistible in a multi-racial country has... yet to be decided. It is quite wrong to think that the majority group in a mixed state is necessarily the most powerful, still less that it is necessarily irresistible.' The statement was aimed as much at South Africa, his power base, as at his Rhodesian audience. He was to argue repeatedly that higher African wages, assured urban residence by right, and an end to job restriction would raise

Kwame Nkrumah of Ghana and Gamal Abdul Nasser of Egypt – early leaders of African Independence. (Africa Week)

Kwame Nkrumah, Prime Minister of Ghana, opens the conference of Independent African Nations in Accra, Ghana, April 1958. (Associated Press/ africanpictures.net)

Gamal Abdul Nasser, President of Egypt, 1954–1970. (INPRA/africanpictures.net)

Patrice Lumumba, first Prime Minister of the Congo (Democratic Republic) with
U. N. Secretary General Dag Hammarskjold, July 1960. (INPRA/africanpictures.net)

The Betrayed Leader: Patrice Lumumba
was murdered in January 1961 with the
connivance of Belgium and the US.
(INPRA/africanpictures.net)

Alhaji Abubakar Tafawa Balewa, first
Prime Minister of Nigeria at independence on 1 October 1960. He was killed in
the first coup of January 1966.
(INPRA/africanpictures.net)

In 1988, halfway through the Algerian War of Independence, Ferhat Abbas announces the formation of an Algerian Government in Exile. (Trace Images – Associated Press/africanpictures.net)

A constant backdrop of violence: the first President of Algeria, Ahmed Ben Bella, attends the funeral of Algerian troops killed in a border conflict with Morocco, 1963. (Trace Images – Associated Press/africanpictures.net)

Nigerian (Federal) soldiers race along the airstrip on the news that the Biafran government has surrendered. (INPRA/africanpictures.net)

Ian Smith signs the Instrument of UDI, 11 November 1965, with his white cabinet looking on. (INPRA/africanpictures.net)

productivity and markets while lowering real labour costs. The Anglo-American Group of companies was a principal key to South African economic power. Outside South Africa the Group also operated in South West Africa, Rhodesia, Zambia, the Congo, Angola and Tanzania. At the beginning of the 1970s the *Investors' Chronicle* described Anglo-American international diversification as follows: 'More like a government than a Company. Its shares are proof against all but the most far-reaching economic trends. They are really an investment in the Western capitalist system.'[16]

Britain maintained especially close ties with South Africa after it left the Commonwealth in 1961. Thousands of white South Africans had been born in Britain and qualified for British passports and hundreds of thousands more had relatives and close friends there while the culture of English-speaking white South Africa was oriented toward Britain, which allowed the 'kith and kin' argument great play during the years of South Africa's isolation. The South African economy, moreover, was more important to Britain of its Western trading and investment partners than to any other country. Britain, whether under Conservative or Labour governments, showed great reluctance to take measures against South Africa and when it left the Commonwealth in 1961 passed the South Africa Act which maintained the new republic's privileged access to British markets that had depended upon Commonwealth preferences. In his first speech as Prime Minister on 12 November 1963, Sir Alec Douglas-Home said: 'I believe that the greatest danger ahead of us in the world today is that the world might be divided on racial lines. I see no other danger, not even the nuclear bomb, which could be as catastrophic as that.' Unfortunately, subsequent Conservative and Labour policies in relation to the White South did not appear to bear out this concern. When the Labour Party came to power under Harold Wilson in 1964 he announced that the government would adhere to the UN arms embargo though current contracts (for Buccanneer aircraft) would be met. In fact his government showed itself half-hearted at best in applying the UN arms embargo to South Africa although in 1966 it did withdraw Britain's only warship, a destroyer, from the Simonstown base at the Cape. In 1968 the President of the British Board of Trade, Anthony Crosland, told the UK South Africa Trade Association (UKSATA): 'It has always been my government's view that political differences should not be allowed to interfere with the growth of trade.' That year Britain sent 14 trade missions to South Africa; in 1969, 20. In spite of South Africa's role in breaking sanctions against Rhodesia, Crosland said: 'We have made it clear that we cannot contemplate any economic confrontation.' Sir Alec Douglas-Home, in opposition, visited South Africa in 1968 and said there that if the Conservatives were returned to power, they would resume the sale of arms to the Republic. In March 1970, the chairman of the Conservative Party, Anthony Barber, visited South Africa to say: 'As far as the supply of arms for the external defence of the Southern Atlantic is concerned, P. W. Botha (then South Africa's Defence Minister) and I are at one.' These and other British politicians made it clear where their sympathies lay.

US involvement in South Africa, both as investor and trader, grew substantially through the 1960s; in particular the US was interested in the country's wide range of minerals. Between 1960 and 1970 the average world rate of return on overseas investment was 11 per cent but in South Africa US capital earned 18.6 per cent. In the post-Sharpeville years a consortium of US banks arranged a revolving loan of US$40 million for the South African government. By the end of 1966 US investment had risen to US$601 million, equivalent to 13 per cent of total foreign investments in the Republic. US earnings from investments in 1960 came to US$50 million; by 1966 they had risen to US$124 million. The rates of return on US South African investments during the 1960s were phenomenally high, roughly double those elsewhere: in 1963 – 20 per cent, 1964 – 18.9 per cent, 1965 – 19.1 per cent, 1966 – 20.6 per cent, 1967 – 19.2 per cent, 1968 – 17.2 per cent.[17] Like British companies in South Africa, US companies paid their Africans abysmally low wages. 'Investment in manufacturing accounted for 50 per cent of US direct investment in South Africa in 1969. It earned a return of over 13 per cent, against a worldwide average of 10.8 per cent. Yet the average African wage in manufacturing enterprises (foreign and local) for the same year was R49.8 – R30 below Assocom's (Associated Chamber of Commerce) Poverty Datum Line for a family of five.'[18]

West German involvement in South Africa also grew steadily over these years. In 1962, again a demonstration of Western sympathy if not solidarity with the beleaguered white regime, the Deutsche Bank led a consortium of banks guaranteeing a £4 million loan to the South African government. Through the 1960s collaboration between West Germany and South Africa increased in trade, investment and the supply of arms, though the latter was secret and indirect. Three hundred West German companies established subsidiaries in South Africa and an average of 3,000 Germans a year emigrated to the Republic. France also became heavily involved in South Africa during the 1960s, breaking its earlier 'acceptance' that the Republic was in Britain's sphere of influence. Through the decade its investments and trade increased substantially and it was the only major power openly to break the arms embargo. In addition, France acted as a clearing-house for South African trade contacts with French-speaking Africa. By 1969 France had become the leading supplier of arms to the Republic: these included submarines, helicopters and Mirage jets. In reverse, by 1970

South Africa had become France's leading arms customer. Responding at the end of the decade to France's assistance with arms, Prime Minister Vorster said: 'We shall never forget that France was and still is prepared to accept our word that we have no aggressive intentions... France, having accepted our word as a self-respecting country, sold us arms of a high standard, such as aircraft and submarines.' Japan of the major trading nations also played a significant role in sustaining the South African economy. For trade reasons, the Japanese had been elevated to the anomalous status of 'honorary whites' by South Africa, for Japan was a major customer for its minerals. Between 1965 and 1969 the South African share of Japan's total imports rose from 23 per cent to 36.8 per cent; of chrome from 12 per cent to 30 per cent; of manganese ore and concentrate from 6 per cent to 29 per cent. By 1969 Japanese monthly exports to South Africa ran at US$23.2 million, its imports at US$24.9 million, and South Africa was Japan's main African trading partner.

These major powers might ritualistically condemn apartheid; this did not deter them from providing the South African regime, by trade and investment, with the economic support that was essential to its survival.

SOUTH AFRICA AND THE UNITED NATIONS

Article 19 of the United Nations Declaration of Human Rights adopted by the General Assembly of the UN on 10 December 1948 reads: 'Everyone has the right to freedom of opinion and expression; this right includes freedom to hold opinions without interference and to seek, receive, and import information and ideas through any media and regardless of frontiers.' South Africa did not sign the Declaration and subsequently felt under no obligation to honour it. Following the Sharpeville massacre of 21 March 1960 the UN Security Council met and called upon South Africa to abandon apartheid. In November 1962 the UN General Assembly called upon member states by 67 votes to 16 with 23 abstentions to break diplomatic relations with South Africa, boycott its goods and refrain from exports to South Africa, including arms. The West ignored the call. The Special Committee against Apartheid was established. Above all the considerations of the South Africa question, and the West's response to calls for action to end apartheid, lurked the belief in Africa and elsewhere that had the colours of the oppressor and the oppressed been reversed the West would have been in the forefront demanding action. In 1963 the Security Council instituted a voluntary total arms embargo against South Africa. In response, the British government immediately announced that in future it would only sell arms that South Africa required for its external defence. Commenting on this issue, Fenner Brockway, by then the doyen of the British Labour Party's left wing, said: '... United Nations action could undoubtedly be decisive in ending the fundamental human wrong of racial oppression. We must accept the probability, however, that the United Nations will not act. Power is with the industrial countries which are identified with the economy of South Africa and, notwithstanding all their disavowals of apartheid, it is this that will be the determining factor. We confess we have little hope for the near future as we look at Southern Africa.'[19] He was correct. The UN paid a good deal of attention to South Africa during 1963. On 11 October the General Assembly, by 106 to one (South Africa), called for the immediate and unconditional release of political prisoners, and an immediate end to all political trials, including those under the Sabotage Act, and on this occasion even Britain voted for the motion. Twice during the year the Security Council resolved that the policies of South Africa constituted a grave disturbance of international peace; however, the Security Council did not use the word 'threat', substituting 'disturb' for it at the insistence of Britain and the United States, since the employment of the word 'threat' implied, under the UN Charter, the need to employ enforcement measures. Although sanctions were frequently discussed, apart from the arms embargo they were at best half-heartedly applied or more often ignored entirely.

The use of sanctions against Rhodesia from 1965 onwards, after the Unilateral Declaration of Independence (UDI), was resolutely bypassed by South Africa for had sanctions brought about the downfall of the Smith regime in Salisbury there would have followed far more vociferous demands for their use against apartheid South Africa.

In 1965 the General Assembly established a UN Trust Fund for South Africa. In 1966 it proclaimed 21 March (Sharpeville Day) as International Day for the Elimination of Racial Discrimination (to be observed annually). In 1967 a UN Educational and Training Programme for Southern Africa was established: it would provide scholarships for students from Namibia, South Africa, Rhodesia and the Portuguese territories of Angola and Mozambique. In 1970 the UN strengthened the arms embargo and urged member states to terminate diplomatic and other official relations with South Africa. Critics of the United Nations often took it to task or derided it for passing resolutions that had little hope of being implemented and in the case of the major Western powers were generally entirely ignored, yet the steady passing of such resolutions ensured that the injustices of the South African system were constantly brought to the attention of the international community.

Even as the United Nations increased pressures upon it, South Africa increased its hold over South West Africa in defiance of the world body. German South West Africa had been invaded and occupied by South African forces in 1915 and in 1920 the territory had been entrusted to South Africa to administer as a Mandate on behalf of the League of Nations. In 1946 the newly formed United Nations invited its members to place their mandated territories under its Trusteeship system and all except South Africa complied with the request. South Africa organized a referendum among chiefs in South West Africa and on the strength of this demanded that the territory should be integrated into the Union. Only Britain supported the move. Thereafter, South Africa had refused to recognize UN jurisdiction over South West Africa and had entered into a long-lasting dispute with the world body that would only finally be resolved with the independence of Namibia in 1990. In 1955 the International Court of Justice (ICJ) confirmed the right of the General Assembly to adopt resolutions on South West Africa. Meanwhile, African opposition to South Africa's control of the territory was growing: in 1959 the first liberation movement, the South West African National Union (SWANU) was formed; in 1960 this was followed by the South West African People's Organization (SWAPO). In 1964 the South African-appointed Odendaal Commission reported and recommended the creation of Bantustans in South West Africa and proposed a five-year economic and social plan. In 1966 the United Nations General Assembly adopted Resolution 2145 which revoked the Mandate and changed the country's name to Namibia. SWAPO, which had sent its first group of guerrillas into the country the previous year, had its first clash with the South African Defence Force (SADF) and the armed struggle was under way. In 1967 the United Nations set up a Council for Namibia to administer the territory and in 1969 the Security Council recognized the right of the General Assembly to revoke the Mandate. Despite these UN pressures to prise Namibia from its control, in 1969 the South African parliament approved a South West Africa Affairs Bill to adjust the administration of South West Africa and, in effect, turn it into a fifth province of the Republic. In 1971 the ICJ gave an advisory opinion that South Africa was illegally in South West Africa. The confrontation between South Africa and the United Nations over Namibia had another 20 years to run.

THE HIGH COMMISSION TERRITORIES

The three British protectorates of Basutoland, Bechuanaland and Swaziland were collectively known as the High Commission Territories and administered by a British High Commissioner from Mafeking in South Africa. Implicit in the 1909 Act of Union had been the British recognition that the three territories would eventually be incorporated into the Union of South Africa, provided this was acceptable to their peoples – which it never was – and South Africa had long worked upon the assumption that incorporation of the three would eventually take place. They had escaped that fate in part as a result of their own determination, preferring British imperial control as the lesser evil. The three territories were landlocked and heavily dependent upon South Africa. During the six years of Prime Minister Malan's rule in South Africa (1948–54) Britain had begun the process of moving the three territories towards independence and after South Africa's withdrawal from the Commonwealth in 1961, its relations with the three had to be reorganized on the basis of them being foreign states. The three territories had long been treated as 'cinderellas' by the Colonial Office and by the 1960s the British tended to imply that they were only in the three territories for altruistic reasons although this was belied by its actual conduct. In Basutoland, for example, during the period 1960 to 1966 when it became independent, the British insisted that aid to the colony should pay. This attitude was sharply rebuffed in the *New Statesman*: 'It is clear that if Basutoland's economic advancement is made dependent on the Union (of South Africa's) Nationalist government, the territory will continue to stagnate. Its politically ambitious and active African leadership, frustrated by economic barriers, may well become embittered. They will blame Britain for not being prepared to spend even £2.12 million in order to provide the prerequisite for economic, and therefore social, advancement.'[20] When Basutoland did become independent as Lesotho in 1966 it faced apartheid South Africa with a dilemma. South Africa had always wanted to absorb Lesotho but since Verwoerd was then busily promoting the idea of Bantustans his government was obliged to accept the independence of Lesotho, even though its territory was entirely surrounded by South Africa. Lesotho had no resources; it was a labour reserve and its biggest annual revenue came from the remittances of its workers in the South African mines.

Like Lesotho, Bechuanaland (later Botswana) had been conditioned by Britain to expect that any requests to London for development assistance would be pared to a minimum: 'Educationally, the Batswana are probably more backward than any other people in Africa which has been under British rule; they are challenged only by the Swazi for this dubious distinction. Certainly in Bechuanaland as a whole the schools are, in the opinion of experts, worse housed and worse equipped than any in British-administered Africa.'[21] Indeed, the British pose of being appalled by apartheid was revealed in its stark hypocrisy by its educational record in Bechuanaland. In 1960 £55,152 was spent on the education of 411 white children, or £134.2 per white child per year, while by contrast £268,683 was spent on the education of 36,273 African children, or £7.4 per African child per year. The point here is not only that 18 times as much was being spent on the education of every white child enrolled as on every black child, but that it is hard to think of a worthwhile education which could be given on only £7.4 per head per year.[22] When Bechuanaland became independent as Botswana in 1966 it found it had an inescapable role as a route of flight and as a sanctuary for anti-apartheid refugees.

Labour conditions were especially bad in Swaziland in the period before independence and wages were often lower than those paid to Africans in South Africa. Strikes occurred in several industries during 1962 and particularly on the sugar plantations – the Ubombo Ranches – where working conditions were generally appalling and wages abysmal. In May 1963 the biggest strike in the country's history took place at the Havelock asbestos mine which then accounted for most of Swaziland's revenue and foreign exchange earnings. Pre-strike wages on the mine were 3/5d a day and the miners demanded £1. Ninety-five per cent of the workforce, 1,350 men, stopped work and after a week of negotiations the government appointed a one-man commission to look into the miners' grievances. Meanwhile, disaffection had spread to the capital, Mbabane, where the Democratic Party held a mass meeting of domestic workers and labourers. The meeting demanded that the Resident Commissioner (governor) should institute a general inquiry into Swazi wages, improve 'intolerable working conditions', and fix a national minimum wage. At that time domestic servants earned between £2 and £5.10s a month, worked unlimited hours and had to find their own accommodation.

The Havelock strike, which began on 20 May, remained peaceful until 8 June when the police arrested 12 alleged ringleaders. They were almost all members of the Ngwane National Liberation Congress (NNLC), an offshoot of the old Progressive Party. Following the arrests, 2,000 strikers demonstrated against the police who dispersed them with tear gas. On 9 June a mass meeting of 3,000 in the Mbabane township protested against the arrests and also against the country's new constitution and called for a general strike in Mbabane. This took place on Monday 11 June; it spread and led to a riot in the prison and the escape of 10 prisoners. The government response was to enlist whites as special constables, promise an inquiry, take emergency powers and bring in police reinforcements from Bechuanaland. Britain airlifted a battalion of Gordon Highlanders from Kenya to Swaziland and they were at once used alongside the police to break the Havelock strike. Within a week of their arrival the *Times of Swaziland* announced, 'Strikers go back to work – Swaziland returns to normal.' African leaders protested at Britain's handling of the strike and Tom Mboya demanded that British troops should quit Kenya, which Britain was then using as a base, 'to oppose our brothers'. Two years after the Havelock strike comparisons were to be made about the readiness of Britain to rush troops to Swaziland to break a strike and the 'impossibility' of sending troops to Rhodesia to prevent treason. One optimistic comment upon the use of British troops suggested, 'In one probably unforeseen way, their presence has given all three Territories a new insurance against South African aggression. For if British troops can be flown in to break a strike, world opinion would never again accept the arguments that they could not be flown in to meet any South African threat.'[23] What Britain was capable of doing and what Britain was prepared to do in Southern Africa were very different things, separated by a vast gulf of economic and racial self-interest.

Britain's efforts to prepare these three territories for independence were minimal as well as being designed not to upset South African susceptibilities. For example, Britain gave assurances to Dr Verwoerd that the broadcasting stations which were to be established in the three territories prior to independence would not broadcast political material considered to be 'hostile' by Verwoerd; would limit their range so as to cover only a minimum of South African territory; and would not compete with the Republic's Springbok Radio commercial network as an advertising medium.[24] Such conditions demonstrated a pusillanimous subservience to South African bullying; they also raised acute issues of neo-colonialism, for what controls would Britain maintain after independence? In general, the British attitude towards these three small vulnerable countries was one of disinterest in their independent futures, parsimony in preparing them for independence and appeasement of South Africa. A senior British official in Basutoland reacted to UN criticisms of British rule in the three territories by saying, 'We never wanted these territories in the first place. They've been nothing but an embarrassment and financial drain on us, and now we're getting kicked for carrying and protecting them all these years.'[25] It would be difficult to find a more revealing comment by a colonial official about Britain's real attitudes as opposed to its vaunted imperial-colonial mission.

Botswana and Lesotho came to independence in 1966, Swaziland in 1968 and all three had to learn the precarious task of living next door to the apartheid giant: Botswana had borders with South Africa, Namibia and Rhodesia and a tiny ferry crossing over the Zambezi to Zambia; Lesotho was entirely surrounded by South Africa; Swaziland was three-quarters surrounded by South Africa and shared its fourth border with Portuguese Mozambique. Their independent prospects hardly appeared encouraging. South Africa had achieved one significant breakthrough with black Africa when Malawi agreed to exchange diplomats with the Republic and was prepared to accept substantial aid as well (see chapter 11 above). But Banda, who found himself at odds with the rest of independent Africa as a result of this initiative, represented a one-off achievement for Pretoria's 'outward looking' policy that would not be repeated. When the three High Commission Territories came to independence they did not, as Pretoria had hoped, follow Malawi's lead even though their geographical position made them semi-prisoners of the Republic. One aspect of this breakthrough had not been foreseen: Malawi's diplomats had to be treated as other diplomats (in effect as honorary whites) and use hotels and other facilities normally reserved for whites only. It was plain that if such concessions were to be made to more foreign blacks they would eventually also have to be made to South African blacks as well.

By the late 1960s, despite the shock of Sharpeville and leaving the Commonwealth at the beginning of the decade, South Africa's position appeared invulnerable. It had become a principal target for Western investment and was able to shrug off African condemnations of its policies as unimportant, the angry bleating of regimes most of which seemed unable to cope with their own problems. Furthermore, the informal organization of South Africa, Rhodesia and Portugal (SAPRO) to resist black advance added to Pretoria's sense of security. Rhodesia and Portugal provided a cordon sanitaire between the Republic and independent Africa to the north, though this alliance would have collapsed by 1975. In any case, defence and security had become central considerations of the government. The South African defence budget had risen from £18 million in 1958–59 to £60 million in 1962–63 and to £115 million in 1965–66. Its security forces were as much concerned with maintaining internal control on behalf of the white minority as they were in facing an external threat though there were unmistakable signs that an external threat was beginning to develop. The security forces steadily tightened their grip on the country and were given ever more draconian powers, so that their right to detain suspects for 12 days eventually became the right to do so indefinitely.

Twenty years after the victory of the NP under Malan in 1948 South Africa did some stocktaking. The government itself was all-powerful, white opposition had dwindled while black opposition was underground, imprisoned or exiled. The Johannesburg Stock Market was enjoying a boom and Western countries were competing to increase their share in South Africa's trade and investment. It was legitimate to ask, despite condemnations from without, whether apartheid might not in fact succeed. Prime Minister Vorster appeared to believe this when he claimed: 'The day will come when people will visit South Africa, not only for its wildlife and scenery; but to see how it is that people of different colours live in peace in one geographical area.' Alongside this calculated optimism, P. W. Botha, the Minister of Defence, warned in November 1968: 'All South Africans were in the front line... we must realize once and for all that we will live in danger for many years to come, and we must realize that not only our soldiers, but all our people must be prepared to fight for all we hold dear.'

Writing in the generally sympathetic London *Daily Telegraph*, Frank Taylor said: 'After 20 years of apartheid the prospect of a self-supporting, politically independent Transkei (to name but one) is as remote as ever. The hard fact is that the ratio of Africans to whites *outside* the homelands – that is in the urban centres of "white" South Africa – is rising every year instead of falling.'[26] The policy of creating industries on the Bantustan borders so that labour did not need to leave its homeland was not working. As Dr J. Adendorf, the General Manager of the Bantu Investment Corporation – the strategic government agency to foster development in the Bantustans – said of Bantustan progress, 'At the present rate of development the Bantu homelands will never be in a position to absorb the increases in Bantu population and assure decent living standards.' He, if anyone, was in a position to know and, as always, the real concern was how to offload the growing black population from white South Africa. The answer was plain enough: it could not be done.

By 1968 white South Africa was increasingly aware of the growing guerrilla threat on its borders. In 1966 SWAPO, led by Sam Nujoma, launched its war against South African occupation of Namibia. In 1967 a joint ANC/ZAPU guerrilla group made a foray into Rhodesia from Zambia. Vorster warned of the Communist menace and said that in time an army would be created for a full-scale attack upon South Africa. In July of 1968 SWAPO claimed some victories for its guerrillas in the Caprivi Strip; at first the SWAPO claims were denied by the South African government but later it admitted that considerable activity had taken place. The country was becoming steadily more militarized and in May had published a Bill to create a R100 million Armaments Development and Production Corporation (ARMSCOR) as a state enterprise. By this time the South African arms industry was sufficiently advanced that an arms embargo could only have an impact upon the upper end of the arms business for South Africa was not yet able to produce such sophisticated weapons as submarines or aircraft. The increasingly close military-arms tie-up between South Africa and France was well developed by 1968. General André Beaufré, a leading French military intellectual, greatly pleased his South African audience when he wrote in the South Africa Foundation's publication *Perspectives* of April 1968: 'In the sense that Europe is a projection of Asia, so is South Africa the European Cape of the African continent. The common fate of these two projections throughout their history has been to remain different from the continental mass, Asia or Africa, and to maintain an individual civilization.' Inadvertently, perhaps, the General had touched upon the white's most acute dilemma: were they Africans or were they Europeans?

A split occurred in the ranks of the National Party at this time with the emergence of the so-called *Verkramptes*, hard-line members of the party who would not contemplate any concessions to the black majority. Dr Albert Hertzog and Dr Andries Treurnicht emerged as the leaders of this group, to form the *Herstigte Nasionale Party* (HNP). They were determined to keep the NP on its strict apartheid lines. Opponents of apartheid briefly hoped to see a major breach develop in the monolithic ruling party but this was not to be. P. W. Botha, the Minister of Defence, rallying to the support of the Prime Minister, said in April: 'The security of the Black man depends on the White man, and as long as the country is led by John Vorster the safety of the White man in South Africa is guaranteed.' Further, Vorster, in an effort to prevent the split in Afrikaner ranks widening, included Treurnicht in his cabinet, a decision that helped cause the events of 16 June 1976 (the Soweto uprising) since Treurnicht was the architect of the ruling that 'Afrikaans was the medium of instruction in black schools' that sparked the explosion.

On the whole, the ruling NP could feel reasonably secure at the end of the decade. It is true that another cloud had arisen on its horizon: sport. The government's refusal to allow the Coloured cricketer Basil D'Oliveira to tour South Africa with the MCC led to the cancellation of the tour in 1969 and the British Minister of Sport, David Howell, had followed this up by saying he did not think Springbok cricket teams should come to Britain in 1970: 'I have no time for any sport based on racial considerations.' Sport would develop into a more important issue during the 1970s. At the end of the decade, always emphasizing its value to Western defence, the South African government floated the idea of a South Atlantic Treaty Organization (SATO) and NATO joining in a Greater Atlantic Treaty Organization. Pretoria made approaches to Argentina and Brazil as possible SATO partners. Defence would become of greater importance during the 1970s.

The Decade in Retrospect

The first overriding concern of all African leaders during the 1960s was to get the Europeans – the colonialists – out of Africa. The entrenched nature of European colonialism was more than simply a physical presence on the continent, it was also a state of mind, as exemplified by the Portuguese belief that the primary function of Africans was to work for the Europeans and that only by so doing could they aspire to become civilized. By holding on so grimly to their African colonies the Portuguese in fact served notice that they needed their colonies and that, of course, was the basis of all colonialism – exploitation. When the British conceded independence to India they did not, as has sometimes been implied, see this as the beginning of total world decolonization; instead, they turned to Africa as an alternative lifeline, a number of imperial fiefs to be properly developed for the first time, to serve British interests. The British did not know what wealth Africa might produce because up to that time they had broadly neglected the continent in favour of other regions of their Empire. Harold Macmillan put his finger on the African problem in 1960 when he said, 'Africans are not the problem in Africa, it is the Europeans.' The Africans, above all, needed to throw off the humiliation that imperialism had imposed on them.

The Europeans might respond to the pressures of a new world order by decolonizing their African empires, yet despite sometimes grandiose claims that they had always intended to prepare their African subjects for independence, they at once demonstrated an extraordinary cynicism towards the weak new states that emerged from their empires, and never more so than in the Congo (K) as that benighted country descended into chaos. Those states that attempted to follow genuinely radical paths were not only opposed by the West but undermined as well until their experiments in true independence collapsed. On the other hand, states that were content to accept Western tutelage, such as Gabon, were protected when the need arose, as was President M'ba by the French. The West never envisaged truly independent African states going their own ways; rather, it sought dependent client states to be manipulated according to its strategic and economic requirements. The result was to be decades of support for tyrants such as Mobutu, leaders who were happy to act as Western agents as long as they themselves were maintained in power. The Cold War, then at its height, provided the West with the excuses it needed to justify its conduct in supporting unsavoury regimes. But that was only part of the equation; the colonial powers may have conceded political control but they had no intention of relinquishing their economic stranglehold upon the continent. Furthermore, the combination of independence and the Cold War made it possible for powerful new actors to enter the African scene – the United States, the USSR, China and the newly formed European Community. Africa had, as it thought, shaken off the shackles of imperialism only to find it faced even more formidable players who regarded the African continent as a chessboard for their international confrontations. Prior to independence African nationalists faced the one enemy in the form of the imperial power. After independence they faced two sets of enemies: the old imperial powers, determined to safeguard their economic and other interests; and the new Cold War warriors who were prepared to subvert Africa in any way that suited their policies. There were plenty of catastrophes – the Congo disaster and the Nigerian civil war providing the most striking examples – but there was also the confrontation with white racialism in Rhodesia, the Portuguese territories and, above all, South Africa, racialism that was to be enormously prolonged by Western support provided through a fog of hypocrisy.

Against this background of international interventions the new states of Africa sought to create a semblance of continental unity: they built up a number of regional economic unions, none of which were to be very effective since they each assumed a level of intra-national co-operation that did not exist, and then established the Organisation of African Unity, which survived over the coming decades only because it aspired no higher than to meet the lowest common denominator of mutual interest without demanding any sacrifices of newly achieved power that none of the emergent leadership would have been prepared to make anyway. The failure to achieve unity should not have surprised anyone. Instead, each new state embarked upon parallel searches for internal political stability on the one hand and economic development with external aid on the other.

The search for political stability followed a familiar path: the rejection, or part rejection, of inherited political systems, the creation of one-party state structures, the need to balance tribal and sectoral pressures for a share of political – and therefore patronage – power, and the further need to come to terms with military participation in government. As the one-party state became the norm in Africa so the coup replaced the election while varying degrees of oppression, including the curtailment of human rights, the reduction of most meaningful forms of democracy and limitations upon free speech, including the press, also became the norm in too many of the new states.

Every new state sought rapid economic progress as the only way to satisfy the expectations of the people as a whole and development, development strategies, five-year plans, aid, loans and grants, and technical assistance added a new dimension, not to say vocabulary, to government activities. Impossible targets were set and huge debts were incurred while a new breed of 'neo-colonialists' in the form of aid experts, United Nations agencies, World Bank teams, non-government organizations and a bewildering variety of would-be advisers descended upon Africa to manage an economic renaissance that had been beyond both the capacity and intention of the former colonial powers. These new advisers and aid donors established the parameters of development to be followed and began to create a system of aid dependence that would last to the end of the century while African leaders who were fully alive to the dangers of the aid trap were nonetheless prepared to fall into it provided such dependence also helped maintain them in power. Small economies – and almost all those of Africa fell into this category – need both protection and government assistance if they are to thrive but, as always, the large dominates the small, and the external advisers and donors began to insist, exerting pressures that would become irresistible over the years, that Africa should open its small weak markets to the exports of the big strong producers, a tactic designed to keep Africa as the source of raw materials rather than manufactured products.

As the decade came to a close a summary of developments, good and bad, included: the emergence of the one-party state as the most favoured form of government; the increasing power and ambition of the military; the fragile state of most economies and the growth of aid dependence; the black-white confrontation in the South that included a number of liberation wars; and the increasing impingement on the continent of Cold War pressures. Such developments induced a growing sense of realism: that most African states had little power, many problems and scant capacity to influence world events or the economic trends that most affected them. On the credit side was the fact that most of the continent had become independent, that it had created a number of structures such as the OAU, which reinforced a sense of African identity and solidarity, and that despite the limitations upon its tiny economies it had achieved a respectable level of economic growth. If Africa entered the 1970s with a sense of achievement behind it, the problems it faced, as it soon discovered, would tax its leaders to the full. At least a new sense of realism was beginning to replace the euphoria of the independence era.

PART II

The 1970s

Decade of Realism

CHAPTER FOURTEEN

Patterns
of Development

The 1970s were to witness huge upheavals through much of Africa: wars, economic and political experiments, the emergence of tyrannies and, everywhere, the pervasive manipulative influence of the dominant Western powers, with the Communists providing an alternative court of appeal. By 1970 the euphoria, which had accompanied independence, had passed; African leaders now had to discover how to steer their countries through an international minefield in which virtually all the levers of economic and political power lay outside their control. In North Africa the death of Nasser marked the passing of an era; in Libya the young Gaddafi decided to take on the oil majors and in the process gave the Organization of the Petroleum Exporting Countries (OPEC) 'teeth'; in the west Morocco embarked upon a path of imperialism whose outcome was still undecided at the end of the century. The two superpowers brought the Cold War to the Horn as the reign of Emperor Haile Selassie, Africa's great survivor, finally ended in tragedy. Three African tyrants – Uganda's Amin, Central African Republic's Bokassa and Equatorial Guinea's Nguema – did their best to justify all the accusations of barbarism that the continent's white critics were so quick to level against it. A number of countries – Algeria, Nigeria, Tanzania, for example – embarked upon development strategies that gave rise to the hope that at least some of Africa's new states would break away from aid dependence upon the West, although elsewhere on the continent aid came to be accepted as an integral part of every development strategy. Both Britain and France seemed intent on proving that Nkrumah's accusations of neo-colonialism were justified with Britain constantly coming down on the wrong side for the wrong reasons and France intervening militarily and economically in its former colonies as though that status had never changed. There were brave attempts by radical leaders to steer their countries into development paths that would not be dependent upon the West; they rarely succeeded. At least a dozen countries were affected by a more or less permanent state of warfare – sometimes low-intensity guerrilla activity, at others escalating into major set piece battles as in the Horn. In Rhodesia the end of the decade would coincide with the emergence of an independent Zimbabwe. The collapse of the Portuguese Empire in 1974–75 brought immediate if only temporary peace to Angola and Mozambique before both countries would again be submerged in even more brutal civil wars, while brooding over the whole Southern African scene was the entrenched apartheid state. Much bitterness would be revealed as various states embarked upon policies of authenticity: changing names, nationalization, expropriating property and expelling metropolitan expatriates were gestures of repudiation signalling the African desire to throw off the remaining evidences of colonialism; but few of these gestures worked. Colonialism had gone deep and countries such as Mali that tried to break free were forced by economic necessity to turn back to the former metropolitan power for economic assistance and survival. This was provided but the price to be paid was a high one.

A brief survey of events in a number of individual countries follows to fill in the background for the decade as a whole.

ARAB NORTH AFRICA

Gamal Abdul Nasser died of a heart attack on 28 September 1970 to bring an era in Egypt's history to an end. Vice-President Anwar Sadat succeeded him and, despite predictions that he was only a stopgap president, quickly consolidated his power. The 1970s, in fact, were to prove a momentous decade for Egypt. In July 1972 Soviet military advisers, a heritage from the Nasser era, were expelled from Egypt and Egyptians manned their military installations. In August the government announced plans to merge with Libya, one of those Arab unions that never came to anything, and relations between the two countries subsequently deteriorated. During 1972–73 there was growing unrest, especially among the student population, until the Yom Kippur War, launched by Egypt, took the world by surprise. When Egyptian forces crossed the Suez Canal on 6 October 1973, Sadat transformed his own position and the entire situation in the Middle East. Although the Israelis held their own, after the initial reverses, the Yom Kippur War was the first Israeli-Arab war in which the military honours were even rather than an all-out victory for Israel. A post-war agreement of 18 January 1974 between Egypt and Israel returned a strip of land on the Sinai side of the Suez Canal to Egypt, whose prestige had been restored, while a now confident Sadat had overnight become the hero of the Arab world. He granted an amnesty to political opponents and restored diplomatic relations with the United States. US President Jimmy Carter (1977–81) worked hard and with success to broker a peace between Egypt and Israel.

However, once Cairo was seen to be pursuing a bilateral peace with Israel so as to regain control of the Sinai Peninsula, Egypt became progressively isolated in the Arab world. In November 1977 Sadat did the unthinkable when he visited Israel and addressed the Knesset (Israeli Parliament). On 26 March 1979, the outcome of the Camp David meetings, a treaty was signed between Sadat for Egypt and Menachim Begin for Israel under whose terms Israel would withdraw from Sinai over the succeeding three years. The two countries established diplomatic relations in February 1980 and by recognizing Israel's right to exist Sadat isolated himself in the Arab world. The Arab League withdrew its headquarters from Cairo and Egypt's membership was suspended.

Few would have predicted in 1969 that the young Muammar Gaddafi who came to power in Libya by means of a military coup would still be ruling Libya at the end of the century. He was to enjoy the great advantage of large oil revenues and a small population so that he always had a surplus of funds for external adventures, and as the world soon learnt external adventures were meat and drink to him. Three basic Gaddafi policies became apparent during the 1970s: the first, taking control of Libya's oil; the second, the pursuit of Arab nationalism at home and in the region; the third, the implementation of a cultural revolution. It was Gaddafi who gave OPEC 'teeth' in the early 1970s; before that time the organization, which had been set up in 1961, had made no impression. Under Gaddafi Libya became a militant supporter of the Palestinians, pushing for greater action on their behalf than other Arab states were prepared to do. Gaddafi proposed a union with Egypt in 1972 and another with Tunisia in 1974; neither came to anything. Gaddafi's radicalism was genuine enough; it would have been more effective had he been less erratic and unpredictable in his behaviour. As soon became apparent, both Arab and African leaders came to mistrust Gaddafi's ambitions in much the same way that an earlier generation had mistrusted those of Nkrumah. Gaddafi supported revolutionary and guerrilla movements in Ethiopia, Rhodesia, Portuguese Guinea, Morocco and Chad (as well as other radical movements outside Africa) and from 1972 to 1979 provided Uganda's dictator Amin with substantial assistance as well. In April 1973 Gaddafi called for a cultural revolution in Libya that involved the rejection of imported cultures, whether from east or west, and the construction of a society based on the Koran. That year saw the beginning of Libya's long involvement in Chad's civil war when Libya claimed and occupied the 50,000 square mile Aozou Strip of northern Chad. In 1976 the General National Congress of the Arab Socialist Union (ASU) was transformed into the General People's Congress (GPC). On 2 March 1977 Gaddafi announced major changes in the GPC and the country was renamed The Socialist People's Libyan

Arab Jamahiriya with all power vested in the people. In 1979 Gaddafi resigned his official posts to concentrate upon 'revolutionary work'. By that time, whatever people thought of him, Gaddafi had become a factor to be reckoned with in both the Arab Middle East and Africa. He was unpredictable and interfering but he had large oil funds at his disposal.

When the Tunisian leader Habib Bourguiba was re-elected President unopposed in 1974 he was at the height of his influence. The following year the assembly made him President for life. But he had already been in power since independence in 1956 and there was growing discontent, especially at deteriorating economic conditions. The *Union Générale Tunisienne de Travail* (UGTT) (General Union of Tunisian Workers) initiated a number of strikes through 1976 and though the government offered a social contract that linked rises in pay to inflation this was not enough to stop the strikes or the demands for higher wages. Labour troubles came to a head on 26 January 1978 when the UGTT called a general strike. Rioting broke out in Tunis and a number of other cities, the army was used to restore order, 51 people were killed and several hundreds injured. The government imposed a curfew and declared a state of emergency. Habib Achour, the militant UGTT leader, and 30 others were arrested for subversion. They were tried amidst widespread claims that the trials were unfair. Achour was sentenced to 10 years in prison and all but six of the others also received prison terms. This explosion of labour unrest was the worst crisis the government had faced since independence. Nonetheless, the government won the 1979 elections although voter turnout was down to 81 per cent rather than the normal 95 per cent. By the end of the decade there was growing uncertainty about the country's political direction, which was exacerbated by speculations about the eventual succession to Bourguiba who was then nearly 80.

On the Atlantic coast of North Africa, Spanish or Western Sahara (the former Rio de Oro) was to become the focus of ugly antagonisms and warfare once Spain relinquished the territory as it did in 1976. When Morocco became independent from France in 1956 it had at once laid claim to Spanish Sahara on the grounds that the territory had formerly been a part of Greater Morocco. Its troops had made incursions across the border at that time but had been repulsed by the Spanish colonial forces. In 1960 Mauritania became independent and advanced claims of its own to Spanish Sahara. In 1963 large phosphate deposits were discovered in the north of the territory at Bou Craa and mining began under the Spanish in 1974. The indigenous people of the territory, less than 100,000 in number, formed a liberation movement, the Popular Front for the

Liberation of Saguia el Hamra and Rio de Oro (POLISARIO), which campaigned for an independent Saharan Arab Democratic Republic (SADR). POLISARIO rejected both the Moroccan and Mauritanian claims to the territory. In 1975 Spain entered into an agreement with Morocco and Mauritania that it would withdraw in February 1976 and divide the territory between the two African states. When Spain withdrew the following year Morocco occupied the northern two-thirds of Western Sahara and Mauritania occupied the southern third. POLISARIO, based in Algeria and receiving a certain amount of support from the Algerian government, formed a government in exile and commenced guerrilla actions against the two African countries that it regarded as invaders. The war for control of Western Sahara was to have a major impact upon both Morocco and Mauritania.

At the beginning of 1973 King Hassan of Morocco was unpopular and politically isolated. In order to improve his political standing and ensure the long-term safety of his throne, Hassan resorted to a series of nationalist moves that had a wide appeal. These included the confiscation of foreign-owned land (mainly French), the extension of the country's territorial waters, the despatch of troops to the Syrian front in the Yom Kippur War and, most popular of all, the claim he advanced to Spanish Sahara. When it became clear that Spain simply wished to withdraw from its colony, both Morocco and Mauritania prepared for action. On 15 October 1975 a UN Mission to Spanish Sahara reported that the majority of the people wanted independence. In response to this report King Hassan mounted a brilliant public relations exercise: he ordered 350,000 unarmed Moroccan citizens to march into Spanish Sahara and claim it for Morocco. The march took place on 6 November 1975 and the marchers penetrated several miles into the territory before they were halted by Spanish troops. On 9 November Hassan called the marchers back home; the gesture had served its purpose and was wildly popular in Morocco. Once Spain had withdrawn, Morocco occupied the northern two-thirds of Western Sahara, and soon found that the war against POLISARIO was to be both costly and long lasting. By 1979 it was absorbing 25 per cent of Morocco's annual expenditure and in the 1980s led to a breach between Morocco and the OAU.

In the first years of the 1970s Mauritania embarked upon a radical policy: it reviewed its post-independence agreements with France and left the franc zone to create its own currency. Then in 1974 the government nationalized the *Société Anonyme des Mines de fer de Mauritanie* (MIFERMA), which was responsible for mining the country's major mineral resource of iron ore and provided 80 per cent of export earnings. Foreign, mainly French, interests controlled MIFERMA. At the same time Mauritania joined the Arab League. This process of radicalization reached its climax in 1975 at the congress of the *Parti du Peuple Mauritanien* (PPM) when Ould Daddah presented a new charter that would turn Mauritania into an Islamic, centralist and socialist democracy. The charter received massive support including that of two opposition parties. The first half of the decade was also a period of great hardship as a result of the long Sahel drought that reached a climax in 1973 when large numbers of the national herd died and many nomads were forced away from their traditional life into the shanty towns of the cities so that by 1975 the country's nomadic population had been halved.

The politics of Mauritania from 1975 to 1979 were to be dominated by the Western Sahara question. The division of Spanish Sahara, which had been agreed between Spain, Morocco and Mauritania in November 1975, allotted the southern province of Tiris el Gharbia to Mauritania but when Mauritanian troops occupied the province in 1976 they met fierce resistance from POLISARIO. Tactically, POLISARIO was probably wrong to concentrate its effort against the weaker of the two occupying powers but that is what it did. Moreover, it carried the fight into Mauritania, mounting attacks upon the railway line that linked the vital iron ore mine at Zouerate to the port at Nouadhibou. In June 1976 POLISARIO mounted a successful raid upon Nouakchott, the Maritanian capital. In response to this unexpectedly fierce resistance, Mauritania had to expand its small army from 1,500 to 12,000 and later to 17,000 men. Even so, Mauritania was unable to control the region of Western Sahara that had been allotted to it and instead became increasingly dependent upon Morocco while the POLISARIO war was generally unpopular with the people of Mauritania. By 1978 the country faced growing problems: it was unable to defend itself effectively from POLISARIO attacks while its economy was in ruins. Ould Daddah was overthrown in a bloodless coup: the constitution was suspended, the national assembly and the PPM were dissolved and a Military Committee for National Recovery (CMRN) was formed under Lt-Col. Moustapha Ould Salek. POLISARIO announced an immediate truce to assist the new government while Morocco moved 9,000 troops into the Mauritanian part of Western Sahara. A period of political instability in Mauritania followed and then in 1979 Mauritania renounced all claims to Western Sahara.

THE SAHEL BELT

The Sahel region consists of those countries lying to the immediate south of the Sahara desert and stretches from Senegal on the Atlantic to Sudan in the east. The Sahel includes parts of Senegal, Mauritania, Mali, Upper Volta, Niger, Northern Nigeria, Chad and Sudan. The region is semi-arid, part desert, part savannah and links the Sahara to the more fertile lands farther south. It is essentially pasture land over which nomads graze their herds and where overgrazing has contributed to making droughts more severe when they occur. The drought which began in 1968 and intensified through to 1973 led to at least 100,000 deaths, the near extinction of a number of crops and the loss of between 50 and 70 per cent of some cattle herds. At the same time the Sahara desert advanced southwards by up to 60 miles as increased desertification took place. Another severe drought occurred in 1983–84. In the aftermath of the first drought the Permanent Inter-State Committee on Drought Control in the Sahel (CILSS) was formed in September 1974 comprising Cape Verde, Chad, The Gambia, Guinea, Guinea-Bissau, Mali, Mauritania, Niger, Nigeria, Senegal and Upper Volta. Some of these countries were only covered by Sahel conditions in part, Nigeria being the most obvious example. The effects of the 1973 drought were especially devastating in the four giant countries – Mauritania, Mali, Niger and Chad. In Mauritania a large part of the national herd – cattle, sheep, goats, camels – was destroyed, with cattle numbers reduced from two million in 1970 to 1.3 million in 1976. Mali's agricultural production was sharply reduced and output of the staples – millet and sorghum – fell from a normal 700,000 tons a year to 525,000 tons while rice output fell from 174,000 tons in 1971–72 to only 100,000 tons. In Niger cattle numbers were estimated to have fallen by two-thirds between 1972 and 1975 while fishing harvests from rivers and lakes fell by a third. Chad, by that time heavily involved in its civil war, also had its cattle herds devastated. Though not considered to be part of the Sahel, Ethiopia experienced a major drought in 1973 and this played a significant role in the downfall of Haile Selassie because of the inept way in which the government handled the subsequent famine in Tigre and Wollo provinces where an estimated 200,000 died. There were allegations of widespread corruption in the handling of relief supplies and a marked rise in food prices that was reinforced by a sharp increase in the costs of all imported goods and especially of petroleum products following the OPEC price rises at the end of 1973. In 1976 a Club of the Friends of the Sahel was formed. It prepared a report, Sahel Development Plan (1978–2000), whose object was 'to enable the Sahel States to achieve food self-sufficiency whatever the climatic hazard'. By 1985, however, the CILSS had failed to achieve its primary aim of food self-sufficiency for the region and food production as a percentage of actual needs had fallen from 98 per cent in 1960 to 60 per cent in 1984.

Poverty across the Sahel belt, remoteness and the desire of politicians to break the French stranglehold on their economic systems contributed over these years to make for political upheavals. Moussa Traoré became Mali's undisputed head of state in April 1971. He improved relations with France (after his predecessor

Keita's more aggressive anti-French socialism) but he did not break relations with the USSR. Traoré faced several coup attempts during the early 1970s and unrest among the military, the civil service and the students who remained loyal to Keita. The government found it was unable to reform state enterprises without the co-operation of the civil service, which was withheld, and there were no willing foreign investors. In June 1974 the government held a referendum on a new constitution and claimed a 99 per cent vote in favour of its proposals, which included a return to civilian rule. The effect was spoilt, however, when the government announced that it would remain in power for a further five years while a new political party was formed. This party, the *Union Démocratique du Peuple Malien* (UDPM), was announced in 1976. The death of the former ruler Keita in detention in 1977 provoked a series of anti-government riots. In 1979 a constituent congress of the UDPM was held and a national council of the party was chosen. This was followed in June by presidential and legislative elections in which the official list of candidates received 99 per cent of the votes.

President Hamari Diori ruled Niger from independence in 1960 to 1974 during which time French influence was pervasive; the French maintained a presence in the country and a military garrison at Niamey much as though the colonial era had not come to an end. President Pompidou visited the country in October 1972 and his appearance led to anti-French demonstrations by students while President Diori, agreeing with the students, said publicly that France's attitude towards Niger was paternalist and outdated. He criticised SOMAIR, the French mining consortium, which had failed to reach its targets in extracting the country's rich uranium deposits. Diori's conversion to mild radicalism came too late and in April 1974 he was overthrown in a coup that brought the Army Chief of Staff Lt-Col. Seyni Kountché to power as President. Kountché was considerably more radical than his predecessor: he tackled the problem of endemic corruption and tried to deal more effectively with the impact of the Sahel famine. He established a *Conseil Militaire Supreme* (CMS), demanded the withdrawal of French troops and exerted pressure upon SOMAIR to accept a 33 per cent government holding. A decree of 27 March 1975 banned foreigners from participating in a number of business activities. Then, in February 1976, Kountché sacked four of the top military men in his government and created a mainly civilian government.

In Chad the rebel *Front de Libération National du Tchad* (FROLINAT) (Chad Liberation Front) became steadily more powerful during the early 1970s under the leadership of Goukouni Oueddei and Libya became its principal backer, providing offices for it in Tripoli. Following an attempted coup against him, President Tombalbaye broke diplomatic relations with Libya. Thereafter

Gaddafi openly backed FROLINAT and provided it with tanks and anti-aircraft missiles. Although under Goukouni's leadership FROLINAT achieved some substantial successes and captured a number of northern towns such as Bardai and Faya-Largeau, the movement like many others split into a number of factions. Goukouni was too independent for Gaddafi who switched his support to a rival group under Ahmed Acyl. Another faction, the *Forces Armées du Nord* (FAN) (Northern Armed Forces), emerged under the leadership of Hissène Habré and this gradually became the dominant arm of FROLINAT. In 1973 Libya moved troops into the Aozou Strip. This region of approximately 50,000 square miles adjoined the southern border of Libya and contained rich uranium deposits. Libya based its claim on a 1935 Franco-Italian protocol that, however, had not been ratified. In 1975 the army overthrew Tombalbaye and Gen. Félix Malloum became President of the Supreme Military Council. The war continued indecisively to 1978 when Malloum met Habré in Khartoum and the two men agreed a ceasefire, which, however, collapsed almost at once. The Chad army then suffered a series of reverses at the hands of FAN under Habré. In mid-1978 France, which had withdrawn its forces from Chad in 1972, sent a substantial number of troops to support the government of Malloum; Libya responded by sending between 2,000 and 3,000 troops in support of FROLINAT. In February 1979 Habré ousted Malloum in a coup and this led in turn to a civil war in the south of the country between Muslims and blacks. Chad's neighbours now became seriously alarmed at the possibility of the war spreading into neighbouring countries and their pressures, as well as those of France, persuaded Gaddafi to withdraw – at least for the time being. The war would continue through the 1980s.

East of the Sahel, Africa's largest state, Sudan, was to enjoy its best decade since independence. When he came to power in 1969 Gaafar Nimeiri inaugurated a policy of Sudanese Socialism. In 1971 the Communists led by Maj. Hashim al-Ata carried out a coup on 19 July, temporarily ousting Nimeiri who went into hiding. However, a popular uprising in favour of Nimeiri brought an end to the takeover in three days. Nimeiri's popularity then soared and relations with the West improved though he did not break off relations with the Communist countries. In presidential elections that October Nimeiri obtained four million votes against 56,000 nos. Then, in March 1972, Nimeiri achieved his greatest success when the Addis Ababa Agreement with the Anya Nya rebels brought the civil war to an end and gave regional autonomy to the South. Nimeiri then embarked upon a pragmatic policy that included a number of important development projects. He excluded from government the right-wing parties and these then organized themselves in the National Front (NF). In 1977 he entered into a secret agreement with Sadiq al-Mahdi, who enjoyed considerable popular support, for a policy of National Reconciliation, with the Sudanese Socialist Union (SSU) as the sole legitimate party. Nimeiri was to retain his appeal to the people and his grip on politics until the end of the decade.

In Kenya, through the 1970s until his death, Kenyatta became increasingly autocratic, a role that appealed to the remaining white settlers who liked 'strong government' by 'good old Mzee'. The National Assembly was largely bypassed while effective power was wielded by a triumvirate of ministers under Kenyatta: Mbiya Koinange, the Minister of State in the President's office; Njoroge Mungai, Minister of Foreign Affairs; and Charles Njonjo, the Attorney-General. In the elections of 1974 Kenyatta was returned unopposed as President but of 158 members of the assembly 88 lost their seats to be replaced by other KANU candidates under the one-party structure. There was mounting unrest during 1975 that included bomb explosions in Nairobi. Then, in March, came the murder in mysterious circumstances of Josiah Kariuki, probably by a government 'hit' squad. At that time Kariuki was the most popular radical figure in the country and the focus of anti-government criticism. A parliamentary committee investigated his death, but the names of two leading politicians mentioned in the report as being linked to his death were deleted at Kenyatta's insistence and no charges were brought. Accusations of corruption were increasingly levelled at the Kenyatta family, and especially at Mama Ngina, the President's wife. Elections scheduled for 1977 that might have revealed the extent of anti-government feelings were cancelled. On 22 August 1978 Kenyatta, aged 82, died peacefully in his bed at the Mombasa State House. Despite predictions of trouble, especially in the British press, and suggestions that a bloodbath would ensue after Kenyatta died, nothing of the sort happened. Kenyatta's body was flown to Nairobi to lie in state until what was to be the grandest and most solemn funeral witnessed anywhere in independent Africa took place. Daniel arap Moi, Vice-President since 1967, succeeded to the presidency smoothly, according to the constitution and a campaign to secure his acceptance that was brilliantly masterminded by Charles Njonjo who became a powerful 'kingmaker' in the process. Moi began his presidency well. He demoted members of the Kikuyu old guard and appointed Mwai Kibaki, a younger, more radical Kikuyu, his Vice-President. He announced immediate elections and indicated his determination to tackle the endemic corruption that appeared to have become part of national life. If anything, Moi became more pro-West in his external policies than his predecessor. The press became noticeably more outspoken during this honeymoon period. By 1980, however, criticism of Moi's government in the National Assembly and from students increased sharply. Despite attempts by Moi to attract him back into the ranks of

KANU, Oginga Odinga, who had been sacked as Vice-President by Kenyatta in 1966 for his 'radical' views, instead launched an attack upon land grabbing and the 1980s seemed set for widening political conflict.

In the tiny states of Burundi and Rwanda Hutu-Tutsi antagonisms were rarely far from the surface. In April 1972, in an attempt at a comeback, Ntare V mounted an unsuccessful coup against President Micombero of Burundi only to provide him with an excuse to blame the Hutu and carry out an extensive purge; this escalated into a number of bloody massacres in which at least 100,000 Hutus were murdered while deliberate efforts were made to eliminate all literate Hutu. A further 100,000 were rendered homeless and many fled as refugees into neighbouring countries. Micombero restructured the government in 1973 by appointing a seven-man bureau with himself as President and Prime Minister. The following year a new constitution turned Burundi into a one-party state under *Union pour le Progrès National* (UPRONA) with Micombero as its Secretary-General. On 1 November 1976 the Deputy Chief of Staff Col. Jean Baptiste Bagaza overthrew Micombero in a coup. Bagaza tried to reconcile the Hutu and Tutsi. He initiated major land reforms that gave Hutu peasants title to land and he reduced the semi-feudal powers of the Tutsi landlords. Yet, despite his efforts, ethnic hatreds resulting from the massacres of 1972 and a longer past of such confrontations remained deeply embedded in the national conscience and the Tutsi continued as the dominant force in the country. Burundi, which was dependent upon coffee exports for its economic survival, was one of the poorest countries in Africa with a per capita income at that time of about US$220.

In neighbouring Rwanda Hutu-Tutsi rivalries had persisted since before independence in 1962 and by 1965 the Hutu were in total control and had turned Rwanda into a one-party state. In the elections of 1965 and 1969 the *Parti de l'Emancipation du Peuple Hutu* (Parmehutu) candidates had been returned unopposed and Gregoire Kayibanda was re-elected President. In 1973 there was an outburst of Hutu-Tutsi violence; at the same time there developed increasing distrust between the Hutus at the centre (the government) and those of the north and on 5 July the army, which was mainly controlled by officers from the north, carried out a bloodless coup and Gen. Juvenal Habyarimana from Gizenyi became the new President. The army then dissolved Parmehutu and suspended the 1962 constitution. The new regime was moderate in its approach to Hutu-Tutsi relations and Habyarimana adopted the slogan 'Peace and national unity'. The policy led to better relations with Burundi. In 1975 Habyarimana formed a new political party, the *Mouvement Révolutionnaire National pour le Développement* (MRND). His aim was to unite the population in economic, social and cultural development. A new constitution was approved by referendum in December 1978 by a 90 per cent vote; President Habyarimana was confirmed in office by a 99 per cent vote.

THREE AFRICAN TYRANTS

The story of Amin's rule in Uganda – 1971–79 – reflects many of the things that went wrong in Africa at that time. Idi Amin was a brutal, virtually illiterate soldier who was able to seize power in a coup and rule Uganda for nine years during which time he became increasingly tyrannical and was responsible for a growing number of massacres and murders. His coup was quickly recognized by Britain under Edward Heath, who had deeply resented President Obote's pressures upon him not to sell arms to South Africa at the January 1971 Commonwealth Summit in Singapore. Amin was also quickly recognized by Israel for his then known pro-Israeli stand, though when he later reversed his attitude to Israel he was supported with troops by Gaddafi. In 1979, when Nyerere helped bring about his overthrow, the OAU, which had scrupulously refrained from criticizing Amin's brutal internal policies, took Nyerere to task for intervening in the internal affairs of a member state.

In January 1971, at the urging of President Nyerere of Tanzania, Obote had gone to the Singapore Commonwealth Summit to oppose plans by the newly elected British Conservative government of Edward Heath to sell arms to South Africa. Before leaving Kampala Obote foolishly asked Amin, then head of the army, for an explanation for his overspending. On 25 January, while Obote was in Singapore, Amin seized power in a bloodless coup. There was considerable evidence to suggest that both Britain and Israel were behind the coup and certainly both were quick to recognize Amin's government and confer legitimacy upon him. Amin visited several European countries in mid-1971 and in Britain was entertained by the Queen at Windsor Castle, a mark of favour conferred upon the simple soldier as opposed to the socialist Obote. Under Amin Uganda became notorious for the brutalities and massacres carried out on his orders and sometimes with his direct participation so that, despite recognition, he was largely isolated by African opinion as he did increasing damage to the continent's image, in the process providing racist white Southern Africa with a wonderful 'justification' for its supremacist policies.

In the early days after his coup Amin was greeted with enthusiasm. After making himself President and head of state he promised to return Uganda to civilian rule after five years. He gave an amnesty to 55 political prisoners and gained popularity with the Buganda by arranging for the body of the late Kabaka, who had died in London, to be returned home for burial. At the same time, however, Amin carried out a series of massacres of Lari and Acholi troops known to be loyal to Obote and he warned the Asian community to be loyal to his government. In August 1972 Amin announced that all non-citizen Asians should leave Uganda within 90 days. The move was popular with many sections of Uganda society and Britain was forced to accept about 30,000 of them. Britain severed diplomatic relations with Amin and imposed a trade embargo on Uganda; Amin responded by nationalizing all British companies in Uganda without compensation. Such a move was popular elsewhere in Africa since any head of state who stood up to the former colonial powers earned a certain kudos. Amin's principal and growing preoccupation was with security, control of the army and the elimination of enemies – actual, potential or imagined. His soldiers acted with increasing lawlessness which went unpunished while purges of those seen as inimical to Amin's power, murders and disappearances became increasingly frequent. In September 1972 pro-Obote soldiers and exiles launched an ill-considered invasion from Tanzania, which proved a disaster. Amin retaliated by bombing Bukoba and Mwanza. By late 1972 Amin had reversed his earlier pro-Israel stand and as a result Gaddafi provided him with arms and troops. In June 1976 an Air France plane *en route* to Tel Aviv was hijacked to Entebbe by PLO terrorists and 200 passengers were taken hostage with the collaboration of Amin and the army. Israel carried out a spectacular rescue: commandos were flown in and saved all but three hostages while killing a number of Ugandan soldiers and destroying military aircraft, to inflict a devastating blow upon Amin's prestige. Between 1976 and 1979 Amin's support in Uganda evaporated and he became increasingly paranoid as he saw plots everywhere. In October 1978, to divert attention from his home problems Amin launched an attack upon Tanzania, devastating the country through which his troops passed in the Kagera salient and reportedly placing troops of doubtful loyalty in the front and then having them massacred from behind. In January 1979 the Tanzanian army invaded Uganda in return in the hope of inspiring a general insurrection to force Amin from power. Two Ugandan exiles, Lt-Col. David Oyite-Ojok and Yoweri Museveni, formed the Uganda National Liberation Army and invaded alongside the Tanzanians. Amin's army retreated to Kampala and though Gaddafi airlifted in 1,500 troops to assist Amin, and 400 of these perished in the fighting in Kampala, which fell to the anti-Amin forces on 10–11 April. Amin fled, first to Libya and then to Saudi Arabia. In May the invaders occupied the West Nile region forcing troops loyal to Amin to flee into Zaïre and Sudan. A period of disorder followed and continued into the 1980s. An estimated 300,000 Ugandans were massacred, murdered or disappeared during the Amin years.

Colonel Jean-Bédel Bokassa, the President of Central African Republic

(CAR), came to power by coup at the end of 1965 and like other leaders of Francophone states tried to lessen the French grip on his country. In 1971 he decided to create a CAR central bank and national currency and break from both the franc zone and French-controlled airline, Air Afrique, then the national carrier. However, he was forced by French pressures to abandon these initiatives and in doing so was made aware of the extent of general economic control exercised by France. In 1973 Bokassa accused France of using its embassy in Bangui to support and promote his enemies; in 1974 he launched another offensive against French influence when he banned French newspapers and nationalized a number of French companies. In order to halt these moves President Giscard d'Estaing visited CAR in 1975 (Bokassa returned the visit later) to restore good relations and maintain France's grip on the economy. CAR in any case was heavily dependent upon French aid. In the meantime, Bokassa had become increasingly megalomanic. In 1972 he made himself President for life, in 1974 Marshal of the Republic. Then, in December 1976, he dissolved the Council of Ministers and announced the foundation of the Central African Empire with himself as its first Emperor. A new constitution provided for a parliamentary monarchy but all power resided in the hands of the emperor and the ministers he appointed. In December 1977 Bokassa had himself crowned Emperor in a coronation ceremony of ostentatious splendour, which cost an estimated 25 per cent of the country's foreign exchange and led to widespread criticism for its extravagance.

By the end of the decade opposition to Bokassa's rule was general and he was seen as capricious, tyrannical and in no sense of any benefit to his subjects. Student riots in 1979 set off wider expressions of discontent and Bokassa was only able to restore order with the help of troops from Zaïre. Then, in May 1979, Bokassa's reputation was damaged beyond repair when a number of school children who had defied him were beaten to death in the market place of Bangui. As a gesture of disapproval France cut military aid but at the time this amounted to very little. In Paris the Central African Empire's ambassador, Sylvestre Bangui, resigned and announced the formation of a *front de libération des oubanguiens* which brought a number of opposition groups together. Then at Cotonou, Benin, on 9 July, the opposition groups united in a common front against Bokassa and on 20 September, when Bokassa was in Libya, a bloodless coup was carried out and David Dacko, the former President who was then the personal adviser to Bokassa, assumed the presidency and formed a government of national salvation, returning the country to its former name of Central African Republic. France sent 700 troops from Gabon in support of the coup since, by then, it had come to the conclusion that Bokassa was too unstable to safeguard its interests in his country.

Equatorial Guinea, consisting of the former island of Fernando Po, renamed Bioko, and the enclave of Rio Muni, became independent from Spain on 12 October 1968. Francisco Macias Nguema became its President. Anti-white demonstrations and incidents led to an exodus of Spanish residents and this, in turn, led to a near collapse of the economy. In 1970 the various political parties were merged into a single *Partido Unico Nacional*, later renamed the *Partido Unico Nacional de los Trabajadores* (PUNT). Over the years 1970 to 1979 Equatorial Guinea was subjected to the dictatorial and arbitrary rule of Macias Nguema who made himself life president in 1972. The cocoa plantations of Bioko provided most of the country's income and these came close to collapse when 20,000 Nigerian contract workers returned home following the end of the Nigerian civil war. A new constitution was adopted in July 1973 with the principal object of reinforcing Fang supremacy over the islands, the Fang being the dominant ethnic group on the mainland. By the mid-1970s Nguema had become brutally tyrannical and treated the tiny country as his personal fief. Mass executions of political prisoners were carried out in 1975 and the Roman Catholic Church was persecuted while Equatorial Guinea became increasingly isolated. Nguema's dictatorship survived as long as it did as the result of an odd combination of foreign assistance, which came from Spain, Cuba, the USSR and China. In 1976 Nigeria evacuated its nationals from the country, forcing Nguema to harvest the Bioko cocoa crop by recruiting workers from the mainland. By that year an estimated third of the population had fled the country and only French firms continued to operate in it. In 1978 Nguema proscribed the Roman Catholic Church. On 3 August 1979 a military coup, led by Lt-Col. Teodoro Obiang Nguema Mbasogo (a nephew of the President), ousted Nguema who was later executed. Obiang opened up the country to foreign contacts and received immediate aid from Spain. His continued refusal to restore the rights of political parties, however, meant that his intentions were doubted and though he invited exiles to return (there were an estimated 130,000 in 1983) few did so.

These three dictators – Amin, Bokassa and Nguema – shared a number of characteristics: ruthless brutality, a bloodthirsty disregard for life that came out in massacres and murders, indifference to international opinion and a total contempt for the people over whom they ruled. They provided excellent anti-African propaganda for white racists both inside and outside Africa. Far worse, however, was the refusal of Africa through the OAU to take action against them after their activities had become notorious, falling back on the provision in the OAU Charter that forbade interference in the internal affairs of a member state. The attitude of external powers, in general, was to turn a blind eye to what happened while the attitude of the former colonial powers was even less excusable. Britain positively welcomed Amin's advent to power since he eliminated Obote who was a powerful critic of Britain's policy towards South Africa. Amin accepted all the attentions the British bestowed upon him and then, in no uncertain terms, gave them their 'come-uppance' when he first expelled the Asians and then nationalized British companies and humiliated Britons living in Uganda. France went along with Bokassa's tyranny for as long as it was possible to do so in order to safeguard its economic interests and then, with total cynicism, supported the coup that overthrew him. Spain, only a minor colonial power in Africa, provided Nguema with aid for some years on the general principal of maintaining a foothold in the tiny country though Equatorial Guinea had little enough to offer. Aid from the three Communist countries to Nguema was no doubt given on the grounds that support for such a maverick state might cause some embarrassment to the West.

WEST AFRICA

The states of West Africa, many of which are very small by international standards, had a great deal in common and yet each faced unique problems of its own. Apart from Portuguese Guinea, they entered the decade of the 1970s as independent members of the international community but their independence was fragile and elusive. Constantly, whether they wished to or not, they were obliged to refer to their former colonial masters whose economic and political interests could not easily be cast off. The majority were one-party states whose military either provided the government or played a significant role in the wings. Their economies depended upon one or more commodities, usually agricultural though sometimes mineral, and there seemed little likelihood that they could break free of an economic dependence that tied them to Europe. Aid and increasing debt had become part of this relationship. A number had embarked upon radical or socialist development paths that caused deep resentment and opposition in the West, which maintained a proprietorial attitude towards Africa, whose objective, always, was control. Those countries that experimented with Marxism or some other form of socialism did so for a complex mix of reasons. These included the desire to throw off Western tutelage and follow an independent path of their own; a genuine ideological commitment to the one major system that was not part of Western capitalism; a belief that had been nurtured during the period of nationalist struggle for independence that only socialism would answer the needs and deal with the poverty of the people.

After a decade of coups Dahomey settled down to a period of collective leadership over 1968–72 but in October of the latter year yet another military coup brought Maj. Mathieu Kérékou to power. He overthrew the collective leadership and set up in its stead a *Conseil National Révolutionnaire* (CNR); Kérékou was to rule for 20 years. He adopted a strong nationalist, anti-French line and made Marxism–Leninism the official ideology. His early years in power were precarious and a major plot to overthrow him was uncovered in 1975. Subsequently, he reorganized the country's structures and renamed the country Benin (in 1975). He created a single party, the *Parti de la Révolution Populaire du Benin*. Relations with France deteriorated sharply and military co-operation was brought to an end. Relations became yet worse in 1977 after an unsuccessful raid had been mounted on Cotonou by mercenaries, a majority of whom were French, led by the notorious Bob Denard.

In Cameroon, a larger, more complex country that had combined Anglo and Franco mandates, a new constitution was approved in May 1972 that abolished separate Anglo- and Franco- state institutions and turned Cameroon into a one-party state. President Ahidjo steered the new united Republic of Cameroon sharply to the left. He established diplomatic relations with Communist regimes in Vietnam and Cambodia and renegotiated the 1960 co-operation accords with France so as to lessen dependence on the West. Cameroon withdrew from the Francophone organization *Organisation Commune Africaine et Malagache* (OCAM) and insisted upon full non-alignment. In 1975 Ahidjo was re-elected President unopposed with 99 per cent of the votes cast. He named Paul Biya, then Secretary-General in the President's Office, as his Prime Minister. A single-party system with a single list of candidates – the *Union Nationale Camerounaise* (UNC) – led to complaints by Anglophone politicians that they were under-represented. Ahidjo was re-elected President in 1980 but by then there was growing discontent with his government, especially among the Anglophone community. Ahidjo resigned in 1982 and was succeeded by Prime Minister Paul Biya.

Félix Houphouët-Boigny dominated the politics of Côte d'Ivoire for more than 30 years from before independence until his death in 1993. Unlike a number of his contemporaries he was always conservative, deeply pro-France and opposed to socialist experiments. By the end of the 1960s increasing student unrest was evidence of a more radical younger generation that opposed Côte d'Ivoire's close tie-up with France although they posed little threat to Houphouët-Boigny's grip on power, which he maintained without difficulty through the 1970s. In 1975, when he was 70, Houphouët-Boigny was re-elected for another five-year term. In 1976, a precaution in the light of the president's age, a constitutional amendment provided for the president of the national assembly to become executive head of state in the event of the death or incapacity of the president. In 1980 Houphouët-Boigny won a fifth presidential term, leading to further speculation about the succession. The economy had grown remarkably through the 1960s and 1970s to provide Côte d'Ivoire and its president with one of the most secure political bases in West Africa. But given Houphouët-Boigny's age, as well as the longevity of his tenure of office, the expectation was for change in the 1980s.

On 20 April 1970 the tiny state of The Gambia became a republic and Sir Dawda Jawara became its first president; he was to face growing opposition during the decade. A former vice-president, Sharif Mustapha Dibba, formed the National Convention Party (NCP) although its aims were similar to those of the ruling People's Progressive Party (PPP). A second opposition party, the National Liberation Party, also appeared at this time but it made little impact and the NCP became the official opposition. However, criticism of the government, for corruption and stagnation, mounted from both the opposition and from within the ranks of the PPP. More radical opposition to Jawara's government emerged at the end of the decade with the appearance of the Gambia Socialist Revolutionary Party (GSRP) and the Movement for Justice in Africa-Gambia (MOJA-G); they rejected the idea of parliamentary opposition and advocated more extreme policies. They appealed to the unemployed, the discontented and the youth, especially those in the towns. When in October 1980 the deputy leader of the paramilitary field force was murdered, the government revealed its sense of insecurity and fear of a possible coup by appealing to its neighbour, Senegal, which sent 150 troops to support the government. The GSRP and MOJA-G were proscribed and their leaders charged with dissidence. The Gambia remained a Westminster-style democracy but the appeal of this system had obviously worn thin.

The 1970s, arguably, were to be Ghana's worst decade during the latter half of the twentieth century. In 1969 Gen. Joseph Ankrah had been replaced by another soldier, Akwasi Afrifa. Civilian elections were held and were won by the Progress Party (PP) of Dr Kofi Busia who obtained 105 seats in the legislature. The PP represented the capitalist middle classes that had always opposed Nkrumah. Busia became Prime Minister on 1 October while three former coup-makers – Afrifa, Harlley and Ocran – shared the presidency. Busia was neither strong nor imaginative and he lasted for little more than two years. On 13 January 1972 he was overthrown as yet another military coup brought Lt-Col. Ignatius Kutu Acheampong to power. Acheampong banned political activity and set up a National Redemption Council (NRC) composed of army and police officers. Acheampong pursued a policy of Ghanaian self-reliance: he repudiated some foreign debts, launched an authenticity programme and an agricultural programme – Operation Feed Yourself (OFY). He kept Ghana non-aligned and made no attempt to return the country to civilian rule. The Acheampong reforms in fact led to massive inflation, which in turn created a huge black market (*Kalabule*), and by mid-1978 the economy was in ruins. On 5 July 1978 Acheampong was replaced as head of state by Lt-Gen. Frederick Akuffo; but he had been closely associated with the policies of his predecessor and made little impact upon the problem of corruption that embraced the members of the Supreme Military Council who were seen to have enriched themselves while presiding over a collapsing economy. On 1 January 1979 political parties were legalized and elections were promised for the following July. The masses of Ghana became increasingly vociferous against both the military and the middle classes who were seen to have bankrupted the country. On 15 May junior officers and NCOs staged an abortive coup and its leader, Flt-Lt Jerry Rawlings, was imprisoned. Three weeks later junior officers and others freed Rawlings and this time, 4 June, they mounted a successful coup. An Armed Forces Revolutionary Council (AFRC) presided over by Rawlings became the country's ruling body. The Rawlings government began spectacularly when on 16 June generals Acheampong and Utuka were executed by firing squad; 10 days later on 26 June generals Akuffo and Afrifa as well as others were shot, bringing to three the former heads of state to be executed. The July elections were held as scheduled. They were contested by five parties and were won by a coalition of the People's National Party (PNP) led by Hilla Limann and the United National Convention (UNC). Limann went on to win the presidential elections comfortably on 24 September. The Limann government lasted for just over two years and suffered from an impossible handicap for it owed its existence to Rawlings and the military and they, rather than the elected government, came to be regarded as the final court of appeal. Rawlings remained immensely popular and Limann's authority collapsed at the end of 1981. On 31 December Rawlings resumed power.

On 22 November 1970 Guinea was subjected to a mini-invasion when 350 Guinean exiles led by Portuguese officers landed from the sea at Conakry in an attempt to overthrow the regime of Sekou Touré. Over two days of fighting considerable damage was done to Conakry, the presidential palace was destroyed, as were the headquarters of the PAIGC, which directed the war in Portuguese Guinea. Harsh repression followed this shock to Sekou Touré's rule; there were many arrests including former ministers and army officers and in January 1971 91 people were sentenced to death. In 1973 the PAIGC leader Amilcar Cabral was assassinated in Conakry and his death raised suspicions of a plot against the regime. Yet another plot surfaced in 1976 to implicate Diallo Telli, the former Secretary-General of the OAU, who was to die in prison the following year, apparently of starvation. The failure of his socialist policies and his general isolation led Sekou Touré to seek a reconciliation with France, which he achieved in the second half of the decade while he also embarked upon a policy of greater economic liberalism. This latter policy followed a massive demonstration in 1977 by the Conakry market women in protest at 'economic police'. Riots occurred in several towns and three local governors were killed. After diplomatic relations had been restored in 1976 France agreed the following year to pay the pensions of 20,000 Guinean ex-servicemen while also curtailing the activities of Guinean exiles in France. French businessmen were then allowed back into Guinea and in 1978 President Valéry Giscard d'Estaing paid an official visit. Touré, meanwhile, was slowly relaxing his grip on politics to allow a wider, more representative expression of views. In January 1979 the country was renamed the People's Revolutionary Republic of Guinea although Touré said his government was prepared to co-operate with capitalists as well as socialists. However, relations with the USSR now deteriorated and, for example, the landing rights allowed to the USSR (which it had used when ferrying arms to Angola in 1975) were withdrawn. The *rapprochment* with the West was accompanied by more open contacts with the country's neighbours, including Côte d'Ivoire and Senegal, while Guinea also began to take a more prominent role in regional organizations such as the Mano River Union, which Guinea joined, and the Economic Community of West African States (ECOWAS). Sekou Touré died unexpectedly, aged 62, in 1984.

Only in 1971, after nearly 10 years of fighting, did Portugal admit that a state of war existed in Portuguese Guinea by which time 30,000 Portuguese troops were facing 7,000 Guinean guerrillas. Gen. Antonio de Spinola, who remained Governor-General to 1974, came to rely more and more on air superiority while also becoming convinced that Portugal could not win the war, a fact that influenced his decision to take part in the 25 April 1974 revolution in Portugal. On 20 January 1973 Amilcar Cabral, the PAIGC leader, was assassinated in Conakry; his naval commander, Innocenta Canida, admitted responsibility. However, PAIGC survived the crisis of Cabral's death and the following month elected a co-founder of the party, Aristides Pereira, as leader. On 24 September 1973 the PAIGC declared the country independent as Guinea-Bissau. The new state was at once recognized by a majority of OAU countries and then by a majority of UN members including the USSR and China. On 2 November 1973 the UN General Assembly by 93 to seven with 30 abstentions voted to recognize the Republic of Guinea-Bissau. Portugal finally recognized Guinea-Bissau's independence on 10 September 1974 and by the end of October had withdrawn all its military forces. The President of the new country to 1980 was Luis Cabral, the brother of Amilcar; his government described itself as 'revolutionary socialist'. Indirect elections for the assembly were held in 1976. Outside the party, whose membership was limited, there were mass structures based upon trade unions, women's and youth movements. There was little evidence of opposition to PAIGC rule through the 1970s: it was, after all, one of the most successful of all African nationalist guerrilla movements. The government followed a strictly non-aligned foreign policy: it accepted military aid from the USSR and East Germany and economic aid from UN bodies, the EC, the Nordic countries, Kuwait and Saudi Arabia. In 1978 Luis Cabral made an official visit to Portugal, which was returned by Portugal's President, Gen. Antonio Eanes, in 1979. The government, however, demonstrated little economic aptitude and neglected the vital agricultural sector. Up to 1980 the PAIGC ruled both Guinea-Bissau and Cape Verde and the two countries intended to merge. But there was growing disaffection in Guinea-Bissau at the disproportionate influence wielded by Cape Verdeans in the government. On 14 November 1980, the Prime Minister João Vieira, whose power had just been reduced by the President, mounted a coup to overthrow Cabral. A new revolutionary council of nine replaced the national assembly and state council, which were abolished. An immediate result of the coup was to reduce the influence of Cape Verdeans and this was taken to mean that a full merger of the two former Portuguese territories would not in fact take place. The islands of São Tomé and Principe, Portugal's other West African colony, became independent on 12 July 1975 with Dr Manuel Pinto da Costa as President and Miguel Trovoada as Prime Minister. Most of the Portuguese then left, their departure precipitating a collapse of the cocoa industry upon which the economy depended. In 1978 Dr Carlos da Graca, a former minister of health, attempted a coup from his base in Gabon; this was suppressed but the government was obliged to call upon Angola to send troops in its support. In 1979 da Costa abolished the post of prime minister though Trovoada retained his other posts. A UN attempt to conduct a census was resisted since it was seen as the prelude to a return to forced labour that had been the practice under the Portuguese. Trovoada fell from favour at the end of the decade and was briefly imprisoned but released in 1981. In December 1981 Principe was the scene of riots following food shortages. The government had pursued an ambiguous foreign policy after independence, proclaiming its adherence to socialism and non-alignment but not Marxism. President da Costa visited China, Cuba and the USSR; he also joined the IMF in 1977 and acceded to the Lomé Convention of the EC in 1978.

When President Tubman of Liberia died in 1971 he was succeeded by his vice-president of 27 years, William R. Tolbert who was subsequently elected President in his own right in 1975. Tolbert opened up Liberia's foreign policy, raised diplomatic relations with the USSR to ambassador level and visited France. In 1973, with Siaka Stevens of Sierra Leone, Tolbert inaugurated the Mano River Union to create a free trade area for their two countries. Liberia participated in a commission on co-operation with Côte d'Ivoire and entered into a defence agreement with Guinea. Liberia became a founder member of the Economic Community of West African States (ECOWAS), which came into being in 1975. In 1979 Liberia hosted the sixteenth annual summit of the OAU, an event that was certainly a contributory cause of the collapse of Tolbert's government. By that time it had become the practice for the annual OAU summit to be hosted by a different member state each year and hosting the event was seen as a mark of national prestige. In Liberia's case the cost of doing so came to just over a third of the annual GDP of US\$329 million and coming on top of nationwide riots of the previous April as a result of the government raising the price of rice, the Tolbert regime began to collapse. In April 1980 Tolbert himself was killed in the bloody coup that saw Master Sgt Samuel Doe seize power. One result of this debacle was a sudden reluctance upon the part of other states to host OAU summits, which, instead, were held at the Addis Ababa headquarters.

During the late 1960s Leopold Senghor attempted to transform Senegal into a one-party state but his moves created increasing unrest including a growth of union activity and student protest. Disturbances in 1968 persuaded Senghor to revive the post of prime minister and in 1970 this went to Abdou Diouf, a young provincial administrator, who now moved to the centre of the political stage. Although Senghor and his *Union Progressiste Sénégalaise* (UPS) won the 1973 elections without difficulty there was further unrest. Poverty was the chief cause. A new political party, the *Parti Démocratique Sénégalais* (PDS) led by Abdoulaye Wade, was formed in 1974 though a quarter of a century was to pass before it would achieve power. At this time Senghor tried to create a three-party system, a form of coalition, but without success. He again won the elections of 1978 when he renamed the ruling party as the *Parti Socialiste*.

The 1970s were a difficult political decade for Sierra Leone. They began badly when a coup was attempted against Siaka Stevens in 1971; this was followed by two assassination attempts against him. As a consequence of these threats Stevens signed a defence agreement with Guinea and Sekou Touré sent troops to support the government and these remained in the country for two years. Brig. John Bangara who had led the coup attempt was executed. In April 1971 Sierra Leone became a republic. Stevens was re-elected President for another five years in 1976. However, anti-government demonstrations occurred throughout the country in 1977; they had been set in motion by protesting students. The government called an election for May 1977 and the opposition Sierra Leone People's Party (SLPP) won 15 seats from the ruling All People's Congress (APC) though the government still had a majority. But the threat to his dominant position led Stevens to argue that one-party rule was the best answer for a disintegrating political system and in May 1978 the House of

Representatives approved by more than the required two-thirds majority a one-party constitution and this was confirmed in June by a referendum in which 2,152,454 votes were cast in favour and only 63,132 against. The opposition SLPP then joined the APC and some of its leading members obtained ministerial posts.

There was a serious coup attempt against Etienne Eyadéma, the ruler of Togo, in August 1970. In January 1972 a referendum gave Eyadéma 867,491 votes to remain as President against only 878 no votes. A personality cult now developed round Eyadéma. In 1974 he launched a policy of authenticity: the phosphate mines were nationalized; foreign personal and place names were given Togolese names – Eyadéma, for example, changed Etienne to Gnassingbé; and Ewe and Kabiye replaced French as the languages of instruction in the schools. Anti-colonial authenticity was generally popular but it did not disguise Eyadéma's tendency to absolutism. In 1976 he increased his personal authority when he reduced the number of members of the political bureau (the cabinet) from 15 to nine while he also nominated all members of the central committee and the government. Plots were discovered in 1977 and 1978 and duly foiled. In November 1979 the *Rassemblement du Peuple Togolais* (RPT) drew up a new constitution, which provided for an elective presidential system and a national assembly of 67 deputies elected from regional lists for five-year terms. In December of that year Eyadéma was elected President under this new constitution with nearly 100 per cent of the votes cast and in January 1980 he proclaimed the 'Third Republic'. He maintained tight political control over all aspects of government and allowed no opposition to appear. The decade, indeed, had demonstrated in classic style the manoeuvres of a strong man closing all the loopholes to guarantee his hold on power.

Upper Volta, the last of these West African states, presented yet another example of what by then was an all too familiar political mix: a military ruler, backed by the army, allowing some power to civilians but finding excuses to curtail it as and when he saw an opportunity to do so. Lt-Col. Sangoule Lamizana came to power in 1966 but in 1970 allowed the country to return to civilian rule with an elected assembly and civilian prime minister. Lamizana, however, remained head of state and government in which he continued to include a number of military men. Gerard Ouedraogo was his civilian prime minister and the leader of the *Union Démocratique Voltaique* (UDV). A confrontation between Ouedraogo and the assembly in 1974 gave Lamizana the excuse to dissolve the assembly, suspend the constitution and restore full military power. Nonetheless, authoritarian military men were rarely as strong as they might seem and growing opposition from the trade unions forced Lamizana to form a new civilian government in 1976 and set up a commission to prepare for an orderly return to democracy. Seven political parties contested the elections in which the UDV won 28 out of 52 seats while in the presidential elections Lamizana had to face a run-off before being re-elected for a further five years. Strikes and mounting opposition to his rule led to Lamizana's downfall in 1980 when Col. Saye Zerbo established a *Comité Militaire de Rédressement pour le Progrès National* (CMRPN) which promptly banned all political activities. Lamizana, at least, was no tyrant and tried to work with the civilians.

If we examine the fortunes of these West African countries through this decade we find that four of them – Dahomey (Benin), Ghana, Togo and Upper Volta – were dominated by the military though with considerable variations between the strong men in Benin and Togo and the more flexible soldiers in Ghana and Upper Volta; in six cases – Cameroon, Côte d'Ivoire, The Gambia, Liberia, Senegal and Sierra Leone – democracy was the rule though the political process was dominated by powerful authoritarian rulers who tried and sometimes succeeded in installing one-party systems; in Guinea the dictatorial survivor Sekou Touré held onto internal power but was forced to return to the French (Western) dominated economic system; finally, the Portuguese territories achieved their independence halfway through the decade and in the case of Guinea-Bissau the PAIGC, which was already a Marxist party, continued its leftward, one-party state orientation. Despite the publicity that military coups and the one-party state received then and later, military regimes were never as secure as they appeared and were constantly obliged at the very least to come to accommodations with civilian politicians.

The Francophone states of West Africa were already recipients of EC aid under the Yaoundé Conventions. Following Britain's entry into the EC in 1973 negotiations took place between the Community and Commonwealth African (as well as Caribbean and Pacific) countries whose economic and trading positions were affected by Britain's new relationship with Europe. These negotiations were conducted in Lomé, Togo, and the First Lomé Convention (Lomé I) replaced the earlier Yaoundé Conventions between the EC and Francophone countries. Lomé I came into force on 1 April 1976. Lomé I provided a framework that linked Anglophone and Francophone Africa with the EC. Under the terms of the Convention about 99 per cent of African agricultural products, except those that directly competed with European agriculture, could enter the EC free of duty. At the same time Lomé I made available a new source of aid to Africa. Lomé II followed in 1979. Although the Lomé Convention was heralded as a new partnership between Europe and Africa in fact its principal result was to tie African economies more closely to the stronger economies of Europe.

EQUATORIAL AFRICA

The Congo, which was renamed Zaïre in October 1971, was always more important for what it failed to do than for what it achieved. The third largest country on the continent, strategically placed in the centre of Africa, it is a storehouse of mineral resources and has huge agricultural, forestry and hydro-electric potential, yet its story from independence to the end of the twentieth century has been a catalogue of disasters: corruption, unnecessary debt, violence, brutal dictatorship and missed opportunities turned Zaïre into a byword for all that went wrong in Africa. An amendment to the constitution in December 1970 made the *Mouvement Populaire de la Révolution* (MPR) into the country's only political organization. The MPR adopted the creed of *Mobutisme*, placing Mobutu above the MPR. All candidates for elections were controlled by the MPR and in 1975 the secret ballot was abolished. Mobutu embraced a policy of authenticity under which names of people and places were changed, he himself becoming Mobutu Sese Seko. Authenticity led to a confrontation with the Roman Catholic Church and Cardinal Joseph-Albert Malala, the Primate and Archbishop of Kinshasa, was expelled. Reconciliation between Church and State, or rather Church and Mobutu, was only achieved in 1980 when Pope Paul John II visited Zaïre. In the meantime, over the years 1971–77, Mobutu systematically eliminated all opposition and took all power into his own hands.

When Angola became independent in 1975 Zaïre supported the *Frente Nacional de Libertação de Angola* (FNLA) but when the *Movimento Popular de Libertação de Angola* (MPLA) emerged as the winner in this first civil war Mobutu became reconciled to its leader Agostinho Neto. The two Shaba wars of 1977 and 1978 posed a major threat to Mobutu. Several thousand soldiers of Tshombe's former Katanga army who had fled into Angola were suspicious of Mobutu's offers of amnesty and had chosen to remain exiles. However, in 1977 they crossed the border into Shaba province, which was disaffected since it never received its share of the wealth generated by its mineral resources. These ex-Tshombe forces – *Front National pour la Libération du Congo* (FNLC) – were not restrained by the MPLA government in Luanda and this allowed Mobutu to claim that they had Communist support. His own forces disintegrated in the face of the invasion and Mobutu had to appeal for outside help; France, which always worked to draw Zaïre into its Francophone orbit, airlifted Moroccan troops into the Shaba province; by May 1977 the invaders had withdrawn. France and Morocco then urged Mobutu to democratize his regime so he reintroduced the secret ballot and allowed 2,000 candidates to contest 270 seats in the legislative council and another 167 candidates to contest 18 elective seats in the political bureau. Mobutu himself was re-elected for another seven-year presidential term. At the same time Mobutu purged his military and 13 senior officers were executed while in Shaba the Lunda suffered further repression for not having opposed the invaders sufficiently rigorously. Then, in May 1978, the second Shaba invasion took place, the invaders this time coming through Zambia from Angola. They were more effective than the previous year and captured the key town of Kolwezi as well as part of the vital railway line. This time France intervened directly with troops and ensured that Mobutu could regain control of the province. Subsequently, a pan-African force of Moroccan, Senegalese and Togolese troops moved into the region and stayed there until May 1979. Mobutu's need to call upon outside help – half his soldiers had not been paid for months – illustrated the fragility of his huge state, which, increasingly, he treated as a personal fief.

During the years of Massamba-Debat's Presidency of Congo (Brazzaville) from 1964 to 1968 a conflict emerged between the youth wing of the *Mouvement National de la Révolution* (MNR), the *Jeunesse de Mouvement National de la Révolution* (JMNR), and the more conservative army with the result that in the latter year Capt. Marien Ngouabi took power in Brazzaville. For a short period the army allowed Massamba-Debat to remain as President before he was dismissed and Ngouabi assumed full powers. Ngouabi created a Marxist-Leninist party, *Parti Congolais du Travail* (PCT) and in January 1970 the country was renamed the People's Republic of Congo. Ngouabi lasted, surviving several coup attempts, until he was assassinated on 18 March 1977 when another, unsuccessful, attempt was made to restore Massamba-Debat to power: he was later executed. The new military head of state, Col. Joachim Yhombi-Opango, promised to continue Ngouabi's policies. He, however, only lasted two years before being deposed and replaced by Col. Denis Sassou-Nguesso. Elections for a national people's assembly and regional councils were held in July 1979 and a referendum gave massive support to a new socialist constitution. Although Nguesso used the rhetoric of socialism, in fact he turned increasingly to the West for economic support and this in reality meant France. Nguesso had to find a balance between the pro-Soviet faction of the PCT and the pro-Western pragmatists. The politics of the Congo at this time were a strange mixture: the adoption of Maxism-Leninism, both as a repudiation of the West and to satisfy the genuine popular demands for socialism, especially from the youth wing of the party; a pragmatic turn back to France for economic reasons; and a series of coups and military rulers who in contradictory fashion kept power in the hands of the military while also supporting a form of popular democracy. The agenda – national independence, throwing off neo-colonialism, surviving economically, and satisfying the expectations of the people – was an impossible one given the country's limited resources.

Gabon, unlike both Congo and Zaïre, enjoyed rapid economic growth through the 1970s. Its most difficult problem was that of accommodating and controlling foreign companies whose investment was wanted but whose concomitant dominant role in a very small country and society was resented. The second problem concerned resentment at the growing gap between the wealthy elite of Gabonese and Europeans on the one hand and the rest of the population. A policy of increasing Gabonese participation in the new wealth creation was implemented from 1973 although Gabon remained firmly oriented to the West, capitalism and foreign investment. In 1968 President Bongo had turned Gabon into a one-party state under the *Parti Démocratique Gabonais* (PDG) and under his direction the country enjoyed a decade of political stability through the 1970s, made possible by a rich if narrow-based mining sector. On a per capita basis Gabon became one of the richest countries in Africa. An extraordinary congress of the PDG was held in January 1979 and this allowed a 'limited dose of democracy' with the result that several leading political figures lost their seats on the central committee. The congress criticized government inefficiency and forbade ministers holding several offices. In reality the criticisms were directed at Bongo himself. Even so, he was able to stand as sole presidential candidate for a further seven-year term in December 1979 and received 99.96 per cent of the votes cast.

THE PERIPHERY OF THE WHITE SOUTH

The 1970s began well for Zambia: copper prices were high, an apparently successful diversification of the economy was taking place and the tenth anniversary of independence was celebrated in 1974 with a real sense of national achievement. But the price of copper then collapsed and the country became increasingly indebted on the mistaken assumption that copper prices would soon recover – which they failed to do. At the same time Zambia undertook an ever more forward role as a front-line state in the confrontation between independent Black Africa and the White South. At the end of 1972 Zambia became a one-party state and in June 1973 Harry Nkumbula, leader of the Zambian ANC, issued the Choma Declaration accepting the one-party state and joining the ruling United National Independence Party (UNIP). By 1978, a consequence of its deepening economic crisis, Zambia was obliged to reopen rail links through Rhodesia although it continued to support the Patriotic Front of ZANU and ZAPU in the final phase of the struggle in Rhodesia. Rhodesia and South Africa retaliated by launching periodic air raids on Zambia.

By contrast, Zambia's neighbour Malawi had become entrenched as black Africa's 'odd man out' because of Banda's continuing and often flaunted relations with South Africa. Banda became progressively more authoritarian through the decade; he would brook no opposition and not permit any person to emerge as a possible successor to himself so that the main opposition came from dissident groups outside Malawi.

Once it was clear that he was losing Lesotho's January 1970 elections, Leabua Jonathan carried out a coup, raising the familiar Communist bogey in relation to his opponents as a means of gaining South African support for his actions. King Moshoeshoe was again put under house arrest and then allowed to go into exile in the Netherlands. The leader of the Basuto Congress Party (BCP), Ntsu Mokhehle, was first imprisoned, then placed under house arrest. Then Jonathan decreed a five-year 'holiday' from politics. During the rest of the year Jonathan carried out a countrywide campaign of repression against his opponents: about 1,000 men took to arms and 500 were killed. In December 1970 the King was allowed to return to Lesotho after he had agreed to a proclamation forbidding his participation in politics. In 1973 Jonathan tried to achieve a compromise with the opposition and created an interim assembly. At first Mokhehle agreed to take part but then changed his mind and fled to South Africa taking his hard-line supporters with him. Other members of the BCP were persuaded to co-operate with the government. There was renewed violence in 1974. The Lesotho Liberation Army (LLA), formed by the exiled BCP, launched attacks on police sub-stations and hundreds of people were killed in the subsequent fighting in the mountains, 200 were detained of whom 35 were later put on trial and 14 found guilty of treason. At the end of the year Jonathan introduced a new constitution, which made Lesotho a constitutional monarchy and gave greater powers to local government authorities. There was further violence in 1978, which continued into 1979, and from South Africa Mokhehle, taking a leaf from Jonathan's book, said he would only take part in elections if the representatives of the Communist bloc (the USSR, Cuba and East Europe) were expelled from Lesotho. At the end of the decade the outlook appeared bleak. The country had been subjected to a decade of violence because of Jonathan's greed for power but in any case Lesotho had almost no economic base except labour to export to South Africa and its hydro potential.

Swaziland emerged to independence in 1968 in the 'deep white south' with apartheid South Africa on three sides and Portuguese-controlled Mozambique on the fourth. A deeply conservative country, Swaziland chose to pursue a low-profile policy in relation to South Africa. In 1973 the old king, Sobhuza II, first proclaimed a state of emergency, then abrogated the constitution and abolished all political parties. From that time onwards legislation was by royal decree. The economy was doing reasonably well and there was a large influx of South African capital that would soon dominate development prospects. An order in council of 1978 established an indirect electoral system; the country was divided into 40 *tinkhundla* (local councils) and these selected members who then chose other members to sit on an electoral college. The system, in fact, ensured the absolute power of the king.

AFRICA IN THE INDIAN OCEAN

Only in 1956 under the *loi cadre* was political activity permitted in Madagascar following the uprising of 1947. In 1957 the *Parti Social Démocrate* (PSD) was formed under the leadership of Philibert Tsiranana who had formerly served as a deputy in France. He was very popular among the *Côtiers*, the latecomers to the island of African origin, as opposed to the Merinas, who were of Indonesian origin and first settled Madagascar. Tsiranana's PSD ruled with little difficulty through the 1960s although by the end of the decade the government faced two broad problems: a deteriorating economy, largely the result of external events such as the 1967 closure of the Suez Canal, the 1968 troubles in France which led to the 1969 devaluation of the French franc; and splits within the ranks of the PSD which were made worse by Tsiranana's long illness when he was unable to mediate between the factions.

Madagascar had remained largely isolated and had taken little part in African affairs up to 1970. The PSD won the September 1970 legislative elections without difficulty since the opposition was divided and ineffective. In April 1971 there was an uprising of peasants in the Toliara region; it was led by the *Mouvement National pour l'Indépendence de Madagascar* (MONIMA) under Monja Jaona. The people were rebelling against repressive local officials. The uprising was put down, further repression followed and this led to a number of deaths. As a result MONIMA attracted more support and became a national rather than just a local movement. In January 1972 Tsiranana won a third presidential term with 99.9 per cent of the votes cast. On 13 May, however, riots that included students, teachers, workers and the unemployed erupted in the capital Antananarivo and the rioters formed the basis for a new political movement – the Federation of the 13 May Movement (KIM). After three days of violence Tsiranana handed full power to Gen. Gabriel Ramanantsoa to restore order. The following October Ramanantsoa held a referendum in which he obtained an 80 per cent vote for reform. Tsiranana was then removed from the presidency. Though personally popular Ramanantsoa faced a deteriorating economy, disunity in the armed forces and growing divisions between the country's two main ethnic groups, the Merinas and the *Côtiers*. At a meeting of the mobile police on 31 December 1974 Ramanantsoa was persuaded to hand over power to another soldier, and he did so on 5 February

1975 to Col. Richard Ratsimandrava who, however, lasted only six days before being assassinated. A period of uncertainty followed before Lt-Cmdr Didier Ratsiraka (a former foreign minister) became head of state and government on 15 June. He established the Supreme Revolutionary Council and inaugurated a socialist revolution: banks were nationalized, as were insurance and shipping companies, mineral resources and the petroleum refinery. The US satellite tracking station was closed down and the major French company *Société Marseillaise de Madagascar* was taken over by the state. Ratsiraka had his policies published as a 'Little Red Book'. In December he won a referendum endorsing his policies by 94.66 of 90 per cent of the votes cast. Ratsiraka's foreign policy included closer relations with the Communist and Arab worlds and providing support for Third World liberation movements. In 1976 he created a new political party, *Avant garde pour la Rénovation de Madagascar* (AREMA) (Vanguard of the Malagasy Revolution), and joined forces with the existing *Front National pour la Défense de la Révolution* (FNDR) (National Front for Defence of the Revolution) although AREMA became the dominant political force in the country. At the beginning of the 1980s Ratsiraka defused growing opposition by releasing Monja Jaona, the leader of MONIMA, whom he persuaded to join the FNDR, which provided an umbrella for all radical movements.

Mauritius became independent in 1968 when the Independence Party (IP) led by Seewoosagur Ramgoolam formed the first post-independence government. Ramgoolam wanted to preserve the communal nature of Mauritian society and believed this could best be achieved by means of coalition governments. He also wanted to diversify the economy away from its then overwhelming dependence upon sugar. In 1970 Mauritius joined the *Organisation Commune Africaine et Malgache* (OCAM). Ramgoolam invited the opposition *Parti Mauricien Social Démocrate* (PMSD) to join the government. However, a new more radical party emerged; this was the *Mouvement Militant Mauricien* (MMM) led by a Franco-Mauricien, Paul Berenger whose main support came from the trade unions. By the end of 1971 the MMM controlled a number of unions including three in the sugar industry, bus drivers and teachers. In August 1971 the dockers, who were mainly MMM supporters, came out on a strike which got out of hand leading Ramgoolam to declare a state of emergency. The government broke the strike and Berenger and other MMM leaders were imprisoned for 20 days. In March 1972 120 leading members of the MMM were imprisoned. These tough measures split the MMM into a pro-government faction and the *Mouvement Militant Mauricien Social Progressiste* which was Marxist oriented. The MMM fought the 1976 election on a platform of making Mauritius a republic, greater centralization and a tougher anti-South African policy. It also demanded the return to Mauritius from the US of the island of Diego Garcia, which had been turned into a US military base. The MMM won 34 seats, Ramgoolam's IP won 27 but he was able to create a coalition with the minority parties and remained in power until 1982. The last years of the decade witnessed growing industrial unrest and strikes, rising unemployment, inflation and devaluation.

France had colonized the Comoros islands in the 1840s. On 6 July 1975 the Comoran Chamber of Deputies made a unilateral declaration of independence (UDI) and the following day elected Ahmed Abdallah as President of the new state. France did not attempt to reverse this UDI but retained control of the island of Mayotte. Opposition to Abdallah was not slow to appear, for he was too dictatorial, and on 3 August he was overthrown in a coup. The leader of the *Front National Uni* (FNU), Prince Said Mohammed Jaffar, became the head of a new national executive council and Ali Soilih, who had organized the coup, became defence and interior minister. Meanwhile, in Mayotte the *Mouvement Populaire Mahorais* (MPM) expelled from the island all those who were thought to favour independence. On 12 November 1975 Comoros was admitted to the United Nations as a unified state even as France prepared to hold a referendum in Mayotte. In reaction to this French move the Comoros national executive council nationalized all French administrative property in the islands and repatriated French officials. On 31 December 1975 France recognized Comoros but did not establish diplomatic relations with its former colony. On 2 January 1976 Ali Soilih was elected head of state. On 8 February the Mayotte referendum returned a 99 per cent vote in favour of retaining links with France. The islands were divided into economic and administrative units of about 6,000 people each, consisting of three or four villages. Land distribution was carried out and the voting age was lowered to 14 years; the Revolutionary Youth Movement became Soilih's most ardent supporters. Soilih made the mistake of trying to modernize what was essentially a conservative society too fast, leaping from colonial and feudal subjugation to a form of progressive socialism. As a result he was overthrown in May 1978 in a coup mounted by 50 European mercenaries who came from South Africa, led by the Frenchman Bob Denard; they brought the country's first president, Ahmed Abdallah, back to power. Soilih was killed. The OAU expelled Comoros from its ministerial council because it had become a mercenary-backed government. In September 1978 the mercenaries were asked to leave. Comoros then received aid from France, Arab countries and the EC. In February 1979 it was readmitted to the OAU. Following a referendum of October 1978 Comoros became a Federal Islamic Republic, allowing a degree of autonomy to each island. France, meanwhile, created the special status of a *collectivité territoriale* for Mayotte, which allowed it one representative in the French Senate and one in the Assembly. Following the 1978 mercenary coup in Comoros Mayotte reaffirmed its rejection of association and maintained its link with France. Comoros continued to claim Mayotte as part of its territory and the UN General Assembly accepted several resolutions that reaffirmed Comoros' claim to the island, a view that was endorsed by the OAU.

The Seychelles became independent of Britain in 1976 with James Mancham of the Seychelles Democratic Party (SDP) as President and Albert René of the Seychelles People's United Party (SPUP) as Prime Minister, an arrangement that only lasted for a year. When Mancham went to London for the 1977 Commonwealth Summit, 60 armed members of the SPUP who had been trained in Tanzania seized power in Seychelles. René denied any prior knowledge of their intentions but did not refuse to be sworn in as President. Mancham's extravagant lifestyle and capitalist policies had made him many enemies. Under a new constitution of 1979 Seychelles became a one-party state while the SPUP had already transformed itself into the Seychelles People's Progressive Front (SPPF).

Although the events in many of these countries appear superficially to be much the same – coups, the formation of one-party states, the insistent intervention in politics of the military – in fact there are wide variations on these themes. Newly independent governments first wished to repudiate colonialism and the colonial power and the easiest, most readily available alternative was to adopt some form of socialism or Marxism, especially as to do so represented not just a break but also a positive denial of everything the metropolitan power stood for. But Marxism, however appealing in theory, did not produce the increased wealth needed to meet national expectations. The result, as we have seen in a number of cases, was that governments were forced to return to the Western fold they had abandoned. And the West then imposed stringent, often punitive, terms as the price of new aid and investment. Benin, Congo, Guinea, Mali, Niger and Togo of Francophone countries were each obliged to turn again to France. The radical movements that criticized over-dependence upon the former colonial powers almost invariably found, if they subsequently became the government, that they had little choice in the matter. It was a question of economics and virtually all the levers of power lay with the West. Few of the new states of Africa were either determined enough or strong enough to defy the pressures that were exerted upon them and follow their own chosen political and economic development paths.

CHAPTER FIFTEEN

Four Different
Development Paths

Four countries – Algeria, Nigeria, Tanzania and Botswana – achieved remarkable if very different economic and political development during the 1970s. Two of them, Algeria and Tanzania, pursued austere socialist paths that demanded a great deal of their people with most of the promise of better times to come set firmly in the future. On the other hand, there was nothing socialist about the bonanza years enjoyed by Nigeria as a result of the oil boom, which followed the Yom Kippur War and fourfold increase in oil prices. Lagos attracted entrepreneurs from all over the world, each hoping for quick returns on investments in what was seen as Africa's largest and most attractive market. Botswana's case was different again. Surrounded by South Africa, Rhodesia and South African-controlled Namibia, Botswana refused to bow to pressures from its racist neighbours and pursued instead a defiant multiracial policy while its huge mineral discoveries transformed the country's long-term prospects.

ALGERIA

At the beginning of the 1970s President Boumedienne embarked upon an ambitious programme of development designed to turn Algeria into an industrial-based economy. At the same time he defined his country's position as non-aligned, socialist and determined to withstand outside interference. Since the overthrow in 1965 of Ben Bella, who was accused of orchestrating a verbal revolution rather than anything else, Boumedienne had already made considerable progress in creating an industrial sector. What he had not succeeded in doing was securing for himself any broad political acceptance; his leadership was always to be from the top downwards rather than based upon grassroots support. His austere dedication to socialist principles was admirable; his understanding of how ordinary people operated less obvious and unlike his contemporary, Tanzania's Julius Nyerere, he was not a teacher. Statistics over these years register encouraging advances on many fronts. Thus, there were 1.7 million children in primary schools in 1969–70, a figure that was raised to 1.9 million with the addition of 6,000 new classrooms by 1970–71. On the other hand, there was a desperate shortage of skills of all kinds so that there were still 48,000 foreigners teaching in primary schools and a further 11,000 in secondary schools.

The government was moving inexorably towards the creation of a socialist society by encouraging workers' participation in management, the distribution of land among landless peasants and further nationalization measures. Petroleum was the key to Algeria's revolution. Oil production of 26 million tons in 1965 had risen to 50 million tons by 1970 while natural gas output over the same period had increased from 1,800 million cubic metres to 2,500 million cubic metres. A confrontation with France, the former metropolitan power, was a prerequisite for Algerian control of the economy and relations with France reached a low point at the beginning of the decade over the question of export taxes on Algeria's oil. The tax reference price for oil had been set in 1965 at US$2.08 a barrel; in July 1969 Algeria revised this upwards to US$2.85 a barrel in a move to control fully its national resources. The quarrel with France lasted through 1971 and, apart from oil, was emphasized by Boumedienne's policy of Arabization and desire to remove the last traces of colonialism as he called for a cultural revolution. A decree of 2 July 1970 established the official use of Arabic numerals and, for example, *Al Nasr*, one of four Algerian daily newspapers, carried two pages of Arabic that year and then published entirely in Arabic in 1972. Court cases (trials) were to be conducted in Arabic. While these changes were taking place efforts were also made, with indifferent results, to reinvigorate the ruling FLN, which was instructed to conduct a campaign of 'moral improvement'.

Negotiations for the nationalization of the oil companies were conducted with France through 1971 and on 24 February the foreign minister, Abdelaziz Bouteflika, insisted that the state would take a 51 per cent stake in the companies at once while natural gas deposits and pipelines were to be fully nationalized. Then, on 13 April, there was a second sharp increase in the tax reference price to US$3.60 a barrel (15 cents a barrel higher than the price negotiated that March by Libya). Compensation for French companies was set at US$100 million, only a third of what they had been demanding. In May, therefore, French companies ceased operations in Algeria and withdrew key personnel. However, on 30 June France's CFP and Algeria's national oil corporation Sonatrach signed a 10-year agreement by whose terms *Compagnie Française des Petroles* (CFP) became a 49 per cent shareholder in Sonatrach. In 1970 Sonatrach exported 9.8 million tons of oil with Germany (4.5 million tons), Brazil (1.6

million tons) and Italy (1.3 million tons) its leading customers. A series of decrees restricted the activities of foreign companies and laid down that from then on only Sonatrach could explore and exploit new finds. At the height of the negotiations with France Boumedienne broadcast over Radio Algeria. He said that he had announced on 24 February that his government would guarantee the provision of oil to France following nationalization. Some French media had responded by claiming they did not trust Algeria to keep its word and had demanded compensation before nationalization. To this Boumedienne replied precisely and clearly to insist that the relationship had to be equal:

> The idea of compensation before nationalisation is therefore fallacious. More important still is the fact that, having personally announced, in the name of the Revolution Command and the Algerian people, that we were prepared to compensate, I now find that today some French circles say: We do not trust these words. If they do not trust the decisions of our country, then they preclude any co-operation between us.
>
> There are other issues besides that of oil. If the French side is really interested in the question of oil, we are just as interested in other questions such as that of our workers abroad; their rights must be preserved and they must be respected. There are other interests such as our exports to the French market; this question must be taken into consideration. There are also the questions of cultural and technical co-operation between Algeria and France: these must be clarified.[1]

There was further friction with France over the treatment of French nationals in Algeria and Algerians in France while the Algerian press was highly critical of the late Gen. de Gaulle and of French policies towards its former African colonies. Throughout these fraught negotiations Boumedienne, skilfully, always talked of future co-operation between the two countries. He was not aiming for a complete break with France but for a fresh and precise definition of their two-way relationship. His aim was to bring an end to the privileged relationship that existed between the two countries since this gave too many advantages to France. Broadly, Boumedienne succeeded in this objective and then turned his attention to the creation of more positive Algerian policies with its Maghreb neighbours. Over the issue of Palestine he was always a hard-liner opposed to any concessions to Israel. Although relations with Africa to the south came very much second to those with the Arab world, Boumedienne had a number of meetings with heads of state from the south including Nigeria, Niger and Cameroon.

On 14 July 1971 the Council of Revolution announced a programme of agrarian reform to include the enclosure of herds, the formation of forestry and alfalfa production units and the elimination of private ownership of water. Large estates were to be abolished and the property of absentee landlords was to be nationalized. Land was to be distributed to landless peasants but in such a way as to allow the maximum use of machinery while avoiding the division of the land into small unviable units. Commenting on this proposed agrarian revolution, Boumedienne said the aim of the revolution was less concerned with the distribution of land and the limitation of ownership than with the creation of good conditions and the full exploitation of the land. Limitation of ownership did not mean ending private ownership but rather working to achieve equality of living standards among sections of the people, abolishing imbalance in individual incomes, providing full employment, and bringing education, medical treatment and social services within the reach of all citizens.

The agrarian revolution dominated government action during 1972. President Boumedienne said the government had waited 10 years to start the revolution so as to prepare the conditions for its success, including the availability of the necessary machinery and personnel. The aim was to increase the irrigated area of land from 300,000 hectares to 500,000 by the end of the decade.

Changing the increasingly static and corrupt FLN proved far more difficult. On 15 December Kaid Ahmed resigned as head of the FLN; he had been head of the party since 1967 but had been unable to win support for it among young intellectuals, students or trade unionists. On the education front schools were unable to keep pace with the population explosion: there were two million children in school in 1972 as opposed to a mere 8,000 (apart from Europeans) in 1963 and by 1972 25 per cent of the national budget was allocated to education. Foreign trade reached a figure of US$3,000 million during the year and US$2,000 million of it or 70 per cent was with the EEC. At the time Algeria was investigating the possibility of associate membership. In a typical response the EEC offered customs exemption for crude oil and natural gas with no limit on quantity but wanted to restrict imports of refined petroleum to 240,000 tons a year, which Algeria regarded as unacceptably low. Algeria had increased its refined capacity from 2.5 million tons in 1968 to an expected 4 million tons by 1973. There were two liquid natural gas (LNG) plants under construction. Targets were being set for every aspect of economic growth. The demand for steel had increased from 300,000 tons in 1968 to 700,000 tons by 1973 while Algerian production of steel was expected to reach 430,000 tons in 1973. Projects due for completion during this hectic year included a tractor and engine factory, a foundry, a wool complex, a textile thread plant and the doubling of the textile complex at Batra. Other developments covered cement, phosphate fertilizer and paper. By 1972 Algeria had come to be viewed as a hard left country in relation to its revolution and its relations with France, in its attitudes to Israel and the Palestine question, in its support for African liberation movements and its reactions to British policies towards Rhodesia and South Africa. It was to play a leading role in North-South relations during 1973.

Algeria played host to both the Non-Aligned Summit of September 1973 and the Arab Summit of November and on both occasions Boumedienne took the opportunity to emphasize his theme that economic independence must precede political independence and he was tireless in calling for both Algeria and the Arab world to take control of their economies. Speaking on Egyptian television on 19 August Boumedienne said: 'The rise of the Arab nation will never... be completed unless we all proceed towards internal construction... It is up to us first of all to ensure control of oil and gas.' Algeria sent two squadrons of combat aircraft to the Yom Kippur War – they reached the front on 7 October – and half a brigade of tanks to Egypt. By hosting the Sixth Arab Summit that November as well as by his prompt support for the Yom Kippur War Boumedienne greatly enhanced his prestige both among Arab states and more generally. The Non-Aligned Conference, attended by 57 heads of state and 105 delegations, was also a triumph for Boumedienne who came to be seen during this year as a formidable spokesman for the Third World. At this conference he pressed his view that the main division in the world was between the industrialized powers and the Third World. He warned that a *détente* between the Soviet Union and the United States threatened to become a source of tension in the relations between the privileged world and the rest of humanity (he was 20 years ahead of events). He said it was up to Third World peoples and leaders 'to provoke a radical transformation in the present situation by counting above all on their potentialities and by mobilizing all their human and material resources for the benefit of their countries'.

Apart from these international activities Boumedienne pressed ahead with the agrarian revolution, which had entered a delicate phase with the redistribution of private land. By this time the first phase of the agrarian revolution could be assessed: 617,867 hectares of publicly owned land had been distributed to 43,784 peasants in 2,500 co-operatives (although the target for this date had been one million hectares and 60,000 peasants). The second phase of the revolution was launched in June 1973 when privately owned farmland was redistributed to poor peasants. Not all the peasants installed in new land were happy: some complained that official assistance was insufficient while others objected to the bureaucracy of the co-operative system. Despite calls for the reform of the FLN, which had begun the previous year, little progress was made during 1973; what was lacking was any substantial input into the party by either the workers or intellectuals. By mid-1973 the Algerian population had reached an estimated 15.3 million and was expected to rise to 19 million by 1980. Between 1970 and 1973 Algeria invested a total of 33,000 million dinars under the Four-Year Plan although only 26,000 million dinars had been projected for this period. A further 54,000 million dinars was earmarked for the 1974–77 Plan and another 46,000 million for 1978–80. A sign of external confidence in Algeria at this time was its ability to raise substantial loans on the eurodollar market: in 1973 these included a loan of $300 million from six US banks, US$100 million from Canada and further loans from the World Bank and Japan. Algeria also signed a contract with the USSR whereby steel production at 400,000 tons in 1973 would be increased to 2 million tons by 1980. By any standards 1973 was a good year for Algeria: on the home front its socialist-economic revolution was steadily advancing; on the international stage Algeria had emerged as a force to be reckoned with.

A shrewd observer of the Arab world[2] provides some interesting insights into Algeria's successes and failures in the mid-1970s. The FLN, which had spearheaded the defeat of the French and the revolution, did not in fact become the ruling force in Algeria after independence, except in name. 'The party still exists but it is little more than a shell. Such "mobilization of the masses" as has taken place, has been through military conscription. The use of the army as an instrument of social and economic progress has been maintained and developed since the revolution… There are elected popular assemblies for the communes and for the higher levels of the governorates or *wilayas*, for which elections were first held in June 1974, but Algeria has no parliament or other national representative institutions… The country is governed and administered by a small, industrious, elite bureaucracy which concentrates on the nation's two most urgent and manifest needs: industrialization and education.'[3] The same commentator continues that a further consequence of the failure of the FLN to develop as a ruling party responsible for 'mobilizing the masses' is that Algerian women have not been emancipated at anything like the pace that was expected during the war of independence. The failure of the FLN during the 1960s and 1970s to make itself an effective ruling party, because the military took on this role, was the basis of the failures to come in the 1980s and 1990s. The army was the victor of the revolution and subsequently was incapable of surrendering the lead role to the FLN with disastrous long-term consequences all round. This, or similar determination by those who won independence struggles to believe that they alone could mastermind subsequent development, caused many problems in post-independence Africa and not just in Algeria.

The immediate task of the 1970s was to take control of the country's resources, most notably its oil and natural gas, and use them as the basis for an industrial revolution and in this respect the Boumedienne government was remarkably adroit. Sonatrach, the state oil company, was the crucial tool of government policy. 'Step by step, this has succeeded in winning control over Algeria's oil resources against the stubborn opposition of the oil companies, especially the French companies, whose position was reinforced by the special privileges they gained in the pre-independence Evian agreements. The struggle culminated in February 1971 when the Algerians expropriated all French interests.'[4] Algeria was to need all the revenues that its oil and gas could yield and its victory over the oil companies and France was all the more courageous when its need for the European markets is understood. Meanwhile, Algeria pursued a tough programme of austerity while maintaining a high level of investment and 'In the last four-year plan of 1970–73 Algeria was probably unique among developing countries in exceeding the planned level of investment'.[5]

Throughout 1974 Algeria established its position as a leading radical country of the Third World, most especially in pursuit of the idea then being floated for a New International Economic Order (NIEO). When he addressed the General Assembly of the United Nations on 10 April Boumedienne urged developing countries to nationalize their natural resources and argued that development aid should not be conditional on the maintenance of extremely low prices for raw materials. He was, as usual, fighting against the economic dominance of the major industrialized countries. The third phase of the agrarian revolution was launched: its objectives were to settle nomads and build primary schools for their children, and to create co-operatives for raising flocks and economic infrastructure in the rural areas. A new Three-Year Plan for 1974–77 was launched. Boumedienne reached the high point of his influence in 1975. His home position was unchallenged even if he was never especially popular himself – he was too austere and remote for general popularity. Algeria's long-term future as an industrialized Third World socialist country appeared to be on course while relations with France improved dramatically when President Giscard d'Estaing came to Algeria on a state visit.

The 1970s saw remarkable progress in Algeria where industrialization was at the centre of government policy. At independence in 1962 the industrial sector had been very small, consisting mainly of food processing, building materials, textiles and minerals; even this limited activity had been slowed down by the departure of the French while for the rest of the decade foreign firms were reluctant to invest for fear of being nationalized. By 1978, however, about 300 state-owned manufacturing plants had been set up although productivity was very low and some plants operated at no more than 15 to 25 per cent of design capacity. Major ambitious projects had been launched including a petrochemical complex at Skikda, and others to produce polyethylene, caustic soda and chlorine and a huge fertilizer plant at Arzew. Parallel with the industrial revolution was the agrarian revolution that Boumedienne launched in 1971. The principal aim of the Second Four-Year Plan (1974–77) was to lay the foundations of an industrial base and 43.5 per cent of investment was allocated to industry. The Plan also emphasized improved agricultural methods, housing, health, and job creation and training. Between 1970 and 1976 the country's GDP grew by an average of 6.2 per cent a year. In June 1975 Boumedienne announced that national elections for an assembly and president would be held and that a National Charter to provide for a new constitution was to be drawn up. The announcement led to an immediate growth of opposition by those who believed these moves were designed to consolidate Boumedienne's power. In March 1976 a manifesto, signed by two presidents of the former government in exile, Ferhat Abbas and Ben Youssef Ben Khedda, criticizing Boumedienne for his totalitarian rule and cult of personality, was circulated. The protesters were put under house arrest and Boumedienne rejected their accusations. The following month the National Charter was published and, after public discussion, received a 98.5 per cent vote of approval in a June referendum. The Charter emphasized the absolute commitment of Algeria to socialism that was specifically adapted to Third World conditions. The Charter also asserted the dominant role of the FLN and made Islam the state religion. A new constitution embodying the charter was passed and in December Boumedienne was elected President with 99 per cent of the votes cast. A National Assembly was elected in February 1977. With his election as president under the new constitution Boumedienne appeared to have secured his position for some time to come but a year later, 27 December 1978, he died of a rare disease. After a period of doubt and speculation Chadli Benjedid, the commander of the Oran military district, became head of state. He said he would continue with Boumedienne's policies but unlike his predecessor he did not monopolize power: he was no revolutionary but a less driven consolidator.

During the fighting against the French the FLN had created a nation by persuading most of the people to support the armed struggle; in the process of opposing the common enemy the majority of the people had come to regard themselves as Algerians as opposed to French colonial subjects. There were divisions, however: between Arab and Berber and between the French-speaking elite and the Arab and Berber peasants. Boumedienne launched a massive education programme and by the early 1970s the government was spending 10 per cent of the country's gross national product on education although all teaching was still carried on in French until 1972. Austerity was the watchword and, for example, only goods needed for development were imported while most basic consumer goods were deemed frivolous and the population was expected to keep its belt tightened. Then, 'In the mid-1970s it seemed to the government and its people that their sacrifices were to be rewarded. The huge rise in oil prices multiplied the state's oil revenues by five or six times in the space of two years. The government instituted a free health service as a present to its people. The rest of its revenues it continued to pour into industrialization. It took over the running of its own oil production and built refineries, liquefied gas plants, steel mills and a large number of engineering industries. By the end of the 1970s it had the biggest industrial base in the continent, after South Africa.

It was at this time that the Minister of Industry, Belaid Abdessalem, made the famous prediction that Algeria was going to become "Africa's first and the world's second Japan".'[6] Michael Field, the author of the above quote, tries to find an answer to Algeria's spectacular failure and descent into civil war at the end of the century and, as he says: 'It is because everybody was so impressed by Algeria in its first 20 years of independence that the disasters of the late 1980s and 1990s came as such a surprise.' There was a switch from unattractive (humourless and austere) success to complete economic, social and political failure and that was far from easy to understand. 'During the period of President Boumedienne, from 1965 to 1978, which is when the institutions of the republic became established, power was in the hands of the President and the military men closest to him.' The regime was a dictatorship, 'But because of its fashionable socialist credentials and the mood of optimism that surrounded the oil states' development projects at that time, it was given a greater reputation for enlightened dictatorial rule than it deserved.'[7] That may be true but it does not explain the subsequent industrial failure. Rather, Boumedienne presided over the creation of a spectacular shell. Thus, the government used its oil revenues to pay foreign constructors to build industrial plants and then announced that Algeria had become self-sufficient in the products the plant produced. But these newly created industries did not operate at a profit and many of the factories were too big and sophisticated to be efficiently managed by a workforce that was simply not equipped with the right skills, despite the government's huge educational programme, to run such establishments effectively. Many of the workers came straight to the cities from a primitive rural background. Most industries were unable to compete with imports into the home market, let alone compete in export markets so the government kept them going with subsidies from its oil revenues and in this way disguised the failure of its industrialization programme to deliver according to expectations. The agrarian revolution also failed to deliver, partly because it was run by bureaucrats, and so, despite good agricultural land, a country that had fed itself under the French began to import essential food. Had Boumedienne lived, he might have had the drive and ruthlessness to correct these failings once they became too obvious to hide but his successor was not in that mould and the FLN, which in its revolutionary days might have been able to set things right, had long been politically ineffective. And so the Algerian dream of the 1970s collapsed in the 1990s.

NIGERIA

When Nigeria became independent in 1960 there were plenty of predictions that it would develop into Africa's leading market and there were adequate reasons for believing that this should be the case. 'The incorporation of Nigeria into the world economy was achieved through the expansion of peasant commodity production. There was little plantation agriculture in Nigeria and a large land-owning class was absent. Commodity production provided the economic foundation for the operations of foreign merchant capitalists and the regional pattern of power and wealth that was consolidated in the 1950s.'[8] Thus, at independence, Nigeria was an agriculture-based economy since industrialization had been discouraged by the colonial regime. However, encouraged by the new oil developments, which provided a base, industrialization soon took off. The average growth of manufacturing output was 13.6 per cent between 1963 and 1967, 10.2 per cent between 1967 and 1972 (the period covering the civil war), and 13.3 per cent between 1973 and 1978. The share of manufacturing in the GDP rose from 5 per cent in 1960 to 9 per cent in 1972 and much of this was concentrated in the consumer sector.[9] 'Apart from textiles, other products experiencing fast growth in the 1970s were vehicle assembly, soaps and detergents, soft drinks, pharmaceuticals, beer, paints and roofing sheets. Six highly protected and subsidized vehicle assembly plants were set up in quick succession.' Car assembly plants included Volkswagen in Lagos and Peugeot in Kaduna; truck assembly included Leyland (Ibadan), Steyr (Bauchi), Fiat (Kano) and Daimler-Benz (Enugu).[10] Apart from oil, economic growth during the 1970s was very mixed. Industrial protection discriminated against agriculture and agricultural exports were discouraged because of the appreciation of the naira as a result of large oil revenues. The changeover from relying upon agricultural commodity exports to over-dependence upon oil exports and their revenues was very rapid, and the great mistake that Nigeria made was to depend increasingly upon oil revenues to solve its problems despite periodic insistence upon policies of diversification that did not take place. In 1960 cocoa, groundnuts and palm produce accounted for 80 per cent of exports; from 1974 onwards, crude petroleum accounted for 90 per cent of exports. Nonetheless, over the 20-year period 1960–80 GNP grew at an average rate of 6 per cent a year. An indication of the uneven nature of Nigeria's development was the extent to which it remained dependent upon expatriates for industrial management. There were, moreover, huge salary differentials with non-Nigerian managerial and professional employees in the industrial sector earning, on average, more than twice as much as Nigerians in the same categories. The Nigerians reacted impetuously to the oil boom and, for example, between 1974 and 1976 the Third National Development Plan was enlarged several times in real terms from an initial projected federal government spending of N3 billion to N8 billion while the flow of imports was so increased in 1975 that delays in berthing at Nigerian ports, and especially at Lagos, ran into months while a queue of several hundred ships formed in the Lagos roadstead. Free spending was the order of the day and by 1976 the balance of payments was in deficit and by 1978, after a fall in oil sales, the government dealt with a negative trade balance by raising loans on the euro-currency market. Oil wealth appeared to have mesmerized Nigerians in general and the government in particular. The rise in oil prices between 1978 and 1981 provided Nigeria with a large extra income and the country responded with alacrity to its increased revenues: Federal outlays went up from N7.6 billion to N14.8 billion for 1978/79 to 1979/80 although this euphoria was quickly dispelled by an oil glut in 1981 and spending had to be cut back sharply.[11]

The end of the civil war saw little desire for vengeance and much fraternizing, a huge and generous relief on the part of Nigerians that the fighting was over and that they were one nation again. The first problem was to restructure society, reintegrate the Ibos, repair the war damage and then tackle development. Gen. Gowon emerged from the war with his prestige greatly enhanced and the government set 1976 as the date for a return to civilian rule although it was far from clear just what constitutional arrangements could be made to ensure national political unity once military control at the centre had been withdrawn. There was another problem that would come to haunt Nigeria in the years that followed: the size, power and ambitions of the army. Prior to the civil war Nigeria had had an army of only 10,000 men; in 1970 it was 250,000 strong. What to do with the army and what the army intended to do on its own account became overriding preoccupations of civilian politicians and military governments alike. From 1970 onwards, as elsewhere in Africa, the army became a part of the political process. At the OAU Summit of September 1970 Haile Selassie was able to announce that reconciliation had been achieved between Nigeria and the four countries that had recognized Biafra – Côte d'Ivoire, Gabon, Tanzania and Zambia – and Gowon responded by saying, 'Now we are all African brothers again.' Nigeria's economy had proved strong enough to carry the country through the war without the need to incur major debt. Nigeria was agriculturally rich, had an industrial sector that was unusually developed for an African country at that time and enjoyed huge and increasing oil revenues. At the beginning of 1970 the government set an oil production target of 1 million barrels of oil a day (b/d) for the end of the year but this had already been reached by April and in May Nigeria became one of the 10 major oil-producing countries: it produced 1.2 million b/d in August and expected to reach 2 million b/d by 1972. BP-Shell, the country's largest producer, then accounted for 500,000 b/d. At that time Gulf, Mobil and Texaco were operating offshore. In 1970 agricultural production still earned more than did oil, though this state of affairs was not to last much longer, and development plans placed high emphasis upon agriculture as a source of revenue and employment. The principal export crops were cocoa, groundnuts, cotton, palm products and rubber. On 1 October 1970 Gowon announced the Second Four-Year Development Plan with the emphasis upon repairing war damage and making the economy more self-sufficient.

The paradox of Gen. Gowon was that while his moderation had made him an ideal war leader, the same quality served him less well in peace. His best post-war achievement was to preside skilfully over the reintegration of the Ibos for he was always good at reconciliation. But he shunned tackling two pressing problems: the increasingly unruly behaviour of the military and the growth of corruption fuelled by the new oil wealth. Over the years 1970 to 1975 Gowon enhanced Nigeria's reputation in continental and international affairs while sidestepping awkward home problems. At the January 1971 Commonwealth Summit in Singapore Nigeria opposed the stated aim of the British to sell arms to South Africa. The government became a militant champion of the liberation movements and opposed fresh British moves to find an accommodation with the Smith regime in Rhodesia. Oil production and its revenues, however, became the dominant theme in Nigeria's public life. Oil revenues leapt from N80 million in 1970 to N270 million in 1971 and the contribution of oil to foreign exchange earnings rose from 41 per cent in 1969 to 58 per cent in 1970 and 71 per cent in 1971. Cocoa remained the most important agricultural cash crop, followed by groundnuts and cotton. As the country's oil-based wealth increased so did its attendant corruption but a federal decree on the problem of corruption, which had been promised, did not appear.

Increasingly, it seemed, Gowon was the prisoner of his 12 state governors and other powerful military figures whose double corruption was to stay in power and enjoy its economic benefits. Nigeria was deeply suspicious of the European Community at this time for as Britain negotiated entry to the EC, which it achieved in January 1973, the Community was offering associate status to Commonwealth African countries. Later, Nigeria would assume the lead in negotiating on their behalf but its conversion to associate status was one of necessity rather than choice. On 1 March 1972 the government announced a series of indigenization measures covering 22 different kinds of enterprise including advertising, broadcasting, road haulage and the retail trade that were to be reserved exclusively for Nigerians as from March 1974. Nigeria, now acknowledged as the leading black nation of Africa, accumulated more wealth during 1973 than at any time in its history and was making its mark as a middle-level power. Its national income had increased by more than five times from £200 million in 1965 to £1,100 million in 1973. But as Chief Obafemi Awolowo, the former leader of the Action Group, said in his capacity as Chancellor of the University of Ife in October of that year: 'A situation such as we now have, under which the good things of life are assured to a small minority of Nigerians and almost totally denied to the vast majority of our countrymen is pregnant with unpredictable dangers for all of us, if allowed to continue for much longer.' He added that although the country had achieved rapid economic growth, it had gained very little economic development. That year the government promised to provide free and compulsory universal primary education (UPE) by 1975. What was clearly not being resolved was the political divide – or divides – that had split the country before the civil war and, despite the reintegration of the Ibos, had not been resolved. The need for new political thinking became ever more urgent as the country began to contemplate a constitution for a civilian Third Republic scheduled for 1976. And the problem of corruption loomed larger all the time for despite repeated calls for the Federal Military Government to give a lead on the subject, nothing was done and it became increasingly clear that Gowon was not the man to take any drastic action against the huge constituency of the corrupt. The possibility of an associate economic relationship with the EC became stronger through 1973 (Britain was now a member of the EC) but Nigeria insisted that any deal had to treat African members as equals. Meanwhile, guidelines were being prepared by the Economic Development Ministry for the projected Third National Development Plan 1975–80 and these stated that a radical departure was essential if Nigeria was to be able to feed its rapidly growing population by the end of the 1980s.

Despite its generally benign reputation, the Federal Military Government (FMG) was in fact a military dictatorship although according to Mr Justice Bello, the country 'enjoyed the most liberal military democracy in modern history'. On 1 October 1974 Gowon announced that the military would not hand power back to the civilians in 1976 as it had promised, in 1972, to do. This was, in part, a reaction to the failure to achieve a consensus about the type of constitution and civilian rule that should succeed a military handover. There were also a substantial number of leading soldiers who were in no sense ready to hand over power to the civilians. As elsewhere in Africa, the military had acquired a taste for power and were ready to persuade themselves that they could rule as well or better than the civilians. Gowon himself had become the prisoner of an increasingly corrupt military elite, including the 12 state governors whom he wanted to change but who refused to step down, and when he committed himself to creating more states he unleashed a series of political claims that he could not satisfy.

One of Gowon's last achievements before his overthrow was the creation of the Economic Community of West African States (ECOWAS), which certainly owed a great deal to Nigerian regional diplomacy, backed by Nigerian oil wealth. ECOWAS was one more African attempt at regional economic integration but in this case it crossed the boundaries between Anglophone and Francophone countries as well as embracing the small Lusophone states of West Africa. The ECOWAS Treaty was signed in Lagos in May 1975 by 15 countries: Benin, The Gambia, Ghana, Guinea, Guinea-Bissau, Côte d'Ivoire, Liberia, Mali, Mauritania, Niger, Nigeria, Senegal, Sierra Leone, Togo and Upper Volta (Burkina Faso), while Cape Verde became the sixteenth member in 1977. The object of the Treaty was to liberalize trade between members and work towards a full customs union over 15 years by 1990. The theory of ECOWAS made a great deal of sense, for if the fragmented economies of West Africa could come together in a working customs union this would give them greater bargaining power with their traditional economic partners in Europe. France was opposed to the formation of ECOWAS and believed, correctly, that a strengthening of regional ties would reduce its influence. In fact, it need not have worried. ECOWAS' prospects were soon shown to be extremely limited: for three years after its launch Nigeria's trade with its ECOWAS partners was a mere 1.6 per cent.[12]

The Third National Development Plan 1975–80, launched in the spring of 1975, was by far the largest African plan to that date and the size of the financial allocation – N32 billion of which N20 billion came from the public sector – was a sign of Nigeria's new-found confidence in its future: the civil war was safely behind it and oil wealth could now be used to place the country firmly on the world economic map. After two preliminary chapters, chapter three – 'Objectives, Priorities and Strategy' – begins with high hope: 'The five national objectives of Nigeria, as identified in the Third National Development Plan, are to establish Nigeria firmly as a united, strong and self-reliant nation, a great and dynamic economy, a just and egalitarian society, a land of bright and full opportunities for all citizens, and a free and democratic society.'[13] Such expressions of purpose are to be found in most plans but in this case there were plenty of grounds for optimism for the wealth existed and there were many able and dynamic Nigerians to make the plan work. In the years 1970–74 the country had experienced an average growth rate of 8.2 per cent. The specific short-term objectives of the Third Plan were: increase in per capita income; more even distribution of income; reduction in the level of unemployment; increase in the supply of high level manpower; diversification of the economy; balanced development; indigenization of economic activity. Nigeria was always open to foreign investment and when he launched the Plan Gowon said: 'I hardly need to add that the foreign businessmen in our midst are as welcome as ever before in the fields which have been clearly defined by law. It is the hope of government that in the promotion of their business activities they will seek to involve competent and reputable Nigerians rather than front men who claim to have influence with governments and government functionaries.' Federal expenditure became all-important at this time. Its share of GDP, including transfers to the states, had increased from 12 per cent in 1966 to 36 per cent in 1977. 'Public expenditure was financed initially from oil surpluses but free spending brought budget deficits which began in 1975–76 and later threatened state investment activity in the oil and steel sectors. The momentum was only maintained by external borrowing in the Eurodollar market. The limits to this form of borrowing, in the shape of two jumbo loans worth US$1,700 million, were quickly reached.'[14] Despite the indigenization exercise, state intervention generally favoured large-scale foreign enterprise while, in response to the new flow of wealth, a rapidly expanding entrepreneur class, which depended upon a mixture of commerce, urban property and the exercise of managerial and administrative skills, appeared and flourished. Growing oil revenues and a strong naira increased pressures to open the economy to outside investment while at the same time encouraging a growth of central bureaucracy presiding over the competition for state expenditure.

There were alternative views as to how Nigeria should use its newfound wealth, though they attracted little attention in the rush to wealth that was taking place. Two academics published *The Socialist Alternative*[15] in 1975, preceding the Third Plan. They argued that while 80 per cent of Nigeria's total arable land remained uncultivated the country was suffering from acute food shortages and that untilled and under-utilized agricultural land was a source of huge waste to the economy. They criticized the industrial sector, which was too small a component of the national economy, as too biased in favour of consumer goods and claimed: 'There is general absence of a serious foundation of heavy capital goods industries for the industrial transformation of the economy. No meaningful industrialization is possible in Nigeria without a basic structure of industries producing machine tools, equipment, heavy machinery, and chemicals. In this connection, the continued absence of an integrated iron and steel industry is probably the most serious indictment of the country's putative industrialization efforts... The textile first strategy of concentration on consumer goods which Nigeria has been using so far to produce soft drinks and cigarettes is clearly neo-colonial diversionary and wrong. No single country has industrialized successfully with that strategy in recent history and Nigeria will not be the exception.'[16] In that the authors would be proved correct. In a section *Objectives of People's Democratic Industrial Evolution* they propose: 'Industry shall be elevated from its present peripheral status to become the dominant sector of the economy. The contribution of industry to total output from its present paltry 8 per cent will be raised to over 40 per cent within a decade. Correspondingly, there will be deliberate reduction of the existing predominant role of primary production in the economy. The structure of employment in the country will be radically shifted from current concentration on agriculture and mining to industry. This will be accompanied by a parallel revolution in agricultural production.' They pointed out, correctly, that the colonial 'export enclave' was still intact and that, if anything, it had grown in size and importance: 'Cash cropping for export is still based on imperialist international division of labour that traps us in primary production while our foreign exploiters push mass-produced manufactures at exploitative prices on the country.'[17] These arguments were sound enough and were being advanced by radical politicians elsewhere in Africa but Nigeria was in the grip of its oil fever and the demand for imported manufactures for those who could afford them outweighed any longer-term considerations about building a sound, broad-based economy. The readiness to spend was greater than the willingness to plan.

By 1975, despite the launch of the country's giant Third Plan, Gowon had run out of steam. Despite his success at rehabilitating the Ibos after the war and the mark he had made on the international stage, he had failed to tackle the most urgent internal problems of politics and corruption. He had been unable, or unwilling, to dismiss and replace the 12 state governors who had come to regard their jobs as lifetime sinecures, he had not carried out his promise to create new states, and finding the task of evolving a new political structure for a return to civilian rule too difficult had instead reneged on his promise to return the country to civilian rule in 1976. There were other problems such as the escalating costs and inefficiency surrounding the proposed World Black and African Festival of Arts and Culture (FESTAC) while the Udoji review of civil service salaries that was envisaged as a way to create a better, less corrupt public service instead turned into a disaster as everyone from house servants upwards demanded dramatic increases of pay and salaries. The result was a military coup, carried out on 29 July when Gowon was in Kampala for the annual OAU summit and had been given the red carpet treatment on his arrival as the head of state of the continent's most powerful black nation. The northerner, Murtala Muhammed (who had been passed over by the military hierarchy at the end of July 1966 in favour of Gowon), became head of state in a bloodless coup. Soon to be given the nickname 'no nonsense Muhammed', the new ruler provided decisive and rapid direction where Gowon had stalled. The Supreme Military Council (SMC) became the centre of government and from this the state governors were excluded and downgraded, merely receiving its directives from then onwards. The 12 state governors were sacked and replaced by men who were appointed to other states than their own in a move to foster greater impartiality in office. The SMC set 1979 as the new date for a return to civilian rule, cancelled the unpopular 1973 census results, postponed FESTAC, which was later cut down to a more manageable size, and created a further seven new states to bring the total up from 12 to 19. It was decided to build a new capital at Abuja in Niger State and radical methods were employed to clear the ports of congestion and reduce the huge lines of waiting ships. Most welcome, at first, was the new government's assault on corruption which turned into the biggest such exercise the country had seen, affecting the judiciary, the police, the army, the universities, the railways and other branches of the public services. The corrupt, the inefficient, the old, those in poor health or holding outside interests were made redundant and in the process the felicitous phrase 'dead wood' was employed to designate those who were to lose their posts. The assets of former corrupt state governors were confiscated. Finally, a 50-man Constitution Drafting Commission under a leading lawyer, Rotimi Williams, was appointed to work on a draft for a Constituent Assembly.

On 13 February 1976 Murtala Muhammed was assassinated during an attempted coup that was led by Lt-Col. Bukar Dimka. Muhammed's deputy, Lt-Gen. Olusegun Obasanjo, became head of state. He maintained Muhammed's programme but lacked his predecessor's ruthless dynamism. A reduced FESTAC was held and provided welcome publicity for Nigeria's leading role in Africa. Under Obasanjo the government instituted (or continued) measures to combat inflation, to indigenize the economy, to promote self-reliance and discipline. It launched Operation Feed the Nation as it became increasingly clear that agricultural output was being outpaced by population growth. Universal primary education, which had been promised by Gowon, was implemented, though with huge imbalances depending upon local resources of teachers and schools, and seven new universities were created. In September 1978 the final version of a new constitution was accepted and the state of emergency, which had been in place since 1966, was lifted. Political parties were allowed to register in preparation for elections in 1979 but they had to meet a basic requirement of having a nationwide (as opposed to purely regional) appeal and in the end of 19 parties only five met this requirement. These were: the National Party of Nigeria (NPN) led by Alhaji Shehu Shagari; the Unity Party of Nigeria (UPN), Chief Obafemi Awolowo; the Nigerian People's Party (NPP), Dr Nnamdi Azikiwe; the Greater Nigerian People's Party (GNPP), Alhaji Waziri Ibrahim; and the People's Redemption Party (PRP), Malam Aminu Kano. There were to be five successive elections during July and August 1979 for local government, state government, state governors, the Federal Legislature and President. The elections were fiercely fought and in the presidential elections Shagari, the most popular candidate, obtained 25 per cent of the votes in 12 but not in 13 states as laid down in the Constitution. Subsequently, the Electoral Commission ruled that a 25 per cent vote in 12 and two-thirds states gave Shagari the victory; this ruling was subsequently upheld by the Supreme Court. On 1 October 1979, after 13 years of military rule, Nigeria returned to civilian rule again and Shehu Shagari became Nigeria's first executive president.

TANZANIA

The Arusha Declaration of 1967, endorsed by the ruling party TANU, had laid down the socialist principles that were to guide Tanzania, while ever since Nyerere had stepped down from the premiership in January 1962 to mobilize the party at the grassroots, he had been propounding a socialist path for the country. By the beginning of the 1970s there was broad acceptance that Tanzania was a socialist country, in intention if not always in practice, but an African socialist country that was creating its own socialist principles suitable to its particular needs and history. Unlike Algeria, Tanzania had no mineral base and was a desperately poor rural-oriented society whose economy depended upon its agriculture. Again unlike Algeria, it was not a military dictatorship but a one-party state democracy and 1970 was to witness the second election under its one-party state constitution. Nyerere, the sole presidential candidate, won 3,456,573 yes votes to 109,828 no votes and 74,388 spoilt papers.

The government designated 1970 Adult Education Year: adult education officers were appointed in every district and 324,664 adults enrolled in literacy classes. There was a rapid extension of *ujamaa* villages during the year (the programme of villageization had been launched in the 1960s) but it suffered from an acute shortage of farm managers, agricultural officers and extension workers. At this time agricultural output from the traditional (peasant) sector accounted for 95 per cent of the whole. The First Development Plan (1964–69) had failed to achieve its targets, partly through lack of enough highly trained manpower and partly due to insufficient funds, for only about 40 per cent of expected finance from abroad had materialized. Of great psychological and international importance, the construction of the TANZAM railway to Zambia by the Chinese was commenced. The international implications of the railway were to be much discussed during the decade since it meant a major economic penetration of East Africa by China, a development that was much resented by the West, which saw this as a threat to its interests. South Africa was even more worried since it saw the railway siphoning off northwards freight that until then had to pass through the south. Western concerns were not lessened by the sheer speed with which the Chinese worked to complete the first stage of the 1,100-mile-long railway; by November 1971 the first 310 miles of track from Dar es Salaam to Mlimba in Central Tanzania had been completed.

The year 1971 was to prove a difficult one economically for Tanzania, which in any case had little leeway to offset economic downturns. The development programme had to be cut back, foreign reserves fell, there was a deficit and the cost of living rose. The government pressed ahead with its socialist programme and the acquisition of all rentable property had an unsettling impact upon the 80,000-strong Asian community, many of whom left the country. A major boost for Nyerere's socialism came with the decision of the 200,000 Wagogo peasants of the Dodoma region to abandon their traditional way of life and adopt in its place the socialist village pattern of *ujamaa*. Their move into *ujamaa* villages took both government and TANU by surprise and led Nyerere to move to the region so as to supervise and help in what was a mass movement of people. A clear divide was developing between the desk-bound bureaucrats in Dar es Salaam, who lauded rural change but themselves remained firmly urban, and the rural peasants who actually did the moving and so changed their lifestyles. Only a relatively few people had moved into the new villages during 1970 but this Wagogo move was on a different scale. They tore down their old houses, took their belongings to the new area and then waited to be settled into villages. There were suggestions that they had been coerced although no evidence was advanced in support of the claim.[18]

In February 1971 TANU published its Guidelines, which among other subjects dealt with trade unions and labour. Clause 13 stated: 'The truth is that we have not only inherited a colonial governmental structure but we have also adopted colonial working habits and leadership methods. For example, we have inherited in the government, industries and other institutions the habit in which one man gives the orders and the others just obey him. If you do not involve the people on work plans, the result is to make them feel a national institution is not theirs, and consequently workers adopt the habits of hired employees. The party has a duty to emphasize its leadership on this issue.' Clause 15 of the Guidelines stated: 'Together with the issue of involving the people in solving their problems, there is also the question of the habits in their work and in day-to-day life. There must be a deliberate effort to build equality between the leaders and those they lead. For a Tanzanian leader it must be forbidden to be arrogant, extravagant, contemptuous and oppressive. The Tanzanian leader has to be a person who respects people, scorns ostentation and is not a tyrant.'[19] Such instructions for model leaders, as well as other TANU policy statements, were to be challenged at the highest level. Sheikh Abeid Amani Karume of Zanzibar came out publicly against two aspects of policy. He objected to a race policy that would allow Asian and European citizens; 'Tanzania is for black Africans and not others,' he said. And he opposed the decision that had emerged from the Arusha Declaration that leaders should not own houses to rent out for income. By the end of 1971, 800,000 rural peasants were living in 3,200 *ujamaa* villages where community living was changing the customs of centuries. In many cases those who had moved were enjoying the social advantages of education, clean water and health services for the first time.

The assassination of Sheikh Karume on 7 April 1972 ushered in an uneasy period of tension between the mainland and Zanzibar. Karume had ruled with an iron hand and made many enemies so that his assassination caused neither surprise nor much sorrow. He was succeeded by Aboud Jumbe as First Vice-President and ruler of Zanzibar; Jumbe was the most senior member of the Revolutionary Council and he acted quickly and decisively to prevent serious repercussions from the assassination damaging Zanzibar. Later in the year a crisis developed with Uganda when on 17 September about 1,000 of Obote's armed supporters crossed into Uganda from Tanzania in an ill-organized and unsuccessful attempt to raise a rebellion against Amin who had been threatening Tanzania over the previous 20 months.

As the socialist revolution was put in place those adversely affected by it had to be placated or helped. In June 1972 Nyerere met a group of West Kilimanjaro settler farmers to tell them that state and co-operative farming were the only two forms of agriculture that would be allowed in the country and that there was no future for large-scale individual farms. In the circumstances Nyerere agreed to approach Britain for a loan to buy them out although he had not accepted aid from Britain over the previous two years because of disagreements with its policies towards Rhodesia and South Africa. In line with comparable Algerian import restrictions (on luxuries) the government passed the Motor Vehicles (Restrictions and Disposition) Bill to legalize its decision to restrict the import of saloon cars, stationwagons, mini-buses, pick-up trucks and kombis, for what was needed for the people were trucks and buses. In May 1972 the National Executive Committee of TANU produced a paper, *Politics is Agriculture*, which stressed the vital importance of agriculture in relation to the population in which the young and old groups were increasing relative to the whole. Between 85 and

90 per cent of the country's total exports consisted of raw or processed agricultural products and to maintain the existing level of imports, exports had constantly to be increased because of changing world market prices. 'For example, in 1965 we could buy a tractor with 5.3 tons of cotton or 17.3 tons of sisal. The equivalent tractor now would cost 8 tons of cotton or 42 tons of sisal.'[20] That was a problem that affected all Africa. Agricultural efficiency had gone down since independence although production had increased because more land was being cultivated, there was increased use of tractors and ox ploughs, new and improved seeds, and there were more farmers as a result of population increase. But, and this was the crucial point, 'Our methods of husbandry have not improved, so that the increases in output are much less than they should be given the labour effort expended.' The population of Tanzania, which had reached a figure of 12,231,000 in 1967, was increasing at an estimated rate of 2.7 per cent a year.

In 1973 TANU adopted a number of new policies likely to test the leadership. The most important and far-reaching of these was the decision to make it compulsory for peasants to move into *ujamaa* villages by 1976. By the end of the year one million peasants were living in *ujamaa* villages and, if the 1976 deadline were to be achieved, a further 10 million peasants would have to move in the space of three years and that represented a massive human relocation by any standards. TANU took the decision to move the capital from Dar es Salaam to Dodoma in the centre of the country although a poll of TANU regional working committees found that 842 out of 1,859 were opposed to the move. Relations between mainland Tanzania and Zanzibar were always difficult and usually strained for the union was not a natural one. Karume's successor, Jumbe, despite the early hope that he would be easier to work with in fact was unpredictable and sometimes harsh with the Zanzibaris. During 1973, for example, he initiated an austere dress code that laid down the length of women's dresses, what could or could not be shown, dresses that showed the contours of the body were outlawed as were see-through materials, wigs and make-up. Regulations for men forbade shorts, bell-bottom or tight-fitting trousers and shirts that exposed the chest; hair length was limited to two inches. Zanzibar enjoyed total autonomy except for 'union subjects' such as foreign affairs.

Tanzania was obliged to import food during 1974 because the country was unable to produce sufficient for its needs after seven years of drought and poor harvests. This failure naturally drew attention to the *ujamaa* programme and the upheavals associated with moving between seven and eight million peasants to new villages, either voluntarily or compulsorily. Moving people was only the first phase of the *ujamaa* concept; thereafter, the people had to be educated and converted to the idea of common ownership and common endeavour for the common good. The end of the process was villages that were also socialist co-operative communities. Even under the best conditions the process was bound to be slow. In some districts the preparations for the moves were well done: sites were properly selected, transport was laid on, assistance was available and discussions were held with those about to move so that they understood what was to happen and why. In other cases the preparations were inadequate and there was little explanation so that instructions from TANU to move were seen as commands and resented. This led the party to issue clarifications in October 1974 so as to minimize the confusion or sense of coercion.

When the first major phase of moving people was completed, the second, more difficult phase of creating *ujamaa* societies began. As President Nyerere said: 'No one can force people to become good socialists – that is a voluntary act.' 'The large-scale villageization simultaneously brought to the forefront the urgency of applying the principles TANU had enunciated as integral to *ujamaa*, especially the equality of the country's citizens and their right to education and health services.'[21] Given that the economy was 90 per cent dependent upon agriculture the success or failure of the programme of villageization was of overriding importance, especially as Tanzania was particularly subject to climate variations and increased world food and fertilizer prices. The country was also adversely affected by the fourfold increase in the price of oil that followed the 1973 Yom Kippur War. By the end of 1974 about three million people had been relocated in *ujamaa* villages, two million were in other 'new' villages, one and a half million in older non-*ujamaa* villages and three and a half million remained in scattered homesteads and hamlets. In 1967 less than 15 per cent of the rural population outside plantations had lived in any type of village. There were great variations between the level of organization and quality of life in the new villages and the government was endeavouring to reach as many as possible with literacy programmes. Village assemblies were created in 1975 and everyone over 18 was a member. A village council of 25 was to be elected by the assembly. The government provided each village with paid personnel to carry out village functions and they were answerable to the village councils. In 1976 TANU was replaced by a single revolutionary party to include Zanzibar – Chama Cha Mapinduzi.

Many plans were upset during 1975 as a result of severe drought and, with all its endeavours to create a socialist society Tanzania was burdened with problems of deep poverty for it was one of the 25 poorest countries in the world and no amount of planning could lift it out of that condition except over a long period of time. Nyerere was re-elected President for another five-year term and suggested that it might be his last. Meanwhile, he showed formidable energy in dealing with Tanzania's day-to-day problems, in supervising the *ujamaa* revolution and in his capacity as chairman of the Frontline States facing the white-controlled South. He had established especially close relations with Botswana, Mozambique and Zambia. In October 1976 the Chinese-built TANZAM Railway was completed and handed over to Tanzania and Zambia. It was a symbol of the two countries' determination to break away from Western tutelage and dependence upon transit routes through the white-controlled South and, as a consequence, was not welcomed by the West.

Early in 1977 Nyerere reviewed the 10 years that had passed since the Arusha Declaration. He pointed out the significant advances that had been made in reducing income differentials between rich and poor, in establishing attitudes for co-operative rather than competitive endeavour, and in the provision of health, education and transport. On the other hand, he was highly critical of the parastatals. 'We are not using our investments as efficiently as we should. Almost all our industrial plants are running well below capacity...' He was equally critical of agricultural production. 'The truth is that the agricultural results have been very disappointing. Modern methods have not spread very quickly or very widely; the majority of our traditional crops are still being grown by the same methods as our forefathers used... The real failure seems to have been a lack of political leadership and technical understanding at the village and district level. Despite the call in *Politics is Agriculture* for all political leaders to learn the basics of good husbandry in their areas, and to join with the peasants in production, we have continued to shout at the peasants and exhort them to produce more, without doing much to help them or to work with them in a relationship of mutual respect.'[22] Nyerere's criticisms pointed up an inherent contradiction in his socialist experiment: the division between the peasants who were exhorted to be socialists in their *ujamaa* villages and the urban population, including the political elite, who had and wished at all costs to retain other prospects. In the late 1980s and early 1990s, once Nyerere had stepped out of the political scene, Tanzania's hierarchy did not take long to embrace a capitalist development path. That lay in the future. As of 1979, of 8,000 villages, 7,126 or 90 per cent of all mainland villages had established their own governments in the form of village assemblies and councils.

BOTSWANA

Ever since the Act of Union of 1910 it had been Pretoria's intention and hope to absorb Botswana (along with Lesotho and Swaziland) into South Africa and though this objective was not achieved the three territories came to independence in the 1960s under the shadow of their powerful neighbour. Botswana was tied to South Africa by the Southern Africa Customs Union (SACU), by the fact that considerable numbers of its men worked in South

Africa, and because it was landlocked and dependent upon land communications through its neighbour. Seretse Khama, Botswana's first President, had learned more than 15 years before independence of South Africa's baleful influence when the British had first tricked him into visiting London and then banished him from his country to appease Pretoria because he had married an English woman, Ruth Williams, and so was guilty of miscegenation. Throughout his presidency Seretse Khama made plain his abhorrence of apartheid and refused to enter into diplomatic relations with his neighbour though, as he explained to the OAU, his country was obliged to trade and have other dealings with South Africa simply to survive.

Throughout the 1970s Botswana pursued a shrewdly independent policy, never surrendering its principles under the frequent pressures exerted upon it by South Africa, but steering a careful path that maximized its independence while not providing an excuse for Pretoria to intervene in its affairs. At independence in 1966 Botswana was rated by the United Nations as one of the poorest countries in Africa, with an economy entirely based upon cattle. That was before the discovery of diamonds and copper. By 1970 the government had reached complex agreements with the international mining community for the development of its new mineral finds and looked set to embark upon an economic expansion that would have seemed unthinkable only four years earlier. Addressing the Non-Aligned Summit in Lusaka, Zambia, in September 1970, Khama said: 'If we appear reluctant to play an active and prominent role in the struggle for the establishment of majority rule throughout Southern Africa, it is not because we are unconcerned about the plight of our oppressed brothers in the white-ruled states of our region. Rather, it is because we are concerned about our particularly exposed position and the severe limitations it imposes on us. We want to see majority rule established not only throughout Southern Africa but throughout our continent. And we are determined to contribute towards the achievement of this noble goal. We are, however, aware that there is a limit beyond which our contribution cannot go without endangering our very independence.'[23]

The pressures South Africa was prepared to exert were brought out during the course of the year as Botswana, with US aid, began the construction of what came to be called the BOTZAM road that would link the centre of Botswana with Zambia at the ferry crossing of Kazungula over the Zambezi. South Africa tried to bully Botswana into abandoning the road but in the face of the government's determination to go ahead with the project, Vorster, the South African Prime Minister, retreated when in June he answered a question in Parliament: 'I have no jurisdiction over links that might or might not be built between independent countries. If the question implies whether that road link will pass over South African territory that, of course, is a different matter and the South African government has made its position clear to the Botswana Government.' In fact, South African bluster had failed to persuade the Botswana government to back down. South Africa also tried to prevent Khama appointing Joe Matthews to his Ministry of Information. Matthews was the son of the late Professor Z. K. Matthews, a former ambassador to the UN. Joe Matthews had recently acted as the representative of the ANC in London and had been a prominent member of the ANC in South Africa until he was exiled in 1960. South Africa regarded him as a communist; Khama said he would make what appointments he chose. The overriding national interest was to reduce dependence upon South Africa while avoiding an open breach and the BOTZAM road represented the desire to establish closer links with Zambia and Tanzania to the north, and beyond them Nigeria. Botswana made plain, in answer to pressures for a dialogue with its neighbour, that it was only prepared to engage in one that was concerned with the attainment of majority rule.

The National Development Plan 1970–75 proposed a growth rate of 15 per cent but stated: 'If mining development occurs to a greater extent than the present cautious estimates envisage the rate of growth may easily reach 20 per cent per annum.' However, it was clear that even with such a high rate of economic growth, three out of every five school-leavers would not find wage employment in Botswana during the Plan period, that agriculture must remain the key to jobs and that mining wealth should be used for rural development. Under the Plan it was determined to develop the livestock industry and increase arable production in basic foods. A World Bank loan for US$25 million was negotiated for infrastructure facilities for the copper-nickel project at Selebi-Pikwe. Botswana did not want its new mining industry to be dominated by South African interests and worked to create a consortium of US, Swedish, West German, Australian, British and Canadian mining interests to finance and operate the Selebi-Pikwe complex. However, it was not able to keep Harry Oppenheimer's Anglo-American Corporation (AAC) out of the diamond developments although it obtained good terms; the AAC became the dominant partner in Bamangwato Concessions, which controlled the new diamond mines. By this time it was becoming apparent that Botswana was a storehouse of minerals. The biggest known coalfield in Southern Africa was discovered at Palapye and could be the source of thermal power for the country while it was known that huge water resources were locked up in the Okavango swamps. Other minerals included brine deposits in the Nata river delta that could produce pure salt and soda ash for industrial use at Makgadigadi. Meanwhile, the national cattle herd, centred in the east of the country, was being expanded too rapidly so that over-grazing was destroying the land. There were huge imbalances in terms of individual wealth: 12 per cent of farmers owned 60 per cent of the cattle, 60 per cent of owners had fewer than 40 beasts and 23 per cent of the people on the land had no cattle at all.

As the country's mineral wealth was exploited, Botswana faced the problem of a two-society development between those working for government or in the mines and towns for wages and the poor in the rural areas and shanty towns. The industrial sector was tiny and consisted of little more than an abattoir and meat canning plant and a few small factories producing furniture or clothing. President Khama stressed that Botswana was a country of farmers and cattle ranchers and that mining was a peripheral bonanza, but bonanza or not the mining boom came to dominate economic considerations. The government was to receive dividends from 15 per cent of the copper-nickel project as well as royalties and corporation income tax, which together were expected to yield an annual income of R4 million. At the same time the government was responsible for R53 million of borrowing to cover the Selebi-Pikwe infrastructure which included a dam, power station, road and rail links. Government policy was to spread the mining wealth and restrict the wages of miners so as not to allow the emergence of a wage elite. Roan Selection Trust (RST) had an 85 per cent stake in Selebi-Pikwe and the Botswana government had the other 15 per cent. Sir Ronald Prain, Chairman of Botswana RST, said it was the first time a country had secured loans for a project in excess of its GDP and forecast that in 10 to 20 years Botswana's per capita income would be among the highest in the developing world. On 26 May 1972 the De Beers Orapa diamond mine, the second biggest kimberlite pipe in the world, was opened; it was expected to yield net profits of R8 million a year with an output of 2.4 million carats of mainly industrial diamonds. Despite the mineral boom only seven per cent of the population had a cash income while the non-mining industrial sector was very small and growing very slowly. Cattle were still the basis of the economy with beef exports earning R10 million a year from a national herd of 1.5 million. It was planned to expand the herd to 2 million head.

Despite the excitement of mineral developments Botswana remained isolated in a deeply disturbed region in which all its neighbours had white minority governments. On a visit to Tanzania in 1973 Khama gave a speech on 28 August in which he said: 'We have made clear on a number of occasions that despite our extremely exposed position in our region of Africa we are not prepared to sell our souls for the sake of good relations with our powerful neighbours. We have recognized the need to co-operate with them on certain matters, but only to the extent that is absolutely necessary for our national survival.'[24] Later that year (November) Botswana, to South Africa's anger, voted for a UN resolution supporting the legitimacy of liberation struggles 'by all available means, including armed struggle'. The economy continued to boom. The Orapa mine proved more profitable than expected, a new diamond pipe was discovered, coal was mined at Morupule (78,000 tons) and this was expected to rise to 200,000 tons by 1977, and in early 1974 copper and nickel production got under way at Selebi-Pikwe, which was expected to provide 2,000 local jobs. In 1969–70 total exports (mainly beef) earned R13 million; by 1973–74 exports were expected to earn R70 million. It was estimated that expenditure on the 1973–78 Development Plan would come to R215 million.

On the political front Khama's Botswana Democratic Party (BDP) won the 1974 elections, taking 27 of 32 seats; the President said he had no intention of creating a one-party state and repeated his commitment to creating a non-racial society in Southern Africa. Khama played a role in the *détente* exercise initiated by South Africa and at the end of the year Botswana established diplomatic relations with Beijing. The result of the oil price rises led the government to give higher priority to the BOTZAM road so as to create an alternative oil supply route through Zambia. The Arab oil embargo on South Africa led Pretoria to cut oil supplies to Botswana by 30 per cent at the end of 1973 leading the government to fear this would hold back the mining operations at Selebi-Pikwe and Orapa. Saudi Arabia agreed to meet Botswana's oil needs provided the oil was not shipped through South Africa.

As Botswana's mineral resources were opened up at Selebi-Pikwe and Orapa social and labour tensions inevitably developed: at Selebi-Pikwe there was resentment at the racialism of the white miners and management; at Orapa (in 1972) 400 miners went on strike against management policy that favoured employing black miners from South Africa. In 1975 over 1,000 miners struck at Selebi-Pikwe demanding wage parity with South African miners. Botswana now had to face the problems associated with organized labour. There were other problems. In 1977 a three-year study by Derek Hudson of the Bank of Botswana showed that Botswana had one of the most unequal distributions of wealth in the world. Diamonds continued to boom. Orapa, which had gone into production in 1972, was the world's second-largest diamond pipe and very profitable. The mine was run by Debswana, a combination of De Beers Consolidated Mines and the Botswana government. In 1975 the original agreement was renegotiated and the government's shareholding was raised from 15 to 50 per cent, and royalties and taxes were placed on a new variable basis, with the result that government revenues from dividends, taxes and royalties amounted to 75 per cent of the profits. Diamonds had become the country's leading export and the principal source of government finance. Two new diamond pipes, DK1 and DK2, 40 kilometres from Orapa, went into production in 1977 and another rich diamond pipe was discovered at Jwaneng in 1978 and was scheduled to go into production in 1982. However, the high hopes for Selebi-Pikwe were scaled down as the mine ran into technical problems and Anglo-American shelved plans to develop the soda ash deposits that had been discovered at Sua. Taking stock at the end of the decade, Botswana had done extraordinarily well. It had moved from the position of one of the poorest countries in Africa to one with a bright economic future possessing one of the continent's strongest currencies. Development, however, was one-sided and apart from the mining sector and the cattle business the rest of the economy was badly under-developed: manufacturing was negligible and arable farming had hardly taken off. Moreover, the new prosperity had not filtered down to the majority of the rural population.

CHAPTER SIXTEEN

Oil and Israel; A New International Economic Order

President Boumedienne of Algeria played a leading role in the events of the early 1970s that led to the demand for a New International Economic Order (NIEO). Though the demand was the direct result of the October War of 1973 between Israel and its Arab neighbours and the subsequent fourfold increase in the price of oil, the search for a more equitable international order that he was to spearhead went back further and related to the history of exploitation from which the whole of ex-colonial Africa was still suffering. In a Memorandum submitted by Algeria to the Conference of Sovereigns and Heads of State of OPEC Member Countries (dated March 1975) the point is made that access to economic power should be given to those countries which were absent from Bretton Woods because they were then colonies and so excluded from the process of establishing and running the prevailing economic order. As a result they were still excluded from the economic decision-making process in 1975. As the memorandum pointed out, in increasing numbers these countries were emerging with their own resources and their great potential as well as their legitimate desire to take their part in the processes connected with major economic and monetary decisions:

> Will the developed countries draw the inevitable conclusions from the fundamental changes that have taken place since Bretton Woods, or will they continue to ignore these changes? Will they accept that Third World countries can mobilize their resources to play a responsible and positive role in international economic relations, or will they persist in ignoring these countries and attempting to leave them in a position without responsibility *vis-à-vis* the vast problems of the world economy, with all the ugly consequences that such a state of affairs is bound to have on the harmony and stability of the world economy?[1]

The oil dominance achieved by the members of OPEC in the aftermath of the

Yom Kippur War was in fact to be short-lived and the turn-around in the market started in 1978 when strikes in Iran against the policies of the Shah began to affect oil production. Furthermore, the West soon recovered from the shocks of 1973–75 once it was realized that the vast accumulations of petro-dollars held by OPEC banks had to be spent and that they could only be spent in the West. 'Recycling' became the new jargon word, one that was much appreciated in the once-anxious West. The debate, sparked off by the oil crisis, was about underdevelopment and that had a long history, which was the product of imperialism.

> The underdeveloped countries are underdeveloped not by accident but because of the activity and influence of the developed countries. The economic conquest of the 'underdeveloped world' began so long ago that few people realize that many present underdeveloped countries were relatively well developed before the onslaught of the West. For example, Chile had a flourishing copper industry in the late nineteenth century that was entirely owned by its own citizens.[2]

In fact, within the capitalist world there are vast inequalities of wealth and income that are sustained by basic mechanisms, which ensure that the gap between needs and resources, both within and among countries, will not be bridged. It was to this whole division of wealth and poverty, control and subjection, that Boumedienne and his Algerian revolutionaries were directing their attention.

In the 1970s Africa was estimated to possess 30 per cent of the non-Communist world's minerals and 20 per cent of its traded oil yet this was not reflected in its economic standing. At the time of the West's rapid imperial expansion during the nenteenth and early twentieth centuries the countries that later came to be called collectively the Third World had neither economies nor military power sufficient to enable them to withstand the colonizing process with the result that they were subsumed in the Western empires or incorporated in their spheres of influence. This was the fate of the African continent. Subsequently, foreign companies that extracted minerals and left little of value in their place became a major obstacle to the economic development of the countries in which they operated and though it has been argued that without the big extractive companies even less development would have taken place, the reverse argument is that since what was extracted were non-renewable resources, it would have been better if these had been left in the ground to be developed when the country possessing them became free. Certainly, not much of the wealth accruing to this extractive process was invested in the countries in which the minerals were found. Moreover, in the post-independence period the roles of aid ministries in donor countries, supported by the World Bank and International Monetary Fund, ensured the continued profitability of extraction by the predatory multinationals since these institutions from their inception promoted foreign private investment in mineral ventures to ensure the continuing profitability of the companies and the continuity of supply to the West. Assistance was never offered to the newly independent countries to assist them in breaking the ties that bound them to the West; rather, aid was geared to bind them even tighter into an economic-financial web from which escape was only possible (if not usually practicable) by some form of socialist revolution. The Communist countries at this time did offer an alternative pattern in which mineral resources were nationalized and government policy was to achieve internal self-sufficiency by expanding indigenous supplies. Those African countries that experimented with socialism faced formidable obstacles: the internal ones they could overcome; the external pressures from the West usually, in the end, proved overwhelming and they were forced back into the Western capitalist camp.[3]

The pattern of mineral supply and demand at this time can be illustrated by the critically precious metal cobalt which is mainly used for jet engines (approximately 70 per cent of cobalt production goes for super-alloys, magnets and steel alloys) and so was of great strategic importance. The United States then consumed approximately 30 per cent of total world production and imported 98 per cent of its total requirements. Zaïre accounted for 60 per cent of world production while a further 15 per cent came from the Communist countries.[4] These facts alone provide a reason for the close support the US always gave to the Mobutu regime in Zaïre. It was never simply a question of where a particular resource was to be found but also of who controlled it. The investment pattern had been established during colonial times: first came the capital inflow and the people with the technological know-how; then the industrial enclave was established and consumer goods (luxuries to the local people) appeared on the scene so that a 'state' within a state was created. Meanwhile the raw materials were extracted and exported as were the greater part of the profits. As a result, the economy of the colony (later an independent developing country) became polarized between the extractive enclave and the rest of the country with an increasing gap in living standards growing up between them. This situation had its own psychological impact and helped foster the belief that all technology and luxury goods must come from overseas. Moreover, expatriates took the important economic decisions, thus emphasizing the gap between the indigenous population, even of its more educated members, and the expatriates who effectively controlled the economy. Processing the extracted minerals is the last link in the chain of control and the extracting companies and the countries out of which they operate have done all in their power to prevent the mineral-producing countries from also processing their own minerals, for it is in the processing that the major value is added to the ore. Moreover, when unrefined ores are shipped out of a Third World country they are often found to contain valuable secondary minerals: copper ores may also contain molybdenum, gold or silver and these secondary metals are obtained without cost and used commercially by the firms that process the ore. Quite apart from the value added by processing, the mining multinationals try to keep the producing countries out of processing so as to protect their control of the industry as a whole. As long as Third World countries are unable to process their ores their bargaining power is limited. To a great extent, the power of the multinationals depends upon their ability to control all aspects of the mining process and most especially the final value-adding processing. During the 1970s the World Bank and IMF became increasingly important in the mineral industry.

> Such institutions are increasingly seen by the developed capitalist countries as mechanisms that serve three inter-related goals: first, they reduce the rivalries among the developed capitalist countries and thus prevent an increase in the Third World's bargaining power. Second, they reduce the power of individual Third World countries by facing them with the power of the whole international capitalist financial and economic community rather than with that of individual mining companies. And third, they keep the Third World countries from developing full control over their mineral resources, either alone or with assistance from the socialist countries.[5]

That formidable indictment of the two UN financial institutions that were supposedly set up to work impartially on behalf of all their member countries gives a clear insight into the way the West subverted to its own ends the most effective international instruments to be created after World War II.

THE OIL REVOLUTION

Four African countries, of which two were in the Arab north, entered the 1970s as oil producers whose economies were largely dependent upon their oil production. These were Algeria, Libya, Nigeria and Gabon though the latter was only a small producer in world terms. In 1977 the percentage share of oil in their GNPs and exports was as follows:

Country	Share of GNP	Share of exports
Algeria	24	88
Gabon	35	85
Libya	60	99.9
Nigeria	30	92

After the Mossadegh debacle in Iran during the 1950s no Middle East country attempted to nationalize any important oil operation until the Algerian government seized a majority share of the French operations in Algeria of *Compagnie Française des Petroles* (CFP) and the French state company *Enterprise de Récherches et d'Activités Petrolières* (ERAP) in 1971. Algeria had already nationalized its US concessionaires in 1967 (when Washington broke diplomatic relations) but their operations were small scale and made little economic impact. However, CFP and ERAP were responsible for most of Algeria's output and were also in a special 'protected' position as a result of the 1965 Franco-Algerian Evian Agreement. When it was apparent that the Algerian-French discussions were making no progress, Algeria unilaterally took control of 51 per cent of CFP and ERAP operations on 24 February 1971. France responded with a boycott but in June CFP came to terms with the Algerian government: Algeria paid the company US$60 million compensation while CFP paid Algeria US$40 million back-payments and accepted a higher price. Five months later ERAP also came to terms with the takeover. The Algerian takeover, though it was seen by outsiders as part of an overall post-independence settlement between Algeria and its former colonial power, nonetheless encouraged the other OPEC producers who collectively began negotiations with the companies in Geneva in January 1972.

Algeria and Libya were the pacemakers in the OPEC revolution of the 1970s. Libya's role in creating OPEC power was extremely important. Algeria was as radical but, in one sense, was engaged in a battle with France, its former metropolitan power. Libya, by contrast, played the role of 'jack the giant-killer' and when it succeeded other Gulf States followed its lead.

Gaddafi's determination to take on the major oil companies in the early 1970s, forcing them into a series of deals that both increased the price paid for Libya's oil and gave Libya a controlling stake in its own resource for the first time, revolutionized the relationship of oil consumers and producers in the Middle East and provided the Organization of the Petroleum Exporting Countries (OPEC) with 'teeth'. In October 1969 the Libyan Minister of Petroleum and Mines, Ezzidin Mabrouk, announced that the government would reappraise the control of Libya's oil wealth. Libya would seek agreements with the oil companies that were 'fair'. In 1970 the government exerted pressures upon the oil companies to accept both higher taxes and an increase in the posted price of crude oil. (The posted price is an artificial rate used for calculating tax and royalties; the market price is lower.) Libya was in a very strong position: it was then the most important single supplier to Western Europe; its geographical location was closer to the markets of the main consumers; and its oil had a low sulphur content which made it especially suitable for refining. Moreover, the government was ready to cut back output, ostensibly as a measure of conservation, as a means of exerting pressure upon the companies. At this time 45 per cent of Libya's exports went to West Germany and Italy and a further 13.8 per cent to Britain.

Gaddafi sought to co-ordinate his oil policy with Algeria, and the two countries agreed a common approach to the oil companies in January 1970. Then, following a visit by Gaddafi and his oil minister, Mabrouk, to Algiers on 19 April 1970, they agreed to the 'creation of a united front to defend their interests in the face of foreign trusts and monopolies'. This was only a beginning. In January 1971 Libya put forward new demands that were equivalent to a further 25 per cent rise in the posted price of oil and the posted price of crude oil was then raised to US$3.45 a barrel. At that time Libya was extracting oil at the rate of 3.1 million b/d. Despite a drop in oil exports during 1971 of 16.7 per cent government revenues had increased by 37 per cent as a result of price increases. The companies now found themselves in a position of constant uncertainty. During the first six months of 1972 they were asked to cut back production the equivalent of 22.3 per cent over the same period for 1971 as a conservation measure. At the beginning of 1973 Libya asked for 50 per cent participation in the Oasis Consortium (Marathon Oil, Continental Oil, Amerada Hess and Shell) and in May, when little progress in the talks had been achieved, the government increased its pressures. On 11 June the government nationalized Bunker Hunt and this move was seen as a warning to the bigger companies. As the government said: 'No power on earth can take from us the right to nationalize our own oilfields or to stop pumping our oil.'[6] On 10 August 1973 terms for a 51 per cent nationalization of Occidental were announced; Occidental had come to terms with Libya on its own. The agreement had a profound impact since Gulf States to that point had been content with 25 per cent stakes. After insisting that the Oasis companies should cut production, they too (though not Shell) came to terms and accepted a 51 per cent deal.

Libya had played its hand shrewdly for the agreements with Occidental and Oasis had separated the leading independent companies from the larger, worldwide corporations which had only limited interests in Libya: Occidental, Marathon Oil, Continental Oil and Amerada Hess were largely dependent upon their Libyan supplies and, therefore, far more vulnerable than the other companies. By December 1973 when the Gulf producers announced a new posted price of US$11.65 a barrel and Libya went one better by raising its price to US$18.76 a barrel (the highest ever in world terms) the battle between the OPEC countries and the companies had effectively been won. Libya had never wavered in its tough stance and its readiness to halt production (whether or not this was a bluff) had forced the pace.

At the Islamic Summit Conference held at Lahore in February 1974, Gaddafi advanced the unique proposal that the oil-producing countries should adopt a three-tier pricing system: the lowest prices to be offered to Islamic states, a middle price to developing countries and the highest price to the industrialized states; but the other oil producers were not interested. Meanwhile, Libya pursued its policy of nationalization through 1974 and on 11 February announced the total nationalization of three US companies – Texaco, California Asiatic and the Libyan-American Oil Company – which had refused to accept the 51 per cent Libyan participation deal of 1973. By the end of the 1970s, Libya, like other Arab producers, was affected by depressed market conditions and the coming on stream of North Sea oil. In 1980 Ezzidin Mabrouk, who had been responsible for Libya's oil for a decade, was replaced by Abdul-Salam Muhammad Zagar because of his failure to speed up the process of total Libyanization. Oil prices peaked in 1980–81 when the spot price for Libyan crude was at a high of US$41 a barrel, but the 1980s were to be a decade of depression in the oil industry and, for example, Libya's oil income, which reached US$23 billion in 1981, dropped to US$10 billion in 1982. In the confrontations of 1971–74 Libya had determined to show it was as tough in negotiations as Algeria and ahead of the other Arab states, especially Saudi Arabia, and in this respect it had succeeded in setting the pace.

ISRAEL

In the late 1950s Israel had initiated an aid programme for black Africa as part of its policy to 'leap over' the hostile Arab states that surrounded it and make friends among the new states of Africa. The aid was at government level and consisted chiefly of technical assistance covering agricultural development, military and police training, public health, the utilization of water resources and community planning. In addition, the Israeli government offered a range of training scholarships and by 1972 more than 7,000 African students had attended courses in Israel. At the same time that government aid was being provided, private industry from Israel had begun to invest in black Africa and, for example, the Black Star shipping line was a joint Israeli-Ghanaian venture. Similar joint ventures had been developed with Ethiopia, Kenya, Nigeria and

Tanzania. In the aftermath of the 1967 Six Day War between Israel and its Arab neighbours, 12 black African states had voted for a UN resolution condemning Israel as the aggressor, 16 had voted in support of Israel and five had abstained. By 1972 Israel had established diplomatic relations with 32 African states and in general African countries were sympathetic to Israel rather than antagonistic and tended to see its problems as similar to their own although attitudes began to change following the 1967 war. Then, after the October 1973 war between Israel and her neighbours, virtually every African state broke relations with Israel, including previously warm friends such as Ethiopia, Kenya and Nigeria, and Israel found its policy of over-leaping the Arab states to find allies in Africa in ruins. As Peter Enahoro wrote in *Africa* (December 1973), 'The survival of Israel became identified with American power. To be opposed to Israel was to be anti-colonialist, anti-imperialist…' Moreover, Israel's growing relations with Pretoria were a mark against it while the cause of the Palestinians came to be equated with the cause of the Southern African guerrillas. Arab pressures upon black Africa to support the Palestinian cause and distance themselves from Israel were intensified during 1972–73, before the Yom Kippur War changed the whole political situation in the Middle East. Libya promised Uganda military and economic assistance and Uganda broke diplomatic relations with Israel at the end of Match 1972. Uganda, under Amin, was something of a special case. There had been Israeli agents in the country since Obote's time and these were believed to be in touch with his supporters. Amin said he was surprised to find 700 Israelis in the country; he had expected 40 or 50. Military advisers who had been in the country since 1964 left hurriedly in the last week of March when Amin announced the termination of the existing defence agreement with Israel. The Israelis, it transpired, had been employed building highly sophisticated military air bases in Uganda, which could be used for air strikes against Egypt.[7] Chad also severed relations with Israel, in its case after Gaddafi had promised to end his support for the Muslim rebels in the north of the country.

At the November 1973 OAU Ministerial Council meeting, in the immediate aftermath of the Yom Kippur War, the Emperor of Ethiopia, Haile Selassie, overtly linked the occupation of Arab lands by Israel with the occupation of Southern Africa by colonialist and racist regimes: 'Africa cannot be assured of continued peace and progress,' he said 'if any part of our continent remains under foreign domination.' The same OAU meeting called for oil sanctions against South Africa, Rhodesia and Portugal. However, apart from this oil boycott, the Arab members of the OAU were asked for other forms of help in return for African support. The Kenyan Foreign Minister asked the oil states to sell oil direct to African countries with what he described as 'fragile' economies at 'concessionary rates' and to channel aid through the African Development Bank.[8] However, although in the end almost every African country fell into line and broke diplomatic relations with Israel, some at least did so under protest. The *Nigerian Tribune*, for example, regretted that Nigeria was not an active participant in the search for peace in the Middle East and condemned the 'folly' of breaking relations with Israel. It said: 'The Middle East crisis is an Arab problem. It is not an African affair. It is not the business of the OAU.' The Assistant Secretary-General of the OAU, Mr Onu, said that peace initiatives should not be a monopoly of the Great Powers although, unsurprisingly, an Israeli spokesman said that by breaking with Israel the African states had 'lost their role in any peace settlement'. By the end of 1973 a common African stand had emerged towards events in the Middle East with the near-complete severance of African diplomatic links with Israel in support of the Arab cause and, in return, the Arab promise to suspend the supply of oil to the white regimes in Southern Africa. Even those African countries that were especially well disposed towards Israel – Côte d'Ivoire, Ethiopia, Ghana, Kenya, Zaïre and Zambia – felt obliged to join the mainstream and break diplomatic relations and though at the time it appeared as though Africa was reacting to the immediate Middle East crisis, in fact the build-up to the breaks had begun in 1972. Arab pressure upon wavering African governments was greatly increased at the Non-Aligned Summit which met in Algiers on 5 November when 17 states broke relations with Israel.

The change in African attitudes towards Israel had been gradual. Through the 1960s the common African view was to accept UN decisions on Israel and Arabs and Africans, therefore, agreed to differ although as early as the 1964 OAU meeting in Cairo President Nasser of Egypt and Ben Bella of Algeria had tried, unsuccessfully, to persuade black African states to support the Arab stand. In 1967, at the time of the Six Day Arab-Israeli War, Guinea had been the first African state to break relations with Israel. From that time onwards African states supported UN Resolution 242 and took the line that while Israel had the right to exist it was illegally in occupation of Arab land. A 1971 African attempt at mediation between the Arabs and Israel – the committee of Ten Wise Men – failed though it came closer than any other attempt hitherto to find a solution. It was Israeli obstinacy over the occupied territories that began to erode African support and switch African sympathies towards the Arab position. The three leading North African Arab states – Algeria, Egypt and Libya – lobbied all members of the OAU intensively and at the 1972 Rabat Summit of the OAU the African members accepted the toughest resolution pertaining to Israel to that date. The following year, at the OAU Summit in Addis Ababa, increased pressure was put upon Haile Selassie to loosen his ties with Israel and

Boumedienne promised to use his influence to end Arab support from Syria, Iraq and South Yemen for Eritrean secession. Up to August 1973 the Israelis thought they could hold the line against the mounting pressures by the Arab states but at the September meeting of the Non-Aligned Movement in Algiers the Arabs achieved a breakthrough when they obtained African backing for a resolution that pledged full support for Egypt, Jordan and Syria in recovering their lost territories. Nigeria's Gowon, however, still held the view that if Africa was to act as a mediator it should retain diplomatic links with both sides. Mobutu broke diplomatic relations with Israel on 4 October, two days before the Yom Kippur War was launched; his move was a bitter blow to Israel, which had been training (or retraining) Zaïre's military. As a result of his gesture Mobutu was the one black African leader to be invited to attend the November Arab Summit, also held in Algiers. The big break came when Israeli troops crossed the Suez Canal during the war for this was seen as an invasion of African soil and a rush of diplomatic ruptures followed. Even the most pro-Israel countries such as Ethiopia and Kenya felt they had to follow the majority. The desire to maintain regional solidarity played a big part in these African decisions. Gowon, as the current chairman of the OAU, felt he could not stand out against the majority; and Houphouët-Boigny of Côte d'Ivoire found he was odd man out as all the other members of the Francophone organization OCAM to which his country belonged had broken their ties with Israel. Then, neither Ethiopia nor Kenya felt they could be totally isolated so they, too, joined the bandwagon. At the OAU Council of Ministers meeting in Addis Ababa over 19–21 November, a resolution for the first time in the organization's history linked Africa with the Middle East problem. In return for this support the subsequent Arab Summit in Algiers agreed to extend the oil embargo to Portugal, Rhodesia and South Africa.

Thus, in the last months of 1973 the African members of the OAU had demonstrated an impressive solidarity with the Arab countries over Israel, although up to that time there had been no equivalent Arab solidarity with the African states over Rhodesia. The question of a *quid pro quo* between Arabs and Africans was to loom large over the next two years. On 7 October, the day after the commencement of the war, Boumedienne in his capacity as chairman of the Fourth Non-Aligned Summit sent a cable to the leaders of Britain, France, the United States and the USSR in which he said:

> Since the conference stresses that force cannot be used to gain territories and since it gives recognition to the national rights of the Palestinian people the Conference asks all States, especially the US, to stop giving any political, economic or financial aid to Israel so that it may not continue its

aggressive expansionist policy. The Conference demands Israel's immediate and unconditional withdrawal from all occupied territories, and undertakes to help Egypt, Syria and Jordan to liberate their territories by every means.[9]

When the war began on 6 October eight African countries had already broken relations with Israel; these were Uganda, Chad, Congo People's Republic, Niger, Mali, Burundi, Togo and Zaïre. After the war broke out a further 17 countries followed suit; these were (in order) Rwanda, Dahomey, Mauritania, Upper Volta, Cameroon, Equatorial Guinea, Tanzania, Madagascar, Central African Republic, Ethiopia, Nigeria, Zambia, The Gambia, Senegal, Ghana, Gabon and Sierra Leone. Ten states retained relations with Israel.

In the last months of 1973 black Africa had demonstrated remarkable support for the Arab position in the Middle East; during 1974, however, the principal concern of the African countries was how to cope with the economic hardships that followed the fourfold increase in the price of oil. Up to that time Afro-Arab relations had been correct, to use the diplomatic term, rather than especially warm though newly independent states had a warm spot for Nasser's Egypt. The two groups had in common their development needs and recent colonial histories and though the Arab League had, for years, sought to obtain African backing for its confrontation with Israel, this had only been achieved in the fraught crisis conditions of 1973. OPEC's use of the oil weapon against the West opened a new phase in relations between the Third World and the developed countries; it also threatened to create a breach between the Arab states and black Africa because the Arab nations as a whole showed little sensitivity to the harm that oil price rises would inflict upon their African allies. The estimated additional cost of oil for Africa's non-oil producers in 1974 was between US$800 million and US$1,000 million, and this was apart from other price rises for imports that necessarily followed the oil hike. Claude Cheyssons, the European Economic Communiy (EEC) Commissioner, pointed out that the 400 per cent increase in oil prices coincided with a 200 per cent increase in the world price of cereals and that the cereal increase alone meant the 19 EEC associates in Africa would have to pay an extra equivalent of 75 per cent of the aid they received from Europe. The question, therefore, that dominated Afro-Arab relations through 1974 was the extent of compensatory finance that the oil-rich states were willing to provide for the African countries most severely affected by the oil price increases. At the Algiers Arab Summit of November 1973 a resolution had been adopted to set up an Afro-Arab Bank with a loan capital of US$100 million (later increased to US$200 million) that would offer loans rather than grants and the smallness of this offer compared with the size of the new oil burden led to angry African criticisms. The OAU General Secretariat responded to the proposal as follows: 'Our Arab brothers mean well but are they also doing well? Why set up another institution when there is one already? We have in mind our African Development Bank, which has to date 39 OAU member-States. The African Development Bank is the only Pan-African financing institution for economic and social development in Africa...' The Arabs, however, clearly wished to keep control of their finances. Arab delays in setting up the new financial institution through to January 1975 meant that hard-hit African countries were obliged to apply directly for aid to the Arab League while the African Development Bank (ADB) was bypassed. Algeria and Libya, the two African Arab oil producers, were more helpful: Algeria contributed a US$20 million loan to the ADB although it specified which countries were eligible for 3 per cent loans while repayments had to be made to Algeria and not to the ADB while Libya set up a separate aid account in the Arab League. There was a forthright Nigerian commentary over Radio Kaduna (11 February 1974):

> Paradoxically, the developing countries, who are in solidarity with the Arabs, the major world oil-producers, are the worst casualties of their own oil weapon. The weapon was aimed at the advanced countries, particularly the United States. True, it hit its target, but because of the inter-relation among the economies of the world and the comparative weakness of the economies in the developing countries the bouncing weapon hit the Third World and its effect has been catastrophic... What the Third World countries really need now is money to offset the oil increases.

Zambia's oil bill doubled from KW36 billion to KW73 billion as a result of the crisis and on 26 February 1974 a leader in the *Times of Zambia* said: 'The Western countries, which generally support Israel, would love it if Africa suffered economic hardship as a result of the let-downs of the Arabs to help us more sensibly. They have been telling us often enough: you can't trust the Arabs. We still trust the Arabs. We are fighting the same battle that they are fighting. But man cannot live by trust alone. He has to have oil at reasonable prices as well.' The apparently reluctant and, some argued, mean response of the oil-rich Arabs to the African need for assistance produced some strong African criticisms of their Arab brothers. Thus, the Kenya *Sunday Nation* of 6 October 1974 (the anniversary of the outbreak of the Yom Kippur War) carried an editorial 'The Arabs and their billions'. 'The larger cost of maintaining "the oil weapon" is borne by the poor nations because it is they who have to drain more and more of their foreign exchange reserves to meet the rising costs of oil and imported manufactured goods without getting anything in return. Still it is the developing countries, particularly in Africa, which have given the greatest moral support to the cause of the Arabs in the Middle East and elsewhere.'

A further comment upon the Arab attitude came from Nigeria in mid-1974 (Radio-TV Kaduna, 25 June 1974): 'The impression has been created that the Arabs have taken and are still going to continue to take black Africa for a ride. In other words, while members of the OAU are taking all reasonable measures to support the cause of the Arabs, the oil sheikhs, on the other hand, appear to pursue a policy "capable of crippling the economy of Africa without showing serious concern".' There was no doubt that by the end of the year Afro-Arab relations were strained and that Africa had experienced a sense of betrayal.

One assessment of the year was extremely gloomy: 'Economically, 1974 was disastrous for the entire continent with the exception of the few important oil-producing countries (Nigeria, Libya, Algeria and Gabon). The continent's overall economy was set back possibly a full decade or more under the combined impact of the fourfold increase in the cost of oil and, perhaps even more, the still deeper input costs of fertilizers and pesticides; the subsequent increases in the cost of manufactured imports; the world-wide inflationary pressures...'[10] In the light of these pressures that arose out of international developments over which they had little control, African leaders became enthusiastic supporters of the concept floated at this time of a New International Economic Order and over this issue, as over many others at this time, Algeria played a leading role. Africa might have been set back by the oil price rises but in international affairs it made its voice felt more strongly than at any time since independence, so much so indeed as to lead the United States to protest openly at the collective African voice in the United Nations. During 1975 Arab aid did become available to Africa through a number of Arab institutions such as the Arab Bank for Economic Development in Africa (ABEDA), the Special Arab Fund for Africa, the Arab African Bank, the Islamic Development Bank and other institutions, but much of the assistance provided went to Arab and other Islamic countries rather than black Africa. The Arab League made clear that it would not support African countries that maintained ties with Israel. As the President of ABEDA, Dr Shazali el Ayari, announced in Brussels: the Bank was not just a technical instrument to provide aid but was 'politically important' and it would not assist 'certain African countries which show hostility towards the Arab world'.[11]

At the time of the oil crisis Nigeria was the only black African country that was both a major oil producer and member of OPEC and had then reached an annual output of approximately 2 million b/d. Although its huge population meant that it could use all the oil wealth it earned, Nigeria was generous in its compensatory aid, more so than richer Arab countries with smaller populations, though, of course, it could be argued that as a black African country it was bound to demonstrate greater solidarity with the hard-hit black African states. Be that as it may, at the end of 1974 Nigeria made available substantial funds to both the IMF and the World Bank: US$120 million to the IMF to be used to finance oil credits; and US$240 million to the World Bank at 8 per cent interest. In the Commonwealth Nigeria was the only developing member to increase its contributions to the Commonwealth Fund for Technical Cooperation (CFTC). On a bilateral basis it provided £2 million to the Sahel countries in the wake of the 1973 drought, US$500,000 to Guinea-Bissau on the occasion of its independence and further aid to Mali, Botswana and Zambia. In West Africa it made substantial grants to Dahomey, Togo and Niger to help balance their budgets. Its total aid in 1975 came to US $80 million and US $35 million in 1980 when its oil income had dropped.

A NEW INTERNATIONAL ECONOMIC ORDER (NIEO)

In May 1974 the United Nations held its Sixth Special Session in Algiers, and the first to study the problems of raw materials and development, 'devoted to the consideration of the most important economic problems facing the world community'. It was very much a Third World occasion and reflected both the excitement and turmoil that the events of the previous months and, most notably, the use of the oil weapon against the developed economies had aroused. African countries in particular were excited by the prospect of a New International Economic Order since, from their point of view, almost any change in the existing order must be an improvement. There was a good deal of naïvety surrounding the *Declaration on the establishment of a new international economic order*[12] by the UN General Assembly for it was a declaration of intent without any means of implementation. The Declaration was accompanied by a Programme of Action whose 10 headings list all the concerns that so obviously divided rich and poor nations at that time and later. These were:

1 Fundamental problems of raw materials and primary commodities as related to trade and development.
2 International monetary system and financing of the development of developing countries.
3 Industrialization.
4 Transfer of technology.
5 Regulation and control over the activities of transnational corporations.
6 Charter of Economic Rights and Duties of States.

7 Promotion of co-operation among developing countries.
8 Assistance in the exercise of permanent sovereignty of States over natural resources.
9 Strengthening the role of the United Nations system in the field of international economic co-operation.
10 Special Programme.

The naïvety attached to this Programme of Action was the assumption that the developed economies would be interested in adopting any part of it.

Nonetheless, these proposals were later spelt out in the *Charter of Economic Rights and Duties of States,* which was voted upon at the UN General Assembly in November 1974. Some 120 nations voted for the Charter, six voted against and 10 abstained. The 16 who voted against or abstained were 'free' Western economies. The Charter was adopted that December. It stipulated that every nation has the right to exercise *full permanent sovereignty* over its wealth and natural resources. This, clearly, was seen as a crucial part of the Charter in the light of transnational activities generally in the Third World, and the recent OPEC experience of the oil companies in particular. The Charter set forth the rights of nations to associate in organizations of primary producers in order to develop their national economies (an obvious endorsement of the operation of the OPEC cartel). In September 1975, the UN held another Special Session on development and international co-operation during which the General Assembly enumerated measures to be taken as the basis for negotiations on the issues of raw materials; energy; trade; development; and money and finance. On this occasion the Assembly called for a restructuring of the UN's own economic and social sectors so that they could deal with problems of economic co-operation and development.

The story of the New International Economic Order is especially interesting because at the time and for a few years afterwards it became a point of reference for all the reasons for confrontation between rich and poor while also, briefly, raising hopes that somehow it would bring about substantial changes in the world power system. The idea of an NIEO was important, therefore, not because it succeeded – it did not – but because it helped emphasize the principal problems that surrounded all North-South issues. These are not questions of compassion, equity or justice, though each has its place, but questions of power. The countries of the North, then and later, wielded approximately 90 per cent of the world's power in terms of the decisions they took and enforced and they did so because they controlled the world economy. And that was why the NIEO failed, because to ask the rich to surrender this power was unrealistic.

The roots of the NIEO idea can be traced back to the writings of Raoul

Prebisch, the Argentinian economist whose name was well known in UN circles during the organization's early days. In *Towards a New Trade Policy for Development*, he attacked the old concept of comparative advantage so much favoured by the capitalist West both then and later, to argue instead that this kept developing countries permanently underdeveloped because it meant that they remained producers of raw materials or one or two commodities. He advocated interventionist policies, which would alter the balance in favour of the developing world. An NIEO would do what Prebisch had advocated. The idea of an NIEO was born in the changed atmosphere of 1973–74 when OPEC briefly threatened to turn the accepted world hierarchy on its head. Even so, the concept of an NIEO was flawed from the beginning, because self-interest does not work towards a one-world community despite all the rhetoric that is paid to the idea. In the initial demands for an NIEO, there was implicit the more realistic threat that the OPEC countries would use the oil weapon to force the advanced economies to make substantial economic concessions to the Third World. These were seen to be in terms of trade and the structure of the international bodies that control the world economy, so that Third World members would have a greater say in the decision-making process. As a result, so the theory went, some of the advantages enjoyed by the advanced economies would be surrendered, or at any rate reduced, in favour of the Third World. Such demands for change – unless backed by oil or other weapons, which the advanced economies cannot ignore – really amounted to a demand for the rich North to show greater generosity in its dealings with the poor South.

In the broadest sense the concept of an NIEO was essentially socialist. It assumed that the better off would, in statesmanlike fashion, surrender advantage for the sake of a wider world harmony and international – as opposed to national – interests. There was, however, little evidence to suggest that the rich North (including the USSR) was prepared to make any such surrender of advantages that were the source of its hegemony, and a great deal of evidence to the contrary. An NIEO, if it were to amount to anything, meant the termination of the existing order of the world economy and its replacement by a new order that had quite different priorities. The concept suffered from the further disadvantage that it was too all-embracing. Demands for an NIEO were on behalf of the oil-rich countries of OPEC; the poor nations of Africa; huge, newly industrializing countries such as Brazil, Argentina and Mexico; small, newly industrializing countries, such as Singapore or Taiwan; as well as the giant India. It was unreasonable to suppose that all their varying needs could be accommodated in the new dispensation. Any demand for redress of an unfair balance by a disadvantaged group is essentially revolutionary. In consequence it is only likely to succeed if accompanied by pressure – 'out of the barrel of a gun' to quote Mao's phrase – and in this case by the sustained pressure of OPEC. In the event the pressure was not, and could not be, maintained long enough to bring about any major changes and, not surprisingly, little came of the demands for an NIEO.

The calls for an NIEO, which became so insistent in the mid-1970s, were based upon two unstated assumptions. The first, that the rich North was heavily dependent upon resources controlled by the poor South (OPEC's exercise of oil power was behind this assumption) and that these resources, therefore, could and, if necessary, would be withheld in order to force the North to agree to a NIEO. The second, that OPEC (which had made the entire dialogue possible in the first place) would maintain its solidarity with the rest of the Third World and continue to use its economic strength as a weapon to force concessions from the North on behalf of the Third World.

Although no NIEO came into being, the dialogue between rich and poor that took place in the mid-1970s set the parameters for all the future North-South dialogues to the end of the century. It also made plain to the developing world that any concessions from the developed nations could only be won by insistent pressures and that gains would be matched, always, by some form of return. Nothing would be conceded simply on the basis of creating a more equitable world system. Africa learnt some harsh lessons at this time: both in its relations with the Arabs; and in the struggle for an NIEO, and these were reflected in the OAU document *What kind of Africa by the year 2000* (see below, chapter 17).

CHAPTER SEVENTEEN

The Growth
of Aid

T he 1970s witnessed a rapid growth of aid to Africa, almost a competition: between the Western donors, especially Britain and France, to demonstrate their concern for the world's poorest continent; between the West and the Communist powers as part of the Cold War; and between the USSR and China whose ideological quarrel sustained their antagonism. In addition, the multilateral agencies, and especially the World Bank, had become leading players in what by this time had developed into a major aspect of international relations. It is worth examining the aid efforts of these various donors, less in terms of the quantity and kind of aid they dispersed, important as this was, than for the ideology behind it.

WESTERN AID

In the middle of the decade (1976), Britain was providing a total of 0.38 per cent of GNP in aid (the average figure for the Development Assistance Committee [DAC] countries was then 0.33 per cent of GNP), and this was a very small total and only just over half the Conference on International Economic Cooperation (CIEC) target of 0.7 per cent. In 1977 gross British Official Development Assistance (ODA) came to £582 million and net transfers to £486 million and of this net total 28 per cent went to Africa. In addition, of 10,000 students and 4,000 trainees in Britain, 49 per cent came from Africa. The greater part of all British aid to Africa went to Commonwealth countries and in the case of a number of small countries, such as The Gambia, Sierra Leone or Malawi, British aid was an essential component of their budgets. Sixty-eight per cent of British personnel working overseas under the auspices of the Ministry of Overseas Development were in Africa. The question of where aid is directed is crucial to an understanding of donor policies. All aid activities should be examined in the light of whether or not they help to bring the recipient to the point at which it can – or at least can begin to – solve its own problems. In these terms, the most constructive aid is that which transfers as much technology as fast as the recipient is able to absorb and use it; or which rapidly boosts a particular sector of the economy to the point at which that sector makes a significantly improved addition to the country's total resources, some of which can then be diverted to other developments. Aid, which, all too often, serves to undermine development, is that with the highest 'humanitarian' content. During the decade the West demonstrated much concern for the poorest or most disadvantaged groups and though this concern sounded constructive it did least to transfer technology and equip the recipient to manage its own affairs.

The basic British strategy, laid down in the 1975 White Paper *More Help for the Poorest*, was to increase the emphasis in favour of the poorest people in the poorest countries.[1] It was a classic example of the humanitarian approach (a sound capitalist policy) and one designed to prolong indefinitely the development assistance needs of the recipients. Now the provision of basic needs may be a worthwhile activity in itself; it does not ensure that the country so assisted will break free from the need for aid. Britain also pushed the concept of appropriate technology, an approach which all too easily degenerated into a question of stimulating British industry to produce simple technological material for use in developing countries instead of demonstrating how these countries could do it on their own. One of the most revealing statements on British aid at this time was the Overseas Development Paper (No. 17) entitled *The Industrial Strategy: The Contribution of the Ministry of Overseas Development*, which was produced by the Ministry and written by the Minister, Judith Hart, in 1978. It begins:

> The purpose of the aid programme is to promote the economic and social development of the developing countries... UK official development assistance (ODA) is being increasingly directed to the poorest people in the poorest countries.

This, as we have already seen, is more likely to prevent a country from making development breakthroughs than achieving them. Paper 17 was clearly intended for British audiences rather than those at the receiving end of British aid. The paper continues:

> There are two basic ways in which the aid programme helps British industry. By helping foster income creation and widely-distributed economic growth in the developing countries, it increases the overseas markets for British goods. In the process it also provides opportunities for aid-financed exports both under bilateral and multilateral aid arrangements.

The Minister could not have been more explicit. After detailing the size of developing country markets, the Paper continues:

> Although developing countries took only 14 per cent of the exports from industrial countries in 1976, they accounted for 64 per cent of the world's population. So a vast expansion of the world market ought to be possible if only the incomes of the people in these countries can be raised. The scope for improving incomes is greatest in the poorest countries, not only because of their poverty (their average GNP *per capita* was only US$167 in 1976) but also because of their size (they contain 1,290 million people).

The purpose of concentrating upon the needs of the poorest thus becomes clear: it is the potential market they offer the West. Though the phrase had yet to come into common usage, what Judith Hart was propounding was laissez-faire *market forces* rather than development aid. One more quote from the Paper deserves attention.

> In addition, the various untied funds, such as the Arab funds, now present possibilities of triangular deals in which aid finance additional to our own is provided to a recipient from which a UK firm can secure orders. We are already co-financing, with various OPEC funds, projects in the poorer Middle East countries, and we are seeking further triangular deals which present a commercial opportunity to British firms.

What these triangular arrangements did for development was less clear. The paper is worth quoting at length because it is one of the most revealing public documents about British aid concepts to have been published. One may admire the Minister for her frankness: it made plain how aid benefited Britain. Whether it developed Africa or other recipients was another question. The only certain conclusion that can be reached about such an aid programme is that it tied the recipient economies even more closely into those of the donors who, in the main, already controlled their 'development'. At this time the flow of British private capital into Africa was eight or nine times as great as the flow of ODA and Britain was concerned, first and foremost, to safeguard and enhance its investments and markets and that was the principal objective of its aid programme.

French aid to Africa was more concentrated than that of the British and more overtly designed to perpetuate France's grip on the economies of its former colonial empire. Moreover, with the exclusion of Britain from the EEC throughout the de Gaulle years and into the 1970s, France had effectively ensured its control of the European Development Fund (EDF), which became an extra arm of French aid to Africa. Indeed, in the early 1960s the openly expressed French attitude towards Africa was that it represented the natural economic hinterland to Europe. In May 1978 the foreign ministers of 20 African countries met in Paris at a preparatory conference for what was to be a Franco-African summit. The French foreign minister, Louis de Guiringaud, told the conference:

> My country is convinced that peace is indispensable to the development of your continent. But, whatever the consequences, sometimes difficult, France has decided to come to the aid of those who, under trial, ask for its help to preserve their independence and their sovereignty, in conformity with agreements that have been concluded.

Although France had no agreement with Zaïre it had just intervened on behalf of Mobutu in the second Shaba war to preserve that province's minerals for the West. What was fascinating about this particular conference was the fact that Mobutu attended the closing session. Zaïre, increasingly, was coming to be regarded in Paris as a part of Francophone Africa. Even in the late 1970s the official French language in relation to Africa has an unmistakable flavour of colonialism about it. An official information document of the time spells out the justification for France's considerable aid programme:

> The clearest commercial advantage that can be evoked by the industrialized nations is that co-operation is a 'good investment', in that it combats world economic imbalances, and strengthens interdependence to everyone's advantage.

The relationship between France and Africa – as between the West generally and Africa – resolved itself primarily into a question of that continent's mineral and other resources. The same document continues:

> There is perhaps not yet sufficient awareness of the food resources offered by vast areas of the uncultivated lands in tropical Africa and which in the future the world economy will urgently need.
>
> The political and cultural advantages of co-operation must not be neglected, even if here discretion is the wisest course if one does not wish to risk rejection; yes, France's weight in the concert of nations can only be increased by the responsibilities of dialogue offered by her friendly relations and her linguistic and cultural links with this group

(Francophone states) of nations: in no way do these hinder assertion of the African or Malagasy identities.

The neo-colonial arrogance and assumptions of superiority – and still more of control – are hard to escape. This same remarkable information document describes co-operation in far more precise terms (in relation to French activities) than is apparent in comparable British documents:

> ...co-operation covers the special relations that have developed between France and a specific area – coloured pink in our old atlases – consisting of 14 states of Africa and the Indian Ocean that became independent around 1959–60, where French is the official language and where decolonization has taken the shape of co-operation. To these republics are now added Mauritius, Zaïre, Rwanda, Burundi...

This astonishing official statement, understandably, infuriated the Belgians since their three ex-African territories – Zaïre, Rwanda and Burundi – had been incorporated into the French area of 'co-operation' just as though the old 'Scramble for Africa' were still on, while from Britain they had 'co-opted' Mauritius (which the British once took from France). In economic terms Francophone Africa had not achieved independence but 'co-operation'. The general level of French aid to Africa was more concentrated than that of the other major donors and unlike Britain, with many more commitments to Commonwealth countries in both Asia and the Caribbean, the overwhelming bulk of French assistance went to countries on the African continent.

Both Britain and France concentrated their aid upon their ex-colonies. Both used their residual imperial connections as the link between themselves and the economies they would 'assist'. Both regarded private investment as aid – the French more or less absolutely, the British with certain reservations although speaking more and more of private flows as though these were designed first to help development in the recipient country rather than earn profit for the source country.

The other most important European donors at this time were West Germany, Belgium, the Netherlands and the Scandinavian countries. West Germany's basic interest in Africa was one of trade and investment; it was unhampered by any recent residual hangovers of empire. In the 1960s West Germany had decided to concentrate its aid efforts upon Tanganyika, formerly German East Africa. A damaging argument had soon developed, following the revolution in Zanzibar and the subsequent union of the mainland and the island to form the United Republic of Tanzania. At the time Bonn had diplomatic representation in Dar es Salaam while East Germany had a Consulate in Zanzibar. Bonn's heavy-handed attempt to apply the Hallstein Doctrine – that a country that had diplomatic relations with West Germany could not also have them with East Germany – was rejected by President Nyerere with the result that Germany suspended its aid offer. It was an inauspicious beginning to West German aid activities in Africa. Although West German aid became a substantial proportion of the total aid flow to Africa, the country's close relations with South Africa became a bone of contention, especially with Nigeria. In June 1978 the West German Chancellor, Herr Schmidt, made his first official visit to Africa; in Nigeria, a country of West German concentration for trade, he failed to agree with his hosts about curtailing West German trade with South Africa and insisted that trading links with the Republic would continue. In Zambia he was again taken to task for West German opposition to UN sanctions against South Africa and his denials of military support given to Pretoria were not believed. The stands taken by West Germany in Africa at this time were among the most conservative and least conducive to change on the continent.

Belgium concentrated its aid upon its three ex-colonies or mandates – Zaïre, Burundi and Rwanda – and in 1976 its ODA came to 0.51 per cent of GNP, considerably more generous than Britain's contribution. One third of its aid went to two Most Seriously Affected (MSA) countries, Burundi and Rwanda, and 41 per cent to Zaïre, which also attracted the bulk of Belgium's overseas private investment. The heavy concentration of Belgian aid in Zaïre was an indication of its high interest in the economy of that country, an interest that was greatly increased at the time because Mobutu had reversed his nationalization policy.

Dutch aid to Africa grew rapidly during the 1970s from US$73.24 million in 1974 to US$327.97 million in 1977. The Netherlands had no residual colonial connection except its long-standing and deep-seated relationship with South Africa. However, with the Scandinavian countries the Netherlands became one of the first countries to achieve a goal of one per cent of GNP provided in aid. Countries of concentration in Africa were Algeria, Ethiopia, Kenya, Nigeria, Sudan, Tanzania and Zambia. The Swedish aid programme, in both its terms and volume, was more generous than most. Sweden claimed four goals for its aid: a growth of resources; economic and social equalization; economic and political independence; and democratic social development. As one of the richest Western countries with minimal historical involvement in Africa, it was considerably easier for Sweden to produce what might be described as ideologically 'pure' aid than was the case for the other major donors. More important, and much welcomed at the time, was Sweden's aid to the liberation movements in Southern Africa. According to an official document, *Sweden's*

440

Policy for International Development Co-operation (Extracts from the Budget and Finance Bill for Fiscal Year 1978/79):

> Particular attention is given to the situation in southern Africa. Increased support is proposed to the so-called front-line states in the area. Sweden's assistance to the liberation movements, refugees and victims of apartheid in Southern Africa has increased substantially during the last year. Approximately Skr60 million will be used during fiscal year 1977/78 for assistance to the peoples suffering under oppressive military regimes in southern Africa.

Both the stand and the language employed set Sweden apart from the major Western donors. Like Sweden, Norway emerged as one of the most generous aid donors during the 1970s: in 1970 its aid as a percentage of GNP stood at 0.22 per cent but by 1977 had risen to 0.82 per cent. Norway's response to demands for a New International Economic Order was to emphasize the achievement of broad economic and social progress and a reduction of the rich-poor gap. Norway, in terms of its economy, was substantially more generous than Britain at this time and the Norwegian government reacted angrily in 1978 when Judith Hart claimed that Britain was the first donor to give grant aid. This was untrue, but the fact of the Norwegian anger illustrated one of the constant problems accompanying all aid efforts: the nationalistic rivalries between the various donors. Such rivalries often inhibited the best aid processes: in a recipient country, where it might make sense for different donors to concentrate upon different sectors, none is willing to undertake the least glamorous or politically least rewarding sectors; and all compete with one another for prestige activities while, too often, failing to work properly together. Denmark's aid contribution was understandably small in relation to the size of its economy; most of its aid in Africa was concentrated upon Kenya and Tanzania and, to a lesser extent, Botswana, Malawi, Zambia and Zaïre. Aid provided by these smaller European countries – the Netherlands, Sweden, Norway and Denmark – was generally well received in Africa since the donors were not perceived to be acting in a neo-colonial fashion.

During the 1970s the US approach to African affairs was largely strategic: to support the positions of its two major Western allies, Britain and France, on the continent; and to counter Communist influence wherever this became apparent. Thus, the US became deeply involved in the Horn of Africa following the overthrow of Emperor Haile Selassie in 1974 when Ethiopia's military Dergue turned to Moscow for support in its wars against Somalia in the east and secessionist Eritrea in the north; and it also became increasingly involved in

Southern Africa when the Secretary of State, Henry Kissinger, began what was to turn into a long lasting US policy of support for UNITA in opposition to the Marxist MPLA government in Angola. In 1976 Kissinger also attempted to broker a peace initiative in Rhodesia with the principal object of preventing a Marxist form of government coming to power there. In two cases, Tanzania and Botswana, the United States was chiefly concerned to appear to be doing something to counter the more spectacular activity of the Chinese construction of the TANZAM railway. It therefore undertook the upgrading of a stretch of road from Dar es Salam to Morogoro and, according to the rumour current in Dar es Salaam at the time, the United States Agency for International Development (USAID) deliberately worked slowly since they were determined to maintain a presence in the country as long as the Chinese were there. More important was USAID's selection as an aid project of the so-called BOTZAM road in Botswana (it was chosen from a long list of possible projects on which it was placed sixteenth) in order to demonstrate that the United States could also build a 'Uhuru' highway.

Africa as a source of minerals was also becoming more important to the United States as the Russian African specialist, L. Valentin, wrote in *Pravda*:

> In US imports, the share of strategic raw materials imported from Africa amounts to 100 per cent of industrial diamonds, 58 per cent of the uranium, 44 per cent of the manganese, which is used in the steel smelting industry, 36 per cent of the cobalt, essential for aircraft engines and high strength alloys, 33 per cent of its oil and 23 per cent of its chromium, used in the manufacture of armour, aircraft engines and gun barrels.[2]

Pravda emphasized the military aspect of the US pursuit of raw materials; but growing dependence on African minerals was a key to American policy in Africa, especially in relation to a country such as Zaïre. Despite these strategic considerations, and the rather artificial black American-African relationship that grew up at this time, there was a general US lack of interest in Africa which was amply testified to in mid-1978 when Senator George McGovern said: 'Africa is not fundamental to American interests, and we cannot do much about it anyway.' The United States was generally much more ruthless than other donors in giving or withholding aid according to the level of support it received, for example in the United Nations, from its aid recipients. Small nations that opposed the American position in the United Nations over Zionism or Korea found their aid agreements running into trouble. These might be delayed or cancelled and, as one US official put it: 'When our Ambassador comes to them and complains about their votes in the UN, and a few weeks later an aid transaction falls through, they get the message.'

Two other substantial donors were Canada and Japan. Like most other Western donors, Canada began to put greater emphasis upon assistance to the poorest, and in Africa concentrated upon rural development and food production. Uniquely among Western donors, Canada was bilingual in English and French and made a point of providing aid equally to Anglophone and Francophone African countries. During this decade Canada enjoyed a high reputation as an aid donor, not least because it was not regarded as a threat and in any event its aid by the mid-1970s had only reached a figure of just over US$100 million a year. Japan was principally interested in obtaining a range of African minerals. Japan's aid programme in Africa began slowly but was stepped up dramatically in 1977, by which year Algeria, Morocco, Egypt, Nigeria, Niger, Gabon, Ethiopia, Kenya, Tanzania, Zambia and Madagascar were all substantial recipients of Japanese aid. By the end of the decade Japan had become a major donor in Africa, on a par with Britain and France; its concern was to find new sources of raw materials for its huge industrial expansion and new markets for its exports.

The growing emphasis placed upon aid to the poorest by Western donors through the decade was in response to the demands for a New International Economic Order. None of the Western donors was interested in changing the existing order – the 16 DAC countries had all voted against the NIEO or abstained in the United Nations General Assembly – but they did feel the political necessity of doing something. An increase in aid, with the emphasis upon the poorest people and countries, was part of their response.

One other major non-Communist source of aid at this time came from the oil states and despite African frustration at what they regarded as a slow start[3], aid disbursements from the oil-rich states were to reach a level of five per cent of GNP in the second half of the 1970s as opposed to the much lower average of 0.5 per cent for the DAC countries. There was, however, a great imbalance in Arab aid disbursements, with Arab states such as Egypt and Sudan being favoured first before non-Arab, non-Islamic states elsewhere in Africa. Even so, by the late 1970s something like 10 per cent of aid to Africa from all sources was then coming from the Arab world.

COMMUNIST AID

Both the Soviet Union and China were already significant aid donors in Africa when the 1970s began and both were concerned with the Cold War dimensions of their aid. Speaking of Soviet aid to Africa, Leonard Brezhnev said that 'the Soviet Union fully supports the legitimate aspirations of young states, their determination to put an end to all imperialist exploitation, and to take full charge of their own national wealth'. And, according to *Polar Star*, it was the Soviet view that the best way for such states to build up a powerful and independent economy lay through the development of their own industry: 'Assistance in the formation and development of this is the main direction of the Soviet Union's co-operation with new African states.'[4] The Soviet Union had agreements for economic and technical co-operation with more than 30 African states. The Russians insisted that their credits had no political, economic or other strings attached to them and, to quote Brezhnev again, 'the Soviet Union does not look for advantages, does not hunt for concessions, does not seek political domination, and is not after military bases'. Had all this been true the Soviet aid performance would have been unique. A statement of Soviet aid principles in the June 1978 issue of *Polar Star* highlighted the most important aspect of Soviet assistance, which was mutual advantage:

> Mutual advantage is an important principle of Soviet economic co-operation with African countries. On the one hand, developing states consolidate their economies with Soviet assistance, and, on the other hand, the USSR receives, as payment for its credits, the commodities necessary for its own economy: minerals, tropical timber, coffee, cocoa, etc. Importantly, in addition to traditional African exports, the Soviet Union is getting increasingly more industrial products from the enterprises built with Soviet technical assistance.

The aim of Soviet aid, which was almost entirely bilateral, was to contribute to a division of labour between the USSR and recipients, so that the former obtained raw materials and light manufactured goods in return for heavy industrial goods. This Soviet approach 'raises the question whether economic co-operation with the Soviet Union implies a real alternative for the developing countries to the economic co-operation with the Western capitalist countries'.[5] Although it was probably the case that Soviet aid did promote a different development pattern to that of aid from the West, the amount on offer was insufficient to make a serious difference. The Soviet Union was mainly concerned to import from Africa such commodities as long-staple cotton, fruit and edible oils, coffee, cocoa and raw hides. As with Western donors, Soviet aid – apart from contributions to multilateral organizations such as the World Bank to which it did not belong – divided into similar categories as Western aid: grants, loans with a considerable grant element, technical assistance and trade credits. Most Soviet aid was capital intensive and led to a considerable demand subsequently for spare parts and maintenance. By the mid-1970s Africa had built more than 350 power projects in collaboration with socialist countries. The main countries of concentration for Soviet aid were Algeria, Nigeria, Ethiopia, Congo, Somalia and Guinea.

China's first real economic impact on Africa came in 1964 when Chou En-lai visited Africa and in Mali enunciated the eight principles of Chinese aid. Between 1954 and 1971 Chinese credits and grants amounted to US$1.112 billion although the figure is misleading since a considerable proportion of the sum represents credits that were never taken up. Even so, the figure represents just over half of all Chinese aid for the period. Up to 1972 the main beneficiaries of China's aid were Mali, Egypt, Sudan, Guinea and Algeria but from that date China expanded its activities to include Togo, Rwanda, Burundi, Ghana, Cameroon and Zaïre. In 1973 it expanded its activities again into Chad, Senegal and Upper Volta, and that year Chinese commitments south of the Sahara made it the chief Communist donor in the region. Once African countries had begun to establish diplomatic relations with China in the early 1970s, the Chinese response was to offer aid. There was no obvious pattern to Chinese aid although the guiding principle at this time was the desire to become a leader of the Third World. The exception was the TANZAM railway. China began the construction of this 1,100-mile rail line in 1970, the year the Russian-built Aswan High Dam in Egypt was completed, and it became the largest single aid project under construction on the continent. It showed China in a favourable light, both with regard to its Communist rival, the Soviet Union, and in relation to the principal Western donors. The sheer size of the TANZAM project (see below, chapter 18) placed China in the forefront of aid donors in Africa and, for a time, persuaded African leaders that there was a viable alternative to Western aid.

By the 1970s the phrase 'trade not aid' had become a constant in discussions about development and in 1962 the UN General Assembly had recognized trade as 'the chief engine of development'. Unfortunately, for Africa, the weakness of its trading position lay in the fact that 70 per cent of its revenues came from the export of primary products and that the control of prices for these products was not in the Africa producer states' hands. This fact made the deliberations of such bodies as UNCTAD of crucial importance to the continent as a whole. The Third United Nations Conference on Trade and Development (UNCTAD III) was held in Santiago, Chile, from 13 April to 19 May 1972. It represented a new global effort to change the existing pattern of world trade in order to assist developing countries and initiate reforms in the international monetary system. The UN had declared the 1970s the Second Development Decade and set a target of boosting the growth of developing countries by at least 6 per cent a year and per capita income by 3.5 per cent. The Secretary-General of UNCTAD, Manuel Perez Guerrero, pointed out that the capital resources transferred by the developed countries as a group to the developing countries were lower as a proportion of GNP in 1970 than they had been in 1960. He said that aid should be defined to include only those flows which are 'concessional' in nature and whose primary purpose is development; and that an equitable sharing of aid obligation required that all developed countries supplied at least a minimum amount of 'official development assistance'. Of the 25 countries nominated as the least developed, 16 were in Africa: Botswana, Burundi, Chad, Dahomey, Ethiopia, Guinea, Lesotho, Malawi, Mali, Niger, Rwanda, Somalia, Sudan, Tanzania, Uganda and Upper Volta.[6]

At a meeting in the Philippines in preparation for UNCTAD IV in 1976, the Manila Declaration was issued calling for measures to be taken by the developed countries and international organizations, such as the World Bank, to resolve and alleviate 'the critical debt problem of developing countries'. However, no agreement was reached on the question of debts at the UNCTAD IV meeting held in Nairobi, although subsequently a number of countries, led by Canada, unilaterally cancelled ODA debts owed by the least developed countries. That year 20 low-income African countries were in debt to the extent of US$6,908 million and of those six owed debts in excess of 35 per cent of their GNPs. Over these years a steady proliferation of organizations concerned with aid and development made their appearance on the international stage and an eloquently dry comment on this process of growth was made in the 1978 Report of the Executive Secretary of the Economic Commission for Africa (ECA), Adebayo Adedeji:

> The year 1978 did not differ in terms of conventional measurements from 1977 or the years before that. Demand and production in advanced countries… continued to affect African exports unfavourably, with the exception of cocoa, coffee, timber, uranium and bauxite. Inflation continued. Debt accumulation continued too. So did imports of food, all with consequent effects on growth rates…

In other words, despite (or because of) all the aid efforts of all the donors, both bilateral and multilateral, the position of the recipients remained as bad and as dependent as ever. The financial operations in Africa of the World Bank and its affiliates, the IMF and the private banks, were very substantial and money was available – at a price – for development purposes. Personnel were also available, on terms of one kind or another, and the UNDP, for example, was heavily engaged in Africa. Yet, despite the size of aid inputs and statistics that revealed marginal increases in growth, higher literacy rates or some other 'development' improvement, developing countries still required massive assistance while, at the same time, the gap between them and the advanced economies grew larger and self-reliance eluded them.

At the end of February 1979, representatives of the Third World met in Arusha in preparation for UNCTAD V, which was scheduled for the following May in Manila. The meeting brought out the weakness of Third World countries. President Nyerere called upon the Third World to forget its differences and speak with one voice in its negotiations with the developed world:

> The truth is that we need power to negotiate, just as we need power to go on strike. So far we have been negotiating as noisy and importunate supplicants. We need to negotiate from a position of steadily increasing power.

It was one thing to pinpoint the weakness of the Third World negotiating position, yet at the end of the decade no African state was on record as saying that it did not want aid or could dispense with it; in most cases it was simply a question of how much they could obtain.

Despite the apparent acceptance by African governments that aid should be an almost indefinite ongoing process, there was much unease among intellectuals at this growing dependence upon donors whose aid was accompanied by prescriptions about the way recipients should tackle their development. By the end of the decade it had become clear that the much-vaunted concept of a New International Economic Order was a dead issue. The West had buried it: first, by the endless discussions held in Paris under CIEC auspices masterminded by Henry Kissinger; and second by increased offers of aid according to the existing pattern. The final *coup de grâce* would be delivered in 1980 with the publication of the Brandt Report.

AFRICA 2000

Meanwhile, at the invitation of the Secretary-General of the Organisation of African Unity, a Symposium on the future development prospects of Africa towards the year 2000 was held in Monrovia (Liberia) from 12 to 16 February 1979. The Symposium was made up of 40 experts from various parts of Africa, drawn from the fields of economics, science, labour, health, diplomacy and research. Their report[7], which was available at the Monrovia OAU Summit that July, became the starting point for the Lagos Plan of Action (see below). First, 20 years after the *annus mirabilis* of independence, the report listed the abysmal state of the economy and development of the continent as a whole. As at the end of the 1970s, Africa's gross national product accounted for only 2.7 per cent of the world product; at US$365 Africa had the lowest average annual per capita income in the world, while its infant mortality rate, at 137 per 1,000, was the world's highest. Driven by an urban-oriented development policy, under-employment and unemployment then affected 45 per cent of the active population. While there was one doctor for every 672 inhabitants of the urban areas, there was only one for every 26,000 inhabitants of the rural areas. Worse still,

> Africa is excessively dependent on other countries, even for food. Trade and commercial structures are still almost invariably in a North-South direction, a legacy from the past which fosters the laws of unequal exchange and its consequences: deteriorating terms of trade, outward-oriented production, little domestic processing of raw materials, and so on.

The Symposium participants emphasized that underdevelopment was not a natural state but that developing countries were the victims of a world economic system that was designed to benefit the more powerful nations. In addition, and more important perhaps, the developing countries were 'the victims of misconceptions and erroneous strategies that have steered them towards ill-suited models of development that are geared neither to human needs nor to a basically endogenous development'. In the light of these considerations, the approach of the Symposium was to persuade Africa to adopt a radical change of attitude. This meant that 'the areas which depend on domestic policies, structural changes and systems of values must be given priority attention so that a new human-being-oriented African development policy can evolve in which the continent can find its own identity and status instead of having them imposed on it'. The development approach envisaged by the Symposium entailed a number of breaks with the past. These included: a break with a number of concepts and habits, starting with excessive mimicry in every field; a break with excessive accumulation of material and financial possessions and with the persistent confusion of growth with development; and a break with the evil of deceitful slogans and paper-thin achievements in favour of a courageous attempt to tackle the embarrassing facts of life so as to be able to start today to prepare the future.

The Symposium placed great emphasis upon science and technology and argued that until 'vigorous autonomous research' geared to Africa's most pressing needs was carried out on the continent, Africa would continue to be at the mercy of the kind of dependence inseparable from 'transfer of technology'. Then the Symposium tackled the question of freedom and justice: 'Only yesterday, the birth of a State that respected basic freedoms was one of the most important demands in the struggle for independence. Has this erstwhile dream now turned into a nightmare?' Africa had to embark upon a strategy that gave it complete control over its own needs. Comparing the achievements of the United States, the Soviet Union, China and the European Common Market, the Symposium condemned the narrow nationalisms of individual African countries and insisted that African unity was a necessity. It called for three specific measures: the creation of an African common market; the free movement of persons and goods on the African continent and the abolition of visas among African countries; and the awakening of African public opinion to the concept of Unity. On the subject of science and technology the Symposium suggested:

> The objective for the year 2000 is to rid the continent of the general approach that currently prevails and which accepts without question the concept and practice of 'transfer of technology' – an expression which the Symposium suggests should be stricken from the international vocabulary.

There were many specific recommendations for action and, in relation to food security, for example, the Symposium argued: 'The Symposium proposed that the degree of a country's dependence for its food imports should henceforth be considered as one of the most significant indicators of its level of development.' Members of the Symposium highlighted the statistics of population increase, infant mortality, education, the movement to the urban centres, decline in the growth of agriculture during the 1970s, in fact all the problems that were regularly rehearsed at donor-recipient or other meetings to consider development on the continent. Development objectives for the year 2000 were summed up as follows:

1 To attain a high degree of self-sufficiency.
2 To democratize national development in order to enjoy the fruits of our efforts more fully and more equitably.
3 To increase and consolidate African solidarity.
4 To carry more weight in world affairs.

The Symposium was important because it brought together eminent Africans other than politicians who were remarkably impartial in their examination of African shortcomings and saw only too clearly the linkage between economic development targets and the need for open politics: that is, democracy, widespread literacy and mass involvement in the development process. In one of its most telling phrases the report called upon African countries to 'break with excessive mimicry in every field'. The Symposium showed a realistic understanding of the continent's problems. The main argument was that any real economic advance for the developing countries of Africa must arise out of their own efforts and would not be achieved through aid or dependence upon outside help.

The Symposium's report became the basis for OAU economic discussions, with the result that in April 1980 an extraordinary summit conference of the heads of state and government of the OAU met in Lagos, Nigeria, and adopted what came to be called the Lagos Plan of Action for the development of Africa up to 2000. The plan called for collective self-reliance and the gradual fusing of national economic policies into regional ones, with the eventual aim of creating an African economic community. Targets were set for food self-sufficiency and industrialization. The Plan of Action was a basic economic blueprint for a move towards pan-Africanism, and was very much in the tradition that had led to the creation of the OAU in 1963. Fundamentally, the high economic ideals and goals set out in the Lagos Plan of Action were recognition of the continent's economic weaknesses and the fact that each country was too small and weak to succeed economically on its own.

THE BRANDT REPORT

In the aftermath of the mid-1970s oil crisis and demands for a New International Economic Order the rich nations of the North, which had no intention of facilitating any basic changes in the world economic system, nonetheless realized that some real concessions – or what passed for concessions – had to be made to the poor countries of the South. The Brandt Report – *North-South: A Programme for Survival* (The Report of the Independent Commission on International Development Issues under the Chairmanship of Willy Brandt) – was the answer. Ten years earlier, another former head of government of a rich country, on that occasion Lester Pearson of Canada, had given his name to a report on the relations between rich and poor; briefly, this had excited hopes that a new relationship between rich and poor could be inaugurated before it languished, largely ignored, on library shelves. Now a former West German Chancellor presided over a similar Commission; and the Brandt Report, published in 1980, was accorded a great deal of publicity. As Willy Brandt said in his introduction: 'Mankind has never before had such ample technical and financial resources for coping with hunger and poverty. The immense task can be tackled once the necessary collective will is mobilized.' The Report contained excellent vignettes of how money used for military purposes could be translated into development achievements and these – for example, the price of one jet fighter (US$20 million) could establish 40,000 village pharmacies – provided splendid quotes for campaigners for change. The Report was thorough and enumerated in depth the areas that required attention: food security, commodity trade and development, aid, appropriate technology, in fact all the headings that made up the development debate. But the Report, despite the North-South composition of its committee, may be seen as the North's answer to demands for an NIEO. The Report's approach is to improve existing structures rather than suggest new ones. A key chapter is headed 'Mutual Interests' and the chapter's subheadings read as follows:

An opportunity for partnership
Understanding interdependence
The transmission of growth
The potential effects of 'massive transfers'
Expanding world trade and markets
Access to markets
Protectionism hurts
Earning more from commodities
Energy, environment, food
Transnational corporations
The financial and monetary systems
Towards a genuine society of nations
Reforms are interconnected
The moral imperatives

On reading such a list the reader could be forgiven for imagining that an NIEO was in fact being proposed. On analysis, however, these add up to a plea for reforms in the existing order, not for an NIEO. One sentence from the Brandt Report reads: 'World Society now recognizes more clearly than ever before its mutual needs; it must accept a shared responsibility for meeting them.' The sentiment may have been well meaning; the cruel events of the 1980s and the continuing growth of the gap between rich and poor turned such an optimistic statement into downright wishful thinking. Each chapter in the Brandt Report ended with a set of recommendations while at the end *An Emergency Programme: 1980–85* set forth four principal elements for action:

1 A large-scale transfer of resources to developing countries.
2 An international energy strategy.
3 A global food programme.
4 A start on some major reforms in the international economic system.

Such targets looked well. What the Report did not do was explain how these targets were to be met, who would provide the means and what kinds of pressure would be exerted upon the rich nations in order to make them share a substantial proportion of their wealth and know-how with the poor. Like its predecessor, the Brandt Report was soon largely ignored.

Immediately, however, the World Bank issued a report, *Accelerated Development in Sub-Saharan Africa: An Agenda for Action* (1981), which was a response both to the Lagos Plan of Action and to the various calls to action that had resulted in the Brandt Report. The Report highlighted the severity and complexity of the problems facing many of the countries of sub-Saharan Africa and accepted the long-term objectives of the Lagos Plan of Action. The Report, like most World Bank publications, presented a meticulous analysis of the problems faced by most African countries and then outlined a series of short-term measures to be backed by the donor community to tackle immediate problems. There was nothing essentially new or original about the Bank's remedies: the earlier chapters in the report discuss measures for accelerating economic growth, always within the context of a Western view of the world economy. Then the Report turns to longer-term issues and begins with population growth and what to do about it; urban growth; resource planning, which covers such subjects as soil conservation, reforestation and fuelwood; and finally, regionalism. There is something oppressively *de haut en bas* about World Bank Reports as, didactically, they tell their readers what they know already. Thus, on the subject of regionalism:

> Regional economic co-operation then, while essential in loosening long-term development constraints facing many African states, will not come easily. It will require changes of great substance, including strengthening of transport links, reduction of monetary and commercial policies that inhibit and distort intraregional trade, promotion of joint projects in industry, education, and research, and regional institutions with adequate staff and budgets that could become major instruments of co-operation and integration.[8]

Then, the final chapter of the Report calls for increased aid to Africa. The *World Development Report 1981* projected a minimal per capita income growth for sub-Saharan Africa from 1980 to 1990 of only 0.1 per cent and there follow suggestions of donor support for programmes of policy reform, foreshadowing one of the main lines that the World Bank would follow in relation to Africa over the next 20 years. The problem inherent in such a World Bank report was the assumption that a non-African institution in Washington could prescribe answers for African development. The prescriptions, as we shall see through the 1980s and 1990s, were essentially Western responses to situations that the West sometimes did not understand and, when it did, determined to manipulate to its own advantage. (The World Bank, despite the composition of its staff and the participation in it as shareholders of the great majority of countries, is overwhelmingly Western oriented in its approach to economic problems and structures.) Finally, though the Report claimed to accept the Lagos Plan of Action as its starting point, it clearly did not accept the far more radical suggestion of *Africa 2000* that there should be a break with the past 'starting with excessive mimicry in every field'. Perhaps, the real tragedy for Africa at this point was that a majority of its political leaders who endorsed the Lagos Plan of Action did not accept the full implications of *Africa 2000* either.

Strategic Highways

The vast size of Africa, 11.5 million square miles, the sparse populations and huge desert or arid regions that are virtually empty of people, the colonial pattern of development that had failed to create an *African* network of highways – whether road, rail or air – to connect the different territories with each other meant that at independence Africa's general problems of development were compounded by the poor communications between countries, and sometimes the virtual absence of any communications at all. This fact made the proclaimed goal of African unity all the harder to achieve. There were no direct transcontinental routes at independence, neither road, rail or air. New highways, or the upgrading and extension of existing ones, therefore, became a priority of the 1960s and 1970s. The concept of strategic highways changes little: they generate development along their paths; they link regions to encourage economic and political contacts; they enable exchanges to take place that formerly were not possible and so bring into closer unity communities or states where earlier interchanges had been limited; and most important of all, they provide routes through neighbouring territories to link landlocked countries with seaports. The 1970s witnessed a proliferation of highways in Africa: some were simply intended to increase development but others, in the south of the continent, were inextricably linked with the needs of landlocked countries, and most especially Zambia, to free themselves from total dependence upon trade routes through the White South.

The continent's transport problems were well illustrated by Zaïre (as it was in the 1970s). The Shaba Province (the former Katanga), for all practical purposes, can be treated as a landlocked country so that transporting its minerals to the sea for export is a major operation. The shortest route to the Atlantic was the 1,000-mile Benguela Railway across the central highlands of Angola which, from the mid-1970s, was closed as a result of the civil war in that country. Secondly, it was possible if political conditions permitted to export Shaba's bulk copper southwards through Zambia, Rhodesia and Mozambique to Beira on the Indian

Ocean. Thirdly, the minerals could have been transported to the Atlantic entirely through Zaïre itself. Zaïre has only two ocean-river ports near the mouth of the Congo River, Matadi and Boma. But between the mouth of the river and Lubumbashi in the heart of the Shaba mining region five trans-shipments between rail and river were needed. There are some 2,966 miles of rail linking the various sections of the river where transport was possible and the main function of the railways was to link the navigable stretches of the huge river network. The Kinshasa–Matadi line was vital, bypassing the early falls and rapids on the river and linking Kinshasa directly to the seaport of Matadi. This 277-mile stretch of rail handled the country's highest tonnage of freight. The main railway system serving Shaba had 1,587 miles of 3 ft 6 in. gauge track that included the various connections between stretches of navigable river. This route, serving the mineral-rich Shaba region, was far less satisfactory and took far longer than did the most direct Benguela railway to the Lobito outlet on the Atlantic Ocean. The whole region, however, was deeply troubled throughout the 1970s.

LANDLOCKED COUNTRIES

Fourteen of the world's landlocked countries were in Africa at this time although when Eritrea became independent in 1993 it cut off Ethiopia's direct links to the Red Sea to turn it into the fifteenth landlocked country on the continent. Five of Africa's landlocked states are in the Sahel region; these, from west to east, are Mali, Upper Volta (Burkina Faso), Niger, Chad and Central African Republic; three are in East Africa – Burundi, Rwanda and Uganda; while the remaining six are in Central and Southern Africa – Zambia, Zimbabwe and Malawi, the members of the former Central African Federation that came to an end in 1963; and Botswana, Lesotho and Swaziland, the former High Commission Territories that achieved precarious independence in the white-dominated South during the latter half of the 1960s. Malawi illustrated perfectly the problems that face even well-endowed countries that are landlocked. Situated in south-central Africa, Malawi has one major mineral resource, bauxite, but this is locked in the great mountain massif of Mulanje in the far south of the country. There is plenty of bauxite worldwide but accessibility is everything. Guinea on the West African coast has large bauxite deposits, as has Jamaica in the Caribbean, and both countries export it. Malawi, whose easiest routes to the sea lay through Mozambique, was seen as too remote as a source of this mineral while other sources with easy access to the sea were available. Thus one of Africa's poorest countries was unable to market its only major mineral resource.

In any case, while the countries of Southern Africa faced the normal difficulties associated with being landlocked, these were greatly exacerbated by the racial confrontations and developing liberation wars that characterized the region throughout the 1970s, especially as South Africa and Rhodesia controlled, and had determined to continue controlling, the most accessible routes to the sea. Much of the history of the landlocked territories of Southern Africa, both as colonies and subsequently, has been concerned with finding the most economical transit routes to the sea for their products and, in times of turmoil, alternative routes.

Central African Republic, as the name implies, is near enough to being the geographic centre of the continent. It has to reckon on a transit time of two months for bulk goods: these travel from Bangui, the capital, down the Ubangui River to its confluence with the Congo, then down to Kinshasa where they may either remain on the river until Boma, alternating between river and rail, and only at Boma will they be transshipped to ocean-going ships for onward passage to Europe. Alternately, such goods can be transshipped at Kinshasa to travel by rail to Pointe Noire in the Republic of Congo for transshipment to ocean-going vessels. The three giant landlocked Sahel countries – Mali, Niger and Chad – suffer from lack of development as a consequence of their remoteness, huge size and sparse populations, and the fact that they do not possess sufficiently abundant or valuable resources to attract the finances required to construct modern highways, whether road or rail. Mali and Niger both have direct access to the River Niger and a route to the sea through Nigeria but here again progress can be slow since large river vessels cannot use the river during the dry season when the waters are low. During the 1960s and 1970s when France intervened in the civil war in Chad the best route of access was through Central African Republic.

The three landlocked countries of East Africa – Uganda, Burundi and Rwanda – depend upon routes through Kenya to Mombasa or, in the case of Burundi, through Tanzania to Dar es Salaam as well. Transit countries, such as Kenya, welcome their roles since they earn substantial fees from handling the traffic of their neighbours, while under international law they are obliged to provide two-way access for neighbouring landlocked states. In Southern Africa much of the post-independence history of Malawi and Zambia, and of Rhodesia during the UDI years, was taken up with the problem of access to the sea and such problems were greatly complicated by the politics of the region: the opposition of the front-line states to apartheid in South Africa meant they needed to find routes that did not pass through the Republic. This persuaded Zambia to go ahead with the construction of the TANZAM Railway. On the other hand, South Africa exerted a number of pressures upon its landlocked neighbours to the north to compel them to use trade routes that passed through its territory. South Africa did not wish to lose their valuable transit fees; furthermore, as long as they had to use routes through South Africa it would be that much easier for Pretoria to exert upon them political pressures to damp down their ideological opposition to its apartheid policies. Finally, Lesotho is the only country within a country in the world and, as such, is entirely at the mercy of South Africa.

THE TRANS-AFRICAN HIGHWAY

At the beginning of the 1970s considerable attention was focused upon the possibility of constructing a trans-African highway that would link Mombasa on Kenya's Indian Ocean coast to Lagos on Nigeria's Atlantic coast. The projected highway would pass through Kenya, Uganda, Zaïre, Central African Republic, Cameroon and Nigeria. It was assumed, though with little supporting data, that linking oil-rich Nigeria with its booming economy and huge population with Kenya, the economic hub of the East African Common Market, would lead to a substantial increase in cross-continental traffic that would benefit the countries lying between the two poles of the highway. In 1969 Japan expressed an interest in helping construct such a highway but since at the time Japan's total aid to Africa only amounted to US$1.1 million the African reaction to this offer was one of suspicion as to that country's intentions. The first difficulty confronting the highway enthusiasts was the fact that the countries though which it was to pass had little in common with each other. The two pole countries, Kenya and Nigeria, were both members of Anglophone Africa though with very different histories. Kenya, moreover, was to be sufficiently engrossed with the problems facing the East African Community throughout the 1970s, especially with the assumption of power in Uganda of Idi Amin, to have much interest in forwarding a highway whose first stretch outside Kenya would come under Ugandan control. The huge northern region of Zaïre through which nearly 1,000 miles of the highway would have to pass was sparsely populated and, for political reasons, neglected by the Mobutu government, which was not anxious to see it become economically strong. Central African Republic and Cameroon were Francophone countries and the regions through which the highway would pass were extremely remote and underdeveloped. Despite the planners, led by the Ghanaian Robert Gardiner who was the Executive Secretary of the Economic Commission for Africa (ECA), the difficulties appeared greater than the attractions. Uganda under Amin could not be relied upon, though that was not at once apparent; Central African Republic was so poor that though it would benefit from the highway, its own contribution in trade movements was likely to be minimal. Mobutu at best was lukewarm towards the idea of such a highway as he saw it detaching the northern region from Kinshasa's control.

Nonetheless, at a time when development was at the forefront of African thinking, the formal idea of such a highway was seized upon by the ECA after a Japanese economic mission to Africa had formulated the idea, which was conveyed to the Kenya government in 1970 by the Japanese ambassador.[1] Japanese enthusiasm to build the highway – there was an active lobby in support of the idea in Japan, Mitsubishi was prepared to construct the road and the Japanese government offered substantial aid for the project – led to the African suspicions of Japanese intentions, especially as up to that time it had shown little or no interest in African affairs. For Japan, however, the trans-African highway meant increased influence and trade on a continent where it sought ever greater quantities of raw materials for its expanding industries. Nonetheless, the proposal to construct a trans-African highway was formally tabled in 1971 by the Executive Committee of the ECA on behalf of the six countries. Robert Gardiner was an enthusiast for the idea and on 1 July 1971 he set up a Trans-African Highway Bureau. The highway was to be 4,400 miles in length and would form part of the existing road network of the six countries through which it passed. On 9 October 1971 nine industrial countries offered help and on 25 October Britain's Overseas Development Administration (ODA) put out a press release to announce that a contract for a pre-feasibility study had been awarded to the London-based firm T. P. O'Sullivan and Partners. Progress thereafter was very slow and little had been achieved by 1974 although Gardiner had hoped to have the road completed by 1976. At that stage it was hoped it might be completed by 1978. The final proposal was for a 4,000-mile highway: Kenya 570 miles, Uganda 410, Zaïre 980, Central African Republic 810, Cameroon 680 and Nigeria 550. The least-developed, most inaccessible stretches would be those passing through Zaïre, Central African Republic and Cameroon. Costs were estimated at between £200 million and £300 million and these had to be scaled down in the light of the aid offers that were forthcoming. The OAU accused the World Bank of a 'negative attitude' and urged it to make a contribution towards the costs while also telling the six countries the road would pass through 'to mobilize all their human and material resources for the execution of the project'.[2]

Unlike the TANZAM Railway, which the West did not wish to promote, the trans-African highway was not controversial from the viewpoint of Western interests and it might well pass through regions where new mineral deposits were to be found. But the problems were formidable. There seemed little prospect that the most economically backward regions of Central African Republic and Zaïre would change and the argument that the road would lead to development in these regions appeared to be based less on evidence than hope. No studies had been carried out to show whether there would be an increased demand in either Central African Republic or Zaïre for goods from Kenya or Nigeria once the road came into operation. Moreover, the political differences between the six countries led inevitably to a consideration of political practicalities: would a quarrel between two of the countries lead to a border closure that would disrupt use of the highway by the others? As Robert Gardiner had said in the early planning stage: 'When you have a road crossing different countries, there may be periods of misunderstanding, and a decision not to allow vehicles to pass from one of the member states.'[3] On the other hand, overcoming political differences was a justification for the highway, which would lead to greater trade, greater movement of people leading to greater unity and understanding; more economic growth along the length of the road; and a greater sense of African strength and oneness. The enthusiasts for the highway were defeated. In 1976 stretches of the existing highways in Zaïre and Cameroon registered an average of only one vehicle in 24 hours and elsewhere of one to 10 vehicles. At the Lagos end 10,000 vehicles a day used the road and at the Mombasa end 6,000, but in between the fall-off in use was huge. By the mid-1970s the project was being abandoned since none of the six countries was sufficiently interested to give the highway the necessary priority. By that time Nigeria was busy promoting the Economic Community of West African States (ECOWAS) and was more interested in the Trans-Sahara Highway. Kenya was coming to terms with the collapse of the East African Common Market; Mobutu was uninterested in developing northern Zaïre; while both Central African Republic and Cameroon needed the trans-African highway to demonstrate its worth before they would take action to promote it. Despite the enthusiasm of its original promoters and the belief that such a highway would promote economic growth, the road was not seen as essential by any of the six countries and lacked the urgency that led to the construction of the TANZAM Railway which was completed in 1976. In the end the dream of a trans-African highway collapsed in the face of political realities.

THE ZAMBEZI FRONTIER

By the 1970s the Zambezi River had become the front line, dividing independent black Africa to the north from white-controlled Southern Africa. Zambia at this time was the most exposed of the front-line states and Kaunda's opposition to UDI in Rhodesia and apartheid in South Africa meant that his country's traditional transit routes southwards were always at risk. Malawi under Hastings Banda had chosen a different path and come to an accommodation with the white South. Tanzania's President Julius Nyerere was the chairman of the front-line states and together with Kaunda spearheaded African opposition to white rule in the South. In 1970 in the two Portuguese territories of Angola and Mozambique the African guerrilla movements were engaged in liberation wars against the Portuguese though this would change dramatically halfway through the decade, following the 25 April Revolution in Lisbon. South of the Zambezi, Rhodesia under Ian Smith would soon be engaged in a full-scale guerrilla war against ZANU forces in the north-east of the country and ZAPU forces in the west and would be obliged to call for help from South Africa. There were four captive territories south of the Zambezi: Namibia which, according to the United Nations, was illegally occupied by South Africa; and the three High Commission Territories of Botswana, Lesotho and Swaziland that were constantly subjected to pressures from Pretoria. South Africa itself was the regional superpower whose white rulers were determined to hold the line against African nationalism. The railway system for the whole region had been developed at the end of the nineteenth century and was designed to bring the countries to the north of South Africa into its economic and political orbit so that a captive state like Botswana that was totally opposed to apartheid, nonetheless, was dependent upon trade routes through the Republic, while Zambia to the north of the Zambezi found that its transit routes all went south.

Under the terms of the Anglo-German Treaty of 1890 Britain had ceded to Germany a slice of northern Bechuanaland (Botswana) to become part of Germany's colony of South West Africa and this was named the Caprivi Strip after the German Chancellor Count Caprivi. The Germans wanted access to the Zambezi under the mistaken notion that this would give them a route to the Indian Ocean. Earlier, in the prelude to the Scramble for Africa, David Livingstone on his second great expedition to Africa had hoped to penetrate deep into the interior up the Zambezi from its mouth on the Indian Ocean but was stopped by the Cabora Bassa gorge and so turned northwards up the Shire River into Nyasaland (later Malawi). These early European expectations of using the Zambezi as a major highway had to be abandoned. Instead, it became a major source of power for Zambia, Rhodesia and Mozambique as the Victoria Falls, Kariba and Cabora Bassa were developed, and a dividing line between the independent black North and white-controlled South from the early 1960s onwards. By the 1970s it was heavily patrolled on the Rhodesian side to prevent incursions by the various Rhodesian, Namibian and South African guerrilla groups based in Zambia and witnessed an increasing number of military incidents.

The River rises in the north-eastern highlands of Angola and sweeps in a great arc into western Zambia, passing through Barotseland before forming the boundary between Zambia and the Caprivi Strip for 100 miles. Kazungula, on the Zambian side of the river, marks the meeting point of the Caprivi Strip, Zambia, Rhodesia (Zimbabwe) and Botswana – the only point in the world at which four countries meet – where there was a ferry linking Botswana to Zambia and the independent black north. Thereafter, the river formed the frontier between Zambia and Rhodesia: at the Victoria Falls a bridge carries the Zambian railway across into Rhodesia and points south; further east the Kariba Dam (the pride of the Central African Federation) created the huge lake of the same name that forms part of the border; then at Feira the river passes into Mozambique's Tete province where at this time an international consortium was constructing the huge Cabora Bassa Dam to provide power for South Africa and give it a stake in Portugal's continuing hold on Mozambique. Until 1974, when the drain of the African wars and consequent disillusionment of the military led to the revolution in Portugal that presaged the collapse of their African empire, the Portuguese had seen the Zambezi, which divides Mozambique in half, as the last line of defence should the FRELIMO forces succeed in fighting their way that far south. The Zambezi, then, had become a strategic and symbolic barrier of the utmost importance and formed the front line between the black North and the white South.

MOZAMBIQUE AS A TRANSIT COUNTRY

Mozambique's location on the eastern flank of Southern Africa gives it a position of unique importance; of all Africa's 'outlet' countries it is the most strategically placed: because of the length of its coastline, the quality and size of its harbours and the number of countries whose outlets to the sea it controls. The Indian Ocean coastline is 1,560 miles long, making Mozambique the natural maritime outlet for Malawi, Zambia, Rhodesia (Zimbabwe), the Transvaal of South Africa and Swaziland. The railways and roads from those countries to Mozambique's ports are vital to its economy because of the transit revenues they earn. This position as a transit country meant that throughout the 30 years from 1964 when the FRELIMO war began, during the UDI years in Rhodesia and Zambia's embattled position as a front-line state, and through the shifting fortunes of war and politics in the region, Mozambique offered essential transit routes to its neighbours. The Lourenco Marques (Maputo)–Transvaal railway reached the Rand in 1894 and by the 1960s was still the shortest and most important transit route for the Johannesburg area, which is the most heavily industrialized in South Africa. Second came the Beira to Salisbury (Harare) railway and the Beira to Blantyre line, each essential respectively to Rhodesia and Malawi. Another line from Lourenco Marques to Gwelo (Gweru) in Rhodesia was completed in 1954. Finally, in the north of Mozambique, the huge natural harbour and port of Nacala was developed as the outlet for the northern provinces of Mozambique and for Malawi. Between them these lines added up to 2,200 miles of track and their strategic importance was enormously enhanced during the years of confrontation that began with UDI in Rhodesia. In addition, major roads were developed from Maputo and Beira to the Transvaal and Rhodesia.

Africa's huge coastline has relatively few good harbours and Mozambique is lucky to have two excellent ones in Maputo and Nacala, though Beira is more problematical since it regularly becomes silted up; between them they serve the countries of the interior and for Zambia, Rhodesia, Malawi, Swaziland and the Transvaal provide the most economic outlets. Beira acted as the sea gateway for Malawi and Zambia (almost entirely prior to UDI in Rhodesia and still thereafter until Smith closed the border with Zambia in 1973). Nacala in the north was the last of Mozambique's ports to be developed; it possesses one of the largest and best natural harbours in Africa and the railway inland was linked to Malawi in 1970.

In November 1975 the civil war in Angola led to the closure of the Benguela Railway and this event forced Zambia to abandon its policy of only exporting its copper to the north; instead, it was obliged once more to export through Rhodesia and Mozambique. Another complication arose in March 1976 when the new FRELIMO government of independent Mozambique closed its borders with Rhodesia, forcing the illegal regime thereafter to use South African routes for all its exports and imports. However, Mozambique could not afford also to close Maputo to South African business. Although, under FRELIMO, Mozambique's ideological inclination was to have as little as possible to do with its white minority neighbours, it too found itself greatly constrained by the politics of the region since a large proportion of its income had always been derived from the freight and port handling charges obtained from its inland neighbours, and especially South Africa, so that a total closure of its ports and railways to South Africa as well as Rhodesia would have precipitated an economic disaster. Under the Portuguese Mozambique had broken UN sanctions against Rhodesia by providing fake certificates of origin for exports of minerals such as chrome and Beira and Maputo had been Rhodesia's main outlets while the bulk of its oil came in through Maputo. After the 1976 border closure all Rhodesia's traffic had to pass through South Africa and the costs were higher. Mozambique, then, was an essential transit country for the white South as well as Zambia and Malawi.

THE BOTZAM ROAD

Prior to independence Botswana's main transport route was the railway to the Cape. In any case, most of its trade and imported manufactures came from South Africa, although the 400-mile railway line that passed through the country from South Africa in the south to Rhodesia in the north-east did give Botswana an alternative white-ruled trading partner. Speaking in Denmark in 1970, Botswana's President, Seretse Khama, described his country's sense of isolation in a white-controlled world:

> Our only common frontier with independent majority-ruled Africa is a narrow disputed one with our sister Republic of Zambia… And these states [the white-ruled ones] are not only our neighbours; for historical and geographical reasons, which are none of our choosing, we also trade with them. Our economies have long been closely interlinked and we depend on their transport systems for our outlets to the world. The main railway connecting South Africa and Rhodesia crosses Botswana and we rely on it not only for our trade with the outside world but for internal communications. It is wholly owned and operated by Rhodesia Railways.[4]

In the early 1970s, as confrontation became a permanent fact of regional politics, the possibility of an outlet to the north that was not under the control of South Africa or Rhodesia became increasingly attractive to Botswana. To create such an outlet meant upgrading an old route that had 'been maintained by the Witwatersrand Labour Association for the transport of labour from Barotseland and Angola to the Rand Mines',[5] a fact that was overlooked by the Pretoria government when it argued that Botswana had no frontier with Zambia.

In the late 1960s the United States had made a loan to Botswana to construct the Francistown–Maun road upon which stands Nata, the turning-off point for Kazungula in Zambia, which was reached by a ferry crossing over the Zambezi. Up to 1969 US interest in Botswana had hardly been noticeable but was now to be increased by two factors: the Communist Chinese had agreed to construct the TANZAM Railway for Tanzania and Zambia and the United States wanted to build its own 'freedom road' in Africa; and President Nixon wished to demonstrate to black pressure groups in America that the United States was busy, on the right side, in Southern Africa. This conjunction of political circumstances led to the US offer to construct the BOTZAM road, which offered just what Washington required. When in 1969 the Americans were looking for a suitable aid project in Botswana, they had been presented with a list of 24 projects in order of priority and they chose number 17, the Nata to

Kazungula road, which was to become known as the BOTZAM. This projected stretch of road would form the northern end of a 625-mile road beginning at Lobatse in the south: the Nata to Kazungula stretch was 180 miles long. In 1972 USAID signed an agreement to provide US$12.6 million for the BOTZAM, a gravel-surface road that would take 32 months to construct and was to include two spur roads at its northern extremity: one of 3.7 miles would connect the road to the Rhodesian border; the other, 40 miles in length, would pass along the south bank of the Chobe River to Ngoma where a bridge crossed the river to the South African base of Katima Mulilo in the Caprivi Strip. This stretch was designed to facilitate traffic from Rhodesia to Katima Mulilo and was included by the US as a sop to Pretoria, which had opposed the road. It was, in consequence, an embarrassment to Botswana whose US-built 'freedom road' would also assist the South Africans maintain their base at Katima Mulilo that, according to the United Nations, was illegally on Namibian soil and posed a direct threat to the independent states to the north. Zambia agreed to upgrade the ferry service across the Zambezi from Kazungula to Kasane and to establish facilities on the north bank to handle heavy traffic. The BOTZAM, from being low on the government's list of priorities, had become the largest aid project in Botswana's 1973–78 Development Plan.

Developments in neighbouring Rhodesia and South Africa's increasing confrontation with the states to the north determined Botswana to break the Republic's economic stranglehold upon the country. From the beginning the BOTZAM was a very political road; in purely economic terms it was never to be very important though its symbolism was crucial to Botswana's desire for closer relations with independent black Africa to the north. During the 1970s the EEC became one of Botswana's major aid donors and the assistance that had been committed by 1977 included a grant of US$10.5 million for work on a segment of the BOTZAM from Francistown to Nata. The Zambian connection, the ferry crossing to Kazungula, was the only geographical route that could release Botswana from the pervasive stranglehold that South Africa exerted upon the country, hence the strategic and psychological rather than economic importance of the road.

South Africa used bullying tactics in an attempt to persuade Botswana not to go ahead with the BOTZAM road but President Khama was not intimidated and Prime Minister Vorster backed down (see the Botswana section of Chapter 15 above). Vorster, who conveniently forgot that the road and ferry crossing had long been used as a route for labour from the north that had been recruited to work in South Africa's mines, had argued that Botswana had no common frontier with Zambia. Not only did South Africa have no case; persistence in its opposition to the BOTZAM road would have drawn unwelcome attention to

South Africa's military presence in the Caprivi Strip, which the United Nations had pronounced illegal. The events of 1973 – the Smith government's decision to close the Rhodesian border with Zambia, the escalation of the guerrilla war in Rhodesia, the Arab oil boycott of South Africa and the Saudi agreement to supply Botswana with oil provided it did not pass through South Africa – each gave point to the BOTZAM road which was then given greater priority by Botswana.

THE BENGUELA RAILWAY

Another highway that assumed great strategic significance in the mid-1970s was the Benguela Railway, which runs from west to east across the centre of Angola. The railway was constructed between 1903 and 1929 and stretches for 838 miles from Lobito on the Atlantic coast of Angola to the Shaba province of Zaïre. The Shaba province is the centre of Zaïre's mineral deposits and mines; an extension of the railway southwards to the Zambian Copperbelt linked up with Zambian railways. In 1973, when Smith closed the Rhodesian border with Zambia and the TANZAM Railway was only half-completed, Zambia urgently needed an alternative route out for its copper and the Benguela Railway appeared to be the answer. At that time 40 per cent of the line's traffic was transit freight from either Zaïre or Zambia and this accounted for 75 per cent of all freight revenues. The political confrontation across the Zambezi gave new life to the Benguela Railway, which had been under-utilized for many years because of the cheaper haulage rates offered for freight going south through Rhodesia and Mozambique to Beira. However, UDI in 1965 led to congestion on the southern routes and, combined with the political confrontation that followed, this worked in favour of the Benguela route, which Zambia then began to use for part of its copper exports. The line assumed even greater significance for Zambia following Smith's closure of the border at the beginning of 1973. Reflecting this change in its preferred exit routes, in January 1975 President Kaunda announced that a new line was to be constructed from the Copperbelt to Solwezi in the north-west of Zambia and thence, through new copper deposits at Lumwana, across the border into Angola to connect with the Benguela Railway at Luso and bypass Zaïre. As a consequence of these events and after an historically slow start, the Benguela Railway entered a new period of prosperity as it served the needs of landlocked Zambia. The prosperity was not to last.

Up to the 1973 border closure between Rhodesia and Zambia, the Benguela Railway was carrying about 15,000 tons of copper from Zambia every month and handling some 8,000 tons of Zambian imports. By May 1974 the tonnage of Zambian imports had climbed to 45,000 a month while its copper exports had risen to 35,000 tons a month with an additional 8,000 tons of lead and zinc exports. By 1975, the year the Portuguese quit Angola, Benguela Railways (owned by the British company Tanganyika Concessions – TANKS) had become the largest single private employer in the country with about 13,000 employees. At that time its steam locomotives were being replaced by diesel engines (the company had embarked upon a major programme of modernization in 1972). But even as the 1973–74 boom for the Benguela line was taking place, the Chinese were constructing Zambia's alternative route to the sea, the TANZAM railway that would give Zambia direct access to the Indian Ocean at Dar es Salaam. The threat to the Benguela Railway posed by the coming of the TANZAM was noted in the TANKS company report for 1973–74: 'The present traffic boom is due to circumstances beyond our control, and it will not be long before a new competing route is opened which will link Zambia to the port of Dar es Salaam.' Meanwhile, TANKS had opened an office in Lusaka and used it to maintain direct contact with the Zambian government, and its directors regularly visited Zambia to confer with officials and ministers.

On the eve of Angola's independence in 1975, it seemed possible that the Benguela Railway would act as a major engine of growth: it provided much-needed jobs while its workshops at Benguela and Nova Lisboa were bases for industrial development. Moreover, Zambia had obtained secret agreements with the Angolan liberation movements not to attack the railway. However, threats to the railway had developed in the last stages of the liberation war against the Portuguese and from August 1975, as the fighting escalated, the railway ceased to provide any services either for Zambia or Zaïre. Bridges were destroyed and for a time UNITA forces held the greater part of the line. On the coast, fighting round Lobito and Benguela see-sawed and the towns changed hands several times. Luso was threatened by anti-government forces and from Luso to the Shaba border trains had to be accompanied by armed guards who travelled in turreted armoured cars ahead of the train while no night travel was allowed on this stretch of line. Just as the strategic-economic importance of the railway had been established for Zambia things fell apart. The withdrawal of the Portuguese in November 1975 meant the use of its ports and railways was suspended. The main military forces of the MPLA were confined to the area round Luanda, the capital, and faced major attacks from the rival liberation movements, the FNLA and UNITA. Cuban forces were sent to support the MPLA government while the Soviet Union supplied technicians and arms. A column of mixed South African and Portuguese troops advanced up the coast from South Africa towards Luanda and newly independent Angola was in deep crisis. By the end of the first Angolan civil war, from independence in November 1975 to March 1976 – the South Africans withdrew from the country on 28 March – the railway was entirely in the hands of MPLA forces from Benguela to Teixeira de Sousa on the Zaïre border.

In May 1976 talks were held between President Agostinho Neto of Angola and President Mobutu of Zaïre to normalize relations between their two countries (Mobutu had backed the rival FNLA movement) and Zaïre traffic was again able to use the line. The Cubans, who by then were in the country in strength, provided engineers to repair damage to bridges and other installations that had been sabotaged. Zambia, whose President Kaunda had been deeply suspicious of Neto, now also recognized the MPLA government, which was anxious to get the railway operating again and earn transit charges from both Zaïre and Zambia. The respite for the railway was brief. In 1976 the TANZAM Railway was officially opened to give Zambia another much-needed outlet. Already, at the end of 1975, UNITA guerrillas were targeting the Benguela Railway in their escalating war against the MPLA government and the railway, despite accords with Zaïre and Zambia, was closed to use in 1976. It was reopened briefly in 1978 but then closed again and remained closed throughout the 1980s. Major plans for its rehabilitation and reopening were drawn up during the 1980s but clearly depended upon an end to the civil war and a political settlement between the MPLA government and the UNITA rebels and this would not, in fact, be achieved until the turn of the century.

THE TANZAM RAILWAY

The TANZAM Railway from Kapiri Mposhi in central Zambia to Dar es Salaam on the Indian Ocean coast of Tanzania was more than 1,100 miles long and was by far the largest and most spectacular Communist and Chinese aid project on the African continent at the time of its construction. According to Western estimates there were at one time as many as 18,000 Chinese working along the line of the TANZAM, which was completed in 1976. In 1978 running and technical difficulties occurred and had to be rectified but in view of the size of the project and the speed of its execution, these were hardly surprising. As the events of the 1970s revealed the extent to which Zambia was almost totally dependent upon exit routes to the south, so the strategic and economic implications of the line to Dar es Salaam became clearer.

Zambia's dependence upon the southern system of transport routes after independence was principally due to the fact that up to 1924 the territory had been the 'property' of the British South Africa (BSA) Company. The BSA Company ruled Northern Rhodesia, controlled its mineral rights and the railway to the south. There was no alternative route through the Congo, neither could the Benguela Railway compete economically with the route to Beira. In both geographical and political terms, therefore, a railway from Zambia north-east to Dar es Salaam would break the established pattern. This, precisely, was why Western opposition to the TANZAM was so sustained. Britain especially, South Africa, Rhodesia and then the West more generally wanted the southern system to be sustained and for Zambia to remain part of that regional complex. The worst aspect of colonialism from an African continental point of view was the fact that each colony had been developed separately without any consideration of comparable developments in neighbouring territories. In terms of any links resulting from colonial times Tanzania and Zambia might as well have been on separate continents. Until the break-up of the Central African Federation at the end of 1963 and its independence in October 1964, Zambia was trapped, locked in by the Portuguese possessions of Angola and Mozambique on its western and eastern flanks and by Rhodesia to the south. Only after independence and spurred on by UDI in Rhodesia was Zambia free to explore alternatives.

The importance of the TANZAM has to be judged in terms of the traumatic events that affected Zambia between 1965 and 1967: as a result of UDI Zambia's position was changed overnight as it found itself on the front line facing the white-dominated South; initially, Zambia was to suffer more from UN sanctions against Rhodesia, which it applied, than Rhodesia itself. Immediately, for example, as oil supplies that normally came from the south were terminated, Zambia had to rely upon a US/Canadian/British airlift of oil and then fuel brought in drums on trucks along the 'Hell Run' as the road from Tanzania was dubbed until the Dar es Salaam–Ndola oil pipeline had been constructed. Zambia's main export, copper, experienced a three-month time lag from extraction in the Copperbelt to customer. Export sales were then at the rate of between 50,000 and 60,000 tons a month. Following the closure of the Rhodesia border in January 1973, the Zambians believed that Britain and British companies were at least as anxious as the South Africans for Zambia to accept Smith's offer of using the route south when in February he declared the border open again: both Rhodesia and South Africa wanted the freight dues from Zambian copper. A programme on Zambian Radio complained 'the British want us to begin using the routes through the rebel colony. That is their advice to us. They can jump into the sea. In the past they have tried to lead us into economic and political ruin by advising us against vital projects such as the oil pipeline...'[6]

There was great bitterness in both Zambia and Tanzania at the Western refusal to assist in building the TANZAM. Both countries needed the railway for strategic and political survival but the West was more interested in promoting the survival of the white regimes in Southern Africa. On 26 October 1970, at an inauguration ceremony at Dar es Salaam, President Kaunda said:

'Many things have been said against our railway which is perhaps one of the most opposed schemes in the world.' Opposition, Kaunda continued, had come 'from vested interests in white ruled Southern Africa and their supporters elsewhere in the world. Campaigning against the railway had been wide and intense. The railway would be uneconomic, it was argued. We refused to listen. The railway would be too expensive in relation to economic returns, we were advised. We rejected the advice. The railway would take too long to build, it was emphasized rather discouragingly. We ignored the warning. Above all, it was argued that Zambia did not need the railway after all as UDI with all its hardships to Zambia would end in a matter of months.' Possible participants in the TANZAM were discouraged, Kaunda claimed, because the British government did not think the project was necessary and still saw Zambia and Tanzania as falling within the British sphere of influence. 'Zambia was to remain dependent on the white-ruled south for the transportation of her exports and imports. We are to be subservient to white domination for as long as it was in the interests of Western governments regardless of our objectives and interests.'

Kaunda's anti-British diatribe reflected his deep disillusionment with the country that he had turned to first for assistance and whose motives he had believed were honourable until its more or less overt support for the white regimes in the South taught him a different lesson. Work on the TANZAM began in October 1970; on 27 August 1973 the railway tracks crossed the border from Tanzania into Zambia. Deliberate scepticism in the Western press – that the Chinese could not finance the line, that they were incapable of building it properly, that it would fall behind schedule – told more about Western attitudes than Chinese performance and such criticisms became more muted as the line progressed.

Negotiations with the Chinese by Zambia and Tanzania had begun in 1967 and once the agreement had been finalized in 1970 Chinese ships were to appear regularly at Dar es Salaam bringing workers and equipment and the line was then built at a spectacularly fast pace. In October 1975 the line was officially declared open although it had reached the old Zambian line of rail at Kapiri Mposhi in central Zambia months earlier to become part of the whole Zambian network. The *raison d'être* of the TANZAM was always political: to enable Zambia to be independent of the white South and to provide it with an additional exit route that might still be needed after UDI in Rhodesia had come to an end, depending upon Zambia's relations with its other neighbours. South Africa opposed the TANZAM because it wanted to retain as large a part of its northern neighbour's trade as possible for both economic and political reasons.

The more of its trade that it captured and the fewer options available to Zambia the greater would be South African dominance and control over Zambia and the region as a whole. Both Nyerere and Kaunda emphasized that the line would give them greater security and more choice, and make them less dependent upon the South. Its construction, despite all the Western pressures against it, represented a victory over Western neo-colonial manipulation. The railway was not strategic for Tanzania in the way it was for Zambia but it gave promise that the remote southern region of the country could be opened up for agricultural production and mineral exploration. Even as the railway extended southwards there was an immediate and encouraging use of it by people who lived along its path.

The history of the TANZAM Railway reveals the extent of Western sympathies with the white South and the lengths to which the West would go to forestall an African venture that threatened its interests. In 1965, prior to UDI in Rhodesia, Kaunda and Nyerere announced that they had decided upon such a railway and they invited offers of assistance. In July 1965 Nyerere told a press conference that the railway should be built and said: 'I am prepared to accept money from whoever offers it and see it is built.' The two presidents made extensive soundings for aid but in the end only the People's Republic of China offered support on the scale required and this amounted to the largest single economic assistance project financed by China. It was made after much prior manoeuvring.

A World Bank study of such a line had been carried out for Zambia shortly before independence but its findings were lukewarm. The report suggested that the region was already sufficiently served by railways, which was clearly a Western-biased conclusion, given the race politics of the region. Even should the routes to the south be closed to Zambia, the World Bank argued that there were still sufficient existing alternatives. Such a conclusion was either wilfully obtuse or had not taken any account of the politics of the region. The World Bank advocated improved road facilities. A UN report then endorsed the World Bank view and this, too, ignored the political realities. Then Kaunda and Nyerere made joint approaches to Britain, the United States, France and West Germany. Britain did finance a survey by the Maxwell Stamp Company and this was being carried out when UDI was declared and Zambia's needs became pressing. The Maxwell Stamp report was positive: it considered the political aspects, the possibility of carrying copper and agricultural products and argued that it would complement existing lines. It estimated the cost at US$350 million and advocated the expenditure of an additional US$33 million to expand the harbour at Dar es Salaam. The Maxwell Stamp report was subsequently subjected to criticisms by the World Bank, the United Nations and the African

Development Bank, and the three organizations proposed to undertake a further survey. This suggestion was rejected by the two presidents, for by then they had decided to accept the Chinese offer.

Western objections to the TANZAM, accompanied by much denigration of the proposal and delaying tactics, were based upon two considerations: that such a railway would detach Zambia from the South African sphere of influence and that, in strategic terms, it would point like an arrow at the white heartland. Kaunda claimed that Western objections to the line were all based 'on political and ideological grounds'. And in 1969 Nyerere said, 'The world has never seen such a profusion of railway projects in Southern Africa as those which are now being canvassed – all of them… designed to try to stop the TANZAM railway from being built.'[7] In September 1967, therefore, Zambia, Tanzania and China signed an agreement in Beijing: China would build the railway, finance it, supply technical personnel and train local manpower. A survey followed and the final agreement was signed in July 1970. Construction began almost at once and Chinese ships arriving at Dar es Salaam thereafter were given priority for unloading. The West, which had been invited first to build the line, had turned down the chance, deployed endless arguments against the need for it, and then belittled the Chinese capacity to do the job. Now the West saw the line being constructed at speed. Over the years of construction from 1970 to 1975 constant rumours were circulated about the number of Chinese working on the line and though the Chinese probably never exceeded their official figure of 18,000 it was suggested that 45,000 Chinese had been drafted into Tanzania. The West, in classic Cold War mode as it saw China accumulating both influence and respect in East/Central Africa, speculated as to what the Chinese would do when the railway was completed. The Rhodesians were alarmed chiefly because of the impending loss of revenue for their railway system while the South African Prime Minister, Johannes Vorster, saw only the advancing 'yellow peril'; both countries believed that the TANZAM would enable Zambia to escape from the white southern orbit.

The Chinese performance was impressive. China equipped and financed a single-track line of 1,162 miles length that embraced 147 stations, 300 bridges, 21 tunnels and 2,200 culverts. They constructed a 10-track marshalling yard at Dar es Salaam and repair yards at Dar es Salaam, Mbeya and Mpika. The finance to pay for the project came to approximately US$412 million in the form of an interest-free loan with repayment to begin in 1983 while Tanzania and Zambia would bear local costs. The railway would soon be beset by a number of difficulties due to structural faults while the exigencies of UDI forced Zambia to use Rhodesia Railways again in 1978. Even so, it was the politics surrounding the TANZAM Railway rather than its actual construction, dramatic as that was, which revealed so much about Western attitudes towards Africa at that time. The West was more interested in maintaining the economic and political dominance of the white South over the region than in assisting two independent African countries break free of that dominance, an attitude that reinforced the prevalent African accusations of Western neo-colonialism and racism.

The Cold War
Comes to The Horn

The Horn of Africa became entangled in Cold War manoeuvres as early as 1950 when the United States effectively replaced the colonial powers of Britain and Italy as the principal source of external support for the regime of Emperor Haile Selassie in Ethiopia. That year the United States insisted upon a federation of Ethiopia and Eritrea to forestall moves by the latter towards full independence; the USSR by contrast supported independence for Eritrea and the creation of a corridor to give Ethiopia direct access to the Red Sea. The US view prevailed, however, and for the next 20 years Ethiopia was a major recipient of US aid.

The strategic importance of the Horn gave its conflicts a wider significance than they would otherwise have achieved. The Horn of Africa protrudes into the Red Sea and Indian Ocean at the maritime crossroads between West and East, Africa and Asia, and control of the Horn by a major power would enable it to dominate the Arabian Peninsula from the south. At this time the Horn comprised four political entities: Ethiopia, Somalia, Eritrea and the Territory of the Afars and Issas, which became independent from France in 1977 as Djibouti. Ethiopia and Somalia had a long history of antagonism and conflict over their disputed border region; independent Somalia had been formed in 1960 by the union of British Somaliland and former Italian Somaliland. Subsequently it laid claim to the three territories of Djibouti, the Ogaden region of Ethiopia and the Northern Frontier Province of Kenya. In the early 1970s, despite being a Muslim but non-Arab state, Somalia had sought and obtained substantial aid from the USSR and in 1974 was admitted to membership of the Arab League. Ethiopia, as well as Somalia, claimed Djibouti, whose port was vital to Ethiopia's commerce with the outside world. The wars that afflicted the region during the 1970s were extremely costly, not just in terms of the material destruction of infrastructure that took place but also because of the suffering they caused to the most vulnerable sectors of the societies concerned while they retarded the development of the region by a decade or more.

Ethiopia was by far the most important of the four Horn territories. In 1974 it had an estimated population of 27.8 million, one of the largest in Africa, and with Eritrea covered 475,000 square miles with a 500-mile coastline on the Red Sea. It had an ancient history and, apart from the Mussolini interregnum (1935–41), had never been colonized. The great prestige of Emperor Haile Selassie at the beginning of the 1960s persuaded the other African countries to make Addis Ababa the headquarters of the OAU when it was formed in 1963. He, however, presided over one of the poorest countries on the continent: agriculture accounted for 99 per cent of export earnings with coffee the dominant crop while 88 per cent of the population worked on the land. The average per capita GDP (1974) was only US$76. Up to the beginning of the 1970s Ethiopia's foreign policy was Western oriented, mainly due to strong US influence while it maintained close relations with Israel as a nearby non-Muslim country, in part to offset Arab support for Eritrean secessionists. Haile Selassie, however, represented an imperial-feudal tradition whose days were numbered and by the beginning of the 1970s his people were waiting for the 'Old Man' to die so that some radical changes could be implemented.

THE DEVELOPING CRISIS IN ETHIOPIA

On 16 December 1970, reacting to the growing threat from the Eritrean rebels, Haile Selassie declared a state of emergency throughout most of the province of Eritrea, claiming that foreign governments were training people as bandits, supplying them with arms and helping them infiltrate Ethiopia to embark upon banditry, sabotage and subversion within Eritrea. The foreign governments in question were Sudan, which provided rebel Eritreans with asylum, Syria, where the leaders of the Eritrean Liberation Movement (ELF) were based, and Iraq. Support for the Eritreans was also being provided by Saudi Arabia and Yemen and such support had been growing since 1962 when the Ethiopian government had abrogated the federal status of Eritrea to integrate it into a single Ethiopian state. The army was now placed in control of the two ports of Massawa and Assab and the border with Sudan was closed. By 1971 the whole province had been brought under military control; ELF responded by stepping up its guerrilla attacks. In some ways, according to the London *Observer*, the rebellion bore the overtones of the Arab-Israeli conflict. The rebels at this time were mainly Eritrean Arabic-speaking Muslims backed by several Arab countries that resented the Emperor's close relations with Israel. Arms for the rebels were being supplied by Russia while the Ethiopian army was largely American armed and trained.[1] Over Christmas 1970 the Ethiopian air force carried out bombing raids on Eritrean targets and ELF claimed that 1,000 Eritreans had been killed since the declaration of a state of emergency while 37,000 refugees had fled to Sudan.

The roots of the Eritrean struggle can be traced to the Scramble for Africa when Italy, defeated by the Ethiopians at the battle of Adowa in 1896, was able to retrieve something from the disaster by making Eritrea an Italian colony. Growing Eritrean resentment at the Federal connection with Ethiopia that had been created under UN auspices in 1952 became an outright demand for secession in 1962 when the Ethiopian Parliament, which the Eritreans described as the Emperor's rubber stamp, voted to incorporate Eritrea into a unitary Ethiopia. Thereafter, ELF demanded secession and full independence. By early 1971 the war developing in Eritrea was described as 10 times greater than the war then being waged in Chad; it involved two-thirds of the Ethiopian army. Growing Arab support for the Eritreans ensured a commensurate growth of Israeli support for Ethiopia.[2]

The failure of Haile Selassie on the occasion of his eightieth birthday, 23 July 1972, to announce plans for a constitutional transfer of power precipitated a period of uncertainty for by this time the Emperor was uncertain in his actions and his unsteady hand on the tiller of state paralysed decision-making.[3] As a result Ethiopia entered a phase of marking time as it waited for the Old Man to pass on. Opposition to his rule became more vocal and was no longer just confined to modernizing radicals but also included members of the establishment who, aware that change had to come, were busy jockeying for position. Two events exerted particular pressure upon the Emperor's weakening grip on power: the growing rebellion in Eritrea; and the disastrous handling of the drought and famine in Wollo Province. Even so, until the end of 1973, Haile Selassie regarded both the war in Eritrea and the famine in Wollo as distant problems; more important was growing unrest in the army.

By July 1973 an estimated 1,874,000 people in the four northern provinces of Tigre, Wollo, Northern Shoa and Begemder were affected by the drought, while huge losses of livestock were impoverishing the nomads of the region. Massive aid was urgently required and, even so, it would take several years to build up the cattle herds again. The immediate relief efforts were insufficient. There was need for long-term measures to include farm diversification and the development of cash crops other than grain, the encouragement of rural industries, more irrigation, anti-erosion measures, re-afforestation, well-digging, improved grain storage, cattle improvement and nutrition education – in fact, an agricultural revolution to modernize a way of life that had not changed in centuries.[4] By the end of 1973 the impact of the drought upon the country's politics could no longer be ignored: between 50,000 and 100,000 people in central Ethiopia had died and two million more were directly affected by conditions that had been worsening over three years.

Thirteen refugee camps were established in Wollo province and as many as 712,000 out of three million people had become famine victims. Relief was hampered by the inaccessibility of the region. Following student protests in Addis Ababa, the government asked friendly countries for help but its first appeals were low key as it did not wish to admit to a major crisis. However, a great proportion of the medical and food supplies that were poured into the famine area by the government never reached their destinations; instead, corrupt government administrators and their aides sold the relief supplies or kept them. Subsequently, the government acted quickly and most of the profiteers were rounded up for trial. Foolishly, the government did not give the famine wide publicity and so was accused of minimizing the facts. The Ministry of the Interior wanted publicity, the Ministry of Tourism did not, while the government was averse to publicizing the corruption that had been uncovered for fear of giving the country a bad name. In the end the facts came out and did more harm than otherwise they need have done. Writing in *The Times*, Patrick Gilkes argued that though the climate caused the famine, the land system made it worse. Despite government attempts at land reform, the land tenure system and tenant-landlord relations were feudal. In Wollo, of 375,000 landless peasants 150,000 were tenants and of these, according to official figures, over 90,000 paid at least 50 per cent of their produce, with an upper limit of 75 per cent, to their landlords; 27 per cent of the landlords were absent, 40 per cent were deceased and only tenants on government land had the security of a written lease. There was no control over evictions of those who did not possess a lease except an appeal to the landlords in their capacity as local government officials. Land reform had been opposed in parliament, a majority of whose members were landlords.[5] Voluntary donations were made by members of the government and the Emperor to relieve the distress but failed lamentably to match the scale of the crisis.

In the post-World War II era Ethiopia had become a close ally of the United States, which had stepped in to replace older ties with the European colonial powers. The US had initiated currency reforms leading Ethiopia to sever its dollar from the British pound and tie it to the US dollar instead. Thereafter, Ethiopia had become one of the few countries in Africa that appeared to matter to the US. The US had secured a base for itself in Eritrea at Kagnew near Asmara. When, on 2 December 1952, the UN General Assembly passed, by 46 to 10 votes with four abstentions, Resolution 390 which embraced the US-initiated federal formula for Ethiopia and Eritrea against the Russian proposal for Eritrean independence it could be said that the Cold War had come to the Horn of Africa. The subsequent UN Commission found the Ethiopian demands relating to federation excessive and conceded less power to Ethiopia in Eritrea than it had demanded. 'While the Commissioner was drafting the constitution, the British Military Administration (that had been responsible for Eritrea since the end of the war) was convening the Eritrean Assembly. The Assembly adopted the constitution with "minor modifications". Haile Selassie ratified the constitution on August 6, 1952, and the Federal Act on September 11. Hence began the Ethio-Eritrean Federation.'[6] The climate of Cold War secrecy at the time was such that the US base facilities in Eritrea were unknown to Congress. Washington provided military assistance to Haile Selassie's government and this was increased following a secret US-Ethiopian defence pact in 1960. The US paid millions of dollars to the Ethiopian regime as part of the arrangement; the payments were 'rents' for Kagnew and naval bases in Eritrea and were made without most members of Congress knowing about the existence of these 'secret' facilities. Kagnew and the naval bases in Eritrea became controversial in the US Congress when, in 1970, a Senate sub-committee on foreign relations probed into the commitments of the US to Haile Selassie's regime.[7] The sub-committee revealed that US 'aid' to the Haile Selassie government was the highest in Africa since the early 1950s and by 1970 had reached a quarter of a billion dollars. In the light of this US support Haile Selassie felt able, on 15 November 1962, to issue Order No. 27 which 'hereby wholly integrated into the unitary system of administration of Our Empire' Eritrea. The secessionist war followed.

SOMALIA AND THE OGADEN BORDER

'Somalia is probably the one country in Africa where the people can justifiably claim to be of the same origin. The various clan groupings notwithstanding, there is a remarkable degree of homogeneity in the origins of the Somali people. Theoretically, therefore, one might presuppose it should be reasonably simple to devise workable solutions that could cater for the aspirations of all the various groupings in Somalia.'[8] Siad Barre worked on that assumption after coming to power by means of a coup on 1969. By 1973 Siad Barre had provided Somalia with three and a half years of strong government. The economy had vastly improved and a sense of nationhood seemed to have developed. In Mogadishu notices proclaimed: 'We have chosen Scientific Socialism because it is the only way for rapid transformation of the country into a developed and economically advanced nation.' President Barre had preached a fiery new Marxist ideology and had tried to grab his country by the scruff of its neck and impose discipline, dedication and development. A revolution was needed in traditional Somali society most of whose three million people were cattle-rearing nomads.

According to one sympathetic observer of Barre's government at this time, 'Soon the nomads will be driving their cattle to projected state farms and World Bank fattening centres, where the animals will be kept on irrigated pastures and fed modern feedlots until ready for export. President Siad Barre has developed military-style campaigns to eradicate tribalism, and to get the people to work and transform the economy into a modern state.' It was an idyllic picture of reform and even if correct at the time it was not to last. 'No longer is Somalia a banana economy, reeling under the closure of the Suez Canal. Though the banana trade is healthy, with Italy taking its quota and new markets opening in the Arab states, livestock is now by far the most important export and the giant Russian meat factory at the southern port of Kismayo is canning meat to capacity, with plans for vast expansion in frozen meat and corned beef.'[9] Up to 1973 the most successful part of the Barre revolution was the livestock programme, which accounted for 70 per cent of export earnings, while 60 per cent of the population depended upon it. The programme emphasized the introduction of new veterinary services and improved breeding stock.

Perhaps the most important social reform at this time was the introduction of Somali as a written language using the Latin script. The first Somali newspaper appeared in October 1972 and civil servants had to sit a language examination in January 1973 while Somali was now to be the sole language, replacing English and Italian. Small-scale industries were established but agriculture remained the core activity and, apart from cattle, consisted of maize, millet, sorghum, cassava, sugar, sesame seed, bananas and other fruit. US reports at the time indicated the presence in Somalia of 2,500 Russian military advisers and argued that the USSR wanted Somalia to give it a strategic advantage in the Indian Ocean though this US conclusion was denied by the Somali government. Siad Barre had turned away from the West after the revolution that brought him to power to seek aid from Russia and China 'where there would be no strings attached'. He made plain his non-commitment in the Cold War: 'Somalia has told Russia and China that she will not be used as a base in the defence strategy of the Communist powers and that the Horn of Africa cannot be militarily aligned with any of the great power blocs. This is because Somalia does not want to jeopardize her policy of "positive neutrality" and endanger her peacekeeping role in Africa.'[10] However, Barre came to realize that the money, materials, arms and expertise provided with apparent magnanimity by Russia and China had a price after all. There occurred at this time widespread distribution in Somalia of anti-capitalist literature and pro-Marxist and pro-Maoist ideological material.

Despite the successes of his revolution, Barre had to deal with the Ogaden question, which was central to Somali nationalism. Successive Somali governments had disputed the status of the Ogaden region ever since independence in 1960. The Somalis referred to the Ogaden as Western Somalia, regarded it as a Somali region under foreign (Ethiopian) domination and demanded self-determination for it. Ethiopia, on the other hand, took the view that the Ogaden region was an integral part of its territory and regarded Somali claims as acts of aggression against Ethiopian integrity and insisted that Somalia should accept the boundaries as they had existed when it became independent in 1960. This Ethiopian position had been greatly strengthened when the OAU Assembly of Heads of State and Government, meeting in Cairo in July 1964, had passed one of its first and most important resolutions 'that all member states pledge themselves to respect the borders existing on their achievement of national independence'. This resolution had not been accepted by Somalia. Relations between the two countries deteriorated in 1964 when Somalia supported guerrilla incursions across the border. However, in 1967 the Somali government of Mohamed Ibrahim Egal favoured dialogue and a communiqué published simultaneously in Addis Ababa and Mogadishu on 22 September affirmed that Ethiopia and Somalia had agreed to 'eliminate all forms of tension' between them.

However, when Siad Barre came to power in 1969 he determined to reopen the border question and his determination was reinforced by the overthrow of Haile Selassie in 1974. However, he soon discovered that the Dergue, which took over the government of Ethiopia, was no more willing to open the question than had been the old Emperor. In 1977, therefore, the Somali government stopped restraining the various Somali irredentist groups that regularly infiltrated into the Ogaden. The chief group was the Western Somalia Liberation Front (WSLF), followed by the Somali Abo Liberation Front (SALF). As a result guerrilla violence escalated through 1977 and in September the Somalis captured the Ethiopian town of Jigiga and then advanced on Harar. In January 1978 an Ethiopian counter-attack, supported by Soviet and Cuban forces, was launched and in early March Jigiga was recaptured followed by a number of strategic points in the region. Even so, Somali guerrilla forces continued to operate over a wide area of the Ogaden while broadcasts from Mogadishu claimed they had inflicted heavy casualties on the Ethiopians and their Cuban allies.

Meanwhile, the USSR had changed sides. In 1977, as the Marxist-oriented Dergue emerged with absolute control in Ethiopia, the USSR abandoned its policy of providing arms for Somalia and threw its support behind Ethiopia, which it saw as being strategically far more valuable as an ally. On 9 February 1978, Somalia ordered a general mobilization and the following day the US Secretary of State, Cyrus Vance, declared that the US would supply arms to Somalia in the event of Ethiopian aggression, which was a somewhat curious statement given that Somalia had been the aggressor. Only on 21 February did the Somali government admit the presence of its troops in the Ogaden alongside the WSLF guerrillas, by which time Somalia was claiming that Ethiopia had launched air attacks upon its towns. On 8 March, responding to a US peace proposal, the Somali government announced that all regular Somali troops were to be withdrawn from the Ogaden. Somalia then appealed to the great powers to ensure 'the withdrawal of all foreign forces present in the Horn of Africa' and called for 'recognition by the interested parties of the right to self-determination' of the Ogaden people and sought the initiation of a process which would lead to 'a negotiated, peaceful, just and durable settlement'. Ethiopia responded on 11 March that the requirement for a just and durable peace would be the unconditional abandonment by Somalia of all claims to territory in Ethiopia, Kenya and Djibouti. The dispute would continue after the Ogaden war of 1977–78 was over with ongoing Somali support for the WSLF though it denied direct involvement. By May 1978 thousands of refugees from the Ogaden were pouring into Somalia. It took until the end of 1980 for Ethiopian forces to reoccupy almost all the territory of the Ogaden up to the Somali border, having by then expelled most of the WSLF guerrillas. On 4 December 1980, following a visit to Kenya by Mengistu, Ethiopia and Kenya issued a joint communiqué from Nairobi emphasizing their co-operation against what was described as Somali expansionism. The communiqué called on Somalia to 'renounce publicly and unconditionally all claims to the territories of Ethiopia, Kenya and Djibouti'.

Sudan, by contrast, was a substantial player in the Ethiopian-Eritrean war. It provided support for the Eritreans through the 1970s and following an attempted coup against President Nimeiri in July 1976 became far more open in its support once Nimeiri had accused Ethiopia of assisting the Sudanese National Front to attempt his overthrow. However, Sudan did not become belligerent, the government contenting itself with providing back-up support for the Eritreans and through necessity rather than choice becoming the temporary home for many thousands of Eritrean refugees. Nonetheless, a generally hostile Sudan was a factor that Ethiopia had to take into account throughout the years of its revolution.

DJIBOUTI

Throughout the confrontations between Ethiopia and Somalia the tiny enclave territory of Djibouti sat uneasily on the sidelines between its two large neighbours, both of which made claims to it. On 27 June 1977 France granted independence to its Territory of the Afars and Issas, which was renamed

Djibouti, and the leader of the *Ligue Populaire Africaine pour l'Indépendence* (LPAI), Hassan Gouled Aptidon, whose party was supported by Somalia, became the country's president, while Ahmed Dini (an Afar), the Secretary-General of the LPAI, became prime minister. By agreement with the independent government, France stationed about 4,500 troops of the French Foreign Legion in the country 'at the disposal of the government'. Their local expenditure made a major contribution to what was a minuscule economy. This, in fact, consisted largely of trade through the international port of Djibouti, which up to 1976 handled 60 per cent of Ethiopia's imports and 40 per cent of its exports. The Ogaden War of 1977–78 led to a temporary closure of the railway although a recovery followed during the latter part of 1978. Violent disturbances between the Issas (a Somali clan) and the Afars at the end of 1977 led to the arrest of 600 Afars, prompting the resignation of Ahmed Dini and four other Afar ministers from the government: they complained of discrimination against the Afars. In March 1979 Gouled announced that a new party would replace the LPAI. This was the *Rassemblement Populaire pour le Progrès* (RPP). In response Abdullah Mohamed Kamil, who had been head of government under the French prior to independence, formed an underground opposition party, *Front Démocratique pour la Libération de Djibouti* (FDLD). He criticized Gouled for his over-dependence upon France, though the government had few options available to it, and this rivalry paved the way for further dissension in the 1980s.

THE ETHIOPIAN REVOLUTION AND THE FALL OF HAILE SELASSIE

On 27 February 1974 the Ethiopian government resigned after two weeks of strikes, growing disorder and an army mutiny. These were largely the result of a rapid rise in living costs and increasing unemployment. On 26 February, protesting at their low pay, troops had seized control of Asmara. This army mutiny was led by junior officers of the Second Division Infantry. The Emperor sent a delegation to Asmara to treat with the rebels but the Navy and the Air Force had joined the mutiny before any talks could take place. At Massawa junior officers took control of the navy's flagship and Rear Admiral Desta, Haile Selassie's grandson, fled to Djibouti. Much closer to Addis Ababa, mutinous members of the Air Force seized the base at Debre Zeit, only 30 miles from the capital. The Emperor accepted the resignation of Prime Minister Habte-Wold and received pledges of loyalty from his troops in Addis Ababa. In a speech to the troops he claimed that the troubles had been caused by a small group which was supported from outside the country. Although he had recently granted an army pay increase of 25 per cent, he promised a second one. He then appointed

Endalkatchew Makonnen as Prime Minister and the new government immediately announced a further 10 per cent pay increase for the armed forces. By this time, however, the mutineers were in charge of the capital as well as Asmara and it was felt advisable to postpone a meeting of the OAU Council of Ministers. Calm appeared to return to the capital in early March, arrested ministers were released and the students held peaceful demonstrations for elections to be held under interim military rule. The new prime minister announced a cabinet that included members who were regarded as 'progressive', who fulfilled the dual role of reassuring the traditionalists because they came from the great families while persuading the modernists that new policies would follow.[11] The appointments represented a classic compromise decision that could not last in what was rapidly developing into a revolutionary situation as demands for change multiplied.

On 5 March the Emperor announced forthcoming constitutional reforms but two days later the trade unions came out on strike. The Ethiopia Labour Federation demanded a minimum daily wage of E$3 (£0.70) and a revision of the labour laws. The university students called for more radical reforms than the Emperor had promised. The government gave in to all the trade union demands and the strikers went back to work on 11 March. Teachers, however, remained on strike while the university students continued to press for radical changes. Makonnen said his was a caretaker government and that he proposed to put a six-month programme of action into law; by the end of March, however, he threatened to resign unless the armed forces and the public gave him a chance to put reforms into practice. He clearly did not read the public mood accurately and in April was shouted down in parliament by the elected deputies who demanded answers to specific problems such as corruption and what was being done about the drought rather than statements on general policy. One hundred and twenty-five members of the upper house, who had been appointed by Haile Selassie under the terms of the 1955 constitution (then under revision), watched this revolt of the deputies in shocked silence as they now criticized the former government, claiming it had allowed 250,000 people to starve to death. A joint parliamentary session then approved a list of 30 questions to be put to the Prime Minister for answers.

On 28 April the army rebels arrested a number of leading military figures including the commander of the Emperor's bodyguard, the former commander of the Ground Forces and the Deputy Chief of Staff as well as former ministers including the ex-Prime Minister Habte-Wold and his brother. By this time control of events appeared to be in the hands of middle-ranking army and police officers; they made it a condition of their support for the government that former ministers and chiefs of staff should be arrested. About 200 senior figures in all were detained. A peasant revolt erupted in the southern provinces where farms were burned down along a 250-mile stretch of the country's most fertile area of the Rift Valley. About 15 people were shot dead by the police, the regional administration was reduced to chaos and the Governor fled to Addis Ababa. By this time escalating inflation, continuing corruption and the need for land reform were the main causes of the continuing unrest. The old order was increasingly threatened: 'The drought and the unrest in the armed forces have somehow jolted the traditionally docile peasants into political activity. It is aimed primarily at the landlords who have long exploited them but it is now spilling over into a challenge against the police and authorities.'[12] Although the original army mutiny of February 1974 had been about conditions and pay, it introduced the six-month period that saw Haile Selassie progressively lose his authority and in the end his throne. Up to May it still seemed possible that a peaceful transfer of power to another system might have been put in place but the momentum of events now speeded up.

On 28 June the armed forces seized the radio and telecommunications centres and took effective power. This move followed a demand by eight members of Parliament that 25 former cabinet ministers who had been detained ever since the fall of the previous government at the end of February should be released. This demand was made in the face of growing student and junior army officer insistence that the former ministers should be tried for corruption and maladministration. Up to the end of June the army had taken the view that the government of Endalkatchew Makonnen should introduce reforms and bring an end to the exploitation of the majority by the wealthy landowning classes. Now the army made further arrests which, according to *The Times*[13], fell into three groups: the Emperor's closest advisers, who were members of the traditional ruling class, government officials including MPs and administrators. The Emperor's grandson, Prince Eskinder Desta, the Rear Admiral who had fled to Djibouti and subsequently returned to Addis Ababa, was arrested, bringing those in danger ever closer to the Emperor himself. Others arrested at this time included the head of the Security Forces, a Supreme Court Judge and the Finance Minister. The Emperor, meanwhile, continued his normal routine, travelling daily from his Imperial Palace to his office in the Menelik Palace. On 3 July he received leaders of the military and agreed to pass on their demands to the Prime Minister; these included the demand for the immediate surrender of 27 officials whom they had failed to find and 20 of these then gave themselves up. A warning was issued that people should not help the other missing officials or try to dispose of their property. An army manifesto of 13 points, consisting of guidelines for the future government of the country, was issued. It made plain that the Army was determined to play a leading role in the new administration, and would work with the civilian government and act as a watchdog. It said a new constitution that would strip the Emperor of many of his traditional powers should be 'implemented on a priority basis'. While still pledging loyalty to the Emperor, the Army promised better labour relations, aid to the drought victims and the elimination of 'traditional beliefs and customs, which may hamper the unity and progress of Ethiopia'. A 15-man Anti-Corruption Committee was set up with members nominated by the Army and Parliament. Dr Breket Hapte-Selassie, then with the World Bank, and Dr Mesfin Wold-Mariam, a leading geographer and outspoken critic of previous governments, were appointed to the commission, prompting the *Financial Times* to claim that the name Mesfin confirmed earlier reports that leading figures previously out of favour because of their direct or indirect involvement in the 1960 coup attempt were being rehabilitated.

By this time it must have been clear that the Emperor's days were numbered and on 12 September Haile Selassie was toppled from his throne. He had been Emperor since 1934 and before that had acted as Regent during much of the Empress Zawditu's reign (1916–34). In 1923 he took Ethiopia into the League of Nations although membership of the League did not save Ethiopia from invasion by Mussolini's Italy in 1935. During the anti-colonial struggle that followed World War II, despite his conservatism, Haile Selassie came to be regarded as a symbol of Black Africa's ability to take control of its own affairs. The Emperor had seen himself as the Father of African nationalism and both the OAU and ECA were sited in his capital of Addis Ababa. He had proved more adaptable in dealing with international affairs than home affairs where he had to contend with a powerful and conservative aristocracy. During the three months that preceded 12 September his powers had been drastically reduced. On 23 July Endalkatchew Makonnen had resigned his post of prime minister to be replaced by Michael Imru Haile Selassie, a member of the royal family. On 1 August Makonnen had been detained in a wave of new arrests. On 16 August the Emperor's Crown Council and Special Appeal Court were abolished. At that point the Armed Services Committee of the military began to move against the Emperor himself and crowds appeared to demonstrate outside the palace. A report in the *Guardian* recorded the steady loss of power and prestige that the Emperor suffered through August: 'The traditional Establishment has collapsed and its leaders, numbering some 140 people, are now imprisoned at the barracks of the Fourth Division.' Army factions had achieved solidarity and the 'radical' Air Force, guarded by the army, was allowed to fly. In Addis Ababa the Air Force planes flew overhead in precise formation and Army tanks and armoured cars rolled round the Piazza while the Imperial Bodyguard, whose loyalty had been suspect for some time, joined the anti-imperial demonstrators.[14] On 25 August the Emperor's Palace was 'nationalized' and the Emperor was placed under strict surveillance until 12 September when he was deposed and his wealth confiscated. On 26 August the Armed Forces Commission published charges against the Wold government and said ministers were collectively and personally responsible for the failure to combat the four-year drought that had resulted in 250,000 deaths in 1973. The new constitution provided for an Emperor to be titular head of state, a bicameral legislature to include 75 professional people elected by local authorities and municipalities and another 15 to be appointed by the cabinet. The judiciary was to be independent. Political associations were to be permitted provided they were not based on tribal or religious lines. A land law would limit personal holdings, which could not be given to anyone other than those using it to earn a living. All state lands were to become the property of the Ethiopian people.

On 13 September Lt-Gen. Aman Michael Andom was named Chairman of the Armed Forces Committee and Head of the Provisional Government. He was the country's most distinguished soldier. He had served under Gen. Wingate to liberate Ethiopia from the Italians in 1941. In 1951 he served with the Ethiopian contingent in the Korean War and had then been appointed (as a full Colonel) Commandant of the Haile Selassie I Military Training Centre. However, he had fallen out with the Emperor over tactics in 1964 when he commanded the forces in the border dispute with Somalia with the result that he was retired. In the Senate thereafter he had conducted a vigorous campaign for reforms, thus incurring the further displeasure of the Emperor. When the Emperor was deposed on 12 September 1974 the Dergue – the Coordinating Committee of the Armed Forces, the Police and the Land Forces – decided to establish a provisional military government. Over the following two and a half months two vital power struggles were fought out inside the Dergue. The first was between the Marxist radicals and the non-Marxists over the question of military rule, which the Marxists lost. The second concerned reforms: what reforms should be given priority and how to deal with the guilty men – those responsible for the famine disaster, government corruption and mismanagement, and finally, the question of what to do with the Emperor.

On 24 November the military government announced the execution of 60 high-ranking military and civilian officials, including Gen. Andom who had been appointed Chairman of the Armed Forces Committee only six weeks earlier. Andom had been ousted from power a few days before the executions; his house had been destroyed and he may have been killed resisting arrest. Those executed included two prime ministers – Habte–Wold (1961–74) and Endalkatchew Makonnen. A government statement said the 60 people had been executed after being found guilty of numerous crimes, including attempts to disrupt the country's popular movement, perpetuating maladministration and injustice by employing divide-and-rule tactics on tribal and religious grounds, sowing division in the armed forces and trying to incite civil war. A further 140 people remained under arrest and faced similar charges. By this time Haile Selassie had been placed under close guard. No successor to Andom was named immediately, although his deputy-chairman, Maj. Haile Mengistu Mariam, was seen as the most powerful member of the Supreme Military Council. However, on 28 November Brig.-Gen. Teferi Bante was sworn in as Chairman of the Supreme Military Council. There were hostile reactions to the 24 November executions from two African states. The Tanzanian paper *Uhuru* said slaughter was no way to solve Ethiopia's or Africa's problems. President Nyerere had made representations to the rulers of Ethiopia to show restraint when Haile Selassie was deposed. In Zambia the government-owned *Zambia Daily Mail* said the executions were barbaric and should be condemned: 'Unless there is a definite change to a civilized way of life Addis Ababa does not deserve to continue to be the headquarters of the Organisation of African Unity. It has become an embarrassment to Africa.'

The events of November 1974 saw the revolution take a decided turn towards violence and division and the possibility of achieving a national consensus for change correspondingly receded. At the same time the decision of the Dergue to embark upon an all-out military effort to defeat the Eritrean rebels was to have momentous consequences for the army and the long-term future of Ethiopia. Up to this point it had been apparent that the military had no clear-cut revolutionary plan; they had sparked off the revolution with a mutiny for better conditions rather than a blueprint for reforms and thereafter had responded to events. In the process they had sorted out their own leadership, brutally enough, with the result that, as in many revolutionary situations, the most ruthless eventually emerged at the top.

It was Haile Selassie's tragedy that when the challenge to his rule was mounted he was too old and indecisive to know how to react. By clinging to power to the end he destroyed much of his life's achievement and from April to September 1974 it was not clear who was running the country. The Emperor was on his throne but not in control, the Establishment was manoeuvring to obtain the support of the army, which, in its turn, was divided into more or less progressive factions. As things fell apart the ordinary soldiers hoped for a better deal while the officers wanted to modernize the army and had strong reasons for doing so: they feared the Emperor would employ his old tactics of divide and rule; they faced the by then daunting task of bringing the war against secessionist Eritrea to an end; Somalia was strengthening its armed forces with the assistance of Russia and a view to embarking upon an Ogaden adventure; and finally they wished to diversify from dependence upon the US for arms and equipment. There were other disgruntled groups; indeed, the Emperor and the old order had been sitting on a powder keg of developing discontents that now surfaced. Muslims wanted an end to their inferior status, priests wanted an end to the feudal structure of the Orthodox Church, Eritreans looked for liberation and non-Shoans to an end of Shoan dominance.[15] As imperial power collapsed control of the army passed to junior officers, NCOs and privates who tried to create a democratic system of control, which led to the setting up of the Dergue. By September, when the Emperor was deposed, the dominant group in the Dergue were left-wing radicals, although these were divided over what to do with the guilty men and how to convert military rule into some form of participatory democracy. The Dergue was cautious over what to do with Haile Selassie who was widely respected in Africa and the international community beyond the continent. The Dergue needed African goodwill and could not afford to liquidate the Emperor; instead, it isolated him from his throne and the old establishment that had surrounded him. By October a confrontation between the Marxists and the more pragmatic members of the military resulted in a temporary defeat of the Marxists: their leaders were purged from the army, their civilian allies in the trade unions and university were arrested and were lumped together with reactionaries as counter-revolutionaries. The following month the radicals on the Dergue seized the initiative. They were determined to deliver the promises that had been made, especially on land reform, and decided to eliminate the counter-revolutionary activities that had sprung up in the countryside and liquidate the leading members of the old establishment. The result of this decision was Bloody Saturday, 24 November, when some 60 generals, noblemen, ministers and courtiers were executed, including Gen. Andom who had been heading the interim government.

Between Bloody Saturday and the end of 1975 the course of the revolution was determined. Violent opposition to the Dergue followed the massacre of Bloody Saturday at the same time that the war in Eritrea escalated into bitter fighting. Further violence broke out in March 1975 following the nationalization of land. By that time the Dergue described all opposition as counter-revolutionary and dubbed both the Eritrean rebels and leaders of resistance on the land as 'bandits' while the radical students and Marxists were described as reactionaries, spreading 'anti-revolutionary confusion'. On 4 March 1975, the Dergue published a Proclamation of the Nationalization of Rural Land. The measure met a mixed reception: feudal landlords, as was to be expected, opposed it but in many parts of the country, especially in the northern provinces where feudalism was practised less than in the southern lands, comparatively small landowners and tenants also opposed the measure. In addition, the nationalization of the land was opposed by private soldiers since, traditionally, ex-servicemen had received their pensions in the form of land. Now, all land had become the property of the Ethiopian people and generations of feudal injustices had been terminated.[16]

As it put its radical policies in place with single-minded ruthlessness the Dergue appeared to alienate all its earlier supporters. On 18 March a further six leading soldiers were executed on the orders of Teferi Bante, who overruled the court prison sentences. On 21 March a proclamation relieved Crown Prince Merid Azmatch Asfa Wossen, Haile Selassie's successor, of his responsibilities (he had suffered a stroke), and amended Proclamation No. 2 of 12 September 1974 that had deposed the Emperor: 'The sort of future government required by Ethiopia will be determined by the people. The status of the Crown powers given to Merid Azmatch Asfa Wossen and all titles of Prince, Princess and similar royal titles which were awarded to others by him as king have been cancelled.' In April the Second and Third Divisions sent an ultimatum to the Dergue demanding a change to the land reform so as to allow private soldiers to own their own land and that it should initiate talks with the Eritreans. The ultimatum accused the Dergue of causing confusion and called on it to disband itself and send the army back to barracks. The Dergue rejected the ultimatum and arrested some 20 officers and civilians involved in the 'plot'. By May student opposition to the Dergue had reached major proportions and a student boycott of classes was broken by a series of mass arrests while severe penalties were threatened against continued demonstrations. The trade union movement was similarly hostile to Dergue policies.

The intentions of the revolutionary Provisional Military Administrative Council (PMAC) or Dergue became much clearer during 1975: in January it nationalized financial institutions and these were followed later in the year by other business enterprises; the land proclamation of March, which nationalized all rural land, was followed in August by the nationalization of urban land so that the regime had gone a long way towards implementing the political demands of the younger, more radical elements in the country who had contributed substantially to converting the army mutiny of February 1974 into a full-scale revolution. By June 1975 the Dergue had 120 members and a corporate identity had become the norm; however, a triumvirate emerged at the top consisting of the Chairman and Head of State, Gen. Teferi Bante, and two Vice-Chairmen, Maj. Mengistu Haile Mariam, and Col. Atnafu Abate who began to act as a separate cabinet. On 27 August the Dergue announced that Haile Selassie had died in his sleep but since no doctor had been in attendance and there was no post-mortem suspicions arose that he had been poisoned or otherwise put to death. By the end of 1975 the revolution that had been welcomed because it would destroy the old feudal system had fallen into the hands of a military autocracy that by then was leading the revolution from the top. The Dergue became increasingly harsh in maintaining discipline and arrests and the absence of trials shocked many Ethiopians who otherwise were in favour of the changes taking place.

THE ERITREAN WAR

When the Dergue assumed full power in September 1974 it faced Eritrean demands for secession that had been pressed during 12 years of intermittent fighting between government forces and the Eritrean Liberation Front (ELF). Ethiopia's only ports, Massawa and Assab, were both on the Red Sea coast of Eritrea and their retention was seen as a vital strategic necessity. ELF had been formed in 1961, the year before Haile Selassie integrated Eritrea into the unified Ethiopian state; its armed wing, the Eritrean Liberation Army (ELA), was then led by Mohamed Idris Awote and it fired the first shots in what came to be called Africa's longest war in September 1961. The Ethiopian revolution of 1974 provided Eritrea with its chance to gain independence, for up to that time there had seemed no possibility of defeating the Ethiopian army. In 1971, for example, Fred Halliday had written: 'Above all, it is impossible to see how the Eritreans could ever inflict a definitive defeat on the Ethiopian army without a parallel anti-monarchic revolution inside Ethiopia itself. In that sense, the victory of the opposition inside Ethiopia appears to be a strategic precondition for the liberation of Eritrea.'[17] By the 1970s the situation in Eritrea was complicated by the bitter rivalry between the ELF and the Eritrean People's Liberation Front (EPLF) as the two movements struggled for mastery that eventually would be won by the EPLF. Over the years 1975–77, at the height of the fighting against superior Ethiopian forces, the EPLF kidnapped many of ELF's revolutionary cadres, ambushed and otherwise terrorized and killed its leading members. Eritrean hopes that a revolutionary government in Addis Ababa would be sympathetic to its independence were soon dashed when the Dergue decided to intensify the war against Eritrean secession.

In the meantime, the United States began to reassess its relations with Ethiopia. To begin with it was not greatly worried by the socialist measures introduced in the early days of the revolution for almost all political observers had assumed that any successor to Haile Selassie would have to move to the left. However, as the proposed reforms were announced and put in place and most especially the nationalization of land, banks, insurance companies and certain basic industries, Washington began to realize that Ethiopia was about to abandon the capitalist path. The Dergue, facing war on two fronts – Eritrea and an increasingly belligerent Somalia – was militarily dependent upon the US, its army being entirely equipped with American weapons, which were the only ones they knew. In March 1975 the US government decided to continue arms sales to Ethiopia, which it regarded 'just not as part of Africa' but as part of 'a greater region that would include the Arabian peninsula and the Persian Gulf and the Indian Ocean'. This decision was very much a Cold War strategic one.[18] However, the continuing move to the left of the Ethiopian revolution led US policy-makers to undertake a comprehensive reappraisal of the US-Ethiopian relationship and over 4–6 August 1976 the Senate Sub-Committee on African Affairs, chaired by Senator Dick Clark (D-Iowa), held hearings on Ethiopia and the Horn. Most experts also saw Ethiopia and the Horn as part of a wider region that comprised the Middle East and Persian Gulf as well as Africa. A majority on the committee agreed that Ethiopia had not totally slipped away from the US sphere of influence (though this might occur) and Secretary Schaufele said the PMAC was not yet 'systematically or instinctively anti-United States'.[19] At the same time most US experts continued to oppose Eritrean independence, although they recognized that Haile Selassie had been at fault in ending the federation, and favoured a reinstatement of the federation between Ethiopia and Eritrea. At the same time, the hope was expressed that Somalia could be weaned away from its Soviet alliance to become a surrogate for Washington.

The decision to intensify the war against the Eritrean secessionists, arguably, spelt the long-term defeat of the Dergue itself since, as became clear over the following decade, the war was unwinnable. Immediately, the new campaign restored the army's initiative although at the cost of between 2,528 and 3,500 Ethiopian soldiers killed. This major assault did not destroy the Eritrean capacity to resist; rather, it inflamed Eritrean nationalism when 300,000 people were driven from their homes and 50,000 crossed into Sudan as refugees to join the 450,000 already there. When the Dergue prevented either the Red Cross or NGOs taking food to the refugees the effect was to harden Eritrean resolve. At this time the ELF and EPLF reluctantly formed a joint command though it was not to last.

In February 1977 the PMAC, at Mengistu's instigation, carried out another purge that included the execution of Gen. Teferi Bante, its chairman; Mengistu, who had long been seen as the most influential member of the Dergue, finally became its chairman. This event was seen as the defining point of the Ethiopian revolution in both East and West. The left-wing radical wing of the Dergue had finally triumphed. This was confirmed in April when PMAC closed down various US institutions in the country including the Kagnew Military Base, the Military Assistance Advisory Groups (MAAGs), the Naval Medical Research

Unit (NAMRU) and the USIS. In May Mengistu led a PMAC mission to Moscow where a 'Declaration of the Basic Principles of Friendly Mutual Relations and Co-operation', the prelude to a full friendship treaty, was announced. Ethiopia at once began to receive massive supplies of weapons and other economic assistance from the USSR and other socialist countries and this marked the end of Ethiopia's dependence upon the US for military assistance and the beginning of an Ethiopian alliance with the socialist world. Later that May US President Jimmy Carter 'cut off military assistance and sale credits to Ethiopia'. He cited the violation of human rights as the reason for his action.

THE OGADEN WAR

The Ogaden war between Ethiopia and Somalia (1977–78) demonstrated the cynicism of Cold War politics as the United States switched its support from Ethiopia to Somalia and the USSR did the same thing in reverse, deserting its Somali ally for what it saw as the greater African prize of Ethiopia. The huge involvement of the two superpowers in the Horn contributed nothing to solving regional problems, but only served to emphasize African vulnerability and big power opportunism.

The Somali drought of 1975 was the worst in memory, affecting the pastoral nomads of the northern region who comprised 75 per cent of the population. The disaster forced the government to put its Five-Year Development Plan on hold, incur large debts and concentrate on relief measures. The government handled the crisis efficiently. Siad Barre was a far more complex character than later appraisals of his performance suggested and was the only person after independence to come near to uniting the Somali clans in a single national system. Like all Somalis, he was fiercely determined to safeguard the country's independence and he took care to balance the growing Somali relationship with the USSR that he established in the early 1970s by promoting closer ties with the Arab world, which he consolidated in 1974 when Somalia was admitted to membership of the Arab League, despite Arab suspicion of Somalia's socialism and ties with the Soviet Union. The Somali armed forces were equipped with Soviet arms, yet the government denied BBC claims that it had given base facilities to the USSR. At the same time that the USSR was seen as the country's principal external ally, Somalia cemented good relations with China, which undertook a road-building programme in the country and welcomed a Somali delegation to Beijing in May 1975 to discuss co-operation in the fields of forestry and agriculture. Had such a visit been to a Western country it would have passed unremarked; since it was to Communist China the Western media elevated it into an ideological alignment.

When in the 1950s the US negotiated for a military base in Eritrea it acted in the role of Cold War 'aggressor' in the Horn and became the principal external support of Ethiopia. At that time the USSR, supporting Eritrean independence, was on the defensive. When Siad Barre came to power in Somalia and initiated a socialist revolution, the USSR saw its chance to obtain a foothold in the Horn, although, as it later discovered, Barre was always his own master, was suitably wary of Russian and Chinese friendship and kept open his options with the West. As the confrontation between Somalia and Ethiopia escalated in 1977 and it became clear that the USSR was switching sides, Somalia expelled its Soviet experts and advisers (in November 1977) and abrogated its Treaty of Friendship with the USSR of 11 July 1974. Meanwhile, until 1975, Cuba had supported the Eritrean secessionists in their fight against Ethiopia; however, as Russia saw the possibility of a greater regional prize as an ally in Ethiopia rather than Somalia, following the Ethiopian revolution, and proceeded to become Mengistu's principal supporter, it then cynically pressured Cuba into deserting the Eritrean liberation struggle and switching its support to Ethiopia. Once Ethiopia had entered into an alliance with the USSR and was 'lost' to the West, the US turned again to Siad Barre and worked to woo Somalia back into the Western camp while, for his part, Barre needed Western support to balance the Soviet desertion. In 1977, therefore, the West calculated that an offer of arms would be sufficient to bring Barre back into its camp and the US and other Western powers 'promised' both military and other economic assistance if Somalia would embrace their moves against the Ethiopian revolution. The Saudi monarchy promised between US$330 million and US$500 million to Somalia 'on the condition that Somalia join the movement to eliminate Russian influence in the Red Sea'.[20] In the straitened circumstances in which it found itself, Somalia was eager to accept these Western overtures and began issuing pro-US statements. However, the US found itself in a dilemma since, by the end of 1977, there was too much evidence of Somali aggression in the Ogaden conflict, including Somali warplanes that had been shot down by the Ethiopians, for Mogadishu to deny its support for the WSLF guerrillas. Even so, the US feigned neutrality although it had given Somalia assurances that it would 'come to their aid' if they attacked Ethiopia. Saudi Arabia, moreover, had encouraged Somalia to count on Western support. In the event none of substance was forthcoming. 'The Soviet Union, Cuba and other socialist countries provided unequivocal support to Ethiopia, decisive in the victory over Somalia in March 1978. The US and its NATO allies were caught in a dilemma when the tide began to turn against Somalia. They would have liked to have "openly" intervened on the side of Mogadishu but were apprehensive of the condemnation such an intervention would evoke from many African states which had clearly noted Somalia was the aggressor.'[21] Somalia complained that the West had failed it, but continued to seek Western support since it then had no option.

COMPARISONS

Somalia's Barre and Ethiopia's Mengistu had a good deal in common. Both were revolutionaries and political opportunists, both seized power when their countries required strong leadership to supervise major changes and both were to discover during the 1980s, as many revolutionaries had found before them, that the best of revolutionary intentions could be defeated in the end by the innate conservatism of the people they aspired to lead. When Barre seized power in 1969 he claimed to have done so to combat 'tribalism, corruption, nepotism and misrule'. He dissolved the National Assembly and set up in its place the Supreme Military Council which instituted military rule. His politics were Marxist inspired and authoritarian; he was then shunned by the Western powers and so turned for aid to the USSR. Although he was a political Marxist Barre was also a practising Muslim who often invoked God in his speeches. He worked hard to gain acceptance from the Arab Muslim world and succeeded in this aim when in 1974 Somalia was invited to join the Arab League. In 1976 Barre attempted to give his regime increased authority when he established the Somali Revolutionary Socialist Party (SRSP) on Soviet lines. The party provided the National Assembly with a single list of candidates nominated by its Central Committee but Barre retained effective power in his own hands. He was to be unanimously elected President by the People's Assembly in 1980 and again in 1986. His undoing began when he pushed the Somali claim to the Ogaden region of Ethiopia, although given the strength of Somali irredentism, he may not have been able to resist doing so even had he wanted to. Barre took advantage of the revolution in Ethiopia when in 1977 he committed his army to supporting the WSLF in their Ogaden campaign. He had grossly under-estimated the realpolitik of the Russians and the relative value to Moscow of Somalia and Ethiopia as an ally. His Soviet backers deserted him in 1977 for what they saw as the greater prize and in 1978 he faced defeat by the Ethiopians with the aid of their new Russian and Cuban allies.

When the Ethiopian revolution began with the army mutiny of February 1974 Mengistu, who was an ordnance officer in charge of military supplies, played no part until he was sent to Addis Ababa as the representative of the Third Division to sit on the Armed Forces Coordinating Committee where he found that many of the officers competing for power were his seniors. Although several senior officers were to be given the titular position as Head of State it soon became clear that real power lay with the Armed Forces Coordinating

Committee; following the deposition of the Emperor on 12 September 1974 the Committee turned itself into the Provisional Military Administrative Committee (PMAC) or Dergue. Mengistu was elected as one of the two vice-chairmen. He was a charismatic speaker and quickly made his mark; he coined the phrase 'Ethiopia tikdem' (Ethiopia first). He had the qualities required of a dictator: he was single-minded, hard working, dedicated and ruthless. In November 1974 when 60 top ranking soldiers and others, including Gen. Andom, were executed, the purge that destroyed them was carried out by forces loyal to Mengistu. He, however, did not push himself forward but allowed Gen. Teferi Bante to become head of state, a post he held for the succeeding two years. In February 1977 Mengistu organized a second putsch against his opponents on the Dergue; Teferi Bante was executed and this time Mengistu seized supreme power and became head of state. He allowed no dissent and though the Dergue turned Ethiopia into a Marxist-Socialist state, dissident groups, including those that adopted Marxist-Leninist policies, were eliminated. Like Barre, Mengistu needed to legitimize and civilianize his regime while retaining control in his own hands. In December 1979 he established a commission to find the correct solution; this was named the Commission for the Organization of a Party of the Workers of Ethiopia (COPWE). However, more than two-thirds of its members remained military men. Gradually its Central Committee took over the functions of PMAC and Mengistu saw that his own supporters were in a dominant position on both committees. These two contemporaries who presided over the revolutions in their respective countries saw their achievements unravel during the 1980s and each was forced into exile in the early 1990s.[22]

Unlike the military coups and takeovers that characterized the politics of Africa at this time, the revolution in Ethiopia unfolded along classic lines: it was neither the instant overthrow of a regime by a rebellious army promising to reform a corrupt system nor was it the replacement of one military group by another that considered its turn to rule had come in a newly independent state that was still searching for the most appropriate form of government. The Ethiopian revolution followed a pattern of escalation akin to the French Revolution. It began with gathering protests against the injustices of a long-established and deeply entrenched feudal system that came to a head in strikes, student protests and an army mutiny, though their demands were still for change within the system.[23] Thereafter, for a matter of months, the Emperor was left on his throne while his powers were whittled away. The moderates were then replaced by the first group of radicals, 'guilty' men of the old regime were executed, the Emperor was first isolated and then deposed and there followed a period in which different revolutionary factions struggled for supremacy, until in 1977, in a second brutal putsch, Mengistu, the Ethiopian 'Robespierre', finally emerged at the top to wield undisputed power, enabling him to impose a radical revolution on Ethiopia.

COLD WAR MANOEUVRES

It was in keeping with his character that Siad Barre, a fervent Somali nationalist as well as revolutionary and political opportunist, should seize the opportunity offered by the unfolding revolution inside Ethiopia in early 1977 to provide all-out military support for the WSLF guerrillas fighting in the Ogaden region in the hope of achieving one of his people's irredentist claims and bolstering his own position at the same time. By early 1977 the WSLF was sending ever larger guerrilla units across the border into the Ogaden where they were making substantial gains of territory. In July Barre sent regular army units across the border to support the WSLF thereby changing long-standing guerrilla skirmishing into a full-scale military assault. By that time, however, the Russians were already withdrawing their support from Somalia and providing military assistance on a far greater scale to Ethiopia. 'In entering the fray as the committed partisan of one side (Ethiopia) and repudiating its former friendship with the other side (Somalia), the Soviet Union – unlike all the other contestants – was making a calculated strategic decision in which national sentiment or sympathy with a struggle for independence had no part and provided no justification.'[24] It was in May 1977, a few weeks after the Dergue ended its arms agreement with the United States, that the USSR and Ethiopia negotiated a secret military agreement in Moscow. No details were published but informed estimates put the arms aid programme at US$400 million. In fact, Soviet military input over the following 12 months came to something in the order of US$1 billion worth of arms and by September crated MiG fighters and tanks began arriving in Addis Ababa. Russian troopships brought thousands of Cuban troops to Assab and by February 1978 between 10,000 and 11,000 Cubans were in Ethiopia, most of them in the Ogaden region, supported by 400 Russian tanks and 50 MiG fighters. At the height of the Soviet arms build-up between December 1977 and January 1978 an estimated 225 Soviet transport planes – Antonov 22s and Tupolov 76s, equivalent to between 12 and 15 per cent of the Russian military transport fleet – were engaged transporting arms to Ethiopia. Further, dozens of Russian and East European cargo vessels, escorted by Soviet naval units, were bringing materiel to Massawa and Assab, including tanks, planes, missiles and 120-mm artillery pieces. According to the Somali Minister of Information, Abdisalam Hussein, military personnel from East Germany, Czechoslovakia, Poland and Hungary were also involved in the Ogaden war.[25]

The Soviet effort in support of the Mengistu regime was one of its biggest military aid efforts anywhere and its role was later to extend to the war in Eritrea as well.

On 12 January 1978 the US President Jimmy Carter accused the Soviet Union of 'dispatching' Cubans to Ethiopia. The Russians responded by pointing to the US link to Somalia via Saudi Arabia and Iran. The previous December the *Washington Post* had described close US-Saudi relations in Africa through 1977 while Saudi sources were quoted estimating that Riyadh had provided Somalia with US$200 million to purchase arms in the West at a 'bargain rate' to replace Soviet equipment.[26] In June 1978 US intelligence sources estimated that Russian war materiel had reached 61,000 tons, transported by 36 freighters and an air ferry of 59 planes. At the height of their involvement, the total number of Cubans engaged in the fighting in Ethiopia was variously estimated at between 11,000 and 19,000 men. After the Ogaden victory their numbers were reduced by 2,000 to 3,000. The Cubans, who played an important role in several parts of Africa at this time and had an influence out of proportion to their international strength, first attempted to mediate between Ethiopia and Somalia before becoming militarily involved in the Ogaden war. Early in March 1978, Fidel Castro announced that Cuban officials had held a secret meeting with Somalian and Ethiopian leaders in Aden in March of the previous year to avert hostilities in the Ogaden; when this failed, and following the Somali invasion of the Ogaden Province, the Cubans assisted the Ethiopian forces to turn the tide of invasion, although at first denying any front-line involvement. In April the British Foreign Secretary, Dr Owen, attacked Russian and Cuban attitudes towards Eritrean secession and claimed that the Cubans had supported the Eritreans for years with both advice and training. The Cubans rebutted Dr Owen's remarks as an example of 'singular arrogance'. Later that month, Mengistu made an official visit to Havana, although it was believed that he had already been there secretly in October 1977, to ask for Cuban help. Eritrea was at the centre of his talks with Castro. In July 1978, Cuba announced that it had cut its forces in Ethiopia by about 25 per cent to between 12,000 and 13,000. The following month, despite initial reservations about taking part in an Ethiopian attack upon the Eritrean rebels, the Cubans did become involved in the fighting against the Eritrean secessionists and Cuban pilots were engaged, flying MiG 21s against guerrilla mountain strongholds. When Castro visited Addis Ababa in September 1978 he received a tumultuous welcome.

The defeat of Somalia in the Ogaden war faced the country with massive problems and though, as Barre's personal physician Dr Cahill, an American and confirmed Somali supporter, suggested, the Somali people 'have learned to endure drought and expect periodic famine. The loyalty of the clan usually sustains the needy, and an intense national pride prevents them from easily seeking, or readily receiving, outside assistance'.[27] They were certainly in need of such assistance by the end of the decade when a vast influx of starving women and children from the war-torn Ogaden crossed into Somalia. The same author, forgetting that the original aggression came from Somalia, depicted the plight of the refugees: 'The men in these families are gone; some have been killed in the sputtering Ogaden war, many in bombing and strafing raids that have characterized Cuba's and Russia's contribution to the overt Ethiopian effort at permanently depopulating the contested area; other men continue to fight in one of the Somali Liberation Front units; while a few remain in the bush with their dying livestock.'[28] In mid-1978 there were 80,000 refugees in Somali camps, but by mid-1979 the number had risen to 220,000; thereafter they arrived at the rate of 1,000 a day and by January 1980 there were over 500,000 refugees inside the Somali borders. Dr Cahill took issue with the US role in relation to Somalia when he argued that the US, in its post-Vietnam war mode, seemed 'determined to permit a Russian-Cuban offensive in the Ogaden as long as it doesn't pass a geographic line imposed by colonial powers, a line never accepted by the Somali people and irrelevant to the pattern of nomadic life essential for survival on the Horn'. He continued: 'Is our fear of overseas entanglements so great that we will impotently watch while Russia dominates the Horn, and with it the Red Sea, and all that it represents to the West? Should we passively accept the insults of an Ethiopian regime that has eliminated a large portion of its university students and resolves political differences by murder? Have we lost the courage even to condemn?'[29] Cahill's is an interesting tirade: at heart a Cold War warrior he yet wanted to persuade the US to support Siad Barre despite Barre's clear culpability in first attacking Ethiopia.

The political alignments and changes that occurred in the Horn during the 1970s were bewildering in their reversals, but though the two superpowers became heavily engaged, the wars – between Ethiopia and Somalia and Ethiopia and Eritrea – were nationalist rather than ideological and this was despite the socialist policies advocated by the two principal political leaders, Mengistu and Barre. It was the outsiders, the US and USSR plus Cuba, who provided a Cold War dimension to these African struggles and they did so, of course, because for them the Horn was only one piece in a world jigsaw that they were contending to bring within their control. By the end of the decade both Ethiopia under Mengistu and Somalia under Barre faced a long haul to reconstruct their countries after the devastation of war. In the case of Ethiopia the Eritrean war had yet to run its course; in the case of Somalia the framework of Barre's socialist revolution had been largely shattered and he faced a decade in which clan rivalries would again move to the centre of Somalia's political life, though they had never been far from the surface. In both cases the ordinary people in one of the poorest regions of Africa had been rendered even poorer and, as they would discover, more dependent upon external assistance and that, as they had already found, only came at a price.

CHAPTER TWENTY

Rhodesia

By the end of the 1960s the white Rhodesians were beginning to realize that UDI had not solved their problems; instead, an escalating guerrilla war was making white control increasingly precarious while their beleaguered status rendered them more and more dependent upon South Africa. In June 1969, the Rhodesian Secretary of Defence said: 'Should terrorist infiltration continue on the increasing scale evidenced to date, it will be necessary for further money to be found to maintain the army at the standard that will be required to meet this emergency.' His statement set the tone for the 1970s. Further, the Land Tenure and Constitution Acts strengthened racial barriers in Rhodesia and established apartheid as the basic philosophy of the government. In any case, land under the Land Apportionment Act of 1930 was divided roughly 50–50 between the 230,000 whites and the five million blacks. The new Land Tenure Act extended the power of the minister to enforce racial segregation. On 2 March 1970 the government proclaimed Rhodesia a Republic and scheduled elections under a new republican constitution for 10 April. The British Foreign Secretary, Michael Stewart, said the Republic, like UDI, was illegal. The United States said that it would not recognize the Republic and on 9 March announced the closure of its consulate; other countries followed suit. At the United Nations Britain attempted to get a quick resolution passed through the Security Council condemning Rhodesia's assumption of republican status in order to outflank any tougher resolution but this manoeuvre failed as African countries delayed the debate until on 12 March another, tougher resolution was introduced, backed by Russia and Poland, which condemned 'the persistent refusal of the government of the United Kingdom to use force' and called for sanctions against South Africa. The resolution was vetoed by Britain and the United States. A further resolution of 19 March at least stiffened sanctions. Although the Rhodesian Government claimed an immigrant boom, the figures did not bear this out. In 1960 there had been 214,000 whites while natural increase had added another 30,000 and new immigrants a further 82,000 so that the population ought to have stood at 326,000 whites by 1970. In fact it was only 234,000 as 90,000 whites in the meantime had left the country so that it had lost the equivalent of all the new immigrants plus an additional 10,000.

The return to power in Britain of a Conservative government under Edward Heath in June 1970 raised hopes in white circles of a favourable settlement in Rhodesia. By October it had become clear that the Heath government was initiating new talks with the Smith regime and Smith insisted that Britain must negotiate with Rhodesia as a sovereign independent state. On 10 November 1970, the Foreign Secretary, Sir Alec Douglas-Home, told the House of Commons that preliminary talks were in progress to ascertain whether detailed negotiations could begin. Following Britain's row with the African members of the Commonwealth at the January 1971 Singapore summit over its announced intention of resuming the sale of arms to South Africa, Smith described Heath and Douglas-Home as 'very reasonable gentlemen'. Meanwhile, his government announced that a new Property Owners (Residential Protection) Bill would be debated the following March; it was opposed by the 25,000 Asians and Coloureds against whom it was aimed since it would allow their removal from any residential area the President declared to be exclusive. Whites defended the Bill on the grounds that it promoted racial harmony. However, the Bill was dropped from the agenda for the Rhodesian Parliament that opened on 2 March as a tactical move to improve the chance of talks with Britain that Sir Alec Douglas-Home appeared about to initiate. Meanwhile, a survey of 200 white sixth-form boys and girls in Salisbury showed that half wanted to leave Rhodesia and half of these did not want to return: their reasons were repression, people afraid to express themselves, too insular, sport-mad, narrow minded, no scope in advanced technology and the future too dependent upon politics.

Lord Goodman, a sort of multiparty ombudsman solicitor and trouble-shooter for British governments, visited Rhodesia early in June 1971 on behalf of the Foreign Secretary for talks with members of the Smith regime. Smith was under pressure to seek a settlement with the British Conservative government, which was seen as more sympathetic to Rhodesia than its Labour predecessor. In Britain there was opposition to any settlement that did not adhere to the five principles; for example, in July an interdenominational group of churchmen in London insisted that a settlement must embody the reality as well as the form of the five principles. The talks continued through the summer. Then in November the Foreign Secretary announced that he was to visit Rhodesia for substantive talks. In a letter to *The Times*,[1] Sir Bernard de Bunsen, Chairman of the Africa Bureau (with 10 signatories), said: 'In the view of the Africa Bureau the five principles can only serve as a basis for negotiation with men who genuinely wish to see African political advance; all the signs since 1965 have been that the Rhodesian Front wishes to perpetuate White minority rule...' After detailing events, the letter continues: 'Against such a background no agreement concluded between the British Government and the Smith regime alone could be acceptable to either the British people or the majority of the people of Rhodesia.' The *Guardian* said of the proposed settlement: 'Unless he has reliable grounds for thinking that Mr Smith has retreated a long way from his previous stands, Sir Alec's announcement must look like the second step on the slippery slope towards a sell-out. The first step was Sir Alec's willingness to have "one more try" to settle with the Rhodesian Front even though Labour's experience and the subsequent apartheid legislation in Rhodesia both showed that negotiations on the basis of the five principles were doomed to futility.'[2] As the talks approached, Lord Acton and Garfield Todd, the former Prime Minister of Rhodesia, said: 'The British Government has not grasped the fundamental truths about Rhodesia. The White Rhodesians are not prepared to accept majority rule ever. The Black Rhodesians do not want independence under a Rhodesian Front government. They have not asked for the lifting of sanctions. The White electorate will gladly accept the removal of sanctions. They have not asked for the lifting of sanctions.'[3]

On 15 November Sir Alec Douglas-Home, who had already told the House of Commons that an agreement had to be consistent with the five principles, arrived in Salisbury for settlement talks and agreed a formula with the Smith regime although this was to be subject to the findings of a commission that they were acceptable to the people of Rhodesia as a whole. The settlement proposals were presented to the British Parliament on 24 November 1971 and were based on the Republican Constitution adopted by the Smith government in 1969. Certain modifications were made, which included a proposal for a new roll of African voters to be created with the same qualifications as those for the European voters' roll. When the number of voters registered on the African higher roll equalled 6 per cent of the number of voters then registered on the European roll, two additional African seats would become due; and when the number of voters registered on the African higher roll equalled 12 per cent of the number of voters then registered on the European roll, a further two additional African seats would become due, two at a time, for each such proportionate increase of 6 per cent in the number of voters registered on the African higher roll, until 34 additional African seats had been created... The complications of this process, which was laid out at length, led Dr Claire Palley to suggest in an article of 28 November in the *Sunday Times* that the settlement would mean that African majority rule would not be achieved in the lifetime of present White Rhodesians (which, after all, was the object of the 1969 Constitution) and that 2035 was the earliest at which an African majority could be achieved in the Assembly and even that majority would still only represent the wealthy minority of Africans who would have qualified for the vote. These 1971 proposals provided for no external safeguards whatever, before, during or after the test of acceptability.

In Dar es Salaam, President Nyerere said: 'If they have agreed, then they have agreed a sell-out.' Smith said: 'We have the happiest Africans in the world.' At the United Nations the General Assembly voted 94 to 8 to reject the Douglas-Home-Smith settlement terms. That December Lord Goodman, a major architect of the settlement, said: 'The African is not profoundly discontented although he is increasingly resentful of the situation.'

THE PEARCE COMMISSION

The Douglas-Home-Smith agreement included the provision for a commission to sound out opinion in Rhodesia as a whole and though this was not the intention, the Pearce Commission marked a watershed in white Rhodesian fortunes, which were to deteriorate thereafter. Opposition to the settlement inside Rhodesia and outside rose rapidly once its terms were known, leading to the formation of the African National Council under Bishop Abel Muzorewa to co-ordinate African opposition, which from December 1971 became very active. The Smith government insisted that a settlement could be reached and denied all allegations that Africans were being obstructed from holding meetings or expressing their views. When demonstrations occurred because of restrictions the security forces were ordered out and strong measures were taken against all demonstrators while Smith argued that Africans were showing their unsuitability for the concessions made to them. Optimistically, Smith told the *Rhodesia Herald* that he thought ratification of the agreement and the lifting of sanctions would be achieved by April 1972 and that he believed support from Europeans and Africans would be overwhelming.[4] Acceptance of the agreement was conditional on the Pearce Commission sounding out both white and black opinion.

Lord Pearce, a former Lord of Appeal, was selected by Sir Alec Douglas-Home as chairman of the Commission (he was not the Foreign Secretary's first choice). While his appointment led to criticism in Britain that he was too old and right wing, such critics were to be confounded. The other members of the Commission were Sir Glyn Jones, the former Governor of Nyasaland, Sir Maurice Dorman, the former Governor of Sierra Leone, and Lord Harlech, the former Ambassador to Washington. On 20 December 1971 Pearce told a press conference in London that his terms of reference were 'to satisfy themselves' that the Anglo-Rhodesian terms 'have been fully and properly explained to the population of Rhodesia' and 'to ascertain by direct contact with all sections of the population whether the people as a whole regard these proposals as an acceptable basis for independence.' Later, when carrying out his mission in Rhodesia, Pearce complained that the regime infringed the terms of the settlement to allow normal political activity by arresting and imprisoning such people as Garfield Todd and his daughter Judith, and Mr and Mrs Chinamano. The Commissioners continued their tours of Rhodesia until mid-February 1972.

The Pearce Report was published on 23 May 1972 and stated: 'We believe that taking into account the explanation given by the Rhodesian authorities, the activities of those opposing or promoting the proposals, the distribution of our simplified version of the proposals and the explanation given by the Commission at meetings and over the radio, the great majority of those who gave us their opinions had a sufficient understanding of the content and implications of the proposals to enable them to pass judgement on them. We are satisfied that the proposals have been fully and properly explained to the population of Rhodesia.' Having made this plain, the Report continued: 'We are satisfied on our evidence that the proposals are acceptable to the great majority of Europeans. We are equally satisfied, after considering all our evidence including that on intimidation, that the majority of Africans rejected the proposals. In our opinion, the people of Rhodesia as a whole do not regard the proposals as acceptable as a basis for independence.' The Report had found that of 120,730 people of all races interviewed, 107,309 Africans rejected the proposals. Reacting to the Report, Sir Alec Douglas-Home said there must now be time for reflection and Smith said the Commission Report was mistaken. The failure of the Pearce Commission to endorse the Douglas-Home settlement proposals, as he had hoped, and so bring an end to sanctions, led Smith to announce that there would be no further talks with Britain on constitutional matters.

White Rhodesians, who had been led to believe that the Pearce Commission would endorse the settlement proposals, were stunned by the result. Never before had their clearly expressed will been so decisively overruled, but then never before had so many Africans been asked what they thought. Opening the annual debate to renew sanctions on 9 November 1972, Sir Alec Douglas-Home said the aim was not to bring Rhodesia to its knees but to bring it back into the comity of nations. He said that as a result of the proposals of November 1971 and of the findings of the Pearce Report he believed that there was a growing awareness in Rhodesia of the need for compromise. The Europeans endorsed it emphatically by accepting the November proposals. The African National Council had since declared in favour of compromise and on a negotiated settlement. However, African distrust of Britain had been increased by the Heath government's attempt to do a deal with the Smith regime. The situation in Rhodesia was to change dramatically at the end of 1972. On 21 December ZANU guerrillas attacked Altena farm in the north-east of the country to signal a new phase in the guerrilla war and from this time onward all white farms became potential targets.

The performance of Sir Alec Douglas-Home over Rhodesia can be seen as the last effort of a disappearing British attitude that still saw the Empire, or what remained of it, in white race terms. Heath had given Sir Alec a free hand as Foreign Secretary to deal with Rhodesia as he saw fit and the latter believed that Smith was a prisoner of his own hard-liners. In November 1970 Smith had begun a secret correspondence with Sir Alec, emphasizing that in the proposed forthcoming talks Rhodesia would not be negotiating from weakness. He wanted a settlement, as long as terms were acceptable, which for him meant continuing white control. When Joshua Nkomo met Sir Alec he argued that there could be no settlement outside NIBMAR (No Independence Before Majority African Rule) while Sir Alec wanted a compromise settlement so as to avoid a bitter race war. What Sir Alec either never grasped or ignored was that a compromise with Smith was not a compromise but a clear victory for him. Although Smith conceded the principle of majority rule, the timetable for this goal was unacceptable to Africans whose mistrust of Smith was total. 'Clauses about a Declaration of Rights and a commission to investigate racial discrimination did not alter the fact that the basis of the settlement was an amended version of Smith's 1969 constitution. The white population were of course in favour, but the African leaders – Nkomo, Mugabe, Muzorewa and Sithole – were united in their opposition. Smith's belief, shared by Douglas-Home, that the agreement would be acceptable to the African population was unrealistic.'[5] In a letter of 3 December 1971 to Lord Pearce, Douglas-Home said: 'I would like you to be certain from the start that my feeling is exactly [the opposite], namely that all those who will be talking to Africans should say quite clearly that the proposals are sponsored by Her Majesty's Government who consider them just and fair. I thought that on that point you would like to know my view.'[6] At the time, the Conservative right wing and others felt that the Commission should have gone to Rhodesia at once, but its members had to be assembled and Christmas intervened. They believed the time lag gave African nationalists time to organize opposition. The Commission arrived in Salisbury on 10 January 1972. Pearce personally saw as many leaders of African opinion as he could while other members of the Commission went into the bush to meet villagers. Pearce was not appreciated by the Rhodesian 'right'. After two months Pearce returned to Britain and presented his report to Douglas-Home on 4 May and it was published on 23 May. On relinquishing office in 1974 Douglas-Home wrote, revealingly, to Miles Hudson, 'I think that Rhodesia is the only real disappointment which I take away with me but even then in a lurking hope that 1970 will not be too wide of the mark when the settlement comes.'[7] His hope, still, was on behalf of the white minority.

ESCALATING GUERRILLA WAR

On 9 January 1973 Smith closed the Rhodesian border with Zambia, a move that was seen as a sign of weakness rather than strength, and during the year that followed it became clear that the initiative had passed to the guerrillas. Later that month Sir Alec Douglas-Home said: 'When a government which is pursuing racial policies inside a country has freedom fighters coming from outside, this is a situation I have warned time and time again is bound to lead to conflict. My fear all along, through all these years, has been that there would be eventually a front on the Zambezi between the southern half of Africa and the north. This is something we must all try to avoid.' Sir Alec saw no irony in his statement though his efforts to achieve a settlement that would have left Smith in control would certainly have increased the violence that he feared. By 1973 South Africa had between 2,000 and 5,000 troops permanently in Rhodesia and by September of that year, for the first time, more whites were to emigrate than come into the country as new settlers.

When Smith closed the border with Zambia following an upsurge in cross-Zambezi guerrilla activity, his government said Zambia's 27,000 tons a month of copper exports that passed through Rhodesia would be allowed to continue, but that no imports would be permitted to go north. Zambia, however, decided to stop sending its copper through Rhodesia. At the same time Zambia suspended all currency dealings between its banks and either Rhodesia or South Africa. For its part, South Africa was refusing to allow goods destined for Zambia to pass through its ports. Commenting on the border closure, Hugo Young[8] said that Rhodesians were increasingly aware of the need for a settlement; guerrillas were operating inside as well as across their borders while drought was an unconcealed natural disaster. The closing of the Zambian border would increase Rhodesian economic difficulties. 'If as some people consider possible, these developments eventually give Mr Smith enough support among Rhodesian whites to come once more to the conference table, he will find that London is not devoid of ideas to accommodate him. The government would like nothing better than to get rid of Rhodesia...' He continued: 'Britain has kept the 1971 offer on the table, despite its rejection by the Rhodesian people by a margin of four to one. To keep it there, the Foreign Office adopts a posture of ignominious silence concerning the five and a half million Africans for whom it is still the trustee... A full battery of pass laws is being enacted.' Young's indictment of the

British government was scathing and concluded: 'The Foreign Secretary's response to these events is the truest measure of how far he is willing to go to get a settlement. He does not say that these are terrible betrayals of the settlement now on the table: for that would offend the Rhodesians. He says, wagging a reproving finger, that the Africans had it coming to them as soon as they rejected his settlement. They have, in other words, only themselves to blame.' Despite the closure of the border, guerrilla activities inside Rhodesia seemed unaffected. Casualties mounted during January and February and included white farmers. On 19 January Smith admitted that the guerrillas had been 'quietly and methodically undermining the local population'. And, he claimed, had used intimidation and witchcraft to mislead a 'simple and gullible people'.

In February the United Nations sent a four-nation group to assess the problems faced by Zambia because of hostile action by Rhodesia. In its report to the Security Council the group said it would cost Zambia £50 million to set up alternate transport routes to those through Rhodesia. A Security Council Resolution was passed by 13 votes to two abstentions (Britain and the United States) condemning economic blackmail and military threats against Zambia 'in collusion with the racist regime in South Africa'. At this time the Rhodesian regime began to impose collective fines on tribes that helped the guerrillas. There were a number of casualties on the Zambian side of the border as a consequence of mines laid by the Rhodesian military. Early in the year the Rhodesian government introduced new race legislation that included influx control and tougher pass laws. It established regional African Authorities for Matabeleland and Mashonaland that constituted a major step towards apartheid. Allan Savory, an outspoken white MP who broke away from the Rhodesian Front to form his own Rhodesia Party, warned that 'brute force and tough talk' would lose the war. He said: 'It is essential to have the active support of the African people – the side that wins this wins the war.' When in April 1973 the Foreign Secretary warned against violence, the ANC's Bishop Muzorewa, generally regarded as a pacific man, replied tartly: 'In advising Africans not to use the gun, Sir Alec Douglas-Home should realize that the use of the gun has always been a last resort in all problematical situations. Frustration leads a people to resort to violent measures.' The British government persisted in its support for the 1971 proposals, which, Heath told the House of Commons on 8 May, remained 'on the table' and should form the basis of any future settlement. In Rhodesia Smith said he rejected the view that a settlement according to the 1971 proposals was no longer possible. By this time the Rhodesian government needed a settlement more than did the British government. Sir Roy Welensky, the former prime minister of the Central African Federation, said any talks were now bound to fail. He warned that a very grave situation (for white

Rhodesians) was developing and called on Smith to take Africans into his government. The National Association of Coloured People representing Rhodesia's 16,000 people of mixed descent withdrew its support for the settlement proposals in June 1973 because of the discriminatory measures that had been introduced over the preceding year.

By mid-1973 Rhodesians had come to accept the guerrilla war as a permanent part of their lives while the country was increasingly dependent upon South Africa. At the annual RF Congress that September the Chairman, Des Frost, spoke of curbing the black population as more whites were seen to be leaving the country than entering it. Meanwhile, Smith had begun talks with Bishop Muzorewa, insisting however that he should accept the 1971 British proposals even though these had been widely rejected by those who were interviewed by the Pearce Commission and then rejected by Smith himself. However, it was becoming clear to Smith that he had to make some broader accommodation with the Africans. The talks continued through to May 1974; then Smith sought talks with both Nkomo and Sithole, suggesting parity power-sharing, but Sithole was rapidly losing what little influence he still had and Nkomo only talked of majority rule. During the year the Rhodesian government published a dossier *Anatomy of Terror*, which was 'designed to portray African nationalists solely as terrorists bent on the destruction of law and order for the benefit of their communist masters in Russia and China. In this way the war could be represented as black anarchy without reference to white injustice, and such a representation could therefore justify the government's cure – a more positive dose of law and order "because this is what the African really understands".'[9]

The war escalated steadily through the year and when the Rhodesian security forces disrupted guerrilla communications across borders, they simply moved deeper into the country and relied on the support of the local Africans. The guerrillas were becoming more determined, better trained and harder to combat. The Rhodesian service chiefs asked for more money to sustain the combat and Lt-Gen. Peter Walls, the Army Chief, said morale was 'satisfactory' but that poor pay and conditions could lead to an exodus of experienced men. The government introduced draconian measures that included the death penalty for aiding and abetting guerrillas and prison sentences up to 30 years. Economic sanctions were the only pressure being exerted upon the illegal regime although Western countries evaded many sanctions altogether. However, economic growth was limited and this contributed to demands for a settlement. At the same time there was an exodus of young whites. The African National Council, led by Bishop Muzorewa, which was the one black political organization that had been allowed to operate, became increasingly provoked by the Smith government as it arrested senior ANC members.

DÉTENTE

A great deal of diplomatic activity was to occur in 1974, following the 25 April Revolution in Lisbon that led to the fall of the Caetano government. The three front-line leaders, Presidents Kaunda, Khama and Nyerere, tried to work out a peaceful solution to Rhodesia with the assistance of South Africa, which attempted to play the role of 'honest broker'. One result of South African pressures upon Smith was the release of leading nationalists, including Nkomo and Mugabe. Faced with a range of adverse economic indicators, Smith warned Rhodesians in his 1974 New Year's speech that the guerrilla campaign would get worse. The government mounted a 'Settlers 74' campaign to attract one million immigrants, but the figure soon had to be reduced to 10,000; the Minister of Information and Tourism, P. K. Van der Byl, said bleakly that the security situation discouraged immigrants. In May, after talks between the government and Bishop Muzorewa's ANC had broken down, the *South African Star* said: 'This is admittedly not the easiest time for Mr Smith to reach a settlement... the point is that the best time is already past: from now on Rhodesia's chances are likely to worsen. The options are no longer fully open. Rhodesians must shake themselves out of their dream of perpetual white supremacy.'

Both ZANU and ZAPU had had chequered careers although by 1972 they appeared to be emerging from a long period of difficulties to play more active roles as the fighting inside Rhodesia began to escalate. ZANU established a military base inside Rhodesia for the first time in 1972 when its tactics were to attack isolated white farms. In March 1973 ZANU and ZAPU had agreed to set up a political council to control a joint military command. Through 1973 the guerrilla war grew in intensity, especially in the north-east of Rhodesia where ZANU held the field. Although the two movements were banned inside Rhodesia, the ANC, which had been formed by Bishop Abel Muzorewa and the Rev. Canaan Banana in December 1971 to persuade Africans to reject the Smith-Douglas-Home settlement terms, was not. Despite the fact that the ANC had succeeded in achieving a massive 'No' for the Pearce Commission, it had remained in being to become the only legitimate means of expressing African opinion. By December 1973 the regime was obliged to pass measures to prevent young men opting out of their military service for religious reasons. Early in 1974 the government increased the size of the regular army while other measures made plain that the guerrilla threat had come to be regarded as the top priority. The call-up was having a serious impact on the manpower position of the private sector. Rhodesian fears increased in early 1974 as the FRELIMO war in neighbouring Mozambique escalated. While the government had tried to keep news of guerrilla activity out of the news, with partial success, during 1973, by 1974 this was no longer possible. In March 1974 Rhodesia lost three aircraft, including a Canberra bomber. On 24 April *The Times* carried an article which said: 'The situation in Rhodesia is not as serious as at the height of political terrorism in places such as Palestine, Cyprus and Kenya' but the implication was that it soon would be. Then came the Lisbon Revolution which dramatically altered the situation for the whole of Southern Africa. The most immediate result for Rhodesia was that it ceased to have value as a buffer between South Africa and independent black Africa. J. B. Vorster, the South African Prime Minister who had just won the April elections in his country, felt he had a free hand and embarked upon his *détente* exercise, with the object of forcing Smith to come to terms with his nationalist opponents and so relieve South Africa of further responsibility for the Rhodesian regime.

As Vorster launched his *détente* exercise the talks between Smith and Muzorewa came to an end after 10 months when Smith offered the Africans a further six seats in parliament to bring their representation to 22 to 50 whites; otherwise they would have to accept the 1971 proposals. The ANC unanimously rejected the offer. The RF chairman, Des Frost, said of their rejection: 'The ANC succeeded in stopping progress at the time of the Pearce Commission and they are obviously doing the same thing again. They do not want a hand of friendship, they want the whole body.'[10] Then on 4 July Harold Wilson, once more Prime Minister of Britain, told the House of Commons that the proposals put forward by the previous government had been withdrawn: 'There will be no consideration of any deal with the Rhodesian regime until we know that the proposals put forward are approved by the majority of the Rhodesian population.'

Meanwhile, at the end of May, Smith met Vorster in South Africa to discuss the impact of the Portuguese Revolution. They said: 'We are not concerned whether Mozambique has a White or Black government. All we are concerned about is that there should be a good and stable government in that territory.' This meeting in fact represented the parting of the ways between Smith and Vorster: Smith still saw the Zambezi as the continuing front line but Vorster saw this as the Limpopo. Rhodesia had become expendable. Vorster's *détente* exercise might have foundered in October 1974 when an OAU resolution in the UN called for South Africa to be expelled from the world body but South Africa was saved by US, British and French vetoes. Vorster then made a number of bold statements clearing the way for his *détente* exercise, among them telling the Cape Town Senate that there had to be a peaceful settlement in Rhodesia. Pik Botha, South Africa's UN representative, gave a speech in which he admitted that unsavoury racial incidents took place in South Africa and were inexcusable and said, 'We shall do everything in our power to move away from discrimination based on race or colour…' Vorster followed this with a statement aimed at Black Africa: 'Give South Africa a six months' chance by not making our road harder than it is already… if you give South Africa a chance, you will be surprised where we stand.' This statement, however, caused consternation in South Africa's white ranks and Vorster had to tell his home audience that his statements only applied to South Africa's neighbours. Kaunda then spoke glowingly of Vorster's 'voice of reason' and spelt out what had to be done: the decolonization of Rhodesia and Namibia. Pretoria, or Vorster, were ready to pay the price of deserting Rhodesia in order to give South Africa a new lease of life.[11] The South African government now exerted huge pressures upon the Smith regime to come to terms with the nationalists: the railways suddenly became congested and Vorster said he would withdraw the South African police contingents from Rhodesia as soon as 'terrorism' ended. Smith, who had been told by his police and army chiefs that the long-term outlook in the guerrilla war was bleak, did not protest publicly.

The nationalists, especially the ZANU radicals, came to the talks reluctantly, as did Smith. Robert Mugabe, out of Smith's jail at Vorster's request, denied that he had ever wanted to negotiate and claimed he had been 'forced' to do so by Kaunda, Khama, Nyerere and the FRELIMO leader Machel. Since Nyerere refused to accept Mugabe as ZANU's president at that time, the first meeting was only between Kaunda, Vorster and Nkomo. A second meeting to include Mugabe was convened a month later. It was no more successful. The talks broke down within days to signal the end of Vorster's ambitious response to events in Portugal. He was never to be in as strong a position again. The talks ended in December, the gold price peaked and South Africa entered a depression while criticism of Vorster mounted. Even so, Vorster insisted that more talks would have to take place since 'The alternative is too ghastly to contemplate'. The Rhodesians welcomed the collapse of the talks and the RF chairman, Des Frost, said, 'Let's be honest. This was something the South Africans started. It wasn't something, as far as I know, that we started.'[12] However, outward Rhodesian bravado cloaked an increasingly desperate situation inside the country. In his diary for 1 December 1974, Ken Flower, the Rhodesian Security Chief, wrote: 'Things are on the decline in Rhodesia. In spite of increased Security Force successes we are not keeping pace with terrorist recruiting. Indeed, we have lost the goodwill of the Africans in the forward areas and over much of the rest of Rhodesia as well… but strangely there appears to be a better prospect of settlement now than ever before; although how can the whites in Rhodesia reverse the trends of the past decade or more? Or if they are going to be forced into change will there be sufficient goodwill, and enough sincerity, to reach a lasting accommodation?'[13]

Despite the 1974 failure, in February 1975 Vorster exerted fresh pressures upon Smith and withdrew the South African Police from their border duties on the Zambezi and, at the same time, withdrew the 2,000 police inside Rhodesia from anti-guerrilla activities, despite the escalating war. By July 1975, with more talks in prospect, the Rhodesian Minister of Information, Van der Byl, revealed the South African withdrawal and complained that the move had strained the Rhodesian forces and made black Rhodesians 'more arrogant'. This play for white support in the Republic led the South African Minister of Justice, Jimmy Kruger, to announce that the 200 South African Police still in Rhodesia would be withdrawn. South Africa did not wish, he said, to become involved in an 'internal struggle between Rhodesians'. Such pressures forced Smith to embark on further talks.

On 25 August Vorster and Kaunda met at Victoria Falls to chair a meeting between Smith and the nationalist leaders. Nkomo appeared willing to enter into a deal. Vorster, apparently optimistic, returned to Cape Town. Smith returned to Salisbury and announced the failure of the talks, playing to the hard right gallery over Vorster's head. Both Vorster and Kaunda, for their own ends, had hoped to force Smith and the nationalists respectively to do what they did not wish to do; in fact Vorster had not 'controlled' Smith and Kaunda had failed to control the Zimbabwe nationalists. Smith now warned against further attempts to make him compromise and on South African television stated that Vorster's withdrawal of the South African Police from Rhodesia had been 'wrong'. He said that negotiations had been made difficult because the nationalist leaders 'believed that the South African government was pressuring us to come to an agreement with them'. He added that Salisbury–Pretoria relations were 'under some strain… mainly as a result of the campaign against us by the press media in South Africa – which has made the average Rhodesian believe that the South Africans are prepared to ditch Rhodesia'. Smith's message to Vorster was clear: to stop any more pressures upon Rhodesia. *Détente* was over.[14]

MORE WAR AND MORE TALKS

Smith may have scuppered *détente* but other developments continued to narrow his options. Mugabe replaced Sithole as the leader of ZANU in 1976 when the commander of the ZANU Liberation Army (ZANLA), Josiah Tongogara, joined Mugabe's delegation at the Geneva conference convened by the British. Mozambique became independent on 25 June so that Rhodesia lost a sympathetic neighbour and instead faced a hostile border that was 700 miles long and ideal for guerrilla incursions from ZANU bases sited inside Rhodesia's neighbour. When, at the end of the year, South Africa sent a military column to invade Angola, the war in Rhodesia resumed on a bigger scale than ever. The war would become increasingly intense from this time until the end of the decade, imposing greater strains on the white minority whose isolation became far more pronounced following the Portuguese withdrawal from Mozambique and Angola and the South African 'disengagement' from Rhodesia's defence.

In January 1976 ZANU mounted a new offensive in the north-east. In April the Zimbabwe People's Revolutionary Army (ZIPRA) (ZAPU's military wing) began infiltrating into northern Rhodesia from Zambia and Botswana. In August the crack Selous Scouts raided Zimbabwe National Liberation Army (ZANLA) camps deep inside Mozambique. ZANU and ZAPU agreed to form a Patriotic Front to put their case to the international community. Meanwhile, Dr Kissinger, the US Secretary of State, had entered the picture as chief Western negotiator. As Ken Flower recorded:

> It took three months for Kissinger to come out in the open, three months during which he was preparing his *quid pro quo* with Vorster: American support for anti-Marxist forces in Angola and no further pressure on Vorster over Namibia, provided that Vorster increased his pressure on Smith and thus cleared America's name in black Africa.[15]

In Salisbury that September Kissinger put on a show about how much he and his wife admired Smith. He thought he had secured a deal. On Friday 24 September Smith announced his acceptance of the Kissinger proposals on the radio: 'The American and the British Governments, together with the major Western powers, have made up their minds as to the kind of solution they wish to see in Rhodesia and they are determined to bring it about. The alternative to the acceptance of the proposals was explained to us in the clearest terms, which left us no room for misunderstanding.' Smith had been offered a package deal: sanctions to be lifted, an aid package to follow, and terrorism to stop. Smith continued, 'backsliding' in Flower's words: 'It will be a "majority rule" constitution and this is expressly laid down in the proposals. My own position on majority rule is well known. I have stated in public many times, and I believe I echo the views of the majority of both black and white Rhodesians when I say that we support majority rule, provided that it is responsible rule.' In the following days, in his own inimitable way, Smith conveyed to his white electorate that any change would be ephemeral. All Kissinger's negotiating skills were no match for Smith's obduracy.

Smith might hold out, twisting and turning to prolong white control, but in the second half of 1976 the situation was steadily deteriorating. Flower's Central Intelligence Organization (CIO) made a remarkably accurate assessment of the

Rhodesia situation. It painted a picture of a country suffering severe strain in every quarter and argued that the solution had to be political. The CIO argued: 'Rhodesia is being increasingly subjected to various forms of external and internal pressure which are seriously affecting the country's security, politico/economic and social structure.' The assessment listed the problems as: the terrorist capacity to recruit; the kill rate was not equal to the recruiting; the blacks wanted the nationalists to triumph; without a future guaranteed the whites would continue to emigrate; Britain, the EC and now the US were pushing for majority rule; Rhodesia was wholly dependent upon South Africa which in turn was being pressured to exert pressure upon Rhodesia to accept majority rule; Zambia (post-*détente*) was committed to assisting the guerrillas; Mozambique was providing full support; Tanzania was switching the training facilities it had developed for FRELIMO to use by the Rhodesian terrorists; and Soviet support for the nationalists was being increased.

During 1977 neither cross-border raids by Rhodesian forces into Mozambique nor bombing ZAPU camps in Zambia slowed down the war. Lt-Gen. Peter Walls argued publicly for negotiations, saying the whites could not win the war. The Smith government then began to seek an internal settlement. The United States became directly involved in the Rhodesia question as a result of Dr Kissinger's 1976 roving diplomacy; he had persuaded Smith to accept the Pretoria agreement endorsing majority rule. Subsequently, when the Geneva talks collapsed at the end of the year, Kissinger left further initiatives to Britain. When Dr David Owen succeeded Anthony Crosland as Britain's Foreign Secretary in 1977 he favoured joint US–UK action while also insisting that Britain should assume direct responsibility during a transition period to Zimbabwe independence. He worked closely with the US Ambassador to London, Andrew Young, who said: 'I would say that President Carter sees there can be no future for Southern Africa unless there is a rationally-negotiated peaceful and meaningful agreement.' In July a joint Anglo-US approach was made in Lusaka to the Patriotic Front, which had been recognized by the OAU as the only representative body of black Rhodesians, but the approach was turned down; the Patriotic Front argued that it was wrong to seek an agreement for an independence constitution before securing Smith's surrender. He had described the Patriotic Front as Public Enemy Number One. The front-line presidents insisted upon the complete dismantling of Smith's army, which was to be replaced by guerrilla forces, but their demand was flatly rejected by Vorster when Owen and Young arrived in Pretoria for talks. He said he would only support what was acceptable to Smith.

An article in the *Daily Telegraph* quoted Rhodesia's two leading generals:

As General John Hickman, Rhodesian Army Commander, said at the weekend, 'the most important battle the guerrillas could win would be the destruction of national morale.' General Hickman, one of a new breed of increasingly vociferous military commanders, warned the politicians that while morale of troops in the field was very high, when they returned home they were given a different picture... Today, General Peter Walls, Commander of Combined Operations, and another of the military school which feels increasingly obliged to speak out, says the whole of Rhodesia must be regarded as an operational area.[16]

In other words, the two leading generals were saying the war could not be won. Ten days after the appearance of this article in Britain, Ken Flower recorded in his diary:

John Hickman has just come to see me, late at night, seeking advice on what to do in response to approaches from the Nationalists. Peter Walls is more heavily involved: all of which is symptomatic of the desperately uncertain time in which we live because the government won't give a steer as to where we're supposed to be going. Or, to be brutally frank: they're determined to hang on to power at any cost.[17]

Once Smith had rejected the Anglo-American initiative launched by Owen and Young, who insisted that the Patriotic Front had to be part of any settlement, he resumed negotiations for an 'internal settlement' with Muzorewa, Sithole and Chief Chirau. The Operations Co-ordinating Committee (OCC) advised the government that the war was being lost and that a political settlement was essential. South Africa's Pik Botha told Smith that 'a peaceful settlement is no longer possible and there will have to be losers'. As the war intensified towards the end of 1977, the Rhodesian Security Forces intensified their attacks upon targets in Mozambique that included ZANU camps at Chimoio and Tembue. Such attacks were more a policy of despair than sound military strategy though they may have given comfort to Rhodesians who saw that something was being done. They did not affect the fighting inside Rhodesia.

While the Anglo-US negotiations with the Patriotic Front continued, the announcement on 15 February 1978 of a successful 'internal settlement' in Salisbury opened a new chapter in the increasingly tortuous Rhodesian story. The Patriotic Front saw the settlement as a betrayal by 'Smith's Black collaborators', refused to take seriously Smith's promise to hand over power to the majority and regarded the agreement as a ploy to 'divide and rule'. Smith agreed to introduce a form of majority rule though with provisions that effectively ensured a continuation of white control. The agreement made no difference to the fighting in the north-east of the country. Ken Flower provides an invaluable 'insider' view of the growing crisis for the embattled whites in his autobiographical account of these years, *Serving Secretly*. As he described the situation in 1978: 'For many years now the consensus of opinion in CIO and Special Branch had been that it was more important to accommodate African nationalism than to over-concern ourselves with the communist threat as it was represented in parts of the Western world.'[18] Despite his much-vaunted internal settlement, Smith also conducted secret negotiations with Nkomo through 1978 but these were brought to an abrupt halt when on 3 September Nkomo's ZIPRA guerrillas, using a Russian Sam-7 ground-to-air missile, brought down an Air Rhodesia Viscount shortly after take-off from Kariba for Salisbury. Thirty-five people were killed and of 18 survivors on the ground 10 were massacred by guerrillas before rescuers could reach the scene. Twenty-four hours earlier Rhodesians had welcomed the official release of news of Nkomo–Smith negotiations; but in reaction to the Viscount disaster they demanded an end to the talks. If they expected international sympathy, the Rhodesians were mistaken. 'Any illusions they might have retained that they were fighting a war, not terrorism, were shattered, and as they waited in vain for condemnation of ZIPRA's action from Britain, the United States or anywhere else, they began to realize they were completely alone in their grief and anger.'[19] And though white ministers demanded retribution and martial law, Gen. Walls responded that only the military would decide military tactics: in other words, they would not impose martial law. The fact that the military could respond in this way demonstrated the growing gap in political-military thinking and Smith's declining control over events. Although Smith signed an agreement with Muzorewa, Sithole and Chief Chirau to form a transitional government to precede majority rule, the internal settlement never achieved credibility while the transitional government failed to stop the war or curb guerrilla recruiting and Muzorewa lost authority when his minister, Byron Hove, resigned.

OILGATE

A major scandal, revealing the duplicity of successive British governments and the complicity in breaking sanctions by Britain's two largest companies, the oil giants BP and Shell, was uncovered by Martin Bailey, a Granada TV journalist in 1977. As the revelations became public the Foreign Office was obliged to hold an official inquiry and on 10 May David Owen appointed Thomas Bingham QC to conduct it. The previous April a BP spokesman had said, 'We have never broken sanctions – United Nations, British or any other.' On 23 May, President

Kaunda announced that the oil companies had just held a conference in Zurich 'at which they decided to destroy all the important papers so that we would not have evidence with which to present our case to court'.[20] A Shell spokesman dismissed Kaunda's allegations but Bingham later confirmed that such a meeting had taken place. Kaunda was cynical about the British government investigation, convinced the inquiry was designed to delay real action to tighten oil sanctions. Why had the British not yet discovered the facts? he asked. 'My little nation with its limited means has been able to learn so much about how oil is reaching the Smith regime and how UN sanctions are being broken, that it is inconceivable to me that British intelligence services should not have known all about it.' Zambia decided to boycott the Bingham inquiry.[21] At the same time the Zambian government filed writs for damages against the oil companies in the High Court in Lusaka and in outlining the case against the oil companies claimed £4,000 million in damages. Zambia stressed that its motive was political and not financial. The United African National Congress (UANC) also wanted to sue the oil companies but ZANU-PF and PF-ZAPU did not pursue the matter although they claimed that the oil companies were playing an important role in sustaining the Smith regime. Robert Mugabe said, 'The West talks of wanting peace – but in reality props up the minority regime through sales of oil.' And Joshua Nkomo expressed the nationalist frustration with Britain when he said at a press conference: 'Inquiry! Inquiry into what? This is the British way of tackling things. They know what is happening.' Plenty of fears were expressed that the inquiry would not 'get' the full facts or would be prevented from publishing by the Foreign Office. However, the situation was changed radically when the 'Sandford file' that belonged to Arthur Sandford, who was a London-based BP executive dealing with Southern Africa, fell into the hands of the inquiry. It was probably a deliberate leak. When David Owen, the Foreign Secretary, saw it he was extremely angry to discover the companies' involvement in sanctions busting. Another key source of information was the Portuguese Jorge Jardim, the head of the Sonarep refinery at Lourenco Marques (Maputo); he had left Sonarep and gone into private business, and extracts from his documents showed that both the head offices of the two oil companies and the British government had been deeply implicated in the sanctions scandal for over a decade. The documents revealed Shell and BP discussing how to persuade the British government they were not breaking sanctions and outlined how oil swap arrangements with Total were made. A BP memorandum on 'Rhodesia's Freight Services', prepared by John Rounce in February 1974 in Cape Town, provided a precise explanation of what happened: 'BP and Shell continue to market products in Rhodesia as a consolidated venture. Supplies to support the marketing activity are effected from South Africa primarily through "Freight

Services", who act as forwarding agents, buying product from BP and Shell SA and reselling to the Rhodesia Government procurement agency Genta for allocation to marketers.' The 'Rounce Memorandum' then went on to explain that 'devious supply arrangements have thus been made to visibly dissociate the oil companies from any first hand and identifiable part in supply operations'.[22] The leaking of these documents made it much more difficult for the government to refuse to publish the Bingham Report since to do so would have led to accusations of a 'cover-up'.

Granada's *World in Action* did a two-part special (31 July and 7 August 1978) on how Shell and BP broke sanctions. Then, on 27 August, the *Sunday Times* ran a front-page lead under the headline 'BP confesses it broke sanctions – and covered up'. The article gave precise details of how this had been managed. As a result of this story Shell shares dropped by 20p and BP shares by 28p within four days. As Peter Kellner was to reveal in the *Sunday Times* '... I realized that we had an unparalleled tale of corporate and government deceit. We had quite remarkable evidence of the complicity of Ministers and civil servants – a story which exposed how Britain's closed system of government could conceal a scandal of international proportions.'[23] Despite these revelations, the Chairman of Shell, Michael Pocock, told shareholders: 'We have no reason to feel ashamed of the record and action of our subsidiary company in South Africa... I feel proud of them.' While somewhat more circumspect, BP said that over 13 years 'mistakes' had been made. Apart from the oil companies, the oilgate scandal clearly shamed Labour politicians: on one occasion when questioned about the sanctions breaking, Denis Healey shouted angrily at reporters while Harold Wilson on another broke off a television interview. George Thomson, who as Commonwealth Secretary in 1968 had had talks with the oil companies, became the main target of attack and in self-defence issued a detailed personal statement: 'I have exercised my rights as a former cabinet Minister to consult the appropriate papers... they confirm that I conveyed in writing to the Prime Minister [Wilson] and other Ministers most directly concerned a full account of all that passed at my meetings on behalf of the government with the oil companies.'[24] The fact that he informed his colleagues did not exonerate either Thomson or the others, including Wilson. Despite these revelations no one in government, the civil service or the oil companies was ever charged with sanctions busting despite their many public denials.

The Bingham Report had overseas consequences. In Zambia, which had suffered extensively as a result of UDI, it caused a major stir. Kaunda told reporters: 'I am so angry that I cannot describe how I feel.' He said that successive British prime ministers had lied and cheated over the oilgate scandal and that it was worse than Watergate in the United States because the result of the oil getting through to Rhodesia had cost thousands of lives. The oilgate scandal revealed British political hypocrisy at its worst: contempt for the Africans who got killed; the determination to continue making money out of a war situation that was Britain's responsibility; blatant racism as Britain secretly bailed out the white Rhodesians while sanctimoniously claiming that it adhered rigidly to UN sanctions. The revelations added profoundly to the deep distrust in which Africans held the British. Oilgate, in any case, was part of a wider pattern of sanctions busting that was always supported by Portugal (to 1975) and South Africa, while many Western businesses were only too ready to benefit from breaking sanctions.

ZIMBABWE INDEPENDENCE

In April 1979, following a white referendum which accepted the principle of majority rule, without Patriotic Front participation, elections were held in Rhodesia under the terms of the internal settlement Constitution and on 1 June Bishop Muzorewa became Prime Minister of Zimbabwe-Rhodesia. Conservative observers from Britain under Lord Lennox-Boyd had reported that the elections had been free and fair but the front-line Presidents opposed the elections and international recognition of Rhodesia was withheld. Moreover, Lord Chitnis, a British Liberal peer who observed the election, reported that it 'was nothing more than a gigantic confidence trick designed to foist on a cowed and indoctrinated black electorate a settlement and a constitution which were formulated without its consent and which are being implemented without its approval'.[25] On a visit to the United States in July, Ken Flower recorded in his diary: 'On the one hand some of us have been doing what we can to fortify the Bishop (Muzorewa) – and ourselves – in the belief that the next three months should see the uplift of sanctions, and recognition. On the other hand there has been enough weakening of the Bishop's position already, through the defection from his party. And the white politicians have been up to their old tricks of divide and rule – a luxury which we can no longer afford when the country is bleeding to death – someone killed each hour of the twenty-four, and the war costing a million dollars a day.'[26] Meanwhile divisions were emerging in the Patriotic Front between Mugabe and Nkomo; this was to be expected for there was no trust between the two men and the Front was an artificial creation that was not of their choosing.

On 1 August the Commonwealth Heads of Government Meeting (CHOGM) assembled in Lusaka. Margaret Thatcher, Britain's newly elected Conservative Prime Minister, and her Foreign Secretary, Lord Carrington, represented Britain. Under intense Commonwealth pressure, which had been most carefully orchestrated by Australia's Malcolm Fraser, Jamaica's Michael Manley, Tanzania's Julius Nyerere and Zambia's Kenneth Kaunda, Margaret Thatcher was persuaded to agree to hold a constitutional conference in London to resolve the Rhodesia question. This was held in Lancaster House from 10 September to 21 December when an agreement was finally signed. In temporary alliance, Britain, South Africa and the front-line States exerted pressure on the leaders of the Patriotic Front to end the war and on Smith to concede defeat. The Zimbabwe-Rhodesia delegation accepted the British proposals on 21 September and Bishop Muzorewa agreed to stand down as Prime Minister, against the wishes of his delegation. The conference came to the verge of collapse in October but continued on a knife-edge with Mugabe especially distrustful of the British proposals. On 11 December Lord Soames, who had been appointed as the Governor of Rhodesia for the transition to independence, flew to Salisbury. On 14 December Eddison Zvobgo, for ZANU-PF, had said 'no' to Carrington, and Mugabe was on his way to catch a flight to New York, to reject the cease-fire and drum up support to continue the war when he was recalled to take a phone call from President Samora Machel of Mozambique. Machel told him bluntly to sign and indicated that if he didn't all he could expect in Mozambique would be political asylum, for by this time the country was suffering from Rhodesian raids, damaged communications and food shortages and it needed the war to come to an end.[27]

The agreement was signed at Lancaster House on 21 December. Legality was restored under a British Governor (Lord Soames) and sanctions were lifted. Elections were to be held the following February/March for a 100-seat parliament in which 80 seats would be contested on an open roll by Africans while 20 seats would be reserved for whites. Immediately, following his arrival in Rhodesia, Lord Soames was dependent upon the Rhodesian military to hold the ring while the guerrillas came in to assembly points and arrangements for the election were made. Calculations in London, as always in relation to Rhodesia wide of the mark, suggested that either Muzorewa could win again or that the Patriotic Front could obtain a narrow victory. The Foreign Office made plain that Mugabe was not their choice. A small Commonwealth contingent was sent to oversee the ceasefire although it had no force at its command had either the Patriotic Front or the Rhodesians decided to return to the bush and renew the war.

Between January and April 1980, 20,000 guerrillas came to 16 assembly points to accept the ceasefire. For a time ZANU-PF and its armed wing ZANLA ignored the ceasefire and there was widespread intimidation. Lord Soames faced a dilemma and Rhodesian forces were redeployed. On 13 January Nkomo returned to Rhodesia, followed by Mugabe on 27 January. The Governor then took wider powers and ignored Rhodesian requests that he should ban or restrict political parties practising intimidation or continuing to break the cease-fire. Combined Operations, or COMOPs, confronted Soames and the British officials but Rhodesian officials said that events would have to run their course. The elections were held over five days from 27 February and the results were announced on 4 March: ZANU-PF (Mugabe) 57 seats, PF-ZAPU (Nkomo) 20 seats, United African National Congress (UANC) (Muzorewa) three seats, Rhodesian Front (Smith) (on reserved white roll) 20 seats. South Africa reacted to Mugabe's victory by launching an anti-Mugabe destabilization campaign, which lasted through to independence on 18 April although Pretoria had to decide how far it would go.[28] The results led to immediate panic among the white population but on the evening of 4 March Soames, Mugabe and Walls broadcast to the nation. Soames called for no violence and a stable government and Walls appealed for calm and peace. Mugabe said: 'Let us join together. Let us show respect for the winners and the losers... There is no intention on our part to victimize the minority. We will ensure there is a place for everyone in this country. I want a broadly based government to include whites and Nkomo.' To the South Africans he said: 'We offer peaceful co-existence. Let us forgive and forget. Let us join hands in a new amity.' And to the world: 'Zimbabwe will be tied to no one. It will be strictly non-aligned.'[29] The speech owed a good deal to Kenyatta's famous address to the white farmers at Nakuru on 12 August 1963. Following this speech many whites who had prepared to leave stayed and members of the civil service who had handed in their resignations now withdrew them. Nkomo, like almost everyone else, had badly miscalculated the tribal factor and the appeal of Mugabe who was generally seen as the man who had done most to win the war; instead, he had relied on his charisma and had rejected the idea of a coalition, believing that ZAPU could win on its own. Mugabe asked Soames, or another British representative, to stay on after independence but Britain said 'no'. 'Why did the British refuse?' asked Flower. 'It seems that they were so relieved to have fluked a solution that their only consideration now was to get the hell out of Zimbabwe while the going was good and relinquish their responsibility for a country which had been a thorn in their side for a long time.'[30] This would seem a just criticism of British conduct.

Gen. Peter Walls, who had commanded the Rhodesian Army against the guerrillas, offered to serve the new government at independence, despite being an avowed anti-Marxist, and was retained by Mugabe. After a few months, however, he resigned when Mugabe refused to promote him to full General. He then left for South Africa, after disclosing that he had asked the British Prime Minister, Margaret Thatcher, to annul the election result when he learned that ZANU-PF had won. The story is revealing on several fronts. First, it was remarkable that Mugabe was willing to retain his services after an official death toll of 30,000. It also revealed much of Rhodesian assumptions about British attitudes that, after the settlement, he should try to persuade Mrs Thatcher to annul the election. And more revealing still than either of those two aspects, it tells us a great deal of white Rhodesian myopia. The Rhodesians often boasted that they 'understood the African' although in company with the British and the Russians they were wholly unprepared for a Mugabe victory. They had made a similar miscalculation about the African 'they understood' at the time of the Pearce Commission and their assumption at that time that the Africans would endorse the proposed settlement.

Joshua Nkomo was deeply humiliated by the election result. He had recently had himself made 'President for Life' of ZAPU and now had to argue that Mugabe had won the election by intimidation and rigging by China, Mozambique, Tanzania, Britain and the United States. However, Nkomo had rejected Mugabe's offer of the presidency of Zimbabwe because he felt the position lacked power. Had he accepted, he might have been able to prevent the loss of life that followed the ZANU–ZAPU compact. The outcome of the election was also a bitter blow for South Africa, which had spent US$300 million supporting the Rhodesian war against the nationalists and then had invested heavily in the election against ZANU. Further, South Africa was then attempting to create a 'Constellation of African States' but Zimbabwe would not take part. Mugabe advocated socialist policies and was an outspoken critic of apartheid. He was determined to reduce Zimbabwe's dependence upon South Africa and on 1 April, prior to independence, had joined the Southern African Development Coordination Conference (SADCC) whose principal objective was to lessen the dependence of all its members upon South Africa.

Independence for Zimbabwe represented a major African victory over the forces of white reaction in the southern part of the continent. The war had cost 30,000 lives (official estimate) and probably a good many more while at least one million Africans had been uprooted during the course of the struggle.

The End of
Portuguese Africa

As the 1970s began, Portugal only exercised direct control over those parts of its three African territories that were not already under the control of the freedom fighters. The ultra-conservatives were in the ascendant at home, determined to hold Portuguese Africa, no matter what the cost. Portugal, it is true, did make some moves towards granting a limited degree of autonomy to the territories, and in 1972 altered the Organic Law affecting Africa so as to make the 'provinces' of Angola and Mozambique into states; this change would give a limited number of people in the territories a greater say in their internal affairs so long as this did not disrupt the greater unity of the 'Portuguese Nation'. There was right-wing disquiet at even these modest changes, since the right had no desire to see any form of autonomy granted to the African territories. It might have been argued that Portugal was too poor to sustain the vast expense of her African wars. In fact these wars illustrate the classic argument about colonies: they paid, and for Portugal they were economically so important that she dared not lose them.

The Portuguese territories of Africa Freedom Movements – the MPLA (*Movimento Popular de Libertação de Angola*), FRELIMO (*Frente de Libertação de Mocambique*) and the PAIGC (*Partido Africano da Independência da Guiné e Cabo Verde*) met in Rome during June 1970 to focus attention and increase support for their fight to end Portuguese colonialism. In a joint declaration they stated: 'In order to oppose this situation, the colonialists of Lisbon are facilitating penetration of powerful economic interests of imperialist powers to ensure that their interests should consider their fate as linked to that of Portuguese domination. They become the defenders of the cause of Portugal's colonialism, expressing themselves through the policies of their governments, and thus create conditions for an increasing internationalization of the confrontation. The direct and massive aid from NATO – not to speak of the military and economic support Lisbon receives from the governments of the United States, West Germany, Britain and France – is a decisive factor in Portugal's ability to continue her colonial wars.'[1]

In 1970 the period of service for conscripts in the Portuguese army was increased to four years. Fatal military casualties admitted by Portugal were 500 a year although the liberation movements claimed the figure was much higher. By this time there was growing opposition in Portugal to a policy that seemed without end: urban guerrillas, the Armed Revolutionary Action Group, used explosives to damage troop-carrying liners about to leave for Africa; and there was growing student opposition to the wars. The biggest drain upon the country was manpower; over 80,000 young Portuguese were living clandestinely abroad to avoid conscription.

In June 1970 Prime Minister Vorster of South Africa visited Portugal: he promised continuing co-operation and Portugal's Prime Minister, Marcello Caetano, said that, despite ideological differences, they would continue to co-operate. As it was, the increasing inability of the Portuguese to contain the situations in Mozambique and Angola had become deeply worrying for South Africa and Rhodesia. Portugal had been able to maintain its African wars for so long because it was sustained by its Western allies – Britain and the United States, and the other principal members of NATO, especially West Germany and France. The Mozambican Dan van der Vat, writing in *The Times* at the end of 1970, said: 'The supreme irony of a war which still remains a thoroughly nasty affair for both sides is that it has taken the creation of FRELIMO to produce, after more than four and a half centuries of stagnation, a sudden upsurge of development by the Portuguese so that they can justify their claim to be able to offer the Africans more than FRELIMO ever could.'[2] By 1972, Portugal had total military forces of 204,000 men of whom 150,000 were deployed in Africa: 60,000 each in Angola and Mozambique, and 30,000 in Portuguese Guinea (Guinea-Bissau). Normally, armies are associated with the politics of the right. In the case of Portugal, however, two factors were of crucial importance: first, a significant proportion of the officer class who had spent years of their professional careers fighting in the African wars could see clearly what Lisbon either failed to see or wilfully ignored – that it could not win the wars; and secondly, the bulk of the soldiers were not professionals at all, but young peasant conscripts who found no difficulty in identifying with the peasant aspirations of the Africans they were sent to fight. They simply wanted to go home. In early 1974 Gen. Antonio de Spinola was to focus army discontents, although he was no radical, when he published his book *Portugal and the Future*, in which he stated that there was no military solution in Africa.

On 2 December 1970, Caetano announced the creation of local legislatures and administrative structures for Angola and Mozambique. He advanced the concept of autonomous self-governing states united through a central government in Lisbon. This concept was, apparently, to include Brazil to form a Portuguese Commonwealth. FRELIMO's Marcellino dos Santos denied that the Caetano proposals could benefit the people. They were only designed to reassure Portugal's allies and make them think Lisbon was introducing reforms. Caetano had tried to reinforce the myth that Angola and Mozambique were overseas provinces of Portugal but his changes would not alter the course of the war. These wars were ruthless affairs, and the Portuguese military, with its huge conscript forces, came increasingly to dominate Portuguese life. Yet, despite the sophisticated weapons, the size of the armies and the high expenditure, Portugal retreated steadily as the 1970s advanced.

GUINEA-BISSAU

By the beginning of the decade, most of the interior of Guinea-Bissau was already in the hands of the PAIGC while the Portuguese held the towns and the coast. Gen. Spinola, the Governor-General of the colony, enjoyed air superiority but little else. There was to be heavy fighting throughout the year. Only in 1971 did Portugal admit that a state of war existed: its 30,000 troops were facing 7,000 PAIGC guerrillas and Amilcar Cabral had undisputed control of the only liberation movement in the territory and received widespread backing from Africa. By 1972 Portugal had expanded its forces and the 30,000 white troops had been augmented by 15,000 black or mulatto forces drawn from the local population. There was a steady rate of casualties. By this time the Portuguese were clearly on the defensive: they maintained fortified posts that held between 150 and 1,000 men and these were isolated from each other.

The PAIGC carried out intensive international lobbying through 1972 in preparation for its intended declaration of independence in 1973; it obtained promises of support for such a declaration from Communist, African and Non-Aligned nations. It held elections among 58,000 registered voters in those parts of the country it controlled during April and July for a National Assembly. The PAIGC faced a major setback when on 20 January 1973 Amilcar Cabral was assassinated in Conakry, Guinea, where he had his headquarters. The PAIGC naval commander Innocenta Canida admitted responsibility having been 'turned' by the Portuguese. Aristides Pereira, a close colleague of Cabral, was elected Secretary-General of the PAIGC in his place on 28 January. The struggle continued without pause, however, and the Portuguese now lost air superiority as the PAIGC began to shoot down their planes with ground-to-air missiles. In November 1972 the UN General Assembly had described the PAIGC as 'the sole and authentic representative of the people of Guinea-Bissau and Cape Verde'. Writing in the *Observer* at the beginning of 1973, Colin Legum argued that the guerrilla pressures upon the Portuguese were far heavier than upon the Rhodesians or South Africans. 'After 11 years of fighting three colonial wars – in Guinea-Bissau, Mozambique and Angola – the Portuguese still show no signs of being able to bring any of them to an end. Their situation in Mozambique had deteriorated considerably in the last 18 months, especially in the strategically important Tete province, which is wedged between Rhodesia and Malawi. It is the Portuguese failure to beat off FRELIMO's attacks in that sensitive corner of Southern Africa that has caused so much anxiety in recent months to Mr Smith and Mr Vorster. The real threat Portugal faces in the immediate future, however, is not in southern Africa but in its "colonial" extension, Guinea-Bissau. That is the part of Portuguese Africa to watch.'[3] By that time the PAIGC dominated life in most of the country.

On 24 September 1973, Guinea-Bissau declared its independence and was at once recognized by a majority of the OAU and a majority of UN members, including the USSR and China. On 2 November 1973 the UN General Assembly voted 93 to seven with 30 abstentions to recognize the Republic of Guinea-Bissau, which was admitted to the UN at the end of the year. Thereafter, the General Assembly refused to accept the Portuguese delegation as representing Angola, Mozambique and Guinea-Bissau – the latter then had its own UN representative – and voted to this effect by 54 to 14 with 21 abstentions. Guinea-Bissau was then admitted to the OAU as its forty-second member. These developments gave the PAIGC a huge psychological boost while UN recognition was also seen as an encouragement to the independence movements in Angola and Mozambique. On a visit to Lagos, Aristides Pereira told reporters that Guinea-Bissau needed financial aid to consolidate its independence. Nigeria responded with a gift of N500,000 (£320,000). The war, however, continued.

Following the 25 April 1974 Revolution in Lisbon, talks between the new government and the PAIGC were held in London during May. Then, at the end of August, at a meeting in Algiers, Portugal and the PAIGC signed an agreement, which brought to an end 400 years of Portuguese rule. The Portuguese agreed to recognize Guinea-Bissau on 10 September and to withdraw all their military forces by the end of October. There were to be no reprisals. Maj. Pires, the PAIGC representative at the Algiers meeting, said that the agreement was 'the natural and logical outcome of the liberation struggle' and that the next step was to work for the liberation of the Cape Verde islands. In fact, though the PAIGC had represented both territories at the talks, Guinea-Bissau and Cape Verde were to go their separate ways. On 9 September Gen. Spinola signed a document, which officially ended Guinea-Bissau's status as an overseas territory of Portugal.

It had been a textbook struggle with the party mobilizing the masses rather than liberating them from above. The PAIGC instituted social reforms in the areas that it liberated during the long war and throughout the war the PAIGC maintained remarkable unity; this, it was agreed, owed a great deal to the leadership of Amilcar Cabral. After independence had been achieved the greatest problem facing the new state was its poverty. A slow *rapprochment* with Portugal followed.

The Portuguese gave independence to the Cape Verde islands, where there had been no fighting, on 5 July 1975 under a PAIGC government, for when pre-independence elections were held on 30 June, 85 per cent of those qualified to vote did so and 92 per cent of these voted for a PAIGC government. The first President of Cape Verde, Aristides Pereira, was a founder member of the PAIGC and had become its Secretary-General in January 1973 following the assassination of Cabral. A commission was set up to consider a Cape Verde–Guinea-Bissau Federation. On 12 January 1977 a Council of Unity was established to search for a formula of unity to bind the two countries but in fact by then it was becoming clear that they would remain two separate states. In 1980, following the November coup in Guinea-Bissau, the unity proposal collapsed and in Cape Verde the ruling PAIGC was renamed the PAICV (*Partido Africano da Independência de Cabo Verde*).

MOZAMBIQUE

The Central Committee of FRELIMO issued a communiqué after its meeting of 9–14 May 1970 in which it confirmed the election of Samora Moises Machel as acting President and Marcellino dos Santos as acting Vice-President until the next Congress. These appointments replaced the Council of the Presidency, which had been set up in April 1969 following the assassination of Dr Eduardo Mondlane, FRELIMO's first leader. The communiqué emphasized the importance of political education and stressed that military victories were the result of political work. Meanwhile, the Portuguese had embarked upon the construction of the massive Cabora Bassa Dam in Tete province, leading Zambia's President Kaunda to declare that Zambia would 'do all in its power' to get international support withdrawn from the project. He claimed that though ostensibly economic the dam was political, designed to spread South Africa's military influence further north. Once South Africa had invested so much money in the scheme it would have to send troops to defend it. Kaunda said Zambia was telling countries intending to participate in the dam that it was 'a question of conscious and deliberate decision: Are they going to support apartheid by spreading it further north or are they going to invest their money elsewhere?'[4] The Italians subsequently decided to withdraw from the dam consortium. In South Africa, however, it was claimed that despite international objections the dam would go ahead and though FRELIMO guerrillas were infiltrating Tete province near Cabora Bassa the Portuguese military was not worried.[5] In contrast to this optimism, FRELIMO claimed that the struggle in Tete was developing fast and that the Portuguese were trying to depopulate the area by moving people into 'protected villages'. In June the Portuguese army, under Gen. Kaulza de Arriaga, launched a major campaign against FRELIMO.

These Frelimo claims were substantiated in 1971 when refugees from the fighting in Tete began to arrive in Malawi where the refugee population reached a figure of 5,000; as a result Malawi-Portuguese relations deteriorated. FRELIMO activities in Tete province increased through 1971 and included attacks upon the railway that supplied Cabora Bassa. After FRELIMO had cut the Blantyre–Salisbury road that crossed Tete province, President Banda informed the South African government of the threat to its communications and Pretoria responded by sending four planeloads of arms and three Ferret scout cars to Malawi. By that time armed FRELIMO bands had begun moving over Malawian territory. A further blow to the Portuguese in 1971 came with the withdrawal of the Roman Catholic White Fathers from Mozambique because, they said, they could no longer support the policies of the Catholic hierarchy which upheld the colonial regime.

Despite Portuguese attempts to persuade themselves and the outside world that they were in full control of the situation in Mozambique, this was belied by the facts. In mid-1971 they placed Tete province under a military governor. More generally, defence expenditure revealed the extent to which its African wars were absorbing more and more of Portugal's political and economic attention. Defence expenditure for the overseas provinces had jumped from R115,500,000 in 1961 (35.6 per cent of government spending) to R280,000,000 (40.7 per cent of total expenditure) by 1970 and no end appeared to be in sight. Portugal imposed a blockade on goods for Zambia passing through Beira, prompting Kaunda to accuse Portugal of threatening an invasion of Zambia. He said that over 21 months there had been 40 border incursions by the Portuguese and that 50 Zambian civilians had been killed, injured or kidnapped.

According to a special correspondent of the *Rand Daily Mail* writing in February 1972, in the space of a year FRELIMO had turned the Tete province into a third front. Their prime target was the Cabora Bassa Dam. No road in the 65,000 square kilometre Tete province could be guaranteed free of mines, railway lines were sabotaged repeatedly, ambushes of road transport had become increasingly common and the area had become a battleground for classic guerrilla war actions. Moreover, FRELIMO guerrillas were widely regarded as heroes by the local people. The Portuguese admitted that there were about 2,000 guerrillas in Tete and had deployed 10,000 troops to deal with them. These guerrilla activities were causing anxiety in both Rhodesia and Malawi. Ian Colvin[6] estimated the strength of the FRELIMO guerrillas between 1,500 and 3,000 in Tete where there had been none three years earlier. The road to Cabora Bassa had been tarred so that it was difficult to mine but ambushes remained a danger. In February 1972 Admiral H. Biermann, the Commander-in-Chief of the South African Armed forces, visited Mozambique to consult Gen. Deslardes, the Portuguese Chief of General Staff about the situation in the territory. At the end of the same month Smith visited South Africa and discussed the Mozambique war with Vorster. Their conclusion was inescapable: that Mozambique had to be defended in the long term if South Africa was not to risk a hostile state on its Indian Ocean border that would cut off Rhodesia from the sea. In June 1972 Will Hussey, writing in the *Johannesburg Star's* Africa News Service, said: 'It must be stated clearly, now, though it may irk the Portuguese, that the state of the war in Tete is serious and carries grave military and political dangers for all of southern Africa in the long term.' And Gen. Kaulza de Arriaga, Commander-in-Chief of the Portuguese forces in Mozambique, warned in December 1972, in the official *Portuguese Digest Mozambique and the Political-Strategic Outlook*, that 'the battle against terrorism' in Mozambique was the key to the survival of Western influence in the world. He went on to argue that South Africa was an object of 'Communist neo-imperialism' to control the world. 'Thus the battle for southern Africa would perhaps be the decisive one; and that battle has already begun. Tanzania… serves as the bridgehead… From this bridgehead the fundamental objectives are Mozambique and the Republic of South Africa.' Such exaggerated claims about communist aims formed a major part of the white minority arguments in defence of their struggles against nationalist guerrillas at that time.

Portuguese morale in Mozambique declined through 1973: FRELIMO was making steady advances, the Rhodesian border had become less secure as the war across it intensified while the guerrillas were approaching the line of the Beira Corridor. Gen. Kaulza de Arriaga, who had spoken confidently of defeating FRELIMO at the beginning of the decade, required another 10,000 troops and these were transferred to Mozambique from Angola. By the end of the year FRELIMO forces had successfully moved into the Tete province where an outer circle of protected villages (*aldeamentos*) surrounded Cabora Bassa, which had its own defensive garrison, and crossed the Zambezi to open new fronts in Manica and Sofala provinces. At the same time FRELIMO was consolidating its administration in the northern territories under its control.

Portuguese problems were compounded during the year by the news of the Wiriyamu massacre that received worldwide attention. According to a report in *The Times*[7] a huge massacre had occurred in December 1972 at the village of Wiriyamu in Tete province when 400 Africans were killed by Portuguese troops in reprisals for aiding the guerrillas, causing 5,000 people to flee into Malawi. The Portuguese government denied that any massacre had taken place. However, news of the massacre led to opposition demands in the British Parliament for the cancellation of the forthcoming visit of Dr Caetano to celebrate the 600th anniversary of the Anglo-Portuguese alliance. The Heath government refused to cancel the visit but further evidence was forthcoming at the United Nations. Father Adrian Hastings, a Roman Catholic priest who had first revealed the evidence of the massacre, appeared before the UN Decolonization Committee on 20 July and claimed that it was only one of many massacres over recent years. Gen. Arriaga responded in an interview in *Die Welt* by claiming that there had been two cases of military excesses and that the soldiers responsible had been punished. According to *Le Monde*[8] Arriaga said Portugal was in the midst of a defensive war, yet during 10,000 military operations over the previous two and a half years only 10 cases of excesses had been reported. Writing in the *Diario de Lourenco Marques*, Mgr Alvim Pereira, the Archbishop of Lourenco Marques, clearly came down on the side of the Portuguese government when he defended the Church hierarchy who were accused of not denouncing the reported massacre. He said the Church in Mozambique was entirely free of the Portuguese government but that the question of political independence was outside the sphere of the Church, which could not take a stand on it. He wrote, 'Some would like the Mozambique hierarchy to condemn the Portuguese Government for its policy of integration, and place itself on the side of the so-called liberation movements.' The Archbishop continued, this attitude 'has been taken up by various foreign priests and a few Portuguese and has earned for some expulsion from Mozambique and even prison... Independent of the personal position of each priest, the Church cannot show itself against or in favour of the independence of any territory'. The Archbishop then went on to the attack: after stating that the Mozambique bishops had been accused of 'not being on the side of the so-called liberation movements' he said that they could not be on their side 'on any grounds, even if only because of the atrocities which these movements have perpetrated'. He regretted that people believed the alleged Wiriyamu massacres so easily and used them to attack Portugal.[9] The affair and the way it was defended did Portugal considerable harm.

Meanwhile, both South Africa and Rhodesia were demonstrating increasing unease at the advance southwards of FRELIMO forces and the inability of the

Portuguese under Gen. Arriaga to stop them. Rhodesia made great efforts to secure its eastern flank. In January 1974 Max Hastings revealed in the *Evening Standard* that the Rhodesian Army (400 troops of the Rhodesian Light Infantry) and the Special Air Services were carrying out sweeps in Mozambique to search out terrorist bases. By this time the Portuguese campaign to win 'the minds and hearts' of the eight million Mozambicans had come too late. The 250,000 whites were becoming increasingly restive. In order to increase its size and effectiveness the army was 'Africanized' up to the rank of captain and new all-African commando units were deployed for search-and-destroy operations against the guerrillas. There was some evidence of a change of policy in Lisbon early in 1974 when the government recognized the black nationalist 'Third Force' group of small professionals who were given permission to form a pressure group in Lisbon, the *Grupo Unido de Mocambique* (GUM). The Cabora Bassa Dam remained the key to the Portuguese plan to integrate Mozambique with the white economies of Rhodesia and South Africa. The dam was on schedule for an operational opening in 1975.

During February 1974 FRELIMO increased the intensity of its campaign in the Tete province, targeting the Beira–Malawi railway that brought supplies for the Cabora Bassa Dam. Writing in the *Rand Daily Mail*[10] Dennis Gordon argued that the next six months would see whether Portugal could halt the advance or the war would reach South Africa's doorstep: 'FRELIMO opened its "fourth front" of the war in the Beira district last June. Since then, terror activity has spread south rapidly. If FRELIMO breaches the Beira-Umtali (Rhodesia) axis, where there has been terrorist activity since the new year, the movement will be on the last leg of its plan to "liberate" the whole country.' A few weeks later Will Hussey, writing in the *South African Star*,[11] said that even its most ardent detractors grudgingly admit that the FRELIMO guerrilla attack in Mozambique was making formidable strides. The tactic of intensifying the war with frequent, widely separated attacks plus landmines tied up 60,000 Portuguese troops.

Suddenly the situation changed dramatically with the 25 April Revolution in Lisbon (see below) and a date for Mozambique's independence was set for 25 June 1975. The agreement to this effect was signed by Portuguese and FRELIMO leaders on 7 September 1974 in Lusaka, Zambia. There was to be an interim government under a FRELIMO prime minister with six of nine ministers appointed by FRELIMO. Rear-Admiral Crespo was appointed Portuguese High Commissioner until independence. On hearing of the independence agreement the white settlers formed the Mozambique Popular Movement and mounted a revolt in Lourenco Marques on 7 September; this was led by former Portuguese commandos, the 'Dragons of Death' and a right-wing group FICO (I stay), which briefly obtained control of the airport, the power station and the oil refinery. They also claimed to have seized control in the towns of Beira, Nampula, Quelimane and Vila Cabral. They released 200 former members of the secret police. In Lisbon the new Chief of Staff, Gen. Francisco da Costa Gomes, ordered the troops to 're-establish peace and tranquillity'; he said the agreement with FRELIMO would be upheld. FRELIMO, for its part, told its supporters to refrain from provocation. Portuguese military strength in Lourenco Marques was increased from 600 to 10,000 and some FRELIMO forces were flown in from Tanzania. On 20 September in Lourenco Marques the interim government was sworn in: Joaquim Chissano, number three in the FRELIMO command, became Prime Minister with six FRELIMO and three Portuguese ministers making up his cabinet. An 80-minute speech by Samora Machel was read to the new government: 'It is necessary to liquidate the superiority complexes and inferiority complexes created by centuries of colonialism.' Machel indicated that there would be no room for ideological opposition; that attempts would be made by South Africa and Rhodesia to form a mercenary task force to cause problems; and that FRELIMO now accepted the Cabora Bassa Dam and would co-operate with the Portuguese in removing mines on the access roads to the project.

THE SIGNIFICANCE OF MOZAMBIQUE

The Portuguese went over to the offensive in 1970 with a massive assault on FRELIMO on three fronts; they employed 35,000 troops and 15,000 tons of arms and ammunition and were assisted by South Africa whose helicopters transported the troops to front-line positions. They claimed to have killed 651 FRELIMO for 150 Portuguese dead and also claimed that in 1970 as a whole 7,000 FRELIMO members and sympathisers had surrendered and over 1,800 had been captured. For its part, FRELIMO claimed that Portugal never admitted to more than 10 per cent of its casualties. Despite these claims to have delivered a major defeat to FRELIMO in 1970, the following year the Portuguese had to begin all over again. Gen. Kaulza de Arriaga launched a second major campaign early in the year yet by May 1971 the security position in Tete had become so bad that the whole province had to be placed under the rule of the military governor. The Tete war drew in the Rhodesians whose forces operated far into the province in pursuit of terrorists. Traffic through Tete from Rhodesia to Malawi was sufficiently interrupted for insurers to declare it a war risk. At the end of 1971 FRELIMO claimed to have launched 800 operations in the two months of October and November; to have destroyed 107 camps and posts; to have killed 3,000 Portuguese and destroyed 344 military vehicles; to have shot down four aircraft and five helicopters; to have destroyed

15 war-boats on the Zambezi, sabotaged dozens of kilometres of railway line and blown up 20 trains. They claimed to control one quarter of the country. Accepting the propensity of combatants to exaggerate their achievements, it was nonetheless plain that FRELIMO rather than the Portuguese army was in the ascendant. By 1972 Portugal had increased the size of its armed forces from 50,000 to 60,000 of whom half were black and said they had eliminated one fifth of the FRELIMO forces. Yet in September 1972 FRELIMO opened a new front in the Manica–Sofala area bordering Rhodesia. By this time the Cabora Bassa Dam area was ringed with triple defences while the Portuguese were trying to control the peasant population in the war zones by the rapid extension of the system of *aldeamentos* (protected villages); they settled one million peasants in 500 *aldeamentos* of which 120 were in the Tete province where a further 85 such villages were being created.

Portugal hung on to its African possessions for their economic value but by the 1970s was exhausting itself in the fight to keep them. Portugal embarked upon a new policy in 1972 when it thrust a measure of economic independence upon Angola and Mozambique and demanded cash payments for imports. In consequence, Mozambique faced growing shortages. That year Ian Colvin wrote in the *Daily Telegraph*, 'Mozambique could be described as the sick man of southern Africa.' A major blow to Portuguese pretensions came when the White Fathers decided to withdraw from Mozambique because they found it 'impossible to apply their principles of the Africanization of the Church'. Father van Asten, Superior General of the Order in Mozambique, said, 'In countries where the Church is officially persecuted and forcibly reduced to silence it still has a worthwhile witness to bear, but in a country like Mozambique where the regime openly proclaims itself Catholic and the Protector of the Church and yet in practice uses it for aims that have nothing to do with the Gospel, a Church that is unable to speak out is the reverse of a witness to its mission.' In response to this statement, the colonial government expelled all the White Fathers. Dr Rui Patricio accused the White Fathers of 'inviting the inhabitants of Mozambique to rebel and join the nationalist movement FRELIMO'.[12]

At the beginning of 1973 FRELIMO had control of most of Cabo Delgado and Niassa provinces where the Portuguese were confined to a few garrisons; they were also deploying guerrillas all over Tete province. Then in June FRELIMO opened a new front north of Beira. By early 1974 FRELIMO was operating astride the Beira–Rhodesia railway and the real front had moved south close to the Save river and within 100 miles of the South African border. The settlers became seriously worried, cabled Lisbon and demonstrated in Beira. Portugal rushed out military reinforcements and 150,000 villagers in the Beira district were moved into *aldeamentos*. As the *Rand Daily Mail* stated: 'The stark fact is that if the FRELIMO push south is not stopped on the Umtali–Beira axis, the whole country will be in danger of terrorism. Portugal is not winning the war in Mozambique.'

Following Gen. Spinola's speech of 27 July 1974, recognizing the right to independence of Portugal's African colonies, the settlers began to leave the country at the rate of 1,000 a week and white troops abandoned their garrisons after making agreements with local guerrilla groups. FRELIMO tried to persuade the settlers to stay. When Portugal suggested some form of federation with its colonies, Machel said: 'We are not going to discuss independence with the Portuguese. That is our inalienable right.' The final agreement for independence in 1975 was reached on 7 September 1974. Although FRELIMO made clear that the 220,000 settlers were welcome to stay, the majority in fact left. The right-wing settlers had looked for three things: support from South Africa; support from Rhodesia; and support from other whites in Mozambique. When they did not receive any such support they panicked and the exodus into South Africa mounted.

An independent Mozambique altered fundamentally the strategic situation in southern Africa. It meant that both Rhodesia and South Africa were outflanked; it meant that African nationalist guerrillas and arms could, for the first time, have direct frontier access to South Africa; it began the process whereby South Africa started militarily and psychologically withdrawing into a 'laager' while being forced to rethink its entire policy towards black Africa as well as towards Rhodesia and Namibia. There could be no going back.

ANGOLA

The war in Angola developed steadily, if unevenly, through the early 1970s. Writing in the *Daily Telegraph*[13] John Miller said that by then the nine-year-old struggle was pinning down 60,000 Portuguese troops, that travel outside the capital Luanda had to be in convoys and that the guerrillas were building up their strength in the east of the country. Writing in *West Africa* Basil Davidson claimed that the guerrillas were slowly winning the war: 'There is no doubt, I think, that the Portuguese have lost the strategic initiative in the east, retaining only the brief tactical initiatives of the kind they exercised when I was there. When judged only by the key area of Muie and its surrounding forests, guerrilla penetration to the West is real and effective.'[14] Unlike Mozambique, Angola had three liberation movements: the FNLA (*Frente Nacional de Libertação de Angola*); the MPLA (*Movimento Popular de Libertação de Angola*); and UNITA (*União Nacional para a Independência Total de Angola*). Through the first half of the 1970s the MPLA was by far the most aggressive in the field. However, by the time of the April 1974 Revolution in Portugal, the war in Angola remained more open and less decided than that in Mozambique.

African efforts to unite the liberation movements had only limited, temporary success. Acting under an OAU mandate the Presidents of Zaïre and the Congo brought Agostinho Neto, the leader of the MPLA, and Holden Roberto, the leader of the FNLA, together in June 1972. They did not, however, invite Jonas Savimbi, the leader of UNITA, who was suspected of working with the Portuguese against the MPLA. A very tentative agreement was reached and subsequently ratified at the Rabat OAU summit later that June. In December a further move to unify the two movements was attempted at a meeting in Kinshasa of the foreign ministers of Zambia, Tanzania, Zaïre and Congo at which Neto and Roberto agreed to place their armies under the overall command of a Supreme Council for the Liberation of Angola. In fact, these meetings were more about gesture politics than any real intent to achieve unity: the leadership, ideologies and intent of the two movements were simply too far apart for such overtures to be successful. Furthermore, both the MPLA and the FNLA were troubled by internal dissensions; FNLA was the more affected when a number of its leading members defected to the Portuguese. The MPLA opened a new front in the region of Mocamedes and Huila.

The Cunene River scheme for hydro-electric generation and irrigation was launched in 1972 and, like the Cabora Bassa project in Mozambique, was a joint Portuguese-South African venture also designed to draw South Africa into the 'defence' of Portugal's interests in the region. The Cunene formed the boundary between Angola and South African-controlled Namibia and the agreement provided for an expenditure of 17.48 million escudos which made the project larger than the Cabora Bassa Dam. The first stage was designed to control the flow of the Cunene along its entire length: there was to be a dam at Ruacana Falls and the Gove Dam, and irrigation for Ovamboland in northern Namibia. The Gove Dam would create a lake 178 kilometres in length and would provide electric power as well as water for irrigation. A generating station at Ruacana with a capacity of 240–300 MW per hour would provide electric power for the Namibian mines at Tsumeb and Grootfontein, as well as for the fishing industry at Walvis Bay. It was, in other words, to be of greater value to South Africa than to Angola.[15]

During 1973 the Portuguese were under less pressure in Angola than Mozambique and this enabled them to transfer 10,000 of their troops from Angola to the latter country. Zambia and Tanzania, which had broken diplomatic contact with the FNLA, resumed relations with Holden Roberto, and his movement was re-adopted by the OAU Liberation Committee. The Portuguese were able to expand both industrial activity and the oil industry during the year although the Portuguese themselves remained reluctant to invest in Angola. The three guerrilla movements and the Portuguese each exaggerated their military achievements, yet the guerrilla performance that year was not especially successful. Despite continuing efforts on the part of the OAU to persuade the three movements to work together they remained divided as to ideology and the political ambitions of their three leaders. President Mobutu of Zaïre, always a political weather-vane, took a stronger anti-Portuguese stand through the year and worked more closely with Tanzania and Zambia, the two leading front-line states.

Angola's oil production from the Cabinda enclave was both a principal economic source of strength for the Portuguese and also an indication of the future resource dependence of an independent Angola. Exports for 1972 from Cabinda Gulf (in barrels) were as follows:[16]

Canada	16,526,536
US–Trinidad	13,451,138
Japan	9,934,099
Portugal	3,618,570
Spain	1,926,141
Luanda refinery	600,743
Denmark	506,445

Following the 25 April Revolution in Lisbon, before Portugal's decolonizing intentions had become clear, the suspicion grew that Spinola hoped to hold onto Angola for its wealth. This suspicion was reinforced by the appointment of a right-wing Governor-General, Silvino Silveiro Marques. It was claimed that he had been appointed to reassure the whites, but he did not reassure the blacks. In July fierce black-white rioting erupted in Luanda and many Africans were killed. The Governor was dismissed as a result and a local military council took control of the country. On 29 July the MPLA and FNLA agreed to meet in Zaïre to set up a common front for independence negotiations. But the whites became increasingly vocal in their protests against a 'sell-out' to the liberation movements. However, the MPLA/FNLA unity meeting was postponed by disputes within the MPLA. An MPLA congress in Lusaka was attended by 165 supporters of MPLA President Dr Neto, 165 supporters of his rival Daniel Chipenda and 70 delegates from Brazzaville led by Joaquim Pinto de Andrade. The congress lasted from 12 to 21 August but ended without agreement. Dr Neto called for a united Angola but refused to agree to co-operate with other political parties in any future government. The MPLA and UNITA reached unofficial peace agreements with the Portuguese Army but the FNLA under Holden Roberto continued to fight.[17]

In October, after the fall of Spinola, the FNLA declared a ceasefire to end 13 years of war. The struggle for ascendancy in Angola now got under way. Roberto was backed by Zaïre's Mobutu while the Americans regarded him as neutral; their principal concern was to safeguard the high level of foreign investment in the country, especially the oil in Cabinda. Complex manoeuvres followed and a fragile common front was formed by the liberation movements in Kinshasa to deal with a delegation from Lisbon. Mobutu and the Portuguese wanted to back the FNLA and the Chipenda faction of the MPLA. Neto did not attend these meetings. During November further violence erupted in Luanda in which 50 people were killed and 100 injured. By this time the differences between the three liberation movements were steadily widening. FNLA influence was confined to the northern coffee-growing region and it had again lost the support of the OAU. Holden Roberto was always in Zaïre rather than in Angola with his forces and the FNLA, like the MPLA, was weakened by splits. By this time the MPLA had made the widest international impact although its main Angolan support was confined to the region around Luanda. Its close links with the Communists ensured US opposition and the split between the Neto and Chipenda factions had yet to be resolved. The third liberation movement, UNITA, which had been formed in 1964 when Jonas Savimbi broke with Holden Roberto, was then operating in the south of the country. As the prospect of Angola being split by civil war to secure the succession to the departing Portuguese developed, Savimbi extended the influence of UNITA in the centre and south of the country and gathered support from white settlers. These manoeuvres continued to the end of the year while cynics looked greedily at Angola's great wealth: diamonds, coffee, iron ore, oil. 'No one knows how rich the country is going to be. But we know it is going to be very rich indeed. Possibly the richest country in the continent per head of the population after South Africa.'[18] Angola's coming independence was going to be deeply troubled and the liberation war, which had ended with the 13 October FNLA ceasefire, would in fact merge into a civil war between the different nationalist factions and was destined to last to the end of the century.

The differences between the liberation movements were deep: part ideological, part a question of power, part tribal. They were temporarily suspended in January 1975, following a meeting between the three movements in Nairobi, which enabled them to present a united front to Portugal at Alvor in the Algarve later that month when Neto, Roberto and Savimbi represented their movements and Portugal agreed upon 11 November as the date for Angolan independence. On 31 January a transitional government was established in

Luanda. The unity was short-lived. On his return to Luanda on 4 February, Neto was greeted by a crowd of 100,000; he called for unity. From Kinshasa Roberto rejected the idea of people's power and communism. Then Chipenda's wing of the MPLA staged a revolt in Luanda and merged with Roberto's FNLA. In March fighting broke out between the MPLA and the FNLA. In April a joint OAU/UN mission tried but failed to bring the liberation movements together again. Instead, dissension and fighting increased for the rest of the year. By June the fighting between the three movements had spread to the capital but by 12 July the MPLA, with Soviet assistance, had driven the Western-backed FNLA and UNITA out of Luanda and then controlled 12 out of 15 provinces. Roberto had returned to Angola for the first time since 1961 to lead the FNLA in its attack upon Luanda but without success. By August the fighting had spread to most parts of the country and South African troops had entered the south of Angola. On 19 September Portugal announced that it would withdraw all its troops by 11 November and most of them had left the country by the end of October. UNITA and the FNLA announced they would set up a government at Huambo in the south of the country until the MPLA had been driven from Luanda. On 11 November the Portuguese made a hurried departure from Angola with nothing settled. The MPLA proclaimed the People's Republic of Angola with Agostinho Neto as President. In Ambriz the FNLA and UNITA proclaimed the Popular and Democratic Republic of Angola with Holden Roberto as President. As the civil war intensified the US offered direct assistance to both the FNLA and UNITA, while the USSR increased its assistance to the MPLA; by 11 November the USSR had airlifted some 16,000 Cuban troops into the country in support of the MPLA. At independence the MPLA had the decisive advantage: it controlled the capital and most of the towns and won international recognition as the government. South Africa, however, was preparing for a major intervention against the MPLA. The departure of the Portuguese signalled the end of the liberation struggle and the beginning of years of civil war that would see the two superpowers, the Cubans, South Africa and mercenaries all involved in a struggle that would continue to 2000.

THE PORTUGUESE RETREAT

By 1972 the world wondered at Portugal's determination to carry on a conflict it could not win but the Portuguese response was that it could not do otherwise. The Portuguese had long been taught that their country's future lay in Africa and that without Africa it would become a nonentity in Europe. Opponents of this view argued that if the same effort that went into holding onto the African colonies were to be used instead to develop Portugal itself the country would be far better off. The change in the Organic Law which governed the African colonies was not very far-reaching and amounted to little more than designating the overseas African provinces of Angola and Mozambique as states with marginal autonomy that would allow them a greater say in their home affairs, largely over economic matters. The change would not be permitted to disrupt 'the essential unity of the Portuguese nation'. When the hard right responded to this new 'soft' line in Africa by re-electing for the third time Admiral Americo Thomaz as President for seven years – he was an old associate of Salazar – left-wing urban guerrillas reacted with violence. Hours before Thomaz was sworn in as President, 30 bombs were exploded in various parts of Lisbon, as well as in Coimbra and Oporto and, among other damage, put the power network out of action.

The priority that had been accorded to African development during the wars meant that in 1972 the economic growth rates in both Angola and Mozambique passed that of Portugal for the first time. At the same time Portugal's home problems were multiplying and Caetano blamed emigration, inflation and housing for Portugal's ills. An estimated 1.5 million Portuguese were living permanently abroad, mainly in France, Germany and the US, while the population at home stood at 8.8 million. The annual rate of emigration stood at 180,000 of whom about 30,000 a year went to Angola and Mozambique; many of the others were draft dodgers or soldiers who had finished their service but feared a second call-up. Despite increasing military service to four years, the army remained short of manpower and in order to induce soldiers to serve for a third time in Africa they were offered a 10 per cent pay increase and further family allowances. When Rhodesia's Ian Smith visited Lisbon in October 1972 and expressed his alarm at the adverse turn of events in the Tete province of Mozambique, Caetano publicly rebuked him, without mentioning his name, when he said: 'Some neighbours with less experience of guerrilla warfare than ourselves do not conceal their fears, and are playing the enemy's game.' Resentment of Rhodesia made sense only if Portugal's concept of multiracialism was to carry conviction among the Africans; in fact, dependence on a so-called southern African bloc made a mockery out of Portugal's policy which, for all its ambivalence, was in no way akin to apartheid.[19]

Opponents of Portugal's African policy were arrested during a peace vigil in Lisbon on New Year's Eve, December 1972. On 15 January 1973 the Prime Minister, Marcello Caetano, said he would not talk with terrorist groups. Liberals in the Portuguese Parliament were defeated by the right-wingers who controlled the assembly, although the country's politics were becoming increasingly stormy as the African wars dominated public life. The Secretary of

State for Information, Moreira Baptista, said Portugal was at war and nothing should be allowed to weaken the national effort: 'We shall continue the fight for freedom of thought.'[20] Herminio Palma Ignacio, a revolutionary of 30 years and the leader of the League of Revolutionary Unity and Action (LUAR) in Portugal, said that revolution would come to Portugal before the freedom fighters succeeded in the colonies and claimed that when the government of Portugal had been overthrown they (the revolutionaries) would bring an immediate end to the African wars. By 1973, although Caetano appeared to be in firm control of events there was growing and widespread opposition to his policies. Britain tried to bolster Portugal's stand by agreeing to celebrations in June 1973 to mark 600 years of Anglo-Portuguese alliance: the Duke of Edinburgh was to visit Portugal over 5–8 June and Caetano was to return the visit in Britain over 16–19 July. These arrangements led to a storm of protests in Britain from anti-apartheid groups. In September 1973 the PAIGC proclaimed the independence of Guinea-Bissau, which was then admitted as the forty-second member of the OAU and recognized by 70 countries while in November the General Assembly of the UN adopted a resolution by 93 to seven with 30 abstentions to welcome 'the recent accession to independence of the people of Guinea-Bissau'.

The government vetoed all criticisms of its African policies during the October 1973 elections with the result that the opposition candidates withdrew before election day. The number of deputies was raised from 140 to 150 with Angola and Mozambique being allotted 12 instead of 10 deputies each. The Angolan Legislative Assembly had 32 elected to 21 nominated members while in Mozambique there were 20 elected and 30 nominated members. Neither assembly had a majority of black members. In order to qualify for the vote Africans had to be over 21, literate in Portuguese and pay a minimal sum in taxes; the fact that so many blacks remained disenfranchised demonstrated how little Portugal had done to bring about the *assimilado* policy that it boasted was its unique gift to Africa. By this time the financial drain on the Portuguese economy of the long drawn out wars in Africa was creating a massive annual trade deficit of £400 million. Following the Yom Kippur War in the Middle East (1973) the Arab states imposed an oil boycott on Portugal as a reprisal because Lisbon had allowed the US to use the Azores as a staging post for military supplies being sent to Israel. The boycott cut Portugal's oil supplies by 60 per cent.

After a desperate year in which all the signs pointed to the coming collapse of Portugal's African policies, Gen. Antonio de Spinola, the Deputy Chief of Staff, published his book *Portugal and the Future* in February 1974. In it he said: 'Today Portugal is living through one of its gravest hours, perhaps the gravest hour of its history. An exclusive military victory was no longer viable in the African wars... We must smash the myth... that we are defending the West and Western civilization... We must also smash the myth... that the essence of the Portuguese nation is the civilizing mission...' Portugal's African policy was unlikely for long to survive the publication of this book.[21] Spinola also said that Portugal had to give frank recognition to the principle of self-determination in the framework of a united but outward-looking and reformed Portugal. Spinola favoured some form of federation but as he was to discover it was too late. An attempt to overthrow Caetano on 9 March resulted in the dismissal of Spinola and Gen. Francisco da Costa Gomes but the attempt was a forerunner of the April Revolution.

The coup of 25 April 1974 was staged at dawn. The Caetano government was arrested and President Americo Thomaz and Premier Marcello Caetano were flown to Madeira and later exiled to Brazil. The news of the coup was received with enthusiasm and few mourned the downfall of Caetano. The *Movimento das Forças Armadas* (MFA) (Movement of Armed Forces), which had staged the coup, handed over the government to a Junta of National Salvation and Gen. Spinola became the acting President. He promised elections within a year, the release of political prisoners, freedom of expression and the press, while exiles such as the socialist Dr Mario Soares and the communist Alvaro Cunhal were allowed home, the latter to head the Communist Party, which was allowed to operate freely. Cunhal became a minister without portfolio while Soares became Foreign Minister. Soares warned that the white settlers in Angola (500,000) and Mozambique (220,000) might try to carry out unilateral declarations of independence. Some of the whites in Africa dissociated themselves from the Junta and its newly appointed territorial administrators. South Africa, on the other hand, was quick to recognize the Spinola government. Gen. da Costa Gomes became immediately responsible for Portuguese Africa and within two weeks of the coup the Portuguese holding key posts in Angola and Mozambique had been replaced. He made it clear in Luanda that any attempt by the white minority to seize power would not be tolerated. Thus, the longest dictatorship in modern history, which had begun in 1926, and the oldest colonial empire in the world came to an end on 25 April 1974 when nameless army officers calling themselves the MFA seized power and 800 men took control of Portugal over 24 hours.

On 19 May Spinola announced the suspension of military operations in Africa. The PAIGC, represented by Aristides Pereira, entered into talks with the new government, represented by Dr Soares, in London on 25 May. In Mozambique, however, FRELIMO continued its military operations. A period of uncertainty now followed as divisions appeared between the middle-of-the-road politicians and the more radical MFA, which opposed Spinola's centrist policies. This division led to the resignation of Premier Palma Carlos and four other ministers and the MFA then chose Col. Vasco Goncalves as Premier on 14 July. Criticism of Spinola increased and he was accused of adopting a personality cult. He was accused of only wanting self-determination for the colonies rather than full independence. The left was firmly committed to total decolonization. The government repealed the first Article of the 1933 Constitution, which defined Portugal as a single state made up of home and overseas provinces. On 27 July Spinola gave a broadcast in which he said the time had come to recognize the right of people to take their destiny in their own hands and he announced 'the immediate initiation of the process of decolonization of overseas Portugal'.[22] Despite this speech Spinola was rapidly losing favour with the young officers of the MFA; he was seen as too conservative and too loyal to friends of the old regime. He sealed his fate when he released several right-wing figures from detention because of 'lack of evidence against them'.[23] On 10 September 1974, following his recognition of independence for Guinea-Bissau, Gen. Spinola gave a speech in which he used the fateful words the 'silent majority' and spoke of a slide towards chaos. The effect of this speech was to bring the right back into action and it started to regroup. The crisis came on 28 September when Gen. Spinola was prepared to sanction a rally in his support mounted by a regrouped right wing, which had adopted the phrase 'silent majority' as its catchword. Clashes between right and left followed and rumours spread of a counter-coup. Spinola bowed to left-wing pressure and called off the rally. Some 200 arrests were made by COPCON (Continental Operations Command), which supported the MFA; those arrested included Gen. Kaulza de Arriaga. Gen. Spinola, who was not implicated in the plotting, resigned on 30 September and was replaced by Gen. da Costa Gomes while Vasco Goncalves took over Defence. By the end of the year the MFA had effective control of the country.

The PAIGC and the struggle in Portuguese Guinea was the most decisive event leading to the 25 April Revolution in Portugal. MFA analyses of Portugal's situation focused first upon developments in Guinea where the influence on the young officers of Amilcar Cabral had been profound. 'The year [1974] began with the fiercest fighting the colonial army had known. Heavy artillery bombardments by the PAIGC and their capture of the Copa camp heralded what could have become certain military victory by the end of 1974 had the April coup not intervened and prompted an immediate though unofficial cease-fire.'[24] In the south of the continent, after five centuries of colonial rule, Mozambique won its struggle for independence under FRELIMO whose tenacious struggle under Mondlane and then Machel had forced the pace and the revolution in Portugal that overthrew Caetano. The date for independence was set for 25 June 1975. The FRELIMO victory signalled a major change in the balance of power in Southern Africa. Angola, the largest and richest of the Portuguese African possessions, also won the right to independence in 1974 although in this case the changeover was far less straightforward than in either Guinea-Bissau or Mozambique and the agreement signed on 15 January 1975 by representatives of the Portuguese government and the three liberation movements – MPLA, FNLA and UNITA – that promised independence for 11 November that year owed more to events in Mozambique and Guinea-Bissau that had precipitated the April Revolution than to liberation pressures in Angola itself.

Few had foreseen the sudden collapse of Portuguese colonialism. The Portuguese government had long disguised from the Portuguese people the true position in Mozambique after FRELIMO launched its decisive southward offensive in January 1974. Lisbon's propaganda had also fooled most Western political and military commentators. In March 1975 Portugal produced its own figures of the human and economic costs to Portugal of its three African wars. From May 1961 to 30 April 1974, 4,788 Portuguese servicemen had been killed in action and of these 1,523 had been recruited in the colonies (not all black); the figures for the three territories were: Angola 1,526, Mozambique 1,606, Guinea-Bissau 1,654. A further 2,341 were killed in accidents and 545 died of disease. The total cost of the wars was estimated at 120,000 million escudos (US$5,000 million).[25] The Portuguese did not produce any figures for African casualties. The liberation movements over the years had claimed a higher rate of Portuguese casualties than these figures suggest.

Portugal's exit from Africa in 1975 was undignified and disorderly. It left behind a developing civil war in Angola while a mass exodus of whites was taking place from both Angola and Mozambique, to give the lie to Portugal's claims to non-racialism and integration. Portugal's new 'radical' rulers showed little more understanding of Africa than had their hard-line predecessors. At the end of 1975 Portugal had little continuing contact with its former colonies and no influence over events either immediately preceding or following independence. The last Governor-General of Angola left without handing over to a recognized successor government. Furthermore, as the Portuguese quit Angola they opened the way for major interventions by the Cold War superpowers, the US and USSR, and had done nothing to prevent this development. Thus, not only did the departing Portuguese fail to make a reasonable handover of power but appeared to welcome the big power interventions as a defeat for the liberation movements that had defeated and humiliated metropolitan Portugal.

Although Maj. Melo Antunes, the architect of decolonization, repeatedly warned of the dangers of Vietnamization (in Angola) this did not occur for three reasons: the pressures of the US anti-involvement lobby in the wake of the American withdrawal from Vietnam; the failure of South Africa to assess correctly the scale of military intervention required for it to achieve its 1975 invasion objective of overthrowing the MPLA government in Luanda; and the inability of the FNLA and UNITA to unite in opposition to the MPLA.[26] 'In reality, Portugal left Angola with its tail between its legs. More shaming than the war itself, which could with justification be blamed partly on foreign powers, was the behaviour of its white Mozambicans and white Angolans who had been held out for generations as examples of integrated settlers and who were supposed to consider themselves more as African than Portuguese. Only a handful stayed in either country, or were prepared to make any sacrifices for "their" new, independent nations.'[27]

As a consequence of the Portuguese withdrawal from Southern Africa and the emergence of two Marxist-oriented governments in Angola and Mozambique, South Africa lost the 'cordon' of white-controlled territories that had separated it from black Africa to the north. Pretoria, therefore, had to rethink its strategies in relation to its neighbours and the first casualty of this rethink was Smith's Rhodesia whose usefulness to South Africa came abruptly to an end. The result was to bring the end of white minority rule in Rhodesia appreciably closer while, for the first time, South Africa was brought into direct contact, along its 500 kilometre border with Mozambique, with the possibility of black liberation movements having direct access to its territory. The Soweto uprising of 1976 was, in part at least, inspired by events in Angola and Mozambique. At last the winds of change were blowing directly across South Africa's borders.

Namibia

From the viewpoint of an increasingly embattled South Africa, Namibia occupied a strategically vital position as a buffer between the Republic and Angola and Zambia to its north. Covering 318,000 square miles of territory Namibia was half as large again as France with a population of just on one million people. Its thousand-mile northern border stretched from the Atlantic along the whole of southern Angola and then western Zambia for the 300 miles of the Caprivi Strip to the Kazungula ferry crossing from Zambia to Botswana at the point where the four countries – Namibia, Zambia, Rhodesia and Botswana – meet. The Caprivi Strip is a geographical anomaly, carved out of northern Bechuanaland in 1890 by the British and ceded to Germany so as to give German South West Africa access to the Zambezi; by the 1970s, when confrontation between South Africa and its northern neighbours was steadily escalating, the Strip enabled South Africa and Rhodesia jointly to encircle Botswana while the huge military base that South Africa established at Katima Mulilo on the Strip acted as a direct threat to Zambia. The Namibian economy could be conveniently divided into two sectors: the south, which was the area of white settlement (including segregated reserve areas for Africans), was the principal area of economic activity and included the territory's huge mining wealth; and the north, where the majority of the African population lived, which was almost entirely dependent upon subsistence agriculture.

In Namibia South Africa behaved like any other colonial power and was to hold on to its colony for as long as it was able to do so, in the process denying all demands for majority rule. In addition, the colonial grip that Pretoria exercised over Namibia was reinforced by the apartheid policies that South Africa imposed at a time when these policies were coming under increasing pressure from the rest of the world community, led by the United Nations. As long as South Africa defied world opinion and refused to leave Namibia it was, in a sense, asserting its determination to remain outside the world community. If it was right to apply apartheid inside South Africa then Pretoria could not do less than apply it to Namibia. As a result, by the 1970s South Africa was in defiance of world opinion as represented by the United Nations by holding on illegally to its 'mandate' from the former League of Nations while refusing to move the territory towards independence as all the other former mandatory powers had agreed to do. Namibia's rejection of South African occupation was expressed in 1968 by Andimba Toivo ja Toivo, SWAPO's co-founder and the regional secretary for Ovamboland, in a statement he made from the dock on being sentenced to 20 years prison by a South African court under the retroactively applied Terrorism Act:

> My lord, we find ourselves here in a foreign country, convicted under laws made by people whom we have always considered as foreigners… It is the deep feeling of all of us that we should not be tried here in Pretoria… We are Namibians and not South Africans. We do not now, and will not in the future recognize your right to govern us, to make laws for us in which we had no say; to treat our country as if it were your property and us as if you were our masters. We have always regarded South Africa as an intruder in our country… Only when we are granted our independence will the struggle stop. Only when our human dignity is restored to us, as equals of the whites, will there be peace between us.[1]

When, eventually, South Africa slowly conceded first that Namibia was a UN responsibility and that South Africa had no permanent rights in the territory and, second, that it was prepared to withdraw from the territory, did South Africa also signal its desire to rejoin the world community.

A BRIEF HISTORY

South West Africa had been colonized by imperial Germany in the course of the Scramble for Africa. The colony was overrun early in World War I when South African imperial forces, led by Generals Botha and Smuts, entered the territory in January 1915 through the ports of Walvis Bay and Lüderitz. Under the terms of the Treaty of Versailles Germany surrendered its colonies to the allies and in December 1920 German South West Africa was designated a C Mandate and entrusted to South Africa to administer on behalf of the newly formed League of Nations. In fact, the Mandate was granted to Britain (George V) to be administered through the Union of South Africa with the obligation 'to promote to the utmost the material and moral well-being of the inhabitants of the territory' so that, in terms of international law, Britain always had a responsibility for Namibia until it eventually achieved independence in 1990.

South Africa administered the territory as though it were an integral part of the Union (much as the main imperial powers, Britain and France, treated their African mandates). During the 1920s and 1930s South African policy was to convert the mandate into a fifth province. In 1922 Walvis Bay, which South Africa had held throughout the German colonial period, was transferred to the South West Africa administration. In 1924 the South West Africa Naturalization of Aliens Act allowed all German adult males to become naturalized. In 1926 a Legislative Assembly was created with 12 elected (white) and six nominated members and an executive committee with authority over roads, bridges, taxation and agriculture. From its inception this assembly lobbied for accession to the Union. This persistent lobbying led the permanent Mandates Commission of the League of Nations in 1933 to object to the suggestion that South West Africa should be joined to South Africa, forcing South Africa to announce in 1937 that it had no such plans.

Following World War II, the mandates of the defunct League of Nations were made Trust Territories of the newly formed United Nations, and in 1946 the UN invited its members to place their mandates under the Trusteeship system. All did so except for South Africa, which, instead, organized a referendum among the chiefs of South West Africa and on the strength of the result demanded that the territory should be incorporated in the Union. Only Britain supported this South African move. Subsequently, Pretoria refused to place South West Africa under the UN or to recognize UN jurisdiction, claiming instead that the Mandate of the League of Nations was at an end. From 1946 onwards South African control of the territory was to be challenged every year in the UN General Assembly. In 1949 South Africa virtually incorporated South West Africa in the Union and the government stopped providing the UN with annual reports of its administration, a move that was tantamount to annexation. Economic integration followed and most of Namibia's wealth, derived from its vast mineral resources, was diverted to South Africa. On 10 December 1959 mass protests against apartheid were held in the capital, Windhoek, and the police fired on the demonstrators, killing or wounding 60 people, an event that signalled a major growth of nationalist opposition. Prior to this event the Ovamboland People's Congress (OPC) had been formed in 1957 in Cape Town, by Namibians working in South Africa, under the leadership of Andimba Toivo ja Toivo. The Congress changed its name to the Ovamboland People's Organization in June 1960 when it extended its activities outside Windhoek. In 1964 it changed its name again to become the South West African People's Organization (SWAPO) and though other movements such as the South West Africa National Union (SWANU) were also formed SWAPO became the main focus of opposition to South African rule. In its early years –

to 1966 – SWAPO sought change by peaceful means but in that year, following the failure of the International Court at The Hague to find against South African occupation of Namibia, SWAPO launched its armed struggle. In 1964 the South African-appointed Odendaal Commission reported and recommended the division of Namibia into 10 self-governing homelands or Bantustans covering 40 per cent of the territory, a recommendation that spelt the break-up of Namibia as a single entity.

In 1966 the UN General Assembly passed Resolution 2145 terminating the Mandate and stating that South West Africa was the direct responsibility of the United Nations. The world body changed the territory's name to Namibia and established the Council for Namibia, which came into being in 1967. South Africa, however, ignored the UN resolution and persisted in its application of apartheid to Namibia. As the UN resolution had stated, South Africa had 'consistently and relentlessly pursued a policy of racial discrimination... in flagrant violation of the spirit of the Mandate entrusted to it by the League of Nations'. The first clash between SWAPO guerrillas and members of the South African Defence Force (SADF) occurred in 1966 and the armed struggle was under way. South Africa now built up its military potential in Namibia in anticipation of the pressures which it expected to be mounted against it, establishing a desert warfare centre for its troops at Walvis Bay and other military installations including a huge military air base capable of handling the largest jet aircraft at Katima Mulilo on the Caprivi Strip in defiance of the terms of the Mandate. By 1968 South Africa was applying all its laws to Namibia and had divided the country into 10 Bantustans as well as one central white region. In 1969 South Africa passed the South West Africa Affairs Bill, which incorporated South West Africa into the Republic, effectively making it the fifth province of South Africa.

Throughout the period after 1946 the United Nations worked hard to detach Namibia from South African control. It had little power and its authority was constantly thwarted by the major Western powers whose interests in terms of trade, investment and Cold War strategy led them to pursue a status quo strategy that favoured South Africa. In 1949, after South Africa had deleted references to the Mandate from the South West Africa Constitution and given whites in the territory direct representation in the South African Parliament, the United Nations submitted the issue of sovereignty to the International Court of Justice (ICJ) at The Hague to begin the long legal battle over Namibian sovereignty that would last to independence. In 1953 the UN General Assembly resolved to supervise the Mandate by means of a Committee on South West Africa and in 1955 the ICJ confirmed the right of the General Assembly to adopt resolutions on South West Africa. This long period of wrangling between the

UN and an intransigent South Africa set the scene for the 1970s, for by the beginning of the decade the South African government had been locked in a confrontation with the United Nations for a quarter of a century. It then regarded Namibia as both an integral part of the Republic and a necessary bulwark against the growing pressures from independent black Africa to the north.

THE 1970s

Two events set the stage for the 1970s: the 1971 ruling of the ICJ and the strike of 1972. In 1969 the Security Council had voted 13–0 (with two abstentions) to withdraw its administration from Namibia. Then, in 1971 the ICJ found that South Africa was occupying Namibia illegally. This decision marked the opening of a 20-year battle between South Africa and the world community, represented by the United Nations, during the course of which, step by step, South Africa would be forced to concede its position until finally agreeing to implement UN Resolution 435 and allow Namibia to become independent. South Africa rejected the 1971 ICJ ruling that it should withdraw its administration from Namibia but almost at once faced massive internal unrest in the form of a strike against the contract labour system, which forced the government to send troops into Ovamboland and establish martial law.

When the ICJ gave its judgment on 21 June 1971 by 13–2 that South Africa was illegally in Namibia and that it was incumbent on all UN member states to 'refrain from any acts' and in particular 'any dealings with the government of South Africa implying recognition of the legality of, or lending support or assistance to such presence and administration', South Africa's Prime Minister J. B. Vorster cited the minority judgment of Britain and France as 'a strong protest against the violation of law contained in the majority opinion'. Following the judgment, the UN Security Council adopted a resolution on 20 October 1971 by 13 votes in favour to two against (Britain and France) that affirmed Namibia to be the direct responsibility of the UN. In March 1972, the UN Security Council sent the Secretary-General (Kurt Waldheim) to initiate contacts 'with all parties concerned'. Dr Waldheim's mandate was 'to establish conditions to enable the people of Namibia, freely and with strict regard to the principles of human equality, to exercise their right to self-determination and independence'. Writing in the *Observer*[2] Stanley Uys said that Dr Waldheim had presumably evoked some kind of encouraging response from Mr Vorster, but his government-sponsored itinerary had an 'almost comic imbalance'. In Ovamboland he had announced that it was not within his terms of reference to investigate the causes of the strike. Instead, he had been taken on a sightseeing tour, met government-nominated African councillors and visited a modern hospital and hydro-electric scheme. The Council for Namibia issued a statement on 12 July 1972 denouncing the South African decision to 'grant self-rule' to Ovamboland and reaffirmed its opposition to the fragmentation of Namibia through the establishment of Bantustans. Dr Waldheim made his formal report to the Security Council on 16 November 1972 and expressed the hope that it provided 'a useful basis' on which to decide further action. Prime Minister Vorster, however, refused either to dismantle the embryo Bantustans then being established in Namibia or to define his government's attitude to independence for Namibia. In December 1973 the Security Council voted 15–0 to halt further talks with South Africa over Namibia. It appointed Sean McBride as Commissioner for Namibia and recognized SWAPO as the 'authentic representative of the people of Namibia'. The Waldheim initiative came to nothing because the Western powers were unwilling to force a real confrontation with South Africa.

THE OVAMBO STRIKE

In December 1971 between 15,000 and 20,000 contract workers went on strike and by January 1972 had almost brought the country to a standstill. The strike began on 13 December 1971 in the Windhoek Municipal Compound and spread to involve workers in 20 different areas of the country. Almost all the mines, including the giant US-controlled Tsumeb mine which employed 4,000 men and represented the lifeblood of the economy, came to a standstill. The Ovambos, who accounted for 45 per cent of the population and 90 per cent of the workforce, made up the overwhelming majority of the strikers. The South African Minister of Bantu Affairs, M. C. Botha, met employers in Pretoria in December when they decided to revise the contract system and abolish the South West Africa Native Labour Association (SWANLA), which had controlled work opportunities and wages since 1933; in future conditions would be determined directly between employers and employees. No mention was made at this meeting of higher wages or the African right to collective bargaining. The strikers set out their demands in a pamphlet of 12 January 1972. These included the improvement of employment agreements to cover: liberty for Ovambos to do the work they want to do and of which they have experience and knowledge; freedom to change jobs without 'fear of landing in jail', freedom to have their families with them; the rate for the job irrespective of colour and equal treatment for all; employment bureaux in all tribal regions and towns; mutual respect between employer and employee; sufficient pay for workers to buy their own food and provide for transport needs; an identification card instead of a passbook; and the removal of the 'barricade' – the police post at the Ovamboland border.

A ban on meetings that was imposed by the Ovamboland Legislative Council was largely ignored. The *Rand Daily Mail* commented as follows:

> With great expedition 13,000 contract workers have been sent back to Ovamboland to live out a limbo existence until such time as the conflict can be resolved... The territory's R90 million-a-year mining industry – the mainstay of its economic viability – has virtually ground to a halt... If most of the Afrikaans newspapers are a barometer, Nationalists within and outside the territory seem content – even eager – to view the Ovambo walk-out as some sort of victory for White enterprise. The cheeky kaffir has tried to buck the system, and has been put in his place. When the hunger pangs start, he'll be back, cap in hand. Meanwhile, South West can exist without him.
>
> That is simply not so. Frantic attempts by the mines to recruit workers from other tribes have met with a notable lack of success...[3]

The aftermath of the strike saw the South West African economy hit, South Africa stepping up its programme of Bantustans, with one new homeland government announced since the Waldheim visit when the Caprivi Legislative Council was opened in March while the various African groups – SWAPO, SWANU and chiefs' groups – found a new sense of unity. The new labour recruiting system, which replaced SWANLA, caused confusion among white officials and businessmen and aroused opposition in the African township of Katutura outside Windhoek. Other recruiting centres were opened in Ovamboland.

A detailed study of mining in South Africa and Namibia[4] demonstrated how close the system was to modern slavery, how hard the white mine owners worked to keep it that way to guarantee maximum profits and how powerful was the Ovambo case for change in the work structure that existed in South West Africa at that time.

> In 1971 and 1972... the Ovambo contract workers launched a remarkable protest action. At mines, farms and other workplaces throughout Namibia, then a South African colony, the Ovambo people joined the campaign for a people's contract, withdrawing their labour and returning home to their families in the north of the country until changes were made. At a great meeting at Oluno, Ondongwa on 10 January 1972, their grievances against the injustices of the contract labour system were set out

in a series of speeches and documents, which rank alongside any other twentieth-century distillation of the need for human rights and dignity.[5]

The author continued to show how the migrant labour system was a modern form of slavery. There was no meaningful contract between employer and employed. Ovambo men could only leave their 'homeland' in the north for another part of the country if they had taken a contract and this took the form of an agreement between an individual and a labour recruiting organization belonging to the mining companies, including De Beers and supported by the colonial state. There was no equity in the contract and 'The people taking contracts had no say whatever in any of the terms and conditions'. A report to the De Beers managers at Oranjemund itemized the many injustices of the system of 'Kontrak', which, the report stressed, the Ovambo had christened 'the Draad', the fence or prison. The system meant the people were not free to change jobs in pursuit of better wages or conditions. 'If they left their jobs before the expiry of the term of contract they were in breach of master and servant and pass laws and could be rounded up, jailed or even forcibly returned to their employer. The contract was so restrictive that they could not even return home in time of family sickness or emergency.'[6] Humiliating health checks were less about health than the ritual subordination of black Africans by colonial officials and whites working for foreign-owned mining companies.

British management was deeply involved in the mining industries of South Africa and Namibia and complicit in these repressive measures. 'In 1974 John MacKenzie, the general manager at Oranjemund, decided to try to do something about the overall situation (for blacks employed at the mine) and drafted a Consolidated Diamond Mines (CDM) company charter to summarize appropriate goals and objectives. The draft caused great anxiety at Anglo/De Beers' head office, with the British De Beers' director P. J. R. Leyden and his boss Julian Ogilvie Thompson detailing their worries about it. The two men flatly opposed the proposal to increase the number of black and coloured employees housed in married quarters as a key corporate aim.'[7] Rather than ameliorate conditions, by 1976 Anglo was asking for cuts in the mine housing budgets. 'This meant that even CDM management's modest plans for modification of the hostels and a few token houses where some senior blacks could live with their families came under threat.' In 1979 the mineworkers' grievances flared up again following the suicide of a miner who had been refused permission to go on leave on compassionate grounds. It is a long, miserable story with some reasonable managers seeking better conditions for their black workers and being refused even their modest proposals by Anglo-American and De Beers who ruthlessly refused to agree to any improvements.

'The list of human rights' infringements and grim conditions at Oranjemund belie the manipulated images of De Beers' unforgettable worldwide advertising campaigns.' The mining profit margins were huge and since its inception the Oranjemund mine had sold diamonds worth £5,000 million: its working costs were low, thanks to the ruthless control of labour, and its revenues high. A final comment on conditions at the vastly profitable Oranjemund mine from 1920 onwards showed how appalling they were for black miners working a 10-hour day with a 20-minute lunch break when cold tea and a loaf of brown bread were consumed in the open. 'They lived isolated from their loved ones, in atrocious single-sex compounds. There were no proper dining-room facilities, the workers had to collect their meals from the mess in metal buckets then take them back to their rooms and eat out of those buckets in the dormitories. Sporting and recreation facilities were virtually non-existent for blacks – there were one or two dirt soccer pitches and a few dartboards, but certainly nothing comparable to the conditions that the whites had. At the world's richest diamond mine, the majority of people who worked there were simply being exploited, and De Beers grew very, very rich as a result.'[8]

Mining became the *raison d'être* of Namibia from 1920 onwards as its vast diamond and other mineral resources were uncovered. The original investments in mines have been recouped several times over: 'For example, the diamond industry, bought for R7 million in 1919 by Sir Ernest Oppenheimer, has yielded pre-tax profits of R500 million to CDM of SWA and De Beers over the last 10 years (to 1974), while the Tsumeb Corporation, purchased by a consortium of US and UK mining companies for R2 million in 1945, yields average annual profits of R12–20 million.' 'In 1973, the pre-tax of Consolidated Diamond Mines increased from R100.7 million to R153.4 million, with the dividend lifted from R4.65 to R5.50 a share.' 'The profits of the South West Africa Company, the third major mining company in the territory were £916,000 in the six months to 31 December 1973, largely due to the strength of the market in the company's main product zinc.'[9] 'Although there are no accurate figures, these companies together have capital assets with a total value in excess of the annual GDP of the territory ... The total production value of the mining industry in 1973 was R250 million, the major but undisclosed element being gem diamond production at Oranjemund.' Statistics provided by the South African government showed, in 1969, nine larger operating mines, 13 medium-sized mines and 34 smaller mining and quarrying operations. It is little wonder, apart from strategic reasons, that Pretoria was so determined to hold onto Namibia. The same authors continue: 'Many of the international mining houses with subsidiaries in Namibia interlock at a higher level in terms of both equity and directors: some with the mammoth Anglo-American Corporation, which controls De Beers

Consolidated Mines; notably Charter Consolidated Ltd, Selection Trust Ltd, Falconbridge Nickel Mines (Canada), Johannesburg Consolidated Investment Ltd.'[10] This roll call of mining corporations, which were all doing very well out of Namibia, provided a powerful reason for maintaining the status quo – and that meant keeping the blacks in a position of total subservience. At the same time, Pretoria was aware of the gathering external pressures that threatened its control of Namibia and towards the end of 1973, in an attempt to bolster overseas economic support for South Africa's administration in Namibia, the South African Department of Mines decided to amend the conditions of mining and prospecting grants as applied to overseas companies. Up to that time overseas firms were able to obtain only a 50 per cent participation in any mining grant, with the majority of the mineral rights being held by the administration. Henceforth, overseas mining companies would be able to obtain up to 75 per cent of any mining grant, only needing to take on local participation when the prospecting stage had been reached.[11]

From 1970 onwards it was official US policy to discourage investment in Namibia. The former assistant secretary of state David Newsom, giving evidence before the House Committee on Africa, distinguished between US investment in South Africa and Namibia. That in South Africa the US government 'neither encourages nor discourages'. But, 'We adopt a much more restrictive policy with respect to Namibia, particularly because of our position that South Africa's presence in the territory is illegal since the termination of its Mandate in 1966. Since May 1970, we have followed a policy of discouraging further American investment in the Territory and have advised potential investors that we will not intercede to protect their investment against claims of a future legitimate government of the Territory. The Export-Import Bank and OPIC [Overseas Private Investment Corporation] provide no facilities for activities in Namibia. Any American firms which have decided to invest there since 1970 can be presumed to have done so in spite of their awareness of US policy.'[12] In 1973 US investment in Namibia was valued at US$45 million to US$50 million. About 90 per cent of this was accounted for by the Tsumeb Corporation in which Newmount Mining Corporation and American Metal Climax jointly owned a controlling interest. 'The number of American interests in Namibia is extensive, given the limited nature of the territory's economy, and there is probably much more of it than has been ascertained to date, particularly with the over 300 US companies operating in South Africa that have direct or indirect operations in Namibia.'[13]

Apart from mining, the manufacturing and construction sectors were small scale and 'closer integration of Namibia and South Africa springs largely from the interlocking ownership of much of the industry but it is also a result of increasing intervention by South African parastatal organizations, and Afrikaner-owned financial interests'. The South African Iron and Steel Corporation (ISCOR) operated two mines in the territory – a tin mine and a zinc mine – while large sums of South African and foreign money had been spent up to that time (1973) on prospecting for oil.[14] At the same time, animal husbandry accounted for 98 per cent of the value of commercial farming output and was worth R60 million a year. Cattle ownership by whites in 1971 came to 1.8 million head, with 502,000 exported in 1972, with the bulk railed to South Africa for an average price of R82 a head. There were three abattoirs in Namibia and in 1972 130,000 head of cattle were slaughtered in them with 90 per cent exported to Europe. The other principal export product was the wool from karakul sheep that had been introduced into the territory by the Germans in 1908. One other major source of wealth was to be found in Namibia's coastal waters, which are a rich source of pelagic fish of several varieties. The industry was based on the harbour of Walvis Bay, which had nine canning and processing factories in 1973. That year 705,937 tonnes of fish were landed at Walvis Bay. When the Namibian and South African fishing catches are combined the fishing industry was the sixth largest in the world; the catch from South African waters was consistently lower than that from Namibian waters.

SWAPO

Sam Nujoma and Andimba Toivo ja Toivo were the joint founders of SWAPO. In 1960 SWAPO decided to make Nujoma its external representative and he left Windhoek, evaded the police and made his way to Dar es Salaam where President Nyerere provided him with a letter to serve as a passport. In June 1960 Nujoma appeared before the UN Committee on South West Africa. He returned to Dar es Salaam where he set up SWAPO headquarters in March 1961. In 1966 Nujoma chartered a plane and flew to Windhoek to challenge the South African claim that anyone was free to move in and out of the country. He was briefly imprisoned before being expelled to Zambia. On 26 August that year SWAPO launched its armed struggle with attacks on targets in northern Namibia; this provoked the South Africans to arrest SWAPO personnel inside Namibia, including Toivo ja Toivo who was to be imprisoned in 1968 where he remained until 1984. In 1969 Nujoma launched the People's Liberation Army of Namibia (PLAN). In October 1971 he gave evidence before the UN Security Council where he made a good impression. Despite the South African strategy, launched in 1975, to bring about an internal settlement by working through minority parties in Namibia, Nujoma stuck to the UN formula, which sought independence for Namibia 'through free and fair elections under the control and supervision of the UN'. At the end of the decade Namibia still faced another 10 years before it would achieve independence under Nujoma as its first President.

In 1966 the United Nations formally recognized the South West African People's Organization (SWAPO) as the legitimate liberation movement representing Namibia. As a military organization SWAPO was never likely to win a war against the South Africans. On the other hand, a slow yet steady escalation of guerrilla activity took place in the Caprivi Strip during the late 1960s and early 1970s (when Angola was still under Portuguese rule) and SWAPO had to operate from Zambia. The pressures it created were sufficient to oblige South Africa to establish its first fighting unit of black police, armed with automatic weapons, which operated in the Caprivi Strip. Although SWAPO actions were militarily insignificant they did establish the fact that a war of liberation was in progress and they did force South Africa to deploy an increasing number of troops along the country's northern border. SWAPO guerrilla activity was sufficient to make parts of the Caprivi Strip 'no go' areas. Following Ian Smith's closure of the Rhodesian border with Zambia in January 1973, South Africa moved substantial extra forces into the Caprivi Strip. The South West Africa Territorial Force (SWATF) was specially created by South Africa to fight this colonial war in the north of Namibia.

During its many years in exile SWAPO's external wing worked through the UN Council for Namibia and in Lusaka, where SWAPO had moved its headquarters from Dar es Salaam, through the UN Namibia Research Institute whose role was to enable SWAPO to prepare for independence by obtaining training for its exiled personnel. Following Angola's independence in 1975 SWAPO was able to increase its activities once it had established bases in southern Angola and these became regular targets, as well as excuses, for South African military incursions across the border from Namibia. From 1976 onwards the guerrilla war in northern Namibia and southern Angola cost an estimated 1,000 casualties a year for both sides combined and involved between 30,000 and 40,000 combatants. The struggle, inevitably, took its toll of the SWAPO leadership. Divisions surfaced in 1975 when a split occurred and some 50 SWAPO members led by Andreas Shipanga were arrested in Zambia and then detained in Tanzania. Later, after they had been released, Shipanga formed the breakaway SWAPO Democrats. In 1979 Peter Katjavivi was dismissed from the ruling hierarchy and in 1980 another SWAPO leader, Mishake Muyongo, defected. Despite such upsets Nujoma remained SWAPO President and continued to control the majority of its forces. As early as December 1975, 5,000 Ovambo had crossed the border into Angola to obtain military training and by the late 1970s Cuban instructors were providing SWAPO with military training in Angola. By 1980 South Africa had established 40 bases along the Namibia–Angola border and a further 35 bases elsewhere in Namibia and the government had embarked upon a policy of forced removals of the population and the creation of 'protected villages' so as to control the people and deny support to the guerrillas. In March 1980 – an indication of the increasingly sophisticated weaponry at its disposal – SWAPO shot down a South African plane in southern Angola. By 1981 SWAPO had an estimated 8,000 guerrillas in Angola or operating in Namibia. Inside Namibia SWAPO was never banned outright although it was closely watched and harassed by the South African authorities.

Although for most of the 1970s the guerrilla war was small scale with occasional escalations of activity, it had three effects: it tied down increasing numbers of South African troops in the north of Namibia; it spread the war across the border into Angola; and the publicity from it ensured continuing international pressures upon Pretoria. At the end of the decade, war incidents increased from 500 in 1978 to 900 in 1979. In May 1978, for example, the South Africans raided deep into Angola to attack the Namibian refugee camp at Cassinga, killing 612 refugees and 63 Angolan soldiers as well as wounding a number of civilians. Parallel with the war was the long-drawn-out duel between the United Nations and South Africa, with the world body trying to prise control of the territory from Pretoria, while South Africa manipulated minority groups in Namibia so as to create an 'independent' state associated with South Africa. In this contest the South African government responded as little as possible to UN pressures but as much as was necessary to maintain a dialogue with the international community since any form of dialogue with an increasingly hostile outside world was seen to have propaganda value for a beleaguered Pretoria. This South African defiance of the UN while it applied its own solutions to Namibia became a regular aspect of the Southern African scenario through the decade. The UN appeared ineffective.

In 1973 South Africa convened an Advisory Council for South West Africa under the chairmanship of Vorster, a move that was widely opposed inside Namibia, and which was rejected by SWAPO and by the Paramount Chief of the Herero people, Chief Clemens Kapuuo. Further, the National Convention of non-whites, which grouped SWAPO, SWANU, the National Unity Democratic Organization (NUDO), the Damara Executive Council and the Rehoboth Volkspartei, said the nominations being received by the government were not representative of the country's black people. There were many protests and refusals by tribal groups to nominate representatives to the Council. The first session of the Council was presided over by Vorster in the former Police Divisional Headquarters in Windhoek on 23 March 1973. At the conclusion of the meeting Vorster described their deliberations as 'very successful'. In August the government suffered another setback when a massive boycott reduced to a farce the first elections for the Legislative Council of the new Bantustan of 'Ovambo' in northern Namibia. When polling took place only six of the 56 seats were contested and none of the candidates represented the main opposition parties – SWAPO and DEMCOP (the Democratic Cooperative Development Party). Government supporters filled the 35 nominated seats and members of the pro-government Ovambo Independence Party were returned unopposed to 15 seats. The government favoured the independence of Ovambo as a region while SWAPO and DEMCOP sought independence for Namibia as a whole. In reaction to these moves and following pressures from SWAPO and independent African states, the UN Security Council voted 15–0 on 11 December to halt further dialogue with South Africa on the issue of the independence of Namibia and appointed Sean McBride as Commissioner for Namibia.

The new UN Commissioner for Namibia announced on 28 March 1974 that he intended to establish a Namibia Research Institute in Lusaka and rejected the idea of fresh UN overtures to South Africa at that time. South Africa clamped down on SWAPO activities in Namibia. In the meantime, on 15 February an official silence on police activity in Namibia was imposed. The Administrator of South West Africa, Mr Ben van der Walt, said 'circumstances are such at the moment that it is no longer necessary for me to issue press statements in connection with police action against possibly offensive activities of the SWAPO Youth League'.[15]

The withdrawal of the Portuguese from Angola at the end of 1975 changed significantly the freedom to operate of SWAPO, which was then able to establish bases in southern Angola. Thereafter, the war against SWAPO in Namibia became inextricably intertwined with the civil war in Angola and South African incursions into Angola would sometimes be directed against Angolan (MPLA) government targets and in support of the rebel UNITA forces, and sometimes against SWAPO bases. Once South Africa had decided to intervene in Angola it abandoned its policy of *détente* with independent Africa. At first the intervention (at the end of 1975) by flying columns threatened SWAPO, which had built up relations with UNITA. Jonas Savimbi, UNITA's leader, supported the South African intervention against the MPLA government and, in turn, had the backing of Zaïre and Zambia in requesting South African military intervention. However, the rapid collapse of the South African invasion – MPLA had substantial help from the Cuban troops already in the country – meant that South Africa had discarded its former policy of not intervening militarily; it had lost any earlier advantages to be derived from *détente* with black Africa; and had broken the terms of the Mandate by using Namibia as a military launch pad. South Africa had not bought time for itself against the liberation movements; instead, for the remainder of the decade the MPLA was largely on top of the military situation in Angola. As a consequence, South Africa had to expand its forces in Namibia. In 1976 it designated Kavango and Caprivi as security areas as well as Ovambo so that 55 per cent of the territory's population was placed under martial law. In December 1976 the UN General Assembly denounced repressive measures by South Africa, called on the Security Council to impose mandatory sanctions against the Pretoria regime and recognized the justice of SWAPO's military campaign. From this point onwards South Africa backed UNITA in southern Angola, in order both to harass the MPLA government and to deny the SWAPO forces in Angola access to Namibia.

AN INTERNAL SETTLEMENT?

In 1975 constitutional talks were held in Windhoek (at the Turnhalle) between the South West Africa Legislative Assembly and representatives of the tribal authorities. These led (18 August 1976) to proposals for the establishment of an interim government and an independent South West Africa/Namibia by 31 December 1978. The United Nations, however, rejected the proposals. Over two years the Turnhalle Conference met to discuss the territory's constitutional future although SWAPO would not take part but, instead, demanded direct negotiations with South Africa under UN auspices after South African military forces had withdrawn from Namibia. In March 1977 a draft constitution for a pre-independence interim government proposed a three-tier system to include a multiracial central administration and the final division of the territory into 11 ethnic governments – 10 Bantustans and a white region. The leader of the white delegation, Dirk Mudge, declared that South African military forces would remain in Namibia after independence while South Africa said that Walvis Bay would revert to South Africa. These proposals were repudiated by both the OAU and the UN Council for Namibia and were later abandoned. The UN response to these South African proposals was the creation of the five-nation Western 'contact group' consisting of Britain, the United States, France, Canada and West Germany. South Africa maintained an ambivalent attitude: while arguing that the UN had no jurisdiction over Namibia and that Pretoria would impose its own solution, it was always prepared to continue talking with the UN and the Western contact group in order to demonstrate that it was not totally isolated and possessed legitimacy. This South African need to talk, without any intention of yielding to UN demands, had become a psychological necessity for

Pretoria although it had the effect of undermining its claim to total sovereignty over Namibia. Having given the impression that it would accept the UN–contact group proposals, including UN-supervised elections, South Africa then announced in September 1978 that it would pursue its own solution and hold elections in December 1978 for a Namibian constituent assembly. These elections were subsequently boycotted by SWAPO, SWAPO Democrats and the Namibian National Front and of 50 seats 41 went to the Democratic Turnhalle Alliance (DTA).

This period of South African pseudo-negotiations with the UN was characterized by Western reluctance to take any overt actions that would force Pretoria's hand. 'The African Group at the UN, in an attempt to introduce more effective pressure, presented a draft resolution to the Security Council in June 1975 proposing an arms embargo against South Africa. It was blocked by vetoes cast by Britain, France and the United States. However, there was growing concern among the three Western members that Pretoria's refusal to consider any solution could lead to greater pressure on them to impose sanctions.'[16] It was for this reason that the contact group was created. It did not seriously attempt to bring about change but, with South Africa, tried to give the impression that progress towards an independent Namibia was somehow under way. In essence it was a charade. Meanwhile, South Africa made plain that it would never accept a SWAPO government. When, on 20 September 1978, South Africa announced that it would proceed with its own internal settlement, the UN responded by adopting Security Council Resolution 435 on 29 September, which formalized acceptance of the UN Action Plan on Namibia. This set out a framework for the achievement of Namibian independence and followed with the creation of a UN Transition Assistance Group (UNTAG) to help the Special Representative achieve the independence of Namibia through fair elections, the so-called Waldheim Plan. At the same time the Security Council declared null and void any unilateral measures taken by South Africa in relation to the electoral process.

Intense UN–contact group–South African negotiations continued over the years 1978–81, following the passing of Resolution 435. SWAPO, however, called for an end to the Western mediating role since it saw this as biased in favour of South Africa. For the three years 1978–81 on-off negotiations at least suggested that a settlement could be reached. In May 1979 South Africa's Foreign Minister Roelf 'Pik' Botha declared that there was 'no hope' of breaking the existing deadlock over an internationally acceptable settlement. Then in January 1981 the United Nations brought matters to a head and called a conference at Geneva, which was attended by SWAPO, South Africa (including the Namibian internal parties), the Western contact group and the front-line states (Angola, Botswana, Mozambique, Tanzania, Zambia and Zimbabwe). Those attending the conference had 'accepted' the terms of Resolution 435; it was, apparently, a question of working out the details and mode of implementation. The plan envisaged a ceasefire, the creation of demilitarized zones along the Namibian borders with Angola and Zambia, the reduction of South African forces in Namibia from 20,000 to 1,500, the deployment of a UN force of 7,500 to supervise the South African withdrawal and the SWAPO forces, followed by UN-supervised elections for a constituent assembly that would work out an independence constitution. This programme was to take place during 1981; in fact, the South Africans walked out of the conference within a week and the plan collapsed. The UN, however, kept Resolution 435 'on the table'. In 1980, accurately as it turned out, South Africa's Gen. Magnus Malan predicted that South Africa would be able to hold on to Namibia for another 10 years. The possibility that this prediction would prove correct was enormously strengthened in 1981 when the United States decided to link the withdrawal of Cuban troops from Angola to the implementation of Resolution 435 in Namibia. South Africa promptly endorsed the US decision by announcing that it would not consider implementing Resolution 435 until Cuban troops had been withdrawn from Angola.

Throughout these talks and political manoeuvres the SWAPO guerrillas had steadily escalated the war. Early in the 1970s the South African military had begun to take over from the police in combating SWAPO. In 1974 SADF strength in Namibia was 15,000 men; by 1976 it had risen to 45,000 and by 1980 to 80,000. These figures included mercenaries, members of UNITA, 'Bantustan' units and SWA territorials. The cost for South Africa over this period rose commensurately. South Africa's military strategy in Namibia was conditioned by the struggle waged by PLAN, the military wing of SWAPO. The war intensified dramatically, following Angolan independence in 1975. As a result PLAN combatants were able to extend their activities by crossing the Angolan-Namibian border to operate over a 1,000-mile area of northern Namibia and establish SWAPO bases and refugee camps in Angola. The South African aim was to separate SWAPO from the local Namibian population and so prevent civilian assistance being given to the liberation movement. Like the Portuguese in Mozambique, in the mid-1970s the South Africans launched a programme of forced removals in the north of Namibia and these population removals were carried out by the army. A one-kilometre strip was cleared along the Namibia–Angola border to create a free-fire zone. The clearance was accompanied by the wholesale destruction of villages and crops. In 1976, for example, the UN Commissioner for Namibia estimated that South African troops had uprooted 40–50,000 villagers over a three-month period. Then came the Soweto uprising in South Africa. 'As news of the Soweto uprising in South Africa during the summer of 1976 reached Namibia, black students throughout the territory were inspired by these events. They boycotted examinations held under the terms of the Bantu Education Act. Leaflets attacking Bantu Education as the "instrument of the homelands policy" were circulated.'[17] SWAPO leaders in Namibia were frequently arrested as the war escalated. Over March/April 1978, virtually the entire leadership of SWAPO was arrested following the assassination of the Herero Chief Clemens Kapuuo, and in April 1979 over 50 top SWAPO officials were arrested and detained under proclamation AG21, prior to the announcement that a tribally based national assembly was to be established. A prominent American church leader who visited Namibia in 1979 said: 'The evidence of South African Army brutality among all segments of the population is so overwhelming, pervasive and capable of documentation that it makes a mockery of the South African government's claim to be "responding to the request of the Ovambo people for protection".'

South Africa had launched a 'hearts and minds' campaign in 1975 and by 1977 the campaign was well under way. Articles in the South African press, especially *Paratus*, the journal of the SADF, described the success of the programme: soldiers assisting the people of Caprivi, educating in schools, training black farmers, teaching blind children; operating government computers and running essential services in Ovamboland. It was a propaganda picture that did not convince. 'The South African Administrator General explained the motives for this activity at a press conference in May 1979. Counter-insurgency consisted of 80 per cent winning support from the people and 20 per cent winning the war against SWAPO, he said. In keeping with this philosophy, South African teachers, doctors, farmers and tradesmen were assisting the SADF. From Katima Mulilo in the east to Ruacana in the west there were teams of national servicemen at work.'[18] While this 'hearts and minds' programme was being carried out an area along the border was cleared of 20,000 people and the Ovambo, Kavango and Caprivi districts became security areas. South African policy inside Namibia was to cripple SWAPO by mass arrests, detentions without trial and bannings, and the widespread use of torture was reported and confirmed. The introduction of compulsory military service in 1980 led to a mass exodus of Namibians into Angola where by September 1981 an estimated 73,000 Namibians, or nearly six per cent of the population (which then stood at 1,212,000), had fled into exile. 'From the evidence of suffering inflicted on the Namibian population, it is abundantly clear that the withdrawal of South Africa's troops and administration, and the holding of United Nations-supervised elections, are the only way to achieve the goal desired by most Namibians.'[19]

South Africa:
The Critical Decade

S ixteen years were to pass between Sharpeville and the next landmark event, the eruption of violence in the black townships, which burst in Soweto (south-west townships) outside Johannesburg in June 1976. The violence spread across the country to involve Indians and Coloureds as well as Africans and presented the government with its most serious crisis in two decades. During the 1960s and early 1970s the apartheid state seemed omnipotent: Mandela and Robert Sobukwe were in prison; other leaders such as Oliver Tambo were in exile; and neither armed struggle nor peaceful political protest appeared able to make any significant headway. When the architect of the Bantustan policy, Prime Minister Dr Hendrik Verwoerd, was assassinated in September 1966, he was succeeded by J. B. Vorster, an equally ruthless if more pragmatic exponent of White supremacy. White liberal opposition was at best ineffective and at worst supine while those Western powers with stakes in the Republic of South Africa that would have provided the leverage to force change – Britain, the United States and the European Community – did not wish to take any actions that would seriously jeopardize their investments and profits. As a result, these years were filled with hypocrisies: annual condemnations of apartheid accompanied by code language that signified no change but business – and profits – as usual. But South Africa's apparently all-powerful white state structure was based upon brittle foundations and by the mid-1970s faced growing African challenges from within and without. By 1974 all but a handful of African colonies had achieved independence and the barrier consisting of white-controlled Angola, Mozambique and Rhodesia, which guarded South Africa from direct contact with independent black Africa to the north, was about to collapse.

The overthrow of the Caetano government in Lisbon and the rapid agreement by Portugal thereafter to withdraw from Angola and Mozambique in 1975 not only altered the entire political outlook for the region but also gave an immense boost to black aspirations inside the Republic. The continent's black revolutions were at last succeeding on South Africa's doorstep.

In 1969 a highly articulate black student, Steve Biko, led a breakaway from the National Union of South African Students (NUSAS), which was multiracial, to form the more radical all-black South African Students Organization (SASO) and went on to form the Black Consciousness Movement and set up the Black People's Convention (BPC). Since the Black Consciousness Movement apparently fitted in with its race separation theories the government at first allowed it considerable leeway. Then came the Soweto uprising. The protest began with school children in Soweto who opposed the introduction of Afrikaans as a language of instruction in the schools; Afrikaans was seen as the language of the oppressors. The main riots erupted on 16 June 1976 and lasted for three weeks. Soweto had become a sprawling city of a million blacks that was difficult to control at the best of times; in 1976 it became a battleground between rioters and police. The riots spread to other townships on the Rand, to Pretoria, Natal and the Cape and drew in Indian and Coloured youths as well as blacks. The riots were a spontaneous outburst against a system that dehumanized the black majority. They continued to break out to the end of the year and many black youths fled the country to join the ranks of the ANC or PAC in exile. The year of Soweto was another South African turning point, admitted to be so even by conservative whites.

South Africa now became increasingly politically volatile. It had taken 16 years from the events of Sharpeville to Soweto, but would take only eight years before major violence swept the country again in 1984. The government reaction to Soweto was the usual clampdown by the security forces and in October 1976 18 black movements including the Black Consciousness Movement were banned and 50 of their leaders arrested and detained. Even so, the government was forced to make concessions: electricity was extended to the townships and the use of Afrikaans as a medium of instruction in the schools was dropped. The Soweto uprising marked the emergence of a black generation that had become deeply radicalized and was ready to turn to violence rather than just accept the dictation of the white minority. Altogether, the unrest lasted for a year and the final death count was in the region of 500.

The events of 1976 turned out to be the beginning of a process rather than a one-off explosion of violence; from this time onwards permanent, smouldering antagonism was likely to erupt at any time. A new generation of radicalized black youths was to become the focus of the new explosion, which occurred in 1984. Between these two events (of 1976 and 1984), however, the government continued to implement its apartheid policies and though it improved conditions for Asians and Coloureds and began to relax what was quaintly described as 'petty apartheid', the process of forcing the population into the homelands continued unabated. Four homelands became 'independent' over the five years after Soweto: Transkei (1976), Bophutatswana (1977), Venda (1979) and Ciskei (1981), although the international community resolutely refused to recognize their independent status. Finally, in 1978, the ruling National Party was rocked by the Muldergate scandal that forced Connie Mulder, the powerful political figure that many thought would succeed Vorster, to retire from politics altogether and ended Vorster's career as well. P. W. Botha, who had served as Minister of Defence through the 1970s, became Prime Minister in September 1978.

The 1970s, then, witnessed the steady erosion of South Africa's options. At the beginning of the decade the apartheid state seemed invulnerable. Namibia was its colony. The Portuguese had their armies in both Angola and Mozambique while in Rhodesia Smith was successfully defying Britain. These three territories formed a cordon sanitaire between South Africa and independent Africa, leaving Pretoria 'free' to pursue its apartheid policy and impose it on Namibia as well. The three former High Commission Territories – Bechuanaland, Basutoland and Swaziland – had by 1970 each achieved independence as, respectively, Botswana, Lesotho and Swaziland and though the development of its mineral wealth and its ferry crossing over the Zambezi to Zambia at Kazungula gave Botswana a measure of freedom to act, it was still greatly dependent upon South Africa for trade, and subject to heavy pressures if it attempted too hard to act on its own. Lesotho and Swaziland were virtual captives of South Africa. By 1980 much had changed. Angola and Mozambique were independent and the cordon of states separating South Africa from the rest of the continent had collapsed; Vorster's policies – dialogue, *détente*, military intervention in Angola – had each failed; and both the economy and the politics of South Africa had become subject to external pressures that had been unthinkable in 1970. When black African states issued the Lusaka Manifesto in 1969 a key passage stated: 'Our objectives in Southern Africa stem from our commitment to the principle of human equality. We are not hostile to the Administrations of these States because they are manned and controlled by White people. We are hostile to them because they are systems of minority control, which exist as a result of, and in the pursuance of, doctrines of human inequality. What we are working for is the right of self-determination for the people of those territories.' In 1969 the white racists of South Africa could dismiss such sentiments as black pipedreams; by 1980 they began to take on an aspect of reality for South Africa itself.

BRITAIN AND THE SALE OF ARMS TO SOUTH AFRICA

The return to power in June 1970 of a Conservative government in Britain under Edward Heath was greeted with relief in Pretoria since his party was generally far more favourable to the South African white minority than had been Labour under Harold Wilson. Within days of coming to power, Heath's Foreign Secretary, Sir Alec Douglas-Home, announced that Britain would resume the sale of arms to South Africa that had been stopped, if reluctantly, by the Wilson government. Heath justified the resumption of arms sales to South Africa when he addressed the Lord Mayor's Banquet on 16 November 1970. After ritually condemning apartheid, he said:

> But the abhorrence of apartheid is a moral attitude, not a policy, and it is certainly not a categorical imperative against any contact with South Africa and the South Africans. There are some who believe that apartheid in South Africa will be brought to an end only by the use of force. This is emphatically not the view of Her Majesty's Ministers. A racial war in Southern Africa, whatever its eventual outcome, would be catastrophic in its consequences for Africa. Nor do we believe that isolation of South Africa would help bring to an end her apartheid policies. It would do exactly the opposite. We believe, with deep conviction, that the moderate and liberal forces within South Africa that are working against apartheid will be best assisted by the maintenance of economic, social and cultural contacts between the rest of the world and South Africa.

In Washington that December, however, Heath found the Nixon administration against the resumption of arms sales to South Africa. A US National Security Council study favoured an unconditional embargo. The study found three flaws in the British argument: the type of arms requested by South Africa under the existing Simonstown Agreement – patrol aircraft, fighter aircraft and naval patrol craft – would make no impression upon any Russian naval presence; the Soviet threat was in the north of the Indian Ocean, far from South African influence; and arms sales to South Africa would act as a powerful stimulus for increased Russian penetration of Black Africa.[1] Heath was due to attend his first Commonwealth heads of government meeting to be held in Singapore in January 1971 and the Commonwealth countries, especially Tanzania and Zambia, hoped that Britain would not make a decision until they had had the chance to influence Heath. The Singapore Conference from 14 to 22 January witnessed a confrontation between Britain's Heath and other Commonwealth leaders, especially Presidents Kaunda, Nyerere and Obote, about the British decision to sell arms to South Africa upon which Heath appeared to be determined. The Conference established an eight-nation study group to examine the security of maritime trade routes in the South Atlantic and Indian Ocean. However, the group had not yet met when Britain announced that it would allow the sale of seven Wasp helicopters to South Africa. In the debate that followed in the House of Commons, former Labour ministers denied that there was any obligation under the Simonstown Agreement to sell arms to South Africa. The sale of these helicopters in fact was as much a political gesture of solidarity as an arms transaction of real significance. When Labour was returned to power in 1974 it announced that it would maintain an arms embargo against South Africa. Meanwhile, the South African role in Western defence and the relevance of the Simonstown naval base or South African relations with NATO were increasingly questioned. For its part, South Africa speeded up its drive to become independent of Britain for its arms and decided in principle to build its own ships, according to its Defence Minister P. W. Botha.

The pressures upon the Heath government not to sell arms to South Africa were a foretaste of a wider range of pressures to be exerted upon South Africa during the decade that would come from many quarters. Typical of them was a resolution of the UN General Assembly (by 91 votes to 22 with 19 abstentions) to suspend South Africa from the UN for the rest of the 1974 Assembly. When this was put to the vote in the Security Council on 30 October it received 10 votes in favour, three against (Britain, France and the United States, and they vetoed the resolution) and two abstentions. The debate in the Security Council had been conducted since 18 October and the South African representative to the UN, Mr R. F. 'Pik' Botha, had argued unconvincingly that discrimination should not be equated with racialism. Duma Nokwe of the ANC told the Security Council that there was no meeting point between South Africa and the rest of the world as long as apartheid existed, and that South West Africa (Namibia) was being subjected to the same racist policies as the Republic. The government of South Africa, he said, was a 'racist military regime, which did not represent the majority of the people'. Ivor Richard for Britain said his country totally condemned apartheid but did not believe expulsion would remedy the situation: 'The objective is not to purge the United Nations. The object is to persuade the South African Government to change its policies.' South African reactions to Botha's performance at the UN were scathing: 'If Botha thinks he can get away with bluffing the UN that discrimination based on the principle of different ethnic groups is not the same thing as discrimination based on race and colour, he might just as well pack his diplomatic bag...'[2] In reaction, the South African government withheld its annual subscription.

POLITICS

As external pressures mounted upon South Africa so internally did its harsh repression excite growing anger. One of the great scandals of the apartheid era was the ethnic cleansing that took the form of mass removals. By 1974 not less than 2,884,000 people had been affected by the population removals that were part of official policy and were carried out under various apartheid laws. At a very different level white South Africans found their precious sporting fixtures were coming under threat. The South African anti-apartheid activist, Peter Hain, had already organized Britain's 'Stop the 70' campaign against the visiting South African cricketers; in 1971 he visited Australia during the early part of the Springbok rugby tour of that country to urge opposition. Sports boycotts were to become an increasingly successful feature of anti-apartheid activities during the 1970s and, for example, on 19 April 1973, the New Zealand Prime Minister, Norman Kirk, announced that the South African rugby tour of New Zealand had been cancelled. He said the tour would have divided the people of New Zealand and that a third of the police would have been required to control a single game. Students became an increasingly irritating factor for the Pretoria government. Thus in February 1973 Vorster announced that eight leading members of NUSAS had been banned under the Suppression of Communism Act, following an interim report from the Parliamentary Committee investigating the organization's activities. Such banning of an ever-wider range of dissenters was by then a routine aspect of South African life. Robert Sobukwe, the former president of the banned Pan-Africanist Congress (PAC), was prevented from leaving South Africa by the Minister of Justice, who refused to relax a banning order confining him to the Kimberley district. Sobukwe had been sentenced to five years in prison for leading anti-pass demonstrations in 1960 and sent to Robben Island. Legislation was subsequently passed to enable the government to keep him in detention on the island after his sentence was completed. He had finally been released in 1970 but restricted to the Kimberley district. There was also at this time growing conflict between some of the churches and the state. A case that received great publicity centred upon the Dean of Johannesburg, the Very Rev. Gonville ffrench-Beytagh, who was arrested on 20 January 1971 and detained for questioning. He was accused of safeguarding publications on behalf of the banned ANC and the South African Communist Party (SACP). Colin Winter, the Bishop of Damaraland in Namibia, preached against imprisonment without trial. On 25 February the government carried out widespread raids on church offices in Cape Town, Johannesburg, Durban and Port Elizabeth. Grants made by the World Council of Churches (WCC) to guerrilla groups were central to this growing church–state conflict. Writing in *The Times*, John Sackur recalled how the Dutch Reformed Church had, on the orders of Dr Verwoerd, broken with the WCC in 1961. Vorster had made similar demands to other churches in 1970 though he did not get the same response. The extreme step of arresting the Dean of Johannesburg on political charges made plain Vorster's determination to take a tough line with the churches.

This was the age of the Bureau of State Security (BOSS), the secretive instrument of repression that had been established in 1969. It was a paradox of the Afrikaners that though they used the laws ruthlessly to control those in the state that they regarded as potential or actual enemies of their supremacy they were also sticklers for the law so that deviations from the law could and would be challenged. Mr Justice Potgieter had completed a report on BOSS in August 1970 but it was only tabled in the House of Assembly 18 months later, in February 1972. It recommended that BOSS should become a department under the control of the Prime Minister. Full details of BOSS' functions had not been disclosed but these covered state, police, security and military intelligence matters and BOSS was answerable only to the Prime Minister and its head, Gen. Hendrik van den Bergh, and did not fall under Parliament, Treasury or the Public Service Commission. The Potgieter Commission's report also recommended that BOSS be given Parliamentary authorization to tap telephones and intercept mail. BOSS was shrouded in extreme secrecy and was seen as one more instrument of Afrikaner state control.

A government inquiry early in 1972 focused upon 'Four Left Groups'. A commentator wrote of the inquiry: 'Though by Western standards the Institute of Race Relations, and the other three organizations, the National Union of South African Students, the University Christian Movement and the Christian Institute, are eminently respectable, perhaps Vorster is right to fear them. For they are among the last groups of people who still preach and often practise multiracialism in South Africa. In particular, the work of the Institute of Race Relations is galling to the Nationalists. The Institute has been fighting the low wages paid to Black workers by attempting to stir up the consciences of South African and American industrialists...'[4] The investigation caused a political furore and was described by another commentator as 'both a smear and a blatant piece of political gimmickry'. The government was clearly directing attention away from its economic difficulties and its inability to deal with them.[3]

It had become an accepted part of the South African lifestyle at this time that there were always ongoing trials for treason, defying banning orders or other dissident activities against the state and a disproportionate amount of time in the South African courts was devoted to so-called treason trials at various levels. Winnie Mandela, the wife of the imprisoned ANC leader, Nelson Mandela, was sentenced early in 1973 to six months in prison for failing to comply with banning orders against her; on appeal she won her case. The Dean of Johannesburg, the Very Rev. Gonville ffrench-Beytagh, also had his appeal allowed against a five-year sentence under the Terrorism Act and left the country for England. In Pietermaritzburg, after a long trial, 13 accused were found guilty of treason. Louwrens Muller, the Minister of Police, announced that only 13 out of 205 police convicted in 1972 on charges of culpable homicide, intent to do grievous bodily harm, and assault were dismissed from the force.[5] Censorship was another weapon of a government that tended to see enemies intent on undermining its authority on all sides. It was reported in 1974, for example, that of 1,283 films submitted to the Publications Control Board, 507 were subjected to exhibition to persons of a particular race or class only, 395 had to be cut before screening, and 129 were prohibited outright while 885 publications and 34 'other objects' were banned. These latter included 'T' shirts with the motif 'Black is beautiful'.

One of the constant fears that drove the ruling Afrikaners was the fact of their dwindling population in relation to all the other races in South Africa. Thus, between 1961 and 1970 the total white population of South Africa increased by 662,836. Natural increase accounted for 395,634. The remaining 263,756 were immigrants but only 0.4 per cent of the immigrant children subsequently went to Afrikaans schools.

The small Progressive Party, whose lone MP, Helen Suzman, had become famous for her role as a white conscience, did at least portray an alternative, more humane white approach to the race divide that made South Africa such an uncomfortable and brutal place for its non-white majority. In October 1971 Colin Eglin, the Progressive Party leader (not in Parliament), and Helen Suzman went on a tour in independent Africa. At a luncheon in Ghana one of the guests asked Mrs Suzman: 'Don't you realize that in making a trip of this sort, putting across a view that South Africa is not quite a totalitarian state – that even though you are an opponent of the regime, you are allowed to go outside and say what you like – don't you see that you might well be an unwitting agent of the regime?' Mrs Suzman denied this. She was then tackled on the issue of press freedom. A newspaper in Tanzania coupled Mrs Suzman with Harry Oppenheimer as opposed to apartheid but enjoying the approval and material support of the 'capitalist West'. The editorial continued: 'Now it is a social truism that it is he who holds economic power that rules. Political leaders in the bourgeois world are often little more than loyal envoys of financial moguls. In South Africa, then it is Helen Suzman and her kind, and not John Vorster, who really rule. The Pretoria regime would collapse overnight without the support of big business.' The Progressive leaders had a two-hour meeting with President

Nyerere. He told them he was completely committed to the Lusaka Manifesto, and that while this provided for dialogue on condition that there was a change of direction in South Africa over apartheid policy, as there had been no such change of direction Tanzania remained utterly opposed to dialogue.[6]

Prior to a general election (for whites) on 24 April 1974, the National Party hurried a number of bills through Parliament with the aim of reassuring the all-white electorate that even after 26 years of unbroken rule, the NP remained in control. Security was becoming of increasing concern to the electorate as South Africa's white community gradually came to realize that African guerrillas were having an increasing impact in Angola, Mozambique and Rhodesia. They had taken for granted that without help from Moscow and Beijing (according to the anti-Communist propaganda to which they had long been subjected) Africans were incapable of organizing effective resistance and, therefore, that once inside the borders of a white-ruled country their supply lines would be severed and their forces rapidly rounded up. It was becoming clear that this was not the case. Vorster and the National Party won the election, taking 122 of 169 seats (they had held 118 of 166 seats in the previous Parliament); the United Party dropped from 47 to 41 seats. The Progressive Party, which had been represented by Helen Suzman alone since 1961, won 10 seats and Colin Eglin now became its leader in the House.

The development of the homelands (formerly called Bantustans) took up a good deal of Vorster's attention during the decade. In 1971, in particular, he was anxious to present a good image of South Africa abroad and divert attention from the adverse ruling of the International Court of Justice over Namibia and he embarked upon a tour of the homelands. However, he could not conceal during this tour the basic inequalities of the allocation of land between the races, and the consequent inequalities of economic opportunity. Neither was he able to reply satisfactorily to the challenge to apartheid presented by the existence of South Africa's two million Coloured people. On this occasion he visited Tswanaland, North Sotho, Machangana and Venda. There was much debate about the homelands during that year with Vorster trying to define just what the homeland policy should be. This debate was carried to London in October when three homeland leaders – Paramount Chief Kaiser Matanzima of Transkei, Chief Lucas Mangope of Tswanaland and Chief Gatsha Buthelezi of Zululand – visited England. While Matanzima and Mangope had accepted the principle of separate development, Buthelezi declared himself a non-racialist, challenged the whole dogma of separate development and refused to seek independence for Zululand. Buthelezi, who was the government-appointed head of the Zulu Territorial Authority, was rapidly building a reputation for outspokenness. He told the *Sunday Times* that he questioned the sincerity of the government when it said it wanted self-determination for Zulus.[7] The following year, on a visit to Malawi in July, Buthelezi told an audience at Mzimba in Northern Malawi that he doubted there would ever be independent so-called Bantu homelands. He said the South African government hardly ever consulted Africans and therefore their policies were imposed by sheer force.[8] Chief Matanzima of Transkei, on his return from the United States, said he had come back 'more determined than ever to work towards a consolidation of African-occupied southern Africa'. On the government side the Minister of Bantu Administration and Development, M. C. Botha, said that no more land would be allocated to the African homelands than that stipulated under the Act of 1936, and that if African leaders continued to demand more they would only have themselves to blame for delays in their progress to independence. In January 1973, Chief Buthelezi told the Zulu Parliament that he would cease negotiating with the government on its proposals to consolidate the Zulu homeland into six widely separated blocks of territory. Buthelezi, who had decided to 'work' the homelands system, continued to refuse to accept 'independence' and through the 1970s, a period of major oppression in South Africa, he made a substantial impact arguing over policy with the Pretoria government. Homeland leaders spoke out frequently during 1973 about the difficulties facing their people and the growing anger amongst the young over their poverty, lack of opportunity and subjection to white interests. Chief Kaiser Matanzima called for non-whites to have a meaningful share of political power and warned that African youth was moving towards black power. Co-existence would only be possible, he argued, under a system of one-man, one vote with representation for all races in Parliament. Matanzima's arguments were echoed by the leaders of Bophutatswana and Lebowa. The Minister of Bantu Administration criticized such statements by homeland leaders as irresponsible and creating the impression of threats, although in a more emollient afterthought he said such sharp and provocative utterances should be treated with self-control and sympathy.

THE ECONOMY: SET IN A MOULD

In 1971 Harry Oppenheimer, the chairman of Anglo-American, blamed the country's growing economic problems on apartheid. He claimed that economic advancement for Africans would also result in much more rapid advancement for whites. Writing in the 1970 Anglo-American review, he said: 'Rapid progress with what we call African advancement would do more than raise material standards for all sections of the population. It would help powerfully to harmonize the natural and reasonable aspirations of the majority of the people with the structure of the economy and the stability of the State. It would do more than any dialogue with other African States, important and valuable though such a dialogue would be, to defeat the sterile policy of isolating South Africa by the right wing element in South Africa and by the left wing element abroad.' Stanley Uys, commenting on Oppenheimer's statement, said that in asking for better wages for Africans, Mr Oppenheimer did not say whether he included those working in gold mines. Their average pay was 69 cents a shift (40p). White miners were paid 19 times as much. South Africa was a major exporter of a wide range of minerals. The most important foreign exchange earners were gold, diamonds, platinum, copper, uranium, asbestos, manganese, vanadium, iron, antimony, nickel, coal and chrome. These and other minerals already provided about two-thirds of South Africa's merchandise exports. Dr A. A. Maltitz, President of the Chamber of Mines of South Africa, discussed the problem of the greater use in industry of non-whites. This course, he argued, 'is unfortunately fraught with political difficulties, but I am convinced that an improved use of labour can be attained within the framework of government policy and on a generally acceptable basis'. He argued that white men could assume more supervisory jobs and non-whites could move up into certain tasks previously carried out by whites. The industry had offered to guarantee that no white employees would be retrenched as a result of such changes. The white worker could remain in highly paid employment and his status would be enhanced.[9] Despite such 'debates' neither Oppenheimer nor any other 'progressive' white was actually prepared to challenge the political system and increase wages for their black workers.

Although the differential in pay for white and black miners in 1971 was huge, white trade unions complained that the government was failing to apply its job reservation principles to the full. The Director of the South African Institute of Race Relations, Fred van Wyk, said that two of the country's biggest employers of labour, South African Railways and the Post Office, had accepted the fact that, if the demand for services during the next few years was to be met, more non-whites would have to be used in skilled and semi-skilled occupations. The *Rand Daily Mail* blamed 'industrial apartheid' for the fact that white people were losing their jobs and that the real rise in white wages over the past 10 years had been only 2.34 per cent according to a University of South Africa survey. 'Artificial labour restrictions and excessive expenditure on ideological projects have pushed up the rate of inflation which has eroded the ordinary man's buying power. Thus is white South Africa cutting off its nose to spite the black worker's face.' Such critiques of the industrial system became ever more frequent as a steadily increasing number of people realized that apartheid and full economic growth were incompatible.

In January 1973 the Johannesburg Chamber of Commerce fixed a poverty line for an African family of five at R8.15 a week. The Chairman of its Non-European Affairs Committee said that African heads of families should be paid R100 a month.[10] In Natal at that time the poverty line was calculated to be about R83 a month. In 1970 the Natal University School Research Department reckoned that only 15 per cent of African families in Durban were not living in poverty and that since then a sharp rise in the cost of living had occurred. At the beginning of 1973, over the New Year, a 600-mile pilgrimage from Grahamstown to Cape Town focused attention on the migratory labour system. Those who supported the pilgrimage pointed out that men were forced to leave their wives and children in their homelands and live in 'single' hostels in order to get work, causing much unhappiness and deprivation. If women wished to go to work they often had to leave their children with grandparents. The march was supported by a number of leading churchmen. Early in 1974, in the aftermath of the Yom Kippur War when black African states, overwhelmingly, had supported the Arab-OPEC stand, South Africa contemplated petrol rationing. Its supplies – together with those of Portugal, Rhodesia and Israel – were embargoed. Speed limits and other measures to cut consumption were enforced. At that time South Africa obtained 40 per cent of its oil from Iran and produced a further 10 per cent in its SASOL plants. The economy was 20 per cent dependent upon oil and 80 per cent dependent upon coal and other fuel sources.

The Anglo-American Corporation (AAC) deserves study. It was at the heart of the South African economy and Harry Oppenheimer, the ruler of this vast industrial empire, claimed to be progressive. He talked of the need to train and include Africans, he supported the Progressive Party financially, and often attacked government policies, though never too severely. And throughout these years he and his vast empire benefited enormously from the apartheid system that so conveniently allowed him to keep black mineworkers' wages at a minimum while conditions for the workers in his mines were often atrocious. In the 1970s the US$15 billion AAC empire dominated the South African economy. AAC controlled 1,000 companies in South Africa alone and its operations could be divided under two main headings: mining, industrial and other operating companies; and finance and investment companies. Its holdings included three of the top four mining houses, six of the top 10 finance houses, the largest investment trust, the second-largest property company, the second-largest merchant bank, the largest transport company and the fastest-growing car company. Minerals, however, represented the core business. In the 1970s Anglo produced 40 per cent of South Africa's gold (which was equivalent to 30 per cent of the non-Communist world's production), 40 per cent of the world's industrial diamonds and over 30 per cent of its gem diamonds. Member companies accounted for 40 per cent of world vanadium production, 15 per cent of coal and 4 per cent of uranium. It was also a substantial producer of copper, platinum and manganese. In 1979 the group's total assets were estimated at more than US$3 billion and the assets of the parent company alone at US$1.7 billion while net income stood at US$700 million and over US$350 million for the parent company. Profits on investments were above 20 per cent. There were three major (non-subsidiary) associates: De Beers Consolidated Mines, Charter Consolidated, and Minerals and Resources Corporation (MINORCO). De Beers, the largest diamond-mining company in the world, achieved net profits of US$900 million in 1978. Charter Consolidated was responsible for mining finance and owned assets worth US$500 million; it owned 6 per cent of Anglo while Anglo owned over a third of Charter Consolidated. MINORCO was primarily a mining investment company and owned assets worth US$300 million; it was 40 per cent owned by Anglo.[11]

The Anglo empire spread like an octopus over Southern Africa: diamonds and iron ore in Namibia; copper, nickel and diamonds in Botswana; copper in Zambia; diamonds in Angola and Zaïre. In West Africa, gold and diamonds in Ghana and Sierra Leone, while it had other companies throughout the world. Cheap labour in South Africa was the key to Anglo wealth. The homelands and the pass system physically separated the miner from his family, so that he need only be paid enough to cover his own subsistence while his family eked out a marginal existence in the homeland. 'The apartheid system was created by the white settler community to keep black labour cheap and under control, and to parcel out black labour, and the spoils from its exploitation, among competing white settler demands.'[12] By the early 1970s, part of a deliberate policy, less than 25 per cent of the labour in the gold mines was from South Africa. Instead, migrant labour was drawn from the surrounding countries – Malawi, Lesotho, Mozambique and Botswana – since such miners were easier to control than local labour and if they went on strike could always be sent back home. In 1975 the average annual earnings of Africans in mining and quarrying was approximately US$800, compared with US$1,100 in manufacturing. In contrast, white workers earned more in mining than in manufacturing: US$6,600 against US$5,300. But the bottom line, as Oppenheimer was on record as stating publicly, was simply: 'Black nationalism is a major danger to the unity, security and prosperity of South Africa.'[13] For all his progressive talk, Oppenheimer's interests were best served by the status quo.

EXTERNAL PRESSURES FOR CHANGE

At the beginning of 1971 the US Polaroid Corporation sent a four-man investigating team to South Africa. The Corporation had been criticized for supplying photographic equipment for the production of identity cards carried by black South Africans. A group of employees, calling themselves the Polaroid Workers Revolutionary Movement (PWRM), demanded that all contacts with South Africa should cease. Instead, the Corporation sent a team of two white and two black employees on a 10-day tour of South Africa. As a result of their findings, Polaroid decided that it would no longer trade direct with the South African government, that there had to be a dramatic improvement in salaries and other benefits for non-white employees and that non-whites should be trained for senior jobs. It would also set aside part of its South African profits for non-white education. Polaroid was urged by black South Africans 'not to walk out' of the country. One of the consequences of what came to be called the 'Polaroid experiment' was that other foreign companies began to pay attention to differentials and to pay better wages to black employees in defiance of apartheid practices. The South African government faced a dilemma. It registered its official anger and alarm that Polaroid should attempt to interfere with its domestic policies but it was no more anxious than employed blacks that the company would withdraw and feared that a wrong move in relation to Polaroid could trigger off a foreign company exodus.[14] In Britain, meanwhile, a campaign had been mounted against Barclays Bank DCO for its involvement in South Africa, signalling a new trend in both the United States and Britain where students and activists targeted firms operating in South Africa as supporters of apartheid.

In mid-January 1973 African factory workers in Durban went on strike for higher wages and by 8 February 65,000 African workers in Natal were on strike with 100 factories affected; about 16,000 of the strikers were employed by the Durban City Council. On 6 February 20,000 textile and engineering workers joined the strike and organized protest marches. The police, who until then had refrained from direct action, began to make arrests and use tear gas to disperse the strikers. About 350 strikers were arrested and fined R50 or given 50 days in prison though later R35 or 35 days in prison was suspended for three years. Shortly after the Durban strikes, the government faced a much greater challenge in the form of the Adam Raphael revelations about the low wages paid by top British companies to their black workers in South Africa.

In March 1973 the low wages paid to black workers in South Africa were brought to world notice by the journalist Adam Raphael writing in the *Guardian*.[15] The immediate result of the Raphael revelations was some relatively substantial pay increases for African workers. On the other hand, the actual position of the African urban wage earner remained unchanged. He was without rights or security and hemmed in by discriminatory legislation and customs that were unaffected by the wage increases. Overseas firms, it was clear, could do little to change the laws in South Africa but a considerable amount to alter customs and conventions, which formed a major part of the structure of apartheid. Raphael revealed that the majority of British companies in South Africa were paying substantial numbers of their African workers below the officially recognized subsistence levels. He investigated 100 British companies and showed that in some cases they were paying wages that were low even by South African standards. The minimum subsistence level (Poverty Datum Line – PDL) had been set at £10–£11 a week for an African family of five. This represented the lowest level calculated at which to avoid malnutrition. As a Research Officer for Johannesburg's Non-European Affairs Department put it, 'If your income is below the Poverty Datum Line your health must suffer.' British companies whose subsidiaries were paying below the PDL included such well-known names as Associated Portland Cement, Tate and Lyle, Metal Box, Courtaulds, General Electric, Reed, Chloride Electrical, Associated British Foods and British Leyland. Some companies claimed that the low wages they paid were supplemented by feeding and housing benefits, which were provided free. But Whites Portland Cement (70 per cent owned by Associated Portland Cement) paid an extra 76p a week to workers living outside the Lichtenberg Plant compound while African workers in the plant earned £3 a week. Of the British companies that replied to the (Raphael) investigation, only three – Shell, ICI and Unilever – were paying all their employees above the PDL. No British company was paying over £13 to £15 a week, the figure calculated as the Minimum Effective Level (MEL) needed for an African family to lead a decent life as opposed to the PDL, which did not allow for medicine, education, savings, holidays, furniture, blankets or other similar necessities.

The Raphael revelations provoked reactions ranging from anger and surprise to contrition. Jim Slater of Slater Walker promised an immediate investigation into conditions on the company farms and said he would raise wages. Whites Portland Cement said it wanted to raise wages but could not do so because of the competition situation. Considerable action followed in face of widespread adverse publicity. Chloride Group said it would drop its profits to raise wages. Slater Walker increased wages by 100 per cent and its action led to widespread reforms in the timber industry. Whites increased pay following a South African government increase of £1 a ton in the price of cement. A major debate took place in Britain and 100 Labour MPs signed a motion 'noting with disgust the low wages paid by British firms'. On 4 April it was decided that a House of

Commons Sub-Committee should look into the wages and conditions of African workers employed by British firms in South Africa. The South African government made it clear that the Sub-Committee would not be allowed into the country, even before a formal request had been made. During a foreign affairs debate, Dr Muller, the South African Foreign Minister, said his government was not concerned if British companies wished to improve wages but was concerned when attempts were made to send a parliamentary committee to South Africa to investigate a purely domestic situation. This would be interference in South African affairs.[16] Arthur Grobbelaar, general secretary of the Trade Union Council of South Africa (TUCSA), said in reaction to the *Guardian* report: 'British companies are no worse than German, American or any other foreign firms. They are all just as bad as, or worse than, South African companies.' In Bonn a list of 24 German firms in South Africa, alleged to pay their African workers below the PDL, was published. On the whole German firms came off well, but only in comparison with their competitors. In Washington the State Department issued a booklet setting down guidelines for payment to black workers by US firms in South Africa. It advised a wage of at least R100 (£57) a month, which was above the PDL and aimed at reaching the MEL. Congress was to be asked to legislate concerning 320 US companies known to pay their black workers in South Africa less than the subsistence level. The Bill was to be introduced by Charles Diggs, the black Democrat Representative who was leading the wages campaign in the US.

This wages row reopened the debate on whether all investment in South Africa should be stopped and existing investments be withdrawn. Pressures to stop or withdraw investments were mounted in Britain by the National Union of Teachers (NUT), Scottish local authorities, the British Council of Churches (BCC) and the WCC Programme to Combat Racism. Chief Buthelezi criticized these advocates of withdrawal and said this was a good way to precipitate revolution. Reg September, the chief ANC representative in Europe, welcomed the campaign for higher wages but said that logically it had to be linked to investment. Helen Suzman objected to investment withdrawal and said: 'I am certain that the continued economic expansion of South Africa will prove to be the strongest weapon against apartheid.' According to the *Rand Daily Mail* 700,000 African workers were promised pay increases averaging R7–R8 extra a month and the largest group to benefit were the 400,000 gold- and coal-mine employees who worked for companies belonging to the Chamber of Mines.[17]

In May the British House of Commons Trade and Industry Sub-Committee under the chairmanship of the Labour MP William Rogers began hearing evidence from British companies with South African operations on the wages and conditions of their African employees. It was like a roll call of the leading

British companies of that era and included Associated British Foods, Associated Portland Cement, Barclays Bank, British Leyland, British Steel Corporation, Consolidated Goldfields Ltd, Dunlop Holdings, General Electric Company, Great Universal Stores, ICI, Marchwiel Holdings Ltd, Metal Box Company, Pilkington Brothers, Rio Tinto Zinc, Slater Walker, Tate and Lyle, Unilever. Marchwiel Holdings (involved in building, civil engineering and coal mining) paid very low wages: R29 a month in construction and R27 in mines for a 50-hour week while its minimum wage for a 59-hour week was R33. African workers for Pilkington at Port Elizabeth were paid between R21 and R65 a week while fringe benefits were worth up to R20 a month. Sir Val Duncan, the chairman of Rio Tinto Zinc, agreed that wage rates could be doubled without any sizeable effect on profits, but added: 'It is difficult totally to dissociate from the community in which you are operating.' Wage rates in the Palabora Mining Company in which Rio Tinto Zinc (RTZ) held a 39 per cent interest were R346 a month for white workers and R52 for black workers. RTZ assets in Palabora amounted to about 7 per cent of the group's total invested capital but provided 43 per cent of its total profits in 1969 and 22.9 per cent in 1972. The evidence of company spokesmen varied: Associated Portland Cement blamed price control by government; the lowest wage they paid was R11.04 a week; British Steel was paying 27 cents an hour for a 45-hour week (R12.5). Consolidated Goldfields Chairman Donald McCall blamed the white trade unions for preventing the company paying better wages. Its African workers in Durban were paid R57 a month. Dunlop Holdings claimed it paid all its African male workers above the PDL but not on a family scale. GEC agreed that 25 per cent of its workers were obliged to work a 50-hour week to reach the PDL level. Tate and Lyle's minimum rate for a factory worker was R43.85 a month; in the agricultural division average monthly earnings ranged from R18.20 for a casual worker to R65 for grade 10 – a handyman or estate clerk. Unilever gave equal pay for equal work and minimum wages were related to the PDL and MEL, and take home pay for all workers, after deductions, was above the PDL. Harry Oppenheimer commented on these wage revelations in the AAC annual report and said that the growth of the South African economy had been held back because productivity and earnings of black workers were 'artificially held back by lack of training, by an outmoded industrial structure, or by legal prohibitions'. The economy had reached a stage where the 'improvement of these matters became an urgent need in order to prevent stagnation'. He said that US and British efforts to raise African wages were valuable but South Africans would have to solve their own problems themselves.[18] Oppenheimer had a habit of making such comments upon the state of the South African economy and what was wrong with it but did so as though he were an outsider

J. B. Vorster of South Africa and Ian Smith of Rhodesia – always uneasy partners.
(Cape Argus – Trace Images/africanpictures.net)

Portuguese Troops in Luanda, Angola, August 1975. A show of force shortly before total withdrawal. (Jim McLagan – Cape Argus – Trace Images/africanpictures.net)

MPLA child soldiers: a sad but familiar sight in too many African countries.
(Jim McLagan – Cape Argus – Trace Images/africanpictures.net)

Britain's Foreign Secretary, Jim Callaghan, visits Uganda in an attempt to improve relations with that country's volatile dictator Idi Amin. (INPRA/africanpictures.net)

South Africa's Prime Minister J. B. Vorster and Zambia's President K. D. Kaunda meet at Livingstone during the détente exercise in 1975. (Jim McLagan – Cape Argus – Trace Images/africanpictures.net)

Presidents Kaunda and Nyerere at a ceremony marking the Tanzam railway crossing the border from Tanzania into Zambia. (Trace Images – Associated Press/africanpictures.net)

Helen Suzman, Progressive Party, for many years a lone white voice for justice in the South African Parliament. (David Goldblatt – South Photographs/ africanpictures.net)

As Prime Minister of South Africa through the 1970s J. B. Vorster dominated the region. (Cape Argus – Trace Images/ africanpictures.net)

Uganda's brutal dictator, Idi Amin (1971–1979) gave Black Africa a bad name. (Cape Argus – Trace Images/ africanpictures.net)

These bleak tin shacks set in the middle of nowhere were considered appropriate housing for Blacks (Bantu) by the apartheid regime. (Cape Argus – Trace Images/africanpictures.net)

A Black Sash protest in South Africa. (Gille de Vlieg – South Photographs/ africanpictures.net)

looking in rather than the greatest beneficiary of the system as it existed.

Although the South African government had vetoed a British parliamentary sub-committee visiting South Africa in the wake of the Adam Raphael furore, it said that a British TUC delegation, led by the recently retired General Secretary Vic Feather, could do so. Mr Grobbelaar, the General Secretary of TUCSA, said the main purpose of the visit would be to determine whether change from within the Republic was possible. 'The TUC's starting point is that change must come – and if it cannot come from within, the leadership will be under pressure to bring it about from outside.' This would consist of 'support for guerrilla movements, determined efforts to ban emigration, arms boycotts and pressure on British industrialists to withdraw their investments might be among the results'. A special opinion poll conducted for the *South African Sunday Times* revealed that a majority of South African businessmen felt that the introduction of black skilled labour into white areas was essential for the development of the economy and would not threaten the position of white workers. Over 90 per cent of businessmen favoured African workers becoming skilled artisans and only 3 per cent were firmly against. One result of the *Guardian* campaign for higher wages was that employers said that if they must pay their black workers more they must be allowed to make them more productive; this meant relaxing the colour bar, which was already under pressure. African labour, increasingly, was becoming the dominant factor in the labour market. The ratio of black to white workers was approximately five to one and the gap was growing. *Volkshandel*, the official organ of the *Afrikaanse Handels Institut*, which represented Afrikaner businessmen, questioned the economic feasibility of separate development in an editorial: 'Cultural, church and political leaders who see the future as separate, politically independent and economically self-supporting black nations must be disillusioned by the hard facts.' South Africa was economically indivisible and decentralization had not succeeded in reversing the flow of black labour to white areas – the urban African was not merely a permanent resident but was also in the great majority at urban growth points.

On 11 September 1973 the police opened fire at Carltonville killing 11 African miners who were protesting against labour conditions. Western Deep Levels was one of Anglo's most modern mines. Commenting upon the tragedy, the *Guardian* made the point 'that rebellions are born out of rising hopes rather than out of despair. The living conditions at other mines (and in parts of Black Africa) are much more desperate'.[19] A further comment upon this mine tragedy came from another journalist: 'For once the employers have not tried to blame a tragedy of this sort on agitators. Instead, within hours of the clash, a company executive admitted that bad labour policies may have been a major cause of the unrest at the mines. Such a statement from Anglo American has vast implications. The giant company's array of gold, diamond and coal mines employ 165,000 Africans and as the largest private employer of black labour, its decisions send ripples throughout the whole South African economy.' Commenting on the anger at the tragedy in Botswana (two miners were from there) and Lesotho (five miners, and the government stopped recruitment for the South African mines), the author quoted a Botswana Cabinet statement which said it was 'a sad commentary on South African society that 11 men should have lost their lives for no other reason than that they, denied any bargaining machinery, were moved by a deep sense of frustration to demonstrate against the discriminatory terms of their employment. Botswana has repeatedly expressed its fears that the continued denial of fundamental rights to the black man by the South African Government will result in violence.'[20]

When the TUC delegation led by Vic Feather arrived in South Africa, he at once dismissed the idea that his team had come to look at wages; it had come to examine the question of trade union rights for black workers and, he made clear, the TUC would support any moves in that direction. David Loshak, writing in the most conservative and generally pro-white South African British paper, the *Daily Telegraph*, said: 'That the government, politically so hostile to the known views of the TUC men, even the right-wingers among them, and as anti-British Afrikaners still deeply troubled by Boer War resentments and memories of internment in World War II, should not only allow such intervention but actually encourage it, is of major significance. Furthermore, the influential *Afrikaanse Handels Institut*, representing some of the most powerful employers, has invited the TUC back. The delegation's report, due in December, is thus likely to have far-reaching effects on the South African labour scene.' The South African soft line was due to the ILO resolution of June 1973 that called for a world boycott of South African goods. 'Clearly as Britain is South Africa's biggest trading partner, this would damage both countries. Mr Feather's team and Mr Vorster's, therefore, had a mutual interest in co-operating to avoid it... South Africa also fears that an antagonized British trade union movement might discourage or seek to prevent the emigration of skilled whites to South Africa, immigrants the country sorely needs.'[21]

Challenges to South Africa's labour practices were constantly emerging at this time. Vorster told employers that they might take steps to improve the productive use of non-white labour, and he told the TUC that he wanted to see greater collective bargaining for black workers, provided it developed in an orderly way. Vorster, carefully, was changing his approach to black-white labour relations in reaction to growing realities that could not be ignored. The TUC report was issued on 15 December 1973. It made four principal recommendations: Continuation of opposition to British investment in South Africa, unless British firms show 'in a practical way' that they are encouraging and recognizing genuinely independent trade unions for African workers; that the TUC's General Council should discourage the emigration of white workers to South Africa; that the ICFTU and TUC should establish a 'focal point' in South Africa, to plan and assist 'on a massive scale' the organization of Africans into unions and that funds be raised to employ full-time black organizers; that these two bodies should mobilize international support for African trade union organizations and a sum of £100,000 be collected. Other reforms advocated included: provision of universal free education; introduction of the rate for the job; provision of trade training opportunities on a massive scale. The South African *Star* headlined 'TUC Report Stuns South Africa' and described its recommendations as 'potentially explosive' and said they would be likely to be regarded as an interference in South Africa's internal affairs. The *Star* asked: 'Does it mean to help promote exclusively African unions or to promote African rights within non-racial unions?'[22] The reaction of Anglo American was to say it did not believe black trade unions were necessary in South Africa. A spokesman for the group said a survey showed that 97 per cent of black workers at three representative mines 'were aware they could air their grievances through the works committees'. According to the Labour correspondent of the South African *Star*, 1973 marked 'the emergence of the hitherto silent majority – the country's millions of African, Coloured and Asian workers'. Strikes in Natal won wage increases for at least 150,000 workers and many more got higher pay because of employers' heightened awareness or to prevent strikes. 'Employers and unions were forced to reassess their attitudes to black workers, particularly on the question of representation.'[23] The average wages for black workers in gold- and coal-mines were 50 per cent higher as of 1 January 1974 than a year earlier while Africans in Durban were being trained as crane operators for the first time and given more scope in the car assembly industry. Early in 1974 the British House of Commons Sub-Committee to study wages and conditions in British companies in South Africa published its report, having received submissions from 141 companies. It urged companies to adopt a 'code of conduct' for the improvement of African conditions and urged the British Embassy in South Africa and the Department of Trade and Industry to abandon their 'fairly passive role' and keep a close watch on companies' employment practices. The committee listed 63 companies that were paying minimum wages below the PDL.

Thus, 1973 was a turning point in perceptions of the South African economy and the impact upon it of apartheid. The Church of England Board for Social

Responsibility, for example, produced two memoranda on investment in South Africa, the second of which commented that the evidence of the preceding nine months had greatly strengthened the view that shareholder action was a viable policy: keep investments in South Africa and use them as levers for change. Turmoil in the labour market and clear indications that black labour would no longer accept its servile role in the South African economy had a marked effect upon investment flows. South Africa had always depended upon inward investment as a crucial ingredient in its development. By the latter years of the decade it began to see a real change in the readiness of external business to put its money into a country that no longer seemed as secure as apartheid had kept it for so many years. 'For the first time ever, the first quarter of 1977 saw a net *outflow* of long-term capital. The estimated outflow for the whole of 1977 was R1,000 million (cf. a net inflow of R1,900 million in 1975) in a staggering turnabout of almost R3,000 million.'[24] Such figures gave the South African ruling establishment real pause to think.

DIALOGUE AND *DÉTENTE*

No other country on the African continent was so closely monitored from outside as was South Africa. There were a number of reasons for this scrutiny. It was potentially and actually the most powerful country on the continent; it was the repository of major Western investments and an important trading partner, especially for Britain; its policy of apartheid made it the focus of deep antagonism for black Africa in particular and the world community more generally; moreover, at a time when the Cold War was at its height, South African intransigence and Western reluctance to exert upon it the pressures that it might have employed gave ample scope to the USSR to support guerrilla movements and win propaganda victories against the West. The question, then, was whether change, which almost everyone except the most myopic saw to be inevitable, could come about peacefully or violently. Could white South Africa save itself by coming to terms with its black majority before catastrophe engulfed the whole of Southern Africa? Vorster, ruthless racist though he might be, saw that at the very least he must try to come to an accommodation with independent black Africa and so, at the beginning of the decade, he embarked upon his 'outward-looking policy', seeking to establish a dialogue with Black Africa.

Malawi under its idiosyncratic ruler Hastings Banda was the only Black African country to enter into diplomatic relations with South Africa, which it had done as early as 1967, and this was seen as a major breakthrough in Pretoria. But the question soon arose: if other black states were to follow Malawi's example, how many black diplomats, enjoying a kind of honorary white status, would South Africa be prepared to accept? Certainly, 1970 was an encouraging year for dialogue. Apart from Malawi, the Malagasy Republic signed a loan agreement with South Africa for R4.5 million for development, especially tourism. The Foreign Minister of Mauritius, Caetan Duval, also favoured close relations with the Republic. Then a more important breakthrough was achieved in West Africa. The prestigious Francophone leader, President Houphouët-Boigny of Côte d'Ivoire, favoured dialogue with South Africa and quipped that the only invasion of that country he supported would be one by African diplomats. President Kofi Busia of Ghana also came out in favour of dialogue. On the other hand, Tanzania, Zambia, Kenya and Uganda opposed dialogue and Somalia's President Siad Barre appealed to French-speaking African leaders to withdraw any offer to hold talks with South Africa. The *South African Star* said that South Africa's over-enthusiastic welcome of the Côte d'Ivoire proposal for dialogue had seriously compromised any chance of success. The Portuguese view that the proposals from Abidjan were a firm reply to the stand taken by Zambia's President Kaunda had also done the Abidjan initiative harm. Other Francophone states were more cautious. Leopold Senghor of Senegal and Haile Selassie of Ethiopia were opposed to the move.[25]

In April 1971 a major row between Vorster and Kaunda was conducted by published correspondence, with Vorster suggesting that Kaunda had been trying secretly to do a deal with South Africa and Kaunda denying it. In the end Kaunda published all the correspondence that had taken place, and this bore out his, rather than Vorster's, version of events. The general view in the South African press was that Vorster had tried too hard to discredit Kaunda whom he saw as the chief obstacle to South African dialogue with other African states. An excellent appraisal of Vorster's dialogue efforts and problems was made at the time by the journalist Derek Ingram and is worth quoting at length.[26]

> Vorster is now switching to a strategy that aims at isolating the hard core of countries which oppose the ideas of a dialogue with South Africa. For more than three years Zambia has been the Number One target for conversion. The country occupies the key geographical position in the centre of Southern Africa, lying between Portuguese Angola to the west and Portuguese Mozambique to the east. Apart from Zambia the whole of this area, which includes Rhodesia, Malawi and Botswana, lies within what can be regarded as a White sphere of influence... In Angola and Mozambique the Portuguese were trying to hold the line firm.
>
> Malawi had adopted a friendly posture towards Pretoria. But the line was broken by Zambia, and Zambia in turn was giving aid and comfort to

Botswana (the two have a common frontier point South Africa disputes), which borders half of South Africa. 'Pacification' of Zambia would reap a double dividend. Botswana, under President Sir Seretse Khama, by no means pursues a soft line towards South Africa. Sir Seretse is a close friend of Dr Kaunda and is sustained by the fact that his country neighbours Zambia. If Zambia took a more dove-like line Botswana would be isolated and forced to do likewise.

In his article Ingram pointed out that Vorster 'gave the impression that President Kaunda had been trying to do a deal with South Africa, whereas all the evidence is that it was South Africa that had been trying to do a deal with Zambia. In fact, Vorster himself stated that Dr Verwoerd had initiated the contacts two years earlier – in 1966'.

Vorster put in a lot of time and effort to woo Kaunda and his uncharacteristic move in revealing private correspondence to Parliament appears to have been made because he realized that he had come to the end of the road with Kaunda.

Angry at this failure, Vorster had dubbed Kaunda a 'double-dealer'.

On 16 August 1971 President Banda of Malawi arrived in South Africa to be greeted with full military honours. His programme included a state banquet hosted by State President Fouché and dinner with the Prime Minister at the President Hotel in Johannesburg. Over four days Banda visited all the Bantustan leaders, the Chairman of the Coloured Persons Representative Council and the South African Indian Council. Outside Soweto's administration offices Banda said to several thousand cheering Africans, mostly schoolchildren: 'I do not like this system of apartheid, but I prefer to talk. If I isolate South Africa, if I boycott South Africa, I isolate you, my people, my children.'[27] His visit was the high point of the dialogue initiative; in the years that followed, Malawi would become increasingly isolated in relation to the unfolding events in Southern Africa. One of the early dialogue breakthroughs had been with the Malagasy Republic but following the coup of June 1972 that brought the military to power in Antananarivo, the new Foreign Minister, Didier Ratsiraka, broke all relations with South Africa. Reactions in South Africa to this event were conflicting. The *Sunday Tribune* said, 'Now that the Prime Minister seems to be joining the right wing retreat into darkness, not even the best disposed of Black states could afford to keep company with South Africa – as Malagasy has now made clear.' On the other hand, *Die Hoofstad* attacked the 'cynical unpatriotic jubilation in the English press' at this set back to the government's outward-looking policy.

With the collapse of dialogue Vorster turned to *détente* with the front-line states that, whether they wanted it or not, were steadily becoming involved in a widening conflict across the whole region. At the heart of the *détente* exercise was the problem of what to do about Smith's Rhodesia. In 1970 Henry Kissinger, the US Secretary of State under President Nixon, had favoured maintaining the political balance in Southern Africa in support of the whites. The collapse of Portuguese power in Southern Africa altered the situation irrevocably while Soviet/Cuban intervention in Angola in 1975 altered the position still further. As a result, Western policies in Southern Africa were in ruins. Kissinger needed to implement a new policy and essentially this was to sacrifice Smith's Rhodesia to buy time for South Africa; and to counterbalance the successful Soviet/Cuban intervention in Angola by demonstrating a new Western concern for black aspirations in the region. In a speech to his constituency on 6 November 1974, foreshadowing the *détente* exercise he was about to launch, Vorster appealed to political commentators to give South Africa a chance. If they did, he said, they would be surprised where South Africa would stand in about six to 12 months. Earlier that year, the spark to set off policy changes throughout Southern Africa came in the form of the 25 April Revolution in Lisbon, which overthrew the Caetano 'dictatorship'. As a result the premise upon which South Africa had operated ever since Sharpeville – that there was a cordon sanitaire consisting of Angola, Rhodesia and Mozambique between itself and Black Africa – had disappeared. The Portuguese withdrawal from Angola brought an independent black-ruled state to the borders of Namibia, South Africa's illegally held colony where it was already waging a war in the border region of Ovamboland that would now escalate. The Portuguese withdrawal from Mozambique meant Rhodesia's flank had been turned and instead of Smith having a friendly Portugal on his eastern border, that ally had been replaced by a FRELIMO government that would, as it at once did, assist his guerrilla opponents. As a consequence an exposed Rhodesia became overnight a liability rather than an asset for South Africa.

Détente would provide a way out for both South Africa and the front-line states since both sides wanted a peaceful solution. Such a solution could only be obtained at a price and for South Africa the price was the betrayal of Smith's Rhodesia. *Détente*, then, was an exercise designed to persuade Smith that UDI could no longer be sustained and that he had to come to terms with majority rule. Smith was not prepared to play. South Africa withdrew its police and troops from Rhodesia and Vorster went all out to achieve good relations with Mozambique, not least because South Africa needed the ocean outlet provided by Maputo. Pragmatically, FRELIMO accepted this South African policy as it could not afford to close Beira to Rhodesia as well as Maputo to South Africa. After it became clear that Smith would not abandon UDI to suit South Africa's new strategy, Vorster in turn abandoned his support for Rhodesia and gave up his attempt to achieve *détente* with the front-line states since they still insisted, as they had to, that *détente* must also presuppose the abandonment of apartheid. Vorster then turned to his third alternative: using South Africa's military power to install pro, or at least neutral, governments in its black neighbours. The result was the South African military incursion into Angola.[28]

Vorster was immediately statesmanlike in his approach to Mozambique: like Smith before him, he wanted to secure his eastern flank. 'A Black government in Mozambique holds no fears for us whatever,' he said. He would not support the abortive white counter-revolution in Maputo and in response to the economic and other chaos in Mozambique during the transitional period said: 'I don't like it. Unrest in any part of the world gives cause for concern, especially in a neighbouring country. Whoever takes over in Mozambique has a tough task ahead of him. It will require exceptional leadership. They have my sympathy and I wish them well.'[29] In an important speech to the South African Senate on 23 October to which the diplomatic corps had been invited, Vorster said: 'Southern Africa is at the crossroads and should choose now between peace and escalating violence.' The cost of confrontation, he said, would be 'high – too high for Southern Africa to pay'. Of Rhodesia he said, 'It is in the interests of all parties to find a solution,' although Smith could have been excused for suggesting Vorster meant in South Africa's interests. He was more ambivalent about Namibia: 'South Africa would not withdraw suddenly.' At no time in all the *détente* negotiations over 1974/75, until he abandoned the exercise for intervention in Angola, did Vorster in any way contemplate ending apartheid. Similarly, the African states had no intention of abandoning the 'unfinished African revolution' – that is, the achievement of majority rule in the south and the end of racial discrimination.

Crucial to the new situation in Southern Africa would be Western policy reappraisals, hence the Kissinger mission to 'resolve' the Rhodesia question, accompanied by a greater readiness in the West, if not to mount pressures upon South Africa, at least to be less ready actually to support its position. Until 1974 the image of South Africa had been that of a stable white-ruled country, largely invulnerable to external pressures for change. This image was now greatly weakened: at home the homeland leaders were becoming increasingly outspoken and defiant as were students and Coloured leaders; abroad, the collapse of Portugal's African Empire revealed South Africa suddenly to be far more vulnerable to outside pressures. There was now a real chance that it would be isolated and that former Western friends would become less accommodating. This was borne out in 1975 when France placed an arms embargo on South Africa. White political figures began to throw doubts on the permanency of apartheid. Theo Gerdener, a former Minister of Interior who had become the leader of the Democratic Party, said, 'No white minority in Southern Africa could any longer remain standing on its own… I have warned that whites who believe that white supremacy can be maintained for ever must think again.'

In the retrospect of history the claims of a Communist (Soviet) threat appear less startling than at the time; in particular, the role of US Secretary of State Henry Kissinger needs to be re-examined in order to separate what he claimed at the time from what actually appears to have happened. Thus, the Soviet Union only reluctantly backed Cuban intervention in Angola and tried to put limits upon it. The US official version of events depicted the war in Angola as a major new challenge to US power by an expansionist Moscow, newly confident following the US defeat in Vietnam. In his memoirs Kissinger wrote: 'My assessment was if the Soviet Union can interfere 8,000 miles from home in an undisputed way and control Zaïre's and Zambia's access to the sea, then the Southern countries must conclude that the US has abdicated in Southern Africa.' In fact the real picture was substantially different. Castro had already sent military advisers, earlier in 1975, to assist the MPLA. He decided to send troops to Angola on 4 November in response to the South African invasion that was already under way. At the time Washington claimed that South Africa had invaded in order to prevent a Cuban takeover of the country. In fact the US knew South Africa's covert invasion plans in advance and co-operated militarily with its forces, contrary to Kissinger's testimony to Congress and what he later said in his memoirs. Castro decided to send troops to Angola without informing the Soviet Union and deployed them at his own expense from November 1975 to January 1976 and only then did Moscow agree to arrange for a maximum of 10 flights to help Cuba. In the end Cuba deployed 30,000 troops in Angola and effectively defeated the 'secret' invasion by South Africa when its column reached the outskirts of Luanda. Cuban intervention was also credited with the MPLA's victory over the two factions backed by the US and China, UNITA under Jonas Savimbi and the FNLA under Holden Roberto. Cuba, in fact, proved a headache for Moscow, which under Brezhnev did not want 'adventurism'. The MPLA leader, Agostinho Neto, complained in 1975 of Moscow's lacklustre support for he hoped the war in Angola would become 'a vital issue in the fight against imperialism'. A National Security Council meeting of 27 June 1975 under the US Secretary of Defence, James Schlesinger, suggested that Washington 'encourage the disintegration of Angola', implying that Washington's main interest in the nation was Cabinda, the oil-rich enclave surrounded by territory of the Congo and Zaïre. At that meeting Kissinger indicated that the CIA's oversight committee had authorized actions for both money and arms. Robert Hultslander was the CIA chief of station in Luanda from July to November 1975, when the US evacuated its mission. He said that US officers on the ground believed that the MPLA was the 'best qualified movement to govern Angola'. His assessment lost him his foreign service career 'when he refused to bend his reporting to Kissinger's policy'. He said: 'Instead of working with the moderate elements in Angola, which I believe we could have found within the MPLA, we supported the radical, tribal "anti-Soviet right".'[30] Such revelations cast a new light on the events of that time.

The failure of his *détente* exercise led Vorster to adopt his military approach to his neighbours: first the intervention in Angola and later the policy of destabilization that became a feature of the 1980s after he had fallen from power. On 14 May 1975 Vorster finally revealed details of his visit to Côte d'Ivoire and talks with Houphouët-Boigny over 22–24 September 1974 when they had discussed improving relations between South Africa and independent African states. At the beginning of 1975 the OAU uneasily continued to back the October 1974 initiative by the Presidents of Zambia, Tanzania, Mozambique (Samora Machel) and Botswana to find a peaceful solution for the problems of Southern Africa although there was growing opposition to the contact. The OAU, while supporting the initiative, was simultaneously strengthening the liberation movements in case the initiative failed. Smith, meanwhile, was holding back from negotiations about a settlement in the hope that a white backlash against Vorster would develop in South Africa for 'betraying' the white Rhodesians. By 15 March 1975 there had been 15 South African-Zambian meetings. There were also growing divisions in the black Rhodesian ranks while Mugabe distrusted Kaunda's manoeuvres, a distrust that never really changed. On 12 February 1975 Vorster flew to Monrovia for talks with President William Tolbert. The transcript of their talks was leaked to *The Times* by the President's brother, Stephen. When, 10 days after the details of the meeting had appeared, Vorster answered questions in Parliament, his main concern was over a statement by Tolbert when Vorster told him: 'We do not want an inch of South West Africa's territory and I would be only too pleased to get South West Africa off our back.'

President Sekou Touré of Guinea condemned the Monrovia talks: 'To hold a dialogue with the supporters of apartheid is to add to the racists' injury to Africa, an injury inflicted by Africa itself.' Touré called on all African governments to 'reject all proposals for dialogue with South Africa until the day when the indignity which now soils our continent through apartheid completely disappears'.[31] By March 1975, especially as the excitement of the Portuguese colonial collapse in Southern Africa opened up new possibilities, there was a danger that Africa would split between those who favoured and those who opposed dialogue. Kaunda throughout was careful to inform the OAU Chairman (Somalia's Siad Barre) and other African leaders of the moves he was making with regard to South Africa. Smith was determined to sink the Pretoria–Lusaka initiative. He was helped in this by the continuing guerrilla struggle, which he emphasized by arresting ZANU's Ndabaningi Sithole on charges of actively encouraging the recruitment of guerrillas. It was at this point, to force Smith to do a deal, that Vorster told him he was withdrawing his forces from Rhodesia. By April 1975 the Lusaka 'four' – Zambia, Tanzania, Botswana and Machel (still waiting to assume the presidency of an independent Mozambique) – found themselves under increasing attack from critics in the OAU as well as all the southern liberation movements. These critics were temporarily stalled when Vorster gave an undertaking to Kaunda that all South African forces would be withdrawn from Rhodesia by the end of May. Then on 7 April the OAU Council of Ministers met in Dar es Salaam and President Nyerere produced what became known as the Dar es Salaam Declaration. Part of the conclusion reads: 'African objectives in southern Africa are unchanged. They are: independence for the whole country on the basis of majority rule in both Rhodesia and Namibia; and an end to apartheid and racial discrimination in South Africa. Africa's strategy should be to separate the two issues as far as practical, and to give priority to ending the colonial situation in Rhodesia and Namibia.' Following the Dar es Salaam Declaration, Vorster told the South African Parliament that '*détente* and dialogue' were over.[32]

In any case, dialogue or *détente* was bound to be over once South Africa intervened in Angola. The intervention is well documented.[33] In March 1975 Savimbi visited a European capital to meet a senior BOSS official to request aid, which was refused. On 14 July South African troops crossed the Namibian border into Angola where they overcame MPLA and UNITA resistance and then attacked SWAPO bases. On 21 August Savimbi met a South African general in Namibia when he obtained a promise that South Africa would provide UNITA with military instructors and train 6,000 of its troops. These trainers arrived in Silvo Ponto, central Angola, in September. At that time the South African objective was to help hold Nova Lisboa (Huambo) for UNITA as MPLA forces were then advancing southwards. After a clash with advancing MPLA forces the South African instructors at Silvo Ponto requested reinforcements and a huge shipment of equipment in C-130s was flown in to the town. More South African troops moved across the border into Angola. Then, on 9 October, Pretoria ordered the formation of the 'Zulu' column that was to be its main strike force. On 14 October Operation 'Zulu' began and it moved up the Angolan coast. By 26 October the 'Zulu' column had taken Sa da Bandeira from the MPLA; two days later it took the town of Moçamedes, on 3 November Lobito and on 5 November Benguela. On 10 November Savimbi flew to Pretoria to see Vorster to tell him that Kaunda and other conservative African leaders hoped that the South African forces would remain in Angola after independence on 11 November; Vorster, who was also under pressure to do so from Washington, agreed. On 11 November Pretoria ordered 'Zulu' to advance to points just short of Luanda; however, the column suffered heavy casualties at the hands of the MPLA outside Novo Redondo and though the South Africans took the town on 14 November their commander requested Pretoria for reinforcements, but the request was refused. The 'Zulu' commander was recalled while his troops remained in Novo Redondo. The MPLA, meanwhile, much to the embarrassment of Pretoria, put four captured South African troops on show at a press conference. Nigeria, which up to this point had refused to recognize the MPLA government, now did so on the grounds that South Africa had invaded its territory. On 20 December Savimbi was again obliged to fly to see Vorster after he had said he was about to withdraw; Savimbi managed to persuade him to keep his troops in Angola, but only for a short time. Britain and France warned South Africa that they would be unable to support it at the UN Security Council debate on Angola scheduled for January. On 31 December Kaunda changed his stance and said South Africa should withdraw its forces from Angola by 9 January 1976. On 22 January South Africa decided to withdraw and on 4 February 1976 announced that all its troops had been withdrawn to within 50 kilometres of the Namibian border and remained in Angola only to protect the Cunene Dam. On 25 March all South African troops were withdrawn into Namibia.

The Angola invasion was a disaster and humiliation for South Africa. It had kept its intervention strictly limited (2,000 troops) but this still led to a huge Communist presence in Angola, which changed from being part of the cordon sanitaire guarding South Africa into a hostile state under a Marxist-style government. Moreover, the African states of the region ceased to see South Africa as invincible while Malawi, Lesotho and Botswana began to withdraw their labour. The debacle was a contributory cause of the next disaster, the Soweto uprising of June 1976. The retreat from Angola marked the end of Vorster's political predominance. He had initiated dialogue in 1970; proceeded to *détente* in 1974; then switched to a more aggressive intervention policy in Angola in 1975. And each in turn had failed. From 1976 onwards Vorster was on the defensive. Especially galling for Vorster, who had spent years claiming to act as a bastion for the West against the advance of Communism, his actions had done much to ensure that such an advance took place. The Russians had much to gain and little to lose in Southern Africa at this time. As Yuri Kornilov wrote in Tass, 11 October 1976: 'The Soviet Union's stand on the problems of Southern Africa is clear and definite: the Soviet Union has no, and cannot have any "special interests", neither in south nor in north, nor in any other part of Africa. The USSR does not look for any benefits for itself there. It only strives for the sacred right of every people to decide its own destiny, for the right to choose its own way of development. This is our unwavering principle, which the Soviet people will never abandon.' The Russians, who were blamed by the West for far more than they ever managed to achieve, could be forgiven for this flight of high-sounding principle. In part, however, it was a response to a speech made by Kissinger in Lusaka the previous April in which he said the US would work for majority rule throughout the region. In the circumstances, the USSR had to emphasize that the United States and Britain were primarily interested in preserving the position of the 'imperialist monopolies'. Although African states such as Zambia were wary of the Communists, they had no interest in upsetting the Russians or Cubans in Angola since the West had begun to change course precisely because of the Soviet threat in the region. The Soviets, in other words, had become an excellent source of pressure for change and the Africans were doubtful about the apparent changes in Western policy.

THE SOWETO UPRISING

The barbaric division between black and white that apartheid maintained had been explained in coldly logical terms by its principal architect, Verwoerd: 'There is no place for him (the black) in the European community above the level of certain forms of labour. What is the use of teaching a Bantu child mathematics when it cannot use it in practice?' In 1969 the hard-line Afrikaners, who became known as the *Verkramptes,* split from the National Party because of Vorster's 'concessions' to blacks to form the *Herstigte Nasionale Party* (Refounded National Party – HNP) under Albert Hertzog and though they had been easily defeated by Vorster in the 1970 election, they remained a force to be reckoned with. Vorster's 1970 victory allowed him to proceed without hindrance with his policy of dialogue. As events in Portugal in early 1974 foreshadowed the coming end of the Caetano regime, Vorster called an election for that April, which he again won easily, so that he could proceed with his new policy of *détente.* However, when the economy slowed down in 1975 as a result of world recession HNP pressures were increased. Then, when news of the Angola intervention became known on 22 December 1975, two months after the 'Zulu' column had been sent into Angola, only to be recalled weeks later, HNP pressures upon the government became even more demanding in the wake of the Angola debacle. 'Having exerted fairly massive pressure on Smith to surrender white rule in Rhodesia, the government was now running away from "black Communists", its tail between its legs, leaving white South African prisoners behind. It was a scenario tailor-made for the *verkramptes*.[34] In January 1976, in an attempt to appease the hard-right *Verkramptes,* Vorster brought Dr Andries Treurnicht into his government though not the cabinet. Treurnicht was the most outstanding of the *Verkramptes* still in the NP who stood uncompromisingly for Afrikaner dominance and exclusivism and as such was a constant reminder that Vorster was deviating from the true path. Vorster made Treurnicht Deputy Minister of Bantu Education and believed he had sidelined him. The Ministry for some time, under his predecessor Punt Janson, had been involved in a departmental battle over the use of Afrikaans as a medium of instruction in Bantu schools. There was massive African resistance to the idea. Treurnicht at once insisted that African children would have to be taught maths and history in Afrikaans.

On 17 May 1976 black pupils of Orlando West Junior Secondary School in Soweto came out on strike against the Afrikaans ruling. Treurnicht refused to back down. On 14 June Leonard Mosala, a Soweto urban councillor, warned that if the Afrikaans medium ruling was not relaxed immediately 'it will lead to another Sharpeville'. He was right. On 16 June the shooting started. Soweto, in any case, was a powder keg constantly bedevilled by a huge crime wave, and many who lived there saw it as a 'ghetto' or 'concentration camp'. According to a survey 75 per cent of those who lived in Soweto saw it as their only home and refused absolutely to regard their designated homelands as home. At this time black unemployment was rising by 100,000 a year while twice that number were entering the labour market and despite the advances of 1973 – the wage increases that had followed the international pressures associated with the *Guardian* report – the position of black labour generally was no better. The cost of wage rises had to be met in one of three ways: lower profits, loss of white jobs or – what actually happened – a cutback in black employment. White employers had demanded higher productivity from their black workers to enable them to economize on the total black labour they employed. The result was increasing unemployment, which was made worse by recession and inflation that between them had eroded the value of the wage increases won in 1973. By 1976 blacks were faced with soaring food and transport costs and the opposition of a white working class grimly determined to defend job reservation in its favour.[35] Young blacks in the schools saw almost no job prospects ahead of them and reacted to the Treurnicht ruling as the last straw; their placards, when they turned out to demonstrate, described Afrikaans as the 'oppressors' language'. The ruling had taken no account of the fact that few teachers knew Afrikaans; it was purely doctrinaire.

Some 15,000 schoolchildren marched towards the school where the strike had begun on 16 June: they were met by a line of armed police who opened fire and an unknown number of children were killed or injured. The police estimate was 25 dead and 200 injured. The children fled and proceeded to riot, smashing Bantu Administration offices, liquor shops or other property associated with white authority. The police responses were savage and included the beating and torture of children. The riots spread to other Johannesburg area townships. The police attempted to isolate the townships: they used helicopters to drop tear gas and co-ordinate their operations but this was not always possible since the townships were often obscured by smoke clouds from the many fires that had been started. The day after these riots erupted Treurnicht said it was for the 'Bantu's own good' that he learned in Afrikaans but a few days later M. C. Botha, his minister, announced that Afrikaans had never been compulsory and that the ruling would be relaxed. The riots then spread to the townships of Natal and some rioters appeared on the edge of white suburbs and in the centre of Johannesburg. After eight days of rioting there was a lull; 176 rioters had been shot dead and several thousand had been injured. Then on 27 July a wave of arson against African schools began in the Transvaal, Orange Free State and Natal. The Soweto Students' Representative Council (SRC) condemned the arson and called for a return to school, but it had lost control of the situation. On 4 August spontaneous violence erupted in the townships across the Rand while in Soweto the students attempted, with only limited success, to prevent workers going to Johannesburg. On 11 August the rioting spread to the townships round Cape Town and later to Port Elizabeth. Addressing a NP audience, Jimmy Kruger, Minister of Police, said: 'He (the Bantu) knows his place, and if not I'll tell him his place.' On 23 August a three-day general strike was called in Soweto; the following day, assisted by the police, hundreds of Zulu hostel dwellers rampaged through Soweto. The same day unrest broke out among the Coloured population of Cape Town where students held solidarity demonstrations. The police resorted to tear gas and bullets. Vorster and Kruger praised the conduct of the police and Vorster said, 'There is no way of governing South Africa other than by the policy and principles of the National Party.' The schoolchildren attacked the shebeens – the illegal drinking houses and beer halls – in protest against their parents' generation for avoiding a confrontation with the whites and turning instead to drink. The *Rand Daily Mail* identified 499 individuals who had died in the troubles although unofficial estimates suggested a figure of well over 1,000 and 10 to 20 times that number injured. Many youths fled the country to join the ANC. Soweto was a massive turning point. As the country began to recover from the upheaval, the Johannesburg *Sunday Times* said: '16 June proved that the main debate in South Africa is between the effective power of the Nationalist government, on the one hand, and the potent but unchannelled power of the black urban masses on the other.'[36] In Parliament the conservative white opposition leader, Sir de Villiers Graaff, said: 'The old order has gone – it was destroyed in the economic and racial shambles created by this government. It was choked in the smoke of Soweto and many other black and brown townships… Anyone who does not realize this is sleeping through a revolution.'[37]

GROWING ISOLATION

The failure of *détente*, the Angolan debacle and then Soweto each worked to increase South Africa's isolation. The buffer states had fallen away; Britain had finally cancelled the largely irrelevant Simonstown Agreement; France had decided to impose an arms embargo; Washington had left South Africa high and dry in the middle of its Angolan intervention. The only plus arising out of these years – one that followed the events surrounding the Yom Kippur War – was a close alliance with Israel: but that country was not an ally that assisted the South African image. By 1977 South Africa found itself under greater pressures for change than ever before in its modern history, leading Vorster to tell his colleagues that South Africa could no longer rely upon Western support in the event of violent conflict. How, then, could the government meet demands for change? The year did witness the beginning of mild change in the area of what came to be known as petty apartheid but otherwise Vorster had run out of steam with the result that his government intensified repression while offering consultation with its external challengers. It was not a policy that could work.

The front-line Presidents had a clear set of objectives: to bring an end to minority rule in Rhodesia and Namibia, and in the long run South Africa itself, if possible by minimal violence and negotiation, otherwise by armed struggle. During 1976–77 there was a steady build-up for war and at last the liberation armies were emerging as credible military forces. Vorster was sincere in his desire for peace, for a long-drawn-out war would have the effect of radicalizing the governments on South Africa's doorstep. The focus of diplomacy at this time was Rhodesia. The arrival of the Democrat Jimmy Carter in the White House in 1977 dealt a further blow to South African hopes. In May of 1977 President Carter sent Vice-President Walter Mondale to meet Vorster in Vienna where he informed him formally that South African-US relations were at a watershed. Thus, suddenly, South Africa faced isolation from the West, prompting the Foreign Minister to say, 'We cannot negotiate on our destruction, either now or tomorrow.'[38] By this time South Africa was coming to be seen more and more as a world problem. Up to 1976 the West had believed that compared with the rest of the continent (despite its internal crises) South Africa was an essentially stable and safe place for Western investment. This perception was destroyed by the events of 1974–77. The wariness of multinational investors was increased by Nigeria, which accelerated economic disengagement from South Africa by compelling Western multinationals to make a choice between doing business with Nigeria or South Africa, but not both. Oil and its huge potential market made Nigeria an increasingly attractive trading partner.

South Africa, on the other hand, was increasingly on the defensive. The US Carter administration began to call for majority rule in South Africa. Then Soviet President Podgorny visited Zambia, Tanzania and Mozambique to emphasize the growing Soviet influence and interest in the region. In the light of this steadily more hostile external environment, the government began to seek internal allies and endeavoured to split the Coloured and Asian communities away from the Africans by offering separate parliaments for the two groups, a policy that reached its climax, or rather nadir, in 1984. The way the young Black Consciousness leader, Steve Biko, was treated by the police in custody aroused world condemnation. He died of brain injuries after being transported in a police vehicle 800 miles, naked and in manacles, in September 1977. Despite, or perhaps because of, this outcry, the government went in for further repression in October when the Christian Institute and 17 other organizations including the Black Consciousness Movement were suppressed. Fifty of their leaders were detained and two publications that catered for an African readership – *The World* and *The Weekend World* – were banned. A defiant Vorster rejected all outside pressures and pursued an increasingly tough line against any opposition. The white opposition was divided. The old United Party finally collapsed, some of its members joining the Progressive Party, which renamed itself the Progressive Federal Party, while the majority of UP members regrouped under the banner of the New Republic Party. Hertzog's HNP found itself outflanked by Vorster's ultra-tough line. Despite all the setbacks, Vorster won a landslide majority in the November 1977 elections. During the last years of the decade (1977–80), although there were no new eruptions comparable to Soweto, black rejection of government policies became more obvious and more open and, for example, the election for a government-sponsored Community Council in Soweto attracted a derisory turnout of only six per cent. Chief Buthelezi, meanwhile, had linked his Zulu cultural and political movement, Inkatha, with the Coloured Labour Party and the Indian Reform Party to form the South Africa Black Alliance, which called for a multiracial convention to devise a new constitution for a non-racial South Africa. In May 1978 the radical Azania People's Organization was founded.

Defence became central to all government planning. The South African military budget had grown in proportion as pressures were mounted upon the Republic. In 1960 the military budget stood at R44 million; by 1966–67 R255 million; by 1974–75 R500 million, this latter rise reflecting the armed struggles in Angola, Mozambique and Rhodesia. By 1977 the budget had leapt to R1,300 million and by 1978 to R2,280 million. Following Zimbabwe's independence in 1980 it went up again to R2,465 million. Writing in *The Times* at the beginning of the 1970s, Dan van der Vat said that South Africa's armed forces were the most powerful military machine in Africa south of the Sahara. Apart from a non-combatant Coloured Corps, recruitment and conscription were confined to whites whose ultimate role was the preservation by force of white rule in the face of an internal black uprising. At that time South Africa's aim for self-sufficiency in arms had nearly been achieved; only warships and long-range reconnaissance planes had to be imported from either Britain or France. The Defence Force relied upon three layers of recruitment: the Permanent Force (10,000 Army, 5,000 Air Force and 3,000 Navy); the Citizen Force of conscripts who had to serve 9–12 months and then went onto an active reserve – at any time the Army had 22,000 Citizen Force conscripts serving with it (the Air Force 3,000 and the Navy 1,250); and finally, the Kommando Force of about 78,000 who trained at weekends and held annual camps.[39] The suspicion persisted all through the 1970s that there were secret, informal links between NATO and South Africa, which was one way Western countries such as Britain, France and West Germany could assist South Africa indirectly. During the decade South Africa built up its nuclear capacity with Western (US) and Israeli assistance. In 1976 the then President of the South African Atomic Energy Board, Dr A. J. A. Roux, said, 'We can ascribe our degree of advancement today in large measure to the training and assistance so willingly provided by the US during the early years of our nuclear programme, when several of the Western world's nuclear nations co-operated in initiating our scientists and engineers into nuclear science... even our nuclear philosophy, although unmistakably our own, owes much to the thinking of American nuclear scientists.'[40] On 22 September 1979 South Africa exploded a nuclear device in the Southern Atlantic. The US State Department asserted that it had 'no corroborating evidence' to verify the explosion and 'no independent evidence' to link it to South Africa. As defence became an increasing burden once the cordon sanitaire had disappeared while growing internal unrest meant ever more 'policing', so the government was obliged to depend more and more upon black troops. The SADF, under Gen. Magnus Malan, called for a total strategy for survival and the General hinted at the need to change social policies. At the end of the decade the length of call-up for white youths was extended while the possibility of military service for women was discussed. South Africa's long hostile borders now allowed increased infiltration by guerrillas, forcing the government to deploy anti-insurgency units along extensive stretches of its borders with Botswana, Mozambique and Swaziland.

By 1976 South Africa was deeply affected by the world recession that had assisted the rise of black unemployment to 600,000 or 12 per cent of the total black labour force, while foreign investors were beginning to avoid South Africa as an investment destination. Examining the 1977 South African budget, introduced by the Finance Minister Owen Horwood, *The Economist* said: 'Buried within Mr Horwood's public borrowing figures, there is an assumption that shows dramatically South Africa's economic plight today: for the first time in recent years, the government recognizes it cannot bank on inflows of foreign capital. The reasons can be spelled out only too starkly: Angola 1975, Soweto 1976. In the past the Republic could count on an average net inflow of capital of c. 3% of GNP each year, worth about US$1 billion at today's prices... Now South Africans will have to learn to live with only the thinnest trickle of foreign capital...'[41]

Vorster's long political reign ended in the far-reaching scandal of Muldergate. Following newspaper allegations of unauthorized expenditure by the Department of Information, made in June 1978, the Director of Information, Dr Eschel Rhoodie, resigned. Connie Mulder, one of the most powerful figures in the government who was expected to succeed Vorster, was the Minister of Information and he too resigned although retaining his other portfolio of Plural Relations. On 20 September Vorster announced that he was to resign as Prime Minister on health grounds and seek election as State President. In the contest for the leadership of the NP that followed, Mulder, who stood, was weakened by the allegations of corruption in the Information Ministry, and was defeated by P. W. Botha, the Minister of Defence, who became Prime Minister on 28 September. Meanwhile, a one-man Commission of Inquiry by Justice Anton Mostert, ignoring a request not to do so by the Prime Minister, held a press conference to allege that there had been improper expenditure of millions of rand by the Information Department. This statement forced Mulder to resign from the cabinet. It was followed by the appointment of a judicial Commission of Inquiry under Justice R. P. Erasmus. The Erasmus Commission delivered its first report in December 1978 to reveal that the Ministry of Information had deployed huge sums of money in a secret operation to gain control of the English-language newspaper group, South African Associated News. This effort had failed; however, even more money had been spent secretly to establish a pro-government English language newspaper, *The Citizen*. The operation was extended to obtain influence in various US, UN and other overseas publications.

This first report placed the main blame on Mulder, who then had to resign his parliamentary seat, Gen. Hendrik van den Bergh, the recently retired head of BOSS, and Dr Rhoodie, who fled to Europe. Further investigations compromised Vorster and the members of his cabinet. From hiding in Europe, Dr Rhoodie gave a BBC TV interview in which he produced a photocopy of a document authorizing these secret expenditures, signed by the Finance Minister, Owen Horwood. Rhoodie also insisted that Vorster had known of the operations. The second Erasmus report exonerated Vorster but failed to kill the allegations and Mulder was obliged to resign his membership of the Transvaal National Party. Finally, in June 1979, the third Erasmus report was leaked to the press; it stated that Vorster had 'full knowledge of all irregularities' of the Department of Information activities. This proved the end of the Vorster era. He had been elected State President when Botha became Prime Minister in September 1978. On 4 June 1979 he resigned, totally compromised by the Muldergate scandal that had devastated the NP. Dr Rhoodie was extradited from Europe back to South Africa, where he was tried and briefly imprisoned. The scandal died at the end of 1979; Botha by then was firmly ensconced as Prime Minister.

The three 'outward' policies that Vorster had essayed over the decade had failed in turn. The dialogue of the early 1970s had not worked because, whereas Vorster wanted to persuade black Africa to come to terms with South Africa, black Africa had only been prepared to enter into a dialogue about dismantling apartheid. *Détente* had not worked for the same reason. The front-line states, especially Zambia, wanted *détente* to lift the economic and physical strains of confrontation, but not on South Africa's terms, which again – effectively – were to accept the apartheid state. Thirdly, Vorster had switched to military intervention in Angola. This proved a disaster for South Africa although, wisely, Vorster had never committed South Africa's full military strength to the intervention. Yet, although Angola represented a huge rebuff, this did not prevent South Africa embarking upon a policy of destabilizing its neighbours through the 1980s. It was a policy of despair, for despite South Africa's preponderant strength in relation to its neighbours, to exist in a state of perpetual tension with black Africa to its north meant permanent isolation on the continent to which, in other circumstances, South Africa had so much to contribute.

Prime Minister Botha faced the 1980s presiding over a very different NP and South Africa than the apparently inviolable white regime Vorster had come to rule in the 1970s. A final twist to the decade came on 18 April 1980 when Rhodesia became Zimbabwe under Robert Mugabe.

The Decade in Retrospect

The 1970s witnessed substantial advances in African self-confidence as a number of African countries forged their own development paths while making it plain to the former colonial powers that while they were prepared for amicable and mutually satisfying two-way relations, they did not intend to be dominated by them, either politically or economically. Such intentions were easier to proclaim than to maintain. The Cold War became a major factor in two African theatres: the Horn, where US and Soviet rivalry and readiness to switch sides between Ethiopia and Somalia ensured that a regional war became an international confrontation; and in Southern Africa, where the collapse of the Portuguese Empire brought the ubiquitous Henry Kissinger onto the scene as a would-be political fixer, and raised the stakes in Angola to the level of another superpower confrontation. Elsewhere in Africa the politics of democracy and freedom from colonial oppression, which had seemed so exciting in the 1960s, gave way to the restrictions that came with the one-party state, rule by the military and the increasingly familiar dictator figures such as Amin, Bokassa, Nguema or Mengistu. Africa's problems were not made easier by the overbearing attitudes of the former metropolitan powers who, too often, seemed to be waiting for African initiatives to founder on inexperience or lack of expertise so that die-hards from the past could say, as they often did, 'I told you so, they were not ready for independence, we should have stayed longer.'

Some form of socialism was the obvious alternative to the systems bequeathed by the departing colonial powers and in at least two countries – Algeria and Tanzania – socialist development paths were adopted and appeared to be achieving remarkable breakthroughs towards the creation of greater equality for their societies. Elsewhere, socialist rhetoric was more in evidence than socialist policies though when these were tried they were too often frustrated, either by outside pressures from a West determined to keep Africa in its Cold War camp or by elites whose concern with power was personal rather than national. At least, during this decade, the outside world watched Africa, anxious to gauge its strengths and wary of it operating as a single continental block, though the dream of African unity remained a dream. Like other Third World countries, Africans embraced the concept of a New International Economic Order (NIEO) that emerged from the 1973 Yom Kippur War/OPEC crisis and for a few short years argued about new possibilities that would never be realized. By the end of the decade a new realism had emerged and the highly competent group of experts who produced *Africa 2000* condemned the narrow nationalisms that were emerging throughout the continent, arguing instead for collective action and a renunciation of the crippling dependence upon aid that was becoming so marked a feature of the continent's relationship with the developed countries.

Kwame Nkrumah, famously, had said, 'Seek ye first the political kingdom,' an injunction that had been eagerly and successfully followed but, far more uneasily through the 1970s, African leaders tried with less success to obtain control over their economic kingdoms. By the end of the decade, as adverse terms of trade, rising debt, rapidly increasing populations and limitations upon infrastructure drove most African countries to seek ever more aid, the donor nations of the West relaxed as they saw few chances that Africa would escape their economic controls, and the Brandt Report of 1980, with all its pious calls for a more equitable world, was little more than a Western-inspired public relations exercise to compensate for the West's ruthless despatch of the real egalitarianism contained in the NIEO concept.

The greatest changes occurred in the south of the continent, when in 1975 the Portuguese finally departed from Angola and Mozambique to destroy a military balance, which to that date had supported a status quo that worked in favour of the maintenance of apartheid in South Africa. Smith's Rhodesia then became expendable and Africa celebrated the emergence of an independent Zimbabwe in 1980. Above all, South Africa, whose apartheid regime appeared immovable in 1970, found by 1980, after a decade of shocks to its system, that it would face the new decade isolated in Africa and threatened with increasing hostility from its erstwhile Western supporters. South Africa was the most advanced economy on the continent; during the 1980s it would have to choose between maintaining rigid apartheid or developing its economy to its full potential, for the two policies were not compatible.

PART III

The 1980s

Basket Case?

Introduction to the Decade:
The OAU Tries to Cope

W hen the 1980s began there were 51 independent African states, the whole continent, save for Namibia which remained under South African control, yet the roll call of African states, which ought to have been a source of strength to the continent, hardly seemed so against the many problems that beset it. Crises would escalate, die down, then re-emerge. The year 1982, for example, was an especially fraught one. The Organisation of African Unity (OAU) witnessed a growing division among its members over the question of an independent Sahrawi Arab Democratic Republic (the former Spanish Sahara) and Morocco's claim to the territory. There was mounting African anger at the West's readiness to accommodate South Africa over Namibia and, more generally, over apartheid. And overshadowing everything else was the world recession whose impact upon the continent's weak economies deprived Africa of any room for political manoeuvre on the international stage. The majority of African economies were underdeveloped and were still heavily dependent upon external trade, investment and aid, and African leaders simply could not afford to quarrel with the West as the slump in commodity prices continued and they required Western economic assistance to survive, a fact that a manipulative West understood all too well. Despite virtual continent-wide independence, Africa was still struggling to free itself from the legacy of colonialism. The inherited colonial boundaries were to cause frictions between states while state structures that had been imposed by the departing colonial powers remained fragile and were often ignored or otherwise subverted by successor governments of doubtful legitimacy. The decade witnessed major armed conflicts, all of which were part of the ongoing unravelling of the colonial heritage.

Like the United Nations, its greater prototype, the OAU suffered from the same problems, although it had no Security Council and did not have to contend with big powers wielding a veto. It had to settle for the lowest common point of agreement: the perennial issue of creating an OAU defence force bore this out. Since its foundation the OAU had seen the fight against colonialism in all its forms as its primary task and to this end had established the Coordinating Committee for the Liberation of Africa, which was based in Dar es Salaam, Tanzania. The Committee's task was to assist the various liberation movements and, by the 1980s, especially those concerned with the white regimes in Southern Africa. At least the fight against colonialism, unlike other problems the OAU faced, was shared by all its members. With the collapse of the Portuguese African Empire in the mid-1970s, when first Guinea-Bissau, followed by Mozambique, Cape Verde, São Tomé and Principe, and finally Angola became independent, a total of 49 countries had achieved their freedom and 48 of them, but not South Africa, had joined the OAU. Then the Seychelles and Djibouti became independent in 1976 and 1977 respectively, but for another 13 years 'confrontation' by the front-line states with South Africa was to continue, although Zimbabwe became independent in 1980, 15 years after the Unilateral Declaration of Independence (UDI) by the Smith government in 1965. Finally, at the very end of the 1980s, Namibia would achieve its independence.

ECONOMIC PROBLEMS

During the 1970s and 1980s, despite confrontation between the front-line states and South Africa, the OAU paid increasing attention to Africa's economic weakness and the need for joint action to promote the continent's social, infrastructural and economic development, and to this end the OAU adopted a number of joint strategies and plans of action. The years 1973–75 had seen the fourfold increase in the price of oil, the rise of OPEC power (with its adverse economic impact upon Africa) and the United Nations Sixth Special Session held during May 1974 in Algiers, which launched the idea of a New International Economic Order (NIEO). The OAU, meanwhile, had launched its 1973 Declaration on Cooperation, Development and Economic Independence. This was followed, in 1979, by the Monrovia Strategy for Economic Development of Africa with its remarkably prescient accompanying paper, *Africa 2000*, leading to the 1980 Lagos Plan of Action.

These plans for continental action, unfortunately, were rarely translated into more concrete activities on the ground. There was no dearth of African politicians and intellectuals who saw what needed doing but their proposals were generally disregarded by individual countries whose development programmes were more narrowly focused. In 1986 the OAU produced its African Priority Programme for Economic Recovery. Africa's problem over these years was, quite simply, its poverty. There was no shortage of ideas about recovery or co-operation but in individual countries there was little capacity to mobilize resources and this was reflected more generally across the continent as a whole. Moreover, despite being the world's poorest region Africa did not remotely attract the amount of international support for reform that it required. Furthermore, the international community tended too often to see Africa as a politically troubled continent in which investment would be at risk. Against this background, African leaders met in Addis Ababa in 1990, at the end of the decade, to adopt a new declaration 'on the Fundamental Changes taking place in the World and their Implications for Africa: proposals for Africa's Response'. At this meeting in Addis Ababa Africa's leaders insisted that the continent's development was their responsibility (a recognition, in part at least, that the era of constant injections of aid was coming to an end). They stated their determination to rationalize the various economic groupings on the continent and establish an African Economic Community. This 1990 declaration represented a new step towards collective action on continental development and led to the 1991 Abuja Treaty Establishing the African Economic Community. These commitments sounded fine, yet in 1989 the United Nations Economic Commission for Africa warned: 'Africa may begin the next millennium with a greater proportion of its population being innumerate, illiterate and unskilled, than it did at the beginning of the post-independence era in the 1960s.'

WARS AND REFUGEES

Although economic problems usually dominated OAU considerations of continent-wide collaboration, human rights and Africa's apparently unstoppable wars were also cause for major concern. In January 1981 a meeting of Ministers of Justice approved an African Charter on Human and People's Rights, which, subject to ratification by a majority of OAU members, would establish a Commission to investigate violations of human rights. In July 1987 the Assembly of Heads of State approved the establishment of an African Commission on Human Rights, after the African Charter on Human and People's Rights (approved in 1981) had been ratified by a majority of member states. The range of Africa's wars witnessed endless human rights abuses and worked against the achievement of real unity and yet, perversely, strengthened an artificial sense of unity since African leaders were loath to criticize one another, thereby parading the continent's weakness to the outside world.

In the course of the decade at least a dozen African countries were troubled by civil wars or wars with their neighbours. Following the overthrow of Idi Amin in 1979, Uganda passed through a period of instability and civil war until

1986 when Yoweri Museveni emerged as victor over the civil strife in which more people had lost their lives than during the Amin decade. Throughout the 1980s South Africa pursued its 'destabilization' policy against its 'frontline' neighbours by launching periodic cross-border raids that included attacks into Angola, Botswana, Mozambique, Zambia and Zimbabwe. In Zimbabwe over the years 1982–87 Robert Mugabe entrenched his power, based upon his Mashona supporters, by carrying out what came to be called the 'Dissidents' War' as he broke the power of the Ndebele, the political base of his rival Joshua Nkomo. In 1984 the division between North and South in Sudan, that for a time President Nimeiri had managed to control, descended again into civil war, which this time round would continue to the end of the century. In Angola the 1987–88 battle of Cuito Cuanavale between the forces of the MPLA government, aided by the Cubans, and the forces of UNITA, aided by the South Africans, led to a humiliating retreat for the South Africans that was a defining event in the developments leading to Namibian independence and the 1990 decision of South Africa's President de Klerk to abandon apartheid. In August 1988 a fresh outbreak of killings (since those of the 1970s) occurred in Burundi; they affected the commune of Murangara in Ngozi Province, Ntegi in Kimundu Province and an estimated 10,000 people, mainly Hutus, in the Bujumbura area. The army was Tutsi-officered and all arms were under its control. About 65,000 Hutu refugees crossed into Rwanda. The relatively small scale of this uprising demonstrated the iron grip exercised over the country by the Tutsis at this time. The long-simmering discontents against the system that Siad Barre had imposed in Somalia came to a head in 1988 with the outbreak of a civil war that would lead to Barre's fall in 1991 and continue through the first half of the 1990s. In Liberia, at the end of the decade, the 10-year rule of Samuel Doe was brought to a brutal end as the little country became engulfed in a civil war that would last to 1997. Eritrea's war of secession from Ethiopia continued throughout the 1980s and by the end of the decade Eritrean persistence, aided by other defiance of Mengistu's rule through much of Ethiopia, had brought the secessionists appreciably closer to achieving their independence from Addis Ababa.

African rhetoric about the effects of colonialism, which continued through the 1970s and into the 1980s, often irritated the former metropolitan powers which accused Africans of blaming colonialism for problems of their own making. Sometimes this was true. Yet, too often, colonial decisions were at the root of problems that erupted many years after independence had been achieved. This was the case in relation to the short five-day war between Burkina Faso and Mali that occurred in December 1985. Upper Volta (later Burkina Faso) had been carved out of French West Africa by the French colonial authorities in

1919. In 1932, however, the territory was divided between its three colonial neighbours – Côte d'Ivoire, Mali and Niger. It was reconstructed as a single territory in 1947. As a result of this colonial division and restructuring Upper Volta's three neighbours each had its own interpretation of the border regions. From the year of independence in 1960 onwards Mali laid claim to the Agacher Strip, which had been allotted to Upper Volta and was believed to be rich in minerals. At the end of 1974 the Malian claim led to a border dispute between the two countries, diplomatic relations were broken off and Mali sent troops to occupy the Strip. During 1975 the OAU acted as mediator and apparently settled the dispute to Upper Volta's satisfaction. The dispute, however, continued to fester and the two countries did not resume diplomatic relations with one another. In 1983 the dispute was referred to the International Court of Justice (ICJ) at The Hague. The quarrel came to a head in 1985 (by which time Upper Volta had renamed itself Burkina Faso). Further African attempts at mediation followed and the Non-Aggression and Defence Aid Agreement (ANAD) of the *Communauté Economique de l'Afrique de l'Ouest* (CEAO) sent delegations to both countries to hear their cases and urge them to keep the peace. Algeria and Nigeria also attempted to mediate. Burkina Faso and Mali, however, prepared for war. Mali moved troops to the disputed area and a government official claimed, 'Our armed forces have done their duty.' On 25 December 1985 fighting between the troops of the two countries broke out along their joint border as both countries claimed the whole Agacher Strip. The fighting was sporadic but caused an estimated 300 deaths on both sides over five days. Burkina Faso announced that it had bombed the Malian town of Sikao and that its troops had destroyed four of Mali's tanks and routed its infantry. In its turn Burkina Faso suffered a Malian air raid on Ouahigouya where 13 people were killed and 35 wounded. Burkina Faso accused France of aiding Mali. Libya and Nigeria offered their services to mediate the dispute. Then in January 1986 President Sankara of Burkina Faso and President Traoré of Mali were reconciled at an ANAD summit held in Yamoussoukro, Côte d'Ivoire, where heads of state of Niger, Mauritania, Senegal and Togo, as well as President Houphouët-Boigny of Côte d'Ivoire, the host, brokered a peace. Burkina Faso and Mali agreed to withdraw their troops from the border region. They each administered part of the disputed territory while they waited for a judgment from the ICJ. This was delivered in December 1986: the Court ruled that the Agacher Strip should be divided equally between the two countries and both were satisfied. In this instance the neighbours of the two disputing countries had acted with commendable speed to end the conflict.

In 1970 there were about one million refugees in Africa, by 1980 three and a half million. Then, during the 1980s, the figure rose steadily, reflecting the continued disturbed state of Africa until by the end of the decade the number of refugees had reached five million, equivalent to a third of the world's total refugee population. This figure was regarded as conservative. In addition, an estimated 10 million people were displaced within their own countries. All the principal causes leading to large numbers of refugees were present: political instability and civil wars, persecutions, droughts, famines and floods. As a consequence, Africa had become a major target for relief activities by the United Nations High Commission for Refugees (UNHCR) and other non-government organizations (NGOs); even so, only about 40 per cent of the continent's refugees received international assistance. Many refugees who fled from war situations came to areas that lacked resources of food and water or the infrastructure that would enable them to be properly serviced.

Throughout the decade the countries of the Horn – Ethiopia, Eritrea, Somalia and Sudan – were beset by both civil and interstate wars while the Ethiopian policy of resettlement and villageization led hundreds of thousands of people to flee from new environments to which they could not adjust. The heavy fighting in Eritrea and the Tigray Province of Ethiopia led to further massive migrations and these were made worse by drought conditions. Yet even as Ethiopia's problems led to a mass exodus of its people, a large contra-flow of refugees from the wars in Sudan and Somalia entered Ethiopia. In 1989, according to UNHCR records, there were 385,000 Sudanese and 355,000 Somalis registered as refugees in Ethiopia and of these 45,000 Sudanese and 6,000 Somalis arrived in the country during that year. By the end of the decade the civil war in Sudan had created some 2.8 million displaced persons within the country and a further 425,000 refugees in Ethiopia and Uganda. Tackling such a vast human problem was never easy and relief efforts often collapsed because of poor logistics, lack of available resources or attacks upon relief columns. For example, a UN relief effort 'Operation Lifeline' brought temporary relief to 100,000 Sudanese in the South who were close to starvation before the effort had to be abandoned in late 1989 because of persistent attacks on the relief columns. At the same time that it faced these problems, Sudan itself became the principal destination for Eritrean and Tigrayan refugees fleeing the effects of both war and famine. By the late 1980s there were an estimated 663,000 Ethiopian refugees in Sudan and of these only about half (349,000) were in reception centres assisted by the UNHCR while the remainder had settled themselves along the border or had found their way to urban centres such as Khartoum. Sudan was also the recipient of refugees from the civil war in Chad with as many as 120,000 in the mid-1980s though the figure had dropped to no more than 24,000 by the end of the decade while in the far south some 63,000 refugees from Uganda had been received and subsequently repatriated.

The civil war in Somalia gathered pace during 1988 to create a new flood of refugees in the Horn: about 355,000 moved into Ethiopia while others who fled to Djibouti in the north or Kenya in the south were treated harshly and in some cases forcibly repatriated. Both countries discouraged refugees from entering the neighbouring territory, forced them to return to Somalia or refused to accord them refugee status. Some Somalis fled from Kenya to Uganda or Tanzania to avoid being deported back to Somalia. At the same time there were large numbers of Ethiopian refugees in Somalia – they had mostly been there throughout the decade – though their numbers were disputed since the Somali government inflated the figures in order to obtain maximum relief supplies while independent observers downgraded the numbers. Thus, while the Somali government claimed assistance from the UNHCR and the World Food Programme for 840,000 refugees, most qualified observers suggested less than half that figure was the true number, between 350,000 and 365,000 since up to 400,000 of the original refugees had voluntarily repatriated themselves to Ethiopia.

As a result of Museveni's triumph in Uganda where he restored central government and peace, about 320,000 Ugandan refugees decided to return home although another 300,000 had been displaced internally; continuing rebel activity ensured constant internal displacements. In its turn Uganda was host to 50,000 refugees from Sudan and a further 118,000 from Rwanda although many of the latter had been living in Uganda since the 1950s. Tanzania was a generous host country to refugees and in the late 1980s had more than 265,000. They came from Burundi, Rwanda, Mozambique, Zaïre and South Africa. Although they were provided with settlements the government encouraged them to develop self-sufficiency. The largest group consisted of 156,000 Hutus from Burundi, which they had fled in the wake of the 1972 massacres. Some of the most recent incomers into Tanzania at this time were from Mozambique, which they had fled since the mid-1980s to escape the RENAMO war.

The Resistencia Nacional Mocambicana (RENAMO), Mozambique National Resistance, fought against the *Frente da Libertaço de Mocambique* (FRELIMO) government which came to power in Mozambique in 1975 through to the peace of 1992. Then, in 1994, RENAMO took part in nationwide elections. RENAMO was set up in 1975/76 by Ken Flower, the head of the Central Intelligence Organization (CIO) in Salisbury, Rhodesia, under the illegal Ian Smith government, as a means of destabilizing the new FRELIMO government that supported the Zimbabwe African National Union (ZANU), which then maintained a number of base camps in Mozambique. The original members of RENAMO were recruited from Mozambicans who had fled from the war into Rhodesia. When Rhodesia became independent as Zimbabwe in 1980, the new government of Robert Mugabe at once withdrew support from RENAMO, but by then Flower had already persuaded the South African government to take responsibility for supporting RENAMO, which it was willing to do since it saw the movement as a means of destabilizing its neighbour.

The disturbed state of Southern Africa through the 1980s – South Africa's policy of destabilizing its neighbours, civil wars in Angola and Mozambique, the Dissidents' War in Zimbabwe and the continuing liberation struggle in Namibia – between them contributed to create large numbers of refugees in the region, both within countries affected by this strife and across borders. By the end of the decade, as increasing cracks in the apartheid system developed, exiles began to return and hopes were raised that relocated people would soon be able to return to their former areas within South Africa. The biggest source of refugees in Southern Africa was Mozambique, which, throughout the decade, was torn by the RENAMO war. Casualties from this war were horrific: at least 100,000 were killed, a further 500,000 died of starvation while many thousands were maimed. By the end of 1989 about 1.3 million Mozambicans had fled to other countries to escape the war. In April 1990 it was estimated that 4.3 million people had become dependent on foreign humanitarian aid and of these, two million were displaced within Mozambique with 500,000 of them inaccessible to relief efforts because they were isolated by RENAMO forces. At the beginning of 1990 Malawi was host to 812,000 Mozambican exiles most of whom had arrived in the country since 1986; during 1989 they had been arriving at the rate of 15,000 a month and represented a huge burden for one of Africa's poorest countries. Swaziland was also host to 28,000 Mozambicans by the end of the decade while another 60,000 had resettled themselves along its border. Another 78,000 refugees had crossed into Zimbabwe. In Angola on the other side of the continent the war between the MPLA government and UNITA led to massive dislocation, high casualties and large numbers of internal and external refugees. As the war intensified from 1985 onwards some 438,000 Angolans became refugees in neighbouring countries while a further 638,000 rural people were displaced within Angola. In addition, another 400,000 rural dwellers were prevented from farming because of the conflict and so became dependent upon food aid and about the same number moved to urban areas where they settled in 'vertical' shanty towns of poor apartment blocks. The war displaced about two million Angolans, or one fifth of the population, with neighbouring Zaïre and Zambia receiving the highest number of refugees. More encouraging was the planned return of Namibians to their country when in 1989 it became clear that independence was at last about to be achieved. Following the US-brokered settlement of 1989 a mass repatriation of Namibian refugees got under way: 33,000 from Angola, 3,700 from Zambia, 1,600 from Cuba and the balance from some 40 other countries.

There were further refugee problems in West Africa: Algeria (in the Tindouf area) was host to refugees from the war between Morocco and the POLISARIO in Western Sahara; the border dispute between Senegal farmers and Mauritanian pastoralists uprooted 255,000 people of whom 65,000 became refugees, while 90,000 Senegalese in Mauritania and 100,000 Mauritanians in Senegal were returned to their countries of origin even though many of them had been living in the other country for years. The civil war in Liberia that started in 1989 had produced 180,000 refugees by April 1990. The upheavals resulting from these refugee movements created enormous economic burdens throughout the continent.[1]

PARTICULAR CONFLICTS

Throughout the 1980s certain conflicts demanded and obtained a great deal of attention from the OAU or neighbouring states though all too often with little apparent success; lack of success in resolving these conflicts had more to do with their intractable nature than incompetence on the part of would-be mediators. The root cause of these conflicts – in Western Sahara, Chad, Namibia, South Africa – could be traced back to the pre-independence dispositions made by the colonial powers.

The seventeenth Assembly of Heads of State, due to meet in July 1980, postponed a decision on admitting the Sahrawi Arab Democratic Republic (SADR), which had been proclaimed by POLISARIO (Popular Front for the Liberation of Saguia el Hamra and Rio de Oro) in Western Sahara (former Spanish Sahara) which was claimed by Morocco after Morocco threatened to leave the OAU if any such recognition were granted. In September 1980 the OAU Committee on Western Sahara announced a six-point ceasefire plan to include a referendum to be organized by the OAU assisted by the United Nations. In June 1981, at the Eighteenth Assembly of Heads of State, Morocco agreed to hold a referendum in Western Sahara. In February 1982 the Committee on Western Sahara empowered President Daniel arap Moi of Kenya to conduct negotiations for a ceasefire between Morocco and POLISARIO. However, at a meeting of the Ministers of Foreign Affairs, the admission of a representative of the SADR prompted a walkout by 19 countries. Then, during March and April 1982, the ordinary business of the OAU was disrupted because boycotts by supporters and opponents of POLISARIO meant that three ministerial meetings lacked a quorum of members and subsequent discussions by a special group of nine countries failed to resolve the deadlock. The dispute was to disrupt the working of the OAU throughout 1982 and the Nineteenth Assembly of Heads of State that was to be held in Tripoli, Libya, had to be abandoned when it failed to achieve a quorum due to the boycott by 19 states. A five-member committee was set up to try to convene another summit before the end of the year but only in June 1983 did the Nineteenth Assembly finally convene in Addis Ababa. The SADR representatives agreed not to attend in order to avoid a boycott of the meeting by their opponents although they said they would attend the next Assembly of Heads of State. The Assembly repeated its call for a referendum to be held in Western Sahara and for direct negotiations between Morocco and SADR. The Twentieth Assembly was held in Addis Ababa during November 1984 and Nigeria then became the thirtieth OAU member to recognize the SADR, thus giving the SADR the necessary majority, and a delegation representing the SADR was admitted to the Assembly. Morocco immediately withdrew from the OAU (the withdrawal to take effect after a year) and Zaïre gave its support to Morocco by also withdrawing from the meeting. The dispute highlighted the weakness of the OAU. A powerful member – Morocco – that was transgressing the key OAU principle of self-determination for its own 'imperial' reasons of aggrandisement, was not able to exercise a veto, so it simply resigned from the organization. It did not rejoin and the SADR dispute was to continue with equally ineffective UN mediation attempts to resolve it until the end of the century.

The civil war between north and south in Chad also occupied the OAU through the decade. This war was hugely complicated by the interventions of Libya and France, the former intervening in the north where it aimed to annex the uranium-rich Aozou Strip, and the latter assisting the official government in the south in order to prevent Libya's Gaddafi obtaining a stranglehold on the country. As in other such wars these interventions prolonged the conflict rather than solving it. In January 1981 the OAU held a conference to consider the relations between Chad and Libya; it condemned Gaddafi's proposal that the two countries should merge and demanded the withdrawal of all foreign forces from Chad (Libyan and French) and decided to send an African force to maintain peace and subsequently to supervise elections. In November 1981 the first members of the OAU peacekeeping force, consisting of troops from Nigeria, Senegal and Zaïre – arrived in Chad to replace the Libyan troops which had been supporting the government against the opposition. In February 1982 the OAU Committee on Chad established a timetable for a ceasefire, negotiations, a provisional constitution and elections in Chad, and announced that the OAU peacekeeping force's mandate would be terminated at the end of June.

The long-running Chad dispute had wider repercussions for the OAU whose well-meaning attempts at mediation did little to bring the conflict to an end or prevent Libyan and French intervention. Chad, as well as the SADR, caused the abandonment of the Nineteenth Assembly of Heads of State due to be held in Tripoli, Libya, in November 1982 since there was a dispute as to who should represent Chad. Gaddafi opposed the presence of President Hissène Habré in favour of the former Chad President, Goukouni Oueddei, but this led 14 moderate states to boycott the meeting. Talks held in Addis Ababa by the rival Chad factions in January 1984 came to nothing, mainly because of the refusal to attend by President Habré. In July 1986 the OAU resolved to continue efforts under the OAU Chairman to bring about a reconciliation between the parties in Chad and to further this aim a council of 'wise men', comprising former African heads of state, was established to mediate, when necessary, in disputes between member countries. In July 1987 the OAU renewed the mandate of the special OAU committee, which had been attempting to resolve the dispute between Chad and Libya, and called a meeting for 24 May 1988 to discuss the sovereignty of the Aozou region. On the eve of the summit, however, Col. Gaddafi, who had boycotted all previous OAU ad hoc meetings, announced that he would not attend. Then on 25 May Gaddafi announced that he was willing to recognize the Habré regime in Chad. Following mediation by Togo, Chad and Libya issued a joint statement on 3 October 1988 expressing their willingness to seek a peaceful solution to their territorial dispute and to co-operate with the OAU committee that had been appointed for the purpose. By the end of the decade it appeared likely that Gaddafi and Habré would come to more or less amicable terms but this was not to be since in November 1990 Habré was forced to flee from Chad when Idriss Deby took power.

Although it made pronouncements about Namibia the OAU had little impact upon events there for the South African grip on the territory was as firm as ever when the 1980s began. In response to a situation it had little power to alter, an OAU meeting of Ministers of Foreign Affairs of February 1981 supported proposals for an intensified guerrilla war by SWAPO in the Caprivi Strip while calling for mandatory sanctions against South Africa to persuade the Pretoria government to negotiate on Namibian independence. In reality, developments in Namibia depended upon the United Nations and the Western Contact Group and when in 1989 the situation had at last changed sufficiently for the United Nations to prepare a UN Transition Assistance Group (UNTAG) to supervise the independence process, the immediate OAU contribution to the process, in February, was for its Council of Ministers to criticize the UN Security Council's decision to limit the size of UNTAG. Then, in July, the Assembly of Heads of State urged the UN to ensure that the coming Namibian elections would be fairly conducted. After some cliff-hanging crises Namibia did become independent in March 1990 but it was a US/UN achievement and the OAU contribution had never been more than marginal.

Throughout the 1980s, as events unfolded in Southern Africa, the pressures of the front-line states, the wars in Angola, Mozambique and Namibia and the widening gap that was becoming ever more apparent between the demands of an expanding South African economy, essential to the country's development, and the rigid demands of apartheid that were totally incompatible, constituted between them the real forces for change. That change was finally signalled in 1990 first by President de Klerk's speech of 2 February when he unbanned the ANC and then on 21 March when Namibia became independent. In the preceding 10 years, however, South Africa had pursued its policy of destabilization against its neighbours with cross-border raids that, apparently, demonstrated its overwhelming military and regional hegemony. Destabilization had a disastrous impact upon both Angola and Mozambique, where it reinforced the wars in those two countries and made any meaningful economic progress impossible. The repeated RENAMO attacks upon the Beira Corridor as a supply line to Zimbabwe made that country increasingly dependent upon South Africa. In response to these South African tactics the Southern African states were obliged to increase their military expenditure through the decade and remained vulnerable to South African raids and economic pressures. Apartheid and the consequent confrontation between South Africa and its neighbours acted as major impediments to economic development in the region. In May 1986 the Twenty-second Assembly of Heads of State of the OAU called for comprehensive economic sanctions against South Africa, and strongly criticized the governments of the United Kingdom and the United States for opposing sanctions. In February 1987 the OAU Chairman, President Sassou-Nguesso of Congo, undertook a tour of Europe to discuss the possibility of a negotiated settlement in Chad, the political situation in South Africa and African debt. In July 1987, once again, the Assembly of Heads of State reiterated its demands that Western countries should impose economic sanctions on South Africa. These and comparable OAU initiatives served only to emphasize Africa's inability to take decisive action to solve its problems and its continuing dependence upon the former colonial powers and the United States to exert pressures for change. Following de Klerk's dramatic speech of February 1990 and the real possibilities for change that had suddenly opened up, the OAU set up a monitoring group to report on events in South Africa and urged the international community to continue imposing sanctions upon South Africa.

Where the conflicts were on a smaller scale and major external powers were not involved, the OAU had a greater chance of mediating successfully, as it attempted in the conflict between Mauritania and Senegal that erupted in 1989.

Following a border incident in April Mauritanians resident in Senegal (there were an estimated 300,000) were attacked and their businesses ransacked. Similar attacks were then made against Senegalese in Mauritania where some 30,000 resided. By early May 1989 several hundred people, mainly Senegalese, had been killed in Mauritania. Later that May the Chairman of the OAU, President Traoré of Mali, undertook a mission of mediation to try to resolve the ethnic conflict that had arisen between the two countries. In September the newly elected OAU Chairman, Hosni Mubarak of Egypt, and the newly appointed Secretary-General of the OAU, Salim Ahmed Salim, attempted to mediate and in November a mediation committee comprising representatives of six countries visited Mauritania and Senegal. Further OAU attempts at mediation were initiated in early 1990 but these were cut short by military action on the Mauritania–Senegal border. Later initiatives were equally unsuccessful and by July 1990 all transport links as well as telephone links between the two countries had been suspended. As with so many conflicts mediation was not supported by power to enforce a solution.

ECONOMIC QUESTIONS

Awareness of the continent's economic weakness was a matter of abiding concern to the OAU throughout the decade. At its May 1980 summit the OAU had resolved to take steps towards the establishment of an African Common Market by the year 2000 and adopted the Lagos Plan of Action as a move in this direction. In November 1984 the OAU Assembly concentrated its attention upon economic matters: it discussed Africa's balance of payments problems, debts and the drought which was affecting many countries. An emergency fund was established to combat the effects of drought and initial contributions were made to it of US$10 million each by Algeria and Nigeria. In July 1985 the Twenty-first Assembly of Heads of State was held in Addis Ababa and devoted its time to economic topics. The result was the Addis Ababa Declaration in which members reiterated their commitment to the Lagos Plan of Action. They adopted a priority programme to cover the next five years and emphasized the need to rehabilitate African agriculture, agreeing to increase agriculture's share of public investment to between 20 and 25 per cent by the year 1989. The meeting also expressed its concern at Africa's heavy external debt, which was expected to reach a total of US$170,000 million by the end of the year, and called for a special conference of creditors and borrowers to seek a solution to the problem and an increase in concessional finance resources. In May 1986, at a special session of the UN General Assembly called to consider the economic problems of Africa, the OAU, represented by its Chairman, presented a programme prepared jointly with the ECA calling for debt relief and an increase in assistance for agricultural investment. By November 1987, when a summit was held in Addis Ababa, Africa's external debt was estimated at US$200,000 million. This meeting, though only attended by 10 heads of state and government, issued a statement requesting the conversion into grants of past bilateral loans and a 10-year suspension of debt service payments, reduction of interest rates and the lengthening of debt maturity periods. The meeting also asked that creditors should observe the principle that debt servicing should not exceed a 'reasonable and bearable' percentage of a debtor country's export earnings. A contact group was established to enlist support for an international conference on African debt. However, the Assembly recognized that no conference on debt was likely to be held until 1989, owing to the reluctance of creditors to participate.

In July 1989 the Assembly of Heads of State again requested that an international conference on Africa's debts should be held. The Assembly reviewed the implications for Africa of recent socio-economic and political changes in Eastern Europe, and of the European Community's progress towards monetary and political union. Addressing the fiftieth ordinary session of the Council of Ministers in Addis Ababa in July 1989, the chairman (Zimbabwe's Foreign Minister) Nathan Shamuyarira, said: 'We would like to feel that the steps we have outlined and the measures proposed will play an important part in consolidating our economies and making sure that the decade of the 1990s is not lost like the decade of the 1980s as far as economic development is concerned.' At the close of the 1989 summit, Egypt's President Hosni Mubarak referred to Africa's foreign debt, which by the end of 1988 had surpassed US$230,000 million, representing 24 per cent of its total income, and called for an international conference to discuss the crisis confronting the continent.

THE NORTH-SOUTH INTERFACE

By the mid-1980s development prospects in Africa, especially in the vulnerable Sahel and equatorial regions, appeared at best to be at a standstill, at worst to be in accelerating decline. The question was, why? World recession during the decade had had a devastating impact on fragile economies largely dependent upon commodity exports while the small size of most African economies provided them with scant room to manoeuvre or resources to fall back upon in bad times. Further, African development strategies were often over-ambitious and over-rigid. Moreover, they had usually been planned by outsiders, who took too little account of local conditions, and were over-dependent upon income derived from particular export staples. Much of this income was not ploughed back into the economy but used for ruling elite purposes such as presidential grandeur or unnecessary and often ultimately dangerous military establishments. International aid had become a major problem: partly because donors too often insisted that it should be channelled into developments that suited their views of how Africa should develop; still more because, by the 1980s, aid had come to be seen as a permanent addition to national budgets and was in consequence relied upon so that it developed a dependency attitude that undermined real efforts to achieve self-reliance; and, most insidious, because corrupt rulers and their elites regarded aid not as a means of development so much as a resource to bolster their hold on power since it enabled them to tax their people less and have a scapegoat when developments went wrong.

Other factors weakened Africa's ability to deal with crises: these included the results of coups and political corruption and pyramidal hierarchies that referred all decisions to the head of state. The independence of judiciaries was undermined, ministers were not restrained but often acted as laws to themselves, while the freedom of the press which had been so vital to the earlier independence struggles was progressively shackled by governments that only wanted the media to act as mouthpieces for the official line. These processes, moreover, were readily assisted by Western (and sometimes Soviet) support for dictatorial regimes on the ostensible grounds that Africa was 'different' and needed strong governments but in reality because dictatorial regimes were more likely to safeguard their interests in return. In any case, power-hungry elites, whether civilian or military, were uninterested in development as such but only in manipulating the system to maintain their grip on power. There were exceptions – Nyerere in Tanzania, Masire in Botswana, Kaunda in Zambia, Rawlings in Ghana – but the corruption of power for its own sake had become pervasive through most of the continent. Thus, the high rhetoric of the 1960s had changed into a 'big brother' syndrome that elevated national leaders above the law.

The deteriorating economic position of Africa as a whole can be illustrated by the decline in food production for personal consumption: 'By 1984 per caput production of food for own consumption had fallen, on official estimates, to little more than 75 per cent of the average quantities produced for the market in 1960–65. A still largely agrarian continent was reduced, for the first time in history, to helpless dependence on food imports, and for those imports it could no longer afford to pay.'[2] Debt escalated through the decade and African countries accumulated ever more loans from abroad, often at very high rates of interest. The result was an ever-rising debt-service ratio (the percentage of export earnings which have to be used to service foreign debt before export earnings can be used to buy imports) from a reasonable 4.6 per cent in 1974 to a huge 20.3 per cent in 1983 and this ratio continued to rise for the rest of the decade. A further burden arose out of the high rate of population increase, often as much as three per cent or more a year. This level of increase placed added strains upon all aspects of development, not least on food resources at a time when food production for home consumption was declining. Some governments and leaders worked hard to overcome the impact of these trends; others appeared to accept them as the lot of the continent. Too often leaders appeared unable or unwilling to grapple with these obstacles and focused their attention upon international rather than home developments.

Africa's ability to tackle its development problems was often undermined by the attitudes of the developed world, and most particularly the former colonial powers, whose interests were best served, as they believed, by creating and maintaining a dependence mentality. The terms of trade between Africa and the developed world remained one of deepening inequality or 'unequal exchange' to Africa's disadvantage. Thus, while in 1972 Tanzania could buy a seven-ton truck for 38 metric tons of sisal, by 1982 it had to pay 134 metric tons of sisal for the same truck. Throughout the decade wealth extracted from Africa was greater than inputs of wealth, whether in the form of payments, investment or aid. In any case, the 1980s witnessed a new world 'conflict' of which Africa was only a part whereby the wealth disparities between the rich developed countries of the North and the poor, mainly ex-colonial territories of the South steadily widened. Indeed, the coming North-South confrontation emerged with increasing clarity during the decade. It was highlighted by the African-European relationship because of the sharp and growing power disparity between the two and because the richest nations seemed totally disinclined to close the gap; rather, they appeared to want to maintain the gap since the alternative of assisting Africa to close it would lessen their own influence and power.

AN UNEASY DECADE

Summarizing the 1980s, Colin Legum wrote: 'After a disappointing decade, the Organisation of African Unity began to turn a corner in mid-1990. It saw the approaching end of its long struggle in support of Namibia's independence and more dramatically, the beginning of the end of Apartheid in South Africa. These two developments promised the fulfilment of the OAU's commitment at its founding in 1963 to achieve the complete liberation of the continent from colonial and White minority rule. After mediocre leadership for a decade, the new Secretary-General, Salim Ahmed Salim, Tanzania's former Foreign Minister, who had been elected by a convincing majority in his contest with

Oumarou, the incumbent, lost little time in stamping his authority on a somewhat moribund organization.'[3] However, the decade's ongoing problems were still very much alive and included: Chad and Libya, Mauritania and Senegal, the SADR dispute (with Morocco remaining outside the OAU), the civil wars in Sudan, Angola and Mozambique. The outgoing Secretary-General, Ide Oumarou, denied that the OAU was in 'deep trouble', as suggested in many quarters, but admitted the organization did not have sufficient credibility with regard to political instability in a number of African countries. He claimed that the OAU could have a more active role in 'the management of conflict situations' in the wake of the East–West rapprochment that heralded the end of the Cold War. However, he added, Africa's problems originated mainly from within the continent: 'If we sought internal solutions then we could solve or soften the impact of foreign intervention in our conflicts.' At the 1989 OAU summit the idea that the organization should establish an African Defence Force was raised once again – the concept had become something of a hardy perennial – but sufficient delegates opposed the idea to make it a non-starter. On this occasion, President Daniel arap Moi of Kenya roundly condemned the idea: 'As far as I am concerned this is a dream. Why? Because before we Kenyans and Nigerians agreed to send observers and troops, the OAU pledged it would pay, but the result was that the Kenyans and Nigerians were to foot the bill. The OAU did not pay a single cent.' The problem was a familiar one. Like the idea of a Defence Force, the OAU Defence Committee, primarily concerned with co-ordinating training and equipment for African armies and consulting on security problems, was really moribund. OAU committees included: the Liberation Committee, the Refugee Committee, the Congress of African Trade Unions, while there were regular policy meetings to consider Namibia, South Africa, Afro-Arab Cooperation. There was also a Pan African News Agency (PANA). The structures for action were all in place, the requisite meetings were held and thereafter, as a rule, little action followed.

The decade proved a hard one for the continent as a whole. Beginning 20 years after the great surge of independence in the early 1960s, the events of the 1980s taught Africa just how vulnerable it was to external pressures, how its small economies remained over-dependent upon external aid and investment for their survival and how urgent was the task of achieving some form of unity that would promote continental self-reliance. The violence that characterized much of Africa through the decade led Western critics of independence for the continent to argue that Africans could not govern themselves and should not have been given independence so soon. The contrary was the case. Only after the colonial powers had withdrawn was it possible for African countries, individually and collectively, to begin addressing problems that had only been disguised or papered over by the colonial presence. If Africa was weak, this in large measure resulted from the distortions that colonialism had imposed on the continent: the consequent lopsided economic development, and the artificial creation of colonial states that defied the natural regional developments, which might otherwise have emerged. Succession governments had been obliged to work within the bequeathed political systems; they had never had the chance to develop systems in their own manner so that any post-independence attempt to do so inevitably produced disruptions and sometimes conflict and many of these problems of adjustment came home to roost in the 1980s.

The Arab North

Authoritarian rule was the order of the day in North Africa at the beginning of the 1980s. In Morocco, despite the trappings of democracy, King Hassan did more or less what he wished. Algeria was a one-party state still dominated by the FLN and the army, the victors of the independence struggle against France. Only Tunisia observed genuine democratic practices, though the ageing Bourguiba exercised wide authority even though there were increasing signs of unrest at his clinging on to power. In Libya the idiosyncratic and ultimately dictatorial Gaddafi controlled every facet of policy. Both Sadat and his successor Mubarak in Egypt favoured personal, populist rule rather than genuine democracy. It was in any case an uneasy decade for the Arab world as a whole; its attention was focused on the continuing crisis over Palestine and Israel and the states of North Africa tended to turn in upon themselves and became less engaged in African affairs than thay had in the immediate years after independence. Arab aid for Africa, it is true, had been hugely increased in direct response to the events of 1973 and the fourfold increase in the price of oil but most of this aid, channelled to Africa through the Arab Bank for Economic Development in Africa (ABEDA), came from the oil rich Gulf States and the 1980s were to witness a fall in such aid as recession cut back international demand for oil.

The five North African Arab states had been members of the OAU since its inception but their participation in African, as opposed to Arab, affairs had sharply diminished and though periodic gestures towards Arab-African solidarity were made, the interchange between these states and sub-Saharan Africa had become formal rather than especially warm or close. There were exceptions. Throughout the decade Libya intervened in Chad to turn a civil war into an international confrontation. Egypt, whose leadership role in the 1960s had made it highly popular throughout the continent, was more preoccupied with the after-effects of its Camp David Accords with Israel than upon its relations with the rest of the Arab world.

Only two Arab states could claim to have been nations for centuries and this gave to each of them a stability that was lacking in the states that had been artificially created on the demise of the Ottoman Empire. These two were Egypt, with its 5,000-year old history, and Morocco. Increasing indebtedness became a problem at this time. Morocco had no oil and so the high oil prices worked against it although it received some grants from Saudi Arabia. It incurred substantial debts over the late 1970s and early 1980s for major infrastructure adjustments in relation to its phosphates industry, which provided the bulk of its export earnings, and during 1983 was obliged to request a rescheduling of its US$14 billion worth of debts. During 1985–86 first Algeria and then Tunisia became deeply indebted but instead of rescheduling, which would have excluded them from commercial money markets, they embarked upon refinancing operations: that is, more borrowing. In 1987 Egypt had to reschedule its debts. Morocco, at least, learnt its lesson. When it rescheduled in 1983 debt-servicing was taking two-thirds of its export earnings but after nine years of regular rescheduling it had reduced its debt-service ratio to 33 per cent of export earnings, which it could manage, and so was able to announce in 1992 that it would not need to reschedule again.

Afro-Arab co-operation, which had reached its height during the OPEC crisis of the 1970s and had been established on an apparently firm basis in 1977 at Cairo, in fact lapsed through much of the 1980s. The natural differences in aims, concerns and backgrounds between Arabs and Africans meant that an alliance of interests had to be worked at constantly if it was to bear fruit. Following the election of President Mubarak of Egypt as chairman of the OAU for 1989–90, his Minister of State, Boutros Boutros-Ghali, said it was an opportunity to revive earlier Afro-Arab co-operation. In an interview with the *International Herald Tribune*[1] Boutros-Ghali said President Mubarak could 'play a role' in reinforcing the co-operation that had been established in Cairo in 1977. He made the point that 'more than 70 per cent of Arab territories are in Africa and more than 80 per cent of the Arab population live in the continent. A better co-ordination between the OAU and the Arab League may help in the synchronization between the African and Arab world. Furthermore, we both have non-alignment in common'. In February 1990, the new OAU Secretary-General Salim Ahmed Salim told the OAU Council of Ministers that it was important not to lose sight of the common destiny that links African and Arab peoples. Increased co-operation between them could set an example for North–South co-operation. He proposed the creation of 'concrete co-operation programmes'. Nothing practical was to follow. In March 1989, in a gesture towards greater co-operation, the OAU Council of Ministers had reaffirmed its support for the creation of an independent State of Palestine although this was a modification of its stronger resolution of 1973.

During this period the states of North Africa became increasingly concerned with the deepening cultural crisis in Islam. The revolution that had brought the Ayatollah Khomeini to power in Iran provided the impetus, though a number of other factors were at work, to increase an Islamic rejuvenation that, however, was seen in many quarters as a rise in Islamic fundamentalism. During the nineteenth century the spread of Western imperialism had undermined Islam by subordinating it to Western power, consumerism and political ideas with the result that a decline in Islam as a cohesive force in the region had followed. At the end of World War I the Middle East had also come under Western influence, not quite colonized but divided into European spheres of influence and, after 1945, that of the United States as well. The creation of the State of Israel in the geographic centre of the Arab world had acted as a spur to this Islamic revival and by the 1980s, when the European empires had come to an end, change was heralded by the growth of fundamentalism: the determination to revert to a stricter form of Islam. The new fundamentalists clashed with the modernizers and secularists who provided the core of the North African political class. These latter had embraced a materialist, semi-Westernised life-style and did not wish to return to the restrictions that fundamentalism would impose upon them. It was the failure of this secular, modernizing leadership to spread the new wealth to their whole populations that provided the opportunity for the fundamentalists. Angry young men rejected the turn to the West, the failure to solve the Palestine issue, the tyranny of entrenched elites and leadership; they believed that only a reversion to fundamentalism could sweep away this leadership and revitalize Arab-Islamic society.[2]

EGYPT

Through the 1980s Egypt was entirely preoccupied with Arab-Middle East affairs and no longer played the role of bridge to sub-Saharan Africa, which it had filled with such success in the 1960s and 1970s. As President Sadat discovered, the Camp David Accords did not settle the Palestine question while his economic policies were unpopular. Moreover, Sadat violated conventional proprieties and ignored growing corruption in high places. As a result, Islamist and leftist opposition to his regime increased. In September 1981, responding to the growing opposition, Sadat had some 1,500 of his critics, including highly respected individuals such as Umar Tilmisani of the Muslim Brotherhood and the journalist Muhammad Heikal, arrested. He then nationalized all the private mosques to deprive populists of their pulpits. He was assassinated on 6 October 1981. His successor, Hosni Mubarak, worked through the 1980s to rehabilitate

Egypt with the rest of the Arab world, following its almost total isolation as a result of the Camp David Accords. Mubarak faced an intensified campaign by fundamentalists to have the Sharia (Islamic law) fully adopted as part of the legal system. Immediately on coming to power, Mubarak had 2,500 people arrested in connection with the assassination of Sadat but most of these were soon released. He enlisted the support of the moderate Islamists and the Brotherhood to oppose the advance of the extremists. In April 1982, five people were executed for the assassination of Sadat but no disturbances followed. In September 1984, 174 of 301 who had been arrested in connection with the Sadat killing were acquitted of plotting to overthrow the government while 16 were sentenced to hard labour for life. Thereafter, Mubarak followed a moderate line with regard to Islam. Only in 1989 was Egypt's isolation that had followed Sadat's recognition of Israel brought to an end when it was readmitted to the Arab League. On the home front Mubarak faced huge problems which included rapid population increase (close to one million a year), high unemployment, periodic shortages of basic foods, a foreign debt of US$50 billion to be serviced, over-bureaucratization, the reluctance of foreign companies to invest in Egypt, a frustrated younger generation and the steady growth of militant Islamic fundamentalism. Nonetheless, by the end of the decade Mubarak was riding high as Egypt re-entered the mainstream of Arab politics.

THE MAGHREB COUNTRIES

An advance in the long-projected Maghrebi Union took place in June 1989 with the formation of a joint Parliament, shared by the five member states (Algeria, Libya, Mauritania, Morocco and Tunisia). Morocco and Algeria finally agreed on the border demarcation between their two states. However, this apparent move towards greater integration looked less promising towards the end of 1989. There were two postponements, as doubts about the union surfaced, before the *Union du Maghreb Arabe* (UMA) (Arab Maghreb Union) Summit was held in Tunis over 22–23 January 1990. The agenda included strengthening relations with other regional groups and especially the European Union. The leaders agreed to give UMA a greater role in co-ordinating their regional policy and international relations. It was agreed to set up a permanent secretariat although this went contrary to the founding principles of UMA, which had been intended as a loose structure avoiding a large, expensive bureaucracy. Despite the summit, the members of UMA appeared lukewarm in their endorsement of the union and resistant to giving it powers to resolve problems. These included Morocco's policy in Western Sahara (SADR), Algerian-Moroccan relations, Gaddafi's foreign policy and the dispute between Mauritania and Senegal.

MOROCCO

The Moroccan claim to Western Sahara dominated that country's relations with its immediate neighbours and Africa through the OAU for most of the 1980s. In February 1976 Spain, in effect, had handed over Spanish Sahara to Morocco and Mauritania and both countries had at once sent troops to occupy the parts of Western Sahara contiguous to their own territories. POLISARIO had fought against both countries, so successfully in the case of Mauritania, which was ill-equipped and too poor to conduct a war outside its own territory that it was obliged to give up its claim in 1979 and withdraw. Fighting between the Moroccan forces and POLISARIO reached a climax over the years 1979–81. At issue, once Mauritania had withdrawn from the contest, was the Moroccan claim to a part of the territory, which had a certain historical basis, and the POLISARIO demand for a democratic election to decide the future of the territory. The consequent Sahara War exposed the weakness of the OAU. In 1980 Cuba recognized the Sahara Arab Democratic Republic (SADR) as proclaimed by POLISARIO and Cuba's action was followed by recognition from a further 36 countries, most of them African. The future of SADR was then debated by the OAU and though member countries were fearful of dividing the organization, 26 of the 50 members recognized SADR, and this ought to have meant SADR's admission to the OAU. Morocco, however, insisted that SADR's admission required recognition by two-thirds of the membership, yet despite this the OAU did admit SADR to membership in 1982. Morocco and 18 other countries that supported its stand then walked out to present the organization with its greatest crisis since its foundation. The crisis was apparently resolved in June 1983 when the SADR delegation voluntarily abstained from taking its seat and Morocco then ended its boycott. In 1984, however, Mauritania, one of the original claimants to Western Sahara, recognized the SADR whose delegate then did take its seat in the OAU. At this point Morocco left the OAU.

The OAU and the UN now saw the Western Sahara as a colonized territory whose people should be able to determine their future by means of a referendum. Although Morocco again agreed to take part in a referendum about the future of the territory, it subsequently found ways repeatedly to defer the referendum, which it was to do successfully to the end of the century. POLISARIO, which by the beginning of the 1980s had 10,000 troops (although only half of these would be engaged in fighting at any given time), used hit-and-run tactics against centres of population, forcing the phosphate mines at Bou Craa to operate at reduced capacity. At this time (the early 1980s) POLISARIO appeared to be winning the war while Morocco was reduced to maintaining garrisons in the centres of population, yet King Hassan continued to receive wide support for the war which by then had become a Moroccan nationalist crusade. In 1981 POLISARIO switched its bases from Algeria to Mauritania and, following an attempted coup in Nouakchott, the Mauritanian government broke diplomatic relations with Morocco. By 1982, however, Morocco had obtained control over the principal centres of population in Western Sahara – El Aiun, Smara, Bojador – and the huge phosphate deposits at Bou Craa. The Moroccans now built defensive lines in the form of endless sand walls round the triangle of these towns and Bou Craa. The first phase of the walls was completed in 1982. In 1984 they were extended to the Mauritanian border and ran for more than 600 kilometres.

The war became highly sophisticated. Morocco accused Algeria and Libya of providing POLISARIO with Soviet-made missiles, which were used to shoot down Moroccan planes. In October 1981, for example, a Moroccan Hercules transport and a Mirage F-A fighter were brought down by SAM-6 or SAM-8 missiles at high altitudes. The Moroccans suggested that Cuban or East German 'advisers' working with POLISARIO were responsible for firing the missiles. The war continued through the decade with varying degrees of intensity. In November 1987, for example, POLISARIO issued a communiqué claiming that 63 Moroccan troops had been killed and 91 wounded in a desert battle. A Moroccan army communiqué, in reply, stated that 245 guerrillas and 72 Moroccan soldiers had been killed in two battles. This fighting immediately preceded the arrival of a UN mission to ascertain the prospects of holding a referendum. POLISARIO then declared a truce. In August 1988 Morocco and POLISARIO accepted a UN plan for a ceasefire and a referendum to give the people of Western Sahara the choice of independence or integration with Morocco, but after nine months the truce and the UN effort broke down. At the end of September 1989 POLISARIO mounted a series of attacks on Moroccan positions and on 7 and 11 October waged substantial battles against the Moroccans at Guelta Zemmour and Hamza. Both sides claimed they had inflicted heavy casualties on their opponents.

The war continued on a reduced scale in 1990. Algeria, the most involved outsider, pressed for a solution according to UN and OAU resolutions. Further negotiations conducted during June in Geneva led the UN to announce that a referendum would be held in 1991 at an estimated cost of US$250 million. By the end of the decade Morocco was no closer to solving the Western Sahara question in its favour and though it had large numbers of troops stationed in the territory at considerable expense, it had fallen out with the OAU as a result of its unilateral action which was in flagrant violation of UN resolutions as well as against the wishes of the inhabitants of Western Sahara. Neither did it appear to be obtaining any benefits from the creation of the UMA even though in 1988

Algeria had suddenly ended its support for POLISARIO to resume diplomatic relations with Morocco as part of a move to make the UMA work.

ALGERIA

President Houari Boumedienne of Algeria died of a rare disease on 27 December 1978 and, following an interregnum, Col. Chadli Benjedid was elected President. Benjedid pursued a less austere policy than his predecessor; opponents of Boumedienne including Ben Bella, who went into exile, were released from prison. The process of switching from the French language to Arabic was speeded up. In the legislative elections of 1982 the ruling FLN received 72.65 per cent of the votes. The Algerian role in obtaining the release in 1981 of the American hostages who had been seized in Iran at the time of the Islamist revolution in that country led to a brief period of good relations with the US but the goodwill was soon dissipated when the US sold tanks to Morocco at a time when Algeria and Morocco were at loggerheads over Western Sahara. During the first half of the 1980s Algeria solved a number of outstanding border disputes with Niger and Tunisia although in the west it continued its support for POLISARIO so that the quarrel with Morocco retarded progress on the creation of a greater Maghreb Union. At least in the early 1980s it appeared that Algeria's economy would continue successfully along the lines of the socialist revolution established under Boumedienne.

A clash between the secular FLN, which had ruled Algeria since independence, and increasing demands by fundamentalists for a more Islamist-oriented state came to dominate the politics of the decade. When the government had tried to appease Islamic sentiment during the 1970s it had met opposition from both the Army, which saw itself as the guardian of the revolution, and the Berbers, who regarded moves towards fundamentalism as an Arab attempt to oppose their own moves towards cultural assertion. Growing militancy culminated in clashes between secular students and fundamentalists in November 1982 when about 200 fundamentalists were arrested. Subsequently 5,000 people attended a Friday prayer meeting in Algiers, which turned into a protest meeting. President Benjedid warned that secular forces could be mobilized against Muslim extremists should this be necessary. This particular crisis ended in May 1985 when 30 of those who had been taken into custody received prison sentences of 3–12 years, 60 were acquitted and the rest released after receiving sentences for less than the time they had already been in detention. Thereafter, Benjedid maintained a low-key approach to the fundamentalists and for a few more years the government appeared to contain the fundamentalist pressures. On the political front Benjedid had won the presidential elections of 1984; he was sole candidate, with 95.4 per cent of the vote. In 1985 Benjedid visited Washington and achieved a rapprochment with the United States. Tension with Morocco was also eased following a meeting in May 1987 between King Hassan II and President Benjedid. More emollient than his prickly predecessor, Benjedid managed to improve relations with Libya. However, Algeria's relations with France were always difficult and in 1987 a dispute over the price of Algeria's natural gas exports led to considerable friction. By this time Benjedid was moving away from socialism and central planning and embarking upon a series of economic reforms.

Growing discontent with both the political and economic restraints of socialism persuaded Benjedid to begin liberalizing the system; but he had embarked upon his changes too late and in 1988 the worst riots seen in Algeria since 1962 occurred and led to 500 deaths. Although the government blamed the Islamic fundamentalists, the true reason for the unrest was economic hardship resulting from the fall in oil prices. The government used the military to suppress the disturbances but also responded to the unrest by improving consumer supplies. These riots signalled the end of three decades of old-style socialist centralism as Algeria, under a more pragmatic leadership, seemed ready to turn the country into a pluralist society. The government's commitment to market liberalization and a shake-up of the bureaucracy was deeply worrying to the many people who feared for their jobs in the huge state sector. A new national constitution, published in 1989, dropped all mention of socialism and introduced political pluralism or multipartyism and conceded the right to strike. In July 1989 the National Assembly passed a political associations law that required political parties to avoid programmes based on language or religion while a second law required a political party to obtain a minimum of 10 per cent of votes in a constituency to qualify for registration. However, these laws were regarded as favouring the continuance of FLN dominance at the expense of the Muslims and the Berber minority. In 1990, true to its older radical tradition, Algeria refused to support the US multinational force against Iraq. The process of democratization was speeded up in 1990: exiles were allowed to return home and a large number of political parties appeared – 25 had been registered by mid-year. On 12 June 1990 elections for town councils and provincial assembles were held and the *Front Islamique du Salut* (FIS) (Islamic Salvation Front) made sweeping gains and took 54 per cent of the votes against 28 per cent for the ruling FLN. It now appeared that Benjedid's reforms – political relaxation and a return to multipartyism – had produced a major confrontation between secular politics and Islamic fundamentalism. The groundwork had in fact been laid for the catastrophe of the 1990s.

The meteoric rise of the FIS was the outstanding event of the last years of the decade. Mouloud Hamrouche had been appointed Prime Minister by Benjedid on 9 September 1989 and, after announcing his government, had promised liberal reforms and a greater say for the opposition. He also admitted that the economy was in a state of disintegration and vowed to improve the investment climate of the private sector. His programme was approved by the Legislature by 281 to three on 30 September. Hamrouche had also changed the composition of his government, replacing ministers with military and party backgrounds with technocrats, a move made easier by the earlier decision of Benjedid (in March) to make the military withdraw from the FLN Central Committee. Although strict conditions had been applied to new parties, which could not be based upon a single region or a religion, this did not hold back the rapid spread of FIS influence. A further law stated that a party gaining over 50 per cent of the votes in a constituency would obtain all the seats. At the time this was seen as favouring the FLN. But by March 1990 Hamrouche was constrained to reverse this law when it appeared that the FIS would obtain a landslide. By then it had become apparent that the FIS posed the old FLN and the reforming government with its greatest challenge. The FIS had widespread support, was suspected of anti-democratic tendencies and was committed to the introduction of Sharia. Many Algerians agreed with FIS demands for a fairer society and more religious observance, but many also feared that polarization of the two sides would take place and did not want to see the curtailment of individual freedoms that went with FIS Islamic ideas, and especially as these applied to the position of women. As the new decade began the ruling FLN found itself on the defensive, the Berber minority, represented by the Culture and Democracy Party, was fearful that government Arabization policies would threaten its own distinct culture while the FIS was garnering nationwide support for an Islamist revival.

The much-lauded socialist experiment that the FLN had launched under Boumedienne appeared to fall apart during the 1980s and determining what went wrong is far from easy. 'Algeria was once the most admired country in the Arab world. There were few who loved it or enjoyed going there – it was too hard and unsmiling for that – but for what it had achieved it was respected. People believed it was going to be a success.'[3] The Algerian struggle against France in the 1950s and early 1960s had been tough and uncompromising and, as such, an inspiration to other independence struggles at that time. But in the process, in which perhaps one million Algerians had been killed, the country had become inured to hardship. The FLN had created the new Algerian nation in the cauldron of the war against France and could subsequently rely upon the sense of unity that had emerged from the struggle. The creation of a centrally planned socialist state under Boumedienne during the 1970s unravelled in the

1980s. 'What makes Algeria particularly interesting is that it displayed all the different faults of the Arab countries. Its government suffered from the hypocrisy, corruption and ruthlessness of the other Arab governments, and in running its economy it combined inflexible socialism with over-ambitious development schemes and, later, a short-sighted desire to win favour with its own people. It so happened that the effects of all its mistakes and shortcomings hit the country at the same time, and in a particularly acute fashion, and in a very short period brought it to ruin.'[4] The FLN in all practical senses was a dictatorship but admirers of the country's post-independence achievements were too ready to overlook this fact because its socialism was fashionable, especially during the years when Algeria was in the forefront of demanding a New International Economic Order and was using its oil wealth to launch major development projects. As a result it was regarded as an enlightened dictatorship.

The process of heavy industrialization implemented through the 1970s was financed by oil wealth, but the industrial plants that were purchased from foreign contractors in fact were not profitable. There were a number of reasons for this. Most of their products were unable to compete with cheaper imports or as exports. The principal reason lay with the lack of indigenous expertise capable of making the newly established plants develop and expand naturally to pay their way. Moreover, in order to safeguard its socialist experiment the government used its oil revenues to finance the losses, which the new industries incurred. At the same time that this industrial revolution was put in place, agriculture was neglected. Two events occurred at the end of the 1970s, shortly after the death of Boumedienne, to have a major impact upon Algeria. The first of these was the Iranian revolution that brought the Ayatollah Khomeini to power and signalled a growth of Islamic fundamentalism right across the Arab world. The other event was the second major rise in oil prices that took place over 1979–80. At the end of the 1970s, relaxing the austerity to which it had accustomed the Algerian people, the Boumedienne government had increased social spending. The oil price rise allowed Benjedid to spend more lavishly. The government relaxed import restrictions and luxury goods such as bananas, foreign cheese, washing machines, refrigerators and cars appeared in the country and were subsidized by a process of adjusting prices. Moreover, to finance its expansive consumer-oriented policies, the government began borrowing on the international market in 1984 and then, when the oil price collapsed from US$30 a barrel to US$10–15, increased its borrowing still further. Government borrowing was accompanied by a rise in unemployment and by the end of the decade as many as 25 per cent of the male workforce were unemployed while among the 17–23 age group as many as 70 per cent were unemployed. The young unemployed, more than any other factor, threatened the government's ability to control the situation. These young unemployed had no money, were bored and bitter and felt they had little future. They were ripe for revolution.

By 1988 the Islamic politicians were becoming more prominent and influential and were instrumental in prolonging the riots of October. Abbasi Madani and Ali Belhadj, the leaders of FIS, which at this point was still in embryo form, were university lecturers and would preach in mosques when allowed to do so. Tradesmen and unemployed workmen now joined the ranks of FIS in growing numbers and became more aggressive in their demands for change. As a result, by June 1990, when the first free vote since independence was allowed for the town councils and provincial assemblies, FIS won 54 per cent of the vote. In the aftermath of this victory, the FIS shut kindergarten schools (to keep mothers at home), turned cinemas into mosques, separated the sexes on buses, had separate counters established in post offices for men and women and had verses of the Koran posted up in the streets. But though the FIS made plain the direction it intended to take, the public as a whole was not greatly impressed. However, in the run-up to the June 1991 national parliamentary elections, FIS tactics, which included using municipal buses to transport their supporters to meetings and denying polling cards to opponents, demonstrated clearly that a real confrontation between FIS and the FLN was about to take place. One outcome of any dictatorship is to teach opponents to adopt equally dictatorial methods.

TUNISIA

Tunisia had become more secularized than any other Arab state in Africa. During the 1980s the main problems faced by its government were economic or concerned with the succession to Bourguiba rather than about Islamic fundamentalism. The decade began uncertainly: Bourguiba, the hero of independence, was old, while divisions in Tunisian society were becoming more marked. In February 1980 the Prime Minister Hedi Novira suddenly became ill and was replaced by the Minister of Education, Mohamed Nzali, who proved a more tolerant leader than his predecessor. He took back into government some ministers who had resigned in 1977 over the government's approach to the growing economic discontents of that time and the confrontation with the *Union Générale Tunisienne de Travail* (UGTT) (General Union of Tunisian Workers) when six ministers had resigned in sympathy with the sacked Minister of the Interior, Tahar Belkhodja. This labour unrest of 1977–78 had been the worst crisis the government had had to face since independence. As a result, in July 1979 the National Assembly had made its first tentative move towards political liberalization. At the extraordinary meeting of the *Parti Socialiste Destourien* (PSD) (Destour Socialist Party) of April 1981, which had been called to examine the 1982–86 Development Plan, President Bourguiba said he was not opposed to the emergence of other political parties as long as they rejected violence and religious fanaticism. His statement was interpreted as a clear move towards multipartyism.

In December 1981 Habib Achour, the leader of the UGTT who had called the general strike in January 1978 and, following widespread riots and disturbance, had been imprisoned for subversion, was now released and resumed the leadership of the UGTT. In mid-1982 the one-party system was brought to an end. In November 1983 the *Mouvement des Démocrates Socialistes* (MDS) and the *Mouvement d'Unité Populaire* (MUP) were officially recognized. Sharp rises in food prices and an end to subsidies on flour and other staples led to riots at the beginning of 1984. The army restored order but at the cost of 89 deaths, nearly 1,000 wounded and 1,000 arrests. Other causes of unrest included growing fundamentalist opposition to the government and high levels of unemployment. A crisis with Libya came close to a violent confrontation when Gaddafi expelled 25,000 Tunisian workers and Tunisia retaliated by expelling a number of Libyans.

By 1986, however, the dominant political question was the succession to the ageing Bourguiba. The elections of November 1986 were won, unopposed, by the ruling Patriotic Union, which was led by the PSD, since the new opposition parties boycotted the election on the grounds that its fairness had not been guaranteed. A year later, on 7 November 1987, Gen. Zine al-Abidine Ben Ali (whom Bourguiba had appointed prime minister a month earlier) replaced the President on the grounds that he was no longer able to carry out his functions (he was then 84 years old). The new President removed from office favourites of Bourguiba and entrenched his own position. The deposition of Bourguiba was welcomed by Algeria, Tunisia's closest African ally, as well as by France and the United States, its most important Western backers. The move came at a time of deteriorating political conditions in the country. One of Bourguiba's last actions as President had been to initiate moves against Islamic fundamentalists whom he saw as a major threat to stability. During 1988 President Ben Ali pursued a policy of reconciliation: this included an amnesty for some political figures and the calling of elections for April 1989. The PSD was renamed the *Rassemblement Constitutionnel Démocratique* (RCD)(Constitutional Democratic Rally). A press freedom law was passed in July 1989. Ben Ali worked to improve relations with Libya and Egypt with the result that Libya relaxed its border controls to allow Tunisians to seek work in Libya for the first time since the 1985 expulsions. Ben Ali was returned unopposed in the 1989 elections with 99 per cent of the vote and the RCD won 141 seats in the assembly. A mid-year amnesty led to the release of 5,400 political prisoners. By 1990, however, President Ben Ali faced growing opposition from the Islamic Nahda Party (which was fundamentalist) and had not been granted political recognition.

Tunisia possessed one of the more sophisticated economies in Africa and from 1987 began to adopt a policy of economic liberalization while also seeking to establish stronger ties with the European Community. Its main foreign exchange earners were petroleum, phosphates, clothing, tourism and agricultural products. However, agriculture was in decline in terms of its contribution to GDP: in 1988 this stood at only 11.8 per cent while the sector employed 21.6 per cent of the work-force. Its principal products – grapes, olives, dates, oranges, figs – were all exported as were fish and crustaceans which earned three per cent of foreign exchange. Manufacturing accounted for 14.1 per cent of GDP and employed 16.3 per cent of the workforce; its principal products were clothing, food, iron and steel, phosphates-related activities and vehicle assembly. By the end of the 1980s the tourist industry had become the second largest in Africa after Egypt. This economy was geared to supply the markets of the European Community and Tunisia had become increasingly anxious about the long-term effects of a single European market. Nonetheless, at this time, Tunisia was classified as a middle-level developing country with a per capita income of US$1,260. Its debts, however, were too high: at US$6,899 million they were equivalent to 71.9 per cent of GNP.

LIBYA

Gaddafi's role during the 1980s, infuriating as it was to both his African neighbours and farther afield on the continent, and even more his capacity to anger the world's number one superpower the United States, tells us a good deal about African attitudes to the West and still more about Western attitudes towards Africa. Armed with his surplus oil wealth, Gaddafi did what no other African leader was able or willing to do: by supporting terrorist or revolutionary groups around the world he acted like a big power and that was his principal crime in the eyes of the West, and especially Washington. While, apparently, it was acceptable for the United States to support the Contras against the legitimately elected government of Nicaragua, it was not acceptable for Gaddafi to support the Islamic Moro National Liberation Front in the Philippines. It was his usurpation of a big power role that was unforgivable.

Gaddafi's relations with Africa to the south were a complex mixture of motives and Libya's oil wealth provided him with a surplus that allowed him to intervene with offers of aid not available from any other African state. His uncertain volatility made him at best an awkward person with whom to deal while his readiness to stand up to and defy the West, especially the United States, gave him an acceptable cachet of approval that money alone would not have provided. An American appraisal of Gaddafi in 1983 stated: 'Virtually all African and Arab moderate regimes are targets of Libyan-supported subversion. Unable to persuade or bribe other states into submitting to a Qadhafi-led "Islamic revolution", and unable to use his army to force stronger states to submit to his will, Qadhafi has armed, funded, and trained a wide range of dissident groups to achieve his ends. Subversion has become the principal tool by which he hopes to fulfil his ambitions.'[5] Later in the same (anonymous) article, the author continues: 'Virtually every state in Africa and the Middle East has been the object of Qadhafi's meddling.' It should be pointed out that many of Gaddafi's actions in Africa were comparable in both style and scope to those of major powers; they were concerned with the spread of Libya's influence and the propagation of ideas in which Gaddafi believed (just as the major powers tried to extend their influence throughout the years of the Cold War).

Gaddafi's activities in a dozen African countries through the 1970s and 1980s included Sudan, Chad, Ethiopia, Eritrea, Niger, Tunisia, Egypt, Algeria, Morocco, Mauritania and Somalia. Libya was an important source of finance for POLISARIO in Western Sahara. During the early 1970s Gaddafi supported liberation groups such as that in Portuguese Guinea (as did half the states of Africa through the OAU), and by the mid-1970s was supplying money, arms and training for liberation movements in Eritrea, Rhodesia, Morocco and Chad. He also provided aid for sympathetic regimes such as those in Togo, Uganda or Zambia. Accusations of subversion against Gaddafi often implied a capacity to undermine that was inherently unlikely. Leaders such as Jerry Rawlings in Ghana, while happy enough to receive aid from Gaddafi, were as a general rule quite capable of safeguarding their own political interests. He played a significant role in persuading a number of African countries – Chad, Congo, Mali, Niger – to break diplomatic relations with Israel at the time of the 1973 OPEC crisis, threatened to boycott the OAU and suggested that its headquarters should be moved from Addis Ababa unless Ethiopia broke relations with Israel. He provided Zambia with aid after Kaunda had closed its border with Rhodesia.

In September 1976 Gaddafi produced new maps purporting to show that 52,000 square miles of territory belonging to Algeria, Chad and Niger were really part of Libya. Algeria and Niger took no action but Chad closed its border with Libya since part of the territory consisted of the Aozou Strip that lay to the immediate south of Libya. By 1977 a number of African states were sufficiently disturbed by the direction of Libyan policies that they attempted to exercise restraint upon Gaddafi; this was notably the case in relation to Chad when at the OAU Gabon summit meeting of July a group was formed consisting of Algeria, Cameroon, Mozambique, Gabon, Nigeria and Senegal to mediate the border dispute between Libya and Chad. In the same year Gaddafi withdrew his support from the Eritrean rebels and aligned himself firmly with the military Dergue of Haile Mariam Mengistu in Ethiopia. This was surprising since Ethiopia was Christian while the Eritreans were mainly Muslims. Gaddafi, however, wished to exert pressure upon what he saw as an alliance of Egypt, Sudan and Saudi Arabia against him. In May 1977 Mengistu visited Tripoli to discuss financial aid for his arms purchases from the USSR. At this time Libya was maintaining more than 30 embassies throughout Africa and a constant stream of African leaders visited Libya whose financial assistance had become an important factor for the continent's often embattled economies. Over 1978–79 Gaddafi saw the collapse of his Ugandan axis as Amin's tyrannical regime imploded. Libya airlifted between 1,500 and 2,500 troops to Kampala as the Tanzania-supported invasion force reached the Ugandan capital. The Libyan troops arrived too late to affect the outcome, for by then the Ugandan army was disintegrating and Amin was obliged to flee. Some 400 of 1,500 Libyan troops who attempted to defend the capital were killed and the rest were expelled back to Libya. This adventure proved a humiliating defeat for Gaddafi.

During the 1980s Gaddafi's principal involvement to the south was in the civil war in Chad in support of his claim to the Aozou Strip although he also continued his interventions elsewhere. By this time, however, African countries had become increasingly wary of his offers of friendship. Early in 1980 Libyan forces were involved in an attack upon Gafsa in Tunisia in support of opponents of Bourguiba while later that year, first President Leopold Senghor of Senegal accused Gaddafi of supporting a coup attempt against him, then President Sir Dawda Jawara of The Gambia made a similar accusation and both countries broke diplomatic relations with Libya. In 1981, Nigeria expelled the staff of the Libyan 'People's Bureau' although it continued to maintain diplomatic relations with Libya while other countries – Uganda, Niger and Mali – accused Libya of plotting against them. Somalia severed diplomatic relations with Libya for its 'animosity to the Somali people'. A consequence of this growing hostility to Gaddafi's destabilizing activities and interference was a humiliation for Libya when in 1982 a number of African leaders objected to holding the OAU annual conference in Tripoli since to do so would automatically mean that Gaddafi would become chairman of the organization for the ensuing year.

Gaddafi blamed the United States for using its influence to pressure African states into taking this line. In March 1982, after consultations with Congress and certain governments, President Ronald Reagan decided to ban the import of

Libyan oil and prevent certain listed items being exported to Libya. A Department of State communiqué stated: 'We are taking these measures in response to a continuing pattern of Libyan activity which violates accepted international norms of behaviour. Libya's large financial resources, vast supplies of Soviet weapons, and active efforts to promote instability and terrorism make it a serious threat to a large number of nations and individuals, particularly in the Middle East and Africa.'[6] (A list of proposed sanctions followed.) In 1983 Gaddafi visited Lagos as part of a tour of West Africa, when he also visited Benin and Upper Volta (Burkina Faso). In 1984 all five Libyan diplomats in the Indian Ocean island of Mauritius were expelled, accused of interfering in the island's affairs. The broad pattern of Gaddafi's activities did not alter although his ability to offer inducements did as the price of oil plummeted during the 1980s from the all-time high it had achieved at the beginning of the decade.

By the 1970s substantial numbers of French troops were in Chad to support the government while between 2,000 and 3,000 Libyan troops backed the FROLINAT opposition movement in the north. In February 1979 Hissène Habré ousted President Malloum in a coup to set off a civil war between Muslims and black southerners. Chad's neighbours became increasingly worried at Libya's growing involvement in the country, few trusted Gaddafi's intentions, and the pressures they exerted added to those of France induced Gaddafi to withdraw from Chad in 1981. An OAU force led by Nigerians intervened to peace keep in 1982. The war was to continue throughout the decade and witnessed renewed interventions by both Libya and France. During 1985, having broken its agreement with France of September 1984 that both countries should withdraw their forces from Chad at the same time, Libya consolidated its grip in the north while Habré strengthened his hold over the central government.

Of all Gaddafi's interventions in Africa, apart from those concerning his immediate Arab neighbours, none was so important or so long lasting as that in Chad. During the two decades of the 1970s and 1980s of recurring civil war in Chad between the Muslim north and black south, Gaddafi became ever more deeply involved: first, in support of the northern insurgent groups against the government, which had inherited power from the departing French in 1960; then, as a claimant to the Aozou Strip which occupies the northern extremity of Chad to the immediate south of the Libyan border. This long civil war included three separate French interventions as well as US financial support for Gaddafi's opponents, and brought misery and disruption to one of the remotest, poorest countries in the world. Chad was a textbook illustration of how colonial decisions could continue to influence developments long after independence. In the case of Chad they resulted from the artificial creation of this huge country of just under half a million square miles that brought together but did not unite totally disparate peoples in terms of their ethnicity, culture and religion, and failed to settle the Franco-Italian border dispute concerning the Aozou Strip that formed the basis of Gaddafi's claim. Only towards the end of the 1980s did it appear possible that a resolution to the conflict might be found. Thus, in May 1988 Gaddafi announced his willingness to recognize the Habré government and to launch a 'Marshall Plan' to reconstruct the war-damaged areas of Chad while, at least for the time being, Habré appeared ready to accept the *de facto* Libyan control of the Aozou Strip. On 3 October 1988 Libya and Chad resumed diplomatic relations even though Libya retained control of the Aozou Strip to which Chad had not renounced its claim. The following year (31 August 1989) Libya and Chad signed an agreement in Algiers under which they would try for a year to resolve their differences before going to arbitration; in the meantime the Aozou Strip would be administered by an African observer force.[7] In December 1990 Habré was ousted in a coup and replaced by Idriss Deby. This change led to an immediate improvement in relations between Chad and Libya, which then provided support including arms for the new Deby government. The two countries agreed to submit the border dispute over the Aozou Strip to the International Court of Justice (ICJ) at The Hague and it went before the court in 1992. On 3 February 1994 the ICJ ruled by 16 to one in favour of Chad's claim to the Aozou Strip. Gaddafi accepted the Court's decision and on 31 May 1994, at a ceremony in Tripoli, Libya and Chad signed a joint communiqué, which formally handed over to Chad the Aozou Strip; Libyan troops had been withdrawn from the Strip over the preceding few days. Gaddafi and Deby signed a 'treaty of friendship, neighbourly terms and co-operation' in Tripoli on 3 June and Deby called for a new era of co-operation between Chad and Libya. One of Africa's longest and most costly confrontations had come to an end and, to the surprise of his many critics, Gaddafi had accepted the ruling of the ICJ without any attempt to reverse it.

LIBYA'S RELATIONS WITH THE MAJOR POWERS

During the 1980s Libya succeeded, as no other small state, in infuriating the major powers, beginning with the United States. Gaddafi gave a bravura performance as though his special task was to demonstrate how Libya had an equivalent role in the world to that of the big powers in supporting selected causes. As much as anything his actions were a criticism of the all-pervasive influence that they exercised.

Throughout the decade tensions between Libya and the United States were high and reached crisis proportions in 1986 with the US bombing of Libya, and again in 1988–89 with the Lockerbie crash. In August 1982 the US

Mediterranean fleet exercised in the southern Mediterranean off Libya's coast though no incident occurred. Early in 1983 the US sent four airborne warning and control systems planes (AWACS) to Egypt because it feared a Libyan invasion of Sudan was intended. Whether or not US demonizing of Libya during the 1980s was justified, the results were not always what the State Department could have intended. Despite Gaddafi's unpopularity with his neighbours, whether Arab or African, or their often deep suspicions of his motives, his ability to infuriate the United States was enjoyed by countries that too often felt humiliated by their dependence – and sometimes subservience – to the Western powers. As a result, Gaddafi's anti-US tirades and pinpricks gave him a standing and popularity that otherwise he would never have achieved. In the October 1983 issue of the Department of State Bulletin, a lengthy article 'The Libyan Problem' provided a US critique of Gaddafi. 'The Libyan regime contributes to instability in a wide range of states in Africa, the Middle East, and elsewhere in a manner disproportionate to Libya's small population. Its enormous oil wealth is at the disposal of an absolute ruler, Muammar al-Qadhafi, whose ambition is to expand his power beyond the limits of Libya by persuasion, force or subversion in the name of his self-styled revolution.' It was the extension of Gaddafi's activities into Latin America, where he provided arms and other assistance to the Sandinistas in Nicaragua and the Salvadoran guerrillas, as well as giving support to leftist groups throughout the region, that infuriated Washington. The State Department claimed that Libya was trying to undermine the position of the United States. In a speech of 1 September 1983 (the fourteenth anniversary of his coup) Gaddafi said: 'When we ally ourselves with revolution in Latin America, and particularly Central America, we are defending ourselves. This Satan (the United States) must be clipped and we must take war to the American borders just as America is taking threats to the Gulf of Sidra and to the Tibesti Mountains.'[8]

Over the years 1975–83 Libya's military forces were increased from 22,000 to 85,000 while Libya spent huge sums on the acquisition of arms. Prior to 1973 arms had come from the West. In 1974, however, Gaddafi had signed a major contract with the USSR to be followed by further agreements in 1977, 1978 and 1980, the agreement of the latter year being worth US$8 billllion. By 1983, of US$28 billion of arms purchases, US$20 billion came from the USSR. On the other hand, the US State Department was doubtful that Libya had the military personnel to handle all these weapons although by this time there were 4,000 foreign advisers in the country, half of them from the USSR. Relations between the US and Libya were cool through 1985, but deteriorated sharply at the end of the year, when the US accused Libya of two bomb attacks at Rome and Vienna airports on 27 December. In January 1986 President Reagan imposed further sanctions on Libya and made support for terrorism the principal reason for his move. A US report of 1986 suggested Gaddafi had secretly given US$400 million to the Sandinistas in Nicaragua and sent a team of advisers to Managua. The kernel of the US case against Gaddafi was his supposed support for terrorism around the world, including targets in the United States. In a speech of June 1984 Gaddafi had told a Libyan audience that 'we are capable of exporting terrorism to the heart of America'. And in another speech on 1 September 1985 (the sixteenth anniversary of his coup) Gaddafi said: 'We have the right to fight America, and we have the right to export terrorism to them...'[9]

In March 1986 a US task force on terrorism under the chairmanship of Vice-President George Bush argued that military action could be used as a deterrent against future acts of terrorism. As it was, between 1981 and January 1986 US naval forces had carried out exercises off the Libyan coast on no less than 18 occasions, seven of them including operations inside what Gaddafi had called the 'line of death' across the mouth of the Gulf of Sidra. On 24 March, from the Sixth Fleet task force of 30 ships, planes from carriers began a total of 375 flights over the Gulf while three ships led by the cruiser *Ticonderoga* crossed the 'line of death' and remained in what were claimed as Libya's waters for 75 hours. Libyans and Americans each fired a number of missiles and two Libyan ships were sunk. On 5 April the explosion of a terrorist bomb in a West Berlin discotheque, La Belle, frequented by US servicemen provided the excuse Washington had been looking for. The bomb killed a US sergeant and a young Turkish woman and injured 230 people including 50 US service personnel. President Reagan blamed Gaddafi for the bomb: 'Our evidence is direct, it is precise, it is irrefutable.' As a consequence, over 14–15 April, US military planes from bases in Britain and the Sixth Fleet in the Mediterranean bombed Tripoli and Benghazi in retaliation for Libya's alleged responsibility for terrorist activities in Europe. Libyan casualties were 130, civilian and military, including Gaddafi's adopted daughter. Gaddafi accused President Reagan of being 'the world's number one terrorist'. The repercussions from this raid continued for several years: the standing of Gaddafi was strengthened – he had not been eliminated – while that of the US suffered from accusations of bullying and terrorism as well as ineptness.

Despite his unpopularity, Gaddafi's defiance of the United States was generally popular in the Third World. He had become to Washington what, a generation earlier, Nasser had been to London, a permanent thorn in the flesh, with the result that Washington was constantly on the lookout for an excuse to punish Gaddafi and if possible topple him from power. In the week following the raid, five US oil companies departed from Libya. By September 1986 at the Non-Aligned Summit in Harare, Gaddafi was sufficiently back to his old form to tell members that most of them were aligned to the West and that the movement was irrelevant.

During the 1980s a number of Libyan nationals in Europe who refused to return home were assassinated by Libyan 'hit-squads'. Britain, France, West Germany and the US therefore regulated the activities of the Libyan People's Bureaux in their countries. Britain's relations with Libya through the 1970s had generally been poor. In an effort to improve these, the British Minister of Health, Kenneth Clarke, visited Libya in February 1983 at a time when there were about 8,000 Libyan students studying in Britain and English was the second language in Libyan schools. However, the Libyans regarded London as a centre for dissident opposition movements and were fearful that opponents of the regime such as the National Front for the Salvation of Libya would influence an increasing number of the Libyan students in Britain. In consequence the Libyan regime began to organize its own followers in Britain and told them to eliminate opposition to Gaddafi. In September 1983 the anti-Gaddafi National Front for the Salvation of Libya held its first demonstration in London and the pro-Gaddafi revolutionary committees among students at once organized a counter-demonstration. There followed a steady escalation of violence between the two sides and this came to a head in 1984. In February 1984 representatives of the revolutionary students took over the Libyan People's Bureau in St James's Square, London, and orthodox Libyan diplomats were sent home. At a press conference on 18 February four revolutionary committee men who had taken over the Bureau 'accused Britain of harbouring people bent on undermining the Libyan revolution and pledged to eliminate all Gaddafi's opponents in the country. Though no one in Britain appeared to take them at their word or even to understand what they were driving at, the quartet stated uncompromisingly that, the "sole purpose of the takeover" was to escalate revolutionary activities in Britain.'[10]

An anti-Gaddafi demonstration outside the Libyan People's Bureau in St James's Square on 17 April 1984 led to a tragedy when a number of shots were fired from the Bureau against the demonstrators and WPC Yvonne Fletcher was killed. The British police besieged the Bureau for 10 days, after which the occupants were allowed to return to Libya under diplomatic immunity.

In the following year Gaddafi attempted to improve relations with Britain while the general British approach to Libya, despite the shooting of WPC Fletcher, was business as usual. In April 1986 Britain's Prime Minister Margaret Thatcher supported the US raid on Libya, not least because Gaddafi had supported Argentina's Gen. Galtieri during the Falklands War and had also provided assistance to the IRA in Northern Ireland. Despite this, Gaddafi was conciliatory towards Britain for the balance of the 1980s, perhaps because of low world demand for oil and the consequent weakness of the Libyan economy. However, this more ameliorative attitude did not last. Libya opposed the Gulf War against Iraq at the beginning of the 1990s and subsequent deteriorating relations with Britain culminated, on 17 June 1991, with a meeting of the General People's Congress (GPC) when Gaddafi said: 'To hell with Britain and relations with it until the day of judgement... To hell with Britain and America, as children would say.'[11] Any hopes of rapprochment disappeared once the US, Britain and France had been convinced that the Lockerbie bomb of 21 December 1988 that destroyed Pan Am Flight 103 with a total loss of 270 lives was a Libyan terrorist act. An article in the London *Sunday Telegraph* of 16 April 1989 implicated Libya in the bombing. This coloured their relations with Libya through the 1990s.

Gaddafi's relations with France were equally strained over the decade. The Libyan intervention in Chad caused permanent tension with France until a settlement of the dispute was finally reached at the end of the 1980s. In Tunisia, following the Gafsa incident of February 1980, when guerrillas raided the Tunisian mining town of that name to incite a rebellion and Tunisia blamed Libya, France sent military forces to support the Tunisian government. In reaction, Libyan mobs burned the French embassy in Tripoli and its consulate in Benghazi. This affair brought to the surface Gaddafi's deep resentment of French neo-colonialist activities. Relations were further set back in 1984 following an agreement by the two countries to withdraw simultaneously from Chad. The French kept their side of the agreement but the Libyans remained in Chad, much to the chagrin of France's President François Mitterand who was left looking foolish. Yet another cause of Franco-Libyan tension was the destruction of the French flight UTA 772, which exploded over Niger in 1989 as the result of a bomb, killing 171 people. In 1991 France issued arrest warrants for four Libyans that it claimed were responsible for the bomb outrage.

Libya's relations with the USSR were more circumspect; the principal tie between the two countries was the purchase of Soviet arms by Libya. This relationship was to change as world demand for oil collapsed so that Libya no longer enjoyed the surpluses that had enabled it to purchase large Soviet arms shipments. In 1983 the USSR proposed a full treaty of friendship between the two countries, for Moscow needed the sale of arms to Libya to continue. However, the Soviet intervention in Afghanistan from 1979 to 1988 posed a difficult problem for Gaddafi since he made a point of insisting upon Muslim solidarity. An American appraisal of Libyan-Soviet relations at the beginning of the 1980s made these closer than the reality: 'Libya is the foremost Soviet arms customer, and in recent years Qadhafi has increasingly provided the Soviet armed forces access to Libyan facilities. Libya serves Soviet aims without a formal relationship, for Soviet arms find their way through Libya to subversive groups and terrorists whose arms serve Soviet interests.'[12] During the Libyan confrontation with the US in 1986, the USSR was careful to keep at arm's length. Moscow had not ratified the treaty of friendship it had proposed in 1983 when Maj. Abdul Salam Jalloud had visited Moscow. By the end of the 1980s the USSR was pressing Libya for the immediate settlement of debts for arms, a sum of approximately US$5 billion. Thus, Libya's relations with the USSR and the Communist bloc were deteriorating just as the Cold War came to an end.

By the end of the 1980s Libya had more enemies than friends yet Gaddafi had an unique capacity to reverse bad relations, at least to his own satisfaction, and in 1989 he contrived to move Libya out of the isolation into which his policies had forced it. He initiated a process of conciliation towards Libya's Arab neighbours: he lifted restrictions on foreign travel for Libyans, which proved highly popular; participated in moves to make UMA more effective; concluded a peace accord with Chad; achieved a reconciliation with Egypt; and managed to improve relations with both France and Italy. At home Gaddafi needed to protect his position as undisputed leader in the face of the growth of militant Islamist groups; he did this by breaking up the army and replacing army units with General Defence Committees, which assumed control of the 'Armed people'. Although this move had a powerful propaganda impact outside Libya it brought the military under the control of People's Committees and eliminated the possibility of a coup so that all real power rested with Gaddafi. Nonetheless, Islamic opposition to Gaddafi became an important factor in January 1989 when clashes occurred at al-Fatah University in Tripoli between pro-fundamentalist students and the security forces. The disturbances were quelled but further violence erupted on 20 January between members of the Revolutionary Committee and worshippers at a Tripoli mosque, and 4,000 people attending mosque services in the city were arrested. In fact Islamic radicalism had existed underground throughout the 1980s although any political expression of it resulted in severe punishment including public executions. The greatest support for such radicalism was found among young people. Possibly Gaddafi's biggest breakthrough in 1989 was the rapprochment with Egypt. At the Casablanca Arab League Summit of 24–26 May, which Gaddafi had attended under pressure from Algeria's President Benjedid, Gaddafi and Egypt's President Mubarak embraced. Since Libya's relations with Algeria and Tunisia had also improved Libya agreed to assist funding UMA.

The Horn:
Continuous Warfare

The endless fighting that characterized the Horn of Africa throughout the 1980s – the Eritrean war of secession from Ethiopia, the civil war between North and South in the Sudan and the clan warfare that escalated steadily in Somalia – provided ample justification for those who sought to dismiss Africa as a hopeless geopolitical mess. It was, after all, the decade during which Africa came to be referred to as a 'basket case'. Only rarely were appropriate questions asked: why such wars, why so long, what were the root causes of the conflicts? In part, the answer lay with political leaders who pinned their reputations to a victory that was unattainable; they only saw, with classic short-sightedness, that any surrender to a different point of view was bound to be interpreted as a surrender of their power. In part, the dilemma went far deeper. Every African country, with the single and in this case ironic exception of Somalia, had agreed with the 1963 OAU ruling that the newly emerging states of the continent should accept their inherited colonial boundaries and this ruling had become a commandment set in stone. Yet in the three conflicts in the Horn, Eritrea would eventually break away from Ethiopia and the northern part of Somalia (the former British Somaliland) would proclaim its independence, although in the case of the Sudan nothing had been resolved by the end of the century.

SUDAN UNDER NIMEIRI

Sudan's Permanent Constitution was amended in 1980 in order to allow the introduction of regional governments in the northern part of the country and five regions were established. These were the Northern Region, the Eastern Region, the Central Region, Kordofan Region and Darfur Region while a separate administration was set up for Khartoum. Under the Southern Provinces Regional Act 1972, the South had become a self-governing region comprising the three provinces of Bahr El Ghazal, Equatoria and Upper Nile.

These had been subdivided in 1976 into three additional provinces – Lakes, Jonglei and Eastern Equatoria. A framework of self-government was created including a parliamentary system. An elected legislature (the Regional Assembly) and an executive – the High Executive Council – were established. Following the Addis Ababa Agreement, which had led to the Southern Province's Regional Act, the South enjoyed a special status in the Sudan and for a time North-South relations were to run smoothly. However, in June 1983 Nimeiri decreed the creation of three regions in Southern Sudan and a Presidential system of guided democracy was established in them, and the three provinces of Bahr El Ghazal, Equatoria and Upper Nile were transformed into three regions with partly elected and partly appointed legislatures. Executive power in each region was vested in a Governor appointed by the President. The Governor for each region, who was assisted by a deputy and five ministers responsible to him, was alone responsible to the President. The proposal for this division originated in Equatoria with Joseph Lagu whose object was to end Dinka domination of the South. Hostility to the Dinka was a permanent concern of the other weaker ethnic groups in the South and as one non-Dinka member of the Sudan Socialist Union (SSU) told the Regional Assembly, 'It took the Sudan 50 years to get rid of the British; it took Southerners 17 years to get rid of the Arabs; it will take you (Southerners) 100 years to get rid of the Dinka.'[1] Lagu had also insisted that the 'division of the South into regions would bring leaders from Upper Nile and Bahr El Ghazal nearer to their people, which was bound to improve development in these areas'.

A reflection on tribalism in Africa at this time by Southern members of the Fourth National Assembly highlighted the tensions that dominated Southern politics:

> Tribalism is still a very strong force in African politics. It was the main obstacle to the African Liberation Movement, and the tribal chiefs the main reactionary force... Nobody will deny tribalism in the Southern Political Leadership since 1972. The Solidarity Committee notes the monopoly of the Dinka tribe in some public institutions... It is at this point that we stand with Joseph Lagu... The question before every citizen of the South is whether the Dinka domination can only be avoided by re-dividing up the Southern Region... Today in Africa, tribes are not preferably accommodated in autonomous regions as a solution to problems their differences pose. Instead, concern of political leaders in Africa is how to integrate them into modern nations, states and societies within a democratic framework.[2]

In late 1983, when his popularity was in freefall, Nimeiri tried to pacify his critics and silence the opposition by the manipulation of religion. He Islamized the laws by replacing all the statutes with the principles of Sharia, a move that angered many people and especially those in the non-Muslim South. Discontent in the South had steadily increased since the end of the 1970s and, after Nimeiri announced his plan to re-divide the southern region, discontent turned into resistance with the formation of the Council for the Unity of Southern Sudan (CUSS). This, in turn, led to the formation of the Sudanese People's Liberation Movement (SPLM) and its military wing, the Sudanese People's Liberation Army (SPLA). The SPLM/SPLA was not a secessionist movement but sought progressive change for the Sudan as a whole. To many Southerners Nimeiri's plan appeared simply a way of weakening them in relation to the central government in Khartoum so that Khartoum would get the greater part of the new revenues from the oil that had been discovered. The US company Chevron was to extract the oil and construct a 1,500-mile pipeline from south-central Sudan to Port Sudan on the Red Sea. In the south it seemed that the oil would bind Washington to the north. As the Vice-President of Standard Oil said: 'We get the feeling that Washington is determined that Sudan should not be lost.' However, by this time Nimeiri's regime was collapsing and he was trying to divert attention from his internal problems by suggesting that Ethiopia intended to invade the Sudan. In an article in *Newsweek* Hilary Ng'weno, the editor-in-chief of the Nairobi *Weekly Review,* wrote:

> A human tragedy of major proportions is in the making in Sudan, where President Jaafar Nimeiri seems determined to plunge the country back into bloody Civil War. Nimeiri decided last year to split the Southern end of the country into the three regional provinces, thereby weakening the local power structure and bringing the region more directly under the control of his regime in Khartoum. He did this over the objection of most of the political leaders in the South and in flagrant contravention of the solemn peace treaty that ended Civil War between the North and the South in 1972.[3]

In the period immediately preceding the coup that toppled Nimeiri it seems likely that the US and other Western powers encouraged a propaganda campaign to get rid of him. Further, it seemed almost certain that US Vice-President George Bush was involved in the reshuffle that brought Gen. Sewar El Dahab to the most prominent position in the Sudan military. He was appointed Defence Minister and Commander-in-Chief of the Armed Forces on 16 March 1985, just a few days before Bush visited Khartoum.[4] Nimeiri was overthrown on 6 April and Sewar El Dahab became interim ruler. It was admitted in some Western media that the coup of 6 April took place in accordance with a plan made jointly by the generals who took power and Sudan's regional and global allies. According to *Africa Confidential* Dahab and other generals 'made arrangements in advance with Egypt and possibly the United States, in order to pre-empt moves by middle rank officers and civilians'.[5] The Sudanese were glad to see Nimeiri go but were not happy at a continuation of military rule. Even so, 30 political parties and 77 trade unions emerged. Exiles returned and hundreds of political prisoners, including Communists, were freed. By July the US had become uneasy when Sudan's new rulers concluded a military pact with Libya; Gaddafi now agreed to co-operate with regard to the southern problem. As the Sudanese Defence Minister said, the Libyans 'promised that they would no longer aid the southern rebels'.

AFTER NIMEIRI

Ali Mazrui commented on the fall of Nimeiri that 'In the streets of Khartoum in 1985, young people protested against President Jaafar Nimeiri and forced the army to intervene and bring Nimeiri down after more than 15 years in power. Civilian rule was later restored.' Possibly it was the young people but civilian rule would not last very long. Immediately, the Transitional Military Council (TMC) ruled Sudan for a year before elections were held in April 1986. Sadiq al-Mahdi's Umma Party (UP) won 99 seats, Osman al-Mirghani's Democratic Unionist Party (DUP) won 63 and the National Islamic Front (NIF), led by Dr Hassan al-Turabi, won 51 seats. In the south voting in 37 of 68 seats was suspended because of violence. Sadiq al-Mahdi became Prime Minister of a coalition government. In July he held talks in Addis Ababa with the American-educated Christian Dinka, John Garang, who was the leader of the SPLA, in an effort to end the civil war. The talks came to nothing. In 1988 al-Mahdi was re-elected prime minister by the assembly, obtaining 196 of 222 votes cast. The three main parties – UP, DUP and NIF – agreed to implement an Islamic code although al-Mahdi stressed this should not infringe the rights of non-Muslims. In August 1988 the worst floods in the country's history rendered two million people around Khartoum homeless. Sadiq al-Mahdi's government was overthrown in a bloodless military coup on 30 June 1989 by army officers who had been pressing for peace in the south; negotiations had been stymied under the coalition because the NIF wanted to impose Sharia on the south. The new government, headed by Gen. Omar al-Bashir, was welcomed by Egypt and, more discreetly, by Britain and the US. Garang, however, mistrusted Bashir because he wanted to leave the question of Sharia to a national referendum, which would give Muslims an automatic majority.

The US was an important factor in the political calculations of Sudan's leaders throughout the decade. In the mid-1980s and later, the US provided Sudan with substantial aid: US$67 million in 1988, US$77.4 million in 1989. This aid kept the government afloat but did little for the ordinary people. Garang meanwhile had expanded his base of support. In 1987 he persuaded the Nuer to join him: their organization, Anya Nya II, was heir to the first Anya Nya that had directed the civil war that ended in 1972. Garang won other support as well and for a time appeared to be developing into a formidable war leader. In January 1988 his forces occupied Kapoeta on the Uganda border in the extreme south of the country. The costs of the war were massive and by the summer of 1988 three million people were close to starvation and 385,000 had crossed the border into Ethiopia. Refugees were dependent upon internal relief organizations for their survival and US aid officials accused the Khartoum government of genocide in the south. However, the politics of aid were always devious; thus the US restrained its criticisms of Khartoum's policy towards the south for fear of driving it into the arms of Libya's Gaddafi. By February 1989 the US State Department reported that between 100,000 and 250,000 had died of starvation in the south as the military on both sides in the conflict intercepted relief supplies. What soon became apparent after the June 1989 coup was that with the backing of the NIF, which moved swiftly to repress other political parties, Sudan was set for military rule and Islamist politics. By March 1990 it was apparent that the new regime had turned to repression and on 22 April, according to the government, there was an attempted coup. This failed and four days later 28 senior army officers were executed by firing squad. They had been opponents of the application of strict Sharia.

THE ROOTS OF THE CONFLICT

One over-simplistic explanation for Sudan's long-drawn-out civil war has been offered by Huntington in his *Clash of Civilizations* in which he argues, 'Cleft countries that territorially bestride the fault lines between civilizations face particular problems maintaining their unity. In Sudan, civil war has gone on for decades between the Muslim north and the largely Christian south'. Later in his book, he says, 'The bloodiest Muslim-Christian war has been in Sudan, which has gone on for decades and produced hundreds of thousands of casualties.'[6] Huntington clearly wants Sudan to fit his thesis of the clash of civilizations yet many others accept his explanation that the north-south conflict is basically a religious one. In relation to Eritrea, fighting its secessionist war against Addis

Ababa, he argues, 'In Sudan during the 1980s the government adopted increasingly extreme Islamist positions, and in the early 1990s the Christian insurgency split, with a new group, the Southern Sudan Independence Movement, advocating independence rather than simply autonomy.' Always emphasizing the religious divide, Huntington underestimates the realpolitik that dictates political strategy in a war situation. Thus he says, 'In Africa Sudan regularly helped the Muslim Eritrean rebels fighting Ethiopia, and in retaliation Ethiopia supplied "logistic and sanctuary support" to the "rebel Christians" fighting Sudan. The latter also received similar aid from Uganda, reflecting in part its "strong religious, racial, and ethnic ties to the Sudanese rebels". The Sudanese government, on the other hand, got US$300 million in Chinese arms from Iran and training from Iranian military advisers, which enabled it to launch a major offensive against the rebels in 1992. A variety of Western Christian organizations provided food, medicine, supplies, and, according to the Sudanese government, arms to the Christian rebels.'[7]

It is true that the war in Sudan is usually described in terms of a struggle between Islam and Christianity with the side effect, no doubt pleasing to Christians who see the struggle in this light, of suggesting that the southern Sudanese have no coherent religions of their own. Instead, they are referred to 'with depressing regularity as "Christian and animist" (or sometimes even "Christian animist"). "Animism" is an archaic term with little descriptive value. In its original sense it referred to a theory of the origin of primitive religion. It has since been adapted as a pseudo-scientific replacement for "pagan", to avoid the latter's pejorative overtones acquired from centuries of Christian propaganda.'[8] The same author goes on to examine the wide range of problems that have acted to separate north and south. These include a habit of the centre versus the periphery derived from slavery and slave raiding in the past; the inequalities of development during the colonial period; the introduction of militant Islam during the nineteenth century; Britain giving independence in 1956 before disparities in development between north and south had been sorted out; northern nationalism creating an Arab-based state; the growing southern awareness of its strength in resources that were generally exploited by the north for the north; and the impact of the Cold War that included a massive flow of arms into the region. As Douglas Johnson argues cogently:

> The final paradox of Sudanese independence was that it was thrust upon the Sudan by a colonial power eager to extricate itself from its residual responsibilities. It was not achieved by a national consensus expressed through constitutional means. A precedent was set that has haunted Sudanese politics ever since: the precedent of taking the popular will for

granted, and therefore circumventing agreed legal procedures in all major constitutional issues. The first post-independence Constituent Assembly was dissolved in 1958 rather than allow it to take a decision on federalism; the referendum in the South was aborted in 1982 rather than let the people of the South register their opposition to the subdivision of the Southern Region; parliamentary government was overthrown in 1989 rather than let it reach a compromise over the Islamic state. Those acts were all committed by Sudanese leaders; but they learned from Britain at the very inception of the Sudan's independence the rewards for ignoring democratic and constitutional procedures.[9]

Development or the deliberate withholding of it from the south by the north is at least as important a divisive factor as is religion and Khartoum ever since independence has shown itself more concerned to extract the south's resources with a minimum return to the south than to build a modern comprehensive state. In these circumstances it was hardly surprising in 1983, when the civil war was resumed, that the SPLA attacked the two most profitable developments in the region, the Jonglei Canal project and oil extraction. Nonetheless, the SPLA fought to change the government of the Sudan and not to secede.

At the same time that the north-south conflict developed into an endless war of attrition, the government in Khartoum, with the support of the West and the conservative Arab states, allowed the Eritrean nationalist movements to menace the Ethiopian regime as long as it maintained friendly relations with the USSR. By 1983–85, in any case, the Ethiopian offensives against the Eritreans had pushed hundreds of thousands of them over the border into Sudan. There existed a close link between Eritrea and Sudan. 'The peasants of western Eritrea look to Sudan principally for sales and purchase of necessities which include food, other consumer items, seeds, tools etc. The normal currency for transactions... is the Sudanese pound... Moreover, the trade with Sudan is mainly explained by the fact that the two economies are complementary to each other, and even if there had not been a war, the people of western Eritrea would still have bought and sold on the Sudanese market and might have been as dependent on it as they are today.[10]

ETHIOPIA

By 1980, with massive Soviet and Cuban assistance, Mengistu had re-established his control over the whole country except for Eritrea. The wars in the Ogaden, Tigray and Oromo provinces that had escalated during the late 1970s had degenerated into ongoing guerrilla actions. At this point, the most favourable for such action, Mengistu might have inaugurated successful policies to unite the country, but he failed to do so. In 1984, despite massive international aid, one million people were to die as a result of the famine. The fighting was to continue throughout the 1980s while policy increasingly became the prerogative of Mengistu alone since he had eliminated his rivals to make himself effective dictator of Ethiopia. The greatest, most consistent challenge to Mengistu's regime throughout the 1980s came from Eritrea whose Eritrean People's Liberation Front (EPLF) pursued its objective of secession with the single-minded determination of all true freedom fighters. They still, however, had a long war to fight. Their alliance with the revolting province of Tigray that lay between Eritrea and Addis Ababa was to prove strategically crucial to their eventual success.

On 12 September 1984, on the tenth anniversary of the revolution, the Workers' Party of Ethiopia (WPE) was inaugurated. In retrospect, Western fears of Soviet influence and Communism in Africa appear hugely inflated but at the time the West feared that the Ethiopian revolution would encourage revolutionary movements throughout the region and that Ethiopia would become 'a Soviet showcase in Africa as a whole' and that this would 'not be desirable for the West, since what happens in Ethiopia affects not just the Horn of Africa, but the Red Sea, such conservative Gulf States as Saudi Arabia, and the countries through which the Nile River flows, including Egypt and Sudan'.[11] This was to extend the 'domino theory' with a vengeance. Mengistu was to survive for as long as he did as a result of Soviet support but when that was withdrawn at the end of the decade, he faced a series of increasingly severe defeats as his forces were driven out of most of Eritrea and the Tigrayan rebels took control of their province and then, in early 1991, launched what turned out to be the last, decisive offensive against the regime in Addis Ababa.

Economically Mengistu's rule was a disaster and quite apart from the famine of 1984 and lesser famines in subsequent years, the imposition of Marxist orthodoxy simply did not work but was rejected by the Ethiopians as a whole. Instead, Mengistu only succeeded in making Ethiopia both poorer and more backward than it had been when the revolution had been carried out in the 1970s, for although at that time there had been real elements of the popular will at work, by the 1980s it had become a revolution imposed from above for which there was little popular consent.

The war in Tigray was both separate and yet crucial to the eventual success of the Eritrean war. In 1979 the Tigray People's Liberation Front (TPLF) had captured several towns in Tigray and cut the road which connected Addis Ababa and Eritrea; the towns were recaptured by Ethiopian forces although the

TPLF retained control of the countryside. The Ethiopians, therefore, ravaged the countryside yet despite high Tigrayan casualties the Ethiopian army failed to reoccupy Western Tigray. There was a similar campaign in 1983 and then in 1984 Tigray was badly affected by the famine. Throughout the decade Tigray was central to the war since it lay athwart the road to Eritrea, and the defeat of the EPLF was Mengistu's first priority. The war in Tigray escalated in 1987 and famine returned to the region in 1988 but the Ethiopian army was unable to regain control of the province though it continued to hold the towns. In the spring of 1988 the Ethiopian military faced a double defeat: its forces were badly mauled in northern Eritrea by the EPLF while the TPLF mounted a second offensive in Tigray and the Ethiopian army was reduced to defending the road through Tigray to Eritrea while abandoning its attempts to hold the rest of the province. A year later, in March 1989, the TPLF broke out of its home province to invade Gondar, Wollo and Shoa in what was to be the final stage of the war.

One bizarre and provocative side issue was the operation to 'save' the Falasha Jews from Ethiopia. Preparations to save the Falashas had got under way in the United States in 1981 under the aegis of the extremist American League for Defence of Ethiopian Jews, which then began work in Sudan, and though some Sudanese politicians opposed the move they were forced to back down by US pressures. In early 1985 the 'rescue' operation was carried out and some thousands of Falashas were persuaded to cross into Sudan whence they were airlifted via Italy, Belgium or Switzerland to Israel. They came to about 10,000 all told. The whole operation was deliberately provocative to Ethiopia. At the same time Israel became involved in the war but though it provided some support to the EPLF and TPLF, its real interest was in the propaganda rescue of the Falashas. 'The Israeli government was aware that Haile Selassie's regime oppressed national minorities including the Jews. But still it fully supported the regime and raised no issue about the plight of the Falashas.'[12] Its concern for the Falashas when Mengistu was in power was clearly motivated, in part, by considerations of US support. However, the new Sudanese government that came to power under Sewar El Dahab on the fall of Nimeiri soon demonstrated that it was not to be a puppet of US pressures and 'made clear that it was not going to collaborate with the US and Israel against Ethiopia by organizing and effecting the exodus of the Falashas to Israel. In fact it established a Commission of Inquiry with the declared intention or prosecuting those who were involved in the affair.'[13]

In May 1989 a major coup attempt by senior army officers nearly ended the Mengistu regime. It was put into operation when Mengistu was on a state visit to East Germany (DDR), forcing him to cut short his visit and hurry back to

Addis Ababa. There was substantial fighting between military loyalists and the coup makers. After the collapse of the coup Mengistu initiated a nationwide hunt for the coup-makers: 15 generals were executed and eventually 176 Army, Navy and Air Force officers, including 24 generals, were court-martialled in Addis Ababa. Although Mengistu had survived, the opposition to him and his policies had become widespread and he only had two more years in office ahead of him. The end for the Mengistu regime was signalled during 1989 when it became clear that, as a result of Mikhail Gorbachev's new policies, the USSR intended to bring to an end its ongoing commitments to the Dergue. In any case, the war with Eritrea appeared to have no end while the implementation of Marxism had brought upon the Ethiopian people hardship rather than relief. By that time the USSR had provided Ethiopia with an estimated US$10 billion in aid. During September, as the final 3,000 Cuban forces left Ethiopia, an attempt to negotiate a settlement was tried at Jimmy Carter's Centre for Conflict Resolution in Atlanta but it failed: the EPLF wanted independence, Ethiopia insisted on the integrity of the state. Then, in February 1990, the EPLF launched a final offensive and attacked Massawa, and the Soviet Navy offshore did not assist the Ethiopians. The EPLF then laid siege to Keren and Asmara, the government's final outposts in Eritrea. The TPLF, meanwhile, had gained control of all Tigray; it established a united front, the Ethiopian People's Revolutionary Democratic Front (EPRDF) with the Ethiopian People's Democratic Movement, a largely Amhara organization, and other revolutionary groups. The EPRDF took the offensive and by early summer its armies were within 60 miles of Addis Ababa. The final collapse came the following year when, on 21 May 1991, Mengistu resigned and fled to Zimbabwe. On 25 May the Eritreans captured Assab to give them control of the whole province. On 27 May the Ethiopian Army surrendered to the rebels and the EPRDF entered Addis Ababa to bring the rule of the Dergue to an end.

ERITREA

The Eritrean war of secession was one of the longest and hardest fought in Africa. The Ethiopian army mounted eight major offensives against Eritrea between 1973 and 1988 and was driven back each time with heavy losses. In 1982 Operation Red Star involving 140,000 troops resulted in 40,000 dead and wounded; despite their apparently overwhelming military strength, backed by the Soviets and Cubans, they failed to capture the northern strongholds in Eritrea. In 1987–88 the EPLF launched a series of attacks on the Ethiopian army, inflicted heavy casualties and broke through its front. On tour of the front line Mengistu arrested a number of officers and had Brig. Gen. Taiku

Taye shot in front of his men *'pour encourager les autres'* although the incident led to a collapse of morale. On 17 March 1988 the EPLF launched a general offensive and in a series of battles claimed to have killed 18,000 Ethiopians, captured a further 6,000, wiped out an armoured brigade and taken several cities, including Af Abet, a principal Ethiopian depot and garrison town. The defeats of early 1988 were sufficiently severe to force Mengistu to call for volunteers throughout Ethiopia and to demand that every Ethiopian should contribute a month's wages or pension towards the costs of the war. More to the point, he reached an agreement with Somalia to restore diplomatic relations, which allowed him to airlift troops to the north from the 150,000 stationed on the Somali border.

The EPLF did not attempt to hold onto the towns it had captured but withdrew its forces to the countryside. By the end of 1988, despite the calls to the nation to rally behind the war effort and the transfer of troops from the Ogaden front to the north, the Ethiopian army was demoralized and on the defensive, holding its last line in Eritrea from Asmara to Massawa on the Red Sea. Parallel with these defeats the regime adopted increasingly brutal tactics. It decreed that the territory along the coast to the north of Massawa was a free-fire zone and anything mobile in it was attacked from the air: this was the grazing area for Eritrean nomads and the policy was to starve them into submission. Elsewhere in Eritrea the Ethiopians adopted scorched-earth tactics and systematically devastated the countryside. According to relief agencies, from March to August 1988 between 350,000 and 500,000 Eritreans from Massawa to Keren were forced to flee their homes. During the famine of 1984 and the second one of 1988 Mengistu prevented foreign relief agencies working in Eritrea and stopped Ethiopian agencies from doing so as well. The famine of 1988 affected seven million people throughout Ethiopia. In April 1988 Mengistu expelled all foreign aid workers from the northern provinces on 'security' grounds, claiming that Ethiopian relief organizations could handle the crisis. Although it had begun as a Marxist organization the EPLF gradually softened its stance through the 1980s, particularly as the USSR was giving its full support to Ethiopia while Sudan and Saudi Arabia were prepared to assist the EPLF. It changed its attitude further as it witnessed the failure of Marxism elsewhere in Africa. However, it was distrustful of outside supporters, except for Somalia which had been unwavering in its solidarity. The EPLF always managed to obtain the weapons it required, including large amounts of arms captured from the Ethiopians.

THE ORGANIZATION OF THE EPLF

During the 1980s the EPLF developed into one of the most efficient of all the liberation movements that Africa spawned in the second half of the century. The organizational outreach of the EPLF was not limited to Eritreans within Eritrea; an important source of political and financial support as well as recruitment was among Eritreans who had fled the country. These included refugees in Sudan, those who had moved into Ethiopia as well as the Eritrean communities in the US and Europe. Refugees accounted for the largest number of Eritreans outside the country and the great majority of these came from the Muslim communities. Sudan acted as the main transit route to other continents and at the time of liberation there were over 600,000 in Sudan. EPLF strength was derived, in part, from the destruction of the other liberation movement, the Eritrean Liberation Front (ELF), and this was assisted by the EPLF alliance with the TPLF. 'The defeat of the ELF in the 1981–82 civil war was also a product of military co-operation between the EPLF and the Tigray People's Liberation Front (TPLF), an important component of the EPLF's strategy of seeking allies among political groups opposed to the Dergue.'[14] Despite the break in their relations in the mid-1980s, the strength of the TPLF in Tigray, which was a major staging post for Ethiopian offensives against Eritrea, and military co-operation between it and the EPLF in the late 1980s and in the final assault on the Mengistu regime, the alliance was of the utmost strategic importance. This alliance made possible EPLF operations deep into Ethiopia. The EPLF became a highly centralized and disciplined military and political organization with spheres for initiative allocated to the cadre, battalion, brigade and divisional commanders. The EPLF also faced a non-military challenge in the 1980s, that of famine, and succeeded in turning this challenge into opportunities for its development, particularly in the arena of international legitimization, so that it expanded its governmental role in dealing with the problem despite Ethiopian opposition.

US POLICY TOWARDS ERITREA

US 'plans' for Eritrea that had been formulated and changed from the 1950s onwards depended upon what happened in Ethiopia. The EPLF realized that it could not assume automatic US support for an independent Eritrean state once Mengistu had gone and that Eritrean independence, in the end, would be determined by the Eritreans alone. Chester Crocker, US Assistant Secretary for African Affairs, was a consistent critic of President Carter's African policy and had opposed Andrew Young's line that in the light of African nationalism, US policy should back African solutions to African problems. Instead, he said, 'African nationalism is fuelled by an infusion of communist military equipment.' He continued: '... in Africa's increasingly militarized context, a policy of support for African solutions may in fact amount to support for military solutions imposed by other external powers'.[15] Policy-makers in Washington understood that states or movements in developing countries could be authentically anti-imperialist only in alliance with the world revolutionary movement, especially the USSR and the socialist community. In the Carter years analysts began to advocate support for 'communist' states in Asia and Africa which 'demonstrate independence from Moscow and willingness to contribute to overall stability'. At the same time these analysts called for measures to 'restrain and... isolate' revolutionary democratic regimes like those of South Yemen and Ethiopia.[16] Increasingly, through the 1980s, the EPLF came to distrust the policy objectives of both the US and USSR. Cold War complexities always had to be taken into account. Thus, in 1980, 'Egypt supplied the EPLF with Soviet-made weapons it had acquired when it enjoyed good relations with the USSR. It provided them to the EPLF pursuant to an understanding with Washington on this matter.' Similarly, 'The Ba'athite government of Iraq, formerly abused in the EPLF media, now provided material support, including pharmaceutical and medical assistance. In 1980, Iraqi transport planes were to fly wounded EPLF fighters from Kassala, Sudan, to Baghdad for treatment.'[17]

Crocker advocated a policy based on US interest and argued that even food be used 'as a tool for the promotion of... US interest – either developmental or political'. His Africa policy recommendations for the 1980s included the following statement: 'In the coming decade, policy makers will need to develop a more careful calculation of the means-ends relationship in African policy. At the same time, the case for an activist regional policy must be based more explicitly on clearly defined American interests that can be understood and supported at home.'[18] The Reagan administration saw support for the Eritreans as a means of countering Soviet and Cuban support for the Ethiopian regime. Peter Duignan, of the Hoover Institution, said: 'Our basic objective ought to be to push the Ethiopians back to their old borders. They don't belong... in Eritrea.' This was to reverse the US line of 20 years previously when it had supported Haile Selassie's federation. 'The US now took several other steps which were a threat to Ethiopia. These were the establishment of a base at the Kenyan port of Mombasa, the increase of military assistance to the Sudan, the supply of sophisticated weapons to Saudi Arabia, and the escalation of US military presence in North Yemen... The forces in collusion with US imperialism included the EPLF in Eritrea and the TPLF in northern Ethiopia.

The EPLF had once again resumed parading as a "Marxist" organisation. The TPLF also claimed to be "Marxist" and socialist oriented.' The author of these statements makes the following point about US policy. 'The policy planners in Washington fully realized that "Marxist" or "socialist" was of no consequence as long as these movements were anti-Soviet.'[19]

The EPLF leader Issayas Afewerki said in an interview in April 1984 that the EPLF would negotiate a settlement in Eritrea but not necessarily with the 'present regime' in Ethiopia. Eritrea under the EPLF 'can allow' Ethiopia 'an outlet to the sea' and establish 'economic, social, cultural and other ties'. This would not be possible with the present (Mengistu) regime but 'with a genuine government that does represent the Ethiopian population'. In 1985 President Reagan asserted that in Ethiopia '... 1,700 Soviet advisers are involved in military planning and support operations along with 2,500 Cuban combat troops'. According to the *New York Times*, one of 'Reagan's five trouble spots' was Ethiopia, where 'Eritrean rebels seeking secession or substantial autonomy are fighting Soviet-backed government forces. Government is also fighting insurgents in Tigre'.[20] By 1989 the defeat of the Ethiopians appeared certain and this was assured when in 1990 Massawa was captured and the EPLF invested Asmara. Issayas Afewerki could say with conviction early in the year that 'victory is only months away'. Even so, the EPLF stood by its promise that it would not proclaim an independent Eritrea until the issue had been submitted to the people by referendum. The final offensive came in 1991. 'After 30 years of armed struggle and 20 years of intense military conflict, Eritrea had attained *de facto* independence and had facilitated the establishment of a government in Addis Ababa that was not opposed to an independent state. Independence had great costs: around 65,000 fighters had died, 10,000 were disabled, an estimated 40,000 civilian deaths were directly associated with the fighting and around 90,000 children were left without parents.'[21]

SOMALIA

At the end of the 1970s the Carter Administration in the US decided to back Somalia as part of its Cold War manoeuvring in the Horn. In August 1980 Washington and Mogadishu concluded an accord under which the US installed a military base at Berbera and supplied Somalia with millions of dollars of credits for the purchase of defensive arms. Subsequently, according to *Newsweek*, the Reagan Administration was prepared to seek 'expanded military assistance for the Somalis and not being too fussy whether some of the weapons find their way to Somali insurgents operating inside Ethiopian territory'. Early in 1981 the Reagan Administration considered 'ending Somalia's diplomatic isolation on the question of the Ogaden by backing Somali territorial claims within well defined limits'.[22] Thereafter, as another commentator points out, 'For a decade from 1978, even as Barre hardened repressive measures, the US spilled US$800 million into the country, one quarter for military "aid", in exchange for its own military access to ports and airports. Somalia's former colonial master, Italy, contributed US$1 billion from 1981 to 1990, more than half of which went for weapons. The value of foreign aid to Somalia soared to US$80 per person, the highest rate in Africa and equivalent to half the gross domestic product.'[23] Such figures demonstrate just how easily poor countries that are deemed to be strategically important by the major powers can obtain weapons of war.

Border confrontations between Somalia and Ethiopia continued through the 1980s with the Barre government supporting the Western Somali Liberation Front (WSLF). In turn Mengistu supported the Somali National Movement (SNM) as well as the Democratic Front for the Salvation of Somalia (DFSS), both of which had been formed in 1981. In neither case did these forces pose real threats to the regimes. Somalia's insistence upon self-determination for Ethiopia's Somali population of the Ogaden kept Somalia isolated, since its policy went against the general OAU principle of inviolable borders. Thus, at the 1981 OAU summit Somalia found little support for its stand. In 1985 the DFSS seized a strip of land on the Ethiopian border; however, the movement then became rent with dissensions and the Ethiopians arrested its leader, Col. Abdullah Yusuf. In 1986, following a conference between Ethiopia and Somalia in Djibouti, Ethiopia agreed to scale down its support for the DFSS. A principal complaint of northerners in Somalia (as with southerners in Sudan) was simply that their region was neglected by the government in Mogadishu, which concentrated upon development in the south. The SNM fed upon this discontent and the threat it posed to government became important in 1987. Meanwhile, the government had to face a new refugee problem. Some refugees had returned to Ethiopia voluntarily during the first half of the1980s but a massive new influx took place in 1986 comprised of Ethiopians fleeing Mengistu's villageization programme and up to 840,000 had to be accommodated.

During 1987 dissidence in the north increased dramatically and the SNM launched a number of attacks from bases in Ethiopia against government positions in the north. In May 1987 the SNM claimed for the second time in the year that it had captured Hargeisa, Burao and Berbera. This claim, however, was denied in Mogadishu and was not borne out by the facts. However, fierce fighting in 1988 reduced Hargeisa and Burao to rubble; an estimated 50,000 people lost their lives and 400,000 refugees fled into Ethiopia. In Hargeisa, which was a government centre, 14,000 buildings were flattened and a further 12,000 heavily damaged. When in mid-July government forces recaptured Burao they found it had been wrecked. This phase of the war in the north was estimated to have cost the government the equivalent of 40 per cent of its annual revenue. By November 1988 government forces were generally in control though there was more fighting in Hargeisa. The government forces did not feel secure and Somalia was reported to be importing nerve gas from Libya.

The situation did not improve in 1989. Barre attempted to improve his image in the wake of the 1988 civil war in the north by visiting a number of Arab countries while his Prime Minister, Muhammad Ali Samate, visited Western Europe and the US. But the SNM continued to gain control of more of the north and Barre's authority began to disintegrate. On 30 August 1989 the government announced it was prepared to hold multiparty elections although this did not halt the decline in Barre's fortunes. Despite his efforts to win foreign support, the granting of an amnesty for those involved in the May-July uprising of 1988 and the release of some prisoners, Barre did not offer the SNM either a cease-fire or talks and by the end of the year the SNM was laying siege to a number of northern towns while Barre was becoming increasingly isolated. His regime by then had become notorious for repression. At the end of 1989, the problem was what would happen when the Barre regime collapsed as everyone then assumed would soon happen. In January 1990, the American human rights group Africa Watch claimed that government forces had killed between 50,000 and 60,000 civilians over the previous 19 months and driven about 500,000 into exile. The majority of these were Isaqs from the dominant northern clan. Barre's position continued to deteriorate through 1990 as most of the country came under the control of various, often unconnected, rebel groups. The SNM controlled most of the north, the United Somali Congress (USC) was active in the centre of the country and the Somali Patriotic Movement (SPM) in the south while the capital, Mogadishu, was increasingly terrorized by armed gangs. Barre's government, indulging in human rights abuses, faced growing internal instability and declining foreign support and now lacked any capacity to solve problems. In May 1990 the publication of the 'Mogadishu Manifesto' number one, signed by 114 prominent politicians and intellectuals, called for Barre's resignation. A second, similar manifesto followed and in June 45 signatories of the first manifesto were arrested. On 6 July presidential guards fired on the crowd in the Mogadishu football stadium when it jeered at a speech by Barre and 60 people were killed. By December 1990 the USC had taken control of parts of Mogadishu, 500 people were killed in two days of fighting and the President was reported to be holed up in a bunker under siege from rebel forces.

In January 1991 he fled the country, leaving chaos and civil war behind him.

> President Barre's mark on Somalia's star-crossed future was indelible. His
> army abandoned 40,000 weapons and hundreds of millions of live rounds
> to the guerrillas. Vast arms and weapons dumps were parcelled out among
> clan leaders, putting into their hands the ability to rule Somalia by force, as
> warlords. The toys divided, these new warlords could begin reaching for
> power for the sake of their clan – just as Barre, the exemplar, had done
> with his. And they could perpetuate their own terror.[24]

Throughout the 1980s an inexorable determination towards violence
characterized the Horn. Ethiopia faced both a civil war and the Eritrean war of
secession; Somalia experienced steadily escalating clan warfare; in Sudan there
was both a north-south civil war and a subsidiary civil war between the tribes of
the south. These wars and confrontations were made immensely more complex
and were prolonged as well by the interventions and manoeuvres of the US and
USSR and their allies who pursued Cold War interests that did nothing to
encourage peace in the region. Furthermore, the wars were inter-related: Sudan
supported Eritrean secession; Ethiopia assisted the SPLA in the south of Sudan;
Somalia constantly threatened the Ogaden region of Ethiopia. At the end of the
decade all three countries – Sudan, Ethiopia and Somalia – experienced major
changes. In Sudan the military coup that brought Gen. Bashir to power
introduced a new period of military rule and a sharp hardening of Islamist
attitudes that forestalled any solution to the north-south conflict. In Ethiopia the
collapse of the Mengistu regime finally led to the emergence of an independent
Eritrea in 1993. In Somalia the collapse of Barre's rule was the prelude to a
decade of clan warfare and a new kind of international intervention.

West Africa:
Nigeria and Ghana

During the 1980s a pattern of interwoven conflicts developed across the whole of West Africa: on the political front this took the form, on the one hand, of a struggle between the civilian-military establishments that had come to power after independence and would go to almost any lengths to hold onto their power and, on the other hand, the forces of grassroots democracy that, despite endless setbacks, fought to achieve a greater say for the people as a whole. On the economic front all the countries of the region, including Nigeria the most powerful, strove, usually in vain, to shake off external market controls so as to follow the development paths of their choice. The result was a state of almost perpetual upheaval countered by repression at home and a deepening suspicion of external forces from abroad, which was made all the worse by growing economic depression and constant failure to meet development targets.

Although the one-party state structure, 'populist' military dictatorships and other anti-democratic forces had been strongly entrenched by the ruling elites, the people demanded – and supported their demands by a growing resort to protest in many forms – a return to full democracy so that even the most autocratic leaders were obliged to make periodic gestures towards greater democratic involvement in the process of government even though these leaders, such as Abdou Diouf of Senegal, constantly tried to fob off their people with limited rather than full participation in the processes of government. It was a Western myth, largely fostered by the departing colonial powers, that Africans preferred strong authoritarian rule to democracy. This was never the case but the myth suited the interests of the Europeans, who wanted to perpetuate their influence, and the Cold War warriors, who needed to justify providing support for autocratic regimes that would safeguard their strategic and financial investments on the continent. The task for democrats was to prise control from the civilian and military powerbrokers who had seized it at or shortly after independence and would go to great lengths to retain it. By the 1980s outsiders who suggested that dictatorial regimes were somehow appropriate for Africa appeared to have forgotten that the nationalism of the 1950s and 1960s that had led to the end of the European empires had been soundly based upon democratic principles.

NIGERIA

By virtue of its size and huge population Nigeria was always destined to dominate West Africa and for most of this period it was ruled by the military. Lt-Gen. Olusegun Obasanjo had succeeded as military head of state on the assassination of Murtala Muhammed in the abortive coup attempt of February 1976. Obasanjo promised to return Nigeria to civilian rule in 1979 and much of his three-year period in office was taken up with working out a new constitution and a proper distribution of powers between the centre and the (then) 19 states to come into place in 1979. The ban on political activity was lifted in September 1978 and within two months 50 political parties had emerged. These had to be assessed by the Federal Electoral Commission (FEDECO) and pass a test of nationwide as opposed to regional acceptance. In the event only five parties were accepted as fully national parties. These were the Yoruba-based Unity Party of Nigeria (UPN), led by Chief Awolowo; the National Party of Nigeria (NPN), based upon Kaduna in the north with Shehu Shagari as its presidential candidate; the People's Redemption Party (PRP), also northern-based and led by Aminu Kano. The other two parties – the Nigerian People's Party (NPP), led by Nnamdi Azikiwe, and the Greater Nigerian People's Party (GNPP), led by Waziri Ibrahim – had begun as a single party and then split. These five parties contested the elections, which were complex since five separate elections (local, state, state governors, legislature and presidential) had to be fought simultaneously. The NPN gained 37 per cent of the seats in the House of Representatives, 36 per cent in state assemblies and 38 per cent in the Senate, and won seven of 19 governorships. The UPN came second. In the presidential elections Shagari won the most votes (5.7 million) with 25 per cent of the votes in 12 states but not in 13, and this led to an immediate challenge that he had not won two-thirds of the 19 states as stipulated in the constitution. FEDECO, however, ruled that he had won on what his opponents saw as a technicality.

Shagari was sworn in as President of the Second Republic on 1 October 1979. The question then and for the rest of the century was whether the federal concept could work successfully to overcome the deep regional and ethnic differences that lay at the heart of all Nigeria's political problems. Only the NPN had managed to perform on a truly national scale and, arguably, the anger at

Shagari's win, whether on a technicality or not, was really the anger of regional-based parties that only his party had achieved a national showing. Shagari's term of office, from 1979 to 1983, was dominated by the way the parties constantly looked to what would happen the second time round in 1983. There was the question of how the federal framework set up by Obasanjo would work. There was, as always, the matter of political spoils – who obtained what offices. There was widespread corruption and the question of the management of the economy – how and for whom. Shagari was not to have an easy ride.

The Second Republic lasted just over four years until the military resumed control at the end of 1983. The government faced severe problems throughout this period: Shagari's credibility was at issue since his electoral win was rejected by his political opponents; there were the constant regional pulls against the federal centre; on the economic front over-dependence upon oil would lead to a severe economic downturn when the oil price plummeted in 1982 to produce a foreign exchange crisis, financial panic and a consequent foreign reluctance to invest. On the social-religious front, between December 1980 and 1982 the sermons of the populist preacher Alhaji Muhammad Marwa (Maitatsine) led to serious rioting in the north, causing many deaths. The rioting was brutally suppressed and Maitatsine himself was killed. He had appealed for an Islamic-based system of justice – Sharia – and an end to 'western-oriented corruption' and he had found a ready following. In October 1982 the police arrested 16 of Maitatsine's followers in Maiduguri, leading to rioting in Kano and Kaduna during which the police killed hundreds of dissidents. In November the sect was banned. However, the movement renewed its activities in February–March 1984 when over 1,000 people lost their lives in the disturbances and in 1985 when another 100 people were killed in Gombe. By that time Gen. Buhari was in power and he blamed the troubles on religious extremism rather than underlying economic deprivation.

The government obtained 90 per cent of its revenues from the oil industry and in order to redeem its election promises embarked upon some massive federal spending projects that assumed a continuing high oil price. This policy led to a programme of rapid investment, a 'boom' import-led economy and a scramble for wealth that was led by politicians and businessmen. The gap between rich and poor widened dramatically. Then came the collapse in oil prices of April 1982 and oil export earnings slumped through 1983, accompanied by a loss of foreign investor confidence. Subsequent government measures to control imports and limit the export of foreign exchange led to widespread corruption and financial malpractices. As a consequence Nigeria found it had become a debtor nation and was forced to turn to the IMF for assistance. As always, the poor suffered most from the crisis and this led to growing resentment against the government. Nigeria's clear commitment to Western free enterprise and dependence upon Western investment undermined its public condemnations of apartheid in South Africa, which were regarded largely as rhetoric, while its intervention in the civil war in Chad at this time was seen as little more than political opportunism, though supposedly done to limit the spread of Libyan influence.

Early in 1983 Nigeria expelled some two million foreign workers, the majority from Ghana but also from Cameroon, Chad and Niger. It was a panic measure in response to the deteriorating economic situation and did much to undermine Nigeria's standing in West Africa. The expulsions led to huge problems in Ghana while doing nothing to solve Nigeria's economic problems. The year was dominated by the elections that were due to be held over August–September. The NPN party machine achieved a triumph for the ruling party and Shehu Shagari won 47 per cent of the votes cast (12.2 million) although the other presidential candidates together obtained one million more votes than Shagari. The NPN won 60 of 96 seats in the Senate, 264 of 450 in the House of Representatives and 13 of 19 state governorships. As usual in a Nigerian election there were accusations of widespread corruption. Shagari was sworn in for his second term on 1 October to find he was presiding over a country that was divided rather than united as a result of the elections. All elections in Nigeria are bitterly contested and their results hotly disputed. This is not just a question of corruption but arises rather from the nature of the power structures of the country and its ethnic divisions: the people have not been persuaded of the fairness of the federal solution to Nigeria's politics.

Shagari, who had been closely associated with Nigeria's first prime minister, Abubakar Tafawa Balewa, and was a founder member of the Northern People's Congress, was a consummate politician. He was trusted for his sincerity and made an ideal presidential candidate. 'He became President in 1979, at a time of great political tension and economic crisis. He found it difficult to hold together the divisive political forces in the face of a looming economic crisis. Though his regime collapsed in an orgy of recrimination and accusations of corruption, he remained personally untainted and still liked and respected by the majority of his people... He saw his principal task was to preserve democracy by sticking to the letter and spirit of the law even if the process was cumbersome, slow and painful.'[1] By the end of 1983, however, the economic situation provided the soldiers with an excuse to intervene and this they did on New Year's Eve of 1984 to return Nigeria once more to military rule. Shagari was retired on 31 December 1983 along with many other civilian leaders. He was never considered to have enriched himself and was released from detention in 1986 though banned for life from politics.

THE RETURN TO MILITARY RULE: BUHARI AND BABANGIDA

When the army seized power on 31 December 1983 under Maj.-Gen. Muhammed Buhari, a northerner from Kaduna state, the new leader emphasized the corruption of the NPN government. All political institutions were banned or dissolved and the Supreme Military Council (SMC) was reinstated. The coup appeared to be widely popular but Nigeria had once more come full circle. The new regime faced two immediate problems: what to do about the economy; and how to deal with corruption. Negotiations with the IMF broke down during 1984 and the government then initiated its own austerity programme. At the same time, special tribunals were set up to deal with former politicians, governors and others, and many were given sentences for corruption. One objective was to recover the huge sums of money that had been smuggled out of the country. Two days after the military coup Umaru Dikko, who had been Minister of Transport and Aviation, fled the country to Britain. He was accused of large-scale corruption, hoarding of essential commodities and enriching himself but when charged by the government with having stolen one billion naira, he replied: 'Whatever money a politician makes goes back to the people because he wants their votes. The military are only talking about money because they can only think of their own bank accounts.' The government made an unsuccessful attempt to abduct him from Britain – in a crate from Stansted airport – but he was found and released. The incident led to a break in Anglo-Nigerian relations when both countries withdrew their diplomats. Bad management of the economy forced the government to resort to barter trade with its oil; at the same time the regime became increasingly authoritarian and imposed severe restrictions upon the media. In May 1985, for a second time, another 700,000 foreigners, including 300,000 Ghanaians, were treated as scapegoats for the state of the economy and expelled from the country. By mid-1985 the government had virtually resolved itself into a two-man show run by Buhari and his Chief of Staff Maj.-Gen. Tunde Idiagbon. In July Idiagbon gave a speech in which he called for greater economic retrenchment and more public discipline while at the same time banning all political debate.

Despite its initial welcome, the Buhari regime lacked charisma. The accusation was levelled at Buhari that few of those convicted of corruption belonged to the NPN and that apart from the ex-governor of Kano, no prominent northerners had been found guilty of corruption. During 1985 Buhari became notably more authoritarian while failing to come to grips with the country's economic problems. Although 2,500 political detainees were released, the government retained powers of detention without trial. Buhari's responses to the continuing economic crisis were negative: 'Buhari also clamped down on press freedom (using the notorious clause 4) and other political liberties. He tried to impose his iron discipline on doctors, trade unionists and other professional bodies that tried to resist his austerity measures. But criticism continued, so in July he banned all political debate. This last despairing measure to crack down on civil liberties opened the way to another coup.'[2] On 27 August 1985 the Army declared Buhari deposed and Maj.-Gen. Ibrahim Babangida, the Chief of Army Staff, took control. Both Buhari and Idiagbon were detained and a number of senior officers were retired. Despite his austere, unpopular rule, Buhari was to emerge again as a presidential candidate in the elections of 2003.

A new Armed Forces Ruling Council (AFRC) was established and Babangida, like his predecessor, faced a continuing economic decline and was obliged to initiate further economy measures. In January 1986 he announced that the armed forces would hand back power to the civilians in 1990. Religious or sectarian unrest in Northern Nigeria that would recur for the rest of the century persuaded Babangida to take Nigeria into the Organization of the Islamic Conference (OIC) that February. Repeated clashes between Muslims and Christians highlighted the country's religious divide; in April 1987, therefore, the government established an Advisory Council on Religious Affairs (ACRA) consisting of both Muslims and Christians. As the date for a return to civilian rule approached the military demonstrated an increasing reluctance to give up power – an attitude that became a recurring theme of the country's politics to the end of the century. The government postponed a full return to civil politics until 1992 but proposed a transitional period to begin in 1987 and the establishment in 1988 of a constituent assembly to draft a new constitution. Thereafter, local and state elections were scheduled for 1990 when two political parties were to be allowed to come into being. Elections for a bicameral legislature and the presidency would finally be held in 1992.

In May 1989 President Babangida lifted the ban on political activity as a prelude to the proposed Third Republic. Much political activity followed and 13 associations applied to be one of the two political parties to be registered by the national government. However, in October Babangida refused to recognize any of them; instead he began to construct the framework for the two parties he intended to create in a form of 'guided democracy' scheduled to begin in 1990. Anti-government riots at the end of 1989 forced Babangida to cancel visits to the US and Italy planned for early 1990. Then riots followed the sacking of Lt-Gen. Domkat Ya Bali from the defence portfolio. He was a Christian and his sacking raised fears that Muslims were to be favoured at the expense of Christians. On 22 April 1990 a coup attempt was mounted by middle-rank officers who attacked Dodan Barracks in Lagos (the effective seat of military government) and took control of Radio Nigeria but after 10 hours of fighting the coup collapsed. The event again highlighted north-south rivalries and Christian fears of Muslim domination. On 27 July Maj. Gideon Orkar, the coup leader, and 41 other soldiers were executed.

Having stepped down as head of state in 1979 Obasanjo employed part of his time during the 1980s running an Africa Leadership Forum or 'think tank' that held 'Farm House Dialogues' to discuss a range of social and political topics. Some of their discussions were published in 1991.[3] Discussions concerning the state of Nigeria provide some important insights into the country's problems relating to development, the military, centralism, relations between north and south and corruption. 'It was argued that while the Nigerian economy has grown appreciably in the past two decades, the growth has not been transformed into development' and that 'a more meaningful approach is to see development as "people inspired, human centred and citizen anchored"'.[4] In relation to rural development the Forum was scathing: 'Rural areas are characterized by their depleted work-force, their rudimentary and inefficient mode of production, their general lack of basic infrastructure and social amenities such as safe potable water, all season access roads, telecommunications, electricity, schools, medical facilities, good houses and recreational facilities, the paucity of processing factories, markets, banks, storage depot and machine repair shops and their low level of health care delivery, nutrition, hygiene, education and social awareness. For those reasons rural areas are normally unable to fully harness their abundant natural resources.'[5] The statement says just about everything that needs saying about the neglect of rural areas – and not just in Nigeria.

On the subject of centralization in the Nigerian Federation another commentator draws attention to the impact of the military: 'Centralist by organization and outlook, relatively unimpeded by local or regional claims and pressures, frequently guided by the ideals of nationalism or national greatness, and standing to advance their own careers considerably', successive military governments in Nigeria have sought to promote integration '... by means of far-reaching and comprehensive – but not revolutionary – programmes of consolidation and centralization.'[6] Awareness of the complexities of problems always appears to outpace the capacity to resolve them.

One of Nigeria's most acute problems concerns its ever-growing population related to its resources and capacity to develop them. The rate of population growth is alarming: in 1953 the population stood at 31 million, in 1963 at 56 million, by 1985 an estimated 98 million. Thus, over 32 years the population increased by 42.3 million or 76 per cent. 'In traditional Nigerian society, the wealth of an individual was assessed by the sheer size of his household. The household included several wives, numerous children, many relations as well as a significant number of indentured labourers' while 'Another index of a man's wealth and status was the size of his herds of cattle, sheep and goats. Essentially then, the household was, in the past, the pivotal basis for assessing a man's social relevance and importance.' In many respects, despite increasing urbanization and other changes, such criteria still stand. At the end of the 1980s, 'Those within the 0–15 years age bracket constitute about half, or more precisely 47 per cent, of the population while those aged 64 years and above account for about 2 per cent. The consequence is that every productive Nigerian is unwittingly saddled with the responsibility of feeding, housing, clothing and educating a child.' (In developed countries, the ratio was two to three to one child.) For this burgeoning and comparatively young population to be productive, adequate health facilities and services were required – and too often were not available. Much of Nigeria's population had little or no chance of securing access to educational institutions even on the assumption of spectacular improvements in the country's overall economic performance and the surpluses that were created would always be instantly consumed by a population that was growing exponentially. The Dialogue pointed out how '... 27 years after the 1963 census, Nigeria has not been able to conduct an acceptable head count. In spite of the numerous and known benefits and advantages of a national census, it is sad to note the inability of succeeding governments, military and civilian, to successfully conduct a census exercise. Participants (in the Dialogue) agreed that the crux of the problem lies in the perception of the census exercise as a major factor in the distribution of amenities and the imposition of tax.' As a consequence any counts were subject to fraud since no one trusted a Nigerian government, civilian or military, to be impartial.[7]

GHANA

Flight Lt Jerry Rawlings took part in the junior officers' and NCOs' coup attempt of 15 May 1979 and was imprisoned for his pains. But three weeks later, on 4 June, his followers freed him and this time they mounted a successful coup. On 16 June Gen. Acheampong and Maj.-Gen. Utuka were executed by firing squad and on 26 June Gen. Akuffo, Lt-Gen. Afrifa and other high-ranking officers were also shot so that three former heads of state had been executed in a dramatic 'house cleaning' operation. This did not stop at the top. Tribunals headed by NCOs were set up to mete out summary justice to those accused of hoarding, profiteering and corruption. Rawlings insisted that the soldiers would return to barracks once elections, as set by the previous regime, had been held.

Five parties contested them and in the event a coalition was formed consisting of the People's National Party (PNP), led by Hilla Limann, and the United National Convention (UNC). In separate presidential elections Limann won comfortably and was sworn in as President on 24 September. The Limann government lasted little more than two years and suffered from an impossible handicap: that it was seen to owe its existence to Rawlings and the military who came increasingly to be regarded as the final court of appeal. Rawlings himself retained his immense popularity. Limann's administration was a weak one and in the course of 1981 its authority visibly collapsed. On 31 December 1981 Rawlings again seized power and created a Provisional National Defence Council (PNDC), which would rule by decree. The 1979 constitution was suspended and the years 1982–84 became a time of upheaval with democratization and mass participation (the ideological tenets of the Rawlings administration) counterbalanced by dissension in the army, which was Rawlings' power base.

Rawlings was a new phenomenon in West Africa: young, dashing and handsome, he achieved huge popularity when in 1979 he swept away the corrupt old order that had become a byword. He was highly critical of the political and economic bankruptcy of the old regime and he had emerged as the spokesman for a new radical populism. His overthrow of the incompetent Limann administration, which had signally failed to combat corruption or deal effectively with the economy, heralded his 'second coming'. He said, on his return to power, that he would restore democracy in which the needs of the people were heeded by the government and that this was not just a question of abstract liberties but 'it involves above all, food, clothing, shelter and the basic necessities of life'. He told the members of the PNDC to see their appointments only as 'a chance to serve the people sacrificially'. While Rawlings wanted mass participation in democracy as well as to democratize the army, his approach was not shared by everybody and inevitably he provoked conflict. There were ethnic confrontations to be faced and Rawlings, with a Scottish father and Ewe mother, came to rely more and more on his Ewe people for support and was thus unable to escape the tribal nature of Ghana's politics. PNDC leaders from non-Ewe groups were forced out, sometimes accused of plotting, and a number of coup attempts were reported. Furthermore, Rawlings found that the People's Defence Committees, which he had set up to decentralize power and encourage mass participation, were exceeding their powers and gradually he reduced their authority. Then the students, faced with economic hardship and austerity measures, became increasingly antagonistic to Rawlings.[8] Later, when he abandoned his earlier Marxist approach to the economy and turned to the IMF for more orthodox assistance he embarked upon a paradox for it was a contradiction in terms to proclaim a revolution and expect the IMF to forward it.

Opposition to Rawlings came from many different groups in Ghana and especially those he had ejected from power at the end of 1981 in favour of 'people's power' since this was anathema to them. The opposition became all the greater with the revolutionary implemented Western-style economic recovery programmes (ERPs). A coup attempt in 1982 highlighted the fragility of his position. In any case, democratization was a double-edged weapon: people's summary justice that bypassed the courts and an increasingly hostile and vociferous student body forced Rawlings and the PNDC to rethink some of their policies. During much of the 1980s difficult relations between the PNDC and the army were to be paralleled by a slow but relatively successful economic recovery programme that enjoyed the endorsement of the World Bank and the IMF.

When Rawlings broadcast on the morning of the second coup, he said: 'Fellow Ghanaians, as you will notice, we are not playing the national anthem. In other words, this is not a coup. I ask for *nothing less than a* REVOLUTION – something that will transform the social and economic order of this country.' His revolution had three objectives: to restore the economy, to eliminate corruption and to promote the interests of the little man.[9] Rawlings had appointed Kwesi Botchway, a lawyer, economist and academic, as Secretary for Finance and Economic Planning and 'By December Botchway was ready and in a nation-wide broadcast on 30 December 1982 he announced the basic principles and outline for a four-year ERP. The devaluation issue was presented as a subsidy on specific exports – timber, minerals, cocoa, coffee and manufactured goods – while imports, apart from oil and basic foodstuffs, were to be surcharged.'[10] In January 1983 Nigeria announced that it was expelling all foreign workers without valid immigration visas and in just over two weeks 1.2 million Ghanaians were evacuated home from Nigeria. 'Over the next few months, in an exercise which amazed the international aid agencies, Ghana managed to reabsorb into national life nearly one-tenth of her normal population.' It was a stunning achievement and it was carried out just as Botchway presented his first budget. 'It was under these circumstances that on Thursday 21 April the Secretary for Finance and Economic Planning, Dr Kwesi Botchway, announced the toughest austerity budget of any government since independence. The minimum daily wage was nearly doubled from 12 cedis to just over 21, and the prices of rice, maize and sugar remained unaltered, but virtually everything else went up by between 100 and 300 per cent as government subsidies were slashed to reduce the budget deficit and import surcharges were imposed on all but the most basic essentials.'[11]

It was not surprising, even when Rawlings had turned to the World Bank and IMF for assistance with the economy, that such a radical and revolutionary figure should attract the deep antagonism as well as subversive activities of the United States whose policy then and later was to oppose any regime that sought genuine independence from Western tutelage. 'An ominous and unpredictable element in the opposition to Rawlings and the PNDC during the early years of the revolution was the clandestine involvement of the United States' Central Intelligence Agency (CIA). Early in 1983 documents came into the hands of Special Security Adviser Capt. Kojo Tsikata, which showed clear CIA involvement with dissident Ghanaians who were trying to destabilize and overthrow the PNDC regime. It came at the height of US attempts to subvert the Nicaraguan government, with whose revolution the PNDC felt a strong sense of solidarity.' Ghana's close links with Libya and Rawlings' anti-imperialist rhetoric put him among the select group of *bêtes noires* of President Ronald Reagan's foreign policy. In most of the abortive coup attempts against the PNDC in 1983 and 1984 the hand of the CIA was to be found lurking somewhere, providing weapons, money or contracts through their offices at the US embassy in Accra or in Lomé.[12] The story did not end there. In 1985 a Ghanaian, Mike Soussoulis, was arrested in Washington on charges of helping a dissident African-American officer of the CIA. At the same time, however, documents that had fallen into the hands of the PNDC named US CIA agents as well as Ghanaians working for the CIA. The government was therefore able to arrest a number of Ghanaians in Accra who had been working at the US embassy. They admitted passing information and were tried and sentenced to prison terms. There followed the extraordinary spectacle of a spy swap in which eight Ghanaians were stripped of their citizenship and exchanged for Soussoulis who arrived home in December 1985 to a hero's welcome. Reacting to the US bombing of Libya in mid-April 1986, Rawlings said uncompromisingly: '... if the US wants to assume this position of power over the rest of the world, then we should all have a say in who gets sent to the White House. The US seem to need help in order to understand the reality of international affairs.' In 1991 Rawlings was to attack Saddam Hussein for invading Kuwait, prophetically it would seem, in relation to the US war of 2003 that would overthrow him. 'It was not so much for his violent resolution of a territorial dispute that he condemned Saddam, but rather for his betrayal of Third World independence by playing into the hands of the United States and allowing the US government the opportunity to intervene in world affairs wherever it saw fit.'[13]

THE GHANA ECONOMIC 'MIRACLE'

Rawlings executed a major U-turn when he decided to adopt an orthodox 'Western' approach in tackling the country's economic problems. This meant a rapprochment with the World Bank and the IMF. By 1984 the economic position was improving but this meant meeting demands from the TUC for higher wages. Much of the decade saw a contest between the demands of popular radicalism and mass participation on the one hand, and the need for Ghana to come to terms – by accepting an IMF-inspired economic reform programme – with the economic realities of the world in which it lived on the other hand. In part, this meant a choice between rhetoric and orthodoxy. During 1985, when economic recovery was going quite well, Rawlings listened to his economic advisers and then launched ERP Mark II against powerful opposition from the PNDC and the Committee of Secretaries. Although he had originally hoped to implement a Marxist economic programme, Rawlings had allowed himself to be persuaded by Kwesi Botchway to realign economically towards the West leading to his acceptance in 1983 of IMF conditions and a devaluation of the cedi. As a consequence of this decision, Rawlings ran the economy on orthodox lines and, for example, brought about a rapid expansion of local food production. One critic of the original approach to the economy under Rawlings, argued that 'In Ghana … only belatedly did the PNDC begin to address the deteriorating social conditions that preceded the crisis of 1983 and agreements with the World Bank and IMF, by means of the Programme of Action to Mitigate the Social Costs of Adjustment (PAMSCAD).' According to the Commonwealth Expert Group (CEG 1989), Ghana lost over half its doctors between 1981 and April 1984 and in 1983, for example, only one of the graduates of the University of Ghana Medical School at Korle Bu remained in the country while one-twelfth of the country's nurses left in 1982 and cutbacks in financing health in Ghana at the height of the economic crisis in 1982–83 resulted in inadequate infrastructure for the basic health programme.[14] Health was only one of the sectors that required massive recovery assistance.

Although economic recovery under Rawlings during the 1980s was impressive, yet at the beginning of the 1990s Ghana still had a long way to go to achieve its true economic potential. Total external debts stood at US$3,078 million in 1989 (equivalent to 59.9 per cent of GNP) while debt servicing was equivalent to 48.9 per cent of export earnings. Rawlings had defended his resort to the World Bank and IMF in 1987 as follows: 'Given the resources at our disposal, and the current international economic atmosphere, we could not have come all this way without the financial support of the World Bank, the International Monetary Fund, and other countries. But we have not swallowed hook, line and sinker all the prescriptions of the multi-national financial institutions.'[15] He was sufficiently justified when in February 1989 the fifth Consultative Group for Ghana meeting in Paris pledged US$900 million in aid. However, the contradictions of a revolution that owed its recovery to the world's leading international financial institutions could not be glossed over. The liberalization and improvement of the economy was matched by increasing restrictions on free speech at home. Leading members of the Ghana Bar Association, for example, were arrested to prevent the delivery of a series of lectures about former high court judges who had been killed in 1982.

Despite international financial assistance, 1989 was a difficult year for Rawlings and Ghana as the PNDC kept to its reform programme. Although there was expansion of output in major sectors of the economy, world prices for gold and cocoa fell drastically to reduce Ghana's foreign exchange earnings. The activities of the 18 District Assemblies, which the PNDC had created, confirmed its belief that a genuinely democratic system could only be built on the foundations of local government structures. However, evidence of renewed corruption in high places had an unsettling effect. There were hints of discord within the PNDC and Rawlings used the tenth anniversary of the 4 June Revolution to say: 'Some of us are showing signs of losing our self-discipline and are being attracted to the old ways of the powerful in our society. June 4th must remind us that such arrogance will breed a reaction, often uncontrollable reaction, from the downtrodden.'[16]

On 22 September 1989 Lt-Gen. Arnold Qainoo was relieved of his post as GOC of the Ghana Armed Forces although he retained his position on the PNDC and was made Chairman of the New National Planning and Development Commission. Apparently Rawlings had been forced to act against Qainoo as the result of a petition from the ranks that he should remove Qainoo if he wanted to avoid trouble.[17] A number of arrests took place in rapid succession, including that of Maj. Courage Quashigah, Squadron Leader Akapo and others in connection with 'activities which could have jeopardized the security of the State'. The aim of the plotters had been to assassinate Rawlings during a visit to Ho, the Volta Regional capital. Until that time Quashigah had been intensely loyal to Rawlings and had foiled two coup attempts in 1982. He was, moreover, an Ewe as were several other plotters. The media then launched a campaign to discredit Quashigah.

Although on several occasions during 1989 Rawlings highlighted the inequalities of the international economic order, he continued to eschew more radical solutions for Ghana. In his January 1990 speech to the nation, Rawlings expressed careful optimism about the momentous events then taking place in Eastern Europe. The PNDC remained close to the countries holding out against the new changes, especially Cuba and China, which offered a US$80 million interest-free loan for projects employing Chinese technology. In February 1990 the PNDC sponsored an Investment Promotion Conference at which the International Finance Corporation representative, Mr Houvaguimian, said Ghana had to make more concessions: 'Success in attracting foreign investment depends on matching the incentives and tax conditions offered by other countries competing for foreign investment, since profit-maximization is the force driving foreign investors.' In reply, Rawlings was equally blunt: 'The PNDC would always welcome investment that was for mutual advantage, it would not tolerate the use of the Investment Code to defraud Ghanaians.' He called for a code to control transnational corporations and left World Bank officials aghast.[18] This Rawlings line exposed both the World Bank and other International Financial Institutions (IFIs) but it also laid bare the dilemma of developing Africa and its weakness: Africa needed the investment more than it could afford to wait for the IFIs to reform themselves.

By the end of the decade it was legitimate to ask just how successful the IMF-sponsored economic recovery had been. In his New Year's broadcast to the nation on 2 January 1990, Rawlings said: 'I should be the first to admit that the Economic Recovery Programme has not provided all the answers to our national problems. In spite of all the international acclaim it has received, the effects of its gains remain to be felt in most households and pockets.' After eight years of recovery and macro-economic growth, the vast majority of Ghanaians were still very poor.[19] Pressures for a return to party politics grew during the year and in July a national seminar on democracy was held and a new Movement for Freedom and Justice launched a campaign for a return to democracy. Rawlings said he would not oppose a return to democracy if that was what Ghanaians wanted. Outside Ghana Rawlings had achieved great popularity among ordinary people who wanted to see genuine change in their countries. These included the people of Côte d'Ivoire and Togo as well as in Burkina Faso, especially under its own revolutionary leader Capt. Sankara who became a close ally of Rawlings. This popularity arose especially from his stand against corruption and readiness to bring to justice – people's justice – the country's former leaders. Rawlings had also established close relations with Libya's volatile leader Gaddafi, to the considerable irritation of Washington.

OTHER DEVELOPMENTS IN WEST AFRICA: ECONOMICS, COUPS AND DEMOCRACY

Small size was never any bar to political upheavals and a number of the countries of West Africa, which were small in both size and population, were politically volatile and subject to recurring upheavals. In Benin President Mathieu Kérékou came to power by coup in 1972 and initiated a strong anti-French line while making Marxism-Leninism the country's official ideology. He survived a French-inspired raid on Cotonou in 1977 that was led by the notorious French mercenary Bob Denard. He would remain firmly entrenched through the 1980s yet, despite adopting a Marxist line, Kérékou discovered that relations with France remained the most important external factor for Benin and these were to improve after 1981 when François Mitterand came to power in France. The decision of Nigeria in 1984 to close its border with Benin in order to reduce smuggling produced recession and hardship and provoked student unrest when the government announced that students would no longer be guaranteed jobs by the state. By 1986 the continuing deterioration of the economy forced the government to approach the IMF and begin a move towards Western economic norms in order to overcome its problems. Kérékou then began to cultivate good relations with conservative Côte d'Ivoire while cutting his links with Libya. Growing dissatisfaction with Kérékou's rule and widespread corruption led to a number of strikes and student protests in 1989, prompting Kérékou to move towards multipartyism in 1990 when he renounced the Marxist-Leninist policies he had initiated in 1974. He called a national conference to draft a new constitution. Presidential and parliamentary elections were held in March 1991 and after 18 years in power Kerekou was defeated by his Prime Minister, Nicephore Soglo, who became the country's new President.

Upper Volta began the 1980s with a military coup that replaced President Sangoule Lamizana (who himself had come to power by coup) with Col. Saye Zerbo, who established a *Comité Militaire de Redressement pour le Progrès National* (CMRPN), which banned all political activities. It was an all too familiar development. Three troubled years of confrontation between government and unions followed. On 7 November 1982 another coup by NCOs led to a brief year under a new *Conseil de Salut du Peuple* (CSP) under Surgeon Maj. Jean-Baptiste Ouedrago. Then on 4 August 1983 yet another coup brought Capt. Thomas Sankara to power. He established a *Conseil National de la Révolution* (CNR) and really was a revolutionary. He appointed Blaise Compaoré, who had assisted his coup, Minister of State to the Presidency. He initiated a series of radical reforms including a purge of the armed forces and the creation of 'people's tribunals' to try former officials accused of corruption (in this he copied Jerry Rawlings in Ghana). In 1984 he renamed the country Burkina Faso. Sankara's radicalism had a growing impact upon Francophone Africa and he established close relations with the only radical leader in Anglophone Africa, Jerry Rawlings; the two men discussed a possible union of their countries. However, by 1987 the coalition of the left that Sankara led began to disintegrate and a power struggle between Sankara and Compaoré ensued. On 15 October 1987 the commando unit that had brought Sankara to power assassinated him and 13 of his close associates and Compaoré seized power and proclaimed a 'popular front'. His coup was welcomed by neighbouring Côte d'Ivoire and Togo, both of which had feared Sankara's radicalism. Compaoré initiated economic reforms that included state capitalism. He encouraged the business community and began negotiations with the IMF (these had been suspended under Sankara) and with France. A draft constitution that would create a multiparty state was announced in 1990. However, Compaoré failed to achieve good relations with most of his neighbours – he gave secret support to Charles Taylor, the Liberian rebel leader – and found that his image was permanently tarnished by his murder of the popular Sankara.

In 1982 President Ahmadou Ahidjo, who had been President of Cameroon since independence in 1960, resigned, to be succeeded by his Prime Minister Paul Biya. However, Ahidjo remained as chairman of the only party, the *Union Nationale Camerounaise* (UNC) and this produced a state of friction with his successor that was only resolved when Ahidjo retired to France in 1984. In January 1984 Biya was re-elected President with 99.88 per cent of the votes cast. Later that year there was a coup attempt by the republican guard but Biya was saved by the loyalty of the army. A total of 46 plotters were later executed. In 1985 Biya renamed UNC the *Rassemblement Démocratique du Peuple Camerounais* (RDPC) finally ending the Ahidjo influence. Moves towards greater democracy were initiated in 1986 with local elections up to department level that included a choice of candidates. A general election for the National Assembly was held in April 1988 and of 180 elected members, 153 were new. Biya, however, was sole presidential candidate and received 98.75 per cent of the votes cast. Growing demands for greater political freedom and a return to full multipartyism led Biya to allow multiparty elections in 1992 which were only narrowly won by Biya's RDPC.

The former Portuguese islands of Cape Verde became independent in 1975 as one of Africa's poorest mini-states. It faced two major problems: what political relations it should establish with Guinea-Bissau on the mainland (the two colonies had acted as one in opposing Portuguese rule); and the urgent needs of its minuscule and unsustainable economy. In January 1977 a Council of Unity had been set up to work out a formula of unity between the two states but already by then it was becoming clear that they would go their separate ways. However, three years later in November 1980 a coup in Guinea-Bissau led to the overthrow of its President Luis Cabral (who was a Cape Verdean) and this ended the unity talks. Early in 1981 the Cape Verde branch of the PAIGC, the joint political party with Guinea-Bissau, renamed itself the *Partido Africano da Independência de Cabo Verde* (PAICV). President Pereira was re-elected in February 1981 and articles in the constitution relating to Guinea-Bissau were deleted. Relations with Guinea-Bissau that had been broken at the time of the coup were resumed in June 1982, after Cabral had been released from detention, following mediation by President Samora Machel of Mozambique. Cape Verde suffered from drought through the 1980s and this limited development while the economy depended upon regular inflows of aid. Cape Verde, which was a one-party state from independence through to 1990, maintained good relations with Portugal and the US. In March 1990, however, the PAICV altered the one-party state constitution to allow multiparty elections, which were held in January 1991. The ruling PAICV was defeated by the new *Movimento para a Democracia* (MPD), which gained 68 per cent of the vote and 56 of the 79 seats in the National People's Assembly.

President of Côte d'Ivoire since independence in 1960, Felix Houphouët-Boigny was one of the longest serving of all Africa's first independence leaders. In September 1980, aged 75, he won his fifth presidential election but faced the new decade during an increasingly difficult time for his country. By then Houphouët-Boigny had come to be seen as a political survivor from a past age. The rapid economic growth that Côte d'Ivoire had enjoyed during the 1960s and 1970s, which had made it the success story of Francophone West Africa, was replaced by stagnation. The economy, which had become dependent upon the export of agricultural commodities, had become vulnerable. There was a coup attempt in 1980. Increasingly, Ivorians wanted to know who would succeed Houphouët-Boigny, but he was in no hurry to name his successor and maintained the status quo throughout the 1980s, though only at the price of student unrest, the passing of a series of anti-corruption laws in 1984, careful control of the press and the absence of any real political debate. In October 1985 Houphouët-Boigny was re-elected President – he was sole candidate – with 100 per cent of the votes. The following month 546 *Parti Démocratique de la Côte d'Ivoire* (PDCI) candidates contested 175 seats for the assembly and only 64 of the sitting members were returned. In July 1986 Houphouët-Boigny appointed a new cabinet that included a number of younger ministers. A crisis arose in 1987 when the secondary school teachers union (SYNESCI) criticized government policy and a number of government-supported teachers seized the union headquarters. Three union leaders were arrested and others were sent to military camps for re-education, a form of treatment most people would associate with the Chinese People's Republic rather than with the most conservative Francophone regime on the continent.

Meanwhile, Houphouët-Boigny had been building his vast Basilica (then estimated to cost US$150 million) at his birthplace of Yamoussoukro, the capital designate, and in April 1989 when he visited the Pope in Rome he offered it to him. The project was criticized both inside and outside Côte d'Ivoire because it was felt the money could have been better spent on the country's development. In 1990, though still in power aged 85, Houphouët-Boigny was increasingly embattled as he faced growing demands for change and was forced to legalize the opposition parties and agree to multiparty elections. Unrest came from students, teachers, farmers and professionals and protests were met with force that included the use of tear gas and firing on the crowds. In May 1990 army recruits went on a rampage in Abidjan; then air force personnel seized the airport and were joined by soldiers. Houphouët-Boigny faced the worst crisis of his long political career. The French garrison was alerted and the troops returned to barracks, but only after concessions about their conditions had been promised by the government. In the October 1990 presidential elections, for the first time, Houphouët-Boigny was opposed by Laurent Gbagbo, the head of the *Front Populaire Ivoirien* (FPI) although he only obtained 15 per cent of the votes. Later, in multiparty elections, the PDCI still won 163 seats while the FPI won nine and three other small parties one seat each. During 1990 Côte d'Ivoire was put under further strain by the influx of refugees from the civil war in neighbouring Liberia. In September 1990 Pope John Paul II visited Côte d'Ivoire: he dedicated the Basilica at Yamoussoukro (by then the cost had risen to US$200 million) and reluctantly accepted it as a gift to the Vatican.

Despite these troubles, Côte d'Ivoire proved to be one of Africa's more successful, diversified economies. It derived the greater part of its wealth from the export of agricultural commodities that were equivalent to 36 per cent of GDP. It was the leading world cocoa producer, a major coffee producer and also exported cotton, palm oil, rubber and sugar. Its manufacturing, mining and construction sectors accounted for 20 per cent of GDP but only employed 10 per cent of the workforce. Diamonds were the only mineral of consequence with an output of 600,000 carats in 1990. Offshore oil discovered and exploited in the 1970s had raised false hopes but production diminished sharply during the 1980s. By 1990 the per capita income at US$790 was one of the highest in Africa. But adverse terms of trade forced the government to begin the 1990s with an austerity programme.

By 1980 there was growing opposition in The Gambia to the continued rule of its President Dawda Jawara and the People's Progressive Party (PPP). The opposition had become more radical with the emergence of two parties – the Gambia Socialist Revolutionary Party (GSRP) and the Movement for Justice in Africa – Gambia (MOJA-G). Both parties rejected the idea of parliamentary opposition and advocated more extreme anti-government measures and both appealed to the unemployed and discontented youth. In October 1980 the deputy leader of the paramilitary field force was murdered. The government reacted swiftly to forestall a possible coup and appealed (under the terms of a defence agreement) to Senegal, which sent 150 troops to prevent a revolt. The GSRP and MOJA-G were proscribed and the leaders of MOJA-G were arrested and charged with sedition. The Libyan embassy was closed on the grounds that it maintained contacts with the dissidents. A second, much greater threat to the government arose on 30 July 1981 when Jawara was absent on a trip to Britain. Kukoi Samba Sanyang who had long been an opponent of the PPP joined forces with disaffected members of the field force to seize power. They took control of key points, but in Banjul, the capital, they forfeited any chance of support by issuing weapons indiscriminately and releasing convicts to create widespread violence. Jawara flew back to Dakar and again invoked the assistance of Senegal, which despatched 3,000 troops to The Gambia. The rebels were defeated but 1,000 lives were lost and a further 1,000 dissidents were detained under emergency regulations. Damage to property amounted to £10 million and the country's hitherto peaceful image was badly damaged. Treason trials lasted to 1984 and though a number of the rebel leaders were condemned to death none were executed.

In the elections of 1982 the PPP took 27 seats, the National Convention Party (NCP) under Sharif Mustapha Dibba three and independents five. In the presidential elections Jawara obtained 137,020 votes and Dibba 50,136. The principal charge levelled at the government through the decade was that of corruption. In the elections of 1987 the PPP took 31 of 36 directly elected seats although the opposition accused the government of electoral irregularities. In 1988 another abortive coup was launched by disaffected Gambians in league with exiles from Senegal. The presence of Senegalese troops in The Gambia through the 1980s posed an interesting political problem. In 1982 the two countries had created the Confederation of Senegambia but by 1989, like so many other moves towards union in Africa, the arrangement was clearly not working and after Senegal had withdrawn its troops that August the Confederation was dissolved in September. The Gambia celebrated 25 years of independence on 18 February 1990. In January 1991 The Gambia and Senegal signed a treaty of friendship and co-operation to replace the defunct confederation.

Long the *bête noire* of Paris, Sekou Touré ruled Guinea from independence in 1958 to his death in 1984. During the 1970s Touré had worked to restore good relations with France and had achieved this in the latter years of that decade. In 1979, having renamed Guinea the People's Revolutionary Republic of Guinea, Touré announced that his government would co-operate with capitalists as well as communists but relations with the USSR then deteriorated as Guinea pursued more open relations with its neighbours Côte d'Ivoire and Senegal and became an active member of the Mano River Union and ECOWAS. On 3 March 1984 Touré died unexpectedly aged 62 and a month later on 3 April the army carried out a coup to pre-empt whatever succession might otherwise have taken place. The military leaders were Col. Lansana Conté, who became President, and Col. Diarra Traoré, who became Prime Minister. The country reverted to its former name of the Republic of Guinea. The new *Comité Militaire de Redressement National* (CMRN) was faced with a declining economy and a civil service in revolt at restructuring that had been started under Touré. Conté adopted a more open style of government and reversed the repression of the Touré years. In July 1985, when Conté was attending an ECOWAS meeting in Togo, Col. Traoré attempted to seize power in a coup of his own but was thwarted by soldiers loyal to Conté. Traoré and 100 of his supporters were arrested. Ismael Traoré, the half-brother of Sekou Touré, and Diarra Traoré were secretly executed while another 60 were tried and sentenced to death although an amnesty was granted to a total of 67 prisoners in 1988. Conté's position had been strengthened by the coup attempt against him and he was able to carry out reforms to bring the economy more in line with Western capitalism. On 1 October 1988 Conté announced plans for a return to civilian rule: a two-party framework was to be put in place over a five-year period. The slow pace of these democratic reforms led to unrest that exploded in anti-government demonstrations in Conakry during September 1990. The people's anger was increased by the economic reforms that had removed subsidies on basic commodities, resulting in huge price rises. Guinea was also affected by the civil war in Liberia, which forced thousands of Guineans to return home.

Until 1980 the PAIGC was the ruling party in both Guinea-Bissau and Cape Verde since the two countries intended to merge into one. But there was growing resentment in Guinea-Bissau at the undue degree of influence wielded by Cape Verdeans in the government and on 14 November 1980 the Prime Minister João Vieira mounted a coup to overthrow Luis Cabral. A revolutionary council of nine members replaced the national assembly and state council, which were abolished. The coup reduced the influence of Cape Verdeans and in the islands this was seen as a sign that the proposed merger of the two countries would not take place. There was a political shift to the right. In May 1982 the government postponed elections and in July, following rumours of a coup plot, a number of politicians who had been prominent prior to the 1980 coup were arrested. A new constitution in 1984 strengthened the position of Vieira as head of state although in 1985 senior army officers supported yet another coup plot, this time by Vice-President Col. Paulo Correia. Although the plot failed it weakened Vieira's position by demonstrating the range of opposition to him. Correia and five other plotters were executed in 1986. From 1983 onwards the government liberalized the economy and by August 1986 had abolished trading restrictions and allowed private traders to import and export goods. The main requirement, however, was to woo Western donors so as to obtain aid and by 1989 the policy had succeeded to the extent that nine nations and 10 international organizations guaranteed sufficient financing to allow Guinea-Bissau to achieve a four per cent growth rate. The elections of June 1989 gave the ruling party a renewed mandate and Vieira was re-elected President with Col. Iafai Camara, the Minister of the Armed Forces, as Vice-President. In September 1990 the PAIGC agreed to begin a move back to multipartyism. A PAIGC congress met in January 1991 and approved 'integral multipartyism' and President Vieira told the 425 delegates that in future the PAIGC would no longer be the ruling force in the country. Multiparty elections were scheduled for 1992. Heavily dependent upon aid for its survival, Guinea-Bissau was one of Africa's smallest economies with a per capita income of only US$180 in 1990, one of the lowest in the world.

On 12 April 1980 a group of soldiers led by Master Sgt Samuel K. Doe stormed the Executive Mansion in Monrovia and killed President William R. Tolbert of Liberia. Doe, who later promoted himself to General, became Chairman of the People's Redemption Council (PRC), which suspended the constitution and all political parties. Although for a time the PRC governed in conjunction with a 17-man council drawn from former political parties, in July 1981 full military rule was inaugurated. Prior to this, the government had doubled army and civil service pay and carried out much-publicized executions by firing squad of 13 leading members of the previous regime. The decade witnessed a steady deterioration of public life in Liberia including mounting corruption, political unease and increasingly arbitrary rule. Having promised a return to civilian rule by 1985, Doe allowed elections to be held that year although amidst widespread allegations of fraud and malpractices and in October, after a two-week delay, it was announced that Doe had won 50.9 per cent of the presidential vote and his National Democratic Party of Liberia (NDPL) 21 of 26 seats in the Senate and 51 of 64 seats in the House of Representatives. The opposition refused to take their seats. On 12 November, the exiled Brig.-Gen. Quiwonkpa re-entered the country to mount a coup but was killed by troops loyal to Doe. In the heavy fighting that took place between 600 and 1,500 people were killed. From 1985 to 1990 troubles mounted for Doe who had not achieved international respectability, frequently changed his ministers while the economy collapsed amid allegations of corruption. A coup attempt in December 1989 failed and hundreds of Liberians then fled to Côte d'Ivoire. In January 1990 a regional revolt in the north-east of the country heralded a decade of civil war.

In the presidential and legislative elections of 1979, President Moussa Traoré of Mali was returned for a further term with 99 per cent of the votes. A period of unrest followed and lasted to 1982 when further elections were held for the assembly, still on a single-party list. During 1983/84 Mali, like other Sahel countries, suffered from drought and had to depend upon famine relief from abroad. In fresh presidential elections of 1985 Traoré as sole candidate obtained 98 per cent of the vote. He then distanced himself from day-to-day politics and in 1986 recreated the post of Prime Minister and relinquished the portfolio of Defence. However, he soon moved back centre stage and resumed the portfolios of Prime Minister and Defence once more. The economy was stagnating and the government was obliged to adopt World Bank/IMF reforms – partial privatization to attract foreign investment. Further economic reforms were backed by France, as well as the World Bank and IMF; these covered trade, investment regulations, the grain market and the banking system. In 1990 Traoré was obliged to make concessions to growing demands for greater political freedom and in April the ruling *Union Démocratique du Peuple Malien* (UDPM) agreed to allow non-party leaders to speak freely and also allowed four new journals to be published. On 26 March 1991 Traoré's government was overthrown by the military after two months in which pro-democracy demonstrations had met violent repression and up to 150 people had been killed. The coup was widely welcomed. A National Reconciliation Council headed by Lt-Col. Amadou Traoré was set up. In April a transitional government was formed and the UDPM was dissolved. Local and legislative elections were held in January 1992 and presidential elections in April when Alpha Oumar Konaré, the Secretary-General of the *Alliance pour la Démocratie au Mali* (ADEMA) became the first president to be elected in a multiparty system since independence.

Mauritania had renounced its claims to Western Sahara in 1979 allowing the government to deal more adequately with the country's internal problems. In 1980, the then Prime Minister Lt-Col. Mohamed Khouma Haidalla announced the abolition of slavery in the country where an estimated 100,000 slaves still existed even if technically they could free themselves. In January 1980 Haidalla replaced Mohamed Louly as president. There were coup attempts against Haidalla in March 1981 and February 1982. Then on 12 December 1984, when he was attending a meeting in Burundi, Haidalla was deposed in a bloodless coup by prime minister Lt-Col. Maawiya Ould Sid'Ahmed Taya. In 1985 Taya implemented Western market economic reforms in the hope of attracting finance from the World Bank and Western donors. It was a troubled decade for

Mauritania. There was black resentment at the programme of Arabicization and this exploded in riots and civil unrest during October 1986 in Nouakchott and Nouadhibou, the two principal cities, and an 'Oppressed Black African Manifesto' was issued. In response the government emphasized the Islamic rather than the Arab nature of Mauritanian society. A coup plot that was uncovered in 1987 was ethnically based and highlighted the tensions that existed between the dominant Moors and the blacks. In January 1990 Arabic was made official for all government business. The return of 200,000 refugees from Senegal put increased strains on the economy: clashes between the Senegalese and the substantial Mauritanian immigrant population in northern Senegal had erupted as a result of worsening economic conditions in that country.

Libyan involvement in Niger's neighbour Chad through the 1980s led Niger to seek closer relations with Tunisia, Algeria and Morocco, and the need for allies increased when Gaddafi accused the Niger government of persecuting the Tuaregs. Slow moves towards a more constitutional form of government included village council elections in 1983 that were intended to lead to choosing regional councils. There was an abortive coup attempt against President Seyni Kountché in 1983. During 1984/85 Niger suffered from drought and conditions were made worse when Nigeria closed their joint border. In May 1987 the government adopted a draft 'national charter' that provided for non-elective consultative institutions at national and local levels. After a year of ill health President Kountché died in Paris in November 1987 and his Chief of Staff Col. Ali Saibou became head of state. He adopted a more open style of government and appealed to exiled Nigeriens to return home, and announced an amnesty for all political prisoners. He instructed the *Conseil National de Développement* (CND) to draft a new constitution and he then lifted the ban on political organizations and formed a new ruling party, the *Mouvement National pour une Société de Développement* (MNSD). He also increased the number of military personnel in the council of ministers. By 1989 Saibou appeared to be widely popular and on 24 September a new constitution was approved by referendum with 99.28 per cent of the votes cast. An election was held for the 93-seat assembly. Disillusionment followed when the limited nature of the democratization process became apparent and during 1990 strikes and demonstrations led to violence while professional and government employees demanded pay increases. Saibou bowed to popular pressure and legalized political pluralism leading three underground parties to emerge into the open. Saibou faced one of the oldest political problems: offer a little democracy and more will at once be demanded. In November 1990 there was a general strike and the unrest continued into 1991 until on 29 July a national conference of Niger was convened. This bypassed attempts by Saibou to maintain control, for the delegates proclaimed the conference to be sovereign. They elected their own president, the historian André Salifou. The conference sat until 3 November and set a date for multiparty elections in 1993.

By 1980 political reform in Senegal was overdue when President Sedhor Senghor announced his retirement. In January 1981 Abdou Diouf, whom Senghor had been grooming for top office, became President. He lifted restrictions on political activities and launched an anti-corruption drive. Diouf won the elections of 1983 convincingly and subsequently strengthened his position by dismissing some of the ruling *Parti Socialiste* (PS) power brokers. In 1985 the opposition *Parti Démocratique Senegalais* (PDS) of Abdoulaye Wade joined with other parties to create the *Alliance Démocratique Senegalaise* (ADS) under the leadership of Abdoulaye Bathily: both he and Wade were then arrested for unlawful demonstrations. Opposition to Diouf mounted as it became clear that he was opposed to electoral reforms. The presidential and legislative elections of 1988 resulted in violence, although Diouf again won decisively. Under a subsequent state of emergency opposition leaders were arrested and tried on charges of inciting violence. Political unrest lasted into 1989 and then at an extraordinary congress of the *Parti Socialiste* in March Diouf announced the establishment of an executive committee in the PS to reform the electoral code and draft a 'national democratic charter'. Senegal under Diouf was feeling its way warily towards a more open system of government.

In Sierra Leone during the first half of the 1980s, under Siaka Stevens, there was a steady deterioration of the economy, growing corruption in both national and local government and agitation for Stevens to step down. Stevens promised to step down in May 1982 after a new house of representatives had been elected, although in fact he formed a new government. Political violence and rioting occurred in 1983 and 1984 as well as strikes by teachers and council workers in 1984 and 1985. In the latter year Stevens announced his choice of successor, the head of the armed forces, Maj.-Gen. Joseph Saida Momoh, and following endorsement by the All-People's Congress (APC) party convention and a presidential election in October Momoh became President in November 1985. Momoh enjoyed a short period of popularity but was soon under attack for his inability to solve the country's economic problems. In January 1987 student demonstrations led to the closure of three universities; in March a coup attempt was followed by a number of arrests and the discovery of a large cache of arms. By April 1989, when Sierra Leone celebrated 28 years of independence, the country was in apparently permanent economic crisis: its refineries only operated at 40 per cent capacity for lack of oil to process while its diamonds and gold were regularly smuggled out of the country instead of providing revenue for the government. In 1990 the devaluation of the leone created a price spiral although determined efforts by the government to halt the economic decline at least produced a substantial aid packet from the European Community. Momoh, however, set his face against a return to multiparty politics. By the end of 1990 the country faced a new problem as an increasing flow of refugees from the civil war in Liberia crossed into Sierra Leone, foreshadowing a decade that would see Sierra Leone descend into a civil war of its own.

President Etienne Eyadéma of Togo had come to power by coup in 1967 and in 1969 had formed a single party, the *Rassemblement du Peuple Togolais* (RPT). Still in power in 1979, Eyadéma allowed the RPT to draw up a new constitution which provided for an elective presidential system and national assembly. On 30 December 1979 Eyadéma was elected President with nearly 100 per cent of the votes cast. In January 1980 Eyadéma proclaimed the 'Third Republic' and announced amnesties. Despite his new constitution, however, Eyadéma maintained tight political controls and did not allow opposition to surface. During the first half of the decade Eyadéma appeared more confident of his position and though close to being a dictator in real terms, he operated a relatively open and successful economic policy.

The elections of March 1985 were open to more than one candidate so that 216 RPT candidates contested 77 seats. However, bomb outrages in Lomé during August 1985 led to a crisis and subsequent wave of repression and in November the government accused Ghana of complicity in the bomb outrages, while accusations of torture were levelled at the government. Pressures for greater political freedom grew in the latter 1980s and in September 1987 a 'terrorist commando unit' attempted to carry out a coup and tried to seize the Lomé military barracks (which was the home of the President). The government accused both Ghana and Burkina Faso of complicity in the coup attempt and the border with Ghana was closed. In order to safeguard Eyadéma France sent 250 paratroopers to Togo – according to the terms of a secret agreement – and Zaïre also sent 350 troops. French concern was perhaps heightened since in November Lomé provided the setting for the Franco-African summit. In December Eyadéma was re-elected President with 99.95 per cent of the votes cast. In 1989 Eyadéma carried out an anti-corruption drive and a number of senior government figures were dismissed. Increased demands for greater democracy were made through 1990 and in elections to the assembly several independents were returned. Anti-government demonstrations took place in October against a background of a sharp deterioration in economic conditions as coffee and cocoa prices fell.

A clear pattern emerges from the events that recurred with almost monotonous regularity in most of these West African countries. They had small if not tiny economies in world terms and these were constantly in trouble since they were dependent on the one hand upon commodity exports and had little control over prices while on the other they had, by the 1980s, become both heavily indebted and reliant upon aid. Those countries that had opted for a socialist development path almost always found that they had to revert to the Western capitalist way and invoke the aid of the World Bank and IMF in order to survive. On the political front the majority of the rulers were extremely authoritarian if not downright dictators and they used every possible stratagem to hold onto power while conceding as little as possible to the demands of their people for greater democracy. When genuine, as opposed to rhetorical, revolutionaries appeared in the persons of Rawlings in Ghana and Sankara in Burkina Faso they were both resented and feared by their neighbours who saw their ideas of 'people power' threatening their positions. Finally, the weapon of the coup had become entrenched. During the decade there were 11 successful coups and 19 attempted coups (though there were almost certainly more that were planned and then abandoned) apart from major disturbances. Upper Volta/Burkina Faso experienced no fewer than four coups, Nigeria two, while both The Gambia and Mauritania faced three coup attempts each. Although not remarked upon at the time as much as it deserved, the constant demands for greater democracy and the readiness of dissidents to face imprisonment or worse at the hands of repressive regimes gave the lie to claims that were too readily made in the West that Africa and Africans did not understand or want democracy.

East and
Equatorial Africa

The great swathe of East and Equatorial African countries that stretch across the continent from Zanzibar on the Indian Ocean to Equatorial Guinea on the Atlantic includes Kenya, Tanzania and Uganda; Burundi and Rwanda; Central African Republic and Chad; the Republic of Congo, Gabon and Equatorial Guinea; and Zaïre (later, the Democratic Republic of Congo). Through the 1980s they faced similar problems: declining economic conditions and growing debts; civil disturbances and wars; dictatorial leaders and their supporting elites fighting to retain power and keep at bay the people's demands for democracy; and the insidious organizing pressures of aid donors and non-government organizations, the former colonial powers and the United States, whose objective – always – was to maintain a controlling influence.

EAST AFRICA: KENYA, TANZANIA AND UGANDA

By 1980, the honeymoon, which President Daniel arap Moi had enjoyed with the Kenyan people since he succeeded Jomo Kenyatta in 1978, had worn off and criticism, both in the national assembly and from students, was increasing sharply. Oginga Odinga, whom Moi had tried unsuccessfully to attract back into the KANU fold, had launched an attack upon land grabbing, and during 1981 there were increasing disputes among government supporters. Moi lacked the charisma of his predecessor: a Tugen from the minority Kalenjin group, his political career had begun in 1955 when the British appointed him to the legislative council. Thereafter, he had been the deputy leader of KADU until it disbanded itself to join the ruling KANU at the end of 1964; he had served Kenyatta faithfully as Minister of Home Affairs and then as Vice-President from 1966 to 1978. On becoming president he had employed the catchword 'Nyayo' – footsteps – to indicate that he would follow the path laid down by Kenyatta. He then launched an anti-corruption campaign and worked to lessen

Kikuyu political dominance. On 1 August 1982 the air force mounted a coup in Nairobi and seized key points in the city, which they held for a day until the army and the general service unit (GSU) regained control. Officially only 159 people were killed though the number of deaths was much higher; some 2,000 air force personnel and 1,000 civilians were detained. The coup leaders claimed that corruption and restrictions on freedom were the reasons for their action. Twelve airmen and the two leaders who had fled to Tanzania, and were later repatriated to stand trial, were sentenced to death. By 1983 Moi saw Charles Njonjo, the influential Attorney-General and 'kingmaker' of 1978 who had ensured Moi's succession to Kenyatta, as over-powerful and set about destroying him. He was accused of being a 'stooge' of a foreign power working to replace Moi and was publicly disgraced. A commission of inquiry sat for a year taking evidence that was largely circumstantial and inconclusive; then Moi 'pardoned' Njonjo although his political and public career was at an end.

Moi increased his grip on power in 1986 when control of the civil service was transferred to the President's office, as was the power to dismiss the Attorney-General, the Auditor-General and judges, thus lessening the independence of the judiciary. A new system of voting that was an open invitation to intimidation was introduced: voters had to queue publicly behind the candidate of their choice. By 1987 Kenya was attracting increasing international odium for its poor human rights record. KANU won the elections of 1988 although known opponents of Moi such as Odinga were prevented from standing and Moi was returned unopposed as President for the third time. In the post-election reshuffle the popular Vice-President Mwai Kibaki was demoted. However, early in 1989 Odinga appeared to have been reconciled with Moi when he called on all Kenyans to support the government. In May of that year the Vice-President, Josephat Karanja, was accused by party leaders of arrogance, forced to resign and then expelled from KANU. In June Moi released all political prisoners including Odinga's son. At the same time he attacked the *Daily Nation* for its political reporting and Arab countries for opposing his decision to resume diplomatic relations with Israel. By the end of the decade Moi was no longer able to ignore the growing demands for a return to multiparty politics. The murder, in February 1990, of the Foreign Minister, Robert Ouko (a Luo), damaged the government's already tarnished image since it was seen as a political killing. In June 1990 two former politicians of standing – Kenneth Matiba and Charles Rubia – applied for a licence to hold a public meeting to discuss a return to multiparty politics. They were consequently harassed, then detained without trial. By 1991, however, the government was moving reluctantly towards a return to multiparty politics although Moi kept insisting that such a move would lead to a reversal to tribalism.

*

In Tanzania after Julius Nyerere was returned as President for the fifth time with 93 per cent of the votes cast in 1980 he announced that he would not stand again in 1985. Prime Minister Edward Sokoine retired for health reasons and was replaced by Cleopa Msuya. A coup attempt was mounted against Nyerere in January 1983 leading to the detention of 20 soldiers and nine civilians. Nyerere later launched an anti-corruption drive that resulted in more than 1,200 arrests. Economic decline during the decade led to a growing realization that the programme of *ujamaa* and villageization was not working, in part because the bureaucracy had been unable to provide the necessary support. There were increasing shortages of basic consumer goods while the lack of foreign exchange became more acute. Disappointed in the failure of his socialist policies, even though he still had the support of the majority of Tanzanians, Nyerere stood down in 1985 and was succeeded as President by Ali Hassan Mwinyi in October. At first Mwinyi made only minimal changes in policy; before long, however, he inaugurated a major departure in economic policy when he accepted IMF proposals and economic restructuring, thus signalling the end of Nyerere's brave attempt at grassroots socialism. Tanzania, thereafter, moved back into mainstream, orthodox Western-style economics. Even so, Nyerere had made a lasting and unique impact upon both Tanzanian and more generally African politics. 'He ruled his country for 25 years and tried to involve all his people in his own homespun brand of socialism. Though his economic policies were not successful, he did create a moral and social climate superior to most of the rest of Africa and he gave his people good educational standards and a strong belief in his philosophies and themselves.'[1]

Ali Hassan Mwinyi had become President of Zanzibar in January 1984; he calmed a politically explosive situation on the island whose politics were always volatile and supervised a return to prosperity, achievements which brought him to the attention of Nyerere. As a result he was Nyerere's choice as successor in 1985 and was duly elected by 1,731 to 14 votes in a special congress of the ruling Chama Cha Mapinduzi (CCM) in August 1985 before he went on to win the presidential elections in October. Tanzania was facing an economic crisis and Mwinyi quickly came to terms with the existing realities when, pragmatically, he turned to the IMF and began to liberalize the economy although he met heavy criticism from the left for abandoning the CCM's socialist principles. In 1989 a rift developed between Nyerere, who had remained chairman of the CCM, and Mwinyi as president since Nyerere was still opposed to any deal with the IMF. He was, however, becoming increasingly isolated on this issue. Despite this difference, Nyerere acknowledged Mwinyi's successes in tightening up the administration: he had made 'the new government look like a government' he said. In February 1990 Nyerere, the architect and intellectual defender of the one-party state, said publicly that Tanzania should consider multiparty politics again. On 29 May Nyerere announced that he intended to resign as chairman of the CCM in favour of Mwinyi. In the elections of October Mwinyi was returned unopposed as president with 95 per cent of the vote. He appointed John Malecela (the former High Commissioner to Britain) as his Prime Minister. By this time many voices were raised in favour of multipartyism and in March 1991 Mwinyi set up a presidential commission to seek the views of the people. The government also relaxed the leadership code as laid down in the Arusha Declaration. By then it was clear that the Nyerere era of the one-party state was over. Despite its poverty and periodic disorders in the troubled island of Zanzibar, Tanzania had enjoyed a remarkable record of stability through the Nyerere years from 1961 to 1985 and then under his successor Hassan Mwinyi.

Milton Obote was one of a very few African leaders ousted in a coup who, after a decade in exile, made a successful comeback. He returned to Uganda in 1980 to lead his Uganda People's Congress in the December elections which he won, taking 68 of 126 seats although the results were widely regarded as having been rigged. Yoweri Museveni, whose Uganda Patriotic Movement had contested the elections, never got on with Obote and after his defeat he took to the bush and built up the National Resistance Army (NRA). Although 1981 and 1982 could not be regarded as years of civil war, there was much violence aimed at the government and many complaints of unruly behaviour and indiscipline on the part of Obote's army. The violence increased dramatically during 1983 and in the area north of Kampala an estimated 100,000 refugees from the escalating violence in the north of the country found themselves targets for an army that was clearly out of control. By 1984 guerrillas opposed to the government were attacking targets ever closer to Kampala so that the civilians in central Uganda were the people who suffered the most as a result of the increasing lawlessness and breakdown of central control. Obote appeared less and less able to exercise control over the army while frequent army forays against the guerrillas north of Kampala failed to eliminate the threats posed by these dissidents with the result that a general sense of insecurity increased. Obote had some limited success in a policy of reconciliation, at least with the Democratic Party, but by 1985 the economic recovery was faltering. Having made his political return, Obote showed little capacity to get on top of an increasingly lawless situation in which anti-government rebels successfully attacked government targets, acts that invited government reprisals rather than any policy. In the west of the country Museveni's NRA went on the offensive. In July the army mounted a coup and Obote fled to Zambia. A military council was established under Gen. Tito Okello; it appointed Paulo Muwango, Obote's Vice-President, as Prime

Minister, a move that caused great anger, especially in the ranks of the NRA which, in any case, was excluded from the new government. The anger increased when the army recruited former Amin soldiers into its ranks. As a result, the military council dismissed Muwango after only a month in office. On 17 December 1985 Museveni signed a peace pact with the military council but this was broken almost at once and after a lightning campaign the NRA took control of Kampala on 26 January 1986 and Museveni was sworn in as President of Uganda on 29 January. Once Museveni had been sworn in as President, Okello's army disintegrated. The NRA showed a restraint that was unique in 16 years of on-off civil wars and massacres to which Uganda had been subject and this added to the appeal of Museveni's National Resistance Movement (his political wing). By the end of March the NRA had taken the whole country with little loss of life, leading Museveni to declare that the war was over, though in this he was premature.

Opponents of Museveni mounted periodic attacks through 1986 and 1987 and in mid-1987 the Federal Democratic Movement brought its alliance with Museveni to an end and joined with the Ugandan People's Democratic Movement in the hope of ousting him from power. A further violent complication arose with the appearance of a religious sect in the north of the country where some 6,000 followers of the prophetess Alice Lakwena rose against the government; they were defeated by the NRA in November although 1,490 were killed in the fighting. Prolonged fighting always debases ideals and this was true of the NRA. Museveni's 'National Resistance Army, which started with the highest ideals, soon found itself in a life and death conflict with several groups of guerrillas and the methods it adopted to win the guerrilla war were just as vicious and inhumane as those of previous regimes. Museveni found it difficult to discipline his own commanders or find a political solution and peace formula agreed by all Uganda's diverse groups.'[2]

Although Museveni tried to persuade the rebels to lay down their arms with repeated offers of amnesty, resistance continued to 1989. In February of that year he held the first elections to the National Resistance Council, though it only had limited powers; even so, the voters were given considerable freedom of choice and 14 ministers were ousted. Real power lay with Museveni alone and in October 1989 he announced that democratic elections and a return to civilian rule would be delayed until 1995. Museveni became chairman of the OAU for the year 1990/91. In 1990 he said, 'Leaders must be elected periodically. They must be accountable. There must be a free press. There must be no restriction on who participates in the democratic process.' This statement of principles was at variance with Museveni's actions. He refused to promote multipartyism, and said, 'There is no reason why a single political party cannot be democratic,' although experience clearly suggested otherwise. At least by the end of the decade most resistance to Museveni had either died out or been crushed.

Over the Amin years and through to Museveni's establishment of full control Uganda had suffered fearful casualties from its civil wars. An estimated 300,000 Ugandans had been killed under Amin from 1971 to 1979, especially among the Acholi and Lango tribes. In 1985 Paul Ssemogerere, the leader of the Democratic Party, claimed in Britain that 500,000 people had died between 1980, when Obote returned to power, until his overthrow in 1985 and in 1986 Museveni claimed that a total of 800,000 Ugandans had been killed under Amin, Obote and Okello. By that time there were about 100,000 Ugandan refugees in neighbouring countries. Uganda entered the 1990s facing twin problems: continuing rebel activity and unrest, especially in the northern and eastern provinces; and falling world coffee prices which threatened the economic recovery programme. At the same time Museveni was obliged to keep a careful eye on the NRA in order to check potential rivals and though a number of exiles were allowed to return to Uganda their demands for multipartyism presented Museveni with new challenges.

BURUNDI AND RWANDA: PERMANENT TRIBAL INTERFACE

Jean Baptiste Bagaza, a Tutsi soldier who had toppled Michel Micombero in a coup in 1976, introduced a new constitution in Burundi in 1981 and was responsible for land reforms that forced Tutsi landlords to hand over land to Hutu peasants. He vested greater power in the *Union pour le Progrès National* (UPRONA) (Union of National Progress). The first elections for a national assembly were held in 1982 and in July 1984 Bagaza, as sole candidate, was elected head of state by direct suffrage with 99.63 per cent of the votes. All too soon, however, Bagaza became increasingly autocratic, overriding those who opposed him. In the mid-1980s he embarked upon a conflict with the Roman Catholic Church, which was seen as a supporter of the Hutus, and had priests deported or detained. In September 1986 he announced the nationalization of Catholic seminaries and placed other restrictions upon the Church. His quarrel with the Church in a highly religious country was not popular, neither was his increasing autocracy. Bagaza was deposed by the army on 3 September 1987 and Pierre Buyoya replaced him as president. Buyoya suspended the 1981 constitution and all the organs of UPRONA, lifted the restrictions on the Catholic Church and released 600 political prisoners. Buyoya was also a Tutsi, as were most of the army. He accused Bagaza (who was out of the country at a French-speaking summit in Canada) of corruption, violations of the constitution and of pursuing an economic policy that was only geared to help certain groups.

In place of the National Assembly which he had dissolved, Buyoya established a *Comité Militaire pour le Salut National* (CMSN) (Military Committee of National Salvation). However, tensions between Hutu and Tutsi were again mounting while Buyoya failed to give ethnic relations the attention they always required. The explosion came in August 1988 when Hutu massacres of Tutsis were met with much more extensive revenge killings: these took place in the commune of Marangara in Ngozi province and at Ntegi in Kimundu province while an estimated 10,000 people, mainly Hutus, were killed in the Bujumbura area. The army, Tutsi officered, also had all arms under its control. About 65,000 Hutus crossed into Rwanda as refugees.

The relatively small scale of the uprising by the Hutus demonstrated how absolute Tutsi control of the country was at that time. In an attempt to restore unity Buyoya appointed a Hutu, Adrien Sibomana, as Prime Minister and a cabinet that had a Hutu majority for the first time. As a result of these measures reconciliation of a sort followed and 40,000 Hutus who had fled the country returned in 1989. In 1990 the government issued a Charter of National Unity, which gave equal rights to the country's three ethnic groups, the Hutu, Tutsi and Twa. Although both Bagaza and Buyoya were Tutsis they each inaugurated changes that favoured the Hutu majority at the expense of the Tutsi minority.

Over the years 1976–90 Rwanda made huge economic strides. 'It had come a long way from 1976, when it had a per capita income lower than that of any of its neighbours. By 1980, however, the World Bank estimated that the per capita income of Rwanda was higher than that of any of its neighbours. By 1987, Rwanda had the lowest debt, the lowest inflation rate, and the highest rate of growth of the Gross National Product (GNP) of any country in the region.' This record was especially impressive in agriculture, re-afforestation and infrastructure developments. 'Between the early 1960s and the early 1980s, Rwanda was one of only three sub-Saharan countries that succeeded in increasing total food production per capita.'[3] By the end of the 1980s, however, the World Bank was citing Rwanda as one of the three worst performing sub-Saharan countries when it came to food production. By then there was hardly any land left for crop expansion. In the absence of any technological breakthrough, and in the presence of an increase in sheer numbers, soil fertility was decreasing. 'The Second Republic began to unravel from about the end of the 1980s. The context of that development was both internal and external. The *external dimension* feeding the post-1985 resource crunch in Rwanda accelerated with the multiplication of forces that fed it: coffee prices plummeted from 1989, a Structural Adjustment Programme was imposed from outside in 1990, and military spending rose dramatically following the RPF [Rwandan Patriotic

Front] invasion, also in 1990.'[4] Also by the end of the 1980s, Rwanda had one of the highest densities of NGOs and internal voices of protest were reinforced by these NGOs as well as by the assembly of Francophone states and the Vatican. Up to 1989 Habyarimana considered that any political change could only be effected through the one-party system; yet by July 1990 he was prepared to agree to a separation of party and state and possibly a move to multipartyism. However, whatever he might have done was pre-empted by the RPF invasion of October 1990. 'On the eve of the RPF invasion of October 1990, the Rwandan polity was healthier than many others in the region. It had a better record of dealing with political opposition than did most countries in the region of the Great Lakes, Tanzania being the notable exception… The unexpected factor, rather, was the critique from without – the critique which stemmed from the RPF and which articulated the aspirations of the mainly Tutsi diaspora. This, indeed, is where the difference with Tanzania was telling. While Tanzania was the one state in the region that did not drive entire groups into political exile, independent Rwanda was the one state whose very birth was linked to the phenomenon of group exile leading to a mushrooming diaspora.'[5] Whatever its achievements the Second Republic failed completely to answer the question of how to reintegrate the Tutsi diaspora in the country. Rwanda had to be a nation embracing both Hutu and Tutsi and that was an outcome the Hutu could not envisage.

Habyarimana dominated the politics of Rwanda throughout the decade. He had seized power from President Gregoire Kayibanda in 1973 and in 1975 had formed the *Mouvement Révolutionnaire National pour le Développement* (MRND) (National Revolutionary Movement for Development) with the proviso that every Rwandan became a member of it at birth. Elections in December 1981 returned the first elected legislature under the single-party (MRND) system and presidential elections in December 1983 reconfirmed Habyarimana as President. The country faced growing tensions between Hutu and Tutsi through the decade and relations with Uganda plummeted when 45,000 Rwandan Tutsis resident there were expelled. Rwanda closed its border and other refugees sought asylum in Tanzania. About 110,000 Rwandan refugees were registered with the UNHCR and as many again were unregistered. The Central Committee of the MRND said the economy was not equipped to absorb more refugees even though these were their own people. By the end of the decade population pressures, soil erosion and the collapse of world coffee prices forced Habyarimana to introduce an economic austerity programme. Then, on 21 September 1990, he announced a charter for the introduction of a multiparty system.

On 28 April 1991 Habyarimana announced a multiparty system would be introduced that June and on 10 June he signed a new multiparty constitution that provided for separate legislative, executive and judicial branches of government and for a prime minister while the presidential tenure of office was to be limited.

Over 30 September–1 October between 5,000 and 10,000 Tutsi exiles in Uganda, who described themselves as the Rwandan Patriotic Front (RPF), crossed the border into Rwanda. The RPF was led by Maj.-Gen. Fred Rwigyema, who had been a leader in the Ugandan army, but he was killed in the fighting that followed. The invasion was an attempt to restore Tutsi control over Rwanda. Habyarimana appealed to Belgium for assistance and the Belgian government sent 600 paratroopers, France a further 300, and Zaïre 500 troops that were later increased to 1,000. There was fighting through October until the rebels agreed a ceasefire. The government then insisted that there was no available land for the 70,000 exiled Rwandans then in Uganda. Further incursions from Uganda occurred on 12 December and on 4 January 1991 and sporadic fighting was to continue through 1991.

CENTRAL AFRICA: CHAD AND THE CENTRAL AFRICAN REPUBLIC

For Chad the 1980s was a decade of unremitting civil war with Oueddei Goukouni in the ascendant from 1980 to 1982 only to be ousted by Hissène Habré who dominated the situation for the rest of the 1980s, to be ousted from power in his turn at the end of the decade by Idriss Deby. These principals were assisted or impeded by French interventions and withdrawals, US financial support, the Libyan invasions from the north and an OAU peacekeeping effort with troops supplied by Nigeria, Senegal and Zaïre. The war was greatly prolonged as a result of Gaddafi's interventions. There was a major reaction to Gaddafi's northern invasion when in June 1981, meeting in Nairobi, the OAU agreed to establish a peacekeeping force, which France and the United States promised to finance. It was mounted the following December and comprised 2,000 Nigerian troops, 2,000 from Zaïre and 800 from Senegal under Nigerian command. When the OAU then persuaded the Libyans to withdraw, the result was to leave many of their weapons in the north for Habré to commandeer so that he was able to pursue his struggle with Goukouni effectively: by June 1982 he had taken N'Djamena and by October had established his government in the capital, forcing Goukouni to flee. Thus the position of 1980, when Goukouni held the capital and appeared to control the government, was now reversed: Habré controlled the capital while Goukouni was back in the north where, with renewed Libyan intervention on his side, he attempted to reverse his defeat. In

June 1983 Gaddafi increased his support for Goukouni to provoke a new French intervention – under pressure from Washington whose principal interest was to contain Gaddafi – and so France sent 2,800 troops to Chad. These were deployed across the country along the 15th (later 16th parallel) from east to west to create what became known as the Red Line to prevent Goukouni's forces penetrating further south. At this point anti-Habré violence erupted in the extreme south of the country, temporarily diverting Habré's energies from the main war and causing a number of refugees to flee into neighbouring countries. Later in the year Habré successfully repulsed the Libyans with heavy losses. In September 1983 Habré attended a Franco-African summit in France at which he criticized France for not being prepared to fight the Libyans (the French forces remained stationary on the Red Line and would not advance northwards to engage the Libyans). The war continued through 1984 with heavy loses on both sides. Habré dissolved FROLINAT (*Front de Libération Nationale du Tchad*) and replaced it with the *Union Nationale pour l'Indépendence et la Révolution* (UNIR) in an effort to create a more evenly balanced north-south government, but the change made no difference. Further opposition to Habré's rule in the south met with brutal government repression and caused a flood of refugees into Central African Republic. This fighting continued until April 1985.

In September 1984 France and Libya agreed to withdraw all their troops from Chad simultaneously. By 10 November all 3,300 French troops had left the country while the Libyan forces remained in the north, forcing President Mitterand to admit that he had been fooled by Gaddafi. France offered to send its troops back to Chad but Habré refused the offer since he did not trust French motives. During 1985 Habré consolidated his power in the south. In the north, however, Libya had 4,000 troops by October and in February 1986 they launched an offensive across the 16th parallel, the Red Line that France had established. Habré appealed to France, and French bombers from Central African Republic attacked Libyan targets in the north. France then established an air strike force in Chad. The United States, which had carried out its air strike against Libya in April 1986, now provided Habré with US$10 million in aid. By mid-November 1986 US arms for Chad were arriving in Douala (Cameroon) while France had sent back to Chad 1,000 troops to support its air units and these were once more deployed along the 16th parallel. In December Habré launched an offensive against the Libyans at Bardai and in the Tibesti Mountains. Apart from dropping supplies to Habré's forces, France would not commit its troops to ground fighting despite Habré's strongest appeals, even though it had 4,000 troops stationed in Central African Republic. The US, however, promised a further US$15 million in aid. By this time, after 20 years of warfare, the Chad economy was in ruins. France tried to dissuade Habré from attacking the

Libyans but in mid-December Goukouni's forces, which meanwhile had switched sides to Habré, inflicted a major defeat upon the Libyans. Habré moved north to follow up this victory over the Libyans and in the new situation France decided to support Habré. In early 1987 Habré launched a major attack upon the Libyans and after quitting most of the towns they controlled, the Libyan forces were badly defeated at Fada where 784 of their soldiers were killed and 100 Russian tanks were destroyed. In response to this defeat Libya built up its forces to 15,000 while France sent another 1,000 troops to support Habré. In March 1987 Habré's forces under the command of Hassan Djamous captured Ouadi Doum, Libya's base for air strike aircraft; 3,600 Libyans were killed and 700 captured while a further 2,000 died of thirst as they fled in the desert. The Libyans now retreated from Faya-Largeau while between 2,000 and 3,000 of their troops had become isolated across the border in Darfur province of Sudan, and Habré at last appeared to be in control of the whole country. Many of the Libyan troops were conscripts who had been pressed into the Islamic Pan-African League; they had gone to Libya, where the war was deeply unpopular, to seek work.

A precarious rapprochment between Libya and Chad was achieved in 1988 although Goukouni, who had depended upon Libyan support ever since 1981 when he had proposed a union with Libya, refused to accept the new situation. However, he was deserted by Achiek Ibn Oumar, the most important of his supporters, who returned to N'Djamena in November 1988 taking most of his troops with him. On 10 December 1989 Habré won a presidential election with 99 per cent of the vote for a seven-year term. This, however, was his last triumph. He had underestimated Idriss Deby, another aspiring ruler of Chad, who meanwhile had been building up an army of his own in Darfur. He invaded Chad in November 1990. France, whose relations with Habré had always been equivocal, refused to provide help at this crucial point and probably saw Deby as a more amenable leader for Chad than Habré. Habré went to lead his troops against Deby but was heavily defeated and fled, first to Cameroon and then Senegal. Deby assumed power in N'Djamena and the war, or series of wars, finally came to an end.

There had been high casualties over the 20 years of fighting though numbers were always hard to quantify, with figures ranging between 50,000 and 80,000 although they may well have been much higher. The three French interventions were not popular in France. It was a senseless war, less about ideology than power. Both France and the US appeared more interested in checking Gaddafi than in assisting Chad solve its problems, while Gaddafi, always a troublemaker, wanted the Aozou Strip and had oil wealth to pay for his interventions as Chad became more deeply impoverished as the fighting continued.

A decade of fighting among warlords assisted by the interventions of France and Libya had done little for the people of Chad except impoverish them still further. The dominant figure for the decade was Habré, a man more suited to war than peace. 'Of all Chad's warlords Hissène Habré was the most aggressive, determined and consistent... His ruthless determination and organizational skill brought him victory for a time, but the battle was long and ferocious against a host of rivals, particularly Goukouni Oueddei backed by his powerful Libyan allies. When Habré took power in N'Djamena for the second time in June 1982, he convinced France and the US that the survival of Chad depended on him alone and he won their grudging support. It was when he lost the support of France, in December 1990 that he was pushed from power by Idriss Deby.'[6] Deby had originally thrown in his lot with Habré in 1978 and created an alliance between his own Zaghawa tribe and Habré's Daza tribe. He became the Chief of Staff of the *Forces Armées du Nord* (FAN) and led the campaign that restored Habré to power in 1982. In 1983 he repulsed Goukouni's forces but by then he was becoming too popular and Habré sent him on a higher officers' education course in Paris. When Deby returned to Chad, Habré made him his military adviser. However, in 1988 Habré gave most offices and positions to his own Daza supporters to become less dependent upon Deby, who saw his influence declining. Then, on 1 April 1989, Deby was accused of plotting against Habré; with his loyal troops he fought his way out of N'Djamena and retreated to Darfur. Later, from Lagos, he accused the Habré government of tribalism, extortion and injustice. He visited Libya and informed Gaddafi of Habré's plans and troop dispositions. In March 1990 Deby moved into Chad from Sudan and embarked upon the campaign and battles with Habré's forces that led to the latter's downfall.

The coup of 1979 that deposed Bokassa, who had crowned himself Emperor of Central African Republic, brought David Dacko, who had been personal adviser to Bokassa, to the presidency; his elevation to this office was backed by 700 French troops flown in from Gabon. Dacko, who was seen as having been too close to Bokassa, lasted less than two years. During 1981 he faced increasing unrest and opposition until on 1 September the military, led by Gen. André Kolingba, carried out another coup. Dacko's rivals – he had just suppressed all opposition – issued a letter of support for Kolingba who became head of state. Kolingba suspended the constitution and banned all activities by political parties. He called for a privileged relationship to continue with France and wanted France to pay the salaries of the civil service for at least a year so as to leave him free to reorganize the economy. This, at least, was a frank admission of the country's heavy dependence upon France. Kolingba set up an entirely military regime and claimed 'when we have order everything else will follow'. His reluctance to set a date for a return to civilian rule soon created discontent and in March 1982 a former prime minister, Ange-Félix Patassé, mounted a coup attempt against him. Only in 1985, after four years of military rule, did Kolingba begin a process of limited democratization when in September he appointed civilians to a majority of the posts in government. There were other minor coup attempts and student unrest but Kolingba did not have any of those convicted of offences executed. In May 1986 Kolingba created a single party, the *Rassemblement Démocratique Centrafricain* (RDC). In November of that year a referendum confirmed Kolingba in power for a further six years and also approved a draft constitution that would give wide powers to the President. The return from France of the exiled Bokassa in October 1986 embarrassed the government; he had been sentenced to death in absentia. He was retried on a number of charges including murder and cannibalism and again sentenced to death; however, in 1988 Kolingba commuted the sentence to hard labour for life.

In July 1987 Kolingba authorized the first legislative elections in 20 years. Growing demands over the following years to reform the single-party system led Kolingba to call an extraordinary general meeting of the executive committee of the party early in 1990 at which he rejected multipartyism, which, he said, was to accept 'political systems which seemed to work in other countries'. However, he did agree to share power with a prime minister and appointed Edouard Frank to the post on 16 March 1991. On 22 April, despite his earlier rejection, Kolingba promised to revert to democracy and multiparty rule and on 7 June set up a national commission to revise the constitution and lay the groundwork for pluralism; in August he agreed to legalize three opposition parties. Central African Republic continued to be dependent upon France for aid and investment. The economy, apart from diamonds and coffee, was agrarian based and there was little industrial development. Periodically, eruptions of anti-French sentiment occurred – expressions of frustration at the all-pervasive influence of the former colonial power.

EQUATORIAL AFRICA

The Republic of Congo, despite a sharp post-independence shift to the left, had maintained close links with France (Brazzaville had acted as the capital of French Equatorial Africa in colonial days). In 1979 the *Parti Congolais du Travail* (PCT) had deposed Col. Joachim Yhombi-Opango and replaced him as President with Denis Sassou-Nguesso. He faced the problem of maintaining a balance between the pro-Soviet faction of the PCT and the pro-Western pragmatists. In addition, he had to balance the tribal rivalries that existed between north and south. He solved the first problem by posing as a left-wing Marxist while following Western-style economic liberalism. In May 1981 Sassou-Nguesso visited Moscow where he signed a treaty of friendship and co-operation with his hosts, and made Congo one of the first Francophone countries to do so. At the same time he maintained close links with France. In July 1984 he was unanimously elected President for another five years by the central committee of the PCT and was also given greater presidential powers. In July 1987 20 senior army officers were arrested for plotting. They came from the northern Kouyou tribe (from which his predecessors Ngouabi and Yhombi-Opango came) while Sassou-Nguesso was from another northern tribe, the Mboshi. Pierre Anga, a former politician, was also involved in the plot: he was responsible for distributing arms to people in Owendo opposed to the government, and in fighting during August and September 60 people were killed.

Despite the country's left-wing stance it never received much aid from the USSR. France continued as the main source of aid, as the main trade partner and the principal exploiter of the Congo's oil resources. Moreover, relations with France had improved after François Mitterand became President of France at the beginning of the decade and in 1983, after a period of suspended diplomatic relations, these were restored with both the US and Britain. In 1989 Sassou-Nguesso was re-elected head of the PCT. In 1990, on a visit to Washington, he agreed a treaty with President Bush guaranteeing protection to private American investors in the Congo. In July 1990 the PCT Central Committee voted to end the one-party system and at the end of the year it abandoned Marxism as its official creed and turned instead to social democracy. On 1 January 1991 opposition parties became legal and after a year of growing pressures President Sassou-Nguesso was forced to appoint Gen. Louis Sylvain Goma as prime minister (8 January 1991) and hold a national conference. The conference declared itself sovereign, rewrote the constitution and appointed a new prime minister, André Milingo, to head a transitional government of national unity. It set a date in mid-1992 for multiparty elections. As Congo was clearly turning to the market economy, Cuba withdrew its troops after 14 years. Sassou-Nguesso, though still President, had greatly reduced powers.

Albert-Bernard (in 1973, encouraged by Gaddafi, he became a Muslim and changed his name to Omar) Bongo came to the presidency of Gabon in 1967; he was re-elected as sole candidate in 1979. Through the 1980s he faced increasing political opposition, largely expressed through the *Mouvement de Redressement National* (Morena), which emerged in 1981 and attracted the support of students and the younger generation and had offices in Paris. Morena accused the Bongo regime of corruption and called for multiparty elections. Bongo's response was repression. Economic conditions deteriorated through the decade and in January 1985, for example, a wave of looting was directed against the Lebanese community in Libreville. Later that year the government carried out a census of foreigners: the borders were closed and illegal immigrants expelled. Employers were instructed to give priority to Gabonese when they recruited staff and financial restrictions were placed upon immigrants wishing to leave or re-enter Gabon. Overall, there was little effective opposition to Bongo through the 1980s despite the efforts of Morena. Generally, Gabon played a moderate role in African affairs though, apparently under the influence of Gaddafi, Bongo converted to Islam. Ties with France were more important than any other relationship: France was the principal source of both aid and investment and also maintained a military presence in Gabon. In 1989 the government announced a programme to study and preserve the country's native languages since these had been neglected in favour of French for even moderate, pro-France Gabon felt nationalist revulsion against too much overt French influence.

Discontent with the system exploded in January 1990 when five students on strike were shot dead by the police, setting off full-scale riots in Libreville. In February Bongo tried to placate the opposition by the device of turning the ruling *Parti Démocratique Gabonais* (PDG) into an all-embracing *Rassemblement Social Démocrate Gabonais* (RSDG) but this did not reduce popular discontent. In March Bongo called a national conference and confirmed the findings of a special commission, which backed democratization. He announced that he favoured moves towards a multiparty system. In May the central committee of the PDG and the national assembly approved amendments to the constitution that would lead to a multiparty system while Bongo resigned as Secretary-General of the PDG since, he claimed, the post was no longer compatible with that of head of state. However, the mysterious murder of Joseph Rendjambe, the leader of the *Parti Gabonais du Progrès* (PGP), led to violent demonstrations in both Libreville and Port-Gentil. French troops evacuated French citizens from Port-Gentil while in Libreville rioters burned public buildings and property belonging to Bongo. When elections were held in September 533 candidates from forty parties contested 120 seats. After fraud, re-runs, cancellations and additional rounds the ruling party (the PDG) obtained 62 seats, 55 went to the opposition parties and three to allied independents. Gabon, like much of Africa at this time, was making painful moves back towards full democracy.

The tiny state of Equatorial Guinea (former Spanish Guinea) suffered under the brutal and despotic rule of Macias Nguema from independence in 1968 until his overthrow by his nephew, Teodoro Obiang, in a coup of 3 August 1979. Obiang was proclaimed President on 11 October. The country at once received economic aid from Spain, which had suspended assistance to his uncle. Obiang embarked upon a policy of achieving better and deeper relations with France and sought membership of the franc zone. Like his uncle, Obiang was guilty of flagrant human rights abuses. There were coup attempts against him in 1981 and 1982, and again in 1986. Legislative elections were held in 1988 and several opposition members were given life sentences for alleged plotting against Obiang that September. In June 1989, as sole candidate, Obiang was elected president for another five-year term. Despite growing pressures and demands for real democracy during 1990 and 1991 Obiang refused to respond to calls for the establishment of a multiparty system.

ZAÏRE

President Mobutu Sese Seko's corruption and political manipulations to maintain his position as undisputed master of Zaïre throughout the 1980s were successful. But he was laying the groundwork for the disasters that would affect the country at the end of the 1990s. An attempt to persuade Mobutu to reform was made at the end of 1980.

> Thirteen members of parliament sent a 52-page letter to President Mobutu in December 1980 demanding political reforms. By this time, Mobutu had already managed to clip the parliament's wings, thanks to diminished concern with the human rights situation in the Congo by Washington, then distracted by its Cold War priorities in the Horn of Africa and Afghanistan, as well as by the Iranian hostage crisis. For their audacity, members of the Group of 13, as the dissident parliamentarians became known, were jailed, tortured and banished to remote detention centres. In spite of this repression, most of them continued to fight for democracy.[7]

In April 1981 Nguza Karl I Bond, his Prime Minister, went to Belgium where he resigned and then launched an attack upon the country's corruption. More persistent opposition in Belgium came from the *Union pour la Démocratie et le Progrès Social* (UPDS) (Union for Democracy and Social Progress) while some MPs in Kinshasa who supported the UPDS and criticized Mobutu were detained and only released as a result of overseas pressures. However, demands for a more democratic system during the years 1980–85 never seriously threatened Mobutu's hold on power. In 1985 by dividing party and government functions of the *Mouvement Populaire de la Révolution* (MPR) he strengthened his position further.

Under Mobutu Zaïre pursued a high-profile foreign policy. Relations with Israel were restored in 1982, troops were sent to Chad as part of a peacekeeping operation in 1983 and in 1984 Zaïre suspended its membership of the OAU in support of Morocco's walkout over the Western Sahara question. In 1986 Zaïre quarrelled with the front-line states over allegations that it was allowing the CIA to supply arms to *União Nacional para a Independência Total de Angola* (UNITA) in Angola through Zaïre (UNITA was backed at that time by apartheid South Africa). Through the 1970s and into the first half of the 1980s the IMF attempted to bring order to the country's economy by imposing financial discipline, but its measures were unacceptable to Mobutu who broke with the Fund in 1986. Mobutu's anti-Communism, as well as the geographic position of his vast country in the centre of Africa, made him a natural choice as an ally for the United States. He always supported the opponents of the *Movimento Popular para a Libertação de Angola* (MPLA) in Angola and allowed Zaïre to be used as a conduit for CIA aid to both Holden Roberto's *Frente Nacional de Libertação de Angola* (FNLA) and Jonas Savimbi's UNITA throughout the 1970s and 1980s. Corruption appeared central to all public activities in Zaïre: 'In 1987, a Zaïrean academic said despairingly: "If things go on in this way in Zaïre, there will be no morality left." They have gone on; and they have got worse. How have individuals responded to a situation of chronic repression and violence and the disintegration of social and economic institutions?'[8] This despairing comment was representative of many Congolese under the man who gained the reputation of the most corrupt ruler in Africa.

A row with Belgium dominated the politics of 1989. At a time when the Belgian government offered to reschedule Zaïre's debts, Belgian journalists claimed that Mobutu was corrupt and that aid to Zaïre was misappropriated. In angry response, Mobutu rejected the rescheduling offer and ordered the 15,000 Zaïreans then in Belgium to return home. A Belgian judge ordered the seizure of all Mobutu's assets in the country in compensation for the nationalization of a Belgian company back in 1973. However, when Mobutu threatened to break diplomatic relations with Belgium, Brussels rescinded the judge's order. The row continued, however, until Mobutu threatened to make France its major trading partner. Belgium then caved in and agreed to cancel all Zaïre's public debt as well as a third of its commercial debt and rescheduled the balance interest-free over 25 years. At the time Zaïre was doing well economically and as a result of these transactions was able to announce in June 1989 that it had paid off all its IMF debts. Mobutu was able to win such a confrontation because his country was seen as a storehouse of mineral wealth over which neither

Belgium nor the West as a whole wished to lose control. By 1990, as the structures of the Cold War collapsed and demands for democracy mounted throughout Africa, Mobutu came under huge pressure to institute changes. In January 1990 Mobutu called for a dialogue between state and people to consider the country's institutions. In May, 100 demonstrating students were massacred by troops at Lubumbashi University. Later, Mobutu announced his resignation as chairman of the MPR so that he could 'rise above' party politics. He established a special commission to draft a new constitution by April 1991 and allowed the free operation of political parties.

Endgame in
Southern Africa

The 1980s proved to be the last decade of apartheid and with its passing the politics and economics of the region changed out of recognition. These changes that ushered in the last decade of the century were preceded by a crescendo of violence and few at the beginning of the 1980s believed that the apartheid state had only 10 years to run. In South Africa anti-apartheid violence reached a climax in the years 1984–86, following President Botha's constitutional reforms of 1983 that still excluded the black majority from any share in power. The front-line states were subject to military incursions by South Africa throughout the decade. In Angola UNITA, supported by South Africa and the United States, waged war against the MPLA government; in Mozambique South Africa supported the rebel movement *Resistencia Nacional de Mozambique* (RENAMO); in Namibia it fought an increasingly difficult rearguard action to maintain its control. In 1990, however, the new South African President, F. W. de Klerk, recognizing the inevitable, signalled the end of apartheid and universal suffrage in his speech of 2 February. On 21 March Namibia finally shook off South African control to become independent.

THE FRONT-LINE STATES

South Africa had long used its economic strength to dominate its neighbours. Through the Southern African Customs Union (SACU), formed in 1969, it incorporated Botswana, Lesotho and Swaziland, as well as Namibia, into its orbit while the mining giant, the Anglo-American Corporation and its subsidiaries, extended AAC control far beyond South Africa into Botswana, Lesotho, Namibia, Zambia and Zimbabwe. The Republic's rail and port infrastructure serviced vital imports and exports for the countries of the interior while migrant workers from the peripheral states went to work in South Africa's mines (in the mid-1980s 280,000 such migrants sent home remittances worth R538 million).

The Southern Africa Development Coordination Conference (SADCC) was formed in 1980 in order to counter this all-pervasive influence, following a meeting at Arusha, Tanzania, by the front-line states. The object was to find ways in which the countries bordering South Africa could reduce their economic and transport dependence upon that country. The original members were Angola, Botswana, Lesotho, Malawi, Mozambique, Swaziland, Tanzania, Zambia and Zimbabwe. SADCC was formed in response to a precise challenge: that of dominant South African power throughout the region. Of its members, only Malawi had recognized South Africa diplomatically, although Botswana, Lesotho and Swaziland were seen as the Republic's 'economic prisoners'. SADCC had an immediate impact during its first year: in November 1980 it held a donor conference in Maputo and raised pledges from the industrial countries of US$650 million for its development projects. The goal of SADCC was 'to liberate our economies from their dependence on the Republic of South Africa, to overcome the imposed economic fragmentation, and to co-ordinate our efforts toward regional and national economic development' according to the Lusaka Declaration of 1 April 1980 that saw the formal founding of SADCC.[1] The Lusaka Declaration stressed that economic liberation was as important as political freedom and analysed dependence as follows:

> This dependence is not a natural phenomenon, nor is it simply the result of a free market economy. The nine states and one occupied territory (Namibia) of Southern Africa were, in varying degrees, deliberately incorporated – by metropolitan powers, colonial rulers, and large corporations – in the colonial and sub-colonial structures centring on the Republic of South Africa. The development of national economies as balanced units, let alone the welfare of the people of southern Africa, played no part in the economic integration strategy.

SADCC, despite this disclaimer of the colonial powers, was nonetheless dependent upon Western capital injections to further its anti-South African agenda and only in 1987 did the USSR and other Communist countries consider providing aid. At the SADCC heads of state meeting in Maputo, eight of nine leaders (Hastings Banda of Malawi did not attend) agreed that, 'South Africa can invade and occupy sovereign states, blow up vital installations, and massacre populations at no apparent cost to its relations with its major allies… Some of the friends of South Africa who provide the racist regime with the capital, technology, management skills, and deadly weapons necessary to carry out such a policy also seek to improve their relations with SADCC.' The best way to do so, they added, was to 'use their influence to check the aggression being waged against SADCC member states'.

All the SADCC states were liable to South African destabilization raids and other tactics. Pretoria met what it called the 'total onslaught' of the Soviet Union with its 'total strategy' under which it justified the destabilization of its neighbours. South Africa's white leaders equated the 'red peril' with the 'black peril' and claimed that South Africa was defending Christian values while its insistence upon the Soviet threat had two advantages: 'On the one hand, all criticisms of apartheid can be dismissed as communist-inspired. On the other hand, it allows South Africa to demand that the West support it as a bastion against communism, despite any distaste for apartheid; when the West attacks apartheid it only aids Moscow.'[2] However, the total strategy, which placed the entire country on a war footing, that allowed destabilization was based upon a fallacy since destabilization was most likely to lead to more calls for Soviet support because Britain and the United States were on South Africa's side and would not oppose its policy of destabilization. South Africa saw providing support to RENAMO in Mozambique as the best way to stretch Zimbabwe's resources and lessen its capacity to cause problems for South Africa since RENAMO constantly targeted the railways to Beira and Maputo upon which Zimbabwe relied for its imports and exports. Proof of South Africa's support for RENAMO after the Nkomati Accord was passed secretly to the ANC by Derek Hanekom, later Lands Minister in Mandela's cabinet. During the 1980s South Africa invaded three capitals (of Botswana, Lesotho and Mozambique) and four countries (Angola, Swaziland, Zambia and Zimbabwe); its agents attempted to assassinate the prime ministers of Lesotho and Zimbabwe; it backed the rebel movements RENAMO in Mozambique and UNITA in Angola; disrupted oil supplies to six countries; and attacked the railways that affected Angola, Botswana, Malawi, Mozambique, Swaziland, Zambia and Zimbabwe.[3]

Once Zimbabwe became independent in 1980 it replaced Zambia on the immediate front line facing South Africa across the Limpopo. Throughout the decade, however, President Kaunda played a leading role in co-ordinating opposition to the apartheid state and from 1985, when Nyerere stepped down as President of Tanzania, became chairman of the front-line states. It was Zambia's misfortune that confrontation so engaged President Kaunda that he neglected the economic growth and well-being of Zambia to the extent that his country became one of the most indebted in the world (on a per capita basis) while his own popularity as the founding father of independent Zambia slumped.

Robert Mugabe's victory in the pre-independence elections in Zimbabwe of March 1980 was a severe blow to South Africa. 'For the South Africans the outcome was a particularly bitter blow. They had invested US$300 million in the Rhodesian war against the nationalists and they had invested heavily in the election campaign against ZANU.'[4] Further, South Africa sought to create a Constellation of Southern African States (CONSAS), which they would dominate economically and technologically. Other front-line leaders might prove malleable, but not Mugabe, who advocated Marxist-Leninist policies, was an outspoken critic of apartheid and determined to lessen his country's dependence on South Africa. He at once became a leading member of SADCC. 'Zimbabwe's geographical and historical ties to South Africa, including the fact that it inherited Pretoria as its largest trading partner at independence, left it particularly vulnerable to economic destabilization. Joining the SADCC 17 days before independence was a recognition of this harsh reality. It was also a public statement that it wanted to do something about it.'[5] Zimbabwe, nonetheless, had to take South Africa's grip on the region into account. At independence 19 per cent of Zimbabwe's total trade was with South Africa and 41 per cent of all Zimbabwe's manufactured exports went to South Africa, 60 per cent of these under a preferential trading agreement of 1964. Abrogation of the agreement would cost Zimbabwe Z$50 million a year and the loss of 6,500 jobs. On the eve of independence, therefore, Mugabe said: 'We must accept that South Africa is a geographical reality and, as such, we must have some minimum relationship with it.' South Africa began by cutting off fuel supplies to Mugabe's Zimbabwe so that the rehabilitation of the Beira–Mutare oil pipeline and the Beira railway became a top priority. At the height of the RENAMO war, between 27 February 1986 and 9 September 1987, the railway was sabotaged on average just over once a week.[6] From July 1985 onwards Zimbabwe deployed troops in Mozambique to assist FRELIMO against RENAMO and guard the Beira Corridor. In September 1987 a government official estimated the cost of maintaining 10,000 troops in Mozambique at US$1.5 million a day although that included the salaries of the soldiers. During the 1980s, while it played a significant role as a front-line state, the ZANU government of Mugabe also fought the 'Dissidents' War' at home (1982–87) whereby the power of Nkomo's ZAPU was broken as an opposition to pave the way for the creation of a de facto one-party state.

SOUTH AFRICA'S TWO FLANKS: ANGOLA AND MOZAMBIQUE

South Africa became deeply embroiled in Angola from 1975 when it made its immediate post-independence invasion of the territory. Pretoria feared the MPLA government's Marxist orientation and Moscow links and saw a Marxist Angola as a threat to the region. Moreover, South Africa sought to remain in Namibia for economic and strategic reasons despite its international obligation to grant Namibia independence. In order to weaken the Angolan government, if not overthrow it, South Africa supported the insurgent movement of UNITA throughout the 1980s. Over the years 1975 to 1987 it made major efforts, including armed incursions, to assist UNITA in its bid to seize power in Luanda but the up-and-down unreliability of UNITA and the substantial military assistance provided by Cuba for the MPLA thwarted this South African design. By the end of the decade rising South African casualties and the defeat (or stalemate) it sustained at the battle of Cuito Cuanavale made the policy unsustainable and forced South Africa into serious negotiations over Namibian independence. South African incursions into Angola were substantial in scale and cost: over December 1983–January 1984, for example, Operation Askari saw the SADF penetrate 300 kilometres into Angola to capture Kassinga and bomb Lubango and other towns. The SADF pulled back after suffering heavier losses than expected and being privately warned by the Soviet Union not to escalate the conflict.[7]

Angola sustained a contradictory relationship with the United States throughout these years. On the one hand, the United States was Angola's most important trading partner for its oil (which Chevron largely controlled) and the United States' fourth trading partner in Africa as a result. At the same time Washington refused to recognize the MPLA government and gave its support to UNITA and South Africa in their attempts to undermine it, even as US oil payments to Luanda were used to buy arms and pay for the Cuban troops Washington wanted to force to leave the country. This complex relationship represented one of the many hypocrisies of the Southern African situation. When President Reagan's government provided assistance for UNITA and Jonas Savimbi visited Washington where he met the President and had talks with the State Department, the Soviet Foreign Minister and two senior generals met with Angolan government officials and then warned that the USSR might increase its military aid to Angola if Savimbi obtained more aid from the US.[8] In any case, by the mid-1980s two wars were being fought in Angola: the civil war between the MPLA government, backed by the USSR and supported by the presence of some 20,000 Cuban troops, and UNITA, in its turn supported by Zaïre, the US and South Africa; and a second war between SWAPO, with bases in southern Angola, and South Africa, which made frequent incursions across the border from Namibia to destroy SWAPO and ANC bases.

Fighting in Angola was widespread. 'By the early 1980s, UNITA forces were entrenched in rural areas across much of southern and central Angola, and were beginning to expand their operations into the north. By the mid-1980s, they had reached the Zaïrean frontier and begun to use Zaïre as a rear base for guerrilla activities in northern Angola… Following the repeal of the Clark Amendment in July 1985, the United States resumed covert assistance to UNITA, thereby once again establishing a de facto alliance with South Africa.'[9] The MPLA government was undermined because it lacked popular participation, suffered from a dearth of qualified personnel and faced the spread of a US-backed UNITA insurgency and a growing debt burden. Both sides in this long war used increasingly brutal tactics and 'Savimbi maintained an iron grip on power and brooked no criticism whatever'. On the other hand *Forças Armadas Populares de Libertação de Angola* (FAPLA) (the People's Armed Forces for the Liberation of Angola) never posed a threat to the government of dos Santos. 'The common threat posed by UNITA and South Africa may provide part of the explanation. The efficient security services, developed with East German assistance, were doubtless another dissuasive factor. Even more important, the presence of large numbers of Cuban troops in the country until 1991 provided a security shield, not just against UNITA and the South Africans, but against potential internal plotters as well.'[10] Oil wealth not only sustained the MPLA government but also reduced the readiness of Western countries, eager for a share in prospecting for future fields, to criticize the government while also reducing its need to depend upon aid.

Oil, indeed, was crucial in setting the parameters of the Angola that would emerge in the 1990s. 'The economic well-being of the sophisticated elite which ruled Angola after the end of the liberation wars of the 1970s was enhanced throughout the 1980s by the growing supply of crude petroleum. The oil revenue cushioning Luanda from the austerity which the collapse of the colonial economy had inflicted on the countryside was also the economic fuel which made the war particularly ferocious… It can, and perhaps should, be argued that it was oil which kept the severe Angolan civil wars running for 25 years.'[11] At the same time, while Washington welcomed destabilizing activities in Angola, 'corporate America remained keen to do business with Angola, selling aircraft, electronic equipment, computer and oil-drilling technology'. President Reagan prevented the United Nations from restraining South Africa's frequent incursions into Angola and though these ostensibly were in pursuit of Namibian guerrillas, they were also aimed at Angolan army targets while the US worked through third parties to ensure a continuing supply of weapons reached Savimbi. South Africa, loudly proclaiming its role in resisting the Soviet 'total onslaught', was able to use Russian support for the MPLA government as a weapon to play upon US fears of the spread of Communism and so ensure continuing US support for the apartheid state.

By the mid-1980s, therefore, the wars in Angola had become inextricably intertwined with the worldwide confrontation of the Cold War so that, reversing its earlier policy, the US House of Representatives voted in 1986 to provide UNITA with US$15 million in aid. In November 1987 a growing battle developed around the strategic town of Cuito Cuanavale in south-east Angola to which South African forces in support of UNITA were laying siege. By January 1988 about 6,000 South African troops were deployed against 10,000 MPLA, supported by Cubans. The battle became one of the biggest set pieces in Africa since World War II. The South Africans lost air superiority to the Cubans and their force was in danger of being trapped. The battle marked a turning point for the region since it destroyed the myth of South African military invincibility and persuaded Pretoria that it could not dominate the region by military means. In April 1988 the USSR and Cuba agreed to the long-standing US insistence upon 'linkage' – that is, the withdrawal of Cuban troops from Angola as part of a package for Namibian independence. The two sides then held a number of meetings over the remainder of 1988 in London, Brazzaville, Cairo, Geneva and New York to produce an agreement that was signed in New York on 22 December 1988 between Angola, Cuba and South Africa. Under its terms the 50,000 Cuban troops (its numbers had been greatly increased in the last phase of the war) were to be withdrawn over 27 months to July 1991; South Africa was to implement UN Resolution 435 leading to Namibian independence in 1990; and South Africa was to withdraw all its forces from Angola while the ANC, with an estimated 10,000 freedom fighters in the country, was to do the same. This US-brokered agreement excluded any peace between the MPLA government and UNITA. However, an initiative to end the MPLA–UNITA war was mounted by President Mobutu of Zaïre who brought President dos Santos and Jonas Savimbi together on 22 June 1989 at his palace at Gbadolite. But the 'Gbadolite handshake' did not work and the war resumed. The US increased its aid to UNITA and by 1990 an estimated 100,000 Angolans had been killed in this war while 900,000 faced famine.

The US approach to the problems of Southern Africa during these years was epitomized by Chester Crocker who had been named Under-Secretary of State for African Affairs in the new Reagan administration. He largely determined US policy in the region. In a speech of August 1981, he said: 'We are concerned about the influence of the Soviet Union and its surrogates in Africa,' and he then added that the US needed South Africa's minerals.[12] In November 1982 Crocker remarked that the major purpose of the US policy of 'constructive engagement' was 'to reverse the decline in security and stability of southern Africa which has been under way now since the early and mid-1970s'. Crocker's top priority was to stop Soviet encroachment in Africa and he spoke of the Soviet Union aiming to thwart goals of shared future prosperity through its surrogates in the region. In this regard he became almost mesmerized by the Cuban presence in Angola. It was Crocker who invented the concept of 'linkage' whereby Namibian independence would depend upon the withdrawal of the Cubans from Angola while his policy of 'constructive engagement' did not also include any contacts with the ANC or other anti-apartheid groups. However, despite eight years of constructive engagement Crocker was only able to broker the 1988 settlement as a result of two factors out of his control: the first, the military setback suffered by South Africa that convinced Pretoria it could not prevail militarily; and second, the decision of Mikhail Gorbachev to end confrontations with the United States and disengage from Angola.

NAMIBIA

The United Nations had been exerting pressure upon South Africa to quit Namibia ever since its foundation in 1945. Over the years 1978–81, using the Western contact group consisting of the US, Britain, France, West Germany and Canada, the United Nations carried out intense negotiations with South Africa on the basis of Resolution 435, which was passed on 29 September 1978 and called for internationally supervised elections in Namibia (the so-called Waldheim Plan). SWAPO, however, called for an end to the Western mediating role since it saw this as biased in favour of South Africa. In a Security Council debate of 30 April 1981 the Africa group brought to a vote four resolutions each imposing mandatory sanctions against South Africa under Chapter VII of the UN Charter, leading the US, Britain and France to use their vetoes a total of 12 times. Then President Reagan brushed aside the contact group mechanism and adopted the policy of linkage. Subsequently, 'The Crocker mission was conducted with great skill and tenacity but the premise – linking a Namibian settlement to Cuban withdrawal from Angola – put the cart before the horse and thus inhibited progress until developments in Soviet policy prompted Cuban withdrawal.'[13] Linkage of the Cubans to Resolution 435 by the US was of enormous value to South Africa, for up to that time it had not been a South African demand. It ran counter to the policy of the other four on the contact group and was also counter to majority opinion in the Security Council. Thereafter, the US made it the cornerstone of its policy towards Namibia. By the end of 1983 France and Canada had withdrawn from the contact group which then ceased to exist.

In 1984 Angola, South Africa and the US signed the Lusaka Agreement, which established a joint military commission to monitor the Angola–Namibia border. In 1985, however, South African troops crossed into Angola, claiming to be in pursuit of SWAPO guerrillas. That year South Africa created a Transitional Government of National Unity (TGNU) in Namibia that was widely condemned by the international community, which refused to recognize its validity. In November 1985 the US and Britain vetoed a resolution for mandatory sanctions against South Africa because of its continued occupation of Namibia. By 1986 South Africa admitted to having 35,000 troops in Namibia (75 per cent locally recruited) although SWAPO claimed that South African forces were 100,000 strong. South Africa was mounting a so-called 'hearts and minds' campaign in Ovamboland where many atrocities were committed; the South African strategy was to drive a wedge between SWAPO, mainly recruited from the Ovambo, and other smaller ethnic groups. In 1987 the People's Liberation Army of Namibia (PLAN) resumed attacks on white farms for the first time since 1983. On 20 December 1988, the Security Council established a small mission, UN Angola Verification Mission (UNAVEM), to verify Cuban withdrawal from Angola. In January 1989 the Security Council adopted a number of resolutions enabling the process set out in Resolution 435 to be activated and approved a budget for the UN Transition Assistance Group (UNTAG), whose personnel began to arrive in Namibia. There was a brief and bloody setback in April 1989 when hundreds of SWAPO fighters infiltrated across the Angolan border to establish bases in Namibia during the transitional period. They suffered very heavy casualties at the hands of the South African forces and fighting continued into May before the South African forces returned to barracks. On 6 June 1989 President de Klerk of South Africa declared an end to apartheid in Namibia and an amnesty for guerrillas returning home from Angola. In November elections supervised by 1,695 UN-trained personnel were held and of 700,000 registered voters more than 90 per cent took part and SWAPO won a clear majority with 57.3 per cent of the votes cast. Constitutional talks were held early in 1990 and were completed in time for independence on 21 March 1990.

MOZAMBIQUE

Mozambique did not possess mineral resources like Angola and at independence its economy was based upon agriculture and fisheries while it depended upon two external factors for a major part of its income: remittances from its workers in South Africa and Rhodesia; and its railways and ports, which served the landlocked countries of the interior. FRELIMO emerged as the only political party at independence and represented the will of the people in a way that the MPLA had never been able to do in Angola. RENAMO (the National Resistance Movement of Mozambique), which did much to devastate the country through the 1980s, was created by white Rhodesia with the sole purpose of destabilizing a potentially dangerous enemy. Even so, FRELIMO managed to maintain a remarkable sense of unity so that it weathered the trauma of Machel's death in 1986.

At the beginning of the 1980s Mozambique appeared to be making reasonable economic progress although this was something of a delusion for outside the towns FRELIMO's writ hardly ran as RENAMO became increasingly active.

Originally, RENAMO had been the creation of Ken Flower, the head of the Central Intelligence Organisation (CIO) of Rhodesia, who set it up in 1976, using disaffected members of FRELIMO. In 1980 South Africa undertook to finance and support RENAMO. Although at the time of Zimbabwe's independence RENAMO had been reduced to little more than banditry, it became increasingly active in 1981 (as South Africa provided it with resources) and began to attack transport communications and especially the Beira Corridor which was vital to Zimbabwe. This renewed activity led FRELIMO to recall former commanders and to arm the people of Maputo as the threat posed by RENAMO grew. FRELIMO, though espousing Marxism, was always pragmatic rather than ideological and in 1982 Mozambique began to court the United States and exert pressure upon South Africa to stop supporting RENAMO. In 1983 the US State Department admitted openly that South Africa was providing the bulk of RENAMO's finances and arms while Chester Crocker suggested that it might be possible to 'pluck Mozambique from the Soviet orbit'.

President Machel continued the tentative shift to the West in April 1983 when he visited Portugal, France, Britain, Belgium, the Netherlands and Yugoslavia to present his country's case against South Africa. This softer line towards the West arose in part from necessity and in part as a result of Mozambique's membership of SADCC whose second top-level meeting of November 1980 had been held in Maputo.

In the years 1980–84, although providing overt support for RENAMO, South Africa also made overtures to Mozambique but, 'FRELIMO believed that to be truly independent Mozambique had to break away from its economic subjugation to South Africa, Rhodesia and Portugal. This objective was supported by current thinking among other Third World countries and among the grouping of non-aligned states that at the time was particularly influential.' Such an attitude had been encouraged by the precipitate withdrawal of most of the Portuguese in 1975.[14] However, a combination of circumstances – drought, failed economic policies and the RENAMO war – forced Machel to agree the Nkomati Accord with South Africa on 16 March 1984. The two countries agreed 'not to allow their respective territory, territorial waters or air space to be used as a base by another state's government, foreign military forces, organizations or individuals which plan to prepare to commit acts of violence, terrorism or aggression' against the other country. What this amounted to in fact was that Mozambique would withdraw its support from the ANC, and South Africa would cease providing support to RENAMO. Subsequently, however, while Mozambique stood by the terms of the Accord South Africa did not. Already in December 1984 Machel accused South Africa of dishonouring its side of the Accord and there was plenty of evidence that it continued to support

RENAMO through 1985. In June 1985, at a meeting in Harare between Machel, Mugabe and Nyerere, Zimbabwe and Tanzania agreed to assist Mozambique fight RENAMO, a promise that subsequently led to the stationing of substantial numbers of Zimbabwean troops in Mozambique, especially along the Beira Corridor, and a more limited number of Tanzanians along the railway from Malawi to the Mozambique port of Nacala. The Nkomati Accord represented the high point of South Africa's policy of destabilization against its neighbours and was seen in Pretoria as a major victory. The *Sunday Times* said the Accord was the result of 'diplomacy backed by unchallengeable military superiority'.

Rubbing salt into Mozambique's wounds the South Africans suggested that their businessmen could revitalize the broken Mozambican economy to prove the advantages of white capitalism over socialism and destroy SADCC in the process. South Africa expected to act as the conduit for any foreign capital destined for Mozambique because it was the 'natural' economic centre of the region. This view had already been put to Machel by Margaret Thatcher on his visit to London in October 1983 when she said any British capital investment would be routed through South Africa. The United States and West Germany made the same point.[15] It is not clear exactly why South Africa entered into the Nkomati Accord since it did not keep it. Partly, perhaps, through arrogance for it had forced Machel to do what he must have hated doing. And partly, perhaps, it reflected a split in the South African cabinet between the hard-liners who only wished to destabilize the country's neighbours and the moderates or liberals who harked back to the earlier idea of a constellation of states controlled by Pretoria. Pik Botha called on Western countries to 'help Mozambique' with investment routed through South Africa. When the Mozambican Chamber of Commerce sent a delegation to the United States, it found that the Americans would try anything to ensure that their initial investments should go through South Africa and Portugal.[16]

One result of these complicated relationships was that in 1985 Machel was able to ask Britain's Prime Minister, Margaret Thatcher, for military assistance and she felt obliged to comply for several reasons: because Machel had pressured Mugabe into accepting the Lancaster House agreement of 1979; because he had signed the Nkomati Accord; and because on the eve of his visit to Downing Street in September 1985 documents had just been captured by FRELIMO forces when they attacked the RENAMO base at Gorongosa that proved South Africa had not kept its side of the bargain. As a result a BMATT (British Military Assistance Training Team) was sent to Mozambique in 1986 to help train FRELIMO troops for the war against RENAMO. It was one of the many ironies in the whole Southern African scenario that the Thatcher government should provide military training for the FRELIMO army fighting RENAMO which was supported by apartheid South Africa that Thatcher did all she could to protect. At one level it could be seen as a British attempt to store up credits against the day when apartheid finally collapsed. Britain would have done better to pressure South Africa into abandoning its support for RENAMO.

Following a summit in Malawi between the leaders of Mozambique, Malawi, Zambia and Zimbabwe in October 1986 that led to the expulsion of RENAMO bases in Malawi, the plane carrying Machel back to Maputo crashed in circumstances that have never been adequately explained and Machel was killed. However, his death did not cause the disintegration of FRELIMO as it might have done and Joaquim Chissano, then Prime Minister, succeeded to the presidency.

The civil war escalated steadily for the rest of the decade and by 1988 one million Mozambicans had fled to become refugees in Malawi (650,000), Zambia, Zimbabwe, South Africa and Swaziland. At the same time a further four million people had become displaced inside the country and large districts had become 'no go' areas outside government control. The Beira Corridor was always an essential highway for Zimbabwe although it had been partly closed for a time in the early 1980s, though trains could use the line provided they had heavy military escorts. Zimbabwe then committed 3,500 troops to assist the Mozambique government keep the corridor open. South Africa's strategy was to use RENAMO to close the corridor so as to force Zimbabwe to use transport links to the sea through South Africa. In the mid-1980s massive financial and technical aid for the rehabilitation of the railways (the Beira line from Mutare in Zimbabwe to Beira on the Indian Ocean, and the Limpopo line from Chicualacuala on the Zimbabwe–Mozambique border to Maputo) was provided by Western aid donors through SADCC. At the same time Zimbabwe increased the number of its troops in Mozambique to approximately 10,000 (a fifth of its army) to assist the Mozambique government in guarding the Beira Corridor, the Tete Corridor (linking Malawi through the Tete province of Mozambique to Zimbabwe) and the Limpopo railway in the south. By 1989 the FRELIMO government had entered into peace negotiations with RENAMO, a process that was given a boost when de Klerk delivered his speech of 2 February 1990. At the 1989 FRELIMO party congress Chissano announced the abandonment of Marxism-Leninism so that early in 1990 the US officially recognized that Mozambique was no longer a Marxist state, a precondition for receiving US aid.

While Savimbi in Angola based his claims and determination to keep fighting upon the premise that the MPLA had not been endowed with full legitimacy at independence, 'By contrast, however much RENAMO sought to destroy Mozambique's infrastructure and eliminate FRELIMO cadres, it never seriously entertained the belief that it could itself challenge FRELIMO's historical place in contemporary Mozambique.' It could only legitimize itself as a party if FRELIMO recognized it as such. 'Savimbi wanted total power; Dhlakama (the leader of RENAMO) wanted a share of the spoils.'[17] By the end of the decade the FRELIMO government only exercised authority in major coastal towns and some garrisoned towns inland while RENAMO had substantial support or exercised control in the northern and central provinces across the Zambezi. By 1990 Mozambique had suffered three decades of devastating warfare and the country was in ruins with approximately a quarter of its population refugees, either inside or outside Mozambique.

THE REST OF THE FRONT LINE

Malawi under Hastings Banda had persisted in its isolated stand in relation to South Africa, and Rhodesia until 1980, though there was little evidence that it had benefited the economy. On the other hand, Malawi had joined SADCC as a founder member and hosted the organization's November 1981 meeting. Although relations with Mozambique were uneasy – Malawi had maintained especially close relations with the Portuguese prior to 1975 – Machel visited Malawi in October 1984 when the two countries signed a general co-operation agreement. However, in July 1986 Mozambique accused Malawi of assisting the RENAMO guerrillas. In September Banda denied these allegations in a meeting with Machel, Kaunda and Mugabe at which Machel warned that he would close the border if such help continued. After the air crash in which Machel died South Africa claimed that documents found in the crash wreckage revealed a plot by Mozambique and Zimbabwe to overthrow the Malawi government. Events in Mozambique forced Banda to reconsider his policies. In April 1987 Malawi committed 300 troops to assist FRELIMO and the Tanzanians guard the strategic Nacala rail link from RENAMO attacks although this new accord was endangered later in the year when a civilian Malawi aircraft was shot down over Mozambique. By July 1988 Malawi was further affected by the war in Mozambique when it found itself acting as unwilling host to 650,000 Mozambican refugees, an event that saw a real shift in Malawi's support from RENAMO to FRELIMO.

Ever since its independence in 1966 Botswana had resolutely opposed apartheid and refused to establish diplomatic relations with South Africa although it was always obliged to pay careful attention to South Africa's preponderant regional power. Under Seretse Khama and his successor Quett Masire, Botswana pursued a non-racial approach to politics and enjoyed universal suffrage while, generally, managing to avoid full-scale confrontations with its neighbour.

During the 1980s, however, it became a target country for South African destabilization tactics and in 1981 joined with Lesotho, Swaziland and Mozambique to denounce South African tactics. In July of that year Machel visited Gaborone. There was already a Soviet embassy in Gaborone and Botswana then began to purchase arms from the USSR. This produced a series of press attacks upon Botswana in South Africa and the accusation that it was becoming a Communist base. Late in 1981 President Masire accused the US of backing South Africa's 'intransigent attitude' and warned that South Africa was preparing to attack Botswana. Early in 1982 he warned that South Africa wanted to turn Botswana into another Lebanon.[18] Despite huge pressures from Pretoria, for example, to enter into a non-aggression pact with South Africa that was designed to curb any ANC presence in Botswana, or the May 1986 cross-border raid at the time of the Eminent Persons Group visit to South Africa, Botswana had the satisfaction during the second half of the 1980s of seeing its currency, the pula (backed by its diamond wealth), becoming stronger on the international money markets than the rand. Already by 1984 diamonds accounted for 76 per cent of Botswana's exports. Indeed, Botswana had been skilful in the way it had ensured maximum returns for the country for De Beers had been involved from the beginning and the government was always wary of South Africa exercising too much control over its diamonds. When the size of the Botswana deposits became clear this greatly strengthened the government's hand. Diamond prices were kept high by a marketing monopoly that included the USSR. Botswana was able to insist on a series of renegotiations with De Beers and got from it one of the best mineral exploitation contracts in the world. Debswana was a 50–50 joint venture from which the Botswana government received 75 per cent of the profits. Despite South African pressures Botswana allowed the ANC to remain in the country, though not to use it as a base for attacks upon South Africa, and it had an open-door policy for refugees from the Republic.

Lesotho under Chief Jonathan had a troubled independence especially after Jonathan had aborted the 1970 elections, which he was losing. He boosted his position by periodic attacks upon the apartheid policy of his giant neighbour whose territory completely surrounds Lesotho. Jonathan's main political opponent, Ntsu Mokhehle of the Basutoland Congress Party (BCP), had become exiled in South Africa from where his Lesotho Liberation Army (LLA) launched periodic attacks into Lesotho. These attacks acted as a destabilizing factor upon Jonathan and as such suited the South African government. Violence by the LLA had first erupted in 1978 and continued into 1979. From South Africa Mokhehle said he would only take part in elections if representatives of the Communist bloc were expelled from Lesotho. After further confrontations in 1982 and 1983 Jonathan promised to hold new elections. His own popularity declined sharply through 1984 and 1985 and at the beginning of 1986 South Africa effectively blockaded Lesotho after Jonathan had refused to sign a joint security pact or expel members of the ANC. On 20 January 1986, Jonathan was deposed by Maj.-Gen. Justin Lekhanya and placed under house arrest. He died in April 1987 while in South Africa for medical treatment. Jonathan's role had been unimportant in real terms though he did manage to act as a constant irritant to South Africa.

Deeply conservative and pro-Western, Swaziland nonetheless proclaimed its neutrality in international affairs, much to Pretoria's satisfaction since its eastern border with Mozambique meant, had Swaziland chosen such a course, that it could have acted as a dangerous conduit for ANC forces passing through into South Africa. Swaziland improved its relations with Marxist Mozambique after the signing of the Nkomati Accord in 1984. In an attempt both to neutralize and bind Swaziland closer to it, South Africa proposed in the late 1970s to transfer to Swaziland the adjoining KaNgwane Bantustan or homeland of the Swazis then in South Africa and another area, the Ingwavuma region of KwaZulu that would have given Swaziland direct access to the Indian Ocean. Whether South Africa really intended to do anything of the sort is doubtful but the prospect of Swazliand regaining its 'lost lands' persuaded King Sobhuza II to enter into a secret security agreement with South Africa in 1982, following which the Swazi authorities harassed the ANC and expelled its representatives from the country. Following strong white and black opposition, South Africa dropped the land transfer proposals in 1984. This did not appear to affect Swaziland's close relations with South Africa. After the signing of the Nkomati Accord, the Swazi government disclosed its secret agreement with South Africa and over the following year deported more than 200 alleged members of the ANC to Zambia or Tanzania. Defying the rest of the front-line states at the January 1985 SADCC meeting, which was held in Mbabane, the Swazi prime minister defended his country's close links with South Africa. Later that year at the Commonwealth summit at Nassau in the Bahamas, Swaziland was the only country to support Margaret Thatcher's opposition to Commonwealth sanctions against South Africa. Despite this record, South Africa was not deterred at the end of 1985 from raiding border villages for supporting the ANC and continued to raid into Swaziland over the next three years.

The British role in Southern Africa was crucial to any resolution of the apartheid-fuelled confrontations of the region. Seven of the nine SADCC countries, as well as Namibia, had been British colonies and Britain had always had strong links with Mozambique, much of whose development had been financed from London. But it was always firmly biased towards South Africa and the Thatcher government in particular, though claiming to oppose apartheid, went to great lengths to defend the South African position and maintain a regional status quo. 'No other country has stronger links with the southern African region than Britain. Given the consequences of South Africa's regional policy, Britain's especially strong links with South Africa heighten its responsibilities towards the whole region, to help resolve the interlinked issues of apartheid, conflict, and economic decline ... Of all the elements of Britain's long and complex colonial history in Southern Africa, its history in South Africa, especially its role in laying the foundations for apartheid, is perhaps of greatest significance to present-day southern African affairs. Although apartheid was introduced by the National Party after it first came to power in 1948, nevertheless the foundations of disfranchisement and institutionalized racial discrimination at all levels of society had already been laid' by Britain when it agreed the peace treaty with the Boers in 1909 that betrayed the black populations of the Boer Republics and effectively prepared the ground for lasting white-minority rule in the most economically powerful nation of the region.[19]

SOUTH AFRICA

Despite the 'Muldergate' scandal that ended the political career of Vorster, and the many problems that white South Africa had faced through the 1970s, the regime entered the new decade as strongly entrenched as ever. P. W. Botha, the new Prime Minister, tried to soften the government's policy by eliminating 'petty apartheid' although retaining core apartheid – the denial of equality of rights to the black majority. But the impossibility of making apartheid work in a state where the white minority depended on the black majority for the smooth functioning of the economy meant that the system began to break down through the 1980s as black opposition to apartheid erupted on all fronts. A central source of South Africa's strength had always been its huge and lucrative mining sector that historically had attracted British, American and other investments. At its core was the giant Anglo American Corporation with tentacles all over Southern Africa and big interests in Botswana, Zambia and Zimbabwe as well as Namibia. Its subsidiary De Beers dominated the non-USSR diamond mining and marketing and its interests included Angola and Tanzania. The story of mining exploitation in South Africa is one of the least defensible aspects of that country's history[20] although Anglo's Harry Oppenheimer, by judicial statements deploring apartheid and with donations to the Progressive Party, attempted to present an acceptable mining face to the world, though few were fooled by it.

In 1979 a mysterious flash in the South Atlantic was interpreted as a South

Robert Mugabe with Lord Soames who attended the Zimbabwe Independence Ceremony, 1980. (Jason Laure – iAfrika Photos/africanpictures.net)

Robert Mugabe won the 1980 elections to become Zimbabwe's first Prime Minister. (Jason Laure – iAfrika Photos/ africanpictures.net)

Joshua Nkomo, popular leader of the Ndebele who never achieved his ambition to become President of Zimbabwe.

(Cape Argus – Trace Images/africanpictures.net)

Agostinho Neto, doctor, poet and leader of the MPLA who became first President of Angola 1975–1979. (Jim McLagan – Cape Argus – Trace Images/africanpictures.net)

Leader of Unita, Jonas Savimbi would not accept second place. Only his death in 2002 brought peace to Angola. (Cape Argus – Trace Images/africanpictures.net)

President Hastings Banda of Malawi: he was the only Black Leader to make a state visit to apartheid South Africa in 1971. (Cape Argus – Trace Images/africanpictures.net)

Woman of Lesotho, a tiny beleaguered nation surrounded by South Africa.
(Stephen Pryke – The Media Bank/africanpictures.net)

Lesotho: An arid land that has been overgrazed while its men sought work in the
South African mines. (Rodney Barnett – South Photographs/africanpictures.net)

P. W. Botha, the 'Great Crocodile', ruled South Africa throughout the 1980s, seen here with his wife. (Guy Tillim – South Photographs/africanpictures.net)

Andries Treurnicht, leader of the C. P., opponent of J. B. Vorster. (Paul Weinberg – South Photographs/africanpictures.net)

Olusegun Obasanjo, President of Nigeria 1999. (Africa Week)

African nuclear test; the US, safeguarding its ally, said that its monitoring service had not detected anything but the denial was not believed and South Africa was suspected of having become a nuclear power. Later, in 1993, President de Klerk admitted that South Africa had a number of nuclear bombs or warheads and agreed to destroy them. UN Resolution 558 of December 1984, which requested all states to stop importing arms, ammunition or military vehicles produced in South Africa, was passed unanimously.

In 1982 the UN General Assembly proclaimed an International Year of Mobilization of Sanctions against South Africa. In 1984 the General Assembly rejected the new South African racially segregated tricameral constitution. By 1985, as violence escalated throughout the South African townships, the Security Council condemned the Pretoria regime for killing defenceless Africans. Despite these expressions of UN disapproval, the coming to power of President Reagan in the US and Prime Minister Thatcher in Britain tilted the diplomatic battle at the United Nations in South Africa's favour for much of the decade. From 1985 onwards there were specific calls for the release of Nelson Mandela while three attempts to extend mandatory sanctions to South Africa – in 1985, 1987 and 1988 – were vetoed by Britain and the US while France abstained. Altogether, there were 45 Western vetoes on South African questions between 1974 and 1988. During all this turmoil education remained strictly segregated and the government spent seven times as much on the education of a white child as on a black child. A telling sign of the breakdown of apartheid was the increasing urbanization of Africans and though some Africans were recognized as 'urban insiders' legally entitled to live in the metropolitan areas permanently, the pass laws were still used in an attempt to keep others out; but it had become a losing battle. In 1984, for example, 238,894 Africans were arrested for pass law offences but neither such arrests nor other measures could stem the flow of Africans into the urban areas. As a result, accepting what it could not prevent, in 1986 the government repealed a total of 34 legislative enactments that between them constituted the pass laws, and announced an 'orderly urbanization'. Further, the government repealed other segregation laws, bans on multiracial political parties and inter-racial sex and marriage and ceased the reservation of particular jobs for whites only. At the same time it opened up business centres in cities to black traders and desegregated some hotels, trains, restaurants and other public facilities. One of the most telling pressures upon the ability of the whites to maintain control was the country's changing demography: in 1936 whites represented 21 per cent of the population, by 1960 19 per cent, by 1980 16 per cent and by 1985 15 per cent while officials predicted that the figure would have fallen to only 10 per cent in 2005.[21]

The South African government was on the defensive throughout the decade.

The so-called Soviet 'total onslaught' could only be countered with a 'total strategy' at every level. In 1982 the chief of the SADF, Gen. Constand Viljoen, announced a new 'area defence system' to meet the growing 'area war' assault by the ANC. This 'legitimized' attacks upon the front-line states. The police and the military worked together in maintaining internal order and by and large the police were seen as more repressive than the soldiers. Thus, after 800 children, some as young as seven years, had been arrested following school boycotts, Brig. Jan Coetze, the Soweto Police Chief, said: 'We are cracking down. We will not allow 5,000 stupid students to disregard law and order in Soweto and South Africa.'[22] The same Coetze had remarked the previous July, 'In our operations, the South African Police and the South African Defence Force operate as one unit.' The apparent relish with which senior policemen such as Coetze spoke of dealing with Africans was partly aimed at their black populations in the hope – unrealized – of intimidating them, partly it was a form of defiance aimed at an increasingly hostile world and partly, perhaps, a cruel gesture of despair as even the most obtuse members of the police must have begun to realize that the situation was getting beyond them. Police violence reached its height during the disturbances of 1985–86. 'The incidence of violence in South Africa involving the police has now reached almost pathological proportions. Police are easily provoked into drawing lethal weapons, their treatment of suspects and arrestees is frequently disgraceful and their use of unnecessary force in respect of minor offenders has become so common as to be considered normal conduct.'[23] The police budget, meanwhile, rose steadily.

Following the Nkomati Accord South Africa had begun to speak of itself as the regional power whose interests always had to be taken into account so that, for example, it had the right to demand the withdrawal of the Cubans from Angola, according to its Foreign Minister Pik Botha.[24] Further, the more the US and the USSR paid attention to South Africa, the more they confirmed its belief in itself as the regional superpower. However, in the long run the state of the economy would dictate what should happen. 'Before the political turmoil of the mid-1980s, South Africa was a net importer of capital. However, during the first half of the 1980s, a foreign debt had begun to be accumulated and when, in August 1985, President Botha declared that the government would not be pressured into abolishing apartheid, and foreign banks began to call in their loans, the country was turned into a net exporter of capital.'[25] Constant violence and the absence abroad or in prison of black political leaders led to the rise of Bishop Desmond Tutu as a spokesman for the oppressed, and a gentle churchman was transformed into a political orator. He had risen rapidly in the Anglican Church, had been made Bishop of Lesotho in 1976 and now used his church platform to speak out against apartheid. When in 1984 a government commission attacked the South African Council of Churches (SACC) for identifying with the 'liberation struggle' Tutu, its Secretary-General, said: 'Until my dying day I will continue to castigate apartheid as evil and immoral...' He was awarded the Nobel Peace prize in 1984 for his non-violent approach to apartheid and was elected Archbishop of Cape Town on 14 April 1986. Meanwhile, the constant police brutality that was shown night after night on television in Britain over 1985–86 had a significant impact upon British public thinking. Many British people who to that time had usually adopted a 'kith and kin' sympathetic approach to the plight of the white South African minority began to change their attitudes. They did not, perhaps, become anti-apartheid activists but they certainly no longer defended the white position and the change represented an important shift in British thinking.

When he came to power after the Vorster era, P. W. Botha intended to act as a new broom. Apartheid, as it had been applied up to that time, was no longer working and Afrikaners, he said, 'must adapt or die'. The essential was change, 'rapid, visible change: the replacing of outdated political principles, the restructuring of race relations, the rejection of racial domination (*baaskap*), the removal of humiliating discrimination and injustice, equal opportunity and rights, fewer restrictions – and a new disposition'.[26] Botha's 'vision', if that is what it amounted to, was clouded by his belief that South Africa was experiencing the full onslaught of Marxism, and so with Gen. Magnus Malan, then head of the SADF (Botha had previously served as Minister of Defence), he devised the 'total strategy' to meet the Marxist onslaught and this meant co-ordinating military activity, foreign policy and domestic, social and political administration in order to ensure security and internal unity. South Africa would use force as and when necessary. This total strategy demanded that the neighbouring front-line states, as they had come to be called by the beginning of the 1980s, must either co-operate or knuckle under and in order to encourage them to follow a path acceptable to South Africa international law could be set to one side in the interests of national security. The logic of such an approach led naturally to the cross-border raids and destabilization policies that South Africa pursued throughout the decade. However, the modest reforms that Botha attempted split the National Party into the *Verkrampte* and *Verligte* camps of hard-liners and enlightened with the former breaking away from the NP to form the new Conservative Party under Andries Treurnicht. The Conservatives were not sufficient in numbers to challenge the NP although the 18 who formed the party represented 20 per cent of the white electorate. Nonetheless, 'The disintegration of Afrikanerdom had begun'. 'The policy of the Botha administration was a complex attempt to adapt to changing circumstances without sacrificing Afrikaner power. It included efforts to neutralize South

Africa's neighbours, to scrap apartheid symbols and practices that were not essential to the maintenance of white supremacy, to draw English-speaking citizens into the party, to win the co-operation of big business, to intensify the ethnic and class cleavages among the subject peoples, and to suppress domestic dissidents.'[27] This policy represented a tall order by any standards but it contained too many contradictions and was bound to fail as it did.

Britain had always been the principal source of investment in South Africa and remained so throughout the apartheid years. British interest in Southern Africa was essentially in the Republic and its policy there was to protect its trade, investments and loan finance; to maintain access to South Africa's strategic minerals; and prevent the mass exodus of those whites who qualified for British passports (an estimated 800,000) to Britain. In 1984, for example, direct private investment by British companies in the SADCC region totalled £100 million, about 3.6 per cent of the value of British direct investment in South Africa, while British trade with South Africa was nine times greater than its trade with all the SADCC countries combined. In 1980 there were 1,200 British companies in South Africa as opposed to 350 from West Germany and 340 from the United States. In 1982 British private investment in South Africa amounted to US$6,342 million, that from the US to US$2,800 million and from West Germany to US$260 million. Foreign direct investment in South Africa had begun to tail off following the 1976 Soweto uprising, forcing South Africa to increase its borrowing. During the 1980s there was a growing and complex disinvestment trend, most marked among US companies. The International Chamber of Commerce estimated that over 500 foreign companies sold their South African holdings between 1985 and 1989. They were concerned to project a more positive public image, to maximize foreign currency returns on investments and to keep enough control over their former subsidiaries to allow re-entry into South Africa at a later date.[28] According to the UN Commission on Trans-National Corporations, of the 535 with more than 10 per cent interests in South Africa, 216 were British-based and they were slower than US transnationals to disinvest. Even so, between 1985 and 1989, 132 British transnationals did disinvest while another 16 reduced their equity interest. Britain's total investment in South Africa, direct and indirect, was estimated as follows: 1986 – £8,586 million; 1987 – £7,924 million; 1988 – £6,400 million. Britain provided approximately 40 per cent of all foreign investment and 80 per cent of the European Community total.

South Africa's debt crisis really became severe in 1985 when the state of emergency led US and European banks to refuse to 'roll over' their loans. Even the British government was urging change by the late 1980s. Addressing the Royal Commonwealth Society in London during May 1988, Sir Geoffrey Howe, the Foreign Secretary, said: '... the sooner white South Africans accept the need for negotiation and change, the greater the odds that change will be peaceful and democratic... The South African Government have to take the lead. Dialogue cannot take place against a backcloth of violence and repression'. At a public meeting in London an ANC spokesman told Lynda Chalker, the Foreign Office Minister, that 'it has to be understood that Britain's international anti-sanctions crusade is widely viewed in South Africa, by people of all political persuasions, as a policy which protects the South African government and undermines the right of the disenfranchised South African people to determine their own future'.[29] At the 1989 Kuala Lumpur Commonwealth Heads of Government summit, Britain still stood out against pressures upon South Africa and issued its own unilateral communiqué after signing the official consensus communiqué. Even Margaret Thatcher changed her stance on her visit to South Africa in November 1989 when she said: 'I do not see how, in the modern world, it is possible to achieve political stability except on a basis where all adults have the vote.'[30]

President Reagan was as active in his support of white South Africa as his political ally Margaret Thatcher. 'US foreign policy is riddled with contradictions. Sanctions are right for Nicaragua or Poland, but not South Africa. The MPLA should be pressed to include UNITA in the government, but no pressure should be put on white South Africa to include the ANC in government. It was hardly surprising that constructive engagement and linkage pleased Pretoria.' One Johannesburg newspaper correspondent talked of 'South Africa's new ally, Mr Ronald Reagan'.[31] It was soon clear that constructive engagement under Reagan was wholly one-sided in support of South Africa. His instinctive sympathies lay with a global philosophy of assisting and installing pro-Western governments and holding back the Soviet threat. 'All he knows about Southern Africa,' one of his own officials privately commented, 'is that he is on the side of the whites.'[32] By the end of 1984 it was clear that Western policies were buying time for South Africa while it was impossible to continue the fiction that US engagement was constructive. On the other hand, the Soviet threat or 'total onslaught' was always exaggerated by the South Africans. Although Moscow had had a long-standing interest in the region through the South African Communist Party's early involvement with the black union movement and the ANC, that interest rated a lower priority than either the Middle East or the Horn. Already by 1986 a shift in Soviet-South African policy was discernible when Russia began to make plain its determination to achieve a rapprochment with the United States and consequently wished to eliminate points of confrontation, whether in Africa or elsewhere.

THE CRUCIAL YEARS: 1983–87

Following the 1983 referendum that established Coloured and Asian 'parliaments' and at the same time split the National Party, *The Economist* commented: 'No government which has recently introduced a racially classified parliament, segregated local government, and a segregated welfare state can seriously expect the world to believe it is intent on dismantling apartheid.' The attempt to have tame council elections in the townships was a fiasco: there was a 5 per cent poll in Soweto, 11 per cent in Port Elizabeth, 15 per cent in the Vaal Triangle, 19 per cent in Durban, 20 per cent on the East Rand. Few respected black leaders put themselves forward for election and most of those elected were regarded as quislings. The government also proposed that townships should be financially self-supporting since they had their own councils and that they should raise their own revenue from rents, which was asking for trouble. 'And so it was that while the whites applauded the reforms, the blacks mobilized opposition to them. In August 1983 more than five hundred community, church, professional, sports, workers', students', women's, and youth organizations formed an alliance called the United Democratic Front (UDF) to campaign against the new constitution and the "Koornhof Bills".'[33] Piet Koornhof, the Minister of Cooperation and Development, had introduced three bills that set up black councils to run their 'own affairs' of the townships, granted urban status only to those who had jobs and 'approved accommodation'. Under the new constitution there were to be three uniracial chambers: a House of Assembly of 178 whites voted by whites; a House of Representatives of 85 Coloureds elected by Coloureds; and a House of Delegates of 45 Indians elected by Indians. A joint session meant an automatic white majority. A cabinet drawn from the three chambers would deal with general affairs while uniracial ministers' councils were to be responsible for 'own affairs'. The State President, elected by a college of 50 whites, 25 Coloureds and 13 Indian members of Parliament, appointed the cabinet and the ministers' councils. He could dissolve parliament at any time and was responsible for the 'control and administration of black (that is, African) affairs'. When the elections under this new constitution were held in August 1984 only 18 per cent of the Coloureds and fewer Indians voted.

Botha's clumsy attempts at divide and rule led, predictably, to revolt. 'The 1984 insurrection was more intense and lasted longer than any previous one. For three years it raged, resulting in more than three thousand deaths, thirty thousand detentions, and untold damage to property and the national economy. The government had to mobilize the army and declare two states of emergency to bring it under control, and even then it was only partially repressed.'[34] Black anger was met with white repression and escalating violence and it was Botha's good fortune that 'The Thatcher government in Britain, the Reagan administration in the United States, and Helmut Kohl's Christian Democrats in West Germany were all disposed to share in some measure Botha's contention that the black nationalists in his country were violent radicals being manipulated by Moscow and to look favourably on a reform programme that would neutralize them and bring in the "moderates".'[35] The Botha cabinet now split between the reformists and the securocrats. The former – Chris Heunis, the Minister of Constitutional Affairs, and Pik Botha, the Foreign Minister – over-persuaded Botha to commit himself to reform in a clear statement; believing they had succeeded, Pik Botha flew to Vienna for a June meeting with American, British and West German diplomats at which he told them to expect a dramatic statement from Botha at the Natal Congress of the NP the following August. Meanwhile, there were vigorous demonstrations against apartheid in every city and nearly every homeland. At the end of 1984 official figures listed 175 dead in the disturbances and many strikes and acts of sabotage. The figures for 1985 were far worse: 879 deaths and 390 strikes involving 240,000 workers. The protests continued into 1986 and in the townships many of the newly elected councillors resigned to be replaced by informal groups. Between July and December 1985 the rate of killing was 3.3 persons a day.

At Durban on 15 August 1985 with the largest-ever international press corps in attendance Botha delivered his much-heralded 'Rubicon' speech and contrary to the expectations that had been aroused conceded nothing at all, telling the assembled press that he was not to be 'pushed around'. At that time 67 per cent of South Africa's US$16.5 billion foreign debt was made up of short-term loans that could be called in at any time. The US Chase Manhattan Bank now did so and its example was followed by other banks; South Africa faced demands for US$13 billion in loans to be repaid by December. The rand fell in value by 35 per cent in 13 days and South Africa became a siege economy. Later in 1985 the Commonwealth Heads of Government met in Nassau (Bahamas) where Thatcher stood alone against the rest of the Commonwealth in resisting demands for sanctions against South Africa. It was however agreed that an Eminent Persons Group (EPG) led by Malcolm Fraser of Australia and Gen. Obasanjo of Nigeria should visit South Africa to meet all shades of opinion and try to move the country towards real reforms. When the EPG appeared to be making significant progress in 1986, Botha ordered attacks on ANC bases in Botswana, Zambia and Zimbabwe on 19 May and the EPG at once left the country. Even so, 'Its results were surprising. The EPG quickly established that there was both a widespread desire among ordinary people for a negotiated settlement and, on the face of it, enough potential common ground among all major political groups to get negotiations going.'[36] As the violence began to subside, Adriaan Vlok, the minister of law and order, admitted (12 February 1987) that 13,300 people, many of them children, had been detained under the emergency. Other estimates suggested 29,000 while 43 people had died in police custody and 263 had been hospitalized. There had been widespread use of torture and violence against detainees, including children.

The violence of these years had given new impetus for demands to apply sanctions to South Africa. In mid-1985 the front-line states Angola, Botswana, Mozambique, Tanzania, Zambia and Zimbabwe backed the call for sanctions against South Africa and called upon Western countries to broaden and intensify pressures on South Africa. Lesotho also made clear its support for sanctions although Malawi and Swaziland maintained silence. Then on 31 January 1986 the annual SADCC conference called for co-ordinated pressure, including sanctions, to be mounted against South Africa. The argument that had arisen in the early 1970s that US companies could stay in South Africa and promote reforms wore increasingly threadbare during the 1980s as pressure groups – churches and students for example – persuaded an increasing number of institutions such as universities to disinvest from companies operating in South Africa and by the end of 1985 disinvestment by US state and local governments had led to US$4.5 billion being withdrawn from companies involved in South Africa. Substantial sanctions were imposed in late 1986 by Canada, Australia, New Zealand, the United States and the Scandinavian countries, while lesser measures were adopted by the EEC. In 1987 Sweden and Norway imposed full trade embargoes while 48 Commonwealth countries agreed to 'widen and tighten' sanctions. Reacting to these growing anti-apartheid pressures, US companies began to disengage from South Africa: 40 in 1985, 50 in 1986. In 1985, President Reagan said South Africa had 'eliminated the segregation we once had in our own country' but the anti-apartheid movement was so incensed that he felt obliged to impose limited sanctions on South Africa in order to pre-empt demands for more. The strategy did not work for in October 1986 Congress passed the Comprehensive Anti-Apartheid Act over the president's veto to ban new investments, bank loans, to end South African-US air links and to prohibit a range of South African imports. Congress also threatened to cut off military aid to allies suspected of breaching the international arms embargo on South Africa.[37]

The whole apartheid structure was imploding and so one National Party MP with the impeccable Afrikaner name of van der Merwe wrote an article in 1985 entitled 'And what about the black people?' in which he said: 'It has long been clear that political rights cannot be withheld from black people forever... Large numbers of black people (as many as 60 per cent) will not be able to be accommodated physically or politically in the homelands and will, therefore, have to exercise their political rights in South Africa.'[38]

The ANC had represented the core opposition to the apartheid regime throughout the years: the oldest black political party on the African continent, dating from 1912, it had always believed in a democratic multiracial society and during the worst oppressions of the apartheid era stuck to that ideology. In the 1980s it found its position outside South Africa becoming increasingly difficult to maintain. Once in power in Zimbabwe, Mugabe had turned on ZAPU, which was a close ally of the ANC and had close South African links, while following the Nkomati Accord Mozambique and Swaziland were closed to it as well. The ANC, therefore, began to concentrate more upon operating inside South Africa where two powerful allies in the form of the UDF and the Congress of South African Trade Unions (COSATU) became formidable anti-apartheid organizations during the decade. The ANC shifted its position during the second half of the1980s but did not change its ideology about the type of democracy and society that it favoured. Its strategy, to reach the 'new South Africa' through negotiation was about the only thing the ANC had in common with the government. The NP, on the other hand, had elaborated a democratic vision that was anathema to the ANC. It was founded on concepts such as 'group rights' and 'minority protection' from 'majority domination' and NP ideas for a new South Africa would do little to redress the legacies of apartheid. The ANC, then, came to embrace the South African Communist Party (SACP) and the trade union federation (COSATU), a tripartite alliance that symbolized the unity forged by different groups in the struggle against apartheid. 'Formed in 1985 by a merger of a number of smaller unions, the UDF-aligned COSATU became instrumental in the latter half of the 1980s in the mobilization of workers for strikes, boycotts and stay-aways.'[39]

In September 1985 a group of South African businessmen led by Gavin Relly, chairman of Anglo American Corporation, flew to Lusaka to meet Oliver Tambo and other ANC leaders to talk of the future South Africa. Then in July 1987 61 white South Africans led by F. van Zyl Slabbert went to Dakar for three days of talks with members of the ANC led by Thabo Mbeki. Such contacts broke through the absolute divide that had existed up to that time between the ruling whites and the 'demonized' ANC. COSATU, like the UDF, was formed on 1 December 1985 and was born out of the political turmoil of the time. It began its existence, after four years of negotiations, with 33 black unions and a membership of 558,000. It proclaimed its non-racial, anti-apartheid credentials and demanded the repeal of the pass laws and the existing state of emergency, the withdrawal of troops and police from the townships, the unconditional release of Mandela and other political prisoners, the dismantling of the homelands and the end of the migrant labour system. It worked closely with the UDF and by 1989 had a paid-up membership of 925,000.

Another, very distinct political player emerged during the 1980s in the person of the Zulu Chief Mangosuthu Gatsha Buthelezi. He built up his Inkatha Movement, which he had established as a Zulu cultural organization, into a political party. Buthelezi was concerned both with national power and Zulu regional power in the new South Africa. Increasing violence between members of Inkatha and the ANC or its allies of the UDF and COSATU became a feature of the late 1980s and into the 1990s and accounted for more than 4,000 deaths in Natal over the last years of the decade, with further violence to follow in the 1990s. Buthelezi, who had 'worked' the homeland system, was tainted with accusations of collaboration with the apartheid government. 'The sharp increase in violence in the townships surrounding Durban during 1983 led to allegations of collaboration between Inkatha and the state. Township dwellers, violence monitors, and journalists cited examples of how Inkatha "impis" received direct help from the police, with transporting "impis" to scenes of violence, police declining to interfere when residents were attacked, and systematic inability on the part of the police to arrest those responsible for attacks.'[40] One of the most incisive critics of the whole apartheid system was Allan Boesak, a minister of the Dutch Reformed Mission Church and President of the World Alliance of Reformed Churches. In a book titled *If This Is Treason* he argued that neutrality was not possible. 'More particularly: in a situation where there is a constant struggle for justice and human dignity and against structures promoting iniquity, neutrality is not possible. On the contrary, neutrality is the most revolting partisanship there is. It is to take the side of the powerful, of injustice, without accepting responsibility for it.' He deals with the argument that Africans in power might behave as badly as the whites and therefore that the whites are justified in holding onto power.

> But this is a false dilemma. The question is not so much what shall we do *one day* if a black government should do something wrong. The question is what are we doing *right now*, while this white government is doing what it is doing... Saying 'yes' to co-operation with the very government that maintains this violent system without first fundamentally changing it is taking responsibility for the continuation of violence. The choice for violence, therefore, has not been made by those who resist the perpetuation of the system in the hope of working for a better society, but precisely by those who have abandoned the struggle for a better society by strengthening the present one. [41]

Boesak became a major thorn in the side of the government; one of his principal arguments was that the violence came from the government side and that the oppressed had every right to answer it with violence.

By the end of the decade most options for South Africa looked bleak. As the journalist Allister Sparks pointed out, there was the possibility of producing a generation of black youth so brutalized and desensitized by its violent encounters with white South Africa's repressive forces that it would lose all sense of life's values. On the other side, there was no northern country to which the whites could withdraw, with the result that 'White South Africans will change only when the perceived consequences of changing seem less painful than the perceived consequences of continuing as they are. And that is a matter of perceptions rather than of reality'.[42] Further, as a result of Afrikaner dominance, 'Three decades of power and deferential treatment had wrought its own changes. The poor whites had come in from the cold, had been cosseted into middle-class prosperity and were enjoying the warmth. The spread of capitalism was doing its corroding, corrupting work. The ethnic fire of the Afrikaner cracker's belly was going out, to be replaced by the acquisitiveness and consumer culture of an urban bourgeoisie.' It was to the poor whites that Treurnicht, with his adherence to rigid apartheid, appealed.

Luckily for South Africa as a whole the whites did begin to see that change would be less painful than holding on to a system that was collapsing about their heads. Moderate Afrikaners moved towards the liberals and the process of change was lubricated by overwhelming economic pressures as South African big business made plain that if it had to choose between the future expansion of business and maintaining apartheid, then it was ready to ditch apartheid. And so at last, after a century of conflict and pain, the whites accepted that a real accommodation with the black majority was essential to their own survival. As early as 1981 Botha had announced that Mandela's release would be considered if he would give guarantees not to commit acts that violated the laws. Mandela rejected the suggestion and said, 'Only free men can negotiate. Prisoners cannot enter into contracts...' What is fascinating about the 1980s is the increasing awareness on the part of the whites that they could not perpetuate their system; they could only buy time for it to continue a little longer. By the middle of the decade the largest white exodus since Sharpeville was under way with about 50,000 leaving the country on what came to be called the 'chicken run', with a majority heading for Britain. About 1.7 million whites then qualified for foreign nationality.[43] The Israelis, surrounded by hostile Arabs, compared themselves with the white South Africans, surrounded by a majority of hostile blacks. 'Diplomatically isolated though she was, South Africa could rely on the support of Israel. Prime Minister Golda Meir had made the analogy with the Afrikaner clear when she said: "It is not as though there was a Palestinian people in Palestine considering itself as a Palestinian people and we came and threw them out and took their country away. They did not exist.'"[44] That was denial on a grand scale but it gave the hard-liner Afrikaner a certain comfort. In fact, even if some whites held out to the bitter end for the maintenance of white domination, the decision to abandon apartheid was taken in 1986 when the Urban Areas Act, which was the basis for the pass laws and influx control, was abolished to be followed by the repeal of the Mixed Marriages and Immorality Act and the Prohibition of Political Interference Act.

The government faced formidable demands for change, which it only appeared able to counter with repression. In the townships the 'young comrades' were more in control than the government while opposition to apartheid was orchestrated by church leaders such as Desmond Tutu and Allan Boesak. As the 1987 election approached, the NP suffered a number of defections by its more liberal members, the most notable being Denis Worrall, a former ambassador to London. By 1988 the signs multiplied that the National Party government under Botha had lost its way. It had attempted timid and wholly inadequate reforms whose main effect was to unleash forces it had no idea how to manage except by repression. Moreover, its policies wrought devastation throughout the region. As the ECA estimated in 1989, 'South Africa's military aggression and destabilization of its neighbours cost the region US$10 billion in 1988 and over US$60 billion and 1.5 million lives in the first nine years of this (1980s) decade.'

In January 1989 President Botha had a stroke, and F. W. de Klerk, who had been in Parliament for 17 years and had held a number of portfolios as well as being chairman of the Transvaal National Party, the most important provincial power base, was elected leader of the ruling National Party. Elections for the tricameral parliament were held on 6 September: the NP won 93 seats (a drop of 30 from the 123 it had held in the previous parliament); the Conservative Party increased its seats from 22 to 39 and the Democratic Party gained 12 on its former 21 seats. The Asian and Coloured electorates were more concerned to boycott the elections than return members. Black defiance continued and on the day of the elections the Mass Democratic Movement (MDM) called a general strike. A new group, known as the 'new nationalists', composed of businessmen and younger, more radical members of the NP who advocated an end to apartheid and negotiations with the ANC, emerged. On the far right the *Afrikaanse Weerstandsbeweging* (AWB) (Afrikaner Resistance Movement) under the leadership of Eugene Terre'Blanche opposed any concessions and prepared for violence. Perhaps the greatest irony of all for South Africa and its whites was the degree to which they depended upon the black majority: 'For all its military might, it is the peculiar weakness of white South Africa that it is totally dependent on the people it represses.'[45]

When de Klerk came to power in 1989 he announced his commitment to change though no one knew what or how much change he intended to implement. In October he released eight political prisoners including the veteran leader Walter Sisulu. Then on 2 February 1990 he gave his speech to the Cape Parliament in which he unbanned the ANC and 33 other black political organizations and announced his determination to end apartheid. A week later he released Nelson Mandela and on 2 May 1990 held the first ever negotiations with the ANC. It is a mistake to imagine that people suddenly change the political and racial views which they have held for a lifetime. They do not. President de Klerk and those closest to him had not undergone any Pauline conversion on the road to Damascus. Rather, they had been brought to reverse the policies of a lifetime because these policies were no longer working; not only were they not working but the whole political edifice which had been so painstakingly created by Malan, Strijdom, Verwoerd and Vorster was on the verge of collapse.

CHAPTER THIRTY

Development
Standstill

T he most optimistic assumption about the expansion of the world economy advanced by the *World Development Report 1981* forecast virtually no growth in per capita income for the African continent as a whole. In its *Accelerated Development in Sub-Saharan Africa: Agenda for Action*[1] the World Bank begins chapter two as follows: 'When the sub-Saharan States won independence some 20 years ago, they faced formidable constraints to development. These included under-developed human resources, political fragility, insecurely rooted and ill-suited institutions, a climate and geography hostile to development, and rapid population growth. And while the governments have scored considerable achievements, the legacy of history and the facts of geography continue to hamper African economic progress.' Such prognostications hardly augured well for the coming decade.

One of the most critical problems of the preceding 20 years had been the scarcity of trained manpower and the consequent need to depend upon expatriates and a range of volunteers under the auspices of the steadily proliferating non-government organizations (NGOs). At the same time aid, which in its various forms had come to be seen as a necessary prop for governments during the 1970s, became a potent symbol of their dependence during the 1980s. The decade, indeed, was to prove especially difficult for Africa as the continent was buffeted by the effects of world recession, falling commodity prices, a series of devastating natural disasters, and brutal wars in Ethiopia and Angola that involved the two superpowers as part of their many Cold War confrontations. These adverse factors were compounded by growing disenchantment among Western donor nations with the aid process generally, coupled with an increasing tendency to insist upon ever more stringent conditionalities for the aid they did provide. From the sale of arms to both warring factions in a civil war to the sale of goods that did not meet standards laid down as a minimum for health in an 'advanced' country, Africa was constantly seen as an easily manipulable market for extra profits by the so-called 'donor' countries that made it a condition of their aid that such markets were opened to their unwanted or surplus goods. Belief in a free market, Western style, always meant the freedom of the rich to penetrate the markets of the poor rather than real two-way trade.

The concept of development has distorted the West's relations with Africa; instead of viewing African countries as poor countries battling with various problems, the West at this time and later came to view them in an exclusive 'development' phase: 'they are developing; they want to develop; we, the donors, will aid their development; and, as donors, we assume they approach problems of development in the same way as do we the donors'. It was a one-sided equation that did not work. There were many reasons for this: the disparity in power between the two sides; the determination of the donors (principally the West) to further their own political and economic agendas by means of aid and the equal determination of the recipients (from a far weaker power base) to use aid for their own political purposes. These combined to create misunderstandings and suspicions on both sides. Thus, while the stated purpose of aid donors was to assist development, recipients (that is, the ruling elites) on the other hand saw aid as a means to satisfy their supporters rather than to use it in the broader national interest. The equation would change substantially at the end of the decade: 'While Western creditors – self-described as the donor community – had been content to push the IMF-designed Structural Adjustment Programme as a standard reform package around the African continent through the decade of the 1980s, the collapse of the Soviet bloc saw demands for political reform take the front seat.'[2]

The most advanced economies, working in combination through the Group of Seven and the European Union or using their voting power in multilateral organizations such as the World Bank or International Monetary Fund, impose their will upon the world economic system whenever they are able to do so while at the same time working together to prevent the emergence of any system perceived to be antithetical to their interests. The nearest that Third World countries ever came to upsetting this Western-dominated economic order was in the mid-1970s at the time of OPEC power and the proposal to establish a New International Economic Order. The process of economic manipulation has been especially marked in Africa. Aid, the creation of debt, the World Bank and in particular the IMF have each come to be used as mechanisms by means of which the advanced economies direct development in the African recipient countries. Thus, the original purpose of the IMF – to maintain monetary stability by sharing the burden of adjustment between surplus and deficit countries – has long been abandoned. In the first place this has happened because the IMF is unable any longer to control its most powerful members. Instead, the Group of

Seven uses the IMF as its instrument to instruct and control the poor nations so that the IMF, which ought to have acted as a guardian of the poor, has instead become a policeman for the interests of the rich. As a result of IMF pressures through the 1980s a number of African countries felt obliged to put in place IMF-inspired structural adjustment programmes (SAPs), whether or not these really suited their circumstances. SAPs were the price to be paid for debt rescheduling and further aid. The lesson was obvious: as long as they remained indebted small African economies would be subject to IMF-dictated economic regimes. The free market arm of Western economic imperialism consisted of the transnational corporations. In Thatcher's Britain, for example, the *Sunday Times* exposed a multi-million dollar marketing drive by British American Tobacco (BAT) to sell cheap and highly addictive cigarettes in Africa – an easy, regulation-free market – with levels of tar and nicotine far above those permitted in the West. A corporation letter to the country's head of medical services stated, 'BAT Uganda does not believe that cigarette smoking is harmful to health... we should not wish to endanger our potential to export to these countries which do not have a health warning on our packs.'[3] Essentially, the donor–recipient relationship was (and remains) one of control. As one shrewd observer noted: 'The main reason why the one-party state was adjudged a failure in Africa is not principally because it was undemocratic – which it was, at least in Western eyes – but because it presided over widespread economic failure.'[4]

During the 1980s, the last decade of the Cold War, donor countries (really by then the West only) forced African countries to accept World Bank and IMF-dictated SAPs. Only if such programmes were accepted would the usually reluctant recipient country then be given the IMF 'seal of approval' and only when this had been given could the country in question then obtain the aid it required (if it was lucky) from the principal donor nations. In effect, the IMF told African countries what policies to follow: privatization, lowering tariffs against Western manufactures, cutting subsidies on such vital commodities as sugar, flour and cooking oil that most affected the poorest sections of the community, so that the recipient could more easily repay its debts. These harsh IMF conditionalities, never envisaged in the original structures of the IMF, imposed political conditions upon the recipients that amounted to blatant interference in their internal affairs, and whether or not these conditions were acceptable to the majority of the people was beside the point: they had to be put in place as the price for continued aid.

The external pressures exerted upon individual African states by the donor community as a whole were matched internally by the determination of the new elites to ensure their control of their country's limited resources for their own ends. Having battled their way to the top in societies of strictly limited resources of all kinds, few of these elites were possessed of any genuine socialist outlook that would spread such resources for the good of the new state at large. Rather, they sought to control economic power and indulge a conspicuous consumption that was the badge of having 'arrived'. All societies produce elites that cling grimly to the attributes and symbols of their power but in a society where the available resources are strictly limited such elites tend to stand out as especially selfish and necessarily opposed to the development of the state as a whole. This is equally true when there is a revolution or coup: the new rulers at once see the advantages of maintaining the old system for their personal benefit. They have not overthrown the former government because of its elitism but because they did not have an adequate share of the limited available resources. Just as the white minority in South Africa saw the coming end of apartheid as inevitable yet clung on as long as possible to a system that benefited it, so also do the entrenched elites in other African states see the long-term effects of their selfishly narrow approach to development yet do nothing to change it. The old Africa that was colonized by the European powers was essentially patrimonial: the chief looked after his tribe or group. The new post-colonial Africa, despite much contrary rhetoric, operates on much the same lines where the 'Big Man', who may well be a government minister, is equally expected to look after his own group.

> In a neo-patrimonial system, political accountability rests on the extent to which patrons are able both to influence and meet the expectations of their followers according to well-established norms of reciprocity. Although in Africa most of the political leaders at independence were new (young graduates), rather than 'traditional' (chiefs) elites, the parameters of the neo-patrimonial systems which developed after independence owed a great deal to what might be called 'traditional' principles of legitimacy. Among those (principles of legitimacy) the most significant had to do with a notion of accountability which involved a direct link with the delivery of resources to clients. In other words, the legitimacy of political leaders was perceived by all (from top to bottom) to rest on their ability to provide for their own personal constituents.[5]

In other words, patrons had to meet their obligations to their own groups or 'clientele' rather than act impartially as national leaders and they are able to do this by the way they use and deploy aid provided supposedly for national rather than more limited sectarian purposes. Working upon a national basis of poverty, competition for limited resources becomes fierce and this forms the basis of political rivalries for power. Leaders need to spend ostentatiously to demonstrate their power and ensure that adequate resources (from a limited pool) are channelled to their supporters. A natural consequence of such power or influence considerations is the neglect of investment in economic activities that will benefit the state as a whole. 'The crisis which crippled African countries in the eighties was thus a result of the combined effect of diminishing economic wealth and the dissipation of political accountability which it brought about. As political elites competed in an increasingly desperate bid to have access to central power – still the fount of most resources – force became widespread.'[6] In the West such practices are seen as corruption although this is too easy a way of dismissing a system that is only partly understood. In an African patrimonial society such practices are regarded as the necessary discharge by the elite of its duties towards its supporters.

In 1982 at the height of the world debt crisis Tom Clausen, the World Bank President, said of the world's poorest nations, many of them in Africa, that they were 'battered by global economic conditions beyond their control' as they were hit by the recession in the industrialized countries, faced falling prices for their export commodities and demands for increased interest rates on their debts. Zambia, to take one example of the changing terms of trade, had enjoyed high expectations in 1974 when its principal export copper peaked at £1,400 a tonne and with cobalt provided over half the government's revenue. By mid-1982, however, the price of a tonne of copper, which cost more to produce because of higher energy costs, higher wages and ageing machinery, had fallen to a low of £684. Similarly, the economies of countries such as Côte d'Ivoire and Kenya that were dependent upon agricultural commodities such as cocoa, coffee and tea were equally damaged by Western recession. Although Africa's various regional economic groups such as ECOWAS, *Communité Economique des Etats de l'Afrique Centrale* (CEEAC) or SADCC aimed to improve trade among member states, in fact they made only a marginal impact since the economies of their individual members remained directed overwhelmingly to Europe and their former metropolitan powers. Moreover, their industrial and manufacturing sectors were too small and unsophisticated to compete with either European or US manufactures. Against this gloomy background African prospects for rapid industrialization fell away while both aid and export revenues remained static and no funds were available for major development projects. In theory, therefore, it was an ideal time to implement 'back to the land' policies although such attempts in the past had quickly been abandoned when economic conditions picked up. According to the *World Development Report 1982*, 'Countries neglect agriculture at their peril – a rapidly developing agriculture is a necessary condition for economy-wide structural transformation and industrialization.' However, before any effective agricultural growth could be achieved, most countries had to reverse the trend of the 1960s when agricultural output had declined by 0.2 per cent a year and the 1970s when it fell by 1.4 per cent. Large-scale migration from the rural areas to the towns had both deprived the rural areas of an essential part of their workforce and created new social problems in the towns. At the same time the problem of debt for sub-Saharan Africa was escalating and by 1982 the total of external debts consisting mainly of loans from the World Bank and its soft arm the International Development Association (IDA) or bilateral loans from governments had reached US$98,000 million. At the end of 1980, for example, Nigeria's debts stood at US$5,000 million, those of Côte d'Ivoire at US$4,265 million and in both cases more than half these debts were on commercial terms. In 1982 Zaïre required US$771 million simply to service its debts and then owed US$175 million from the previous year in which it had failed to meet its debt repayment obligations. Funding to help a country overcome a balance of payments crisis produced no long-term returns as did funding for development projects and the decade saw an increasing number of countries – Ghana, Kenya, Malawi, Sudan, Tanzania, Zaïre and Zambia – turn to the IMF for rescheduling exercises. Meanwhile, Africa faced an ever-growing population that swallowed up many of the gains from successful developments while estimates suggested that the 1982 population of sub-Saharan Africa, then standing at 353 million, would rise to 1,411 million by 2020. Some real advances had been achieved and, for example, life expectancy at birth had increased by an average of 10 years or 25 per cent over two decades.

THE ROLE OF THE WORLD BANK

By 1990, after years of expanding activity, the World Bank had become the largest source of aid for Africa. It described the structural obstacles to development as follows: human resource deficiencies (inadequate training and education); poverty; environmental degradation; rapid population growth unmatched by comparable development; and the urgent need to speed up agricultural development and increase food production. The World Bank saw seven major areas as the keys to African progress: population control; environment; agriculture; the social dimension of adjustment; food security; education; and women in development. The Africa sections of the World Bank annual reports during the decade make gloomy reading. That for 1982, for example, records that four countries of East Africa experienced a marked decline in agricultural production: Zimbabwe by 19 per cent, Zambia by 11 per cent for its two export crops of tobacco and cotton; while Madagascar and

Ethiopia had less steep declines. The East African region's capacity to import was sharply affected by the severe decline in world market prices of copper (15 per cent), cotton (14 per cent), sugar (49 per cent) and tea (4 per cent). The combined index of six major primary commodities of the region, accounting for 52 per cent of total exports, fell by 10 per cent. The balance of payments situation in the region was grim and was reflected in the increase of arrears on external payments and a widespread decline in official external reserves. Western Africa suffered from depressed markets for commodities, high interest rates and stagnating levels of official development assistance. The region had been deeply affected by world recession since 1979. Growth of GDP for the region over 1980–82 showed increases in average per capita incomes in only two countries – Cameroon (26 per cent) and Congo (Brazzaville) (40 per cent) due to oil exploitation. In Côte d'Ivoire, Togo and Sierra Leone GDP grew at rates less than the population and in nearly all the other 18 countries, including Nigeria, a net decline in per capita incomes was registered. 'One of the potentially most damaging effects of the crisis is that its persistence and severity make it difficult for governments to carry out structural-adjustment policies needed to foster long-term growth.'[7] The recurrence of the word 'crisis' in relation to African economies became a commonplace of reports through the decade.

In the following year's report, the Bank explained, 'The economic crisis in the countries of the Eastern Africa region, detailed in the *Annual Reports* of recent years, continued largely unabated during the past fiscal year (1984). Per capita income declined in the region as a whole and dropped substantially in a number of countries. Exogenous factors, as usual, played their part in contributing to these declines; but, most cruelly, what may turn out to be, for several countries, the worst period of drought in this century deepened the difficulties of the year.'[8] As always, Africa was mainly dependent on its exportable commodities and the World Bank noted that the beginnings of economic recovery in the industrial countries had not brought about a general increase in the prices of the region's major export commodities: copper rose 7.5 per cent in 1983 above the1982 price, cobalt fetched half the price of recent years, the price of coffee fell below the 1982 level or that of any year from 1976–80. Copper, cobalt and coffee accounted for over half the region's exports. The Bank noted that over the previous two years there had been a turn around in the willingness of governments to reconsider domestic economic policies: 'major efforts have been made to implement financial stabilization policies and to design adjustment policies that aim at renewed growth. This is particularly true in the case of Madagascar, Somalia, Zaïre and Zambia. But achievements under stabilization policies were not without costs – investment and per capita income have declined. These declines were the result of many factors, and they were exacerbated by the fact that efforts at stabilization were undertaken during a time when the external economic environment was especially difficult.'[9]

The World Bank's efforts at self-exculpation ring false: the weaker the African economies, the more determinedly were they pressured into structural adjustments that the Bank and the IMF insisted upon. Dependence upon aid donors is made plain when it is pointed out that several, mostly low-income countries (Burundi, the Comoros, Djibouti, Ethiopia, Lesotho, Malawi, Rwanda, Somalia and Tanzania, for instance) depended almost entirely on official development assistance (ODA) for net capital inflows. This, moreover, was the case at a time when there had been no recent increases in ODA to offset the effects of the worldwide trade recession. In 1982, for example, ODA to Eastern Africa amounted to US$4.3 billion, indicating that absolute stagnation had taken place since 1980. The net flow of commercial loans to the region fell sharply at this time, declining from about US$950 million in 1980 to about US$350 million in 1982. The picture was much the same for Western Africa where prices for iron ore, uranium, phosphate rock and oil were depressed, with adverse effects in Liberia, Mauritania, Niger, Nigeria and Togo. Nigeria, the largest and potentially richest country in the region, was in a state of financial crisis for most of fiscal 1984 since both the production and price of oil dropped sharply so that export earnings and government revenues, as well as the external current account and the government fiscal position, weakened dramatically. Nigeria's capacity to import dropped considerably as trade credits dried up under the impact of accumulated trade arrears. The drop in imports was equal to 5 per cent of Nigeria's GDP and induced a decline in national income equivalent in real terms to 7.4 per cent.

There was little improvement in terms of trade for Eastern and Southern Africa during 1985 while the decline in aid flows continued and drought caused havoc in several countries. There is a relentless quality about World Bank-speak in such circumstances: 'Nonetheless, it can be said that most countries now appear to have a better recognition of their need to revise the economic strategies of the past. Several have made real progress in formulating and in initiating the implementation of programmes of financial stabilization and economic reform. Progress in these areas is reflected in the fact that eight countries currently have active standby agreements with the IMF, and six countries have been assisted by World Bank operations in support of policy reforms.'[10] With regard to Western Africa, the same report noted that world markets remained depressed for its commodities – uranium, oil, iron ore, cotton and rubber – and that West Africa was principally tied to Europe for its trade in such commodities. The term 'crisis' was applied to the region as a whole and most countries, according to the World Bank, responded to the difficult situation by putting into motion measures aimed at improving internal efficiency. *Toward Sustained Development in Sub-Saharan Africa: A Joint Program of Action* (World Bank 1984) made clear that without adequate external aid, African countries can hardly achieve the structural changes needed to resume economic growth. But little aid was forthcoming and so those countries in need stagnated. During 1985 a successful consultative group was set up for Senegal and donors indicated 'they might be willing to commit some US$500 million annually in assistance'. Other groups were being planned for Mauritania, Guinea, Benin, The Gambia, Guinea-Bissau, Liberia, Mali and Togo. By the mid 1980s it had become clear that the pattern of aid to Africa was largely in the hands, and under the direction, of the World Bank and the IMF and that structural adjustment programmes were coming to dominate the aid process although a good deal of 'back-sliding' was to be expected.

It is worth looking briefly at particular economic problems in individual African countries. In the two decades after independence Côte d'Ivoire had come to be regarded as one of Africa's success stories. Yet by the mid-1980s the World Bank suggested that its economy had been destabilized by the cocoa and coffee boom of 1975–77 that led it to embark on an ambitious public investment programme. This resulted in a budget deficit imbalance of 17 per cent in 1980 and a consequent reform programme in 1981. The deficit remained high during 1980–83 as a result of drought and deterioration in the terms of trade. Interest payments increased from 3 per cent of GDP in 1979 to over 10 per cent in the early 1980s though they improved over the period 1984–86 due to better terms of trade and cuts in the public investment programme.

A quite different problem in Ghana concerned the flow of finances out of the rural areas to the urban areas, a factor working against rural development.

> For example, in Ghana it is widely recognized that commercial banks have served to mop up and transfer rural savings to the capital markets of the Accra-Tema metropolitan area, the national capital, and to a lesser extent to other large metropolitan areas such as Kumasi and Sekondi-Takoradi. Such capital drained from cocoa and food producers has been reallocated for foreign monopolies and other business interests which are located in the non-indigenous economy, that is, those economic sectors with very few spin-off effects on the petty commodity sector of the national economy.[11]

The pattern constantly changes and in the case of Kenya the picture is modestly encouraging. The annual rate of GDP growth slowed to 3.5 per cent over the years 1980–85, which was a period of drought, political uncertainty, including a coup attempt, and falling terms of trade (among the worst in Africa).

In 1986, however, growth recovered to 6.4 per cent with higher coffee prices (for export) and lower oil prices (imported). During 1981–84 the budget deficit was cut as a result of cutbacks in development expenditure. But in 1987 declining terms of trade and higher public expenditure produced another economic downturn. In the case of Malawi, its structural problems stemmed from its undiversified economy: tobacco, tea and sugar from an estate sector accounted for 75 per cent or more of its exports so that it was greatly susceptible to external price fluctuations. For the years 1980–86 it had a growth rate of only 2.5 per cent, which was below the level of population growth.

Following the collapse of copper prices in 1975, the government of Zambia relied upon large increases in foreign borrowing and arrears in repayments to make up for the loss of copper revenues while the second oil shock at the end of the 1970s meant that Zambia's terms of trade fell by a further 25 per cent during the 1980s. A growth average of only 0.3 per cent over the last years of the 1970s became negative in the 1980s and by 1985 imports in real terms were at only 25 per cent of the 1974 levels while gross investment had fallen to 10 per cent of GDP and per capita income was down by 35 per cent. By 1987 Zambia's external debt had reached US$5.7 billion or four times GDP and debt-service obligations were equivalent to 70 per cent of exports, including repayment of arrears. By this time Zambia was facing the prospect of the depletion of its copper reserves during the 1990s.

Africa's growing awareness of its individual and continental economic weaknesses led to the adoption by the 1985 OAU summit of a five-year (1986–90) African Priority Programme for Economic Recovery (APPER). African leaders argued that their economies had been penalized by an unjust and inequitable international economic system aggravated by continental disasters such as droughts and floods as well as domestic policy shortcomings. One result of the APPER initiative was the convening of a special session of the UN that adopted the United Nations Programme of Action for Africa's Economic Recovery and Development (UNPARED). Much attention was also accorded to the issue of debt, which by then constantly hampered African development. By this time (1985–86) a dual pattern had emerged: on the one hand, African politicians demanded of the World Bank and other international institutions a more equitable approach to world economic problems that would better serve African interests; on the other, despite the Bank's capacity to analyse Africa's problems with apparent impartiality, they remained deeply suspicious of its remedies and the IMF-inspired structural adjustment programmes that had become the principal feature of the donor world's reaction to African problems.

In 1985 the protracted economic stagnation in Ethiopia, Madagascar, Tanzania, Uganda, Zaïre and Zambia caused the per capita income in those countries to fall below levels reached in 1970. The terms of trade for the East African region fell by 6 per cent and were 30 per cent below the levels for 1978–80. The primary cause of this collapse was the second oil price rise and by 1985 per capita incomes on average were 4.6 per cent below the average for 1982–84. The inflow of foreign resources also declined in 1985 and disbursement of concessional and non-concessional medium- and long-term loans (net of amortization) dropped for the fifth year in succession to reach only 40 per cent of the peak volume achieved in 1980. The problem of servicing foreign debt intensified for several countries and hampered their efforts at stabilization and adjustment while Madagascar, Somalia, Sudan, Tanzania, Zaïre and Zambia accumulated substantial arrears and each of these countries except Tanzania had to renegotiate its debt at the Paris or London Club at least once during the first half of the 1980s.

Stabilization and adjustment, the two most familiar jargon words used by World Bank officials, meant adopting policies such as ending subsidies for basic foods, which made repayment of debts easier but life for the ordinary people harder. A total of 19 structural adjustment efforts under World Bank supervision were approved between 1980 and 1986 in Burundi, Kenya, Madagascar, Malawi, Mauritius, Sudan, Tanzania, Uganda, Zaïre, Zambia and Zimbabwe. The World Bank noted encouraging progress on several fronts, though 'the implementation of some difficult reforms was interrupted by the continuing fall in export prices, political uncertainties, and declining net inflows of aid and loans'. By this time, it appeared, African development and World Bank instructions as to how it should be achieved had become inseparable. Debt moved to the top of the agenda. It had a significant impact upon almost all African countries but in different ways. Some countries, such as Kenya and Mauritius, managed their debt well and so continued to have access to new credit on conventional terms while others such as Malawi and Zimbabwe had serious debt-servicing problems but restored a measure of credit worthiness by undertaking economic reforms. But a third group of countries was not able to meet its scheduled debt-servicing obligations and for 1986–90 30 per cent of the group's debt-servicing would be owed to multilateral institutions with the IMF accounting for 61 per cent. These countries included Madagascar, Somalia, Sudan, Tanzania, Zaïre and Zambia. As the World Bank commented: 'Since multilateral debt-service payments cannot be rescheduled, those high ratios will increase the difficulties to be faced by this group of countries in coping with its debt burdens.'[12] Of 21 West African countries, which were all borrowers over 1984–86, Cameroon had a per capita income of US$1,800, Nigeria US$730, Côte d'Ivoire US$610, Liberia US$470 and Mauritania US$450 while the rest ranged from US$380 for Senegal to a low of

US$140 for Mali (no figures were available for troubled Chad which was devastated by civil war throughout the decade). Despite all the interventions and prescriptions offered by the World Bank and the IMF the problems did not change: adverse terms of trade for commodity exports, diminishing inflows of capital, increasing indebtedness.

The *World Development Report 1986* summarizes the state of sub-Saharan Africa halfway through the decade. First it deals with debt. The total long- and short-term liabilities had increased from US$38.5 billion in 1978 to approximately US$80,000 billion in 1984, an increase from 30 per cent to 50 per cent of the region's combined GNP. Total debt service, which was US$6.4 billion in 1983, had risen to US$7.9 billion in 1984 while the debt-service ratio at 21.6 per cent in 1984 had risen to 33.2 per cent in 1985 for the continent as a whole. Although debt repayments were not the fundamental cause of Africa's low growth, the report argued, the debt problem had become increasingly acute for three reasons: the proportion of debt payments not eligible for rescheduling (that is, loans from multilateral organizations) was rising rapidly; rescheduling in any case was costly; and net financial flows to sub-Saharan Africa had fallen substantially. Ten countries rescheduled debt at the Paris Club in 1983, 1984 and 1985 so that rescheduling had become a continuous process. Worse than that, several countries did not reschedule at the Paris Club primarily because they were unable to reach agreement with their creditors on adjustment programmes and most of these countries were additionally hampered by their arrears to the IMF, which technically prohibits rescheduling negotiations. So the report posed the question: can African countries grow fast enough to meet existing debt obligations and maintain adequate domestic investment? The prospects seemed poor. In order to reverse Africa's decline concessional lending would have to go hand in hand with policy reforms and recipient governments should clearly outline the programmes of adjustment they intended to follow.

The report was especially concerned with agriculture. The neglect of agriculture was general in much of Africa. One reason was the high level of taxes imposed by African governments on export crops: thus, in Togo the farm price for coffee was a third of the border price; in Mali cotton and groundnut farmers received half the border prices, in Cameroon and Ghana cocoa producers received less than half. In many African countries marketing boards, a leftover of colonial times, acted as taxation agencies for governments and the money was used to industrialize or for other purposes rather than being put back into the agricultural sector. One result of this high taxation was the emergence of parallel markets as peasant farmers ensured that a proportion of their crops evaded the system. The main losers in such a situation were the governments, which lost taxes when farmers sold export crops unofficially. They would have done better to impose lower taxes. Once farmers engage regularly in smuggling commodity crops across borders to avoid high taxes, the government both foregoes revenues and begins to lose control of the farming sector.

Africa's food problems were often ascribed to an over-emphasis on non-food crops. However, data from 1960–70 and 1970–82 gave a different picture to show that countries that experienced satisfactory growth of one type of crop also experienced satisfactory growth of the other. In 25 of 38 African countries, the rate of growth of both food and non-food production fell in 1970–82 compared with the 1960s. In six countries both growth rates increased. In only five did the rate of growth of food production increase while that of non-food fell. In two countries – Kenya and Malawi (which were self-sufficient in food) – the food production rate slowed down while non-food production increased.[13] When farming becomes unprofitable farmers lose the incentive to care for their land; taxes, therefore, should be moderate and agriculture, like any other industry, needs nurturing. The table rating the standing of countries in the development league showed that of the 36 low-income economies listed in the 1986 report, 23 were in Africa while of the 40 lower-middle-income countries 14 were in Africa.

Deteriorating political and economic conditions in South Africa during 1986 and 1987 and Pretoria's escalating pressures on its SADCC neighbours damaged their economies, which were always highly dependent upon South Africa for trade. South Africa was the major supplier of food, oil, spare parts, motor vehicles, machinery and other manufactured goods for the region. It owned or controlled up to 40 per cent of manufacturing activities in neighbouring states while approximately one million migrants from the SADCC countries worked in South Africa. About 85 per cent of SADCC's foreign trade passed through South Africa. Zimbabwe, at this time, was producing an exportable surplus of one million tons of grain and with the help of the Food and Agriculture Organization of the UN (FAO) had overcome the threat of locusts. In May 1987 Zambia abandoned its IMF recovery programme, whose draconian impact was causing political unrest, and imposed a price freeze and price controls. Most countries of the region were experiencing an erosion of their standard of living. Some governments were paying greater attention to the problem of population explosion and the need to control growth and relate increased productivity to increased wellbeing. Educational levels remained below those of other regions in the developing world and the shortage of skilled manpower acted as a further impediment to development. Both Zaïre and Zambia faced domestic political problems as a result of implementing, or trying to implement, reforms and both countries questioned the adequacy of the aid they were receiving. Debt remained the primary problem and in the case of four countries – Mozambique,

Sudan, Tanzania and Zambia – arrears in repayments exceeded US$500 million.

The FAO focused its attention upon Africa in 1986 in an attempt to reverse the prevalent neglect of agriculture. In January the FAO launched a crash programme to provide urgently needed farm inputs in the Sahel and other regions. The Agricultural Rehabilitation Programme for Africa (ARPA) helped channel a total of US$175 million to 25 countries: ARPA included supplying farmers with seed and fertilizer, repairing irrigation systems and rebuilding cattle herds. At the same time the FAO prepared an Africa-wide programme to eradicate the cattle disease rinderpest. The continent was constantly subject to natural disasters and diseases such as drought, flood, rinderpest, grasshopper and locust plagues. At that time only 6.5 per cent of Africa's farmland was irrigated and the FAO provided help for a new era of irrigation development. The Fourteenth FAO Regional Conference for Africa was held in Yamoussoukro, Côte d'Ivoire, in September 1986 and a broad consensus on the causes of the African food crisis and ways to resolve it was reached. The FAO Director-General told the conference that Africa could meet almost all of its food requirements but for that to happen new development policies, new international trade relationships and, most of all, new financial and material resources would be needed. Africa was then recovering from the drought and famine during 1983–85. The return of good rainfall undoubtedly helped but the bumper harvests of 1986 were also due to a concerted effort by the FAO to restore crop, livestock and fisheries production. At the FAO's Fifteenth Regional Conference for Africa, held in Mauritius in April 1988, many African countries were in crisis. The Director-General told the conference: 'There is no question that the new locust plague which has swooped down on the continent is exceptionally vast. International and regional action is more essential now than ever before.'[14] He may have been right to say so but it was a familiar refrain that Africans constantly heard from a range of development institutions.

In 1986 the World Bank produced a major report on Africa, *Financing Adjustment with Growth in Sub-Saharan Africa, 1986–90* whose theme – that Africa's attempts to help itself would fail without additional resources in the form of new aid and debt relief – was probably more acceptable to Africa than the accompanying remedies. 'Many African governments are now making significant progress in structural adjustment. But they still have much to do to correct the accumulated policy distortions of the past.' Such statements, smug and all-knowing, must sometimes have annoyed those on the receiving end of them as much as did the Bank's and IMF's prescriptions for adjustment. The analysis and policy suggestions that follow all too often ignore the political realities on the ground.

Governments were commended for having started to reduce the over-valuation of their currencies – one way in which agriculture had been penalized. They had increased agricultural prices and lowered real urban wages. They had reduced public spending, with its bias toward expanding employment in urban areas. These moves may have made sense in theory; it is doubtful whether their authors really understood the political pressures exercised by Africa's rapidly growing town populations upon fragile governments. Declining imports and investment threaten to undermine structural adjustment in low-income Africa, the report says, and then adds that to continue its progress toward economic adjustment, low-income Africa will need at least US$11 billion a year of concessional flows during 1986–90 but allowing for known and expected aid commitments, a gap of US$2.5 billion remains. The report points out that one general rule should be observed: *no donor country should be a net recipient of resource flows from any African country undertaking credible economic reforms.* That advice to the donors certainly made sense; the report does not specify how donors are to be persuaded to follow such a rule of thumb. A sign of the developing multilateral approach that would characterize the 1990s was the emphasis upon donors working together. Donors, we are told, must act more in concert with each other and with recipients. The report suggests six ways to improve co-ordination:

> First, donors must be willing to work within adjustment programmes designed by African governments. Second, they should better harmonize decisions on aid and debt relief together. Third, the major participants should discuss the elements of the required financial package in advance of full-scale aid co-ordination meetings. Fourth, to provide effective support for medium-term adjustment, donors should be more willing to give medium-term indications of aid. Fifth, instruments should be established to monitor progress toward economic reform and toward implementing governments' and donors' agreements, Sixth, the multilateral agencies must assume a larger role in orchestrating donor assistance – both in designing adjustment programmes and in financing them. The World Bank and the IMF, in particular, must work together with African governments, first to develop adjustment and investment programmes aimed at restoring growth, and second to assess the requirements for, and sources of, external aid.[15]

This set of principles is clearly a blueprint for control of the entire aid process.

For the first time since World War II, a whole region had suffered regression over a generation. The fall in the investment rate during the 1980s reflected both a decline in domestic and foreign savings. Domestic savings averaged about 15 per cent of GDP until the mid-1970s. By 1984, however, the rate had fallen to a low of 6 per cent. This was the result of a fall in per capita incomes and an increase in public sector deficits due to unchecked budget deficits and losses from state-owned enterprises. Fourteen countries rescheduled debts over 1984–85 and in some cases the new arrangements were just the latest in a series. Over the same period several countries fell deeper into arrears with their repayments. The report argued that if Africa's decline was to be reversed, action was needed on three fronts. 'First, the region needs more resources for investment... both foreign and domestic. Second, it must use new and existing resources more efficiently. Third, it must curb its growth in population.'[16] Restraints imposed on budgets by adjustment programmes can best be seen in the deterioration of public services such as road building and repairs, education and health. Fewer resources mean less efficiency. Although health conditions in sub-Saharan Africa had improved over the previous few decades, they remained among the worst in the world and in most African countries access to health care is extremely limited. What comes across with increasing clarity over the decade in all the pronouncements and reports emanating from the World Bank is the remoteness of the institution from the problems on the ground that it pontificates about so grandly. It is not that African leaders did not understand the causes of their declining economies but rather that they had to deal with complex political problems on the ground that were rarely understood fully by visiting missions from the multilateral institutions. In 1982 President Nimeiri of Sudan explained how the IMF had insisted that before it could provide assistance he had to cut subsidies on sugar, petrol and bread. He explained that if he did so he would have riots in Khartoum, Port Sudan and Atbara. The IMF insisted. He cut the subsidies on sugar and petrol. Severe riots duly followed. The IMF said: what about bread? So he evaded cutting the price by resorting to a stratagem and decreed that the size of all loaves had to be reduced. The IMF then let him off the hook and provided some assistance. It is a revealing story: the IMF demanding actions that produce riots; the head of state being forced to resort to tricks. It is little wonder that the IMF is generally loathed throughout Africa.

The year 1988 is a good one for taking stock of Africa's economic plight after the best part of what can only be described as a disastrous development decade. According to the UN International Fund for Agricultural Development (IFAD), African states still reported in 1988 that 'both economic and quality of life indicators have either remained at unacceptably low levels or continued their downward spiral in such categories as trade earnings, amount of official development assistance, private capital inflows, incidence of malnutrition and child mortality, as well as levels of food imports, industrial output and under- and unemployment'. The region's per capita income had declined more than 12 per cent since 1970 and in some cases, for example Chad, by as much as 30 per cent. The poorer countries of Africa were even poorer in 1988 than at independence in the 1960s while Africa had ceased to feed itself in the 1980s: whereas in 1974 it imported 3.9 million tonnes of cereals, by 1985 it was importing 10.2 million tonnes. The principal causes of this poor performance divided between external and internal factors. The major external factors were continuing adverse terms of trade and declines in foreign aid and investment. The principal internal factors were poor soils, harsh climatic conditions, poor human and physical infrastructure, rapid urbanization and population growth and inappropriate public policies. Over 1980–85 there had been no growth in exports but an annual decline of 5 per cent as against a growth rate of 9.8 per cent for the years 1965–89, and despite the benefits offered under the Lomé Conventions for access to the European market, protection and restrictive agricultural practices in the European Community (its CAP policy) and in the United States had resulted in an over-supply of agricultural commodities and a consequent weakened demand for African exports. Between 1980 and 1984 the continent's debt service payments had increased from 18 per cent of export earnings to 26 per cent while by 1985 sub-Saharan Africa paid over 30 per cent of its export earnings to service its debts.

The rapid urbanization of the continent presented another set of social and political problems. By the mid-1980s more than 42 per cent of all urban-dwellers in sub-Saharan Africa lived in cities of 500,000 or more (the figure had been 8 per cent in 1960) and it was estimated that by 2000 there would be 60 or more cities with populations in excess of one million inhabitants. People migrating to the cities did so in search of jobs, access to education and better medical care and the supposed attractions of urban life; too often, however, they arrive to disappear into urban slums. Whenever structural adjustment programmes are applied and cutbacks result, or are necessitated by lack of funds, it is the health, education and infrastructure sectors that are hit first and hardest. A major reason for economic decline has undoubtedly been the neglect of agriculture by governments who see their potentially dangerous urban populations as the first priority for attention in the form of food subsidies and higher wages. Between 1973 and 1984, for example, only 10 sub-Saharan countries increased food production on a per caput basis. Most of the problems came back to poverty and lack of funds and by the late 1980s Africa was mainly dependent upon official aid flows rather than private source flows. In 1980 the net inward flow of private source finances stood at US$1,500 million; by 1985 the net outward flow was US$700 million.

The tone of the 1989 World Bank Report was suddenly upbeat. It claimed that in aggregate sub-Saharan Africa's GDP had grown by 2.6 per cent over 1985–88, counteracting the general perception that 'Africa is a continent still in unrelenting decline'. This growth, however, had not been reflected in per capita incomes, which were 15 per cent lower than they had been a decade earlier. In other words, this modest rise in GDP had done no more than permit the African economies to stand still. Agriculture, the report argued, had grown by 4 per cent between 1985 and 1988. As always, the first concern of the World Bank was policy reforms. 'By the end of fiscal 1989, the number of countries implementing policy reforms to effect structural adjustment had increased to nearly 30. In many countries that have had strong and sustained reform programmes and which have not been affected by strong external shocks, for example, in The Gambia, Ghana, Guinea, Mauritius, Tanzania, and Togo, there are encouraging signs of growth in output generally well above the average for the region as a whole and above that achieved in the early 1980s.'[17] There was an increase in aid flows. Aid over 1984–87 increased by 9 per cent over the early years of the decade. The region's share in worldwide ODA went up from 23 per cent in 1980 to 30 per cent in 1987 while low-income countries in the region received US$36 per capita in aid compared with US$25 per capita in 1983. However, the impact of aid was threatened by a population growth averaging 3 per cent a year that could increase to 4 per cent if fertility rates were not brought down. And another problem concerned the degradation of the environment with an alarming rate of desertification taking place, as well as deforestation, ground water loss and air and water pollution.

According to the World Bank this modest recovery continued in 1990 when GDP rose by 3.5 per cent as opposed to 2.5 per cent in 1988 while countries dependent upon concessional ODA did better at 4.2 per cent as opposed to 3.4 per cent in 1988. The region was also helped by an increase in non-oil commodity prices in 1988 and oil in 1989. Pressure was maintained to make countries adopt structural adjustment programmes although structural obstacles to development were seen as particularly profound in Africa, and long-term efforts to overcome them were necessary on a broad front, ranging from human resource development and poverty alleviation to environmental protection, slowing the growth of population, and quickening the pace of agricultural development. As the report conceded, agriculture is the primary source of growth in sub-Saharan Africa and even when full account is taken of environmental constraints, the scope for expanding agricultural production remains considerable. On education the report said: 'Although school enrolments have been vastly expanded over the past three decades, too often this expansion has come at the expense of educational quality.'[18] Of the 42 countries listed as low-income economies in the *World Development Report 1990,* 27 were in Africa.

During the 1980s a distinct pattern emerged in the relationship between the donors and their African recipients and it was a disturbing pattern because it highlighted all that was wrong about what ought to have been a genuine two-way partnership for development. The donors always *knew* what had to be done. Structural adjustment programmes (SAPs) or economic recovery programmes (ERPs) were devised in Washington or Paris by teams of highly competent economists but never on the ground in Africa, just as an earlier generation of 'experts' had devised five-year plans for newly independent African states. If these planners for Africa had been impartial their remoteness, their production of solutions from on high would not have mattered so much, but they were not impartial. From their early beginnings the World Bank and the International Monetary Fund had been hijacked by the West whose principal countries, led by the United States, controlled the voting power and soon came to see these international financial institutions as instruments for imposing Western economic policies upon Africa. Part of the motivation was the Cold War and it was both Africa's fortune and misfortune to emerge to independence at the height of this ideological confrontation. Still more, however, Western capitalism saw Africa as a region that had to be firmly corralled into its own orbit and this became most apparent during the 1990s when the Cold War had come to an end. It was, in any case, a one-sided battle for all the advantages lay with the donors who, in the final analysis, dispensed or withheld favours. Most African economies were small and fragile and they needed some form of government protection or intervention. Donor policies, however disguised, had as their ultimate aim opening up Africa to Western economic penetration and control and during the 1990s, with the constraints of the Cold War removed and reinforced by the new Western capitalist ideology of globalization, the donors at last came close to achieving their objectives.

None of this excuses the failings of African leadership. Gen. Olusegun Obasanjo, who had already served as head of state for Nigeria, made the following observations at the beginning of the 1990s:

Despite over a quarter of a century of political independence, Africa's aspirations and hopes remain unfulfilled. This has not been, however, a period of unmitigated failure in the history of the continent; there have been successes in education, public health, import substitution industries, and in the continuing process of decolonization. The problems of development, peace and security, the health of the world economy, and improving the environment are interrelated global issues; they do not admit of piecemeal solutions.

And yet all countries find that in the absence of true global co-operation, they have to tackle particular aspects of them. At the national level in Africa, the inadequacy of information, data, and resources render the problems daunting. Regionally they are overwhelming.[19]

Obasanjo speaks with the authority of an ex-head of state and one, moreover, who had stepped down and handed over power to the civilians exactly as he had promised. If, as he suggests, many of Africa's and the world's problems require 'true global co-operation' then much of the onus must rest with the most powerful nations and in terms of Africa's problems this means the major donors. Unfortunately that co-operation has been conceived not in terms of achieving greater global equity but rather as a means of extending their influence and economic control.

A classic World Bank appraisal *Poverty, Adjustment, and Growth in Africa*, written by Ismail Serageldin in 1989, sets forth the problems admirably: 'To reduce poverty in Africa in a long-term, sustainable manner, economic growth is absolutely essential. Growth can increase people's incomes, support education and health expenditures, generate investment and employment opportunities, raise living standards. But without growth, as indeed we have seen from the African experience in the later 1970s and the 1980s, living standards will become further and further depressed – and it is the poorest in society who will be hurt most.'[20] Few would disagree with the author's emphasis upon the need for growth; the problem, however, must be the manner in which growth is achieved. He goes on, more controversially, to argue: 'Despite the profound difficulties – economic, social, and political – involved in economic reform, there is now a strong consensus within Africa and within the donor community on the need for adjustment.' There may have been such a consensus among the donors, for good reasons of their own; there was little evidence of a similar consensus among African leaders or governments. They may have consented to adjustment reforms but almost always they did so under protest because only by agreeing World Bank or IMF programmes could they obtain the aid they so desperately needed. The seriousness and depth of the African crisis through the 1980s was real enough and international awareness of the crisis was expressed by a series of World Bank in-depth studies: *Accelerated Development in Sub-Saharan Africa: the Agenda for Action* (1981); *Sub-Saharan Africa: Progress Report on Development Prospects and Progress* (1983); *Towards Sustained Development in Sub-Saharan Africa: A Joint Program of Action* (1984); *Financing Adjustment with Growth in Sub-Saharan Africa, 1986–90* (1986). Yet one looks in vain for any sense that the World Bank was planning and working *with* the people of Africa.

Always, these reports and appraisals carry with them a sense of Bank conviction that it knows the answers, if only the Africans would be sensible enough to accept its judgements. Nowhere is there evidence of doubt or even the possibility that African leaders might know better than the Bank how best to develop their countries and their people. And in the background, driving Bank decisions, are the major Western donors whose primary consideration has ever been to spread their influence and look after their global financial interests.

The most revealing statement made by Serageldin is the following: 'Despite 25 years of development programmes and projects supported by multilateral and bilateral aid institutions, two-thirds of the rural population and a third of the urban population of sub-Saharan Africa remain below the absolute poverty level. Infant mortality rates averaged 104 per thousand in sub-Saharan Africa in 1985, compared with 71 per thousand for all the developing economies. In that same year, child death rates were estimated at 18 per cent in sub-Saharan Africa, twice as high as in all developing economies.'[21] What never appears to occur to either the writer or the World Bank as a whole is the possibility – given the huge attention lavished upon Africa's problems – that perhaps their approach was the wrong one.

Poverty and debt go together and once an African country had become sufficiently indebted it was at the mercy of donors who used debt as a lever to enforce upon the debtor country policies it would never otherwise have adopted. Under pressures of crisis, governments that are forced to service onerous debts and repay loans are obliged to cut back on those aspects of development which are the most important: social spending – education, health, housing, clean water – instead, increasing the production of commodities for export to their donors or liberalizing trade barriers so that the advanced economies can the more easily move into positions of control. Since, on the World Bank's own admission, basic needs are not being met in much of Africa, should it not be asked whether the years of bilateral and multilateral aid have not been woefully misdirected?

African dependence upon aid in all its forms had become ingrained by the late 1980s and the growth of this dependency was largely due to the activities of the World Bank and the IMF's 'seal of approval' that conveniently provided individual donors with a shield when they might otherwise have been prevailed upon to pursue separate policies of their own. But though external factors have had a devastating impact upon African development this cannot excuse the shortcomings of African leaders and elites whose behaviour in the 1980s was far removed from the socialist rhetoric of the 1960s. Inefficiency, corruption, greed and self-serving elites have all played their part in Africa's woeful development performance. State structures are too often rigid and inefficient and provide minimal services to the public while the notion of a government working in the 'national interest' is far removed from the sectarian regimes that cater to specific groups (the clients of the ruling elite) and are sustained in power by their external backers, who provide aid, or withdraw it, depending upon how the rulers protect the national and corporate interests of the donors. As an African participant in a 1988 Nairobi conference put it succinctly: 'The development strategies followed by African countries during the two to three decades of their political independence has gradually led the continent into its present destitution... Worse still, all plans designed by those concerned with development, whether social or economic, indicated that without exception, the present policies, plans and strategies are incapable of bringing about any growth recovery in the foreseeable future.'[22]

The Decade in Retrospect

The word 'crisis' occurs all too often as the descriptive term for Africa's problems during the 1980s. The independence euphoria had passed; nationalist heroes had turned into repressive dictators; economies were stagnant and living standards falling; civil wars and violence in much of the continent appeared to be endemic; experiments in self-reliant socialism were collapsing in the face of subversive Western pressures. Yet, emerging from this depressing scenario were some hopeful signs as a new realism led African leaders at Addis Ababa in 1990 to assert that development was Africa's responsibility, as opposed to the donor world to which they had looked with such dependence up to that time. There were new moves to resuscitate a sense of African unity as the first tentative steps were taken to create an African economic union. After the long decades of struggle, apartheid in South Africa had at last collapsed and President de Klerk's speech of February 1990, in which he unbanned the ANC, and the subsequent release of Nelson Mandela heralded a new beginning for that deeply troubled country. Most encouraging of all, persistent demands for democracy were challenging the roles of autocratic rulers from one end of the continent to the other.

Wars and civil violence were a permanent feature of the Horn of Africa – Ethiopia, Eritrea, Somalia and Sudan; of Southern Africa – Angola, Mozambique, and South Africa destabilizing its neighbours as things fell apart within its own borders; while, more generally, the continent as a whole had become heavily militarized with the helmeted soldier in battle fatigues clasping his Kalashnikov one of the continent's most potent symbols. Ethnic or tribal divisions in many countries – the Congo, Zaïre, Ghana, Nigeria or Uganda – lay at the heart of divisions threatening national unity and in many cases had emerged as stronger forces than the appeals to nationalism of an earlier generation. In the Arab North the growth of Islamist fundamentalism posed new threats to stability while in countries such as Nigeria or Sudan clashes between Christians and Muslims were employed as political weapons by the power hungry.

Above all, it was in the economic sphere that Africa suffered endless setbacks, partly due to factors beyond its control, partly the result of mistaken policies. Few countries escaped what appeared to be a permanent economic blight upon the continent of rising debts, unfavourable terms of trade for export commodities, declining agricultural output (campaigns to persuade people to go 'back to the land' never worked), manipulation by aid donors, falling incomes, natural disasters and general stagnation for economies most of which had such small bases that they had no reserves to fall back upon. In a state of semi-permanent economic crisis, Africa turned to the international financial institutions (IFIs) – the World Bank and IMF – for assistance but did so with reluctance and suspicion. Few African countries either wished to apply the structural adjustment programmes (SAPs) so readily put forward by the World Bank and IMF or believed that these were in their best interests; but SAPs were the price to be paid for much-needed aid. There were exceptions and for a time during the 1980s the revolutionary Jerry Rawlings of Ghana became the 'darling' of the IFIs because he had accepted their adjustment programmes, though he came to doubt their efficacy later. Elsewhere, country after country, with varying degrees of reluctance, felt obliged to seek World Bank assistance because they could see no alternative way out of their economic troubles. One result of Africa's economic collapse was the end of most experiments in socialist self-reliance: countries such as Guinea or Mali that had attempted to break free of the West's economic stranglehold were drawn back into the capitalist fold, patted on the back for being sensible, and then, once more, provided with aid – strings attached. In Tanzania the collapse of Nyerere's *ujamaa* experiment, the continent's most famous attempt at home-grown socialism, signalled one more defeat for African self-reliance. On the other hand, Zaïre's Mobutu, a past master at brinkmanship, engineered a confrontation with Belgium, which he successfully blackmailed into providing more aid and forgiving a large slice of his debts because his country possessed a fabulous range of minerals that the West would do virtually anything to control. And so, at the end of the decade, as at the beginning, Africa remained woefully dependent upon the West for its economic survival and though its leaders were only too aware of their dependency they could not find a way to escape from it.

On the political front insistent demands by increasingly determined opponents of one-party, dictatorial or military rule moved the continent slowly yet inexorably towards more open, democratic forms of government. Reluctant autocrats were obliged to make concessions to these popular demands and tried to buy off their critics with limited moves towards full democracy; but the little they offered was never enough and increasingly determined masses lost their fear of oppressive leaders and began to force them, step by step, to concede power to the people. It was a relative process but by the end of the decade the signs were clear: the days of the charismatic, one-party 'dictator' were coming to an end. Progress, however, was slow and the counter-revolutionaries usually had the army on their side and the coup remained a principal weapon of political change. At the same time, there was fear of real radicalism and in West Africa Thomas Sankara of Burkina Faso and Jerry Rawlings of Ghana were regarded with deep distrust by their more conservative neighbours, as well as the West, because they might actually succeed in giving real power to the people. The efforts of the CIA to destabilize and discredit Rawlings more than justified the ongoing accusations of neo-colonialism against the West that were still made by African leaders.

At the beginning of the independence era Kwame Nkrumah had warned of Western neo-colonialism; at the end of the 1980s it was as strong or stronger than ever. Western reluctance to exert pressures upon the whites of Southern Africa, its use of aid as a weapon to force reluctant governments to fall in with Western economic strategies, its manipulation of the World Bank and IMF as instruments with which to extend economic control and its readiness to support any regime that did not threaten its vested interests all indicated how far Africa still had to progress before it could achieve real independence. As Africa entered the final decade of the twentieth century it was collectively weaker than at the beginning of the 1960s when the world waited to see what the new Africa would do. But the accumulated experience of 30 years of 'freedom', an awareness of the relentless pressures it faced from outside and a growing understanding that real advances could only come from within the continent opened up the possibility that the last years of the century could witness a different Africa begin to emerge.

PART IV

The 1990s

New Directions and
New Perceptions

CHAPTER THIRTY-ONE

The End of
the Cold War

The end of the Cold War was a global turning point: the bipolar world of the two superpowers that had provided neat parameters for lesser nations was replaced by a unipolar world dominated by the United States. The Third World necessarily disappeared and though it was not at once apparent, Africa, the poorest region of the Third World, found itself more marginalized than ever. Francis Fukuyama, who suggested in his book *The End of History and the Last Man* that the end of the Cold War and the collapse of Communism meant the spread everywhere of neo-liberal democracy, was propounding a concept whose attractions for a triumphalist West were anathema to much of the rest of the world. He said of Africa: 'In sub-Saharan Africa, African socialism and the post-colonial tradition of strong one-party states had become almost totally discredited by the end of the 1980s, as much of the region experienced economic collapse and civil war. Most disastrous was the experience of rigidly Marxist states like Ethiopia, Angola and Mozambique. Functioning democracies emerged in Botswana, The Gambia, Senegal, Mauritius, and Namibia, while authoritarian rulers were compelled to promise free elections in a host of other African countries.'[1] Another judgement suggested that if the Cold War had been 'won', the success had been achieved by the United States rallying a whole new international economic structure to the cause: 'When the American economy faltered, the European and Japanese economies which American policy had cultivated were able to take up the slack... We can already say that the real significance of the Cold War, which has dominated the lives of most people now alive, has been to play the role of catalyst in the creation of the extraordinary global economy which will dominate our future.'[2] What are described here are the foundations of the new orthodoxy of globalization that emerged in the 1990s. Meanwhile, as the author reminds us in passing, the wars of the Soviet succession in Africa's formerly 'Marxist' states of Angola, Mozambique, Ethiopia and Somalia could trace their origins to the Cold War. Throughout the Cold War 'the Soviet "threat" served four main purposes: it provided a pretext for Western military intervention and covert action abroad as "defence" against Soviet expansion; it allowed repressive governments to be supported on the excuse that they were bulwarks against communism; it allowed clampdowns on domestic dissent to take place by referring to infiltration by the enemy; and it allowed huge profits to be made by military industry, which produced the weapons demanded by a permanent arms race.'[3] The repressive and hypocritical nature of the West's response to the Cold War led, among other results, to the supply of vast quantities of arms to some of the world's most oppressive dictators as well as the support and sponsorship of anti-socialist guerrilla movements such as Savimbi's UNITA in Angola or direct military interventions to defend dictators against popular opposition – all in the name of freedom and democracy. Whatever else the Cold War achieved or failed to achieve in Africa, it left the continent awash with a range of deadly weapons. This was certainly the case in Somalia by the end of the 1980s. 'Mogadishu's arms markets had grown unchecked since the eve of the dictator's (Siad Barre) collapse, when merchants quickly took clients to inspect their clandestine weapons stock. Now the market teemed with criminals and self-appointed defenders and excited boys, the whole scene smelling of gun oil and testimony to an all-pervasive gun culture fed for decades by Italian, Soviet and American "friends". Here in microcosm was the true wealth of the Barre regime.'[4] The collapse of the Soviet-dominated system as well as the failure of socialist economies to achieve sustained development created an ideological vacuum. The West attempted to fill the vacuum and used such institutions as the World Bank and IMF as their instruments to this end as they attempted to persuade the former members of the now defunct Third World to accept the Western doctrines of neo-orthodox economics and democratic politics though whether they will succeed in any permanent sense in non-Western cultures remains to be seen. At least the Cold War had presented countries with a choice or choices.

> During the Cold War a country could be non-aligned, as many were, or it could, as some did, change its alignment from one side to another. The leaders of a country could make their choices in terms of their perceptions of their security interests, their calculations of the balance of power, and their ideological preferences. In the new world, however, cultural identity is the central factor shaping a country's associations and antagonisms.[5]

More than anything, for the small, weak countries that had made up the Third World, the end of the Cold War led to a loss of certainty: where did African states now stand in the new world order? The end of the Cold War confrontation meant the disappearance of the Third World and the emergence in its place of the South, which was the weaker, less influential half of the new North-South divide. Russia, the core of the old Soviet empire, joined the North as the new member of the Group of Seven, to transform it into the Group of Eight; Russia's former East European satellites queued up for membership of NATO and the EU; the Soviet Republics of Asia became members of the South and in this new line-up all the advantages lay with the advanced economies of the North while the South found that it was of even less account than it had been as the Third World when its members were able to exercise choices.

A brief period of euphoria followed the end of the Cold War and collapse of the Communist system.

> One widely articulated paradigm was based on the assumption that the end of the Cold War meant the end of significant conflict in global politics and the emergence of one relatively harmonious world... The expectation of harmony was widely shared. Political and intellectual leaders elaborated similar views. The Berlin wall had come down, communist regimes had collapsed, the United Nations was to assume a new importance, the former Cold War rivals would engage in 'partnership' and a 'grand bargain', peacekeeping and peacemaking would be the order of the day.[6]

Things did not quite work out like this; instead, the United States proclaimed a 'new world order'.

When in 1990 US President George Bush Snr proclaimed a 'new world order' he implied a world controlled by the North that in its turn would be led by a United States no longer constrained by its confrontation with the USSR. The South was soon to discover that, from its point of view, the passing of the Cold War had introduced a more difficult and dangerous era and this change became quickly apparent once the immediate euphoria had worn off. The end of the worldwide confrontation between the two superpowers and their allies alerted the former Third World to the realization of what in fact had already been emerging during the brutal, recession-dominated 1980s: that it was largely expendable. From about the middle of 1989 Third World leaders expressed increasing fears that their case – for aid, better trade conditions and a more equitable world order – would go by default as a triumphalist West turned its attention to the new and vastly more satisfying problem of reincorporating Eastern Europe, including the successor states to the Soviet Union, into the Western capitalist system.

Africa had been deeply affected by Cold War confrontations ever since 1956, when the USSR had agreed to finance the Aswan High Dam in Egypt after the

West withdrew its offers of aid, and in 1960, when the superpowers became involved in the collapse of the former Belgian Congo. Throughout the years of the Cold War the real threat to Western interests in Africa came not from Communism or the USSR but from nationalism, which among other policies threatened to take over colonial economies and run them on socialist lines. 'The principal "threat" they posed was to Western control over their economic resources – the fear that a country's resources might be primarily used to benefit its people. Nationalist movements and governments were invariably labelled as communist to justify action against them.'[7] Thus, the West opposed leaders that the African political process brought to the fore if they appeared likely to threaten Western interests. The Communist threat provided a convenient cloak under which to take action against them and ensure a more pliable leadership came to power. In South Africa the white apartheid regime, with help from Israel, made nuclear weapons, a fact that was known in Washington and approved by silence; the whites, after all, were on the right side in the Cold War and constantly proclaimed their fight against Communism. In 1993, President de Klerk announced that these weapons had been destroyed, but an interesting reflection on the nuclear question comes from Huntington as follows: 'The ability to build nuclear weapons cannot be destroyed, however, and it is possible that a post-apartheid government could construct a new nuclear arsenal to insure its role as the core state of Africa. Human rights, immigration, economic issues, and terrorism are also on the agenda between Africa and the West.'[8] That, indeed, poses a very different scenario about future African relations with the North of the new world order.

The Congo crisis of 1960–65 saw the first direct and major UN intervention in black Africa that included, at its peak, 20,000 troops as well as civilian administrators. The Prime Minister of newly independent Congo, Patrice Lumumba, had appealed to the UN to provide a peacekeeping force and the UN in responding hoped to prevent a US–USSR clash. The Cold War had come to black Africa. But the UN was not impartial. 'However, the UN secretary-general, Dag Hammarskjold, interpreted the UN mandate in accordance with Western neo-colonialist interests and the US Cold War imperative of preventing Soviet expansion in the Third World.' The first result of this UN stance was the murder of Lumumba in January 1961 for he, most obviously, was an enemy of Western economic and political interests. After five years of brutal civil war the coup of 24 November 1965 brought Mobutu to power and his emergence as a strong man was popular because he held out the promise of peace. The coup was backed if not entirely engineered by the CIA to ensure a Congo leader who would safeguard Western interests. 'As an externally backed autocracy, the Mobutu regime was a pure product of the Cold War. It originated in the cold strategic calculation of Western powers that leaders with no social or political base were preferable to those with strong national constituencies, to which they were accountable. Since the latter reflected the militant nationalism and anti-imperialist positions of their supporters, they had to be discredited in the eyes of world public opinion.'[9] Subsequently, the key US premise in supporting Mobutu for 30 years was the need to use the Congo as a base from which to promote Western interests in Central and Southern Africa. The consequence of this US support was 30 years of dictatorship and state kleptocracy and only at the end of the Cold War, when Western support for Mobutu wavered, was he obliged to give in to opposition demands for a sovereign national conference. Even so, he staved off any real democracy until his end in 1998. US and other Western support for this corrupt regime was presented as a necessary Cold War policy; in the post-Cold War era the need to uphold such regimes disappeared.

It became obvious during 1989 that the USSR was disengaging from its active support for African socialist regimes. In a series of meetings with the US through 1988 it helped broker the peace deal that led the Cubans to quit Angola and the South Africans to agree to Namibia's independence; and in 1989 Gorbachev informed the Ethiopian leader, Mengistu Haile Mariam, that he could expect no more arms or aid. Thus, by 1990 the Soviet Union had extricated itself from military involvement in Africa and the decline, or in Africa's case, disappearance, of superpower rivalry and confrontation meant that, almost overnight, Africa had become of far less interest, both strategically and economically, to the superpowers and, as one cynical commentator said, 'African states were transformed from Cold War pawns, into irrelevant clutter.' Africa soon began to realize that in the new post-Cold War climate it was being marginalized and that the West, since Russia could now be discounted, would only intervene or assist where it had direct economic interests or some specific strategic consideration, for example, to prevent large-scale emigration. It was a bleak prospect for countries that had come to rely upon economic support in the form of aid over the years of the Cold War. This reality was forced home in 1992 when the unwillingness of the North to help the South was highlighted in the UNDP's *Human Development Report* which contrasted the refusal of the West to write off Africa's debts with its readiness to reduce the debts of Poland by 50 per cent, despite the fact that Poland's per capita income was five times that of the average for Africa. The contrast was striking. Africa clearly faced a period of neglect.

Aid had been the principal link between the developed countries and Africa through the Cold War and African ability to exploit the rivalries of the two sides had assisted it to obtain substantially more aid than otherwise would have been the case; moreover, through the 1960s and 1970s the aid donors had provided assistance with very few restraints upon the manner in which it was used, with the result that recipients came to regard aid as an additional source of finance that gave them considerably more political room in which to manoeuvre than they could otherwise have hoped to wield. This state of affairs now came to an end. 'The end of the Cold War and the apparent triumph of liberal ideology have drastically altered the international context in which Africa is seeking to manage its present dependence.' As a result, the amount of aid that most Western countries are prepared to allocate to Africa has been radically reduced. 'Finally, the age of bilateral aid has faded, as most countries now adhere to World Bank lending principles.'[10] At least, during the Cold War African leaders were not simple pawns of the East–West power struggle but had learnt how to play the two sides off against each other as leaders such as Mobutu or Sassou-Nguesso had demonstrated, enhancing their own political positions in the process. After 1990 less aid was provided for the obviously dictatorial regimes but this did not mean more for reforming regimes. In fact there was an absolute decline: while aid flows to Africa had increased by 4 per cent a year during the 1980s, between 1990 and 1996 official financial assistance to sub-Saharan Africa fell in real terms by 21 per cent or US$3 billion. The conflict between East and West had largely been played out in the Third World and Western 'fear' of Communism was the principal motive for aid. Moreover, it was recognized that poverty was the most likely breeding ground for Communism so that development assistance was seen as a weapon for containing the spread of Communism while at the same time extending Western, capitalist interests. 'The Cold War then provided the main rationale for the war on poverty and legitimized the spending of vast resources on peoples in far-away places.'[11] The ingrained Western assumption that Third World countries would follow First World development patterns was part of the whole aid process. Only the alternative Communist model threatened to upset this development pattern that otherwise would deliver Third World countries into the capitalist camp. Once the Communist threat had been removed aid could be reduced since the recipient countries had nowhere else to go. Moreover, 'The collapse of Communism as an alternative development model rendered Western countries much more powerful *vis-à-vis* Africa and the South in general, and much more stringent conditions could now be attached to development assistance without fear of losing allies to Communist influence. It is at this juncture that we can locate the emergence of the good governance agenda.'[12] It should be added that prior to this juncture the West had shown little concern as to the kind of governance pursued by African countries, good or bad. Many regimes that lacked home support had been propped up by Western aid during the Cold War; they soon discovered that they no longer mattered. The more we examine the process of development, both during the Cold War and in its aftermath, the more apparent it becomes that Western aid was not designed to assist genuine development of recipients at all but to promote Western interests: first, negatively, in the sense of confining and controlling the alternative of Communism; and second, positively, in the sense of drawing the recipient countries into the Western economic system in which they would be little more than pawns.

Between 1962 and 1988 the bulk of US aid to Africa went to half a dozen countries such as Kenya, Liberia and Zaïre that were particularly friendly towards the United States but whose records on human rights or democratic principles did not bear close scrutiny. The same applied to Britain and France, the principal ex-colonial powers. The removal of the Soviet deterrence freed the United States in the exercise of violence, whose deployment would no longer be likely to lead to a superpower conflict. In the immediate aftermath of the Cold War an American couple who specialize in war themes commented as follows: 'Unfortunately for all concerned, friends and enemies alike, American elites, both political and military, are deeply disoriented not only by the end of the Cold War, but by the split-up of the Western alliance, the economic rise of Asia, and, above all, by the arrival of a knowledge-based economy whose global requirements are by no means clear to them.'[13] Working out what the Americans are after has become a priority for countries worldwide and not just in Africa. Its negative policies were easily discernible: 'Following the collapse of the Soviet Union, the US reduced or eliminated military aid to long-term allies like Kenya, Somalia, Liberia, Chad and Zaïre. The US further reduced its presence in Africa by closing nine aid missions and 15 intelligence posts and redirecting aid personnel to new priority assignments in Eastern Europe and the former Soviet Union.'[14] Following the US lead, Britain closed its embassies in Congo, Gabon and Liberia while France in especially ruthless fashion would not send troops in 1990 to help stop the army and air force mutiny in Côte d'Ivoire, the most faithfully pro-France of all its former colonies under the aged Félix Houphouët-Boigny. France was coming to regard its African allies as an economic liability and so France, along with Britain and the US, called for political and economic liberalization.

Once the Cold War was over the only effective alternative economic policy to the Western model, the Soviet one, had been discredited and had collapsed. Moreover, no African country was sufficiently independent to embark upon a development path of its own that did not require, or could dispense with, Western aid. The position is explained succinctly as follows: 'Alternative economic policies have become marginalized or come to be regarded as unfeasible, and an influential body of opinion now holds that although the imposition of structural adjustment programmes has caused widespread suffering and might jeopardize the survival chances of democracy, African countries have in reality no other option.'[15] This indeed places Africa in a strait-jacket and only two or three countries – South Africa, Nigeria, perhaps Egypt – have any chance of breaking free of such an externally imposed system. The same author, quoted above, continues: 'Some countries – for example, Uganda and Mozambique – are finding that the conditions applied by the IMF to control money supply and reduce government deficits prevent them using additional assistance to fund recurrent costs, including social development expenditures. The effect is that if extra funds are forthcoming from donors, the rules require these to be channelled into uses other than enhancing and expanding services for the poor.' A decade of structural adjustment programmes had not produced a single convincing success in terms of development and since that is the case it is time that recipients of these programmes, usually unwilling recipients, understood that the purpose of such programmes is to ensure that the donors get their money back rather than to achieve any development *per se*. And so we come to the new orthodoxy of the 1990s: good governance.

Western support for the concept of good governance only appeared as the Cold War came to an end and it appeared with quite remarkable speed. The Communist alternative effectively collapsed in 1989 and by mid-1990 the principal concepts being advanced by the Western donors were good governance linked to aid conditionality. Unsurprisingly, the West's sudden belief in good governance was not matched by the African leaders, who were expected to accept new principles of government that would reduce their power or sideline them altogether; nor were the masses, who were becoming increasingly restless under the old one-party autocratic systems and revolting against them, likely to embrace good governance as it was so suddenly thrust upon them by their former exploiters. Democracy would be greatly assisted if first the donors withdrew their support from the dictators, then it might be possible to consider good governance and what was meant by it as opposed to the kind of democracy that the people themselves would like to institute. In any case, it was soon obvious that good governance was a tool to be used for the exercise of continuing control over recipient countries. In effect, they were told, only if they accepted good governance as the West defined it could they expect continuing development assistance. Thus, Africa was still to be reformed and developed by the advanced economies of the West in ways that suited its purposes. In this way the donors, having 'won' the Cold War, could now move onto a new platform of moral high ground from which to dispense development and democracy to Africa. The assumptions behind the Western proposed good governance are entirely arrogant: Africa's performance has to be constantly vetted though there is no one to vet the behaviour of the West. Not only was this sudden switch to good governance as the guiding principle of its relations with Africa reminiscent of the high hypocrisy of nineteenth-century missionary endeavour, but the West legitimized its hypocrisy by organizing a high-powered Commission on Global Governance composed of the great and the good, from both sides of the divide, to prepare a report *Our Global Neighbourhood* that would apply to the South but clearly not to the North whose powerful members would continue to go their own ways. The report is worth reading if only for the range of proposals that will automatically be ignored, as were earlier proposals in other publications such as the Brandt Report of 1980.

Following a meeting in Stockholm in 1991, a document was produced entitled *Common Responsibility in the 1990s: The Stockholm Initiative on Global Security and Governance* which, in its turn, led to the establishment of the Commission on Global Governance chaired jointly by Ingmar Carlsson of Sweden and Shridath Ramphal, the former Secretary-General of the Commonwealth, from Guyana. Their report, *Our Global Neighbourhood*, was published in 1995. By the time the report appeared – it was to be a guide for the post-Cold War conduct of international relations – there had already occurred the first Gulf War of 1991, ethnic cleansing in the Balkans, the breakdown of the international rescue operation in Somalia and the massive genocide in Rwanda. Optimistically, the report claimed, 'There is no alternative to working together and using collective power to create a better world' although immediate post-Cold War behaviour patterns would suggest otherwise. As with other such reports, the information and statistics provided make fascinating reading. Thus, for example, between 1945 and 1989 there were 138 wars causing 23 million deaths, all fought in the Third World; and between 1970 and the end of the Cold War in 1989 weapons worth US$168 billion were transferred to the Middle East, US$65 billion worth to Africa, US$61 billion worth to the Far East, US$50 billion worth to South Asia and US$44 billion worth to Latin America. The main suppliers of these arms were the US and the USSR, accounting between them for 69 per cent, followed by Britain, France and West Germany. In this way these five leading powers had armed and thereby facilitated wars in those regions. The implied question was simply, would they now desist from this lucrative trade? *Our Global Neighbourhood* is in the tradition of many UN documents, including its original Charter, the Pearson Report and the Brandt Report, and by implication it asks whether the world of the 'new order' would behave any better or any differently to that of the Cold War, which had just passed. As it pointed out, realistically and somewhat hopelessly:

When the Cold War ended in 1989, it appeared reasonable to contemplate a serious, new look at prospects for demilitarizing international relations. Cold War rivalry – which had fuelled military budgets, powered the search for new weapons' technologies, and fastened a reliance on military solutions to conflicts – was over, and it seemed that a new era of global harmony might be possible. That amount of euphoria was short lived, however. Although the tide of democracy was rising, it could not stem the subsequent outbreak of a host of cruel and devastating civil conflicts. In 1991 and 1992, 11 major wars broke out and the human death toll in all 29 of the ongoing wars reached six million.[16]

At that point in time, however, there seemed to be no alternative to a Western-dominated, liberal economic democratic system for all since the collapse of the Communist system and the general destruction of its credibility lent great weight to Western arguments that 'democracy', preferably as advanced by the West, was the only political answer to the world's many problems.

Yet it soon became plain that the now all-powerful West, led by the United States, was less interested in either development or democracy when these values were conceived entirely on behalf of the people they affected, despite all its preaching about them over the years, than it was in exercising control over their economies so that these should be firmly drawn into the Western system by means of globalization. Control and not freedom was what the West sought and it soon came to see that 'the maintenance of order requires a lowering of newly acquired expectations and levels of political activity'.[17]

In the wake of the Cold War new orthodoxies and attitudes surfaced in the West: racism directed at immigrants, the acceptance that the poor are 'always with us' that downgraded the idea of eliminating poverty with development assistance, and demands for good governance, ostensibly as a prelude for aid, in fact as an argument for interference and intervention. Part of the helplessness of Africa as well as the contempt for its plight that surfaces so easily in the West was illustrated early in 1992 by the extraordinary revelation that the World Bank's chief economist had proposed increased pollution for Africa. In an internal Bank memorandum Lawrence Summers suggested: 'I've always thought under-populated countries in Africa are vastly under-polluted. Shouldn't the World Bank be encouraging *more* migration of the dirty industries [to such countries]? I think the economic logic behind dumping toxic waste in the lowest-wage countries is impeccable.'[18] Subsequent apologies by the Bank and the claim by Summers himself that he was merely indulging in an intellectual exercise to sharpen debate could not erase the effect of this appalling indiscretion. As *The Economist* pointed out, Summers was equating the value of human life with income per head, on which basis he could conclude that 'one

Englishman is worth the lives of 100 Indians'. When such attitudes surface in the World Bank it is hardly surprising that such institutions had become so distrusted in the Third World, and continued to be distrusted by the new South. The West may have triumphed in the Cold War and, as a consequence, adopted a lofty language about spreading democracy and good governance. Under the surface, and sometimes blatantly on the surface, its attitudes were arrogant and neo-imperialist.

South Africa:
The Last Hero

The prologue to the 1994 elections lasted for four years and was a period of tortuous political infighting, violence and double-dealing before the final surrender of power by the whites. After the initial excitement that greeted President de Klerk's speech of 2 February 1990 and the subsequent release of Nelson Mandela, the year became more troubled as both sides manoeuvred for political advantage, although the government repealed the Separate Amenities Act and said it did not regard independence for the six non-independent homelands as a continuing option. Towards the end of the year, Oliver Tambo, the ANC's President-in-exile for 30 years, finally returned to South Africa. On 17 March 1990, in a move to counter white opposition to his policy, de Klerk called a nationwide white referendum on his reform policy and negotiations with the ANC, and said he would resign if he lost. As Mandela commented: 'In the end 69 per cent of the white voters supported negotiations, giving de Klerk a great victory. He felt vindicated; I think the margin even swelled his head a bit. His hand was strengthened, and as a result, the Nationalists toughened their negotiating position. This was a dangerous strategy.'[1] Despite the hopes for change that had been raised it was a year of violence. Already, by March 1990 more than 3,000 people had been killed in the preceding three years in Inkatha–UDF clashes. Mandela saw it as his priority to stop the killing. That March the death toll was 230 with hundreds more wounded, hundreds of houses destroyed and 12,500 people forced to flee to refugee centres. Talks between Mandela and Buthelezi to stop the violence were cancelled as a result of ANC pressure, for its distrust of Buthelezi was profound. Subsequent anti-government demonstrations were met by severe police violence, resulting in many deaths, while continuing black-black violence in Natal, between Inkatha and ANC supporters, led to over 1,000 deaths in the first half of the year. During July, August and September Inkatha launched an offensive against the ANC in the Transvaal townships (leading to another 800 deaths) and obliging the government to launch Operation Iron Fist. There were also right wing demonstrations against the government by the Conservative Party and the *Afrikaanse Weerstandsbeweging* (AWB) (Afrikaner Resistance Movement). Buthelezi argued that he was a national leader who transcended the tribal divides of South Africa, although the evidence did not support his claim. Since he did not command support like Mandela, his control of Inkatha was vital because it enabled him to cause sufficient trouble to ensure a place for himself at the negotiating table. By 1990 there was clear evidence that Inkatha had earlier received support from the government as an inducement to attack the UDF and ANC so as to hold them in check. The government was then working to create a Third Force to disrupt negotiations by fermenting Inkatha–ANC violence. The possibility of a right-wing white backlash was always present. There was the incursion by Eugene Terre'Blanche and his AWB into Bophutatswana, which had the contrary effect of ending homeland rule, while in 1994 Gen. Viljoen warned Mandela of a plot by white extremists to organize an uprising. In May the ANC agreed to assist the government in curbing violence and in August it agreed to end the armed struggle (launched in 1961) 'in the interests of moving as speedily as possible towards a negotiated peaceful political settlement'. In return, the government released political prisoners, agreed to the return of exiles and amended the security legislation. Despite these moves, deaths at the hands of the police were higher in 1990 than in earlier years: between 2 February and 31 July 129 people were killed by the police and in one incident in March at Sebokeng township 17 people were killed and 400 injured.

The activities of the hard right wing whites added to the unrest and violence. The Conservative Party (CP) threatened strikes and demonstrations and on 26 May at a rally of 50,000 whites at the Voortrekker Monument outside Pretoria their leadership urged them to fight. The homelands, originally referred to as Bantustans, had been established under a number of acts from 1951 to the 1971 Bantu Homelands Constitution Act. Four homelands had been declared independent by South Africa: Transkei (26 October 1976), Bophutatswana (6 December 1977), Venda (13 September 1979) and Ciskei (4 December 1981). None of the four had been recognized as independent by the international community. The other six homelands were Lebowa, Gazankulu, KwaZulu, Qwaqwa, KwaNdebele and KaNgwane. De Klerk had already said that independence for the remaining six was no longer on the political agenda and in fact their brief histories as symbols of division under apartheid were about to be terminated.

The rest of the apartheid laws were repealed during 1991, fighting between Inkatha and the ANC continued and the government was forced to admit that it had previously financed Inkatha, which was a devastating blow to Buthelezi's standing. The ANC held a conference with 2,500 delegates attending in July at which Mandela was elected President. Another 1,200 deaths resulted from

ANC–Inkatha fighting during the first half of the year and though several attempts to achieve an accord between the two were tried all failed and the violence continued. Over 20–21 December the all-party conference, the Convention for a Democratic South Africa (CODESA), met in Johannesburg with representatives of 19 political organizations including the government present, although it was boycotted by right-wing white groups, the Azanian People's Organization (AZAPO) and the Pan-Africanist Congress (PAC). The world community began to ease sanctions against South Africa while the groundwork was being laid for substantive talks between government and the various opposition political parties, though manoeuvring by government led to charges of bad faith from the ANC. Township violence continued through the year and between July 1990 and August 1991 there were 2,000 violent deaths from Inkatha–ANC clashes, 1,200 of these dating from January 1991. In August, 2,000 members of the AWB demonstrated against a National Party meeting being addressed by de Klerk; the police opened fire on the demonstrators and killed one. In an earlier period Verwoerd had taken pains to conciliate English-speaking South Africans, correctly judging that most had as little enthusiasm for majority rule as any Afrikaner. 'Indeed, as late as 1991, when the ANC was clearly going to be a major force in any government, only 7 per cent of English-speakers (as against 5 per cent of Afrikaners; hardly a major difference) wanted a normal parliamentary system in which blacks had full rights.'[2]

In May 1992, after a four-month interruption, the multiparty conference held its second plenary session at the World Trade Center. Known as CODESA 2, the talks had been preceded by secret meetings between ANC and government negotiators and a final session between Mandela and de Klerk; yet no agreement was reached. According to Mandela, the government seemed to think that the longer the ANC had to wait, the more support it would lose. CODESA 2 broke down over four issues: the government's insistence upon an unacceptably high percentage of votes in the assembly to approve the constitution (a back-door veto); entrenched regional powers that would bind a future constitution; an undemocratic and unelected senate that had veto power over legislation from the main chamber; and a determination to make an interim constitution negotiated by the Convention into a permanent constitution.[3] There now occurred a tragedy that could have led to catastrophe. 'In May 1992 the much-admired young leader of the communists Chris Hani was murdered by two far-right gunmen, one of whom, Clive Derby-Lewis, had been a Conservative Party MP. Hani had, as Mandela had hoped, abandoned his earlier Stalinist hard line in favour of a democratic socialist attitude, and commanded the allegiance and affection of the young to a degree second only to Mandela himself. His death, and the manner of it, caused an outburst of grief and anger.'[4]

The ANC mounted a defiance campaign in August at a time when the gulf between de Klerk and Mandela appeared to be widening alarmingly. Then, on 7 September, 70,000 ANC protesters marched to the main stadium in Bisho, Ciskei, and when a group of marchers attempted to run through an opening in a fence in order to take a different path to the town, the poorly trained homeland troops opened fire on the marchers killing 29 and wounding over 200. Now Bisho and its homeland defenders became a byword for brutality. Then on 26 September, and not before time, de Klerk and Mandela met: they signed a Record of Understanding that set the mould for subsequent negotiations. It established an independent body to review police actions, created a mechanism to fence in the hostels and banned the display of 'traditional weapons' at rallies. Its real importance, however, was to break the constitutional deadlock of CODESA 2. The government finally agreed to accept a single elected constitutional assembly which would adopt a new constitution and serve as a transitional legislature for the new government. In response, Inkatha withdrew from all government/ANC negotiations. In November the National Executive Committee of the ANC agreed a power-sharing deal that would allow all parties gaining 5 per cent or more votes a share in the cabinet of national unity. It was during this hectic year that Mandela and his wife Winnie, who had become both notorious for her behaviour and a power in her own right, agreed to separate. An estimate of July 1992 put at 7,000 deaths in township violence since de Klerk's speech of 2 February 1990. During the first six months of 1992 there had been 1,181 deaths according to the police although Human Rights Watch set the figure for deaths to 30 September 1992 at 2,762. Inkatha was seen as the main aggressor. Despite the deep suspicion of each other that led to the breakdown of talks, it was becoming clear that the ANC and the government needed each other if a workable political solution was to be found. Despite repeated setbacks through 1992, continuing violence, periodic expressions of distrust or bad faith from either side and ANC accusations that de Klerk was unable to control either the police or military, who were seen to be well to the right of government, nevertheless, by February 1993 the ANC and government appeared to have worked out a formula for advance. Yet while they were close to agreeing constitutional arrangements, the question of what role Buthelezi should play became more and more important. It seemed at that time that he was determined to wreck any agreement since he saw himself being marginalized because his Inkatha power base, which represented only a part of the Zulu nation, was too small to carry national weight.

'Although few people will remember 3 June 1993,' Mandela was to write, 'it was a landmark in South African history. On that day, after months of negotiations at the World Trade Center, the multiparty forum voted to set a date for the country's first national non-racial, one-person-one vote election: 27 April 1994. For the first time in South African history, the black majority would go to the polls to elect their own leaders.'[5] In July 1993 the multiparty forum agreed on a first draft of an interim constitution. Elections to regional assemblies would take place at the same time as national elections and the regional bodies could draw up their own constitutions consistent with the national constitution. Chief Buthelezi wanted a constitution drawn up before the elections. A second draft interim constitution that August gave greater powers to the regions but failed to placate either Buthelezi or the Conservative Party, with the latter describing the resolutions as hostile to Afrikaner interests. A group calling itself the Afrikaner Volksfront, led by Gen. Constand Viljoen – a former Chief of the South African Defence Force – was now formed to unite conservative white organizations around the idea of a *volkstaat* or white homeland. In October parliament passed legislation to create a transitional executive council. Mandela made a direct appeal to the United Nations with the result that the UN, the US and the Commonwealth withdrew all economic sanctions against South Africa. The national territory of South Africa was re-divided into nine regions: Western Cape, Eastern Cape, Northern Cape, Orange Free State (which became the Free State in 1995), Northwest, KwaZulu/Natal, Eastern Transvaal (later Mpumalanga), Northern Transvaal (later Northern province) and PWV (Pretoria, Witwatersrand and Vereeniging – later Gauteng).The homelands were to be absorbed into these new regions. The central parliament was to comprise a house of assembly of 400 members elected by proportional representation, half on national and half on regional lists, while an upper house of 90 would be chosen by the regional assemblies. The Interim Constitution, under which South Africa was to be governed for five years from the April 1994 elections, was finally endorsed on 18 November 1993 by the delegates to the multiparty negotiations. Chief Buthelezi, however, warned that the Inkatha Freedom Party (IFP) would resist the Interim Constitution and reduce it to the 'rubble of history'. In December the Transitional Executive Council (TEC) was established to give the African majority a legal role in central government for the first time in the country's history. It was opposed by the Freedom Alliance consisting of Inkatha, the Conservative Party under Ferdi Hartzenburg, and Gen. Viljoen of the Afrikaner Volksfront, as well as the leaders of the two nominally independent homelands, Lucas Mangope of Bophutatswana and Joshua Oupa Gqoza of Ciskei. Despite this opposition, it was agreed that South Africa would be ruled for a five-year interim period after its first one-person-one-vote election by a Government of National Unity (GNU) comprising five parties – the ANC, the NP, the PAC, the CP and Buthelezi's IFP – with Nelson Mandela as President. According to calculations made at the time a 22-member cabinet would consist of 14 ANC ministers, four NP, two PAC and one each for the other two parties. 'The new constitution, approved on 18 November 1993, provided for universal suffrage and a cabinet constitution, and was – once more in an echo of the Act of Union – only capable of amendment by a two-thirds majority of the popular vote. It was, all things considered, an extraordinary achievement, the voluntary relinquishment of power (with, certainly, internal violence and outside pressures acting as potent incentives) by the white minority... South Africa emerged from the shadow of apartheid badly injured, but alive.'[6] There were still hurdles to overcome.

Early in 1994 the government and the ANC held talks with the Freedom Alliance to persuade its various member groups to take part in the elections, but without success. Ciskei, however, subsequently broke ranks and then on 14 January withdrew from the Alliance. Then the PAC suspended the activities of its armed wing, the Azanian People's Liberation Army (APLA), and at the deadline finally said it would take part in the elections. On 29 January the TEC announced plans for a 10,000-strong national peacekeeping force. In mid-March the militant section of the Afrikaner extreme right suffered a severe reverse. The Bophutatswana army and police mutinied against Chief Mangope who fled. Some 2,000 Afrikaner extremists then invaded Bophutatswana to restore Mangope and to take over all or part of the homeland for a *Boerestaat*. However, the Bophutatswana forces attacked the Afrikaner invaders and de Klerk sent units of the South African army to restore order. Buthelezi, however, held out for the first three months of 1994 and fears that Inkatha could wreck the elections continued into mid-April by which time 10,000 people had died in the violence of the preceding four years. Finally, on 19 April, Buthelezi dropped his opposition to the elections and agreed to let his followers take part. He did so despite having failed to obtain most of the 'guarantees' he had sought though it was agreed that the Zulu monarchy should be legally accommodated in the provincial government. Over the last seven days leading up to the elections the killings stopped and the elections took place in an uninterrupted calm. 'It was a powerfully impressive spectacle, witnessed with keen interest by the rest of the world, to see millions of South Africans of all races queuing patiently together to register their votes.'[7] During the run-up to the elections the ANC had prepared its *Reconstruction and Development Programme* (RDP), an ambitious blueprint for social change covering jobs, housing, health, free education, the redistribution of land, cuts in food taxes and affirmative action, and a simpler election version called *A Better Life for All*. The party was all too aware of the high expectations of the people that it would have to satisfy. Mandela had already embarked upon his mission to win over the whites: 'I told white audiences that we needed them and did not want them to leave the country. They were South Africans just like ourselves and this was their land too. I would not mince words about the horrors of apartheid, but I said, over and over, that we should forget the past and concentrate on building a better future for all.'[8]

In the elections the ANC won 62 per cent of the vote, the NP 20 per cent and control of Western Cape, Inkatha 10 per cent and was 'credited' with a 51 per cent victory in KwaZulu/Natal. On 9 May the assembly elected Mandela as President of South Africa. Thabo Mbeki was elected First Vice-President, F. W. de Klerk Second Vice-President. On 10 May, Mandela was inaugurated as President of South Africa in the court of the Union Buildings in Pretoria in the presence of the largest gathering ever of international leaders the country had seen. In his speech Mandela said: 'We, who were outlaws not so long ago, have today been given the rare privilege to be host to the nations of the world on our own soil. We thank all of our distinguished international guests for having come to take possession with the people of our country of what is, after all, a common victory for justice, for peace, for human dignity.' South Africa then joined the OAU, rejoined the Commonwealth, which it had left in 1961, joined the Southern African Development Community (SADC), previously the SADCC, and resumed its UN seat. In September 1994 Britain's Prime Minister John Major made an official visit to South Africa and in March 1995 the Queen made a state visit followed by a return state visit to Britain by Mandela in July 1996.

The hard tasks now had to be tackled. 'From the moment the results were in and it was apparent that the ANC was to form the government, I saw my mission as one of preaching reconciliation, of binding the wounds of the country, of engendering trust and confidence.'[9] At the grassroots the problems were huge. As a member of Alexandra township responded to a question about the new government's record in December 1994: 'Satisfied? How can you ask if I am satisfied with this government?' And as another said: 'The government must start doing something concrete.'[10] During the apartheid years the white minority in South Africa held all the levers of political and economic power and could be seen as an extension of the rich developed North set down in a poor country of the South and able to control the black majority by means of the apparatus of apartheid. Following the elections of April 1994 this situation was turned on its head: South Africa became (what it always was in fact) a poor developing country with a rich white elite in the middle of it. The *Human Development Report 1998* highlighted the extent of the economic divide between black and white in South Africa. Under apartheid, consumption patterns of black and white were separated – by both unequal income distribution, but also by unequal access to basic services and suppression of living standards. Government house building came to a halt in the early 1980s at a time when the housing backlog was estimated at about 600,000 units. By 1998 it was 2.5 million units. Unequal access to public infrastructure meant the black population was barely able to meet basic needs. Among top objectives for the new South Africa was to meet basic needs for all – housing, water, transport, electricity, telecommunications, a clean and healthy environment, nutrition, health care and jobs. In 1995 alone there was a marked increase in access to services among black households: the share with electricity increased from 37 per cent to 51 per cent, those with a telephone from 12 per cent to 14 per cent, those with piped water from 27 per cent to 33 per cent, those with a flush toilet or latrine from 46 per cent to 51 per cent and those with refuse removal by the local authority from 37 per cent to 43 per cent. 'In one survey, however, pensioners said electricity might consume up to a quarter of their income, yet they could no longer imagine living without it. And because other spending could not be cut, they sought credit.'[11]

The implementation of the RDP was far more difficult than had been anticipated: there were neither the resources nor the personnel to implement it in full and in 1996 the Ministry for RDP was abolished. Joe Slovo, the first minister of housing, died in January 1995 and though he had tried to provide mass housing, his programme, as well as that to extend electricity, had partly stalled. The government had to rethink its plans and in June 1996 Trevor Manuel, the Minister of Finance, announced a new plan for growth, employment and redistribution (GEAR) which emphasized the privatization of state assets. GEAR was criticized by both COSATU and the Communist Party because it had been adopted without debate or consultation and would mean fewer jobs would be created. On 9 May 1996 de Klerk announced that the National Party would withdraw from the GNU. His NP cabinet colleagues were shocked and Leon Wessels thought he had not tried hard enough to make the GNU work. Some ANC ministers were also angry and suggested, 'Breaking it up was one of de Klerk's greatest disservices to the country.'[12] Although de Klerk can take credit for the realistic and pragmatic way he ended apartheid, he was not possessed of any greatness of character. The withdrawal of the NP left Mbeki as sole Vice-President and by this time he had taken over most aspects of running the country as Mandela became increasingly aloof from day-to-day government. He saw the break with the Afrikaners as inevitable and useful. And though Mandela had no regrets about the departure of de Klerk, he wanted to bring his old black rivals of Inkatha and the PAC into power-sharing. He was acutely aware of how narrowly South Africa had escaped civil war in 1992–94 and saw increasingly that his role should be that of peacemaker. Mbeki's position was now increasingly secure and Mandela was treating him as his political heir. Cyril Ramophosa, his chief rival who had overseen the preparation of the constitution, left parliament to become Deputy Chairman of New African Investments Ltd (NAIL). He denied a serious clash with Mbeki and said he would return to politics in 10 years. A second rival, Tokyo Sexwale, the Premier of Gauteng, had also been a contender for president but had been sidelined by Mbeki and quit politics in 1997 for business.

The Truth and Reconciliation Commission (TRC), which was set up in 1995 under the chairmanship of Archbishop Desmond Tutu, was always bound to be controversial. It was also cathartic, not just for those who came before it but also for others who watched its proceedings. It was not about justice, though many Africans who had suffered under apartheid must have found this difficult to understand, but about reconciliation by persuading people to admit their crimes against their fellows. One failing of the TRC was its inability to investigate the human rights abuses that South Africans had committed in neighbouring countries such as Namibia. Many members of the ANC thought that the formula, finally agreed by de Klerk, that the Commission could grant individuals amnesties on condition they showed their actions had been politically motivated, was far too generous. Two years of hearings revealed horrific stories of torture and assassination – more than many had imagined – yet despite these revelations de Klerk still denied that the government had given the security forces a licence to kill.[13] The report of the TRC provides a benchmark against which future white behaviour as well as the conduct of governments may be judged. It is a historic record of a brutal regime whose primary motive was to maintain a racial minority in power. And it is a reminder of how easily power and the desire to retain it can corrupt and destroy a people's integrity. How much this exercise in exposing truths that a majority of the whites wished only to hide or ignore will assist the new South Africa to forge a racially integrated future remains to be seen. Throughout the sittings of the TRC it was clear that a new non-racial South Africa was an ideal that had yet to be created. The gaps remained – the poverty statistics that separated the majority from the minority – and though black Africans may have gained confidence since the elections of 1994, they have not, in most cases, gained very much else. Whites, who appear to think they have made the supreme sacrifice by the act of rejecting apartheid, behave as though there is nothing else they can do, complaining instead that they are at risk from mounting violence.

Inevitably, in the years from 1994 there were racial incidents – whites objecting to blacks coming to 'their' schools, the ratepayers of Johannesburg's wealthiest suburb of Sandton objecting to an increase in rates despite the poverty of nearby townships, objections to affirmative action and so on. The resistance of hard-line former supporters of apartheid was, perhaps, understandable or at any rate to be expected. Nonetheless, it was and remains essential for the wealthy, privileged whites to realize that if the new South Africa is to work they have to give to it more than the grudging acceptance of the end of apartheid. A press article of July 1995, began as follows: 'Like the nobles of feudal Europe, white South Africans are retreating behind fortifications. On the leafy avenues in Johannesburg's richer suburbs, defensive walls around the houses are climbing upwards, usually topped off with what South Africans call siege architecture: crenellations, electric fencing or just plain razor wire.'[14]

Reconciliation in the light of the apartheid years could be neither easy nor simple. The thousands of victims of torture and those who had lost relatives and friends did not want forgiveness to obliterate what had happened. Mandela believed that apart from Hitler's genocide of the Jews, 'there is no evil that has been so condemned by the entire world as apartheid'.[15] Mandela went out of his way to meet former enemies and his charisma and charm clearly bowled many of them over, though not Botha, the old 'crocodile'. He made his peace with the Afrikaner churches: 'The men all wanted to touch me. The women all wanted to kiss me. The children all wanted to hang on my legs.' He gave a lunch for Percy Yutar, the Rivonia trial prosecutor who had been renowned for his vindictive, hectoring tirades, and Yutar said of the occasion: 'It shows the great humility of this saintly man.'[16] Forgiveness for most people is very hard but Mandela achieved it in a spectacular fashion that contributed enormously to the South African transition.

It was inevitable that as the ANC settled into its role as the ruling party of South Africa, strains would develop with its former allies, COSATU and the SACP. The issue most likely to cause tensions was that of free market growth and its impact upon the large numbers of unemployed, with COSATU attacking the GEAR strategy as 'Thatcherite'. The greatest concern of ordinary members of the ANC, its wide constituency throughout the country and its two allies – COSATU and the Communist Party – was how the party would deliver services, shelter, employment, alleviation of poverty, safety and security effectively. More ominous for future harmony was the suggestion advanced in 1997 (prior to the ANC conference) by Peter Mokaba, who was a deputy minister and member of the ANC executive committee, that the Communist Party should be dropped from the tripartite alliance and that the ANC should be converted into a party of free market capitalism. The Communist leader, Charles Nqakula, who could only take 14 delegates to the ANC national conference as non-voting members, claimed that many ANC members were also card-carrying members of the Communist Party. As he said on the eve of the conference: 'We have to ensure the ANC retains its character as a movement of workers and poor people in rural areas and townships. At the same time, we have to jealously consolidate the space the ANC has created in its ranks for the progressive democrats. As party delegates, as members of the movement, we have to make sure the ANC does not veer away from its original mission of raising the standard of living of the disadvantaged.'[17] Times, however, were changing, as Nqakula had rightly feared. The ANC was moving away from the championship of the poor and dispossessed and it was clear that its pragmatic free market economic policy would remain in place. Others, too, feared its flirtation with capitalism, the 'secret weapon' of the whites. Mandela's parting speech as President of the ANC at the December 1997 conference was in part, perhaps, designed to spare Mbeki the need to say such things. He said the ANC was being thwarted by those 'committed to the maintenance of white privilege' and he warned against the dangers of corruption and greed; he attacked other African countries where 'predatory elites that have thrived on the basis of looting the national wealth', and he called for a moral renewal to achieve an African renaissance. He warned against political careerism to make money and he criticized white businessmen for the slow pace of transformation and black empowerment. He blamed the media for perpetuating old hierarchies and neglecting black viewpoints. He warned against an Afrikaner 'counter revolutionary network' trying to subvert the economy and use crime to make South Africa ungovernable. There was a predictable white press reaction in both South Africa and Britain, claiming that Mandela had destroyed his earlier reputation for conciliation, yet the fury of the reaction was only commensurate with the accuracy of Mandela's accusations.

Mandela's foreign policy was a curious blend of straightforward resolve and naïve hopefulness that the reconciliation, which he had practised so successfully in South Africa, could work as easily elsewhere on the continent. Refreshingly, he refused point blank to give in to American pressures when he insisted upon allowing visits from the heads of state of Cuba, Iran and Libya, for those three countries, on Washington's black list for supporting terrorism, had each given aid to the ANC in the dark days when apartheid appeared to be set in stone. It was a duty he owed and repaid. He was criticized for not applying far greater pressure to the military regime of Gen. Abacha in Nigeria to prevent the execution of Ken Saro-Wiwa in 1995. He argued for a 'softly softly' approach although later he denounced the Nigerian government when the country had been suspended from the Commonwealth. He attempted to mediate a peace in the Congo when Laurent Kabila's forces were in striking distance of taking Kinshasa and ousting Mobutu and appeared not to understand the geopolitics of the situation on the ground. He also wanted to mediate with Indonesia about the war in East Timor and the endless war in Sudan. On the other hand, a compliment to the emergence of a democratic South Africa, the country played host to the Non-Aligned Movement summit in 1998 and the biennial Commonwealth Summit in 1999, both of which were held in Durban.

Ex-President de Klerk now bowed out of politics. Back in 1989, when he became President, he had adopted a pragmatic approach to South Africa's race divide for by then apartheid was clearly untenable any longer as a policy. He was deeply influenced in his decision to come to terms with the African majority by external events and 'According to Willem (de Klerk's brother), the principal reasons for F. W. de Klerk's dramatic change of policy were the end of the Cold War, which removed both the (largely illusory) Soviet threat and the (rapidly crumbling) US support'.[18] On a visit to Britain in 1997 de Klerk defended his record and claimed that under his leadership the NP abolished apartheid. In August 1997 he resigned the leadership of the NP leaving a party deeply divided. He denied he had ever thought Africans inferior to whites, only different: 'The two things are not the same. Times have changed and we now firmly believe in a single, unified state. But 20 years ago the hope was for separate development, parallel improvements for all races.' And waxing eloquent about the future, he argued: 'The whole continent needs a success. We can provide it. I don't want to import pollution, but we have vast open spaces. They provide a fine environment for basic industry. We can provide the infrastructure for the whole continent. We can provide the building industry with bricks and not just copper but copper wire and the covering of copper wire. We are going to privatize the mines. The commercial centre of Africa will soon be neither London nor Paris but Johannesburg.'[19] It was an odd swansong and somehow suggested that deep down de Klerk thought the whites were still running South Africa. Following de Klerk's resignation, the National Party continued on its downward slope until it finally merged with the ANC.

The economy was the key to the future. Just as the economic imperatives of development had persuaded the white business community to abandon apartheid so in the post-apartheid age its correct management would provide the means whereby the expectations of the people could be met. The South African economy is one of the most widely developed and sophisticated in the South as a whole and the best developed on the African continent. In the long run it ought to meet adequately the needs of all the people, but given its history – geared to the needs and supremacy of the whites and linked by investment to Britain and the United States – there were many problems and adjustments to be made before it could meet the expectations of the black majority. The strength of the economy had encouraged the white minority to hold onto power. The requirements for expansion led white businessmen to undermine apartheid. The transition to full democracy required black empowerment. The country is blessed with immense actual and potential economic capacity: it possesses huge mineral resources; can feed itself in normal times though subject to periodic droughts, and produce a surplus of agricultural products, both staples and commodities, for export; has some of the world's finest offshore fisheries and the best developed business-commercial infrastructure on the continent. Further, its road and rail system is not only geared to serve its own needs but those of its neighbours to the north as well. It has never achieved its full potential because of the inhibitions imposed by the apartheid system and in the latter 1980s also by sanctions.

The pressures the economy faced in the new South Africa were formidable. Thus, at the beginning of 1995, when the civil service advertised 11,000 posts for managers, clerks and cleaners, more than 1.5 million applicants came forward. That year Trevor Manuel, the Minister of Finance, highlighted the need to unbundle the conglomerates that in the apartheid 1980s had acquired a range of companies cheaply as expatriate corporations disengaged. Exchange controls had prevented them from investing their surplus revenues outside South Africa with the result that they invested inside the country in activities away from their core businesses and also, within the limited framework of South Africa, became increasingly antagonistic to competition. The willingness of international business to reinvest in South Africa under Mandela's presidency became both the touchstone of the country's new acceptability and the measure of its economic success. By the end of 1997 British companies had invested R6 billion since 1994 most of which, they claimed, had created real business. This investment was on top of the R12 billion already invested in the country. At the same time, major South African companies were investigating the possibility of flotations on the London Stock Exchange and two mining conglomerates, Gencor and Billiton, led the way. The new government was unhappy that its companies were seeking primary stock exchange listing in London. By the beginning of 1998 an estimated 150 US companies had returned to South Africa, following the abolition of sanctions, although the major US pension funds that had disinvested did not return. Manufacturing accounts for a quarter of South Africa's GDP and provides employment for about 14 per cent of the labour force. The principal manufactures are wide-ranging and include food, beverages, soaps, paints, pharmaceuticals, refined petroleum, iron and steel, transport equipment, metal products, non-electrical machinery, paper and paper products and construction. After more than a century of heavy exploitation, South Africa remains a storehouse of minerals and these have long constituted the lead sector in the economy. In the 1990s mining contributed 9 per cent of GDP though only employing three per cent of the labour force. Gold, diamonds, coal and the platinum group of ores are the leaders though gold output, after a century of predominance, was in serious decline.

Anglo American had long been the country's premier industrial corporation so that its lead always had a significant impact upon industry as a whole. During October 1998 it unveiled a plan to bring all its assets under the control of a single company and transfer its main stock exchange listing from Johannesburg to London. This move came as a psychological blow to the South African economy just as the country sought to make a fresh impact upon the international business scene. The stock market evaluation of Anglo American then stood at £6 billion. When the move to London was carried through it caused consternation in South Africa where it was regarded as both a snub to Mandela and a blow to the Johannesburg Stock Exchange. Given the history of Anglo American, which had been identified for the best part of a century with the mining structures upon which the South African economy had been based, this move from Johannesburg to London, as soon as it was possible for the company to do so after the end of the apartheid restrictions, came as a wounding blow to the new South Africa, especially as two-thirds of Anglo assets remained in South Africa. The National Union of Mineworkers (NUM) described the Anglo American move as 'passing a vote of no confidence in the economy of South Africa and its government'. Other major companies were expected to follow suit. Gwede Mantashe, the General Secretary of NUM, said: 'We are unhappy about the move because it is sending the wrong signals. Why should international investors be excited about coming to South Africa when all our major companies are going to have their primary listings in London?'[20] Anglo American, he said, was shifting from creating jobs.

Although agriculture contributes less than five per cent to GDP its importance to the economy cannot be exaggerated. The agricultural sector employs 13 per cent of the labour force. South Africa is self-sufficient in food and a substantial exporter. However, possession of the land is wound inextricably into the history of the Afrikaner in South Africa and they possess more than 80 per cent of the arable farmland. A future political problem, highlighted by events in Mugabe's Zimbabwe at the end of the century, will undoubtedly be some form of land redistribution. As it came to grips with economic realities, the new ANC government had to modify many of its earlier ideas about the economy. 'One lesson quickly learned by the ANC leaders was that their previous vaguely socialist ideals would have to be modified. By 1994 few informed people believed that a centralized, state-controlled economy could work; the examples of the only surviving Marxist countries, Cuba and North Korea, were enough to prove the point.'[21] Such logic was all very well but was a market-oriented economy going to solve the problems of expectations?

The emergence from the 1994 elections of a victorious ANC forming a South African government under Mandela created a totally different atmosphere in the region. South Africa joined the Southern African Development Community (SADC) and in 1995, largely due to South African pressures, Mozambique was invited to become a member of the Commonwealth. Speaking at the 1995

SADC summit, South African Foreign Minister Alfred Nzo said that membership of SADC was the realization of 'a dream South African democrats have had for a very long time. That dream is to participate as a good neighbour in the affairs not only of the region, but of Africa as a whole. South Africa is very anxious to contribute whatever it can to the stability of the region – economically, politically and security-wise. The SADC is an important vehicle for achieving that goal.'[22] Pretoria discovered quickly enough, however, that the other SADC members were afraid that their small economies would be swamped by South Africa's large one and by 1998 the government was working on a comprehensive offer of market access for its SADC partners, which would assist the move towards a free trade agreement among the 14 SADC members. It was an irony for Pretoria that its SADC partners, in terms of their desire for access to its market, were in the same relationship to South Africa as it was to the EU and the same kind of protectionist arguments were likely to surface.

Meanwhile, South African business was looking eagerly for opportunities in Africa to the north that had been denied it during the apartheid era. In the year following the end of apartheid South African businesses made major investments in 19 African countries covering operations in aviation, breweries, electric power, hotels, mining, railways and ports, and telecommunications. In what one newspaper described as a new Great Trek, South African companies were taking over from American and European corporations, which had become disillusioned with working conditions in Africa. The television company, Multichoice, over two years became Africa's biggest provider of pay TV channels broadcasting to 40 African countries up to and including Egypt. Other companies that rapidly extended their operations northwards were Standard Bank and South African Breweries. A major beneficiary of this outward investment was Mozambique, which had established a promotion agency for foreign investment in 1993. By 1997 US$346.2 million had been invested in 449 projects and the two lead countries providing this investment were Portugal and South Africa, ironically the two countries from whose economic clutches Mozambique had once aspired to break free. As optimists began to speak of South Africa as the springboard for investment in the whole continent, the former editor of the *Rand Daily Mail*, Allister Sparks, added a timely caution to the debate: 'There is, too, a sensitivity towards the neighbouring countries. There is the sense of a debt owed to them because of the heavy price they paid for supporting the ANC during the apartheid years, but it is coupled with a reluctance to appear arrogant or domineering as the continent's most powerful economy.'[23]

The many problems South Africa faced kept coming back to the relationship between black and white that remained central to the country's history.

Speaking for the benefit of whites whom many blacks felt had made no effort to transform and had retained all their former privileges, Thabo Mbeki said: 'The white population I don't think has quite understood the importance of this challenge... If you were speaking of national reconciliation based on the maintenance of the status quo because you do not want to move at a pace that frightens the whites, it means that you wouldn't carry out the task of transformation.'[24] During the latter part of Mandela's presidency, Mbeki had already become effective day-to-day ruler. The first post-1994 elections were held on 2 June 1999 when 16 million of 18 million voters took part. These elections were seen as free and fair. The ANC obtained 266 seats out of 400, just one seat short of the two-thirds majority required to amend the constitution. The ANC had obtained 66.4 per cent of the vote. The NP, meanwhile, had become the New National Party under Martinus van Schalkwyk but it only obtained 28 seats while the Democratic Party obtained 38 seats to become the official opposition. The Inkatha Freedom Party obtained 34 seats and remained in the coalition government with Buthelezi continuing as Minister of Home affairs. On 16 June Mbeki was sworn in as South Africa's second black president. There was an immediate problem when Winnie Mandela contested the position of deputy president, but after securing only 127 of 3,500 votes stood down in favour of Jacob Zuma.

Mandela paid tribute to his successor but warned him to allow dissent. Mbeki, then aged 55, was closer to ANC tradition than had been Mandela. He was aware that the heroes of the struggle had passed; he had to get down to the hard political task of satisfying his supporters and keeping promises. In his new cabinet Mbeki kept two key white figures in place – Trevor Manuel as Finance Minister and Alec Erwin at Trade and Industry – which was taken as a sign that he intended to maintain Mandela's economic strategy. He pressed on with the policy of privatization of state assets. Following Mandela's earlier efforts, Mbeki worked hard to secure a peaceful settlement in the Democratic Republic of Congo (former Zaïre) and in 2000 was ready to commit South African troops as peacekeepers. He tried, with less success, to prevent arms passing to Savimbi's UNITA in Angola. At the end of the century as the crisis in Zimbabwe worsened, Mbeki was urged to condemn the land seizures that were taking place there. He refused publicly to criticize Mugabe and took plenty of time before stating that land occupations would not be allowed in South Africa. He said he preferred to use 'quiet diplomacy' with Mugabe. He attempted to raise funds internally to pay for land seizures in Zimbabwe, a move that was interpreted as a sign that he might not stand firm on the rule of law in South Africa if something similar was attempted there. Land reform was moving very slowly and of 60,000 claims by blacks for land appropriated by whites only a few hundred had been settled by 2000. At the end of the century about 86 per cent of all rural land remained in the hands of 60,000 white commercial farmers while 14 million Africans tried to survive on 14 per cent of the land.

By the turn of the century South Africa was in a position in which it could easily overstretch its resources. 'Some critics urged Mbeki to abandon talk of South Africa playing a role in the rebirth of Africa, and instead to distance himself from the tragedies unfolding elsewhere on the continent and assert the claim that South Africa was a different case.'[25] Mbeki was much criticized over his statements in support of dissident scientists who questioned whether HIV was linked to AIDS and for suggesting an indigenous cure might be found. On the other hand, there was wide sympathy for his view that AIDS be considered in the context of poverty. However, his stand diverted attention from the problem of AIDS in South Africa where in 2000 an estimated 4.2 million people were infected with HIV. Overwhelming evidence forced Mbeki to alter his stand. The huge rise in crime during the 1990s became a major factor in politics and the events in Zimbabwe led to an increase in white emigration over 1999–2000. White businessmen objected to legislation designed to force companies to make their workforces representative of the country's demographic divisions. An increasing number of young white males saw no prospect of jobs in South Africa and emigrated. The government had to face criticisms of the TRC for the amnesties granted to notorious whites such as Craig Williamson and members of the security forces responsible for murders of activists such as Ruth First in the 1980s. Further, demands for reparations by blacks remained unresolved and the TRC recommendations were not published by the government. In mid-2000 a wider Democratic Alliance was formed by the merger of the Democratic Party under Tony Leon and the New National Party under Martinus van Schalkwyk: Leon became the leader and van Schalkwyk the deputy leader of the new party. The government was criticized for a large arms deal in which it allocated R30,000 million for the purchase of arms from Britain and Sweden; the weapons were said not to be necessary and there were also accusations of corruption, with the result that four official inquiries were launched in 2000.

Assessments of Mbeki's performance at the beginning of the new century were mixed. He faced huge problems: crime, which in part was seen to be a legacy of apartheid and refusal to obey the law; unemployment, housing, education and health. None of these problems could be easily or quickly overcome. At the same time large sectors of the population had electricity and clean water for the first time, while there were many new health clinics in rural areas. Corruption was another problem. 'A special investigative unit, established by the Mandela administration, uncovered much corruption, but was threatened with disbandment by the government, which disliked its public image. The Mbeki government failed to set a strong example, and resources continued to be wasted through a mixture of inexperience, lack of expertise, mismanagement and corrupt practices.'[26] On the other hand, the economy remained the strongest in Africa and there had not occurred an outflow of investment resources, despite the move of major companies to the London Stock Exchange, as had been feared.

By the end of the century Mandela had been more widely acclaimed than any other living politician: a hero for South Africa and an icon for a continent that all too often appeared the source of disaster stories. Yet, behind the image of a living legend there had always been a steely politician who had negotiated his way through the minefields of 1990–94 with masterly skill. In 1993 he had, with de Klerk, been jointly awarded the Nobel Peace Prize. In his speech of acceptance in Norway he had paid tribute to de Klerk: 'He had the courage to admit that a terrible wrong had been done to our country and our people through the imposition of the system of apartheid. He had the foresight to understand and accept that all the people of South Africa must, through negotiations and as equal participants in the process, together determine what they want to make of their future.' However, when asked how he could accept the prize with de Klerk whom he had criticized so severely, he said: 'To make peace with an enemy, one must work with that enemy, and that enemy becomes your partner.'[27] Mandela's great achievement was to persuade black Africans not to seek to exact revenge for all the horrors of apartheid. There have been many judgements of Mandela and there will be many more in the future. The historian Welsh writes: 'In his own person, Nelson Mandela combined much diverse South African history, Khoikhoi, Xhosa and English. A Thembu aristocrat, brought up to accept the obligations and privileges of leadership, he was heir to the Thembu traditions of accommodating oneself to events, reasonable discussion only giving way to action as a last resort.'[28] In February 1999 Mandela addressed the final session of parliament in Cape Town before he retired as President at the 2 June elections. He called for a 'new patriotism' to counter the enemies of reconciliation. He summed up five years of achievement since he had become president. He said: 'For a country that was the polecat of the world... the doors of the world have opened, precisely because of our success in achieving things that humanity as a whole holds dear. Of this we should be proud.' Having parted from Winnie, Mandela married Graca Machel, the widow of the former President of Mozambique, who had witnessed plenty of suffering in Mozambique. She said of his achievement:

He symbolized a much broader forgiveness and understanding and reaching out. If he had come out of prison and sent a different message, I can tell you this country could be in flames. So his role is not to be underestimated too. He knew exactly the way he wanted to come out, but also the way he addressed the people from the beginning, sending the message of what he thought was the best way to save lives in this country, to bring reconciliation... Some people criticize that he went too far. There is no such thing as going too far if you are trying to save this country from this kind of tragedy.[29]

The new South Africa that bids to lead the continent in a renaissance owes its ability to adopt such a role to the moral leadership provided by Mandela.

Whatever South Africa's relations with the United States, Britain, the European Union or Asia, its future lies in Africa where its performance as the regional economic and political superpower will have a profound impact upon the continent's development in the twenty-first century. At home, the 'trick' for the ruling ANC must be how to use the white minority and integrate it into the new South Africa so that its expertise and energies are used to the benefit of the whole population; the success or failure of this integration process will determine the success or failure of the country as a whole. Integration is one of the hardest of all political exercises. By 1998, the euphoria generated during the first year of the new Rainbow Society had given place to white worries about what they stood to lose and black worries about what they had yet to obtain. Ex-President P. W. Botha said he would never apologize for apartheid and denounced the assault on the Afrikaner by the country's new rulers. 'I am not guilty of any deed for which I should apologize or ask for amnesty,' he said. 'In many circles the Afrikaner is being isolated to be punished for all the unfavourable events in the history of South Africa.' Botha blamed the British and the Soviets: 'The Afrikaner was a victim of (British) colonial greed... the recent conflicts in which we were involved were primarily against Soviet imperialism and colonialism.'[30] Such attitudes were to be expected from the old hard-liners of apartheid; the question is whether such attitudes will truly disappear as South Africa faces the new century and whether the country's new rulers can manage the trick of integration.

CHAPTER THIRTY-THREE

Democracy

T he question as to whether or not African countries are democratic in the way the West defines democracy assumed great importance during the decade that followed the end of the Cold War. This new Western interest in the politics of Africa did not have a great deal to do with the intrinsic worth of democracy as such; rather, the emphasis upon democracy provided a useful means of exercising control over African economic policies. How African governments handled the complexities of running 'democratic' states was often treated with indifference in the West; what mattered was their acceptance of norms applied externally because only this way could political leaders ensure the continued flow of the all-important economic assistance upon which their regimes depended for survival. In any case, 'democracy' in Africa is still under discussion. 'Seen from the perspective of human history, therefore, the idea of popular democracy based on mass enfranchisement is still relatively new. Likewise there is a very short collective experience of different voting systems and rules to ensure that the democratic process gives as faithful a reflection as possible of the people's wishes.'[1] It is not that Western-style democracy cannot be made to work; the question is: do the ruling hierarchies want it to work? During the carve-up of the continent by the European powers in the nineteenth century, Africa mattered to Europe but the African people did not. At the beginning of the new century Africa's resources and how to control them matter to the US, the EU and the transnational corporations but not the African people or the way in which they would develop if left to do so on their own. All states, whatever the political system, tend towards tyranny. The best that can be said of a democratic system is that it resists or offers a degree of protection against the tyranny of the state. Africans want and understand democracy as much as any of their external critics who argue that they prefer 'strong government', if by democracy is meant participation in the multiple decision-making processes that govern their lives. Almost all democracies come to be controlled by hierarchical groups – political parties, the rich, the establishment – where real power lies and decision-making takes place while the voters, the ordinary people, periodically have the chance to endorse or reject but almost never to control. In the developing world, 'where political and other forms of corruption are more obvious and the conditions of life for the masses are far less tolerable than in the US or Britain, the response to such abuses is often more explosive'.[2] This was borne out through the 1990s when mass protests, rioting and demonstrations often leading to significant amounts of violence preceded political changes that introduced a greater degree of democracy. Elites always try to manipulate or subvert democracy to their own ends and while paying lip service to the principle they restrict the process if there is any danger of it giving real power to the people. During the 1990s, moreover, there was a violent backlash against democracy by Africa's authoritarian rulers, which was encouraged by the lack of any genuine support for democracy or human rights in Africa by the major world powers. An important perception of Africa in the 1990s suggested that economic stagnation worked in favour of authoritarian rulers since it made it easier for them to exercise their power, at least until the masses revolted. The acceptance by reluctant rulers of a democratic – or more democratic – constitution, either as a result of internal pressures or the external demands of aid donors, often led to a long battle in which the ruler attempted to claw back the concessions he had made. In several countries (Namibia in 1999) the ruling incumbent persuaded, or tried to persuade, the National Assembly to set aside a two-term limit on the presidency so that he could continue in power. In many countries, as a result of such manoeuvres, the people have become deeply cynical about the constitutional promises made by their rulers, suspecting, all too often correctly, that they will never give up power. Democracy in Africa cannot be treated in isolation from the wider international community, since 'The present international political agenda is dominated by the twin imperatives of economic liberalization and democratization, the two being in practice intimately connected.'[3]

During the Cold War Western rulers often saw democracy in poor countries as a breeding ground for Communism: 'To allow political freedom to flourish in the "third world" suddenly appeared as a hazardous strategy, and a fundamental reordering of development priorities occurred during this period.'[4] The same author goes on to argue that the World Bank and IMF imposed structural adjustment programmes (SAPs) in Africa to create a free market and a minimal, technocratic and highly efficient state that must be shielded from the 'distributional demands of its citizens'. Since the end of the Cold War meant the disappearance of any credible alternative to the capitalist development model, the result was a triumphant West assuming there was no alternative to its political model either. And so there was a sudden surge of political morality in the West with Britain's Foreign Secretary Douglas Hurd suggesting that the promotion of good government was a 'moral imperative'. Prior to 1990 the West used aid as a tool in its confrontation with the Communist world; post-1990 it commandeered the moral high ground and assumed it had the right to control development and insist upon democracy in the South. This brings us to the good governance debate.

Certain governments and international organizations never stop talking of democracy although the procedures they actually use are always authoritarian. In his book *Deterring Democracy*, Noam Chomsky advances the thesis that though the United States pays lip service to democracy in the Third World, it is only too ready to undermine it if there is any chance that it will lead to radical people's choice – that is, a development pattern geared to the needs of the people that would necessarily put a stop to US/European/corporate investment designed to remove wealth from Africa (or anywhere else in the South). 'In the client states of the Third World, the preference for democratic forms is often largely a matter of public relations. But where the society is stable and privilege is secure, other factors enter... If a country satisfies certain basic conditions, then, the US is tolerant of democratic forms, though in the Third World, where a proper outcome is hard to guarantee, often just barely.'[5] The proper outcome referred to above is, always, one that favours and, indeed, accepts Western tutelage. Western economic controls are largely operated through the World Bank and IMF where the G7/8 states account for 40 per cent of the voting power and can always rely upon enough support from some of the smaller OECD countries to maintain an absolute majority so as to control the policies of these institutions. The whole of sub-Saharan Africa, on the other hand, controls only 4 per cent of the votes and consequently must submit to policies drawn up by the West in its interests. Development is not separate from democracy, as donors would maintain, but intertwined with it, at least if we accept in principle that development is about the welfare and advancement of the mass of the people. This is not to say that the West has everything its own way: 'What happened after independence was the Africanization of politics, that is, the adjustment of imported political models to the historical, sociological and cultural realities of Africa. This is still going on today: the so-called democratic transitions are being reinterpreted locally.'[6]

In 1995 a document prepared by the French Ministry of Foreign Affairs indicated that there 'were signs that authoritarian governments in Africa were taking vigorous counter-measures to halt the advance of democracy. In spite of the impressive size of popular pro-democracy pressures which were sweeping the continent and despite the general spread of multiparty political movements, some of which had actually toppled governments from power'.[7] Sometimes, it seems, that in direct proportion as politicians, institutions and aid donors talk of the necessity of democracy in the developing world (Douglas Hurd's moral imperative), in fact they operate to another agenda. The concept of good governance appears principally to be designed to sanction the right of Western countries to intervene in the countries of the South in order to promote and ensure the adoption of their vision of development and democracy, 'while simultaneously marginalizing alternative interpretations. As such, the good governance discourse also serves to shield the West from democratic scrutiny. The rich countries are automatically regarded as democratic and able to democratize the third world as part of the larger development effort.'[8]

In the early 1990s, almost at the drop of a hat as it were, the West discovered what it had failed to notice throughout the years of the Cold War: that poor or corrupt governance was the principal reason for the failure of its development policies in Africa (and elsewhere). The remedy, therefore, was good governance as a precondition for sustainable economic development. The consequence of this discovery was the establishment of the Commission drawn from the great and the good of both North and South that produced *Our Global Neighbourhood*. This lengthy document offers a blueprint for a better world. Its style – a rolling blandness – makes plain that its authors know what the world needs while hypocritically including prescriptions that they must equally have known would be ignored by the major powers. In the end, therefore, it is a series of prescriptions for *them*, the world's poor or disfranchised, telling the people of the developing world what they must do to achieve acceptability with the powerful. There are too many statements as follows: 'The threat to liberty in any part of the global neighbourhood needs to be seen as a threat to the entire neighbourhood. Action against attempts to violate the right to liberty is a common responsibility.' This statement does not encompass the questions: who defines liberty; who decides; who intervenes, who prevents intervention? On democracy it is blandly superficial: 'The spread of democracy has been one of the most heartening trends in recent years. It is democracy that can ensure that a country's affairs are conducted – and its development directed – in ways that respond to the interests and wishes of the people.' There is much praise for democracy with little attention paid to whether it actually delivers answers. Of the military it claims correctly that dominant military establishments are always a threat to democracy and in Africa there are many military establishments that have threatened successfully both the democratic and the autocratic traditions with equal impartiality. (The Commission does not examine the role of the military of the major powers.)

The Commission is at its best when examining the way the United Nations works and here, perhaps, it comes to the nub of the democratic problem. It suggests, quite correctly though without hope, that in time the permanent members of the Security Council should give up their vetoes. The United Nations has never been democratic because from its inception the big five powers insisted upon their right to a veto. The General Assembly, of course, could be democratic with one-country one-vote. Broad assertions of principle read well but their implications are rarely followed through. Thus, 'Empowerment depends on people's ability to provide for themselves, for poverty translates into a lack of options for the individual.' The question, as far as Africa is concerned, is whether democratization empowers or is the best route for Africa to take. There is much disenchantment with the democratic process and the apparent inability of politicians to deliver on promises, and deep resentment of politicians who, having won elections, neglect large sectors of their people. None the less, the Commission insists: 'It is fundamentally important that governance should be underpinned by democracy at all levels and ultimately by the rule of enforceable law.' The difficulty for any commission of this nature with its international team is that it cannot afford to say anything that anyone would reject, so it ends up with a consensus of well-meaning platitudes. Its final comment on democracy reads as follows: 'Democracy provides the environment within which the fundamental rights of citizens are best safeguarded and offers the most favourable foundation for peace and stability. The world needs, however, to ensure the rights of minorities, and to guard against the ascendance of the military and corruption. Democracy is more than just the right to vote in regular elections. And as within nations, so globally, the democratic principle must be ascendant.'[9] Implicit in the entire report of the Commission is the assumption that these principles, which bear all the hallmarks of Western theory and practice, have to be applied to countries of the South, whatever their own traditions may be.

What do Africans think about the endless exhortations from the West generally and aid donors in particular to be democratic and adhere to good governance or adopt neo-liberal economic policies? As one perceptive critic of Africa suggests: 'Although present political transitions in Africa are important, and the desirability of democracy is in principle not to be denied, an assessment of the prospects for greater democracy demands that we approach the task of explaining contemporary African politics from a different analytical angle.'[10] Many of the expectations at independence have been confounded and much of the aid that has been directed to Africa has apparently failed to produce the intended development while African states are regarded as having failed to make their chosen political systems work. There are clear indications in a number of African countries that bypassing the state in a number of mainly illegal fashions has become the norm. The old Africa worked on patronage – the chief looking after his followers – and patronage remains the driving force in

African politics and patronage requires means – in other words, wealth for distribution among the patron's followers. The poor expect their patrons to demonstrate their wealth with ostentation and act as their role models. Thus, 'abuses of power are tolerated so long as the patron is able to meet with adequate largesse the (insatiable) demands which are made upon his person'.[11] As a Zambian minister is quoted as saying: 'If I don't support people from my own region, who else will?' Providing state employment for followers is not just the norm in much of Africa, it is the way the system works and all the pressures for democratization or other changes demanded from outside have made no impact upon the practice which, at some levels, may be seen as the lifeblood of African politics. Nepotism in Africa overrides Western prescriptions about equal opportunities and is no more seen as corruption than the 'old boy' network that, certainly to the time of C.P. Snow, was part of the British establishment norm: 'the Establishment in England has a knack of looking after its own', he said. Nepotism, moreover, acts as a brake upon radical youth in its attempts to undermine the existing system. Since the achievement of independence, 'sharing the spoils' has been a crucial aspect of African politics and one of the reasons why the one-party state had its attractions: those who did not belong to the ruling party were automatically excluded from any share in the spoils.

By the 1990s, however, there were fewer spoils to go round and that, perhaps, may encourage those who think the system can be altered. Even when African states have turned away from the one-party state and adopted more open democratic practices, the leaders of the new political systems, as a rule, turn out to be the old leaders resurrected in a new guise and it is worth pointing out that this phenomenon has also occurred all through the former Communist world. It may appear cynical, but also be close to the truth, to suggest that the only way of producing new political leaders is through military coups by radical young officers. However, circumstances are changing. 'African politicians today cannot expect to draw support by pointing to their anti-colonial credentials or by exploiting Cold War rivalries. The ideologies of nationalism, development, or "authenticity" have exhausted their appeal and there is need for a fresh approach. Legitimization depends now on the adoption of the currently fashionable notions of liberalization, pluralism, democracy, human rights, rule of law, good governance and even structural adjustment.'[12] This suggested 'legitimization', however, differs from early bases for national leadership for the ideologies that have exhausted their appeal as suggested above were at least home-grown reactions to the former colonial situation whereas the current set of prescriptions have all been suggested and where possible applied from outside. There is as yet little evidence that leaders who embraced democracy during the last decade of the twentieth century were in fact any more democratic than their predecessors; rather, they were, like most politicians, prepared to make the new system that was emerging work to their advantage.

Development and democracy are on 'offer' from the West as a package deal, the one dependent upon the other, and the package assuming the eventual Westernization of Africa. Superficially, at the beginning of the new century, 'Democracy in the sense of accountability and fair elections is increasingly the international norm against which states must measure themselves, eagerly or otherwise'.[13] This is certainly true when Africa is viewed through Western eyes but as Robert Mugabe seemed so desperate to prove at the end of the century, after two decades of power, regime survival can override all other considerations. This raises one of the most significant questions about the aid process: is it about development or is it about maintaining clients in power? 'Taken together, aid dependency and elite visions of democracy go a long way towards explaining why, since the return of democracy, the wishes of external supporters appear to have taken clear precedence over the needs and demands of domestic constituencies.'[14] Despite endless criticisms from the West aimed at the African political process since the end of the Cold War, the activities of African politicians in securing jobs or channelling funds to their own supporters or ethnic communities are little different from the 'pork barrel' politics of the United States. Nkrumah's generation of African politicians learnt precisely how to use imported Western democratic processes during their independence struggles. Later, they perverted them to create one-party authoritarian structures but they, as with a later political generation, needed political support bases and these, overwhelmingly, were found in their own tribal or ethnic groups. Once their nationalist charisma had worn off they turned increasingly to such support bases.

Now if politics is about delivering to 'your' own community, then membership of the opposition in the Western political sense is useless since such an opposition does not command any of the resources that may be distributed. In a situation where the winner takes all, not just in terms of political power but also in control of all patronage resources, those who have been excluded will either join the ruling party to share in the spoils or, if exclusion appears likely to be permanent, turn to violence. A political party is not seen as part of a national political process so much as part of the machinery needed to help the 'big man' distribute favours. There may be exceptions:

A few, like Nelson Mandela, may in fact embody the highest virtues of the Protestant work ethic. The fact remains, however, that the ability of such exceptional leaders to move the political system beyond its present rationality is limited, not primarily because of a lack of ambition but much more fundamentally because of the nature of existing forms of political legitimacy. In the end, there is an inter-locking neo-patrimonial logic between the deep ambitions of the political elites and the well-grounded expectations of their clients.[15]

All this suggests that attempts to force Africa to adopt Western-style democracy will be unsuccessful; the forms may be adopted, the practice will be African. As another commentator points out,

> Efforts to combine the requirements of the market economy with the demands of popular sovereignty have ended in failure. There can be no doubt that most of the hopes raised by the promise of democratization have now been dashed, in spite of the substantial achievements of the movements of the early 1990s in the fields of freedom of the press and freedom of association… With South Africa providing the only really important exception, the process of democratization has been captured, under the guise of competitive elections, by the authoritarian groups already in control of state power (notably in Côte d'Ivoire, Togo, Cameroon, Gabon and Kenya), or it has given rise to new regimes whose weakness offers little promise of future stability (Mali and Benin) or produced others which cannot easily be considered genuinely democratic (Central African Republic, Congo until 1997, Equatorial Guinea, Zambia, Chad), or else democracy has been snuffed out by the intervention of the armed forces (Nigeria, Niger, Burundi).[16]

This formidable indictment of the process must give pause for reflection: will the collapse of the democratization experiment simply mean that weak African states revert to authoritarian governments and elites whose survival will depend upon Western aid? At this point it is worth looking at some individual cases.

THE STATE OF DEMOCRACY ON THE THRESHOLD OF THE TWENTY-FIRST CENTURY

At the beginning of the twenty-first century 44 of Africa's 54 states were described as multiparty republics while 10 had other forms of government as follows: a one-party republic, Morocco a multiparty monarchy with Western Sahara annexed to it, Eritrea a transitional government, Somalia a transitional government, Uganda a non-party republic, Congo (Brazzaville) a transitional government, Lesotho a multiparty monarchy, Swaziland a non-party monarchy and Comoros a transitional government. How much did these descriptive forms represent the actuality?

If we travel quickly through the continent in 2001 the picture is understandably uneven for what critics of Africa so often forget is that the continent consists of 54 countries, more than a quarter of the membership of the United Nations. In North Africa Algeria had just emerged from a decade of brutal civil war, still not resolved, between the secular government representing the much reduced FLN backed by the army, and the Islamists whose coming electoral triumph at the beginning of the 1990s had been aborted by the army. In April 2001, however, the government faced major rioting in Kabylia, the main Berber-speaking region, which continued for three months leading to 60 deaths and more than 2,000 wounded in clashes between young protesters and the police, with despair at economic deprivation the main motive for the violence. Armed Islamist groups continued to defy the government and large sections of the countryside remained insecure with massacres of civilians taking place in areas that supposedly had been pacified. The Francophone press criticized President Bouteflika for his attempts at dialogue – his 'concorde civile'. There was no obvious end in sight for this long-lasting confrontation. In neighbouring Morocco there was growing impatience with the regime of the new King, Mohammed VI, at the continuing political stagnation as well as the poor economic conditions. The people were beginning to question the King's commitment to reform and his failure to overcome resistance to change by powerful vested interests. In July, on the second anniversary of his accession to the throne, the King reaffirmed his personal commitment to reform and said he wanted to promote the country's different regional and cultural groups and establish a royal institute to 'protect, revive and improve' Berber culture. Restrictions on the press, however, remained in place. In Tunisia the main political concern was whether Zine el-Abidine Ben Ali would amend the constitution to enable him to stand for the presidency again. In March almost 100 moderate figures signed a petition opposing any amendment to the constitution that would allow Ben Ali a fourth term. In November Kalel el Taief, a former close political ally of Ben Ali, was arrested after giving an interview in which he said the country was ruled by a mafia linked to the president's family and that the people were scandalized at the widespread corruption that was prevalent and angered at the lack of civil liberties. These three country vignettes reflect the overall political situation to be found in the Arab north of the continent.

The countries of former French Equatorial Africa – Central African Republic, Chad, Niger, Republic of Congo, Gabon and Cameroon – continued down well-marked political paths and democratization at best played only a limited role in determining events. In May a coup attempt was launched in Central African Republic against the regime of President Ange-Félix Patassé by supporters of the former president, André Kolingba, and there followed 10 days of fighting in Bangui. Libya, now in a new role as guardian of legitimacy (Gaddafi, not for the first time, was reinventing himself) despatched troops to assist Patassé. In November, the President faced another coup attempt, this time by his army commander, General François Bozize; after being dismissed the General had launched an unsuccessful coup attempt and was forced to flee to Chad. In May presidential elections in Chad returned Idriss Deby to power with 67 per cent of the vote; he had been ruling Chad since overthrowing Habré in 1990. He faced a rebellion in the north of the country that had been smouldering since 1998. In Niger the government of President Mamadou Tandja, which had been elected in 2000, was troubled by corruption and general fatigue while the country was also seen as being vulnerable to penetration by terrorists in the aftermath of the 11 September attacks in the United States. In the Republic of Congo President Sassou-Nguesso still worked to consolidate his position after the coup and civil war of 1997 that had brought him back to power with the covert if not overt support of France. In Gabon elections were held in December and provided a massive victory for the ruling Gabonese Democratic Party (PDG) in both legislative and municipal elections that emphasized the political dominance of the apparently indestructible President Omar Bongo, who had been continually in power since 1967. The opposition appeared resigned to defeat. Finally, Cameroon was preoccupied with the ongoing conflict between the minority Anglophones and majority Francophones, a sort of steady state relationship.

Benin, which had established a reputation for frequent coups in the 1960s, came to be regarded as a model of democratization in the 1990s. Maj. Mathieu Kérékou seized power in 1972 and inaugurated a policy of Marxism-Leninism. By the end of the 1980s opposition to his rule was growing, not least because of economic breakdown. In response to this popular opposition, Kérékou announced the abandonment of Marxism-Leninism and then agreed to allow a national conference of the 'active forces of the nation'. This was held in February 1990 and attended by 500 delegates. The conference declared itself to be sovereign and voted to abolish the existing structure of government, laying down that the president should be elected by universal suffrage. The conference then designated Nicephore Soglo as interim prime minister and in the succeeding months civilians in effect took control of the state so that Benin became the first African country to experience a civilian coup. As a result, a one-party state, dominated by the military, was forced by public pressure to return to multiparty democracy. Subsequently, after the formation of numerous parties and alliances, Soglo was elected President and Kérékou made a dignified exit. However, Kérékou made a political comeback in 1996 by winning the presidential elections. On his victory he undertook to strive for national unity. Soglo's defeat was due to his failure to adequately address social and economic issues. In the legislative elections of March 1999, opposition parties took 42 seats, the pro-Kérékou parties 41 seats. In 2001 Kérékou again won the presidential election with 84 per cent of a low poll since his rivals for the office, Soglo and Adrien Houngbedji, withdrew from the contest, alleging vote rigging.

The story of Côte d'Ivoire in the 1990s was markedly different. During the 1960s and 1970s Côte d'Ivoire was regarded as the great success story of Francophone Africa under the remarkable and enduring leadership of President Félix Houphouët-Boigny who, despite his dictatorial side, derived his political legitimacy from his leading role in the nationalist debates with France that led to independence for the francophone states in 1960. He had, moreover, always been a close ally of France. But he stayed too long: 'The same is true in country after country. Houphouët-Boigny started as a modernizer who had to display some Big Man traits to be effective; he ended as a Big Man hollowing out the hard-won treasures of his modernization. They all stay too long. That in itself is sufficient justification for democracy.'[17] In fact Côte d'Ivoire had long been an under-managed, as opposed to real, democracy that allowed Houphouët-Boigny to rule in his dotage and run the economy into the ground. Côte d'Ivoire had outdone Ghana in development during the 1960s and 1970s but from the late 1980s experienced a decline as precipitous as had been Ghana's a decade earlier. Houphouët-Boigny had obtained investment from Paris and Wall Street and Côte d'Ivoire was the first African country to enter the Eurodollar market, 'But in his dotage he [Houphouët-Boigny] so canted the government budget – maybe half a billion on the appalling cement replica of St Peter's in his home village – that it verged on bankruptcy.'[18] Thus, through the megalomania of a once successful leader a success story collapsed. In the latter part of 2000 a major crisis arose following presidential elections that brought the long-time opposition leader, Laurent Gbagbo, to power against the challenge of the military ruler Gen. Robert Guei. The power struggle between Gbagbo and Guei brought the country to the brink of civil war. During 2001 an attempted coup received support from Burkina Faso in alignment with the people of the north of the country, many of whom were Burkinabes. Gbagbo tried the path of reconciliation and France became active in attempting to bring about a political reconciliation between the different factions – Paris did not want to see the collapse of its showcase country – but civil violence spread and continued into the following year.

The Democratic Republic of Congo (the former Zaïre) has been in a state of crisis for years (see chapter 37 below) and by 2000 faced possible disintegration with the help of its predatory neighbours. It did make some minimal moves towards democratization in the early 1990s, as a consequence of external events rather than by design on the part of President Mobutu. 'For all practical purposes, the Mobutu regime as a system of personal and dictatorial rule ended on 24 April 1990, when internal and external pressures finally convinced him to replace the one-party system with multiparty democracy.'[19] The change was relative, Mobutu reacting to forces he could not resist entirely but, as he soon demonstrated, could so manipulate that he was to remain in power for another seven years. He was supported in his determination to hold on because of the weak democratic tradition that existed in the country – or, more accurately, did not exist, a divided opposition and a hierarchy determined to hold on to its privileged position at all costs. The so-called transition to democracy under Etienne Tshisekedi over 1992–93 generated optimism that was never to be realized. Tshisekedi argued for reform and change and told his political adversaries (those who supported the Mobutu regime that had enriched them) that he pardoned them for any wrongs they had done him. Their response was contempt. Tshisekedi found himself in the position of leading a caretaker government to whom an endless stream of supplicants came for preferment. The transition to real democracy did not take place. When in 1997 Mobutu was finally forced to flee the country and was replaced by Laurent Kabila, the latter refused to work with the Congo's democratic forces but relied, instead, upon the support of the Rwandans and Congolese of the diaspora who had backed his bid for power. Mobutu had so debilitated and corrupted the body politic of the Congo that in the 1990s, first under his malignant hand and then under the grotesque and greedy Kabila, democracy had no chance. As the state imploded individuals tried to grab what they could for themselves while the idea of implementing a democratic system that would sort out the state in the hope of producing a more equitable, democratically controlled system seemed a non-starter.

Few of the small states of West Africa had an easy economic passage through the 1990s and in most cases democracy was at best fragile in practice. At the beginning of the twenty-first century Burkina Faso had to deal with the return of 200,000 of its citizens from the north of its troubled neighbour Côte d'Ivoire. Legislative elections of January 2001 in Cape Verde brought an important change of government: a decade of rule by the Movement for Democracy (MPD) was ended and the former ruling party – the African Party for the Independence of Guinea and Cape Verde (PAIGC/PAIVC) won a majority of seats and its leader José María Neves became prime minister. Then, in the February presidential elections Pedro Pires of the PAICV emerged victorious. In another of West Africa's mini-states, The Gambia, President Yahya Jammeh decided in July to lift the ban on the political activities of the parties, which he had overthrown in his military coup of 1994, opening the way for democratic challenges in the scheduled presidential elections for that October. When these were held on 18 October they were marred by violence. Jammeh, supported by the Alliance for Patriotic Reorientation and Construction (APRC), won another five-year term with 52.96 per cent (242,302 of 509,301 votes cast) while his closest rival, Ousainon Dalboe of the United Democratic Party (UDP), obtained 149,448 votes, 29.34 per cent of the total. In Guinea-Bissau a shaky government presided over a volatile political situation as President Kumba Yalla was urged by the UN Peace-Building Support Office in Guinea-Bissau to pursue a policy of national reconciliation following a difficult confrontation with the armed forces. The neighbouring state of Guinea was deeply affected by the civil wars in both Liberia and Sierra Leone and suffered from cross-border incursions into its territory from both these countries and there had developed a major refugee crisis in the Gueckedou area close to where the three countries meet. President Lansana Conté responded forcibly to these incursions and had at his disposal a loyal army that was also much stronger than those of Guinea's two neighbours. On the home political front Conté planned constitutional changes that would permit him to stand for a third presidential term and have this extended to seven years. His political opponents claimed that he was perpetuating a dictatorship. On 12 November 2001 he held a referendum on these proposals, which were approved by 98 per cent of the votes in a 20 per cent turnout of voters. Other changes allowed the government to appoint local officials, who hitherto had been elected. International donors were upset by these moves, since they had been pressing for decentralization; however, because Guinea faced 'considerable difficulties' the international donor community remained supportive.

Liberia and Sierra Leone had experienced a decade of brutal civil wars whose devastation and death tolls seemed greatly out of proportion to their small populations. Both countries entered the new century in turmoil though in the case of Sierra Leone, with a substantial UN force on its soil, the possibility of achieving a more settled situation seemed greater than in Liberia (see chapter 36 below). The year 2001 was the last in office for President Alpha Oumar Konaré, who had won Mali's first multiparty elections in 1992 and had generally won plaudits for the moderation of his rule. By the end of the year some 80 political parties were preparing for the succession struggle though in the end they would join together in coalitions. In neighbouring Mauritania the Democratic and Social Republican Party was firmly in the saddle and won the legislative and local elections of that year. At the end of 2001, Senegal's first President, Leopold Sedar Senghor (1960–80), died. He had laid the foundations of the country's democratic system when he voluntarily stood down in 1980 at a time when few heads of state contemplated doing anything of the sort. His immediate successor and protégé, Abdou Diouf, who was out of the country, returned for Senghor's funeral, and the incumbent president, Abdoulaye Wade, 'claimed' to be Senghor's spiritual successor. In Togo President Gnassingbe Eyadéma shared with Gabon's Bongo the perhaps dubious distinction of having been continuously in power since 1967 and was regarded as the continent's leading 'unreconstructed' dictator. Although he announced that he would not run in the 2002 presidential elections, no one believed him. In the tiny island state of São Tomé and Principe the 2001 presidential elections were pronounced free and fair by observers. President Trovoada was not permitted to run a third time and Fradique de Menezes obtained 56 per cent of the vote to defeat Pinto da Costa, the leader of the *Movimento de Libertação de São Tomé e Príncipe* (MLSTP) (Movement for the Liberation of São Tomé and Principe). Menezes was leader of the *Ação Democratica Independente* (ADI) (Independent Democratic Action) party and he was sworn in that September. In December he dissolved the legislature and set elections for March 2002.

After 20 years in power, Jerry Rawlings stood down as President of Ghana in January 2001, following the presidential elections of the previous December that had been won by John Agyekum Kufuor, the leader of the National Patriotic Party (NPP). The NPP also gained narrow control of the legislature, winning 52 of the 100 seats and six months after Kufuor's accession to power Ghana's democracy seemed relatively stable. Many Ghanaians, however, had doubted that Rawlings would go quietly. It is true that Rawlings had said in 1998, 'My time is up. I want to obey the Constitution.'[20] Cynicism about such statements was to be expected however, for too many African heads of state had made similar pronouncements and then found excuses to remain in power. Rawlings, moreover, had liquidated three previous heads of state, killed several inconvenient judges and put opponents in prison and such legacies are not easily forgotten. Judgements on Rawlings (as with other dictatorial figures in Africa) are mixed: 'In the beginning, there was no doubt that Rawlings was a military man: he acted just like a typical African despot. But in 1992 he very noisily took off his uniform and organized democratic elections which he unsurprisingly swept; slightly more surprisingly, particularly given the evidence to the contrary, the elections were sanctioned by the international community. The dose was repeated in 1996, although local dissent, at least, was louder.'[21] In 19 years Rawlings got Ghana back on track and, despite his very shaky record on human rights, he did take a number of vital decisions that benefited the country rather than a presidential supporting elite.

On the other side of the continent, the little states of Burundi and Rwanda experienced a decade of civil war and massacres: at the turn of the century South

Africa's elder statesman Nelson Mandela was trying to mediate reconciliation in Burundi while Rwanda was still trying to recover form the horrific events of 1994. In Somalia, which had experienced an equally traumatic decade of civil strife, the Transitional National Government (TNG) that had been established in 2000, despite recognition by the UN, had failed to establish its authority even over the whole of Mogadishu, let alone outside it. In June 2001, Kismayo produced a regional administration that declared its support for the TNG. However, no reconciliation had been achieved with the faction leaders and warlords who refused to accept the reconciliation proposed in 2000 at the Anta conference. A referendum of June 2000 in Uganda had seen 90 per cent of voters retain the country's no-party 'Movement' advocated by Yoweri Museveni although pluralists condemned the referendum for creating a de facto one-party state. In the legislative elections that followed, the pro-no party 'Movement' won 230 of 292 seats although 50 MPs, including 10 ministers, were defeated. Then in March 2001, after a bitter campaign, Yoweri Museveni won a landslide presidential election victory, obtaining 69.3 per cent of the vote as opposed to 28 per cent for his opponent Kizza Besigye. Irregularities, mainly on behalf of Museveni, did not affect the outcome.

No other region of the world has seen so much constitution making – or re-making – as Africa over the last 40 years and the new constitution worked out by the Constitutional Commission for Eritrea (CCE) following the end of its war of independence from Ethiopia in 1991 is worth examination. The constitution had to serve the basic aims of nation building, equitable development and stability, the building of democracy, the protection of human rights and the assurance of popular participation. However, the CCE also stressed the need to balance the rights of citizens with their duties to national unity, such that basic freedoms had to be guaranteed by a 'democratic political culture' and economic and cultural development. Stress was also placed on the need for firm and strong government and governmental institutions in order to create the social, economic and cultural foundation for the growth of democracy which 'has to develop gradually, taking root through a process of struggle and change'. A multiparty system and competitive elections were viewed in a rather negative light and were described as 'procedural as opposed to an essential' aspect of democracy. There was need for strong leadership with clear vision for development.[22] Eritrea's new head of state Issayas Afewerki, the former war leader, became president, commander-in-chief of the armed forces, chairman of the national assembly and secretary-general of the People's Front for Democracy and Justice (PFDJ) so that all effective power lay in his hands. There were some 'Orwellian' aspects to the creation of this constitution as one critic suggests: '…the need to create national unity devoid of past ethnic and religious tensions.

The framework for this has been a relatively authoritarian government modelled on the policies and practices of the EPLF, and a recognition that whereas the EPLF instilled nationalist sentiments and values in its members, unreconstructed sub-national loyalties lurked in the hearts of broader Etritrean society.'[23] A good deal of reconstruction was clearly intended. In essence this constitution represented the transition of a successful liberation movement turning itself into an exclusive ruling party. By 2001, following the war over borders with Ethiopia at the end of the 1990s, opposition to President Afewerki's autocratic rule surfaced. A group of critics, the 'G15' including Mahmoud Sherifo, a former minister who had chaired a committee to prepare for elections for December 2001 (which were indefinitely postponed), drafted a report favouring political parties. However, when pre-publication copies were distributed to members of the National Assembly in February, President Afewerki dismissed Sherifo, who had been regarded as unofficial vice-president, and later had 11 of the 15 who were still in the country arrested. Dissent was clearly not to be part of Eritrean politics.

At the end of the 1980s donors began to exert serious pressures upon Kenya's President, Daniel arap Moi, to democratize but Moi, like other tenacious leaders, was to weave and obfuscate issues for another decade before he was finally voted out of power. At the beginning of the 1990s he referred to democracy campaigners as 'unpatriotic people with borrowed brains'. However, in November 1991, donors suspended aid to Moi's regime worth approximately US$1 billion, leading him to accept the reintroduction of democratic elections that December. With considerable skill Moi managed so to divide the opposition that he retained power and political control, winning the 1992 elections and surviving through the decade at the end of which he still claimed that he was the one to change the country, 'even after 20-odd years of misrule'.[24] In June 2001 Kenya's first coalition government was formed when Moi appointed Raila Odinga, leader of the National Development Party (NDP), to the cabinet as Minister of Energy and another NDP member as Minister for Planning. In November he made Uhuru Kenyatta, the son of Kenya's first President, Minister for Local Government. He was trying to breathe new life into KANU against his resignation (under the terms of the constitution) that had to take place in 2002: he hoped by these appointments to keep control of the party. The elections of December 2002 finally brought an end to both Moi's long rule and his influence. The National Rainbow Coalition (NARC), led by Mwai Kibaki, won 132 seats in the legislature against KANU's 68, and Kibaki was elected President with 3,578,972 votes (62.3 per cent). It was the first time since the establishment of the multiparty system in 1991 that the opposition had united to present a credible challenge to Moi. According to *African Business*, 'The change has been a subtle but profound alteration in the attitude of the people themselves. The NARC is a coalition of all the various peoples of Kenya and all the different classes. In previous elections, bickering and infighting among opposition parties handed victory to KANU on a plate. By uniting together, the people have succeeded in toppling the massive edifice that KANU represented... The emphasis has changed from leaders to people. Now the people will lead and will dictate terms to those they select to represent them.'[25] Given past experience, this may well be too sanguine a view; at least the democratic situation in Kenya had taken a marked turn for the better. Organizing opposition to longstanding incumbents is never easy. 'A number of factors explain the victory of unpopular incumbents in countries such as Kenya, Ghana and Côte d'Ivoire. One important reason in all three countries was the failure of the opposition to maintain unity and to fight the president on a single platform.'[26] At last NARC had managed to remedy that fault in Kenya.

Africa's four Indian Ocean territories – Comoros, Mauritius, Seychelles and Madagascar – have undergone varied political fortunes since independence. In 2001 Comoros faced a continuing stalemate over the island of Anjouan's determination to secede that dated from 1998. In Mauritius, the most stable and economically successful of the four, elections in 2000 saw the return to power of Anerood Jugnauth of the Mauritian Socialist Movement (MSM) as Prime Minister, and Paul Berenger of the Mauritian Militant Movement (MMM) as his deputy, a combination that worked well. The island seemed set for a further period of reasonable economic progress. In Seychelles President Albert René of the *Front Progressiste du Peuple Seychellois* (FPPS) (Seychelles Popular Progressive Front) was re-elected for a third and final term. He had originally come to power by means of a coup in 1977 (the year after independence) but had transformed the island into a multiparty democracy in 1991. Madagascar began the new century dangerously. The close presidential election results of December 2001 led to six months of confrontation and near civil war over the first half of 2002 before Didier Ratsiraka finally accepted defeat and retired to France and Marc Ravalomanana became President.

Democracy had never had an easy ride in Lesotho and at the end of 2001 the ruling Lesotho Congress for Democracy (LCD) was preparing a new electoral role for elections the following year while the opposition was riven with factions. Even so, the LCD also suffered from internal fighting and 27 members broke away to form the Lesotho People's Congress. It seems almost a rule of thumb that the smaller an African country, the greater the likelihood of political fragmentation. In Mozambique the RENAMO opposition still refused to accept the 1999 election results that had returned FRELIMO to office. In Namibia, President Sam Nujoma had persuaded the National Assembly to change the constitution so that he could stand for a third presidential term in 2000, which he did successfully; then, early in 2001, he announced that he was prepared to run for a fourth term in 2005 although later he said he would not do so. In Swaziland the issues of democratization and liberalization continued to dominate the political scene, with the monarchist establishment pitted against the political reformers. The Constitutional Review Commission, which had been established in 1996, submitted a private report to the King in August 2001. This act in itself aroused controversy since most of the commissioners were not allowed to see it and assumed that it had been 'doctored'. It argued that the absolute monarchy should continue and that political parties should remain banned although it did make provision for a bill of rights. The previous June the King had announced a decree enabling his government to ban any book, magazine or newspaper without providing reasons. No person or court could challenge any matter pending before the King. There was to be no bail for a range of crimes. However, pressures from the United States and COSATU in South Africa forced the King to revoke this decree although controls of the press continued unabated.

At its third congress in December 1990, Angola's ruling party, the MPLA, formally abandoned Marxism-Leninism and a constitutional revision law was enacted in May 1991, coinciding with the Bicesse Accords (peace accords between the government and UNITA) agreed in Portugal. The law of May proclaimed a democratic state based on the rule of law and respect for human rights; it introduced a multiparty system. Other laws passed at the same time regulated associations, political parties, the right of assembly, the press and the right to strike. In April 1992 a new electoral system was devised and a National Press Council established. These new laws preceded the first ever multiparty presidential and parliamentary elections in September 1992. When Jonas Savimbi failed to win the presidential election he returned to the bush in October and resumed the war. Dos Santos had not won the election with an outright majority but since Savimbi had returned to the bush the second round was postponed and later cancelled. The war over 1992–94 was exceptionally brutal and bitter and an estimated 100,000 people lost their lives. Those UNITA deputies who had won seats in the 1992 elections only took their places in the assembly in 1997. There had been a lull in the fighting from the end of 1994 but it was resumed in 1999, causing the abandonment of democratization and decentralization, at least for the time being. Hyper-inflation in May 1996 caused an outburst of public anger, leading dos Santos to replace his economic ministers, although subsequent demonstrations were ruthlessly suppressed. The collapse of the peace process meant that Angola continued to operate under a system of sub-national government based entirely on the nomination of officials from above. 'The provinces have provincial governments, headed by governors, who are appointed by the head of state and are considered his representatives at the provincial level.'[27] Civil war, half-war, fear and destruction prevailed in Angola throughout the 1990s so that the presidential system, which had been developed under the one-party state, was given a new lease of life. The party was marginalized following the breakdown of the peace process in late 1992 and the president became all-powerful. The regime had accepted the democratic reforms of 1991 under pressure to end the war but when this flared up again, it became possible for the government to abandon the process and this suited both the president and the ruling elite. Only after the death of Savimbi on 22 February 2002 did the prospect again open up for a possible peace process that might last.

Botswana can be regarded as the democratic and economic success story of Africa. It had been democratic ever since independence in 1966 although the political process had always been dominated by the Botswana Democratic Party (BDP) which had won every election up to 2000, under Seretse Khama from 1966 to 1980, Quett Masire (1980–98) and then Festus Mogae. At the beginning of the new century Transparency International rated Botswana in 26th place in the world and the highest in Africa while Moody's Investors Service gave it the highest credit rating in Africa.

By the 1990s the people of Malawi had become increasingly restless under the long dictatorship of Hastings Banda who had ruled the country more or less autocratically ever since independence in 1964. In October 1993 Banda became seriously ill and had to go to South Africa for medical treatment. In his absence the office of the president announced the creation of a three-member presidential council that would assume executive power in Banda's absence. In November this council reshuffled the cabinet and took away from Banda his ministerial responsibilities. The National Assembly passed a constitutional amendment bill to repeal the life presidency that had been conferred on Banda while also reducing the age qualification for a prospective presidential candidate from 40 to 35 and laid down that prospective candidates need not be members of the Malawi Congress Party (MCP). The Assembly also repealed the right of the President to nominate members of the legislature exclusively from the ranks of the MCP and lowered the voting age from 21 to 18. Banda, meanwhile, made a rapid and unexpected recovery and returned to Malawi on 7 December to resume the presidency and the presidential council was discharged. In February 1994 the MCP announced that Banda would be its presidential candidate for the elections set for that May. On the eve of the elections the National Assembly adopted a provisional constitution. Banda's long domination of Malawi finally came to an end with the elections of 17 May when Bakili Muluzi of the United

Democratic Front (UDF) obtained 47.3 per cent of the votes, Banda 33.6 per cent and Chakufwa Chihana of AFORD 18.6 per cent. Muluzi became Malawi's second president and in June he announced an independent commission of inquiry into the deaths of Dick Matenji, the former secretary-general of the MCP, and others in 1983 – it had long been suspected that they had been assassinated or murdered on Banda's orders. In January 1995 Banda was placed under house arrest. John Tembo, who had been a rival of Matenji's for the eventual succession, and was accused of a hand in his death, had been regarded as Banda's choice, and two police officers were arrested and the three plus Banda were put on trial. However, the trial was adjourned because Banda was too ill to attend; the trial was later abandoned. These events signalled the destruction of Banda's authority and in January 1996 an MCP newspaper published a statement by Banda in which he admitted he might unknowingly have been responsible for brutalities perpetrated under his regime and apologized for any 'pain and suffering' inflicted on Malawians during his presidency. It was a humiliating comedown for the once all-powerful president. The country reverted to a multiparty democratic system.

Discontent in Zambia at the dire state of the economy and unrest among workers and students characterized much of 1989. There was rioting on the Copperbelt in July. In April 1990 the ruling party, UNIP, rejected proposals for multiparty politics but in May Kaunda announced that a referendum would be held on multipartyism in October and public meetings to discuss it would be allowed. In June, an announcement that the price of maize was to double set off rioting in Lusaka in which some 30 people were killed. In July the Movement for Multiparty Democracy (MMD) was formed. The MMD was led by Frederick Chiluba, chairman of the ZCTU and a long time critic of Kaunda, and Arthur Wina, a former Finance Minister. Kaunda said that the proposed referendum was to be postponed to August 1991 in order to facilitate full electoral registration. Wina demanded that the referendum should be held in December. The National Assembly proposed a multiparty system which Kaunda at first opposed but he gave way a month later and appointed October 1991 for multiparty legislative and presidential elections. Despite rumours in the run-up to the elections – Kaunda accused international observers of a conspiracy to remove UNIP from power – the elections took place on 31 October and the observers said they had been conducted fairly. Chiluba obtained 75.79 per cent of the votes cast, Kaunda 24.21 per cent. In the legislative elections the MMD won 125 seats to UNIP's 25. Kaunda stood down gracefully and Frederick Chiluba became Zambia's second president, an office he held for 10 years. The MMD was an elite movement of trade union leaders and business leaders that had built up a mass following. The fact that during the elections both Chiluba and Wina felt able to go abroad to seek promises of aid lent some credibility to Kaunda's suggestions of international support for his opponents. They were treated like a government in waiting. 'The massive victory (of the MMD), however, conferred little legitimacy on the government, and by the time President Chiluba started his second term in office all illusions of Zambia as a pioneer of democracy had been shattered. Not only had the constitution skewed the election results, but the press had also been subjected to increasing intimidation and censorship during the election campaign.'[28] In 1996 international observers refused to go to Zambia since to do so would give legitimacy to what was seen as a flawed process. At the beginning of 2001 Chiluba seemed determined to seek a third term as president but to do so required a constitutional amendment supported by two-thirds of the National Assembly and opposition to any such move mounted in the ranks of the MMD. In May 2001 Chiluba backtracked and said he would not seek a third term. In August Levy Mwanawasa was chosen as MMD presidential candidate and he promised to tackle corruption. The elections, which were held in December, were fiercely contested, and Mwanawasa, who was presumed (wrongly as it turned out) to be a puppet or front man for Chiluba, won though with a minority of the total votes cast.

Three other countries should be mentioned. Zambia's neighbour to the south, Zimbabwe, entered the new century in a state of deepening crisis as its President, Robert Mugabe, resorted to increasing violence and denial of the rule of law to hold onto power (see chapter 38 below). In Nigeria President Obasanjo won a second term in the elections of 2003 and, hopefully, the long period of military dominance was a thing of the past. In South Africa the search for a viable opposition to the ANC led to the formation of the Democratic Alliance. The hope, expressed by a range of African observers, was that the new South Africa would act as the driving force in an African renaissance. 'The experience of South Africa where, uniquely on the continent, Western and African notions of identity both have deep historical roots, will be an interesting test case of the extent to which Western-style democracy evolves in Africa.'[29]

When we have stripped away all the external factors of pressure and interference – and these are many – the responsibility for African democracy, in whatever form it takes, remains with the African people. They face formidable tasks: greed of rulers and the determination of politicians to hold onto power at almost any cost; the endless pulls of rival ethnic groups; the manipulations of elites whose fortunes are tied to the preservation of tyrants in power. The return to democracy in the 1990s, where it took place, was fraught with dangers and setbacks, yet the determination of the African masses to bring an end to one-party dictatorships was an encouraging aspect of the continent's politics, even when victories were subsequently whittled away or overthrown by the old power mongers of the one-party state era.

Unfortunately, too often, democracy did not deliver the expected rewards and so was followed by disillusion and discontent. Why, it has often been asked, do democratically elected governments not deliver policies that the mass of the people want? Too often, those who obtain power do not work on behalf of the poor majority but in the interests of middle class or elitist groups to which they themselves belong. Many revolts leading to a form of democratization were less against the existing system than they were for better economic conditions. Poverty was the driving force for change and had economies been better managed and wealth more equitably distributed the chances are that existing power structures would not have been challenged. If we consider external pressures for democracy, which often come from such international institutions as the World Bank or IMF, it is time they were reformed and made truly democratic rather than based upon voting related to financial contributions while it comes ill from the major Western powers – the US, Britain and France – to argue for democracy when they insist upon their undemocratic vetoes in the UN Security Council. For democracy to be meaningful it must empower people to participate in the process of bettering themselves. One optimistic appraisal of change in Africa is as follows: 'Most notably, the societies which have been subject to such extreme destabilization are continually developing new strategies of an extraordinary diversity and inventiveness, which offers proof that Africa, so often said to be governed by age-old tradition, is in fact a place of unrivalled change and mobility.'[30] The argument too often applied to Africa is that 'strong' leaders (that is, dictatorial figures) are necessary to bring about necessary change and consequently that the luxury of political rights – democracy – has to be deferred to some indefinite future. It is an argument that has suited many authoritarian rulers – in Africa and elsewhere – but its appeal has been eroded by the performance of such leaders when in power. 'Africa has a chance, but only as the old leaders – and, let us hope, their legacies – die off; only as the nations begin to recognize that open societies are the vital ones, that agriculture does not detract from a nation's dignity, and that human development may make people worse subjects, but wonderfully better citizens.'[31] Democracy has to be fought for every day.

Civil Wars:
Algeria, Somalia, Sudan

T he 1990s witnessed more than a dozen wars in Africa, most of them civil, some ongoing like that in Sudan. They were explained in multiple ways: religious divides, ethnic differences, ideological confrontations, unfair distribution of national wealth, but in reality they were about power – who had it and who lacked it. The three countries considered here had much in common: their populations were predominantly Muslim, they were each members of the Arab League, they belonged to the geographic northern belt of African countries and their governments had demonstrated marked determination to break their former colonial connections. There the similarities ended. Algeria had fought a bitter independence war against France and had emerged as one of the most politically radical countries in Africa. Sudan was distinguished from the rest of colonial Africa as a condominium of Britain and Egypt and was sharply divided along ethnic lines between the Arab north and the black south. Somalia was ethnically more homogeneous than any other African country and compensated for this apparently unifying factor by dividing on clan lines. Diversity, as ever, was the rule.

ALGERIA

From independence to the end of the 1980s Algeria was a one-party state though state power never resided in the hands of that party – *Front de Libération Nationale* (FLN) (National Liberation Font); rather, the party was an instrument of state policy while the centre of power, always, was the army. Neither was the FLN an ideological party in the sense of being committed to a particular creed. Its job was to safeguard the Algerian state.[1] During the 1990s Algeria was to suffer from brutal confrontations and massacres, essentially between the secular state authorities and the Islamist 'fundamentalists' who sought a greater say in the running of the state than the army-backed government was prepared to allow. Although the confrontation that turned into civil war resulted from the growth of fundamentalist Islamic forces – the concept of fundamentalism has to be treated warily – the challenge to government arose out of the failure of the one-party state of the FLN to satisfy the economic and political needs of the people. In 1988 Algeria witnessed the worst rioting and social unrest since independence in 1962, and that was the measure of the government's failure. That October riots erupted in Algiers, Annaba, Oran and other cities and continued for a number of days with government buildings and state-owned shops being especially targeted. The disturbances were suppressed by the army and resulted in 159 deaths (the official figure) but as many as 500 according to other estimates. Although the government blamed fundamentalists for the riots, a more likely explanation was simple popular dissatisfaction with harsh economic conditions. Discontent with the state of the economy could be traced to the austerity measures, including a 30 per cent devaluation, that had followed the 1986 fall in oil prices, and factions within the FLN that had also opposed the measures. When the riots had subsided the government quickly increased consumer supplies and at the same time promised constitutional reforms; it was these latter, implemented in 1989, which opened the way to multipartyism. Up to this time, Algeria had been ruled by a closed political hierarchy so that the eruption of Islamist claims for a role in the state was seen as a major threat. 'The state is a very tightly run dictatorship which has long claimed, and has largely succeeded in maintaining, a monopoly over public life.'[2]

The *Front Islamique du Salut* (FIS) was founded in February 1989 and legalized the following September; it rapidly emerged as a major political force, able to mobilize large numbers of supporters and commanding a nationwide appeal. The riots of 1988 were especially directed at President Chadli Benjedid who, with his surrounding cronies, was seen as deeply corrupt: 'We don't want butter or pepper, we want a leader we can trust.' Despite the discontents with a failed economic system, the FIS did not advance any economic policy of its own although it drew its support from the poorest and most deprived sections of the community. Ironically, in the light of subsequent European judgements as to what was happening in Algeria, the Islamists did not aim to overthrow the FLN state structures but wanted to advance their interests within the existing system. By the end of the 1980s demands for economic reform had become something of a crusade, enabling the adroit Benjedid to pose as a reformer as he changed the constitution to allow multiparty politics for the first time since independence. By September 1989 five political parties (apart from the FLN) had registered while within the FLN a power struggle had developed between President Benjedid and the old party hierarchy. The Gulf crisis of 1990, following the Iraq invasion of Kuwait, led to massive pro-Iraqi demonstrations in Algeria with the FIS as well as secular nationalists opposing any US presence in the Gulf.

Benjedid continued to carry out political reforms through 1990 and exiles, including former President Ahmed Ben Bella, were allowed to return to Algeria. In the town council and municipal elections of June the government and FLN suffered a huge setback: 65 per cent of the electorate voted with the FIS obtaining 54 per cent of the vote while the FLN managed only 28 per cent. The FIS took control of 32 out of 48 wilayats, mainly in the densely populated coastal regions. The result led to a split in the FLN and the resignation of Prime Minister Mouloud Hamrouche who had miscalculated how the elections would turn out. President Benjedid committed himself to elections for the National Assembly early in 1991. The end of the Cold War meant the disappearance of the alternative Soviet model for nationalist Algeria, and France at once began to reassert its influence, by attempting 'to force upon the Algerian government its own preferences in economic policy, and to induce it to spring a pluralist constitution upon a society entirely unprepared for this transition as a pretext for legalizing the Islamists as the essential preliminary to instrumentalizing them against the nationalism of the FLN.'[3] France, it may be argued, had never forgiven the FLN for the defeat of 1962. However, when the political experiment in multipartyism went wrong and the FIS escaped Benjedid's control and the army intervened, Paris became 'secularist' and supported the subsequent repression.

During the Gulf crisis public opinion throughout the Maghreb became overwhelmingly pro-Iraq and Saddam Hussein became a popular Arab hero. The Western press assumed this attitude to be the result of Islamic fundamentalism but in fact it was the reaction of the great majority of the Arab people. In Algeria the crisis helped radicalize public opinion and united much of the Algerian nation. The FIS depended upon the unemployed youth of the towns for its main support and from 26 May 1991 onwards it began to fill the streets and squares of Algiers with its followers in a series of peaceful protests. Certainly at this stage, in mid-1991, the principal complaint of the FIS was the attempt by the Hamrouche government to gerrymander the elections for the National Assembly, a complaint shared by others apart from the FIS. Meanwhile, the government carried out a number of economic reforms designed to move Algeria towards a full market economy. The FIS, however, faced internal factional problems and split between the moderates under Abbasi Madani, and the radicals under Ali Belhadj. The FIS objections to the electoral reforms, which led to a general strike and demonstrations gave the army an excuse to proclaim a state of emergency on 5 June 1991, which it maintained through to September, by which time the FIS leadership had been arrested and the party – apparently – disbanded.

The elections, which had been postponed from early 1991 as originally promised, were finally held on 26 December and to the dismay of the government and FLN, the FIS made huge gains, winning 188 of 430 seats in the National Assembly while it led in 150 of the remaining seats where a second round of voting would be held. The FLN had won a mere 16 seats (as opposed to 295 in 1987) while the socialists took 20 seats. The principal factor working in favour of the FIS was the perception that the Benjedid regime was totally decadent. In the two weeks following the elections the army decided that Benjedid was leading the country to disaster and would have to go. The second round of voting was set for 15 January 1992, when the FIS would only need 30 seats more to obtain an absolute majority. Fearing these results, the armed forces took control of the country, forced President Benjedid to resign on 11 January, cancelled the elections and declared a state of emergency. It then created a *Haut Comité d'Etat* (HCE) (High State Council) and invited the long-exiled Muhammad Boudiaf, who had impeccable nationalist credentials but had been 28 years in Morocco, to return to Algeria and head the HCE. When the Western media reacted to these events by describing a 'military-backed' regime they ignored the fact that governments in Algeria had always been military-backed and that of Benjedid more than most. Before he introduced his democratic reforms, Benjedid had got himself elected in 1988 under the old one-party, dictatorial rules. 'The public reaction of Western governments and commentators to the suspension of the electoral process in Algeria following President Benjedid's resignation on 11 January 1992 was a profoundly mixed one. Relief at the fact that Algeria was not about to become "a second Iran" very quickly gave way to disapproval of the manner in which this prospect had been conjured away at the last moment, as numerous editorialists in London and Paris and no doubt elsewhere indulged themselves in vigorous criticism of what they had not hesitated to call a "military coup".'[4] The West faced one of its classic dilemmas: it wanted, or pretended to want, democracy in Algeria provided the democratic process produced a 'safe' government from the West's point of view but it came round to accepting the army's intervention if this prevented Islamic fundamentalism. Then, when the FIS was deprived of its electoral victory, Western media argued that it should have been allowed to take power. The security forces proceeded to dismantle FIS party structures and arrested about 9,000 of its members who were interned in camps in the Sahara. On 4 March the FIS was banned. Violence followed these draconian measures and by October 150 people had been killed, mainly in urban areas.

Boudiaf was not as compliant as the army and old hierarchy had hoped. He tried to move the government back to its experiment with democracy by creating a new mass movement, *Rassemblement Patriotique,* and launching an anti-corruption campaign. He was assassinated on 29 June and though the

Islamists were blamed for his death the people believed Benjedid rather than the FIS was responsible and that it was done to forestall the anti-corruption campaign. The appointment of Boudiaf as President had undermined the FIS claim to be the heirs to the historic FLN since he was an old revolutionary and had helped create the FLN. Boudiaf was replaced by Ali Kafi with a strong prime minister, Belaid Abdessalam, who tackled urban terrorism by creating special courts and laying down severe punishments. By this time violence was supplanting political manoeuvres. Unfortunately, Algeria had a long history of political violence – 50 years of fighting the French colonialists in the nineteenth century and a bloody independence struggle that had cost a million lives – and now violence replaced politics as the weapon of confrontation. Violence escalated through 1993. Some 210 security personnel had been killed in 1992 and by October 1993 about 1,000 Islamist sympathizers, whether members of the FIS or not, had been killed while a further 3,800 had been brought before the courts with 240 of these being condemned to death. The Islamists targeted prominent figures such as intellectuals and soldiers while the government responded by placing all responsibility on the FIS.

The government became increasingly unpopular as it failed to control the violence; it also became increasingly internationally isolated. On 23 March 1993 it broke diplomatic relations with Iran and then withdrew its ambassador from Sudan, accusing both countries of supporting the Islamist extremists. It tried to create a common anti-extremists front with Tunisia and Egypt. Its relations with Morocco had also deteriorated after King Hassan criticized the military suspension of the electoral process. The conflict escalated during 1994. The HCE chose Liamine Zeroual, a former general and defence minister, as President. Zeroual favoured the readmission of the FIS to the constitutional process and attempted to hold a dialogue from which no one should be excluded. He released a number of FIS prisoners and in September 1994 had Abbasi Madani and Ali Belhadj transferred from Blida prison to house arrest. Madani had intimated that the FIS would respect a pluralistic political system resulting from any future elections. The FIS would not renounce violence, however, and the dialogue did not materialize. The Islamist opposition split into two factions: the *Groupe Islamiste Armée* (GIA) (Armed Islamic Group), mainly centred upon the city of Algiers; and the *Mouvement Islamiste Armée* (MIA) (Armed Islamic Movement), which drew its strength from the east and west of the country. Foreign nationals were now targeted and more than 60 killed, persuading most countries to withdraw their nationals from Algeria. The government launched a new campaign against the GIA. The French government decided to expel FIS supporters from France. By the beginning of 1995 estimates suggested that as many as 40,000 people had been killed in the three years since January 1992.

In January 1995 the FIS, FLN, *Front des Forces Socialistes* (FFS) (the Socialist Forces Front) and the Hamas party met in Rome where they agreed on the need to end the violence and form a government of national unity to supervise elections. The government, however, rejected these proposals although they had the backing of France, Italy, Spain and the US as well as a majority of anti-government groups inside Algeria. The GIA demanded that the country's leaders should be punished. Presidential elections were held in November 1995 and Zeroual was elected with a comfortable majority. He attempted further negotiations with the FIS leaders. By this time Algeria was subject to mounting international criticism for human rights abuses; there was growing concern at the increasing numbers of extra-judicial killings by security forces, which appeared to be condoned by the government. Many of the killings and massacres were conducted in barbaric fashion, billions of dinars worth of property had been destroyed and the army had also destroyed hundreds of thousands of acres of forest to deprive the Islamist guerrillas of cover. Members of the government divided between the *eradicateurs* who favoured all-out repression of 'political Islam' and the conciliators who argued that repression and security alone would not work. A compromise with the FIS was needed. The killings and massacres continued in 1996 and there were few witnesses and less information divulged by the government as to what was happening or what its retaliatory measures amounted to.

Algerians acknowledged Zeroual's political skills but he failed to stop the killings and by February these were reckoned at a weekly rate of 100 to 150. Every city now had its 'no go' areas and foreigners were warned away from the centre of Algiers. The fundamentalists attacked newspapers and television and killed many journalists who were regarded as pro-government. In April Zeroual initiated talks to map out a new political-constitutional course of action. He proposed a ban on political parties based on religion or language and laid down that a party should draw its support from across the nation and not just from one region. The president was only to be allowed to serve two terms of five years. The parties reacted cautiously and the FIS, which had not been invited to take part in the talks, rejected the proposals as did old supporters of the former president, Chadli Benjedid. Nonetheless, the proposals were endorsed by a national conference in September and the new constitution was approved by referendum in November in which 80 per cent of the country's 16.4 million voters took part to give an 86 per cent endorsement. There was to be a second chamber or upper house that would severely limit the powers of the lower chamber – an indirectly elected Council of the Nation – with two-thirds of its members drawn from local and regional assemblies and the rest 'national personalities and experts' approved by the President. Meanwhile, in May GIA made headlines when it kidnapped and subsequently executed seven Trappist monks. In August the bishop of Oran was killed by a car bomb; the incident raised fears in the French community in Algeria, then estimated at about 1,000. Up to that time about 40 French people had been killed since 1993. GIA regarded France as the main external supporter of the Algerian government. Evidence provided by human rights groups suggested that by 1996 government death squads as well as the GIA were responsible for the various massacres taking place. By this time the army had effectively privatized the war by arming 200,000 civilians as 'communal guards' or 'self-defence groups' and there were 550,000 men under arms in Algeria.

The war of the 1990s was fought between the forces of a government that had lost its credibility and was seen to have failed to satisfy the political and economic needs of the people, and the Islamic fundamentalists who saw themselves as an older, more radical alternative to the secular, one-party state that had ruled Algeria since 1962. By 1997, the repercussions of the war were being felt increasingly in Europe and suspected Algerian terrorists were being arrested in France, Germany and Italy. The savage tactics employed by the GIA were increasingly criticized by mainstream Islamists, including the FIS, but to no effect. As Ali Yahya, a leading human rights lawyer, said in Algiers: 'There is no military solution because the crisis is primarily a political one, and must be resolved by talks.' The prime minister claimed that 80,000 people had been killed since the violence began although the FIS said the figure was 120,000. Figures had become relatively meaningless; what mattered was that the rate of killing went on unabated. April 1997 was an especially brutal month with village massacres and train bombs. The area worst affected by atrocities such as throat-cutting massacres in villages was the Mitidja plain south of Algiers. It became increasingly clear that at least a proportion of these massacres could be attributed to the security forces rather than the fundamentalists. More disturbing, no one ever seemed to be brought before a court of law. As Amnesty International reported: 'There is just a statement, released to the press, that the killer or killers had been killed.' A certain European unease surfaced at the extent to which France supported the Algerian government: on the one hand it was suggested that the Algerian authorities were able to exert many pressures on the French government but, on the other hand, France managed to carry its EU partners with it so that EU policy towards Algeria was largely left to Paris. In the parliamentary elections of June 1997, the *Rallé National Démocratique* (RND) with 36.3 per cent of the vote won 156 seats in the assembly while its ally, the once all-powerful FLN, only obtained 15.3 per cent of the votes and 62 seats. Only 41.78 per cent of the electorate had voted. An estimated 5,000 people were killed between these elections and the end of September. Information about the violence was hard to come by and massacres often occurred near army barracks, yet neither the army nor the police intervened until the killers had gone, a fact that reinforced the argument that the army was either directly responsible for the massacres or willing to stand aside while they were perpetrated. By that October an estimated 12,000 Algerians had simply disappeared.

Discussions of the violence in Algeria by outsiders were always in terms of who was responsible for it rather than why it was taking place. In any case, the inability of the government to stop the violence put it on the defensive. By 1999 both the government and the Islamists were accused of terrible atrocities. Presidential elections were due in April 1999 and the day before they took place six of the seven candidates withdrew, accusing the authorities of initiating a massive fraud in favour of the former Foreign Minister Abdelaziz Bouteflika, who was the candidate favoured by the army. In the event, Bouteflika gained 73.8 per cent of the votes cast, with 60.25 per cent of eligible voters participating. Bouteflika quickly made contact with the FIS and in June the *Armée Islamique du Salut* (AIS) agreed to make the ceasefire, which had been in place since October 1997, permanent and to co-operate with the government against the GIA. The FIS leader, Abbasi Madani, was still under house arrest but the FIS constitutional council endorsed the agreement. A referendum of September 1999 rendered a 98.6 per cent vote in favour of the Bouteflika peace initiative, which included a civil concord offering amnesty to Islamic militants not implicated in mass killings. There was opposition to the civil concord and one French language paper called it a 'shameful capitulation to Islamist violence'. There has been much debate about the nature of the Algerian civil war. As one commentator said: 'Not the least striking aspect of the Algerian crisis is the absence of a consensus as to its nature. There is not only disagreement as to the rights and wrongs of the conflict and uncertainty as to who has been responsible for which particular acts of violence but also, and above all, a fundamental disagreement over the character of the conflict itself.'[5]

In January 2000 a new agreement was reached between the government and the AIS to give full amnesty to its 3,000 fighters. AIS agreed to disband permanently though for a time some of its fighters were to be enrolled in an 'auxiliary unit' to fight the GIA. The ban of the FIS remained. Although Algiers and the major cities were calm, the countryside remained insecure with approximately 200 killings occurring every month. Meanwhile, Bouteflika worked to improve Algeria's overseas image: he went on a state visit to France in June; in July Spain's premier José María Aznar visited Algeria and US officials came to discuss political, economic and military issues. Despite many confrontations since independence, France and Algeria needed each other. Algeria wanted France to break the diplomatic isolation in which it had been stuck for most of the 1990s while France needed better relations with Algeria for both commercial and strategic reasons, especially as the United States had been demonstrating a growing interest in Algeria since 1998 and was seeking military co-operation. This worried Paris. 'Thus, following US Defense Secretary William Cohen's declaration in February [2000] that the US government intended not merely to continue but to expand military co-operation with Algeria, Paris immediately dispatched a senior official to Algiers to discuss *French* military co-operation with Algeria. And no sooner had the US Sixth Fleet held joint exercises with the Algerian navy in early May than Vice-Admiral Paul Habert, the French naval commander for the Mediterranean, visited Algiers for urgent talks.'[6] Algeria, it seemed, was coming in from the cold, at least as far as its strategic position was concerned.

By this time an increasing number of Algerians were calling for the army to withdraw from its domination of the political scene so that a true civil government could come into being. December 2000 witnessed an upsurge in violence when 300 civilians were killed by GIA in the first half of the month. The reaction in the private press was that Bouteflika's peace initiative had failed. Violence in the form of massacres and bombs in Algiers continued in 2001 and was attributed to Islamist groups. There was continuing criticism of the civil concord in the Francophone press, especially after 11 September and the 'eradicateurs' criticized Bouteflika for maintaining the dialogue with the Islamists. The authorities, on the other hand, declared that they felt less isolated after the 11 September attacks in the United States because there was greater understanding in the West of their own battle against terrorism. President Bouteflika made two visits to Washington and joined the US coalition against terrorism. However, many Algerians condemned the bombing of Afghanistan.

In the elections of 30 May 2002, the FLN, reversing their humiliation of 1997, won 199 of 389 seats in the new National Assembly while the RND was reduced to 46 seats. It seemed at least possible that the FLN was making a recovery as the dominant factor in Algerian politics. Given the changed world situation, following 11 September, and US interest in closer ties with Algeria shadowed by a determined French push to improve its relations as well, European criticisms of the Algerian political structure may well become less evident. In any case, European interest in Algeria has always been geared more to economics than to politics and if Algeria was prepared to enter into closer military ties with the US its less than satisfactory political performance – from a Western point of view – could be overlooked without much difficulty. Despite the moves towards democracy initiated by Chadli Benjedid, which acted as the tinder to launch the civil war of the 1990s, by the early part of the new century though violence was still continuing the Islamist opposition had become muted, at least for the time being, and the power structure in Algeria still consisted of the army, the presidency and – following the elections of May 2002 – a somewhat rehabilitated FLN once more in the political saddle. At the beginning of March 2003, President Jacques Chirac of France made a state visit to Algeria – the first since independence in 1962 – to a hero's welcome. Partly, this was due to his stand against the United States and Britain going to war with Iraq; but partly, also, for an embattled country, it represented a welcome recognition of a government that had been isolated and treated with semi-pariah status for 10 years.

SOMALIA

The Algerian civil war had been fought between Algerians alone, without external interference; this was not the case in Somalia. During the 1980s Siad Barre had become increasingly autocratic and isolated while his poor human rights record alienated international opinion. By 1990 he had not only failed to eliminate the Somali clan system but had produced a situation in which there was escalating fighting both between clans and between clans and government. The country was reduced to a state of anarchy and Barre was losing control. By mid-1990 the government was forced to impose a curfew in Mogadishu while Barre was obliged to promise political reforms and elections for 1991, but it was too late. By the beginning of January 1991 the dissident United Somali Congress (USC) controlled large parts of the capital and on 27 January the USC announced that it had taken control of the government. Barre fled under army protection and went into exile in Nigeria, leaving behind him a civil war situation that would last for the rest of the decade.

The two principal players in the unfolding drama that Barre left were Gen. Farah Aideed and the businessman Ali Mahdi Mohammed. Aideed had been Somalia's ambassador to India from 1984 to 1989 as Barre, who did not trust him, wanted him out of the way. In 1989 Aideed went to Italy where he became the leader of the dissident faction there. He returned to Somalia in 1991, after Barre had been forced to leave the country, to discover that his rival Ali Mahdi Mohammed had been proclaimed interim president. Factional fighting had increased rapidly on the departure of Barre and Aideed now emerged at the head of the faction that controlled most of Mogadishu. Aideed was shortly to achieve a high international profile, following the arrival of some 28,000 US marines at the end of 1992 whose stated purpose was to ensure that humanitarian aid reached the huge number of Somalis who had become refugees as a result of the clan warfare and were close to starvation. Aideed's forces repeatedly prevented the marines from gaining control of Mogadishu with the result that violence between his faction and the US forces escalated steadily through 1993. The US marines, who were technically part of the wider UN operation, made the mistake of demonizing Aideed. A UN resolution ordered his arrest but he was never captured despite enormous US efforts and in the end he was seen to triumph when the United Nations brought its mission in Somalia to a close. However, Aideed's success in defying both the Americans and the UN did not continue after the withdrawal of the UN Operation in Somalia II (UNOSOM-II) and he himself was mortally wounded in the faction fighting in 1996.

Aideed was always a warlord rather than the statesman that post-Barre Somalia required. Ali Mahdi Mohammed was a businessman and pragmatist rather than a warlord. In 1990 he had been one of 114 private citizens who signed a letter condemning Barre's policies and had then been obliged to flee the country to avoid arrest. Outside Somalia he raised money to finance the USC, which had offices in Rome. He returned to Somalia towards the end of 1990 by which time the USC had established a foothold in Mogadishu. He was not a military man or fighter and saw his role as one of raising funds for the USC. On 27 February 1991 he had been put forward as a compromise candidate to be interim president. Mohammed's presidency was endorsed by six guerrilla groups though not by Aideed or by other factions outside Mogadishu who had not been consulted. Even so, he was sworn in as President of Somalia on 18 August 1991 for a two-year term. However, Aideed at once contested his presidency and in September a power struggle for control of Mogadishu erupted between the followers of the two men. The situation deteriorated through 1992 as famine and starvation affected a growing number of the population. Armed bands, acting independently, controlled their own areas and held people and food relief supplies to ransom.

The United Nations became involved in mid-1992 in the hope of restoring order and ensuring that relief supplies reached their proper destinations but its failure to do so persuaded US President George Bush (senior) to authorize the use of 28,000 marines (under UN auspices) in Operation Restore Hope to protect relief columns from the depredations of clan groups. The US-led United Nations Task Force (UNTAF) arrived in Somalia in December 1992 and in January 1993 began to search for weapons in Mogadishu and other centres of population. On 7 January the US Commander, Gen. Robert Johnson, announced that his troops had opened up supply routes to the famine-affected areas and that a 'new phase' in Somalia was about to begin. In Mogadishu, almost at once, the marines came up against sniper fire and other forms of resistance and it was clear that the various parties vying for political control did not intend to accept US mediation. Gen. Aideed, who was soon to be denounced by the US authorities in Somalia, had formed the Somali National Alliance (SNA) with a military wing, the Somali Liberation Army (SLA). One of the first marine actions was to destroy an SNA arms cache and kill 30 Somalis. On 13 January the US forces suffered their first casualty when a marine was shot dead. Marine 'policing' action now became more aggressive. By the end of the month there were 24,000 US marines and a further 13,600 troops from other countries in Somalia under the UN umbrella. Tensions quickly developed between the US and the UN over the role of the American forces. Washington wanted to withdraw its forces from Somalia by April 1993, which clearly gave them little time to accomplish anything worthwhile, but the UN argued they should remain longer to help control the situation. At the end of February Aideed went on the offensive with his SLA, following a rumour that the US favoured one of his rivals. The SLA barricaded streets in Mogadishu, fought running battles with the US marines and attempted to storm the US and French embassies. At the same time, about 100 people were killed in street fighting between the SNA and the supporters of Gen. Mohammed Siyad Hersi Morgan, a son-in-law of Barre. During March the United States began to pull out its troops and the UN Secretary-General, Boutros Boutros-Ghali, named 1 May as the date for the peacekeeping operation to be handed over to the UN (by the Americans) to become UNOSOM-II. The US agreed to leave 5,000 troops as its contribution to UNOSOM-II, bringing its strength up to approximately 20,000 troops, apart from 2,500 civilian staff. Fighting in the southern town of Kismayu in March required the US to send 500 marines to restore order and bolster the US-Belgian garrison. The operation resulted in 100 Somali deaths. On 15 March a national reconciliation conference was convened in Addis Ababa and both Mohammed and Aideed attended. By the end of the month the conference had agreed to establish a Transitional National Council as a temporary Supreme Authority. In May the US-led UNTAF handed over authority to the UN and UNOSOM-II came into effect under the command of a Turkish general. UNOSOM-II had 20,000 troops from 35 countries and the authority to act anywhere in Somalia and use whatever means were required to disarm the warring factions, maintain peace and safeguard relief workers.

UNOSOM-II had an uneasy history and its operations in Somalia reflected little credit on the United Nations. Troops from several of the participating countries were accused of brutality and atrocities. In the north, meanwhile, the self-proclaimed state of Somaliland (former British Somaliland) behaved as an independent country and on 5 May 1993 elected Mohamed Ibrahim Egal as its president. On 5 June a street battle in Mogadishu resulted in 23 Pakistani casualties and Pakistan called for retaliatory action against Aideed. The United States sent reinforcements from the Gulf and the Security Council in New York condemned the unprovoked attack on UNOSOM forces. UNOSOM then launched a series of attacks on SNA. While this action may have given a certain satisfaction to the countries whose troops had been targeted, it could hardly be described as peacekeeping. Following US air attacks upon SNA targets, Aideed accused the United States of attacking civilians. On 13 June Pakistani troops fired on demonstrators in Mogadishu, killing 10 and wounding 50. There appeared to be little restraint on the part of UNOSOM forces and not much evidence of control from above.

The UN then made the mistake of ordering the arrest of Aideed and UNOSOM mounted a massive manhunt for him in Mogadishu in which 31 UN soldiers were killed as the manhunt proceeded. Then the death of three Italian soldiers led to demands by the opposition in Rome for the withdrawal of the Italian contingent while Italy blamed US belligerency for the deaths. By this time there was growing criticism of the US contingent for its 'macho' attitude in Somalia and especially that of Adm. Jonathan T. Howe, the US Special Representative in Somalia. A second operation to capture Aideed was mounted on 12 July with no more success although it resulted in 54 deaths and 174 wounded. In August the elite US Rangers raided a house in which they thought to find Aideed but instead took UN and French aid workers prisoner. By this time the US forces appeared to be acting as though their operation was a vendetta against Aideed rather than part of a larger UNOSOM operation. Two hundred Somalis were killed on 9 September when a US helicopter fired on a crowd in Mogadishu; there were seven UN casualties. On 22 September 1993, the UN Security Council adopted Resolution 865 that would bring the UNOSOM-II operation to a close in March 1995. In October a battle in Mogadishu led to the deaths of 300 Somalis and 18 US marines, while a US pilot and a Nigerian soldier were taken prisoner. On 9 October Kofi Annan, the UN Assistant Secretary-General for Peacekeeping Operations, visited Mogadishu and decided that the UN casualty rate was too high; he subsequently argued for 'some sort of judicial process' to investigate Aideed's responsibility for UN deaths. In effect, this represented a UN climb down, an admission that the demonizing of Aideed and the attempt to arrest him had been a failure, especially for the United States which had pushed the policy. On 27 October UN Secretary-General Boutros Boutros-Ghali announced that the UN would reconsider Resolution 837, which had authorized the arrest of Aideed. US President Bill Clinton called for the creation of a new Somali government and announced that all US troops would be withdrawn from Somalia by 31 March 1994. Germany, France, Belgium and Sweden announced their intention of also withdrawing early in 1994. Pakistan, on the other hand, said it was prepared to commit 5,000 troops to UNOSOM-II. In November the UN formally abandoned the search for Aideed and instead set up a Commission of Inquiry into responsibility for attacks upon UN forces. The UN renewed the UNOSOM mandate until 31 May 1995.

The end of 1993, which had been a disastrous year for the reputations of both the UN and US in Somalia, saw the withdrawal of a large proportion of the US, German, Italian and French forces. On 4 February 1994, in another softening of its earlier stand, the UN emphasized that its mandate was peacekeeping and reconciliation as opposed to enforcement. Violence continued throughout the first half of 1994 as UN troops were withdrawn. Aideed and Mohammed remained the two principal contenders for power. The problem throughout the country, which neither the US nor the UN had resolved, was how to disarm the various militarized groups. By 25 March 1994, after the withdrawal of the US and European contingents, UNOSOM-II was reduced from 29,000 to 19,000 troops drawn mainly from Africa and Pakistan. Aideed and Mohammed met in Nairobi, Kenya, during March and agreed to form a government of national reconciliation although the agreement was soon abandoned. There was more fighting in Mogadishu in May when Aideed's forces captured the airport. In March 1995 the last UNOSOM-II forces were evacuated from Somalia by an international fleet and 1,800 US marines. The enterprise had been a disaster for the UN. Faction fighting continued to the end of 1996. On 1 August 1996 Aideed died of wounds received in a battle in Mogadishu a week earlier. His death threw the future of the SNA into doubt though immediately his son, Hussein Aideed, became the SNA leader.

At the end of 1996 Somalia remained divided among its factions; fighting periodically erupted in Mogadishu and elsewhere; the country was physically ruined; tens of thousands of people were maimed. The outside world that had briefly taken an interest in its problems had ceased to be interested. Thus, instead of Somalia providing the first example of a peacekeeping operation under the 'new world order' proclaimed by President Bush in the immediate euphoria following the end of the Cold War, it had led to the humiliation of both the UN and US and put in jeopardy any further effective UN peacekeeping operations. There had been little co-operation between the various peacekeeping forces and the most obvious lesson for the UN was how little its members either respected it or were prepared to ensure its success. The above is a chronological account of the operation in Somalia, but it is worth examining a few of the problems that had to be dealt with or – as too often was the case – were not dealt with adequately.

In the first place any peacekeeping operation requires at least a minimal desire amongst the combatants to find a solution to their confrontation. This, clearly, was not the case in Somalia. The Somali combatants had not asked for

UN intervention, despised and resented UN efforts, and when the UN forces did attempt to intervene in Mogadishu fought them grimly, inflicting sufficient casualties to make UNOSOM-II change both its tactics and its objective. What did interest the Somali warlords was the relief food that UNOSOM was mandated to deliver to those in need. The inability to deliver food to the hungry became the problem in Somalia rather than any lack of food supplies. Sometimes the ships bringing food to Mogadishu were turned away by mortar fire as the militias fought for the incoming spoils. Mohammed Sahnoun was appointed by Boutros-Ghali as his special representative in Somalia in April 1992, yet in October the Secretary-General dismissed him for making high-profile complaints about UN incompetence. Throughout the UN operation too much attention was paid to public relations and not enough to what was actually happening on the ground. The US intervention with its high-sounding title – Operation Restore Hope – was geared to the US big power image while President Bush's bombastic claims that the troops were doing 'God's work' in Somalia, on a mission at which Americans 'cannot fail', was simply handing hostages to fortune.

The relief operation ought to have been relatively simple to handle. The relief agencies had been loud in their demands for military intervention since the supplies they provided were constantly looted. Since Somalia possessed two good ports and reasonable airports and highways the operation of relief did not face the kind of problems that existed in the south of Sudan. In fact, famine deaths had peaked by October–November 1991 and were in decline when the Americans arrived. A US government-commissioned report found that the US intervention may have saved 10,000–25,000 lives (plus 40,000 during the August–December 1992 airlift of relief food) while the number of lost lives 'due to delays in undertaking earlier decisive action' was between 100,000 and 125,000.[7] Such calculations give a rough idea of the size of the problem.

The American journalist Scott Peterson, in his vivid account of the Somali fiasco, describes the arrival of the US marines and the way in which their man on the spot, Robert Oakley who had only arrived two days earlier, stage-managed the arrival and in order to do so effectively had sought the support of the warlords so that he 'may have actually' elevated the status of the warlords at a time when their authority was ebbing. As one cynical UN official explained, 'George Bush doesn't want a war at Christmas'. This immediate US decision not to disarm the warlords caused the first rift with the UN Secretary-General. Thus, while Lt Gen. Robert Johnson, the marine commander, confirmed this decision: 'I think the belief that we can disarm Somalia is totally naïve', Boutros-Ghali complained publicly that President Bush had promised him disarmament. The aid agency *Médecins sans Frontières* added to the dispute when it said the new US stance 'fitted in with its ambitious timetable to start withdrawing American troops as early as January and its commitment to "zero casualties", an approach influenced by the lack of conviction behind a media-driven intervention'.[8] Close examination of the US intervention makes clear how little it had to do with resolving problems in Somalia and how much it was geared to internal US politics at the tail end of Bush's presidency and, as a Pentagon official said, 'The best thing about Somalia was that it saved us from Bosnia'. A plan that envisaged rushing 28,000 marines to Somalia in December and beginning their withdrawal in January suggests an almost total lack of understanding of what was happening on the ground. At the same time Boutros-Ghali, though later he fell out bitterly with the Americans, wanted a massive US intervention to cover the abysmal failings of the UN operation at that time.

In the end the UN and the US committed themselves to disarm Aideed and became involved in a battle – or series of battles – in Mogadishu that provided Aideed's forces with perfect conditions in which to take on a superior enemy force while proving a disaster for both the UN and the US marines. When the Americans departed they claimed, with astonishing self-delusion if not hubris, that they had 'brought Somalia back from the brink of self-destruction'. Peterson describes the daily US press briefings as fabrications and double-speak. He says of Dave Stockwell, the US information spokesman, 'He knew that we knew that he had been ordered to fabricate the truth as necessary – to revise recent history – so that UNOSOM-II or at least the American role, was bathed in the warmest possible glow.'[9] The warlords were in control when the UN and then the US went into Somalia and they were still in control when they departed. The much-vaunted mission to Somalia turned into a tragedy as well as a public relations disaster with the Americans and the UN blaming each other for what went wrong while going against all the rules laid down for conducting peacekeeping operations as they demonized Aideed and used unacceptable force. Not only did they inflict heavy casualties upon the people they had come to protect and succour, they did not even succeed in their objective. One final comment by Peterson is worth recording: 'The myth that American troops were bullet proof Rambos would be broken forever in Somali minds.' Shocked by a similar realization – and reluctantly admitting that the relief mission had in fact turned to war – President Clinton would end the manhunt and withdraw US forces six months later. The front lines of 'peace enforcement' were to be abandoned. The pullout precipitated the retreat of the 14 other Western contingents, irreversibly undermining the UN's nation-building dream.'[10] This fiasco would ensure the non-participation of the US in the even greater looming calamity in Rwanda.

Now, if the US intervention in Somalia can be faulted, so too can the way in which the UN operation was deployed. In his book *Unvanquished* the former Secretary-General of the United Nations, Boutros Boutros-Ghali, makes plain in only semi-diplomatic language the extent to which he blamed the Americans for what went wrong. At the same time, he reveals something of the constraints upon his power, none of which hindered the United States. Boutros-Ghali addresses the issue of the failed state: 'By 1992 Somalia had become a "failed state". For the past half century, it had been assumed that nations emerging from colonialism and gaining entry into the United Nations would achieve "statehood" as a permanent condition; it was never envisaged that statehood could be lost.'[11] Here at any rate was a problem that applied to other states in Africa during the 1990s and not just Somalia. The difficulties of mounting an effective UN peacekeeping operation when the necessary military forces have to be drawn from some 35 countries are clearly illustrated by the behaviour of Italy in relation to Somalia.

> Because Italy was the former colonial ruler of Somalia, it should not, according to UN practice, contribute troops to serve there. But I had been in desperate need of troops for the UN operation in Mozambique, and in order to get an Italian contingent there, I was compelled to accept Italian forces in Somalia. This was a mistake. The United Nations established policy was correct. Once on the ground in Somalia, the Italian forces, under instructions from Rome, pursued their own agenda at the expense of the common UN effort.[12]

Not only did the Italians conduct unilateral talks with Aideed but, according to Boutros-Ghali, were suspected of tipping him off as to UN movements.

Trouble with the Italians was as nothing compared with the Secretary-General's problems with the United States and, in retrospect, it is clear that the subsequent American determination to prevent Boutros-Ghali continuing for a normal second term as Secretary-General was at least in part due to the number of leading American politicians he had crossed swords with over Somalia. Throughout the Somali crisis the United States and Boutros-Ghali were at loggerheads: every US move, he concluded, was designed not with Somalia but with the US Congress and electorate in mind and as he concludes, plaintively, 'It was clear that the United States, having failed to disarm the Somali factions at the start, was under strong congressional pressure to get itself out of the resulting mess.'[13] Certainly, a great deal of blame was aimed at the UN by the US and vice versa. What also emerges from this debacle is the sheer difficulty of organizing an effective peacekeeping initiative in a country whose principal actors did not want it in the first place while the main supporters of the UN, who alone could provide it with the operational thrust it required, in fact each pursued their own political agendas rather than working together to make the UN operation a success.

During the remaining years of the decade, from 1996 when UNOSOM was withdrawn from Somalia, and into the new century, the Somalis worked to create regional administrations. In August 1999 a Somali Peace Alliance was launched. The northern Republic of Somaliland, still unrecognized, benefited from the use of the port of Berbera to import relief food for eastern Ethiopia and, in March, from the lifting of the livestock ban imposed by Saudi Arabia in 1998. By 2000 there were signs of recovery. In May a Somali reconciliation and government conference opened at Arta in Djibouti. A 245-member Transitional National Assembly was finally chosen in August under a complex clan-based system, and on 27 August Abdiqasim Salad Hasan, a former deputy prime minister and minister of the Interior under Barre, was sworn in as President. The regional Intergovernmental Authority on Development (IGAD), the Arab League, the United Nations and the European Union endorsed the results. However, it could only claim to be half a settlement since 14 clan leaders and warlords stayed aloof as did the Republic of Somaliland and the separate administration of Puntland, who between them condemned the conference as unrepresentative. The Transitional National Government failed to extend its authority over the whole of Mogadishu or outside it and though not much progress was made at reconciliation there was far less fighting. Following the events of 11 September 2001, Somalia, as a collapsed state, was identified by the US as a possible haven for Osama bin Laden. Despite its status as a failed state at the beginning of the new century, Somalia appeared less violent and somewhat less troubled than when it played unwilling host to the UN, the US marines and military forces from another 35 countries, a fact that should give pause to advocates of intervention.

SUDAN

By 1997 Sudan was generally isolated in the Arab world; its relations with the West, which had cut off virtually all aid, were poor, and those with the US were positively bad. The United Nations estimated that to the end of 1989 500,000 people had died since the resumption of the civil war in 1983. Outside Sudan the tragedy of this long-lasting war was largely ignored by the international community, and no serious attempts to halt it were mounted. By 1992 seven million Sudanese suffered from food shortages and three million were either refugees or displaced within the country, while many violations of human rights were regularly reported. Sudan was ruled by Omar Hassan al-Bashir, the soldier who had led the bloodless coup against the government of Sadiq al-Mahdi. Bashir created a Revolutionary Command Council for National Salvation (RCC-NS). Over 100 army officers, seen as opposed to the coup, were arrested. Although Bashir claimed that his coup was a national one, he did not hold talks with the southern leader John Garang and it soon became apparent that he was a supporter of Islamic fundamentalism. He insisted that Sharia should be applied nationwide. In April 1990 Bashir had 28 army officers executed on the grounds that they were plotting a coup. A second coup attempt was launched in September 1990 but by the end of the year Bashir appeared more secure. He continued the war against the Sudan People's Liberation Army (SPLA) in the South.

Talks between the government and the SPLA were held during 1993 in Abuja, Nigeria, and Nairobi, Kenya, but they came to nothing. In May 1993 the UN identified 1.5 million people in the South who required food aid, 600,000 of whom were wholly dependent upon UN supplies. In October 1993, the military Revolutionary Command Council dissolved itself and Sudan reverted to civilian rule with Bashir as its president. In the South there was fierce fighting between rebel factions and this led to a new exodus of refugees into Uganda. In February 1994 the government launched a massive military operation against the SPLA while the UN appealed for humanitarian aid to meet the needs of another 100,000 displaced people. Further peace talks in Kenya produced no results. During 1995 the war continued but at a lower intensity and made few international headlines although the London-based Africa Rights group accused the government of launching a campaign of genocide against the Nuba people of Kordofan Province. By 1996 there was a possibility that Uganda would become embroiled in the war when the Khartoum government accused it of assisting the SPLA and Kampala in return accused Khartoum of assisting the Christian fundamentalist rebels (the Lord's Resistance Army) in northern Uganda. Renewed fighting in January 1997 caused a new wave of refugees to cross into western Ethiopia.

A rapid sequence of events unfolded when, on 13 January, President Bashir called for a Jihad against the enemies of Islam. His call followed reports that the SPLA (then estimated to number 30,000) had captured the towns of Kurmuk and Quissan 600 kilometres south-east of Khartoum and were threatening the Damazin power station, which supplied the capital. Khartoum University was closed so that students could 'join the army and fight "Ethiopian aggression"' since the government now accused Ethiopia of attacking Kurmuk and Quissan. On 17 January Maban in southern Blue Nile Province fell to the rebels and on 21 January Garang claimed that SPLA troops had killed 300 government soldiers at Aba Shameina, south of the Damazin Dam, and a further 150 at al-Keili. On 26 January government forces attacked a rebel base near the Uganda border and this led President Yoweri Museveni to ask the OAU to declare the Sudan civil war a colonial conflict, so as to permit other African countries to supply material aid to the rebels. In February Nelson Mandela, the President of South Africa, announced he was to hold talks with Bashir (he had already held talks with Garang). The SPLA captured Yei and took 1,000 prisoners and on 25 March Garang claimed to control the whole southern border of the country. The general picture was deeply confusing and both sides were suffering heavy casualties. The government lodged a complaint at the UN that both Uganda and Ethiopia had sent troops to fight in Sudan and there seemed a real possibility that the war would spread. On 22 April, after a battle between government and Uganda forces, the Uganda government admitted that its forces had entered Sudan. Meanwhile, the government signed a peace agreement with six southern factions that had broken their ties with the SPLA. The government promised that it would hold a referendum on self-determination for the South after four years and that it would suspend legislation to impose Sharia on the South and grant an amnesty for members of the six groups. These were: South Sudan Independence Movement (SSIM); Bahr el-Ghazal group of the SPLA; Bor group; Equatoria Defence Force; Independence Movement; and United Sudanese African Parties. Garang described the agreement as 'a sham'. On 10 May Presidents Bashir and Museveni met in Nairobi with President Moi in the chair in an attempt to achieve a Sudan-Uganda reconciliation. Moi proposed that the Intergovernmental Authority on Development (IGAD) comprising Djibouti, Eritrea, Kenya, Ethiopia, Somalia, Sudan and Uganda should act as a forum. However, the fighting continued throughout May and Khartoum acknowledged the loss of Rumbuk.

Border tensions with Eritrea and Ethiopia increased dramatically in mid-year. On 9 July the government accepted a framework for peace negotiations at the annual IGAD summit. This IGAD Declaration included the separation of religion and the state, the principle of self-determination for the largely non-Muslim South and the recognition of Sudan as multi-ethnic. Bashir, however, said that the framework was not binding and Garang riposted that he would not negotiate unless the framework was accepted as binding on both sides. The SPLA, meanwhile, was making further advances and opened a new front in Upper Nile State. Bashir met Mandela in Pretoria in August and both called for a ceasefire in Sudan; Mandela offered to host talks between Bashir and Garang at the end of August but Garang failed to turn up. At the end of October talks did begin in Nairobi under IGAD auspices but were adjourned on 11 November without any progress having been made. It was agreed to resume them in April 1998. On 10 December 1997, the US Secretary of State Madeleine Albright held a meeting in Kampala with members of the National Democratic Alliance based in Eritrea and John Garang of the SPLA after the United States had imposed economic sanctions on Sudan in November for its alleged support for terrorist activities and its bad human rights record.

The government, meanwhile, held gubernatorial elections in 10 southern states under the agreement with the six breakaway factions. The southern states were to be administered by the former rebel Riek Machar over a four-year period with the assistance of 10 elected governors. By the beginning of 1998 the SPLA appeared to have control over wide areas of the South although the situation was fluid and towns and regions frequently changed hands. Sudan continued to be isolated internationally. A power struggle developed – it had long been predicted – between Bashir and Dr Hasan al-Turabi, the leader of the National Islamic Front, causing Bashir to declare a three-month state of emergency on 11 December 1999 and suspend the National Assembly. While attending the UN Human Rights Commission in Geneva (March 1999) Garang stated the objective of his organization was to end the civil war and achieve a peace by the creation of two separate but confederal states. The most important developments in 1999 concerned oil with the completion of preparations to export oil from the Hegliz field in the Muglud Basin. The first shipment of oil to Singapore represented a major breakthrough for the government. Immediate output was expected to be between 40,000 and 60,000b/d. The 1,600-kilometre pipeline to the Red Sea was vulnerable to sabotage.

Throughout 2000 Bashir and al-Turabi were in conflict. At the end of the year Bashir was re-elected President for another term of four years. In order to achieve reconciliation with the SPLA Bashir argued for a move towards democracy and the creation of a secular state. Al-Turabi strongly objected to the latter suggestion. At the same time Bashir emphasized the need to face the military situation in the South. In July Bashir issued a decree pardoning those who had raised arms against the state. In September al-Turabi called for an end to the war, and accused the President of abandoning the cause of Islam. Fighting continued widespread over much of the South and included action round the Bentu oilfield. Ongoing IGAD meetings in February, May and December reached no conclusions. Western aid agencies assisting displaced people in the South pulled their operations rather than sign separate memoranda with the government and the SPLA. The United States sent two officials in March and a delegation in September to assess the peace process in the South, the internal political difficulties and Sudan's links with terrorism. Sudan protested against a visit without official permission by Susan Rice, the US Assistant Secretary of State for African Affairs, to assess humanitarian aid and report on human rights violations in SPLA-controlled areas. In October the US blocked Sudan's election to the Africa seat on the UN Security Council because of its alleged links with terrorism.

During 2001 IGAD made no progress in its attempts to resolve Sudan's North-South differences, which appeared as intractable as ever. The fighting continued, large numbers of people were displaced, military operations escalated and the United States angered Khartoum by allocating US$10 million to the SPLA to pursue its cause in the civil war. Christian aid organizations claimed that oil companies operating in southern Sudan had forced people to move from their tribal areas. The government declared its control over the oilfields and turned down the SPLA proposal to link peace with a halt in oil exploration. In March Garang visited France in an attempt to dissuade Total from exploration in the south of Sudan. The United States approved a law to compel oil companies to reveal oil exploration in Sudan before registration on the US Stock Exchange. China signed an agreement with Khartoum to establish petro-chemical activities in Sudan. Oil had now become a major issue in the war. The SPLA accused the government of using oil revenues to purchase weapons for use against the South. In June Talisman Oil Corporation announced it would continue with oil exploration and production reached a level of 200,000b/d to yield the government an annual revenue of US$400 million, that was equivalent to 40 per cent of oil revenues. Oil was clearly transforming Sudan's economy and also providing the government with the revenue it would need to pursue the war. Relations with the United States remained tense and despite Khartoum expressing its willingness to co-operate with the United States against terrorism, following 11 September, Washington extended its sanctions against Sudan for another year and cited Sudan as one of three countries in line for possible military action in the US war on terrorism.

The recital of Sudan's war scenario over this decade wearies by its sameness – year after year the same story: towns are captured and lost, the government launches a major military initiative, the SPLA gains ground, large numbers of refugees are created, aid agencies come and go, peace talks never make progress and all the while the horrific statistics of the dead and maimed steadily increase. In mid-2002, however, the peace talks at last seemed to have succeeded. Five weeks of talks in Machakos, Kenya, resulted in an unprecedented agreement between the Khartoum government and the SPLA. The government agreed to allow a referendum in the South after a six-year interim period to allow people to decide whether they wanted to remain part of Sudan. The constitution would be rewritten to ensure that while Sharia law could be used in the North it would not infringe the rights of non-Muslims in the South. However, despite the apparent breakthrough at Machakos the talks continued into 2003 and were not helped by President Bush signing the Sudan Peace Act under whose terms the President could impose sanctions against Sudan if in the opinion of the US government the Sudan government was not serious about the peace process. The act caused fury in Khartoum. It also illustrated how US pressures have become ubiquitous, at least in any country where the United States has particular interests: in the case of Sudan, oil and fundamentalism and possible links with Osama bin Laden.

The war in Sudan – Africa's longest war – has defied any attempts at intervention although Sudan's neighbours (Eritrea, Ethiopia and Uganda) have been involved on the fringes. Moreover, the nature of the terrain, the size of the country and the inability of either side to prevail decisively, even after winning particular victories, may at last have convinced both the government and the SPLA that neither can win. If that is the case, can they at last work out a solution: either a total split into separate countries or a genuine federal state that would retain Sudan's integrity as a single state but allow real control over its affairs to the South, something that so far governments in Khartoum have always refused to contemplate. At least at the beginning of the twenty-first century it seemed possible, to put it no higher, to hope that decades of devastating warfare might have finally convinced the two sides that a peace would be beneficial to both.

Genocide and Border
Confrontation

The genocide that destroyed a million Rwandans and shocked the world in 1994 left a scar on Africa as it did upon the conscience of the West that could have prevented it but chose not to do so. And the brutal border war that erupted in 1998 between Eritrea and Ethiopia, two countries whose leaders only a few years earlier had together fought to bring about the downfall of Mengistu, evoked comparisons with European trench warfare. Why, in both cases, was there such ferocity? The answer in either case is not easy to find. What legacies provoked planned and deliberate genocide and what deep resentments could turn allies into enemies overnight? The fragility of state structures, the precarious nature of ethnic alliances, the legacies of colonialism which are still working their way through the system may each be cited as contributory causes yet none is sufficient to explain the nature of these violent eruptions. The violence that characterized much of Africa through the 1990s gave the impression that the continent was the surface of a vast volcano where explosions could break the surface almost anywhere as the whole gradually settled down and came to terms with realities that had long been under wraps.

GENOCIDE IN RWANDA

Colonialism as such may not be to blame for the genocide of 1994 yet it played its part and set the scene for what was to follow. The Belgians, who acquired Ruanda-Urundi from Germany at the end of World War I, regarded the Hutus as a serf class and in order to politicize the differences for their own purposes of colonial rule conducted a census and found that 14 per cent of the population was Tutsi and 85 per cent Hutu. Thereafter, as the administering power, the Belgians systematically favoured the Tutsis while the Hutus were largely denied education except for those training for the Catholic priesthood. During the 1950s, Belgium, like the other colonial powers, came under UN pressure to decolonize and to hand over power to a democratic political structure. Then, according to a UN Trusteeship Report of March 1961, 'The developments of the last 18 months have brought about the racial dictatorship of one party' the report warned, and 'An oppressive system has been replaced by another one... It is quite possible that some day we will witness violent reactions on the part of the Tutsis'. Between Belgian colonial convenience – divide and rule – and United Nations insistence upon democratically regulated independence, the parameters for later disasters were set.[1]

'The Second Republic began to unravel from about the end of the 1980s... a Structural Adjustment Programme was imposed from outside in 1990, and military spending rose dramatically following the Rwanda Patriotic Front (RPF) invasion, also in 1990.'[2] Already at this time, the result of earlier massacres and Hutu-Tutsi confrontations there were registered with the UNHCR 266,000 Tutsis in Burundi, 82,000 in Uganda, 22,000 in Tanzania and 13,000 in Zaïre. By the 1990s a crucial element in Rwanda's overall problem was shortage of land. 'In the absence of any technological breakthrough, and in the presence of an increase in the sheer numbers, soil fertility was decreasing. In response there was a shift away from cereals and beans towards root crops: the food basket was becoming protein-poor and starch-laden.'[3] In the face of the RPF invasion, the Hutu army that stood at only 5,000 in 1990 grew to 30,000 over the two years to 1992 and its growth was paralleled by the formation of Hutu extremist political parties. President Habyarimana, despite negotiating with the Tutsis, was as determined to maintain Hutu supremacy as the Tutsis were to re-establish theirs. Furthermore, there was an external factor at work: the problems of 1990–94 were heavily influenced by Uganda where there was also a crisis of indigeneity. By permitting the RPF to invade Rwanda from its soil, Uganda was exporting its crisis and getting rid of non-Ugandans as in 1972 it had got rid of its Asians. Waves of Tutsi had left Rwanda on three occasions – 1959–61, 1963–64 and 1973 – and a significant proportion of them had settled in Uganda, though they all believed they had the right of return to Rwanda. By 1990, however, Habyarimana's government could and did maintain that there was no land for them to return to. When the Tutsi-dominated RPF invaded Rwanda from Uganda over 30 September–1 October 1990 under Maj.-Gen. Fred Rwigyema (who was killed in the first week of fighting) Uganda sealed its border to prevent further Tutsis joining the RPF. The government of Rwanda appealed for help to Belgium (which sent 600 paratroopers), France (300 troops) and Zaïre (500, later increased to 1,000 troops). By the end of October Tutsis were being rounded up in Kigali. Uganda's President Museveni claimed the rebels had agreed to a ceasefire but though President Habyarimana offered peace talks he insisted that there was no longer any available land for the Tutsis in Rwanda. Over December 1990–January 1991 more Tutsi rebels crossed the border. A settlement appeared to have been achieved in February 1991 when President Mwinyi of Tanzania presided at a meeting of Habyarimana and Museveni in Zanzibar. A border ceasefire between Rwanda and Uganda was agreed but sporadic fighting was to continue throughout the year. Uganda, which had close ties with the Tutsis, was unable even if it had been willing to stay out of the conflict. Representatives of the RPF and government met in Paris in June 1992 to work out an accord and one was signed that August. In October the government agreed to set up a transitional cabinet to include all political parties and the RPF and an agreement was signed in Arusha on 9 January 1993. However, it was then repudiated by Habyarimana's ruling *Mouvement Révolutionnaire National pour la Démocratie et Développement* (MRNDD) (National Republican Movement for Democracy and Development) and by the end of that month a new round of ethnic killing had broken out. By February hundreds of people were being killed and an estimated one million people had fled their homes to escape the conflict and become refugees. The RPF launched a new offensive from Uganda and recaptured Ruhengeri, which it had taken for a brief period in 1991. This new RPF offensive was condemned by Belgium, France and the United States and more French troops (in addition to the 300 already in the country) were sent to support the government. Both sides were guilty of atrocities during this new phase of fighting. Following a fresh cease-fire on 21 February, France withdrew its troops to Central African Republic. On 8 May the government announced a nine-month programme to demobilize 13,000 troops and 6,000 gendarmes. A buffer zone was established between government and RPF forces, to be monitored by a Military Observer Group (MOG) that had been created in 1992. On 30 May the government agreed to assist the return of 650,000 refugees, but the negotiations were broken off on 25 June amid accusations on both sides that the other was preparing a new military offensive.

Back in October 1990, the United Nations had created a UN Assistance Mission in Rwanda (UNAMIR), which had a force of 2,500 troops to help maintain the peace following the initial RPF invasion. Its presence up to 1993 did not appear to have prevented any of the violence. In March 1994, after negotiating another truce, the RPF ambushed and killed 250 government troops. In Kigali the government reacted by claiming that 500,000 people had fled from the new violence in the north of the country. By this time the tensions that preceded the explosion of April must have been apparent to almost everybody. An interesting contrast was made between Rwanda and South Africa: 'If Rwanda was the genocide that happened, then South Africa was the genocide that didn't. The contrast was marked by two defining events in the first half of 1994: just as a tidal wave of genocidal violence engulfed Rwanda, South Africa held elections marking the transition to a post-apartheid era. More than any other, these twin developments marked the end of innocence for the African intelligentsia… the civil war profoundly changed all those who took part in it. The Rwanda Patriotic Front (RPF) went into it as an army of liberation and came out of it as an army of occupation. The Habyarimana regime entered the war pledged to a policy of ethnic reconciliation and came out of it pledged to uphold Hutu power.'[4] Journalists who visited RPF-controlled areas in 1992 and 1993 all agreed on one thing: that a desolate calm prevailed in these areas; they used the adjective 'eerie' to describe the feeling. A Kampala-based journalist, Catherine Watson, writing in1992, said: 'In contrast, the area under the RPF is eerily calm. One of the most densely populated regions of Africa in peacetime, it now holds a mere 2,600 civilians grouped by the RPF into two "safe" villages.'[5] The RPF admitted that only 1,800 Hutu peasants were left in an area which had had a population of about 800,000 before the war, and according to another Uganda journalist, Charles Onyango-Obbo, 'The rebels have asked all civilians to leave, because they don't want the responsibility of caring for them and fear infiltrations. Privately, some officers say they hope that as the number of displaced people swells, pressure will grow on Habyarimana to reach a settlement in the war.'[6]

The RPF invasion of 1990 inevitably raised the spectre in Kigali of a return of Tutsi power and led the Foreign Minister, Casimir Bizimunga, to accuse the invaders of seeking 'a reversal of history', which could only mean 'forced labour and feudal servitude' for the Hutus. On the other hand, the Hutus had come to see the Tutsis as a race alien to Rwanda. For those who believed in Hutu Power, the Hutu alone comprised the nation and the Tutsis were not part of it. The extreme Hutus who believed in Hutu Power felt they had to reverse Habyarimana's attempt to rehabilitate the Tutsi as an ethnic minority in Rwandan society and treat the Tutsis as alien incomers to be rejected. The foremost representative of these views was the radio station *Radio et Télévision Libres des Mille Collines*, followed by the newspaper *Kangura*. Hutu Power was reinforced by the belief that the aim of the RPF was not simply rights for all Rwandans but power for the Tutsis. Propaganda, therefore, highlighted the threat of the Tutsis seeking 'power' and the government argued that it had to keep Tutsi power or domination over the Hutus at bay. The extreme propaganda of the Hutus suggested again and again that the Tutsis aimed to kill them. The RPF, for its part, resorted to the widespread displacement of Hutu civilians, to pillage and even the conscription of Hutus for forced labour. While the Tutsis used displacement as a weapon to persuade the government to reach a compromise, the Hutus resorted to massacres to achieve their dominance.

Thus, when Habyarimana signed a power-sharing protocol at Arusha on 9 January 1993, the extreme Hutus resorted to a massacre of Tutsis at Gisenyi as a clear message to their own government not to share power with the Tutsis.

Juvenal Habyarimana, who had come to power in a bloodless coup in 1973, found by 1990 that he was becoming increasingly unpopular – like too many politicians he had stayed too long – and so, in answer to pressure for reforms, he introduced measures on 21 September designed to lead to a multiparty system. His plans were thrown into confusion by the RPF invasion at the end of the month. However, after the defeat of the RPF and their retreat back to Uganda, Habyarimana went ahead with his reform programme and on 10 June 1991 Rwanda 'became' a multiparty state. Habyarimana had hoped to persuade the Tutsis, or some of them, to return home and take part in multiparty elections but instead they launched a second invasion and were clearly intent only on seizing political control on behalf of their own ethnic group. These complex manoeuvres and events acted as the prelude to 6 April 1994 when the plane carrying Presidents Juvenal Habyarimana of Rwanda and Cyprien Ntaryamira of Burundi was shot down over Kigali and both presidents were killed. They were returning from a meeting in Tanzania with regional presidents at which they had been examining solutions to the rising Hutu-Tutsi violence. The assassination was later attributed to extremist Hutus opposed to any accommodation with the Tutsis. In Kigali the presidential guard went on the rampage and those immediately killed included the prime minister and three Belgian soldiers attached to the United Nations. Within two days the fighting had become general; in the north government forces and the RPF engaged directly with each other.

The killing in Kigali appeared to be indiscriminate and targets included ministers, nuns, priests and Belgian, Bangladeshi and Ghanaian peacekeeping troops. Many of these killings, by the presidential guard, were thought to be revenge killings for the murder of the president. Belgian and French troops prepared to evacuate their nationals and the Red Cross reported an initial 1,000 casualties. Paul Kagame, leading the RPF, which had reached the outskirts of Kigali, said it would restore law and order. French troops took control of the airport and supervised the evacuation of the 3,000 foreigners waiting to leave. Most of the people slaughtered in Kigali during this first week were Tutsis. Eight hundred Belgian paratroopers arrived. By 12 April the RPF army, 20,000 strong, was fighting its way into Kigali where it caused panic in the government. The deaths of Habyarimana and the Prime Minister, Agathe Uwilingiyimana, removed the two people who had publicly championed ethnic reconciliation; but Hutu extremists did not believe, or want to believe, in ethnic reconciliation. The history of the previous three decades gave them reason to think this way: the massacres of 1972, for example, had seen 200,000 Hutus including many school-children and intellectuals killed while in neighbouring Burundi in 1993 the Tutsi-controlled army had murdered the country's first Hutu president.

The government army of 30,000 now began to disintegrate; a week after the death of the two presidents an estimated 10,000 people had been killed in Kigali alone. On 13 April RPF Radio Muhabura announced that the northern region of Mutara had been liberated. As the chaos escalated the United Nations force (UNAMIR) began to leave the country, some of its members in panic, using the excuse that the government had not given them control of the airport. Accurate figures for casualties were impossible in such a fluid situation but according to Human Rights Watch of New York about 100,000 people altogether had been killed between 6 and 19 April while it appeared that a campaign of killing had been planned by Hutu extremists many weeks in advance, prior to the death of Habyarimana. Human Rights Watch claimed that 'army officers trained, armed and organized some 1,700 young men into militia affiliated with the president's political party'. The Security Council met on 21 April. 'While the secretary-general requested more than a doubling of the size of the contingent (already in Rwanda), from the original 2,500 to 5,500, the major powers hesitated: led by the United States, the Security Council decided to leave behind a derisory force of only 270 soldiers. The message to the government was clear: implement the Arusha Agreement or else the UN will pull out and the RPF take power.'[7] In the prevailing circumstances the government, whatever its intentions, could not implement the Arusha Peace Agreement of 9 August 1993 that led to the establishment of UNAMIR, as the UN Security Council knew full well. It was indulging in total hypocrisy. The failure of the UN to send more troops to Rwanda at this juncture, when it was increasing its presence in Bosnia, raised awkward questions about the racial bias of its policies and drew from Boutros Boutros-Ghali the sarcastic reference to 'the rich man's war'. By early May an estimated 200,000 people had been killed in three weeks of slaughter while 500,000 refugees had crossed into Tanzania. On 17 May the Security Council reversed its policy and voted to increase the size of UNAMIR to 5,000 although neither the US nor the EU were prepared to send any troops.

Two names now surfaced: the *Interahamwe* (those who attack together) emerged as one of the extremist militias drawn from the ranks of the MRNDD; and a second group, the *Impuzamugambi* (those with a single purpose). They came from the extremist wing of the MRNDD, the Coalition for the Defence of the Republic (CDR). These groups had been in training prior to 6 April. A private radio station owned by members of the President's inner circle had begun a campaign against the Tutsi and Hutu opponents of the President and after 6 April its campaign became more virulent. In a sense two parallel wars were taking place: the RPF war against the government to give control of the country to the returning Tutsis; and the Hutu extremist actions against all Tutsis as well as Hutu moderates. By June an estimated 500,000 people had been killed. On 19 July the RPF, which by then controlled Kigali and most of the towns, announced that it had won the civil war and would form a government according to the 1993 Arusha Agreement but excluding the former ruling MRNDD. France of the major powers intervened in June with an initial force of 150 men (expected to rise to 2,000) and used them to relieve beleaguered Tutsi communities and to establish a safe haven for the displaced population in the south-west. By this time one million Hutu refugees were pouring into Zaïre near the town of Goma. Although they claimed to be strictly neutral, the French were regarded as rescuing the Hutu government or enabling it to escape the retribution of the Tutsis. The French withdrew in September by which time the UNAMIR had been increased to 2,500 troops. As the RPF established its control over the country, the UN Security Council established (8 November 1994) the International Criminal Tribunal for Rwanda (ICTR) to prosecute those responsible for genocide. The Security Council (as we shall see) had denied genocide was taking place when to admit it would have meant sending a force to stop it. By the end of 1994 the RPF government was pushing a policy of reconciliation although through 1995 a quarter of the population remained outside the country as refugees. At the same time militant Hutu guerrillas infiltrated the country to destabilize the new regime. While the prisons and detention centres were full of people suspected of involvement in the genocide, the *Interahamwe* militants were busy in the cross-border refugee camps, recruiting. RPF relations with UNAMIR were poor because the UN body appeared to be more concerned with possible violations of human rights by the RPF than with bringing those responsible for genocide to justice. Problems continued through 1996 for though the RPF was highly efficient it only represented the Tutsi minority and there was little indication of any Tutsi-Hutu rapprochment. By August 1997 most of the two million refugees had returned home and large numbers of them, especially from the north-western provinces of Ruhengeri and Gisenyi, had taken up arms and joined the *Interahamwe*, which had been recruiting, training and arming sympathizers in the refugee camps in eastern Zaïre. There were a growing number of incidents in the north-western provinces during 1997 and, as a visitor said, it was 'like a volcano'. Violence continued through 1998 and it was clear by then that the RPF had no solution to Hutu-Tutsi confrontation; rather, the RPF government 'controlled' a country seething with antagonisms and discontent.

No accurate figures for the genocide of 1994 exist though eventually 800,000 was settled upon as a reasonable estimate for the toll of four months' slaughter although the total has sometimes been put at one million. A report commissioned by the United Nations and published in 1999 blamed the United Nations for having failed to act on the eve of genocide and then for failing to halt the killings once they had begun. Warrants were issued throughout the year by the ICTR leading to the arrests in several countries of people accused of perpetrating genocide. One such arrest was of Georges Ruggio, a Belgian who had worked as an announcer for the Hutu radio station *Mille Collines*; he was sentenced to 12 years' imprisonment by the ICTR in Arusha. A life sentence was imposed by the same court on the former Prime Minister Jean Kambanda and upheld on appeal by the UN appeals court in The Hague. These were high-profile cases. Another 125,000 remained in prison or detention centres accused of genocide and awaiting trial. The process of retribution was slow. Arguments about the 'whys' will continue for many years. One argument advanced by Hutus was that killing Tutsis, all Tutsis, was not genocide but necessary in a war situation where 90 per cent of the Tutsis sympathized with the invading RPF. According to François Xavier Nkurunziza, a Hutu lawyer, the dilemma was how so many Hutu had allowed themselves to kill. He said: 'Conformity is deep, very developed here. In Rwandan culture, everyone obeys authority. People revere power, and there isn't enough education. You take a poor, ignorant population, and give them arms, and say "It's yours. Kill." They'll obey.' This is too simplistic a view but not to be ignored. During the RPF advances and victories over 1990–93 many thousands of Hutus were displaced. Thus, 89,000 displaced Hutus in 1990 rose to 350,000 by May 1992 and to 950,000 following the RPF February offensive of 1993.[8] Robert Kajuga, a founding member of the *Interahamwe*, said: 'It's a war against the Tutsis because they want to take power, and we Hutus are more numerous. Most Tutsis support the RPF, so they fight and they kill. We have to defend our country. The government authorizes us. We go in behind the army. We watch them and we learn.'[9] His statement, 'We have to defend our country' describes accurately the divide that previous massacres and confrontations had brought about. The invading RPF, though they had originated from Rwanda, were no longer seen as citizens of Rwanda by the Hutus but as foreign invaders. When the genocide is analysed in this way it becomes apparent how easy genocide may become. In 1994 the UN was faced with a clear choice. Lawlessness had increased rapidly from February when people had been killed in front of the UN troops who did not intervene. Then, 'The slaughter of the prime minister and the 10 Belgian soldiers sent to protect her, right inside the UN compound, presented the UN with a clear choice: either increase the size of the United Nations Assistance Mission in Rwanda (UNAMIR) force and change its mandate, or pull out. The UN chose to all but pull out.'[10] In a war the demonizing of opponents makes easier the task of justifying extreme measures against them – that is, atrocities. What was clearly deeply troubling about the Rwanda genocide was that people whose professions are most associated with valuing life such as doctors, nurses, priests and teachers became involved in taking it. The Roman Catholic Church was the originator of the Hamitic hypothesis – that the Tutsi had come from elsewhere and imposed themselves on the Hutus and this view was adopted by the Belgians as the colonial power. The Church provided the lay personnel who permeated every local community and helped distinguish Hutu from Tutsi in every neighbourhood: without the Church there would have been no 'racial' census in Rwanda.[11] In 1994 Tutsi power replaced Hutu power in Rwanda, at least for the time being, while it was abundantly clear that only an armed peace between the two groups was possible into the foreseeable future. As with all major crimes, the originators seek to implicate as many people as possible in what they are doing. They appear to have had little difficulty in doing this in Rwanda but were greatly helped by a history of massacres stretching back over four decades.

In his short term as Secretary-General of the United Nations, Boutros Boutros-Ghali faced two especially fraught problems in Africa: the first in Somalia, the second in Rwanda. When the peace agreement had been successfully concluded in Arusha on 9 August 1993, the Security Council was asked by the parties to the agreement to establish UNAMIR to monitor the peace agreement and assist in maintaining the security of Kigali as well as providing humanitarian assistance and help with refugee repatriation. Boutros-Ghali appointed Gen. Romeo Dallaire of Canada as force commander and Jacques-Roger Booh-Booh, a former minister of Cameroon, as the Secretary-General's special representative in Rwanda. In January 1994 Gen. Dallaire sent a cable to the United Nations to report an informant's claim that weapons were being stockpiled by Hutu forces in preparation for mass killings of Tutsis. Dallaire requested permission to seize the weapons. The request was refused by the UN Department of Peace Keeping Operations (DPKO) because the mandate did not cover such action. However, on 12 January, on UN instructions, Dallaire relayed this information to the ambassadors of Belgium, France and the United States; thus, the powers, which could have acted to stop genocide, had been informed. Then came the deaths of the two presidents on 6 April and two explanations were advanced to cover this event: that they had been killed by Hutu extremists who opposed the concessions they were making to the Tutsis; or, as Hutu leaders claimed, it was the Tutsis. Whichever explanation was accepted their deaths set off the genocide. Following the killing of the 10 Belgian soldiers guarding the prime minister, Belgium panicked and its foreign minister asked Boutros-Ghali to withdraw all UN forces from Rwanda since Belgium had decided to withdraw its entire contingent, which was the biggest part of the UN force at that time. They were, as Boutros-Ghali says, suffering from the 'American syndrome'. He asked them to leave their heavy weapons behind to be used by the remaining UN troops but they took them all with them. On 13 April Boutros-Ghali sent a letter to the Security Council to say the Belgian withdrawal made it difficult for the UN operation to continue unless they were replaced by another well-equipped contingent. He said he had requested the force commander and his special representative to draw up plans for the withdrawal of the UN mission unless it received additional forces. The United States, Britain and France reacted indignantly to his suggestion. US Ambassador Madeleine Albright suggested a 'small, skeletal' operation be left in Kigali 'to show the will of the international community' and that 'later, the Council might see what could be done about giving an effective mandate'. It is difficult to think of a more pusillanimous response to a major crisis than this from the world's only superpower.

However, the United States withdrew still further from the possibility of any commitment for on 3 May, as massacres raged in Rwanda, President Clinton signed PDD 13 – Presidential Decision Document (later renumbered 25) which 'dealt a deadly blow to co-operative multilateral action to maintain peace and security. Entitled "The Clinton Administration's Policy on Reforming Multilateral Peace Operations", the new rules were so tightly drawn as to scope, mission, duration, resources, and risk that only the easiest, cheapest, and safest peacekeeping operations could be approved under them and many current UN operations could not. It was the end of what Madeleine Albright two years earlier had declared to be a policy of "assertive multilateralism". A headline declared, THE US WASHES ITS HANDS OF THE WORLD.'[12]

Following the publication of PDD25, Albright argued with the Security Council that the new Clinton conditions should apply before Resolution 918 of 17 May, which increased the strength and expanded the mandate of UNAMIR, was carried out. This meant a ceasefire had to be in place; the parties agree to a UN presence; and UNAMIR should not engage in peace enforcement unless what was happening in Rwanda was a significant threat to international peace and security. Were troops, funds and equipment available and what was the exit strategy? Thus, the US advanced serious objections to a large peace enforcement mission in Rwanda. Recalling Somalia (a key US consideration) Albright said 'the parties to the conflict would use force to oppose such a mission'. These objections, Boutros-Ghali argued, were hypocritical when, by then, everybody knew that the enlarged mission was to prevent genocide. As the Secretary-General argues in his memoirs: 'The behaviour of the Security Council was shocking; it meekly followed the United States' lead in denying the reality of genocide. Although it was a clear case of genocide, US spokesmen were obviously under instructions to avoid the term in order to avoid having to fulfil their treaty obligations under the 1949 Genocide Convention. US representatives simply said that "acts of genocide may have occurred and need to be investigated".[13] The United States would not even jam the hate radio station *Mille Collines* because to do so would be too expensive. On 27 May Boutros-Ghali saw Clinton in the Oval Office but he evaded talk of Rwanda. 'On that same day, May 27 1994, I told the press that Rwanda was a scandal. It is genocide... and more than 200,000 people have been killed, but the international community is still debating what to do.' Later, Boutros-Ghali said, 'The US effort to prevent the effective deployment of a UN force for Rwanda succeeded with the strong support of Britain.'[14] Boutros-Ghali's account of the indifference, obstruction and refusal to admit that genocide was taking place on the part of the United States, which was determined not to become involved, ably supported by Britain, makes disgraceful reading. Dallaire complained bitterly at the inaction of the Security Council and pointed out that an early and determined effort to get troops and resources on the ground could have saved so many lives.

The French initiative, Operation Turquoise, was launched on 23 June 1994, and authorized by Security Council Resolution 929 to continue until 21 August 1994. The French sent 2,500 troops to establish a 'humanitarian protected zone' in south-west Rwanda that covered about one fifth of the country's territory. This French action was controversial since some observers claimed that the French were using their area of operation to provide a refuge for France's Hutu friends who had launched the genocide. Others pointed out that the French zone served to protect large numbers of civilians threatened by the slaughter. By 1 August UNAMIR was still a long way from the target of 5,500 troops authorized on 17 May. Nineteen countries had originally pledged 30,000 troops but endless wrangles ensued as troops from one country had to be matched to resources from another country. At the beginning of August there were still fewer than 500 troops on the ground as the French began to withdraw. By August the RPF had established control over most of Rwanda. 'The RPF's swift advance and inflammatory broadcasts by its radio stations caused masses of Hutus to flee into neighbouring Zaïre.'[15] The saga of Rwanda, as told by the UN Secretary-General, revealed both the United Nations and the permanent members of the Security Council at their worst.

The American journalist Scott Peterson provides a grim picture of genocide in action. 'No system of genocide ever devised has been more efficient: the daily kill rate was five times that of the Nazi death camps. Extremist Hutu officials, army commanders, and militia thugs conspired to eliminate all Tutsis and moderate Hutus and to draw every Hutu into complicity... The daily death rate *averaged* well more than 11,500 for two months, with surges as high as 45,000. During this peak, one murder was committed every two seconds of every minute, of every hour, for days; an affliction befitting the apocalypse.'[16] Peterson suggests that three pillars upheld the Rwandan genocide: Hutu fear of the Tutsis and consequent detailed preparations to exterminate the 'Tutsi' problem; the acquiescence of the Catholic Church as those preparations became irreversible; and the French government role in propping up the doomed regime – even during the genocide – with cash and weapons. French policy was to uphold a pro-French Hutu regime even as it was collapsing, and France had clear complicity in genocide. France, Peterson argues, saw itself losing a cultural battle to the Uganda-UK backed Tutsi. He should have added a fourth condition: the indifference and determination of the United States and Britain to do nothing. Although the world had condemned genocide ever since 1945 and was committed through the United Nations to take action should genocide arise, in the case of Rwanda the major players stood by and did nothing. So determined was Washington not to become involved in another Somalia that 'The bosses of some Security Council ambassadors received telephone calls from Washington, requesting that they "lay off" the Rwandan issue, and certainly shy away from using the word "genocide".'[17] In the end, all the members of the UN Security Council appeared more concerned to placate Washington and fall in with the US view on Rwanda than take – or try to take – appropriate action, with the UN calling genocide a 'humanitarian' crisis. In Rwanda the Secretary-General's special representative, Jacques-Roger Booh-Booh, described the killing as a 'free for all' despite the evidence to the contrary. *The Washington Post* commented at the height of the killing: 'As terrified UN peacekeepers evacuated Rwanda, other nations consoled themselves with the hope that the butchers would grow weary of the killing. This once seemed to us a likely prospect too, but it does no more. The savagery continues unabated. Anguished international onlookers, including Americans, now comprehend more fully the awful consequences of standing on the sidelines.'[18] Fuller comprehension, unfortunately, did not bring more action.

In compensation for not acting to stop the genocide, the United States did a great deal to succour the huge numbers of refugees who had fled to the neighbouring countries, especially Zaïre, with its 'Operation Sustain Hope'. Then came the apologies. In May 1998 Kofi Annan, by then Secretary-General, made a visit to Rwanda and admitted that 'the world failed Rwanda at that time of evil' and 'must deeply regret this failure'. Annan had been beaten to the task by Bill Clinton, slickest of all US presidents, who landed at Kigali airport on 25 March 1998 and spent three and a half hours there. He did not leave the airport and the engines of Air Force One were not switched off, presumably in case the

President had to leave in a hurry. The President, who had forbidden his diplomats to use the G word during the Rwandan holocaust, now used it 12 times in a speech in which he said: 'We did not act quickly enough after the killing began. We did not immediately call these crimes by their rightful name: genocide.'[19]

BURUNDI

Burundi may not have indulged in genocide, though that is debatable, but over the years 1993 to 2000 some 200,000 people were killed in its civil war. President Pierre Buyoya held Burundi's first ever multiparty presidential elections on 1 June 1993. He was defeated by Melchior Ndadaye, the first Hutu to become president. Tutsis immediately demonstrated against his victory and the army attempted to carry out a coup at the time of Ndadaye's inauguration. That attempt failed but on 21 October the army carried out a successful, bloody coup in which President Ndadaye was killed. Massacres followed in many parts of the country and by the end of the month, according to the UNHCR, more than 500,000 refugees had fled the country – 342,000 into Rwanda, 214,000 into Tanzania and 21,000 into Zaïre. By mid-November estimates suggested that as many as 150,000 people had been killed. The OAU created a force of 200 soldiers to protect ministers while relief agencies tried to cope with the refugees whose numbers had risen to 800,000 of whom 100 a day were dying. By 21 December 1993 about 1.5 million out of a population of 5.6 million had fled their homes to escape violence and by then up to 150 a day were dying. On 13 January 1994 the National Assembly appointed Cyprien Ntaryamina, also a Hutu, as President. About 100,000 refugees then returned home. The violence continued. According to the findings of an international commission the greater part of the army, which was Tutsi, had been involved, actively or passively, in the first unsuccessful coup attempt and then in the second successful one. Estimates of deaths to this point ranged wildly from 25,000 to 200,000. President Ntaryamina was killed on 6 April 1994 in the plane he shared with Rwanda's Habyarimana but while that event was the spark that set off the genocide in Rwanda it did not lead to a similar breakdown in Burundi. The speaker of the assembly, Sylvestre Ntibantunganga, became president. However, Hutu extremists in Burundi now began to make contact with their counterparts in the refugee camps outside the country, which soon contained many exiles from Rwanda. Burundi experienced a state of low-intensity civil war through 1994 in which unofficial Tutsi militia were supported by the army. Hutu guerrilla groups recruited supporters from the refugee camps and violence increased during the second half of the year so that by the end of the year the United Nations reported that three to four soldiers were being killed daily and about 200 civilians weekly.

In February 1996 the UN warned that civil war was taking place in many parts of Burundi and recommended that the world should take preventive action rather than wait for another bout of genocide. There were signs that neighbouring countries were prepared to intervene to prevent further killing. On 25 June 1996, at a regional summit in Arusha, Burundi reluctantly accepted the principle of international intervention although the next month Prime Minister Antoine Nduwayo reversed this position and came out against any international peacekeeping operation. Following a massacre of 300 Tutsis at Bugendera in mid-July, another coup was mounted by the army on the 25th of the month and Pierre Buyoya was installed in his former job. He said: 'We have done this to avoid genocide. We want to restore peace and protect the population.' In reaction to the coup, Burundi's neighbours – Kenya, Rwanda, Tanzania, Uganda, Ethiopia and Zaïre – imposed sanctions. In mid-September Hutu rebels claimed that 10,000 people had been killed since the coup. By 1997 Buyoya was carrying on an all-out war against the Hutu rebels and defence expenditure for the year had increased by 70 per cent over 1996. Many Hutu peasants were moved into 'regroupement camps' to prevent them assisting the guerrillas. The fighting and massacres continued into 1998. Fighting around Bujumbura, the capital, broke out in January and continued through to April by which time 20,000 people had been forced to leave their homes. On 7 April 1998, Human Rights Watch (New York) published a report accusing both the government and the Hutu rebels of responsibility for 'a massive campaign of military violence' which had resulted in thousands of civilians being killed, raped or tortured. By the late 1990s on-off civil war appeared to have become the norm with no solution in sight. Between 1993 and 1999 the Tutsi army–Hutu rebel killings had accounted for some 250,000 lives. 'The fighting nowadays is low-intensity, but it remains vicious, marked by massacres and arbitrary killings.'

A process of negotiations had been started in June 1998; at Arusha in January 1999, though little progress had been made, President Museveni of Uganda suggested that the sanctions imposed by neighbouring states in July 1996 should be lifted. Further talks were conducted in July. In May 1999 five soldiers were found guilty of the murder of the country's first elected president, Melchior Ndadaye, and six ministers in 1993 and were sentenced to death by the Supreme Court while a further 28 were sentenced to prison. By this time about 300,000 peasants had been moved into 'regroupement camps' where the conditions were so awful that aid workers would not stay and the UN Security Council called on the government to abandon the policy. The government replied that it would do nothing until the rebels abandoned their 'genocidal agenda'. The peace talks were set back when former Tanzanian President Julius Nyerere, who had initiated them, died. Nelson Mandela replaced Nyerere as chief negotiator in 2000. He criticized Buyoya's rule and the latter promised to curtail Tutsi domination of military and political life in Burundi. In April 2000 Buyoya promised to dismantle the 'regroupement camps'. On 28 August 2000 a power-sharing agreement was reached at Arusha between the government, the military and a number of political parties, both Hutu and Tutsi, and signed in the presence of Mandela, US President Bill Clinton and a dozen other heads of state. Buyoya had to balance any agreement against army pressures and the fact that three Hutu guerrilla groups had been absent from the meeting as had several Tutsi groups. Although figures frequently changed, the consensus at the end of the century was that about 200,000 had died in the civil strife since 1993 while about six per cent of the population had been displaced. In February 2001 the peace negotiations collapsed when a majority of the participants refused to accept Buyoya as head of an interim three-year transitional government.

ERITREA AND ETHIOPIA GO TO WAR

In 1998 an unexpected war erupted between Eritrea and Ethiopia. Their two leaders, Issayas Afewerki of Eritrea, and Meles Zenawi of Ethiopia, had worked together to bring an end to the regime of Mengistu in Ethiopia at the beginning of the decade. Now they fell out and the subsequent war between their two countries, which lasted from 1998 to 2000, was bitter, costly in lives and resources. It was fought nominally over a few small stretches of border territory. In fact, it was about more than territory, and not least because the emergence of an independent Eritrea had deprived Ethiopia of its Red Sea coastline and reduced it to the status of a landlocked country. The apparently good relations between the two countries were broken in May 1998 when a border dispute led to violence. Following the deaths of several Eritrean soldiers near the border town of Badme in the Tigray province of Eritrea on 6 May, Eritrean forces seized an area then under Ethiopian control but claimed by Eritrea. Clashes occurred at a number of points along the border and led to several hundred casualties during the month. In June Ethiopian aircraft attacked Asmara airport and in retaliation Eritrean planes bombed Makelle and Adigat. Sporadic confrontations took place over the rest of the year while both sides purchased arms from China and Eastern Europe.

In June 1998, after the first hostilities, the Ethiopians began to round up Eritreans with military training or members of the Eritrean People's Front for Democracy (PFD) to expel them to Eritrea and by December both Eritreans and Ethiopians of Eritrean origin had been deported. Many people were displaced on both sides of the border and there were accusations of mistreatment. Trade between the two countries came to a standstill and Ethiopia diverted its imports and exports through Djibouti. Several problems were behind the confrontation: Ethiopia was angry at the cost of access to the port of Assab, while Eritrea was angry because Ethiopia had insisted that all trade between them had to be conducted in dollars after Eritrea had launched its own currency, the nafka, in 1997. Perhaps the root of the quarrel was the reduction of Ethiopia to a landlocked country by Eritrea, which had been a part of greater Ethiopia: in other words, anger at loss of empire. The OAU, the United States and Rwanda joined in trying to find a peaceful resolution of the dispute but to no avail; Eritrea would not withdraw from territory it had occupied after 6 May, insisting that it had only deployed troops inside its own territory. The US was concerned to resolve the conflict since otherwise it threatened its policy of containing Sudan but it made little progress as both sides adopted increasingly hard stances. At the end of 1998 there was an uneasy stand-off between the two countries and though both their economies were adversely affected, that of Eritrea was harder hit if only because it had so little to fall back on. The port of Assab, whose principal function was to service Ethiopia, was near standstill while the trade gap was widening dangerously with the government's huge increase in military spending.

What had begun as a straightforward quarrel between Eritrea and Ethiopia threatened to include Djibouti, Sudan and Somalia and demonstrated both the fragility and underlying hostilities that existed throughout the Horn. In February 1999, after eight months of relative quiet, Ethiopian forces launched a major attack to retake Badme (which Eritrea had seized in May 1998) and then push on 30 kilometres into Eritrea. A subsequent Ethiopian attempt to take Zalembessa failed, however, as did an Eritrean effort to retake Badme. Eritrea tried again in May and June with no greater success. Casualties over these months were heavy on both sides, estimated at 30,000 each. Ethiopian planes bombed both Assab and Massawa and there were artillery exchanges along much of the front, which some journalists compared with the trench warfare of 1914–18. The OAU spearheaded peace efforts and produced a framework that required observers and the demarcation of the border with UN help, with both combatants redeploying their forces outside the occupied areas. The conflict continued while these negotiations were conducted. Eritrea provided support for the dissident Djibouti Front for the Restoration of Unity and Democracy (FRUD) and encouraged it to sabotage the railway to Addis Ababa. Eritrea also provided arms and training for the Oromo Liberation Front (OLF) in southern Ethiopia and sent 1,500 fighters to assist OLF through Somalia (by agreement with Hussein Aideed). This move led to joint Ethiopian-Kenya security operations and was almost certainly counter-productive since it strengthened Ethiopian anger at Eritrea. In any case, Hussein Aideed changed sides and in October 1999 paid a visit to Ethiopia. Ethiopia claimed to have killed or captured 1,100 OLF fighters and was joined by Sudan in supporting external Eritrean opposition groups. Meanwhile, 10 Eritrean opposition groups, drawing support from Eritrean Muslims, had launched the Alliance of Eritrean National Forces (AENF) in Khartoum. Later, however, an improvement in relations between Sudan and Eritrea forced the AENF to relocate to Ethiopia. By December 1999 Ethiopia had expelled a total of 65,000 Eritreans. Amnesty International criticized the scale and methods used in these expulsions. At the same time, some 22,000 Ethiopians had left Eritrea. The Ethiopian economy was adversely affected by this confrontation: partly because of the rise in military expenditure, and partly because donors held back aid in an effort to force an end to the fighting.

There was a lull in the fighting during the first months of 2000 and both sides said they accepted the peace framework negotiated by the OAU although disagreements remained about its implementation. However, proximity talks, which had been sponsored by the United States and Algeria, collapsed in May and despite a UN Security Council arms embargo, Ethiopia launched an offensive and achieved major gains. These included the recapture of Zalembessa and Bada; in addition, its forces penetrated deep into Eritrea to take Senafe and Barentu. Faced with defeat, Eritrea withdrew from the areas it had seized in 1998. Then, under international pressure the two countries agreed to a ceasefire on 18 June. A formal peace treaty was signed on 12 December: this allowed a 4,200-strong UN peacekeeping force to be deployed in a 25-kilometre security buffer zone inside Eritrea until the demarcation of the border had been completed. By the end of December half the peacekeeping force was in place. Repatriation of prisoners began before the end of the year while Ethiopia demobilized 50,000 troops. Despite the peace both sides continued with a war of propaganda and each supported the other's dissidents: Ethiopia provided backing for the AENF and Eritrea continued its support for the Oromo dissidents (OLF). Neither side provided any details about the costs of the war although more than 70,000 soldiers had been killed. Both countries had spent several hundred million dollars purchasing aircraft from Russia and other arms from China, Libya and Israel. The social and development programmes of both countries had clearly suffered as a result of the war. Thus, the final Ethiopian advance in May 2000 had badly disrupted the planting season in western Eritrea as thousands of people had fled to escape the fighting while the numbers needing food aid had risen to one million. And in Ethiopia, according to the IMF, the war had caused a sharp fall in expenditure on health, education and development.

In 2002 the Permanent Court of Arbitration at The Hague issued its ruling on the disputed frontier. This gave Eritrea substantial territorial awards in the western sector of the border and handed some gains to Ethiopia in the centre, including all the disputed towns and villages, such as Zalambessa, Alitena and Badme. Ethiopia had cause to celebrate, Eritrea less so, although the government claimed it had obtained the land that it sought. Relations between the two countries, following the ruling, remained tense. The gains, either way, hardly warranted the loss of 70,000 lives.

Failed States and the Return
of the Imperial Factor

The idea of the 'failed state' achieved currency in the late 1990s and the term may be loosely applied to any country where the accepted mechanisms of control no longer operate effectively over the whole territory and all the people. Both the cause but also the result of a failed state may be civil war although the collapse of central power in relation to the peripheries of the state may also create this condition. It is by no means easy to settle upon a satisfactory definition of a failed state: civil war, certainly; rule by a corrupt elite concerned only with its own aggrandizement to such an extent that the population simply ignores the centre and operates independently; breakdown into local power centres, a development most likely to encourage the rise of warlords. Above all, and for whatever reason, a large proportion of the population cease to look to central government to solve or even to try to solve their problems. Once the condition has been accepted, the question then arises: can the people themselves reverse the situation and put a working state structure together again; or will it only be possible to recreate a reasonably functioning state with help from outside? Such outside help may come in the form of peacekeepers or peace enforcers in a civil war and these may be drawn from several sources – the United Nations, regional forces or intervention by a major power. In any case, and all too often, breakdown invites interventions that are predatory as with Democratic Republic of Congo, and neighbours more interested in helping themselves to its resources or pursuing some other political agenda of their own than in assisting the state to recover its authority. In terms of international politics, the failed state acts as an open invitation to interference or straight intervention and as such attracts the major powers. It is no accident that the term has come into vogue in the media of Britain, France or the United States. To speak of a failed state automatically suggests that help is needed and external assistance always comes with a price tag of its own.

A number of states in Africa, where breakdown appears to have been accepted as a semi-permanent condition, have been designated as failed states –

Angola, Burundi, Liberia, Rwanda, Somalia, Sierra Leone or Sudan – are examples. And this brings us to the factor of external intervention. Why did the United Nations and the United States intervene in Somalia and then quit when the job was unfinished and why did France intervene briefly in Rwanda in 1994 when the other major powers were determinedly finding excuses not to do so? As always, the answer to such questions resolves itself into one of interest and despite such discrepancies there were unmistakable signs in the late 1990s and into the twenty-first century of the emergence of a new form of imperialism. Sometimes, goaded by a public opinion led by 'aid' NGOs demanding that something should be done – the relief of poverty, the forgiveness of debt – there has been a return to nineteenth-century arguments about moral responsibility; more often, realpolitik prevails and interventions are guided by the self-interest of the big powers. Whatever the reasons, there is a discernible readiness on the part of Britain and France in particular, and the United States in a somewhat different fashion, to debate publicly reasons for intervention. Four countries are considered here: Sierra Leone where Britain reinforced a shaky UN operation; Republic of Congo (Brazzaville) and Côte d'Ivoire where France was busy (covertly in the first case, overtly in the second); and Liberia where people have called for the United States to come to the rescue. Whatever their problems, Africans should pause when the big powers proffer assistance. They should recall how they used to regard the Christian missionaries: 'When the missionaries arrived in Africa, they had the Bible and we had the land; later we found that we had the Bible and the missionaries had the land.'

SIERRA LEONE

The tragic collapse of Sierra Leone into anarchy in the late 1990s could be foreseen at the beginning of the decade. In 1991 Sierra Leone was affected by events in neighbouring Liberia when border fighting led to some 5,000 deaths as Charles Taylor and his National Patriotic Front of Liberia (NPFL) tried to gain control of the diamond-producing region of southern Sierra Leone. On 30 April 1992 a military coup brought Capt. Valentine Strasser to power. By this time the dissident Revolutionary United Front (RUF) had been formed and operated from across the border where it had established bases in Liberia. Thereafter, Sierra Leone was to be engulfed in a civil war that developed steadily for the rest of the decade. Strasser was ousted in another coup of 1996. Later, following elections, Ahmed Tejan Kabbah of the Sierra Leone People's Party (SLPP) was elected president and, following negotiations with the RUF leader Foday Sankoh, a temporary peace was achieved between the new government and the RUF. It did not last. A third coup was mounted in 1997, this time by Johnny

Paul Koroma, and Kabbah was forced to flee the country. Subsequently ECOWAS sent a peacekeeping mission (ECOMOG) that was led by a contingent of Nigerian troops to restore order. ECOWAS was already involved in peacekeeping efforts in neighbouring Liberia. Meanwhile, Britain gave its support to the exiled President and Kabbah was invited to attend the Commonwealth Heads of Government Meeting (CHOGM) held at Edinburgh in October 1997.

By 1998 Sierra Leone faced an uncertain future. In February ECOMOG forces, principally Nigerian, fought their way into the centre of Freetown to dislodge the military regime of Koroma, which was forced out of Freetown and much of the rest of the country, and President Kabbah was restored to power. In Britain a political storm arose over what came to be known as the Sandline Affair, or the 'Arms for Africa' affair and whether or not the Foreign Office knew that Sandline International, a British security company, had provided arms and other military assistance to the exiled Sierra Leone government. Sandline was doing precisely that in breach of the UN embargo on supplying arms to any party in the Sierra Leone dispute. Kabbah returned to Freetown on 10 March and faced the task of political reconstruction and economic and social rehabilitation in a situation of general collapse. About 1,300 supporters of the rebel Armed Forces Revolutionary Council (AFRC) were detained and 30 of them were executed, while others received prison sentences. Koroma managed to escape although the former head of state, Joseph Momoh, was sentenced to 10 years imprisonment.

Other rebels fled into the interior and sought to escape across the border into Liberia. These rebels joined the RUF that they had earlier been fighting when it threatened the Koroma regime, demonstrating thereby their principal (perhaps only) motivation, which was to obtain power and a share in the country's spoils. The RUF then intensified the war. Foday Sankoh, who had been detained in Nigeria, was sent back to Freetown where he was sentenced to death. By October the ECOMOG forces, assisted by village militias (*kamajors*), were achieving substantial successes against the rebels who were pushed to the eastern and southern borders of the country. President Kabbah, who received international financial support for the task, was beginning to re-establish a fully functioning administration and repair the huge damage to the country's infrastructure after seven years of civil war during which 1.5 million people out of a total population of five million had been displaced. By the end of the year, however, the RUF had reorganized itself and been reinforced by several hundred Ukrainian mercenaries while also receiving financial aid from unidentified sources (almost certainly the Charles Taylor government in Liberia).

At the end of December the RUF and the former Armed Forces Revolutionary Council launched a major onslaught upon Freetown. They were driven back by ECOMOG forces within two weeks but not before some 3,000 citizens had been killed and huge damage had been inflicted upon the city. The rebels remained within 20 miles of Freetown and appeared to have control over about 60 per cent of the country. Since repeated attacks upon their positions failed to dislodge them, Kabbah came under mounting pressure to restart negotiations. Nigeria was the mainstay of ECOMOG but at a cost of 900 lives and US$1 million a day. It now signalled that it wished to withdraw. Britain was the other source of financial support for the government. The two countries combined to persuade President Kabbah to reopen negotiations with the rebels and a national consultative conference was held in April. Liberian representatives also attended the conference at which President Kabbah rejected rebel demands for a total amnesty for their atrocities, a share in the government and the release from prison of Foday Sankoh. These objections, however, were overruled at a later meeting in Lomé, Togo, on 18 May. Here, under external African pressures, it was agreed as follows: a ceasefire should begin on 24 May and fresh talks on 25 May; that both sides should retain the territory they held, that humanitarian relief agencies should be given access to rebel-held areas, prisoners should be released and the United Nations be asked to deploy monitors to supervise disarmament and the rehabilitation of combatants. A peace agreement that was signed on 7 July provided for the release of Sankoh, who was to be given vice-presidential authority in the government, an amnesty for war crimes and rebel participation in the government. The agreement represented a major surrender to the rebels. There was immediate international condemnation of the blanket amnesty and, in any case, violent clashes continued in the north of the country. Relations between the former rebels and the 6,000-strong UN force that had been assembled rapidly deteriorated: the former rebels were afraid of being arrested to face charges of war crimes and also resented the UN refusal to pay for surrendered weapons.

The accord between government and rebels, which lacked any trust on either side, deteriorated until, on 7 February 2000, the UN Security Council voted to increase the UN peacekeeping force from 6,000 to 11,000 troops. In fact, by the end of 2000 there were 13,000 troops in the country, the largest peacekeeping force in the world. This build-up had been necessary to replace the ECOMOG force, which was withdrawn. The accord finally collapsed in May 2000 when the RUF abducted 500 troops of the UN Mission in Sierra Leone (UNAMISL). Full-scale fighting between the Sierra Leone army and the RUF followed. On 8 May 10,000 people in Freetown marched on the house of Foday Sankoh who was still nominally vice-president. Police fired on the crowd and Sankoh managed to escape. The shooting of the demonstrators and the obvious inability of the UN force to control the situation led to the deployment of 1,000 British troops. The rebels were forced onto the defensive and suffered a series of defeats. On 17 May Sankoh was captured in Freetown and President Kabbah announced that his immunity from prosecution was to be lifted so that he could stand trial. By 28 May all the UN hostages taken by the RUF had been released. Fighting continued to August when the RUF replaced Sankoh with Issay Sessay as their leader. The RUF now said that it was ready to commit itself to a peace agreement but this was aborted when the West Side Boys (WSB), a militia nominally allied to the government, kidnapped 11 British soldiers. Five were released on 30 August and the rest on 9 September when British troops stormed the WSB headquarters, killing 25 and capturing others. In November Britain sent a further 500 troops to Sierra Leone in reaction to the escalating crisis and a realization that the rebels would not honour any ceasefire. As long as the rebels controlled the diamond region they were likely to continue fighting. On 10 November the rebels agreed another ceasefire but the Kabbah government said 'it had no intention of relaxing its stance'.

Britain had begun by sending substantial forces apparently solely to rescue Commonwealth citizens. Subsequently, these troops were used to strengthen the UN forces, which had suffered the humiliation of having 500 troops taken hostage. By the end of the year the bulk of the British force had been withdrawn although 300 troops were to remain to retrain the Sierra Leone army. The diamond region, which remained under RUF control, provided it with the financial means to continue the war. Sierra Leone was the classic example of a small country that could easily, and repeatedly, become the prey of warring factions and would-be warlords and in this respect was the perfect candidate for the status of a 'failed state'. In February 2001 elections were postponed because of the security situation with the agreement of the UN and Britain. In March the UN Security Council voted to extend the UNAMISL mandate and increased its strength to 17,500. At the same time it criticized the RUF and other groups for their human rights violations. On 18 May the RUF and pro-government *kamajor* militias signed an agreement to end all hostilities; this followed a month-long offensive by the *kamajor* militias that had driven the RUF forces far back into the diamond fields. At the end of May the RUF and *kamajor* disarmed 2,500 soldiers and the RUF freed 600 child soldiers. The RUF demanded the creation of a transitional government by the end of September, insisting that it was no longer going to fight, but the government dismissed the demand. The government said it would only hold elections when all arms had been surrendered. In September the UN Secretary-General, Kofi Annan, announced that 16,000 RUF and pro-government militia troops had been disarmed although a further 9,000 combatants remained to be disarmed. In September 100 of the remaining 550 British troops were withdrawn from the country. By the end of the year the 17,500 UN peacekeeping force was operating at full capacity while 30,000 rebel and militia fighters had given up their arms although the process of disarming the rebels in the eastern part of the country was yet to be completed.

In January 2002 President Kabbah officially declared the civil war to be over; an estimated 50,000 people had died in 10 years of fighting. UNAMISL claimed that the disarmament of 45,000 fighters had been completed. A war crimes court was established. Sierra Leone troops, assisted by British military advisers, were deployed near the country's sensitive borders with Liberia and Guinea. In February Britain's Prime Minister, Tony Blair, visited Sierra Leone and told British troops that they had given the country 'a chance to get back on its feet again'. In March President Kabbah ended the four-year state of emergency. In May Kabbah easily won the presidential elections, beating Ernest Koroma of the All People's Congress by a comfortable margin; his SLPP won 83 of the 112 seats in the Assembly. In July a Truth and Reconciliation Commission (modelled on that of South Africa) was set up.

The war in Sierra Leone raised many questions that had not been answered when officially it came to an end. They concerned the efficiency – or otherwise – of the United Nations in its peacekeeping activities, what should be expected of regional intervention forces such as ECOMOG, and how long Britain would be required to prop up the government of Sierra Leone once the fighting was over. The RUF of Foday Sankoh was able to operate as long as it did because of the complicity of Burkina Faso whose President Blaise Compaoré traded arms in return for the diamonds that the RUF controlled, while it suited Liberia's Charles Taylor to support the RUF since he, too, wanted a share in the diamonds. The RUF did not obtain its arms only from Burkina Faso. At the height of the fighting in 2000 a British airline and a Gibraltar-based arms trader were accused by the United Nations of exporting arms to the rebels in Sierra Leone. Foyle Air, the company at the centre of these UN accusations, admitted that it had delivered 67 tons of military equipment that included Sam-7 missiles, guided anti-tank rockets, 3,000 Kalashnikovs and 25 rocket-propelled grenade launchers from Ukraine to Burkina Faso. Thereafter, the company did not 'know' what had happened to the arms. When the arms eventually reached the RUF in Sierra Leone they were paid for by money earned from the illegal sale of diamonds.[1] This single incident illustrates how easily arms can be smuggled into a war zone against a proclaimed arms embargo and raises many questions about the attitudes of the big powers towards arms sales that fuel such wars: the five permanent members of the UN Security Council account for approximately

80 per cent of arms sales worldwide. The most worrying question of all must be: how long can Sierra Leone survive on its own once all the UN forces and British support have been withdrawn? Or must it depend indefinitely upon the willingness of Britain to intervene when necessary to prop up its legitimate government? If this proves to be the case it represents the creeping return of the imperial factor into Africa.

CONGO (BRAZZAVILLE)

Pascal Lissouba won the presidential elections of August 1992 against the former military general, Denis Sassou-Nguesso, who had been in power since 1979 but had been forced by popular pressure to abandon Marxism and the one-party state and hold open elections. At that time Lissouba did not feel secure since the regular army was dominated by officers from Sassou-Nguesso's Mbochi tribe who were loyal to the former head of state. Lissouba, therefore, formed his own militia from the loyal Zoulou. In May 1993 indecisive legislative elections were followed by violence, which continued into 1994 and by February an estimated 300 people had been killed. In June 1997 a full-scale civil war broke out between supporters of Lissouba and supporters of Sassou-Nguesso. The outbreak had all the appearance of a determined bid to return to power on the part of Sassou-Nguesso. The situation was to be affected from the start by the fact that French troops were already in Brazzaville preparatory to evacuating expatriates from neighbouring Zaïre where the Mobutu regime was facing collapse. On 5 June fighting broke out in Brazzaville after the army had cordoned off Sassou-Nguesso's house as part of an attempt to disarm his independent Cobra militia. On 7 June Lissouba accepted an offer from the Mayor of Brazzaville, Bernard Kolelas (who was also a contender for supreme power), to attempt to find a solution to the crisis. President Omar Bongo of Gabon offered his services as a mediator in what clearly was developing into a dangerous conflict. On the same day, a French soldier was killed in fighting in Brazzaville and France announced that it would send additional forces to reinforce the 450 French troops already there. By 9 June Brazzaville had been cut in half by the rival groups, both of which were using heavy weapons. A further 400 French troops arrived in Brazzaville and President Chirac appealed to Lissouba and Sassou-Nguesso to end the fighting. Both did order a ceasefire on 11 June but this broke down on the following day. French air force planes evacuated foreigners and by 15 June some 5,000 foreign citizens had left, most being ferried to Gabon. On 17 June a three-day ceasefire was agreed to allow the French troops to withdraw. On 21 June the UN Secretary-General, Kofi Annan, asked the Security Council to approve a force of 1,600 international troops to secure Brazzaville airport.

Fighting continued, despite the ceasefire, and there were reports of atrocities against civilians, as well as looting, by both sides in the conflict. According to French military sources 2,000 people had been killed by the end of June with overall casualties reaching 10,000. The fighting continued throughout July and by 23 July estimated deaths had reached 4,000.

Meanwhile, as peace talks were being conducted in Libreville, Gabon, Lissouba had asked the Constitutional Court to postpone the presidential elections, which were due on 27 July, and to extend his mandate to its expiry date on 31 August. Sassou-Nguesso opposed any extension, which, he said, would lead to further fighting. Instead, he demanded the formation of a national government. The Libreville talks broke down on 19 July and on 22 July the Constitutional Court postponed the presidential poll, a decision that produced a furious response from the Sassou-Nguesso camp. Fighting continued through August and spread to the north of the country where Sassou-Nguesso's forces captured Ouesso, the main town. A peace plan was advanced by President Bongo of Gabon to be rejected by Sassou-Nguesso on 21 August and Lissouba on 23 August. The government radio accused Bongo of favouring Sassou-Nguesso who was his son-in-law. Thirty-nine parties and groups that supported President Lissouba or the opposition *Mouvement Congolais pour la Démocratie et le Développement Intégral* (MDDI) (Congolese Movement for Democracy and Full Development) signed a power-sharing agreement although the *Forces Démocratiques Unies* (FDU) (United Democratic Forces) did not sign even as heavy fighting engulfed Brazzaville. The agreement came into effect on 31 August, the expiry date of Lissouba's presidency, and provided for a government of national unity and the continuation of existing political institutions for an indefinite transitional period. Lissouba appointed Kolelas, who was the leader of the MDDI, as Prime Minister and gave him a mandate to form a government and bring an end to the three-month-old civil war. By mid-September casualties were estimated at between 4,000 and 7,000 dead while 800,000 people had fled the devastated capital. However, no end to the war appeared in sight.

Lissouba visited Paris where he announced that he would not negotiate with Sassou-Nguesso whom he described as a 'common rebel'. Sassou-Nguesso's Cobra militia, meanwhile, was fighting government forces in the north of the country. Interviewed on *Radio France Internationale*, Sassou-Nguesso said he believed there had to be a transitional government to reorganize the state and 'organise credible elections'. A meeting of eight African leaders in Gabon called for a UN peacekeeping force and appealed to the warring sides to cease fighting. Lissouba sent Kolelas to this summit while he went to Kinshasa to meet the newly installed President Kabila. Kolelas struggled to make his new government work in what by then was a largely dysfunctional Brazzaville where fighting prevented ministers from getting to their offices. Sassou-Nguesso's party refused to take up the five seats they had been offered in the coalition government. Kolelas proclaimed his aims as the restoration of peace, post-war reconstruction and new presidential elections. The war reached its climax in October when Sassou-Nguesso's forces launched a massive offensive in Brazzaville; one by one the key points in the city fell and Kolelas' government, which had never looked convincing, collapsed. The Cobra militia celebrated their victory by a wave of looting in a city strewn with corpses. A triumphant Sassou-Nguesso explained the civil war, without irony, in terms of 'tribalism, regionalism, intolerance and political violence. In order that history does not repeat itself, we ought to attack the problem at the root and henceforth work for national reconciliation and unity to finally give birth to an indivisible and happy democratic Congo,' he told his first press conference.[2] The first problem facing Sassou-Nguesso was that of dismantling the various militias representing factions and elite groups that had sprung into being over the preceding years. On 25 October 1997 the Executive Secretariat of the *Forces Démocratiques et Patriotiques* (FDP) (Democratic and Patriotic Forces) announced that Maj.-Gen. Denis Sassou-Nguesso was President. He was sworn in at the Parliament building which was one of the few public buildings still standing.

The immediate and urgent question for Sassou-Nguesso was recognition by Africa and the position that France would adopt. Throughout the conflict France had maintained an apparently ambiguous attitude to the conflict though in fact the French government favoured a return to power of Sassou-Nguesso. His quick victory owed much to the intervention on his behalf of Angola whose President dos Santos had sent troops to help Sassou-Nguesso capture Pointe Noire, the centre of Congo's oil industry and the key to the country's economy. Dos Santos, of course, wanted a 'return' for his support in the form of the suppression in the Congo of any bases for UNITA or for the separatists of Angola's Cabinda enclave. With the fall of Mobutu in Zaïre, Congo Brazzaville had become the last fuel and weapons base for UNITA. The greater part of Brazzaville's 800,000 population, meanwhile, had dispersed in the bush or become refugees across the river in Kinshasa. France denied that it had intervened on behalf of Sassou-Nguesso in the civil war. Its sole object, Paris insisted, had been to support Omar Bongo's efforts at mediation. On the other hand, Elf Aquitaine, the French oil multinational that handled Congo's oil, had clearly favoured a return to power of Sassou-Nguesso, who had always looked favourably on its monopoly position. French denials of support for Sassou-Nguesso were not matched by the official reaction to his installation as President. A Foreign Ministry spokesman, Jacques Pummelhardt, said 'It is a good thing' and 'it is essential for war ravaged Congo to commit itself wholeheartedly to the path of nation'.

Pummelhardt then, to distract attention from France's role, denounced the 'savage occupation' of the country by the Angolan forces which had backed Sassou-Nguesso.[3] The Angolan intervention was part of Luanda's effort to eliminate all outside sources of support for UNITA. Towards the end of the civil war Lissouba was reported to be hiring UNITA mercenaries. Other mercenaries, with connections to French intelligence, had been leading Sassou-Nguesso's Cobra militia.[4] Sassou-Nguesso had always been a reliable ally of France, even in his Marxist days, and had been treated as a VIP when in opposition to Lissouba he had visited France. The French government now sent medical aid to Brazzaville and signalled its support for the new regime. The situation remained complex and dangerous. On 28 October, three days after the inauguration of Sassou-Nguesso as President, dos Santos announced that the Angolan troops would only be withdrawn after an agreement with the Congo government. When Sassou-Nguesso announced his new government in early November, he claimed that UNITA troops and other mercenaries had assisted Lissouba. Although the new Minister of the Interior, Pierre Oda, said that only security forces could carry arms, banning the various militias was not going to be easy. Cobra soldiers demonstrated and demanded incorporation in the regular security forces. Lissouba's militia, the Zoulous, were given an ultimatum to come out of the bush and lay down their arms. Angolan support in the form of 1,000 crack troops had probably swung the balance in favour of Sassou-Nguesso. They were still in the Congo in 1998 despite calls in the US Congress for their withdrawal. Britain and the United States, which had been loud in their condemnation of the illegal coup in Sierra Leone in 1997, kept remarkably quiet about what, in real terms, was a coup by warfare carried out in Congo by Sassou-Nguesso. Clearly, they did not want to upset France and its President, Jacques Chirac, or interfere in a region which they considered came under France's sphere of influence.

Lissouba blamed Chirac for his political fall and Congo's oil was the key to the Paris line. Elf Aquitaine dominated the Congo's oil industry, which it controlled with other French companies. When Lissouba came to power the Congo only retained 15 per cent of the oil revenues, the rest being kept by the companies. After becoming President, Lissouba changed the system governing the country's oil. He introduced competition by persuading other oil majors such as Exxon and Shell to come in or increase their stakes and he negotiated a 33 per cent take for the Congo government. Elf, the main beneficiary of the previous system, set out to destroy the new one and, according to Lissouba, used Sassou-Nguesso and enlisted the support of Chirac. Shortly after Lissouba's overthrow, the oil companies renegotiated the Lissouba oil deal with the new government and had the 33 per cent national share of profits reduced to 20 per cent. While the fighting was taking place Chirac had telephoned Lissouba from Paris to demand that he appoint Sassou-Nguesso as vice-president and head of the armed forces, a request that would have put him in an all-powerful position. When Lissouba demurred on constitutional grounds, Chirac reportedly said, 'Chuck your bloody constitution in the dustbin'.[5] Further, again according to Lissouba, a pan-African peacekeeping force, prepared by the French Prime Minister, Michel Rocard, was set to intervene when pressure from Chirac aborted the plan.

In the end, oil and French economic and political interests in Congo ensured French support for Sassou-Nguesso and the destruction of the democratic process which had been inaugurated in 1992 after 14 years of Sassou-Ngueso's autocratic rule. Despite its stated belief in democracy and its opposition to Marxism, France preferred the dictatorial Sassou-Nguesso, provided he would safeguard its interests, to the democratically elected Lissouba who wanted a greater share of the country's oil resources to be used for the Congo rather than be expatriated to France. The relationship between France and Sassou-Nguesso reveals a great deal about France's role in Africa and power-hungry African leaders. Sassou-Nguesso was quite prepared to reduce his country's legitimate take from its oil by reducing a reasonable (and still moderate) 33 per cent dividend on oil to 20 per cent in order to ensure French support for his seizure of power while France had been prepared to undermine the democratic process in Congo so as to maximize its exploitation of the country's major resource. Commenting on the French attitude towards its former colonial territories six years after the events described here, the *Financial Times* said retrospectively that, 'France's passive attitude towards the violent overthrow of President Pascal Lissouba of Congo was widely criticized. Mr Lissouba's government had looked favourably on US energy companies exploiting offshore oil reserves, much to the anger of French companies. A successful uprising led by Congo's former military dictator, Denis Sassou-Nguesso, was barely criticized in Paris, and French companies resumed their prime position once Mr Lissouba was overthrown.'[6]

CÔTE D'IVOIRE

The long years of Houphouët-Boigny's rule and the apparent stability he achieved (the velvet glove and iron fist alternating) had produced the impression of a more stable society than was actually the case. This impression had been greatly enhanced by one of the most successful, agriculture-based economies in

West Africa and the fact that Houphouët-Boigny had encouraged the sizeable French community to remain. France, as a result, had come to view Côte d'Ivoire as the showpiece of Francophone Africa. By the end of the 1990s, however, this cosy view of the country was about to change.

In 1998, with two years still to go before elections were due, pre-election manoeuvres had nevertheless got under way and an alliance appeared to be forming between the ruling Democratic Party of President Bédié, who had succeeded to the presidency in 1993 on the death of Houphouët-Boigny, and the opposition *Front Populaire Ivorien* (FPI) (Ivorian Popular Front) of Laurent Gbagbo. The alliance had a good deal to do with the fact that the other popular contender for power, a former prime minister under Houphouët-Boigny, was Alassane Ouattara. He had been 'constitutionally' disqualified from running for the presidency under nationality and citizenship clauses because it was claimed that he was a Burkinabe rather than an Ivorian. Although the economy performed well at this time, with a 1998 growth rate of six per cent, debt servicing had become a near crippling burden demanding 50 per cent of foreign exchange earnings.

The crisis came at the end of 1999 when, on 24 December, West Africa was shaken by what until then had been unthinkable: a coup in Côte d'Ivoire. A military junta overthrew the government of President Henri Konan Bédié. The coup, apparently, had begun at a barracks meeting by an elite para commando unit, which had not been paid for serving with the UN in Central African Republic. However, what might have been no more than a mutiny over pay soon developed into a full-scale takeover as the airport, TV-radio station and president's office were seized, suggesting that careful planning was involved. Gen. Guei, a former chief of army staff, was brought out of retirement, possibly against his will, at first to act as spokesman for the mutineers. However, he announced the removal of the head of state and the dissolution of the National Assembly, the Constitutional Council and the Supreme Court. These institutions were replaced by a nine-member National Committee of Public Safety; later it was announced that Gen. Guei was to be the new head of state. Bédié and his family fled to the French Embassy using an underground passage from state house, whose existence suggests an even closer liaison between France and the rulers of Côte d'Ivoire than might have been expected. Bédié then broadcast, calling for resistance to the coup though none was forthcoming. Despite the tunnel there had been no French response on behalf of Bédié and the only pro-Bédié Frenchman appeared to be President Chirac's African Affairs Adviser, Michel Dupuch. France did however send reinforcements to its base in the country in case of any threats to the French community. Bédié went into exile in Paris. Prior to the coup the economy had been slowing down while revenues from commodities, the principal exports, were slumping. The IMF had assisted this decline by suspending payments because it was unhappy at 'governance'. The coup appeared to be well received in the country and though France, the United States, the EU and the OAU condemned it, they contented themselves with calling for as short a period of military rule as possible. Every one of Côte d'Ivoire's neighbours had experienced one or more coups; now the success story of Francophone West Africa was in trouble.

Although Guei was accorded a measure of goodwill, people were wary that the army had become involved as the country's power broker. The most influential figure in the new regime, briefly, was Alassane Ouattara, but he faced much opposition in the south because of his Burkinabe connections. Guei, who may have thought otherwise to begin with, decided to run for the presidency in the forthcoming elections. In August 2000 a referendum was held that entrenched the concept of *Ivoiricité* with a substantial majority, which was a further blow to Ouattara's political chances. An assassination attempt against Guei in September was blamed on two generals sympathetic to Ouattara. In October, as the presidential elections approached, the courts again ruled that Ouattara could not stand for the presidency with the result that his party, *Rassemblement Démocratique Républicain* (RDR), boycotted them. This left two main contenders for the presidency: Gen. Guei and Laurent Gbagbo. They had collaborated in order to exclude Ouattara from running; now they fell out. Guei, in classic military style, sacked the electoral commission and proclaimed himself the winner. His prime minister, Souleymane Diarra, resigned in protest while thousands of Gbagbo's supporters took to the streets to demonstrate and sections of the army deserted Guei who was obliged to flee the country instead of swearing himself in as president. Diarra reinstated the electoral commission and pronounced Gbagbo the winner with 59 per cent of the votes to Guei's 31 per cent. Ouattara's supporters called for fresh elections. He met with Gbagbo and both men appealed for calm although Gbagbo maintained the ban on Ouattara, with the result that his RDR boycotted the parliamentary elections of December. Gbagbo's FPI won the elections and the RDR came in second place. However, the exclusion of Ouattara and his RDR from political life threatened a breakdown of the country's political structure and split Côte d'Ivoire between north and south along ethnic and religious lines, with the north predominantly Muslim and the south predominantly Christian. The north also played host to several million migrants from Burkina Faso and Mali who habitually worked the coffee and cocoa plantations. By this time the economy was in free fall.

The dramas that had characterized the last half of 2000 led to heightened tensions in 2001 for though Gbagbo had successfully faced down Gen. Guei and the army, the exclusion of Ouattara from politics had edged the country close to civil war. An attempted coup in January was rumoured to have the support of Burkina Faso while the rise of anti-northern feelings in the south had led thousands of Burkinabes to leave the country. Gbagbo tried to damp down the growing north-south split as did France, which saw its showcase Francophone country collapsing. Gbagbo, however, would not do the one thing that could have diffused the rising tensions: that is, recognize Ouattara's Ivorian nationality, no doubt fearing that Ouattara would win the presidential elections. In June Gbagbo called together a National Reconciliation Forum. Bédié, Ouattara and Guei returned from abroad to take part although Ouattara needed a good deal of convincing, though in the end he felt it would be politically counter-productive to boycott it. An uncomfortable lull followed and continued into 2002. Finally, in September the tensions exploded when army mutinies broke out simultaneously in five cities. The outbreak failed in Abidjan but was successful in Bouaké in the centre north of the country and Korhogo in the far north. The revolt had been sparked off by 750 army recruits who had been told they would be dismissed from the army. The uprising took place on 19 September. Both Gen. Guei and the Interior Minister were killed when President Gbagbo was out of the country. The Defence Minister, Lida Moise Kouassi, said on television that the government had brought the situation under control and only pockets of resistance remained. This soon proved to be incorrect although, in the way of coups, there were lulls while the different factions gathered their forces and decided on what actions to take. At first Gbagbo, who was on a visit to Italy, said he would delay his return until he had had an audience with the Pope. In Bouaké the rebels took control of police and military bases. In Abidjan paramilitary police set fire to dozens of houses around the military base on the grounds that they needed to secure the area but, perhaps, it was no accident that most of the people whose houses were destroyed were Muslims from neighbouring countries. In Korhogo the mutineers handed out guns to civilians.

Gbagbo now cut short his visit to Italy and returned to Côte d'Ivoire. Claims by the government that it had regained control were increasingly unrealistic. In Abidjan, after hours of gunfire, Interior Minister Emile Boga Doudou and a number of senior military officers had been killed while Ouattara, fearing he would be blamed for the uprising, sought asylum in the French embassy. France airlifted in reinforcements to its base in the country, ready to protect its 20,000 citizens. Sgt Alfred Camin in Bouaké said: 'We mutineers are ready to negotiate under the aegis of France, which must assure the application of agreements.'[7] The United States then sent 200 Special Forces soldiers to rescue American children trapped in a school in Bouaké that catered for the children of missionaries serving in various West African countries. President Gbagbo pledged to launch a full-scale assault to free Bouaké. Speaking from the French embassy, where he had taken refuge, Ouattara accused the government of trying to kill him after the uprising and said: 'It is clear they are using the situation to try to liquidate and eliminate people in my party.'[8]

At the end of September African leaders met in Accra, Ghana, to prevent what by then had come to be called a conflagration from spreading across West Africa. Loyalties in the region are complicated. Ivorians believed that Burkina Faso was supporting the rebels yet both countries belonged to ECOWAS and Nigeria, its leading member, sent three jet fighters to be used by Gbagbo in putting down the rebellion. Ghana also offered military assistance. Gbagbo, however, wanted to 'cut off the rebels' head' by striking at Burkina Faso where he believed the rebels had bases. Mali also had many citizens working in the north of Côte d'Ivoire and, like the Burkinabes, its citizens had often suffered from xenophobic attacks by the Ivorians. At this time the current Chairman of ECOWAS, President Abdoulaye Wade of Senegal, was considering raising a force of 3,000 to 4,000 men to help Gbagbo regain control of his country, under the auspices of ECOMOG, the ECOWAS Monitoring Group. By the end of September about 600 people has lost their lives while the French had managed to remove 2,000 French citizens and other foreigners, especially from Bouaké. The French rescue operation, however, obstructed the government's efforts to recapture the northern towns and, according to the Defence Minister, Kida Kouassi, the 'invisible hands' of the French had put pressure on President Gbagbo not to pursue the rebels as strongly as he wanted and that French troop movements had made it impossible for the government forces to be reinforced and supplied.

Ouattara, who had been Houphouët-Boigny's prime minister from 1990 to 1993, could be the key to a solution. Although born in Côte d'Ivoire he had Burkinabe ancestors and each of Houphouët-Boigny's successors made that an excuse to bar him from standing against him. They feared Ouattara because he was a Muslim and they constituted the single largest voting bloc in the country. Since most Muslims live in the north of the country and large numbers of Malians and Burkinabes, who are also Muslims, reside and work in the north, this creates a potential divide from the largely Christian south.[9] The dangers of a north-south split along ethnic and religious lines became all too apparent once the uprising had begun. Meanwhile, Thabo Mbeki of South Africa had joined the other leaders in Accra. President Gbagbo, in response to the ECOWAS offer of troops, said he only wanted logistical help in crushing the rebels. Gbagbo rejected peace proposals, arguing that the rebels should disarm first, and according to the Togolese foreign minister the Ivorian authorities 'believe that their government is legitimate and should not be considered on the same levels of legitimacy as the rebels'. By early October as many as 150,000 people had been displaced by the fighting in Bouaké against which the government had launched an offensive. One result of the fighting was an exodus of thousands of Malian and Burkinabe immigrants back to their own countries. The rebels held on to Bouaké and then suspended talks with the West African mediators, accusing Angola of flying in troops to back the government. A spokesman for the rebel *Mouvement Patriotique de Côte d'Ivoire* (MPCI) (Patriotic Movement of Ivory Coast), Cherif Ousmane, said that 500 Angolan troops had arrived in Abidjan and that the MPCI suspended all participation in any mediation until they had left the territory. Having rejected one ceasefire agreement because of the Angola scare, the rebel leader, Tuo Fozie, signed a ceasefire agreement in Bouaké on 17 October. By mid-October the rebels had seized most of the northern half of Côte d'Ivoire and, following the ceasefire, French troops had taken up positions along the front line to monitor it. A stalemate characterized the following month, with neither side gaining any positive advantage. By early December, however, the country appeared to be closer to outright civil war after new rebel groups appeared in the west of the country and both sides accused one another of massacring civilians. France, with 1,000 troops in the country, was appreciably nearer greater involvement in the conflict. The defence minister, Bertin Kadet, denying government responsibility for a massacre, urged France, the United States and the European Union to intervene to halt the fighting and, speaking on state-controlled television, said: 'One shouldn't wait until there is another Rwanda to intervene. In order to finish with these aggressors and free our country, I want to appeal solemnly for a general mobilization of Ivorians beneath the flag.' He called upon 20- to 26-year-olds to sign up with the army.[10] By late December France had become more fully committed to intervention. In Paris the government decided to double the number of its troops in Côte d'Ivoire to 2,500 after a fierce battle between rebels and troops of the French Foreign Legion in the west of the country. The Legionnaires had put to flight a rebel group that was pursuing routed government forces near the town of Duekoue. The increased French involvement was widely seen as a move to shore up the position of Gbagbo. While the rebels accused France of waging a colonial war, Paris insisted that its role was still one of peacekeeping. However, on the insistence of Gbagbo, the French ambassador in Abidjan, who opposed deeper French involvement in the conflict, was removed by Paris.

Following the widespread condemnation of its intervention in Rwanda in 1994 it appeared that France had abandoned its long-standing tradition of direct and indirect intervention to bolster client governments in Francophone Africa. The decision to send troops to Côte d'Ivoire, even with UN blessing, was seen as a return to the old policy. Fighting in the west of the country erupted in January

2003 where the *Mouvement Populaire Ivoirien du Grand Ouest* (MPIGO) (Popular Ivorian Movement for the Far West) seized control of the town of Neka. The French Minister for Foreign Affairs, Dominique de Villepin, visited Côte d'Ivoire on 3 January. In Abidjan he had talks with Gbagbo who promised to observe the October ceasefire and to send home foreign mercenaries from Israel and South Africa. De Villepin also visited Bouaké for talks with the leaders of the northern-based rebel group, the MPCI. The rebels also agreed to abide by the October ceasefire and to attend peace talks in Paris on 15 January. Fighting continued in the west of the country.

Peace talks between representatives of the governments of Côte d'Ivoire and France and the three rebel groups began on 15 January in Marcoussis, south-east of Paris, and concluded on 24 January with a tentative agreement for the establishment of an interim 'government of national reconciliation' representing all parties and rebel groups, as well as an amnesty and new measures to overcome the ethnic friction that was at the root of the conflict. The 2,500 French troops, then in Côte d'Ivoire, would, together with troops from several West African states, oversee disarmament. The agreement was approved at Marcoussis at a meeting attended by 10 African leaders and international donors and was jointly chaired by President Chirac of France and Kofi Annan, the UN Secretary-General. The plan was thrown into doubt at once when mobs besieged the French embassy in Abidjan, accusing France of humiliating Côte d'Ivoire by brokering a peace agreement that was too kind to the rebels. Gbagbo did not, as he had promised, deliver a television address supporting the power-sharing agreement. The French government had pushed Gbagbo too far and de Villepin almost accused him of playing a double game by accepting peace terms in Paris while ordering his supporters onto the streets in Abidjan. 'Ivory Coast humiliated in Paris' was the front-page headline (27 January) in *Notre Voie*, a newspaper run by Gbagbo's ruling party. As France discovered, 'With 16,000 French residents barricaded in their homes and 2,500 French soldiers under attack from supporters of a government they were deployed to defend, Paris faces the prospect of being drawn into all-out civil war.'[11]

The conflict was broadly about north-south ethnic differences. One in four of the country's 14 million population have foreign roots and while many have been in the country for decades, others were more recent incomers, attracted by the country's stability and economic boom. Much of the blame should rest at Gbagbo's door because of his use of the concept of *Ivoiricité* – giving priority to Ivorians – that had led to attacks upon minorities. At issue after Marcoussis was the promise that the MPCI should get the defence and interior ministries in the new government. The protesters made plain that they did not want the rebels in the government at all. By mid-February with renewed fighting, the Marcoussis agreement appeared to be dead. It seemed clear by this time that the rebels were financed by Burkina Faso. French policy was uneasily poised between wanting to achieve a return to stability as quickly as possible in Côte d'Ivoire, since that would best suit French interests, and reluctance to support Gbagbo who was keen 'to extract Ivory Coast from the long-established stranglehold of French business interests'.[12] As with many other African countries, Ivorian 'independence' has only benefited a few Ivorians and their external (French) patrons. Too often, when a crisis arises, African governments turn to their former colonial powers for a way out. 'The continuous dependence and reliance on former colonial powers confirms what (Frantz) Fanon said, that "there is no new entity born of colonialism". Herein lies the problem.'[13]

LIBERIA

Following the 1980s, a decade of increasingly corrupt rule under Samuel Doe, an uprising was launched against him at the end of 1989. The rebels called themselves the National Patriotic Front of Liberia (NPFL); they were led by Charles Taylor, a former Doe minister who had fled Liberia in 1984, accused of corruption (his nickname was 'superglue'), taking US$900,000 with him to the United States. Taylor manifestly did not possess the credentials of a crusader against a corrupt regime. He wanted his share of the loot and was after power. Taylor had escaped from prison in the United States in odd circumstances – he was about to be extradited to Liberia – and returned to Africa where he obtained the backing of Libya and Burkina Faso for his onslaught upon the Doe regime. He established a base in Côte d'Ivoire with the support of Houphouët-Boigny where he created the NPFL. Taylor's rebels launched their attack from Côte d'Ivoire at the end of 1989 and by mid-1990 the civil war had engulfed Liberia. Doe himself was seized and killed by Prince Yormie Johnson and his rebel group and thereafter the rival factions reduced Liberia to chaos and years of fighting. The Economic Community of West African States (ECOWAS) prepared a military intervention force under the command of the Ghanaian soldier Lt-Gen. Arnold Qainoo, and its Monitoring Group (ECOMOG) established itself in the capital of Liberia, Monrovia. This was the first attempt at regional peacekeeping in West Africa and ECOMOG was to remain involved in Liberia until the civil war came to an end and elections were held in 1997.[14] The 1997 elections resulted in victory for the principal contender for power, Charles Taylor, who won the presidential election while his party, the National Patriotic Party (NPP), took 49 of 64 seats in the House of Representatives and 21 out of 26 seats in the Senate. Normalization of political life in 1998, the year after the elections, was uncertain at best. Taylor did not keep to the peace agreement that had been worked out with the other warring factions but packed the administration and reformed the security forces with his own followers from the NPFL. He worked to crush opposition by force and intimidation while his relations with the ECOMOG forces that were still in the country to oversee the peace were strained.

Meanwhile, he had begun to provide support for the RUF rebels in neighbouring Sierra Leone. In the course of 1999 Taylor became more deeply involved in Sierra Leone and was condemned by the international community for his destabilizing activities in the region. In part his interference in Sierra Leone and also Guinea was retaliatory since both countries had committed military forces to ECOMOG whose presence in Liberia Taylor deeply resented. More important, he wanted access to the diamond-mining region of Sierra Leone across the border, which was then controlled by the RUF.

Taylor's hold on power was now challenged by dissidents based in Guinea. During August and September they launched armed attacks in Lofa county. They called themselves the Joint Forces for the Liberation of Liberia and they were made up of elements of former rebel factions. On 17 September Taylor signed a peace accord with Guinea's President Lansana Conté at Abuja in the hope of curtailing the dissident activities and in October the last ECOMOG forces were withdrawn, enabling Taylor to enter 2000 with some sense of security. He maintained his grip on power through a circle of corrupt associates protected by loyal armed guards. He controlled the diamond export trade and this was boosted by events in Sierra Leone where Taylor supported Foday Sankoh and the RUF. This policy backfired when Britain persuaded the EU to block the first tranche of US$55 million EU aid to Liberia. In February 2001 rebels launched an attack, which was backed by Guinea. Taylor's government, under international pressure, announced that it was closing the RUF offices in Monrovia. In March the UN Security Council gave Liberia two months to convince it that it had stopped supporting the RUF; otherwise, sanctions would be imposed. The ambassadors of Guinea and Sierra Leone were declared persona non grata and given seven days to leave Liberia. On 19 March Liberia closed its borders with Sierra Leone. Despite these measures, UN sanctions were imposed in May because the Security Council did not believe that Liberia had really cut its ties with the RUF. The sanctions were to last for 12 months and they included a ban on the all-important diamond exports. In October an Amnesty International report accused the government of brutal treatment of its opponents.

During 2002 Taylor's many crimes against his people caught up with him as an increasing number of people revolted against his corrupt and brutal government. In January tens of thousands of Liberians fled the north of the country as fighting escalated between government forces and rebels of the Liberians United for Reconciliation and Democracy (LURD). At this stage the rebels were thought to be led by Doe's former chief of staff Charles Julu. Fighting broke out in other parts of the country where LURD was gaining support. In February Taylor declared a state of emergency. In March LURD said it was ready to conduct peace talks with government or opposition, but not with Taylor himself. Taylor ignored these offers and sought to destroy his enemies by force although this was to prove increasingly difficult because the international arms embargo prevented his government obtaining fresh arms. In May the UN Security Council renewed sanctions against Liberia for another 12 months because Taylor's government had 'not yet complied fully' with its demands to end its support for the RUF rebels. Towards the end of September the Liberian government claimed major successes against LURD and lifted the state of emergency. Taylor said that all areas occupied by LURD forces had been retaken except for parts of the northern city of Voinjama. This apparent government success proved illusory.

In early June 2003, while attending a Liberian peace summit in Ghana, Taylor said that he might step aside if it would bring peace to Liberia. He had just been indicted for war crimes in Sierra Leone. He told the conference: 'I will strongly consider a process of transition that will not include me. If President Taylor removes himself for the Liberians, will that bring peace? If so, I will remove myself.' It is doubtful that many in his audience believed him. By that time some 200,000 Liberians had died in the civil war of the previous decade while the two rebel movements, LURD and the Movement for Democracy in Liberia, controlled two-thirds of the country and had several times fought their way into the outskirts of Monrovia. By mid-June about a million people had crowded into Monrovia, facing the city with potentially disastrous health and food shortage problems. A Liberian man, Anthony Washington, explained his country's plight: 'We got no order. We don't know who's a rebel and who's a government man. We don't know who to run from, or where to run to next.' This is the Liberia Taylor's greed for power has created. The rebels were supported by his three neighbours – Côte d'Ivoire, Guinea and Sierra Leone – because he had armed and supported rebels in their countries.[15] Despite these pressures Taylor had publicly withdrawn his promise to step down. By this time aid workers and Liberians were calling upon the United States to intervene to end the anarchy although Washington showed no inclination to do so. There were 100 marines in Monrovia to guard the American embassy. Following shelling, angry crowds accused the United States of failing to protect Liberians from fighting in the capital. At this point in the Liberia story, an interesting debate surfaced among the major Western powers as Britain, France and the

United Nations urged Washington to intervene. Why, if Britain and France have sent forces to help their former colonies in Sierra Leone and Côte d'Ivoire, should the US not help Liberia? The conflicts in the three countries had been linked as rebels moved back and forth across borders.[16] By mid-July 2003 all the signs pointed to a final bloody confrontation in Monrovia before the final collapse of the Taylor regime.

The wars in these four countries – Congo, Côte d'Ivoire, Liberia and Sierra Leone – had much in common. They occurred in small countries where ethnic divisions were acute or could easily be elevated into lethal antagonisms. The conflicts had more to do with power-hungry warlords seeking control than any more ideological question of a ruling philosophy on behalf of the people as a whole. In each case the structures of government proved fragile and unable to withstand the pressures they faced. And in each case increasingly desperate populations appealed for outside intervention and turned 'naturally' to their former metropolitan powers, a fact that tells volumes about the brainwashing capacities of the colonial powers: if they achieved nothing else they created a sense of dependence that has not yet begun to disappear.

The Congo:
Africa's Great War

Deeply troubled since its creation as a personal fief by Belgium's rapacious king, Leopold II, the independent Congo was born in bloodshed only to be treated again as a personal fief by the equally rapacious Mobutu before rising demands for democracy at the beginning of the 1990s signalled the coming end to his rule. Democracy, however, had to wait as the Congo came near to disintegration under the pressures of its predatory neighbours. The struggle for multiparty democracy in the Congo that threatened the Mobutu regime at the beginning of the 1990s may have been part of a continent-wide rejection of military rule and the one-party state yet, as its leader Etienne Tshisekedi and his supporters were to discover, they had a long way to go. Major examples of Mobutu's rearguard reactions to demands for change over his last years include the massacre of Lubumbashi University students in 1990, the instigation of looting and violence by the military in 1991 and 1993, the massacre of Christian demonstrators demanding the reopening of the National Conference in Kinshasa in 1992, the instigation of ethnic cleansing in the Shaba and Kivu provinces in 1992–94, the refusal to deal with the danger posed to the country by the Rwandan refugee camps under the control of Hutu extremists over 1994–96 and finally the use of white mercenaries in a last-ditch effort to save his regime in 1996–97.[1]

In 1992, apparently bowing to popular pressure, Mobutu saw the formation of a democratically elected government under Tshisekedi who was to learn much about frustration if he achieved little else. 'During the three months in which his government was formally unchallenged as the executive power of the state, from 30 August to 30 November 1992, he was unable to start fulfilling his promise to the people. His adversaries, the forces of the status quo, responded to his olive branch with utter contempt, and exploited his patience to obstruct his administration.'[2] In fact, Tshisekedi and his cabinet functioned like a caretaker government rather than a regime that was going to change anything, and a caretaker government waiting for the Mobutuists to resume control. On 6

December 1992 the National Conference dissolved itself to be succeeded by a 453-member High Council of the Republic (HCR) with Archbishop Monsengwo as its president. It was empowered to amend and adapt the constitution and organize presidential and legislative elections. In January 1993 the HCR, which had declared Tshisekedi head of government, also declared Mobutu guilty of treason and threatened impeachment unless he recognized the legitimacy of the transitional parliament. Strikes and disorder followed this pronouncement while Mobutu attempted to reassert his authority and worked to divide the various forces ranged against him. He reconvened the dormant national assembly as a rival to the HCR and then created a conclave that appointed Faustin Birindwa prime minister. By September 1993 Mobutu was insisting that Tshisekedi's mandate had been superseded while his supporters insisted that he was still prime minister. In January 1994 Mobutu announced the dissolution of the HCR, the national legislative council, the dismissal of the Birindwa government and a contest between Tshisekedi and Molumba Lukoji for the premiership. In 1995, expert as ever in the game of playing for time, Mobutu used the presence in the country of 2.5 million refugees from the Rwanda genocide war as an excuse for postponing elections.

In April 1996 it was announced that a referendum on a new constitution would be held in December and would be followed by presidential, legislative, regional and municipal elections in 1997. In fact, none of these events took place for by the end of the year the security situation was collapsing. In August Mobutu flew to Switzerland for treatment for cancer and was to be away for four months. His absence, added to the chaos in eastern Zaïre as a result of the Rwanda refugee crisis, marked the turning point of Mobutu's long rule. Having established a national elections commission (the *Commission Nationale des Elections*) (CNE), Mobutu had proceeded to marginalize it as he did with anything designed to encourage the emergence of democracy. 'One by one, each of the major components of the institutional framework of the transition – the legislature, the executive and the electoral commission – failed to help effect the democratic transition in the Congo. The original framework adopted at the *Conférence Nationale Souveraine* (CNS) (sovereign national conference) was called into question by the Mobutu camp, which used its control of the security forces and other organs of state power to block the democratization process.'[3] Meanwhile, Rwandan Hutu militiamen who had fled Rwanda in 1994, fearing Tutsi retribution, had mingled with the refugee camps to turn these into bases for recruitment and rearmament. From 1996 the Hutu militias began carving out strategic territory for themselves in eastern Zaïre with support from locally based Hutus and members of the Zaïrean armed forces (*Forces Armées du Zaïre*) (FAZ), killing and expelling local Tutsis and other ethnic groups in the process.

They were assisted in this course because there already existed widespread resentment of local Tutsis resident in South Kivu province who were known as the *Banyamulenge*. An aspect of the ethnic complexity of this region was the long-running dispute as to whether the *Banyamulenge* were entitled to citizenship of Zaïre. In October 1996 the governor of South Kivu ordered the *Banyamulenge* to leave the province in a week and though the order was subsequently suspended it caused great alarm with the result that Tutsi militias were formed and were at once supported by the Tutsi-controlled Rwanda government and Uganda. They proceeded to attack the Hutu forces and their FAZ allies. The Tutsi rebels were joined by various other groups of ethnic dissidents and these formed the *Alliance des Forces Démocratiques pour la Libération du Congo-Zaïre* (AFDL), which made the somewhat unlikely figure of Laurent Desiré Kabila its leader. Kabila had been an aide to Lumumba and an opponent of Mobutu since the 1960s. By November 1996 the AFDL forces controlled significant areas bordering on Rwanda, Burundi and Uganda including Goma and Bukavu. Mobutu's continued absence meant that his regime was not co-ordinated properly to meet the AFDL threat. By the end of the month the AFDL controlled most of Kivu Province.

The career of Mobutu is a case study in tyranny and corruption and his last years showed him visibly and increasingly on the defensive under intensive pressure from democratic forces demanding change. The economy was collapsing and inflation soaring. It was against this background that he opted to introduce a multiparty system and announced his resignation as chairman of the *Mouvement Populaire de la Révolution* (MPR) so that he could 'rise above' party politics. This situation prompted his apparent embrace of democratic processes at the beginning of the 1990s. Had he managed, as he tried, to co-opt Tshisekedi as his prime minister, he might have survived longer but he failed to do so. Outsiders often refer to tyrannies as though these are the fruits of one person's endeavours but this is never the case. 'One may equally wonder whether Marshal Mobutu, whose authority for so many years was uncontested, was not for a substantial period the hostage of what we have called a "board of directors", consisting in his case of the Equatorian clique from his home province, and the military barons of the government.'[4] All tyrants, in fact, surround themselves with a clique bound to the tyrant by complicity and corruption, and Mobutu was no exception to this rule. In Mobutu's case control of the economy was exercised by smuggling out of the country officially sanctioned counterfeit banknotes and the President was 'able to choose whether to change some of these banknotes into dollars or to use them for paying the army'.[5] By the 1990s, if not well before, Zaïre under Mobutu had become a regime based upon state kleptocracy solely concerned to promote the interests of the ruling clique to the detriment of the general welfare.

Mobutu's long reign was assisted by the fact that the United States, Belgium and France, in pursuit of their own regional interests, ignored all Mobutu's shortcomings and went along with his outrageous system until it became convenient or necessary to ditch him. Mobutu's economics were based upon a system of political patronage networks that made it unnecessary to put large resources into public services that would provide the elite with only limited returns. When, finally, the Mobutu regime collapsed the system of patronage became localized, allowing regional leaders to continue for themselves the process of manipulation that formerly had kept Mobutu in power. Once his immediate entourage saw that Mobutu was doomed they deserted him. 'Mobutu's propaganda machine and his external backers had created the image of a strongman without whom the Congo could not be held together. On 16 May 1997, Mobutu's generals dispelled the myth when they informed the field marshal that they could no longer guarantee his own security in the country.' He retreated to Gbadolite where the crew of his presidential jet refused to fly him out of the country on the grounds that it belonged to the state. Humiliatingly, therefore, he was flown out of Zaïre in a military transport upon which some of his soldiers fired as it took off.[6]

Beginning his political career as a protégé of Lumumba and a Marxist, Kabila had been implicated in the Simba massacre of civilians in Stanleyville in 1964 before he had formed his own political party, the *Parti de la Révolution Populaire* (PRP) which opposed Mobutu for 30 years although from 1964 to 1996 Kabila had fought a wholly ineffective campaign against Mobutu from his stronghold in the Fizi mountains on Lake Tanganyika. According to Che Guevara to whom Kabila played host in 1965, there was little of the revolutionary about him. As Guevara said, 'He displays none of the required discipline of a dedicated revolutionary and is too addicted to drink and women.' In the intervening years he had become a trader in ivory and gold. Despite this dubious reputation, Kabila did manage to lead a broad coalition against Mobutu and in October 1996 his PRP joined with three other parties to form the AFDL. When he emerged victorious in 1997 as Mobutu's forces disintegrated, outside observers attributed his victory mainly to the support of the Tutsi troops from Rwanda and Uganda rather than to his own followers. Little was known of him in 1997 except that he was to the 'left' in politics. Presidents Museveni of Uganda and Kagame of Rwanda had proposed making Kabila the leader of an instant Congolese liberation struggle, no doubt also believing they would subsequently be able to manipulate him. Mounting a revolt from eastern Zaïre was hardly difficult in 1996 since, apart from general Congolese dissatisfaction with everything about Mobutu, the whole region covering eastern Zaïre, Burundi,

Rwanda and Uganda was in turmoil as a result of the 1994 genocide in Rwanda and the large numbers of Rwandans who had become refugees. By November 1996 Kabila had established his claim to lead the AFDL, which had made some substantial advances. Despite this, Kabila had no vision for a future Congo and had been forced into a leadership position by the politics of Zaïre's neighbours.

AFDL forces entered Kinshasa on 17 May 1997 and Kabila announced the establishment of the Democratic Republic of Congo (DRC) replacing the name Zaïre. In a broadcast to the nation Kabila said he would do everything possible to 'guarantee peace, national unity, and the security of the people and their property'. The population of Kinshasa welcomed the AFDL troops and Tshisekedi's *Union pour la Démocatie et le Progrès Social* (UDPS) (Union for Democracy and Social Progress) welcomed the new regime on 19 May. Kabila's new government was recognized by Angola, Rwanda, Uganda and Congo (B); Western countries indicated support but withheld recognition. Kabila promised maximum co-operation with relief agencies looking after the refugees. He entered Kinshasa on 20 May and quickly made clear that there was no place for Tshisekedi in his transitional government. There were protests at Tshisekedi's exclusion and on 26 May Kabila banned demonstrations. On 29 May he took the oath of office including full executive presidential powers. In June he announced his government priorities and said the administration would be run on socialist lines. His priorities were the construction of roads, the establishment of mechanization centres to modernize agriculture and the electrification of the whole country. On 7 September Mobutu died in Morocco. Whatever his capacities and real aims, Kabila faced general chaos and a breakdown of law and order in a country that had some 240 ethnic groups or tribes, a renewal of secessionist ambitions in Shaba and predatory Western companies moving in to profit from the economic chaos left behind by Mobutu. The corruption and greed of President Mobutu had been on such a scale that he and his supporters were deemed to be responsible for the new political term 'state kleptocracy' or rule by theft. As the rebellion, which got under way in 1996, gathered momentum at the beginning of 1997 it was perhaps fitting that Mobutu sought to bolster his crumbling regime with the assistance of mercenaries. In fact they did him little service and in March 1997 quit Kisangani in the face of the oncoming rebels and fled the country. Mobutu's chief of staff, Gen. Mahele Lyoko Bokungu, had made contact with the rebels and said he saw no reason to put a city of five million at risk for one man. On 16–17 May, Mobutu's presidential guard, including his son Capt. Mobutu Kongolo, went on the rampage in Kinshasa killing those they regarded as traitors, including Gen. Bokungu. About 177 people were killed in all. On 16 May, the minister of information, Kinbiey Mukumba, announced that Mobutu 'had decided to leave the capital' and had 'ceased all intervention in the affairs of state'.

By early 1998 it was already becoming clear that Kabila, though he had been given the benefit of the doubt, was not the man to solve DRC's problems, which included armed groups that were a law to themselves, and the eastern border area, which formed the crux of the problem. Hutu militants were launching attacks upon Rwanda from bases in Kivu, other ethnic groups in North and South Kivu simply defended themselves against all comers while former FAZ soldiers were out of control. Kabila did not enjoy a wide support base and his victory had clearly been due to the *Banyamulenge* backed by Rwanda and Uganda. Now, however, the Tutsis in Kinshasa overplayed their hand, behaving too much like victors, to cause deep resentment. Kabila should have sought the backing of the country's best-known opposition figure, Tshisekedi, but he was unsure of himself and fearful of Tshisekedi's influence so he subjected him to four months' internal exile. Tshsekedi and his UDPS were based upon Eastern Kasai. Kabila did what his predecessor Mobutu had done and filled posts with his family or extended family from Shaba, his home base. He resented and then opposed the UN team that was investigating alleged human rights abuses, most notably massacres of thousands of Hutu refugees in 1997, forcing the team to withdraw in April. Aid donors who had promised half the US$1,500 million needed for an immediate reconstruction plan had only provided US$100 million by mid-year. Meanwhile, the rate of inflation increased.

In July, fearing a coup by his Tutsi supporters, Kabila began removing them (whether Rwandan or *Banyamulenge*) from key posts in the military. As popular sentiment against the Tutsis increased, the *Banyamulenge* moved back to their South Kivu homeland. In order to balance the Tutsis whom he feared, Kabila provided training camps for Hutu extremists to the dismay of the RPF government in Kigali. On 2 August military units in Goma and Bukavu mutinied and after two weeks these rebels announced the formation of the *Rassemblement Congolais pour la Démocratie* (RCD) (Congolese Democratic Rally). The core of the RCD consisted of the Tutsi (*Banyamulenge*), supported by Rwanda and Uganda. The RCD drew support from other disaffected groups. A Bakongo professor, Ernest Wamba dia Wamba, became the RCD president. Meanwhile, on 4 August the rebels carried out a daring manoeuvre: using civilian planes captured at Goma airport they transported several thousand of their best troops to the Kitama military base near Matadi on the Atlantic coast. Most of the soldiers then at the base were ex-FAZ undergoing 're-education' and they joined the rebels. They quickly occupied the vast Inga Dam and then pushed on to Kinshasa airport. Kabila faced forces that were superior to his own, which in any case were of doubtful quality, and so appealed to Angola and Zimbabwe to come to his aid. They responded with highly seasoned troops and air force units. The Angolans attacked the rebels in the rear from Cabinda and the Angolan and Zimbabwean air forces bombed the rebel column, forcing them to retreat into northern Angola. Other neighbouring countries – Namibia, Congo (B), Central African Republic, Sudan, Chad and Gabon – pledged support for Kabila and provided aid or small military contingents. In the east, however, the rebels seized control of a vast area centred upon Kisangani and stretching to the Sudan border in the north and Shaba in the south. With so many countries involved, even if only on the periphery, the revolt was developing into a major African war.

As yet there had been no intervention from outside the continent though the three powers with most interests in the Congo, the United States, Belgium and France, watched uneasily the unfolding of a drama over which they had no control. The readiness of Congo's neighbours to intervene was heavily influenced by the country's vast store of mineral wealth and it soon became clear that they had some of these resources in mind at least as much as providing assistance to one or other side in the conflict. Angola was interested in oil, Zimbabwe acquired stakes in the country's cobalt and copper, Namibia obtained access to diamonds, Uganda to gold. 'The main players in Congo are seen by many as greedy warlords with ready made armies at their disposal and a clear interest in enriching themselves. Continued war could be their best way of doing this.'[7] By the end of 1998 the war had developed into a complex, all-Africa conflict with six of Congo's neighbours involved to a greater or lesser degree on one or other side. Rwanda and Uganda, and to a lesser extent Burundi, supported the rebels. Angola, which wanted to ensure that Kabila did not provide future bases for Savimbi's UNITA, supported Kabila. Zimbabwe's Mugabe sent 12,000 troops to support Kabila, partly to help a fellow 'Marxist', partly to 'protect' his mineral interests in the country. Namibia also sent troops to support Kabila. By the end of the century the Congo conflict had been dubbed 'Africa's Great War' and, whatever the original reasons for intervention by its neighbours, the huge mineral wealth of DRC made it one of the richest prizes on the continent. It began to look increasingly like a war of warlords whose principal aims were to acquire control of segments of the country's mineral wealth rather than to assist the Congo become a united, stable nation after the long Mobutu era. Given its vast size, potential wealth and strategic position straddling the centre of the continent, a long war in the Congo involving its neighbours threatened to destabilize half Africa. Since the time of Leopold II, the Congo's mineral wealth had been jointly monopolized by the country's rulers and their foreign business partners rather than used for the benefit of the Congo's people who remain amongst the poorest in the world. One result of this partnership in greed has been to persuade ordinary people that only money is worth achieving: 'To be considered in Zaïre, you got to have money!' How to get it then becomes the question and in a state with no law acting as a framework the search for money goes outside the law to become the norm of behaviour.[8] As the war continued it became clear that Rwanda and Uganda were attempting to alter DRC boundaries to their advantage. Thus, 'Rwanda and Uganda, later on joined by Burundi, took advantage of the disintegration of the Congolese state and armed forces to create territorial spheres of interest within which they could plunder the Congo's riches.'[9]

As 1999 began, the civil war was being fought in the east of the country where a new group, the *Mouvement de Libération Congolaise* (MLC) (Movement for the Liberation of the Congo), was formed under Jean-Pierre Bemba. In mid-January yet another group of resistance fighters appeared. These, known as the Mai-Mai, with aid from Burundi, attacked Bukavu. In retaliation, the RCD massacred 500 civilians in a village near Uviva in southern Kivu. As the war continued – it appeared increasingly open-ended – the countries that had intervened began to count the costs in terms of both money and casualties, finding moreover that their interventions were not popular with their own populations. In consequence, five nations – Angola, Namibia and Zimbabwe on the one side, Rwanda and Uganda on the other – met on 18 January in Windhoek, Namibia, and agreed the first stage of a ceasefire. In March the OAU appointed Zambia's President Chiluba as its peace co-ordinator. In April Col. Gaddafi convened a meeting at Sirte in Libya at which President Kabila met President Museveni of Uganda and the two men signed a peace agreement under whose terms Uganda undertook to train 1,500 Congolese troops as a way to replace its own troops in eastern Congo. Kabila, who was both vain and arrogant, was not an easy man to deal with and had ordered that he should be called 'the creator, the thinker, the initiator, the main craftsman and chief architect', a habit of personal superlatives borrowed from China and North Korea. At the end of May Rwanda announced a unilateral ceasefire while the Kinshasa government called for the withdrawal of 'uninvited forces'. A split now occurred in the RCD and Wamba dia Wamba was demoted though he maintained a separate power base in the Kisangani area. In July both the RCD and MLC announced substantial gains with the MLC taking Gbadolite and the RCD laying siege to Mbuji-Mayi, the diamond-producing centre in eastern Kasai crucial to Kabila's revenue. However, under pressure from Rwanda, which, in turn, was under pressure from the US, the RCD and MLC signed the Lusaka accord and accepted a ceasefire. The Lusaka accord grew out of a June meeting that had been convened by South Africa and Tanzania. On 11 October the joint military commission (JMC) that had been formed to monitor the peace by the OAU chair, Gen. Lallali Rachid of Algeria, met in Kampala. The meeting was attended by all the warring parties, the OAU, the UN, the EU and Zambia. Its first task was to send back to Rwanda ex-soldiers of the Rwanda army and *Interahamwe*; Kabila saw this as a precondition for further progress. The Lusaka accord had laid down a timetable that required the withdrawal of all foreign troops by February 2000. The UN was to provide 500 peace monitors. In December the OAU appointed the former Botswana president, Quett Masire, as facilitator of the peace process. The three rebel groups, the RCD, the breakaway RCD-Mouvement de Libération under Wamba dia Wamba and the MLC came together in Uganda to form a coalition. By this time (December) the ceasefire had broken down.

Rwanda, at best a reluctant peacemaker with members of both the *Interahamwe* and former soldiers of the Hutu Rwanda army in DRC, decided to protect its frontiers by occupying eastern areas of DRC and continued to assist the rebels against Kabila. On the other side, both Angola and Zimbabwe were increasing their presence and support for the Kabila government. In fact, in early 2000 the peace accord was broken almost all the time in Shaba, Kivu and Equateur provinces. Kabila offered an amnesty to any rebel who was willing to accept his authority but the offer was turned down by the MLC and RCD. Another ceasefire was agreed on 8 April, but the introduction of UN peacekeepers was delayed because the opposing forces refused to withdraw to established positions to allow the UN forces to be deployed. An SADC emergency meeting, scheduled for August in Lusaka, collapsed when Kabila refused to accept Masire as mediator. Kabila was also angered because his allies, Angola and Zimbabwe, would not call for the withdrawal of Rwanda and Uganda. Kabila then suspended the Lusaka accords and called for direct negotiations with Rwanda, Uganda and Burundi and rejected UN peacekeepers. Kabila's intransigence could be related to the success or failure of his troops: they had been gaining ground so he did not make any concessions; in August and September they lost ground. New peace initiatives were attempted at the end of 2000. Early in 2001, however, RCD and Rwandan troops moved south to capture Pweto on Lake Mweru causing 3,000 Zimbabwean and Congolese troops to flee to Zambia, leaving the way open to Lubumbashi, the capital of Shaba and Kabila's major stronghold.

The minerals of eastern Zaïre acted as a magnet to Uganda and Rwanda and their mining and illegal export financed military operations. At the height of the coltan boom in December 2000, revenue from the export of this mineral amounted to over US$1 million a month. In the same year, according to official statistics, the RCD exported gold and diamonds worth US$30 million. 'After "blood diamonds", gold and oil, "coltan", short for columbite-tantalite, a rare ore containing tantalum, has joined the rogues' gallery of African subsoil resources fuelling wars on the ground. Coltan is a crucial element in the manufacture of mobile phones, PlayStations or any item that needs a capacitor to maintain the electric charge of a computer microchip.'[10] Its rarity – and abundance in eastern Congo – has turned it into one of the most sought-after ores. It is coltan rather than diamonds or gold that has kept the Rwandan war machine operating in the Congo war and has played a big part in attracting Congo's neighbours to become involved in its war. For years the price of coltan was US$30 a pound but in December 1999 it soared to US$210 before settling at a more modest US$155. Since, apart from Australia, DRC has some of the richest coltan deposits in the world, the rebels declared a monopoly on coltan exports. It is the mineral riches of DRC that explain why six of its neighbours were so keen to become involved in its civil war. Thus Kabila's allies, Angola, Zimbabwe and Namibia, were granted offshore oil concessions, as well as diamond mines, cobalt and rare timber. The supporters of the rebels – Rwanda and Uganda – were taking 'pay' for their assistance in diamonds, timber, coffee, gold and tantalum. Uganda, which backed the rebels in the main DRC gold region of Bunia, has no important gold reserves but since the war has registered as a gold exporter. Rwanda's intervention in support of the RCD has been largely financed by the tantalum and diamonds it was able to extract. The RCD president, Adolphe Onusumba, justified the illegal export of these DRC ores, saying: 'I mean – we are at war. We need to maintain the soldiers. We need to pay for services.'

By 2001, after three years of war, the government, with the aid of Angola and Zimbabwe, controlled the west of the country, about a third altogether, while the north, east and south-east were in the hands of the rebels supported by Rwanda, Uganda and Burundi. Kabila said that no peace process could be implemented unless all foreign forces withdrew unconditionally. Neither Museveni nor Kagame would agree to this and the latter in particular was concerned that the Hutu enemies of the Tutsis would use bases in Congo from which to attack Rwanda under his rule. As long as Kabila refused to address Rwanda's security concerns there would be a stalemate. However, on 16 January Kabila was assassinated by a member of his presidential bodyguard. He was succeeded as president by his son Joseph who showed himself to be more flexible than his father. Following his inauguration as President, Joseph Kabila went on an overseas tour to France, Belgium and the United States. He also met Paul Kagame of Rwanda and the UN Secretary-General Kofi Annan. In March he met ex-president of Botswana Quett Masire, the chairman of the peace process whose efforts to end the war had been blocked by Laurent Kabila.

In April 2001 the United Nations published a report that condemned the 'looting' of DRC that had been carried out by the leaders of Rwanda and

Uganda and their associates. The main thrust of the report suggested that the countries intervening on behalf of the rebels were less concerned with their stated reasons for intervention – their security – than they were determined to profit by the exploitation of DRC's resources. The report noted how the Rwandans and Ugandans had stripped those parts of DRC, which they occupied, of large amounts of its most precious minerals – diamonds, copper, cobalt, gold, coltan – as well as timber and ivory. The coltan in particular was required as a component in the manufacture of delicate, sophisticated goods such as mobile phones and US fighter aircraft. The report also noted that about one-third of the 12,000 elephants in the Garamba national park had been slaughtered over four years for their ivory. On the other hand, it glossed over the activities of Kabila's allies – Angola, Namibia and Zimbabwe – despite their equally voracious efforts in stripping the country of resources. Their depredations were 'legal' because they had been sanctioned to help themselves by way of payment for their assistance.

In April 2001 Joseph Kabila allowed UN monitors into the country to patrol the front line between government and rebel forces. Masire was able to resuscitate the peace process in May. Kabila met Kagame and assured him that *Interahamwe* attacks on Rwanda from DRC would be stopped and that the rebel Hutus would be disarmed. On 12 May Security Council ambassadors visited the country and recognized Kabila as the formal head of state and referred to the RCD and MLC organizations as rebels: it was an important step in legitimizing Kabila's position. Kabila lifted restrictions on opposition activities (Tshisekedi had already returned to Kinshasa in late April). He also took steps to open up the economy: the Congolese franc was floated, commercial courts replaced military tribunals and the control of diamond trading was relaxed. As a result there were indications from the donor community that it would be prepared to consider new flows of aid and perhaps a moratorium on interest payments on DRC's US$14 billion debt. Namibia now withdrew its 1,800 troops from DRC. Yet, despite these encouraging developments, heavy fighting erupted in Rwanda over May and June when Hutu extremists crossed the border into Rwanda and Burundi. These Hutu activities rebounded upon the RCD, which was revealed as quite unable to control them. After talks in November, it was agreed to hold further talks in Sun City, South Africa, in January 2002. Meanwhile no less than 443 political groups had registered with the government though exactly what role they would eventually be permitted to play was not clear. Joseph Kabila's position was far from strong. He had no real power base, had been brought up in Tanzania and spoke little French or Lingala. He was dependent upon the Angolans, whose principal concern was to deny Savimbi and UNITA bases in

DRC, and Zimbabwe, which appeared to regard DRC first and foremost as a source of wealth. Although considerable improvements or reforms had been initiated under the second Kabila during 2001, the government had little control over the economy. Inflation, which had stood at 554 per cent in 2000, remained extremely high and it was essential to find money to pay the armed forces.

In January 2002 representatives of the government and the various rebel groups met at Sun City to continue the Inter-Congolese National Dialogue (ICND) to establish a broadly representative transitional government to bring an end to the war and prepare the country for elections. These new peace moves faced a setback in March when RCD forces seized Moliro on the Zambia/Tanzania border, causing the Kinshasa government to quit the talks in Sun City. The UN condemned the RCD action and when its forces had given up Moliro the talks were resumed. Half an accord was reached in April because, despite pressure from South Africa's President Thabo Mbeki, Kinshasa excluded the RCD and entered into an accord only with the MLC, which was led by Jean-Pierre Bemba and backed by Uganda. The Kinshasa government hoped to isolate the RCD and its Hutu supporters and that way limit the war to the eastern region. Quett Masire, the chairman, criticized the agreement and the Rwandans were furious with the result that by the end of April Rwanda was sending troop reinforcements across the border to the RCD. A brutal massacre was carried out by members of the RCD in Kisangani in May and served both to demonstrate the unreliability of the RCD and their Hutu backers and suggest that Kabila's decision to isolate them may have been the correct one. Meanwhile, the withdrawal of the Ugandans in the north-east was followed by heavy tribal fighting, prompting the Rwandans to argue that any withdrawal of their forces would leave a vacuum that would lead to increased ethnic violence. The stalling of the peace process led the UN to extend the mandate for its mission in DRC (MONUC) and increase the numbers of their monitors. The position of the Kinshasa government was strengthened when it received substantial restructuring loans: US$750 million from the IMF, US$410 million from the World Bank and US$44 million (grant) from the IDA. Following considerable South African pressure, negotiations between the Kinshasa government and the RCD were resumed and an agreement was reached on 30 July in Pretoria between President Kagame of Rwanda and President Kabila of DRC. Kinshasa undertook to disarm, arrest or repatriate the Hutu rebels in the Congo and in return Rwanda agreed to withdraw its 22,000 troops. The Rwandans remained nervous at leaving the territory on their border under the control of the RCD.

There was considerable doubt as to whether this peace deal would hold; after four years of fighting in which a number of peace deals had been overthrown no one was sanguine. An estimated 2.5 million Congolese were reckoned to have died, mainly of starvation and disease, by the time this accord was signed in Pretoria. Sceptics pointed out the difficulties: after four years of warfare in a region that at the best of times is difficult to control, there were endless confrontations taking place. The RCD rebels faced a number of enemies as well as splits in their own ranks. The Mai-Mai fighters control swaths of the countryside and the local people, who had suffered extensively at the hands of these different groups held them in fear or contempt. A key figure in this complex situation was the leader of the second-largest rebel faction, the MLC, Jean-Pierre Bemba who enjoyed the support of Uganda. Although he promised to come over to the government side in 2001 he had yet to do so in July 2002. He had earlier made a fortune during the heyday of Mobutu's kleptocracy. Unlike other wars, this in the Congo was well, if illegally, financed, reflecting the country's vast wealth that is its real attraction. Laurent Kabila obtained aid from Angola and Zimbabwe by promising diamond concessions to senior generals. Mineral concessions were also the big attraction on the rebel side with coltan, gold, diamonds, timber and coffee the chief rewards. Both sides in the conflict resorted to extreme brutality including rape and torture, and the war did immense damage to the environment. The Rwandan insistence that it stay to ensure that the *Interahamwe* did not return to Rwanda was less than convincing and they were suspected of wanting to annex parts of eastern Congo. Nonetheless, on 17 September the Rwandans began to withdraw their troops and the last 2,000 Zimbabwean troops also began to leave. The Kinshasa government banned the Democratic Liberation Forces of Rwanda whose purpose was to represent the interests of Hutu exiles in DRC. On 10 September the DRC and Uganda signed a separate agreement and Ugandan troops then began to withdraw from the north-east of the country. By early October most of the foreign troops had left the DRC.

Unfortunately for DRC, the withdrawing forces had left behind networks to continue plundering the wealth of the country. A second UN report of October 2002 revealed the existence of criminal cartels working with corrupt DRC government officials to perpetuate the pillaging that had been started by their armies. The report to the UN Security Council named 54 people, including senior military and political officials in Rwanda, Uganda, Zimbabwe and DRC itself, as the leaders of new 'elite networks' to exploit the country's minerals, timber and wildlife. Emmerson Mnangagwa, the speaker of Zimbabwe's Parliament and President Mugabe's preferred successor, was named as the key strategist for the Zimbabwean branch of this network. Other senior figures named included the Rwandan army chief-of-staff, James Kabarebe, the DRC Minister of the Presidency, Augustin Katumba Mwanke, and the Ugandan army chief-of-staff, Maj.-Gen. James Kazini. The report said: 'The looting that was previously conducted by the armies themselves has been replaced by organized systems of embezzlement, tax fraud, extortion, the use of stock options as kickbacks and diversion of state funds.' The report named 29 companies as well as the 54 individuals involved in the pillaging, spread from Africa to Belgium to the United States. The accusations were devastating yet wholly unsurprising.[11]

The security position declined in October when pro-government militias took advantage of the withdrawal of Rwandan and Ugandan troops; the town of Uvira on Lake Tanganyika fell to the Mai-Mai opposition militia until it was recaptured six days later by RCD troops. As thousands of refugees fled the renewed fighting, Kabila and Kagame met under the auspices of President Mbeki to review the July peace accord and discuss a power-sharing agreement. In November representatives of the movements engaged in the war met in Pretoria to negotiate a shared transitional government. This laid down that Kabila should be the president of DRC for two years and should be assisted by four vice-presidents representing the RCD, the MLC, unarmed opposition parties and the governing party. Democratic elections would be held at the end of this period.

The great powers most seriously concerned with Africa – the United States, Britain and France – repeatedly demonstrated their unwillingness to intervene to uphold the values they preach: democracy, human rights and peace. They stayed resolutely on the sidelines during the four years of the 'African Great War' although this would not have been so reprehensible had they not also been involved on the periphery. It took the UN Security Council nearly two years to June 2000 before it accused Rwanda and Uganda of aggression in the Congo and ordered them, under Resolution 1304, to withdraw. Meanwhile, and despite their non-democratic credentials, 'Uganda and Rwanda continue to obtain US foreign aid and loans from the Bretton Woods institutions. Given the punishment administered to Iraq for its invasion of Kuwait and the billions of dollars spent in the Balkans to stop Serb aggression against other national groups, the people of the Congo cannot but feel bitter about the double standards in international response to aggression and state-sponsored terrorism.'[12] According to an independent publication in Kampala, 'The interests of the people of DRC never featured anywhere on the agenda. The Lusaka agreement treated Rwanda and Uganda with kid gloves. It was only when their armies turned their guns on each other, and in the process killed and maimed hundreds of thousands of DRC civilians, that the world woke up to the carnage in Kisangani.'[13] Throughout the Congo war the main interest of the United States and other Western powers has been to maintain access to the resources of DRC, to sell their weapons of war and to support their useful allies – Uganda and Rwanda, which act as conduits for the extraction of DRC resources. As perhaps the Congo's leading intellectual-activist, Nzongola-Ntalaja is worth quoting once more: 'Having prevented UN action to stop the genocide (Rwanda in 1994), US policy makers and other major players in world politics feel so guilty with respect to Rwanda that they seem prepared to let the Tutsi-dominated regime there get away with murder. Add to this the seal of approval granted to Museveni and Kagame as two of Africa's "new breed of leaders", and you understand why they feel so bold in taking actions such as invading the Congo.'[14]

The Final Act of the Inter-Congolese Dialogue was signed in Sun City on 3 April 2003. It included the All-inclusive Agreement on the Transition in the Democratic Republic of the Congo, which provided for peace and reunification of the country. By the time this was signed there had been five years of war and possibly three million people had died. The signatories included 24 Congolese leaders, the most significant of whom were Leonard She Okitundu for DRC, Adolphe Onusumba for the RCD and Olivier Kamitatu for the MLC. The signing was in the presence of President Thabo Mbeki of South Africa, the leaders of Zambia, Zimbabwe and Botswana as well as the facilitator, Sir Ketumile Masire and a Special Envoy of the UN Secretary-General. Whether the agreements would in fact bring in an era of peace remained to be seen. The event was overshadowed by news of renewed fighting in eastern Congo and the absence from the ceremony of President Kabila and the leader of the MLC, Jean-Pierre Bemba, although both had made clear their support. On 5 April Joseph Kabila was sworn in as the 'new' President of DRC. The Agreement provided for the post of president and four vice-presidents, a transitional government composed of 36 ministers and 25 vice-ministers and a national assembly, the posts to be distributed among the parties to the agreement according to an agreed formula. The Agreement also provided for the first democratic elections in the Congo since 1960. Three days after the signing of the agreement a large number of civilians were massacred in eastern Congo as a result of inter-ethnic violence. And there was little sign that either Rwanda or Uganda intended to retire from their involvement in the country. The agreement represented the concerted effort of Congo's neighbours to bring about a peace, especially on the part of South Africa and Botswana. The problems faced by the Congo were enormous, not least the habit of disintegration that had set in with the assistance of the country's predatory neighbours.

It seemed likely during the first half of 2003 that while the Agreement might apply reasonably successfully to the greater part of the country, collapse or at least ongoing ethnic violence in the east would provide an excuse for all those who sought to undermine the Agreement. One assessment of the situation held out little hope for a peaceful settlement in the east: 'Eastern Congo seems to be the epitome of a hollowed-out state succumbing to the violent assaults of private actors such as ethnic militias, warlords and military-commercial syndicates. While the economic function of local warfare and its interconnection with global markets is clearly at work, "war as a continuation of economics by other means" is just one aspect underlying the current state of Congolese affairs.'[15] It is easier for a weak centralized state to operate through patronage rather than structures that will be ignored. In 2003 Kabila hardly commanded any structures in eastern Congo and was unlikely to find much assistance in establishing them, either from the various local interest groups or from the region's two neighbours, Rwanda and Uganda, whose continuing involvement seems unlikely to be curtailed in the foreseeable future.

As though to emphasize just how complex any peace in the Congo would be, the withdrawal of Rwandan troops was immediately followed by an eruption of fierce fighting between two of the region's ethnic groups, the Lendu and Hema. The existing UN Mission in the Congo was quite inadequate to deal with the situation and France signalled its willingness to lead a peacekeeping force with a substantial number of its own troops. Britain's Prime Minister, Tony Blair, then announced that Britain would be willing to contribute to such a force. At the time the UN mission, MONUC, had a total of 3,800 troops in the Congo and of these only 700 were in Bunia where the fighting was taking place. By the end of May 2003, a French-led UN mission had been agreed, with British participation but, as the Lendu survivor of a Hema massacre said: 'I am pessimistic. People have been coming here, white and black, from all over the world, but they never bring peace.'[16] The UN, criticized for its ineffectiveness, complained that it only had a small force to patrol an area the size of Sierra Leone. In New York, the French argued for a mission that would allow their troops to open fire to protect civilians. Rwanda and Uganda opposed the French proposals. The general savagery of the massacres that occurred suggested that either an overwhelming peacekeeping force should be provided for the area, and that seemed unlikely, or that the conflict continue long enough to threaten the entire peace process with its transitional government. Even so, perhaps representing an advance, the European Union announced its first military mission outside the continent of Europe on 4 June, which was to send to the Congo a 1,400-strong peace keeping force comprising French, Belgian and British troops. The EU force would replace 750 UN peacekeepers from Uruguay and its mandate was to run to September. Whether an EU force comprised principally of troops from the three former colonial powers would be well or badly received and sufficient in numbers to impose a lasting peace remained to be seen. No UN operation in the Congo since 1960 has either distinguished itself or solved the problems on the ground. Perhaps, but only perhaps, an EU operation could do better. While a spokesman for the European Commission conceded that the risks were high, Glenys Kinnock, the international development spokeswoman in the European parliament for the British Labour Party, said: 'This is a positive step with the EU pulling together on an important security issue: the need to avoid the danger of genocide in Congo. It will set an important precedent because we are always being told to react in areas where we are the major donor.'

How effective will an EU intervention be? It raises interesting questions about motives. For four years, until the French offer of intervention, the Europeans studiously ignored the developing Congo tragedy where entanglements appeared to offer more problems than rewards. The change of attitude requires explaining. The West's record in the Congo from King Leopold's brutal genocidal regime through the years of Belgian rule to the crisis of 1960 and the murder of Lumumba has been universally bad while its support for Mobutu, who claimed to be anti-communist, sat on a storehouse of minerals and gave the CIA a base from which to interfere in Angola, was shameful in its self-serving hypocrisy. Has a real change of heart and motive occurred in the West? There is both irony and danger in the spectacle of the two greatest former imperial powers in Africa – Britain and France – deciding to work together to sort out the Congo. This sudden Anglo-French interest in saving the Congo needs to be appraised with care. There are now unmistakable signs from both Britain and France that they are embarking upon a new phase of scramble, the neo-imperialism of the twenty-first century. The old colonial predators may claim that they are going back to Africa to save it from itself, but is there another agenda? Western corporate greed has fuelled the fighting in the eastern Congo ever since 1998 and the interest in this remote region is the mineral coltan and the other resources of this rich area rather than any sudden sense of duty to prevent massacres and genocide. Both Rwanda and Uganda, predators in their own right, have opposed the French peacekeeping mission and many in the region remember the 1994 French intervention in Rwanda in support of the murderous Hutu regime and would prefer not to see French troops in the region again. The collapse of the Congo state created a power vacuum while the Congo's resources have attracted both regional and external powers to intervene in a country that has experienced more interventions with less benefit to its people than any other on the continent.

Mugabe's Zimbabwe

Following his election victory in March 1980, Robert Mugabe addressed a divided and apprehensive Rhodesia in a statesmanlike and conciliatory speech in which he said:

We will ensure there is a place for everyone in this country. We want to ensure a sense of security for both the winners and the losers... I urge you, whether you are black or white, to join me in a new pledge to forget our grim past, forgive others and forget, join hands in a new amity and together, as Zimbabweans, trample upon racism.[1]

In retrospect, it has to be asked whether this was just the politics of a shrewd manipulator whose control of the levers of power had yet to be tested and entrenched or whether, at that time of his political triumph, Mugabe meant what he said. If so, what went wrong over the following 20 years?

The background to the Zimbabwe tragedy at the end of the twentieth century is to be traced to the British arrogance and racism that pervaded the history of Rhodesia, far more so than elsewhere in Africa. Britain allowed the white settlers almost complete freedom to behave as they pleased in Rhodesia, which they turned into their own style of apartheid state as they adopted the attitudes of the ruling whites in their larger neighbour to the south, giving the lie to those Britons who argued for decades that the white racists of South Africa were the Afrikaners rather than the British. In the years since 1960 much rhetoric about the evils of colonialism has come out of Africa to turn such accusations into a political cliché, a convenient weapon to be used when the occasion demanded some form of exculpation for immediate political failures. As a result, attacks upon the legacy of colonialism have come to be dismissed outside Africa as a sign of weakness, endless excuses for the here and now of politics. This is a mistake for though, of course, past colonialism has been used in this fashion, its bitter legacy runs deep and the worst of that legacy is racial and cultural arrogance.

Neither Britain nor France in the years since 1960 have truly understood the damage they did and when the subject of colonialism and its effects is raised they dismiss it as no more than the excusing rhetoric of the weak, that old 'chestnut' again, for seriously to recognize the depth of the anger and hurt that they left behind is also to admit the abomination of the system they controlled at a time when 'empire' is being given a new gloss in the history books. When Britain's Prime Minister, Tony Blair, in his missionary mode, described Africa as a scar on the conscience of the world it is doubtful whether he paused to consider why that was the case.

In a BBC interview of 1984, Lord Soames, who had been appointed Britain's last governor of Rhodesia following the 1979 Lancaster House Conference, reminisced about the election that brought Mugabe to power in the following terms:

> You must remember, this is Africa. This isn't Little-Puddleton-on-the-Marsh and they behave differently here. They think nothing of sticking tent poles up each other's what nots and doing filthy, beastly things to each other. It does happen, I'm afraid. It's a very wild thing, an election.

This passage is quoted in David Blair's book *Degrees in Violence* and the author says how Lord Soames colourfully expressed himself.[2] Colourful is hardly the term to use. At the time of independence it was reported that Soames and Mugabe had achieved a rapport that greatly eased the transition from a white-ruled Rhodesia to an independent Zimbabwe. In retrospect one must wonder how much of Lord Soames' attitude came across to Mugabe at the time. Later, he must have been made aware of this BBC performance. Just the short extract quoted above reveals all the arrogance, sense of racial and cultural superiority and sheer contempt that, all too often, was the stock in trade of white Britons in Africa.

The Zimbabwe crisis at the end of the century raised many questions that were not addressed in the West. It was, of course, about a dictatorial ruler using every weapon at his disposal to hold onto power: these included violence and intimidation of his opponents, altering the constitution or ignoring it; destroying the independent judiciary; and seeking popular support by deploying as weapons the two highly emotive issues of land redistribution and the control of land by the white farmers. But Mugabe was also using as a weapon the deep underlying resentments of past colonialism and the ingrained bitterness resulting from a century of the racial arrogance and contempt that had been second nature to the majority of the white settlers. The fact that, despite the exercise of intimidation, many Zimbabweans willingly voted for Mugabe has to be taken into account. Many people in Zimbabwe and elsewhere in Africa saw him in a totally different light to the British in particular or, more generally, the West. Among other things, he stood for a much-needed and admired defiance of the all-pervasive influence of Western power. Africans, quite simply, had become tired of being told how to govern themselves by non-African outsiders. African unwillingness to condemn Mugabe had as much to do with African resentment of external interference in the affairs of the continent as it did with tolerance of Mugabe's excesses.

The beginnings of the end of century crisis may be traced to a brutal massacre in Matabeleland of November 1987 that helped precipitate a unity agreement between Joshua Nkomo's ZAPU and Robert Mugabe's ZANU-PF. In theory, this healed the split that had divided the two parties since the beginning of the independence struggle in the early 1960s; in practice, it signalled the defeat and subordination of ZAPU to ZANU-PF and an end to Nkomo's ambitions to lead the nation. The two parties agreed to merge and this agreement came into force in April 1988. The new single party was committed to the establishment of a one-party state adhering to a Marxist-Leninist doctrine. Mugabe was to be its leader while Nkomo became one of two vice-presidents and was offered a senior cabinet post along with two other of his ZAPU colleagues. An amnesty brought an end to what had been known as the 'Dissidents' War' and a rapid easing of the tensions, and an improvement in political and security conditions in Matabeleland followed. In September 1987 the reservation in the assembly of 20 seats for whites was abolished and in October the 80 remaining members of the assembly elected 20 candidates, each nominated by ZANU-PF, including 11 whites. Ten candidates to the Senate, also nominated by ZANU-PF, included four whites. In a further change to the constitution the President became an executive as opposed to ceremonial head of state and Mugabe, the sole candidate, was inaugurated in the post on 31 December. Two years later, in November 1989, the House of Assembly voted to abolish the Senate while the single chamber was expanded from 100 to 150 members of whom 30 were to be non-elective (eight provincial governors, 10 chiefs and 12 presidential nominees). Thus, by the end of the 1980s the authoritarian nature of the Mugabe government had become clear. Edgar Tekere, an opponent of the government, founded the Zimbabwe Unity Movement (ZUM) at the end of the decade but it made little headway. Various conflicts during 1990 challenged the authority of the ruling party and, for example, a clash with students in July led the government to close the University of Zimbabwe from October 1990 to April 1991. When the Zimbabwe Congress of Trade Unions (ZCTU) issued a statement in support of the students, its Secretary-General, Morgan Tsvangirai, was arrested and imprisoned for six weeks. Targeting ZUM, ZANU-PF fought the 1990 election on the theme of national unity and though some violence occurred the result was declared 'representative' of the people's wishes and was seen as an overwhelming endorsement of Mugabe and ZANU-PF, which obtained 117 of the 120 seats with voter participation ranging from 55 to 65 per cent. It was an apparently solid endorsement of the new one-party unity created in 1988. Mugabe made few changes to his cabinet and kept three whites in it. There were looming problems for the future, including rising unemployment, while with 50 per cent of the population under 25 appeals to the nationalism of pre-independence days seemed likely to prove an increasingly irrelevant political tactic. Some progress had been made on the land issue. 'By the end of the first decade of independence, a total of 52,000 families, some 416,000 people, had been resettled on the 6.5 million acres of former white land the government had bought for the purpose. This was a worthy enough achievement, but it came nowhere near tackling the scale of the problem: each year the communal areas alone produced an additional 40,000 families, compounding the problem of overcrowding.'[3]

In 1991 Zimbabwe adopted an economic structural adjustment programme (ESAP) and, a nod in the direction of momentous changes elsewhere in the world, Marxism-Leninism was replaced in official discussions by 'pragmatic socialism' and 'indigenous capitalism'. In May there were student demonstrations over increased government supervision of universities. The Commonwealth Heads of Government Meeting (CHOGM), chaired by the host country's President Mugabe, was held in Harare that October and issued the Harare Declaration of Commonwealth principles that reiterated those laid down at the 1971 CHOGM held in Singapore. There was widespread industrial unrest in 1994 although the ZCTU made little progress in its demands, partly due to the resignation of its Secretary-General Morgan Tsvangirai.

The government became increasingly preoccupied with the land issue through the decade. The Land Acquisition Act (LAA) was drafted following the expiry of the Lancaster House provisions that protected white ownership of land and was passed into law on 19 March 1992. The new law permitted the compulsory purchase of 5.5 million hectares of the 11 million hectares then still held by the white farmers. The stated intention was to use the purchased land to resettle small-scale farmers from the communal areas. The Act did not specify fair compensation. In April 1993 the government announced that it was to acquire 70 farms covering a total of 190,000 hectares; there was an immediate outcry and an appeal by the Commercial Farmers Union (CFU). In March 1994 it transpired that a former cabinet minister and other senior politicians had acquired leases to some of these farms. Mugabe abrogated the leases and announced a detailed study of the land tenure and land lease system. In mid-

1996 Mugabe requested financial assistance from Britain to pay for land sequestrations.

Although discontent with the government was increasing, ZANU-PF won the 1995 elections decisively; considerable violence was reported, however, and eight opposition groups boycotted the election. Even so, there was a 57 per cent voter turnout and ZANU-PF received 82 per cent of the votes and won 118 seats of the 120 seats of which 55 had been uncontested. Most international monitors agreed that the elections had been free and fair though they also enumerated various shortcomings. In a reshuffle of his cabinet, Mugabe increased its numbers by 13 against the wishes of the World Bank and IMF on the grounds of increased expense. Presidential elections were held in March 1996: Mugabe won with 92.7 per cent of the votes cast as opposed to his two opponents – Bishop Muzorewa with 4.7 per cent and Ndabaningi Sithole with 2.4 per cent – although the turnout of voters had only been 31.7 per cent. When Mugabe reshuffled his cabinet in May, Dennis Norman, the white Minister of Agriculture, resigned. Over August–September thousands of civil servants went on strike for salary increases and then over October–November nurses and junior doctors went on strike. ZANU-PF formally announced that it was abandoning Marxism-Leninism. As the economic situation deteriorated over 1997–98 the government was criticized for its arrogance at a time of economic hardship. A major corruption scandal surfaced in 1997 concerning unfair tendering for official contracts and the use of ministerial funds to finance the construction of houses for ministers and Mugabe's wife. Mugabe was obliged to admit that corruption existed in government ranks. Many of the increasing number of discontents that surfaced at this time were economic but there was also growing anger at the government for its perceived arrogance and corruption. The much-anticipated Land Redistribution Bill came into effect in mid-November 1997. It listed 1,503 white farms that were designated for compulsory purchase and uncompensated reallocation to 'the landless people of Zimbabwe'. The farms listed included some of the largest and most profitable in the country, including one that was described as the most productive tobacco farm in the world. In response, the farmers threatened a reduction in agricultural output of up to 25 per cent that would be worth Z$6,000 million over the next three seasons.

Land reform during the decade was implemented in chaotic fashion: 'No attempt was made to consult farmers, rural communities, or even the government's own agricultural specialists.'[4] As land became the most important political issue during the 1990s, so the language employed by Mugabe in defence of the takeover from white farmers became more extreme. Addressing the ZANU-PF central committee in September 1993, Mugabe bitterly denounced

Western governments that criticized his land policies: 'How can these countries who had stolen land from the Red Indians, the Aborigines and the Eskimos dare to tell us what to do with our land?'[5] This was not simply rhetoric; the anger and feeling behind such words is too easily ignored. However, much of the righteous justification for these land policies was undermined by the fact that the black elite loyal to Mugabe continued to get their hands on the land to leave 'the redistribution exercise contaminated with corruption'. Britain, which had provided £44 million for land resettlement, now cut off further support. By 1997 it was legitimate to ask: how much did Mugabe control the 'war veterans' or how much was he their prisoner? The 'war veterans' were the young men who invaded white-owned farms and threatened the farmers with violence, in some cases forcing them to leave their farms. He had unleashed a demand and with it a sense of grievance that could not be bottled up or contained.

By the beginning of 1998 Mugabe and his government were deeply unpopular and the economy was in crisis. A sudden increase in food prices, following the collapse of the currency the previous November, led to riots and looting in Harare on 19 January. The currency collapse was the result of a government decision to compensate ex-combatants from the independence war; it had meant an additional unscheduled expenditure of Z$3,600 million which came on top of a budget deficit of Z$15,000 million. As a consequence, the World Bank and IMF suspended their balance-of-payment and structural adjustment support. Demands for Mugabe to step down followed and in February a two-day strike organized by the ZCTU achieved a 75 per cent turnout. In September a conference of 12 leading aid donors (the World Bank, UNDP, FAO, EU, Britain, USA, Australia, Denmark, Germany, Japan, Norway and Sweden) met in Harare. The conference approved the principle of land redistribution provided it was financially sustainable, transparently fair and geared to the reduction of poverty. This represented perhaps the last opportunity for Mugabe to engage realistically with the international donor community. However, no action was taken following the conference and the proposed technical support unit was never formed. In November, without warning, the agriculture minister, Kumbrai Kungai, announced the seizure of 841 white-owned farms; Mugabe wrote to the 841 farmers to say that their properties were immediately forfeit without compensation. There was an immediate response from the IMF, which declared that discussions on loans to Zimbabwe had ended 'as of now'. Without external funding, the land redistribution was unenforceable and the named farmers were still in possession at the end of the year, uneasily awaiting the government's next move. On the other hand, the withdrawal of donor money merely accelerated the next stage of the operation, which was seizure without compensation.

In a move that might appear the height of folly for a government that was already facing so many problems at home, Zimbabwe decided to support President Kabila of Democratic Republic of Congo (DRC) in his civil war. In August 1998 6,000 troops, fighter aircraft and attack helicopters were sent to DRC to assist Kabila against the rebels who were supported by Rwanda and Uganda. The cost of this operation was Z$60 million a month and led to a 46 per cent increase in the defence budget. The government argued that it was necessary for the security of its commercial contracts. Kabila granted Zimbabwe mining concessions in payment for its support. Another, more personal reason involved the antipathy that existed between Mugabe and Mandela, with the latter advocating that SADC should attempt a peacekeeping role. Mugabe, with Angola and Namibia, wished SADC to support Kabila and that is what the three countries proceeded to do. This involvement in the Congo war added to discontents at home. The war was not Zimbabwe's business and the huge costs increased the economic hardships already being suffered at home where it was extremely unpopular. In October there were demonstrations in Harare against a 67 per cent increase in fuel prices; in November two successful national strikes were organized by the ZCTU, forcing the government to call for talks with business, labour and civic authorities to resolve the economic troubles. During the year the Zimbabwe stock exchange lost 60 per cent of its value. The IMF, which had been committed to a US$176 million standby loan, took Zimbabwe off its agenda while it awaited information on the financial impact of the Congo war, the land acquisitions and general financial targets. By the end of the year the Zimbabwe dollar stood at 62 to the pound sterling, inflation was running at 47 per cent, interest rates were at 50 per cent, unemployment had reached a new high and the country's reserves were at their lowest on record. On 17 December the *Sunday Standard* carried a story to the effect that a number of senior army officers had been arrested for inciting colleagues to join in a military coup against the regime.

The economic crisis deepened in 1999 with rising unemployment, inflation passing 70 per cent, fuel and commodity shortages and a foreign exchange crisis. The IMF refused to alter its stand and insisted that the government must assert greater control over spending, inflation and the growing deficit before it would act. On 12 January, Mark Chavunduka, the editor of the *Sunday Standard*, was arrested for exposing the attempted coup of the previous December. He and a colleague were imprisoned and tortured. When four Supreme Court judges appealed to the President to confirm that he was committed to the rule of law, Mugabe's response was to launch an attack upon the judiciary and call for the resignation of the judges. A subsequent demonstration in Harare of lawyers and activists demanding 'zero tolerance of any erosion of human rights' was tear-gassed by the police. In May the government appointed its own Constitutional Commission headed by Judge Godfrey Chidyausika to hold a series of open consultations about a new constitution. Its draft proposals were tabled in November although several of the commissioners complained that dissenting views concerned with curtailing the powers of the President had been suppressed. Mugabe subsequently amended the proposals further 'to reflect what the people want' and announced a constitutional referendum for early 2000. Meanwhile, a new political party, the Movement for Democratic Change (MDC) was created to combine workers, trade unionists and peasant farmers. The MDC was led by the ZCTU chairman, Gibson Sibanda, and Morgan Tsvangirai. A pause in constantly mounting tensions occurred when the old political warhorse Joshua Nkomo died on 1 July. Mugabe decreed him a hero's funeral and then in October announced plans to compensate civilian victims of the Gukurahundi military campaign of the 1980s in Matabeleland. By mid-year the unpopular intervention in the Congo war, where 10,000 troops were then deployed, was costing the country Z$2.3 million a day and defence spending was again increased. The release of figures of the depredations of the AIDS epidemic added to the gloom: the country's growth rate had been reduced from 3.3 per cent in 1980 to one per cent and AIDS was killing 1,700 people a week.

The referendum to agree amendments to the constitution that would increase the powers of the President was held on 12 February 2000. It became a popular expression of opposition to Mugabe and his government, the amendments being defeated by a 55 per cent 'no' vote. Mugabe accepted the result but then launched a campaign of intimidation against suspected or known opponents and the subsequent violence did further damage to Zimbabwe's international reputation. The referendum defeat was probably the final turning point for Mugabe who saw this (or said he saw it) as the work of white farmers supported by Britain. What had become clear was his dual determination to hold onto power by any available means and dispossess the white farmers. The 4,500 white farmers became the main target of government anger. They owned 11 million hectares of the best land while 16 million hectares were shared by more than a million black farmers. The government now condoned the mass invasion of white farms by landless squatters, many of whom claimed to be veterans of the 1970s war of liberation. By the beginning of March 2000 142 white-owned farms had been occupied, often violently, and early in April a white farmer, David Stevens, was killed. Mugabe blamed the colonial past for the land crisis and called on Britain to compensate the farmers. Relations between the two countries deteriorated sharply and were not helped when British diplomatic bags were opened in Harare airport. The British Foreign Office called the action 'uncivilized and paranoid'. At the April Euro-African Conference in Cairo the

British Foreign Secretary, Robin Cook, raised the possibility of funding a land compensation scheme with Mugabe in return for a commitment to the rule of law by ZANU-PF. The Zimbabwe Farmers' Union obtained a court ruling that the farm invasions were illegal although the Attorney-General, Patrick Chinamasa, dismissed it as unenforceable. Nonetheless, the government rushed through legislation that legitimized the seizure of designated farms without compensation.

The legislative elections were held at the end of June and the preceding campaign was tense and resulted in 31 deaths, mostly of government opponents. Opposition rallies were constantly harassed and attacked by government supporters, leading the British Foreign Office Minister, Peter Hain, to describe the attacks as 'thuggery licensed from on high'. Nonetheless, MDC rallies attracted enthusiastic crowds. John Nkoma, chairman of ZANU-PF, said ZANU-PF would form the next government regardless of the ballot and that 'President Mugabe is an institution'. In the event, there was a 65 per cent turnout of voters: the MDC obtained 47.06 per cent of the vote and 57 seats, ZANU-PF 48.45 per cent of the vote and 62 seats although it also controlled the 30 non-elective seats. International monitors said intimidation had been high in the rural areas. On 14 July 100 white-owned farms were designated for immediate seizure and a further 2,197 were listed for appropriation by the end of the year. The veterans who invaded the farms were led by Chenjerai 'Hitler' Hunzvi. Thabo Mbeki, the President of South Africa, attempted to restrain Mugabe but to no avail. Then on 29 September South Africa's former president, Nelson Mandela, publicly criticized Mugabe's 'use of violence and the corroding of the rule of law'. In November a ruling of the Zimbabwe Supreme Court that the land resettlement was unconstitutional and illegal provoked Mugabe into attacking the judiciary: he said the government was at war with the whites. The economy continued to decline throughout the year: foreign reserves fell, there were continuous shortages of petrol and electricity and rises in the costs of most basic requirements, including food. In August the Zimbabwean dollar was devalued by 24 per cent. The Minister of Finance, Simba Makoni, said Zimbabwe's involvement in the Congo war had cost the country Z$10,000 million since 1998 and was unsustainable. In his November budget he cut military expenditure by 13.4 per cent. Tourism, a mainstay of the economy and the third foreign exchange earner after agriculture and mining, slumped drastically with 200,000 fewer visitors than in 1999. The Congo war may have been a drain on the official economy but Zimbabwean involvement was maintained. 'Both at home and abroad, the Congo intervention was seen as a sign of Mugabe's growing megalomania. Opinion polls showed it to be deeply unpopular. Western governments queried the need for providing Mugabe with financial assistance for land reform if he was prepared to squander money on foreign adventures.'[6] However, the army in the Congo was deeply corrupted and all kinds of people were making money out of the intervention. General Vitalis Zvinavashe won contracts to haul supplies to the Congo and, to keep the army happy, special allowances were paid to all soldiers serving there and both officers and other ranks were encouraged to make their own deals. 'There are fortunes to be made in the Congo,' said Col. Tshinga Dube on television. 'They import everything there, even potatoes and cooking oil,' he added, 'so why rush to conquer the rebels?'[7]

The policy of farm seizures was pursued relentlessly in 2001 and by June 95 per cent of all white-owned farms had been listed for resettlement and by the end of the year 4,874 farms were either occupied or under threat. These seizures were carried out by the 'war veterans' and clearly acquiesced in by the police who did nothing to stop them and were accompanied by considerable violence. Apart from the white farmers, thousands of black farm workers were displaced and lost their jobs. According to a report of September by the human rights organization, the Amani Trust, the farm invasions had led to the deaths of 27 black farm workers, assaults on 1,770 and the eviction of 20,000. Although some farms were staked out for small-scale cultivation, many of the most productive were given to leading politicians and ZANU-PF supporters. Meanwhile, after a campaign of harassment, the Chief Justice, Anthony Gubbay, was forced from office and two other judges retired early. Thereafter, the Supreme Court, with a ZANU-PF majority, declared the government land seizures to be legal. Morgan Tsvangirai, the MDC leader, was constantly harassed.

In May Nkosana Moyo, the Trade and Industry Minister, fled the country. A relief to many people came in the middle of the year when on 4 June Chenjerai 'Hitler' Hunzvi died of an AIDS-related illness. Pressures against any person or institution seen as antagonistic to the government were applied relentlessly. The independent *Daily News* was threatened by the Minister of Information, Jonathan Moyo, who said it was a threat to security and would be 'silenced'. A short time later its presses in Southerton, Harare, were blown up with anti-tank mines that were available only to the army. Since the IMF continued its refusal to provide financial assistance to Zimbabwe, Mugabe called for it to be reformed and said that balance-of-payments support should be paid to developing countries 'whether human rights have been violated or not', a point that would be appreciated through most of Africa where the politicization of the IMF by its principal Western donors was deeply resented. In September President Gaddafi of Libya guaranteed oil supplies worth US$90 million to Zimbabwe, but at a price in the form of grants of land and equities in the country. Also in

September, President Obasanjo of Nigeria persuaded Mugabe (as he thought) that a restitution of the rule of law in the land resettlement programme would open the way for £36 million from Britain for compensation. Mugabe subsequently did nothing and the presumed offer fell away. In June fuel costs were increased by 70 per cent, adding to food and transport costs while the Zimbabwe dollar, which was pegged at 55 to the pound sterling, was trading at the rate of 430 to the pound by the end of the year. With a death rate from AIDS of 2,000 a week, Zimbabwe seemed about to become the first state in the world to report a zero population growth while life expectancy was predicted to fall to 27 by 2010.

The presidential elections were set for March 2002 and Mugabe was to be challenged for the presidency by Morgan Tsvangirai. His rallies were to be routinely interrupted by ZANU-PF 'war veterans' or prohibited under various regulations by the police. Desmond Tutu, the former Archbishop of Cape Town, said, 'Zimbabwe was sliding towards dictatorship'. On 18 February the EU imposed 'smart sanctions' on Mugabe and 19 of his leading supporters; these included a prohibition on travel and the freezing of overseas bank accounts. On 3 March the Commonwealth deferred a decision on whether or not to suspend Zimbabwe until after the election so that it could first study a report on how these had been conducted. Over the two days of the election it was found that there were 50 per cent fewer polling stations in the urban areas (the MDC strongholds) than in the 2000 election while there was an increased number of polling stations in the rural areas from which ZANU-PF drew most of its support. As a result, only 28 per cent of the registered voters had been able to cast their votes by the end of the second day of polling. The MDC appealed to the High Court and there was a part-extension of polling time for a third day. The result, after two revisions of the count, gave Mugabe 56.2 per cent of the vote to Tsvangirai's 41.9 per cent, a margin of 463,000 votes. However, according to the Helen Suzman Foundation of Johannesburg, 700,000 votes had been 'discovered' and added to Mugabe's vote. African countries were quick to accept the result. Observers from South Africa declared the election free 'to a degree'. The EU observer mission had been withdrawn after Zimbabwe expelled its leader, the Swede Pierre Schori, though the Commonwelth mission remained. The United States declared the result flawed and did not recognize Mugabe as President. There was continuing violence after the election as retribution was visited upon constituencies that had favoured the MDC.

On 8 September 2,900 of the remaining white farmers were ordered off their land without compensation and prime farms were appropriated by politicians and friends of the President. Earlier, a state of disaster had been declared on 1 May and by August a third of the population was at risk of starvation. In an outrageous statement, Didymus Mutasa, a close confidant of Mugabe and a former Speaker of the Assembly, said 'we would be better off with only six million... of our own people who support the liberation struggle'.[8] By the end of the year about two million Zimbabweans had emigrated or migrated illegally into neighbouring countries. Mugabe, however, appeared as entrenched in control as ever.

No matter how Mugabe's actions were regarded and condemned, the case for land reform was unanswerable. The question, however, was in what manner should it be implemented. By 2000 it was clear that Mugabe blamed the British and believed they were working with the white farmers. The Lancaster House Conference of 1979 had written into the constitution a clause that protected the white farmers from any compulsory purchase for 10 years. It is impossible to say whether the absence of such a clause would have made any difference for Mugabe 'wanted a Zimbabwean government to be able to seize land compulsorily from white farmers and pay no compensation. He got the exact reverse – a constitution that protected farmers by ruling out compulsory land acquisitions and guaranteeing full compensation. Moreover, these clauses would be set in stone and shielded from amendment for 10 years. Mugabe signed up to this reluctantly, in order to bring peace to his country.'[9] Much of the land acquired went to rich, powerful blacks in place of whites and was not divided into peasant farms. For small farms to work, especially for people who had not farmed for years, huge back-up services would also be required and these were clearly not catered for under the land seizures.

Britain's relations with Zimbabwe have never been easy, neither were they much better with Rhodesia even before Smith made his unilateral declaration of independence. As Harold Macmillan came to realize on his visit to Rhodesia in 1960, the Central African Federation had been a mistake. And if in the late 1990s Tony Blair found Mugabe difficult to deal with so earlier had Harold Wilson found Smith just as awkward a proposition. Bad Anglo-Rhodesian, Anglo-Zimbabwean relations appeared to have entered the political bloodstream of the two countries. Mugabe was always deeply suspicious of Britain's motives and given its record during the UDI years he had reason to be so. Britain, moreover, always used its bilateral assistance, despite claims to the contrary, as a lever to influence policy. In the early 1990s Britain was the largest aid donor to Zimbabwe and one of its two main trading partners. This fact ought to have made possible a sensible solution, acceptable to both sides, of the land issue, yet by the end of the decade the relationship had collapsed into one of two-way name-calling. Was this simply due to the intransigence of Robert Mugabe, or the arrogance of Britain, or the anti-Mugabe machinations of the white farmers? The Blair government clearly understood nothing about Africa when it came to power in 1997 and did not begin to appreciate how to handle the Zimbabwe situation and was ham-handed, to put it no worse, in its dealings with Mugabe. Alienation would seem to be the appropriate word to use and it stretched back a long way.

Blair and Mugabe met at the Commonwealth Edinburgh summit of October 1997 and apparently took an instant dislike to one another and given their totally opposed characters – the charismatic, moralizing, sincere, heart-on-sleeve Blair and the dour, intellectual, narrow-visioned, race-conscious Mugabe – this is not surprising. Blair, moreover, was reluctant to acknowledge the assurances about financial assistance that John Major had given Mugabe on the land issue. Then Clare Short, Labour's Minister for the Department for International Development (DIFID), entered the picture when she wrote a letter to the Zimbabwean Agriculture Minister in November 1997: 'I should make clear that we do not accept that Britain has a special responsibility to meet the cost of land purchase in Zimbabwe. We are a new government from diverse backgrounds without links to former colonial interests. My own origins are Irish and as you know we were colonized not colonizers.'[10] This letter caused outrage in Zimbabwe and was released to the press. If the deliberate intent had been to create bad relations between Britain and Zimbabwe Short could not have done better than first deny any sense of responsibility for what, by any criteria, was a major leftover problem of British imperialism and then add her absurd personal Irish connection as though this could excuse her government attempting to evade its responsibilities. In 1999, on the eve of the farm invasions, the Foreign Secretary, Robin Cook, clearly as ignorant on the subject of Zimbabwe as Clare Short, tried to persuade Lord Carrington to intervene on his behalf though the latter had resigned as Foreign Secretary in 1982. This escapist suggestion was vetoed by the Foreign Office. Blair paid little attention to Zimbabwe until 2000 when he was at last obliged to take note of what was happening. At Edinburgh Mugabe had wanted Britain to pay for land reform in accordance with the 1979 Lancaster House promise – to which he had only reluctantly acceded – that he believed to be an unconditional commitment. The Conservatives had paid over a total of £44 million, the last tranche in 1995. However well or badly that money had been spent, a great deal more was clearly required if the land resettlement problem was to be completed. DIFID under Clare Short, however, regarded land reform as a development project rather than an obligation from the imperial past. Between them, Blair and Short had sent indifferent and hostile signals to the prickly Mugabe that he would neither forget nor forgive. The British, with all their 'experience' in Africa, managed to demonstrate a bewildering ignorance of how the continent worked. When Peter Hain, who had risen to fame as a young man demanding a boycott of South African cricketers in the 1970s and by 2000 was a minister and rising star in New Labour, delivered an attack upon Mugabe through the *Daily Telegraph* (8 March 2000), in choicely undiplomatic language, he said: 'The political leadership is bankrupt... the politics pursued by Robert Mugabe are economically illiterate, indeed innumerate – after 20 years, Zimbabwe is all but on its knees, and there is only one group responsible for that – the ruling party,' he was signalling loud and clear that Labour washed its hands of any further attempt to find a solution and left the white farmers to their fate. Stan Mudenge, Zimbabwe's Foreign Minister, described this outburst as an 'unprecedented anti-Zimbabwe crusade'.[11] By the 2001 Labour Party Conference Blair was comparing Mugabe with Osama bin Laden. What neither Blair nor Hain understood was that they had made it almost *de rigueur* for other African leaders to support Mugabe against these attacks from the former metropolitan power. Subsequent British government or media attacks upon Mugabe appeared petty and useless in face of a man who knew exactly what he wanted and was fighting for political survival.

In due course, when Mugabe has passed from the political scene he will leave behind mammoth problems both of rebuilding a shattered economy and of healing the bitter divisions that his policies have created. Following the defeat of his referendum in 2000, Mugabe blamed the white farmers and the MDC, and on ZBC television addressed the white farmers as follows: 'Our present state of mind is you are now our enemies, because you really have behaved as enemies of Zimbabwe and we are full of anger. Our entire community is angry and that is why we now have the war veterans seizing the land.'[12] What was difficult for Mugabe to explain was the fact that he and ZANU-PF had been in power for 20 years and had not solved the land issue. Could it be that he had not bothered and only saw the land issue as a vital political concern when his popularity was plummeting and he needed a popular cause to rekindle support? 'Land for Mugabe was a political weapon. He had used it successfully during the war to help him gain power; he used it now to help keep him in power. With a population growing ever more disgruntled and restless after 18 years of his rule, it was the last political card he had to play.' As the same critic also claims: 'The colonial regime under which Mugabe grew up, however, engendered in him an abiding sense of bitterness. Rhodesian whites were generally contemptuous of the African population, treating them as an inferior race, demanding unfailing obedience to white rule. "We feared the white man," Mugabe recalled. "He was power. He had guns." Fear and distrust of white society were part of everyday life, deeply ingrained.'[13] Undoubtedly, the bitterness and distrust from the past were playing their part in the events unleashed by Mugabe at the turn of the century.

President Sam Nujoma listens with a smile as South African President F. W.
de Klerk addresses the Namibian nation during the independence celebrations.
(Andrew Ingram – Cape Argus – Trace Images/africanpictures.net)

President Sam Nujoma's guard of honour stand to attention as he inspects them
during the Namibian independence celebrations. (Andrew Ingram – Cape Argus – Trace
Images/africanpictures.net)

Nelson Mandela and F. W. de Klerk in an uneasy alliance that brought the new
South Africa into being. (Gideon Mendel – South Photographs/africanpictures.net)

Confrontation: Archbishop Desmond
Tutu, the charismatic priest whose
preaching against apartheid had a huge
impact. (Benny Gool – Oryx Media
Productions/africanpictures.net)

Muammar Gaddafi of Libya and
President Jerry Rawlings of Ghana in
conclave. (Africa Week)

President Nelson Mandela of South Africa and President Joaquim Chissano of Mozambique established a cordial, close relationship. (Cape Argus – Trace Images/ africanpictures.net)

Thabo Mbeki succeeded Nelson Mandela as President of South Africa in 1999. (John Robinson – South Photographs/africanpictures.net)

Olusegun Obasanjo of Nigeria and Thabo Mbeki of South Africa, architects of NEPAD, with Britain's Tony Blair. (Africa Week)

Writing in *African Affairs*[14] Stephen Chan contrasts the cultural nationalism of Zimbabwe with the racial and cultural exploitation of the British and makes the point, too often overlooked by aid donors laying down principles, that the new middle class in Zimbabwe was no more interested in land seizures on behalf of the peasants, as opposed to for themselves, than were the former white settlers concerned with land for the peasants – they made sure they had the best for themselves. Thus, the black elite in Zimbabwe expects to replace the white elite while the peasants are expected to remain peasants and serve the interests of the new elite. Hardly anywhere in Africa have the post-independence elites worked to create egalitarian societies, as naïve aid donors have often assumed; they wished only to replace the settler or colonial elites with themselves and this is true of Zimbabwe. At the same time, well-organized peasants make good political cannon fodder. Regimes such as Mugabe's survive, despite all pressures, not only because they repress or restrict opposition but because sufficient numbers of people support them. 'The regime may be morally wrong, but be regarded as intellectually right. The regime's critique of globalism – and British pressure – strikes chords unappreciated in Whitehall, and the inappropriate depiction of white farmers as British agents illustrates a wider critique rather than narrowing and vulgarizing it… Mugabe may be bad, and it may be sad, but he is certainly not mad. Nor has he succeeded only by force of himself. Mugabe is not Zimbabwe; despite his need to rig elections, significant numbers of Zimbabweans voted willingly for him; Mugabe is supported by many Zimbabweans. This simple fact is passed over and not discussed by most authors.'[15] Most Western critics of Mugabe forget the corroding influence of colonialism and, especially in Southern Africa, the abiding contempt for Africans expressed by Europeans whose racism was necessarily encouraged by the need to justify holding on.

When the Commonwealth summit, which had been postponed as a result of 11 September 2001, met at Coolum in Australia early in 2002, the African members pulled the proposed tough British statement on Zimbabwe to pieces so that a watered-down mild criticism was all that survived. The conference did agree that John Howard of Australia, Thabo Mbeki of South Africa and Olusegun Obasanjo of Nigeria should act as a committee to report back to the Commonwealth after the Zimbabwe elections had taken place. There had clearly been no meeting of minds between the British and the African heads of government in Australia where Blair only seemed concerned to line up the white Commonwealth in his support. This was clearly demonstrated when, on his return to South Africa, Thabo Mbeki wrote in the ANC weekly newsletter that critics of the Commonwealth decision on Zimbabwe were possessed by a 'stubborn and arrogant mindset that at all times the white world must lead'. He continued: 'Those inspired by notions of white supremacy are free to depart if they feel that membership of the association reduces them to a repugnant position imposed by inferior blacks.'[16] These words, coming from Thabo Mbeki, who spent many years in Britain and is seen as balanced, diplomatic and tolerant, should set alarm bells ringing, above all in Blair's Britain where the Prime Minister had announced that he wanted to put Africa at the top of his agenda. Mbeki reluctantly went along with Obasanjo and Howard to suspend Zimbabwe from the Commonwealth.

The next stage in the diplomatic saga saw Britain trying to persuade South Africa, of all countries, to exert upon Zimbabwe the kind of pressure it was no longer able or willing to exert itself. There was an extraordinary historical irony in the spectacle of Britain calling upon South Africa to do anything of the kind. Over the years of apartheid when Africans begged Britain to act, London argued for a 'softly, softly' approach and insisted that change would come from within. Similarly, over the UDI years Africans asked Britain to take effective action against the Smith regime, also in vain. Now, with the position reversed, Britain demanded of South Africa actions against Zimbabwe that it had never been prepared to take against either apartheid South Africa or UDI Rhodesia. Further, London paid scant attention to South Africa's own problems. By early 2000 the crisis in Zimbabwe was causing considerable damage to the South African economy while many thousands of Zimbabwean refugees were coming into the country. At the same time, the breakdown in Zimbabwe was frightening away investors from the whole region and any action, short of invading Zimbabwe, would damage South Africa as much as it did Zimbabwe. Furthermore, South Africa had a land issue that dwarfed anything in Zimbabwe with large numbers of desperately poor rural peasants, often still dispossessed from the apartheid era and waiting for redress through an unbelievably slow court procedure, seeking land while the bulk of the best land remained in the hands of the Afrikaner farmers, the bedrock of the old apartheid state. A wrong move in relation to Zimbabwe could spark off a land crisis that would do irretrievable damage to the new South Africa. None of this appeared to be appreciated in London.

Back in South Africa from his Commonwealth travels, the normally mild Mbeki lashed out at Britain and the United States. The Mugabe-Zimbabwe question is, of course, a race issue. Mugabe said: 'Today, Britain, Australia, New Zealand and America, what colour are they, the people there? Those whites, they are the ones leading in the fight against Zimbabwe, the fight of resisting the completion of the independence struggle.' Race remains at the centre of most arguments between Europe and Africa. Throughout its imperial relations with both South Africa and Rhodesia, Britain was prepared to leave the whites largely to their own devices. Only rarely has Britain shown real concern about black against black violence and it is pertinent to ask whether it would have made such a fuss if the land resettlement programme in Zimbabwe had only been a question of replacing one lot of black farmers with another.

Corruption

External observers of the African scene have bestowed upon the continent a reputation for corruption that suggests Africa is unique in this regard. In fact, Africa is probably no more corrupt than any other region of the world though its sins in this respect have been much highlighted for political reasons. Three broad categories of corruption are considered here: venal corruption – the demand for bribes and payments for services or contracts; patronage corruption – nepotism and the provision of jobs or kickbacks for supporters; and political corruption – the manipulation of elections and constitutions against the existing rule of law to perpetuate an individual's or party's hold on power. In the years since the end of the Cold War the West has taken to lecturing Africa, using accusations of corruption as a weapon with which to manipulate economic and political behaviour.

Western business and venal corruption go together. In the knowledge that Western companies will go to almost any lengths and use most available means in order to secure lucrative contracts and exclude rivals, Africans have naturally responded to such 'institutionalized' greed by demanding bribes or 'sweeteners'. Representatives of Western companies argue that by giving bribes they are simply acting according to the customs of the country with the accompanying implication that they are not corrupt but what else can they do?[1] Corruption in its various forms is to be found in all societies; in some it appears endemic although it is absent from none. The high profile of African corruption, at least in part, results from the inadequacy of the mechanisms to deal with it. Britain, France and Italy, for example, may suffer from as deeply entrenched forms of corruption as any African state but it is never argued by outsiders that it is impossible to deal with these countries because of it. The weak structure of many African states, on the other hand, is a major part of the problem and this is compounded by the fact that they are supplicants for Western aid. This allows would-be donors to lecture African recipients about their shortcomings and use the elimination of corruption as a condition of control. It is open to question whether most donors are concerned about corruption in any ethical sense.

On the other side, African coup-makers, for example, always announce as one of their first priorities the elimination of corruption. Indeed, it is usually cited as a reason for overthrowing the existing regime. Once in power, after token attacks upon the corruption sickness, attacks that often bypass their own supporters, they soon settle into a pattern that differentiates them little from their predecessors. The degrees of corruption present in African states are closely associated with questions of meaningful economic independence, and calls by donors for recipients to tackle corruption never lead to a curtailment of aid though occasionally they are followed by a temporary suspension of it as part of a ritualistic donor-recipient confrontation. One particularly harsh judgement suggests, 'In Africa, for at least four decades, the role of the state has simply been to entrench itself while sucking the people dry.'[2] This may have been the case in some states but too often the state has failed to entrench itself and that is part of the problem. Western pieties about African corruption collapse in the light of Western behaviour. The revelation that US$20 billion of IMF loans to Russia was flown out of the country to be laundered in the US and Europe[3] reveals just how hypocritical are Western attitudes. Nigeria is often cited as the most corrupt country in the world though it would be difficult to better Mobutu's Zaïre in this respect, but when corruption involves 10 per cent or more of the national wealth this may reflect the fact that the state is the main employer, buyer and seller and that much of the incoming revenue is derived from oil companies, for example, or customs rather than internal sources.

Levels of corruption do not appear to have been much affected by either democracy or economic liberalization. In so far as it can be accurately measured, there is probably no more corruption in Africa than in Asia or the West: in Asia it is more discreet, in the West it is principally confined to corporate business dealings. In Africa, on the other hand, it is more overt and is accepted as an integral part of the social-political order. Certain forms of corruption become the norm and, for example, many Africans have enriched themselves while the continent as a whole has failed to develop. Patrimonialism is a crucial aspect of African societies and the patron or 'big man' is expected to look after his followers. 'It is when patrons cease to redistribute their legal or ill-gotten gains to their clients – that is, in effect, to be accountable to them – that their activities become criminal, in the sense of being perceived as illegitimate by those who might have stood to benefit but no longer do.'[4] Here is an aspect of corruption that is especially African. Yet all forms of corruption have to be analysed in the context of the societies in which they occur and usually Western analysis is solely in terms of Western norms as though these alone apply worldwide. If the state, for whatever reason, has been reduced more or less to an empty shell, then the real business of politics has to be conducted outside, or regardless of this shell. In these circumstances corruption as defined in the West is broadly meaningless.[5] Defining corruption, drawing lines between what works and what is merely greedy personal accumulation, is far from simple. When is patrimonialism corrupt? If an action or series of actions makes for the smooth working of the state must they be abandoned if adjudged to be corrupt even if the alternative would result in a less efficient state? The questions that the subject raises are endless. In a very poor country, for example, the petty corruptions at the bottom of the scale, which are necessary supplements to an inadequate wage or salary that is often not paid on time, can be excused, especially if the elites at the top are seen to be hopelessly corrupt. In Africa, 'corruption is not just endemic but an integral part of the social fabric of life. For those at the bottom end of society, like lowly civil servants, the sale of the limited amount of power they possess is virtually their only means of survival. Higher up, extortion is one of the major avenues of enrichment; it facilitates social advancement and the upholding of one's position.'[6] The difficulty here is that systematic pilfering at the lower end of the scale or massive corruption at the top between them weaken the economy as a whole and therefore reduce its contribution to the efficient working of the state. Since officially all African societies have accepted Western norms about corruption they are obliged, periodically, to expose and punish the most blatant examples of corruption when these come to light just as new regimes taking power denounce the corruption of their predecessors.

The report of the Commission on Global Governance, *Our Global Neighbourhood*, which sets out proposals for a new world order, allots the problem of corruption two pages. Corruption is a worldwide phenomenon affecting both the public and private sectors, compromising the processes of legislation and administration, regulation and privatization. Corrupt dealings between the worlds of business and politics at very high levels have come to light in recent years in dozens of countries, both industrial and developing. 'In a number of developing countries, corruption flourished under despotic rulers as well as under democratic regimes. Vast sums that should have been in government treasuries to be spent on national objectives were siphoned off to be invested abroad. The people of these countries were effectively robbed. The great powers that supported corrupt rulers in the full knowledge of their venality must share the blame. So must the banks that help stash away ill-gotten funds and launder the money of drug dealers and other criminals.' These sweeping generalizations by a committee of the 'great and the good' tend to make the reader feel that since all is known, effective action must follow. The problem is, what action? 'Most opportunities for significant corruption in developing countries,' the report continues, 'arise in interactions between their politicians and officials and the business sector in industrial countries.' At this point we come to the role of democracy in combating corruption. 'The strengthening of democracy and accountability is the antidote to corruption. While there are no guarantees against corrupt practices, as so many democracies confirm, a free society with vigorous independent media and a watchful civil society raises the chances of the detection, exposure, and punishment of corruption.' This statement must be considered with care. The principal Western donors, that are so anxious to impose democracy and accountability upon developing countries in Africa and elsewhere, are without exception democracies and claim to have free media. Yet they are also the countries whose business operations in Africa are complicit partners in the corruption outlined above and democracy in Italy has not prevented that country acquiring notoriety for its corrupt practices. There is something hypocritically equivocal about the report, which continues with the remarkable adjuration: 'It is also important that the privatization of state-owned companies should be carried out without any taint of irregularity, so that the process of economic reform, of which privatization forms a part, is not discredited.' African critics of privatization would argue that the very process, when pressed upon their countries by aid donors and the international financial institutions, is a form of corruption since its principal object is to provide an opportunity for the business corporations of the developed world to acquire the best assets of the developing world at knock-down prices against the wishes and instincts of the states that own them.[7] Later, the report deals with multilateral trade and argues that 'Governance would be strengthened through multilateral agreements that define minimum standards of corporate behaviour. It is in no one's interest that standards of safety are allowed to slide to the level that allowed the Bhopal disaster'.[8] In the end, the pontificating of such a report leaves the reader with a sense of unreality, for it does not spell out – and in fairness to its members does not know – how to deal with the problem of human and corporate greed.

A second report of the 1990s was that of the South Commission yet despite the prevalence of corruption in the countries of the South, *The Challenge to the South* only spares one page of text to the subject of corruption. It says: 'Corruption has been on the increase in many countries – in all parts of the world. Circumstances differ and so do the causes. In the West it tends to be associated with big business and such activities as manipulation of the stock markets; in socialist countries and the South over-regulation and the absence of effective systems of public accountability make it tempting to resort to corrupt practices. Over-centralization, limited administrative capabilities, laxity of tax administration, and authoritarian tendencies have combined to provide fertile conditions for corruption in many developing countries.' It continues: 'In the

South, the excessive concentration of economic power in the hands of the government and the corporate sector, poverty, insecurity, and the underpayment of public personnel also account for some of these undesirable practices. So do corrupting influences from Northern sources related, but not confined, to obtaining profitable contracts and to the trade in arms and the illicit traffic in drugs.' These statements set out the problem in matter-of-fact terms as one that is simply a part of the ongoing political-economic scene. The report places much of the blame squarely on the shoulders of governments in the South. 'Regardless of these factors (stated above), governments must bear a large part of the responsibility for corruption in the South. By and large they have not regarded its eradication as a priority, despite its acknowledged economic, social, and political costs.'[9] These two reports are worth quoting at length since they represent the official collective international view of corruption, which they see as a major part of the world in which we live and implicitly do not see much likelihood of changing.

Of course, there are obvious ways in which the incidence of corruption can be decreased. Thus, public officials should be banned from accepting any emoluments apart from their official salaries, such as consultancy fees, and salaries should be sufficient to discourage corruption while they are in office. They should also be banned from paid employment with corporate or other groups that could benefit from their inside knowledge for several years after leaving office and pensions should be adequate to enable them to live without recourse to such employment. Passing such rules is easy; ensuring that they are followed depends upon the willingness of governments to enforce them. An interesting African viewpoint on relations with Europe is to be found in *Congo-Paris*, whose subtitle 'Transnational Traders on the Margins of the Law' indicates its content. It describes the activities of African traders to Paris from the two Congos who smuggle, deal in drugs and break the law in order to service the African diaspora. Their activities are often illegal if not specifically 'corrupt' within the obvious meaning of the word. 'In Europe, traders and others explicitly state that operating outside the law, even in theft, drug-dealing and other activities, is justifiable because: "In the past Europeans looted Africa, now it is the turn of Africans to help themselves to the riches of Europe".'[10] Attitudes such as these are crucial to an understanding of more general Afro-European relations. The ideas advanced in *Our Global Neighbourhood* (see above) provide a global ethic but how, in fact, is this viewed by power-hungry transnational corporations or a unilateralist United States, and whose global values are we discussing?

Africans often accuse the West of double standards and they make a sound case. 'Throughout the long years of the Cold War, the US and its allies were quite happy to exploit the inherent weakness of the Third World countries in pursuit of their own narrow political and corporate interests. Indeed the record of sustained Western-sponsored subversion, manipulation, corruption and repression of human rights in all parts of the Third World over the last 50 years is well documented.'[11] By their sustained support for corrupt and brutal dictators such as Mobutu, the US and its allies have 'contrived both to undermine their own moral authority in the Third World and progressively to weaken their ability to influence events'. As a result, dictators who owed their position to Western support demanded ever greater indulgence and favours, including the misuse of aid as their price for acting as Western stooges. 'The damage done to the reputation of the developed world's leadership has been compounded by its willingness to aid and abet the crimes of Third World dictators and their henchmen both before and after their overthrow.'[12] If leaders of African states, or would-be leaders such as Charles Taylor of Liberia, can behave as though their countries are simply there to be seized as estates for the benefit of the warlord who seizes them and are then promptly recognized by Western governments, this destroys any moral authority the Western world might otherwise claim when it advances the merits of democracy. In 1995, President Chirac of France demanded that his government should make a clean break with heads of state who prevaricated in the face of change and were corrupt or autocratic. French development aid, he argued, should be used in the struggle against crime, corruption and drug trafficking. Given Chirac's personal reputation in relation to corruption or the cynical use of French influence to manipulate African governments to adopt policies favourable to French interests his stand at this time must have caused surprise. He was, of course, reacting to developments then taking place in Africa and, not least, the rearguard actions against the democracy the West had found it expedient to champion. 'There were signs (1995) that authoritarian governments in Africa were taking vigorous counter-measures to halt the advance of democracy, in spite of the impressive size of popular pro-democracy pressures which were sweeping the continent and despite the general spread of multiparty political movements, some of which had actually toppled governments from power.'[13] While President Chirac was indulging his favourite pastime of seizing the moral high ground, Britain and Switzerland were willing to allow the proceeds of the egregious acts of theft of Nigeria's Gen. Abacha to be deposited with no questions asked in their banks and the US and Europe are prepared to grant the right of abode to virtually any foreigner with huge amounts of money.[14]

THE CORRUPTING INFLUENCE OF AID

By the end of the century it was clear that aid had failed its avowed purpose of assisting development and, instead, had encouraged the widespread corruption of government officials and, even more disastrously, had increased African institutional dependency. Donor governments had shown themselves either unable or unwilling to impose any serious conditionalities in regard to either economic or financial matters or politics. 'Aid can deliver bridges, vaccines and training services, but at the same time, it can decimate, demoralize and corrupt a nation's corps of civil servants, teachers and health professionals. Recipients overtly welcome aid, but at the same time conceal their resistance to its rules... Where foreign aid is a major source of jobs and the social wage of health and education services, and where debt repayment puts prior claims on revenues, the importance of aid chains to politics – who gets, what, when, and how – cannot be overestimated.'[15] Those in recipient countries whose positions depend upon the continuing flow of aid will go to great lengths to persuade donors that they are using the aid as the latter intended, no matter what they do with the aid in reality. In many African countries a whole chain of agencies, banks, departments, politicians and individuals have become dependent upon the continuing flow of aid and will go to great lengths to ensure that donors continue to provide it. The donors, for their part, have their own agendas for continuation. Since, after 40 years, donors have failed to work themselves out of their jobs as they should have done, they can hardly continue using the old arguments in support of aid. Instead their rhetoric is no longer about development but rather is centred upon the new orthodoxy of good governance whose lack is blamed for the failures of past development efforts. They argue that the adoption of good governance will be followed by the development that has eluded recipients for so long. Thus, good governance, which in the past was implicit in the aid relationship, became the reason for aid in the 1990s.

Yet despite the new orthodoxy of linking aid to good governance (democracy, trade liberalization, less corruption) there is no evidence that bad governments receive less aid than good governments or that an increase in foreign aid reduces corruption.[16] Aid, especially if it is on any scale and comes to be regarded as necessary for particular projects, inevitably has the effect of undermining the government itself and weakening state structures since the government has ceased to be the source of finances upon which projects depend and those involved in such projects cease to look to their own governments but turn instead to the aid donors. Over the years donors have become increasingly arrogant and prefer to work with minimum interference from governments once they have established themselves in a country. Aid has become big business and like any other business the donors have to keep going or lose their influence. Since this is perfectly understood by recipients a two-way charade is conducted in which donors and local recipients in charge of an aid project work together to the exclusion or downgrading of government influence. This process may be especially marked in countries where aid is the country's second-largest employer after the public sector. The longer aid is used to support a programme or institution of whatever kind, the harder it becomes for either donor or recipient to envisage the aid input coming to an end. As a result, the process of continuation and, therefore, of dependence becomes more or less permanent and correspondingly insidious.

Thus, the West downsizes governments and corrupts African leaders with its aid. While aid ought to be used to support development strategies that increase self-sufficiency and regional integration, in fact the opposite is usually the case. Aid donors insist that recipients abstain from any measures that might increase their financial self-sufficiency and so reduce their dependence on foreign aid. Weak countries, such as Rwanda, are not allowed to give protection to local agricultural and manufacturing enterprises, which have a reasonable potential for competing in its home markets but must give support instead to export-oriented production such as tea and coffee.[17] Aid in return for policy reforms has become the norm and policy reforms are not seen to operate in the interests of the people on whose behalf they are supposedly implemented. 'Since the imposed policies are themselves all too often shown to be hopelessly unrealistic and damaging to the economy and to living standards, to the extent that they can be implemented at all, their effect is to intensify popular discontent. In such a climate of corruption and alienation it is all too common to find that the integrity and effectiveness of institutions and administrations progressively breaks down.'[18]

STATE-SPONSORED CORRUPTION

African governments, like governments all over the world, seek scapegoats for their own failures and aid donors provide easy targets when the need arises. However, a brief look at four countries where corruption appears endemic – Algeria, Angola, Nigeria and Democratic Republic of Congo – shows that while assistance from outside is always welcome, corruption in one form or another is attained without undue effort from within.

In Algeria Abdelhamid Brahimi, who had been Chadli Benjedid's prime minister from 1984 to 1988 when he fell from power, emerged from obscurity in 1990 to announce that FLN corruption in government had cost the country US$26 billion over the years, the equivalent of the entire debt burden. He made this statement deliberately at that time to assist the FIS in the local and regional elections. Meanwhile, the West was presenting Benjedid as the apostle of reforms while overlooking what the rioters of 1988 had known only too well, that 'Benjedid had been the apex of a system of generalized nepotism and corruption for years, and in various ways, such as promoting and "covering" members of his own family – something Boumedienne had never done – had set an example which his subordinates had merely followed with alacrity.'[19] The same author points to the deterioration of Algeria's relations with France. These descended into corruption. France had wanted to establish an exemplary relationship with Algeria, but instead this had declined into a matter of involvement with individuals. From the Algerian point of view 'it is the story of a shift from a form of co-operation between two states, which qualified but did not necessarily cripple Algeria's nascent sovereignty, to a complex and unsavoury system of patronage, reciprocal back-scratching and corruption which rapidly subverted this sovereignty, delegitimized Algeria's rulers in the eyes of their people and helped precipitate and perpetuate Algeria's political crisis.'[20]

In his examination of Angola at the end of the century, Tony Hodges[21] provides a depressing yet understandable picture of the petty corruption at the lower end of the scale where, he says, there is a weak sense of public duty or service among officials, including the front-line service delivery institutions, such as the National Health Service. The problem was made worse in the 1990s by the spread of the practice of public officials demanding bribes or tips (*gasosas*) for the provision of services. 'Low salaries are one of the main driving forces of petty corruption, which has become endemic throughout the public administration, particularly in services with a high degree of contact with the general public, such as the police, health services and education.' A survey by the *Ministro da Administração Pública, Emprego e Segurança Social* (MAPESS) (Ministry of Public Administration, Employment and Social Security) and the *Instituto Nacional de Estatística* (INE) (National Statistics Institute) in 1998, found that 67.5 per cent of those in professional posts and 74 per cent in administrative posts admitted they would be prepared to accept a 'gift' to perform a service. At the same time, other employees exploited positions of authority to extract money for the issuance of documents such as driving licences. In the absence of a bribe the required document can be delayed for months.[22] At the same time, 'There is very little documented information about higher-level corruption, although there is a more or less universal presumption among Angolans that it is deeply entrenched in a system of public administration characterized by arbitrariness and lack of transparency.' The problem was acknowledged at the highest levels by the 1996 legislation that established the *Alta Autoridade contra a Corrupção* to tackle the problem although in fact the authority remained a dead letter.[23] The armed forces loot in lieu of pay, general poverty encourages corruption if only so that people can survive and from on high, as it were, aid donors and NGOs who find Angola a difficult place in which to operate voice their concern about entrenched official corruption.

In his lively, personal account of travelling in Nigeria, Karl Maier, the author of *The House Has Fallen,* provides a vivid account of corruption in Africa's largest black state. At the beginning of his book he quotes a Nigerian, Dr Folarin Gbadebo-Smith who is considering money-laundering, as follows: 'A man who receives stolen goods is called a fence, but what do you call a country that is in the business of receiving stolen goods? They lend Nigeria money, somebody here steals the same amount of money and gives it back to them, and then they leave these poor Nigerians repaying what they never owed. The role of the Western powers has been totally disgraceful.'[24] As he continues, Nigeria's leaders, like the colonialists before them, have sucked out billions of dollars and stashed them in Western banks. The reference to colonialists is important here, for it implies directly that the process of extracting wealth from Africa, which was the starting point of colonialism, now continues with Africans as the prime movers with the West as more passive recipients. Maier continues his examination of the 'Fallen House' with a look at the Nigerian role in the international drugs trade, and the way in which profits are made out of fuel shortages: 'The system of corruption had become so ingrained that entire villages in northern Nigeria depended on the fuel shortages for their livelihood: The longer the lines of vehicles outside the legitimate gas stations in the big northern cities, such as Kano, Kaduna and Zaria, the more numerous the roadside gangs of youths selling plastic jugs full of pink motor fuel.' And so his story continues. Maier quotes M. D. Yusufu, the former inspector-general of police: 'I think Babangida was even worse than Abacha. Babangida went all out to corrupt society. Abacha was intimidating people with fear. With him gone now, you can recover. But this corruption remains, and it is very corrosive to society.' A government commission headed by the economist Pius Okigbo in 1995 found that during Babangida's time in office and during the first several months of the Abacha regime more than US$12 billion could not be accounted for. The author has other stories to tell but overall the picture he paints is one of a society where everybody is trying to make money on the side by more or less corrupt means.

When Obasanjo came to power in 1999 he introduced anti-corruption legislation and suspended controversial oil contracts that had been awarded by the Abacha government as it stepped down. He sent envoys to London,

Washington and other capitals to seek access to Abacha's bank accounts. The Swiss government froze four accounts, three in Geneva and one in Zurich. Abacha and his associates had siphoned off at least US$2.2 billion, which the government hoped to recover. Meanwhile, the new Assembly voted itself a US$25,000–US$35,000 furniture allowance at a time when the minimum wage per month was US$30. As Maier points out, a known incorruptible is not supported for office by his local community 'because he won't eat and he won't let us eat'. This book paints a particular portrait of Nigeria but one that is familiar to people who know the country. When Nigerians are told that their country is regarded as the most corrupt in the world, they reply: 'This is how we do things in Nigeria.'[25]

According to a Congolese, the story of Democratic Republic of Congo (DRC) (formerly Zaïre) is one long tale of corruption. At the top under Mobutu it was a matter of state kleptocracy. Mobutu ensured that his supporting clique all became corrupt and, therefore, were complicit in his corruption and consequently pliable. Lower down the scale survival depended upon corrupt practices of one kind or another. Further, the mineral wealth of the Congo has corrupted almost every outsider who has become involved in the country – Belgium, France, the US, the neighbouring states, multinational corporations – each after their 'share' of its wealth. Once money was seen as the 'goal' that everyone pursued in order to be anyone then how it was obtained became of secondary importance. Moreover, if the leaders and 'big men' are seen to be overtly corrupt, why not everyone else? Whatever the role of outsiders, they cannot operate without the willing complicity of Congolese nationals. The corrupted and the corrupters feed on each other and such a society breeds plenty of people who want to be corrupted. At the end of the Mobutu era corruption had reached an all-time high. 'The corrupters, of course, have no respect for diplomatic niceties such as national sovereignty and territorial integrity that may stand in the way of short-term profitability. They make deals with whoever controls a mineral-rich territory, including warlords and invaders, as they have done in the Congo with the AFDL, Rwanda, the Ugandan warlord Brig. James Kazimi, both wings of the RCD and the MLC. For the African partners, all that does matter is the amount of money foreign businesses are prepared to pay up front to win lucrative contracts, and the percentage of earnings that will later go back to political authorities or warlords.'[26] Corruption and wealth on the scale of the Congo will draw participants into the scramble for a share from all over the world. 'In one transaction in May 1997, the AFDL received an initial payment of US$50 million from Consolidated European Ventures of the Lundin Group of Vancouver, Canada, for a copper and cobalt investment deal worth US$1.5 billion, with the remainder US$200 million to be paid over four years.'[27]

Africa's endless wars are natural breeding grounds for greed and corruption. In a climate of violence and endless uncertainty it is not surprising that people are tempted to take anything they can as a hedge against an uncertain future. In wars, 'Moreover, there is nothing like greed to forge the social networks needed to overcome problems of scale and co-ordination. In other words, the true cause of much civil war is not the loud discourse of grievance, but the silent force of greed.'[28] In war after war – Liberia and Sierra Leone in the 1990s are good examples as was the carve-up of Democratic Republic of Congo by its predatory neighbours – greed is the driving force. If they can, the ordinary people try to distance themselves from the fighting though too rarely do they succeed in doing so. These wars do not serve justice or solve problems, no matter what reasons were advanced for the original involvement of participants. Rather, the warlords manipulate the people into fighting for an apparent cause while they are only concerned with their own enrichment and power. These wars are financed by the illegal sale of looted resources – diamonds, coffee, coltan – and in the background are the Western money-launderers and arms companies who service the warlords and ask no awkward questions.

THE END OF THE RAWLINGS REVOLUTION IN GHANA

The corruption of Rawlings' Ghana can be seen as a classic story of revolutionary zeal turning into autocratic cronyism. At the personal level, Rawlings' 'wild streak' that had made him such a charismatic reformer when he first seized power, in his later career at the end of the century only appeared mean-spirited. By 2000,

> As corruption soared and life became harder, particularly for urbanites, the former foot-soldiers of the 'revolution', increasingly marginalized, became disillusioned; with increasing policy distortion, the alliance with business also frayed. The fall-off of donor patronage tightened the crisis. The unemployed and marginalized youth of Accra and the towns, the trade unions and students – in some respects the very social forces that had propelled the 'Rawlings revolution' almost 20 years earlier – came together with other interests in a 'democratic revolution' to expel the regime.[29]

This scenario typifies the end to which so many reforming regimes come, so much so as to raise the bleak query as to whether the natural state is one of corruption, the revolutionary state merely an aberration from the norm. Prior to Rawlings, Ghanaians had seen the Acheampong regime as deeply corrupt, a corruption shared by the armed forces. The coups of 4 June 1979 and 31 December 1981 were marked by the implosion of the armed forces. 'It was an indication of the malaise in the Ghana Armed Forces that on both occasions only a small handful of ranks and junior officers were able to overthrow the military hierarchy.' Corruption had made it ripe for collapse.[30] Fighting corruption can all too easily become counter-productive because the anti-corruption forces themselves become corrupt. This happened, for example, with the Timber Task Forces (TTF) that were responsible for controlling illegal felling and logging. They became laws to themselves, used violence, raided villages and sawmills and indulged in illegal sales of logs in order to enrich themselves until they were abolished by the Minister for Lands and Mineral Resources.

Aid played its part in subverting self-help schemes to make them dependent instead upon inputs from outside. But, most disturbingly, a regime that had begun by tackling the country's blatant corruption and had made great headway in eradicating a great deal of it, later saw its elite become like their military predecessors, and begin to erode the ascetic image that had been the hallmark of the Rawlings revolution. By the end of the 1990s 'Commissions on state contracts destined for the coffers of the NDC (National Democratic Congress) were alleged to be widespread (estimated at 10–15 per cent of contract values), as were demands that businesses large and small make contributions to the NDC; the price for this was the growing number of abandoned or poorly finished projects.'[31] It is not easy to explain such a descent into the corrupt practices that had justified the Rawlings coups in the first place. There are various possibilities: a deeply entrenched cultural affinity with corruption; lack of any clear accountability in administrative structures; underpaid civil servants improving their lot; or forced privatization providing easy opportunities for quick personal gains? There is also a danger that dictatorial regimes always give rise to, and that is the readiness to ignore the law and act arbitrarily and if the government is doing this in one direction the temptation for ordinary citizens to enrich themselves arbitrarily should not be ignored. In the early Rawlings years whatever corruption took place was carefully concealed but this changed after the 1992 elections for the party (NDC) had opened its doors to moneyed individuals in order to finance its campaign, and these newcomers were not ascetic reformers but carpetbaggers. According to reports of the Serious Fraud Squad corruption and embezzlement became widespread in the District Assemblies. By 1999 activists had become sufficiently disillusioned with the Rawlings government and the NDC that a section of the party broke away to form a separate party, the Reform Movement. By this time the revolutionary party that had fought corruption and eschewed foreign aid had, instead, become dependent upon aid.

When an African state relies upon aid rather than its own resources it becomes an adjunct, a form of local government, in the global, Western-controlled economic order and this had happened to Ghana. Nyerere had warned against this in his 1967 Arusha Declaration but his warning had been largely ignored, including in the end, by Tanzania itself. The Ghana story is especially instructive because the corruption of power was most noticeable in Rawlings, the charismatic, ascetic revolutionary who wanted to clean up his country but found by 1998 that a reform movement inside his own party was calling for an end to corruption and sycophancy. As usual, the international aid community played its part in this transformation. Rawlings' original populism resulted from his emphasis upon the moral rectitude of the poor majority and his attack upon elite corruption. Such an attitude did not endear his Provisional National Defence Council (PNDC) to donors and creditors who were naturally opposed to people's socialism in any form. Once Rawlings had turned to the World Bank, whose darling he became in the 1980s, aid donors and multilateral agencies sighed with relief and corruption once more reared its head.

Forms of corruption vary from country to country. In Kenya, for example, President Moi constantly agreed to economic reforms or human rights improvements as suggested by donors but once the aid had been released ignored or positively reneged on his promises. In this case the real corruption was that of the donors who knew how he would behave yet provided the aid anyway, thus reducing their ethical stands to a hypocritical charade. A Kenya-donor ritual grew up during the Moi years: Kenya was promised aid; the government refused to reform as required; the aid donors threatened to withhold the aid; Kenya implemented 'reforms', that were not subsequently carried out; the aid was delivered. On the other side of the continent in Côte d'Ivoire the austerity measures announced in 1990 led to popular attacks upon elite corruption that was not affected by such measures. The most preposterous corruption of all concerned the megalomania of the country's octogenarian ruler Houphouët-Boigny spending half the country's wealth in the construction of *Notre Dame de la Paix*, a gilded copy of St Peter's (Rome), in Houphouët-Boigny's home village of Yamoussoukro at a cost of US$300 million (the cost had doubled from the original estimate). When the ruler of Guinea, Sekou Touré, died in 1984, the military took control and, while bringing an end to the corruption of the presidential elite, they deregulated the plundering of the state and made corruption open to all. One of Africa's supreme warlords was Charles Taylor of Liberia, known in his ministerial days under Samuel Doe as 'superglue'. His activities helped corrupt Liberia's neighbours Burkina Faso and Sierra Leone. Taylor's ambition was to wrest from Doe the royalties of the world's largest commercial shipping fleet and the rents to be earned from narco-dollars passing through Liberia. Taylor offered a stake in the enterprise to Joseph Momoh, the President of Sierra Leone, but he offered his services to the highest bidder who turned out to be Samuel Doe. Following Doe's death and Taylor's ascendancy in Liberia, he punished Momoh by starting a rebellion in Sierra Leone where, of course, he had his eyes on the diamonds.[32]

SOUTHERN AFRICA

Before Mozambique began getting massive doses of aid in the second half of the 1990s, its public sector management and legal system 'may have been basic and unimaginative, but at least they were not ravaged by corruption, loss of good staff, demoralization, legal decay and rampant gangsterism'.[33] A sad story from Mozambique is that of Francisco Langa, a FRELIMO hero of the liberation war who in 1980 succumbed to accepting a bribe but then committed suicide rather than face his comrades. 'Two decades later, however, officials with big houses and cars flaunt the money stolen from the aid programme. The shift in culture from Puritanism to self-seeking greed has been rapid and dramatic. In the early 1990s Mozambique was the poorest country in the world. 'Steadily corruption became endemic, as people struggled to survive, while all around them were wealthy foreigners and large amounts of aid. And aid workers anxious to get their projects going without being delayed by what they saw as Mozambican "bureaucracy" were only too happy to allow rules to be ignored at the cost of a small bribe or turning a blind eye to some aid being diverted.'[34] By 1999 the issue of corruption had become a topic for debate for it was recognized that the country had become deeply corrupted. During the floods of 2000, the country rose above it.

> We had no reports of significant diversions of aid, and many reports of integrity and selflessness. But Mozambique has established a new and unenviable reputation with donors so there were efforts to avoid a corruption which was now expected. This ranged from the South African decision to send goods rather than money to attempts by a number of small agencies to do their own distribution, allegedly because they feared corruption, but more often because they wanted to control the distribution.[35]

In his book about the machinations of Enron, the US company whose collapse in 2002 represented the biggest corruption scandal in US corporate history, Vijay Prashad recounts a story about its activities in Mozambique and, more important, the efforts of the US government to support it. The US readiness to lecture developing countries about their corruption does not sit well with the following episode. In 1995 Mozambique sought investment to develop its Pande offshore gas field. The best two bids were from South Africa's SASOL and Argentina's Plus Petrol. Then Enron stepped in and worked to replace SASOL and was backed in its attempt by the US. At that time US$1.1 billion of Mozambique's US$1.5 billion budget was financed by foreign aid and of this amount US$40 million came from USAID. John Kachamila, the Minister of Mineral Resources, told the following story which was published in the *Houston Chronicle*:

> There were outright threats to withhold development funds if we didn't sign (the deal with Enron) and sign soon. Their diplomats, especially Mike McKinley (deputy chief of the US Embassy), pressured me to sign a deal that was not good for Mozambique. He was not a neutral diplomat. It was as if he was working for Enron. We got calls from American senators threatening us with this and that if we didn't sign. Anthony Lake (US national security adviser) even called to tell us to sign... Enron was forever playing games with us and the embassy was forever threatening to withdraw aid.

A study commissioned by the World Bank found that many of Mozambique's concerns were warranted. The view of an unnamed State Department official is also quoted: 'This project represents tax revenue, hard currency earnings in a big way for the Mozambique state... If the Mozambicans think they can kill this deal and we will keep dumping money into this place, they should think again.' It was at this time that Anthony Lake wrote to President Chissano to say that the US would not release US$13.5 million in aid funds unless Mozambique accepted the Enron bid.[36] When the subject of African corruption in relation to aid is raised such brutal arm-twisting by the US State Department should be seen as part of a two-way corruption process where all the cards are in the hands of the donor. Reverberations of the Enron scandal continued through 2003 when, for example, six major Western banks including Barclays Bank, Deutsche Bank and Canadian Imperial Bank of Commerce were implicated for their alleged knowledge of what Enron was doing. The United States, Britain, Germany and Canada are among the world's leading aid donors that regularly lecture African recipients about corruption.

Political corruption, the unsanctioned use of public resources for private ends, is regarded as endemic when it becomes open and routine. South Africa since 1994 has certainly not been seen as one of the continent's most corrupt countries by a long way but plenty of petty corruption has been recorded. Pension frauds between 1994 and 1998, in the form of ghost or double claimants, accounted for R5 billion while police corruption (which was endemic in the apartheid era) did not improve: partly this was ascribed to demoralization and disloyalty to the new regime. In 1998 10,000 policemen out of a force of 140,000 were under investigation on charges of bribery, theft, fraud and involvement in crime syndicates. According to the accountants Deloitte and Touche, losses by public sector fraud in 1998 probably exceeded R10 billion. Between 1994 and 1998 the government lost up to R20 billion as a result of corrupt employee behaviour. In 1998 the Special Investigative Unit headed by Judge Willem Heath claimed that the R10 billion it was investigating represented only 5 per cent of the total though this went back to instances of corruption prior to 1994. In 1999 the government-sponsored National Anti-Corruption Summit resolved to establish a National Anti-Corruption Forum. Two years later it was only just ready to function. South Africa's provincial governments are open to corruption and difficult to monitor since departments keep disciplinary procedures secret. Neither does the government welcome civil society anti-corruption initiatives. In November 2000, for example, the Minister of Safety and Security, Steve Tshwete, rejected proposals for a private sector agency to monitor police corruption – the police had its own unit for the purpose. Nonetheless, in 1998 and 1999 the government hosted two major anti-corruption conferences and all political parties, including the ANC, focused on this issue during the election campaigns. The extent of police corruption in South Africa is seen as alarming given the role the police ought to play in rooting out corruption. In early 1999, of the 80,000 cases the Special Investigative Unit under Judge Heath was investigating, only two or three cases had been referred to it by the government, a clear indication that investigating corruption was not a government priority. Thus, while the government was seen to denounce the evils of corruption it was not seen to pursue corrupt practices with any obvious conviction. This reluctance to pursue corruption was borne out in the case of Andrew Feinstein, an ANC MP, whose over-keen pursuit of corruption led to his removal from an investigative committee. This was justified under party discipline: 'Some people have the notion that Public Accounts Committee members should act in a non-partisan way. But in our system no ANC member has a free vote.'[37] The party, clearly, would look after its own. As the same authority claims: 'The political will to punish corruption in high quarters remains inconsistent – and non-existent in certain provincial governments. Though elected politicians have occasionally lost office as a result of corruption accusations, not a single ANC minister or parliamentarian has been charged with or convicted for a corruption-related political offence.'[38]

*

Western critics often take African leaders to task for shielding one another or refusing to criticize individual state or leader deficiencies: the reluctance to condemn Robert Mugabe of Zimbabwe for his land policies at the turn of the century is a good example and implicit in such criticism is the suggestion that Africans cover up the corruption or other shortcomings of their continental peers. This Western attitude is doubly hypocritical. In the first place, most Western governments have been prepared to deal with leaders and governments whose corruption is often notorious when it suits them to do so. More important, however, is the comparable reluctance of Western governments to criticize each other. President Chirac of France and Prime Minister Berlusconi of Italy both have reputations for corruption that would place them high in any pecking order, yet their European counterparts, who readily denounce corruption in Africa, deal with their European counterparts without qualms or complaints.

Some aspects of corruption have a lighter side to them. It was only possible to salute the brazen impertinence of Nigeria's Gen. Abacha as he despatched Nigerian troops under ECOMOG to restore to power the democratically elected government of President Kabbah in Sierra Leone. The notion that it was better to keep the Nigerian ECOMOG soldiers outside the country also played a role in the decision. In any case, 'Kabbah's government was as corrupt and neo-patrimonial as any other, but as in the case of Liberia a former rebel leader had been given legitimate status in order to stop the fighting'. Sierra Leone, indeed, has a long history of corrupt practices to its credit. '...the parallel economy in Sierra Leone, which exceeded the official economy in size, expanded as a consequence of the systematic corruption, theft of state revenues and personalist rule of President Siaka Stevens between 1965 and 1985.'[39] In both Liberia and Sierra Leone, unfortunately, the Nigerian troops became as mired in corruption and self-seeking as the regimes they were supposedly coming to discipline. There is little evidence to suggest that democratic elections reduce corruption though, for a time, they may lead to greater openness so making it easier to spot the corruption that is taking place. Chabal and Daloz, already quoted, suggest that some corruption may be regarded as an habitual part of everyday life, an expected element of any social transaction. 'Provided the beneficiaries of graft do not hoard too much of what they accumulate by means of the exploitation of the resources made available to them through their position, and provided they redistribute along lines that are judged to be socially desirable, their behaviour is deemed acceptable.'[40] In other words, there is unlikely to be much censorship of corrupt practices if their fruits are suitably redistributed to the patron's followers. Condemnation is reserved for cliques who appropriate public resources for themselves purely out of greed.

One final comment is worth making. In developed societies such as those of Europe high levels of corruption can be subsumed by the system and only occasionally do they erupt to become major public scandals. In developing countries where most systems remain fragile and the majority of the people are extremely poor corruption is at once more apparent and often more necessary to the working of the system as a whole. And here it is worth pointing out that there is nothing to prevent those Western countries that so readily condemn African corruption from seeking out the secret accounts of money laundered out of Africa by corrupt rulers to return such funds to the successor governments for the provision of social services such as schools or clinics.

CHAPTER FORTY

Century's End:
Globalization

The 40 years from 1960 (the *annus mirabilis* of independence) to 2000 were a period of momentous changes for the whole African continent. Most African countries achieved their independence in the 1960s, though not the white-dominated South, but freedom, as they soon discovered, was a relative term. Poverty, lack of trained personnel and poor – in some cases non-existent – infrastructure meant a continuing reliance upon the former metropolitan powers for aid and it soon became clear that aid only came with strings attached. It was Africa's misfortune to achieve independence at the height of the Cold War with the result that its newly independent states at once found themselves being drawn into a global confrontation that was none of their concern. The determination of the West to ensure that Africa was attached to its camp was in reality a policy designed to control Africa's resources on the one hand and ensure that African economies remained tied to Western prescriptions on the other. What the West did not want and managed largely to avoid was an 'independent' Africa able to go its own way. Manipulation of weak states, the provision or withholding of aid, the presence of a growing number of expatriates as advisers, and the proliferation of aid agencies and non-government organizations between them ensured that there were more expatriates helping Africa to be independent than ever there had been to administer it in colonial times. This, in sum, was the neo-colonialism that Nkrumah had denounced. The influx of newcomers happened at great speed, with the Cold War as its *raison d'être*. Thus Africa faced both the former colonial powers and the new Cold War warriors – the US, the USSR and China – each in pursuit of its own economic and strategic interests.

African awareness of its weakness was the driving force behind the search for African unity but this failed in the face of the individual nationalisms of the new states whose leaders above all relished their newfound power. In the years that followed, almost all African states experimented with different political forms – the bequeathed Westminster democratic pattern, French-style presidential rule, the one-party state, military rule, populist dictatorship – and many such experiments, inevitably, led to violence. By the 1990s African populations had become tired of overbearing rulers and there was a continent-wide move back to democracy. More than half the states of Africa experienced wars, whether with neighbours or internal civil wars, during these years and the military – the soldier in his battle fatigues clasping his Kalashnikov – became a familiar symbol of the continent. None of this should have been surprising. The rapid withdrawal of the imperial powers, which at best left inadequate structures behind them, created a vacuum that could not easily or quickly be filled. In any case, the return of the imperial powers as aid donors and the arrival of the Cold War warriors put intolerable strains upon the new governments that were ill-equipped to deal with the pressures levelled upon them. It would be quite unrealistic to expect an entire continent that had been relieved of its colonial masters over an incredibly short period of two decades to be able to settle down as viable nation states without upheavals and violence. Empires do not disappear that easily. It is worth considering, even if unproductive, what would have happened had Africa achieved its independence when there was no Cold War confrontation and the major powers had simply left the continent to its own devices.

The last decade of the twentieth century witnessed some remarkable developments in Africa as well as some depressing re-runs of past failures. On the plus side was the final end of apartheid and white minority rule in South Africa to be followed by the uniquely humane presidency of Nelson Mandela while continent-wide demands for greater democracy marked the passing of an age in which dictatorial rulers were any longer to be accepted as the norm. On the debit side was the continuing violence that had come to be seen as the apparent hallmark of much of Africa: civil wars in Sudan, the Congo, Angola, Algeria, Liberia and Sierra Leone that between them encompassed irreconcilable differences inherited from the colonial age, simple power struggles between warlords, ideology against religion and the collapse of state structures. The Cold War may have come to an end but big power interventions had not ceased and Africa remained the world's weakest economic region, aid dependent, and subject to endless pressures to accept World Bank/IMF structural adjustment programmes designed to maintain the West's economic grasp on the continent. Part of Africa's problem has always depended upon external perceptions: how it is seen from outside has done a great deal to perpetuate the straitjacket in which the continent is bound. If the major Western powers insist that Africa is an investment risk such an attitude all but ensures that it does not obtain the investment it needs. People and nations believe what they want to believe and relentless denigrating media coverage of Africa has not helped the continent overcome its problems.

Much publicity has been given to the HIV/AIDS pandemic in Africa and its devastating effects have yet to be fully realized. In South Africa, some 4.7 million of the population in 2002, or one in nine, was HIV positive, with a higher mortality rate among women than men. A study by Statistics SA found that the overall proportion of deaths due to HIV/AIDS had nearly doubled from 4.6 per cent in 1997 to 8.7 per cent in 2001. From a policy perspective the government continued to send out mixed signals on the means to fight the disease.[1] An ILO paper which examines the impact of AIDS upon the working populations of African countries affected by the pandemic comes to a gloomy conclusion about prospects in the early years of the twenty-first century.

The losses of human capital will not be confined to those with the greatest level of education and training so that the costs of the epidemic will be much greater than those normally estimated by economists. Since the system requires many levels and types of skills and capacities – both of men and women – it becomes even more necessary to ensure that mechanisms are strengthened to supply the levels and mix of skills that are needed for development. This is the policy problem: to ensure that skills are created as appropriate and labour supplies maintained as the HIV epidemic threatens to erode them. The problem is compounded by the fact that the epidemic systematically undermines the capacity to achieve these objectives, at precisely the time that labour supplies are most threatened. This is the challenge facing developing African economies...[2]

Here, set out in dry language, is one of the major problems overshadowing advance in sub-Saharan Africa.

The UNDP *Human Development Report 2003* highlights the ongoing problems that most affect development in Africa, beginning with the trade policies in rich countries that remain highly discriminatory against developing country exports. The report looks at the 1980s and 1990s when 'globalization was seen as the great new motor of worldwide economic progress. Poor countries were assumed to be able to achieve economic growth as long as they pursued good economic governance, based on the precepts of macroeconomic stability, liberalization of markets and privatization of economic activity.' These precepts for development proved hugely inadequate for many parts of the world including sub-Saharan Africa. To give one example, 'Poor, remote countries like Mali generally connect to the world economy by producing a few traditional primary commodities. But slow world market growth, unchanging technologies and often volatile and declining world prices for these commodities offer much too narrow a base for economic advance.'[3]

In a relatively upbeat assessment of African economic advance, *Transforming Africa's Economies*, the Economic Commission for Africa (ECA) claimed that Africa made impressive economic progress in the 1990s:

> The climate became more conducive to domestic and foreign investment. Capital markets broadened and deepened. Demand for African manufactured goods increased in Europe and the United States. And in the second half of the 1990s real GDP growth in Africa averaged 4 per cent a year, exceeding the continent's high population growth rate of 2.8 per cent a year. Export growth nearly doubled to 8 per cent a year. Real GDP grew by 3.2 per cent in 1999, up from 3.1 per cent in 1998.[4]

There followed many caveats but like other international bodies appraising African performance, the ECA broadly supports the orthodox line linking development to good governance.

In 2000 The World Bank produced a report, *Can Africa Claim the 21st Century.*[5] Gloomily, it makes the following points: 'Moreover, many development problems have become largely confined to Africa. They include lagging primary school enrolments, high child mortality, and endemic diseases – including malaria and HIV/AIDS – that impose costs on Africa at least twice those in any other developing region. One African in five lives in a country severely disrupted by conflict.' The AIDS pandemic, in particular, is eating into the continent's much-needed and fragile class of educated technocrats and other skilled personnel. As always, defining the problems is easier than prescribing solutions and there is a certain *déjà vu* quality about statements such as 'investing in people is also essential for accelerated poverty reduction'. Of course this is true but the World Bank has been saying such things for years. Africa must increase its competitiveness, reduce its aid dependence and so on. As this report also points out, 'Africa's average output per capita (in constant prices) had changed little by the end of the 1990s from 30 years before' yet the Bank and other external organizations rarely ask why there has been so little change or, even more important, whether the policies they have advocated may have been part of the problem. Having enumerated more problems and posed the question, is it credible to ask whether Africa can claim the twenty-first century, the report suggests that Africans and their development partners must reverse the economic marginalization and exclusion of recent years. This suggestion goes to the root of the matter, for it assumes that Africa cannot solve its problems on its own. Further, given the arguments advanced throughout this book that manipulation by the external 'partners' is one of the continent's main problems, it is time for Africa to face up to the fact that prescriptions from outside – to take the World Bank route – are no more likely to solve the continent's problems in the new century than they were in the century just past. Accompanied by a splendid diagram of inter-connecting circles, the report[6] suggests that Africa should focus development efforts on four groups of issues with strong cumulative interactions as follows: improving governance and resolving conflict; investing in people; increasing competitiveness and diversifying economies; and reducing aid dependence and debt and strengthening partnerships. Such prescriptions read well yet, despite periodic attempts to change its approach, the World Bank has always spoken oracularly as from on high and readers of such a report are left with the sense that there is no African input, no understanding of what is happening on the ground and why. One last quote from this report is worth recording because if the advice it offers is followed it will help to accelerate the collapse of state structures that are doing so much to create Africa's 'failed states'. Having made the highly debatable statement, 'Consensus is emerging that aid should be used to reduce poverty', the report lays down: 'To make aid more responsive to the needs of the poor, its delivery must be deconcentrated to local governments and communities. At the same time, these entities need to be strengthened to improve their capacity to manage development programmes.' Bypassing governments is no solution to Africa's problems however culpable or inefficient such governments may be. It is not the business of aid donors, whether the World Bank at one end of the spectrum or NGOs at the other, to decide that governments should be bypassed and aid be provided independently at the discretion of donors. That way can only lead to greater disintegration of weak states and pave the way for yet more intervention from outside. Those who take it upon themselves to 'aid' Africa are almost without exception believers in the inevitable forward march of globalization and it is to this topic we must now turn.

GLOBALIZATION

Those who argue that globalization is an inevitable process never explain why. If it becomes inevitable, in the sense that it dominates the entire world system of trade and investment, this will be the result of international bullying by the major economic powers, led by the United States, in order to force open all markets to corporate interests. One definition of the process is provided in *Our Global Neighbourhood*.[7] 'The term globalization has been used primarily to describe some key aspects of the recent transformation of world economic activity. But several other, less benign, activities, including the drug trade, terrorism, and traffic in nuclear materials, have also been globalized. The financial liberalization that seems to have created a borderless world is also helping international criminals and creating numerous problems for poorer countries.' It continues: Technological advances have made national frontiers more porous. States retain sovereignty, but governments have suffered an erosion of their authority. They are less able, for example, to control the trans-border movement of money or information. They face the pressures of globalization at one level and of grassroots movements and, in some cases, demands for devolution if not secession at another. In the extreme case, public order may disintegrate and civil institutions collapse in the face of rampant violence, as in Liberia and Somalia. Although many would agree that there is need for global management of population, consumption and the environment, the forces working to globalize the entire world economy are very powerful, driven by corporate greed, while the forces working to control the environment on behalf of everybody are thwarted by the greed of the same forces that would globalize the world economy.

There is no easy overall definition of globalization. The concept emerged in the 1990s following the collapse of the USSR since this removed all constraints from the activities of transnational corporations (TNCs). The USSR had acted as a defence shield for the formerly colonized zones of Eastern Europe and to a lesser extent around the globe and had made possible the rise of the non-aligned movement. 'To most of the world, globalization did not mean the equality of conditions of exchange. But it meant the entry of G-7 goods and finance into their zones just as a few of their compatriots could take their own goods to a limited part of the G-7 markets.'[8] Privatization is the leading policy weapon of globalization and by the end of the century water and power had become crucial items on its list: control of these fundamental resources had to be opened up to corporate ownership. All the instruments governing international trade and economic relations that in any case have long been controlled by the major developed nations, have been advancing policies leading to globalization. For example, 'The overall framework of GATT was to "liberalize" the traffic in goods, to open markets to TNCs and to cutback on the right of states to levy tariffs as a means to manage economic development and equity. It appears that these can be violated by the US, when it suits it, as made clear by its 2002 tariff on imported steel.'[9] Increasingly, global firms 'write' the rules of international economic behaviour and when, for example, a scandal such as that concerning Enron takes place, the West does not rewrite the rules controlling the behaviour of such companies (which it certainly would do if such a company was a Third World one) but rather treats such excesses as a one-off lapse, leaving in place the structure that allowed the scandal to take place.

One view of US wars on drugs and terrorism is that they are designed less to fight these threats than to give it control of strategic areas and resources. What appears unanswerable is the way in which the major economic powers, led by the United States and the EU, have, since the end of the Cold War worked to open all trade and all investment opportunities to penetration by their companies and corporations, regardless, or in spite of, the wishes of smaller countries who need some forms of protection in order to retain any control over their development. 'Market forces' has become one of the catch phrases of the present age but in reality the pattern of a country's trade is intimately linked to its economic and military strength and hence to its international power and influence. The powerful tell the weak to open their markets,[10] yet if the US and the EU really believed in market forces they would end their subsidies to agriculture and allow weak economies to benefit from the one major area in which they have an advantage. The WTO in principle discourages economic integration between nation states in that it theoretically requires that members practice non-discrimination in trade: that is, they accord equal treatment to all other countries which are parties to the agreement.[11] In fact, the WTO, like the other international financial institutions, is dominated by the US and the EU who ignore rules when it suits them to do so while insisting that the majority of weaker members adhere to them at all times. Occasionally they are defeated. In 1998 they attempted to force through the Multilateral Agreement on Investment (MAI) but were overruled as the result of a campaign led by NGOs. Had MAI been agreed it would have given a huge increase in powers to TNCs over elected governments by expanding their investment rights worldwide and empowering companies to sue governments, for example if their profits were diminished as a consequence of national laws. Then there came the scandal of the WTO's General Agreement on Trade in Services (GATS): this particular form of global liberalization aimed to require all countries to allow foreign business equal access to all domestic markets for services, including health and education, as well as tourism and financial services. The EU Commission has described GATS as 'first and foremost, an instrument for the benefit of business'. But, as a leaked DTI memo of 2001 made clear, the case for GATS was 'vulnerable' when campaigners asked for 'proof of where the economic benefits lay for developing countries'.[12] The more globalization is examined the harder it is to argue that it works equitably let alone to the benefit of the world's small economies.

Aid has always been an instrument of policy and increased emphasis upon channelling aid through the private sector is a warning signal that donors are prepared to use aid to boost private business in recipient countries. 'Where a Southern state depends on external aid rather than the national economy for its existence, it effectively becomes a local government in the global political order. Sovereignty is meaningless in a situation where primary government functions – security, economic management, the selection and implementation of public policies – cannot be minimally guaranteed or undertaken unless externally negotiated and financed.[13] Deliberate channelling of aid through NGOs is a way of both bypassing and downgrading the recipient government. Moreover, since NGO funding comes in part from governments they have lost the ability or desire to either criticize donor policies or work on a truly radical basis – as some did to begin with.[14] During the 1990s the World Bank responded to mounting criticisms of the way it worked by a new initiative to promote 'participation' of civil society in formulating government policies in developing countries. It required governments to consult with civil society groups to draw up a national development strategy that would then receive World Bank funding. No real consultations along these lines took place; rather, civil society groups were asked to ratify decisions or policies made by elites. Except in revolutionary situations this is normal, something the World Bank knew only too well. Its proposals were no more than a gesture to appease critics while its basic *modus operandi* would not change.

The genesis of globalization can be found in immediate post-World War II attitudes of Britain and the United States. Clement Attlee, the Prime Minister, Ernest Bevin, Foreign Secretary, and Sir Stafford Cripps, Chancellor of the Exchequer, saw the development of 'our' African resources as of prime importance and a major consideration in planning Britain's economic activities while Field Marshal Montgomery claimed that British living standards could be maintained by Africa's minerals, raw materials, land and cheap coal. The only problem, Montgomery added, was that the African was 'a complete savage' incapable of developing these resources himself. At that time Colonial Office planners were aware that they were grossly exploiting the colonies: 'the Colonial territories are helping so much on balance of payments' as one 1951 file records. Bevin, who in his other role as a leading trade unionist knew all about exploitation, believed that the possibility of presenting British policy as exploitation was 'almost endless' and suggested that 'care and preparation' would be needed to present British policies as promoting development.[15] Little had changed by the end of the century. The basic aim of US foreign policy at the end of World War II was to create an 'open door' in trade and investment where US companies were to be able to secure access to other countries' markets. Both the United States and Britain, still pursuing similar policies, had become ardent advocates of globalization at the end of the century.

In a devastating critique of New Labour's policies towards Africa, Mark Curtis[16] examines the British approach to post-apartheid South Africa which Britain had spent years shielding from the wrath of anti-apartheid activists. 'Following apartheid, the advocates of global liberalization – inside and outside the country – have created a South African economy geared to offering a generally favourable climate for investment by business. At the same time, the threat of radical change that might have principally benefited the majority of the population living in poverty has been staved off.' In other words, South Africa's white business elite that Britain went to such lengths to defend has won after all. Peter Hain, a radical turned poacher, said as minister in the Foreign Office 'where South Africa was once the reactionary pariah of Africa, now it is the radical and progressive model'.[17] Another Labour Minister, Trade Secretary Patricia Hewitt, said, 'We have no doubt about South Africa's attractiveness as a business partner for UK companies.' She has also said, 'We want to open up protected markets in developing countries.' Penetration of its economy had indeed gone deep and by the end of the century British investment in South Africa stood at £11 billion. The British aid department, DIFID, has become the strongest advocate of globalization among development organizations and all the donors appear to have adopted a similar line over globalization. Developing countries, on the other hand, need import protection, domestic subsidies and significant regulation of foreign companies. 'Under New Labour Britain is helping to organize the global economy to benefit a transnational business elite while pursuing policies that are often deepening poverty and inequality. New Labour has, in fact, a very grandiose project, not – as it claims – simply to *manage* globalization, but actively to push an extreme form of economic "liberalization" globally.' So much for the new partnership that Tony Blair says he wants with Africa. Speaking in Cape Town on 8 January 1999, Blair said, 'Real development can only come through partnership. Not the rich dictating to the poor. Not the poor demanding from the rich. But matching rights and responsibilities.' True partnership, it should be stressed, can only be achieved between equals. One last quote from Curtis is in reality a commentary upon the difference between the promise of New Labour and the reality. 'Instead of promoting a one-size-fits-all straitjacket of global economic "liberalization", Britain should champion diverse economic policies suited to local situations.'[18]

The internationalization of economies and finance, and the expansion of technologies, especially communications and information, have been the most obvious aspects of globalization during the period from 1990 onwards. The chief problem posed by this rapid expansion has been a commensurate reduction of democratic decision-making: governments have less control over social and welfare policies as the power of the nation state over economic decisions is downgraded. The evidence is increasing that where government policies concerning welfare come into conflict with the power and practices of TNCs, the latter win the argument. Thus, at the 1998 World Economic Forum at Davos, business leaders expressed dismay at 'excessive government regulation' such as rules covering the workplace and the environment. At the 1999 Davos

Forum, on 5 July, UN Secretary-General Kofi Annan, falling into line with business pressures, launched the United Nations-International Chamber of Commerce (UN-ICC) Global Compact. This relies upon the ability and will (in other words it is voluntary) of transnational corporations to comply with proposed standards concerning human rights, labour conditions and environmental practices. The transnationals are to regulate themselves and there are no monitoring or enforcing mechanisms. In return for this compact the United Nations would support free trade. This shameful surrender was the antithesis of any UN role as the guardian of the weak. At almost the same time as this Davos agreement was reached, on 12 July the annual UNDP *Human Development Report* was published. It detailed how profit-driven economic globalization resulted in the neglect of human rights and social justice for the majority of the world's people. It stated, among other things: 'Multinational corporations are already a dominant part of the global economy – yet many of their actions go unrecorded and unaccounted... They need to be brought within a frame of global governance, not just a patchwork of national laws, rules and regulations.' The UNDP wanted globalization with a human face and in a sense conceded defeat as it all but admitted that the process of globalization was already beyond control. Like the United Nations at Davos, pleas for globalization with a human face are no substitute for controls over governments and corporations that are determined to push the process above everything else. As the UNDP report continued: 'Today, they are held to codes of conduct only for what national legislation requires on the social and environmental impact of their operations. True, they have in recent years taken up voluntary codes of ethical conduct, but multinationals are too important for their conduct to be left to voluntary and self-generated standards.' The UNDP argues that human rights are the key source of ethical principles and, unlike the UN-ICC, stresses the need to strengthen current international human rights regimes and says that not only governments but also that TNCs and the WTO should be held accountable to those affected by their actions.[19] The Secretary-General of the International Chamber of Commerce, Maria Cattaui, responded to the *Human Development Report* in an open letter to the *Financial Times* in which she said the report was 'on the wrong track in calling for a mandatory code of conduct for multinationals' since binding rules 'would put the clock back to a bygone era'. She was of course correct and the last thing the ICC wants is the kind of controls that existed in the past. As transnationals have become bigger and more influential, they have ignored codes of conduct or claimed to be self-regulating. Now, more than ever, codes of conduct are needed just as they are being abandoned. Corporate engineering is not new but it should be understood that corporations are only interested in doing more and better business. This can most easily be achieved with a minimum of restraints. The great argument now and in the coming years is how much restraint can be applied to them on behalf of the people and to what extent they will work to evade such restraints with the connivance of *laissez-faire* governments.[20]

'Privatization is the act of cannibalism made possible by the forces of globalization.'[21] This description may appear dramatic but becomes less so when a poor country such as Mozambique sees its major state assets being bought up by outsiders. The Western push for privatization really means globalization by another name: structural adjustment programmes in Africa that include privatization force small economies to open up their controlled assets to foreign takeovers which are a form of asset stripping. Market fundamentalism was meant to rescue economies from the dead hand of the state and put them in the safe hands of bankers, technocrats and the thrusting new class of entrepreneurs. But as countries such as Ghana, Mozambique and Uganda have found, 'the enrichment of foreign asset-strippers and domestic political cronies disguised as entrepreneurs has been a main outcome of privatization'.[22] In South Africa privatization became a bone of contention between the ANC and COSATU: the main beneficiaries of privatization were the new black business elité.

Globalization has produced some of the fiercest political arguments in many years: broadly, its advocates are the rich, developed West and its opponents the representatives of the South or developing nations and that division at once defines what the argument is about. As one opponent of the process puts it: 'There are essentially three "classes" or "actors" in the world political economy: the advocates and beneficiaries of globalization; the adversaries and exploited classes and states; and those who experience both exploitation and benefits and waver in their response.'[23] Almost all Africa falls into the second category though mining or commodity export enclaves that clearly enrich local classes may favour the process. Adversaries of globalization make up in numbers what they lack in financial power and that goes to the root of the problem. South Africa, with its long-standing links with British and American business, is an interesting borderline case. Arguments about globalization invoke the shades of Fukuyama and the 'end of history' for supporters of globalization argue that it is the last stage in history in which all countries and economies will be linked together in a single market. At the turn of the century three African countries – Algeria, Nigeria and South Africa – were on the margin and liable to be enmeshed in the globalization process but most of the rest had such small economies that, with luck, they were not worth bothering about and so might just have a chance to organize themselves before they lose all control of their economies. The weakening of the nation state is a necessary corollary of the extension of globalization. 'Globalization, defined here simply as the intensification of economic, political, social and cultural relations across borders, has gradually eroded and weakened the integrity of the nation-state as an autonomous, independent actor.'[24] The adjustment policies imposed on African economies by the World Bank and IMF have opened their economies to transnational actors on the one hand while debt has been used as a lever to direct domestic production away from industry and towards primary products for export on the other. 'Moreover, the required privatization of public industries has frequently led to take-overs by foreign companies and multinationals, as sufficient national capital has rarely been available.'[25] Weak states with large resources are a natural target for the globalizers.

THE IMPACT OF GLOBALIZATION UPON AFRICA

The process of globalization faces Africa with huge challenges that, by and large, it is ill-equipped to meet. Countries that are deeply dependent upon aid and desperate to attract investment have little bargaining power and since both aid and investment are largely dependent upon the 'seal of approval' of the international financial institutions and since, in turn, these are controlled by the major *laissez-faire* Western states that are pushing globalization, Africa will find it extremely difficult not to be 'globalized'. One of its main hopes is support from the United Nations. 'The UN approach in economic and social issues is different from that of the WTO and Bretton Woods institutions. The latter promote the empowerment of the market, a minimal role for the state and rapid liberalization. Most UN agencies, on the other hand, operate under the belief that public intervention (internationally and nationally) is necessary to enable basic needs and human rights to be fulfilled and that the market alone cannot do the job and in many cases in fact hinders the job being done.'[26] The same writer adds: 'The North has leverage in the Bretton Woods institutions and the WTO to shape the content of globalization to serve their needs and to formulate policies which the developing countries have to take on.' It is not true that trade liberalization is to the benefit of all; nor has this ever been the case. While some countries gain substantially from liberalization most of the poorest countries have not gained at all and some have lost. The proposal of MAI (considered above) was clearly designed to assist foreign investors to expand their activities and protect them from almost any kind of interference by states that would impose conditions on their operations. Very clearly, as the new century began, most developing countries faced a dilemma: open up to globalization in the hope of obtaining some benefits; or continue by various means to protect fragile economies and risk being bypassed in the global free-for-all. At the top of any agenda for developing countries ought to be the question of greater rights of participation in the decision-making processes of the World Bank, IMF and WTO, though how this is to be achieved is unclear. Despite current claims on behalf of an all-powerful market, the idea that the market knows best and that state intervention in development and industrialization is always counter-productive is not borne out by past history.

Sub-Saharan Africa represents the least economically dynamic region in the world and, according to the World Bank's 1997 report *Global Economic Perspectives and the Developing Countries*, although the region was on the threshold of a period of sustained growth at 4 per cent a year this would not be enough to reverse the region's marginalization. By 2020 sub-Saharan Africa's share of global GDP will only have risen from 1.2 per cent (1997) to 1.7 per cent and will have lost ground to more dynamic countries, especially in Asia. Over the same period, sub-Saharan Africa's share of developing world GDP was expected to fall from 7.6 per cent in 1992 to 5.8 per cent in 2020. South Africa may be the largest, most dynamic economy in the region but that did not alter the fact of belonging to a region that in world terms was marginal. This report had particular relevance for South Africa, which at that time was enjoying a sense of release from apartheid and a new acceptance by the rest of the world. It was, however, in danger of taking apparently attractive decisions that it might later regret. In its search for capital investment and reintegration into the world economic system South Africa appeared too ready to accept uncritically all the Western economic orthodoxies that always work to the advantage of the major economies but often spell continuing dependence if not total manipulation for developing countries. Further, in its desire for racial harmony, was Pretoria too ready to give way to white business pressures at the expense of justice for the majority of its people? At the beginning of the new century South Africa was the one major investment attraction for international business in Africa: while this was of vital importance to its economic development it also laid the country open to globalizing pressures that it might later come to regret.

At the other extreme of the continent, Algeria under Chadli Benjedid in the early 1990s had abandoned socialism and turned back to capitalism. This meant the resubordination of Algeria's economic future to French economic influence so that the retreat from socialism was simultaneously a retreat from nationalism as far as economic and social policies were concerned.[27] According to this writer, Europe deliberately held back support from Benjedid as his political-economic crisis deepened since it wished to force the Algerian government to accept the rescheduling of Algeria's debt and all that that entailed – the obligation to undertake a structural adjustment programme as dictated by the IMF. 'After January 1992, no funds were released until this objective had been attained and the promise of funds was used as a lever to secure compliance. All other policy considerations – stability, democracy, respect for human rights – were sacrificed to this objective.'[28] Thus, the EU sought to impose rescheduling and structural adjustment on Algeria so as to secure its integration into a free trade area dominated by Europe. Paris was the source of this strategy and France expected its EU partners to defer to its 'vital interests'. Such a self-seeking French policy did not assist Algeria achieve peace in its civil war but it did safeguard the French hold on the Algerian economy. Thus, at the height of the Algerian civil war and as the West generally was insisting upon good governance and democracy in the aftermath of the Cold War, in fact it was never serious about promoting these values in Algeria and turned a blind eye to the flouting of these values by the Algerian army.

There have been various attempts to promote regionalism in Africa ever since independence, because it was argued that stronger units would be better able to bargain with the EU or US. In fact, few of these regional arrangements have come to anything and regionalism as such appears to have done little to boost internal African trade. On the other hand, in contrast to this formal approach, there has been a huge growth in Africa of informal trading systems, a form of globalization indigenous to the continent. Unfortunately, regionalism has always suffered because of the fear that a dominant member of the bloc will reap most of the advantages: Nigeria in ECOWAS, Kenya in the East African Community, South Africa in SADC. Such suspicions are understandable but unless they are overcome Africa stands little chance of presenting even a moderate show of unity against globalizing pressures from outside. 'Globalization is generally thought of in terms of multinational companies and the changing relations between nation states and peoples as they become enmeshed in the world economy.' However, a study of transnational trade of second-economy traders between Africa and Europe[29] provides some interesting insights into African entrepreneurial capacities. The story of traders from Congo-Kinshasa and Congo-Brazzaville to Europe focuses on individuals operating in the interstices of these larger national entities and on how they manage to take advantage of the way the world economy now works. A key aspect of globalization, of great importance to Africa, is the size and geographical range of the African diaspora and the close family networks that operate as a result. Drugs, illegal trade, the 'internationalization of the family' represent a significant aspect of Africa's 'private' globalization activities.

During the nearly 60 years since the end of World War II the world has become an unmistakably harsher place. There are many reasons for this: the confrontation of the Cold War, the doubling of the world's population with the commensurate increase in pressures upon resources and what would appear to be a fundamental change for the worse in the power attitudes of the rich, developed nations. During this period the entire continent of Africa became independent to find in both economic and power terms that it was the poorest, least influential region in the world. Ever since the independence era of the 1960s African states have been trying to find their own place in the world while dealing with the leftover problems of colonialism; they have done so in a climate that was rarely favourable to the independence of small states even though so many had appeared on the world scene. Yet in 1945 'everyone was a Keynesian'. 'The idea that the market should be allowed to make major social and political decisions; that the state should reduce its role in the economy; that corporations should be given total freedom; or that trade unions should be curbed and citizens given much less rather than more social protection – such ideas were utterly foreign to the spirit of the time.'[30] Such perceptions favoured small states newly emerging on the world scene; their replacement by the market forces arguments central to globalization has created a world inimical to the freedoms so essential to the growth of a small new state. Privatization ought to make small as well as big markets more successful but in fact the point of privatization, as promoted by the IFIs, has not been about economic efficiency or improved services to the people but about the transfer of wealth from the public purse, where it might be used to benefit the people, to the private purse where it would not do so. Further, by its nature globalization degrades democracy while the post-1990 rise of US unilateralist power and arrogance has threatened or downgraded every institution, beginning with the UN, that opposed, or threatened to oppose, US policies. 'Thus, the only international organizations which have any real influence on world affairs are those economic and financial organizations (the World Bank, IMF, WTO) where, often, decisions are influenced and even prepared by private organizations such as the International Chamber of Commerce, the Club of London (private lending banks), or the various committees dealing with norms and standards. Financially dependent on the developed countries, the World Bank, the IMF and the WTO are effectively under their political control.'[31] This is not an encouraging climate for weak economies struggling to achieve development without surrendering their freedom of action.

We may live in a capitalist-oriented world and most Africans are capitalist-oriented rather than otherwise, but 'What is radically new is its (capitalism's) claiming of the market as the sole foundation of its philosophy and organization, and the sole criterion of its further development, so that a cumulative process is unleashed which it is less and less able to control'.[32] The globalized market, almost by definition, disregards collective needs in an individual country or society. It has to impose the one criterion of market behaviour everywhere and the idea has gown that the market will alone solve all economic and social problems. In opposition to this view, the first aim of all economic and social organization ought to be to satisfy the priority needs of the people, all the people. That, of course, is what the African nationalists of the 1960s claimed and however much they or their successors have deviated from that nationalist aim globalization has further exacerbated their failings as most of them have found themselves in the grip of a process they cannot begin to control. The proponents of globalization have been so successful in their propaganda that no one – even at the top levels – questions it. There is no debate, only a 'take it or leave it' response. 'Unless global pressures for profit maximization and more intense competition are corrected by some worldwide public intervention, they have the effect of making some poorer and others richer. Opponents of globalization, in making their case, may thus counter its ostensible advantages by referring to the new poverty it brings about, especially through the destruction of local economies and the refusal to prioritize the essential needs of the population.'³³

In part, but only in part, Africa is accommodating itself to globalization in so far as it is able to make the decision to do so independently of the pressures that are constantly exerted upon it from the G7/8 and IFIs. On the other hand, much of the continent's population is irrelevant to the process anyway and is hardly touched by the world's formal economy. Over the last decade of the twentieth century this was recognized by the donors who changed their policy from one of promoting development to one of providing 'global poor relief'. In the North the idea of a national economy is coming to be replaced by the concept of an interdependent globalized world. This idea of interdependence applies to Africa in a number of ways. There are vigorous African informal economies that cross borders illegally and encompass a range of activities such as the international drug trade. Ironically, informal activities have been greatly enhanced by the structural adjustment programmes and other conditionalities imposed on African states from outside. An ever-increasing number of African entrepreneurs have opted out of state structures to operate illegally on their own and their activities, in turn, have helped to accelerate the disintegration of central state power and so give rise to the phenomenon of 'failed states'.

It is against this background of globalization and relentless international pressures that the world's weakest continent faces the twenty-first century. The idea of an African renaissance was first mooted by Thabo Mbeki in 1997. If there is to be such a renaissance it can only come from within the continent and must be spearheaded by Africans at every level. A renaissance that makes Africa viable and gives it a meaningful voice in world affairs would be to everyone's advantage. Whether it can be achieved remains to be seen.

An African
Renaissance

The beginning of the new century has witnessed the transformation of the OAU into the African Union, the launch of a New Partnership for Africa's Development (NEPAD) and the South African insistence that the time has come for an African renaissance. At the same time Africa faces the new neo-colonialism represented by the World Bank, the IMF, the World Trade Organization – the international financial institutions – that, whatever their ostensible purposes, have been turned into instruments of Western manipulation and control. The question of how Africa can shake off dependence upon the outside world is quite separate from engagement with that world. Despite the fanfare about NEPAD and the visit to Africa in July 2003 by US President George W. Bush, the West at most is only marginally interested in Africa as Africa, as opposed to what it can extract from it, and if African leaders pause to think about this they should be relieved rather than upset. If past history, both colonial and post-colonial, is any guide neither European nor American interest has done the continent any favours. NEPAD, the launch of the African Union and an African renaissance are closely intertwined as part of the same exercise: how to rid Africa of the weight of external pressures that force it to develop as the West requires instead of in its own fashion.

The African problems that engage external attention have been well rehearsed: poverty, lack of development, aid dependence, debt, corruption, civil wars, lack of democracy, failed states. It is a depressing list. The question for Africa is, how best to tackle these problems? Awareness of their debilitating impact upon Africa's potential for growth has been behind these new continental initiatives. Let us begin with the new African Union. There will have been no point in transforming the OAU into a new African Union unless the core issue of enabling Africa to speak with one voice is tackled. The newly independent nations of Africa rejected moves towards real union in the immediate post-independence era, for understandable reasons, and instead opted for a weak OAU. However, the need for African unity has never been more urgent than today, as the process of world globalization is pushed ever harder by a dominant West, and should be at the top of the continental agenda. Fifty-four weak states will be permanently subservient to Western interests and pressures unless they learn to act as one in relation to the United States and the European Union. Even the strong work together rather than separately. The donor nations, for example, invoke IMF or World Bank conditionalities when they wish to evade one-to-one decisions and the EU bargains as a collective with individual African countries. Given the power disparities between the West and Africa it becomes essential that the African Union (AU) should speak for the whole continent, most especially at the present time when the United States is seeking new bases in Africa. The aims of the African Union, as set out in its charter – unity, harmonization of policies, economic integration – are impeccably correct but are they also meaningless? Africa has made many attempts to achieve regional economic integration and ECOWAS and SADC are at present the best examples of this but what the continent needs is a single economic voice.

The second task for the AU, one that is only too apparent at the present time, is the need for it to take control of peacekeeping in Africa. In troubled Sierra Leone, Africa appeared only too ready to allow the former imperial power, Britain, to do the peacekeeping. When Côte d'Ivoire went up in flames, the African Union's first chairman, President Thabo Mbeki of South Africa, had a unique opportunity to involve the AU in a peacekeeping exercise; instead, he gave his blessing to a Paris initiative under the arch neo-colonialist, President Jacques Chirac. And in the case of Liberia, reeling after 14 years of civil war, the people all clamoured for US intervention to bring them peace even when ECOWAS was organizing a peacekeeping operation. Africa does not lack for soldiers and it is time some of these were placed permanently at the disposal of the AU for peacekeeping operations anywhere on the continent. African independence owed much to United Nations pressures in the 1950s and 1960s and the integrity of the UN is of greatest importance to its weakest members, yet when the United States and Britain arrogantly bypassed the UN to invade Iraq without a UN mandate to do so, Africa was noticeably mute in its response to this deliberate downsizing of the world body, giving rise to the suspicion that it was desperate not to offend the two Western powers because it was relying upon their generosity to make NEPAD work.

And what has the AU been prepared to say, let alone do, about events in Democratic Republic of Congo (DRC), including the predatory activities of the Congo's neighbours, especially Uganda and Rwanda, whose raping of that country's resources and arming of its militias is straight international piracy, while the ethnic violence in the Ituri region of north-east Congo between Lendu and Hema threatens to develop into full-scale genocide? Everyone, it seems, would avoid a rescue operation in DRC and no one seems willing to point any finger of blame at the country's neighbours. At the 2001 Labour Party conference in Britain, Tony Blair in his 'concerned for Africa' mode, said, 'I tell you if Rwanda happened again today as it did in 1994, when a million people were slaughtered in cold blood, we would have a moral duty to act there.' The evidence in 2003 was overwhelming that a comparable slaughter akin to genocide was taking place in eastern DRC and human rights estimates suggested that some four million people had died over the preceding five years. Blair had also said, 'The state of Africa is a scar on the conscience of the world. But if the world as a community focused on it, we could heal it. And if we don't, it will become deeper and angrier.' Given the nature of politics, it is unrealistic to expect that Britain should act alone yet it did take action, but action that would lessen the chances of stopping the carnage. After many delays the UN Security Council voted in July 2003 to impose an arms embargo on DRC yet Britain and the US would not allow this to extend to Rwanda and Uganda, which back the militias killing civilians in eastern DRC. Both Rwanda and Uganda are substantial recipients of British aid and Britain could exert major influence upon them, yet it prefers to turn a blind eye to their activities in DRC. Rwanda has been heavily involved in the DRC's North and South Kivu provinces where its officers have plundered vast amounts of gold, diamonds and coltan while claiming to be fighting against the *Interahamwe* extremists responsible for the 1994 genocide. According to a senior UN official based in Goma, 'Rwanda has been hiding behind the guilt the outside world has for having failed to stop the genocide (in 1994). It has been able to do what it likes in DRC without fear of real criticism – and now four million, maybe more, have died in a conflict fuelled by Rwanda.'[1] Given the West's past record, this reluctance to intervene in DRC is, perhaps, to be expected, despite Tony Blair's brave words. But what of Africa? Article Four – Principles – of the Constitution Act of the African Union lays down

(h) The right of the Union to intervene in a Member State pursuant to a decision of the Assembly in respect of grave circumstances, namely war crimes, genocide and crimes against humanity.

There could not be a clearer case demanding intervention than DRC and there is no ambiguity about the above principle; yet there was no sign that the AU or any member state was prepared to invoke it. Not only did the AU act like its predecessor the OAU and do nothing about the internal affairs of a member state (DRC) but it seemed ready also to condone or ignore the blatant piracy of that state's neighbours. Until Africa is seen to be ready to deal with such crimes on the continent, there can be little hope of an African renaissance that has any meaning.

The NEPAD concept arose out of the October 2001 meeting in Abuja, Nigeria, when African leaders reviewed the dangers of terrorism. They also discussed the New Africa Initiative (NAI) that had been formulated in July 2000 at the final OAU summit in Lusaka. They agreed to rename NAI as NEPAD and establish its headquarters in Pretoria. They envisaged three African commitments: clear accountability and open government; an end to gross human rights abuses; and an end to African wars and the imposition of African peacekeeping. In return, the West would provide more aid for infrastructure, development and education as well as increased investment and the lifting of existing trade barriers. This represented a neat equation and though the initiative should not be decried, it was depressingly similar to past occasions when, in return for promises of good governance, Africa asks for more aid. It is surely a humiliation, to put it no higher, that 40 years after independence Africa is collectively promising to behave well in return for more aid. Libya's Col. Gaddafi put his finger on the blatant neo-colonialism of the NEPAD concept when he said: 'We are not children who need to be taught. They (the colonial powers) made us slaves, they called us inferior but we have regained our African name and culture.' Thus, it has to be asked, will NEPAD do anything other than tie Africa more closely to the West just when it should be breaking free? The only NEPAD initiative that would make ground-breaking sense would be one that brought an end to US and EU subsidies to their farming sectors so that they opened their markets to African agricultural products in the way President Bush asks Africa to open its markets to the more advanced Western economies.

NEPAD presupposes a new relationship between Africa and the North, especially Britain, France and the EU, and the United States. This requires us, first, to look at the old relationship. At the beginning of the 1960s the leaders of newly independent Africa nonetheless recognized that the West was determined to continue controlling the economies of Africa and this has not changed. Poverty, and the manipulation of the poor by the rich, is central to the world's current problems. Almost all international gatherings over the last 10 to 15 years have revealed a hardening of attitudes between North and South with both sides finding confrontation easier than consensus. Moreover, no matter how many initiatives have been launched, for example over debt relief, the rich get richer and the poor poorer, and though we have the knowledge as well as the resources to bridge all the gaps that exist, the rich do not have the will to do anything of the sort. Those who possess wealth and power do not want to equip the poor to rival them. Demonstrations against the annual meetings of the G8, the World Bank and IMF, the WTO or the Davos meeting are symbolic of the yawning divide that separates North and South. Far from altering anything, these demonstrations simply emphasize the fact that the world is divided into two camps: smug power facing desperate poverty. Finding solutions to an unequal relationship always founders on two realities: the first, that the weak have very few weapons to hand with which to confront the strong; and the second, that the strong are always determined, by whatever means, to maintain their advantages. Thus, when we consider NEPAD, we must ask: what does the EU want of Africa and what does the United States want?

The manipulation of Third World states – especially in Africa – has been part of a relentless policy pursued by the United States and the old metropolitan powers Britain and France, ever since decolonization took place. It has been evolved as a form of indirect rule. Aid has been the West's main weapon in this manipulation process and the attitudes that divide the rich donors from their African recipients were formed during the 1960s and have changed little since that time. It is historically instructive that the donors only recognized the value of aid after African countries had become independent; prior to independence, colonies were largely supposed to pay for themselves. As a broad generalization, aid became a weapon of economic management for donors while for recipient rulers it relieved them of responsibilities to their people that could not have been avoided if there had been no aid. The result of decades of aid has been to create aid dependency on the one hand and mountains of debt on the other, which between them deprive African countries of any freedom of economic choice. Further, it is pertinent to ask just what aid has achieved over the last 40 years of the twentieth century and why so many African countries, despite aid, are either no better off or even worse off than they were at independence. It has become difficult for donors any more to justify aid as an instrument of development when so little development has taken place, so instead they have switched the justification to the pursuit of good governance. According to Phoebe Griffiths of the UK Foreign Policy Centre aid provided through the IMF or World Bank has created globalized dependency, which 'means that because most of their revenue is generated externally (whether through aid or mining revenues), African governments are more accountable to the outside world than to their own people'.[2] The most obvious demands for Africa to make in any future aid forum ought to cover three areas: the elimination of debt followed by a clear statement that no more aid is requested; an insistence upon fairer trade which means the elimination of Western agricultural subsidies; and finally, the introduction of democracy in the economic decision-making bodies such as the World Bank – that is, one country one vote rather than weighted voting according to financial contributions. It is naïve to suppose that a NEPAD funded by the West will do anything other than tie Africa more closely into an economic system it cannot control.

At the G8 summit of July 2002 in Canada a deputation of African leaders including South Africa's Thabo Mbeki and Nigeria's Olusegun Obasanjo were invited to attend and present the case for NEPAD. They obtained a firm promise of an additional US$1 billion of aid for Africa (US$22 billion was promised Russia, the former superpower). Now, whatever NEPAD is about, it should not require African leaders acting as supplicants, like Oliver Twist, asking for more. Britain's Prime Minister, Tony Blair, is reportedly a firm supporter of NEPAD, which is an African-led initiative, but just what do statements of support for the initiative mean? Will NEPAD simply legitimize the present North-South relationship under a new name and attract marginally more aid for Africa? Or does it amount to something more valuable? At the March 2002 Monterrey summit in Mexico – the International Conference on Financing for Development with the grand title 'Confronting the Challenge of Financing Development, A Global Response' – which discussed eradicating African poverty and elaborated on the Millennium Development Goals, targets were set for universal education and a two-thirds reduction of child deaths for 2015. President Bush spoke of a 'compact for development', in which US aid would only go to countries that rooted out corruption, restructured their economies and opened their markets. Then reluctantly, under intense EU pressure (since the Europeans did not wish to bear the greater part of the aid 'burden'), Bush agreed a small increase in US aid from US$10 billion to US$15 billion by 2006 (a rise from 0.1 per cent to 0.15 per cent of GDP as opposed to the EU average of 0.33 per cent which was to rise to 0.39 per cent, both far below the target of 0.7 per cent). The inclusion of rooting out corruption in President Bush's 'compact for development' must have appeared unbelievably arrogant to anyone from Africa or elsewhere in the South at a time when the Enron scandal, the largest corporate corruption case in history, was unfolding.

There was a repeat performance for the 2003 G8 summit. On 28 May the Heads of State and Government Implementation Committee of NEPAD met in Abuja, Nigeria, to urge the international community to ensure that African issues remained on the global agenda. However, the British development charity, ActionAid, said Africa had been let down once again by the G8. In its report, *Wishful Thinking,* it concluded that there had been less action since the 2002 G8 launch of the Africa Action Plan than there was before. According to *Wishful Thinking*, 'The United States has blocked negotiations which would have given poor people access to cheap drugs for AIDS. European states, most visibly France and Germany, have refused to dismantle agricultural subsidies which undermine the livelihood of farmers in the developing world'. While the G8 met at Evian in France, at the end of May, another alternative summit,

Summit for Another World, met at Annemasse and Geneva. This ended on 31 May having expressed doubts about NEPAD and claimed it would not constitute a true opportunity for fair relations between Africa and the industrialized world. The head of the Africa Network Forum for African Alternatives (in Dakar), Demba Moussa Dembele, said: 'NEPAD must be rejected by all African people because it is not anything different from structural adjustment policies – in fact it is even worse because we now have African leaders championing it.' The Vice-Chairman of the Southern African Institute of International Affairs in South Africa, Moeletsi Mbeki, said: 'The dependency of African governments seems to be at the centre of the relationship with the G8.' He added: 'After 40 years of self-rule it is sad that the rulers have no idea about how to mobilize African skills and capital to solve some of Africa's problems.'[3]

Almost as soon as NEPAD was born British MPs were suggesting that Britain ought not to support it unless first President Mbeki of South Africa had exerted pressure upon Zimbabwe's President Mugabe to change his ways; this was to revert to classic aid tactics: behave politically as we (the donors) tell you and aid may be forthcoming. In other words, nothing had changed.

An aspect of the New World Order, first proclaimed by George Bush senior, is the democratization and greater accountability of countries in the South. Now accountability and open government is accepted as part of NEPAD, though exactly what is expected is difficult to analyse. In order for it to work, democracy must be an indigenous growth. It cannot be imposed from without. The people of a country have to want it and fight for it themselves, as has been happening over much of Africa in recent years. Similarly, accountability is not to be imposed from outside. Western governments make much of the need for accountability though their own actions are often not accounted for at all. Uniquely, in 2003, the Zambian parliament voted unanimously to lift ex-president Frederick Chiluba's immunity against prosecution for corruption although such actions are still something of a rarity in Africa. Even so, it was in stark contrast to the action of the Italian parliament, which in July 2003 passed legislation to exempt Prime Minister Silvio Berlusconi from prosecution on massive corruption charges. Once more, the world was treated to the spectacle of double standards. What the West insists Africa must do is contemptuously disregarded in Europe. This raises another question about this most uneven of relationships. Should aid donors that claim to believe in democracy only deliver aid to countries that practise democracy (as the West understands it) or should they continue, as they do, to deliver it to tyrannies and so help keep the tyrants in power? And this leads, naturally, to another question: what to do about the decision-makers of major institutions that govern so much that takes place in

Africa. These comprise the United Nations, the World Bank, the IMF and the G8 itself. The United Nations may try to speak on behalf of the poor and least developed yet all-important decisions are subject to scrutiny by the Security Council where the five permanent members have the veto, which enables them to override the wishes of the majority, as they frequently do. The World Bank and the IMF are even less democratic in terms of either transparency or democracy where the weighted voting power of the major donors always enables the West to control policy. At the beginning of the twenty-first century Britain, France, Germany, Japan, Canada, Russia, Saudi Arabia and the United States controlled 46 per cent of World Bank and 48 per cent of IMF voting rights. The US always appoints the head of the World Bank, Europe of the IMF. These institutions above all, since so much of their work concerns the developing world, should themselves be made fully transparent and democratic, with one country one vote, no matter the size of their monetary contributions. The democratic structure of the WTO has been subverted by the rich nations who make key decisions in conclave before open sessions take place. Given such practices in the developed world, why should African countries be expected dutifully to accept Western prescriptions about accountability?

NEPAD raises awkward questions about Western trading practices. For example, would the President of the United States – any President – risk losing votes by insisting upon a reduction of US living standards that would follow if certain measures to achieve a more equitable world trading system were adopted? The most obvious of these would be an end to subsidies to American farmers so as to allow African agricultural products a chance to penetrate the huge American market while also bringing an end to subsidized US cotton undermining African cotton production. Similar considerations apply to the EU with its iniquitous CAP support system for its farming sector. Another cause for concern is the constant Western pressure upon African countries to privatize state assets. Such privatization in a poor country where few of its citizens are able to purchase shares merely ensures that Western companies can move in to buy up the assets whose control may then pass out of the continent. The strong argue for free trade (though in the matter of agriculture they ignore their own precepts) while the poor need protection. Dependence upon commodities accounts for 76 per cent of the continent's agricultural exports. Almost all initiatives emanating from the North require Africa to open its markets to outside competition while ignoring the fact that the North, where it has political groups to protect, does not do the same thing.

The launching of the NEPAD initiative by Africa's two most powerful leaders, Obasanjo of Nigeria and Mbeki of South Africa, certainly did not receive universal approval. In an upbeat appraisal, S. K. B. Asante wrote:

NEPAD is the most significant continent-wide economic initiative to emerge in contemporary Africa. It is an initiative by African leaders, based on a common vision and a firm and shared conviction that they have a pressing duty to eradicate poverty and to place their countries, both collectively and individually, on a path of sustainable growth and development while, at the same time, participating actively in the world economy... What makes NEPAD different is the African political commitment behind it. For the first time, Africa is offering to move away from a relationship of dependency with the developed world and replace it with one of development by equals through co-operation, mutual understanding and partnership in the global economy. NEPAD is an African solution to an African problem; it is also a challenge to the developed world.[4]

The sting is in the tail: is the vision to be shared by the rich West and will it provide the funds and what will be the price? Asante's enthusiasm was not shared by Richard Dowden. He first pointed out that NEPAD is a creed setting out Africa's development aims and governance principles and adopted – in theory – by all 52 countries in the African Union. However, he then suggested: 'But there is a strong suspicion that most African leaders regard it as a new hymn sheet from which they must sing for their aid. Like hymns, the words may be beautiful and the feelings divine but understanding them, let alone following the precepts, are far from the minds of many leaders.'[5]

When in March 2002, Presidents Obasanjo and Mbeki went to Harare as representatives of the Commonwealth to try to persuade Mugabe to make concessions following his flawed elections and, for example, appoint a government of national unity, they came away empty-handed. Subsequently they went to London where they were joined by the Australian Prime Minister, John Howard, and had to make their recommendation as to whether or not Zimbabwe should be suspended from the Commonwealth. Mbeki still wanted to give Mugabe another chance but was constrained as the architect of NEPAD since he wanted to obtain more Western aid for it. When he spoke with Tony Blair over the telephone the British Prime Minister warned him that NEPAD would have little credibility if Africa gave the impression that it would tolerate Mugabe's excesses. So Mbeki endorsed Zimbabwe's suspension from the Commonwealth.

NEPAD suffered a setback in July 2003 when Zimbabwe's Mugabe snubbed a high-level EU delegation to the African Union summit in Maputo. The EU President, Romano Prodi, had come to the summit with the offer of €250 million (£170 million) for a standing African peacekeeping force but he was obliged to admit that he had watered down the offer because 'we face a wall in any contacts, and that wall is Zimbabwe'. The previous April the Europe-Africa summit, due to take place in Lisbon, had been cancelled because of EU resistance to inviting Mugabe. At the end of the Maputo summit Romano Prodi said: 'Lots of ideas are flying around but at the moment we are getting nowhere. On the issue of money for the standing African force, we had a proposal, but for the moment we are just saying we will look at funding if and when a force is created.'[6] The idea of a standing African force had been around for 40 years and had always been treated with extreme caution by African states, many of which opposed the concept altogether. Perhaps the withholding of the EU offer to fund this particular AU operation had less to do with Zimbabwean intransigence than African suspicions of the project and of European interest in it. African leaders have complained more than once that while the UN deploys peacekeeping forces round the world it is very ready to emphasize that Africans should do the peacekeeping in Africa. Certainly, UN peacekeeping efforts in Africa – Congo, Somalia, Rwanda – have been less than rewarding for the reputation of the world body.

The future of NEPAD must be considered in relation to globalization: are the two concepts compatible? A growing proportion of people worldwide, especially in the developing world, oppose globalization yet seem unable to prevent its spread despite all their protests. If NEPAD is to mean anything it must be about altering the balance between rich and poor and globalization – the rapid spread of corporate power – hardly seems the instrument to alter the balance except in one direction only, towards the rich. There have been too many uncritical African responses to globalization as though the process is inevitable when, in fact, it is nothing of the kind. There appears to be a developing consensus in Africa: if you cannot beat it, join it. It is an attitude that turns the state into a conduit for capital rather than an instrument for controlling it so as to ensure that it is used to bring about greater social equity. The West, greatly assisted by the international financial institutions which it controls, appears to have been only too successful in selling the 'inevitability' of globalization to those countries least able to cope with it.

What, then, will constitute an African renaissance? Nelson Mandela first used the term in 1997 and Thabo Mbeki has sponsored the idea ever since. First, any real change for the better in Africa's situation can only be effected from within; if the renaissance relies upon assistance from outside the continent it will be a non-starter. Africa must put Africa to rights; outsiders, whatever their proclaimed objectives, always have their own agendas and these, naturally, favour their particular interests. Moreover, it is inherently unlikely that any renaissance can take place as long as African economies remain in the grip of aid donors and the international financial institutions. Too many African leaders look outside the continent for solutions to their problems instead of relying upon self-transformation. They do so for two main reasons of which one is excusable, the other not. Most preside over such small weak economies that they have only limited room in which to manoeuvre; many, however, are more concerned to keep themselves in power at almost any cost rather than pursue genuine development. The cost, as a rule, is accepting Western capitalist pressures and adopting policies approved by the donors.

The prospects for an African renaissance at the present time are not encouraging for a continent that has a higher proportion of civil wars and failed states than any other region in the world. The best hope for an African renaissance lies with Nigeria and South Africa, the continent's two regional great powers, creating a working axis between them. Thabo Mbeki is President of the most developed and potentially richest country in Africa and he has done much to bring both the AU and NEPAD into existence. South Africa should be the continent's economic powerhouse: it is self-sufficient in food, has the best industrial-commercial infrastructure in Africa (the Johannesburg Stock Exchange is ranked tenth in world terms) and is a storehouse of mineral wealth. It also has substantial military capacity that should be used for peacekeeping and is one of the very few African countries strong enough to pursue a relatively independent foreign policy. Nigeria possesses oil, has Africa's largest market and a highly developed entrepreneurial capacity. It has also, through ECOMOG, deployed its military forces on a number of peacekeeping operations, an activity in which it has built up a certain expertise. Neither country is in receipt of aid, except on the margins, and both are major exporters. If these two states work together to spearhead an African renaissance there is a genuine possibility that it could become a reality.

The problems are daunting and Africa has fallen into a habit of dependence that must be broken. When the two old colonial powers, Britain and France, suddenly show a renewed interest in Africa, as they have done over the turn of the century, the continent should be wary. Both Tony Blair's interest in NEPAD and Jacques Chirac's sudden rescue operation in Côte d'Ivoire reek of neo-colonialism. In a speech delivered in Cape Town in January 1999, Britain's Prime Minister told his South African hosts: 'Real development can only come through partnership. Not the rich dictating to the poor. Not the poor demanding from the rich. But matching rights and responsibilities.' Yet despite such Clintonesque rhetoric there are few signs of any real changes in British-African policy. The same is true of France. The Twenty-second Franco-African Summit was held in Paris over 20–21 February 2003. At this summit Chirac promised increased co-operation for the realization of NEPAD. He urged his colleagues in the developed world to join France's initiative to remove trade barriers to exports from African countries. In stately language he lamented the growing gap between rich and poor and said he saw in NEPAD 'real hope for Africa to fill that gap that is still keeping Africa at arm's length from the global economy'. He avoided mentioning the huge efforts France exerts to maintain CAP.

When a hard right wing US Republican President decides to visit Africa the continent should analyse his every move and promise, with courtesy of course, but also with suspicion. Already, for example, Democratic Republic of Congo, Djibouti, Egypt, Gabon, The Gambia, Ghana, Madagascar, Mauritania, Rwanda, Seychelles, Sierra Leone, Togo and Tunisia have allowed themselves to be bullied by Washington into agreeing to accept the iniquitous US demand that in the case of US citizens committing crimes in their countries that qualify for reference to the ICC, they bypass trial by the ICC and instead send them back to the United States. Much has been said and written since the beginning of the new century about the spread of US worldwide hegemony and this will affect Africa as it will just about everywhere else. As it claims to support democracy Washington in fact extends its influence. At some point this extension of its power must be halted: '... a civilization that purports to be based on the twin pillars of democracy and the rule of law cannot for long impose itself on the rest of the world by systematically betraying those principles.'[7] Meanwhile, increasingly warily, the world adjusts to overwhelming US power. Prior to his July 2003 African trip, President Bush spoke at a US-Africa business summit in Washington. The President outlined his optimism about Africa. Peace and security were the first goals, he said, and then the fight against hunger. But the US could not assist this process if some governments refused to import genetically engineered food. 'The ban of these countries is unfounded; it is unscientific; it is undermining the agricultural future of Africa' (though a cynic might be tempted to substitute America for Africa). He went on to say that another US goal was 'to help African nations develop vibrant, free economies through aid and free trade'. US foreign aid would go to countries whose governments were committed to good governance and invested in health and education. 'Corrupt regimes that give nothing to their people deserve nothing from us.' Present at the Summit was the executive secretary of the UN Economic Commission for Africa, K. Y. Amoako, who called upon the developed countries to reduce and then end their subsidies on agriculture. 'If Africa could freely compete in the agricultural sector, literally millions of women and men could abandon their dependence on aid, revitalize Africa's rural sector and contribute significantly to the global economy.'[8]

When President Bush went on his five-country African trip in July no great enthusiasm was manifested by Africans. The war in Iraq was extremely unpopular in Africa where the US action was seen as bullying and racist. The President's promise of US$15 billion to fight AIDS, after the first welcome, was regarded with suspicion since most of the money, it was suspected, would go back to US pharmaceutical corporations. There was a sense of 'promise fatigue', that too many US promises had not been kept, and there were anti-Bush demonstrations. Oil was very much on the US agenda. Writing in the *Guardian,* Julian Borger said: 'The US is currently importing 1.5 million barrels a day from West Africa, about the same as imports from Saudi Arabia. Meanwhile the US has so far invested US$10 billion (£6 billion) in the West African oil fields this year. The US department of energy expects African oil imports to reach 770 million barrels a year, and US investment in the oil fields to exceed US$10 billion a year.' The US African Oil Policy Initiative Group (an advisory panel) said in 2002 that it considered 'the Gulf of Guinea oil basin of West Africa… as a vital interest in US national security calculations'.[9] Any region thus designated should expect increased US pressures. The same panel, which included Pentagon officials, advised setting up a 'unified command' for Africa. Gen. James Jones, commander of the US European Command with responsibility for African operations, said the US was trying to negotiate the long-term use of a 'family' of military bases across the continent to include large installations for up to 5,000-strong brigades 'that could be robustly used for a significant military presence' and also smaller bases for marines and special forces in times of crisis. An early option, it was hoped, would be Mali while possibly the tiny island state of São Tomé, where large offshore oil has been found, would become the first US base. These reflections alone suggest a US determination to colonize Africa militarily if in no other way. In South Africa, though Bush wanted to talk about Mugabe, Mbeki was only concerned to point out that poverty breeds corruption, lack of democracy, disease, despondency and is thus a fertile breeding ground for terrorism. An editorial in the South African *Mail and Guardian* said:

It would be a mistake to take Mr Bush's compassionate agenda seriously. His tour must be seen for what it is – hard-eyed self-service posing as a mercy mission. African leaders should approach it in the same self-interested spirit. Bush's primary concerns, as they were before the invasion of Iraq, are domestic security, the advancement of corporate America and the securing of strategic assets, mainly oil. The African countries seen as 'pivot states' by US government strategists – primarily Nigeria and South Africa – may have more leverage than usual. Above all, they should raise their voices against glaring US hypocrisy in forcing norms on other countries – increasingly by military means – while regarding itself as above international regulation. The cause of multilateralism was dealt a grievous blow by the Iraqi war, waged in the teeth of overwhelming international condemnation. Africa can exert some beneficial influence in bringing the world's most destructive and irresponsible rogue state back into line.[10]

The US is not often subjected to such strong language and condemnation from Africa; the feelings exist, however, and the US and the West generally should try to understand just how deeply resented their pressures upon the continent can be. It comes back to the question of power. Africa's current (2003) contribution to international trade is 1.7 per cent; its world exports are 2 per cent; its global direct investment 0.9 per cent; its share of global GDP 1 per cent. International relations are all about power: who has it and who does not. Africa has little influence and less power, a fact that attracts the major powers like vultures to a carcase to be exploited. If there is to be an African renaissance it will be achieved by the skilful deployment of what Africa itself controls. NEPAD funded by the West is not the answer.

List of Abbreviations

AAPSO – Afro-Asian People's Solidarity Organisation
ABEDA – Arab Bank for Economic Development in Africa
ACRA – Advisory Council on Religious Affairs (Nigeria)
ADB – African Development Bank
ADEMA – Alliance pour la Démocratie au Mali
ADI – Ação Democratica Independente (São Tomé and Príncipe)
ADS – Alliance Démocratique Senegalaise
AEF – Afrique Equatoriale Francaise
AENF – Alliance of Eritrean National Forces
AFDL – Alliance des Forces Démocratiques pour la Libération du Congo-Zaïre
AFORD – Forum for the Restoration of Democracy
AFRC – Armed Forces Revolutionary Council (Ghana)
AFRC – Armed Forces Revolutionary Council (Sierra Leone)
AFRC – Armed Forces Ruling Council (Nigeria)
AIS – Armée Islamique du Salut (Algeria)
Al Fatah – Movement for the Liberation of Palestine
ALN – Armée de Libération Nationale (Algeria)
AML – Les Amis du Manifeste et de la Liberté
ANAD – Non-Aggression and Defence Aid Agreement
ANAF – Anya Nya Armed Forces (Sudan)
ANC – African National Congress
ANC – African National Council
APC – All-People's Congress – Sierra Leone
APLA – Azanian People's Liberation Army (South Africa)
APPER – African Priority Programme for Economic Recovery
APRC – Alliance for Patriotic Reorientation and Construction (Gambia)
AREMA –Association pour la Renaissance de Madagascar
ARPA – Agricultural Rehabilitation Programme for Africa
ASU – Arab Socialist Union (Libya)
AU – African Union
AWB – Afrikaanse Weerstandsbeweging (Afrikaner Resistance Movement)
AZAPO – Azanian People's Organization (South Africa)
BCC – British Council of Churches
BCP – Basotho Congress Party (Lesotho)
BDG – Bloc Démocratique Gabonais
BDP – Botswana Democratic Party
BMATT – British Military Assistance Training Team

BOSS – Bureau of State Security (South Africa)
BPC – Black People's Convention (South Africa)
CCE – Constitutional Commission for Eritrea
CCM – Chama Cha Mapinduzi (Tanzania)
CDR – Coalition for the Defence of the Republic (Rwanda)
CEAO – Communauté Economique de l'Afrique de l'Ouest
CEEAC - Communauté Economique des Etats de l'Afrique Centrale
CEG – Commonwealth Expert Group
CFTC – Commonwealth Fund for Technical Cooperation
CFU – Commercial Farmers Union (Zimbabwe)
CHOGM – Commonwealth Heads of Government Meeting
CIA – Central Intelligence Agency (US)
CIEC – Conference on International Economic Cooperation
CILSS – Permanent Inter-State Committee on Drought Control in the Sahal
CIO – Central Intelligence Organization (Rhodesia)
CMRN - Comité Militaire de Redressement National (Guinea)
CMRPN – Comité Militaire de Redressement pour le Progrès National
  (Upper Volta)
CMSN – Comité Militaire pour le Salut National (Burundi)
CND – Conseil National de Développement (Niger)
CNE – Commission Nationale des Elections (Congo)
CNL – Conseil National de Libération (Congo (Brazzaville))
CNR – Conseil National Révolutionnaire (Dahomey/Upper Volta)
CNS – Conférence National Souveraine (Congo)
CODESA – Convention for a Democratic South Africa
COMOPS – Combined Operations (Rhodesia)
CONSAS – Constellation of Southern African States
COPCON – Continental Operations Command (Portugal)
COPWE – Commission for the Organization of a Party of the Workers of
  Ethiopia
COSATU – Congress of South African Trade Unions
CPEs – [Communist] Centrally Planned Economies
CPP – Convention People's Party (Ghana)
CPP – Convention People's Party (Togo)
CRUA – Comité Révolutionnaire pour l'Unité et l'Action (Algeria)
CSP – Conseil de Salut du Peuple (Upper Volta)
CUSS – Council for the Unity of Southern Sudan
CUT – Comité de l'Unité Togolaise
DAC – Development Assistance Committee [of OECD]
DFSS – Democratic Front for the Salvation of Somalia
DIFID – Department for International Development (Britain)
DPKO – Department of Peace Keeping Operations (UN)
DRC – Democratic Republic of Congo

DSRP – Democratic and Social Republican Party (Mauritania)
DTA – Democratic Turnhalle Alliance (Namibia)
DUP – Democratic Unionist Party (Sudan)
EAC – East African Community
EACM – East African Common Market
EACSO – East African Common Services Organization
EADB – East African Development Bank
ECA – Economic Commission for Africa
ECOMOG – Economic Community of West African States Monitoring Group
ECOWAS – Economic Community of West African States
EDF – European Development Fund
EEC – European Economic Community
EFTA - European Free Trade Association
ELA – Eritrean Liberation Army
ELF – Eritrean Liberation Front
EPG – Eminent Persons Group
EPLF – Eritrean People's Liberation Front
EPRDF – Ethiopian People's Revolutionary Democratic Front
ERPs – Economic Recovery Programmes
ESAP – Economic Structural Adjustment Programme
FAN – Forces Armées du Nord (Chad)
FAO – Food and Agriculture Organization (UN)
FAPLA – Forças Armadas Populares de Libertação de Angola
FAZ – Forces Armées du Zaïre
FDIC – Front de Défendre des Institutions Constitutionnes (Morocco)
FDLD – Front Démocratique pour la Libération de Djibouti
FDP – Forces Démocratiques et Patriotiques (Congo (Brazzaville))
FDU – Forces Démocratiques Unies (Congo (Brazzaville))
FEDECO – Federal Electoral Commission (Nigeria)
FESTAC – World Black and African Festival of Arts and Culture
FFS – Front des Forces Socialistes (Algeria)
FIS – Front Islamique du Salut (Algeria)
FLN – Front de Libération National (Algeria)
FMG – Federal Military Government (Nigeria)
FNDR – Front National pour la Défense de la Révolution (Madagascar)
FNLA – Frente Nacional de Libertação de Angola
FNLC – Front National pour la Libération du Congo
FNU – Front National Uni (Comoros Islands)
FPI – Front Populaire Ivorien
FPPS – Front Progressiste du Peuple Seychellois
FRELIMO – Frente de Libertação de Mocambique
FROLINAT – Front de Libération Nationale du Tchad
FROLIZI – Front for the Liberation of Zimbabwe

FRUD – Front for the Restoration of Unity and Democracy (Djibouti)
FUA – Frente de Unidade Angolana
GATS – General Agreement on Trade in Services (WTO)
GEAR – Growth, Employment and Redistribution (South Africa)
GIA – Groupe Islamiste Armée (Algeria)
GNPP – Greater Nigerian People's Party
GNU – Government of National Unity (South Africa)
GPC – General People's Congress (Libya)
GRAE – Governo Revolucionario de Angola no Exilo (Angolan government in exile)
GSRP – Gambia Socialist Revolutionary Party
GUM – Grupo Unido de Mocambique
HCE – Haut Comité d'Etat (Algeria)
HCR – High Council of the Republic (Congo)
HNP – Herstigte Nasionale Party (Refounded National Party) (South Africa)
ICJ – International Court of Justice (The Hague)
ICRC – International Committee of the Red Cross
ICTR – International Criminal Tribunal for Rwanda
IDA – International Development Association
IDEP – Institute for Economic Development and Planning
IFAD – International Fund for Agricultural Development (UN)
IFC – International Finance Corporation
IFIs – Independent Financial Institutions
IFP – Inkatha Freedom Party (South Africa)
IGAD – Intergovernmental Authority on Development
IMF – International Monetary Fund
INE – Instituto Nacional de Estatística (Angola)
IP – Independence Party (Mauritius)
JMC – Joint Military Commission
JMNR – Jeunesse du Mouvement National de la Révolution
KADU – Kenya African Democratic Union
KANU – Kenya African National Union
KAU – Kenya Africa Union
KCA – Kikuyu Central Association
KFL – Kenya Federation of Labour
KIM – Federation of the 13 May Movement (Madagascar)
KPU – Kenya People's Union
KY – Kabaka Yekka (King Alone) (Uganda)
LAA – Land Acquisition Act (Zimbabwe)
LCD – Lesotho Congress for Democracy
LLA – Lesotho Liberation Army
LPAI – Ligue Populaire Africaine pour l'Indépendence (French Somaliland)
LUAR – League of Revolutionary Unity and Action (Portugal)

LURD – Liberians United for Reconciliation and Democracy

MAI – Multilateral Agreement on Investment (WTO)

MAPESS – Ministro da Administração Pública, Emprego e Seguanço Social (Angola)

MCP – Malawi Congress Party

MDC – Movement for Democratic Change (Zimbabwe)

MDDI – Mouvement Congolais pour la Démocratie et le Développement Intégral

MDM – Mass Democratic Movement (South Africa)

MDS – Mouvement des Démocrates Socialistes (Tunisia)

MEL – Minimum effective level

MESAN – Mouvement pour l'Evolution Sociale de l'Afrique Noire (Central African Republic)

MFA – Movimento das Forças Armadas (Portugal)

MIA – Mouvement Islamiste Armée (Algeria)

MLC – Mouvement de Libération Congolaise

MLSTP – Movimento de Libertação de São Tomé e Príncipe

MMD – Movement for Multiparty Democracy (Zambia)

MMG – Mouvement Mixte Gabonais

MMM – Mouvement Militant Mauricien

MMMSP – Mouvement Militant Mauricien Social Progressiste

MNC – Mouvement National Congolais

MNR – National Revolutionary Movement (Congo (Brazzaville))

MNSD – Mouvement National pour une Société de Développement (Niger)

MOG – Military Observer Group

MOJA-G – Movement for Justice in Africa-Gambia

MONIMA – Mouvement National pour l'Indépendence de Madagascar

MONUC – United Nations Observer Mission in the Democratic Republic of Congo

Morena – Mouvement de Redressement National (Gabon)

MPCI – Mouvement Patriotique de Côte d'Ivoire

MPD – Movimento para a Democracia (Cape Verde)

MPIGO – Mouvement Populaire Ivorien du Grand Ouest

MPLA – Movimento Popular de Libertação de Angola

MPM – Mouvement Populaire Mahorais (Mayotte)

MPR – Mouvement Populaire de la Révolution (Congo/Zaïre)

MSM – Mauritanian Socialist Movement

MRND – Mouvement national pour le développement (Rwanda)

MRNDD – Mouvement républican national pour la démocratie et le développement (Rwanda)

MTLD – Mouvement pour le Triomphe de Libertés Démocratiques (Algeria)

MUP – Mouvement d'Unité Populaire (Tunisia)

MUZ – Mineworkers Union of Zambia

NACP – National Association of Coloured People (Rhodesia)
NAI – New Africa Initiative
NAMRU – Naval Medical Research Unit (US institution in Eritrea)
NARC – National Rainbow Coalition (Kenya)
NCNC – National Council for Nigeria and the Cameroons
NCP – National Convention Party (Gambia)
NDC – National Democratic Congress (Ghana)
NDP – National Development Party (Kenya)
NEPAD – New Partnership for Africa's Development
NF – National Front (Chad)
NIBMAR – No Independence Before Majority Rule (Rhodesia)
NIEO – New International Economic Order
NIF – National Islamic Front (Sudan)
NLC – National Liberation Council (Ghana)
NLF – National Liberation Front (Chad)
NLP – National Liberation Party (Gambia)
NNDP – Nigerian National Democratic Party
NNLC – Ngwane National Liberatory Congress SWAZILAND
NP – National Party (Afrikaner South Africa)
NPC – Northern People's Congress (Nigeria)
NPFL – National Patriotic Front of Liberia
NPN – National Party of Nigeria
NPP – Nigerian People's Party
NPP – National Patriotic Party (Ghana)
NRA – National Resistance Army (Uganda)
NRC – National Redemption Council (Ghana)
NUDO – National Unity Democratic Organization (Namibia)
NUM – National Union of Mineworkers (Britain)
NUP – National Unionist Party (Morocco)
NUP – National Unionist Party (Sudan)
NUSAS – National Union of South African Students
NUT – National Union of Teachers (Britain)
OAU – Organisation of African Unity
OCAM – Organisation Commune Africaine et Malgache
ODA – Overseas Development Administration (Britain)
ODA – Official Development Assistance
OECD – Organisation for Economic Co-operation and Development
OFY – Operation Feed Yourself (Ghana)
OIC – Organization of the Islamic Conference
OLF – Oromo Liberation Front (Ethiopia)
OPC – Ovamboland People's Congress (South Africa/Namibia)
OPEC – Organization of the Petroleum Exporting Countries
OPIC – Overseas Private Investment Corporation (US)

OS – Organisation Secrète (Algeria)
PAC – Pan-Africanist Congress (South Africa)
PAFMECSA – Pan-African Movement for East, Central and Southern Africa
PAICV – Partido Africano da Independência de Cabo Verde
PAIGC – Partido Africano dA Independência da Guiné e Cabo Verde
(Guinea-Bissau)
PAMSCAD – Programme of Action to Mitigate the Social Costs of
Adjustment (Ghana)
PANA – Pan African News Agency
Parmehutu – Parti de l'Emancipation du Peuple Hutu (Rwanda)
PCT – Parti Congolais du Travail
PDA – Partido Democratico Angolana
PDCI – Parti Démocratique de la Côte d'Ivoire
PDG – Parti Démocratique Gabonais
PDG-RDA – Parti Démocratique de Guinée-Rassemblement Démocratique
Africain
PDL – Poverty datum line
PDS – Parti Démocratique de Senegal
PFD – People's Front for Democracy (Eritrea)
PFDJ – People's Front for Democracy and Justice (Eritrea)
PGP – Parti Gabonais du Progrès
PIDE – Policia Internacional e de Defesa do Estado (Portuguese security police)
PLAN – People's Liberation Army of Namibia
PLF – Popular Liberation Front (Eritrea)
PLO – Palestine Liberation Organization
PLS – Parti de Libération et du Socialisme (Morocco)
PMAC – Provisional Military Administrative Council (or Dergue) (Ethiopia)
PMSD – Parti Mauricien Social Démocrate
PNDC – Provisional National Defence Council (Ghana)
PNP – People's National Party (Ghana)
Polisario – Popular Front for the Liberation of Saguia el Hamro and Rio de
Oro (Western Sahara)
Poqo – 'Blacks Only' – militant wing of the PAC (qv)
PP – Progress Party (Gambia)
PPA – Parti du Peuple Algérien
PPM – Parti du Peuple Mauritanien
PPP – People's Progressive Party (Gambia)
PPT – Parti Progressiste Tchadien
PRC – People's Redemption Council (Guinea-Bissau)
PRP – People's Redemption Party (Nigeria)
PRP – Parti de la Révolution Populaire (Congo/Zaïre)
PRPB – Parti de la Révolution Populaire du Benin
PS – Parti Socialiste (Senegal)

PSD – Parti Social Démocrate (Madagascar)
PSD – Parti Socialiste Destourien (Tunisia)
PTP – Progress Party (Togo)
PUN – Partido Unico Nacional (Equatorial (Spanish) Guinea)
PUNT – Partido Unico Nacional de los Trabajadores (Equatorial (Spanish) Guinea)
PWRM – Polaroid Workers Revolutionary Movement (South Africa)
RCC – Revolutionary Command Council (Egypt)
RCC-NS – Revolutionary Command Council for National Salvation (Sudan)
RCD – Rassemblement Congolais pour la Démocratie
RCD – Rassemblement Constitutionnel Démocratique (Tunisia)
RDA – Rassemblement Démocratique Africain (Guinea)
RDA – Regroupement Démocratique Afar (Djibouti/French Somaliland)
RDC – Rassemblement Démocratique Centrafricain (Central African Republic)
RDP – Restruction and Development Programme (ANC – South Africa)
RDPC – Rassemblement Démocratique du Peuple Camerounais
RDR – Rassemblement Démocratique Républicain (Côte d'Ivoire)
Renamo – Resistencia Nacional Mocambicana (Mozambique National Resistance)
RND – Rallé National Démocratique (Algeria)
RPF – Rwandan Patriotic Front
RPP – Rassemblement Populaire pour le Progrès (Djibouti)
RPT – Rassemblement du Peuple Togolais
RSDG – Rassemblement Social Démocratique Gabonais
RUF – Revolutionary United Front (Sierra Leone)
SACC – South African Council of Churches
SACP – South African Communist Party
SACU – Southern African Customs Union
SADC – Southern African Development Community
SADCC – Southern African Development Coordination Conference
SADF – South African Defence Force
SADR –Sahrawi Arab Democratic Republic
SALF – Somali Abo Liberation Front
SAPs – Structural Adjustment Programmes
SASO – South African Students Organization
SCLA – Supreme Council for the Liberation of Angola
SDP – Seychelles Democratic Party
SLA – Somali Liberation Army
SLPP – Sierra Leone People's Party
SMC – Supreme Military Council (Nigeria)
SNA – Somali National Alliance
SNM – Somali National Movement
SPLA – Sudan People's Liberation Army

SPLM – Sudan People's Liberation Movement
SPM – Somali Patriotic Movement
SPPF – Seychelles People's Progressive Front
SPUP – Seychelles People's United Party
SRSP – Somali Revolutionary Socialist Party
SSIM – South Sudan Independence Movement
SSU – Sudanese Socialist Union
SWANLA – South West Africa Native Labour Association
SWANU – South West African National Union
SWAPO – South West Africa People's Organization
SWATF – South West Africa Territorial Force
SYL – Somali Youth League
TANU – Tanzania (formerly Tanganyika) African National Union
TEC – Transitional Executive Council (South Africa)
TGNU – Transitional Government of National Unity (Namibia)
TMC – Transitional Military Council (Sudan)
TNCs – Transnational Corporations
TNG – Transitional National Government (Somalia)
TNP – Transvaal National Party (South Africa)
TPLF – Tigray People's Liberation Front
TRC – Truth and Reconciliation Commission (South Africa)
TTF – Timber Task Forces (Ghana)
TUCSA – Trade Union Council of South Africa
UAM – Union Africaine et Malgache
UAMCE – Union Africaine et Malgache de Co-opération Economique
UANC – United African National Congress
UAR – United Arab Republic
UCPN – Union des Chefs et des Populations du Nord (Togo)
UDE – Union Douanière Equatoriale
UDEAC – Union Douanière des Etats de l'Afrique Central
UDF – United Democratic Front (Malawi)
UDF – United Democratic Front (South Africa)
UDI – Unilateral Declaration of Independence
UDP – United Democratic Party (Gambia)
UDPM – Union Démocratique du Peuple Malien
UDPS – Union pour la démocratie et le progrès social (Congo)
UDV – Union Démocratique Voltaique
UEAC – Union des Etats de l'Afrique Central
UGCC – United Gold Coast Convention Party
UGTA – Union Générale des Travailleurs Algériens
UGTT – Union Générale Tunisienne de Travail
UMA – Union du Maghreb Arabe
Umkhonto we Sizwe – 'Spear of the Nation' – militant wing of the ANC (qv)
UNAMIR – United Nations Assistance Mission in Rwanda

UNAMISL – United Nations Mission in Sierra Leone
UNAVEM – United Nations Angola Verification Mission
UNC – Union Nationale Camerounaise
UNC – United National Convention (Ghana)
UNCTAD – UN Conference on Trade and Development
UNDP – United Nations Development Programme
UNFP – Union Nationale des Forces Populaires (Morocco)
UNHCR – United Nations High Commissioner for Refugees
UN-ICC – United Nations-International Chamber of Commerce
UNIP – United National Independence Party (Zambia)
UNIR – Union Nationale pour l'Indépendence et la Révolution (Chad)
UNITA – União Nacional para a Independência Total de Angola
UNOSOM-II – United Nations Operation in Somalia II
UNPARED – United Nations Programme of Action for Africa's Economic
    Recovery and Development
UNTAF – United Nations Task Force
UNTAG – United Nations Transition Assistance Group
UP – Umma Party (Sudan)
UPA – Union das Populações de Angola
UPC – Uganda People's Congress
UPDS – Union pour la Démocratie et le Progrès Social (Congo)
UPN – Unity Party of Nigeria
UPP – United People's Party (Nigeria)
UPRONA – Union pour le Progrès National (Burundi)
UPS – Union Progressiste Sénégalaise
USAID – US Agency for International Development
USC – United Somali Congress
USIS – US Information Services
WANS – West African National Secretariat
WCC – World Council of Churches
WPE – Workers' Party of Ethiopia
WSB – West Side Boys (Sierra Leone)
WSLF – Western Somalia Liberation Front
WTO – World Trade Organization
ZANLA – Zimbabwe National Liberation Army
ZANU – Zimbabwe African National Union
ZANU-PF – Zimbabwe African National Union-Patriotic Front
ZAPU – Zimbabwe African People's Union
ZAPU-PF – Zimbabwe African People's Union-Patriotic Front
ZCTU – Zimbabwe Congress of Trade Unions
ZIPRA – Zimbabwe People's Revolutionary Army (military wing of ZAPU – qv)
ZUM – Zimbabwe Unity Movement

Notes

Prologue

1   Edward Mortimer, *France and the Africans 1944–1960* Faber and Faber, 1969, p.29
2   Mortimer, *op. cit.*, p.29
3   Mortimer, *op. cit.*, p.34
4   George Bennett, 'Settlers and Politics in Kenya' in *History of East Africa* vol. II, eds. Vincent Harlow and E. M. Chilver, OUP, 1965, p.331
5   John Middleton, 'Kenya: Administration and Changes in African Life', in *History of East Africa* vol. II, eds. Vincent Harlow and E. M. Chilver, OUP, 1965, p.386
6   Middleton, *op. cit.*, p.386
7   Waruhiu Itote 'General China', *Mau Mau in Action* TransAfrica, 1979 p.6
8   Cyril Ehrlich, 'The Uganda Economy' in *History of East Africa* vol. II, eds. Vincent Harlow and E. M. Chilver, OUP, 1965 p.469
9   J. E. Flint, 'Zanzibar 1890–1950', in *History of East Africa* vol. II, eds. Vincent Harlow and E. M. Chilver, OUP, 1965, p.667
10 William F. Gutteridge, 'Military and police Forces in Colonial Africa', in *Colonialism in Africa 1870–1960*, vol. II 'The History and Politics of Colonialism 1914–1960', eds. L. H. Gann and Peter Duignan, C.U.P. 1979, p.309
11 Gann and Duignan, *op. cit.* p.19 (note)
12 Gutteridge, *op. cit.*, p.290
13 *West Africa*, 17/11/1945
14 Mortimer, *op. cit.*, p.392
15 Middleton, *op. cit.*, p.392
16 Jomo Kenyatta, *Suffering Without Bitterness*, East African Publishing House, Nairobi, 1968 p.47
17 George Bennett, *Kenya: A Political History The Colonial Period*, OUP, 1963, p.112
18 David Rooney, Kwame Nkrumah: *The Political Kingdom and the Third World*, I. B. Tauris, 1988, p.23
19 *West Africa*, 3/11/1945
20 Lord Hailey, *An African Survey*, OUP, 1957, p.204
21 Roger Anstey, 'Belgian Rule in the Congo and the Aspirations of the Evolue Class' in Gann and Duignan, *op. cit.*, p.213
22 James Duffy, 'Portuguese Africa, 1930 to 1960' in Gann and Duignan, *op. cit.*, p.175
23 Duffy, *op. cit.*, p.181
24 Hugh Kay, *Salazar and Modern Portugal*, Eyre and Spottiswoode, 1970 p.215
25 Basil Davidson, 'Africa in Historical Perspective' in *Africa South of the Sahara 1980–81*, Europa Publications, 1980
26 Peter Hennessy, *Never Again: Britain 1945–1951*, Jonathan Cape, 1992, p.432
27 Professor John Gallagher, 1974 Oxford University Ford Lectures, quoted in Hennessy, *op. cit.*, p.216
28 Hennessy, *op. cit.*, p.216

Introduction: Independence

1   Iain Macleod, *Hansard*, 15 July 1960
2   *New African*, February 2000
3   *New African*, February 2000
4   Ludo de Witte, *L'assassinat de Lumumba*, Paris, Karthala, 2000
5   *New African*, February 2000
6   Madeleine G. Kalb, *The Congo Cables: The Cold War in Africa, from Eisenhower to Kennedy*, New York, Macmillan 1982
7   *New African*, February 2000
8   See Guy Arnold, *Historical Dictionary of Civil Wars in Africa*, Lanham, Maryland, Scarecrow Press, 1999
9   Edward Mortimer, *France and the Africans 1944–1960*, Faber and Faber, 1969, p.201
10 Alistair Horne, *Macmillan 1957–1986*, vol. II, Macmillan, p.177
11 Mortimer, *op. cit.*, p.204
12 Mortimer, *op. cit.*, p.341
13 Mortimer, *op. cit.*, p.311
14 Mortimer, *op. cit.*, p.314
15 Mortimer, *op. cit.*, p.333
16 Mortimer, *op. cit.*, p.371
17 David Rooney, *Kwame Nkrumah: The*

Political Kingdom in the Third World, I. B. Tauris, 1988 pp.131–2

18 Michael Scott, *Africa Digest*, vol. IV, No. 5, April 1957

19 *Ghana Times* January 1960 reported in *Africa Digest*, vol. VII, No. 4, February 1960

20 Horne, *op. cit.*, p.177

21 Horne, *op. cit.*, p.182

22 The Daily Service (organ of the Action Group in Nigeria), reported in *Africa Digest*, vol. VII, No. 5, April 1960

23 *Africa Digest*, vol. VII, No. 6, June 1960

24 Peter Hennessy, *Never Again: Britain 1945–1951*, Jonathan Cape, 1992, p.219

Part I The 1960s: Decade of Hope

Chapter One Problems of Independence

1 Frantz Fanon, *The Wretched of the Earth*, MacGibbon & Kee, 1965, p.49

2 Gwendolyn M. Carter, *Independence for Africa*, New York, Praeger, 1960, pp.167–9

3 For discussion of an African 'Personality' see Georges Balandier, *Ambiguous Africa*, Chatto and Windus, 1966

4 Julio Finn, *Voices of Negritude*, Quartet, 1988 (see preface)

5 Balandier, *op. cit.*, pp.264–5

6 Ronald Segal, *The Race War*, Jonathan Cape, 1966, p.104

7 John Hatch, *The History of Britain in Africa*, Andre Deutsch, 1969, p.283

8 Fanon, *op. cit.*, p.177

9 See René Dumont, *False Start in Africa*, Andre Deutsch, 1966, for a discussion of these problems.

10 Christopher Stevens, *The Soviet Union and Black Africa*, Macmillan, 1976, p.196

11 Balandier, *op. cit.*, p.258

12 For a discussion of this problem see Margery Perham, *The Colonial Reckoning* (The Reith Lectures), Collins, 1961

13 See Ruth First, 'Political and Social Problems of Development', *Africa South of the Sahara 1980–81*, Europa Publications, 1980

14 First, *op. cit.*

15 Fanon, *op. cit.*, p.137

16 Fanon, *op. cit.*, p.139

17 Dumont, *op. cit.*, p.141

18 For a detailed study of civil service problems in post-colonial Africa, see A. L. Adu, *The Civil Service in New African States*, George Allen and Unwin, 1965

19 Dumont, *op. cit.*, p.88

20 Segal, *op. cit.*, p.113

21 Eddie Agyemang, 'Freedom of Expression in a Government Newspaper in Ghana', *Reporting Africa*, editor Olav Stokke, The Scandinavian Institute of African Studies, Uppsala, 1971, p.50

22 Dumont, *op. cit.*, p.277

23 Fanon, *op. cit.*, p.135

Chapter Two The Congo Crisis

1 *Guardian*, 10/12/1960

2 *The Times*, 12/12/1960

3 *Observer*, 07/05/1961

4 Frantz Fanon, *The Wretched of the Earth*, MacGibbon & Kee, 1965, p.192

5 Ronald Segal, *The Race War*, Jonathan Cape, 1966, p.91

6 Segal, *op. cit.*, p.93

7 Georges Nzongola-Ntalaja, *The Congo*, p.101

8 Nzongola-Ntalaja, *op. cit.*, p.115

9 Nzongola-Ntalaja, *op. cit.*, pp.126–7

10 Conor Cruise O'Brien, *Observer*, 06/12/1964

11 William Attwood, *The Reds and the Blacks*, Harper 7 Row, 1967, pp.218–19

12 George Thayer, *The War Business*, New York, Simon & Schuster, 1969, p.169

13 *Guardian*, 08/05/1961

14 *The Times*, 22/12/1961

15 *Observer*, 29/08/1965

16 For a detailed history of mercenaries in Africa see Guy Arnold, *Mercenaries: The Scourge of the Third World*, Macmillan, 1999

Chapter Three African Unity and the Formation of the OAU

1 D. K. Chisiza, *Realities of African Independence*, The Africa Publications Trust, 1961

2 *West Africa*, 26/04/1958

3 *West Africa*, 06/12/1958

4   *West Africa*, 13/12/1958
5   *West Africa*, 20/12/1958
6   See Colin Legum, *Pan-Africanisn: A short political guide*, The Pall Mall Press, 1962
7   David Rooney, *Kwame Nkrumah*, I. B. Tauris, 1988, p.214
8   Legum, *op. cit.*, p.130
9   Quoted in Legum, *op. cit.*, p.111
10 Alan Rake, *100 Great Africans*, Scarecrow Press, Metuchen, N. J., 1994
11 Rooney, *op. cit.*, p.224
12 Keith Kyle, *Spectator*, 14/06/1963

Chapter Four The Coup d'Etat and the One-Party State

1   Ruth First, *The Barrel of a Gun*, Allen Lane The Penguin Press, 1970, p.40
2   First, *op. cit.*, p.31
3   J. M. Lee, *African Armies and Civil Order*, Chatto & Windus, 1969, p.19
4   First, *op. cit.*, p.432
5   Lee, *op. cit.*, p.117
6   First, *op. cit.*, p.420
7   *Guardian*, 01/01/1964
8   *West Africa*, 29/02/1964
9   *The Times*, 25/02/1966
10 *Guardian*, 18/04/1967
11 *Africa Digest*, vol. XVI, No. 1, February 1969
12 *Guardian*, 05/01/1966
13 *West Africa*, 21/01/1967
14 Lee, *op. cit.*, p.78
15 *Observer*, 18/12/1963
16 *Economist*, 28/08/1963
17 *The Times*, 24/12/1960
18 *The Times*, 22/12/1958
19 Julius Nyerere, 'Democracy and the Party System' in *Freedom and Unity*, OUP 1967, p.194
20 Nyerere, *op. cit.*, p.203
21 Frene Ginwala, *Spearhead* (editorial), Dar es Salaam, February 1963
22 Tunlikki Pietila, Sanna Ojalammi-Wamai and Liisa Laakso, 'Elections at the Borderland: Voter Opinion in Arusha and Kilimanjaro, Tanzania', *Multi-party Elections in Africa*, editors Michael Cowen and Liisa Laakso, Oxford, James Currey 2002, p.279
23 *Africa Digest*, vol. XII, No. 2, October 1964

Chapter Five Problems of Development

1   I. M. D. Little, *Aid to Africa*, Pergamon Press, 1964
2   Andrew Shonfield, *The Attack on World Poverty*, Chatto & Windus, 1961, p.17
3   Reginald H. Green and Ann Seidman, *Unity or Poverty*, Penguin Books, 1968, p.127
4   Walter Rodney, *How Europe Underdeveloped Africa*, Bogle L'Ouverture Publications, 1972, pp.236–7
5   *Jeanneny Report*, Official text, Paris, 1963
6   See René Dumont, *False Start in Africa*, Andre Deutsch, 1966
7   Basil Davidson, *Can Africa Survive?*, Heinemann, 1974, p.24
8   Davidson, *op. cit.*, p.24
9   Professor Arthur Lewis, *The Legon Observer*, 24/05/1968
10 Dumont, *op. cit.*, p.70
11 Green/Seidman, *op. cit.*, p.32
12 Davidson, *op. cit.*, p.101
13 Paul Lewis, *Financial Times*, 04/04/1968
14 Green/Seidman, *op. cit.*, p.187
15 *The Economist*, 16/03/1968
16 *The Times*, 30/10/1967
17 Dumont, *op. cit.*, p.104
18 *The Times*, 02/09/1964
19 Green/Seidman, *op. cit.*, pp.32–3
20 Dumont, *op. cit.*, p.61
21 Andre Philip, *Bulletin de L'Afrique Noire*, 21/02/1962
22 Common Market correspondent, *Financial Times*, 21/06/1966
23 *Barclays Bank Overseas Review*, November 1962
24 Christopher Stevens, *The Soviet Union and Black Africa*, Macmillan, 1976, p.28
25 Stevens, *op. cit.*, p.74
26 Reported in *Kenya Weekly News*, 10/06/1966
27 Stevens, *op. cit.*, p.74
28 Richard Lowenthal, *Model or Ally?*, OUP, 1977, p.272
29 Davidson, *op. cit.*, p.122
30 *Africa Digest*, vol. IX, No. 6, June 1962
31 *The Economist*, 01/09/1962
32 *The Observer*, 26/08/1962
33 Stevens, *op. cit.*, p.86
34 Guy Hunter, *The New Societies of Tropical Africa*, OUP, pp.181–2

35 Green/Seidman, *op. cit.*, p.95
36 'The Arusha Declaration: Socialism and Self-Reliance', quoted in Julius Nyerere, *Freedom and Socialism*, OUP, pp.235–41
37 *West Africa*, 05/08/1970

Chapter Six North Africa
1 *The Economist*, 19/08/1961
2 Ronald Segal, *Africa Profiles*, Penguin Books, 1962, p.394
3 Peter Mansfield, *The Middle East*, OUP, 1973, p.233
4 Samir Amin, *The Maghreb in the Modern World*, Penguin Books, 1970, p.214
5 Alan Rake, *100 Great Africans*, Metuchen, N. J., Scarecrow Press, 1994, p.376
6 Darsie Gillie, *Guardian*, 31/10/1963
7 Rake, *op. cit.*, p.273
8 Mansfield, *op. cit.*, pp.351–2

Chapter Seven The Nigerian Civil War
1 John Hatch, *The History of Britain in Africa*, Andre Deutsch, 1969, p.269
2 Walter Schwarz, *Nigeria*, Pall Mall Press, 1968, p.xiv
3 Schwarz, *op. cit.*, p.xiv
4 James O'Connell, 'The Political Class and Economic Growth', *Nigeria Journal of Economic and Social Studies*, vol. 8:1 (March 1966), p.129
5 Ali A. Mazrui, *Violence and Thought, Essays on Social Tensions in Africa*, Longmans, 1969, p.129
6 *West Africa*, 03/06/1961
7 Hella Pick, *The Guardian*, 25/02/1962
8 Schwarz, *op. cit.*, p.31
9 Schwarz, *op. cit.*, p.14
10 Clyde Sanger, *Guardian*, 29/10/1963
11 Patrick Keatley, *Guardian*, 22/01/1962
12 *West Africa*, 14/01/1961
13 *West Africa*, 27/03/1965
14 Ali A. Mazrui, *op. cit.*, p.113
15 Olusegun Obasanjo, General, *My Command*, Heinemann, 1980, p.6
16 J. D. F. Jones, *Financial Times*, 05/05/1966
17 John de St. Jorre, *The Nigerian Civil War*, Hodder and Stoughton, 1972, p.57
18 Fed. Min. of Info., PR.610/1966, of 24/05/1966
19 St. Jorre, *op. cit.*, pp.73–74

20 Obasanjo, *op. cit.*, p.8
21 Schwarz, *op. cit.*, p.218
22 Obasanjo, *op. cit.*, p.155
23 Obasanjo, *op. cit.*, p.56
24 *West Africa*, 28/10/1967
25 *West Africa*, 02/12/1967
26 *West Africa*, 07/12/1968
27 St. Jorre, *op. cit.*, pp.316–18
28 See Guy Arnold, *Mercenaries: The Scourge of the Third World*, Macmillan, 1999, for a detailed study of mercenary activity in Africa
29 Margery Perham, 'Nigeria's Civil War', *Africa Contemporary Record 1968–69*, editors C. Legum and J. Drysdale, Africa Research Limited, 1969, pp.1–12

Chapter Eight West and Equatorial Africa
1 Paul Fordham, *The Geography of African Affairs*, (4th edition), Penguin Books, 1974, pp.77–8
2 Fordham, *op. cit.*, p.103
3 Ken Post, *The New States of West Africa*, Penguin Books (revised edition), 1968, pp.43–4
4 Post, *op. cit.*, p.191
5 Douglas Rimmer, *The Economies of West Africa*, Weidenfeld and Nicolson, 1984, p.60
6 Rimmer, *op. cit.*, p248
7 Rimmer, *op. cit.*, p.81
8 Rimmer, *op. cit.*, p.84
9 Alan Rake, *100 Great Africans*, Scarecrow Press, 1994, p.278
10 David Rooney, *Kwame Nkrumah*, I. B. Tauris, 1988, p.205
11 John Stockwell, *In Search of Enemies*, Andre Deutsch, 1978, p.160n.
12 Paul Lee, *West Africa*, 3 articles, 19–25 November 2001
13 John Hatch, *Africa Today – and Tomorrow*, Frederick A. Praeger, 1960, p.50
14 Rimmer, *op. cit.*, p.146
15 John Hatch, *The History of Britain in Africa*, Andre Deutsch, 1969, p.270
16 Ronald Segal, *African Profiles*, Penguin Books, 1962, p.281
17 *West Africa*, 26/08/1961
18 Segal, *op. cit.*, p.280
19 Edith Hodgkinson, 'Benin', *Africa South*

of the Sahara 1980–81, Europa Publications, 1980, p.173

20 Rake, *op. cit.*, p.357

21 Arthur W. Lewis, *Politics in West Africa*, George Allen and Unwin, 1965, p.21

22 Lewis, *op. cit.*, p.23

23 Lewis, *op. cit.*, pp.62–3

24 Rimmer, *op. cit.*, p.215

Chapter Nine The Horn of Africa

1 *East African Standard*, 13/05/1960

2 *The Times*, 24/12/1960

3 James Morris, *Guardian*, 11/12/1961

4 *Observer*, 11/02/1962

5 *East Africa and Rhodesia*, 23/08/1963

6 Norman Bentwich, *The Times*, 17/05/1963

7 See Tesfatsion Medhanie, *Eritrea Dynamics of a National Question*, B. R. Gruner, Amsterdam, 1986, p.19

8 Medhanie, *op. cit.*, p.23

9 Medhanie, *op. cit.*, p.26

10 Kevin M. Cahill, *Somalia A Perspective*, The State University of New York Press, Albany, 1980, p.52

11 Barry Lynch, 'The Somali Democratic Republic. The One that Got Away', in *The New Communist Third World*, editor Peter Wiles, Croom Helm, 1982, p.278

12 *Somaliland News*, 29/08/1960

13 *Africa Digest*, April 1962, vol. IX No. 5

14 *Somali News*, 03/08/1962

15 Barry Lynch, *op. cit.*, p.279

16 Mohamed Omer Beshir, *The Southern Sudan Background to Conflict*, C. Hurst & Co., 1968, p.81

17 Beshir, *op. cit.*, p.101

18 See Ali Mazrui, 'The Multiple Marginality of the Sudan', pp.240–55, in *Sudan in Africa*, editor Yusuf Fadl Hasan, Khartoum University Press, 2nd edition, 1985

19 Mazrui, *op. cit.*, p.242

20 Mazrui, *op. cit.*, pp.244–52

21 *Guardian,* 20/10/1965

22 Roy Lewis, *The Times*, 28/05/1970

23 *Financial Times*, 24/08/1966

Chapter Ten East Africa

1 Ali Mazrui, *Violence and Thought*, Longmans, 1969, p.14

2 Alan Rake, *100 Great Africans*, Scarecrow Press, 1994

3 *The Nationalist*, Dar es Salaam, 12/01/1965

4 John Okello, *Revolution in Zanzibar*, East African Publishing House, 1967, p.24

5 A. Marshall MacPhee, *Kenya*, Ernest Benn, 1968, p.183

6 *Sunday News*, Dar es Salaam, 26/01/1964

7 Mazrui, *op. cit.*, p.5

8 *Africa Digest*, April 1964, vol. XI, No. 5

9 Julius Nyerere, *Freedom and Unity*, Oxford University Press, 1967, p.85

10 *Uganda Argus*, 1/07/1963

11 See Donald Rothchild, editor, *Politics of Integration*, East African Publishing House, 1968, for documents and speeches on East African integration

12 *Uganda Argus*, 11/05/1964

13 Reginald Green and Ann Seidman, *Unity or Poverty*, Penguin Books, 1968, p.142

14 *Sunday Post*, 22/03/1964

15 The photograph is reproduced in *Kenyatta, A Photographic Biography*, by Anthony Howarth, East African Publishing House, 1967

16 MacPhee, *op. cit.*, p.173

17 See William Attwood, *The Reds and the Blacks*, Harper and Row, 1967

18 Ali Mazrui, *On Heroes and Uhuru Worship*, Longmans Green, 1969, p.57

19 Attwood, *op. cit.*, p.215

20 Policy Statement by Bro. Tom Mboya, Kenya Federation of Labour 1960 Annual Conference, Nairobi, p.3 (Quoted in Ioan Davies, *African Trade Unions*, Penguin Books, 1966, p.101)

21 Ioan Davies, *African Trade Unions*, Penguin Books, 1966, pp.163–4

22 George Bennett, 'Patterns of Government in East Africa', *International Affairs*, vol. 45, No. 1, January 1969, p.90

23 See *Independent Kenya*, Anonymous, sponsored by the Journal of African Marxists, Zed Press, 1982, p.12

24 *Independent Kenya*, p.26

25 A. J. Hughes, *East Africa The Search for Unity*, Penguin Books, 1963, p.243

26 Hughes, *op. cit.*, p.243

27 *The Times*, 28/09/1962

28 *Guardian*, 5/10/1962

29 *Kenya Weekly News*, 5/10/1962

30 Cranford Pratt, *The Critical Phase in Tanzania, 1945–1968*, Cambridge University Press, 1976, p.134

31 Pratt, *op. cit.*, p.166

32 Rodger Yeager, *Tanzania: An African Experiment*, Westview Press, 1989, p.73

33 See Julius Nyerere, '*Ujamaa* The Basis of African Socialism' in Nyerere, *Freedom and Unity*, Oxford University Press, 1967, p.162 et seq.

34 *Guardian*, 2/06/1970

Chapter Eleven White Racism in Central Africa

1 *Bulawayo Chronicle*, 17 & 18 February 1949

2 Quoted in Patrick Keatley, *The Politics of Partnership*, Penguin Books, 1963, p.272

3 Speech at Que Que election meeting, 02/03/1956, quoted in Ronald Segal, *The Race War*, Jonathan Cape, 1966, p.85

4 John Hatch, *Africa Today – and Tomorrow*, Frederick A. Praeger, 1960, p.251

5 Theodore Bull (editor), *Rhodesian Perspective*, Michael Joseph, 1967, p.17

6 Richard Hall, *The High Price of Principles*, Hodder & Stoughton, 1969, p.61

7 Hall, *op. cit.*, p.101

8 *Daily Telegraph*, 03/07/1965

9 Hall, *op. cit.*, p.127

10 Hall, *op. cit.*, p.156

11 Quoted in Guy Arnold, *The Last Bunker*, Quartet Books, 1976, p.136

12 Bull, *op. cit.*, p.108

13 Eileen Haddon, 'Rhodesia's Four Years of Sanctions', *Africa Contemporary Record 1969–70*, editors Colin Legum and John Drysdale, African Research Ltd, 1969–70, pp.A4ff

14 Ben Pimlott, *Wilson*, Harper Collins, 1992, p.453

15 Richard Gibson, *African Liberation Movements*, Oxford University Press, 1972, pp.179–80

17 *Observer*, 13/10/1968

18 *Guardian*, 25/10/1965

19 Ken Flower, *Serving Secretly*, John Murray, 1987, p.48

20 Pimlott, *op. cit.*, p.371

21 Martin Loney, *Rhodesia*, Penguin Books, 1975, p.161

22 Hall, *op. cit.*, p.67

23 Kenneth Kaunda, *UNIP Proceedings of the Annual Conference at Mulungushi*, p.iv., *Guidelines*, p.12

24 Hall, *op. cit.*, p.39

25 Jan Pettman, *Zambia Security and Conflict*, Julian Friedmann, 1974, p.41

26 Hastings Banda, *Malawi Hansard*, 16/12/1966, p.67

27 Philip Short, *Banda*, Routlerdge & Kegan Paul, 1974, p.283

28 *Malawi News*, 21/05/1960

28 See Carolyn McMaster, *Malawi Foreign Policy and Development*, Julian Friedmann, 1974, pp.48–49

29 Hall, *op. cit.*, p.32

30 Short, *op. cit.*, p.249

31 Short, *op. cit.*, p.313

Chapter Twelve Portugal in Africa

1 Colin Legum, *Africa South*, July-September, 1960

2 Amilcar Cabral in 'Foreword' to Basil Davidson, *The Liberation of Guine*, Penguin Books, 1969, p.9

3 Patrick Chabal, *A History of Postcolonial Lusophone Africa*, Hurst, 2002, p.31

4 Eduardo Mondlane, *The Struggle for Mozambique*, Penguin Books, 1969, p.50

5 James Duffy, *Portugal in Africa*, Penguin Books, 1962, p.203

6 Hugh Kay, *Salazar and Modern Portugal*, Eyre and Spottiswoode, 1970, p.183

7 Ronald Segal, *The Race War*, Jonathan Cape, 1966, p.83

8 Segal, *op. cit.*, p.66

9 Sid Gilchrist, *Angola Awake*, Ryerson Press, 1968, p.60

10 Chabal, *op. cit.*, p.30

11 William Minter, *Portuguese Africa and the West*, Penguin Books, 1972, p.150

12 Minter, *op. cit.*, pp.134–5

13 Segal, *op. cit.*, p.83

14 Dean Acheson, to the American Society of Newspaper Editors, April 1969

15 Minter, *op. cit.*, p.94

16 Duffy, *op. cit.*, p.204

17 Basil Davidson, *In the Eye of the Storm, Angola's People*, Longman, 1972, p.96 Davidson's wide travels in Portuguese Africa with the liberation movements provided him with many insights into the background of the Portuguese African wars
18 Davidson, *op. cit.*, p.120
19 Gilchrist, *op. cit.*
20 *Observer*, 21/05/1961
21 Douglas L. Wheeler and Rene Pelissier, *Angola*, Pall Mall Press, 1971, p.193
22 Russel W. Howe, *Current*, November 1961
23 *Observer*, 11/02/1962
24 *Flying Review International*, April 1966
25 Quoted in Mondlane, *op. cit.*, p.70
26 Mondlane, *op. cit.*, p.139
27 Eduardo Mondlane, *Socialist International*, 05/03/1965
28 *Figaro*, 24/10/1967
29 Basil Davidson, *The Liberation of Guine*, Penguin Books, 1969, p.21
30 *West Africa*, 17/04/1965
31 Chabal, *op. cit.*, p.9
32 Davidson, *op. cit.*, p.125
33 Basil Davidson, *West Africa*, 02/11/1968

Chapter Thirteen South Africa

1 Ronald Segal, *The Race War*, Jonathan Cape, 1966, p.119
2 Mary Benson, *The Struggle for a Birthright*, Penguin Books, 1966, p.21
3 Benson, *op. cit.*, p.23
4 Govan Mbeki, *The Peasants' Revolt*, Penguin Books, 1964, p.23
5 Brian Bunting, *The Rise of the South African Reich*, Penguin Books, 1964, p.134
6 Quoted in Frank Welsh, *A History of South Africa*, Harper Collins, 1998, p.460
7 Bunting, *op. cit.*, p.132
8 Alistair Horne, *Macmillan 1957–1988*, vol. II (official biography), Macmillan, 1989, p.194
9 Welsh, *op. cit.*, p.449
10 See Laurie Platzky and Cherryl Walker, *The Surplus People: Forced Removals in South Africa*, Johannesburg, 1985, p.10
11 Leonard Thompson, *A History of South Africa*, Yale University Press, 1990, p.200
12 Bunting, *op. cit.*, p.162

13 *Star* (Johannesburg), 26/11/1970
14 Ruth First, Jonathan Steele, Christabel Gurney, *The South African Connection*, Temple Smith, 1972, p.41
15 Thompson, *op. cit.*, p.205
16 *Investor's Chronicle*, 26/11/1971
17 *US Business Involvement in Southern Africa*, House of Representatives, US Government Printer, Washington D. C., 1972
18 Alex Kepple, *South Africa: Workers Under Apartheid*, International Defence and Aid, 1971
19 Fenner Brockway, *The Colonial Revolution*, Hart-Davis, MacGibbon, 1973, p.593
20 James Fairbairn, *New Statesman*, 06/02/1960
21 Jack Halpern, *South Africa's Hostages*, Penguin Books, 1965, p.307
22 Halpern, *op. cit.*, p.310
23 Halpern, *op. cit.*, p.378
24 *Sunday Times* (Johannesburg), 11/08/1963
25 Halpern, *op. cit.*, p.59
26 Frank Taylor, *Daily Telegraph*, 10/04/1968

Part II The 1970s: Decade of Realism

Chapter Fifteen Four Different Development Paths

1 Houari Boumedienne, *Recording*, Radio Algeria, 29/03/1971
2 See Peter Mansfield, *The Arabs*, Allen Lane, Penguin Books, 1976
3 Mansfield, *op. cit.*, p.474
4 Mansfield, *op. cit.*, p.475
5 Mansfield, *op. cit.*, p.475
6 Michael Field, *Inside the Arab World*, John Murray, 1994, p.129
7 Field, *op. cit.*, p.132
8 Tom Forrest, 'Recent Developments in Nigerian Industrialisation', in *Industry and Accumulation in Africa*, editor Martin Fransman, Heinemann, 1982, p.324
9 IBRD, 1979
10 Forrest, *op. cit.*, p.331
11 Douglas Rimmer, *The Economies of West Africa*, Weidenfeld and Nicolson, 1984, p.131
12 *Annual Report*, Central Bank of Nigeria,

1978

13 Federal Government of Nigeria, *Third National Development Plan 1975–80*, vol. I, The Central Planning Office, Lagos 1975, p.29

14 Forrest, *op. cit.*, p.334

15 Ola Oni and Dr Bade Onimode, *Economic Development in Nigeria: The Socialist Alternative*, The Nigeria Academy of Arts Sciences and Technology, 1975

16 Oni and Onimode, *op. cit.*, p.172

17 Oni and Onimode, *op. cit.*, p.191

18 Colin Legum, *Africa Contemporary Record 1971–72*, (ACR), 'Tanzania', p.B206, Rex Collings, 1972

19 Legum, *op. cit.*, 'Tanzania', p.B211

20 Legum, *Africa Contemporary Record 1972–73*, 'Tanzania', p.B255, Rex Collings 1973

21 Legum, *Africa Contemporary Record 1974–75*, p.B284, Rex Collings, 1975

22 Julius Nyerere, *The Arusha Declaration – Ten Years After*, Dar es Salaam, 1977, pp.19–20

23 Legum, *Africa Contemporary Record 1970–71*, 'Botswana', pp.B471–2, Rex Collings, 1972

24 Legum, *Africa Contemporary Record 1973–74*, 'Botswana', p.B308, Rex Collings, 1974

Chapter Sixteen Oil and Israel; A New International Economic Order

1 People's Democratic Republic of Algeria, *Memorandum submitted by Algeria to the Conference of Sovereigns and Heads of State of OPEC Member Countries*, Algiers, March 1975, p.5

2 Michael Tanzer, *The Race for Resources*, Monthly Review Press, 1980, p.244

3 Tanzer, *op. cit.*, provides an in depth analysis of the process whereby control is exercised in developing countries by multinationals and their supporting institutions of the West.

4 Tanzer, *op. cit.*, p.194

5 Tanzer, *op. cit.*, p.71

6 Keesings Record of World Events, November 1973

7 *Africa Digest*, vol. XIX No. 3, June 1972

8 *East African Standard*, 22/11/1973

9 Quoted in Legum, *Africa Contemporary Record 1973–74*, Collings, 1974, p.C80

10 Colin Legum, 'The Year in Perspective', p.xviii, *Africa Contemporary Record 1974–75*, Collings, 1975

11 *Times of Zambia*, Lusaka, 18/09/1975

12 UN Resolution 2626 (XXV) 2229th plenary meeting, 1 May 1974

Chapter Seventeen The Growth of Aid

1 I am indebted to Kogan Page for permission to quote extensively from my book, *Aid in Africa*, published in 1979, in which I analysed aid to Africa through the 1970s.

2 L. Valentin, *Pravda*, 14/08/1976

3 See chapter 16, above, for details of the Arab-African debate on compensatory finance from the oil states to Africa

4 *Polar Star*, June 1978

5 Jens Erik Torp, *The Development Strategies behind the Aid Programme of the Soviet Union to African Countries*, Nordiska Afrika Institutet, 1976

6 For an analysis of UNCTAD III see *Africa Digest*, vol. XIX No. 3, June 1972

7 *What kind of Africa by the year 2000?* (Final Report of the Monrovia Symposium on the future development prospects of Africa towards the year 2000), OAU, 1979

8 The World Bank, *Accelerated Development in Sub-Saharan Africa: An Agenda for Action*, World Bank, 1981, p.119

Chapter Eighteen Strategic Highways

1 Richard Taylor, 'Uhuru Highway', *Africa Magazine*, No. 3, 1971

2 Richard Synge, 'Trans-African Highway', *Third World*, Jan/Feb 1975

3 Richard Taylor, *op. cit.*

4 'Botswana and Southern Africa', address by President Seretse Khama to the Foreign Policy Association of Denmark, 13/11/1970

5 See Lord Hailey, *An African Survey*,

revised 1956, Oxford University Press, 1957, p.1577

6 Reported in *The Times*, 08/02/1973

7 Douglas Anglin, 'The Politics of transit routes in land-locked Southern Africa', in *Landlocked Countries of Africa*, Zdenek Cervenka (editor), The Scandinavian Institute of African Studies, Uppsala, 1973, p.102

Chapter 19 The Cold War Comes to The Horn

1 *The Observer*, 20/12/1970

2 Hugh Hanning, *The Times*, 26/02/1971

3 See Colin Legum, *Ethiopia: The Fall of Haile Selassie's Empire*, Rex Collings, 1975, p.2

4 See *Africa Digest*, vol. XX No 5, October 1973

5 Patrick Gilkes, 'Ethiopia: It Takes More Than Aid To End Starvation', *The Times*, 1/11/1973

6 Tesfatsion Medhane, *Eritrea: Dynamics of a National Question*, B. R. Gruner, Amsterdam, 1986, p.21

7 See US Congress, Senate Sub Committee on United States Security Agreements and Commitments Abroad of the Committee on Foreign Relations, *United States Security Agreements and Commitments Abroad: Ethiopia*, Hearings 91st Congress, 2nd Session, June, 1, 1970

8 Martin Doornbus, Lionel Cliffe, Abdel Ghaffar, M. Ahmed and John Markakis, *Beyond Conflict in the Horn*, Institute of Social Studies, The Hague, James Currey, 1992, p.7

9 Alan Rake, *Gemini News Service*, 20/03/1973

10 A. J. McIlroy, *Daily Telegraph*, 14/04/1973

11 Michael Wolfers, *Guardian*, 5/03/1974

12 Martin Walker, *Guardian*, 15/04/1974

13 *The Times*, 2/07/1974

14 Alan Rake, *Guardian*, 20/08/1974

15 Colin Legum, *op. cit.*, p.4

16 Colin Legum, *op. cit.*, p.74

17 Fred Halliday, 'The Fighting in Eritrea', *New Left Review*, No. 67 (May–June 1971), p.65

18 *US Policy for Sale of Arms to Ethiopia Hearings*, 94th Congress, Ist Session, March 5, 1975 (Washington DC:

Government Printing Office, 1975) p.11

19 Medhane, *op. cit.*, p.79

20 See Colin Legum and Bill Lee, *Conflict in the Horn of Africa*, Africana Publishing Company, New York & London, 1977, p.7

21 Medhane, *op. cit.*, p.99

22 For portraits of these two leaders see Alan Rake, *Who's Who in Africa*, Scarecrow Press, 1992

23 For a detailed history of Ethiopia in the years prior to the revolution of 1974, see Patrick Gilkes, *The Dying Lion, Feudalism and Modernization in Ethiopia*, Julian Friedmann, 1975

24 Legum and Lee, *op. cit.*, p.96

25 *Daily Telegraph*, 1/03/1978

26 *Washington Post*, 20/12/1977

27 Kevin M. Cahill, M. D., *Somalia A Perspective*, The State University of New York Press, Albany, 1980, p.31

28 Cahill, *op. cit.*, p.34

29 Cahill, *op. cit.*, p.42

Chapter Twenty Rhodesia

1 *The Times*, 9/11/1971

2 *Guardian*, 10/11/1971

3 *The Times*, 10/11/1971

4 *Rhodesia Herald*, 7/12/1971

5 D. R. Thorpe, *Sir Alec Douglas-Home*, Sinclair-Stevenson, 1996, p.425

6 Thorpe, *op. cit.*, pp.425–6

7 Thorpe, *op. cit.*, p.428

8 Hugo Young, *Sunday Times*, 14/01/1973

9 Ken Flower, *Serving Secretly*, John Murray, 1987, pp.121–2

10 *The Times*, 4/06/1974

11 R. W. Johnson, *How Long Will South Africa Survive?*, Macmillan, 1977, p.122

12 Johnson, *op. cit.*, p.123

13 Flower, *op. cit.*, p.127

14 Johnson, *op. cit.*, pp.127–8

15 Flower, *op. cit.*, p.164

16 *Daily Telegraph*, 6/07/1977

17 Flower, *op. cit.*, p.191

18 Flower, *op. cit.*, p.213

19 Flower, *op. cit.*, p.210

20 *Financial Times*, 24/05/1977

21 *Guardian*, 8/07/1977

22 Martin Bailey, *Oilgate*, Coronet Books, 1979, p.83

23 Bailey, *op. cit.*, Interview, 18 April 1979,

p.87

24 Bailey, *op. cit.*, p.92

25 Report of Observers on behalf of the British Parliamentary Human Rights Group, *Free and Fair? The 1979 Rhodesia Election,* quoted in 'Zimbabwe', *Destructive Engagement*, editors Phyllis Johnson and David Martin, p.44

26 Flower, *op. cit.*, p229

27 Flower, *op. cit.*, pp.247–8

28 Phyllis Johnson and David Martin, 'Zimbabwe', *Destructive Engagement*, p.43

29 Flower, *op. cit.*, pp.267–8

30 Flower, *op. cit.*, p.269

31 See *Destructive Engagement*, Note 5 to Chapter 2, p.352

Chapter Twenty-One The End of Portuguese Africa

1 See *Africa Digest*, vol. XVII, No. 4, August 1970

2 *The Times*, 23/12/1970

3 Colin Legum, *Observer*, 14/01/1973

4 *Financial Times*, 27/05/1970

5 *South African Star*, 13/06/1970

6 *Daily Telegraph*, 14/03/1972

7 *The Times*, 10/07/1973

8 *Le Monde*, 26/07/1973

9 See *Africa Digest*, vol. XXI, No. 1, February 1974

10 *Rand Daily Mail*, 30/01/1974

11 *South African Star*, 23/02/1974

12 See Elizabeth Morris, 'Portugal's Year in Africa', *Africa Contemporary Record 1971–72*, Colin Legum (editor), Rex Collings, 1972

13 John Miller, *Daily Telegraph*, 03/09/1970

14 Basil Davidson, *West Africa*, 16/08/1970

15 *Africa Contemporary Record 1972–73*, Angola, B482, Colin Legum (editor), Rex Collings, 1973

16 *Africa Contemporary Record 1973–74*, Angola, B527, Colin Legum (editor), Rex Collings, 1974

17 Michael Knipe, *The Times*, 21/08/1974

18 *Sunday Times*, 20/10/1974

19 See Elizabeth Morris, 'Portugal's Year in Africa', *Africa Contemporary Record 1972–73*, Colin Legum (editor), Rex Collings, 1973

20 *Africa Digest*, vol. XX, No. 2, April 1973

21 See Elizabeth Morris, 'Portugal's Year in Africa', A83–9, *Africa Contemporary Record 1973–74*, Colin Legum (editor), Rex Collings, 1974

22 *Daily Telegraph*, 29/07/1974

23 See Elizabeth Morris, 'Portugal's Year in Africa', A71, *Africa Contemporary Record 1974–75*, Colin Legum (editor), Rex Collings, 1975

24 *Africa Contemporary Record 1974–75*, Guinea-Bissau, B670, Colin Legum (editor), Rex Collings, 1975

25 Elizabeth Morris, *op. cit. Africa Contemporary Record 1974–75*

26 See Jane Bergerol, 'Portugal's Year in Africa', A112, *Africa Contemporary Record 1975–76*, Colin Legum (editor), Rex Collings, 1976

27 Bergerol, *op. cit.*

Chapter Twenty-Two Namibia

1 Statement in the Supreme Court of South Africa, Transvaal Provincial Division, Pretoria, 1 February 1968

2 Stanley Uys, *Observer*, 12/03/1972

3 *Rand Daily Mail*, 18/01/1972

4 Laurie Flynn, *Studded with Diamonds and Paved with Gold*, Bloomsbury, 1992

5 Flynn, *op. cit.*, p.41

6 Flynn, *op. cit.*, p.42

7 Flynn, *op. cit.*, pp.44–5

8 Flynn, *op. cit.*, p.48

9 Roger Murray, Jo Morris, John Dugard, Neville Robin, *The Role of Foreign Firms in Namibia*, Africa Publications Trust, 1974, p.42

10 Murray et al, *op. cit.*, p.44

11 *Rand Daily Mail*, 2/11/1973

12 Testimony by Hon. David Newsom on 27 March 1973, before the House Subcommittee on Africa, in US Congress, House of Representatives committee on Foreign Affairs, *US Business Involvement in Southern Africa*, Part III (Washington D. C: Government Printing Office) p.12

13 Murray et al, *op. cit.*, p.202

14 Murray et al, *op. cit.*, pp.46–7

15 *South African Star*, 16/02/1974

16 Phyllis Johnson and David Martin (editors), *Frontline Southern Africa*, Ryan Publishing, 1989, p.150

17 Barbara Konig, *Namibia The Ravages of*

War, International Defence and Aid Fund for Southern Africa, 1983, p.30

18 Konig, *op. cit.*, p.50

19 Konig, *op. cit.*, p.55

Chapter Twenty-Three South Africa: The Critical Decade

1 *Guardian*, 18/12/1970

2 *Financial Mail*, 1/11/1974

3 *Rand Daily Mail*, 7/02/1972

4 Denis Herbstein, *Gemini News Service*, 24/02/1972

5 *Daily Telegraph*, 22/02/1973

6 See *Africa Digest*, vol. XVIII, No. 6, December 1971

7 *Sunday Times*, 5/12/1971

8 *Rand Daily Mail*, 5/07/1972

9 See *Africa Digest*, vol. XVIII, No. 4, August 1971

10 *Rand Daily Mail*, 20/01/1973

11 See Michael Tanzer, *The Race for Resources*, Monthly Review Press, (NY and London), 1980, pp.178–87

12 Tanzer, *op. cit.*, p.182

13 Tanzer, *op. cit.*, p.185

14 *The Economist*, 23/01/1971

15 Adam Raphael, *Guardian*, 12/03/1973

16 *Guardian*, 2/05/1973

17 *Rand Daily Mail*, 31/03/1973

18 *Guardian*, 6/06/1973

19 *Guardian*, 13/09/1973

20 Benjamin Pogrund, *Sunday Times*, 16/09/1973

21 David Loshak, *Daily Telegraph*, 31/10/1973

22 *South African Star*, 22/12/1973

23 *South African Star*, 5/01/1974

24 *South African Star*, 2/04/1978

25 *South African Star*, 19/12/1970

26 Derek Ingram, *Gemini News Service*, 26/04/1971

27 *Guardian*, 20/08/1971

28 See Colin Legum, 'Southern Africa: The Secret Diplomacy of Détente', pp.A3–A15, *Africa Contemporary Record 1974–75*, Colin Legum (editor), Rex Collings, 1975

29 Legum, *op. cit.*, p.A7

30 Jim Lobe (Washington), '1975: Angola, Cuba and the CIA', *West Africa*, 15–21 April 2002, p.22

31 *Conakry Radio*, 22/02/1975

32 See Colin Legum, 'Southern Africa: How the Search for Peaceful Change Failed', pp.A39–40, *Africa Contemporary Record 1975–76*, Colin Legum (editor), Rex Collings, 1975

33 See R. W. Johnson, *How Long Will South Africa Survive?*, Macmillan, 1977

34 Johnson, *op. cit.*, p.177

35 Johnson, *op. cit.*, p.191

36 *Johannesburg Sunday Times*, 12/12/1976

37 *Rand Daily Mail*, 5/01/1977

38 See Colin Legum, 'The Southern Africa Crisis', pp.A3–A32, *Africa Contemporary Record 1977–78*, Colin Legum (editor), Rex Collings, 1978

39 Dan van der Vat, *The Times*, 19/11/1977

40 Phyllis Johnson and David Martin (editors), *Frontline Southern Africa*, p.284, Ryan Publishing, 1989

41 *The Economist*, 9/04/1977

Part III The 1980s: Basket Case?

Chapter Twenty-Four Introduction to the Decade: The OAU Tries to Cope

1 For a comprehensive examination of the refugee problem in Africa during the 1980s, see Nicholas van Hear, 'Refugees and Displaced People in Africa', pp.A47–A58, *Africa Contemporary Record*, vol. 22 1989–1990, Africana Publishing Company, 1995

2 Basil Davidson, 'Africa in Historical Perspective', *Africa South of the Sahara 1989*, p.15, Europa Publications Ltd, 1988

3 Colin Legum, 'The Organisation of African Unity, 1989 to Mid-1990: The End of a Disappointing Decade', p.A23, *Africa Contemporary Record 1989–90*, Marion E. Doro (editor), African Publishing Company, 1995

Chapter Twenty-Five The Arab North

1 Boutros Boutros-Ghali, *International Herald Tribune*, 24/07/1989

2 See Malise Ruthven, 'Islamic Politics in the Middle East' pp.136–47, *The Middle*

East and North Africa 1986, Europa Publications Limited, 1985

3   Michael Field, *Inside the Arab World*, p.126, John Murray, 1994

4   Field, *op. cit.*, p.130

5   'The Libyan Problem', *US Department of State Bulletin*, October 1983, pp.71–8 (US Government Publications)

6   'Libya: US Economic Measures', *US Department of State Bulletin*, June 1982, Department of State, 10 November 1982

7   See Guy Arnold, *Wars in the Third World since 1945* (2nd edition), pp.192–202, Cassell, 1995

8   FBIS 2 September 1983

9   Special Report No. 138, *Libya under Qadhafi: A Pattern of Aggression*, January 1986, US Department of State Bureau of Public Affairs, Washington DC

10 David Blundy and Andrew Lycett, *Qadhafi and the Libyan Revolution*, p.186, Corgi Books, 1988

11 *Keesing's Record of World Events*, June 1991

12 'The Libyan Problem', *US Department of State Bulletin*, October 1983, p.72, US Government Publications

Chapter Twenty-Six The Horn: Continuous Warfare

1   Musaddag Ahmed El haj Ali, 'The Redivision of the Southern Sudan', p.237, in *Decentralisation in Sudan*, editor Al-Agab al-Teraifi, Graduate College Publications No. 20, University of Khartoum, 1987

2   'The Redivision of the Southern Region: Why it must be Rejected?' (Nile Printing Press), pp.12–13, Solidarity Committee of the 4th National Congress

3   Hilary Ng'weno, 'Human Tragedy in Sudan', *Newsweek*, 02/07/1984

4   *New York Times*, 07/04/1985

5   *Africa Confidential*, vol. 26, No. 8, 10/04/1985

6   Samuel P. Huntington, *The Clash of Civilizations and the Remaking of World Order*, p.256, Touchstone Books, 1997

7   Huntington, *op. cit.*, p.275

8   Douglas H. Johnson, *The Root Causes of Sudan's Civil Wars*, p.xvii, James Currey, 2003

9   Johnson, *op. cit.*, pp.29–30

10 Agriculture and Rural Development Unit, Centre of Development Studies, University of Leeds, *Eritrea Food and Agricultural Production Assessment Study Final Report*, p.40, University of Leeds, 1988

11 D. Willis, *The Christian Science Monitor*, 13/09/1984

12 See Tesfatsion Medhanie, *Eritrea: Dynamics of a National Question*, pp.224–5, for the story of the Falashas, B. R. Grunner, Amsterdam, 1986

13 Medhanie, *op. cit.*, p.237

14 David Pool, *From Guerrillas to Government*, p.147, James Currey, 2001

15 See Chester Crocker, 'The Quest for an Africa Policy', *The Washington Review of Strategic and International Studies*, *Washington Quarterly*, vol. 1, No. 2, April 1978, p.73

16 See Donald Zagoria, 'Into the Breach: New Soviet alliances in the 3rd World', *Foreign Affairs*, Spring 1979, p.750

17 Medhanie, *op. cit.*, p.134

18 Chester Crocker, 'Africa Policy in the 1980's', *Washington Quarterly*, vol. 3, No. 3 (Summer 1980), p.74

19 Medhanie, *op. cit.*, p.129

20 *New York Times*, 25/10/1985

21 Pool, *op. cit.*, p.157

22 'A Test in Africa for Reagan's Clout', *Business Week* (New York), p.99, 02/02/1981

23 Scott Peterson, *Me Against My Brother*, p.13, Routledge, 2000

24 Peterson, *op. cit.*, p.16

Chapter Twenty-Seven West Africa: Nigeria and Ghana

1   Alan Rake, *Who's Who in Africa*, pp.257–8, Scarecrow Press, 1992

2   Rake, *op. cit.*, p.239

3   See Olusegun Obasanjo and Akin Mabogunje (editors), *Elements of Development*, Africa Leadership Forum, 1991

4   Obasanjo, *op. cit.*, p.95

5   Obasanjo, *op. cit.*, p.139

6   Rotimi Suberu, 'Integration and Disintegration in the Nigeria Federation', p.92, in *Regionalism in Africa*

Integration and Disintegration, Daniel C. Bach (editor), James Currey, 1999

7 Obasanjo, *op. cit.*, pp.9–16

8 Rake, *op. cit.*, pp.129–31

9 Kevin Shillington, *Ghana and the Rawlings Factor*, p.80, Macmillan, 1992

10 Shillington, *op. cit.*, p.107

11 Shillington, *op. cit.*, p.110

12 Shillington, *op. cit.*, p.114

13 Shillington, *op. cit.*, p.148

14 Fiona Mackenzie, 'Introduction', in *Development from Within. Survival in Rural Africa*, D. R. Fraser Taylor and Fiona Mackenzie (editors), p.11, Routledge, 1992

15 *People's Daily Graphic*, March 1987

16 Jerry Rawlings, 'Accountability Not Negotiable', Accra: Information Services Department, 1989

17 *Africa Confidential*, 'Ghana: Time is Running Out for Rawlings', pp.4–5, 20 October 1989

18 See *Africa Contemporary Record*, vol. XXII, 1989–90, 'Ghana', p.B50, Marion E. Doro, editor, and Colin Legum, consulting editor, Africana Publishing Company, 1995

19 Shillington, *op. cit.*, p.125

Chapter Twenty-Eight East and Equatorial Africa

1 Alan Rake, *Who's Who in Africa*, p.366, Scarecrow Press, 1992

2 Rake, *op. cit.*, p.385

3 Mahmood Mamdani, *When Victims Become Killers*, pp.144–5, James Currey, 2001

4 Mamdani, *op. cit.*, p.147

5 Mamdani *op. cit.*, p.155

6 Rake, *op. cit.*, p.56

7 Georges Nzongola-Ntalaja, *The Congo*, p.185, Zed Books, 2002

8 Janet MacGaffey and Remy Bazenguissa-Ganga, *Congo-Paris Transnational Traders on the Margins of the Law*, p.4, James Currey, 2000

Chapter Twenty-Nine Endgame in Southern Africa

1 See Joseph Hanlon, *Beggar Your Neighbours*, p.19, James Currey, 1986

2 Hanlon, *op. cit.*, p.8

3 Hanlon, *op. cit.*, p.1

4 Eschel Rhoodie, *The Real Information Scandal*, Orbis SA (Pty) Ltd, 1983

5 Phyllis Johnson and David Martin (editors), *Destructive Engagement*, p.67, Zimbabwe Publishing House, 1986

6 Johnson and Martin, *op. cit.*, p.91

7 *The Times*, 6/01/1984

8 *Financial Times*, 31/01/1986

9 Tony Hodges, *Angola from Afro-Stalinism to Petro-Diamond Capitalism*, p.11, James Currey, 2001

10 Hodges, *op. cit.*, p.50

11 Patrick Chabal et al, *A History of Postcolonial Lusophone Africa*, p.162, Hurst, 2002

12 *Financial Times*, 3/09/1981

13 Anthony Parsons, *From Cold War to Hot Peace*, p.120, Michael Joseph, 1995

14 See Malyn Newitt, 'Mozambique', p.195, in Chabal, *op. cit.*, Hurst 2002

15 Hanlon, *op. cit.*, p.145

16 Americo Magain, President Mozambican Chamber of Commerce, quoted in *Noticias,* Maputo, 10/07/1984

17 Chabal, *op. cit.*, p.119

18 *New York Times*, 13/04/1982

19 Susanna Smith, *Front Line Africa: the Right to a Future*, pp.259–60, OXFAM, 1990

20 For a detailed analysis of the South African mining industry see Laurie Flynn, *Studded with Diamonds and Paved with Gold*, Bloomsbury, 1992

21 Leonard Thompson, *A History of South Africa*, p.240, Yale University Press, 1990

22 *Guardian*, 24/08/1985

23 Robin Cohen, *Endgame in South Africa*, p.66, Africa World Press Inc., 1988

24 *Citizen*, 7/06/1984

25 Mats Lundahl and Lena Moritz, 'The Quest for Equity in South Africa – Redistribution and Growth' in Bertil Oden, *The South African Tripod*, Nordiska Afrikainstitutet, Uppsala, 1994

26 Frank Welsh, *A History of South Africa*, p.479, Harper Collins, 1998

27 Welsh, *op. cit.*, p.224

28 Smith, *op. cit.*, p.270 et seq.

29 Plenary Session, British Council of Churches, London, 28/02/1989

30   Interview with *Beeld*, 29/11/1989
31   Hanlon, *op. cit.*, p.24
32   Kevin Danaher, 'The Political Economy of US Policy toward South Africa' [Ph.D. disc., University of California, Santa Cruz, 1982], 5.
33   Allister Sparks, *The Mind of South Africa*, p.332, Heinemann, 1990
34   Sparks, *op. cit.*, p.337
35   Sparks, *op. cit.*, p.348
36   Sparks, *op. cit.*, p.352
37   Thompson, *op. cit.*, p.234
38   S. van der Merwe, 'And what about the black people?' 1985 Pretoria, Information Service of the National Party
39   Bertil Oden, *op. cit.*, pp.60/61
40   Alex Davidson and Pen Strand, 'The Path to Democracy – A Background to the Constitutional Negotiations in South Africa', in Oden, *op. cit.*, p.72
41   Allan A. Boesak, *If This is Treason I am Guilty*, pp.13, 26, 131, William B. Eerdmans Publishing Company, 1986
42   Sparks, *op. cit.*, p.271
43   South African whites who qualified for foreign nationality:
     Britain 800,000
     Portugal 500,000
     Israel 119,000
     Germany 100,000
     Italy 50,000
     Netherlands 40,000
     Belgium 25,000
     US 17,000
     Other 37,000
44   Welsh, *op. cit.*, p.489
45   Sparks, *op. cit.*, p.378

Chapter Thirty Development Standstill

1   The World Bank, *Accelerated Development in Sub-Saharan Africa: Agenda for Action*, p.9, World Bank
2   Mahmood Mamdani, *When Victims become Killers*, pp.152–3, James Currey, 2001
3   See Noam Chomsky, *Deterring Democracy*, p.126, Vintage, 1991
4   Patrick Chabal et al, *A History of Postcolonial Lusophone Africa*, p.90, Hurst, 2002
5   Chabal, *op. cit.*, p.89
6   Chabal, *op. cit.*, p.90
7   The World Bank Annual Report 1983
8   The World Bank Annual Report 1984, p.79
9   The World Bank Annual Report 1984, p.82
10   The World Bank Annual Report 1985, p.88
11   Jacob Songsore, 'The Cooperative Credit Union Movement in North-Western Ghana', quoted in *Development from Within: Survival in Rural Africa*, p.83., D. R. Taylor-Fraser and Fiona Mackenzie (editors), Routledge, 1992
12   The World Bank Annual Report 1986, p.83
13   World Development Report 1986, pp.77–78
14   World Food Report 1986, FAO
15   *Financing Adjustment with Growth in Sub-Saharan Africa 1986–90*, p.5, The World Bank, 1986
16   The World Bank, *op. cit.*, p.11
17   The World Bank Annual Report 1989, p.106
18   The World Bank Annual Report 1990, p.112
19   Olusegun Obasanjo and Akin Mabogunje (editors), *Elements of Development*, 'Background note on the Africa Leadership Forum', p.230, Africa Leadership Forum, 1991
20   Ismail Serageldin, *Poverty Adjustment and Growth in Africa*, p.iii, The World Bank, 1989
21   Serageldin, *op. cit.*, p.14
22   Ngumba Musa-Nda, 'A greater role for local development strategies', 1988, *Regional Development Dialogue* 9(2): 1–11

Part IV The 1990s: New Directions and New Perceptions

Chapter Thirty-One The End of the Cold War

1   Francis Fukuyama, *The End of History and the Last Man*, p.35, Hamish Hamilton, 1992

2   Martin Walker, *The Cold War*, p.354, Fourth Estate, 1993

3   Mark Curtis, *Web of Deceit*, p.76, Vintage, 2003

4   Scott Peterson, *Me Against My Brother*, p.19, Routledge, 2000

5   Samuel P. Huntington, *The Clash of Civilizations and the Remaking of World Order*, p.125, Touchstone Books, 1997

6   Huntington, *op. cit.*, p.31

7   Curtis, *op. cit.*, p.76

8   Huntington, *op. cit.*, p.241

9   Georges Nzongola-Ntalaja, *The Congo*, p.142, Zed Books, 2002

10 Patrick Chabal and Jean-Pascal Daloz, *Africa Works Disorder as Political Instrument*, p.112, James Currey, 1999

11 Rita Abrahamsen, *Disciplining Democracy*, p.19, Zed Books, 2000

12 Abrahamsen, *op. cit.*, p.3

13 Alvin and Heidi Toffler, *War and Anti-War*, p.42, Little, Brown & Co., 1993

14 Abrahamsen, *op. cit.*, p.33

15 Abrahamsen, *op. cit.*, p.142

16 The Commission on Global Governance, *Our Global Neighbourhood*, p.122, OUP, 1995

17 Abrahamsen, *op. cit.*, p.27

18 *Observer*, 1/03/1992

Chapter Thirty-Two South Africa: The Last Hero

1   Nelson Mandela, *Long Walk to Freedom*, p.590, Little, Brown & Co., 1994

2   Frank Welsh, *A History of South Africa*, p.461, Harper Collins, 1998

3   Mandela, *op. cit.*, p.595

4   Welsh, *op. cit.*, p.508

5   Mandela, *op. cit.*, p.602

6   Welsh, *op. cit.*, p.509

7   Welsh, *op. cit.*, p.512

8   Mandela, *op. cit.*, p.606

9   Mandela, *op. cit.*, p.612

10 *The Independent*, 17/12/1994

11 UNDP, *Human Development Report 1998*, OUP, 1998

12 Anthony Sampson, *Mandela*, p.534, Harper Collins, 1999

13 Sampson, *op. cit.*, p.530

14 *Sunday Independent* (SA), 16/07/1995

15 *Sunday Independent* (SA), 6/12/1998

16 Sampson, *op. cit.*, pp.522/23

17 *South African Star*, 16/12/1997

18 Welsh, *op. cit.*, p.502

19 Roy Hattersley, *Observer*, 31/08/1997

20 *Business Report* (SA), 6/10/1998

21 Welsh, *op. cit.*, p.513

22 *Business Report* (SA), 22/08/1995

23 Allister Sparks, *Natal Witness* (SA), 9/08/1995

24 Shaun Johnson, *Sunday Independent* (SA), 14/12/1997

25 Christopher Saunders, 'South Africa: Recent History', p.1060, *Europa: Africa South of the Sahara 2001*, Europa Publications, 2001

26 Saunders, *op. cit.*, p.1061

27 Mandela, *op. cit.*, p.604

28 Welsh, *op. cit.*, p.502

29 Quoted in Sampson, *op. cit.*, p.533

30 *The Independent*, 22/11/1996

Chapter Thirty-Three
Democracy

1   Harry Shutt, *A New Democracy*, p.146, Zed Books, 2001

2   Shutt, *op. cit.*, p.149

3   Patrick Chabal and Jean-Pascal Daloz, *Africa Works: Disorder as Political Instrument*, p.118, James Currey, 1999

4   Rita Abrahamsen, *Disciplining Democracy*, p.27, Zed Books, 2000

5   Noam Chomsky, *Deterring Democracy*, p.332, Vintage, 1991

6   Chabal, Daloz, *op. cit.*, p.51

7   Jean-François Bayart, Stephen Ellis and Beatrice Hibou, *The Criminalisation of the State in Africa*, p.xiii, James Currey, 1999

8   Abrahamsen, *op. cit.*, p.23

9   See The Commission on Global Governance, *Our Global Neighbourhood*, and p.337, OUP, 1995

10 Chabal, Daloz, *op. cit.*, p.xvi

11 Chabal, Daloz, *op. cit.*, p.38. Their book deals with this subject in depth in this pertinent examination of the problems suggested by the title.

12 Chabal, Daloz, *op. cit.*, p.36

13 Nicholas Thompson, Scott Thompson, *The Baobab and the Mango Tree*, p.89, Zed Books, 2000

14 Abrahamsen, *op. cit.*, p.118

15 Chabal, Daloz, *op. cit.*, p.162
16 Bayart, *op. cit.*, pp.4–5
17 Thompson, *op. cit.*, p.118
18 Thompson, *op. cit.*, p.118
19 Georges Nzongola-Ntalanja, *The Congo*, p.8, Zed Books, 2002
20 *Ghanaian Times*, 16/08/1998
21 Thompson, *op. cit.*, p.49
22 David Pool, *From Guerrillas to Government*, p.168, James Currey, 2001
23 Pool, *op. cit.*, p.196
24 Thompson, *op. cit.*, p.165
25 Anver Versi, 'Victory to the People', *African Business*, February 2003, p.13
26 Abrahamsen, *op. cit.*, p.102
27 Tony Hodges, *Angola from Afro-Stalinism to Petro-Diamond Capitalism*, p.61, James Currey, 2001
28 Abrahamsen, *op. cit.*, p.130
29 Chabral, Daloz, *op. cit.*, p.157
30 Bayart, *op. cit.*, p.2
31 Thompson, *op. cit.*, p.118

Chapter Thirty-Four Civil Wars: Algeria, Somalia, Sudan

1 Hugh Roberts, *The Battlefield Algeria 1988–2002*, p.109, Verso, 2003
2 Roberts, *op. cit.*, p.4
3 Roberts, *op. cit.*, p.313
4 Roberts, *op. cit.*, p.104
5 Roberts, *op. cit.*, p.250. The particular merit of Hugh Roberts's book is the analysis he provides as to why things happened the way they did in Algeria, as opposed to many accounts of the civil war that simply record what happened or assume that it was a straightforward confrontation between secular and fundamentalist forces.
6 Roberts, *op. cit.*, p.285
7 Scott Peterson, *Me Against My Brother*, p.52, Routledge, 2000
8 Peterson, *op. cit.*, p.60
9 Peterson, *op. cit.*, p.112
10 Peterson, *op. cit.*, p.144
11 Boutros Boutros-Ghali, *Unvanquished*, p.53, I. B. Tauris, 1999
12 Boutros-Ghali, *op. cit.*, p.96
13 Boutros-Ghali, *op. cit.*, p.100

Chapter Thirty-Five Genocide and Border Confrontation

1 See Scott Peterson, *Me Against My Brother*, p.259 et seq., Routledge, 2000
2 Mahmood Mamdani, *When Victims Become Killers*, p.147, James Currey, 2001
3 Mamdani, *op. cit.*, p.146
4 Mamdani, *op. cit.*, p.185
5 Catherine Watson, 'Rwanda: War and Waiting', *Africa Report*, November/December 1992, p.55
6 Mamdani, *op. cit.*, p.187
7 Mamdani, *op. cit.*, p.213
8 Mamdani, *op. cit.*, pp.196–204
9 Quoted in Lindsay Hilsum, *Observer*, 'Hutu Warlord Defends Child Killings', 3/07/1994
10 Mamdani, *op. cit.*, p.213
11 Mamdani, *op. cit.*, p.232
12 Boutros Boutros-Ghali, *Unvanquished*, p.134, I. B. Tauris, 1999
13 Boutros-Ghali, *op. cit.*, p.136
14 Boutros-Ghali, *op. cit.*, p.138
15 Boutros-Ghali, *op. cit.*, p.140
16 Peterson, *op. cit.*, p.252
17 Peterson, *op. cit.*, p.293
18 *The Washington Post*, 'Stopping Rwanda's Bloodbath', 5/05/1994
19 Peterson, *op. cit.*, p.302
20 *The Economist*, 23/10/1999

Chapter Thirty-Six Failed States and the Return of the Imperial Factor

1 *The Independent*, 16/05/2000
2 *Observer*, 19/10/1997
3 *West Africa*, 22/10–09/11/1997
4 *The Times*, 21/10/1997
5 Baffour Ankrah, *New African*, May 1998
6 *Financial Times*, 20/02/2003
7 *The Independent*, 23/09/2002
8 *The Independent*, 25/09/2002
9 *Observer*, 29/09/2002
10 *The Independent*, 9/12/2002
11 *The Independent*, 28/01/2003
12 *Financial Times*, 20/02/2003
13 See Thomas Jaye, 'Roots of the Crisis', *West Africa*, pp.20–21, issue 4359, 20–26 January 2003

14 For a detailed account of the civil war, see Guy Arnold, *Historical Dictionary of Civil Wars in Africa*, pp.148–56, Scarecrow Press, 1999

15 James Astill, *Observer*, 22/06/2003

16 Rupert Cornwell, *The Independent*, 4/07/2003

Chapter Thirty-Seven The Congo: Africa's Great War

1 Georges Nzongola-Ntalaja, *The Congo*, p.172, Zed Books, 2002

2 Nzongola-Ntalaja, *op. cit.*, p.199

3 Nzongola-Ntalaja, *op. cit.*, p.208

4 Jean-François Bayart, Stephen Ellis and Beatrice Hibou, *The Criminalization of the State in Africa*, p.22, James Currey, 1999

5 Bayart et al, *op. cit.*, p.108

6 Nzongola-Ntalaja, *op. cit.*, p.214

7 *The Economist*, 24/10/1998

8 Richard Werbner (editor), *Postcolonial Subjectivities in Africa*, pp.123–4, Zed Books, 2002

9 Nzongola-Ntalaja, *op. cit.*, p.227

10 *The Independent*, 21/03/2001

11 *The Independent*, 22/10/2001

12 Nzongola-Ntalaja, *op. cit.*, p.227

13 *The Monitor* (Kampala), 3/07/2000

14 Nzongola-Ntalaja, *op. cit.*, p.233

15 Denis M. Tull, 'Reconfiguration of Political Order? The State of the State in North Kivu (DR Congo)', *African Affairs* (The Journal of the Royal African Society, vol. 102, No. 408, July 2003), p.431

16 *The Independent*, 30/05/2003

Chapter Thirty-Eight Mugabe's Zimbabwe

1 Address to the Nation, 4 March 1980

2 David Blair, *Degrees in Violence*, p.165, Continuum, 2003. This book provides a detailed account of the violence, the activities of the 'war veterans' and the developing polarization between Mugabe and his government on the one hand and the white farmers and black political opponents (Movement for Democratic Change – MDC) on the other.

3 Martin Meredith, *Mugabe*, p.121, Public Affairs Ltd (Oxford), 2002

4 Meredith, *op. cit.*, p.122

5 Meredith, *op. cit.*, p.126

6 Meredith, *op. cit.*, p.148

7 Meredith, *op. cit.*, p.149

8 See 'Zimbabwe', *The Annual Register 2002*, pp.288–91, Keesing's Worldwide, 2003

9 Blair, *op. cit.*, p.174

10 Quoted in Blair, *op. cit.*, p133

11 Blair, *op. cit.*, p.137

12 Quoted in Blair, *op. cit.*, p.112

13 Meredith, *op. cit.*, pp.144, 226

14 Stephen Chan, 'Mugabe: Right and Wrong', pp.343–7, *African Affairs*, The Journal of the Royal African Society, vol. 102, No. 407, April 2003

15 Chan, *op. cit.*, p.347

16 *ANC Today*, 8 March 2002

Chapter Thirty-Nine Corruption

1 I have had more than one conversation with European businessmen in Africa who say something as follows: 'You have no idea how corrupt these people are (wherever they may be). I had to pay off the minister, his number two and two civil servants before I could secure the contract.' 'It takes two to be corrupt.' Such a response is not understood. They (the Africans) were corrupt. The businessman was just doing what was necessary to obtain his contract!

2 Nicholas Thompson, Scott Thompson, *The Baobab and the Mango Tree*, p.11, Zed Books, 2000

3 Mark Duffield, *Global Governance and the New Wars*, p.162, Zed Books, 2001

4 Patrick Chabal, Jean-Pascal Daloz, *Africa Works: Disorder as Political Instrument*, p.79, James Currey, 1999

5 Chabal, Daloz, *op. cit.*, p.95

6 Chabal, Daloz, *op. cit.*, p.95

7 See The Commission on Global Governance, *Our Global Neighbourhood*, pp.63–5, OUP, 1995

8 The Commission on Global Governance, *op. cit.*, p.173

9 South Commission, *The Challenge to the South*, pp.51–2, OUP, 1990

10 Janet MacGaffey, Remy Bazenguissa-Ganga, *Congo-Paris, Transnational Traders on the Margins of the Law*, p.81, James Currey, 2000
11 Harry Shutt, *A New Democracy*, p.96, Zed Books, 2001
12 Shutt, *op. cit.*, p.96
13 Jean-François Bayart, Stephen Ellis, Beatrice Hibou, *The Criminalization of the State in Africa*, p.xiii, James Currey, 1999
14 Shutt, *op. cit.*, p.96
15 David Sogge, *Give and Take 'What's the Matter with Foreign Aid'*, p.86, Zed Books, 2002
16 A. Alesine and B. Weder, 1999, 'Do Corrupt Governments Receive Less Foreign Aid?', Paper No. W7108, Cambridge National Bureau of Economic Research
17 Shutt, *op. cit.*, p.97
18 Shutt, *op. cit.*, p.20
19 Hugh Roberts, *The Battlefield Algeria 1988–2002*, p.107, Verso, 2003
20 Roberts, *op. cit.*, p.307
21 See Tony Hodges, *Angola from Afro-Stalinism to Petro-Diamond Capitalism*, James Currey, 2001
22 Hodges, *op. cit.*, p.71
23 Hodges, *op. cit.*, p.72
24 Karl Maier, *This House has Fallen: Nigeria in Crisis*, p.xxii, Allen Lane, The Penguin Press, 2000
25 Chabal, Daloz, *op. cit.*, p.100
26 Georges Nzongola-Ntalaja, *The Congo*, p.236, Zed Books, 2002
27 Nzongola-Ntalaja, *op. cit.*, pp.236–7
28 Duffield, *op. cit.*, p.133
29 Eboe Hutchful, *Ghana's Adjustment Experience: The Paradox of Reform*, p.3, UN Research Institute for Social Development, in association with James Currey, 2002
30 Hutchful, *op. cit.*, p.37
31 Hutchful, *op. cit.*, p.223
32 See Bayart, Ellis, Hibou, *op. cit.*
33 Sogge, *op. cit.*, p.179
34 Frances Christie, Joseph Hanlon, *Mozambique and the Great Flood of 2000*, p.74, James Currey, 2001
35 Christie, Hanlon, *op. cit.*, p.138
36 See Vijay Prashad, *Fat Cats and Running Dogs*, pp.38–9, extract from the *Houston Chronicle*, 'U.S. Foreign Aid as Lever that moved Enron Deal', *Houston Chronicle*, 1 November 1995, Zed Books, 2002
37 Tom Lodge, *Bus Stop for Everyone*, p.147, James Currey, 2002
38 Lodge, *op. cit.*, p.151. His chapter 'Countering Corruption', pp.129–52, gives a finely balanced account of the problem in Mbeki's South Africa.
39 Michael Schulz, Frederik Soderbaum, *Regionalization in a Globalizing World*, p.77, Zed Books, 2001
40 Chabal, Daloz, *op. cit.*, p.99

Chapter Forty Century's End: Globalization

1   The Annual Register, 'South Africa', p.299, Keesings Worldwide, 2003
2   Desmond Cohen, *Working Paper ILO AIDS 'Human Capital and the HIV experience in Sub-Saharan Africa'*, ILO Programme on HIV/AIDS and the World of Work, Geneva, June 2002
3   See *Human Development Report 2003*, UNDP 2003
4   Economic Commission for Africa, *Transforming Africa's Economies*, p.1, ECA, Addis Ababa, 2001
5   The World Bank, *Can Africa Claim the 21st Century?* The World Bank, Washington DC, 2000
6   The World Bank, *op. cit.*, p.39
7   The Commission on Global Governance, *Our Global Neighbourhood*, p.10, OUP, 1995
8   Vijay Prashad, *Fat Cats and Running Dogs*, p.44, Zed Books, 2002
9   Prashad, *op. cit.*, p.149
10 Harry Shutt, *A New Democracy*, p.72, Zed Books, 2001
11 Shutt, *op. cit.*, p.82
12 Mark Curtis, *Web of Deceit*, pp.226–7, Vintage, 2003
13 Eboe Hutchful, *Ghana's Adjustment Experience 'The Paradox of Reform'*, p.245, UN Research Institute for Social Development, in association with James Currey, 2002
14 Curtis, *op. cit.*, p.248
15 Curtis, *op. cit.*, p.235

16 See Curtis, *Web of Deceit*
17 Curtis, *op. cit.*, p.249
18 Curtis, *op. cit.*, p.437
19 See UNDP, *Human Development Report 1999,* OUP, 1999
20 Judith Richter, *Holding Corporations Accountable,* p.146, Zed Books, 2001
21 Prashad, *op. cit.*, p.145
22 David Sogge, *Give and Take 'What's the Matter with Foreign Aid?',* p.126, Zed Books, 2002
23 James Petras and Henry Veltmeyer, *Globalisation Unmasked,* p.31, Zed Books, 2001
24 Rita Abrahamsen, *Disciplining Democracy,* p.8, Zed Books, 2000
25 Abrahamsen, *op. cit.*, p.9
26 Martin Khor, *Rethinking Globalisation,* p.15, Zed Books, 2001
27 Hugh Roberts, *The Battlefield Algeria 1988–2002,* p.222, Verso, 2003
28 Roberts, *op. cit.*, p.325
29 See Janet MacGaffey and Remy Bazenguissa-Ganga, *Congo-Paris Transnational Traders on the Margins of the Law*, James Currey, 2000
30 François Houtart and François Polet (eds), *The Other Davos.* P.7, Zed Books, 2001
31 Houtart and Polet, *op. cit.*, p.27
32 Christian Comeliau, *The Impasse of Modernity*, p.32, Zed Books, 2000 (translation 2002)
33 Comeliau, *op. cit.*, p.83

Epilogue

1 Sam Kiley, *Observer*, 17/08/2003
2 See Anver Versi, 'Who Rules Africa', p.13, *African Business*, No. 290, August/September 2003
3 See Nilla Ahmed, 'G8 Leaders told to fulfil promises', p.31, *West Africa*, issue 4379, 9–15 June 2003
4 S. K. B. Asante, 'Making NEPAD a shared vision', p.30, *West Africa*, issue 4374, 5–11 May 2003
5 Richard Dowden, *The Independent,* 31/05/2003
6 *The Independent*, 15/07/2003
7 Harry Shutt, *A New Democracy*, p.21, Zed Books, 2001
8 James Butty, 'USA hears Africa's trade demands', p.27, *West Africa*, issue 4383, 7–13 July 2003
9 Anver Versi, 'He came, he saw, did he conquer?', p.15, *African Business*, No. 290, August/September 2003
10 Editorial, *Mail and Guardian*, South Africa

Bibliography

Abrahamsen, Rita, *Disciplining Democracy*, Zed Books, 2000

Adu, A. L., *The Civil Service in New African States*, George Allen & Unwin, 1965

Afrifa, Colonel A. A., *The Ghana Coup 24th February 1966*, Frank Cass, 1967

Agricultural and Rural Development Unit, Centre of Development Studies, University of Leeds, *Eritrea food and agricultural production assessment study, Final Report*, University of Leeds, 1988

Al-Teraifi, Al-Agab Ahmed (editor), *Decentralization in Sudan*, Graduate College Publications, University of Khartoum, 1987

Allcock, T. B., et al, *Border and Territorial Disputes*, (3rd edition), Longman, 1992

Amin, Samir, *The Maghreb in the Modern World*, Penguin Books, 1970

Anonymous (sponsored by the Journal of African Marxists), *Independent Kenya*, Zed Press, 1992

Arnold, Guy, *Kenyatta and the politics of Kenya*, J. M. Dent, 1974

—, *A Guide to African Political and Economic Development*, Fitzroy Dearborn, 2001

—, *Historical Dictionary of Civil Wars in Africa*, Scarecrow Press, 1999

—, *Political and economic Encyclopaedia of Africa*, Longman, 1993

—, *World Government by Stealth 'The Future of the United Nations'*, Macmillan, 1997

—, *Modern Nigeria*, Longman, 1977

—, *Aid in Africa*, Kogan Page, 1979

—, *Wars in the Third World since 1945* (2nd edition), Cassell, 1995

—, *The Last Bunker 'A Report on White South Africa Today'*, Quartet Books, 1976

—, *Mercenaries: The Scourge of the Third World*, Macmillan, 1999

—, *The Maverick State 'Gaddafi and the New World Order'*, Cassell, 1996

—, *The Third World Handbook* (2nd edition), Cassell, 1994

—, *The End of the Third World*, Macmillan, 1993

—, *South Africa: Crossing the Rubicon*, Macmillan, 1992

—, *The New South Africa*, Macmillan, 2000

Arnold, Guy and Ruth Weiss, *Strategic Highways of Africa*, Julian Friedmann, 1977

Attwood, William, *The Reds and the Blacks*, Harper and Row, 1967

Bach, Daniel C., *Regionalisation in Africa Integration and Disintegration*, James Currey, 1999

Bailey, Martin, *Oilgate*, Coronet Books, 1979

Balandier, Georges, *Ambiguous Africa*, Chatto & Windus, 1966

Barnett, Corelli, *The Lost Victory*, Macmillan, 1995

Bayart, Jean-François, Stephen Ellis and Beatrice Hibou, *The Criminalisation of the State in Africa*, James Currey, 1999

Bennett, George, *Kenya: A Political History*, Oxford University Press, 1963

Benson, Mary, *The Struggle for a Birthright*, Penguin Books, 1966

Beshir, Mohammed Omer, *The Southern Sudan: Background to Conflict*, C. Hurst & Co., 1968

—, *The Southern Sudan: From Conflict to Peace*, The Khartoum Bookshop, 1975

Blair, David, *Degrees in Violence*, Continuum, 2003

Blum, William, *Killing Hope,* Zed Books, 2003

Boesak, Allan A., *If This is Treason, I am Guilty*, William B. Eerdmans Publishing Company, 1986

Boutros-Ghali, Boutros, *Unvanquished*, I. B. Tauris, 1999

Brandt, Willy (chairman), *North-South: A Programme for Survival* (The Brandt Report), Pan Books, 1980

Brockway, Fenner, *The Colonial Reckoning*, Hart-Davis, MacGibbon, 1973

Brogan, Patrick, *World Conflicts*, Bloomsbury (3rd edition), 1998

Bryceson, Deborah F., *Food Insecurity and the Social Division of Labour in Tanzania 1919–1985*, Macmillan, 1990

Bull, Theodore (ed.), *Rhodesia Perspective,* Michael Joseph, 1967

Bunting, Brian, *The Rise of the South African Reich*, Penguin Books, 1964

Cahill, Kevin M., MD, *Somalia A Perspective*, The State University of New York Press, 1980

Carter, Gwendolen, M., *Independence for Africa*, Frederick A. Praeger, 1960

Cervenka, Zdenek, *Landlocked Countries of Africa*, The Scandinavian Institute of African Studies, Uppsala, 1973

Chabal, Patrick and Jean-Pascal Daloz, *Africa Works Disorder as Political Instrument*, James Currey, 1999

Chabal, Patrick, et al, *A History of Postcolonial Lusophone Africa*, Hurst, 2002

Chan, Stephen, 'Mugabe: Right and Wrong', *The Royal African Society,* vol. 102, number 407, April 2003

Chomsky, Naom, *Deterring Democracy*, Vintage, 1991

Christie, Frances and Joseph Hanlon, *Mozambique and the Great Flood of 2000*, James Currey, 2001

Clark, Trevor, *A Right Honourable Gentleman: Abubakar from the Black Rock*, Edward Arnold, 1991

Cliffe, Lionel & John S. Saul (editors), *Socialism in Tanzania: Politics* (vol. I), East African Publishing House, 1972

Cohen, Robin, *Endgame in South Africa*, Africa World Press Inc., 1988

Comeliau, Christian, *The Impasse of Modernity,* Zed Books (translation 2002), 2000

The Commission on Global Governance, *Our Global Neighbourhood*, Oxford University Press, 1995

Cowen, Michael and Liisa Laakso, *Multi-Party Elections in Africa*, James Currey, 2002

Curtis, Mark, *Web of Deceit*, Vintage, 2003

Davidson, Basil, *Can Africa Survive?*, Heinemann, 1974

—, *Which Way Africa?*, Penguin Books, 1964 (revised 1967)

—, *The Liberation of Guine*, Penguin Books, 1969

—, *In the Eye of the Storm 'Angola's People',* Longman, 1972

Davies, Ioan, *African Trade Unions*, Penguin Books, 1966

De Villiers, Dawid, *The Case for South Africa*, Tom Stacey Ltd, 1970

De Witte, Ludo, *The Assassination of Lumumba*, Verso, 2001

Dickie, John and Alan Rake, *Who's Who in Africa*, African Development, 1973

Doornbus, Martin, Lionel Cliffe, Abdel Ghaffar, M. Ahmed and John Markakis (editors), *Beyond Conflict in the Horn*, Institute of Social Studies, The Hague, James Currey, 1992

Duffield, Mark, *Global Governance and the New Wars*, Zed Books, 2001

Duffy, James, *Portugal in Africa*, Penguin Books, 1962

Dumont, René, *False Start in Africa*, Andre Deutsch, 1966

Fanon, Frantz, *The Wretched of the Earth* (*Les damnes de la terre-1961*), MacGibbon & Kee, 1965

—, *Toward the African Revolution*, Grove Press NY, 1967

Federal Republic of Nigeria, *Third National Development Plan 1975–80*, The Central Planning Office, Lagos, 1975

Field, Michael, *Inside the Arab World*, John Murray, 1994

Finn, Julio, *Voices of Negritude*, Quartet Books, 1988

First, Ruth, *The Barrel of a Gun*, Allen Lane The Penguin Press, 1970

—, *South West Africa*, Penguin Books, 1963

First, Ruth, Jonathan Steele and Christabel Gurney, *The South African Connection*, Temple Smith, 1972

Fisher, Nigel, *Iain MacLeod*, Andre Deutsch, 1973

Flower, Ken, *Serving Secretly*, John Murray, 1987

Flynn, Laurie, *Studded with Diamonds and Paved with Gold,* Bloomsbury, 1992

Food and Agricultural Organisation, *World Food Report 1987*, FAO (UN) Rome, 1987

Food and Agricultural Organisation, *FAO in 1988*, FAO (UN) Rome, 1988

Fordham, Paul, *The Geography of World Affairs* (4th edition), Penguin Books, 1974

Forsyth, Frederick, *The Biafra Story*, Penguin Books, 1969

Fransman, Martin (editor), *Industry and Accumulation in Africa*, Heinemann, 1982

Fraser Taylor, D. R. and Fiona MacKenzie (editors), *Development from Within: Survival in Rural Africa*, Routledge, 1992

Fukuyama, Francis, *The End of History and the Last Man*, Hamish Hamilton, 1992

Gann, L. H., and Peter Duignan (editors), *Colonialism in Africa 1870–1960* (vol. II), Cambridge University Press, 1970

Gibson, Richard, *African Liberation Movements*, Oxford University Press, 1972

Gilkes, Patrick, *The Dying Lion: Feudalism and Modernisation in Ethiopia*, Julian Friedmann, 1975

Graaf, William D., *The Nigerian State: Political Economy, State Class and Political System in the Post-Colonial Era*, James Currey, 1988

Green, Reginald H. and Ann Seidman, *Unity or Poverty?*, Penguin Books, 1968

Gussman, Boris, *Out in the Mid-day Sun*, George Allen & Unwin, 1962

Hall, Richard, *Zambia*, Pall Mall Press, 1965

—, *The High Price of Principles*, Hodder & Stoughton, 1969

Halpern, Jack, *South Africa's Hostages*, Penguin Books, 1965

Hanlon, Joseph, *Beggar Your Neighbour*, CIIR/James Currey, 1986

Harlow, Vincent and E. M. Chilver, assisted by Alison Smith (editors), with an introduction by Margery Perham, *History of East Africa*, Oxford University Press, 1965

Hasan, Yusuf Fadl (editor), *Sudan in Africa*, Khartoum University Press, 1985

Hatch, John, *The History of Britain in Africa*, Andre Deutsch, 1969

—, *Africa Today – and Tomorrow*, Frederick A. Praeger, 1960

Hennessy, Peter, *Never Again*, Jonathan Cape, 1992

Hodges, Tony, *Angola from Afro-Stalinism to Petro-Diamond Capitalism*, James Currey, 2001

Holt, P. M., and M. Widaly, *The History of the Sudan*, Weidenfeld and Nicolson, (3rd edition), 1979

Horne, Alistair, *Macmillan 1957–1986* (vol. II of the Official Biography), Macmillan, 1989

Houtart, François and François Polet (editors), *The Other Davos*, Zed Books, 2001

Howarth, Anthony, *Kenyatta A Photographic Biography*, East African Publishing House, 1967

Huddleston, Trevor, *Naught for your comfort*, Collins Fontana Books, 1957

Hughes, A. J., *East Africa: The Search for Unity*, Penguin Books, 1963

Hunter, Guy, *The New Societies of Tropical Africa*, Oxford University Press, 1962

Huntington, Samuel P., *The Clash of Civilizations and the Remaking of World Order*, Touchstone Books, 1997

Hutchful, Eboe, *Ghana's Adjustment Experience: The Paradox of Reform*, UN Research Institute for Social Development in association with James Currey, 2002

Hutt, W. H., *The Economics of the Colour Bar*, Andre Deutsch, 1964

Itote, Waruhiu 'General China', *'Mau Mau' General*, East African Publishing House, 1967

—, *Mau Mau in Action*, TransAfrica, 1979

Johnson, Douglas H., *The Root Causes of Sudan's Civil Wars*, James Currey, 2003

Johnson, Phyllis and David Martin (editors), *Frontline Southern Africa*, Ryan Publishing, 1989

—, *Destructive Engagement*, Zimbabwe Publishing House, 1986

Johnson, R. W., *How long will South Africa survive?*, Macmillan, 1977

Kanza, Thomas, *Conflict in the Congo*, Penguin Books, 1972

Kay, Hugh, *Salazar and Modern Portugal*, Eyre and Spottiswoode, 1970

Keatley, Patrick, *The Politics of Partnership*, Penguin Books, 1963

Khor, Martin, *Rethinking Globalisation*, Zed Books, 2001

Konig, Barbara, *Namibia The Ravages of War*, International Defence and Aid Fund for Southern Africa, 1983

Lee, J. M., *African Armies and Civil Order*, Chatto & Windus (for The Institute for Strategic Studies), 1969

Legum, Colin, *Ethiopia The Fall of Haile Selassie's Empire*, Rex Collings, 1975

—, *Pan-Africanism: A Short Political Guide*, Pall Mall Press, 1961

Lewis, W. Arthur, *Politics in West Africa*, George Allen & Unwin, 1965

Little, I. M. D., *Aid to Africa*, Pergamon Press, 1964

Lodge, Tom, *Bus Stop for Everyone*, James Currey, 2002

Loney, Martin, *Rhodesia, White Racism and Imperial Response*, Penguin Books, 1975

Lowenthal, Richard, *Model or Ally,* Oxford University Press, 1977

MacGaffey, Janet and Remy Bazenguissa-Ganga, *Congo-Paris Transnational Traders on the Margins of the Law*, James Currey, 2000

MacPhee, A. Marshall, *Kenya*, Ernest Benn Ltd, 1968

Maier, Karl, *The House Has Fallen 'Nigeria in Crisis'*, Allen Lane The Penguin Press, 2000

Mamdani, Mahmood, *When Victims Become Killers*, James Currey, 2001

Mandela, Nelson, *Long Walk to Freedom*, Little, Brown & Co., 1994

Mansfield, Peter, *The Arabs*, Allen Lane Penguin Books, 1976

—, *The Middle East*, Oxford University Press, 1973

Martin, David and Phyllis Johnson, *The Struggle for Zimbabwe*, Zimbabwe Publishing House, 1981

Maxey, Kees, *The Fight for Zimbabwe*, Rex Collings, 1975

Mazrui, Ali A., *Cultural Forces in World Politics*, James Currey, 1990

—, *Violence and Thought*, Longmans, 1969

Mbeki, Govan, *The Peasants' Revolt*, Penguin Books, 1964

McMaster, Carolyn, *Malawi Foreign Policy and Development*, Julian Friedmann, 1974

Medhane, Tesfatsion, *Eritrea: Dynamics of a National Question*, B. R. Gruner (Amsterdam), 1986

Meredith, Martin, *Mugabe*, Public Affairs Ltd (Oxford), 2002

Minter, William, *Portuguese Africa and the West*, Penguin Books, 1972

Misser, François and Osei Boateng, *New African Magazine*, 'Lumumba', February 2000

Mondlane, Eduardo, *The Struggle for Mozambique*, Penguin Books, 1969

Mortimer, Edward, *France and the Africans 1944–1960*, Faber and Faber, 1969

Murray, Roger, Jo Morris, John Dugard, Neville Rubin, *The Role of Foreign Firms in Namibia*, Africa Publications Trust, 1974

Nkrumah, Kwame, *Africa Must Unite*, Heinemann, 1963

—, *I Speak of Freedom*, Heinemann, 1961

Nwanko, Arthur A. and Samuel U. Ifejika, *The Making of a Nation: Biafra*, C. Hurst, 1969

Nyerere, Julius, *Freedom and Unity/Uhuru na Umosa*, Oxford University Press, 1967

—, *Freedom and Socialism/Uhuru na Ujamaa*, Oxford University Press, 1968

Nzongola-Ntalaja, Georges, *The Congo*, Zed Books, 2002

Obasanjo, General Olusegun, *My Command*, Heinemann, 1980

Obasanjo, Olusegun and Akin Mabogunje (editors), *Elements of Development*, Africa Leadership Forum, 1991

O'Brien, Conor Cruise, *Murderous Angels,* Hutchinson, 1968

Oden, Bertil, Thomas Ohlsen, Alex Davidson, Per Strand, Mats Lundhal, Lena Moritz, *The South African Tripod*, Nordiska Afrikainstitutet, Uppsala, 1994

Okello, John, *Revolution in Zanzibar*, East African Publishing House, 1967

Oni, Ola and Dr Bade Onimode, *Economic Development of Nigeria: The Socialist Alternative*, The Nigerian Academy of Arts Sciences and Technology, 1975

Organisation of African Unity (OAU), *What Kind of Africa by the Year 2000? Final Report of the Monrovia Symposium on the future development prospects of Africa towards the year 2000,* OAU (Addis Ababa), 1979

Organisation of African Unity, *The OAU 35 Years in the Service of Africa*, World of Information, 1998

Parsons, Anthony, *From Cold War to Hot Peace*, Michael Joseph, 1995

People's Democratic Republic of Algeria, *Memorandum submitted by Algeria to the Conference of Sovereigns and Heads of State of OPEC member countries*, Algeria Government, 1975

Perham, Margery, *The Colonial Reckoning*, Collins, 1961

—, 'Nigeria's Civil War', *Africa Contemporary Record 1968–69*, Colin Legum and John Drysdale, Africa Research Ltd, 1969

Peterson, Scott, *Me Against My Brother*, Routledge, 2000

Petras, James and Henry Veltmeyer, *Globalisation Unmasked*, Zed Books, 2001

Pettman, Jan, *Zambia Security and Conflict*, Julian Friedmann, 1974

Pimlott, Ben, *Harold Wilson*, Harper Collins, 1992

Pool, David, *From Guerrillas to Government*, James Currey, 2001

Post, Ken, *The New States of West Africa*, Penguin Books, 1968 (revised edition)

Prashad, Vijay, *Fat Cats and Running Dogs*, Zed Books, 2002

Pratt, Cranford, *The Critical Phase in Tanzania 1945–1968 'Nyerere and the Emergence of a Socialist Strategy'*, Cambridge University Press, 1976

Rake, Alan, *100 Great Africans*, Scarecrow Press, 1994

—, *Who's Who in Africa*, Scarecrow Press, 1992

Rasmussen, R. Kent, *Historical Dictionary of Rhodesia/Zimbabwe*, Scarecrow Press, 1979

Richter, Judith, *Holding Corporations Accountable*, Zed Books, 2001

Rimmer, Douglas, *The Economics of West Africa*, Weidenfeld and Nicolson, 1984

Roberts, Hugh, *The Battlefield Algeria 1988–2002*, Verso, 2003

Rodney, Walter, *How Europe Underdeveloped Africa*, Bogle-L'Ouverture Publications, 1972

Rogers, Barbara, *White Wealth and Black Poverty*, Greenwood Press, 1976

Rooney, David, *Kwame Nkrumah The Political Kingdom in the Third World*, I. B. Tauris, 1988

Rothchild, Donald (editor), *Politics of Integration*, East African Publishing House, 1968

St. John Wood, Anthony, *Northern Rhodesia*, Pall Mall Press, 1961

St. Jorre, John de, *The Nigerian Civil War*, Hodder & Stoughton, 1972

Sampson, Anthony, *Mandela 'The Authorised Biography'*, Harper Collins, 1999

Schulz, Michael and Frederick Soderbaum, *Regionalisation in a Globalising World*, Zed Books, 2001

Schwarz, Walter, *Nigeria*, Pall Mall Press, 1968

Segal, Ronald (editor), *Sanctions against South Africa,* Penguin Books – Penguin Special, 1964

—, *The Race War*, Jonathan Cape, 1966

—, *African Profiles*, Penguin Books, 1962

Serageldin, Ismail, *Poverty, Adjustment and Growth in Africa*, The World Bank, 1989

Sesay, Amadu (editor), *Africa and Europe*, Croom Helm, 1986

Shamuyarira, Nathan, *Crisis in Rhodesia*, Andre Deutsch, 1965

Shillington, Kevin, *Ghana and the Rawlings Factor*, Macmillan, 1992

Shonfield, Andrew, *The Attack on World Poverty*, Chatto & Windus, 1961

Short, Philip, *Banda,* Routledge & Kegan Paul, 1974

Shutt, Harry, *A New Democracy*, Zed Books, 2001

Sithole, Ndabaningi, *African Nationalism*, Oxford University Press, 1961

Smith, Susanna, *Frontline Africa The Right to a Future*, OXFAM, 1990

Sogge, David, *Give and Take 'What's the matter with Foreign Aid?'*, Zed Books, 2002

South Commission (chair. Julius Nyerere), *The Challenge to the South*, Oxford University Press, 1990

Sparks, Allister, *The Mind of South Africa*, Heinemann, 1990

Stevens, Christopher, *The Soviet Union and Black Africa*, Macmillan, 1976

Stockwell, John, *In Search of Enemies*, Andre Deutsch, 1978

Stokke, Olav (editor), *Reporting Africa*, The Scandinavian Institute of African Studies, Uppsala, 1971

Tanzer, Michael, *The Race for Resources*, Monthly Review Press, 1980

Taylor, D. R. Fraser, and Fiona Mackenzie (editors), *Development from Within Survival in Rural Africa*, Routledge, 1992

Thayer, George, *The War Business*, Simon and Schuster, 1969

Thompson, Leonard, *A History of South Africa*, Yale University Press, 1990

Thompson, Nicholas and Scott Thompson, *The Baobab and the Mango Tree*, Zed Books, 2000

Thorpe, D. R., *Alec Douglas-Home*, Sinclair-Stevenson, 1996

Toffler, Alvin and Heidi, *War and Anti-War*, Little, Brown & Co., 1993

UNDP, *Human Development Report 1988,* Oxford University Press, 1998

Vambe, Lawrence, *An Ill-Fated People,* Heinemann, 1972

Venter, Al. J., *The Terror Fighter*, Purnell, 1969

Walker, Martin, *The Cold War*, Fourth Estate, 1993

Welsh, Frank, *A History of South Africa*, Harper Collins, 1998

Werbner, Richard (editor), *Postcolonial Subjectivities in Africa*, Zed Books, 2002

Wheeler, Douglas L. and Rene Pelissier, *Angola,* Pall Mall Press, 1971

Wiles, Peter (editor), *The New Communist Third World*, Croom Helm, 1982

Wilson, Monica and Leonard Thompson (editors), *The Oxford History of South Africa II South Africa 1870–1966*, Oxford University Press, 1971

The World Bank, *Accelerated Development in Sub-Saharan Africa An Agenda for Action*, The World Bank, 1981

—, *Adjustment Lending An Evaluation of Ten Years of Experience*, The World Bank, 1988

—, *World Development Report 1986,* The World Bank, 1986

—, *Financing Adjustment with Growth in Sub-Saharan Africa*, 1986–1990, The World Bank, 1986

—, *World Development Report 1990*, The World Bank, 1990

—, *The World Bank Annual Reports* (1983, 1984, 1985, 1986, 1987, 1988, 1989, 1990), The World Bank

Yeager, Rodger, *Tanzania An African Experiment*, Westview Press, 1989

ANNUAL REVIEWS, YEARBOOKS, MAGAZINES AND NEWSPAPERS

Africa Contemporary Record (yearbook) 1968 to 1990, Africana Publishing Company

Africa South of the Sahara (yearbook) Europa Publications

The Middle East and North Africa (yearbook) Europa Publications

The Annual Register (yearbook) Keesings Worldwide

Africa Digest (bi-monthly) 1958–1974, The Africa Publications Trust

West Africa Magazine

African Business

New African

Keesings Contemporary Record

Newspapers and the internet

Index